## THE LONDON INSTITUTE

Library & Learning Resources

SE16SB        Telephone:  020 7514 6527

# E WEEK LOAN

..... be charged for late return
at 5p per day

# CITY LIGHTS

## Urban–Suburban Life in the Global Society

### SECOND EDITION

## E. BARBARA PHILLIPS

New York    Oxford
OXFORD UNIVERSITY PRESS
1996

Oxford University Press

Oxford   New York
Athens   Auckland   Bangkok   Bombay
Calcutta   Cape Town   Dar es Salaam   Delhi
Florence   Hong Kong   Istanbul   Karachi
Kuala Lumpur   Madras   Madrid   Melbourne
Mexico City   Nairobi   Paris   Singapore
Taipei   Tokyo   Toronto

and associated companies in
Berlin   Ibadan

Copyright © 1981 by E. Barbara Phillips and Richard T. LeGates
Copyright © 1996 by E. Barbara Phillips

Published by Oxford University Press, Inc.
198 Madison Avenue, New York, NY 10016

Oxford is a registered trademark of Oxford University Press

Library of Congress Cataloging-in-Publication Data
Phillips, E. Barbara.
City lights : urban–suburban life in the global society /
E. Barbara Phillips. — 2nd ed.
p.   cm. Includes bibliographical references and index.
ISBN 0-19-505689-2
1. Sociology, Urban. 2. Urban economics.
I. Title.   HT151.P513   1996   307.76—dc20   94-13652

9 8 7 6 5 4 3

Printed in the United States of America
on acid-free paper

*To Tim Teninty,*

urbane peasant who defines our division of labor Einsteinishly: "I take care of space, and you take care of time."

*and to Berkeley, California, our adopted hometown,*

where more books are sold per capita
than in any other U.S. city.

# Preface

Historian Arthur Schlesinger, Jr., once remarked that there are only two kinds of historians: "Those who admit their bias and those who shoot from ambush." This applies to social scientists, too, so I begin by stepping out from behind the bushes. Here are my biases and assumptions relevant to writing—and reading—this book about urban–suburban life in the global society.

## WHAT YOU SEE DEPENDS ON HOW YOU LOOK AT IT . . .

Here is my basic assumption: Nobody has cornered the market on knowledge. No one ideology, intellectual discipline, perspective, or guru has a monopoly on truth.

Indeed, people professing THE TRUTH or easy answers scare me. As Schlesinger warned college students in 1989, a belief in absolutes of Truth and Virtue is "the great enemy today of the life of the mind." In Schlesinger's view, and I agree, the greatest and most characteristic American thinkers have been "skeptical, irreverent, pluralistic and relativistic." Hence, this book doesn't offer one way of thinking about an issue. Instead, it aims to show how and why observers disagree on issues relevant to cities and suburbs: *what* they see, the *meaning* of what they see, and *what to do* about what they see.

## . . . AND HOW YOU DEFINE THE PROBLEM DETERMINES ITS SOLUTION

Take the case of urban poverty. Scholars and citizens don't agree on its causes, nature, or cure. The president of the United States and the mayor of Detroit, the urban planner and the sociologist, the banker and the auto worker, the socialist and the conservative, the homeless child and the affluent retiree—all bring different perspectives to the issue of poverty. And they don't agree on how to fight poverty. If, for example, mayors see the problem as lack of money, they may lobby for more federal and state funds. They may try to attract new tax-paying industry to their cities. But if they define poverty as a problem rooted in the unequal distribution of existing resources, the mayors will pursue different policies—ones aimed at changing institutional structures and redistributing existing resources, such as wealth and access to information. In sum, *there is no one right way to define a problem.*

However, *how people define a problem determines how they try to solve it. Or ignore it.* For example, some define the AIDS epidemic in the United States as punishment for what they consider sinful behavior; these taxpayers will resist spending public money to find a cure. Those who believe that homicide rates in cities are increasing due to the availability of handguns and drugs may seek to curb both; others, who think that despair and alienation undergird drug addiction and murderous acts, may attempt either to change the conditions producing such despair or to provide all-encompassing rehabilitation programs. Those who equate gun ownership with personal liberty will fight gun control. But those who equate guns with criminals will fight for gun control. Those who connect murders to the lack of police protection will call for more police on the street. Those who define the number of people under eighteen arrested for serious crimes in the United States—about 2 million in 1992—as an undeclared war against children may pressure lawmakers to fund massive early-childhood-intervention programs; others, defining the same situation as bad kids gone mad, may lobby to fund bigger, more secure prisons. And so on.

This approach means that I see my task as laying out appropriate ways of thinking about an issue, not as peddling a particular point of view. At the same time, I don't believe that all perspectives on the urban world are equally valid. For

**Fig. A**   WHAT'S THE PROBLEM HERE? It all depends on how you see it. Chapters 2 and 3 detail how and why scholars and citizens disagree on what causes urban slums, such as these in Taichung, Taiwan. (Martin Gorosh)

instance, I reject the idea that poor people are poor because they're lazy.

## USE YOUR IMAGINATION!

Focus on these real-life situations:

1. A fifty-nine-member Cultural Affairs Task Force—representing virtually every ethnic, artistic, and interest group in San Francisco—must come to some agreement on how millions of city dollars should be spent on local arts projects.
2. Two lesbian students in a "Social Aspects of Human Sexuality" class tell the professor, a heterosexual male, that he is incapable of un-

derstanding homosexuality and thus incompetent to lecture on lesbianism; they ask the Social Science Department to change professors.

At the heart of both cases are controversial issues of politics, epistemology, and cross-cultural communication. Particularly relevant here is the challenge of understanding and fairly representing people unlike ourselves. Is it possible? Some think not. They subscribe to the *Insider-as-Insighter* doctrine: Outsiders cannot truly understand insiders. This doctrine holds that individuals have a monopoly on knowledge or privileged access to understanding by virtue of their group membership or social position, or lack of it. Filmmaker Spike Lee espoused the Insider doctrine when he said (on *Nightline,* June 21, 1991) that *only* an African-American can make a realistic film about Malcolm X or a black neighborhood in Los Angeles. In other words, the Insider doctrine holds that *only* African-Americans can really understand African-American history, *only* women can truly understand sexual harassment of women, *only* soldiers are capable of knowing the complex emotions of fighting a war, and so on.

But many scholars reject the notion that you have to "be one to understand one." A Vietnamese Buddhist researcher, they say, *can* come to understand Native American history. Likewise, a 5-foot, 2 inch-tall female sociologist *can* develop comprehension of male-bonding rituals among basketball players. Here, I agree. As Henry Louis Gates, Jr., then chair of Harvard's Afro-American Studies Department, said on National Public Radio's *Fresh Air* program (June 8, 1992), "The whole point of being in the academy is that we can explore other cultures with great freedom, with great energy. . . . You don't have to *be* the thing in order to understand the thing that you're studying."

I would go further. In my view, one particular strand of the Insider doctrine—the notion that race or ethnicity is a person's defining characteristic—is wrongheaded and dangerous. First, it is rooted in the white European subjugation of colonial peoples, using their race as a justification for domination. Second, it wrongly assumes homogeneity. Take, for example, the notion of an "African culture." Ghanaian-American scholar Kwame Anthony Appiah, a professor of Afro-American Studies at Harvard, reminds us that the idea of a single African culture is pure fiction—a social construction of nineteenth-century European colonialists. Africans do not share a single culture, race, religion, or color; there are hundreds of different African cultures. Finally, the idea of race/ethnicity as a defining characteristic can be seductive. For urbanites seeking community in an uncertain world, it is a way to distinguish "us" from "them." But hate and murder are the flip sides of brotherhood and sisterhood. Such places as Nazi Germany, Bosnia, Rwanda, and Sri Lanka remind us of the sometimes deadly bonds of kinship. And nearer to home, Christian Identity and like-minded white supremacist groups use hi-tech tools (e.g., dial-a-racist messages and computer bulletin boards) to preach hate, even death, to "them": non-Christians and nonwhites, and some non–northern European Americans.

In my research, I polled journalists on this issue. Overwhelmingly (97 percent), they rejected the Insider-as-Insighter doctrine. My guess is that most social scientists would also reject it. Here's why. First, social scientists would be reduced to conducting research *only* about people like themselves. This means that a male Catholic social psychologist could not conduct research concerning homeless females or WASP elites. Second, many social scientists argue that empathy and imagination are powerful instruments in the outsider's struggle to understand insiders. This is my hope. I think we can, to a significant degree, get inside the shoes and heads of human beings unlike ourselves. Here are a few ways: (1) *doing or reading fieldwork studies* that immerse us in the culture of the insider group. For example, a white anthropologist, Philippe Bourgois, lived in a barrio neighborhood of New York City for several years; his rich description, published in his book *In Search of Respect* (1995), gives readers a sense of how it feels to live in a crack cocaine culture and why it persists; and (2) *reading, watching, and listening to people's stories* that allow us to experience the colors and texture of a particular way of life, group, or historical period.

Frederick Wiseman's documentary films are exemplary. They give viewers an insider's look at various U.S. institutions, including a welfare agency, a mental hospital, and a high school. Likewise, novels and artworks can introduce us to people who think and act differently from ourselves, thus expanding our own little social worlds. Anna Deveare Smith's theaterpieces, *Fires in the Mirror* and *Twilight: Los Angeles, 1992*, brilliantly accomplish this leap of imagination. Both artworks show how real people live with (and make sense of) ethnic, racial, and class conflict. Smith gives voice to her real-life characters without judging them, taking audiences into their minds, hearts, and separate realities.

Smith's performances echo the immortal words of comedienne Lily Tomlin: When asked about acting the movie role of a straight woman in a love scene, Tomlin, a lesbian, quipped, "You don't have to be one to play one." Historian Taylor Branch expressed a related sentiment in *Parting the Waters* (1988), his Pulitzer Prize–winning study of the U.S. civil rights movement: "Truth requires a maximum effort to see through the eyes of strangers, foreigners, and enemies."

Some of the most thought-provoking studies of U.S. life come from outsiders. (*Democracy in America* by the nineteenth-century French visitor Alexis de Toqueville is a prime example.) Why? *Perhaps marginal people make better spies.* Outsiders often see what insiders dismiss as "natural."

Starting in Chapter 1, there are many references to fieldwork and artwork. Hopefully, they will stimulate the imagination, helping you to reach beyond self and to experience a wider range of people and ways of life.

## BEWARE "SELF-EVIDENT TRUTHS"

Overall, the general tone of this book is tentative. As poet William Blake wrote, "What is now true was once only imagined." He might have added that *what now seems self-evident truth may be considered mere nonsense in 100 years . . . or maybe just 10 months.* After all, neither social scientists nor politicians nor poets predicted—or imagined—the upheavals in Eastern Europe that occurred from 1989 to 1991. In the United States, no pundit prophesied that after the Rodney King verdict in April 1992, long-smoldering embers of racial, ethnic, and class hatred would erupt in a volcano of violence in South-Central Los Angeles. In other words, most of what we think we know about reality may soon be obsolete.

Sometimes, time turns the unimaginable into the commonplace. For example, before the 1980s, a few homeless persons camped out on city streets, but they were a rare sight. By the 1990s, scores of people—including children—were living on the street. In just one decade, homelessness had become ordinary, not extraordinary.

And time often reveals new information that changes our interpretation of things. Here's an example close to home: In the first edition of this text, I wrote about the Tasaday, a "small Stone Age tribe living in a Philippine rain forest" who "apparently live a conflict-free existence. Some observers, particularly John Nance, portray the Tasaday as living in a garden of Eden." Well, shortly after Ferdinand Marcos was toppled from power in Manila, the "garden of Eden" was exposed as a hoax. Apparently (an important word!), Marcos's minister of culture, an American-trained anthropologist, had paid a small number of people to *act* like a Stone Age tribe; when he left government, the Tasaday walked out of their caves because they no longer got paid! Yet, the truth remains elusive. Many respected scholars think that the situation is much more complicated and that the Tasaday were not paid actors.

In addition, things that seem self-evident often aren't. Take violence on television. It is generally assumed that violent shows are antisocial. Thus, it came as a shock to students in my "Mass Media" course when 80 percent of their survey respondents, asked about watching *Hawaii-50* (the most violent show in reruns, rated in terms of the number of murders and beatings per hour), said that the most important aspect of the show was the respect and friendship between the two leads. Or take another case—the Anita Hill–Clarence Thomas proceedings before the Senate Judiciary Committee. Emotions ran high, and critics disagreed about who "lied" during the televised hearings. Yet all missed two nonobvious points that concern perception and power. First, during the few days of the televised hearings, viewers saw and heard many more articulate and competent African-Americans than they had during decades of TV sitcoms and crime shows. Second, male definitions of reality—that some sexual innuendo constitutes harmless "just kidding around"—were rejected by women. In the longer run, these perceptions may have deeper consequences on attitudes and behavior than the Senate committee could imagine.

Given this skepticism about the "obvious," as well as a commitment to tentative truths and multiple perspectives, I don't provide definitive answers to anything you may have wanted to know about cities, suburbs, or postsuburban forms. I do not, for instance, say how and why urban riots happen. Nor do I offer a checklist for measuring the quality of city life, although it would be instructive to analyze the assumptions that underlie such value-laden lists. Likewise, I do not promote one particular public policy for dealing with the use–abuse of cigarettes, alcohol, coca products, and other drugs. Instead, my hope is that this book will help readers to choose more intelligently for themselves among competing claims and truths—and value-loaded statements—about how cities and suburbs do work and should work. Alas, there are no easy routes. *We spend our entire lives sifting sense from nonsense, trying to decide which is which.* Hopefully, we keep on questioning the truisms, altering our perspective on life. Here I present (1) information— ammunition for asking better questions about city life—and (2) concepts, visions, and frameworks to better understand information about cities.

## THE PLACE OF URBAN "PROBLEMS"

Are there really any urban problems? A strange question? Perhaps, but nobody talked about problems until this century. People did speak about disagreeable urban conditions and conflicts, but the idea of clearly definable urban problems is recent. It came into style in the early twentieth century as social scientists, eager to play the role of social doctors, began to apply medical language to the city. A city was compared to a human body. Just as people had diseases complete with symptoms and (under a doctor's care) cures, cities had problems that could be cured.

Today, it is common to hear a city diagnosed as sick or terminally ill. More optimistically, an urban area might be described as healthy or showing good vital signs. I avoid this medical terminology for two reasons. First, talk of sick, problem-ridden cities masks an important idea: *There is no agreement on what constitutes an urban problem.* What is defined as an urban problem

depends basically on two factors: (1) who's doing the talking, and (2) the intellectual-political fashion of the times. Both drugs and homelessness, to take just two examples, have been features of American city life for decades. Indeed, some scholars say that the United States experienced an epidemic of narcotics and cocaine use from 1885 to 1920, and that homelessness accompanied the industrialization of cities. But when did they become defined as problems in the United States? Drugs became a "problem" at about the time that drug use spread from lower-class, ethnic neighborhoods to affluent metropolitan homes. Homelessness became a "problem" at about the time that (1) homeless persons spilled over from the nation's skid rows, becoming more visible to affluent urbanites, (2) respectable people, such as families of working poor, joined the ranks of the homeless, and (3) activists, especially the late Mitch Snyder in Washington, D.C., brought the plight of the homeless into America's living room via the nightly TV news. Second, constant talk and photos of urban "problems" encourage one-sided, negative pictures of urban life. If, for instance, local TV news portrays a city as a dangerous, frightening place, more positive images—the city as a center of science, culture, fun, and new ideas—can be wiped out of a viewer's consciousness. Indeed, my students at San Francisco State University found that many grade-school students in suburban schools do not want to visit nearby San Francisco because— paraphrasing their responses—they fear crime, grime, and slime. And where did they get such notions? Mainly from family and television.

*Urban problems can disappear as fast as they appear—at least in the public mind.* Homelessness is a good example. In the 1988 primary campaigns for U.S. president, the urban homeless was a key issue. By the time of the 1992 primaries and the presidential campaign, homelessness as a problem had virtually disappeared—*even as homelessness appeared to be getting much worse in terms of numbers.*

In the future, what conditions will be defined as problems? It's hard to predict. One long-standing condition—secondhand cigarette smoke— was not considered a problem in the United States until the late 1970s. Then, various nongovernmental groups redefined it as a health hazard. These mainly middle-class groups led successful campaigns to restrict or ban cigarette smoking in many urban buildings. (It was not until 1991 that scientists commissioned by the Environmental Protection Agency concluded that secondhand smoke kills 53,000 nonsmokers a year.) Similarly, in the late 1980s, an old form of crime got a new name and new attention: the "hate crime," an assault of harassment based on the victim's religion, race, sexual orientation, or ethnic background. In the early 1990s, some educators sought to redefine urban violence as a public-health problem.

The flip side is this: What conditions are *not* defined as problems? That's harder to determine. If a condition isn't highlighted in the mass media, discussed in class, or mulled over with family and friends, it doesn't get on the public agenda of *what* to think about or *how* to think about it. For example, most of us don't think about homeless people's lack of an address and a telephone number (and consequent inaccessibility to potential employers) as problems. Or the growing salary gap between top managers and their entry-level employees. And so on.

A number of issues affecting urban areas are discussed here, but the discussion is not organized around so-called problems. To do so would ignore the richness of the urban experience and even further emphasize the seamy side of city life (a side already emphasized by contemporary visual media). Even worse, the urban problems approach perpetuates the wrongheaded idea that people agree on what the problems are—which they do not. And even if people *did* agree on what the

**Fig. B**   DRUGS ARE GARBAGE. Does the La Jolla, California, sanitation company mean *legal* drugs—like alcohol and cigarettes? Presumably not. But the definition of what's *legal* or what's a *drug* can change. For example, in the 1920s, alcohol was illegal in the United States. In 1994, the American Medical Association and some federal officials redefined cigarettes as addictive drugs, due to their nicotine content. *How* a substance is defined determines how public policy deals with it. Chapter 11 examines "the definition of the situation," and Chapter 18 looks at the various approaches to "solving" the "problem" of poverty. (Tim Teninty)

problems are, the urban-problems approach gives the false impression that a problem—whether it is people living on the streets, street crime, white-collar crime, savings and loan failures, or joblessness—is local in nature. Yes, a General Motors plant closing in Flint, Michigan, does lead to unemployment there. But unemployment in Flint can be understood only by looking way past the city limits. Which brings us to my next assumption.

## IT'S A SMALL, SMALL WORLD: URBAN–GLOBAL INTERLOCK

In 1986, a nuclear reactor exploded in Chernobyl, a town in the former Soviet Union. Over 135,000 people were evacuated from their homes, but the danger of radiation did not stop at Chernobyl's city limits. Instead, hundreds of miles away in Lapland, many reindeer had to be destroyed because their meat was contaminated. Vegetables and milk in Germany also suffered contamination.

Chernobyl reminds us that it's a small, small world. Neither radioactive fallout nor toxic waste nor polluted water uses passports. Neither does the AIDS virus, illegal drugs, nor valuable information. Earthly boundaries—city, state, and federal—can't contain environmental hazards or nuggets of knowledge.

If our destinies are often tied to strangers in foreign lands, the reverse is also the case. The fate of people all over the world is linked to U.S. public policies, business activities, and individual actions. For example, the employment rate in Angeles, the longtime Philippine home of Clark Air Force Base, depended almost totally on the number of U.S. soldiers stationed there, not on local manufacturing or agriculture; after the eruption of Mount Pinatubo in 1991, the base was abandoned, and Angeles became a ghost town. When a U.S. naval base in the Philippines was abandoned in 1992, so were some 10,000 Amerasian children, thrown away "like a spoiled napkin" (in the words of an Irish priest working there) by their American servicemen fathers. These children live without sanitation or running water in the filthy slums of Olongapo, a dusty town near the former naval base that existed to serve the sailors' pleasure. The populations of Mexican cities near the U.S. border, such as Ciudad Juarez, have exploded as a result of the decision of American corporations to locate factories there. Toxic waste from these American-owned light assembly plants (known as *maquiladoras*) in Mexico seem to be responsible for a rash of birth defects (thirty-one babies born without brains, as of this writing) on both sides of the border: Brownsville, Texas, and Matamoras, Mexico. Singapore's biggest employer is the owner of NBC, the U.S.-identified multinational General Electric.

More and more, there is no hiding place. Maps still divide the world by country, but national frontiers mean less and less. First, borders are often porous and easily crossed. This applies to tourists and terrorists as well as economic refugees. Second, many nations are composed of people with separate cultural backgrounds, thus complicating the notion of a specific "national identity." National identity is further complicated by the existence of millions of refugees. Finally, the whole world is becoming a single economic and ecological unit.

What happens in a remote corner of the globe often has local impact. For example, the ozone level at the South Pole can affect food production near Keokuk, Iowa. Transactions on Tokyo's stock market can affect the price of housing and other investments in Los Angeles. Cheap dollars on the international market can turn a town like Columbus, Nebraska, from bust to boom times; the town manufactures electric products, exported in greater quantities when dollars are cheap. In other words, *U.S. cities—and companies—are part of a global economic system.* This system operates via electronic communications on a twenty-four-hour-a-day basis.

In this timeless, borderless world, managers of planetary enterprises do not necessarily think about the impact they have on nations, let alone cities. For instance, in the 1980s, Detroit's Chrysler grew increasingly dependent on foreign suppliers and partners; American machine-tool manufacturers, hard hit by Japanese competition, grumbled when the car company bought multimillion-

**Fig. C**   EVEN THE LONELIEST TOWN IS NOT ALONE. Far from the madding crowds, residents of tiny Eureka may not think about the impact of national or global policies on their daily lives. Yet their well-being may hinge on decisions made faraway by faceless corporate and government officials, including those who authorized atomic-test blasts in Nevada (affecting cancer rates), those who negotiated international-trade agreements (affecting the price of nearby metals), and those who decide where to construct themeparks (affecting land values, employment, etc.) Chapters 4, 6, and 12 detail some local–international connections in the global village. Chapter 14 discusses electronic forms of citizen input that may bring Eurekans a louder voice in decision making. Chapter 17 examines the fate of one small town in the West that experienced technological change and why "good citizens" there suffered most. (Tim Teninty)

dollar metal-stamping presses from a Japanese rather than an American firm. Chrysler advertised autos "Born in the USA," but it sold—as Chryslers—a large number of cars and trucks made in Japan by Mitsubishi. (Indeed, in 1990, Chrysler owned 12 percent of Mitsubishi.) In a related vein, the Hewlett-Packard Company moved its personal computer group from Silicon Valley, California, to Grenoble, France, in 1990, reflecting the growing importance of the European market.

In this global system, many multinational corporations act like private governments. Multinationals control vast resources, employ intelligence experts, and make decisions that affect who gets what. However, unlike government officials, multinational managers salute no flag. As the then president of one U.S.-based multinational corporation (since gobbled up by the world's largest telecommunications company, AT&T), National Cash Register, told a *New York Times* reporter in 1989, "We at NCR think of ourselves as a globally competitive company that happens to be headquartered in the U.S." For good reason too: In 1992, 53 percent of NCR's reported $7.1 billion in revenue came from non-U.S. sources.

Is it possible for nations—let alone local governments—to reassert significant economic authority in a global system? Most observers think not. Indeed, some claim that global markets boss nations around. That is why James Carville, a Clinton adviser, once quipped that if reincarnated, he'd like to come back as the markets because "they get whatever they want." A *New York Times* headline put it this way: "When money talks, government listens: Who runs the world? In many ways, the global markets do" (July 24, 1994, E3). If so, how can ordinary citizens assert control over their daily lives? This is a key question—with no easy answers. This book offers a range of responses from electronic participation (Chapter 14) and local ordinances (Chapter 12) to a search for community (Chapter 5). It also pays a great deal of attention to two important forces, often in conflict, that are chipping away at both the nation-state and democratic citizenship: (1) ethnic- or religious-based fundamentalism and (2) global capitalism. These opposing forces, called *Jihad vs. McWorld* by political scientist Benjamin R. Barber in his 1995 book, are highlighted here in several places, including Chapter 4 (the world urban system) and Chapter 9 (global identity versus the pull of "lesser loyalties").

## "ONLY CONNECT"

In this global society, it is impossible to separate domestic from international issues. To borrow political scientist Ken Jowitt's term, we have a mesh of "intermestic" issues: issues that are simultaneously domestic and international. For example, U.S.-owned factories on the Mexican side of the border affect the political economy of Mexico, the environment of both Mexico and the United States, and the health of Americans on the U.S. side of the border.

One outcome of this mesh affects us all: *Some social groups, some cities, and some nations will be advantaged, perhaps for decades to come. Likewise, other groups and cities will be disadvantaged by forces far beyond the control of a mayor or city manager.*

Knowing that our local environment is connected to the global environment may be intellectually satisfying. But knowledge doesn't guarantee effective action. How can we *act* locally to have an impact on a global situation? This book notes a number of ways and examples. Here's one: In 1989, the City Council of Irvine, California (fifty-five miles south of Los Angeles, with a population, at the time, of 105,000), decided not to wait until the nations of the world got together to protect the earth's ozone layer. Instead, it offered its own plan. By city ordinance, Irvine prohibits the use of almost all chlorofluorocarbons in most industrial processes and bans the sale and use of Styrofoam food packaging. Can cities actually take the lead, prodding world leaders to act on international problems? Is there such a beast as *municipal foreign policy?* The then mayor of Irvine, California, thinks so. He said that "local communities acting two to five years in advance of states and nations is how change takes place." (In 1989, the Center for Innovative Diplomacy, headed by the mayor of Irvine, called a conference attracting mayors from dozens of U.S. and Canadian cities.) Other leaders and ordinary citizens focus on the opposite side of the spectrum—global approaches to local problems. World citizen Gary Davis, for one, believes that global problems with local impact can best be approached via world government. So, once again, there is a variety of approaches. In this book, I draw some connections—from America's Main Street to Tokyo's Ginza and to Brazil's rain forest—and suggest the range of urban policies that deal with global issues, and vice versa.

This book tries to bring together a wide variety of perspectives on urban phenomena and to suggest some connections between phenomena. In an age of information explosion and extreme specialization, this is not easy for any of us. But let us begin by following the advice—or hope—of novelist E. M. Forster in terms of both people and ideas: "Only connect."

## THINGS URBAN ARE BEST UNDERSTOOD IN A BROADER CONTEXT FROM AN INTERDISCIPLINARY PERSPECTIVE

This book puts urban phenomena in broader contexts. Sometimes this means putting an issue into a national or an international framework. Sometimes it means putting an issue into the framework of general theory before examining its urban–suburban applications. To better understand Los Angeles in the 1980s, for instance, I link its economic fate to worldwide processes, national trends, and regional developments. These include the growth of the global economy, the internationalization of the movement of investment money, shifts in population and power from Frostbelt to Sunbelt, massive immigration, and changes from an industrial to a postindustrial economy.

To expand our vision of things urban, an interdisciplinary approach is essential. When discussing the economy of cities, to take one example, I blend insights from sociology, geography, literature, political science, and other relevant disciplines with economic theory and data. Why? Because economic concepts alone don't tell the whole story. Certainly, they add nothing to our understanding of human reactions to economic change or poverty.

## THE LINK BETWEEN SOCIAL ACTION AND SOCIAL THEORY

Throughout this book, I try to provide a solid theoretical base for action-oriented people. Theory and practice are emphasized because, in my view, *there is no good social action without good social theory.* Case studies highlight individuals and groups who have acted on their urban world. Then their practice is linked to theories about urban life. For instance, I examine how elected officials, such as Chicago's late mayor, Richard J. Daley, and appointed officials, such as New York City's master builder, Robert Moses, exercised enormous influence and power. I fol-

low the progress of lesser-known but important people such as members of Bananas, a group of California women who set out to perform a community service: providing harried parents with information about children's activities—to save them from "going bananas." Bananas learned how the political system works and, with much persistence and hard work, got something done.

My approach—trying to merge practice and theory—comes partly from lessons learned while trying to get things done. For instance, in West Virginia, I learned that fighting a War Against Poverty armed with only false hopes is a losing battle. More recently, through efforts in an urban university and a suburban park system, I learned that an understanding of organizational politics plus a long time line and a hearty laugh are useful for keeping one's resolve and sanity.

I hope that this book will lay the groundwork for better understanding of how cities work and, hence, more effective urban action. My aim is to make world watching less a spectator pastime and more a contact sport.

## REVELATIONS IN ORDINARY PLACES

Taking a closer look at ordinary people doing ordinary things—like riding a city bus—can reveal a great deal about urban life. For instance, when riding a crowded bus, we expect to be left alone. If, perchance, a seatmate strikes up a conversation, we note how unusual this is. The next time, we may bury our heads in a newspaper or stare out the window to avoid conversation. Now, nobody taught us how to stave off urban strangers. Or that rules—not talking to strangers, for example—govern bus behavior. Yet most of the time, most of us follow these implicit rules. *By observing routine activities, we can begin to understand what rules govern urban social behavior and what purposes these rules serve.* Thus, a chapter is devoted to such ordinary actions as walking down a busy street, riding a subway, going to a bar, and standing in a bank's automatic teller machine (ATM) line.

## NAMING AND RENAMING THE WORLD

Ordinary names can reveal much about urban values. Street names, for example, may be a tip-off to local heroes and heroines. Name changes—for example, from "Oriental" to "Asian-American," from "chiropodist" to "podiatrist," from "minority" to "people of color" or "unre-presented people"—reflect changes in the way people define themselves and one another. And the lack of an agreed-on name ("Hello," I'd like you to meet my . . . ahh . . . "lover" . . . I mean . . . "significant other" or "domestic partner") suggests emerging social realities.

Words can also point to the trail of those who came before. In American English, that trail stretches from *adobe* to *zilch*.

Frequently, names in the news are like submerged treasures waiting to be discovered. Take, for instance, the terms *looter* and *welfare*. Who are defined as looters in the United States? Usually poor folks. In April 1992, "looters" stole television sets, clothing, and relatively small-ticket items in South-Central Los Angeles. In contrast, financier Charles Keating, convicted in the 1980s savings and loan debacle that is costing U.S. taxpayers more than $200 billion, was never called a looter. Neither was Ivan Boesky, a Wall Street inside trader who paid a $100 million penalty to the victims he swindled and to the U.S. Treasury.

**Fig. D**  FROM ADOBE TO ZILCH. The language tree at the Ellis Island Immigrant Museum shows a few of the many words that American English borrowed from native and immigrant cultures. Chapters 8 and 9 examine immigration, assimilation, and multiculturalism. (Roberta Tasley)

Similarly, the word *welfare* is not used for rich and poor alike. In the mainstream press, a single mother gets a government "handout" or "welfare." Meanwhile, Chrysler receives a government "subsidy" or "bailout money." Aerospace giant McDonnell Douglas received more than $200 million in secret Pentagon cash payments in 1990. In other words, "welfare" goes to the poor and "subsidies" go to the rich. AFDC may mean Aid to Families with Dependent Children received by some poor. Alternatively, as citizen advocate Ralph Nader defines it, AFDC may mean Aid to Federally Dependent Corporations.

Language is not neutral; it limits our reality. New words can refocus perception and change "reality." As fund-raisers know, there is a world of difference in trying to save a "jungle" or a "rain forest."

Writer Maxine Hong Kingston says that she tries to "change the world one word at a time." I try to walk in her footsteps. For instance, I avoid the word *foreign* because the concept is obsolete. We live in a timeless, borderless world with a global market for ideas, information, and IOUs, all being exchanged in nanoseconds.

## INFO ALERT!

We live in the Information Age. Information should be easy to get, right? Alas, hardly ever. For example, U.S. census data are in the public domain, but bits of census information can take days to track down.

Once census data are tracked down, we should ask: Are the data trustworthy? That's unclear. Why? For two reasons: GIGO and possible politicization. First, GIGO. In computerese, GIGO stands for *Garbage In, Garbage Out*. Unfortunately, GIGO may apply to the 1990 U.S. Census of Population. Lawsuits filed by San Francisco and several other big cities against the U.S. Census Bureau question the manner in which data were collected and the 1991 decision not to adjust for admittedly undercounted groups— estimated at between 4 and 15 million people— particularly big-city homeless and ethnic poor.

Second, demographers and other experts inside and outside the Census Bureau charge that the bureau's integrity is endangered by politicial meddling. These critics, including some respected scholars, contend that what data are collected and when data are released publicly appear to be politically influenced. For example, William O'Hare, director of the University of Louisville's Population and Policy Research Center, claims that a report showing a significant increase in the proportion of low-income wage earners during the Reagan–Bush administrations was revised because it gave information "detrimental to the administration" and because it emphasized "the fact that there was a downturn in the economy during the '80s."

Another problem with census data concerns access, both physical and financial. In the 1980s, some U.S. Census Bureau offices closed to save tax dollars, limiting physical access. Private companies do offer census data online—for a price. Unless funded by a grant, few researchers or community activists can afford to use computer data services. Further, it takes several years to get some census information. Numbers trickle out, and social scientists are forced to use estimates or old data.

In general, it is wise to remain skeptical when evaluating research. Aside from the problem of collecting reliable data, there is another issue: honesty. Even highly respected scientists have been known to falsify data, bury findings that could threaten their institution's reputation, and steal other people's work or words. If such unethical acts did not exist, the U.S. government would not need watchdogs such as the Office of Scientific Integrity, located in the National Institutes of Health.

## UNITY VERSUS DIVERSITY

Why do human beings think and feel so differently? Scholars point to a number of factors. Depending on their field of expertise, some name occupation, religious beliefs, educational background, and age. Some point to family upbringing, social class, unconscious premises, race and ethnicity, physical state, mental abilities, income level, and degree of power. Others say that birth order, oxytocin and other human hormones, or environmental hazards have great impact on a person's body and mind. Still others think that the dominant socio-economic system is the key influence on personality and beliefs.

In the early 1990s, many Americans were sensitized to another influence on a person's mental and emotional life: gender. Televised Senate hearings of sexual harassment charges against (then Supreme Court nominee) Clarence Thomas in October 1991 brought gender issues to center screen. In addition, Deborah Tannen's best-seller, *You Just Don't Understand: Women and Men in Conversation* (1990) spread the idea that men and women in America use different words and inhabit different worlds. For example, linguist Tannen argues that men use conversation as a tool in one-upmanship, trying to get and keep the upper hand, while women use conversation for the opposite purposes: to establish intimacy, give and get confirmation and support, and reach consensus.

Interestingly, Tannen does not address an issue that may *even further* separate people: Is it possible to generalize about the conversational styles of men or women? Do *all* men—whether WASP football player, African-American professor, or Asian-American news reporter—define themselves conversationally in terms of a hierarchy? Do *all* women—whether Hispanic social worker, Euro-American sales executive, or Native American artist—share a desire for intimacy and consensus that is reflected in language use? If not, are we doomed to talk past one another?

Now let's take the opposite tack. By stressing differences, we may forget that we share characteristics, particularly the capacities to think abstractly, laugh, and come to one another's aid. For example, if an elderly person—whatever his or her race, class, or gender—falls on a busy street, we are surprised if passersby do *not* help. As Morton Hunt reminds us in his book *The Compassionate Beast: The Scientific Inquiry into Human Altruism* (1990), "Cruelty is attention-getting, kindness unremarkable."

In addition, a wide range of thinkers—from environmental scientists to global economists—remind us that our fates are intertwined. Neither riches, skin color, beauty, power, prestige, gender, nor personal background has an impact on the direction of winds wafting radioactive air.

Does it take dirty water, natural disaster, or bomb blasts to remind us of our common situation? In the San Francisco—Oakland Bay Area, a deadly earthquake was accompanied by acts of heroism and helpfulness that cross-cut the everyday boundaries separating human beings. In Oklahoma City, a color-blind bomb that killed 167 people brought people of all backgrounds together to share grief. As a local clergyman put it, "When we saw these babies we didn't think 'Oh, it's a black baby, or a Hispanic baby . . . We saw babies . . . what the world has seen is that we are far more alike than unalike." How can we intensify this sense of greater community, emphasizing the cement of our humaneness as well as the strength of our differences? This remains a question worth thinking more about.

Here, I try to pay close attention to *both* sides of the U.S. motto: diversity (*pluribus*) and oneness (*unum*). For example, Chapters 8 and 9 consider ethnic history and the debate over multiculturalism. Some observers argue that unity is just a myth, built on the repression of ethnic diversity by a small Anglo elite and on "Americanization," a bland term for cleansing minorities of their ethnicity. Others fear that diversity equals disunity. Whichever, many factors, including social movements for civil rights and waves of recent immigrants, have helped to rid textbooks of negative stereotypes and to celebrate unique identities. Yet an emphasis on cultural uniqueness can also divide people into deadly opposing camps: "us" and "them." As Martin Luther King, Jr., said, "We are caught in an inescapable network of mutuality."

## ANYTHING ELSE?

Other assumptions and biases can be read between the lines of the following chapters.

Choices (what issues to include? how to present them? which theorists to exclude?) are inevitable. No doubt, some choices were barely conscious, stemming from my own background, life experiences, professional training, and personal reaction to the currents of our times. Because I believe that there is an autobiographical basis—and bias—to the way authors think (myself included), I've tried to acknowledge major influences relevant to this book.

First, *academic training*. An undergraduate degree in history; advanced degrees in international relations, public administration, and interdisciplinary social science. With this background, I probably have a trained incapacity to stay within traditional disciplinary boundaries.

Second, *a fascination with language and maps*. On huge wall maps, our fifth-grade teacher had us trace the geographical journeys of words into English from Scandinavia, ancient Greece, and elsewhere. These exercises alerted me to the stewpot called English. And mapping introduced me to physical space as an important factor in human relations. Several chapters reflect my continuing interest in space, both public and private, as a symbol of social power, economic domination, psychological control, historic preservation, and cultural values.

Third, *chance*. As a child, I had flat feet. A pediatrician advised ballet lessons. I still have flat feet, but I developed a lifelong enchantment with French (the language of ballet), dance, and the arts in general. Hence, there are many references and illustrations from the arts and pop culture in this book.

Fourth, *cross-cultural experience*. My views were influenced by a host of experiences outside the United States—as a political science student in Paris, a U.S. Foreign Service Officer in Africa and India, and a student of classical dance in Tokyo. This book focuses on U.S. cities and suburbs, but I draw on personal acquaintance to compare and contrast urban lifestyles. I also draw on the observations of far-flung friends and former students who happen to be both good observers and good correspondents.

Fifth, *courses and students I've taught*. In large measure, my students' interests shaped and re-shaped this book. My students, ranging in age from eighteen to seventy-eight, helped me to keep current too.

Sixth, *generation and social background*. My formative years coincided with the 1950s, the heyday of U.S. economic and military power. After World War II, optimism was pervasive for many middle-class white teens like myself. We gyrated to Elvis, cooled out to Dave Brubeck, and laughed at Lucy. As Simon and Garfunkel defined it, it was a time of innocence and confidence. People may have been suffering in the Other America, but we were unaware. We oozed faith in the nation's future and our own ability to build a better world. Everything seemed possible! (In that era, French writer Albert Camus captured this upbeat feeling from a slightly different angle, calling the United States "this country where everything is done to prove that life isn't tragic.")

Still, like people of all ages today, I am not immune to trepidation concerning the urban (read: postmodern) condition. We all share a historical moment, perhaps a defining moment: a time of great uncertainty and indeterminacy near the millennium. In these times, some people are attracted to all-encompassing philosophies that offer simple and hate-filled explanations for complex phenomena. That could be predicted. What could not be predicted, and thus has shocked many of us, is the willingness—and ability—of such zealots to commit mass murder against total strangers, whether they are children in an Oklahoma City federal building or commuters in a Tokyo subway. This random violence upsets the taken-for-granted balance of power and plays havoc with our sense of personal security.

In general, however, my tendency is to see glasses as half-full rather than half-empty. Overall, my tone in this book is hopeful. For one thing, I believe we can resist what news analyst Daniel Schorr has called "a tidal wave of deceit and a mountain of manipulation" coming from officialdom, public or private. This sense of hope distinguishes me from the majority of Americans aged ten to twenty-four, who, according to several national surveys, face the future in a fearful and dispirited mood.

At least two other important biases pervade this

book, and for them I am unrepentant. One concerns the role of ideas in public life. In my view, *without reasoned and lively debate over ideas, "public life" is an oxymoron.* I hope that this book will stimulate debate on matters affecting our collective present and future. The other is an unabashed pro-urban bias. I like cities, particularly big ones. I hope my enthusiasm for cities will be apparent. Even rub off a little.

Last, studying today's human settlements can seem overwhelming because the world that helps shape them is so complex and because honest scholars disagree on how they work. There is some help along the way: key terms in bold print; biographical sketches of theorists and practitioners; case studies of real people setting policies that affect metropolitan life or trying to change the way things are done; artworks; graphs, and boxed selections from classic essays or interesting observations related to urban life.

Most especially, you—kind reader—are invited to participate directly in discovering the metropolis. I hope that carrying out the projects listed at the end of each chapter will bring city and suburb alive, encouraging serious discussion and even theory building. I would like to know what you find when doing the projects. Write me in care of Oxford University Press about the projects or anything else related to this book.

So, that is where the book is "coming from," to use the vernacular. From a person shaped by the people, social currents, places, ideas, and media images I've known. Of course, how any of us *interpret* our world depends on all that we have met. That's why I've tried to reveal some of those influences instead of shooting from ambush.

*November 1995*                                      E.B.P.
*Berkeley*

# Acknowledgments

Luckily for me, social science can be a social endeavor. I want to thank colleagues and friends, often one and the same, for sharing their ideas, memories, cities, and neighborhoods with me: Brack Brown, Fred Burke, Neagu Djuvara, Jean Fargo, Martin Gorosh, Sandy Granzow, Carol Green, Susan Hoehn, Karen Hossfeld, Susan and Ernest Koenigsberg, Hans Kötte, Domnica Melone, Susan Robbins, Sandy Robinson, Barbara Shear, Bob Snyder, Carol Sterling, Kay Tiblier, and Linda Weiner. Special tribute goes to José Correa, who showed me his hometown, Cuzco, Peru, with the eyes of a social scientist and the sight of a poet.

My intellectual debts are legion to the late Peter Knauss, Margaret Fay, Bloke Modisane, Lena, and Martha Levitan. Most of all, I want to honor the memory of my parents, Elaine and Charlie Phillips. They fostered the important illusion that I could (and should) do almost anything, except play cards with strangers. Together, they gave me love, security, appreciation for learning, enthusiasm for city life, and fearlessness to take on big projects.

Special thanks to communards at 1043 who talked, even sang: Kit Riley, Kostas Karadininis, Judy Ireland, Stan Politi, Arlene DeLeon, Georges Rey, Gwen Brock, Randy Rydell, Larry Brawn, Carol Watson, Arden Chamberlin-Williams, Brian Fletcher, Pam Radcliff, Geoff Spellberg, Alyson Pytte, John Jekobsen, Paul Levenson, and Noah Siegel. Aside from nouvelle cuisine and old-fashioned camaraderie, they provided a fund of knowledge ranging from Spanish anarchism to Latvian political jokes. Were they equipped, I'm sure that Ibid, Akiba, and Bonkers would have said thanks too—for many a pat while I worked on this book.

Undergraduate students at San Francisco State University critiqued draft sections. Teams at San Francisco State and Stanford University conducted research for "The City" and "Urban Sociology" classes; some of their findings are included here. Student-researcher Suzanne Coshow used computer indexes to the max, with great enthusiasm. My greatest gratitude goes to Deborah Mosca, a crackerjack researcher and much more: tour guide through non-yet-mainstream ideas and finder of long-lost items.

Many helped by finding information or giving wise counsel. Roberta Tasley made sure I didn't detour off the information superhighway. Rich DeLeon suggested lines of thought on urban politics. Karen Paulsell helped navigate the WELL. Andreé Abecassis jogged my associative synapses. Barbara Cohen and Harvey Bragdon offered thoughts on city planning and mass media. Architect-artist Lisa Siegel Sullivan acted as design consultant and intellectual springboard. Painter Lisa Esherick gave me another perspective on urban life. Political sparring partner and standardbearer for standards, Boston-born Mary Lou FitzGerald reminded me of the strength of urban villages: "I come from a tribal society where autonomy is considered ingratitude."

I've never met Scott Simon, Bailey White, Andrei Codrescu, Terry Gross, Harry Shearer, John Hockenberry, or Ray Suarez, all former or current National Public Radio (NPR) reporters or storytellers. Nonetheless, their voices—full of compassion, intelligence, and wit—often inspired and informed me. They served as regular reminders of the urbane spirit.

Berkeleyites went far out of their way to be helpful. Particular thanks go to the reference librarians at the Berkeley Public Library.

The Oxford Street gang—Stan, Metece, Arlene, Rich, Tim, Geoff, Barbara—nurtured ideas. Amy Elaine and Kevin Carlton, Sara Teninty, and Courtney Kibiloski remind me of the urban future we must reclaim for all our children.

Abdulrachman Mohammed Babu has been my dear friend and soulmate across continents and time. He inspired me to open my mind to ideas, no matter how unpopular, and to develop a longer time line.

If there were a medal for support, caring, and endurance during peacetime, it would go to Ilona and Richard Kirby. They nourished my mind, clipping file, and stomach for many years.

My greatest appreciation goes to Tim Teninty, to whom this book is dedicated. His quirky intelligence, quarky humor, and practical skills sustained me. Not to mention that he does Windows. On to the next edition—can stoves be far behind?

# Contents

# PART I
# An Invitation
# to the City

Brack Brown

Oscar Graubner

# CHAPTER 1
# The Knowing Eye and Ear

Once upon a time, so the story goes, a prophet ran through the streets screaming, "We are doomed! In twenty-four hours our city will be flooded." Some people forgave their enemies, kissed their loved ones goodbye, and prepared to die. But others huddled together with a different idea. "Well," one woman said optimistically, "We've got twenty-four hours to learn how to live under water!"

This story suggests that how we respond to cities (and life in general) depends on what's *inside* our heads and hearts, as well as what's *outside* in the street. And how we judge our ability to triumph over flash floods or other urban uncertainties is probably rooted in unconscious mental habits, particularly hope or hopelessness, not logic alone.

If you close your eyes and think about the city, what do you visualize? Sleek skyscrapers? Great libraries and good food? New ideas and world-changing inventions? Walt Whitman's Brooklyn Bridge and Gustav Eiffel's tower? Rappers rhyming? Fans cheering for the home team? Trendy fashions and diverse pleasures? Or do you envision a bomb blast in Oklahoma City and a poison-gas attack in Tokyo? Short-tempered drivers honking in gridlock? People lining up at the soup kitchen? Heatless rooms with rats and roaches? Smells of Lysol and body sweat at homeless shelters? High schoolers hiding guns in the hallways? Chilling crimes and petty irritations? People sleeping, perhaps dying, on the snowy streets of Stockholm and St. Paul? Children living in tenements and tracts, dumpsters and vans? Or estates with signs threatening "Armed Response"?

Perhaps your vision encompasses *both* urban glories and dilemmas. Concerning the urban condition, you may vacillate among confusion, caution, cynicism, and confidence. Possibly, like the "Kids of the Baby Boom" in the Bellamy Brothers' country rock song, your "optimism mingles with the doom." One moment you may despair, thinking about dead radiators, random violence, ethnic tension, a growing gap between rich and poor, and the seeming lack of political vision for urban America—or urban anywhere. You may fear that the future holds a "jagged-glass pattern of city-states" (Kaplan, 1994:72) or nightmarish cityscapes in the style of *Blade Runner*'s (1982) Los Angeles. The next moment you may radiate joy at one of humankind's great inventions—the city—focusing on the enriching diversity of urban life, individuals who make a difference, and institutions that fulfill the promise of urban living.

Maybe you sympathize with E. B. White's quandary: "If the world were merely seductive, that would be easy. If it were merely challenging, that would be no problem. But I arise in the morning torn between a desire to improve the world, and a desire to enjoy the world. This makes it hard to plan the day."

Maybe you think about cities as writer John Gunther did. He once described New York City like this: "It has 22,000 soda fountains, and 11 tons of soot fall per square mile every month, which is why your face is dirty."

You may personally know forgotten neighborhoods—like Mott Haven in New York City's South Bronx—where a safe playground is harder to find than "crackling gunfire and early deaths" (Gonzalez and Dugger, 1991:1). Even if you have only read about such dangerous places, you may wonder, "What *can* I do about it?" Or, aware that crime, the economy, education, and controlling the spread of AIDS are chief public concerns (Kershner, 1993:1), you may ask, "What *should* I do about these issues?"

a

b

c

**Fig. 1.1** METROPOLITAN LIFE. Where else can you hug a bear, watch Uncle Sam play a musical saw, appreciate Robert Bechtle's painting, *'60 T-Bird*, buy sandals (or almost anything) at a street fair, find a Valentine's Day card, skateboard around the square (this one is in Toledo, Spain), and shop with your dog—if leashed (and in Paris)? ([*a*] Brack Brown; [*b*] Michael Schwartz; [*c, d, g*] Tim Teninty; [*e*] Ilona Lynn-Kirby; [*f*] Barbara Cohen)

Possibly you focus on more theoretical questions: How and why are U.S. cities today significantly different from cities of just a generation ago? Since the 1970s, how have economic and demographic changes—a shift from local factories to a global assembly line, a shift from manufacturing cars to processing information, and a massive population shift out of cities to larger metropolitan regions—affected U.S. urban politics and social life? What can people, working together, do to make cities healthier and more humane? How can people in a U.S. **metropolitan area,** say, greater New York City, cooperate with Muscovites and Lagosians to improve their mutual well-being?

You may ask whether it is even possible to make sense out of the changing urban world. After all, key borders that defined the post–Vietnam War era have fallen away: the bipolar distinction of "East" and "West" is gone. The boundaries of time and space are fuzzy, thanks to computers and such. The line between full-time, secure employment and full-time, temporary, insecure work is often crossed. And the once perceived Maginot line between "safe" suburbs and "unsafe" cities is shattered by grisly television images of shooting sprees, kidnap-murders, and other violent crimes committed beyond the city's limits.

Perhaps, just perhaps, by studying the city, we can begin to understand the larger world. As the *New York Times*'s architectural critic remarked,

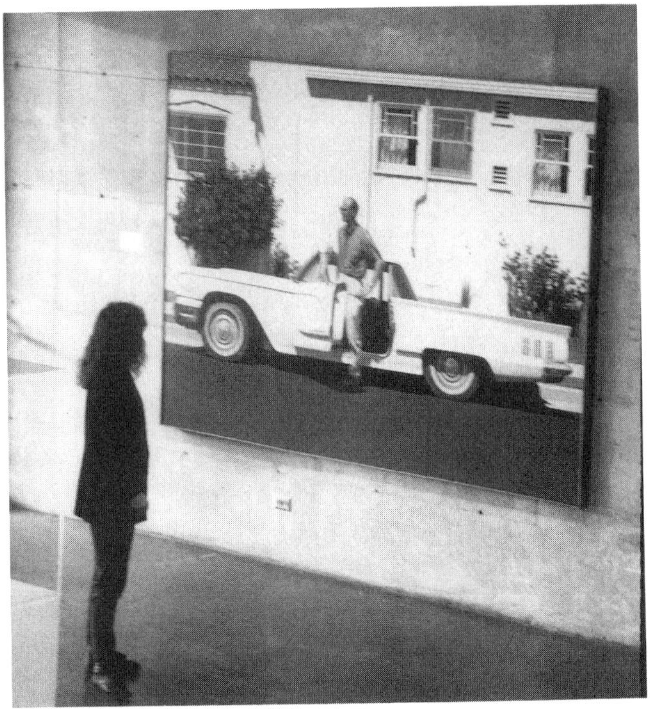

d

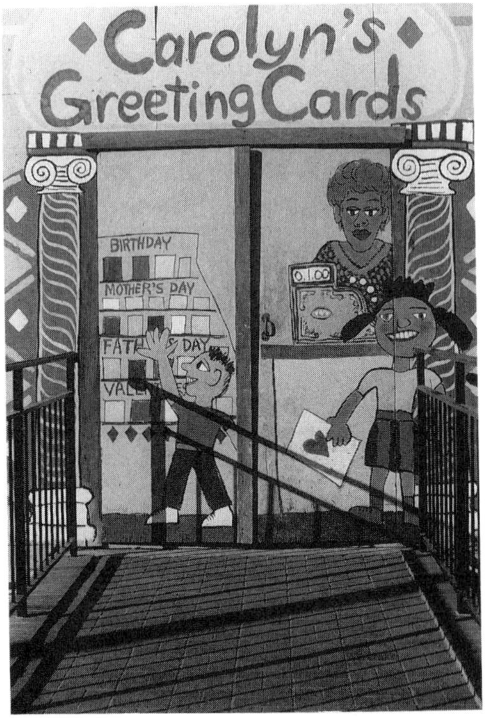


e

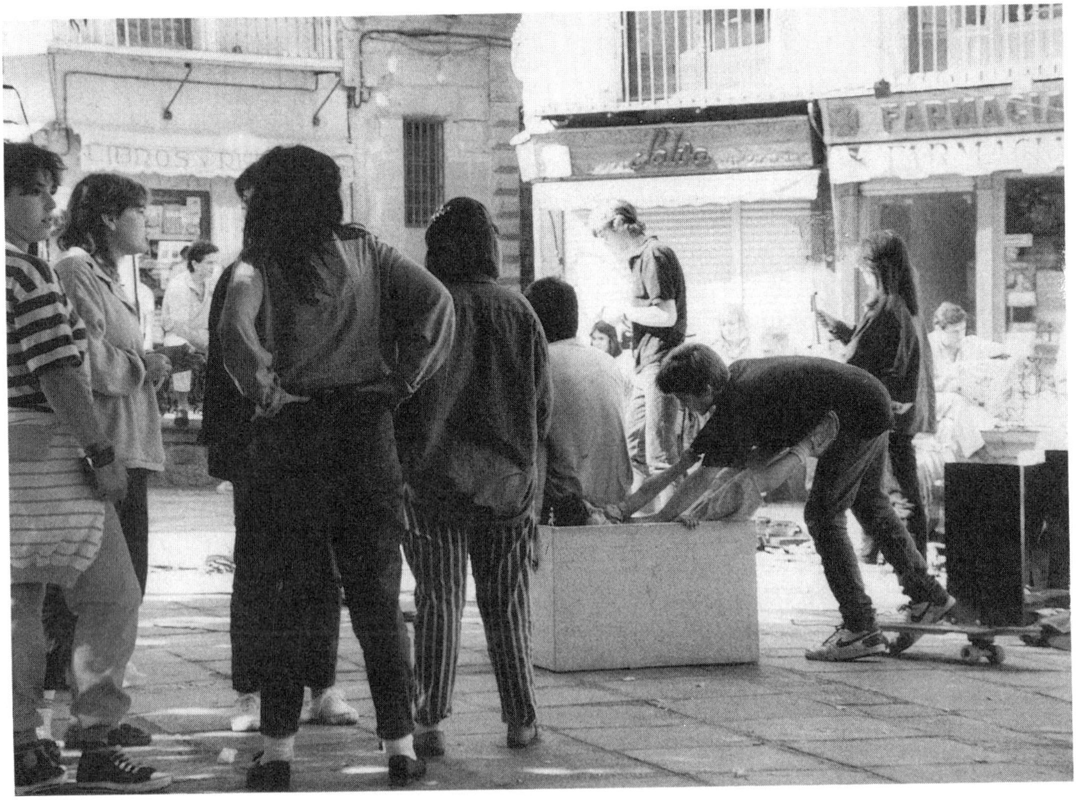

f

**Fig. 1.1** *(continued)*

g

"Anyone who walks down the streets of an American inner city can get a pretty good idea of the new world order. The mix of uses and populations, the porous borders surrounding neighborhoods, the interdependency of skills and services: the city is the most accessible model we have for understanding the shape of the world after the collapse of global bipolarity" (Muschamp, 1993:30).

## TWO PATHS TO UNDERSTANDING THE CITY

### "Acquaintance With" and "Knowledge About" Metropolitan Life

Until the mid-twentieth century, it was conventional wisdom that (1) personal experience and (2) abstract reflection offer two different ways of understanding the world (including cities and suburbs). Then, as insights from physics drifted into social science, this view—of two *totally separate* paths—was shown to be misleading. However, for purposes of discussion, let's first look at each path separately.

Firsthand experience gives **acquaintance with** the city. Direct and concrete, it depends on sense experience: sight, hearing, touch, taste, smell. This mode of understanding is intuitive, nonlinear, and holistic. Psychologists associate it with right-brain thinking.

On the other hand, **knowledge about** the city comes from abstract, logical thought. This mode of understanding is analytical, linear, and rational. It may be mathematical and highly theoretical. The "knowledge about" path to understanding is sequential, ordering information by breaking it down into component parts. Psychologists associate it with left-brain thinking.

Television news, novels, and art can make us feel *as if* we have experienced something ourselves. That is, images and words may *substitute for* personal experience, giving us "unexperienced experience" (Goethals, 1982:54). Word pictures and photographic images often transmit acquaintance with an urban scene: a sense of being there, an immediate emotional reaction. For instance, Jacob Riis's photo allows us to witness the life of poverty in New York City around 1890 (Figure 1.2). Even at one remove, the scene touches our feelings, and that was social reformer Riis's intent—to touch people's hearts, to make them understand emotionally *How the Other Half Lives* ([1890] 1971). More than 100 years later, the bleak underside of New York City remains; only the faces are different. (See Fred R. Conrad's 1991 photos.) Similarly, portraits of South American gold miners and Ethiopian peasants taken by former economist Sebastião Salgado are overwhelming in their ability to bear witness to *An Uncertain Grace* (1990), that is, human endurance and pride amid starvation and virtual serfdom.

In contrast, raw numbers don't tug at our heartstrings. Yet, they can provide a stepping stone to knowledge about cities. (Statistics alone do not give knowledge about cities or anything

**Fig. 1.2** ONE PATH TO KNOWLEDGE. A European immigrant coalheaver's windowless, cold cubicle on West Twenty-eighth Street in New York City around 1890. Danish-born social reformer and *New York Tribune* police reporter Jacob Riis's photos of poverty before the turn of the twentieth century, including this one, give viewers a firsthand acquaintance with New York City's tenement life. A century later, New York City remains a leading port of entry for poor newcomers, and Chinese immigrants live in similar circumstances on Baxter Street. Ironically, when the *Golden Venture,* a crowded freighter carrying a smuggled cargo of undocumented Chinese immigrants, ran aground in June 1993, it was beached near a Queens, New York, park named for Jacob Riis. (Library of Congress)

else; they remain to be *interpreted within theoretical frameworks.* We merely start with numbers. Then we look for relationships that help *explain* the numbers.)

Looking at the statistical data displayed in Table 1.1, we might ask why some cities lost or gained population in the 1980–1990 decade. The numbers themselves do not suggest any explanation. But we might have a hunch or two. Here's one hunch: poverty rates are higher in the population losers than in the gainers. And the hunch

is correct. For example, according to the 1990 census, Gary, Cleveland, Detroit, and Flint (big population losers) all had poverty rates over 28 percent, while Moreno Valley, Plano, Irvine, and Rancho Cucamonga had poverty rates under 9 percent.

To understand *why,* we must put numbers or "factoids" into theoretical frameworks. Here is one: large-scale (macro-level) processes affect population changes. These include the following: (1) *a population and power shift* from older in-

**Table 1.1** The Fastest-Growing U.S. Cities and the Biggest Population Losers, 1980–1990

| The Fastest-Growing Cities | | | | The Big Population Losers | | | |
|---|---|---|---|---|---|---|---|
| | 1980 | 1990 | % Change | | 1980 | 1990 | % Change |
| 1. Moreno Valley, Calif. | 28,309 | 118,779 | 319.6% | 1. Gary, Ind. | 151,968 | 116,646 | −23.2% |
| 2. Rancho Cucamonga, Calif. | 55,250 | 101,409 | 83.5% | 2. Newark, N.J. | 329,248 | 275,221 | −16.4% |
| 3. Plano, Tex. | 72,331 | 128,713 | 77.9% | 3. Detroit | 1,203,369 | 1,027,974 | −14.6% |
| 4. Irvine, Calif. | 62,134 | 110,330 | 77.6% | 4. Pittsburgh | 423,960 | 369,879 | −12.8% |
| 5. Mesa, Ariz. | 163,594 | 288,091 | 76.1% | 5. St. Louis | 452,804 | 396,879 | −12.4% |
| 6. Oceanside, Calif. | 76,698 | 128,398 | 76.1% | 6. Cleveland | 573,822 | 505,616 | −11.9% |
| 7. Santa Clarita, Calif. | 66,730 | 110,635 | 65.8% | 7. Flint, Mich. | 159,611 | 140,761 | −11.8% |

SOURCE: U.S. Census Bureau.

dustrial cities in the Northeast and Midwest to "suburban cities" in the Sunbelt; (2) *an economic-technological shift* in the United States from factory to service-information jobs, often called deindustrialization or massive plant shutdowns, and (3) *a production-consumption shift* from local and national markets to a global economy. Like higher math, these shifts cannot be seen, touched, heard, or grasped concretely. Testable, abstract statements—not personal knowledge—lead to knowledge about these cities' population changes.

Often poets and other artists touch our emotions in ways that statistical tables and abstract theory cannot. Supposedly, novelist John Steinbeck phrased it this way: "History tells us what happened, and fiction tells us how it felt." Such is the case with the photos of Riis and Salgado. Here is another: Nobel Prize winner Saul Bellow's ironic assessment of social mobility in the modern industrial city, excerpted from *The Adventures of Augie March*. It is the obituary of a real estate broker in Chicago, written by the broker's son. The son writes that his father

found Chicago a swamp and left it a great city. He came after the Great Fire [in 1871] said to be caused by Mrs. O'Leary's cow, in flight from the conscription of the Hapsburg tyrant, and in his life as a builder proved that great places do not have to be founded on the bones of slaves, like the pyramids of Pharaohs. . . . The lesson of an American life like my father's . . . is that achievements are compatible with decency. (Bellow, [1949] 1964:104)

Literary artists like Bellow give readers a sense of the richness of life, particularly through the use of detail. Readers feel that they are personally acquainted with the characters and their settings.

Of course, great artists do more than that. They go beyond portraying particular people in specific settings. They represent typical characters in typical situations, that is, general types. As one literary critic notes, "The goal for all great art is to provide a picture of reality in which the contradiction between appearance and reality, the particular and the general, the immediate and the conceptual, etc., is so resolved that the two converge . . . and provide a sense of an inseparable integrity" (Lukacs, 1971:34). Art, then, or great art, offers both personal acquaintance with and knowledge about a subject.

### Rethinking the Two Paths

Artists, philosophers, and scientists don't agree on the functions or procedures of art—or science. Yet, most now say that acquaintance with and knowledge about an object are inseparable. Some even deny the existence of objective reality altogether.

In the twentieth century, artists were among the first to question the notion of scientific objectivity. For example, Pablo Picasso's influential Cubist painting *Les Demoiselles d'Avignon* (*The*

a

**Fig. 1.3** MULTIPLE VIEWPOINTS. (*a*) In his cubist painting *Les Demoiselles d'Avignon* (begun May, reworked July 1907; oil on canvas, 8' × 7'8"), Pablo Picasso shows a new way of looking at "truth"—from multiple points of view. His artistic statement predated Heisenberg's uncertainty principle by nearly two decades. (Museum of Modern Art. Acquired through the Lillie P. Bliss Bequest.) (*b*) In her painting *Venus/Louvre* (1993), Lisa Esherick captures a related notion: that onlookers interpret the famous statue from multiple viewpoints. (John Friedman)

*Young Women of Avignon,* 1907), celebrates indeterminacy and multiple points of view, not certainty or objective reality (Figure 1.3a). Television's cult classic series *Star Trek* echoes this philosophy: the Trekkian theory of life is "Infinite Diversity in Infinite Combination (IDIC)."

Even photos, often assumed to be a clear reflection of reality, are IDIC in nature. As photographer Richard Avedon stated, "All photographs are accurate. None of them is the truth." In addition, photos change their meaning with every viewer; all photos are inherently ambigu-

b

ous, showing appearances without context. For example, when literary critic John Berger and photographer Jean Mohr (1982) showed a photo of a grinning assembly-line worker to various viewers, they got varied interpretations, including "He's happy the day is over" and "It makes me think of the prisoners in the German camps."

Many scholars and artists agree with Berger and Mohr's implicit point: the distinction between acquaintance with (subjective understand-

ing) and knowledge about (so-called objective understanding) is phony. Some argue that objectivity cannot exist; all knowledge is acquaintance with knowledge because every person participates in all acts of understanding in an individual way (e.g., Polanyi, 1958). Others, notably feminist social scientists (e.g., Millman and Kanter, 1975; Keller, 1980; Spender, 1982), say that the separation of subjectivity and objectivity is a "man-made" norm of mainstream/male-stream social science; they claim that a woman-centered theory of knowledge would narrow the gap between subject and object.

Deconstructionist literary critics go even further. They claim that no such thing as a "real world" exists. In their view, human beings inhabit an indeterminate universe where meaning is constantly shifting and thus unknowable. Founder Jacques Derrida (1986) and followers of Derrida's theory (or *dogma,* as opponents call it; see Lehman, 1991) believe that *everything depends on interpretation.* Their conclusion is that one interpretation is no more right or wrong than any other.

Interestingly, the literary deconstructionists repeat principles associated with the quantum physicist Werner Heisenberg: indeterminism and uncertainty. Essentially, the Heisenberg **uncertainty principle** says that it is impossible to know both the location and the momentum of a subatomic particle simultaneously: "Either the energy or its location is determinable at the expense of the other" (Wolf, [1988] 1990:44). Why is this principle of physics so important to literary critics as well as social scientists? Because it implies that (1) observers cannot eliminate themselves from what they observe, and (2) people can't observe reality without changing it. Thus, people cannot study the world *except* from a point of view (Zukav, 1979). If correct, this means that facts cannot be separated from values. It also means that neither scientific certainty nor objectivity is attainable. It means that there is no one way of conceptualizing reality, and that "scientific observations are . . . not value neutral" (Heelan, 1984:xii). In other words, scientists don't "tell it like it is"; they "tell it like they see it" (Von Glasserfeld in Barney, 1977:A13).

*To conclude:* Many thinkers now believe that uncertainty characterizes both science and art. Einstein's theory of relativity, Picasso's cubism and collages, and the New Physics's quantum mechanics call into question the very idea of a real world or objectivity. A historian summarizes this point of view:

Einstein and Heisenberg made it clear that mind and nature—subject and object—are involved in each other and not separate. . . . An objective world that can be "observed" and "understood" if only the imagination can be held in check simply does not exist. Facts are not observations "collected . . . on a wholesale scale" [as Charles Darwin held]. They are knots in a net. (Hardison, 1989:33)

In other words, human observers impose patterns and meaning onto facts.

Ironically, just as social scientists in the United States embraced precise observation and rigorous quantification (traditional research methods of the physical sciences), the physical sciences were leaving these methods behind for new ones that could deal with indeterminacy, irregularity, and unpredictability (the very qualities that many social scientists were trying to leave behind). In effect, there was "a methodological passing of ships in the night: The 'soft' sciences tried to become 'harder' just as the 'hard' sciences were becoming 'softer'" (Gaddis, 1992:A44). Still, many argue that the *ideal* of objective knowledge remains important. In this view, "objective-truth claims are too important, both politically and culturally . . . to give up" (Clifford in Coughlin, 1988:A8).

The debate over how we know what we know has engaged thinkers for at least 2,500 years. And like most questions worth asking, it will undoubtedly continue to be debated long past our lifetimes. Meanwhile, for **heuristic** purposes, we will draw the distinction between personal acquaintance with and knowledge about the world around us. In light of this distinction, let us examine a poem: Carl Sandburg's "Chicago." It may be folk art, not great art—that is a question for literary critics. But we can read it to see what and how it communicates to readers. Here is an excerpt from Sandburg's 1914 word picture of his adopted city:

HOG Butcher for the World,
Tool Maker, Stacker of Wheat,
Player with Railroads and the Nation's Freight
Handler;
Stormy, husky, brawling,
City of the Big Shoulders:
They tell me you are wicked and I believe them, for I
have seen your painted women under the gas
lamps luring the farm boys.

And they tell me you are crooked and I answer: Yes, it
    is true I have seen the gunman kill and go free to
    kill again.
And they tell me you are brutal and my reply is: On the
    faces of women and children I have seen the
    marks of wanton hunger.
And having answered so I turn once more to those who
    sneer at this my city, and I give them back the
    sneer and say to them:
Come and show me another city with lifted head sing-
    ing so proud to be alive and coarse and strong and
    cunning.
Flinging magnetic curses amid the toil of piling job on
    job, here is a tall bold slugger set vivid against the
    little soft cities. . . .

                          (in Williams, 1952:579)

Sandburg's strong images paint a two-sided face
of Chicago: vitality and brutality. A proud,
strong, cunning and crooked, hungry, wicked
city.

Aside from communicating the feel of an industrial city on the move, Sandburg's poem offers insight into the services that Chicago performs: "HOG Butcher for the World," "Tool
Maker, Stacker of Wheat," and "Player with Railroads and the Nation's Freight Handler." Compare that list with a more systematic classification of city functions by Harris and Ullman
(1945). According to these geographers, there are
three different kinds of industrial cities, although
one city may perform all three functions: (1) central place cities—performing central services,
such as retail trade, for their surrounding area;
(2) transport cities—including railroad centers
and ports; and (3) specialized function cities—
performing one particular service, such as mining or meat packing. From the first three lines of
Sandburg's poem, we know that Chicago is (or
rather, was) a city that performs all three functions: (1) central place—"Tool Maker, Stacker of
Wheat"; (2) transport—"the Nation's Freight
Handler"; and (3) specialized function—"HOG
Butcher for the World." Thus, the kind of city
Chicago was can be derived from Sandburg's
poem, as well as from the Harris and Ullman
classification scheme.

Writers, artists, and social scientists often communicate similar messages but use different

methods and styles. The awareness of industrial
city life is more intimate and direct in Sandburg's
poetic vision than in the geographers' scheme.
As a Chicagoan of Sandburg's era, sociologist
Robert E. Park, said in his classic essay on the city
in 1916: "We are mainly indebted to writers of
fiction for our more intimate knowledge of contemporary urban life" (1974:3). Park continued,
however, that urban life "demands a more searching and disinterested study"—a marriage of personal acquaintance with and knowledge about
the city. And that is what Park and the distinguished urban-oriented scholars at the University of Chicago proposed to do in 1916.

## UNDERSTANDING CHICAGO IN ITS HEYDAY, 1890s–1920s

### Using Social Science and Literature as Paths to Knowledge

To novelist Nelson Algren, Chicago is the

most native of American cities, where the chrome-
colored convertible cuts through the traffic ahead of
the Polish peddler's pushcart. And the long, low-
lighted parlor-cars stroke past in a single, even yellow
flow. . . . Big-shot town, small-shot town, jet-propelled
old-fashioned town, by old-world hands with new-
world tools built into a place whose heartbeat carries
farther than its shout. ([1952] 1961:59–60)

Around the time that Park and his University
of Chicago colleagues were studying the city
scientifically—using Chicago as their sociological laboratory—a world literature was being produced in the Windy City. From the beginning of
this century until roughly 1920, Chicago produced writers the same way it had created the
nation's first skyscrapers in the 1880s. Writers
became so numerous in Chicago in the period
1900–1920 that literary critic H. L. Mencken observed that it had nearly taken over the entire
field of American letters. Why was Chicago like a
magnet, attracting writers speaking with a new

**Fig. 1.4** SANDBURG'S CHICAGO. (*a*) The intense energy that characterized Chicago in 1905 is reflected in its street life. This photo was taken at State and Madison Streets, said to be the busiest streetcorner in the world at the time. Note Louis Sullivan's skyscraper, later the Carson Pirie & Scott Company, at the right; Sullivan's Art Nouveau decoration frames the store's display windows. It has been called one of the great works of modern commercial architecture. (*b*) Chicago's five-term mayor, Carter H. Harrison II (whose father also served five terms as mayor), was considered incorruptible, despite the widespread city corruption of his day by financiers such as Charles T. Yerkes (immortalized as *The Financier* and *The Titan* in Dreiser's novels). About himself, Mayor Harrison said, "Chicago is fortunate in having a mayor who keeps his hands in his own pockets." (Chicago Historical Society)

American voice? Why was Chicago also an architect's dream town, with Louis Sullivan's skyscrapers and Frank Lloyd Wright's prairie houses? And why was Chicago a social scientist's town, a lab for urban research? For many of the same reasons.

Nelson Algren suggests that Chicago's great literary scene did not happen accidentally: "Chicago is the . . . city in which a literature bred by hard times . . . once became a world literature. . . . For it was here that those arrangements more convenient to owners of property than to the propertyless were most persistently contested by the American conscience" ([1952] 1961:12–13). "Those arrangements more convenient to owners of property" had been contested even before the turn of the century. Indeed, Chicago was a center of industry and industrial conflict by the 1870s.

## Labor Radicalism, Industrial Progress, and Social Reform

Several events before 1900 give a feel for the conflicting currents in Chicago. First, there was the railroad strike in 1877, which prepared fertile ground for socialist and anarchist organizers among the workers.

Second, there was the Haymarket Square affair in 1886. This was a labor meeting in Haymarket Square, called to protest police violence against locked-out employees at the Cyrus McCormick Harvester Works. As Box 1.1 details, it ended when an unknown person or persons threw a bomb into the crowd. The Haymarket Square affair, according to one urban historian, "symbolized an era in American history; it dramatized the determination of the business interests to maintain the status quo" (Spear, 1967:3).

Third, there was the Chicago World's Fair— the Columbian Exposition—in 1893. Led by the famous architect and planner Daniel Burnham (remembered by his credo, "Make no little plans. They have no magic to stir men's blood."), a group of architects, promoters, and planners constructed a White City, part of the City Beautiful, on Chicago's South Side. It was a monument to industrial progress, showing off the technology that was making the United States a world economic power. An estimated 27 million visitors came from all over the world to see the exposition's midway, the world's first Ferris wheel, and the Woman's Building (designed by a woman, managed by women, and featuring thousands of exhibits exclusively by women). Visitors also slurped one ancestor of fast food: ice cream. This mass-produced, affordable edible became an important treat for workers, and the World's Fair was "an ideal marketing ground" for ice cream (Binford, 1987:9).

Fourth, there was the Pullman railroad strike in 1894. The strike shut down the nation's railroads and brought federal troops to the city. Railroad magnate George Pullman had constructed a model industrial town for his workers just south of Chicago; the privately owned company town was a totally planned community, with decent housing for the workers, attractive shopping arcades, a library, and a hotel. But no matter how lovely the parklike setting and the amenities for workers in Pullman's town, it was still Pullman's town. His ownership and control carried the seeds of industrial conflict, not peace.

And finally, there was a variety of efforts aimed at social reform. These ranged from Jane Addams's work at Hull House on the West Side to attempts to reform City Hall and improve sanitary conditions in the slums, led by local merchants and their wives.

All of this—industrial conflict, attempts at reform, monuments to "progress" and technology —was taking place in the world's fastest-growing metropolis of the era: Chicago. And all of this so shortly after Mrs. O'Leary's cow had allegedly started the 1871 fire that ravaged one-third of the city.

In its heyday, Chicago was many things to many people. It had the reputation of being the most politically radical of all American cities. Among others, it was the town of socialist Eugene V. Debs and Big Bill Haywood, leader of the Wobblies, the Industrial Workers of the World (Box 1.1).

Box 1.1

## CHICAGO'S "OFFICIAL HISTORY"

HAYMARKET RIOT

ON MAY 4, 1886, HUNDREDS OF WORKERS GATHERED HERE TO PROTEST POLICE ACTION OF THE PREVIOUS DAY AGAINST STRIKERS ENGAGED IN A NATIONWIDE CAMPAIGN FOR AN EIGHT-HOUR WORKDAY. RADICALS ADDRESSED THE CROWD. WHEN POLICE ATTEMPTED TO DISPERSE THE RALLY, SOMEONE THREW A BOMB. THE BOMB AND ENSUING PISTOL SHOTS KILLED SEVEN POLICEMEN AND FOUR OTHER PERSONS. ALTHOUGH NO EVIDENCE LINKED ANY RADICALS TO THE BOMB, EIGHT OF THEM WERE CONVICTED AND FOUR HANGED. THREE WERE LATER PARDONED. THE STRIKE COLLAPSED AFTER THE TRAGEDY.

ERECTED BY ILLINOIS LABOR HISTORY SOCIETY AND THE ILLINOIS STATE HISTORICAL SOCIETY, 1972

Haymarket Plaque, placed on a building at the corner of Desplaines and Randolph Streets in 1971. It reads:

On May 4, 1886, hundreds of workers gathered here to protest police action of the previous day against strikers engaged in a nationwide campaign for an eight-hour workday. Radicals addressed the crowd. When police attempted to disperse the rally, someone threw a bomb. The bomb and ensuing pistol shots killed seven policemen and four other persons. Although no evidence linked any radicals to the bomb, eight of them were convicted and four hanged. Three were later pardoned. The strike collapsed after the tragedy.

### What Schoolchildren Learned About Their City

What an elementary school textbook writer chooses to include—and exclude—gives clues to the "official" version of history at a particular time. Thus, examining the content of a grammar school history book can be most instructive. One widely used elementary text in the 1910s and 1920s was Jennie Hall's *The Story of Chicago*, published in 1911 and revised in 1929. Interestingly, this text, distributed to schools by the Chicago Board of Education, contains no mention of certain facets of the city's history: political corruption,

labor history, industrial conflict, or ethnic prejudice and discrimination. One does find Haymarket Square, complete with a line drawing of its hustle-bustle, but the incident that immortalized it—the Haymarket Square affair in 1886—goes unmentioned. Here is what Chicago schoolchildren learned about its function: "There is another place in Chicago besides the market on 14th Street where vegetables are sold. It is Haymarket Square on the west side. . . . Haymarket tells you a story of the many truck gardens near this great city" (250). Yes, but Haymarket, of course, symbolizes quite another story. Indeed, Haymarket was "the great social drama of the era" (Avrich, 1984).

Somewhat ironically, Hall (a teacher at one of Chicago's elite private schools) hoped that her book would be "a finger pointing to real material for study" (303). What is "real material," however, is usually a matter of some controversy. In the following excerpt from *The Story of Chicago*, note particularly how the text handles the problems of the city and the proposed solutions. Compare Hall's "official" textbook version of history to the unofficial competing vision for the Industrial Workers of the World. Clearly, their views of reality do not coincide.

Why did Chicago, built in a swampy wilderness, become a great city? Where will a large city grow up? There must be people living about with things to sell. Good land roads or water roads must lead to her. . . . [In Chicago] land travel met lake travel. That is why we are a railroad center. That is why cattle are brought here. . . . That is why grain comes here. . . . All these industries bring workers. These people need stores, theatres, churches, schools. . . . So the city keeps adding to itself. Soon it comes to need officers to take care of it and its people—mayor, policemen, firemen, board of health, street commissioners. Then it gets into trouble because it is so big. In some places its houses are so close together that people get no sunshine and children no place to play. Some of its tenements are too crowded. The air is smoky from factories. Many of the people are poor. The city need try no more to be large and rich. But it must try to be clean and comfortable and happy. That is the great problem now, and there is much work to be done in solving it. There are many fine public schools in Chicago. . . . Americanization schools help the foreigner to become a good citizen. . . . But there is still much to be done in making the schools as useful to all as they can be. People must be taught to make even better use of . . . the public libraries and the Art Institute. . . . (Hall, [1911]1929:261–264, 287–288)

### What Some People Were Singing About

The Industrial Workers of the World (IWW), nick-named the "Wobblies," were organized in Chicago in 1905. Their goal was to organize unskilled workers in the factories and fields throughout the nation. They focused their efforts on groups considered to be dis-possessed and downtrodden, including textile mill workers in the Northeast, coal and iron miners in West Virginia and Minnesota, migrant workers, and North-west lumberjacks. "Sing and fight" was a Wobblie slo-gan. Many organizers shaped their protests into songs as tools for agitation. About 1909, the first edition of their "Little Red Song Book" appeared, with its cover announcing: "IWW Songs—to Fan the Flames of Dis-content." The most popular union song in the United States, "Solidarity Forever," was written by Wobblie organizer Ralph Chaplin after his return from a coal miners' strike near Charleston, West Virginia, in 1915. Sung to the tune of "John Brown's Body," the song is full of revolutionary fervor. One stanza reveals the Wobblies' view of the new industrial order—class struggle—in which people are divided into two camps: THEM (owners of mines and factories, the capitalists) and US (the exploited workers):

They have taken untold millions that they never toiled to earn,
But without our brain and muscle not a single wheel could turn.

We can break their haughty power, gain our freedom when we learn
That the union makes us strong.

Wobblie organizer Joe Hill was one of the IWW's best songwriters, as well as a leading agitator. In 1914, Hill was arrested in Salt Lake City on a murder charge and executed there. The day before his execution in 1915, he sent IWW head Big Bill Haywood a wire in Chicago: "Don't waste time mourning. Organize." Joe Hill's body was brought to Chicago, where a great funeral procession was held. One of the songs sung by the approximately 30,000 sympathizers was Ralph Chaplin's "The Commonwealth of Toil" (in Fowke and Glazer, [1960] 1961:14–16). Here is the first verse and the chorus:

In the gloom of mighty cities,
Midst the roar of whirling wheels,
We are toiling on like chattel slaves of old,
And our masters hope to keep us
Ever thus beneath their heels,
And to coin our very life blood into gold.

CHORUS
But we have a glowing dream
Of how fair the world will seem
When each man can live his life secure and free;
When the earth is owned by labor
And there's joy and peace for all
In the Commonwealth of Toil that is to be.

## Urban Researchers and Writers: Convergent Goals

The "City of the Big Shoulders" was the cradle of urban research in the United States for many of the same reasons that made Chicago the most stimulating literary scene of its day. As writer Algren put it, it was in Chicago that challenges were made to the existing economic and social arrangements by "a conscience in touch with hu-manity." Social scientists at the University of Chicago who pioneered urban research were an important part of that conscience.

As two University of Chicago sociologists later recalled about this period:

By the time our studies began, the various ethnic neighborhoods were well established. . . . By this time, too, public sentiment had crystallized into rather firm prejudice and discrimination against the new arrivals from Eastern Europe and Southern Europe. . . . Land-lords were taking advantage of the crowded housing situation. . . . The city administration was commonly regarded as corrupt. . . . Many families were desper-ately poor. (Burgess and Bogue, 1964:5)

Sociologists tried to understand the social and economic forces at work in the slums and their effect on slum dwellers. Their objective was sci-entific analysis. But their hope was a moral one, and it was policy oriented: "To dispel prejudice and injustice" and to help change the plight of the slum dwellers.

The numerous poets and novelists inspired or formed by the Chicago scene didn't aim for scientific analysis. Yet, they shared the social scientists' goal: to dispel prejudice and injustice. Here are a few injustices exposed by Chicago's literati. There was the injustice of grain speculators in Chicago's wheat market, exposed by Frank Norris. Norris's *The Pit* ([1903] 1970:41) paints Chicago's Board of Trade building, the global center of the wheat trade, in dark colors: "black, monolithic, crouching on its foundations like a monstrous sphinx with blind eyes, silent, grave."

There was political corruption, exposed by novelist Theodore Dreiser. The story of financier Charles T. Yerkes's buying and selling of Chicago—by corrupting city officials—is told in Dreiser's *The Financier* (1912) and *The Titan* (1914). There were the savage practices at the Union Stockyards, the place that made Chicago "HOG butcher for the World." Socialist Upton Sinclair exposed the unsanitary conditions and adulteration of food at the nation's stockyards in the greatest muckraking novel of all, *The Jungle* (1905). This exposé had public policy impact, too, influencing the passage of the Pure Food and Drug Act by Congress (Box 1.2).

Chicago's urban literature ranged in tone from reformist muckraking to socialist outrage. Some described what they saw as "capitalist decay" and the oppression of the many by the few. Like West Coast writer Jack London, Upton Sinclair saw the evils of capitalism in the new industrial order, represented by Chicago. Sinclair measured what was against what could be in his ideal society under socialism. By contrast, Theodore Dreiser accepted the new industrial order and its corruption as the American destiny, as natural.

There was also a bit of nostalgia for less complex times. Some novelists idealized the Jeffersonian ideal of the small town. Big-city life was sometimes viewed as destructive of human and humane values.

And there was the realization that industrial cities encouraged new standards of behavior. One new norm concerned women. Typically, nineteenth-century fictional heroines were weak and faint-hearted, dressed either in rags or regal gowns. But some Chicago novelists (e.g., Fuller, 1895) understood that such traditional heroines had no place in the city; the new city woman was stronger and more independent, resembling social reformer Jane Addams (the founder of Chicago's Hull House) more than a shrinking violet.

In general, then, writers reacted in two different ways to Chicago and the new republic for which it stood. Some looked backward and oth-

---

Box 1.2

## POLITICS AND THE NOVEL

### The Impact of Upton Sinclair's The Jungle

In *The Jungle* (1905), Sinclair tells the tragic story of Jurgis Rudkus, a Lithuanian immigrant, and his relatives and friends who work at the Union Stockyards and live nearby, in the "back of the yards" neighborhood. There, in what Sinclair called Packingtown, immigrants were victimized by those who had control or influence over them: landlords, real estate brokers, meatpacking bosses, supervisors, and political bosses. Sinclair paints a dreary picture of crushed lives under these conditions. In the end, Rudkus turns to socialism as the only hope for a decent life.

Ironically, very few pages of Sinclair's novel are de-voted to the brutality and smell of the stockyards. But that is what caught the public eye—and stomach. Sinclair's purpose was much broader: to expose what he considered the evils of capitalism, especially "wage slavery," and to make an appeal for socialism. But, as he said of his own work, "I aimed at the public's heart and by accident I hit it in the stomach."

*The Jungle* had immediate political impact, but not what Sinclair had hoped for. President Theodore Roosevelt, who had seen an advance copy of the book, wired Sinclair to visit him in Washington, D.C., to talk about stockyard conditions. Six months later, over violent opposition by the meatpacking industry, the Pure Food and Drug Act and the Beef Inspection Act were passed by Congress.

ers looked forward. Novelists of the Progressive Era (1904–1917) "based their values either on the traditional individualism and amenity of an agricultural and small owner's way of life (which was the ideal of the Progressive movement), or on . . . Socialism" (Kazin, [1942] 1956: 64–65).

Urban research started by the Chicago sociologists, beginning in the Progressive Era, arose from the same mix of responses to the new industrial order. Robert Park, for instance, had nostalgia for the small town in Minnesota where he grew up. At the same time, Park was deeply ambivalent about the limitations of small-town life and the sense of community it supposedly offered. Before teaching at the University of Chicago, he had been a reformist-minded news reporter in the Midwest and publicity person for Booker T. Washington's Tuskegee Institute. Park's colleague, Ernest W. Burgess (who constructed a classic model of urban space, shown in

Chapter 2), was concerned with what he assumed to be a result of urban-industrial life: social disorganization—indicated by crime, delinquency, family breakdown, and so forth.

### The City Beautiful

Urban research . . . social reform . . . big novels. All responses to Chicago, "the capital of the frontier world of acquisitive energy" (Kazin, [1942] 1956:94) and the pulse of the heartland. But what about other professionals and interested parties— how did they react to the expanding industrial city?

Chicago's business executives focused their energy on promoting the city's industrial development and facilitating suburbanization. City planners concentrated their efforts on making the city more beautiful (Figure 1.5).

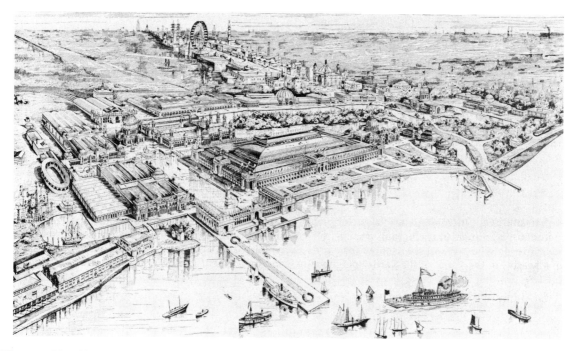

**Fig. 1.5**  BIRD'S-EYE VIEW OF THE CHICAGO WORLD'S FAIR, 1893. The monumental neoclassical architecture of the Columbian Exposition (critics called it a "White City of wedding-cake buildings") inspired the City Beautiful movement throughout America. (Hubert Howe Bancroft, *The Book of the Fair* [Chicago, 1893], p. 71)

It was in the Chicago Plan that the expertise and ideas of planner extraordinaire Daniel Burnham came together with the interests of Chicago's business leaders. Labeling his idea the "**City Beautiful**," Burnham persuaded the influential Chicago Commercial Club to back the Chicago Plan of 1909: a giant, even superhuman-scale, city plan. Burnham's idea was to create romantic parks and lovely waterfront landscapes by Lake Michigan with huge plazas and broad thoroughfares. This was to serve as a contrast to city life. According to Burnham:

Natural scenery furnishes the contrasting element to the artificiality of the city. *All of us should often run away . . . into the wilds, where mind and body are restored to a normal condition,* and we are enabled to take up the burden of life in our crowded streets and endless stretches of buildings with renewed vigor and hopefulness. (Burnham and Bennett in Glaab and Brown, 1983:263; italics mine)

Clearly, Burnham thought the city was a place to escape from.

Interestingly, the Chicago Plan hardly mentioned the "burden of life" on those who carried more than their measure: the urban poor. As the University of Chicago researchers and the novelists had well noted, by 1909 parts of Chicago were one immense slum, housing new immigrants from Eastern and Southern Europe in crowded, overpriced, deteriorated tenements. But only two short paragraphs of Burnham's Chicago Plan are devoted to the problems of the widespread slums. And what were the suggested solutions? The plan, in familiar-sounding language, suggested two ways of dealing with what it termed the "unwholesome district": (1) cutting broad boulevards through it and (2) enforcing sanitation and cleanliness codes.

So, Chicago became a proving ground for Burnham's City Beautiful concept: that cities could be improved physically without any restructuring of economic, social, or political institutions. Most of the improvements that Burnham counseled, aside from the glorious parks for people wishing to flee the city, were meant to spur commerce and industry. For instance, Mich-

igan Avenue and other streets were to be widened to facilitate downtown traffic. "No wonder," writes one of Chicago's biographers, "the cry went up that the Chicago Plan was in reality a scheme to tax the poor for improvements desired by the rich" (Lowe, 1978:173–174).

The Chicago Plan emphasized civic beauty, for Burnham was convinced that human nature craved beauty so much that "people will travel far to find and enjoy it." This vision of human nature and what people need to lead healthy, fulfilling urban lives was distinctly different from what Chicago's novelists and urban researchers believed.

The City Beautiful. The squalor of the slums. Industrial progress and poverty. Chicago was all of these. And it was a poet—Carl Sandburg—who perhaps best captured the promise and the problems of the city. In "Chicago" and other poems, Sandburg drew an image of the Windy City as a wondrous thing, a bold human enterprise. Yet Chicago, this new city, this representative of the new industrial order, corrupts what he considered human emotions. That is, in the shuffle for the almighty dollar and industrial development, Sandburg feared that friendship, mutual caring, and human dignity were lost amid the skyscrapers and the steel.

## Chicago: Microcosm of the New Industrial Order

Sandburg's view of Chicago—and, more broadly, urban industrial capitalist society—echoes the theories put forward by many nineteenth-century social theorists about urban life. And his views resound in the work of the Chicago school of sociology. As detailed in Chapter 5, the University of Chicago urban theorist Louis Wirth viewed "Urbanism as a Way of Life"; several of Wirth's key ideas parallel Sandburg's poetic images.

Alienation. Rootlessness. Superficial relationships. The loss of human connections. Materialism. Money instead of personal relations as the bond of association among people. These were what poet Sandburg and theorist Wirth saw as the price to be paid for living in the modern industrial American city. At the same time, both noted the energy, the greater mobility, and the increased individual freedom that the new industrial city promised. Such were the contradictions in Chicago and in the new American industrial order that Chicago symbolized. Using ideas or images, Chicago's urbanists, poets, political organizers, and novelists alerted their different audiences to the promise and conditions of urban life.

*To summarize:* Chicago's writers and urbanists responded to the new industrial order that Chicago represented. Both described new phenomena, whether in the form of personal images that communicated a firsthand acquaintance with the city or in the form of abstract maps and models. Rooted in the same historical climate, their insights often ran parallel. Some theorists, like Park, had a nostalgic affection for small-town, agricultural communities; they worried about the loss of the sense of community in a big industrial city. Others, like Upton Sinclair, described similar urban conditions but saw the causes of urban problems as part of the economic and social arrangements under capitalism.

These differences in vision remain to this day. So do controversies about civic beauty and about what urbanites need to thrive. This brings us to another poem by Carl Sandburg, "Elephants Are Different to Different People":

Wilson and Pilcer and Snack stood before
  the zoo elephant.
Wilson said, "What is its name? Is it from
  Asia or
Africa? Who feeds it? Is it a he or a she?
How
old is it? Do they have twins? How much
  does it cost
to feed? How much does it weigh? If it
  dies how much
will another one cost? If it dies what will
  they use
the bones, the fat, and the hide for? What
  use is it
besides to look at?"
Pilcer didn't have any questions; he was murmuring

to himself, "It's a house by itself, walls and
  windows,
the ears came from tall cornfields, by God;
  the
architect of those legs was a workman, by
  God; he stands like a bridge out across
  deep water; the face
is sad and the eyes are kind; I know elephants are
good to babies."
Snack looked up and down and at last said
  to
himself, "He's a tough son-of-a-gun outside and
I'll bet he's got a strong heart, I'll bet he's
strong as a copper-riveted boiler inside."
They didn't put up any arguments.
They didn't throw anything in each other's
  faces.
Three men saw the elephant three ways
And let it go at that.
They didn't spoil a sunny Sunday afternoon.
"Sunday comes only once a week," they
  told each other. (1970:628–629)

Our aim is to see the elephant (in this case, the city) in more than three ways—and *not* let it go at that. Wide-angle vision and spirited debate, not sweeping controversy under the rug for the sake of a sunny Sunday afternoon, are essential if we want to reclaim the promise of the city and to deal effectively with urban conditions.

Thus, this book is not full of definitive answers or solutions. Nor is it a tract for a particular point of view. Rather, it is an invitation to open your eyes, ears, heart, and mind to experiencing and reflecting upon the city. I hope to provide tools that will assist you in deciding whether Wilson, Pilcer, or Snack sees the beast most clearly—or whether they all suffer from tunnel vision.

## KEY TERMS

**Acquaintance with**  Personal, direct, intuitive, holistic, nonlinear, concrete, subjective knowledge. Contrast: **knowledge about.**

**City Beautiful**  A movement inspired by architect–

a

**Fig. 1.6**   WALLS THAT TELL STORIES. (*a*) Victor Arnautoff's *City Life* is one of the 1930s federal arts project frescos in Coit Tower, San Francisco. (*b*) Brooke Fancher's mural, *Tuzuri Watu/We Are a Beautiful People* (1987), also in San Francisco, celebrates African-American culture, particularly women writers. ([*a*] Tim Teninty; [*b*] Deborah Mosca)

city planner Daniel Burnham around the turn of the twentieth century. City Beautiful planners believed that people needed to escape from the burden of city life to natural surroundings, such as large parks, and that cities could be improved physically without restructuring basic institutions.

**Heuristic**   A model, assumption, or device that is not necessarily scientifically true but is a useful tool to aid in the discovery of new relationships. For example, classifying people as urbanites or rural dwellers is a heuristic device that assumes that urbanites share common traits in contrast to rural people.

**Knowledge about**   Systematic, abstract, linear, theoretical knowledge.

**Metropolitan area**   A concentrated, dense settlement of people in a core city together with the city's suburban population who are economically and socially interdependent The U.S. Census Bureau uses specific criteria of population size and economic interdependence to define metropolitan areas, as detailed in Chapter 6. Opposite: *nonmetropolitan area.*

**Uncertainty principle**   German physicist Werner Heisenberg's principle: observers cannot know both the position and the momentum of a moving electron with absolute certainty. Interpreted by many scholars to mean that objectivity in doing physical or social science is impossible.

b

## PROJECTS

1. **Understanding the city through social science and art.** Compare the treatment of one U.S. city by artists and social scientists. Taking Los Angeles, for example, what impressions does one get from various films, such as *Boyz 'N the Hood* (1991), *Blue Thunder* (1983), *The Player* (1992), *Welcome to L.A.* (1976), and the movie version of Nathanael West's novel *The Day of the Locust* (1975)? What impressions does one get from looking at statistical data on Los Angeles (e.g., U.S. Census Bureau data, information from realtors, news coverage) related to subjects treated in the artistic works?

2. **An eye-ear tour of one city.** Walk around a city with a notebook, camera, and tape recorder, recording the city's soundscape. Are some areas noisier than others? What sounds typify different neighborhoods? For example, are children's voices everywhere? Are street sellers or knife sharpeners calling out their services in any areas?) Also, note the landscape: What are the city's most imposing buildings, and what functions are performed in them? Are church spires, factory smokestacks, or office buildings the tallest structures? What do bulletin boards and signs advertise? If street murals exist, what do they portray?

3. **Varieties of experience.** This is a group project (for three to five teammates). Together, choose any two- to four-block area of a city or suburb. Then, separately, walk around the area, taking photos and / or writing down observations at different times of the day. Compare your impressions. Did you experience the area in the same way? If not, what might account for the differences?

## SUGGESTIONS FOR FURTHER LEARNING

The tendency in American thought and literature to romanticize rural and small-town life and denigrate urban life is detailed in Morton White and Lucia White's *The Intellectual Versus the City: From Thomas Jefferson to Frank Lloyd Wright* (New York: Mentor, 1964). For an opposite view, that "civilization in the United States survives only in the big cities," see H. L. Mencken, *The Vintage Mencken*, ed. Alistair Cooke (New York: Vintage, 1956).

Works of art that take cities as their settings or subjects are too numerous to mention. Examples that show the range of popular films include the late Willard Van Dyke's early documentary film *The City* (1939), with narration by the late Lewis Mumford; it romanticizes the New England small town, focuses on the lack of humanity in big industrial cities, and calls for new greenbelt communities; Fritz Lang's classic feature film *Metropolis* (1927), whose setting is a robotlike underground city composed of workers and an affluent overground city composed of their bosses; Charlie Chaplin's *City Lights* (1931), a tale of any city (the plot turns on a meeting between the Little Tramp and a millionaire); and *Batman* (1989), which creates "Gotham City," a place of ominous opulence. The novels of small-town America include Sinclair Lewis's *Main Street* (New York: Harcourt, Brace, 1920), set in Sauk Centre, Minnesota, and Sherwood Anderson's *Winesburg, Ohio* (New York: Modern Library, 1947) (in actuality, his hometown of Clyde, Ohio, near Toledo). Both Lewis and Anderson deromanticized small-town life.

Saul Bellow's *The Adventures of Augie March* (New York: Viking, [1949] 1964), James Farrell's *Studs Lonigan* (New York: Modern Library, 1938) trilogy, and Richard Wright's *Native Son* (New York: Signet, 1940) give different views of Chicago life in the post–World War I era. In *The Moviegoer* (New York: Popular Library, 1962), Walker Percy captures what he calls "the genie-soul" of the city:

here is Chicago . . . the buildings are heavy and squarish and set down far apart and at random like monuments on a great windy plain. And the Lake. . . . Here the Lake is the North itself: a perilous place from which the spirit winds come pouring forth all roused up and crying out alarm. . . . This is a city where no one dares dispute the claim of the wind and the skyey space to the out-of-doors. This Midwestern sky is the nakedest, loneliest sky in America. To escape it, people live inside and underground.

Novelist James Baldwin gives another view of the city—the black ghetto of New York's Harlem in *Go Tell It on the Mountain* (New York: Dell, 1952).

Chicago's urban beginnings are the subject of William Cronon's *Nature's Metropolis: Chicago and the Great West* (New York: Norton, 1991). Cronon argues that the Chicago is best understood in an ecological context: the opening of the Great West from the Appalachians to the Rockies. In his view, Chicago's drive for markets and resources helped to create an integrated city–country system that transformed the U.S. landscape. Describing one environmental impact of Chicago's influence, he writes that animals' lives were "redistributed across regional space": livestock were "born in one place, fattened in another, and killed in still a third."

English professor Carla Cappetti describes Chicago's role as a lab for both novelists and sociologists in *Writing Chicago: Modernism, Ethnography, and the Novel* (New York: Columbia University Press, 1993). Commenting on the connection between fiction and social science, she says that "James T. Farrell, Nelson Algren, and Richard Wright not only explored but kept alive the radical possibilities embedded in the discipline of sociology" (16).

Alienation and dehumanization in the modern city is a continuing theme in the drawings collected in Harold Rosenberg's *Saul Steinberg* (New York: Knopf, 1978). But in the paintings of Ralph Fasanella, the city is depicted as a joyous place, with stickball games, as well as a place of aloneness. See Patrick Watson's *Fasanella's City* (New York: Ballantine, 1973).

An excellent study of a city's architecture and its relationship to the social context is David Lowe's *Lost Chicago* (Boston: Houghton Mifflin,

1978); it proceeds from the comment by the architect of the American skyscraper and inventor of Art Nouveau in the United States, Louis Sullivan: "Our architecture reflects us, as truly as a mirror." For a discussion of the controversies surrounding Daniel Burnham's City Beautiful movement and many issues related to Chicago's economic and aesthetic development, see also Garry Wills's excellent, wide-ranging book review essay "Chicago Underground," *New York Review of Books*, October 21, 1993, pp. 15–22.

Books by visual anthropologist–photographer (turned Bay Area brew pub owner) Bill Owens give an intimate view of *Suburbia* (San Francisco: Straight Arrow Press, 1973), *Our Kind of People* (San Francisco: Straight Arrow Press, 1975), and *Working* (New York: Simon and Schuster, 1977).

Of special interest are two documentaries that provide the opportunity to link personal acquaintance with knowledge about city life. In *The Writer and the City* (1970), Alfred Kazin narrates, reading the words of writers about Chicago and New York City, while powerful visual images invade the screen. In *Calcutta* (1968), a section of Louis Malle's prize-winning *Phantom India*, intellect and emotions are both stretched.

Southwestern University in Georgetown, Texas, offers an interdisciplinary course using Chicago as a lab. Offered every other year, the course, "Chicago, 1933–1983," offers students both a firsthand understanding of and systematic reflection about the city. A teaching packet for the course, including bibliographies, is available from the university.

*New Ways of Seeing: Picasso, Braque, and the Cubist Revolution* (video) shows more than 150 works from the much-acclaimed Museum of Modern Art's exhibit in New York City.

Countless studies raise the issues of *what* we know and *how* we know what we know. Unfortunately, few introductory social science texts (gatekeepers of a generation's knowledge) discuss the New Physics, whose works reject the notions of certainty and determinacy. For a thoughtful discussion of the possibility of conducting objective, value-free social science, see Clifford Geertz, *Works and Lives: The Anthropologist as Author* (Stanford, Calif.: Stanford University Press, 1988). The racism and anti-Semitism of some historians who claim objectivity is discussed by Peter Novick in *That Noble Dream: The "Objectivity Question" and the American Historical Profession* (Cambridge: Cambridge University Press, 1988). For examples of the ways in which scientists construct reality, see Walter Truett Anderson, *Reality Isn't What It Used to Be: Theatrical Politics, Ready-to-Wear Religion, Global Myths, Primitive Chic and Other Wonders of the Postmodern World* (New York: Harper & Row, 1990). Anderson's premise is that reality is a human construction based on the structure of language and signs. For a readable and fascinating overview of the relation of scientific notions of objectivity to modern culture, see O. B. Hardison, Jr., *Disappearing Through the Skylight: Culture and Technology in the Twentieth Century* (New York: Viking Penguin, 1989). Hardison argues that modern and postmodern people throughout the world have grown comfortable with fragmentation and contradiction, eschewing the notion of certainty. In *Wild Knowledge: Science, Language, and Social Life in a Fragile Environment* (Minneapolis: University of Minnesota Press, 1992), sociologist Will Wright argues that the idea of knowledge is related to the structure of language and cannot be understood objectively and technically.

A desktop computer system called "Global Jukebox" helps researchers trace the globalization of culture. Folklorist Alan Lomax and musicologist Victor Grauer have put together a multimedia system containing sound recordings, ethnographic films, and taped performances from 400 cultures, making it possible to trace how music and dance styles migrate from one culture to another.

## REFERENCES

Algren, Nelson. [1952] 1961. *Chicago: City on the Make.* Sausalito, Calif.: Contact Editions.

Angus, Paul. 1986. "Scholars note Chicago's contribution to American literary tradition." *Chronicle of Higher Education* (January 8):5–6.

Avrich, Paul. 1984. *The Haymarket Tragedy.* Princeton, N.J.: Princeton University Press.

Barney, Walter. 1977. "Dismantling the scientist's 'objectivity'." *San Francisco Sunday Examiner and Chronicle* (February 27):A13.

Bellow, Saul. [1949] 1964. *The Adventures of Augie March.* New York: Viking.

Berger, John, and and Jean Mohr. 1982. *Another Way of Telling.* New York: Pantheon.

Binford, Henry C. 1987. "I scream, you scream . . . the cultural significance of ice cream." *Mosaic* (Fall):6–9.

Burgess, Ernest W., and Donald J. Bogue, eds. 1964. *Contributions to Urban Sociology.* Chicago: University of Chicago Press.

Conrad, Fred R. 1991. "New York in the nineties." Contemporary photos, text by Sam Roberts. *New York Times Magazine* (September 29):35–39.

Coughlin, Ellen K. 1988. "Anthropologists explore the possibilities, and question the limits, of experimentation in ethnographic writing and research." *Chronicle of Higher Education* (November 30):A5, A8.

Derrida, Jacques. 1986. *Philosphy Beside Itself: On Deconstruction and Modernism.* Minneapolis: University of Minnesota Press.

Dreiser, Theodore. 1912. *The Financier.* New York: Burt.
———. 1914. *The Titan.* New York: Boni & Liveright.

Fowke, Edith, and Joe Glazer, eds. [1960] 1961. *Songs of Work and Freedom.* Garden City, N.Y.: Doubleday, Dolphin.

Fuller, Henry Blake. 1895. *With the Procession.* New York: Harper.

Gaddis, John Lewis. 1992. "The cold war's end dramatizes the failure of political theory." *Chronicle of Higher Education* (July 22):A44.

Glaab, Charles N., and A. Theodore Brown. 1983. *A History of Urban America.* New York: Macmillan.

Goethals, Gregor. 1982. *The TV Ritual.* Boston: Beacon Press.

Gonzalez, David, with Celia W. Dugger. 1991. "A neighborhood struggle with despair." *New York Times* [national edition] (November 5):1+.

Hall, Jennie. [1911] 1929. *The Story of Chicago.* Chicago: Rand McNally.

Hardison, O. B., Jr. 1989. *Disappearing Through the Skylight: Culture and Technology in the Twentieth Century.* New York: Viking.

Harris, Chauncy D., and Edward L. Ullman. 1945. "The nature of cities." *Annals of the American Academy of Political and Social Science* 242:7–17.

Heelan, Patrick. 1984. Foreword to *The New Scientific Spirit,* by Gaston Bachelard. Boston: Beacon Press.

Kaplan, Robert D. 1994. "The coming anarchy." *Atlantic Monthly* (February):44–76.

Kazin, Alfred. [1942] 1956. *On Native Grounds: A Study of American Prose Literature from 1890 to the Present.* Garden City, N.Y.: Doubleday, Anchor.

Keller, Evelyn Fox. 1980. "Feminist critique of science: A forward or backward move?" *Fundamenta Scientiae* 1:341–349.

Kershner, Vlae. 1993. "Crime is now no. 1 concern, state poll says." *San Francisco Chronicle* (November 24):1+.

Lehman, David. 1991. *Signs of the Times.* New York: Poseidon.

Lomax, Alan. 1960. *The Folk Songs of North America in the English Language.* Garden City, N.Y.: Doubleday.

Lowe, David. 1978. *Lost Chicago.* Boston: Houghton Mifflin.

Lukacs, Georg. 1971. *Writer & Critic and Other Essays.* New York: Grosset & Dunlap.

Millman, Marcia, and Rosabeth Moss Kanter, eds. 1975. *Another Voice: Feminist Perspectives on Social Life and Social Sciences.* New York: Doubleday, Anchor.

Muschamp, Herbert. 1993. "Things generally wrong in the universe." *New York Times* [national edition] (April 11):sec. 2, 1+.

Norris, Frank. [1903] 1970. *The Pit.* Columbus, Ohio: Merrill.

Park, Robert Ezra. [1916] 1974. "The city: Suggestions for the investigation of human behavior in the urban environment." Pp. 1–46 in Robert E. Park, Ernest W. Burgess, and Roderick D. McKenzie, *The City.* Chicago: University of Chicago Press.

Polanyi, Michael. 1958. *Personal Knowledge.* Chicago: University of Chicago Press.

Riis, Jacob A. [1890] 1971. *How the Other Half Lives: Studies Among the Tenements of New York.* New York: Dover.

Roe, Colin, and Fred Koetter. n.d. *Collage City.* Cambridge, Mass.: MIT Press.

Salgado, Sebastião. 1990. *An Uncertain Grace. Essays by Eduardo Galeano and Fred Ritchin.* New York: Aperture.

Sandburg, Carl. 1970. *The Complete Poems of Carl Sandburg.* New York: Harcourt Brace Jovanovich.

Sinclair, Upton. 1905. *The Jungle.* New York: Vanguard.

Spear, Allan H. 1967. *Black Chicago: The Making of a Negro Ghetto, 1890–1920.* Chicago: University of Chicago Press.

Spender, Dale, ed. 1982. *Men's Studies Modified: The*

*Impact of Feminism on the Academic Disciplines.* Oxford: Pergamon.

Williams, Oscar, ed. 1952. *A Little Treasury of Modern Poetry.* New York: Scribner.

Wirth, Louis. 1938. "Urbanism as a way of life." *American Journal of Sociology* 44:1–24.

Wolf, Fred Alan. [1988] 1990. *Parallel Universes.* New York: Simon and Schuster, Touchstone.

Zukav, Gary. 1979. *The Dancing Wu Li Masters: An Overview of the New Physics.* New York: Morrow.

Richard Hedman

*urbanists see different aspects of city life, depending on what parts they explore*

# CHAPTER 2
# Thinking About Cities

## WHAT YOU SEE DEPENDS ON HOW YOU LOOK AT IT

Reality is in the eye of the beholder. This truism is whimsically illustrated in Antoine de Saint-Exupéry's tale, *The Little Prince:*

Once when I was six years old I saw a magnificent picture in a book, called *True Stories from Nature,* about the primeval forest. It was a picture of a boa constrictor in the act of swallowing an animal. Here is a copy of the drawing.

In the book it said: "Boa constrictors swallow their prey whole, without chewing it. After that they are not able to move, and they sleep through the six months that they need for digestion."

I pondered deeply, then, over the adventures of the jungle. And after some work with a colored pencil I succeeded in making my first drawing. My Drawing Number One. It looked like this:

I showed my masterpiece to the grown-ups, and asked them whether the drawing frightened them.

But they answered: "Frighten? Why should anyone be frightened by a hat?"

My drawing was not a picture of a hat. It was a picture of a boa constrictor digesting an elephant. But since the grown-ups were not able to understand it, I made another drawing: I drew the inside of the boa constrictor, so that the grown-ups could see it clearly. They always need to have things explained. My Drawing Number Two looked like this:

The grown-ups' response, this time, was to advise me to lay aside my drawings of boa constrictors, whether from the inside or the outside, and devote myself instead to geography, history, arithmetic and grammar. . . . Grown-ups never understand anything by themselves, and it is tiresome for children to be always and forever explaining things to them.

So then I chose another profession, and learned to pilot airplanes. I have flown a little over all parts of the world; and it is true that geography has been very useful to me. At a glance I can distinguish China from Arizona. If one gets lost in the night, such knowledge is valuable.

In the course of this life . . . [whenever I met a grown-up] who seemed to me at all clear-sighted, I tried the experiment of showing him my Drawing Number One. . . . I would try to find out, so, if this was a person of true understanding. But, whoever it was, he, or she, would always say: "That is a hat."

Then I would never talk to that person about boa constrictors, or primeval forests, or stars. I would bring myself down to his level. I would talk to him about bridge, and golf, and politics, and neckties. And the grown-up would be greatly pleased to have met such a sensible man. ([1943] 1970:3–5)

Whether we identify with the imaginative pilot or the sensible grown-ups in Antoine de Saint-Exupéry's modern fable, the point is clear: *What you see depends on how you look at it.* People can look at the same thing and see it through different lenses. Urbanists are no exception. Like other human beings, urbanists filter what they see through lenses. Whatever lens we use, our vision is necessarily limited, for some things are not focused on (like the inside of a boa constrictor), or are seen only partially or with distortion.

Here's a more concrete example: an urban street scene. Walking down a familiar street every day, you may not see birds overhead or hear teenagers singing. You may filter out information that seems extraneous, missing the less visible and ignoring the overall picture.

How people see and make sense out of the world depends on many factors, including their age, sex, social background, past experience, present purposes, and so on. For a moment, let's concentrate on ways of seeing based on different (1) modes of understanding, (2) academic and occupational perspectives, and (3) maps they use.

## Different Modes of Understanding

Schools stress reason and logic, not emotion or holistic thought. We aren't taught to see boa constrictors, or primeval forests, or stars. We are taught to break down wholes into their component parts, to dissect complex phenomena logically. Of course, the sequential, analytic-rational mode is very useful, even essential, to science. After all, as Saint-Exupéry said (tongue-in-cheek), reason helped him to know whether he was flying over China or Arizona.

In his fable, Saint-Exupéry isn't saying that intuition and acquaintance with something should replace reason and systematic thought. Rather, he seems to say: Isn't it a shame that sensible grown-ups have lost the childlike quality of imagining, of seeing beyond the information given! Grown-ups who don't use holistic thought and flashes of intuitive insight are robbed of an entire dimension of understanding.

This brings us to another way of ordering information: academic and occupational perspectives. While useful, they too can lead to partial or distorted vision.

## Academic and Occupational Perspectives

People's perception of the world is influenced by many factors—age, gender, motives, academic training, and so on. An exercise developed by Larry Susskind of the Department of Urban Studies and Planning at the Massachusetts Institute of Technology illustrates these perceptual differences.

Susskind begins by drawing a series of maps on the blackboard. Each represents a different way of seeing a city. Taking San Francisco as our example, Figure 2.1 presents several subjective or mental maps of the city—that is, **cognitive maps.** The bare outline of San Francisco (2.1a) is shared by all; the other maps are not. Figure 2.1b shows how transportation engineers might see the city. From this perspective, San Francisco is a vast array of transport networks: a ferry terminal, bus lines, cable car tracks, underground rapid transit, major arteries, and a street grid.

The environmentalist may see one city (Figure 2.1d), while others may see another. The urban designer (Figure 2.1c) may pick out the Transamerica "Pyramid," the city's most visually dominant structure. A bioregionalist may focus on native plants and ecosystems, mapping what's "Wild in the City" (1984). A sociologist concerned with issues of class and race may focus on neighborhoods of extreme contrast, such as white, affluent Pacific Heights and densely-settled Chinatown (Figure 2.1e); other parts of the city may fade out altogether.

Is it possible that people just don't see parts of the city? Doesn't this exercise using cognitive maps grossly overstate the case? Empirical evidence suggests not. When Kevin Lynch ([1960] 1974) asked Bostonians to draw maps of their city, he found that the interviewees consistently left out whole areas.

And what about unseeable parts of the city? How can we focus on some aspect of city life if it is uncharted? Take, for example, information flows. An important global market in money exchange depends on up-to-the-minute information via telecommunications (Brand, 1987:chap. 12). These information flows may be more important to a local economy than, say, feedgrain or tourism. Yet the journey of information remains unmapped . . . and probably unnoticed.

## Even Road Maps Contain a Point of View

All maps are cognitive maps. They seem to be objective, even natural. But, as Denis Wood points out, every map contains a viewpoint because "Every Map Shows This . . . But Not That." The upshot: "Maps Construct—Not Reproduce—the World" (1992:17, 48).

Even an ordinary state map contains hidden messages: "By promoting automobile transportation [over mass transportation, for instance], state highway maps support the interests of all who profit from the highway system" (Smithsonian Institution, 1993).

*To conclude:* What this implies is that all of us have blind spots. The question is how to reduce them and expand our vision.

a

b

major
—— streets
—— highways
—·—·— BART

c

▲ Landmarks

d

e

Selected Major Ethnic Communities
■■■ Black
▨▨ Hispanic
☐ Chinese

**Fig. 2.1** COGNITIVE MAPS. People with different academic training, occupations, social background, or interests often see a city through different lenses. (*a*) The bare outline of San Francisco. (*b*) How a transportation engineer might envision San Francisco—as a series of major streets, highways, and a mass-transit line. (*c*) Features of the cityscape on which an urban designer might focus. (*d*) The city from the point of view of an environmentalist who wants to preserve open space. (*e*) The same city as perceived by a sociologist, showing a few of San Francisco's many ethnic communities.

## EXPANDING OUR VISION OF THE CITY

One way to reduce the blind spots is to look at urban life from many perspectives and then to combine insights. Alas, this is easier said than done. Hardly anyone today is a Renaissance person who, like Leonardo da Vinci, is a serious student of the social and physical sciences as well as a creative artist.

### Fragmentation of the Social Sciences

The expansion and specialization of knowledge in our high-tech society make it difficult for anyone to study systematically the many facets of any complex phenomenon, including the city. Academically speaking, this proliferation of knowledge has led to a splitting up of the world into specialist **disciplines** and professional territories such as sociology, history, and economics. Subdisciplines (e.g., urban sociology) and hybrids (e.g., economic sociology) have also developed as further responses to the knowledge explosion and to real-world concerns.

This was not always the case. In the nineteenth century (before the knowledge explosion and computerized data banks), influential social thinkers argued vigorously against carving up the world into narrow disciplines. Thinkers who agreed on little else—such as sociology's founder Auguste Comte, Karl Marx, and John Henry Cardinal Newman—agreed that social phenomena are so inextricably linked that studying one small category of the social world was fruitless. Cardinal Newman summed up this point of view in 1852. He wrote that a true university education should provide the power of viewing many things at once as "one whole, and referring them severally to their true places in the universal system, and understanding their respective values, and determining their mutual dependence" ([1852] 1919:137).

Many educators today reaffirm Newman's lofty vision. The president of Dartmouth College, for one, believes that specialization discourages students from becoming educated (Freedman, 1987:47).

Yet, despite such calls for holism, specialist disciplines continue to multiply. This fragmentation can lead to expertise in a specialized area—say, ethnic voting behavior. But scholars risk knowing more and more about less and less.

Some theorists say that there is no rational way to classify the social sciences, for distinctions among them are artificial (e.g., Duverger, 1964). Some call for new college courses, ones that do not package learning into disciplines (e.g., Alexander, 1993:B3). Some, including a high-profile global commission, are pooling ideas on how to restructure the current organization of knowledge. Nonetheless, at present, higher education is organized along disciplinary lines. Thus, there are departments of sociology, history, geography, and so forth. And each discipline has developed particular perspectives on the world it tries to better understand.

What constitutes a discipline's perspective? Its substantive content, **paradigms** for doing research, and research methods. Thus, an economist and a sociologist look at the world through different lenses.

However, times are changing—and so are academics. Increasingly, scholars are becoming **interdisciplinary** or **multidisciplinary**. For example, Adolph Reed is a professor of both political science and history at Northwestern University; his research focuses on urban politics and twentieth-century African-American social thought. Similarly, University of Florida professor Joe R. Feagin draws on insights from political sociology, U.S. history, international economics, and urban geography to understand the "urban real estate game": how corporations decide where to locate, how government subsidies affect urban growth, and how citizens' movements can help control urban redevelopment (Feagin and Parker, 1990).

### Ways of Expanding Our Vision

This book attempts to expand our vision of things urban in several ways: (1) by encouraging both acquaintance with and knowledge about the urban world; (2) by drawing on and trying to connect insights from different disciplines, professional fields, and arts; (3) by presenting a range of ideological perspectives on urban conditions and policies; (4) by examining why honest people disagree about how cities work; (5) by reexamining what seems so obvious, such as the way people walk down busy city streets or behave on subways; and (6) by exploring the links among local, national, and international conditions. My approach will be from the point of view of urban studies. A word about this subject area is appropriate here.

## Urban Studies

**Urban studies** is a relative newcomer to academia. It developed in the 1960s as a response to the needs of academics and practitioners who sought a less piecemeal approach to urban phenomena. It is variously called *urban studies, urban affairs, metropolitan studies,* and *urban–suburban studies;* academics don't agree on what to call it or where to put it. It is sometimes a department, a program, or an entire school. No one label identifies its theorists and researchers. Some call themselves *urbanists* or *urbanologists;* others shrink from such labels.

Whatever it's called, urban studies is a *field of study,* not a discipline. It is often viewed as either a multidisciplinary or an interdisciplinary field focusing on urban-related theory, issues, and policies. In academia, some see it as a promising development; others call it nothing more than "a sphere of rather disconnected interdisciplinary inquiries" (Savage and Warde, 1993:32). Popularly, it is often associated with the attempt to solve urban problems.

As a field of study, urban studies has rather ill-defined boundaries. Neither its physical nor its intellectual boundaries are well delineated. For some, urban studies means the study of cities and suburbs. For others (including myself), it encompasses global theories, data, and perspectives.

Some scholars maintain that it is no longer possible to make meaningful distinctions between things urban and nonurban. They argue, and I agree, that in an interdependent world, ur-

ban life cannot be divorced from rural, let alone national and international, life. I call this the "urban-schmurban" stance.

Ideally, urban studies students are encouraged to achieve interdisciplinarity. As one scholar puts it, "Almost none of the great questions of science, scholarship, or society fit in single disciplines" (Kates, 1989:B1). Brown University, for one, recognizes this: Its collage of thirty-five interdisciplinary centers ranges from Afro-American Studies to the World Hunger Program. So much for traditional disciplinary boxes!

A few scholars are trying to remake urban theory from an interdisciplinary standpoint. For instance, Edward W. Soja (1995), who teaches urban and regional planning, draws on a variety of perspectives—from cultural theory, architecture, and feminism to geographical space—to offer a new mode of thinking about urbanism. Similarly, Michael Peter Smith moves far beyond his original homebase (political science) to reconsider the history of *Urban Theory* (1996).

But synthesizing insights among disciplines is difficult, sometimes impossible. One urbanist describes the recipe for many so-called interdisciplinary studies like this: "Take a physical planner, a sociologist, an economist; beat the mixture until it blends; pour and spread" (Alonso, 1971:169). In other words, synthesizing unlike insights or data sets is like blending oil and water; it won't work.

Without basic agreement on conceptual frameworks—which does not presently exist—interdisciplinarity remains an ideal. Meanwhile, scholars often achieve some degree of integration when they work in an interdisciplinary team.

Most commonly, research team members approach the city from the perspective of their own disciplines. An example will help to clarify the various disciplinary approaches to the same phenomenon: slums.

## DISCIPLINARY PERSPECTIVES: THE EXAMPLE OF SLUMS

According to the *Oxford English Dictionary,* a slum is

**Fig. 2.2**  SLUM. According to the *Oxford English Dictionary*, a slum may be defined as "a thickly populated neighbourhood or district where the houses and the conditions of life are of a squalid and wretched character." People living in areas called slums may not see it that way. (Ben Achtenberg)

a street, alley, court, etc., situated in a crowded district of a town or city and inhabited by people of a low class or by the very poor; a number of these streets or courts forming a thickly populated neighbourhood or district where the houses and the conditions of life are of a squalid and wretched character. (1971:2874)

People concerned with the history and use of language would be interested in the derivation of the word *slum* (British provincial slang), its first recorded usage (1825, in England), and its changing meanings over time (by the 1890s it connoted crime, viciousness, and debauchery—in other words, bad people as well as bad physical conditions). People living in areas called slums (by people who don't live there) would undoubtedly have more pressing concerns than understanding where the word *slum* came from. In other words, what is of utmost importance to one group of people may be of much less concern to another.

This observation also holds true for urbanists: What is of primary importance to people trained in one discipline or field may be peripheral to, even neglected by, those trained in another. To illustrate, we'll look at various disciplinary approaches to slums.

First, a word about disagreements within a discipline or field. Rarely, perhaps never, do sociologists, historians, or others in the same discipline or field share a paradigm or research model. Historically, mainstream social science rejected the assumptions of many contending visions, from creationism and parapsychology to Marxism and feminism, but some scholars continued to work in alternative paradigms. In recent times, there seems to be an opening within mainstream social science, providing room for some of the dissenting outsiders.

## Economics

Economists agree among themselves more than do members of most disciplines. Indeed, "no other social science has a single way of thinking that dominates the field to the overwhelming degree that the neoclassical model dominates economics" (Coughlin, 1993:A8). As one scholar puts it, "80 percent agree with 80 percent of it." (Note: The neoclassical model's bedrock assumption is this: People are rational calculators who act in their self-interest and operate in a free, competitive market.) Still, that leaves 20 percent. Two groups—feminist economists and radical economists—fall into that 20 percent category, questioning neoclassical economics's basic assumption. What follows is a discussion from the neoclassical viewpoint. Then a feminist view is considered. The next chapter includes a discussion of the radical vision.

*Neoclassical or Mainstream Economics* Economics, once called the "dismal science," is primarily concerned with choice: how individuals, global corporations, or societies choose to use their scarce productive resources (land, labor, capital, know-how) to produce and distribute goods and services. Whether economists study a complex economic system, such as that of the United States, or the economic organization of child care in one city, they ask three basic and interrelated questions:

1. *What* goods and services are produced, and *how much* of alternative commodities is produced? For example, does the U.S. economy produce many weapons for national defense and few housing units? A mix of both? Or many housing units and few weapons?
2. *How* are goods produced? For instance, is high technology used? What resources are used?
3. *For whom* are the goods produced? For example, how are certain kinds of housing distributed to the affluent and the poor or to whites and nonwhites?

These questions—*what, how, and for whom*—inform an economist's perspective on the issue being investigated. To answer these questions, economists use a variety of tools, mainly quantitative in nature. In an economics text, for instance, we would expect to find numbers, statistics, mathematical equations, graphs of relationships between factors involved, and econometric projections. It is the rare economist who is trained in or uses qualitative research methods common to anthropology and sociology, such as in-depth interviewing and participant-observation.

Looking at urban housing, one does not have to be a sophisticated economist to understand *what* poor people get: high-density, physically deteriorating slums (or less, a street space). Indeed, it has been said that if all of New York City were as densely populated as parts of Harlem, the entire population of the United States would fit into three of New York City's boroughs (Harrington in Hunter, 1964:37).

Why do the poor live in densely populated dwellings, usually near the center of the city, rather than on the city's fringes? The answer is not so obvious. Here, neoclassical economists' logic and models can help to explain. The key to their explanation is a heuristic device showing the way urban land prices vary in a market-based economy: the **bid rent curve**. Figure 2.3 is a residential bid rent curve. It depicts the relationship between two factors that economic analysts consider essential to explain urban land use: (1) the price of land per square foot and

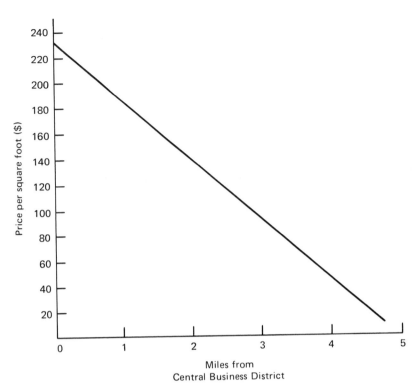

**Fig. 2.3**  ECONOMIC MODEL. This residential bid rent curve shows that the price of land per square foot decreases as the distance from the central business district (CBD) increases.

(2) the distance of the land from the central business district (CBD).

Near the center of the city, land is expensive— the most expensive in the city. In this example, it is $240 per square foot. (Note: Rodeo Drive in Beverly Hills, California, approximates the figure here: $225 per square foot in 1989. In that year, Tokyo's Ginza district had the most expensive retail-store rent in the world, averaging $650 per square foot; the next most expensive location was New York City's Fifty-seventh Street, at $435 per square foot. By comparison, stores on Telegraph Avenue, the street near the University of California at Berkeley's campus, rented for less than $10 per square foot.) Land is expensive near the center because centrally located land is prime land, close to the nerve center of the city, with its corporate headquarters, large department stores, banks, and so forth. At the city's edges, land is

cheaper because it is not as convenient to jobs or amenities. (It is important to note that the recent rise of "postsuburbia," discussed in Chapter 7, calls these assumptions into question.)

*Why* urban slums are found near the center of cities rather than on the periphery, where land is cheaper, is a seeming paradox. Studying this phenomenon, regional planner William Alonso concludes that the reasons are connected to the amount of land affordable by rich and poor. "At any given location," Alonso says, "the poor can buy less land than the rich, and since only a small quantity of land is involved [for living space], changes in its price are not as important for the poor as the costs and inconvenience of commuting" (1973:54). What Alonso claims, then, is that the rich make a trade-off. They are willing to take more trouble and time commuting to work in exchange for living farther away from the city center (where, presumably, it is more comfortable and pleasant).

In Alonso's simple model shown in Figure 2.3, the value of land declines from $240 per square foot at the city's center to $20 per square foot at the city's edge. How does this relationship between the price of land and its location help us understand why the poor live in crowded settlements called slums? The economic analyst would point out that since centrally located land is expensive, any housing built there must try to minimize land costs: by building up or by packing people in. In the case of poor people with little money, both situations occur, resulting in slums.

To answer the *what* question, neoclassical economists frequently employ the concept of supply and demand. In a market economy (also called a *free-enterprise* or *competitive* economy), classical theory holds that goods will be supplied in the marketplace according to people's ability to pay for them. However, in the case of housing, some economists say that there is a large "noneffective" demand—that is, a group of people who want decent housing but can't afford to pay for it. Their logic is this: The laws of the market work to give them only what they can pay for—physically deteriorating housing.

*How* is slum housing provided? With the exception of a small amount of publicly assisted housing, no new housing is produced by the market for poor people. Instead, older housing units are occupied by successively lower-income groups, and this housing eventually "trickles down" to the poor slum dweller. Urban economists call this the **filtering** process. Some economists argue in favor of public policies to provide more housing to upper- and middle-income people on the assumption that more and better housing will then filter down to the poor more rapidly. However, others note than in many U.S. cities the market encourages "trickling up" (gentrification). In this process, lower-income inner-city neighborhoods are rehabilitated for upper-income housing (Palen and London, 1984). As real-estate developers gentrify these neighborhoods, displaced tenants move to places they can afford—slums, in many cases.

*To conclude:* Neoclassical or market economists tend to see the provision of slum housing in a market economy as an outcome of the workings of the law of supply and demand. Such factors as land costs and the journey to work determine the behavior of urbanites, whether as buyers or renters of urban land, as owners of slum property, or as slum dwellers. Crowded, physically deteriorated slum housing, in this way of thinking, tends to trickle down to poor people or trickle up to more affluent people because of underlying market forces. In either case, in this perspective, underlying market forces are the key determinants of who lives on what land.

**Feminist Economics**  Briefly, feminist economists reject the neoclassical model of the rational, self-interested actor. Instead, they focus on economic activities that are more cooperative and social (Bergmann, 1986).

They approach questions about poverty and slums from a different angle than mainstream economists. For example, Trudi J. Renwick and Barbara R. Bergmann (1993) suggest that the U.S. needs a new definition of poverty because, Bergmann says:

Our current definition of poverty is ridiculous. Threats to get single mothers off welfare after two years [as President Clinton suggested] is not going to do it. It's not just a matter of motivation, saying "Get up off your butt and go to work." There's a child-care issue here that is extremely important. (in Coughlin, 1993:A8)

Their proposed redefinition of poverty is based on a basic needs budget, taking into account child-care expenses that a poor, single, working mother must pay to continue working outside the home. Currently, in their view, the federal government's baseline for determining poverty is too low to ensure a minimally sufficient standard of living for working, single mothers. One inference here is that government definitions help determine whether or not single-working-mother–headed families do or do not end up in poverty.

## Geography

Geographers, whether Central American specialists or urbanists, stand on common ground: space and place. Yet, like most social sciences in recent years, geography has experienced increasing specialization and blurred boundaries (Coughlin, 1987:9). Some geographers even joke that their field is the Los Angeles of academic disciplines: It's spread over a large area, it merges with its neighbors, and it's hard to find the Central Business District!

At the same time, scholars from neighboring disciplines, particularly those influenced by three French scholars—historian Fernand Braudel ([1986] 1990), philosopher Michel Foucault (1980), or philosopher-urbanist Henri Lefebvre ([1974] 1991)—are making geography central to their analyses of social life. In the past decade, the geographer's central concepts of space and place have traveled to other disciplines, thereby reinvigorating urban theory. Take, for example, two important sociological works discussed in this book: *Urban Fortunes* (Logan and Molotch, 1987), which discusses the political economy of place, and *The Informational City* (Castells, 1989) which discusses urban spatial structure and the "space of flows."

Mapping is a key tool, but geographers also use mathematical and computer-assisted models, field observation, and other social science methods plus such high-tech tools as satellite observations. Investigating slums, a geographer might map out where they are located in city space or construct a model to predict where they will be located fifty years later.

A starting point for the description of housing patterns in U.S. industrial cities, including the location of slums, is sociologist Ernest W. Burgess's model of urban space. This model, developed by Burgess at the University of Chicago in the 1920s, was central to urban geography for several decades, showing the interdisciplinary roots of much urban theory.

Figure 2.4 depicts the Burgess model of urban space. It suggests that U.S. **industrial cities** (i.e., cities like Chicago that developed in the era of manufacturing) expand outward from the CBD in a nonrandom way—through a series of zones or rings. One implication of this model (discussed in more detail in Chapter 16) is that poor people live in slums because changes in the city's land-use patterns push them there. Briefly, the logic is this: The city's changing environment leads to the sorting and sifting process that segregates individuals by social class, ethnic background and race, and family composition. As a city's population grows, demand for land in the CBD (the city's core) can be satisfied only by expanding outward. Property owners in and around the CBD will let their housing units deteriorate, for they can profit by selling their land to businesses expanding there. The result of this growth process, the Burgess model predicts, is that the poor living in slums near the CBD will be pushed out into new slums a bit farther out from the CBD.

Today, scholars doubt the relevance of Burgess's model to postindustrial cities (Chapter 15). Nevertheless, it is an important intellectual grandparent of land-use models. In addition, the Burgess model is of special interest here because of its interdisciplinary nature; it combines economic assumptions about the way the world works (economic competition for urban space) with patterns of spatial and social order. For instance, it predicts that the higher people move up the socioeconomic ladder, the farther away they will live from the CBD, Zone I.

## Sociology

Sociologists study people: how they act, think, produce things and ideas, and live. They may study social interaction between as few as two individuals or as many as the entire world population. Their major interest lies in better understanding human action. Normally, sociologists are not concerned with one person's action.

Sociologists start with the assumption that things are not always the way they seem. For instance, universities exist, according to their high-principled mottos and public-relations brochures, to expand the frontiers of knowledge and

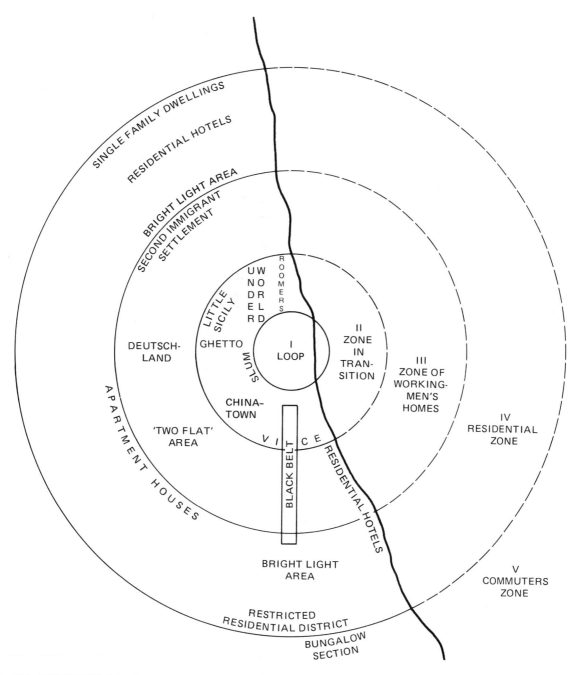

**Fig. 2.4** BURGESS'S CONCENTRIC ZONE MODEL. Applied to Chicago, the zonal model shows that the Loop (Chicago's CBD) is surrounded by low-income neighborhoods in Zone II. (Robert E. Park, Ernest W. Burgess, and Roderick D. McKenzie, *The City* [Chicago: University of Chicago Press (1925) 1974], p. 55. Copyright © 1967 by the University of Chicago. Reproduced by permission of the University of Chicago Press. All rights reserved)

(more recently) to provide career training. Those are their official reasons for existence, their **manifest functions.** Looking below the surface, however, sociologists may uncover some hidden or unintended purposes of universities, their **latent functions.** These include lowering the unemployment rolls by keeping people off the streets and instilling habits useful in the labor market, such as following orders from authority figures. These latent functions can't be seen with the naked eye or discovered by common sense; they emerge as one explores the connections among people, institutions, and ideas.

The sociological perspective attempts to better describe and understand the social forces that mold the lives of individuals, perhaps without their own realization. It can be applied to many events that, on the surface, seem to be purely personal eyperiences.

A sociologist investigating any topic, including slums, might ask the following questions:

1. *What are people doing and thinking here?* For instance, do slum dwellers vote, join church groups, or feel satisfied with their lives?
2. *What kinds of people are here?* What are their social characteristics?
3. *What rules govern behavior here?* In the case of slum dwellers, are they expected to passively accept their substandard housing?
4. *Who says so?* For example, in slum buildings, who or what groups have the power to make rules and enforce them?
5. *Whose interests do these social arrangements serve?* For example, what social functions do slums serve? Do some groups in society benefit more than others from their existence?
6. *What powerful people, institutions, and structures influence these arrangements?* For example, what roles do government agencies and private developers play in creating or eradicating slums?

The work of John R. Seeley represents one approach to the study of slums. Seeley (1970) argues that slums will not—cannot—ever be eradicated because the definition of the word *slum* is relative to how other people live. He reasons that people at the bottom of the social ladder will still be perceived by those higher up as living in slums even if their living conditions are improved. Further, Seeley maintains that in a society where economic and social inequality exists, as in the United States, there are bound to be those who will be labeled "slum dwellers."

In his analysis of slums, Seeley employs a device common to many scientific disciplines: a **typology** or classification scheme. His typology differentiates slum dwellers on the basis of length of residence and reasons for residing in the slums. He distinguishes among four major types of people who live in slums: (1) the "permanent necessitarians" (who live there permanently and by necessity); (2) the "temporary necessitarians" (who aspire to leave the slums but live there out of necessity); (3) the "permanent opportunists" (who stay in the slums primarily because it affords them opportunities to escape the law or live the high life); and (4) the "temporary opportunists" (who want to pursue dominant cultural values like success; these include recent arrivals to the city).

Other sociologists explore face-to-face encounters among slum dwellers, paying special attention to how people interpret each other's actions and bring meaning to their interaction; this approach typifies the symbolic interaction school of sociology. Elijah Anderson's study *Streetwise* (1990) is exemplary. Anderson finds an influential "oppositional" youth subculture in the slum. He says this oppositional subculture is based on gangster respect and the romanticization of violence, not the values of work, love, and hope. For instance, one teenager told Anderson that he had committed murder because he was "just having a bad day." Such a study seems particularly revelant, policywise, in a time when (1) the *majority* of U.S. children (54 percent of whites; 66 percent of people of color) say that they worry about some family member becoming a victim of violent crime (Princeton Survey Research Associates, 1993) and (2) African-American males under twenty-four are "killing and dying in record numbers, and the communities in which they live are paralyzed by the fear of violent crime" (Morganthau, 1993:66).

Other sociologists take another tack, linking government's intervention in local affairs, the growing inability of urban politics to decide who gets what housing to live in, and the global restructuring of urban space. This approach typifies the so-called new urban sociology (Gottdeiner and Feagin, 1988).

And many sociologists combine approaches and methods. French-trained University of California, Berkeley, scholar Löic J. D. Wacquant (1989) combines participant-observation and an analysis of statistical data with macro economic theory to understand Chicago ghetto life. Wacquant says that no one factor can account for the plight of the ghetto, but "there is no denying that the accelerating decline of the inner city finds its deepest roots in the ongoing structural transformation of American capitalism" (1989:510). He adds that public policy has also played a role in perpetuating ghetto life: "the rolling back of state and federal payrolls (for example in the post office) has also reduced access to legitimate channels of upward mobility out of the ghetto" (512).

Whatever approach or method is used (ranging from mathematical models to firsthand participation and observation), sociologists focus on the social forces that shape individual lives. They look for traits that cannot be explained simply by referring to individual psychological states.

## Political Science

Traditionally, political scientists have been concerned with questions of power and governance: Who governs? How do they govern? To what end? Or, as one political scientist so neatly put it, *"Who gets what, how, and why?"*

As in other disciplines, the range of topics within political science is broad. But the nature of political processes and political outcomes is central to the discipline. The research tools of political science include mathematical models, content analysis, attitude surveys, and observation of events.

In the case of slums, political scientists may investigate a number of issues. Some study citizens' attitudes toward government housing policy; others explore the relations between different levels of government (federal, state, local) in establishing housing policy. Still others look at comparative political systems, exploring how different countries handle housing policy. A political scientist exploring power relationships might study conflicts of interest in which local and international decision makers stand to gain personally from land deals to raze slums. And a political philosopher might question the nature of a political system that either allows or perpetuates slums.

One study of slums from the perspective of political science is *Politics, Planning, and the Public Interest* (1955) by Edward Banfield and Martin Meyerson. This study centers on the decision-making process that led to the construction of low-income public-housing projects in Chicago. (These housing units, meant—at least by government definition—to provide standard housing for the poor, came to be known as slums.)

Banfield and Meyerson found that Chicago's aldermen (city councillors) had effective veto power over public housing construction in their wards. The proposed housing projects were going to house poor people, the majority of whom were black. Middle- and upper-class residents of predominantly white neighborhoods vigorously opposed the suggestion that such public-housing projects should be located in their neighborhoods. These affluent whites believed that if the projects came in, crime would increase, property values would decrease, and the aesthetic character of their areas would change. Their opposition to public housing was sufficient to block the original proposal: that public-housing projects be scattered throughout the city. Eventually, much less public housing than originally contemplated was built, and virtually all units were placed in a very few wards that were already nearly all African-American.

Banfield and Meyerson recognize other influences but stress political factors. They focus on the politics of class and race, as well as on what Chicagoans call "clout" (influence and power), rather than on concepts central to other disciplines, such as urban growth over space.

## Anthropology

Since the nineteenth century, anthropologists have made significant contributions to the study of urbanization and cultural change from a cross-cultural point of view. In recent years, they have turned their attention away from folk or so-called "primitive" cultures, such as that of the Trobriand Islands, and have focused on urbanizing and urban cultures. Wherever anthropologists work, their primary method of investigation remains fieldwork.

The late American anthropologist Oscar Lewis used fieldwork methods to get an insider's view of family life in Mexico City. He wanted to find out what it meant to grow up in a slum tenement within a city undergoing rapid social and economic change, such as Mexico City. Using a tape recorder to take down the life histories of one Mexican family, *The Children of Sanchez* (1961), Lewis recorded their personal statements and feelings about a wide range of issues, including religion, kinship patterns, interpersonal relations, and social mobility. But he was interested in much broader issues: the effects of industrialization and urbanization on the peasant and urban masses. He sought to develop a conceptual model of what he called the *culture of poverty*, that is, "a design for living which is passed down from generation to generation" among "those people who are at the very bottom of the socioeconomic scale" (1961:xxiv–xxv).

A generation later, Lewis's culture of poverty model remains hotly contested. Many scholars dismiss it, arguing that chronically poor people's "ingenuity and aspirations are not different from working people's, but that their chances of success are small" (Sharff, 1987:47–48). Political scientist–historian Adolph Reed rejects Lewis's basic assumption that poor people have different behavior or values: "Some percentage of *all* Americans take drugs, fight in families, abuse or neglect children, and have children out of wedlock. These behaviors don't cause poverty. Poor people aren't poor because they have bad values or behave improperly" (in Leopold, 1992:3–4). Reed blames public policy choices—not the victims of poverty—for ghettoization: "It's not as though jobs just up and left the cities. The shape and character of the domestic economy is guided by public policy." Citing a federal bias since the 1940s toward road construction over mass transportation, toward suburbs over cities, and toward owner-occupied housing over rental housing, Reed says, "We let government off the hook for the role it's played in increasing poverty by redistributing wealth upward."

In recent years, a subdiscipline of urban anthropology, urban archeology, has been tapping a rather ingenious source of information: garbage. As the head of a "dig" in Atlanta, Georgia, put it, "People's garbage never lies. It tells the truth if you know how to read it" (in Weathers, Morris, Precourt, and Jones, 1979:81). From a Newburyport, Massachusetts, garbage dig, urban archeologists discovered evidence that nineteenth-century Irish and Canadian immigrants, long presumed illiterate, could read and write. From interviewees in Tuscon, students in the "Garbage Project" found that there was a wide gap between what people say they do and what they actually do. For instance, many vastly underestimated their weekly beer consumption. And according to archeologist William Rathje, head of the Garbage Project and coauthor of *Rubbish!* (1992), there is a gap between good intentions and behavior: Based on their analysis of garbage, the students found that many people buy both healthy fresh vegetables and salty, cholesterol-filled microwave dinners but often throw away the veggies—untouched. (Note: In May 1988, the U.S. Supreme Court ruled that garbage bags outside the home and its immediate surroundings can be legally searched. The ethics of trash searching remains controversial.) From looking at "ecofacts" (food remains, evidence of past environments) and archival records, anthropologists reconstructed one bit of African-American history; they found that in Buxton, Iowa, a coal-mining town from 1900 to 1925, there had been a majority population of African-Americans who prospered and interacted with local whites harmoniously (Gradwohl and Osborn, 1984).

Wherever they go to study people, anthropologists seek "to provide convincing accounts of what is happening to people in varied real life situations and to set these in a broader framework of time and space" (Southall, 1973:4). Their emphasis on the diversity of human experience, as well as the search for common or universal themes, gives anthropologists a particular perspective on the social and material world.

## History

His-story and her-story—the range of humankind's experience over time—is the subject matter of historians. Some focus on a small piece or area of the whole, while other grand (some say grandiose) thinkers try to see patterns throughout the whole of human experience.

Historians have contributed a variety of studies about urban life and culture, starting with the earliest known settlements in the Middle East. To investigate various aspects of urban life, they use a range of tools, including the analysis of written records, oral histories, and, more recently, quantitative techniques such as computer-aided statistical analysis.

One influential historian of urban culture is the late Lewis Mumford (1895–1990). In *The City in History: Its Origins, Its Transformations, and Its Prospects* (1961), Mumford paints a picture of the forms and functions of the city throughout the ages. He also pleads for a "new urban order" that emphasizes "local control over local needs." In his historical tour from the early origins of the city to the contemporary megalopolis, Mumford stops to comment on the development of European industrial cities between 1830 and 1910. First, he quotes his mentor, the Scots planner Patrick Geddes, who influenced a generation of U.S. city planners, and then he offers his own comments on slums:

"Slum, semi-slum, and super-slum—to this has come the evolution of cities." Yes: these mordant words of Patrick Geddes apply inexorably to the new environment. Even the most revolutionary of contemporary

critics [like Friedrich Engels] lacked genuine standards of building and living: they had no notion how far the environment of the upper classes themselves had become impoverished. . . . [Even Engels, the revolutionary critic] was apparently unaware of the fact that the upper-class quarters were, more often than not, intolerable super-slums. (Mumford, 1961:464–465)

Thus, according to Mumford, the new industrial cities not only were bleak environments for the poor, but also were just as intolerably overcrowded, ugly, and unhygienic for the nonpoor.

A pioneering work in U.S. urban history, Arthur M. Schlesinger's *The Rise of the American City, 1878–1898* (1933), makes the claim that innovation and social change are uniquely associated with city life. Schlesinger maintains that overcrowding in slums, intense economic and social interactions in the CBD, and other aspects of urban life lead city dwellers to adopt new lifestyles in order to survive. This theme echoes the findings of theorists from other disciplines, including the Chicago school of sociology.

Other historians trace changes within one city, often using the case study approach to illuminate issues common to other cities or to generate broader theory. Sam Bass Warner, Jr.'s, "If All the World Were Philadelphia: A Scaffolding for Urban History, 1774–1930" (1968), is a case in point. In this article, Warner looks at housing patterns in Philadelphia at three points in time: 1774, 1860, and 1930. Using historical data, Warner argues that at the time of the American Revolution, poor people in Philadelphia lived around the fringes of the city, not near the city's core. He maintains that both racial segregation and the relocation of slums near the CBD in Philadelphia were nineteenth-century phenomena. What caused these changes in settlement patterns? Warner says that improvements in transportation within the city and the creation of large business organizations led to the changing residential patterns. In conclusion, Warner states that the organizing principle of the big city in the nineteenth century became "intense segregation based on income, race, foreign birth, and class" (35).

## Psychology, Social Psychology, and Social Psychiatry

Is there an "urban personality" or an "urban way of life"? Do city folk suffer more mental illness than rural people? What effects does growing up poor, or rich, have on urbanites' beliefs about themselves and others? These are some questions explored by psychologists, social psychologists, and social psychiatrists.

A classic study in social psychology is Louis Wirth's "Urbanism as a Way of Life" (1938). This still controversial essay, excerpted in Chapter 5, contends that city dwellers—whether slum residents or super-rich—share certain characteristics, including indifference to others, sophistication, rationality, and calculating behavior. Presumably, urbanites develop these personality traits in order to defend themselves and preserve their sanity amid the intensity and stimulation of city life.

A generation later, Robert Coles explored the psyches of rich and poor children in both urban and rural America. In so doing, he created a new subdiscipline: social psychiatry. In his five-volume series *Children of Crisis*, Coles uses a mixture of clinical observation, oral history, narrative description, psychiatric approaches, and social comment to look at how wealth, power, cultural background, and historical influences mold the character of children and their expectations of what life can offer them. In the latter two volumes of his study, *Eskimos, Chicanos, Indians* (1977a) and *Privileged Ones: The Well Off and the Rich in America* (1977b), Coles paints a portrait of growing up poor, outside the mainstream of American culture, versus growing up wealthy. He notes striking differences. Rich children, for instance, are routinely trained to believe that their way of life is worthwhile; they grow up believing they're special. In Coles's words, the children of the wealthy have a "continuous and strong emphasis . . . on the 'self'" (1977b:380). In contrast, poor children, some trapped in the slums, are discouraged from being independent and assertive. They are routinely trained by parents and their environment to keep their thoughts to themselves and not to cultivate a sense of being special persons.

## Public Administration

Historically, the professional field of public administration emerged from the discipline of political science in the United States. The field is intimately connected with the efforts to reform the U.S. city. As Dwight Waldo states in his influential study *The Administrative State*, "Much of the impetus to public administration came from the municipal reformers [of the early 1900s], who were genuinely inspired by a City of the Future" (1948:73). Interestingly, in contrast to the intellectual bias against the city held by many social scientists in the first quarter of this century, public administration writers thought that "The Good Life is an urban life. . . . [They] rejected the Jeffersonian idea that cities are sores on the body politic and menaces to democracy."

It is tempting to say that what public administrators do is to manage the public business, carrying out decisions made by political leaders. But this creates a false distinction between administrators and politicians. Early theorists of public administration attempted to distinguish between administration and politics, but current thinkers reject this distinction, demonstrating that administration *is* politics. In other words, the administration of public programs, such as school busing, is a highly political process. Indeed, bureaucratic politics (e.g., the politics of constructing a city or national budget, discussed in Chapter 19) has increasingly captured the imagination of public administration scholars.

In the case of slums, theorists and practitioners in the field have written about a number of issues, ranging from the interface between professionals and their welfare clients to evaluations of government programs designed, in theory at least, to alleviate poverty and slum conditions.

## City Planning and Urban Design

Like public administration in the United States, city planning and urban design are relatively young professional fields. Initially, they were heavily influenced by the ideas and methods of architecture, engineering, and landscape architecture. Today, graduate programs in city planning usually offer training in economics, information science, and policy analysis, as well as the more traditional fare. And reflecting fears of urban terrorism, some programs now offer courses in security techniques, such as ways to protect a city's water supply.

Planning—whether for city growth or social purposes—has not had the acceptance in the United States that it enjoys in many other nations, including England and France. Indeed, as a political scientist puts it, the United States is "the most anti-statist country in the developed world" (Lipset in Burdman, 1995:A11). In large part, this reflects American individualism and nonconformity dating from frontier days, captured in this old backwoods lyric:

I'll buy my own whiskey, I'll drink my own dram,
And for them that don't like me, I don't give a
    damn!

It also reflects many Americans' long-standing preference for private enterprise and reliance on the market to regulate economic matters, including what gets built where. However, with the enlarged reach of corporate business and the expansion of federal, state, and local governments since World War II, more economic and physical (but relatively few social) planners have been added to private and public payrolls.

Wherever they work, city planners and urban designers are, of necessity, political animals. More than most urban professionals, they find themselves at the center of perpetual controversy and in a maelstrom of conflicting demands from numerous groups (Forester, 1988). They can hardly ignore the clout of private developers; citizens' preferences either for preserving the character of the community or attracting new people, business, and money; federal regulation of local programs; the political environment in which they work; and differences in aesthetics and perceived needs among local groups. Even the most functional and aesthetically pleasing (in the planners' minds, at least) design plan remains a plan until both private and public interests decide to fund it and back it.

## Mass Communications

"*Who* says *what* in *which channel* to *whom* with *what effect?*" That was the question a pioneer in the interdisciplinary field of mass communications, political scientist Harold Lasswell (1943), asked years ago that summarizes the field's concerns. Usually, researchers focus on one of the five Ws: *who* (communicators), *what* (message content), *which channel* (medium of communication), *to whom* (audience analysis), or *what effect* (impact).

Since World War II, computers and other electronic media have changed how people work, where they live, and perhaps how they think (McLuhan, 1964; Smith 1980; Meyrowitz, 1985; Zuboff, 1988). Many scholars think that these new communications technologies have had revolutionary consequences, creating a global village, a global economy, and a global culture. Moviemaker Francis Ford Coppola sums up the changes this way: "The communications revolution makes the Industrial Revolution look like a small-time tryout out of town."

Computers and communications technologies have profound political impacts too. One theorist even predicts the end of the nation-state because it is based on territoriality, and computer-based technologies know no such geographical boundaries (Smith in Brand, 1987:239; see Chapter 5 for a fuller discussion).

How does high-techology, fueling an **information economy** (Porat, 1977), affect cities and suburbs? Most scholars agree that the new "high

**Fig. 2.5** ONCE IT LEAVES THE DRAWING BOARD . . . What pleases the planners and urban designers may not suit various interest groups, both public and private. Drawing a plan is only the first step in the long, highly political process of getting it implemented. These drawings, from the *San Francisco Urban Design Plan* (1971), reveal the planners' preference for long vistas of the Bay, unobstructed by tall buildings. (Reprinted by permission of the San Francisco City Planning Department)

technology is deeply modifying our cities and regions" (Castells, 1985:19). But to whose benefit and whose loss? Most probably, divisions between rich and poor cities, between cities and suburbs, and between inner-city neighborhoods will deepen as a result of this information technology–economy gap (Castells, 1985:32). In short, at all levels—from local to international—the information-poor will probably get poorer and the information-rich richer. Why? For interconnected reasons, including the following: (1) the information economy tends to polarize the workforce into the highly paid and well educated versus the poorly paid, and less educated, and (2) the information economy encourages the "electronic home" and "electronic office," which, in turn, stimulate sprawl outside inner cities (Castells, 1985: 32).

The United States (and some other countries, including Japan) has entered the stage of **postindustrialism** or **informationalism**—where more people manage things, serve things, think about things, and communicate about things than produce things. According to many (but not all) scholars, information processing has become the core activity of production, distribution, consumption, and management (Castells, 1989:17).

Particularly relevant to the example of slums are studies dealing with access to information in postindustrial society. Some scholars fear that the information highway is market-driven, narrowcasting (instead of broadcasting) to affluent segments of the population while ignoring the poor, and thus increasing the gap between information-rich and information-poor. From a different angle, political sociologist Claus Mueller (1973) contends that lower-class people in advanced technological societies like the United States lack both the linguistic ability and the conceptual frameworks that would allow them to gain access to necessary information to participate effectively in politics. He argues that the mass media reinforce consumerism and leisure, thus integrating the poor into the political system. Others (e.g., Phillips, 1975; Romano, 1985) maintain that news reportage routinely ignores issues that concern the city's poor and ethnic groups; such issues become defined as non-news and don't even get debated. This suggests that even so-called objective news reports are biased in a subtle way: toward a particular view of the social world—a cosmopolitan, middle- and upper-class, educated view that reflects the news reporters' own outlook on reality.

## Environmental Studies

Deforested jungles, ozone depletion, garbage pile-ups, hazardous waste, oil spills, nuclear accidents, and industrial smog all helped to raise global consciousness of the borderless biosphere. One response is Eco-Rap, a movement devoted to spreading environmental concern through music, spearheaded by Berkeley performance artist and historian Leonard Pitt. Another response is new university-based programs dedicated to the interdisciplinary field of environmental studies. Typically, these programs cover a variety of topics, from risk analysis, conflicts between job loss and environmental destruction, and occupational health to solid waste disposal.

Environmental studies may also include the study of mass migrations and international conflict that can result from environmental degradation. Indeed, according to one observer, the environment is *the* national security issue of the early twenty-first century: "The political and strategic impact of surging populations, spreading dis-

ease, deforestation and soil erosion, water depletion, air pollution, and, possibly, rising sea levels in critical, overcrowded regions like the Nile Delta and Bangladesh . . . will be the core foreign-policy challenge from which most others will ultimately emanate" (Kaplan, 1994:58).

Environmentally speaking, what to do with effluents in affluent industrial cities is a continuing question (Lampard, 1973; Melosi, 1981; Lewis, Kaltofen, and Ormsby, 1991). Recently, environmental studies scholars have been asking these questions, all connected to slums and poverty: *Where* do private corporations and public governments dump toxic wastes? (Answer: often in poor neighborhoods of rich countries heavily populated by people of color, such as East Los Angeles [Lee, 1987] and poor countries, including West Africa's extremely poor Benin.) *Why* do poor African-American urbanites have much shorter life expectancies than whites? (Answer, according to Weissman and Epstein [1989]: numerous factors related to poverty, such as high infant mortality rates, and some related to race, such as racial inequalities in medical care.) And *who* pays the highest price for ecological disruption? (Answer, according to sociologist-engineer-chemist Allan Schnaiberg: the urban poor. Typically, Schnaiberg argues, publicly funded projects, such as suburban freeways, "have subsidized the material progress of affluent suburbanites at the expense of working and poverty-class urban dwellers, whose tax burdens grow and whose social services decline" [1980:337]).

## Literature and the Arts

How often poets, songwriters, and artists speak to the soul, clarifying the human condition in ways that statistics or theoretical models cannot! Those familiar with the poor southern sharecroppers in Walker Evans's photos in James Agee's *Let Us Now Praise Famous Men* ([1939] 1960) and Dale Maharidge and Michael Williamson's *And Their Children After Them* (1989) or the Kinte clan in Alex Haley's *Roots* (1976) can feel poverty's ache. Likewise, we feel like we know the Cuban

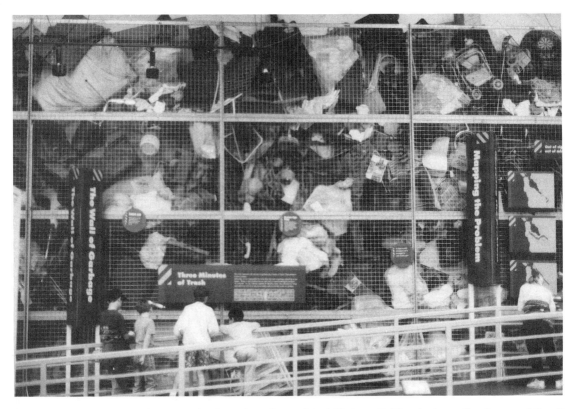

**Fig. 2.6**  GARBAGE MUSEUM. At The Recyclery, located in Milpitas, California (near San Jose and San Francisco), there is a 100-foot-long, 20-foot-high Wall of Garbage representing all the junk dumped in Santa Clara County every three minutes, or one second of all U.S. trash. (Tim Teninty)

immigrants to New York City yearning for success in Oscar Hijuelos's *The Mambo Kings Play Songs of Love* (1989). All these works provide a firsthand encounter with these people and their lives, an acquaintance that touches the emotions as well as the intellect.

Poverty and slum conditions have been a theme in the arts since the Industrial Revolution, which gave us both the word *slum* and the condition called slums. To take but one example, novelist Charles Dickens draws a portrait of Coketown, a new industrial town that could be one of many English cities in the mid-nineteenth century:

It was a town of red brick or of brick that would have been red if the smoke and ashes had allowed it; but as matters stood it was a town of unnatural red and black like the painted face of a savage. It was a town of machinery and tall chimneys, out of which interminable serpents of smoke trailed themselves. . . . It had a black canal in it, and a river that ran purple with ill-smelling dye, and vast piles of buildings full of windows where there was a rattling and a trembling all day long. . . . It contained several large streets . . . inhabited by people equally like each other, who all went in and out at the same hours, with the same sound upon the same pavements, to do the same work, and to whom every day was the same as yesterday and tomorrow, and every year the counterpart of the last and the next. ([1854] 1967:17)

No statistical table can capture the monotonous rhythm of life, the squalor and dirt, and the pervasive gloom of working conditions in nineteenth-century England as well as Dickens's word portrait.

More recently, the urban despair of poor children has been captured in their own words and images. Listen to one twelve-year-old, Shemika Skipworth, speaking about what she knows firsthand—coping with a parent's drug habit:

> You go to the mail pick up your check
> Go and smoke it up on the project step
> Now you're on the streets nowhere to go
> You smoked up your check and you can't go home.
>                                    (in Williams, 1989)

The image of poverty and slums has also been poignantly captured by the movie camera. Yet, most Hollywood movies focus on the social disorder presumed to accompany slum life. *West Side Story* (1961) is a case in point. But on close inspection, the film also shows what sociologist Gerald D. Suttles calls *The Social Order of the Slum* (1968): a well-defined moral order rooted in personalistic relations and provincialism. To be sure, the rules of the gangs (the Jets and Sharks) are not those of middle-class block groups. But they are widely understood by people in the neighborhood, and they serve to regulate daily life.

Other forms of popular culture and folk culture—from graffiti and street murals to bestsellers and rap music—are important sources for understanding people's responses to poverty and slum life. Consider, for instance, one American musical tradition: the blues. The blues speak of melancholy, what early American settlers from England called the "blue devils." Immigrants coming from the villages and small towns of the British Isles to the hills and hollows of the American wilderness apparently suffered from the blue devils of homesickness, and they sang about it. In the words of novelist Thomas Wolfe, the pioneers were "lost and wind-grieved" in the vast, raw spaces of the New World. Later, in the nineteenth century, white and black migrants from the rural countryside to the city started singing the blues. Some sang "The House of the Rising Sun Blues," the story of the poverty that forced poor country girls, perhaps as early as the 1840s, into a life of prostitution in New Orleans.

Freed slaves during the Reconstruction era sang of their kinship with the boll weevil, which "was lookin' for a home, just a'lookin' for a home." And around 1900, when some blacks left southern sharecropping and headed north, they "found the blues waiting . . . at every station down the line. [They had] the *Alabama Blues, The Atlanta Blues, The New Orleans Hop Scop Blues, The Fort Worth Blues and the Dallas Heart Disease, The St. Louis Blues . . . , The Michigan Water Blues, The Wabash Blues, The State Street Blues* (in Chicago), *The Harlem Blues*" (Lomax, 1960:576). And in the textile mill towns, workers sang the "Winnsboro Cotton Mill Blues" or "Cotton Mill Colic": "I'm a-gonna starve, ev'rybody will, / You can't make a livin' at a cotton mill" (Lomax, 1960:287).

By the 1920s, blues singers like Big Bill Broonzy began recording their songs for the whole world to hear. As folk song historian Alan Lomax comments:

> If all the verses of the recorded blues were laid end to end, it would make a lonesome moan that could be heard on the moon. These songs speak plainly, pithily, and powerfully about the emotional disturbances of urban society in the west. The jobless, dispossessed, unwanted predatory Negro [sic] male was the first character in our civilization to experience and express these feelings. Now we are all aware of them, and the big sad wind of the blues sings through the heartstrings from Memphis to Moscow. (1960:576)

More recently, African-American hip-hop and rap artists sing of desperation, not melancholy. In the songs of Ice-T, for example, "The House" down the street is a prison, and no one tries to save kids from their abusive parents. The neighborhoods he chronicles are often "The Killing Fields" where some residents treat an Uzi submachine gun as their best friend.

## MAKING SOME CONNECTIONS

After this brief look at how various disciplines and fields of knowledge might view one urban condition through their own special lenses (and blinders), we might ask whether any common foci appear. And you might wonder, quite sensibly, whether any connections, however desirable, can be made.

Some common themes and factors do emerge from this potpourri of information about slums. For one thing, the impact of economic forces in shaping people's lives is a theme that cuts across many disciplines and fields. Economic logic underpins Burgess's model of urban growth and Alonso's model of residential bid rent. Economic forces are also emphasized in Lewis's anthropological studies of the culture of poverty, Warner's historical look at Philadelphia, Coles's social psychiatric research on children, and Mueller's analysis of communication in mass society. Other factors important to urban life that cross-cut disciplines and fields include the importance of power relations, social organization, information flows, environment, and technology in influencing individual lives.

For another thing, this brief look at perspectives on slums shows that intellectual disciplines may have unique outlooks, but scholars don't stop at disciplinary boundaries. Indeed, some scholars seem impossible to classify! Take, for one, Spanish-born, French-trained, U.S.-published scholar Manuel Castells. He defies national or departmental pigeonholing. Trained as a sociologist in Paris, Castells did research in the 1960s on industrial location, a concern more typical of geography and economics. By 1979, he was professor of city and regional planning at the University of California at Berkeley. Space and social structure remain key to his theory and research, which ranges widely over issues of political movements, the process of urbanization, economic change, and comparative urban life.

Another theme emerges: People living in a certain situation—say, in Appalachian poverty or Philadelphia's slum—may understand their subjective experience differently than "objective" social scientists do. As I've implied by starting this book with a list of personal biases, the notion of an objective, value-free social science is a mythical ideal, not a practical possibility. Worse, it often serves as a cover, turning a professional, upper-middle-class view of what's real into the official definition of reality. This can be especially dangerous when urbanists advise policymakers. Projecting what they think is objectively good for other people (especially people who don't share the same dreams, material possessions, or values), urbanists have often imposed their values on others in the name of objectivity.

Unfortunately, no synthesis of views is on the horizon; the lack of an agreed-upon conceptual framework and the absence of meaningful consensus among urbanists prevent it. Still, we can begin the project of weaving some threads together to better understand the urban world.

As we begin that difficult, long-term project, let us recall Gertrude Stein. Her life as a writer exemplifies the quest to see beyond a mere litany of facts. On her deathbed, Stein turned to her assembled friends and asked, "What is the answer?" After a moment of stunned silence, she asked, "What, then, is the question?" Then she died.

The next chapter suggests some worthwhile questions to ask. It also looks at even more reasons why urban observers disagree on answers.

## KEY TERMS

**Bid rent curve**   Economist's description of how much a residential buyer will bid (pay) for land or rent at varying distances from the CBD of a city.

**Burgess model**   Model or hypothesis constructed by sociologist Ernest W. Burgess concerning the spatial-social structure of the U.S. industrial city and its expansion over time. The hypothesis explains that a city's population is organized in a series of five concentric rings or zones, starting from the CBD.

**Cognitive maps**   Personal, mental maps that usually bear little resemblance to official tourist maps of a city or neighborhood. Images of a city—outstanding features, landmarks, important places, and so on—differ among individuals and social groups.

**Discipline**   A division of intellectual labor associated with higher education. As specialization increased and knowledge about the physical and social world expanded in the nineteenth century, social science split up into disciplines: economics, political science, sociology, and so forth.

**Filtering** The process by which housing passes or trickles down from higher-income to lower-income residents as it ages and becomes less desirable. Thus, a mansion built in 1860 for a very rich family may have filtered down to house a moderate-income family by 1920. By 1980, the same house might have filtered down still further to house four very-low-income families. Opposite: *gentrification.*

**Industrial cities** Cities such as Chicago and Detroit in the United States whose population growth and spatial pattern were influenced mainly by manufacturing and centralizing technologies. Contrasts: Preindustrial cities such as Paris and Tokyo; postindustrial regions such as Orange County, California.

**Information economy** A type of economy built on telecommunication highways that distribute information (which becomes a commodity, like shoes or cars) to be bought and sold. Similar terms: *information society, postindustrial society.*

**Informationalism** A type of social organization, evolved from industrialism, that depends on information processing as its core activity. This term is associated with sociologist-planner Manuel Castells, who argues that cities and regions of the world are being transformed by a combination of technological and economic processes.

**Interdisciplinary** Having a degree of integration among several disciplines. The concepts, methodology, procedures, terminology, or data may be more or less connected among two or more disciplines in an interdisciplinary study. To some, *interdisciplinary* connotes the attempt to bridge disciplines and apply research tools and/or perspectives from more than one discipline; to others, it is synonymous with multidisciplinary studies.

**Latent function** A function or purpose hidden from view and often unintended. For example, a city public works department exists officially to build roads. Its latent function may be to provide patronage opportunities such as jobs for political supporters and ethnic voting groups.

**Manifest function** The officially stated, visible reason for existence. For example, building roads is the manifest function of a city's public-works department.

**Multidisciplinary** Involving more than one academic discipline. In practice, multidisciplinary and interdisciplinary efforts are not always distinguishable.

**Paradigm** A model or patterned way of seeing the world. In the scientific disciplines, the dominant paradigm defines the problems and methods of a research field; it makes legitimate what counts as facts, what assumptions are valid, and what procedures are deemed scientific. Today there are competing paradigms in the social science disciplines.

**Postindustrialism** As distinguished from preindustrialism and industrialism, a society and an economy characterized by high technology, which permits most people to work at jobs in the information and service sectors rather than in the agricultural and manufacturing sectors.

**Typology** A classification scheme composed of two or more ideal types, used to organize data and guide research—for example, four types of slum dwellers, distinguished by length of residence and reasons for being there.

**Urban studies** A multidisciplinary or interdisciplinary field of study whose central focus is the city and its surrounding area. Its intellectual boundaries are not well defined, and programs of urban studies vary in content from one academic institution to another.

## PROJECTS

1. **What you see depends on how you look at it.** Select four individuals of differing occupations and neighborhoods (for instance, a Zone II food server; a downtown business executive, a suburban athletic coach) and ask each one to draw a simple sketch of the city you're in (or near), noting its most important places and outstanding features. Do these cognitive maps differ? If so, how?

2. **Disciplinary perspectives.** Select one urban issue, such as transportation, crime, violence, or unemployment, and examine how basic texts in at least three different disciplines or fields approach it, noting what factors they stress in their analysis. Do themes emerge?

3. **I hear the country singing.** Using the same

issue selected for Project 2, investigate how song-writers have approached it. For example, compare the messages in songs recorded by rap groups and pop singers. In what ways, if any, do these approaches vary from those of the three intellectual disciplines and/or professional fields?

## SUGGESTIONS FOR FURTHER LEARNING

Two books about Paris illustrate the saying "What you see depends on how you look at it": Mort Rosenblum, *The Secret Life of the Seine* (Reading, Mass.: Addison-Wesley, William Patrick, 1994), and François Maspero, *Roissy Express: A Journey Through the Paris Suburbs* (New York: Verso, 1994). Rosenblum's romantic view of Paris comes from his life aboard a 54-foot boat. Maspero's steely-eyed perspective comes from his ride aboard the 37-mile train from Charles de Gaulle Airport to the other side of Paris, where he sees mostly dreary housing and drab, disjointed spaces when he visits each of the thirty-eight stops.

For a closer look at disciplinary perspectives, the best bet is introductory texts. For sociology, as one example, see a best-selling text by Donald Light, Suzanne Keller, and Craig Calhoun, *Sociology* (New York: Knopf, 1989); it presents the sociological perspective in Chapter 1 and discusses urban life in Chapter 9.

For an example of how various perspectives can be fused to obtain a richer view of urban life, see Sharon Zukin, *The Culture of Cities* (New York: Blackwell, 1995). She draws on insights from sociology, political economy, and the analysis of visual form.

For recent thinking about an alternative approach to a discipline, see the essays on feminist economics in Julie A. Nelson and Marianne A. Ferber, eds., *Beyond Economic Man: Feminist Theory and Economics* (Chicago: University of Chicago Press, 1993), and Nancy Folbre, *Who Pays for the Kids?* (New York: Routledge, 1994). The Folbre study of child care calls into question neoclassical economics's assumption of the so-called rational actor. The author wonders what a mother's self-interest is—can she separate her self-interest from that of her own child?

British sociologists Mike Savage and Alan Warde give a history and critique of urban sociology (and the "new" urban sociology) in *Urban Sociology, Capitalism and Modernity* (New York: Continuum, 1993). They believe that "there is no solid definition of the urban" and that the label "urban sociology" is "mostly a flag of convenience." Yet, they try to "identify the common elements" explaining the persistence of their subdiscipline, urban sociology.

For a hands-on experience of how disciplines and fields work, computer software can be helpful. See, for one, a computer game designed by Will Wright, "Sim City" (Lafayette, Calif.: Maxis Software); it allows a player to build a city and make it work. Simulated City players fashion their own cities or play one of eight disaster scenarios.

Reflecting a profound change in the discipline of anthropology, urban places like Fargo, North Dakota—rather than the Trobriand Islands—are becoming common research sites for U.S. anthropologists. One award-winning study, Faye D. Ginsburg, *Contested Lives: The Abortion Debate in an American Community* (Berkeley: University of California Press, 1989), is based on field interviews in Fargo with middle-class women.

Too numerous to mention, of course, are all the works of literary and visual art that expand our vision of the urban world. Here are just a few on one topic: the blues. In *Looking Up at Down: The Emergence of Blues Culture* (Philadephia: Temple University Press, 1989), William B. Barlow traces the blues from its rural roots to its urbanization in Chicago, Memphis, and other regional centers. For poetic commentaries on folk music and personal evocations of the communities that produced the blues, see Alan Lomax, *The Folk Songs of North America in the English Language* (Garden City, N.Y.: Doubleday, 1960), and *The Land Where the Blues Began* (New York: Pantheon, 1993). Lomax himself collected many of these songs as he traveled throughout the United States. Lomax's *Blues in the Mississippi Night* (1990, compact disc) features blues musicians reminiscing about life and music in the Deep South.

A series of eight videotapes produced by the Conference on Literature and the Urban Experience (CLUE) at Rutgers University shows artists, novelists, playwrights, and social scientists giving poetry readings or talking about a variety of topics, ranging from *The Language of the Streets* (James Baldwin) and *The Re-invention of Childhood* (Jonathan Kozol) to *City Limits: Village Values—Concepts of the Neighborhood in Black Fiction* (Toni Morrison).

For an excellent discussion of attitudes toward urban and rural life expressed in U.S. painting, see Sidra Stich's *Made in U.S.A.* (Berkeley: University of California Press, 1987). One section on cities, suburbs, and highways—the "New American Landscape"—argues that in the 1950s and 1960s, U.S. painters called attention to "the congestion and exhilaration of the urban milieu, the comfort and conformity of suburbia, and the fascination and monotony of the highway." Such artists as Robert Bechtle and Robert Arneson "openly exposed the most banal and alienating aspects of the contemporary setting" (45).

Movies alert us to a special kind of alienation: the rage and violence of oppressive urban lives. One powerful film, Matty Rich's *Straight Out of Brooklyn* (1991), is a dynamic and tragic description of life in an African-American ghetto. *River's Edge* (1987), based on a real-life event in the San Francisco Bay Area, vividly portrays the alienation of teenagers in a white working-class suburb.

Peter Gould and Rodney White present cognitive images of places and distances in *Mental Maps*, 2nd ed. (Winchester, Mass.: Allen & Unwin, 1986). David Brodsky offers "Thirteen Ways of Looking at a Freeway" in *L.A. Freeway* (Berkeley: University of California Press, 1981); this study explores the ways in which the southern California freeway defines the way people think about the metropolitan area.

Geographer Mark Monmonier reminds us that maps may reflect unconscious bias. He notes that "a single map is but one of an indefinitely large number of maps that might be produced for the same situation or from the same data" in *How to Lie with Maps* (Chicago: University of Chicago Press, 1991). In *The Power of Maps* (New York:

Guilford Press, 1992), Denis Wood goes further, arguing that all maps necessarily "lie" because, like paintings, they express a viewpoint.

Concerning slum districts, Robert D. Kaplan infers that maps often lie in other ways. In "The Coming Anarchy," *Atlantic Monthly*, February 1994, pp. 44–76, Kaplan says that perhaps 15 percent of the population of the Ivory Coast's capital—Abidjan, often called the Paris of West Africa—live in shantytowns named Chicago, Washington, and so on; few such slums appear on maps. To Kaplan, this suggests that political maps are "products of tired conventional wisdom" and "in the Ivory Coast's case, of an elite that will ultimately be forced to relinquish power" (48).

## REFERENCES

Agee, James, and Walker Evans. [1939] 1960. *Let Us Now Praise Famous Men.* Boston: Houghton Mifflin.

Alexander, Jeffrey C. 1993. "The irrational disciplinarity of undergraduate education." *Chronicle of Higher Education* (December 1):B3.

Alonso, William. 1971. "Beyond the inter-disciplinary approach to planning." *American Institute of Planners Journal* 37:169–173.

————. 1973. "A theory of the urban land market." Pp. 45–55 in Ronald E. Grieson, ed., *Urban Economics.* Boston: Little, Brown.

Anderson, Elijah. 1990. *Streetwise: Race, Class, and Change in an Urban Community.* Chicago: University of Chicago Press.

Banfield, Edward, and Martin Meyerson. 1955. *Politics, Planning, and the Public Interest.* Glencoe, Ill.: Free Press.

Bergmann, Barbara R. 1986. *The Economic Emergence of Women.* New York: Basic Books.

Brand, Stewart. 1987. *The Media Lab: Inventing the Future at MIT.* New York: Viking.

Braudel, Fernand. [1986] 1990. *The Identity of France.* Vol. 1, *History and Environment.* Trans. Sian Reynolds. New York: Harper & Row.

Burdman, Pamela. 1995. "Bombings linked to social malaise." *San Francisco Chronicle* (May 1):A1+.

Castells, Manuel. 1985. "High technology, economic restructuring, and the urban-regional process in the United States." Pp. 11–40 in *High Technology,*

*Space, and Society.* Vol. 28 of Urban Affairs Annual Reviews. Beverly Hills, Calif.: Sage.

———. 1989. *The Informational City: Information Technology, Economic Restructuring, and the Urban-Regional Process.* Oxford: Blackwell.

Coles, Robert. 1977a. *Eskimos, Chicanos, Indians.* Boston: Little, Brown.

———. 1977b. *Privileged Ones: The Well-Off and the Rich in America.* Boston: Little, Brown.

*The Compact Edition of the Oxford English Dictionary.* 1971. New York: Oxford University Press.

Coughlin, Ellen K. 1987. "Geographers are urged to reorient research to central concerns of place and space." *Chronicle of Higher Education* (May 13):9.

———. 1993. "Feminist economists vs. 'economic man': Questioning a field's bedrock concepts." *Chronicle of Higher Education* (June 30):A8–9.

Dickens, Charles. [1854] 1967. *Hard Times.* New York: Dutton.

Duverger, Maurice. 1964. *An Introduction to the Social Sciences.* New York: Praeger.

Feagin, Joe R., and Robert Parker. 1990. *Building American Cities: The Urban Real Estate Game,* 2nd ed. Englewood Cliffs, N.J.: Prentice-Hall.

Forester, John F. 1988. *Planning in the Face of Power.* Berkeley: University of California Press.

Foucault, Michel. 1980. "Questions on geography." Pp. 63–77 in C. Gordon, ed., *Power/Knowledge: Selected Interviews and Other Writings, 1972–1977.* New York: Pantheon.

Freedman, James O. 1987. "The tendency toward specialization has had fragmenting consequences." *Chronicle of Higher Education* (August 12):A47.

Gottdiener, M[ark]. [1985] 1988. *The Social Production of Urban Space.* Austin: University of Texas Press.

Gottdiener, Mark, and Joe Feagin. 1988. "The paradigm shift in urban sociology." *Urban Affairs Quarterly* 24:163–187.

Gradwohl, David M., and Nancy M. Osborn. 1984. *Exploring Buried Buxton: Archeology of an Abandoned Coal Mining Town with a Large Black Population.* Ames: Iowa State University Press.

Haley, Alex. 1976. *Roots.* Garden City, N.Y.: Doubleday.

Hijuelos, Oscar. 1989. *The Mambo Kings Play Songs of Love.* New York: Farrar, Straus & Giroux.

Hunter, David R. 1964. *The Slums.* New York: Free Press.

Kaplan, Robert D. 1994. "The coming anarchy." *Atlantic Monthly* (February):44–76.

Kates, Robert W. 1989. "The great questions of science and society do not fit neatly into single disciplines." *Chronicle of Higher Education* (May 17):B1+.

Lampard, Eric. 1973. "The urbanizing world." Pp. 3–57 in H. J. Dyos and Michael Wolff, eds., *The Victorian City: Images and Realities.* Vol. 1. London: Routledge and Kegan Paul.

Lasswell, Harold. 1943. "The structure and function of communications in society." Pp. 37–51 in Lyman Bryson, ed., *The Communication of Ideas.* New York: Institute for Religious and Social Studies.

Lee, Charles. 1987. "Waste and race." New York: United Church of Christ.

Lefebve, Henri. [1974] 1991. *The Production of Space.* Trans. Donald Nicholson-Smith. Oxford: Blackwell.

Leopold, Wendy. 1992. "Through a glass darkly: Making sense of what happened in L.A." *Mosaic* (Summer):3–4.

Lewis, Oscar. 1961. *The Children of Sanchez.* New York: Random House.

Lewis, Sanford, Marco Kaltofen, and Gregory Ormsby. 1991. "Border trouble: Rivers in peril, a report on water pollution due to industrial development in northern Mexico." Boston: National Toxic Campaign Fund.

Logan, John R., and Harvey L. Molotch. 1987. *Urban Fortunes: The Political Economy of Place.* Berkeley: University of California Press.

Lomax, Alan. 1960. *The Folk Songs of North America in the English Language.* Garden City, N.Y.: Doubleday.

Lynch, Kevin. [1960] 1974. *The Image of the City.* Cambridge, Mass.: MIT Press.

Maharidge, Dale, and Michael Williamson. 1989. *And Their Children After Them: The Legacy of* Let Us Now Praise Famous Men: *James Agee, Walker Evans, and the Rise and Fall of Cotton in the South.* New York: Pantheon.

McLuhan, Marshall. 1964. *Understanding Media: The Extensions of Man.* New York: McGraw-Hill.

Melosi, Martin V. 1981. *Garbage in the Cities: Refuse, Reform, and the Environment, 1880–1980.* Chicago: Dorsey.

Meyrowitz, Joshua. 1985. *No Sense of Place: The Impact of Electronic Media on Social Behavior.* New York: Oxford University Press.

Morganthau, Tom. 1993. "The new frontier for civil rights." *Newsweek* (November 29): 65–66.

Mueller, Claus. 1973. *The Politics of Communication: A Study in the Political Sociology of Language, Social-*

*ization, and Legitimation.* New York: Oxford University Press.

Mumford, Lewis. 1961. *The City in History: Its Origins, Its Transformations, and Its Prospects.* New York: Harcourt, Brace & World.

Newman, John Henry Cardinal. [1852] 1919. *The Idea of a University.* London: Longmans, Green.

Owens, Bill. 1977. *Working [I Do It for the Money].* New York: Simon and Schuster.

Palen, J. John, and Bruce London. 1984. *Gentrification, Displacement and Neighborhood Revitalization.* Albany: State University of New York Press.

Phillips, E. Barbara. 1975. "The artists of everyday life: Journalists, their craft, and their consciousness." Ph.D. diss., Syracuse University.

Porat, Marc Uri. 1977. *The Information Economy: Definition and Measurement.* Washington, D.C.: Office of Telecommunications, Department of Commerce.

*The Power of Maps.* 1993. Washington, D.C.: Cooper-Hewitt, National Museum of Design, Smithsonian Institution.

Princeton Survey Research Associates. 1993. "Newsweek–Children's Defense Fund Poll." *Newsweek* (November 29):65.

Rathje, William L., and Cullen Murphy. 1992. *Rubbish! The Archaeology of Garbage.* New York: HarperCollins.

Renwick, Trudi J., and Barbara R. Bergmann. 1993. "A budget-based definition of poverty with an application to single-parent families." *Journal of Human Resources* 28:1–24.

Romano, Carlin. 1985. "The grisly truth about bare facts." Pp. 37–78 in Robert Karl Manoff and Michael Schudson, eds., *Reading the News.* New York: Pantheon.

Saint-Exupéry, Antoine de. [1943] 1970. *The Little Prince.* Trans. Katherine Woods. New York: Harcourt Brace Jovanovich.

Savage, Mike, and Alan Warde. 1993. *Urban Sociology, Capitalism and Modernity.* New York: Continuum.

Schlesinger, Arthur M. 1933. *The Rise of the American City: 1878–1898.* New York: Macmillan.

Schnaiberg, Allan. 1980. *The Environment: From Surplus to Scarcity.* New York: Oxford University Press.

Seeley, John R. [1959] 1970. "The slum: Its nature, use and users." Pp. 285–296 in Robert Gutman and David Popenoe, eds., *Neighborhood, City, and Metropolis.* New York: Random House.

Sharff, Jagna Wojcicka. 1987. "The underground economy of a poor neighborhood." Pp. 19–50 in Leith Mulling, ed., *Cities of the United States: Studies in Urban Anthropology.* New York: Columbia University Press.

Smith, Anthony. 1980. *The Geopolitics of Information: How Western Culture Dominates the World.* New York: Oxford University Press.

Smith, Michael Peter. 1996. *Urban Theory.* New York: Blackwell.

Soja, Edward W. 1995. *Thirdspace: A Journey Through Los Angeles and Other Real-and-Imagined Places.* New York: Blackwell.

Southall, Aidan, ed. 1973. *Urban Anthropology: Cross-Cultural Studies of Urbanization.* New York: Oxford University Press.

Susskind, Lawrence. 1978. Personal conversation. Berkeley, Calif.

Suttles, Gerald D. 1968. *The Social Order of the Slum: Ethnicity and Territory in the Inner City.* Chicago: University of Chicago Press.

Wacquant, Löic J. D. 1989. "The ghetto, the state, and the new capitalist economy." *Dissent* (Fall): 508–520.

Waldo, Dwight. 1948. *The Administrative State.* New York: Ronald Press.

Warner, Sam Bass, Jr. 1968. "If all the world were Philadelphia: A scaffolding for urban history, 1774–1930." *American Historical Review* 74:182–195.

Weathers, Diane, with Holly Morris, Geoffrey Precourt, and James C. Jones. 1979. "Urban archeology." *Newsweek* 83 (April 16):81–82.

Weissman, Joel, and Arnold M. Epstein. 1989. "Case mix and resource utilization by uninsured hospital patients in the Boston metropolitan area." *Journal of the American Medical Association* (June 23–30):3572–3576.

"Wild in the city: The bioregional mapping of San Francisco." 1984. *Planet Drum Review* 9:11.

Williams, Cecil, ed. 1989. *I Have Something to Say About This Big Trouble.* San Francisco: Glide World.

Wirth, Louis. 1938. "Urbanism as a way of life." *American Journal of Sociology* 44:1–24.

Wood, Denis. 1992. *The Power of Maps.* New York: Guilford Press.

Zuboff, Shoshana. 1988. *In the Age of the Smart Machine: The Future of Work and Power.* New York: Basic Books.

*Mary Swisher*

## DOING SCIENCE

At their best, urbanists make the world more understandable. In their struggle to reach this goal, they think in ways common to all intellectual disciplines. To begin with, they are skeptical. As astronomer Carl Sagan puts it, "skeptical scrutiny is the means, in . . . science . . . by which deep insights can be winnowed from deep nonsense" (1978:xiv).

In addition, urbanists are tentative and humble about their knowledge. Most realize that "most of what we think we know about social reality is going to be obsolete in the near future" (Smith in Coughlin, 1992:A11).

Finally, more often than might be suspected, urbanists bring eagerness and passion to their work. When this happens, it results in what Sagan calls the "romance of science." An ecstatic sense of discovery, of following up on hunches, and of creatively searching for meaning—these are at the heart of doing science too.

Qualities like ecstasy are best experienced firsthand or vicariously through the words and images of inspired communicators, including Sagan. Instead of dwelling on these qualities here, we'll focus on common elements of doing science that can be transmitted from generation to generation: reasoning processes, systematic analysis, and hypothesis construction.

# CHAPTER 3
# Posing the Questions

## Reasoning, Deductive and Inductive

Deductive and inductive reasoning processes represent two ways of gaining knowledge about a subject. **Deductive reasoning** proceeds from general principles to particular examples. A **model** of how something works is speculatively constructed in the theorist's mind, then tested by gathering data. **Inductive reasoning** proceeds from particular instances to the general. A researcher first collects and sifts through pieces of **empirical evidence** and then derives **hypotheses** and generates **theories** about how something works.

In practice, however, the two kinds of reasoning processes are not clearly separate. None of us starts with a blank mind. We have some preconceived notions about how something might work or couldn't work; these models influence how we interpret new information. Without some assumptions or working models, we wouldn't even know what data to start gathering. So, most social science thinking develops as a result of both inductive and deductive reasoning.

This was the case for Ernest W. Burgess. This University of Chicago sociologist started with a hunch: that human communities are organized in ways similar to plant communities along Chicago's lakefront. Then he sent his students out to collect any data they could find—where pool hall hustlers gathered, where the rich and poor lived, what crimes were committed in which neighborhoods, and so forth. On the basis of this empirical evidence, he derived his refined concentric zone hypothesis of urban space.

## Systematic Analysis

Whatever their disciplinary background, scholars are routinely taught how to use the **scientific method.** This name—scientific method—makes doing science sound much more methodical than is usually the case. It also masks the guesswork and creativity involved. Nonetheless, it is the model for doing science in the West, setting the step-by-step procedures for collecting, checking, classifying, and analyzing data. In theory, the scientific method proceeds as follows:

*Step 1.* Defining the problem and stating it in terms of existing research.
*Step 2.* Classifying or categorizing facts, often by constructing categories or typologies (e.g., types of slum dwellers by reasons for residence).
*Step 3.* Constructing hypotheses related to the problem—that is, looking for possible relationships between phenomena or factors. (For instance, in the Burgess model, it is hypothesized that an individual's social status is linked to his or her place of residence in the city: The higher the status, the farther out from the CBD the person lives.)
*Step 4.* Determining what methods to use for data gathering and then gathering the data.
*Step 5.* Analyzing the data gathered to see if hypotheses are confirmed or disconfirmed; relating findings to the existing body of theory.
*Step 6.* Predicting facts on the basis of findings.

In practice, scientific research doesn't usually proceed in such well-ordered, successive steps. First, the steps are often interwoven. For instance, constructing categories entails some prior observation. Second, the scientific method has no provision for intuitive flashes or acquaintance with something. It is a **positivistic** model that assumes that anything worth knowing can be known through sensory experience and verified by procedures outlined in the six steps. But we know, by Einstein's own declaration, that intuitive insight inspired his theory of relativity, a theory that forever changed our way of seeing the universe. Indeed, scientific breakthroughs often result from minds not hemmed in by the reigning paradigms of doing science (Kuhn, [1962] 1970).

As discussed in Chapter 1, the scientific method is now questioned by a host of scholars—philosophers of science, the New Physicists, phenomenological philosophers, and social scientists. Under attack are the scientific method's assumptions that there are causes and effects that can be tested; that objectivity can be achieved; and that subjective insight plays no role in actual scientific endeavors.

To conclude: Currently, the very notion of objectivity is suspect. So is the positivists' clear distinction between facts and values. Today, neither physical nor social scientists agree on what doing science really means. Nonetheless, as noted in Chapter 1, the *ideal* of scientific objectivity may be too important to discard.

## Facts, Hypotheses, and Value Judgments

For a moment, let's play the "as if" game. Let's return to the scientific method *as if* facts can be separated from values, *as if* there are causes and effects that can be tested.

Like other scholars, urbanists are trained to use the scientific method. This method makes clear distinctions among statements of fact, statements of suggested relationships among facts, and value judgments about facts. These are called *empirical statements, hypotheses,* and *normative statements,* respectively. The ability to differentiate among these three types of statements is a prerequisite to critical analysis.

Consider the following sentences that could appear in a government report about homelessness:

1. In Our Town, 100 homeless persons (including 40 children) sleep in shelters located in "The Pits," a Zone II-ish area near downtown that lacks playgrounds and schools.
2. Since no homeless shelters exist in The Heights (a high-income, high-status area), the City Council has probably vetoed the conversion of empty mansions there into homeless shelters.
3. Shelters should be scattered throughout Our Town so that homeless children will have easy access to schools and healthy places to play.

*Statement 1 is presented as an empirical or factual statement.* It appears to be based on scientifically gathered and accurately reported data. These facts can be checked and verified by independent researchers.

*Statement 2 is disguised as a statement of fact, but it is not.* Rather, it is a hypothesis—that is, a statement of relationship between two or more **variables** (factors subject to change). In this case, there are two variables: (1) spatially segregated homeless shelters and (2) the City Council's veto power. Statement 2 can be restated in the form of a hypothesis using these two variables: Our Town's clustered pattern of homeless shelters is a product of the City Council's veto power, used to prevent placing homeless shelters in affluent neighborhoods.

The *independent* variable (the factor that causes or influences something; in this case, the resulting spatially segregated homeless shelters) is the City Council's veto power. The *dependent* variable (the factor determined or influenced by the independent variable) is the pattern of spatially segregated homeless shelters.

Hypotheses must satisfy two requirements: (1) they must be testable, and (2) they must contain a statement of relationship. The statement that "the Devil controls the world" satisfies neither requirement. It is not testable by empirical scientific methods. Nor is it a statement of relationship; it is merely an assertion. By contrast, the suggested relationship between clustered homeless shelters and the veto power of elected officials satisfies both requirements: It can be tested by the scientific method, and it contains a statement of relationship between two variables.

*Statement 3 is neither a statement of fact nor a hypothesis.* It is a normative statement, a value judgment about what *should* be. It is based on the researcher's own values of what is good or bad. One can agree or disagree with a normative statement, depending on one's values.

Separating empirical statements, hypotheses, and normative statements is not always easy (Box 3.1). For instance, the statement that "people on welfare don't want to work" is not factual; it is a hypothesis in disguise. It states a relationship between being poor and being lazy. In this case, the thrust of social science research (e.g., Goodwin, 1972; Hartmann and Spalter-Roth, 1992) shows

Box 3.1

## RATIONAL ANALYSIS

### Hypotheses

Distinguishing between mere assertions and hypotheses is a critical step in rational analysis. For example, the statement that "People are basically evil" (or "good") is a mere assertion. It fails to meet the two basic requirements of a hypothesis: (1) it is not testable by scientific methods, and (2) it does not contain a statement of suggested relationship. By contrast, the following is a hypothesis containing an independent and a dependent variable:

The suicide rate among Protestants is higher than the suicide rate among Catholics and Jews.

This hypothesis suggests a relationship between religion and suicide rate. The independent variable is religion; the dependent variable is suicide rate. It suggests that a group's religious background affects the propensity of its members to commit suicide.

The graphic model below (a bid rent curve) contains an implied hypothesis: a statement of relationship be-

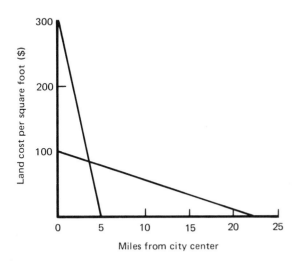

Miles from city center

tween two variables—cost of land and distance of land from the city center. In this model, distance determines land cost or rent: As distance from the city center increases, land cost decreases. Thus distance is the independent variable, and cost is the dependent variable.

The following statement is a hypothesis containing several variables:

Unemployed teenage urban males are more alienated from the political system than unemployed urban teenage females or unemployed rural teenagers.

This hypothesis suggests a relationship between place of residence (urban or rural), sex (male or female), and attitudes toward government. Age is a constant—not a variable—here, for all involved are teenagers. The dependent variable is attitude toward the political system; the hypothesis suggests that attitude toward the political system depends on both sex and place of residence.

The following paragraph contains an implied hypothesis, empirical statements, and a normative statement:

In 1990 there were 5,000 large families (with three or more children) in Our Town living below the poverty line. A child born into a large family was 3.5 times as likely to be poor as a child born into a small family (with fewer than three children). To decrease the number of people below the poverty line, governmental programs should encourage the use of contraceptives by persons who already have two children.

The implied hypothesis here is that family size is related to income level. Family size is the independent variable, and poverty status is the dependent variable. The first sentence of the paragraph is an empirical statement. The last sentence is a normative statement. An alternative normative statement, derived from the same empirical information, is this: To decrease the number of people below the poverty line, government should guarantee large families an annual income.

that welfare recipients prefer working to receiving government assistance, and that the number of welfare mothers unwilling to work is far smaller than believed. Thus the hypothesis is generally invalid or nul.

## WHY SOCIAL SCIENTISTS DISAGREE

Ideally, social scientists seek the truth at all times and apply the scientific method to their research. Why, then, can they look at the same phenomena —say, poverty and slums—and disagree on what they see and what should be done about it?

To explore this knotty question, let us take the example of poverty in urban America. Suppose that the president of the United States declares a war on poverty. Before deciding how best to fight the war, the president appoints a task force of highly respected social scientists. Their mission is to produce a joint report on the causes, nature, and extent of poverty in the nation's cities. Eighteen months and $1.5 million later, the report is submitted for policy action. It contains a majority opinion and three separate minority reports. It is clear that the researchers disagree among themselves on basic issues. To begin with, they disagree on whether or not poverty even constitutes a problem. In addition, those who think it is a problem don't agree on whether it can be solved or on the means to solve it.

Disagreements among task force members might be based on the following kinds of differences: (1) theoretical orientations, (2) disciplinary perspectives, (3) research methods, (4) levels of analysis, (5) ideological assumptions and values, (6) subtle influences, such as the funding source, and (7) attitudes toward social problem solving. These differences can affect what questions a researcher asks, what a researcher finds, how a researcher defines the problem and thus the solution, and/or what the researcher advises doing about it.

### Theoretical Orientations

First, social scientists do not share a theoretical orientation. Within any one discipline, there may

be competing models or paradigms of how the world works. Taking sociology as an example, let's examine how two major theoretical orientations filter the social world through different lenses: structural-functionalism and symbolic interaction. Very briefly, structural-functionalists are concerned with the structures of society and their functions (purposes). They look for the connections among different parts of a social system, assuming that society, like the human body, is organized in terms of systems and subsystems. Just as each system of the body (circulation, defense against disease, etc.) serves different functions and contributes to the whole organism's welfare, so do different institutional structures in society. In this view, systems (both the human organism and the social system) seek equilibrium, balance, stability, and order. Structural-functionalists think that whatever exists—poverty, for instance—serves a social function or it would cease to exist. Critics of structural-functionalism hold that this theoretical perspective is inherently conservative because it focuses on social order (rather than social change) and things as they are (rather than things as they might be).

Symbolic interactionists have a different focus. Instead of social systems or institutions, they focus on *meaning*—how people construct meanings, how they define social reality in different ways. They deal with micro-worlds of social behavior, such as face-to-face encounters and small-group behavior. The language people use to express themselves (both words and gestures) and the way these words and gestures are understood by others are especially interesting to symbolic interactionists. They may explore the subtle ways in which meaning is transmitted between parents and children in the slums or the interpretation of action from the actor's point of view. Researchers in this tradition are routinely trained in qualitative techniques such as participant-observation and in-depth interviewing. Herbert Gans's study of a Boston slum, *The Urban Villagers* (1962), examines the group life of Italian-Americans using the participant-observation research method.

Each theoretical orientation looks at poverty (as a research problem) in a particular way. And

**Fig. 3.1** FACTS DON'T SPEAK FOR THEMSELVES. (© 1976 Richard Hedman)

in large measure, each approach determines what questions will be asked. In turn, what questions are asked influences one's findings about the nature and causes of poverty.

## Disciplinary Perspectives

Urbanists bring their disciplinary perspectives with them when they investigate an issue. The example of slums in Chapter 2 illustrated how various social science disciplines, professional fields, and the humanities might see slums and poverty. Recall that some concepts and research tools cross disciplines, but each one retains its central focus. This means that scholars in the same discipline may differ in their theoretical orientations, and even in their ideologies and methods, but still share a disciplinary perspective that sets them apart from other social scientists.

## Research Methods

Urbanists use different strategies for observing and analyzing facts. Research methods may vary among disciplines, subdisciplines, and theoretical orientations. Most economists today, for instance, use quantitative techniques (econometrics, mathematical equations and models, statistical analysis). Anthropologists, on the contrary, depend primarily on qualitative techniques—direct, intensive observation of social life through fieldwork, or what sociologists call **participant-observation.** This entails observing people firsthand to get an intimate, personal acquaintance with their situation or way of life.

Within a single discipline techniques vary, so much so that researchers often find it difficult to understand one other. This situation is reflected in learned journals. For example, sociologists trained mainly in qualitative methods often find it hard to follow current articles in the discipline's leading journals because so much research today is based on quantitative techniques.

Members of a theoretical school are routinely trained in particular methods. In sociology, for instance, symbolic interactionists are trained in the method of participant-observation. This method encourages inductive reasoning. Theory is grounded in and generated from direct obser-

**Fig. 3.2**   DOING SOCIAL SCIENCE. (Richard Hedman; revised by Lisa Siegel Sullivan)

vation. In contrast, structural-functionalists (and neo-Marxists) are more commonly trained in quantitative research methods and tend to begin with more complete models of how things work, thus applying deductive reasoning to the facts they find.

Comparison—the analysis of similarities or differences among phenomena—is considered by many theorists to be the basic method of the social sciences. But researchers use varying techniques to gather and analyze comparative data. Some study the content of written and other social documents: official statistics, diaries, graffiti, paintings, tombstones, organizational records, TV soap operas, census data, and so on. Others gather information by conducting polls and interviewing random samples of the population (survey research) or setting up controlled experiments. To express the results of these various data-gathering techniques, urbanists use a number of aids: graphs, organization charts, diagrams, flow charts, statistical tables, verbatim conversational reports, narrative description, and abstract models.

Why do the techniques used to investigate and analyze a research problem like poverty make a difference? As philosophers of science point out, the techniques used to investigate a research topic help to determine what the findings will be. Here is one example, discussed in Chapter 14 in greater detail. Two social scientists, political scientist Robert Dahl and sociologist-anthropologist Floyd Hunter, set out to study the same questions: Who runs this town? How are political decisions made at the city level? Hunter ([1953] 1963) used a technique called the *reputational method* to explore the question, asking influential people in Atlanta, Georgia, to assess the relative power of reputed leaders in local decision making. Dahl (1961), investigating who runs New Haven, Connecticut, used *decision analysis*, examining local decisions (e.g., urban renewal) to see who participated in making them. The two researchers found different patterns of influence and power. Hunter found a power structure that was highly centralized and monolithic. Dahl found a pluralistic structure in which various elites shared power. *To a significant degree, the research methods that Dahl and Hunter used helped to determine what kind of power structure each found.*

Each method of investigation has its own strengths and weaknesses. Participant-observation can provide direct acquaintance with poverty; no questionnaire survey can do that. But no direct observation of a few people living in poverty can yield general statements about all people living in poverty; the group under study may be atypical. Then again, a person constructing a questionnaire may miss salient questions without firsthand acquaintance with poverty situations. Similarly, those who depend on official statistics can be misled, even if the statistics represent the best available data. Suicide rates are illustrative. Whether a death is reported as natural or suicide is often problematic; high-status individuals may not be listed as suicides as often as low-status, low-income individuals, for family doctors can list deaths as natural to protect the high-status family from embarrassment, while the poor have fewer means to protect themselves. For these reasons, methodologists counsel social science researchers to use a variety of techniques in their work—for example, to combine fieldwork (participant-observation and interviewing) with survey research and **unobtrusive measures** (i.e., methods that don't influence the research subjects or have reactive effects, such as analyzing the content of documents or TV shows).

## Levels of Analysis

"Science," says astronomer Carl Sagan, "is a way of thinking much more than it is a body of knowledge" (1978:13). For some, doing science means reflecting on a grain of salt; for others, it means trying to understand the entire universe. And for still others, it means trying to make the connections between the grain of salt and the entire universe.

Those who study grains of salt use the micro-level approach, focusing on small-scale phenomena. Micro-sociology is the study of small groups. Micro-economics is the study of the economic behavior of individuals, households, and business firms.

Those who study the universe, so to speak, use the macro-level approach. Macro-sociology is thus the study of large-scale social systems, and macro-economics investigates how fiscal and monetary policies and other large-scale factors keep an economic system working.

Used in combination, the micro and macro approaches can give a very different view of a phenomenon, such as poverty, than either could do alone. Elliot Liebow's study of black streetcorner men in Washington, D.C., *Tally's Corner* (1967), demonstrates the wisdom of using both levels of analysis to explore the same issue. In *Tally's Corner*, Liebow gives an account, based on his participant-observation, of how this group of men spend much of their daily life hanging out on streetcorners in the nation's capital. But he doesn't stop there. He goes on to relate their everyday activities to larger social forces—racial discrimination, structures of economic opportunity, and other factors that shape their everyday lives. Had he looked only at the macro level (the larger social forces that influenced the men's self-perceptions and lifestyles) or only at the micro-social structure (the streetcorner), he could not have traced the interrelationships between individual behavior and structural opportunities. Connecting micro and macro levels of analysis, Liebow finds that the behavior of Tally and his buddies is a response to their failure to reach the goals of the dominant culture—goals that the men share. Liebow concludes that it is a lack of economic opportunity and lack of skills—not distinctive cultural traits (as Oscar Lewis's "culture of poverty" thesis would have it)—or laziness that mold the lives of the twenty-four men who stand around the New Deal Carry-out shop at Tally's corner.

## Ideologies and Values

In 1960, Harvard sociologist Daniel Bell proclaimed *The End of Ideology*. Bell reasoned that in

**Fig. 3.3** NEITHER CONSERVATIVE, LIBERAL, NOR RADICAL. Political ideology may help to explain some attitudes and behaviors. However, attending car worship services is not one of them. (Deborah Mosca)

the then emerging postindustrial society, intellectuals (including urbanists) would not have deep-seated ideological differences. Heralding the exhaustion of political ideas, Bell said that public choices in postindustrial society would be technical, not political, in character. (This vision seemed to underpin Ross Perot's 1992 presidential campaign.)

More than thirty years later, postindustrialism had arrived in the United States, and Daniel Bell had shifted ground. Bell now says that American intellectuals no longer agree on the ends of public policy: "We may be at the end of old ideologies . . . but there are [*sic*] no unified set of beliefs to take their place" (1992:E17). Many theorists and citizens agree with Bell.

Is there a unifying framework on the horizon? Who knows? Perhaps we are witnessing a turning point when new theories are emerging to explain socioeconomic and political organization in a global economy. Meanwhile, many "isms" and "ocracies" compete for preeminence. The range is fairly broad, from nationalism, tribalism, feminism, fascism, communitarianism, conservatism, religious fundamentalism, democracy, and technocracy to environmentalism, libertarianism, democratic socialism, neo-Nazism, and anarchism.

Here, let us focus on a time-honored, tripartite division of political thought: conservative, liberal, and radical. These labels are now used fairly loosely. For instance, a TV newscaster in Syracuse, New York, once described his town as "conservative." Pressed to specify what he meant by this label, he answered, "You know, Syracusans don't get married in drive-in churches or buy everything on credit." What he apparently meant was that *conservatism* refers to traditional social values. To some, including one-time presidential candidate Michael Dukakis, a *liberal* is a person who is "open-minded." To others, a conservative is "a liberal who's been mugged." *Radical* may conjure up the image of a wild-eyed, bearded bomb thrower. And to the nineteenth-century satirist Ambrose Bierce, a conservative is "a statesman who is enamored of existing evils, as distinguished from the liberal, who wishes to replace them with others."

However, these loosely applied labels do have —or have had—more precise meanings. Conservative social thinkers have had a consistent view of human nature for hundreds of years, and a rather pessimistic one at that. Radicals, on the contrary, have maintained a much rosier picture of human motivation, tending to see bad social systems, not inherently bad people. This is a more optimistic view of social change, for it follows that if a social system is altered, the personalities of the people who live under it will also change.

The liberal label once had a very precise denotation. To be a liberal in the nineteenth century meant holding certain ideas about how the social and economic orders did and should work. *Classical liberalism* (also called *laissez-faire economics*) provides the basis for what is today called *economic conservatism*. In other words, a nineteenth-century classical liberal would be called an economic conservative today.

To make things even more confusing, *liberal* has become a code word. As used by conservatives, it often refers to "tax-and-spend" politicians who are "soft on crime" and who support racial "quotas" in hiring.

It is worth mentioning that liberalism, radicalism, and conservatism—indeed, all political belief systems—share one important attribute: All **ideologies** pivot on a view of human nature, a view that can be neither defended nor refuted on strictly empirical grounds. Ideologies, in other words, are more faith claim than science.

**The Liberal and Neoliberal Perspectives** Originally, the liberal perspective saw humankind through the eyes of English philosopher Thomas Hobbes (1599–1679). According to Hobbes, the human condition is one of "the war of all against all." People are driven by personal gain, glory, and selfishness. Their lives are "solitary . . . nasty, brutish, and short." In order to bypass people's assumed selfishness and greed, liberal philosophers assigned all social and political decision making to a mechanism they believed to be neutral and self-regulating: the market of supply and demand.

Over the centuries, liberalism changed significantly. Liberals today tend to be more optimistic about the slow but sure progress of individuals and society. They also think that the market mechanism doesn't always work to prevent major social and economic trauma, such as worldwide economic depression. Yet, through all of these changes, Hobbes's materialist conception of human nature and his atomistic individualism remain at the heart of the liberal perspective.

Before detailing the points of difference between liberals and conservatives today, let's examine their shared assumptions. These assumptions are rooted in the political economy of Adam Smith (1776), and they can be found today between the lines in the many editions of one of liberalism's most well-read works: Paul Samuelson's best-selling introductory text, *Economics*. Liberals, both classical and modern, make the following assumptions:

1. *People act in their own rational self-interest.* Individuals and decision-making units (such as business firms) act in a rational way to maximize their own welfare.
2. *Consumers are sovereign in the marketplace.* Given simple constraints, individuals are free to determine how to use their scarce resources, choosing goods and services from a wide range of alternatives in the marketplace.
3. *The market is self-regulating.* The market mechanism of supply and demand "still works to solve the WHAT, HOW and FOR WHOM questions" (Samuelson, 1964:53).
4. *The "invisible hand" works to serve the public in-*

*terest and bring about social equilibrium.* Adam Smith theorized in 1776 that each individual would act in the general interest "as if guided by an invisible hand." In other words, individual and social interests automatically harmonize; if you do well for yourself, you also benefit the entire community.

5. *A rising tide lifts all boats.* National growth and prosperity benefit all citizens.

6. *Wealth trickles down from top to bottom.* Money invested by business elites eventually filters down to those at the bottom of the social ladder, thereby benefiting everyone. Or as a president of General Motors put it in the 1950s: "What's good for GM is good for the country."

These key assumptions underlie classical liberalism. It is evident that the role of the free market is central to their analysis.

The major area of disagreement between liberals and conservatives today is the role of government in modern American life. Liberals tend to believe that the market does not always work to provide opportunities for those at the lower end of the social ladder. In contrast, conservatives tend to think that the expansion of government regulations and programs—so-called trickle-down government—is the problem, not the solution. Indeed, some liberals hold that "in the global economy, 'trickle down' has been replaced by 'trickle out,' as American savings race to wherever around the globe they can get the highest returns" (Reich, 1991:E15). Thus, liberals hold, government *should* intervene in the competitive market to affect public welfare and help individuals do better for themselves (thus benefiting the entire community). In practice, this means that liberals support the expansion of opportunities for all (through job training, education, etc.) and income redistribution (through tax policy, resource-allocation policies, etc.).

Liberals today also support government intervention to promote economic stability. They want to avoid the unemployment and instability that accompanied the Great Depression of the 1930s. To prevent another ruinous depression and lessen the effects of massive unrest in the 1930s, Lord John Maynard Keynes advocated vast government spending to create jobs for millions of persons out of work and to intervene in the private market. Since the 1930s, Keynesian and neo-Keynesian prescriptions and economic analysis have dominated liberal economic thought. MIT is known as a bastion of neo-Keynesian thinking.

Traditionally, liberals have favored government intervention at the federal level, viewing state and local governments as either incompetent, corrupt, and / or agents of the status quo. In recent years, however, some liberals have changed their tune, stressing grass-roots efforts to achieve social change. Liberals were at the forefront of programs created in the 1960s such as Head Start, a federally funded but locally run antipoverty program.

Generally speaking, liberals view many present facts of urban life—such as poverty and homelessness—as capable of solution or at least amelioration. Their approach to problem solving is to make incremental changes at the edges of social and economic institutions, not to restructure basic institutions. A major tool of liberal social policy is the federal income tax. Liberals view the federal income tax as a key instrument in redistributing goods and services that the market fails to provide for citizens at the bottom (and sometimes middle) of the economic ladder.

Another liberal solution to urban problems concerns government investment in people: sponsoring programs aimed at creating conditions of supposedly equal opportunity for citizens deemed disadvantaged. Federally sponsored Head Start, job training, and affirmative action programs are based on the liberal tenet of providing equal opportunity for all.

Another key liberal assumption bears special notice. An extension of classical liberal thought, it joins liberal politics to liberal economics: pluralist democracy. Liberals assume that power is fairly widely dispersed among a multiplicity of interest groups, each representing its members' self-interest.

The liberals' notion of pluralist democracy in America—where diverse interest groups bargain

**Fig. 3.4** GET THE LIFE JACKETS! Liberals favor government intervention to address some failures of the free market system. (© 1976 Richard Hedman)

and negotiate in the political arena to protect their rational self-interest—helps account for their almost total inattention to or dismissal of the issue of social class. Both conservatives and radicals use the concept of social class in their analysis of society and social problems (albeit in very different ways), but liberals tend to act "as if the subject did not exist" (Hacker, 1973:65). However, many liberals focus on race (instead of class) as a key factor in understanding sociopolitical life in the United States.

During the Reagan–Bush years (1980–1992), liberalism was tarred by conservatives as the *l* word: an obscene term signifying big government, affirmative action, and weak defense. By and large, liberal policy proposals—more funds to cities, more social programs designed to help the poor and so on—were rejected at the polls. One response: neoliberalism. Neoliberals (socalled New Democrats) see themselves as prag-

matists, incorporating ideas they deem sensible from across the political spectrum. Bill Clinton exemplified neoliberalism circa 1992. The *Washington Monthly* is one of their journals.

In brief, then, liberals and neoliberals today tend to sponsor social change within prescribed limits: social change that can be managed and directed by government action, that is incremental in nature, and that does not alter basic economic and social institutions. Liberals view government as the proper agent of managed social change; neoliberals see a larger role for the private sector.

### The Conservative and Neoconservative Perspectives
As outlined earlier, conservatives today remain classical liberals in their economic doctrine. They tend to see big government as the enemy, a threat to individual freedom and pros-

perity. In their view, business interests—if left alone and unhampered by government interference or regulations—would do a better job than government of managing the economy. This preference for the free market to determine social and political outcomes means that conservatives tend to fear big government more than big business. In contrast, contemporary liberals tend to fear big business more.

Again in contrast to liberals, most conservatives today do not favor social reforms. To understand why, we must look at the conservatives' assumptions about human nature and the social order. Basically, conservatives are pessimistic about the human condition. In the words of a classic conservative thinker, Edmund Burke (1729–1797), people have "disorderly appetites" such as pride, avarice, lust, and ambition. Or, in the words of contemporary conservative James Burnham: "man is partly corrupt as well as limited in his potential" (in Hacker, 1973:13). In other words, individuals are deeply flawed, marked with what Christian theologians call *original sin.* It follows that people are not essentially good and that even the best-intentioned social reforms are self-defeating because people are prone to perversity. Given this view of human nature, it also follows that conservatives prize social stability, social order, and authority above all else.

So-called neoconservatives share the basic assumptions of laissez-faire economic doctrine and conservative social thought. This group emerged in the late 1960s in the wake of what they considered to be the excesses of liberalism: the Great Society programs of President Lyndon B. Johnson (including the War on Poverty), New Left politics, and countercultural lifestyles. What makes them "neo" or new conservatives is not their pessimism about human nature or their distrust of the masses, for these are traditional conservative ideas. Rather, it is their perception of the current American situation. They fear a crisis of authority, a breakdown in morality, a loss of family values, and government's inability to govern. The neoconservatives fear liberal and radical proposed solutions to poverty and social injustice more than they fear the injustices themselves (Steinfels, 1979).

Edward Banfield sums up the neoconservative stance in his still controversial books, *The Unheavenly City* ([1968] 1970) and *The Unheavenly City Revisited* (1974). Banfield argues that "social problems will sometimes disappear in the normal course of events" and "government cannot solve the problems of the cities and is likely to make them worse by trying" (1970:257). Further, Banfield discusses class characteristics openly, claiming that "so long as the city contains a sizable lower class nothing basic can be done about its most serious problems" (1970:210).

Banfield, together with some other 1960s urbanists, including Senator Daniel Patrick Moynihan (D-New York) and social scientist Nathan Glazer, form part of the neoconservative core. Their doctrines can be found in the pages of their journals, notably *Public Interest* and *Commentary.*

In the Reagan–Bush era, conservative economics joined hands with neoconservative politics and moral conservatism. As the Cold War of anti-Communism waned, another war galvanized moral conservatives: a cultural-religious war for what was called "the soul of America" (Buchanan, 1992). To neoconservatives, "welfare" seems to connote the destruction of "traditional American values," specifically, hard work; individual enterprise; two-parent, heterosexual families, and productivity. For example, President Bush's press secretary blamed welfare and the "failed liberal social policies" of the 1960s and 1970s for the 1992 riots in Los Angeles.

From the morally conservative standpoint, where did America go wrong? According to Buchanan, the "problems" are pornography, public schools that expelled Christ and the Ten Commandments, rock concerts and rap music, and a breakdown in families (in Wills, 1992:9). His solutions follow directly from his definition of the problems: school prayer, censorship of violent movies and music, and an infusion of traditional values.

In terms of public policy proposals, conservatives, neo or otherwise, continue to reject social programs and what they consider the "liberal do-goodism" that began under Franklin D. Roosevelt. Instead, they encourage the privatization

**Fig. 3.5**  GET SOME NEW BOATS! Radicals call for basic changes in the relationships between social classes in order to meet the problems of people and cities in distress. (© 1976 Richard Hedman)

of public services (e.g., turning prisons and museums over to private enterprise) and the lowering of taxes on investment. These policies are rooted in the free-market, anti-Keynesian ideology of the University of Chicago school of economics. This school of thought is associated with several Nobel Prize–winning economists, including Milton Friedman.

**The Radical Perspective**  The radical perspective is a misnomer. Radicals range from far right, anti-federal-government white Christian supremacist revolutionaries (e.g., Aryan Nations) to far left, anti-corporate revolutionaries (e.g., Peru's Shining Path). Here I focus on only one strand of radicalism: thought rooted in the theories of Karl Marx. Why? Because in social science, his ideas have been both influential and inescapable.

*A note at the outset:* When discussing Marx and

his interpreters, you need a scorecard to know who thinks what. There are at least five varieties of neo-Marxists, and they disagree among themselves on (1) how to interpret what Marx originally said or (2) how best to apply Marx's notions to the contemporary world. Even so, they tend to share a basic notion: Most social problems cannot be solved within the context of the present institutional structure. This radical idea is in contrast to (1) conservatives and neoconservatives, who think that few social problems can be solved (especially by government programs), and (2) liberals and neoliberals, who think that government action can improve social life. Marxists reject the liberal problem-solving approach of incremental change at the edges of basic social and economic institutions. They say that only by going to the roots (*radical* means "root") of economic instability and social injustice can problems be solved. Fiddling around with marginal changes, radicals claim, is like applying Band-Aids to social cancers; superficial responses won't cure the root problem. For Marxists, it is not possible to abolish poverty and leave the present economic system intact. In their view, capitalism and authority structures that grow out of that social-economic-political system are the roots of the problem.

Urban geographer David Harvey (1973, 1989) is a spokesperson for one branch of neo-Marxism. Harvey starts with this assumption: Poverty is a manifestation of social structural problems in monopoly capitalism, the national and international socioeconomic system. In his view, what is needed is not liberal reform or conservative benign neglect of social problems. What is needed is radical restructuring along socialist lines.

Some neo-Marxists point to such conditions as the unequal distribution of wealth and income among social classes and the capitalist state's alliance with business interests and elite groups as forces that perpetuate poverty. Since most neo-Marxists think that government is part of the problem, they don't look to government for the solution.

One Marxist analysis of society proceeds from the following assumptions:

1. *The productive forces in society determine its essential character.* The prevailing beliefs, legal system, politics, and social relationships in a society are determined by that society's mode of production (e.g., the state of technology, the ownership and management of scarce resources, and the authority relations that result from a particular productive mode, such as feudalism or capitalism).
2. *There is no such thing as "human nature."* This follows from the first assumption that the ways people think, relate to other people and their work, and even feel are linked to the prevailing mode of production. For instance, people tilling the soil in preindustrial rural societies, fashioning handicrafts in medieval towns, or attaching left-rear bumpers on an assembly line in capitalist urban-industrial societies necessarily interpret their worlds in

very different ways. People are formed by the productive activities in society. They are not basically "economic animals," as the liberal perspective maintains; rather, they are active agents who transform the material world and master nature. Marx used the term *Homo faber* ("man the maker" or "producer") to express this notion.

3. *Social conflict between classes dominates capitalist societies.* Under the capitalist mode of production, social harmony does not exist (as liberals maintain). Rather, economic and political life is primarily determined by the conflict between two great social classes: those who own or control factories, global finance, information, and other productive forces in society (the bourgeoisie, now including the upper executive and professional corporate sectors) and those who neither own nor control the society's productive forces (the have-nots, or the proletariat, now including clerical workers, the "new working class" of the service economy). Under capitalism, a few "continue to obtain enormous shares of wealth and leisure, while others continue to support themselves and others with their labor" (Gordon, 1977:7). In other words, neo-Marxists see a necessary connection between poverty and wealth under capitalism: Some are poor because others are rich.
4. *Government (the state) under capitalism is not neutral.* Whereas liberals see diverse interest groups bargaining and negotiating for scarce resources in the political arena in the context of a neutral government, some (but not all) neo-Marxists see the state as a tool of the bourgeoisie. Decision making is dominated by those who own and control society's productive forces or by civil servants who act to protect their interests. In short, public policy under capitalism is dominated by urban business and creditor classes.
5. *Under monopoly capitalism today, the self-regulating market mechanism is a fiction.* The theory of the free market as self-regulating neglects the facts of monopoly price-fixing, the creation of needs by advertising, the corporate political economy that tries to avoid competi-

tion in its own interest, and government intervention on behalf of private enterprise (e.g., "welfare for the rich" in the form of business subsidies, tax breaks, and bailouts).

6. *The sum of the private interests does not equal the public interest.* Believing, as classical liberals (conservatives) do, that the "invisible hand" works to ensure social harmony and individual well-being is illogical. It assumes that "the lead of private greed [can be transmuted] into the gold of public welfare" (Wolfson and Stanley, 1969:1).

Democratic socialist Irving Howe briefly addresses points 4 to 6 in this radical critique, saying that the dominant ethic of the Reagan–Bush years was

a heartless Social Darwinism, reinforced by the weary myth that the sum of individual selfishness would be collective beneficence. Mindless chanting for "the free market" filled the air, though in every modern society government and the economy are intertwined. . . . The ideological right kept shrilling that nothing good could come from government, and did its best to prove it. The rich got richer, the poor poorer.

Howe's "solution": "Sooner or later, America will have to address the fact that multinational corporations can carry on production anywhere in the world and can disregard governments that would set standards (minimum wages, child labor laws, Social Security). This systemic problem requires, at the least, enforcement of international labor standards" (1993:A19). Like many before him, Howe suggests that the (multinational) tail may be wagging the (government) dog, not vice versa.

In sum, neo-Marxists and democratic socialists don't expect the capitalist state to change its basic institutional structure. On the contrary, they see government policies and programs— affirmative action and college loan programs, for example—as smoke screens, diverting attention from structural problems inherent under capitalism. In their view, such superficial programs give the populace a false feeling of change, ignoring

the roots of unemployment and alienation. Further, in their view, liberal programs mainly substitute racial conflict for class struggle.

**New Dimensions** By tradition, Marxists, socialists, and syndicalists (e.g., the Wobblies) are considered to fall on the left of the political spectrum, while liberals occupy the center and conservatives the right. Most probably, this left–center–right distinction originated in the seating arrangements of the eighteenth-century French National Assembly; socialists and other radicals took the chamber's left wing, moderates were seated in the middle, and social conservatives of the day on the right.

People still identify political ideologies as left-wing, right-wing, and middle-of-the-road. Yet this one-dimensional view obscures a great deal. First, it overlooks the centralist–decentralist dimension. Decentralists agree with the economist E. F. Schumacher (1973) that "small is beautiful." They tend to be anti-bigness, and pro-self-sufficient, small community. Decentralists of the left and right come together on such concerns as ecological consciousness and the desire to meet human needs rather than to encourage economic growth. By contrast, centralists tend to be pro-bigness: either big government or big business plus big technology. Centralists of the left and right come together on such issues as the preference for large-scale organizations (assumed to be efficient and economical providers of goods and services) and economic growth as a necessary condition of human welfare.

Second, the left–right spectrum may be breaking down on other grounds. According to one-time Republican strategist Kevin Phillips (1992:38), in a time of "economic trauma and disillusionment" like the 1990s, voters ignore ideological boundaries.

*To conclude:* Social scientists (including urbanists) disagree on fundamental issues of political ideology. Personal preferences (e.g., for left- or right-wing politics) influence how they see the world. These ideological preferences also influence how they advise policymakers to cope with the world—or try to change it.

## Subtle Influences on Researchers

Disagreements among urbanists can also stem from another factor: dependence on funding sources. In an era of government- and corporate-sponsored research, it is almost impossible for researchers to be independent intellectuals, answerable to nothing but their own conscience in the long search for knowledge.

Scholars of various ideologies decry the ever-increasing dependence on corporate and government funding sources. The president of the Council of Graduate Schools warns that "this pressure on universities to be research-and-development labs for industry is destroying research universities. It's distorting the values" (in Cordes, 1992:A26). One fear is that "he who pays the piper calls the tune."

## Attitudes Toward Solving Social Problems

Can social science solve social problems? Should social scientists play a key role in formulating social policy? Among themselves, social scientists don't agree, and their opinions often are linked to their ideologies (Box 3.2).

First, a note on the term *social problem*.

One hundred years ago, there were disagreeable social conditions, issues, and conflicts—but no social problems or social ills. The idea that society can be "sick" and need "treatment" for "chronic disease" is relatively recent, probably dating from the early twentieth century. The Chicago school of sociology (Park, Burgess, etc.) was partially responsible for this linguistic change that altered people's way of seeing the world, for they were convinced that urban industrial life led to "social disorganization" and "social pathology." Thus as they studied crime, deviance, juvenile delinquency, and other "pathologies," they helped to transfer medical and clinical language to the realm of urban life (Rule, 1978:16). At about the same time, the new field of psychoanalysis, in an attempt to gain legitimacy, began to apply the medical model to individual behavior. Where people were formerly labeled "sin-ful," "strange," or "eccentric," they now became mentally "ill."

Today we routinely use medical language to describe people and societies. What we often forget is that the medical model of illness and problems is a mere metaphor, a rhetorical device, that masks other ways of seeing and understanding. In particular, seeing disagreeable social conditions as problems conceals the political conflicts of interest that belie social problems: "A conflict, after all, inescapably requires one to take a stand. A 'problem,' on the other hand, is something everyone can safely oppose. . . . Social problem solving . . . is a profoundly political enterprise from beginning to end" (Rule, 1978:18–19, 23).

When problems were merely disagreeable social conditions, they were thought to be approachable through either the market mechanism or the political process. But once something is defined as a social problem, it logically calls for a technical solution. Here is the logic: Just as medical experts are needed to cure physical illness, social experts (social scientists) are needed to cure society's chronic ailments. Using technical experts—urbanists, for example—to solve social problems means transferring issues out of the political arena. This sidesteps public debate. It also turns social scientists into technocrats—as if they were value-free, with no ideological axes to grind. We have already seen how faulty that assumption is.

A case study by sociologist Scott Greer (1961) illustrates the problematic nature of problem solving. Looking at urban traffic and transportation, Greer asks: Whose problem is it? What kind of people, playing what social roles, define the nature of the metropolitan transportation problem? Who is concerned about it? After all, Greer says, traffic may not be a problem to drivers sitting and listening to car radios. Nor is traffic a major concern to suburbanites, who may pay the price of driving slowly through fumes rather than paying for antipollutants. But congestion may indeed be a major concern for downtown business merchants or suburban shopping mall developers. In other words, it is wrong to assume that a social problem is everyone's problem.

Box 3.2

## WHERE YOU STAND DEPENDS ON WHERE YOU SIT

### Handy Guide to Public Policy Proposers and Their Proposals

| Ideological Position | View of Present and Future | Proposals for Future |
| --- | --- | --- |
| Languishing Liberal | Troubled times | More money and programs, racial integration |
| Counteracting Conservative | Crime, centralization, and crumbling civilization | Law, order, soap, haircuts, truth and morality |
| Rabid Rightist | It's getting REDder all the time | Wave flags and stockpile arms (public and private) |
| Primitive Populist | Domination by pointy-headed pseudo-intellectuals | Throw briefcase in Potomac; restore common sense |
| Passionate Pacifist | A garrison state | A peaceable kingdom |
| Rumbling Revolutionary | A repressive, racist, imperialist, capitalist establishment | Confront and destroy The System (other details to be worked out later) |
| *Role-related positions* | | |
| Urgent Urbanist | Decline and fall of cities | More funds and programs, sidestepping states |
| Emphatic Ecologist | Decline and fall of everything else | Control contaminators and restore nature |
| Stultified Student | Entrapment in *their* world | Inner and interpersonal exploration and other relevant learning |
| Tortured Taxpayer | Growing gaps between income, aspirations, and expenditures | Cut, cut, cut, cut |
| Contracting Conglomerator | Cybernation, diversification, and internationalization | Withering of the state |

SOURCE: Michael Marien, "Handy Gride to Public Policy Proposers and Their Proposals," *Public Administration Review* 30(1970): 154. Copyright © 1970 by The American Society for Public Administration and the author. All rights reserved.

Greer advises researchers to analyze what groups in society have power to define a problem, as well as what interest groups benefit most from its solution.

Having looked at the transformation of social conflicts into more neutral social problems, let us touch briefly on a related matter: the proper role of social scientists in solving problems. This issue is rooted in much larger questions: Who should govern? Will government by experts turn out to be government in the interest of experts?

Since World War II, social scientists have become part of a giant knowledge industry. Armed with sophisticated research tools, many social researchers think they can—and should—use their knowledge to build better cities. Even a better world. Indeed, some see themselves as a priestly caste, possessing reason and analytical skills that can lead people into the good society (e.g., Hoult, 1968). Others (e.g., Lindblom and Cohen, 1979) aren't so sure that social scientists should play the role of physician or social engineer. This view is epitomized by the neoconservative urbanist Senator Daniel Patrick Moynihan in his book *Maximum Feasible Misunderstanding* (1969), a stinging appraisal of social scientists as problem solvers in the War on Poverty. Moynihan concludes that social scientists should measure and evaluate the outcomes of public policy, not formulate or implement it. Still others argue that the debate over the proper role of the scientific expert is academic, for professionals, afraid to risk the loss of community standing, are inherently conservative and thus end up serving the ends of those in political power.

How social scientists view their proper role in defining and solving problems is significant because it influences their research. Indeed, urbanist Nathan Glazer (in Scully, 1978:7) claims that problem solving has already supplanted theoretical concerns as the mission of the social sciences. Since the 1960s, he says, there has been a striking shift: away from pure theory toward policy studies aimed at making social institutions more effective.

What is the wider impact of this shift? One implication is that social scientists are now taking the place of novelists and artists as observers and critics of good and evil in social life. In other words, social scientists have become the moralists of our time. This represents a significant departure from what doing science once meant.

## WHAT QUESTIONS TO ASK

"Research shows that . . ." Sounds scientific, but consumers beware: So-called research can support almost any hypothesis, from the most outrageous to the most obvious. Poet Allen Ginsberg (1994) pokes fun at what he considers the obvious: "Research shows that socialism is a failure if it's run by the secret police."

But it is not always easy to know what's outrageous. And sometimes the obvious is wrong. So, how can we discriminate among good or questionable research? Here are some worthwhile questions to ask of any urban-oriented research study in order to assess more critically its "evidence" and the policy recommendations that may flow from it:

1. *Who says so?* What do we know about the author? Specifically, what is his or her (a) disciplinary background, (b) theoretical orientation, (c) practical experience that may be relevant, (d) assumptions and values, and (e) funding sources?

   What is the author's political ideology? Is it explicit or does it hide under the neutral guise of "objective" social science? Can you tell by reading between the lines or by looking at the acknowledgments and footnotes? Is the study or tract published by an organization (or magazine) with a known point of view, such as the American Enterprise Institute (conservative), the Brookings Institution (centrist), the Institute for Policy Studies (radical), the Cato Institute (libertarian), or so-called Patriot groups (far right).

   How do your own values and biases affect your evaluation of information? Specifically, do you automatically accept as objective what some sources, such as the *New York Times* or CNN report but reject as slanted information (perhaps the same information) appearing in a European newspaper or telecast?

2. *What's been neglected?* Is there evidence that might contradict the basic point of the study? Does the author use micro-level analysis alone when macro-level analysis would have added an important dimension, or vice versa? Could the study have been improved by combining several methods of investigation? What points of view seem to be overlooked? These are important questions because in research, as in life, sins of omission can be as deadly as sins of commission.

3. *So what?* Some urban studies may be sophisticated methodologically, but their findings may be trivial, their conclusions relatively meaningless. Hence the "so what?" question: Does the study enrich our understanding of the topic under investigation?

*To conclude:* By routinely asking and trying to answer these questions—Who says so? What's been overlooked? So what?—we can begin to separate sense from nonsense. And we can strengthen our ability to understand and act on the urban world in which we live.

## KEY TERMS

**Deductive reasoning**　The process of reasoning from general principles to particular examples. Contrast: **inductive reasoning.**

**Empirical evidence**  Evidence derived from direct observation and sense experience. Contrasts: *intuitive insight, metaphysical speculation,* and *pure logic.*

**Hypothesis**  A tentative statement suggesting a relationship between two or more variables. A hypothesis is intended to be tested empirically or at least to be testable.

**Ideology**  A set of beliefs and ideas that justify certain interests. An ideological position reflects and rationalizes particular political, economic, institutional, and/or social interests.

**Inductive reasoning**  The process of reasoning from particular examples to general principles. Contrast: **deductive reasoning.**

**Model**  A tentative and limited tool that represents some aspect of the world in words, mathematical symbols, graphs, or other symbols. Models attempt to duplicate or illustrate by analogy a pattern of relationships found in the empirical world. They are used to guide research and build theory in the sciences.

**Participant-observation**  A research method commonly used by sociologists, anthropologists, and journalistic feature writers. The investigator becomes or poses as a member of a group under study in an attempt to gain an intimate, firsthand acquaintance with the group and understand how group members interpret the world.

**Positivistic science** or **positivism**  The philosophical stance claiming that all true knowledge can be derived from sense experience (empirically based knowledge). It rejects intuitive insight, subjective understanding, and metaphysical speculation as bases of knowledge.

**Scientific method**  A method for doing science based on the assumption that all true knowledge is verifiable using empirical evidence. Well-ordered, successive stages—defining a research problem, constructing hypotheses, data gathering and analysis, and prediction of facts—are outlined.

**Theory**  A comprehensive explanation of something. Its functions are to summarize and order information meaningfully, to permit prediction, and to suggest new lines of scientific inquiry. A theory is a generalization that is intermediate in degree of verification between a scientific law and a hypothesis.

**Unobtrusive measure**  A research method that seeks to remove the observer from the event under study and thereby to eliminate possible reactive effects. Examples are content analysis of television programs and archival research.

**Variable** A trait or factor that can vary among a population or from case to case (e.g., sex, size of firm, cost per square foot, social class). Opposite: *constant.*

## PROJECTS

1. **Constructing hypotheses.** Using poverty status as the dependent variable, construct three different hypotheses (with different independent variables) to explain why some people are poor. These three hypotheses should reflect the liberal, conservative, and neo-Marxist points of view.

2. **Reading between the lines.** Examine two works of urban scholarship on the same topic—for instance, slums or urban unemployment. Do the authors agree? If not, why not? Try to analyze their assumptions, research methods, political biases, disciplinary perspectives, and levels of analysis used.

## SUGGESTIONS FOR FURTHER LEARNING

The women's movement in America has encouraged a reexamination of many assumptions underlying social science methods. See, for example, Joyce Nielsen, *Feminist Research Methods* (Boulder, Colo.: Westview Press, 1990), and Mary Margaret Fonow and Judith A. Cook, eds., *Beyond Methodology: Feminist Scholarship as Lived Research* (Bloomington: Indiana University Press, 1991).

For a spirited defense of the free market, see Milton Friedman's PBS television series, *Freedom of Choice* (1980). For a much less sanguine view of capitalism focusing on the stock market, see Oliver Stone's movie *Wall Street* (1987).

There was an outpouring of literature on ideology in the early 1990s. Here are a few examples: How and why the liberal coalition in the United

States disintegrated and what replaced it is the subject of Thomas Byrne Edsall with Mary D. Edsall, *Chain Reaction: The Impact of Race, Rights, and Taxes on American Politics* (New York: Norton, 1992). In *The L Word: An Unapologetic, Thoroughly Biased, Long-Overdue Explication and Celebration of Liberalism* (New York: Morrow, 1992), David P. Barash writes that Cold War liberalism was "energized by the Keynesian recognition that Federal spending was good for the economy." In *God and Other Famous Liberals: Reclaiming the Politics of America* (New York: Simon and Schuster, 1992), F. Forrester Church, a Unitarian pastor and son of the late Senator Frank Church (D-Idaho), writes from a political and religious heritage that buttresses his liberalism. Church scorns evangelist Jerry Falwell for writing that God is in favor of "property ownership, competition, diligence, work and acquisition." Writing from a different angle, Martin W. Lewis gives his viewpoint in his title: *Green Delusions: An Environmentalist Critique of Radical Environmentalism* (Durham, N.C.: Duke University Press, 1992). Geographer Lewis claims that there are at least five main types of "eco-extremism": "antihumanist anarchism," "primitivism," "humanist eco-anarchism," "green Marxism," and "radical eco-feminism."

For a discussion of contemporary theoretical perspectives, particularly the various strands of neo-Marxist theory (including critical theory, structural Marxism, Hegelian Marxism, Braverman's economic sociology, and Wallerstein's historically oriented world systems theory), see George Ritzer's *Contemporary Sociological Theory*, 3rd ed. (New York: McGraw-Hill, 1992).

The subdiscipline of economic sociology is based on the proposition that economic institutions are social, not natural, constructions. For a range of views on how market capitalism works from this perspective, see Mark Granovetter and Richard Swedberg, eds., *The Sociology of Economic Life* (Boulder, Colo.: Westview Press, 1992). A related anthropological study, *Learning Capitalist Culture: Deep in the Heart of Tejas* (Philadelphia: University of Pennsylvania Press, 1990), examines how youth in a southwestern town learn American values through sports, dating, classroom interactions, and so on. Author Douglas E.

Foley, a professor of anthropology and education, uses data gathered over fourteen years of field work.

What books inspired Ross Perot's 1992 presidential bid? He didn't say, but here are two possibilities: Thorstein Veblen's *The Engineers and the Price System* (New York: Kelley, [1921] 1965), a defense of a form of technocracy in advanced technological society, and Robert Boguslaw's *The New Utopians* (Englewood Cliffs, N.J.: Prentice-Hall, 1965), a description of the computer manufacturers, operations researchers, systems engineers, and other technological experts who aspire to transcend present reality.

Christopher Jencks calculates that there was a fourfold increase in U.S. homelessness between 1980 and 1988. In *The Homeless* (Cambridge, Mass.: Harvard University Press, 1994), a model for clear, well-balanced argument, sociologist Jencks discusses both liberal and conservative rationales for homelessness.

For visions of the nature of human beings and their effect on political ideology, see Sheldon Wolin, *Politics and Vision* (Boston: Little, Brown, 1960), and C. B. Macpherson, *Political Theory of Possessive Individualism: Hobbes to Locke* (New York: Oxford University Press, 1962).

Political satire is alive and well on public radio and television. For a sendup of ideologues of many stripes, listen to Harry Shearer's weekly program *Le Show* on National Public Radio and watch Mark Russell's program on PBS. A Washington, D.C.-based musical group, The Capitol Steps, can be heard on NPR and on commercial recordings.

## REFERENCES

Banfield, Edward. [1968] 1970. *The Unheavenly City.* Boston: Little, Brown.
——. 1974. *The Unheavenly City Revisited.* Boston: Little, Brown.
Bell, Daniel. 1960. *The End of Ideology.* New York: Free Press.
——. 1992. "Into the 21st century, bleakly." *New York Times* [national edition] (July 26):E17.

Buchanan, Patrick. 1992. Speech at the Republican National Convention, Houston, August 17.

Burgess, Ernest W., and Donald J. Bogue. 1964. "Research in urban society: A long view." Pp. 1–14 in Ernest W. Burgess and Donald J. Bogue, eds., *Contributions to Urban Sociology*. Chicago: University of Chicago Press.

Burke, Edmund. [1790] 1959. *Reflections on the Revolution in France*. New York: Holt, Rinehart and Winston.

Cordes, Colleen. 1992. "Debate flares over growing pressures on academe for ties with industry." *Chronicle of Higher Education* (September 16): A26+.

Coughlin, Ellen K. 1992. "Following Los Angeles riots, social scientists see need to develop fuller understanding of race relations." *Chronicle of Higher Education* (May 13):A10–A11.

Dahl, Robert. 1961. *Who Governs: Democracy and Power in an American City*. New Haven, Conn.: Yale University Press.

Gans, Herbert J. 1962. *The Urban Villagers*. New York: Free Press.

Ginsberg, Allen. 1994. Poem read at the Tikkun Conference, New York City. Broadcast on *As It Happens*, CBC (January 21), 5:30 P.M. PST.

Goodwin, Leonard. 1972. *Do the Poor Want to Work?* Washington, D.C.: Brookings Institution.

Gordon, David, ed. 1977. *Problems in Political Economy: An Urban Perspective*. Lexington, Mass.: Heath.

Greer, Scott. 1961. "Traffic, transportation, and problems of the metropolis." Pp. 605–650 in Robert K. Merton and Robert A. Nisbet, eds., *Contemporary Social Problems*. New York: Harcourt, Brace & World.

Hacker, Andrew. 1973. "On original sin and conservatives." *New York Times Magazine* (February 25):13+.

Hartmann, Heidi I., and Roberta Spalter-Roth. 1992. "Survey of income and program participation." Washington, D.C.: Institute for Women's Policy Research.

Harvey, David. 1973. *Social Justice and the City*. Baltimore: Johns Hopkins University Press.

———. 1989. *The Condition of Postmodernity: An Enquiry into the Origins of Cultural Change*. Oxford: Blackwell.

Hobbes, Thomas. [1651] 1968. *Leviathan: or the Matter, Forme and Power of a Commonwealth Ecclesiasticall and Civil*. New York: Collier.

Hoult, Thomas F. 1968. "'. . . Who shall prepare himself to the battle?'" *American Sociologist* 3:3–7.

Howe, Irving. 1993. "Clinton, seen from the left." *New York Times* (January 20):A19.

Hunter, Floyd. [1953] 1963. *Community Power Structure: A Study of Decision Makers*. Garden City, N.Y.: Doubleday, Anchor.

Kuhn, Thomas S. [1962] 1970. *The Structure of Scientific Revolutions*. Chicago: University of Chicago Press.

Liebow, Elliot. 1967. *Tally's Corner: A Study of Negro Streetcorner Men*. Boston: Little, Brown.

Lindblom, Charles E., and David K. Cohen. 1979. *Usable Knowledge: Social Science and Social Problem Solving*. New Haven, Conn.: Yale University Press.

Marien, Michael. 1970. "Handy guide to public policy proposers and their proposals." *Public Administration Review* 30:154.

Moynihan, Daniel Patrick. 1969. *Maximum Feasible Misunderstanding*. New York: Free Press.

Phillips, Kevin. 1992. "The politics of frustration." *New York Times Magazine* (April 12):38+.

Reich, Robert B. 1991. "Here's an economy policy." *New York Times* [national edition] (November 3):E15.

Rule, James B. 1978. *Insight and Social Betterment: A Preface to Applied Social Science*. New York: Oxford University Press.

Sagan, Carl. 1978. *Broca's Brain: Reflections on the Romance of Science*. New York: Random House.

Samuelson, Paul A. 1964. *Economics*, 6th ed. New York: McGraw-Hill.

Schumacher, E. F. 1973. *Small Is Beautiful: Economics as if People Mattered*. New York: Harper & Row.

Scully, Malcolm G. 1978. "'Striking change' seen reshaping science." *Chronicle of Higher Education* 16:7.

Smith, Adam. [1776] 1970. *Wealth of Nations*. Baltimore: Penguin.

Steinfels, Peter. 1979. *The Neoconservatives: The Men Who Are Changing America's Politics*. New York: Simon and Shuster.

Toffler, Alvin. 1970. *Future Shock*. New York: Random House.

Wills, Garry. 1992. "The born-again Republicans." *New York Review of Books* (September 24):9+.

Wolfson, Robert, and Manfred Stanley. 1969. "Beyond the invisible hand: Policy advisors and their clients." Syracuse, N.Y.: Educational Policy Research Center. Working draft.

# PART II
# Polis, Metropolis, Megalopolis

*Bank of California*

E. Barbara Phillips

# CHAPTER 4
# From Urban Specks to Global Cities

## THE FIRST CITIES

### Digging into Urban History

Rising like a giant spaceport out of Turkey's Anatolian plain is a 58-foot mound of earth. Until 1961, it was just a big mound lying in the hot sun. Then an international team moved in to excavate and analyze this ancient site, named **Çatal Hüyük** (pronounced Chatal Hooyook, meaning "mound at the end of the road" in modern Turkish). Under the direction of archeologist James Mellaart, the team dug wide trenches into the urban past. As they cut through the mound, they uncovered a prehistoric community—perhaps even a city—constructed about 9,500 years ago or even earlier.

Archeological digs such as Çatal Hüyük and new scientific techniques for radiocarbon dating of ancient artifacts have been overturning long-held theories about why and where cities first came into existence. New evidence has also called into question the dates for the birth of cities, often referred to as the "dawn of civilization." Until recently, it was generally assumed that urban life started in the fertile river valleys of present-day Iraq around 3500 B.C. Newer theories have pushed back the date to 8000 B.C. or earlier. Newer theories also suggest that the earliest city dwellers settled in the hills above the valleys or in places far from the great rivers of antiquity.

But these matters are far from settled. The origins of cities remain controversial. And as archeological teams uncover new mounds in their digs, we can expect even more controversy and theorizing about what prerequisites were necessary for the emergence of urban life.

Controversy and tentative knowledge thus typify scholarly discussions of the earliest cities. In fact, controversy and tentative knowledge seem to be our fate in studying many urban phenomena, whether in ancient earth mounds or modern U.S. cities. For some, this may produce anxiety and a desire to enter another field or discipline, perhaps physics with its laws and certainties. Yet physicists on the cutting edge of research say that they too deal only with tentative knowledge and approximations of truths. Facing the limits of our collective understanding in so many important areas—from the origins of the universe and the birth of cities to the causes and cures for human misery—could throw us into despair. Or it could (and, I argue, should) encourage us to join the long search for knowledge and meaning by seeking better answers to more informed questions.

Let us now begin the search by tracing the roots of urban life and culture through the millennia. En route, let us think about questions that have few definitive answers: Why did people originally form cities? What features do the varied cities invented and sustained by human beings have in common? Why did cities grow and prosper in certain historical periods? What roles do **technology,** social organization, physical environment, and population play in city growth?

### What Is a City?

Before attempting to date the origin of cities, we run into a problem of definition: What exactly is a **city?** The ancient Romans made a sharp distinction between the community of people who banded together to form a settlement, which they called *civitas* (from which our words *city* and *civilization* are derived), and the physical place they formed—an *urb* (from which our word *urban* is derived). The earliest Roman cities were created by a solemn religious ceremony—the banding together of a group of people to form a community at a definite site.

Today there is no precise or agreed-on definition of the word *city*. It has been applied to so many different settlement types that the original Roman use of the word is obsolete. This is one reason why it is so difficult to discuss when the first cities were invented or whether some communities were indeed cities.

In most definitions of *city*, however, there are common elements. These include notions of *permanent residence, large population, high density,* and *heterogeneity.* But how large is large? How densely settled must a community be to be classified as a city rather than a village—200 people per square mile, 400, more? And how differentiated by occupation and kin group must a population be in order to be categorized as heterogeneous? Again, there are no precise criteria.

Another approach is to define a city in terms of its economic character. Using this approach, we can describe a city as a *market settlement,* a place "where the local inhabitants satisfy an economically substantial part of their daily wants in the local market" (Weber, [1921] 1963:66–67).

Yet another approach assumes that a city exists only when there are *cultural ingredients* considered essential to urban life—fine arts, exact sciences, and, in particular, writing. In this view, a collection of people—no matter how large—does not constitute a city unless these characteristics are present.

## The First Urban Settlements: An Overview

Using any of these definitions, should the most ancient sites yet excavated be called cities? It is unclear. Early settlements that might qualify as cities overlap two other settlement forms: agricultural villages and trading posts.

Some add another permanent settlement form: the *preagricultural village.* Indeed, a recently excavated site in present-day Israel is changing archeologists' views of why and when permanent settlements first arose. This site, **Wadi-al-Natuf,** was home to the Natufians (named for the site) about 13,000 to 14,000 years ago. The Natufians were foragers—not farmers—when they built what many archeologists now believe to be the world's first large, permanent habitat with storage facilities, elaborate buildings, and semiunderground houses. These settlements were so complete that, according to archeologist T. Douglas Price, the Natufians had practically "everything but mailboxes" (in Stevens, 1988:B11). Yet archeologists think these settlements were preagricultural villages, not true cities.

Jarmo, in present-day Iraq, is the most widely studied example of a large neolithic agricultural village. Around 7000 to 6500 B.C., an estimated 150 people lived there at a low density, about 27 people per square mile. Perhaps it had the stirrings of a barter economy, a simple division of labor, and some cultural life. But it was not a city by anyone's definition.

Ancient **Jericho** is harder to classify. Some archeologists believe that Jericho is indeed the earliest city. When Dame Kathleen Kenyon and her team of archeologists started digging up Jericho in the 1950s, they found ruined walls that apparently came tumbling down around 1400 B.C., when Joshua "fit the battle of Jericho" in the biblical story. Beneath these ruined city walls, they kept finding remains of earlier Jerichos. Finally, some 70 feet down, they unearthed a substantial settlement, the first Jericho—a Neolithic community, inhabited perhaps as early as 10,000 years ago. Kenyon (1957:65) estimates that it contained about 3,000 residents, called the "hog-backed brick people" after the round houses with humps at the top that they built.

Although Kenyon calls ancient Jericho the first "town" (a settlement bigger than a village but smaller than a city), its status remains controversial. To many, it is a mere trading post.

If Jericho's status is disputed, if Wadi-al-Natuf is viewed as a preagricultural settlement, and if Jarmo is certainly not a city, what is the earliest true city? Perhaps archeologists will find an early site near the Great Sphinx of Egypt. Its age was reevaluated in 1991 by a team of geologists and geophysicists who say that it was carved between 5000 B.C. and 7000 B.C.—that is, millennia before Mesopotamian cities and some 2,500 to 5,000 years earlier than is generally thought (Wilford, 1991:A13). Or was it Çatal Hüyük on Turkey's Anatolian plain?

Çatal Hüyük was probably established shortly after Jericho. Apparently, its population was twice that of Jericho. Residents produced some spectacular artwork and engaged in extensive trade. By some people's definitions, it qualifies as one of the earliest cities.

Bigger and much more sophisticated were a number of cities in ancient Mesopotamia that arose about 3500 B.C. Until the discoveries at Jericho, Çatal Hüyük, and Wadi-al-Natuf, conven-

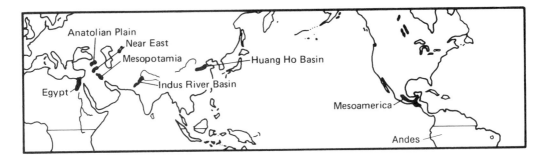

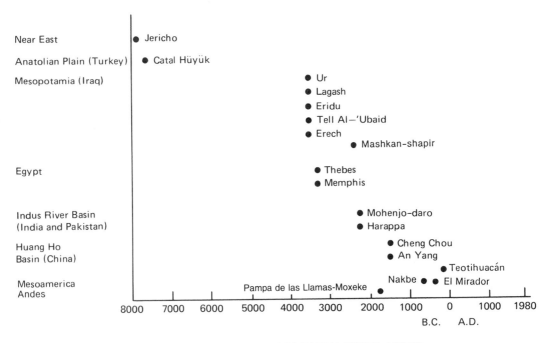

**Fig. 4.1** WHERE AND WHEN EARLY CITIES AROSE.

tional wisdom held that these Mesopotamian cities in the Sumer region were the earliest cities.

Four other centers of early urban civilization have been identified, the first in the Indus Basin in present-day India and Pakistan. Here twin capital cities, Mohenjo-daro (about 240 miles north of present-day Karachi, Pakistan) and Harappa (about 350 miles farther north) flourished around 2300 to 1750 B.C. Physically, these were large cities, about 1 square mile in size (Wheeler, 1953, 1966). Carefully built according to identical

city plans, they housed perhaps as many as 250,000 persons each. And, the archeological record shows, Mohenjo-daro and Harappa were technologically sophisticated centers as well as trade centers.

The second early center of urban life was in the valley of the Huang Ho River in China. The first Chinese dynasty, the Shang, built large cities at Cheng Chou and An Yang in approximately 1300 to 1500 B.C. (Wheatley, 1971). One archeologist estimates that it would take 19,000 workers, working full time, for at least eighteen years to build the massive packed-earth walls that surround An Yang, the largest of the Shang cities.

The third early urban center was in **Mesoamerica**: present-day Mexico, Guatemala, and other parts of Central America. Various Indian cultures, including the Olmec, Maya, and Aztecs, developed large cities with elaborate buildings and political structures. For example, a recently excavated Mayan city of apparent grandeur, Nakbe, existed in what is now a remote tropical forest in Guatemala. Archeologists think that Nakbe reached its population peak between 600 and 400 B.C. On the basis of new finds like Nakbe in 1989, archeologists are revising conventional wisdom about when Mesoamerican city cultures began.

Quite recently, some archeologists added a fourth center of early urban civilization: the Peruvian Andes. That anyone at all lived there is surprising. The area's high altitude and dry cold make it hostile to human beings (Stevens, 1989:8). Yet well-preserved ruins (thanks to the height and dry cold) reveal numerous planned ancient communities, excavated since the late 1970s. Other Andean cities are well preserved due to desertlike conditions. The most exciting site yet excavated, **Pampa de las Llamas-Moxeke,** dates back approximately 3,500 to 3,800 years— to roughly the same period as the Egyptian pyramids and the heyday of Sumerian cities. Located on a desert plain 217 miles north of Lima and nestled between fingers of the Andes Mountains, this site contains features typical of ancient Andean communities: a ten-story, U-shaped temple; a three-story public building to its north; and an enormous plaza between them with a labyrinth of food storage rooms (Pozorski and Pozorski, 1994). The complex social organization needed to build such large monuments, the complexity of the planned site, and the apparent lack of social stratification lead some archeologists to conclude that Pampa de la Llamas was an early city-state.

Why did the ancient Andean civilization disappear? That remains a mystery. So does the disappearance of the largest of the Mesoamerican early cities, **Teotihuacán** ("place of the Gods," so named by the Aztecs when they uncovered it

about 700 years ago), located just outside Mexico City. Established much later than the Andean settlement, about 150 B.C., and flourishing for more than 1,000 years, Teotihuacán's ruins today show an impressive city of pyramid-type structures and religious buildings. At its height, the multiethnic city became a major market and pilgrimage center; it may have had as many as 200,000 residents (Wilford, 1993:B5). Both Pampa de las Llamas-Moxeke and Teotihuacán, however, lacked what some consider a prerequisite for the birth of cities: a fertile environment. Teotihuacán emerged on a high, arid plain, and the ancient Peruvian civilization arose on a low desert plain. Furthermore, some view the wheel and writing as prerequisites of early urban growth. Yet, even at their height, neither the ancient Peruvian civilization nor Teotihuacán had these inventions.

A final puzzle concerns cultural diffusion. Some archeologists think that the Peruvian and Mesoamerican civilizations had common roots: Stone Age chiefdoms in the central Amazon basin about 7,000 to 8,000 years ago (Stevens, 1989:Punch 8). A few think that Teotihuacán borrowed elements from already established urban cultures in Sumer or Egypt. (There are striking parallels, including religious pyramids similar to Mesopotamian ziggurats.) In one ingenious test of the cultural diffusion thesis, explorer Thor Heyerdahl built a reed boat, the *Ra II*, to demonstrate that Egyptian sailors might have reached Mesoamerica centuries ago. It sank.

Cities in Mesoamerica, Egypt, the Indus Basin, the Huang Ho River valley, and the Peruvian Andes were established after those in ancient Sumer. Now our quest to find answers about where and why cities came into existence brings us back to Mesopotamia.

## The Childe Thesis: The Urban Revolution in Mesopotamia

Australian-British archeologist V. Gordon Childe (1892–1957) spent a scholarly lifetime studying the rise of civilization in **Mesopotamia**: the Fertile Crescent located between the Tigris and Euphrates rivers (which flow into the Persian Gulf) in what is now Iraq. In his very readable books, *Man Makes Himself* ([1936] 1952) and *What Happened in History?* ([1942] 1964), Childe details his thesis about what he considers the evolutionary development and progress of humankind from prehistoric food gatherer to food producer in the Neolithic revolution to city builder in the second revolution, the **urban revolution.**

According to the **Childe thesis,** the long march of human development started in the fertile river valleys of the Tigris–Euphrates. At the end of this developmental sequence was the emergence of cities around 3500 B.C.

In brief, Childe's logic goes like this: The transition from hunting and gathering to food cultivation and the domestication of animals—the agricultural revolution—was a necessary precondition for the emergence of village and city life. Agriculture and the consequent production of a food surplus permitted people to stop their nomadic wandering and form settled communities. Thus in Childe's view, agriculture is the key factor in the revolutionary change from nomadic wandering to village life.

In a fertile environment such as the Tigris–Euphrates River valley, the Childe thesis continues, farmers could and did produce and store a food surplus. Population in the agricultural villages then increased, for a constant food supply allowed more people to survive. Over the millennia, larger and larger villages developed. In turn, larger villages led to the need for more complex social organization and social control. To feed the ever-increasing population, intensive agriculture was invented. Eventually, a whole series of technological innovations and political changes followed as a result of larger populations and the need to handle and ensure the food surplus. For instance, the Childe thesis holds that ruling elites or classes developed to oversee the organization of the surplus. These elites invented systems of recording to ensure the surplus, as well as peace and security. This long historical chain of events set the stage for the emergence of cities in Mesopotamia: the urban revolution.

Child's thesis assumes that the urban revolution in Mesopotamia is the product of four inextricably linked factors:

1. *P*opulation. Increased numbers encouraged by the agricultural surplus.
2. *O*rganization. An increasingly complex division of labor, particularly the evolution of ruling religious and secular elites to organize the surplus and a variety of specialists such as craftspeople, metallurgists, and scribes.
3. *E*nvironment. A hospitable physical setting, such as a fertile river valley, capable of producing an agricultural surplus.
4. *T*echnology. Innovations that first brought food cultivation and food surplus and gradually led to such inventions as the wheel and writing.

Thus, according to the Childe thesis, the earliest cities resulted from the interaction between these demographic, environmental, social, and technological factors, easily remembered by their acronym, POET.

Childe uses the term *revolution* on purpose to emphasize a total transformation in a very short period of time. It is as if a chemist slowly added ingredients to a test tube until suddenly the mixture was just right to produce a sudden transformation into a new compound.

What were the Mesopotamian cities like? And how well do they fit the several definitions of a city discussed earlier? The case of ancient **Ur,** the largest of the Mesopotamian cities, is instructive.

The population of Ur was large compared with that of any settlement that preceded it. At its height, Ur's population may have numbered as many as 34,000 within the walled city itself and perhaps as many as 360,000 people in "greater Ur" (Sjoberg, [1960] 1965:36–37). Ur was densely settled. The total area within the wall and moat in 3000 B.C. was 220 acres, and the entire population was compressed into this space.

The population of Ur was socially heterogeneous, reflecting a well-developed system of classes and specialization of function. Wide differences in wealth and power existed between elites and the rest of the population. There were also finely graded occupational divisions, including full-time soldiers, herders, artisans, and musicians. Cuneiform clay tablets from Ur record the specialization of labor at the royal palace: gatekeepers, cooks, stewards, servants, messen-

Box 4.1

## CHILDE'S CRITERIA

### How to Distinguish an Early City from Other Forms of Human Settlement

1. Larger size and denser population (Ur and other Sumerian cities contained from 7,000 to 20,000 persons by 3000 B.C.).
2. Classes of nonfarming specialists, including artisans, merchants, administrators, and priests, all supported by the agricultural surplus.
3. Taxation and capital accumulation (taxes or tithes paid to gods or kings who concentrated the surplus).
4. Monumental public buildings, such as the stately temples of Sumer with their ziggurats.
5. Ruling elites or classes who absorbed, accumulated, and organized the surplus.
6. Exact sciences, needed to predict, measure, and standardize (e.g., arithmetic, geometry, astronomy).
7. The invention of writing or scripts, enabling the "leisured clerks" to elaborate the exact and predictive sciences.
8. Specialists in the arts, supported by the surplus.
9. Long-distance trade in vital materials.
10. Community membership based on residence alone, rather than kinship.

SOURCE: Adapted from V. Gordon Childe, "The Urban Revolution," *Town Planning Review* 21 (1950):9–16. Published in Liverpool at the University Press. Reprinted by permission.

gers, a harem official (hence, a harem), and a royal cupbearer (Adams, 1966:143).

Using conventional criteria, then, Ur may be defined as a city. It was a relatively large, dense, and heterogeneous community. Ur also qualifies as a city in terms of market functions and urban culture. It served as the marketplace for an extended region. Artifacts unearthed at the site show trade with countries as far away as Egypt, Armenia, and Oman in the Persian Gulf. Culture in Ur also advanced to high levels. The city itself was a handsome, planned area with wide streets and large civic buildings. The dominant architectural feature was a **ziggurat**—a pyramid with stepped sides central to the religious functions of the community. Further, residents developed writing, an accurate solar calendar, musical instruments, fine art, and handicrafts.

Reflecting on how radically different Ur and other cities in the Sumer region were from the scattered, humble farming villages that preceded them, Childe generalized about what distinguishes any early city from such villages: ten criteria, deducible from archeological data (Box 4.1). These criteria remain influential—and controversial.

In other words, Childe set out his own list of prerequisites for urban life. All existed in the Mesopotamian cities by definition, for he deduced them from archeological evidence.

## Counterviews on the Origin of Cities: Trade, the Sacred, and the Spirit of the People

Childe's evolutionary thesis dominated scholarship throughout his lifetime. His views became conventional wisdom. It was generally assumed, for instance, that agriculture was invented as populations started to increase—that is, as a response to social stress, or, alternatively, as a response to shrinking natural resources or environmental pressure. In addition, it was assumed that cities emerged after a long linear sequence: from nomadic wanderings to agricultural villages to cities.

Recent discoveries, however, pose new questions about when cities arose. These new findings are causing archeologists to radically revise their theories. Here we'll consider a few of the leading competitors to Childe's thesis, including a still emerging theory.

Shortly after Childe's death, Kenyon's findings at Jericho upset conventional wisdom about the slow progression of agricultural settlements. Later, in 1961, at Çatal Hüyük, archeologist James Mellaart dug deep into something Childe said could not exist: a Neolithic city.

The settlement lies in south central Turkey about 250 miles from Ankara. It is situated on a high mountain plain, not in a fertile river valley. Environmentally, Çatal Hüyük was not particularly favored. In Neolithic times a freshwater lake nearby may have made its environment somewhat more fertile, but certainly far less so than the swampland of Mesopotamia.

Çatal Hüyük's population was probably 5,000 to 6,000 (Mellaart in Todd, 1976:122). Since the mound from which the settlement is being excavated covers only 32 acres, it was densely settled.

While Çatal Hüyük had a somewhat heterogeneous population, there is no evidence of anything like the elaborate class structure of the Sumerian cities. Distinct skeletal types unearthed show that at least two different racial groups inhabited the settlement. Religious buildings suggest the existence of a priestly class, and art and trade artifacts suggest some social differentiation and specialization of functions. But this is far removed from the elaborate Mesopotamian social structure with a royal cupbearer.

Does Çatal Hüyük qualify as a city in terms of its cultural level? In the judgment of Mellaart, it "shines like a supernova among the rather dim galaxy of contemporary peasant cultures" (1967:77). Representational and abstract wall paintings include striking scenes of bulls, people, and cattle, and one macabre room is decorated with vultures and decapitated human beings. Other artifacts reveal rather subtle clay baked seals and fine obsidian daggers. But there was no writing. Thus by Childe's standards—which placed great weight on the invention of writing—Çatal Hüyük falls short of city culture. But in Mellaart's view, it was a stellar cultural achievement even when compared with some cultures today.

Çatal Hüyük would qualify as a city under Weber's definition, for it was a market center. Çatal Hüyük apparently carried on brisk trade with its neighboring region.

In *The Economy of Cities* (1970), amateur urbanist and professional iconoclast Jane Jacobs describes New Obsidian, the "first city." Jacobs's first city is an imaginary creation, but she draws heavily on the discoveries and theories of Mellaart. In fact, New Obsidian closely parallels Çatal Hüyük. Mellaart, the patient archeologist taking years to sort through the dust and rubble, is more cautious about constructing theories than Jacobs. Yet their ideas on the possible role of trade in Çatal Hüyük are similar.

Jacobs's **trade thesis** turns Childe's thesis on its head. In her imaginary scenario, the city becomes the independent variable, explaining the development of agriculture—not the reverse. Moreover, factors that Childe stressed as vital in setting the stage for the urban revolution (a favorable environment, technology, a large population base, and elaborate social organization) are relatively unimportant in her vision. To Jacobs, the first cities arose because of trade. Location was a key factor; early cities had to be located near the source of prized goods such as salt and obsidian. And they had to be situated along trade routes that bypassed geographical barriers. In Jacobs's scenario, the survival of the first city dwellers, the New Obsidianites, was based on exchanges of vital commodities for food from their trading partners, not on agriculture. Furthermore, Jacobs believes that agriculture was invented by ancient city dwellers and diffused by trade. In her view, then, intensive farming didn't lead to the development of cities. To the contrary, *agriculture developed because of cities.*

If correct, the trade thesis does overturn Childe's thesis. It implies that agriculture was not an absolute prerequisite for the rise of cities. It also implies that Childe's notion of slow evolutionary development—a Darwinian concept whereby each stage of life represents an advance over the previous stage—is wrong. In other words, some cities could have been established as cities from the start, without a gestation period of several millennia and without the linear progression from nomadic wandering to food production to settled village life to the rise of cities. Finally, the trade thesis calls into question Childe's list of ten criteria as universal.

Both Childe's evolutionary thesis and Jacobs's trade thesis are called into question by a third competing view of city origins and growth: the sacred meanings-symbolic thesis. In this view, both Childe's thesis and Jacobs's thesis are incomplete because they neglect *nonmaterial* factors in city development.

Urbanist Lewis Mumford, representing this third viewpoint, writes that "early [people's] respect for the dead, itself an expression of fascination with [their] powerful images of daylight fantasy and nightly dream, perhaps had an even greater role than more practical needs in causing [them] to seek a fixed meeting place and eventually a continuous settlement" (1961:6–7). Mumford states that practical needs did draw families and tribes together in campsites, but "the very reason for the city's existence" was sacred in nature: "The first germ of the city, then, is the ceremonial meeting place which has "'spiritual' or supernatural powers" that are endowed with a "cosmic image" (10).

Other scholars in this tradition (e.g., Fustel de Coulanges, [1864] 1955; Adams, 1966) emphasize the idea that a strong ideological core, holding together early urbanites in a sense of community, is a key variable in the origin or growth of cities. In this view, then, what brought people together in settlements in ancient times had to do with much more than physical survival and economic subsistence. As Mumford puts it, "fixed landmarks and holy meeting places called together, periodically or permanently, those who shared the same magical practices or religious beliefs" (1961:8).

Using the religious-symbolic thesis, it could be argued that Çatal Hüyük was a shrine city, attracting the faithful. Its central purpose was to serve as a holy meeting place. If so, many materialist social science theories are called into question, for materialist theories assume that culture (including religion) is a *dependent* variable, reflecting the material base of culture, not an independent variable.

Very briefly, there is yet another point of view,

one that debunks all the foregoing theories. This fourth view, associated with the late architectural historian Spiro Kostof, holds that neither religion, trade, environment, nor the evolution from agricultural village to city was a key to the origin of cities. Economics and environment, in this view, are not nearly as important as the *spirit of people*. According to Kostof (1991), city creating always entails an act of will by a leader or a collectivity.

## An Emerging Theory of Early City Making

By the late 1980s, new excavations in many parts of the world—present-day Russia, Israel, Peru, Guatemala, Iraq, and Western Europe—led archeologists to question, even reject, Childe's evolutionary thesis in favor of a still emerging theory of the origin of cities. According to this emerging thesis, hunter-gatherers had permanent communities thousands of years before the development of agriculture.

Here's the thinking: Stone Age hunter-gatherers were not simple nomadic folk. To the contrary, preagricultural foragers such as the ancient Natufians tended to stay put, establish decision-making hierarchies, develop a system to store the food surplus, trade goods over long distances, and make a variety of tools. Preagricultural, settled foragers were often culturally complex, designing social and political hierarchies. In central Russia, for instance, archeologist Olga Soffer says that "you find enormously rich burials of some individuals and other guys are lucky to get a doggie bag" (in Stevens, 1988:B11).

Why did these complex foraging societies appear? It's not yet clear. Some archeologists point to changes in climate—warmer and wetter weather as the glaciers retreated—that led to the explosive growth of wild grains, which in turn allowed people to store wild resources. Others think that hunter-gatherers settled down because their main food source (mammoths and other large animals) became extinct at the end of the Ice Age, forcing the preagriculturalists to develop more complex forms of social organization in order to store surplus food. Still others say that population increase is the key to understanding why settled communities began. In this view, more complex institutions developed to manage the food surplus and handle the increased social conflict that apparently accompanied nonnomadic life.

There is no consensus on *how* these early complex societies came about (Price and Brown, 1985). But a consensus is developing around this new, still-emerging thesis: long before agriculture, human beings developed complex cultures.

*To conclude:* If correct, the emerging thesis overturns Childe's conventional wisdom. Like Jacobs's trade thesis, it suggests that agriculture was not a prerequisite for the rise of cities, and that there was no slow evolution from nomadic hunting-gathering to farming to settled villages to an urban revolution and early cities. Recent evidence, particularly discoveries about the Natufian culture and ancient Andean civilization, does pose a serious challenge—perhaps a death knell—to Childe's evolutionary thesis. Yet, at this time, there is no definitive conclusion about the puzzles of early agriculture or cities. Indeed, when thinking about the origin of cities, it is wise to recall what Childe himself said on his opening page: "Almost every statement in prehistory shoud be qualified by the phrase 'On the evidence available today the balance of probability favors the view that'" ([1936] 1952:v).

One more thing: The debate about when and where cities really began is essentially a debate over two issues: (1) the definition of a city and (2) when and where *civilization* began. *City* and *civilization* are connected not only through a common Latin root—*civitas*—but also by a belief that cities are produced by civilizations (and that great cities are produced by great civilizations). Indeed, the links between being "civilized" and "citified" go back at least to Mesopotamia. In the ancient city of Babylon, urbanites stood at the "gates of God," for their city was "a visible heaven on earth, a seat of the life abundant—in other words, utopia." (Mumford, 1966:13) Later, during the Roman Empire, to live meant to live in Rome.

## TRYING TO CLASSIFY CITIES

The controversy about the emergence of cities is just one of many current debates on the nature of urban life. We now turn to another. This debate focuses not on the desirability but rather on the success of attempts to generalize about the nature of cities.

### Preindustrial versus Industrial Cities (Sjoberg)

Sociologist Gideon Sjoberg thinks that cities share certain general features and can be classified accordingly. Sjoberg's central hypothesis is that "in their structure or form, preindustrial cities—whether in medieval Europe, traditional China, India or elsewhere—resemble one another closely and in turn differ markedly from modern industrial-urban centers" ([1960] 1965:4–5). In other words, Sjoberg looks for what he calls "structural universals" that typify preindustrial cities and distinguish them from modern industrial cities.

Let's look more closely at the preindustrial city. According to Sjoberg, all cities that utilize animate energy sources (human beings and animals) rather than inanimate energy sources (steam, electricity, nuclear fission, etc.) are classified as preindustrial. This means, in Sjoberg's view, that cities as diverse in culture and context as ancient Ur, the lost cities of Africa, Periclean Athens, seventeenth-century London, and modern Kathmandu "share numerous patterns in the realms of ecology, class, and the family, as well as in their economic, political, religious, and educational structures, arrangements that diverge sharply from their counterparts in mature industrial cities" ([1960] 1965:6).

Sjoberg argues that the demographic and ecological structures of all preindustrial cities are remarkably similar and transcend cultural boundaries. For instance, he notes the common features of small size (under 100,000 inhabitants), cramped conditions (because transportation and building technology are limited, people live close together in low-rise structures within walking distance of central facilities), widespread residential segregation by ethnic and occupational groups (the poorest castes or classes live farthest away from the city center, where the elites are concentrated; special quarters are set aside for particular economic pursuits, such as goldsmithing or pottery making), and little specialization in land use (due to the lack of industrial technology, such as rapid transit, which permits high specialization of land use in industrial cities).

Similarly, Sjoberg hypothesizes that class and status structures in all preindustrial cities have common features. These include a small elite, generally composed of political and religious leaders and sometimes military leaders, educators, and wealthy merchants; a large lower-class group of laborers, artisans, and small merchants; and, commonly, an outcaste group, such as India's untouchables or a slave population. These class and caste barriers were and are nearly impossible to cross, for social position is determined by one's family background rather than one's personal achievements, including education. Thus, he says, there is little mobility within the rigid social structure of preindustrial cities.

**Fig. 4.2** SJOBERG'S PREINDUSTRIAL CITY. Essaouira, Morocco, displays many characteristics that Gideon Sjoberg associates with the preindustrial city, including (*a*) the hiding of female attractiveness and (*b*) governmental and religious structures that dominate the urban horizon. (© Andrée Abecassis, 1980)

a

b

In many other areas—family, the economy, politics, communication, and the nature of education—Sjoberg notes recurring patterns among preindustrial cities. These range from the "purposive adulteration of goods" ([1960] 1965:211) and periodic public festivals that provide entertainment and promote social cohesion (though outcaste groups may be excluded) to the treatment of books as sacred and holy.

While tidy, how useful is Sjoberg's way of approaching the nature of preindustrial cities? Here urbanists disagree. A few consider the concept of the preindustrial city a notable contribution to urban studies. The majority, however, attack Sjoberg for bringing more confusion than clarity to the study of preindustrial cities. Critics charge him with imprecision on concrete historical matters, technological determinism, and neglect of the role that culture plays in city form and structure. In addition, urbanists point to a basic fallacy in Sjoberg's approach: He incorrectly treats all cities before the Industrial Revolution as dependent subsystems within larger feudal societies. This is historically wrong, critics hold, pointing to such ancient cities as Athens, Rome, and Constantinople, which did not exist under feudalism, and such medieval cities as Venice, which were autonomous—not dependent subsystems within feudalism—to support their challenge. As one critic puts it, "The preindustrial city type lumps so many disparate societal systems [feudalism, capitalism, etc.] that its value as an operational instrument seems nullified" (Cox, [1964] 1969:26). Or, in more straightforward terms, it is useless.

## VARIETIES OF WESTERN CITIES: A SAMPLER

Sjoberg's critics are convincing. Thus we will not use Sjoberg's dichotomy to examine the wide variety of cities and urban cultures created over the millennia, including *Lost Cities of Africa* (Davidson, [1959] 1970) and *Victorian Cities* (Briggs, 1963). Instead, here's a sampler of Western cities. This sampler focuses on architecture and town planning in ancient Greek cities; the role of trade in medieval European cities; and the impact of the Industrial Revolution on nineteenth-century Manchester, England.

## The Glory That Was Greece

"Frankly, Scarlett, I don't give a damn" may be the best-remembered exit line of the American cinema. Delivered by Rhett Butler (Clark Gable) in *Gone with the Wind* (1939), it signals more than the hero's rejection of a woman. It brings down the curtain on a way of life embodied by Tara, the stately southern plantation house built during the Greek Revival period of architecture in the United States (1830–1860). In a nation moving toward industrialization after the Civil War, Rhett Butler turns his back on a way of life: an agrarian way of life symbolized by Tara's perfect proportions and pure form in harmony with its natural setting.

Ironically, Greek templelike plantation homes such as Tara (and county courthouses and other public buildings constructed in the Greek Revival period) may be considered some of the many expressions of antiurban tendencies and thoughts in the United States. "The Greek temple," one architectural historian notes, "does not really want to get along with other buildings in a street, but to stand free outside. . . . As revived, it demonstrates the puristic instinct to the utmost" (Scully, 1969:64–65). What's ironic is that the original ancient Greek temples and public monuments crowned the glory that was Greece—an urban glory—and celebrated city life.

In ancient Greece, monumental public buildings —theaters, stadia, gymnasia, and temples— were erected to enrich the beauty of the city. Consistent with the Greek emphasis on collective civic endeavor (detailed in the next chapter), private houses were small and unpretentious. The Greeks devoted their energy to public institutions such as the *agora* (literally, "the place where people get together"), which dominated the city center. The everyday life of ordinary Greek citizens focused on the *agora:* a mixture of markets,

**Fig. 4.3**   THE PARTHENON IN ATHENS. (Alison Frantz)

courts, temple shrines, and government buildings. Here Greeks of the fifth century B.C. could get fish, discuss their leader Pericles's policies toward Persia, pay tribute to their gods and goddesses, and gossip.

In Greek cities before the fifth century B.C., an **acropolis,** such as Athens's famous Parthenon, dominated the city (Figure 4.3). Built on hills with commanding views, these acropoleis consisted of a fortified palace, temple, and fort complex. Later, as the Greeks evolved democratic institutions, the acropolis declined in importance.

Cities built during the height of Greece's glory—the democratic period, particularly Periclean Athens—were constructed mainly on the principles of one architect–town planner, Hippodamus of Miletus, born in the fifth century B.C. Integrating architectural and planning principles, Hippodamus urged the use of simple, functional, and pure forms blended harmoniously with the natural environment. The outcome was not only a magnificent beauty but, according to Thucydides ([411 B.C.] 1956, vol. 1:19), a sense of overwhelming power. In its own day, then, Athens's mix of commanding acropolis and Hippodamian-inspired buildings was recognized as architecture that magnified the city's strength.

Ancient Greeks viewed their cities' monuments from streets laid out in a grid system. The grid, introduced earlier, was continued by Hippodamus in his city plans. Centuries later, it became the dominant scheme in American cities, appearing as early as 1641 in the plan of New Haven, Connecticut.

## Medieval Cities

For complex reasons discussed in the next chapter, the glory that was Greece faded. It was later replaced by the grandeur that was Rome. The vast Roman Empire stretched from the Sahara and the Euphrates to Gaul, creating such grandiose structures as the Roman Forum; the Temple of Bacchus at Baalbek, Lebanon; and the Pont du Gard near Nîmes, France.

What produced and sustained this vast empire and its sparkling cities, particularly its jewel, Rome? According to the eminent Belgian historian Henri Pirenne ([1925] 1956), commerce was the key variable. Roman civilization was built on trade, and the Mediterranean Sea was the crucial element in Rome's maritime empire. Even after the fall of Rome in 476 A.D. to the Goths, Vandals, and other invaders, trade continued on the Mediterranean, and the economy of the Mediterranean commonwealth, created by the Roman Empire, remained unified.

But in the seventh century A.D., this long-lived unity and world order that had survived the fall of Rome collapsed. Islamic expansion changed the face of the world, spreading from the China Sea to the Atlantic Ocean. And in its wake, the Mediterranean Sea, which had for so long united the cultures of eastern and western Europe, became a barrier between them.

According to Pirenne, the closing off of the Mediterranean by the Islamic invasion led to the stagnation of the old Roman cities. But by the twelfth century, conditions stabilized, and western Europe was back on the road to economic progress: "[T]he new Europe resembled . . . more the ancient Europe than the Europe of Carolingian times. . . . She regained that essential characteristic of being a region of cities" (Pirenne, [1925] 1956:73).

Pirenne paints a picture of many medieval towns built around the physical shell of an ancient Roman city. These towns contained an old burg (walled fortress or town) occupied by a Catholic bishop or other religious officials but were surrounded by a new burg, a fortified area for storing goods plus living quarters for traders.

It was in twelfth-century towns operating as autonomous trading centers—Venice and Bruges, for instance—that a new merchant class acted as a catalyst, pushing forward economic and social change. Unlike the vast feudal masses of western Europe, people in these autonomous cities were not tied to tradition. The secular commercial towns encouraged innovation and entrepreneurial activity.

Residents of commercial suburbs were referred to as *burghers* or members of the *bourgeoisie* (from the root *burg* or *bourg*). From their origins in the twelfth century as a fledgling merchant class, they came to dominate England and other nations in the throes of the Industrial Revolution in the eighteenth century. By the nineteenth century, the word *bourgeoisie* had turned into a contemptuous epithet and the overthrow of this class an objective of revolutionary intellectuals like Karl Marx and Friedrich Engels.

## Manchester, England: Symbol of the New Industrial City

Beginning in the late eighteenth century, a series of technological changes in textile machinery in England made possible large-scale, mechanized, capital-intensive industry unlike anything the world had previously seen. In two generations, textile workers who labored on hand looms in their cottages were replaced by an urban-industrial proletariat toiling in giant spinning factories. Many other sectors of the British economy also experienced the Industrial Revolution. Water and steam power replaced hand labor, machinery grew in complexity, and the small-scale familial workplace was replaced by massive industrial establishments.

Engels noted that in 1760,

England was a country like every other, with small towns, few and simple industries, and a thin but *proportionally* large agricultural population. Today [1844] it is a country like *no* other, with a capital of two and a half million inhabitants; with vast manufacturing cities; with an industry that supplies the world, and produces almost everything by means of the most complex machinery; with an industrious, intelligent, dense population, of which two-thirds are employed in trade and commerce, and composed of classes wholly different. ([1845] 1950:15)

"Composed of classes *wholly different*." In Engels's view, that was the key. The bourgeoisie, or capitalist class, formed a relatively small, privileged group. In contrast, a large, oppressed mass —the industrial proletariat—was developing. "What is to become of these destitute millions," Engels asked, "who consume today what they earned yesterday; who have created the greatness of England by their inventions and their toil; who become with every passing day more conscious of their might and demand with daily increasing urgency their share of the advantages of society?" (17) Engels's prescription was socialist revolution.

Manchester is often taken as the symbol of the new industrial city, and few were neutral about it. Like the Chicago painted by Nelson Algren (Chapter 1), "Manchester forced to the surface the problems of 'class' and the relations between rich and poor" (Briggs, 1963:93).

Like Chicago in the 1890s and 1900s, some saw Manchester as a grand city, a symbol of progress and civilization. Engels did not deny the grandeur of parts of Manchester, but he loathed the brutality of the city toward its working-class residents. And he connected "the marvels of civilization" for the few to the "nameless misery" for the many. The price paid for progress under capitalism, in Engels's view, was "brutal indifference," "unfeeling isolation," and "reciprocal plundering" (24).

Manchester was not what a city planner would call a planned community. But Engels thought that private forces—the workings of the capitalist economic system—had patterned the city and its environs in a certain fashion: to serve the interests of the bourgeoisie. Members of the capitalist class, living in villas and breathing the clean air of the suburbs, could catch a horse-drawn omnibus to work and ride along broad boulevards, walled off from human misery by the shops of the petty bourgeoisie. They did not even see the working-class slums.

In many ways, Engels's writing on Manchester prefigures the work of later urban sociologists, as we shall see in the next chapter. According to Engels, the new urbanites

crowd by one another as though they had nothing in common. . . . The brutal indifference, the unfeeling

isolation of each in his private interest becomes the more repellant and offensive, the more these individuals are crowded together. . . . This isolation of the individual, this narrow self-seeking is the fundamental principle of our society everywhere, [but] it is nowhere so shamelessly barefaced, so self-conscious as just here in the crowding of the great city. The dissolution of mankind into monads, of which each one has a separate principle, the world of atoms, is here carried out to its utmost extreme. ([1845] 1950:24)

Thus atomism for all, crushing poverty for wage earners, and the marvels of civilization for those who owned and controlled the industry that made Manchester and other English towns great —such was, in Engels's view, the new industrial city in the capitalistic society.

*A dissenting view:* Recall from Chapter 2 what Lewis Mumford says about "slum, semi-slum, and super-slum" in Manchester. According to Mumford, even Engels didn't realize "the fact that the upper-class quarters were, more often than not, intolerable super-slums" (1961:465). In this view, there were few marvels of civilization for any class to enjoy. The new industrial cities were just as intolerably ugly, overcrowded, and unsanitary for the rich as for the poor.

## AMERICAN URBAN ROOTS

### Specks in the Wilderness

America's first European settlers founded tiny, compact colonial cities, "specks in the wilderness" (Bridenbaugh, 1938:467). Between their founding in the seventeenth century and the American Revolution, these first settlements matured into larger cities. Let's look at late-eighteenth-century Philadelphia to get a feeling for the colonial city.

Historian Samuel Bass Warner, Jr. (1968) characterizes Philadelphia on the eve of the Revolution as a "private city." The vast majority of its 23,700 residents were artisans or independent shopkeepers, contracting out on a daily basis. A small merchant elite engaged in production and trade, and a small underclass of indentured servants, slaves, and hired servants toiled at the bottom of the heap. Most Philadelphians, however, were modest, independent businessmen (and their families) with a privatistic ethic.

Colonial Philadelphia, according to Warner, was a town of abundant opportunity. Workers were in great demand. People could find work, save money, and move into most trades, for the guilds had failed in their attempts to restrict access to their crafts. If there was great social mobility in Philadelphia at the time, what was its cause? Property ownership, in Warner's analysis.

The physical form of colonial Philadelphia was consistent with its social structure. The city was compact—a classic **walking city.** All points were easily accessible on foot. Blocks tended to be economically and socially mixed. The clustering effects of ethnic or occupational groups were not consequential.

The political structure also reflected the privatistic ethic. Citizens wanted little government. The formal city government consisted of a "club of wealthy merchants without much purse, power, or popularity" (1968:9). Its only significant functions were to manage the market and run the local records' court; there were no public schools or public water supply; most streets were unpaved. Philadelphia had independent commissions of assessors, street commissioners, city wardens (in charge of the night watch and street lighting), and a board of overseers for the poor. But these groups accomplished little. Warner concludes that things got done in Philadelphia less through formal government structures than through the clubbiness of a small community that functioned by a set of informal rules and power relationships (a common theme in urban government, as we shall see in Chapter 13).

Warner depicts a city of small-scale entrepreneurs, abundant opportunity, and social fluidity, without the geographic segregation that characterized Philadelphia (and other American cities) in later years. But he points out that Philadelphians were not socially or economically equal by any means. Indeed, the tax list for 1774 shows that the upper 10 percent of the taxpaying households owned 89 percent of the city's taxable property.

The little private city of Philadelphia described by Warner did not have the great extremes of wealth and poverty, the teeming slums, the unhealthy conditions, or the social discord of European industrial cities that emerged shortly thereafter. Nor did it have the urban problems of contemporary Newark, East St. Louis, or Detroit. Nor was much of the American population urban at the time. Indeed, only 5.1 percent of the population was classified as urban by the first U.S. census in 1790. Nonetheless, the predominantly rural intellectuals of the day generally disliked and distrusted the city. As cities grew larger, more heterogeneous, and less tied to rural ways during the nineteenth century, this animosity increased.

## Antiurbanism of the Intellectuals

"The mobs of great cities," wrote Thomas Jefferson in 1784, "add just so much to the support of pure government, as sores do to the strength of the human body." In this negative judgment, he was in good company; few American intellectuals liked cities. Jefferson's blast at city mobs in 1784 is examined closely by Morton and Lucia White in *The Intellectual Versus the City* ([1962] 1964). They identify medical, moral, and political reasons for his antiurbanism at that time and trace the evolution in his later thinking.

One reason why the concentration of people in cities in eighteenth-century America was undesirable was purely medical. Periodically, yellow fever ravaged the early colonial cities, and Jefferson based part of his opposition on medical grounds.

But Jefferson's critique went much deeper. In his views on what made for the good life, Jefferson was somewhat torn between the values of the country squire and those of the city gentleman. As a child of the Enlightenment, he enjoyed the good things of civilized urban life: art, literature, witty conversation, painting, science, and other "elegant arts." Yet he more dearly loved the simple pleasures of the country farmer. Further, he feared the effect of cities on the health, virtue, and freedom of the people: "I view great cities as pestilential to the morals, the health and liberties of man. True, they nourish some of the elegant arts, but the useful ones can thrive elsewhere, and less perfection in the others, with more health, virtue, and freedom would be my choice" (in White and White, [1962] 1964:28).

Another basis for his concern was political stability. Jefferson's writings reflect a fear of the political consequences of city mobs. The words of Alexis de Tocqueville a generation later echo this fear. Tocqueville viewed the largest American cities in the 1830s with alarm, even predicting that the United States and other republics would "perish from [the unruly, self-interested mobs of cities] unless the government succeeds in creating an armed force which, while it remains under the control of the majority of the nation, will be independent of the town population and able to repress its excesses" (in White and White, [1962] 1964:35). Similarly, Jefferson believed that a dispersed agricultural population, tied to the land and concerned with private property, was most conducive to political stability and personal freedom.

Jefferson's antiurban views survived decades of politics and travel to Paris. But late in life, they changed. During the War of 1812, Britain was able to cut off imports from Europe, and the United States, lacking industries of its own, suffered. Jefferson concluded that the United States must develop its own manufacturing (and by implication, cities) rather than face dependency or want in time of war or national crisis.

During and after Jefferson's time, antiurbanism was a dominant attitude among philosophers, novelists, poets, and social critics. Transcendental poet and essayist Ralph Waldo Emerson reportedly shuddered when approaching New York City (population: 200,000 by the 1830s). He wrote: "That uncorrupted behavior which we admire in animals and young children belongs to the . . . man who lives in the presence of nature. Cities force growth and make men talkative and entertaining, but they make them artificial" (in White and White, [1962] 1964:40). Accordingly, transcendentalists "prefer to ramble in the country and perish of ennui, to the degradation of such charities and such ambition as the city can propose to them." Henry David

Thoreau carried the logic of the "cities corrupt—nature restores" philosophy to its logical extreme, repudiating cities, towns, and eventually the society of other human beings. Thus, while Jefferson disliked cities on political grounds, the transcendentalists attacked them on metaphysical grounds.

Meanwhile, major American novelists and poets described the city as a bad dream. Edgar Allen Poe paints a surreal setting in which a nightmarish city, disembodied from space and time, is destroyed:

> And when amid no earthly moans,
> Down, down that town shall settle hence,
> Hell, rising from a thousand thrones,
> Shall do it reverence. (1886:170)

Similarly, Hawthorne, in *The Marble Faun* ([1860] 1950), describes the streets of Rome as "uneasy," "evil," and "stony-hearted" and the city itself as "chilly," "gloomy," "melancholy," "sickly," "dreary," "filthy," and "foul."

American writers, using nightmarish imagery, tended to set their fantasies in Europe, not America. But as America began to experience the first strains of industrialization and urbanization in the 1830s and 1840s, these authors looked with fear at the potential consequences.

How much do the views of novelists and philosophers count? What impact did they have on policymakers and the masses? The Whites argue that the antiurban bias of American intellectuals and writers helped to shape the values and attitudes of Americans for generations. And, they add, part of the difficulty in focusing public policy on urban problems is rooted in the long tradition of antiurbanism.

## From Walking City to Streetcar Suburb

The cities described in nightmarish terms by America's antiurban intellectuals were small and compact by today's standards. Indeed, until the 1850s, even the largest U.S. cities could be crossed on foot in about thirty minutes; hence the name walking city.

Today, as we think about the potential effects

of increased costs and decreased availability of energy on city life, historical studies of the relationship between transport technology and city form take on renewed interest. Speaking in 1895, one observer noted the role of three new technologies: the trolley, bicycle, and telephone. Although their influence on city and country life was "impossible to foresee," the observer said that already they had added 5 to 15 miles to the radius of every large town. "It is by such apparently unimportant, trifling, and inconspicuous forces," concluded the observer, "that civilization is swayed and moulded in its evolutions and no man can foresee them or say whither they lead" (F. J. Kingsley in Banfield, [1968] 1970:25). In other words, a change in transport or communications technology leads to changes in city structure, and no one can totally predict "whither they will lead."

The demise of the compact walking city can be traced to a series of innovations in transport technology. What trolleys, bicycles, and, later, cars did was to expand the limits of the walking city.

The centrifugal forces that ultimately destroyed the walking city were put into motion as early as 1829, when a New York City entrepreneur initiated the first omnibus route in America. A decade later, similar operations had spread to all major U.S. cities. Apparently, these buses were far from comfortable or convenient. A New York City newspaper commented in 1864 that "modern martyrdom may succinctly be defined as riding in a New York City omnibus" (in Chudacoff, 1975:69). Still, the proliferation of bus companies and the rapid increase in ridership testify to the popular desire for improved transportation. Soon the omnibus was followed by horsedrawn buses on rails and commuter railroads, further accelerating the sprawl of the city.

But it was the invention of the electric trolley in 1886, coupled with that of the telephone in 1876, that worked a major change in the structure of cities. These two inventions greatly increased people's ability to work in cities and travel to suburban homes, to live on the outskirts of town and communicate to central locations.

In his study of three Boston **streetcar suburbs,** historian Samuel Bass Warner, Jr., notes that the electric trolley pushed Boston's urban fringe out

to 6 miles in the 1880s and 1890s. By 1900, the old walking city had become primarily a region of cheap housing. Warner concludes that early streetcar suburbanization around Boston produced an urban area characterized by housing segregation, by both ethnicity and class. In addition, the new trolley technology made possible what many builders, large institutions, and upper-class homeowners wanted: the physical separation of work from residence.

*To conclude:* Despite Jefferson's lament, cities continued to grow apace in nineteenth-century America, changing from colonial walking cities to more sprawling places with suburbs reached by streetcars and trolleys. Such technological innovations in the 1880s influenced the shape of housing patterns, as well as other social and political patterns.

## URBANIZATION OF THE WORLD'S POPULATION

American cities grew in population in the nineteenth century, but the majority of people still lived in rural areas. This was true everywhere in the world.

It was not until about the turn of the twentieth century that the first urbanized society came into existence. At that time, Great Britain became the first society in history whose urban population exceeded its rural population. As noted earlier, at the time of the first U.S. census in 1790, only 5.1 percent of the population lived in cities, and in 1850 no society could be called urbanized. Only since around 1900 has there been a profound change in the number of cities worldwide, their size, and the proportion of the world's population that lives in (or around) them. Demographer Kingsley Davis calls this profound change "The Urbanization of the Human Population."

### The Process of Urbanization

Early cities were nothing more than urban specks in a rural world—and small ones at that.

Ancient Sumerian cities and Periclean Athens had populations no larger than those of many contemporary suburbs. Moreover, Ur, ancient Athens, Teotihuacán, medieval Venice, and all cities before the Industrial Revolution accounted for only a tiny proportion of the population of their societies. In other words, being a city dweller and being urbanized aren't the same thing.

**Urbanization** refers to population concentration: "the proportion of the total population [in a society or nation] in urban settlements, or else to a rise in this proportion" (Davis, 1965:41). Urbanization may also refer to the process of becoming urban in terms of social, technological, political, and spatial organization.

Urbanization should not be confused with city growth. Urbanization refers to the *proportion* of an entire society's or nation's population living in urban places. So, it is quite possible for cities to increase in population enormously without urbanization taking place. This can occur if the rural population grows as rapidly as, or more rapidly than, the urban population. For instance, both China and India have several of the world's largest cities, yet neither is an urbanized *society*.

Two factors are crucial in the urbanization process: (1) *out-migration* from rural areas to cities and (2) *natural increase* (population increase due to an excess of births over deaths). The movement of people from rural to urban areas can change the total proportion of people living in cities. Natural increase can also alter the demographic structure of a society. If birth rates are lower or mortality rates higher in cities than in the countryside, they may retard urbanization. Poor sanitation and health conditions in many eighteenth- and nineteenth-century cities led to just such a differential in mortality rates.

## Industrialization and Urbanization in Western Europe and North America

Kingsley Davis concludes that between the sixteenth and eighteenth centuries, the average rate of urbanization was barely perceptible—about $6/10$ of 1 percent a year for the European cities he

examined. Since that time, industrialized nations in Europe and North America have passed through a recognizable pattern of urbanization: an S-shaped curve, beginning slowly, moving sharply upward, then leveling off. In rural preindustrial societies, urbanization proceeds slowly. Then, if the society experiences an industrial revolution, it shoots up. At the most advanced stages, it tends to level off.

Generally speaking, urbanization accompanied industrialization in western Europe and North America. Thus when Britain became the first urban society in human history around 1900, rural migrants to the city were working in the factories and shops of an industrialized nation. This is not the case in many poor countries today.

## Urbanization in Poor Countries

Before examining the dramatic urban population growth in many countries of Africa, Latin America, and Asia, we should note that there is no agreed-on name for these countries. They are variously called *emerging, underdeveloped, less developed, backward, developing, modernizing, economically dependent, South,* and *Third World*. But *Third World* is outdated: Politicians once described anti-Soviet, industrialized nations as the *First World;* the Soviet bloc as the *Second World,* and nations neutral in the struggle between the Soviet bloc and the so-called free world as the *Third World,* a term coined by Charles de Gaulle and used at the Bandung Conference in 1955. With the disappearance of the Second World, the term *Third World* became obsolete. Now it is often used to mean underdeveloped nations. It is also used as a synonym for people of color. Here I use the term **poor countries** because so-called Third World nations display enormous cultural richness and diversity but share an economic situation: mass poverty.

Particularly in Africa, cities are growing rapidly. Indeed, in Africa, the least urbanized continent, some cities double in population every twelve years. Urbanization in Africa is occurring more rapidly than it did in western Europe's and North America's period of rapid industrialization.

**Table 4.1**  The World's Largest Metropolitan Areas, Ranked by 1990 Estimated Population (in millions)

| Urban Area | Country | 1950 | 1970 | 1990 | 2000 | Urban Area | Country | 1950 | 1970 | 1990 | 2000 |
|---|---|---|---|---|---|---|---|---|---|---|---|
| 1. Mexico City | Mexico | 3.1 | 9.4 | 20.2 | 25.6 | 37. Shenyang | China | 2.1 | 3.5 | 4.8 | 6.3 |
| 2. Tokyo | Japan | 6.7 | 14.9 | 18.1 | 19.0 | 38. Philadelphia | United States | 2.9 | 4.0 | 4.3 | 4.5 |
| 3. Sao Paulo | Brazil | 2.4 | 8.1 | 17.4 | 22.1 | 39. Caracas | Venezuela | 0.7 | 2.0 | 4.1 | 5.2 |
| 4. New York | United States | 12.3 | 16.2 | 16.2 | 16.8 | 40. Baghdad | Iraq | 0.6 | 2.0 | 4.0 | 5.1 |
| 5. Shanghai | China | 5.3 | 11.2 | 13.4 | 17.0 | 41. Lahore | Pakistan | 0.8 | 2.0 | 4.1 | 6.0 |
| 6. Los Angeles | United States | 4.0 | 8.4 | 11.9 | 13.9 | 42. Wuhan | China | 1.2 | 2.7 | 3.9 | 5.3 |
| 7. Calcutta | India | 4.4 | 6.9 | 11.8 | 15.7 | 43. Alexandria | Egypt | 1.0 | 2.0 | 3.7 | 5.1 |
| 8. Buenos Aires | Argentina | 5.0 | 8.4 | 11.5 | 12.9 | 44. Detroit | United States | 2.8 | 4.0 | 3.7 | 3.7 |
| 9. Bombay | India | 2.9 | 5.8 | 11.2 | 15.4 | 45. Guangzhou | China | 1.3 | 3.0 | 3.7 | 4.8 |
| 10. Seoul | South Korea | 1.0 | 5.3 | 11.0 | 12.7 | 46. San Francisco | United States | 2.0 | 3.0 | 3.7 | 4.1 |
| 11. Beijing | China | 3.9 | 8.1 | 10.8 | 14.0 | 47. Ahmedabad | India | 0.9 | 1.7 | 3.6 | 5.3 |
| 12. Rio de Janeiro | Brazil | 2.9 | 7.0 | 10.7 | 12.5 | 48. Belo Horizonte | Brazil | 0.4 | 1.6 | 3.6 | 4.7 |
| 13. Tianjin | China | 2.4 | 5.2 | 9.4 | 12.7 | 49. Naples | Italy | 2.8 | 3.6 | 3.6 | 3.6 |
| 14. Jakarta | Indonesia | 2.0 | 3.9 | 9.3 | 13.7 | 50. Hyderabad | India | 1.1 | 1.7 | 3.5 | 5.0 |
| 15. Cairo | Egypt | 2.4 | 5.3 | 9.0 | 11.8 | 51. Kinshasa | Zaire | 0.2 | 1.4 | 3.5 | 5.5 |
| 16. Moscow | Russia | 4.8 | 7.1 | 8.8 | 9.0 | 52. Toronto | Canada | 1.0 | 2.8 | 3.5 | 3.9 |
| 17. Delhi | India | 1.4 | 3.5 | 8.8 | 13.2 | 53. Athens | Greece | 1.8 | 2.5 | 3.4 | 3.8 |
| 18. Metro Manila | Philippines | 1.5 | 3.5 | 8.5 | 11.8 | 54. Barcelona | Spain | 1.6 | 2.7 | 3.4 | 3.7 |
| 19. Osaka | Japan | 3.8 | 7.6 | 8.5 | 8.6 | 55. Dallas | United States | 0.9 | 2.0 | 3.4 | 4.4 |
| 20. Paris | France | 5.4 | 8.3 | 8.5 | 8.6 | 56. Katowice | Poland | 1.7 | 2.8 | 3.4 | 3.7 |
| 21. Karachi | Pakistan | 1.0 | 3.1 | 7.7 | 11.7 | 57. Sydney | Australia | 1.7 | 2.7 | 3.4 | 3.7 |
| 22. Lagos | Nigeria | 0.3 | 2.0 | 7.7 | 12.9 | 58. Yangon | Myanmar | 0.7 | 1.4 | 3.3 | 4.7 |
| 23. London | United Kingdom | 8.7 | 8.6 | 7.4 | 7.4 | 59. Casablanca | Morocco | 0.7 | 1.5 | 3.2 | 4.6 |
| 24. Bangkok | Thailand | 1.4 | 3.1 | 7.2 | 10.3 | 60. Guadalajara | Mexico | 0.4 | 1.5 | 3.2 | 4.1 |
| 25. Chicago | United States | 4.9 | 6.7 | 7.0 | 7.3 | 61. Ho Chi Minh City | Vietnam | 0.9 | 2.0 | 3.2 | 4.1 |
| 26. Teheran | Iran | 1.0 | 3.3 | 6.8 | 8.5 | 62. Chongqing | China | 1.7 | 2.3 | 3.1 | 4.2 |
| 27. Istanbul | Turkey | 1.1 | 2.8 | 6.7 | 9.5 | 63. Porto Alegre | Brazil | 0.4 | 1.5 | 3.1 | 3.9 |
| 28. Dhaka | Bangladesh | 0.4 | 1.5 | 6.6 | 12.2 | 64. Rome | Italy | 1.6 | 2.9 | 3.1 | 3.1 |
| 29. Lima | Peru | 1.0 | 2.9 | 6.2 | 8.2 | 65. Algiers | Algeria | 0.4 | 1.3 | 3.0 | 4.5 |
| 30. Madras | India | 1.4 | 3.0 | 5.7 | 7.8 | 66. Chengdu | China | 0.7 | 1.8 | 3.0 | 4.1 |
| 31. Hong Kong | Hong Kong | 1.7 | 3.4 | 5.4 | 6.1 | 67. Harbin | China | 1.0 | 2.1 | 3.0 | 3.9 |
| 32. Milan | Italy | 3.6 | 5.5 | 5.3 | 5.4 | 68. Houston | United States | 0.7 | 1.7 | 3.0 | 3.6 |
| 33. Madrid | Spain | 1.6 | 3.4 | 5.2 | 5.9 | 69. Monterrey | Mexico | 0.4 | 1.2 | 3.0 | 3.9 |
| 34. St. Petersburg | Russia | 2.6 | 4.0 | 5.1 | 5.4 | 70. Montreal | Canada | 1.3 | 2.4 | 3.0 | 3.1 |
| 35. Bangalore | India | 0.8 | 1.6 | 5.0 | 8.2 | 71. Taipei | China | 0.6 | 1.8 | 3.0 | 4.2 |
| 36. Bogotá | Colombia | 0.6 | 2.4 | 4.9 | 6.4 | | | | | | |

Note: The table is arranged according to urban areas that had populations of more than three million in 1990.

Source: John W. Wright, ed., *The Universal Almanac 1993* (New York: Andrews and McNeel, 1992), p. 329.

The United Nations projects that in the year 2000, the majority of the world's ten largest urban areas will be in poor countries. Every year, according to the UN Population Fund (in Robinson, 1993:A11), 20 to 30 million of "the world's poorest people" migrate from rural to urban areas, especially mega-cities in poor countries such as Mexico (Table 4.1).

According to Davis, a population boom, not rapid urbanization, is the primary cause of urban growth in poor countries. Others are not so sure. Dissenters argue that is is *overconsumption* in the rich countries, such as the United States—not overpopulation in the poor countries—that underlies urban problems in the poor countries. They note, for example, that in 1990, 1 American used as much electricity as 200 people in China.

Indeed, there is wide disagreement about both the causes and the effects of urbanization in poor countries. There are three general perspectives: (1) modernization, (2) urban bias, and (3) economic dependence (Bradshaw, 1987). Briefly, modernization theorists believe that as traditional, agrarian societies modernize, they will experience rapid urbanization, a positive trend that should be encouraged. Urban bias scholars and policymakers claim that government policies are biased in favor of metropolitan areas; these policies promote migration from rural area to city, a long-term negative effect in poor countries. For example, a spokesperson for the UN's Mega-Cities Project states that policymakers worldwide are promoting—not controlling—growth by wrongheaded policies such as subsidizing urban transport, energy, and water (Brennan, 1989). Economic dependence theorists argue that the capitalist world economy, dominated by the advantaged **core** powers (Western Europe, the United States, Canada, and Japan) use areas on the **periphery** (poor, dependent countries such as Uganda, Ethiopia, and Bangladesh) and **semiperiphery** (middle countries, such as Brazil) as sources of cheap labor, raw materials, and environmental dumping grounds. In this view, development and underdevelopment are flip sides of the same coin (Frank, 1969): Industrialized countries became rich by exploiting poor countries. Foreign investment is an obstacle, not an aid, to balanced urban development. It forces farmers into cities by reducing the land available to them, distorts urban labor markets, and increases the poor countries' dependence on the rich countries.

## Worldwide, the Future Is Urban

The scholarly and policy debate about causes goes on. Meanwhile, worldwide urbanization is expected to continue on a massive scale, particularly in poor countries. For example, in 1985, 56.7 percent of the world's 4.9 billion people lived in rural areas. By 2020, it is estimated that the world's population will grow to at least 8.1 billion, but only 37 percent will inhabit rural areas.

Worldwide, large cities will absorb much of the population increase. This is especially so in poor countries. A few statistics show the dramatic growth: In 1900, 12 percent of the world's population lived in cities of more than 1 million; in 2020, 35.4 percent will live in cities of 1 million. Most **mega-cities**—giant metropolises of over 7 million inhabitants by the year 2000—are located in poor countries (Table 4.1).

Metropolises and mega-cities in poor countries face seemingly unmanageable conditions, including high rates of unemployment and underemployment; inadequate sanitation and water; unstoppable migration from rural areas based on the hope for opportunity; overloaded transportation systems; air, water, and noise pollution; and lack of housing. Take, for example, the capitals of Kenya and Mexico. Kenya's population growth in 1988 was the world's highest (nearly 4 percent annually). From 1950 to 1979, the capital, Nairobi, grew 600 percent. By 1988, the city held about 2 million people, with over 250,000 living in rock-bottom poverty: a 6-square-mile squatter settlement of one-room shanties, roads of sewage, and few to no social services. By 1993, bread and sugar were unaffordable luxuries for countless slum dwellers (Lorch, 1993:A4). And by 2000, it is estimated that Nairobi will be home to 6 million people.

As Table 4.1 shows, metropolitan Mexico City's population nearly septupled from 1950 to 1990 (from about 3 million to roughly 20 million), and the UN predicts that its population will top 25 million by the year 2000. What the table does not show is this: Residents of Mexico City and its metropolitan area—the world's largest metro area—endure very unhealthy conditions, including the world's most polluted air (from toxic clouds of industrial emission, fecal dust, and car exhaust). In 1990, Mexico City's air exceeded acceptable ozone levels four out of every five days, and nearly one-third of its residents had no sewer service (Uhlig, 1991:1).

Is there any hope of improving living conditions in mega-cities? Some think so. Janice Perlman, founder of the Mega-Cities Project at New York University, believes that diverse metropolises such as Bangkok, Buenos Aires, and Beijing face many common challenges (e.g., housing poor people, moving garbage around). All can gain by sharing information about creative projects that are "socially just, ecologically sustainable, economically viable and participatory." One example is the so-called magic eyes project in Bangkok, Thailand. An effective advertising campaign encouraged children to pick up massive amounts of street litter and hassle their parents if they littered. Thanks to this low-cost urban success story, litter has decreased in Bangkok.

Perlman notes another factor uniting megacities in rich and poor countries: "Every third-world city has a first-world city in it; every first-world city has a third-world city in it" (in Roberts, 1990:A13). In Lagos, Nigeria, for example, there is posh suburban Ikoyi. In the United States, as Krashaun Scott, an inactive member of the Los Angeles Crips gang, puts it, "South central Los Angeles is a Third World country. There's a south central in every city, in every state" (in Lewis, 1992:B1).

Economic dependence theorists might explain the mix as follows: Standards of living differ enormously *within* a city. In part, these differences occur because a few high-paid managers in poor countries, working in global offices of multinational corporations and their subsidiaries,

create a core inside the periphery or semiperiphery. Meanwhile, low-paid immigrants from poor countries, working in the new sweatshops of Los Angeles, other U.S. cities, or cities in other rich countries, create peripheral areas inside the core (Sassen-Koob, 1984). This brings us to a broader discussion of linkages between cities everywhere.

## THE WORLD URBAN SYSTEM

### Globalization of Cities

Generally, theorists agree that New Orleans, Paris, Lagos, Lima, and New Delhi have quite distinct personalities—yet confront many common practical challenges. Theorists also point to two forces that are *decreasing* cultural diversity among cities while *increasing* their economic interdependence: (1) the *globalization of cultural life,* including the production and diffusion of films, TV series, and news from multinational corporations (e.g., IBM, Sony, CNN, Time Warner), and (2) the *globalization of economic life.*

It is important to note that while cultural and economic life is becoming globalized, the feeling of cultural uniqueness can inspire people to fight physically for a separate identity, as in the case of the East Timorese, Basques, and Bosnian Serbs, to name just three examples. Also, the threat of economic or cultural loss can lead to protectionism. For example, the French curbed the import of U.S. movies in 1993 (Cohen, 1993), and they tried to ban English-language words from their commercial signs.

### The International Division of Labor, Old and New

Citizens and scholars alike have been realizing that a very abstract concept—the internationalization of the economy and culture—is having a significant impact on Main Street. This con-

a

**Fig. 4.4** GLOBALIZATION OF CULTURAL AND ECONOMIC LIFE. (*a*) "American" movies, often produced by multinationals such as SONY, are popular in many cities, including Bangkok (pictured here) and Paris. Hollywood had captured about 80 percent of the European film market by the early 1990s (Cohen, 1993:14). France has tried to protect its movie industry from extinction—and, some say, its culture from corruption—by General Agreement on Tariffs and Trade (GATT) quotas and subsidies, but (*b*) American-style *French* fries are another story. An ad for McDonald's, complete with golden arches, adorns eighteenth-century Parisian rooftops. (*c*) In 1942, Rick's Cafe existed in Hollywood's *Casablanca;* in 1992, it could be found in real-life Amsterdam. ([*a*] Lisa Esherick; [*b, c*] Tim Teninty)

sciousness of connection may be recent, but in the view of economic dependence theorists, the phenomena themselves are not: "For the past three centuries at least, world-economic, political, and cultural forces have been major factors shaping cities" (King, [1990] 1991:1–2). In this view, it was colonialism that shaped cities worldwide.

And, in this view, it was colonialism that created the **old international division of labor**

**(OIDL).** Using the example of British colonialism, here's how the OIDL worked: Peripheral colonies in Africa, India, and elsewhere in the British Empire produced primary products and raw materials (e.g., cotton, tea, rubber) for the core industries in Liverpool and Manchester and the dinner tables of London. In exchange, people in the empire got machine tools, cotton cloth, railway cars, and other manufactured goods from Britain (Taylor, 1985). Under this arrange-

b

**Fig. 4.4**   *(continued)*

ment, Britain's largest cities grew rapidly in the eighteenth and nineteenth centuries; their growth and prosperity depended on Britain's key role in the international economy. Conversely, by the 1930s, Britian's global role had declined greatly, and consequently, so did the economic fortune of its largest industrial and port cities.

By the late 1960s, the old international division of labor was replaced by the **new international division of labor (Needle)**. Here is a key difference between the old and the new: The OIDL depended on *nation-states* such as Great Britain; Needle depends just as much, or perhaps more, on *transnational corporations*. As one scholarly group notes, "of the hundred largest economic units in the world, only half are nation states: the rest are multi-national companies" (Makler, Martinelli, and Smelser, 1982:13).

In a nutshell, the thinking is as follows: Global

and local issues can no longer be separated because there is a new international division of labor. That is, cities everywhere are economically interdependent, linked by a network of giant transnational corporations that engage in production, exchange, finance, and service functions. Theorists of the new international division of labor say that Needle started happening in the 1960s as multinational corporations relocated manufacturing production from high-wage cities in rich nations to low-wage cities in poorer countries (Froebel, Heinrichs, and Kreye, 1980; Henderson and Castells, 1987).

Let's take a key industry—automobiles—to get an idea of how Needle works. The car industry dominated the industrial organization of rich countries after World War II. But the industry has been undergoing a crisis since the early 1970s, and auto makers responded by restructur-

c

ing their global operations. One result was that in the United States, hundreds of thousands of jobs were lost, not only in car manufacturing but also in allied industries—steel, machine tools, electronics, and automotive components—that depend heavily on auto production (Hill, 1987:19). Detroit, Flint, Gary, and Pittsburgh are a few of the many cities that experienced structural unemployment, underutilized plant capacity, and disinvestment. After global restructuring, cars were partially manufactured at various lower-cost industrial sites all over the world, creating the "global factory." And this restructuring was accomplished by a small number of large transnational or multinational corporations ("planetary enterprises," in the colorful language of Barnet and Müller [1974]) that control the auto industry globally; twenty-two firms produced

about 90 percent of all cars in the world in the early 1980s (Tolliday and Zeitlin, 1987).

As a result of restructuring, it is now difficult to buy an "American car" or a "foreign" (a word banished from CNN in favor of "international") car because so many vehicles are "world cars": international hybrids, or products of joint ventures. For example, in the late 1980s, General Motors and Toyota produced 200,000 subcompacts annually in Fremont, California; 50 percent of the cars' content came from the United States and 50 percent came from Japan, and the cars were sold by Chevrolet dealers. Ford's Fiesta was designed as a world car to appeal to consumers everywhere. (Of all American auto makers, Ford Motor Company "has most successfully adapted to the post-mass-production era" by becoming the "most avid in trying to develop a car that can be

**Fig. 4.5**   WHAT NATIONALITY IS THIS CAR? (Lisa Siegel Sullivan)

sold anywhere in the world" and the "most re-sourceful in making transnational alliances with its Japanese competitors [Barnet and Cavanagh, 1994:17]). Parts of Ford's Escort may be made in Europe, Canada, the United States, or Japan. Hondas made in Marysville, Ohio, may be sold in Japan as Japanese cars. Chrysler advertised its cars as "Born in America," but imported Japanese metal stamping presses rather than using U.S. machine tools (Levin, 1990:C1). The "Japanese" Honda, Nissan, Toyota, Mitsubishi, and Mazda may be made in the United States, not Japan.

These data suggest that in an age of globalization, *multilocational, transnational firms are hard to identify as "American" or "not American."* What nationality, for instance, is a auto maker that borrows money from banks in Tokyo, airmails word processing to a back office in Dublin, buys auto tires from a subsidiary in Brussels, assembles parts outside Mexico City, uses a London-based ad agency, and coordinates all of these activities in its suburban New York City corporate headquarters? In today's global economy, the question seems pointless (Figure 4.5).

## U.S. Cities in the World Urban System

It may be pointless to ask which flag an auto maker salutes. In contrast, the following question seems all-important: What impacts will the transnationalization of production, distribution, and corporate organization have on cities everywhere?

Sociologists John R. Logan and Harvey L. Molotch (1987:chap. 7) address this question, focusing on U.S. cities. Taking for granted that "U.S. cities are tied to a transnational system" (257), Logan and Molotch suggest that there are at least five types of U.S. cities, each playing a different economic role within the new international division of labor: (1) headquarters, (2) innovation centers, (3) module production centers, (4) Third World entrepots (warehouses), and (5) retirement centers. To this list I would add one more type: (6) leisure-tourist playgrounds (Table 4.2). Why? Because tourism, by at least one measure, is the largest industry in the world: One out of every fifteen workers worldwide is employed in the tourist industry. By some estimates, it ac-

**Table 4.2** Logan and Molotch's U.S. City Types Plus One Addition

| Type | Examples | Key Functions |
|---|---|---|
| Headquarters | New York City, Los Angeles | Corporate centers: dominance in cultural production, transportation, and communication networks; corporate control and coordinating functions of many large transnational corporations and international banks |
| Innovation centers | Silicon Valley towns, including Santa Clara, Calif.; Austin, Tex.; and Research Triangle, N.C. | Research and development of aerospace, electronics, and instruments; some are (or were) so involved in military contracting that they are "war-preparation centers" |
| Module production places | Alameda, Calif. (military base);* Hanford, Wash. (nuclear waste); Omaha, Neb. (the "800" phone exchange center); Detroit and Flint, Mich. (cars) | Sites for routine economic tasks (e.g., assembly of autos, processing of magazine subscriptions or credit-card bills), some located near a natural resource (e.g., mining center) or government function (e.g., Social Security main office in Baltimore) |
| Third World entrepots (warehouses) | Border cities such as San Diego, Calif.–Tijuana, Mexico; Miami, Fla. | Trade and financial centers for importing, marketing, and distributing imported goods, including illegal goods such as drugs and pirated music; major labor centers because of their large numbers of low-paid workers in sweatshop manufacturing and tourist-oriented jobs such as hotel maids |
| Retirement centers | Tampa, Fla.; Sun City, Ariz. | Home to growing numbers of aging Americans. *Range:* affluent towns that maximize services to less affluent cities dependent on pensions, Social Security, and other public programs to support the local economy |
| Leisure-tourist playgrounds† | Tahoe City, Calif.; Las Vegas, Nev.; Atlantic City, N.J.; Disney World, Fla.; Williamsburg, Va. | *Range:* theme parks, sport resorts, spas to gambling meccas, historical places, and cultural capitals |

*Closed, in large part, since the publication of Logan and Molotch's book.

†This category is my addition.

SOURCE: John R. Logan and Harvey L. Molotch, *Urban Fortunes* (Berkeley: University of California Press, 1987), chap. 7.

counts for about $2 trillion annually, and it accounts for about 10 percent of the world's gross domestic product (Mitchell in Raymond, 1991:A5). In 1990, Americans spent $38.6 billion on lodging, transportation, and restaurants, making the United States the top tourism spender in the world (Elsworth, 1991:F4). Further, revenues from tourism increased every year from 1950 to 1990, even in times of economic recession (Raymond, 1991:A5). Natural wonders, cherished climate, amusement and entertainment, gambling, and/or accessibility to sports are key attractions in or near such U.S. centers as Las Vegas, Lake Tahoe resorts, Honolulu, and Vail, Colorado. Theme parks are another draw. Indeed, in 1990, more people (28.5 million) visited Disney World in Florida than all of Great Britain!

According to Logan and Molotch (1987), each city type contributes to the permanent advantage or disadvantage of individuals and social groups. Specifically, each city type has distinct and unequal consequences for residents in terms of *local rents, wages and wealth, taxes and services, and daily life.* They cite the following examples: Affluent residents of innovation centers have "much of the best of all worlds" because their places are in high demand. Hispanic migrant populations will continue to increase in the entrepot cities, invigorating barrio culture and discouraging assimilation (288). Module production centers and most retirement cities are unlikely to provide income redistribution through taxes. Growing headquarters cities and innovation centers have the highest rates of housing price inflation. Tourist playgrounds, I would add, tend to have a two-tier local economy: many low-wage service personnel (e.g., hotel maids, swimming-pool attendants, amusement-ride ticket takers) and relatively few highly paid top managers.

*To conclude:* There is a **world urban system:** an interdependent system of "people, knowledge, images, and ideas" and, to varying degrees, "capital, labour, and goods" (King, [1990] 1991:2). Cities perform differing economic roles in the new international division of labor, and their roles lead to disadvantages or advantages for residents. Places at the bottom of the urban heap may compete for garbage, nuclear waste, or potential toxic spills, often becoming "contaminated communities" (Edelstein, 1988) such as Love Canal, New York, and Bhopal, India. Meanwhile, world command cities such as New York, London, and Tokyo attract heavy concentrations of top corporate decision makers from finance, industry, commerce, law, and the media. Economic functions are coordinated in the world command centers—headquarters cities—where "500–1000 multinational corporations create a truly transnational economy, one whose primary geographical nodes are the world's cities" (Feagin and Smith, 1987:3).

### Cities in the Global Environment

The explosion of the Chernobyl nuclear reactor in Ukraine in 1986 alerted people everywhere

that an environmental disaster somewhere can be a disaster anywhere. Here are a few examples: People as far east as India and as far south as Ethiopia were breathing soot containing cancer-causing compounds, such as benzene, from burning Kuwaiti oil wells in 1991. American electronic assembly plants in Tijuana, Mexico, create polluted air and water that spill over to U.S. cities. Sulfur and nitrogen oxides, produced during industrial processes, enter the air above northeastern U.S. cities and end up in Canadian earth and streams in the form of acid rain, which can kill fish, weaken trees, and eat stone monuments. Carbon from fossil fuels emitted in industrialized nations (notably the United States and Canada, nations with the highest per capita emission of fossil fuel) contributes to global warming; gases from fossil fuels act like panes of glass in a greenhouse, trapping heat from the sun and raising temperatures, particularly in the middle latitudes of the Northern Hemisphere. Carbon is also released when trees are burned in tropical rain forests, contributing to climatic change in far-flung metropolises. And by 2020, rich and poor countries will each contribute 50 percent shares of carbon dioxide, a gas responsible for about half of the global-warming effect (Smil in Passell, 1990:B5).

Awareness of a shared ecosphere has expanded greatly since the disaster at Chernobyl. Yet this awareness is not matched by political mechanisms to control (or prevent) transnational environmental assaults.

So, what can be done to protect the ecosphere? Once again, there is no agreement. Here is a sampler of views: Biologist Barry Commoner identifies the major problem as a production process that generates pollutants. His solution is to change political decision-making processes that produce poverty and pollution, thereby altering production technologies to prevent or greatly reduce pollutants. Commoner thinks that to the extent that population growth is a problem, it can be controlled by ending the "grossly unequal distribution of the world's wealth." Researchers at the Worldwatch Institute point to the disappearance of cropland due to erosion, overirrigation, and loss of protective ozone. Their partial solution is to find new ways of putting food on people's plates. Ecologists Paul and Anne H. Ehrlich urge population control, warning that population growth is outstripping the earth's supply of food. Economist Julian Simon counterclaims that population growth, in the long run, is positive because it will lead to a cleaner environment and more abundant food for all: More people means more chances for inventing good ideas, and higher population densities allow for efficiencies of scale in production. At the opposite end of the spectrum, members of the U.S.-based organization Earth First! define the problem as modern industrialism. Their solution is to abandon industrialism and return to a hunting-gathering way of life compatible with a healthy land.

*To conclude:* In a remarkably short time, a world of urban specks was replaced by a predominantly urban world. By 1985 more than 40 percent of the world's population (2 billion out of 5 billion) lived in an urban place. By the year 2000, more than 50 percent of the world's population will be city dwellers.

## ANOTHER LOOK

Looking back on this speedy drive-through tour of several millennia of urban history—from early cities in a rural world to urban-industrial cities by the year 1900 and a world of mega-cities by the year 2000—several themes emerge. First, scholars disagree on why and where cities arose. These disagreements have little to do with their disciplinary backgrounds. Clearly, archeologists differ among themselves, as do sociologists and historians. Their dissent turns primarily on the relative weights they assign to various factors associated with the birth and development of cities. Some scholars, notably Childe and Sjoberg, place great emphasis on the role of technology. Others, such as Mumford and Kostof, stress the role of nonmaterial factors such as spirituality in the development of human institutions. This split—between those who think that ideas and culture can act as independent variables in deter-

mining social and political institutions and those who see ideas and culture as dependent upon people's material existence—is deep and irreparable. And it extends to many aspects of urban scholarship.

A second theme concerns conventional wisdom: Today's truth can quickly become tomorrow's folly. New evidence often challenges or changes long-accepted explanations of urban-related phenomena. Such is the case with Childe's thesis. Thus it is wise to consider all urban "truths" as tentative, not timeless.

A third theme concerns language and definitions. Often scholars do not share a definition of a very basic concept, including that of a city. Perhaps the best strategy is to accept dissensus as a given and then try to understand how a particular theorist uses a concept.

Finally, this chapter points up the difficulty of trying to draw boundaries around "urban" studies. Increasingly, we are learning that in order to understand what's happening in Detroit or Singapore, we must understand how the global economy and culture work.

## KEY TERMS

**Acropolis** In early classical Greek cities, a combined palace-fortress-temple complex built on a defensible hill within the city.

**Çatal Hüyük** An early (perhaps the earliest) trade city, dating from about 9500 years ago. It was located on high, arid land in present-day Turkey. Its economy was apparently based on trade in salt, obsidian, and other goods, not agriculture.

**Childe thesis** Evolutionary thesis about the origin of cities formulated by V. Gordon Childe. Childe argued that after a necessary agricultural revolution, cities emerged about 3500 B.C. in Mesopotamia. He linked the development of ancient Sumerian cities to a fertile environment, increasing population, the growth of social organization, and introduction of technology. Although it was once conventional wisdom, many now reject the notion that the urban revolution was a prerequisite for the development of ancient cities.

**City**   No single definition exists. Definitions often assume a relatively large population, high population density, and heterogeneity in terms of job specialization. Alternatively, a settlement may be defined as a city if it performs certain market functions or cultural roles.

**Core, periphery, semiperiphery**   Terms used by economic dependence theorists and world-systems theorists, notably Immanuel Wallerstein. In this view, a worldsystem is an interrelated economic—not political—unit divided into three zones, distinguished by different economic functions in the international division of labor, forms of labor control, political organization, and class structures. Today richer industrial core areas, such as North America and Japan, perform control functions for the world economy. Poorer areas on the semiperiphery (e.g., Brazil) and the poorest areas on the periphery (e.g., Ethiopia, Bangladesh) are sources of cheaper labor and raw materials.

**Jericho**   Ancient urban center in the Near East, located in mid-desert. Scholars dispute the claim that it was the first city.

**Mega-cities**   Giant metropolises with populations of at least 7 million by the year 2000.

**Mesoamerica**   The area in which pre-Columbian (pre-1492) Indian civilizations flourished, now thought to begin about 600 B.C. It encompasses the southern two-thirds of mainland Mexico, Guatemala, Belize, a western strip of Honduras, El Salvador, the Pacific coast of Nicaragua, and northwestern Costa Rica.

**Mesopotamia**   The Fertile Crescent region (in present-day Iraq), where some, notably V. Gordon Childe, believe the first true cities arose about 3500 B.C.

**New international division of labor (Needle)**   Economic interdependence between nations rooted in the specialization of economic tasks carried out through a global network of transnational corporations and cities. It connotes a restructuring of the world economy, starting in about the the late 1960s, with these features: (1) a shifting global market for workers that results in plant closures in rich countries and plant startups in poor countries; (2) the worldwide integration by large multinational corporations of basic economic functions—production, exchange, finance, and corporate servies—arranged in a hierarchical system of cities; and (3) the production of goods for the world market subdivided into smaller fragments, manufactured wherever it is most profitable. Term associated with a groundbreaking book, Fokker Froebel, Jurgen Heinrichs, and Otto Kreye's *The New International Division of Labour* (1980). Contrast: the *classical* or **old international division of labor** (where an integrated world market consisted of a few industrial nations producing capital goods and consumer goods and the vast majority of underdeveloped countries producing raw materials).

**Old international division of labor (OIDL)**   Peripheral zones (colonies) produced primary products and raw materials (e.g., cotton, cocoa, copper) for industries of the core countries (imperial powers) and received finished goods in return.

**Pampa de las Llamas-Moxeke**   The most spectacular site yet excavated of the ancient planned communities uncovered in a desert plain near the Peruvian Andes, dating back 3,500 to 3,800 years.

**Poor countries**   One term for nations with diverse cultures that face a common situation: economic poverty. This name avoids the ideologically loaded, negative term *underdeveloped nations* and the now obsolete *Third World*, a term coined by de Gaulle to refer to nations neutral in the Cold War struggle.

**Streetcar suburbs**   First wave of U.S. suburbs resulting from improved transport technology during the last quarter of the nineteenth century.

**Technology**   Tools and cultural knowledge used to control the physical environment to achieve practical ends. In Sjoberg's typology, it is the key variable in distinguishing city types.

**Teotihuacán**   Largest of the Mesoamerican cities, located on a high, relatively infertile plain near present-day Mexico City. Its population may have reached 200,000.

**Trade thesis**   One thesis of the origin of cities. Unlike V. Gordon Childe, Jane Jacobs and some others claim that trade, not agriculture, was the basis for the emergence of the earliest cities, notably Çatal Hüyük.

**Ur**   Largest of the ancient Mesopotamian cities in the Fertile Crescent. It emerged in a fertile, swampy area of Sumer in lower Mesopotamia between the Tigris and Euphrates rivers. A well-planned, compact city of perhaps 34,000 persons, it served as a religious and organizational center and a distribution point for the agricultural surplus of a larger agricultural area.

**Urban revolution**  Term used by archeologist V. Gordon Childe to refer to what he deemed profound changes in civilization that occurred concurrently with the rise of cities in ancient Mesopotamia.

**Urbanization**  Process by which the proportion of a society's or nation's total population living in urban settlements becomes greater, and the proportion living in rural areas decreases. Some scholars use the concept to refer to the process of becoming urban in terms of social, technological, political, and spatial organization. Urbanization is *not* the same as the growth of cities.

**Wadi-al-Natuf**  What some archeologists think was the world's first large, permanent habitat about 13,000 to 14,000 years ago in present-day Israel.

**Walking city**  A city prior to the introduction of transport technology that expanded its outer limits beyond comfortable walking range. Prior to 1850, all American cities were walking cities: The edge of the urbanized area could be reached in a half-hour's walk.

**World urban system**  Systematic interconnection of interdependent cities in terms of people, knowledge, images, ideas, capital, labor, and commodities.

**Ziggurat**  Religious temple in ancient Mesopotamian cities shaped like a pyramid (with steps rather than smooth sides) with a temple on top.

## PROJECTS

1. **American urban history.** For the city in which you live (or a nearby one), identify and determine the location of key transportation routes and their history. For instance, when were major roads, trolley lines, and highways built? Has this city been affected by water transport or air hubs? What effects on the present form of the city are evident from these early developments?

2. **American urban history.** Select an older inner-city neighborhood. Walk through the area.

Differentiate the architectural styles of the houses: When were they built? For whom? Notice particularly the churches: Do their architecture and size say anything about the ethnic roots of the neighborhood? Do they indicate when ethnic groups arrived (or were present in large enough numbers with enough wealth) to build a church? Are these buildings still used as churches?

3. **Cities and the environment.** Find out what policymakers and scholars believe to be the chief environmental culprits in your area—such as air pollution, toxic waste, or garbage removal. What proposals exist to deal with these conditions? Do they represent a wide spectrum of ideas or not?

## SUGGESTIONS FOR FURTHER LEARNING

Since the mid-1980s, there has been an explosion of new evidence and theorizing about early human settlements. Archeologist Donald O. Henry focuses on the Natufian culture in *From Foraging to Agriculture: The Levant at the End of the Ice Age* (Philadelphia: University of Pennsylvania, 1989). Olga Soffer concentrates on *The Upper Paleolithic of the Central Russian Plain* (Orlando, Fla.: Academic Press, 1985). For an exposition of the emerging theory about culturally complex cultures in the Stone Age, see T. Douglas Price and James A. Brown, eds., *Prehistoric Hunter-Gatherers: The Emergence of Cultural Complexity* (Orlando, Fla.: Academic Press, 1985). In the Americas, Jonathan Haas, Shelia Pozorski, and Thomas Pozorski explore *The Origins and Development of the Andean State* (Cambridge: Cambridge University Press, 1987). Recent evidence from Mesoamerican finds is discussed in Linda Schele and David Friedel, *A Forest of Kings: The Untold Story of the Ancient Maya* (New York: Morrow, 1990), and Kent V. Flannery, *Guila Naquitz: Archaic Foraging and Early Agriculture in Oaxaca, Mexico* (Orlando, Fla.: Academic Press, 1986).

The urban revolution in Mesopotamia is described in compact, highly readable form in two of V. Gordon Childe's books: *What Happened in History* (Harmondsworth: Penguin, [1942] 1950) and *Man Makes Himself* (New York: Mentor, [1936] 1952). For a brief critique of Childe's evolutionary view, see S. N. Eisenstadt and A. Shachar, *Society, Culture, and Urbanization* (Newbury Park, Calif.: Sage, 1987).

Were the ancient Mesopotamians colonialists or traders? Questions about ancient urban states are far from settled. This is clear from the controversies surrounding digs at the Turkish site of Hacinebi Tepe. Starting in 1992, anthropologist Gil J. Stein has directed excavations that may lead to the rejection of conventional wisdom about Mesopotamian trade and colonization. Anthropologist Guillermo Algaze, representing accepted theory, thinks that ancient colonialism sprang—inevitably—from the early urban states. He believes that Mesopotamia (as well as Teotihuacán, Harrappa, and Sumer) expanded in order to get resources and territory. But, based on artifacts, Stein posits that the classic colonial model doesn't work and that Mesopotamian outposts may be trading posts, not colonies.

Elizabeth C. Stone, a codiscoverer in 1989 of Mashkan-shapir, a lost rival to Babylon in the Iraqi desert, writes about the region in *Nippur Neighborhoods* (Chicago: Oriental Institute, University of Chicago, 1987).

A CD-ROM for Macintosh or Windows, "Exploring Ancient Cities" (San Francisco: Sumeria, with *Scientific American*), offers an interactive tour of Petra, Teotihuacán, Pompeii, and Minoan Crete. It features textured maps, a twenty- to thirty-five-minute slide show of each society, and discussions of cultural features, such as architecture, in the ancient cities.

For U.S. urban history, see Howard P. Chudacoff, *The Evolution of American Urban Society*, 2nd ed. (Englewood Cliffs, N.J.: Prentice-Hall, 1981), which is particularly strong on the connection between technological change and the evolution of city form, social and cultural history, and urban politics. Charles A. Glaab and Theodore Brown, *A History of Urban America*, 3rd ed. (New York: Macmillan, 1983), attempt to synthesize material on selected themes in U.S. urban history. One chapter provides a unique look at the bases of construction techniques (e.g., the origin of elevators) that made high-density cities possible. In *America Becomes Urban: The Development of U.S. Cities and Towns, 1780–1980* (Berkeley: University of California Press, [1988] 1990), Eric H. Monkkonen argues that "the United States is urban but not urbane," in part because it lacked a single dominating capital in the beginning. His first chapter, "Writing About Cities," assesses three approaches to urban history: the humanist critique characterized by Lewis Mumford and Jane Jacobs, the statistical approach practiced by Adna Ferrin Weber, and the "new urban history" of the late 1960s associated with Stephan Thernstrom and Sam Bass Warner, Jr.

In *Culture as History: The Transformation of American Society in the Twentieth Century* (New York: Pantheon, 1984), Warren I. Susman includes a chapter on "The City in American Culture," in which he relates this paradox: America, from the start, was more urbanized than most nations in the world, yet it has had a persistent myth of antiurbanism. Susman argues that the city was accepted as inevitable and necessary for progress in nineteenth-century intellectual thought as a result of "revolutions" in American life that affected communications, bureaucratic organization, and intellectual images.

William Cronon's *Nature's Metropolis: Chicago and the Great West* (New York: Norton, 1991) is one of a growing number of studies challenging conventional wisdom about cities and the U.S. frontier. "The central story of the 19th century West," according to Cronon, "is that of an expanding metropolitan economy creating ever more elaborate and intimate linkages between city and country." Chicago's history is bound to frontier expansion, Cronon says, because the city lies on the boundary between the East and the West.

Contemporary research and analysis of cities in agricultural and industrializing counties is reported in *The Urban Edge*, published ten times a year by the World Bank in Washington, D.C. The newsletter lists seminars, training opportunities, and annotated bibliographies of relevant publications.

Case studies of urbanization in various time

periods and parts of the world, including the Chinese Empire, Russia, early Islamic cultures, Latin America, Japan, and medieval Europe, are highlighted in S. N. Eisenstadt and A. Shachar, *Society, Culture, and Urbanization* (Newbury Park, Calif.: Sage, 1987). *Antipode, a Radical Journal of Geography,* often includes articles about urbanization worldwide.

Glenn Firebaugh and Frank D. Beck offer a useful literature review in their article "Does Economic Growth Benefit the Masses? Growth, Dependence, and Welfare in the Third World," *American Sociological Review* 59 (1994):631–653. Their findings contradict many earlier studies that had concluded that the effects of dependence dwarf those of economic growth.

For a sophisticated discussion of the causes and effects of urbanization in poor countries, see York W. Bradshaw, "Urbanization and Underdevelopment: A Global Study of Modernization, Urban Bias, and Economic Dependency," *American Sociological Review* 52 (1987):224–239. Bradshaw uses panel regression analyses to assess the validity of three different interpretations of urbanization in sixty-one poor countries between 1960 and 1980. His extensive references to works by economists, demographers, sociologists, political scientists, and political economists indicate that urbanization and "development" are multidisciplinary topics.

For works typifying the three perspectives on urbanization in poor countries, see the following: (1) *modernization:* Joseph Spengler and George Myers, "Migration and Socioeconomic Development: Today and Yesterday," in *Internal Migration: A Comparative Perspective,* ed. Alan Brown and Egon Neuberger (New York: Academic Press, 1977); (2) *urban bias:* Michael Lipton, *Why Poor People Stay Poor: A Study of Urban Bias in World Development* (Cambridge, Mass.: Harvard University Press, 1977); and (3) *economic dependence:* Michael Timberlake, ed., *Urbanization in the World Economy* (Orlando, Fla.: Academic Press, 1985), and Andre Gunder Frank, "The Development of Underdevelopment," *Monthly Review,* September 1966, pp. 17–31. For a summary of the various points of view, see Charles K.

Wilber, ed., *The Political Economy of Development and Underdevelopment,* 4th ed. (New York: Random House, 1988).

Serious jokester and filmmaker Michael Moore rejects modernization and urban bias perspectives. Moore indicts U.S. multinationals (including NBC's parent company, General Electric) in his first edition of *TV Nation* (July 1994, NBC-TV). He tours Reynosa, Mexico, a town with over 200 *maquiladoras* near the Texas border, with a bilingual guide who explains that the Mexican workers do live in slums and earn little, but have no home mortagages, car payments, and big expenses. Meanwhile, the Americans who manage the factories live in McCall, Texas, and play golf on one of the city's twenty courses.

In *The New State of the World Atlas* (New York: Simon and Schuster, 1987), Michael Kidron and Ronald Segal use statistics from the United Nations and international organizations to produce fifty-seven color maps on such subjects as international urban blight and rich and poor nations. One map, "Our Daily Bread," measures adequate nourishment worldwide; the authors comment (combining the urban bias and economic dependence points of view) that

rapid urbanization [in Africa] has drained human and material resources from the countryside. The new urban elites have acquired a taste for foods, such as wheat and rice, which are not traditional crops and have had to be imported in increasing volume at increasing cost. . . . And policies to keep food cheap for the appeasement of the urban populace deprive farmers of resources and accelerate the drain of population from the countryside. . . . Not least, warfare—whether waged by discontented peoples against the artificial unifications of the state, as in Ethiopia, or promoted by foreign intervention, as in Angola and Mozambique—has devastated vast areas of once richly productive agriculture. (Unpaged note to Map 39)

There is a growing literature on cities in a global society. For key works on core–periphery relations in a global economic system, see Immanual Wallerstein, *The Modern World System* (New York: Academic Press, 1976), who traces the world system and world economy to the late fifteenth and early sixteenth centuries in Europe; Wallerstein's third volume in this series, *The Second Era of Great Expansion of the Capitalist World-Economy, 1730–1840* (San Diego: Academic Press, 1989), examines the postmercantilist era of the European world economy. Anthony D. King, a professor of art history and sociology, explores the historical, cultural, and spatial links between the core and periphery in *Urbanism, Colonialism, and the World-Economy* (London: Routledge, [1990] 1991), paying special attention to British colonial cities and the transformation of built environments on a global scale. Works about contemporary society include Saskia Koob, "The New Labor Demand in Global Cities," in *Cities in Transformation: Class, Capital, and the State,* ed. Michael Peter Smith (Beverly Hills, Calif.: Sage, 1984), pp. 139–171. Joe R. Feagin and Michael Peter Smith present a readable and succinct discussion of "Cities and the New International Division of Labor: An Overview," in *The Capitalist City,* ed. Smith and Feagin (Oxford: Blackwell, 1987), pp. 3–34. A volume of twenty-five articles, ranging from a case study of New York City as a global capital to ecostructures required in a global society, are collected in Richard V. Knight and Gary Gappert, eds., *Cities in a Global Society,* Urban Affairs Annual Reviews (Newbury Park, Calif.: Sage, 1989).

Gerald Sussman and John A. Lent, eds., *Transnational Communications: Wiring the Third World* (Newbury Park, Calif.: Sage, 1991), deals with communication and technology transfer to peripheral and semiperipheral economies. In *Music at the Margins* (Newbury Park, Calif.: Sage, 1991), Deanna Campbell and others explore the continuing debate about pop music: Is it becoming more homogenized or diverse as it spreads from culture to culture?

Opposing views on population and ecology are put forth by Barry Commoner in *Making Peace with the Planet* (New York: Pantheon, 1990) and Paul Ehrlich and Anne Ehrlich in *The Population Explosion* (New York: Simon and Schuster, 1990). The Ehrlichs warn of imminent disaster based on population growth, but Commoner believes that the key culprit is how we produce things and how decisions are made about what to produce—not population growth.

## REFERENCES

Adams, Robert M. 1966. *The Evolution of Urban Society: Early Mesopotamia and Prehispanic Mexico.* Chicago: Aldine.

Banfield, Edward. [1968] 1970. *The Unheavenly City.* Boston: Little, Brown.

———. 1974. *The Unheavenly City Revisited.* Boston: Little, Brown.

Barnet, Richard J., and John Cavanagh. 1994. *Global Dreams: Imperial Corporations and the New World Order.* New York: Simon and Schuster.

Barnet, Richard J., and Ronald E. Müller. 1974. *Global Reach: The Power of the Multinational Corporation.* New York: Simon and Schuster.

Bradshaw, York W. 1987. "Urbanization and underdevelopment: A global study of modernization, urban bias, and economic dependency." *American Sociological Review* 52:224–239.

Brennan, Ellen M. 1989. Remarks. Annual meetings of the Population Association of America, May 3–5. Toronto.

Bridenbaugh, Carl. 1938. *Cities in the Wilderness.* New York: Knopf.

Briggs, Asa. 1963. *Victorian Cities.* New York: Harper & Row.

Childe, V. Gordon. [1936] 1952. *Man Makes Himself.* New York: New American Library.

———. [1942] 1964. *What Happened in History?* Harmondsworth: Penguin.

———. 1950. "The urban revolution." *Town Planning Review* 21:3–17.

Chudacoff, Howard P. 1975. *The Evolution of American Urban Society.* Englewood Cliffs, N.J.: Prentice-Hall.

Cohen, Roger. 1993. "Europeans back French curbs on U.S. movies." *New York Times* [national edition] (December 14):A1+.

Cox, Oliver C. [1964] 1969. "The preindustrial city reconsidered." Pp. 19–29 in Paul Meadows and Ephraim H. Mizruchi, eds., *Urbanism, Urbanization, and Change: Comparative Perspectives.* Reading, Mass.: Addison-Wesley.

Davidson, Basil. [1959] 1970. *Lost Cities of Africa.* Boston: Little, Brown.

Davis, Kingsley. 1965. "The urbanization of the human population." *Scientific American* 213:40–53.

Edelstein, Michael R. 1988. *Contaminated Communities: The Social and Psychological Impacts of Residential Toxic Exposure.* Boulder, Colo.: Westview Press.

Elsworth, Peter C. T. 1991. "Too many people and not enough places to go." *New York Times* [national edition] (May 26):F4.

Engels, Friedrich. [1845] 1950. *The Condition of the Working Class in England in 1844.* London: George Allen and Unwin.

Feagin, Joe R., and Michael Peter Smith. 1987. "Cities and the new international division of labor: An overview." Pp. 3–34 in Michael Peter Smith and Joe R. Feagin, eds., *The Capitalist City.* Oxford: Blackwell.

Frank, Andre Gunder. 1969. *Capitalism and Underdevelopment in Latin America.* New York: Monthly Review Press.

Froebel, Folker, Jurgen Heinrichs, and Otto Kreye. 1980. *The New International Division of Labor.* Cambridge: Cambridge University Press.

Fustel de Coulanges, Numa Denis. [1864] 1955. *The Ancient City.* Garden City, N.Y.: Doubleday, Anchor.

Hawthorne, Nathaniel. [1860] 1950. *The Marble Faun.* New York: Arcadia House.

Henderson, Jeffrey, and Manuel Castells, eds. 1987. *Global Restructuring and Territorial Development.* Newbury Park, Calif.: Sage.

Hill, Richard Child. 1987. "Global factory and company town: The changing division of labour in the international automobile industry." Pp. 18–37 in Jeffrey Henderson and Manuel Castells, eds., *Global Restructuring and Territorial Development.* Newbury Park, Calif: Sage.

Jacobs, Jane. 1970. *The Economy of Cities.* New York: Vintage.

Kenyon, Kathleen M. 1957. *Digging Up Jericho.* New York: Praeger

King, Anthony D. [1990] 1991. *Urbanism, Colonialism, and the World-Economy: Cultural and Spatial Foundations of the World Urban System.* London: Routledge.

Kostof, Spiro. 1991. *The City Shaped: Urban Patterns and Meanings Through History.* Boston: Little, Brown.

Levin, Doron P. 1990. "Chrysler ads belie ties to Japan." *New York Times* [national edition] (August 27):C1.

Lewis, Gregory. 1992. "L.A. riot area likened to third world nation." *San Francisco Examiner* (May 31):B1.

Logan, John R., and Harvey L. Molotch. 1987. *Urban Fortunes: The Political Economy of Place.* Berkeley: University of California Press.

Lorch, Donatella. 1993. "Kenya, asking for west's aid, battles a plummeting economy." *New York Times* [national edition] (June 7):A4.

Makler, Harry, Alberto Martinelli, and Neil Smelser, eds. 1982. *The New International Economy.* Beverly Hills, Calif.: Sage.

Mellaart, James. 1967. *Çatal Hüyük: A Neolithic Town in Anatolia.* London: Thames and Hudson.

Mumford, Lewis. 1961. *The City in History.* New York: Harcourt, Brace & World.

———. 1966. "Utopia, the city and the machine." Pp. 3–24 in Frank E. Manuel, ed., *Utopias and Utopian Thought.* Boston: Beacon Press.

Passell, Peter. 1990. "Economists start to fret again about population." *New York Times* [national edition] (December 18):B5.

Pirenne, Henri. [1925] 1956. *Medieval Cities.* Princeton, N.J.: Princeton University Press.

Poe, Edgar Allan. 1886 *The Complete Poetical Works of Edgar Allan Poe.* Chicago: Belford, Clarke.

Pozorski, Shelia, and Thomas Pozorski. 1994. "Early Andean cities." *Scientific American* (June):66–72.

Price, T. Douglas, and James A. Brown, eds. 1985. *Prehistoric Hunter-Gatherers: The Emergence of Cultural Complexity.* New York: Academic Press.

Raymond, Chris. 1991. "Cultural and economic impacts of increased tourism worldwide offer new opportunities for scholarly research, geographers say." *Chronicle of Higher Education* (May 1):A5+.

Roberts, Sam. 1990. " 'Mega-cities' join to fight problems." *New York Times* [national edition] (June 25):A13.

Robinson, Eugene. 1993. "U.N. calls mass migration global problem." *San Francisco Chronicle* (July 7):A1+.

Sassen-Koob, Saskia. 1984. "The new labor demand in global cities." Pp. 139–172 in Michael Peter Smith, ed., *Cities in Transformation: Class, Capital, and the State.* Beverly Hills, Calif.: Sage.

Scully, Vincent. 1969. *American Architecture and Urbanism.* New York: Praeger.

Sjoberg, Gideon. [1960] 1965. *The Preindustrial City.* New York: Free Press.

Stevens, William, K. 1988. "Life in the stone age: New

findings point to complex societies." *New York Times* [national edition] (December 20):B5+.

———. 1989. "Huge Andean temples 'as old as the pyramids'." *San Francisco Examiner* [Punch section] (November 5):8.

Taylor, Peter J. 1985. *Political Geography: World-Economy, Nation-State and Locality.* London: Longman.

Thucydides. [411 B.C.] 1956. *History of the Peloponnesian War.* Books 1, 2. Vol. 1. Trans. Charles Forster Smith. Cambridge, Mass.: Harvard University Press.

Todd, Ian A. 1976. *Çatal Hüyük in Perspective.* Menlo Park, Calif.: Cummings.

Tolliday, Steven, and Jonathan Zeitlin, eds. 1987. *The Automobilie Industry and Its Workers: Between Fordism and Flexibility.* Cambridge, Mass.: Harvard University Press.

Uhlig, Mark A. 1991. "Mexico City: the world's foulest air grows worse." *New York Times* [national edition] (May 12):A1.

Warner, Samuel Bass, Jr. 1962. *Streetcar Suburbs: The Process of Growth in Boston, 1870–1900.* Cambridge, Mass.: MIT Press.

———. 1968. *The Private City: Philadelphia in Three Periods of Its Growth.* Philadelphia: University of Pennsylvania Press.

Weber, Max. [1921] 1963. *The City.* Trans. and ed. Don Martindale and Gertrude Neuwirth. New York: Free Press.

Wheatley, Paul. 1971. *The Pivot of the Four Quarters: A Preliminary Enquiry into the Origins and Character of the Ancient Chinese City.* Chicago: Aldine.

Wheeler, Mortimer. 1953. *The Indus Civilization.* Cambridge: Cambridge University Press.

———. 1966. *Civilization of the Indus Valley and Beyond.* New York: McGraw-Hill.

White, Morton, and Lucia White. [1962] 1964. *The Intellectual Versus the City.* New York: Mentor.

Wilford, John Noble. 1991. "A very old sphinx may be older yet." *New York Times* [national edition] (October 25):A13.

———. 1993. "Mysterious Mexican culture yields its secrets." *New York Times* [national edition] (June 29):B5–6.

Wide World Photos

# CHAPTER 5
# The Ties That Bind

Poet John Donne expressed his view of the human condition in a memorable phrase: "No man is an island." If, as Donne implies, people are social animals whose fates are intertwined, then why do so many people feel disconnected and alone in the world? What ties people together? How do we prevent insecurity and loneliness? The idea of community is central to such questions of personal security and social connectedness. Although the abstract concept has many

**117**

meanings, "community" hinges on the notions of togetherness and sharing.

Chapters 5 to 9 focus on the ties that bind people together—and tear them apart. This chapter begins with a discussion of the concept of community and then examines a form of community that Aristotle (and many since) held up as an ideal: the polis of ancient Athens. Next, the chapter looks at various explanations of the shift from rural to urban life in western Europe and North America. The effects of this rural–urban shift on human personality are evaluated in terms of their basic assumptions and contemporary relevance. For example, nineteenth-century urban theories predict an *inevitable* breakdown in community within urban-industrial society. Did this happen? That leads us back to the issue of metropolitan community today, a major topic of Chapter 6. Then in Chapter 7, we continue the search for modern community, asking what, if anything, binds people together in large, sprawling urban–suburban areas? Do computer chat groups on the Internet promote a new type of community, one that is both placeless and faceless? And what about community life in the future—in proposed space age cities above the Earth and beneath the water? Chapters 8 and 9 in Part III continue with related questions, particularly: Is it possible to have multicultural, multiethnic societies with unity in diversity?

These five chapters pose many questions—and not merely abstract ones. What makes us feel like insiders or outsiders in a neighborhood or a nation? Why do we tend to trust people like ourselves but mistrust people unlike ourselves? What are the pluses and minuses of hanging out solely with people like ourselves? When do we feel cut off and alone, disconnected from the fates of others?

Finally, can any events bring us—a diverse bunch with varied concerns and interests—together in community? These questions confront us all, often in deeply emotional ways. How beautiful it would be, we may fantasize, to live in peace and harmony like the 1,000 members of the isolated Aché tribe who hunt and gather in the Paraguayan subtropical forest. Can any group in postindustrial society succeed in

building a community based on trust and self-sufficiency?

So many questions, so few answers. . . . Of course, there are many proposed answers to questions of community. The essence of many solutions is this: *If only* we could do X or Y, *then* we could create an atmosphere in which human beings live in harmony. Solutions have taken various forms—altering basic institutions through civil war or revolution; organizing separatist political or religious movements such as those in Hayden Lake, Idaho, northern Italy, and Algeria; and segregating, exiling, or killing people defined as outsiders (e.g., Hitler's Final Solution—a national policy of killing Jews, people with disabilities, gays, and Gypsies [Roma]; "ethnic cleansing" in Bosnia). These often deadly solutions suggest the power of community.

Meanwhile, philosophers and writers wonder aloud whether there are any answers. Are twentieth-century people doomed to be eternally *Waiting for Godot*, in the phrase of playwright Samuel Beckett? Is there *No Exit*, as Jean-Paul Sartre implies?

My purpose here is not to provide definitive answers to the problems of human community because, in my view, there are none. Rather, I hope that by openly discussing issues of community, all of us may make more conscious choices, both in our personal lives and in our collective life.

## WHAT IS A COMMUNITY?

Like love, truth, and other abstract concepts, **community** has no agreed-on meaning. In the discipline of sociology alone, there are at least ninety definitions of the word.

However, in general terms, a human community usually refers to either (1) a group sharing a physical space (e.g., residents of Chicago's Austin neighborhood), (2) a group sharing a trait (e.g., a student or lesbian community), or (3) a group sharing an identity and a culture typified by a high degree of **social cohesion** (e.g., the Amish, the Nation of Islam, and the seventeenth-century Massachusetts Bay Colony settlers). Often, this last group is called a *traditional community*.

## Communities Based on Territory

As just noted, a physical concentration of people —in a neighborhood, city, or nation—may be called a community. If asked "What community are you from?" most of us would probably respond by naming a place—say, Chicago, the West Side, or Austin, depending on the context and geographical knowledge of the questioner. Few would answer with a number—a ZIP code. Yet, as discussed in the next chapter, some researchers think that a ZIP code is the single most important bit of information about people in the United States. It identifies us as birds of a feather: members of residential communities where neighbors share preferences for food, cars, and presidential candidates.

Here we are not concerned with communities based solely on the sharing of space. Rather, we focus on communities rooted in social relationships. In this context, community is based on a feeling of "we-ness"—that is, a sense of shared identity and interdependence. Such a community may or may not share a physical territory.

## Communities Based on Common Culture

Some groups share both a physical territory and a cohesive social existence—the traditional community mentioned earlier. For instance, the Hopi inhabit a common physical space and accept the group's rules and goals.

However, many groups called communities today are not bound to a plot of land. For instance, a close-knit ethnic or religious community (e.g., Armenians, Sikhs, Hasidic Jews) can be widely dispersed. Yet its members share a culture and origins that bind them and set them apart from others in the society.

Similarly, members of an occupational community do not inhabit a common territory. They can be spread throughout the world, and rarely do they share origins. Yet certain occupational groups—lawyers, nurses, soldiers, and priests, to name a few—engage in activities that give rise to a shared culture, attitudes, and values in urban society.

Many consider a professional group (such as doctors) to be a community because it has the following characteristics:

1. Members are bound by a sense of shared identity.
2. Once in the profession, few leave.
3. Members share a language (or jargon) that can be understood only partially by outsiders.
4. Members share values.
5. In a social sense, members collectively reproduce the next generation.
6. Insiders are easily distinguished from outsiders in the professional community.
7. Requirements for membership are the same for all members.
8. The professional group has power over its members. (Goode, 1957)

This list stresses that a professional group is a community without a physical location. Still, it is often called a community because its members have a common identity, culture, and occupational goals.

Many universities call themselves communities. But, as the former president of the University of California, Clark Kerr, once joked in earnest, a university is "a series of individual faculty entrepreneurs held together by a common grievance over parking." Faculty in a university program or department, however, sometimes consider themselves to be a community of scholars.

Nonoccupational groups can also be considered communities if they meet the eight criteria. Examples here include some—but not all—religious, ethnic, political, spiritual, age-based, economic, and gender-specific groups: Alcoholics Anonymous; the AIDS Coalition to Unleash Power (ACT-UP); the Vietnamese-American community in San Jose, California; Dykes on Bikes; paramilitary "survivalists"; and poor people in economically segregated districts. Such groups may constitute **subcultures:** subcommunities that share some cultural elements of the dominant culture, but also have their own symbols, beliefs, and values. Alternatively, they may constitute **countercultures,** or oppositional groups: subcommunities whose beliefs, symbols, attitudes, and values *oppose* those of the dominant culture (e.g., 1960s hippies, today's streetwise youth in city slums).

Some social scientists (e.g., Kahler, 1957) distinguish between communities and **collectivities.** Communities, they say, derive from common *origins,* while collectivities are established on the basis of common *ends.* Using this distinction, occupational groups such as doctors, as well as other nonkin groups, would be considered collectivities, not communities.

## A Sense of Community

A sense of belonging—a we-ness—typifies many traditional communities. But is this sense of community possible today? Many theorists think not. They argue that contemporary urban-industrial or postindustrial society is too large, too diverse, and too individualistic to promote a sense of community except in subcommunities (e.g., ethnic groups) or collectivities (e.g., occupational groups)

Before considering that possibility, let us examine forms of community in times past. We begin with what some scholars believe to be the most highly developed community in the Western world: the polis in ancient Athens.

## THE ATHENIAN POLIS OF ANCIENT GREECE

In the fifth century B.C., Greece was composed of a number of independent, economically self-sufficient, and self-governing political units called *poleis* (singular, *polis*). The word **polis** is usually translated as "city-state," but this is a bad translation. The polis was not much like a modern nation-state, and it was much more than a city.

For this reason, following a historian of the Greeks, H. D. F. Kitto, we use the Greek word *polis.*

By current population standards, a polis was small. Only three poleis—Athens, Syracuse, and Acragas—numbered more than 20,000 citizens. (*Note:* Not all inhabitants were granted citizenship. Slaves, who were foreigners, and other foreigners were not citizens. Further, women had no political rights. Thus a citizenry of about 10,000 persons implies a total population of about 100,000.)

The small population of the polis is important in understanding its ethos. Greek philosophers insisted on this point. Plato wrote that the ideal polis should contain no more than 5,000 citizens (about 50,000 people). Aristotle maintained that the polis should not be too small or too large. He reasoned that it should be small enough so that all citizens could recognize one another on sight and be properly governed. But it should not be too small because it would not be economically self-sufficient. The idea of a metropolitan community numbering several million or a nation-state with over 200 million people, such as the United States today, would have seemed absurd to the ancient Greeks.

By contemporary standards, the physical scale of the polis was also small. Corinth, a commercial center, encompassed only 330 square miles. Sparta, covering 3,200 square miles, was considered enormous. To think in such small terms is difficult today. After all, the Los Angeles metropolitan area, covering over 4,000 square miles, is larger than any ancient Greek polis. Ancient Greeks would not have liked living in a huge modern state like the United States. The Greeks were in contact with one such vast state, the Persian Empire, and they thought it suitable only for barbarians, not civilized people like themselves.

Why did the Greeks live under the small-scale polis system rather than consolidating into larger political units? Surely economic factors and geographical barriers (particularly mountains) contributed to maintaining the polis system; but the "real explanation," according to Kitto (1951:69), was the character of the Greeks: Fearing that differences in scale would become differences in kind, they chose to live in poleis.

## A Communal Way of Life

Most citizens of a polis were farmers. Although agriculturalists, they preferred to live in a town or village, walk to their fields, and spend any leisure time talking to fellow citizens in the public square.

To these ordinary citizens, the polis was a community where all issues of common concern were public, not private. Citizen participation was widespread; about 15 to 20 percent of the citizens in the Athenian polis served the community in some capacity each year, filling offices by lot and rotating administrative responsibilites. Legislation took place in large popular assemblies. (Again, note that slaves and other foreigners were barred from public affairs. Further, women took no public role; they remained secluded in their homes, for Athens was a male-dominated community where men and women had separate spheres.)

From our vantage point, it is hard to comprehend what the Athenian polis meant to ordinary Greek citizens, particularly in the Golden Age of Pericles (ca. 490–429 B.C.). Depending on our political ideology, we see modern government as a mechanism to prevent "the war of all against all" (the classical liberal approach based on Thomas Hobbes's philosophy); as a means of regulating who gets what when the market mechanism of supply and demand needs adjustment (the liberal approach); or as a weapon serving the interests of the powerful against the powerless (the radical approach). But to the Greeks, the polis represented a positive force. It was the only framework in which people could realize their human potential: intellectual, spiritual, and moral.

The democratic leader of the Athenian polis, Pericles, gives a clue to communal life in the polis in his famous Funeral Oration: "Each individual is interested not only in his own affairs but in the affairs of the polis as well. . . . We do not say that a man who takes no interest in politics is a man who minds his own business; we say that he has no business here at all."

Pericles's Funeral Oration and the Athenian Oath of Citizenship (Figure 5.1) indicate the public-spirited attitude of the Greeks. They were social animals, living in and through the polis. For the Greeks, the polis was a community and a way of life. It was an active agent, training the minds and characters of its citizenry. It was a living entity, and citizens were like members of a large extended family. As Kitto concludes, the Greek citizen was essentially an individualist in economic affairs. But in the rest of life, he was essentially communal: "Religion, art, games, and the discussion of things—all these were needs of life that could be fully satisfied only through the polis" (1951:78). This situation stands in stark contrast to current conceptions of self-fulfillment.

*To conclude:* The polis was built on a common cultural life. Its geographic area was compact, so that people identified with their locality, and its population was small enough so that citizens were personally known to one another. Unlike a city or nation-state in urban-industrial society, the polis was a self-sufficient entity with an ethos of public, not private, interest.

The Athenian polis was ancient Greece's crowning glory. Why, then, did it disappear as a way of life? Some accounts of the decline and fall of the polis system focus on the effect of trade and markets. According to economic anthropologist Karl Polanyi (1957), the Athenian polis under Pericles was governed by laws of economic reciprocity. The concept of profit hardly existed. Instead, economic exchanges were seen more as gift giving than as trade; their chief function was to ensure social solidarity, not to redistribute wealth. This system of economic reciprocity faded with the emergence of a market economy (where prices are set by supply and demand) in the fifth century B.C. With the market economy came new ideas—profit and individualism.

In Kitto's view, what destroyed the polis system was progress. The polis was suited for amateurs, not professionals or specialized experts. Indeed, the polis discouraged specialization and efficiency, for its ideal was participation: Every citizen could and should play a role in public affairs. To accomplish this, no role could be very difficult for an ordinary person to play. When life became more complex in the fourth century B.C., new experts were needed. Commerce had expanded on the Mediterranean, and Philip of Macedonia had introduced new military tactics

# FROM THE OATH OF THE ATHENIAN CITY-STATE

WE WILL EVER STRIVE FOR THE IDEALS AND SACRED THINGS OF THE CITY, BOTH ALONE AND WITH MANY; WE WILL UNCEASINGLY SEEK TO QUICKEN THE SENSE OF PUBLIC DUTY; WE WILL REVERE AND OBEY THE CITY'S LAWS; WE WILL TRANSMIT THIS CITY NOT ONLY NOT LESS, BUT GREATER, BETTER AND MORE BEAUTIFUL THAN IT WAS TRANSMITTED TO US.

**Fig. 5.1** ATHENIAN OATH OF CITIZENSHIP. Citizens pledged to transmit the polis's cultural heritage and to improve Athens as part of their civic duty. (Athenian oath as it appears at the Maxwell School of Citizenship and Public Affairs, Syracuse University. Reproduced by permission)

in a war against the poleis. In short, the world was shrinking, and specialized skills—military tactics and commercial skills in particular—were needed to meet the challenges. Athens responded by employing professional soldiers (mercenaries) instead of citizen-soldiers. This act denied the very ideal of citizen participation.

In addition, Athenian education changed. Under Pericles, education was free and available to all citizens; it was part of living in the polis. But to meet the new challenges in the fourth century B.C., education became specialized and available only to those who could pay. Soon divisions between the educated and uneducated appeared, and specialist experts separated from laypersons. At his educational academy, Socrates taught students that government should be left to experts instead of being decided by democratic vote and popular debate; these teachings—not the expression of unpopular opinions—may have led to his condemnation to death (Stone, 1979).

These educational changes had wide-ranging effects. The educated of all poleis now had more in common with one another than with uneducated members of their own polis; this weakened the bonds of community. Further, the division between experts and laypersons destroyed the common knowledge base and culture upon which the polis was built.

It was at this time, the fourth century B.C., that the word **cosmopolis** was coined. It meant that people owed allegiance not to their own local community but to a larger group, the community of humankind. This new notion of cosmopolitanism, signaling the individual's connection to a wider community, helped to break down the traditional sense of community.

*To conclude:* As the educated became cosmopolitan in outlook, the ideal of the polis as a community waned. And as specialized experts in military and commercial affairs arose, the ideal of community gave way to the ideal of cosmopolitan life.

This brief account of the rise and fall of the polis, especially in Athens, suggests that a sense of traditional community could not be sustained in the face of growing complexity and specialization. The preconditions for its existence—a simple, small-scale, self-sufficient, relatively unspecialized local way of life—gave way to a wider world and a more cosmopolitan outlook.

Now let us begin a more systematic examination of some issues touched on in the history of the polis. For instance, does functional specialization necessarily lead to the breakdown of community? Can a sense of traditional community exist in a world shrunk to the point where a moon landing can be telecast to a global audience? Are individualism and loss of community inevitable companions of large-scale, complex society? We turn to urban scholars whose theoretical constructs deal with these very issues.

## CLASSICAL URBAN THEORY

By the 1870s, western Europe had experienced the effects of twin revolutions: the French Revolution and the Industrial Revolution. The giant broom of the twin revolutions was sweeping traditional community into the dustbin of history. The foundations of small-scale rural community—family, social hierarchy, church, relatively simple technology, property in land—were crumbling in the wake of industrialism, urbanism, and industrial capitalism. Great population shifts from countryside to city were in process, and England was on its way to becoming the first

urban society in human history. Thus it is not surprising that at this time the idea of community became a dominant theme in European social thought.

Theorists living through the demise of traditional community formed differing judgments about the new urban-industrial-capitalist order. Ferdinand Tönnies, for one, romanticized the medieval small town as the home of the humane life and mourned the passing of traditional community. Karl Marx, however, viewed the slow transformation from feudalism to industrial capitalism as a positive step, ending what he called "the idiocy of rural life." For Marx, the twin revolutions were liberating forces, freeing the political spirit and setting in motion the forces that would someday lead to a new basis for community—the solidarity of the working classes of the world.

Nineteenth-century theorists viewed the transformation of Europe in different ways, but they interpreted these changes in a similar fashion: *as inevitable evolutionary developments from one form of social organization to another—from rural to urban, from simple to complex, from feudalism to capitalism, from small-scale to large-scale, from religious to secular.* Hence classical urban theory is based on polar contrasts between two forms of social organization and human personality.

### Typologies of the Rural–Urban Shift

Theorists express these polar contrasts in the form of typologies (classification schemes). As noted in Chapter 2, typologies are designed to be tentative models of the real world, not to correspond exactly to every observable case. A typology is composed of two or more **ideal types** that can be used to describe, compare, and test hypotheses, such as the rural and urban types of society.

Despite their unique features, the various typologies of the rural–urban shift share some assumptions. Most important is their evolutionary bias. The shift from rural life to city life is viewed as a one-way street: a unilinear, inevitable, and irreversible development. At one end of the evolutionary process lies simple rural life, and at the other end lies complex modern society. However, a continuum between the two poles is implied.

Let us take a closer look at some of the many rural–urban typologies, examining several classical nineteenth-century formulations and other more recent ones. We begin with the most well known: Tönnies's *Gemeinschaft–Gesellschaft* dichotomy.

## Gemeinschaft and Gesellschaft (Tönnies)

Like other nineteenth-century theorists, Ferdinand Tönnies (1855–1936) based his typology on changes in peasant communities in western Europe. From that vantage point, he constructed a typology contrasting two forms of social organization: community and society. *Gemeinschaft* (community) lies at one end of the continuum, and *Gesellschaft* (society) lies at the other.

According to Tönnies, social life evolves in the following way: from family units to rural villages, to towns, to cities, to nations, and finally to cosmopolitan life. At the beginning stages of this evolutionary development lies *Gemeinschaft*, the traditional community that existed prior to the twin revolutions in Europe.

In *Gemeinschaft* social organization, people are bound together by common values, sacred traditions, and blood ties. They share a physical territory, experience, and thoughts. They are linked by a "reciprocal, binding sentiment." Kinship, land, neighborhood, and friendship are the cornerstones. These key elements are embodied in the family, the primary social unit.

By contrast, kinship, land, and friendship count little in *Gesellschaft*. In *Gesellschaft* (a form of social organization that accompanied the rise of industrialism, capitalism, and cities), there is a lack of close-knit family and friendship ties. Tönnies argues that in this urban-industrial capitalist society, human relations are based on contracts and laws, not binding sentiment. Attachments to land and neighborhood lose their meaning; money and credit become paramount concerns. In-

deed, Tönnies, like his contemporary, Karl Marx, insists on the importance of the money economy in determining human interaction. For Tönnies, people in *Gesellschaft* measure all values, including self-worth, in terms of money. This cash nexus replaces community values based on traditional authority, binding sentiment, religious traditions, and kinship.

As described by Tönnies, *Gemeinschaft* is typified by small rural communities where people know one another and their place in the social system. In contrast, *Gesellschaft* is marked by large urban centers where people are strangers whose place in the social system can shift.

Individualism, not community interest, is the hallmark of *Gesellschaft*. Since no common morality exists in the heterogeneous city, people are free to calculate rationally what is in their own self-interest. The movie *Saturday Night Fever* (1977) illustrates Tönnies's point. Both disco dancer Tony Manero (John Travolta) and his brother, a former priest, follow their own conscience in setting life goals. Neither is bound by family wishes, absolute moral values, or traditional authority. But in *Gemeinschaft*, Tönnies maintains, people do not base their actions on rational self-interest. Instead, they conform to accepted standards of behavior and share a definition of right and wrong.

Why did *Gemeinschaft* evolve into *Gesellschaft*? For Tönnies, *Gesellschaft* arose with the growth of commerce and capitalism. It serves the interests of merchant-capitalists who trade commodities on the basis of contracts, not friendship or blood ties.

How did Tönnies evaluate this movement from the simple rural community to the complex industrial city? Mainly negatively. He romanticized European medieval towns and their feudal institutions—symbolized by church spires, fortifications, and castles—as the source of the humane life. And he believed that the shift from *Gemeinschaft* to *Gesellschaft* meant an inevitable loss of community, a loss he tended to mourn with a sense of nostalgia. At the same time, he noted what he considered *Gesellschaft*'s positive aspects, particularly the rise of cities as cultural and scientific centers.

## Mechanical and Organic Social Solidarity (Durkheim)

French sociologist Emile Durkheim (1858–1917) sees the rural–urban shift in terms of changes in social bonds among people, or social solidarity. At the rural end of the continuum, people are mentally and morally homogeneous. In this form of social solidarity—**mechanical solidarity**—communities are not atomized.

At the other end of the continuum, the urban-industrial end, lies a society characterized by **organic solidarity.** Here the mental and moral similarities among people disappear, the collective conscience (shared beliefs, values, sentiments, and morality) weakens, and the **division of labor** stimulates individualism. People become highly differentiated according to their jobs.

To Durkheim ([1893] 1964), Western civilization was inevitably moving from mechanical to organic solidarity. That is, it was changing from a form of social organization based on unity of thought, beliefs, sentiments, and manners to one based on unity of heterogeneous individuals bound together by functionally interrelated tasks. For Durkheim, the prime force behind this evolution is the increasingly complex division of labor. In organically solid societies such as the United States, tasks are highly specialized. This specialization is reflected in the Labor Department's *Dictionary of Occupational Titles*, which consists of 1,371 pages of job titles known to the federal government,

from artificial eye maker to zyglo inspector (Table 5.1).

Both mechanically solid and organically solid societies, in Durkheim's view, are natural forms of social organization. Both are rooted in social unity; only the type of unity differs. The unity and homogeneity of rural society are replaced by unity consisting of functional interdependence in industrial society. (Tönnies, in contrast, defines *Gemeinschaft* as a natural social form and *Gesellschaft* as artificial.)

What are the consequences of the evolution from rural, mechanically solid society to urban-industrial, organically solid society? Durkheim says that the collective conscience weakens as a society becomes more specialized and differentiated by function. Contracts and a belief in the individual replace the collective conscience. In urban-industrial society, moral order is upheld by contracts and restitutive law, not by a common morality and repressive law. To Durkheim, then, the two forms of social organization can be distinguished by their legal base: "Law reproduces the principal forms of social solidarity" ([1893] 1964:68). In mechanically solid society, the legal system represses offenses against the common morality or collective conscience; such offenses are symbolically repressed because they threaten the moral order. Retaliation and punishment are typical sanctions applied in mechanically solid society. But in organically solid society, few offenses are seen as threats to the entire moral order. In many cases, an offense is handled by making amends (restitution) to the injured party in the form of money.

**Table 5.1**  Job Titles

### What's Your Line?

Reptile keeper, spray-gun repairer, fun-house attendant, peanut-butter maker, experimental rocket-sled mechanic, comedy diver, accordian repairer, bowling alley detective, bank-note designer, astrologer, astronomer, snow-removing supervisors, bottle washer (Machine I), trombone-slide assembler, interpretive dancer, young-adult librarian, net-making supervisor, playground-equipment erector, press-box custodian.

SOURCE: U.S. Department of Labor, *Dictionary of Occupational Titles* (Washington, D.C.: Government Printing Office, 1977).

Here is an example of the difference between repressive and restitutive legal systems. Suppose that you are holding a gun that accidentally goes off, killing another person. Everyone agrees that this was a freak accident. Would a court imprison or exile you? Not in organically solid society, for this action would not be considered a threat to morality. At worst, you could be judged negligent and ordered to pay restitution to the victim's survivors.

This same freak accident in mechanically solid society, however, could be punished in a repressive way. In *Things Fall Apart* ([1959] 1974), Nigerian novelist Chinua Achebe describes just such an incident. In the novel, the gun of an Ibo tribesman accidentally goes off, killing a sixteen-year-old boy. The punishment is seven years in exile, for "it was a crime against the earth goddess to kill a clansman, and a man who committed it must flee from the land" (117).

*To conclude:* Durkheim draws a polar distinction between two forms of social solidarity: mechanical and organic. The law, either repressive or restitutive, provides an index to a society's form of social solidarity. In both forms, the division of labor functions to cement social bonds. In rural, mechanically solid society, the simple division of labor promotes a common morality (collective conscience); in urban, organically solid society, the complex division of labor promotes functional interdependence. As simple, homogeneous, rural society is transformed (by population growth, increased communication, and larger territory), the division of labor evolves toward higher and higher specialization of function. This specialized division of labor can—*but does not necessarily*—lead to social dislocations: If the complex division of labor malfunctions in urban-industrial society, Durkheim warned, it could not play its role of cementing social solidarity. For example, the division of labor can become so complex that people work at very specialized tasks, not knowing how their task fits into any larger whole. Under such conditions, people can experience feelings of anxiety and meaninglessness, not a sense of social solidarity. This point of view, as we shall see in Chapter 18, is especially relevant to contemporary job dissatisfaction.

## Culture and Civilization (Spengler)

Oswald Spengler (1880–1936) was so unlike his predecessors in the typological tradition that the differences deserve comment. Spengler was an obscure high-school teacher, not a respected scholar. But the book he wrote—translated as *The Decline of the West* ([1918] 1962)—had much more popular impact than the writings of Tönnies and Durkheim combined.

Spengler was not a social scientist. The label *agrarian mystic* comes closest to describing him. In *The Decline of the West*, Spengler celebrates the triumph of the will and intuition over reason and intellect, glorifying the notion of destiny and denigrating social science. This brand of mystic romanticism is echoed in Hitler's propaganda of the 1930s, particularly the Nazi film *The Triumph of the Will* (1936), which stresses the superiority of so-called Aryan community over heterogeneous society.

Spengler draws a fundamental contrast between country and city. Clearly, in his eyes, the country is the home of all things bright and beautiful. He refers to rural, preindustrial life as the home of a living, organic entity (culture). In contrast, the city is a dead, mechanical shell, the home of civilization.

To express his evolutionary view of the shift from country to city, Spengler uses the metaphor of the seasons. In the spring of history, there are rural communities typified by intuition and unity. Then comes summer, the time of early urban stirrings. Religion becomes impoverished, mathematical and scientific thought expands, and rationality starts to replace mystical views of the universe. The autumn of a culture's history soon follows. Here is the "intelligence of the city," the height of intellectual creativity. And a cult of science, utility, and prosperity is not far behind; it follows in the winter season, that time of megalopolitan civilization and irreligious cosmopolitanism. It is in winter that civilization finally withers and dies.

Birth, growth, death, and rebirth. That, in Spengler's cyclical view of history, is the evolutionary sequence from culture to civilization and back again to culture.

The central focus of Spengler's analysis is social psychological: the urban and rural personalities. In the preindustrial-rural community, Spengler writes, people interact on the basis of feelings. But in urban-industrial life, money becomes paramount; intellect takes over from intuition; and human interaction becomes shallow.

## Urban Personality (Wirth)

Louis Wirth (1897–1952), a member of the Chicago school of sociology, was not at all attracted by Spengler's antiscientific mysticism. But he was vitally concerned with the social psychology of modern city dwellers. He asked, and answered, the question: Is there an urban personality?

In his still influential essay "Urbanism as a Way of Life" (1938), Wirth argues that **urbanism**—patterns of social interaction and culture that result from the concentration of large numbers of people in small areas—affects the human personality. In his essay, Wirth implies a polar contrast between urban and rural personalities, and he theorizes that the way urbanites think and act is linked to the characteristics of modern cities (Box 5.1).

More specifically, Wirth says that cities are large, dense settlements with heterogeneous populations. These three variables—*large size, high density,* and *heterogeneity*—promote a certain kind of emotional and mental response. Urbanites typically react by becoming sophisticated, rational, and relativistic. They become indifferent and seemingly uncaring toward one another because that is the only way they can protect themselves against "the personal claims and expectations of others." Human interaction becomes "impersonal, superficial, transitory, and segmental" (Figure 5.2).

The lone individual counts for little in the modern city. Thus to accomplish their goals, individuals with similar interests join together to form organizations. Unlike rural folk, city dwellers do not owe their total allegiance to any one group or community. A woman might simultaneously be a member of Save the Whales, a political party, a cousins' club, a baseball team, a church-sponsored social group, and a labor union. Each group represents merely one part of the woman's total interests; none commands her undivided loyalty. Similarly, urbanites relate to one another on the basis of segmented roles—as teachers and students in a classroom, for example, rather than as total human beings who know one another's families, interests, concerns, and so forth.

Like Tönnies, Spengler, and Marx, Wirth insists on the importance of the money economy as a determinant of the urban personality. According to Wirth, the "pecuniary nexus" replaces personal relations as the basis for association in the city. Utility and efficiency replace emotion and intimacy. The result is depersonalization.

For Wirth, then, urbanism leads *inevitably* to specific forms of social action and personal behavior. For example, urbanites come into contact with too many people to interact in any but a superficial way. Wirth implies that the large, dense, heterogeneous city is such a powerful force in people's lives that they react to this entity in similar ways. That is, urbanites—regardless of race, color, creed, or social rank—react to their physical and social surroundings in a typically urban fashion.

## Preindustrial and Industrial Cities (Sjoberg)

American sociologist Gideon Sjoberg ([1960] 1965) is not, strictly speaking, in the rural–urban tradition. His typology (detailed in Chapter 4) contrasts two city types: preindustrial and industrial. But Sjoberg's categories essentially deal with two types of societies, not cities: those his predecessors call rural and urban, mechanically solid and organically solid.

In Sjoberg's view, technology dictates social, political, and ecological organization. Taking energy sources (animate, such as people or animals, versus inanimate, such as steam or electricity) as his key variable, Sjoberg argues that extensive industrialization requires particular economic, social, and political institutions. An industrial

Box 5.1

## SIZE, DENSITY, AND HETEROGENEITY

### "Urbanism as a Way of Life"

#### A Sociological Definition of the City

For sociological purposes a city may be defined as a relatively large, dense, and permanent settlement of socially heterogeneous individuals.

#### Size of the Population Aggregate

Ever since Aristotle's *Politics*, it has been recognized that increasing the number of inhabitants in a settlement beyond a certain limit will affect the relationships between them and the character of the city. Large numbers involve . . . a greater range of individual variation. Furthermore, the greater the number of individuals participating in a process of interaction, the greater is the *potential* differentiation between them. The personal traits, the occupations, the cultural life, and the ideas of the members of an urban community may, therefore, be expected to range between more widely separated poles than those of rural inhabitants.

That such variations should give rise to the spatial segregation of individuals according to color, ethnic heritage, economic and social status, tastes and preferences may readily be inferred. The bonds of kinship, of neighborliness, and the sentiments arising out of living together for generations under a common folk tradition are likely to be absent or, at best, relatively weak in an aggregate the members of which have such diverse origins and backgrounds. Under such circumstances competition and formal control mechanisms furnish the substitutes for the bonds of solidarity that are relied upon to hold a folk society together.

Increase in the number of inhabitants of a community beyond a few hundred is bound to limit the possibility of each member of the community knowing all the others personally. . . . The increase in numbers . . . involves a changed character of the social relationship. . . .

Characteristically, urbanites meet one another in highly segmental roles. They are, to be sure, dependent upon more people for the satisfactions of their life-needs than are rural people and thus are associated with a great number of organized groups, but they are less dependent upon particular persons, and their dependence upon others is confined to a highly fractionalized aspect of the other's round of activity. This is essentially what is meant by saying that the city is characterized by secondary rather than primary contacts. The contacts of the city may indeed be face to face, but they are nevertheless impersonal, superficial, transitory, and segmental. The reserve, the indifference, and the blasé outlook which urbanites manifest in their relationships may thus be regarded as devices for immunizing themselves against the personal claims and expectations of others.

The superficiality, the anonymity, and the transitory character of urban social relations make intelligible, also, the sophistication and the rationality generally ascribed to city-dwellers. Our acquaintances tend to stand in a relationship of utility to us in the sense that the role which each one plays in our life is overwhelmingly regarded as a means for the achievement of our own ends. Whereas the individual gains, on the one hand, a certain degree of emancipation or freedom from the personal and emotional controls of intimate groups, he loses, on the other hand, the spontaneous self-expression, the morale, and the sense of participation that comes with living in an integrated society. This constitutes essentially the state of *anomie*, or the social void. . . .

The segmental character and utilitarian accent of interpersonal relations in the city find their institutional expression in the proliferation of specialized tasks which we see in their most developed form in the professions. The operations of the pecuniary nexus lead to predatory relationships which tend to obstruct the efficient functioning of the social order unless checked by professional codes and occupational etiquette. The premium put upon utility and efficiency suggests the adaptability of the corporate device for the organization of enterprises in which individuals can engage only in groups. The advantage that the corporation has over the individual entrepreneur and the partnership in the urban-industrial world derives not only from the possibility it affords of centralizing the resources of thousands of individuals or from the legal privilege of limited liability and perpetual succession, but from the fact that the corporation has no soul. . . .

The dominance of the city over the surrounding hinterland becomes explicable in terms of the division of labor which urban life occasions and promotes. The extreme degree of interdependence and the unstable equilibrium of urban life are closely associated with the division of labor and the specialization of occupations. . . .

. . . Typically in the city, interests are made effective through representation. The individual counts for little, but the voice of the representative is heard with a deference roughly proportional to the numbers for whom he speaks. . . .

## Density

An increase in numbers when area is held constant (i.e., an increase in density) tends to produce differentiation and specialization, since only in this way can the area support increased numbers. Density thus reinforced the effect of numbers in diversifying men and their activities and in increasing the complexity of the social structure. . . .

The different parts of the city acquire specialized functions, and the city consequently comes to resemble a mosaic of social worlds in which the transition from one to the other is abrupt. The juxtaposition of divergent personalities and modes of life tends to produce a relativistic perspective and a sense of toleration of differences which may be regarded as prerequisites for rationality and which lead toward the secularization of life.

The close living together and working together of individuals who have no sentimental and emotional ties foster a spirit of competition, aggrandizement, and mutual exploitation. Formal controls are instituted to counteract irresponsibility and potential disorder. . . . The clock and the traffic signal are symbolic of the basis of our social order in the urban world. Frequent close physical contact, coupled with great social distance, accentuates the reserve of unattached individuals toward one another and, unless compensated by other opportunities for response, gives rise to loneliness. The necessary frequent movement of great numbers of individuals in a congested habitat causes friction and irritation. Nervous tensions which derive from such personal frustrations are increased by the rapid tempo and the complicated technology under which life in dense areas must be lived.

## Heterogeneity

The social interaction among such a variety of personality types in the urban milieu tends to break down the rigidity of caste lines and to complicate the class structure. . . . The heightened mobility of the individual . . . brings him toward the acceptance of instability and insecurity in the world at large as a norm. This fact helps to account, too, for the sophistication and cosmopolitanism of the urbanite. No single group has the undivided allegiance of the individual. . . . The individual acquires membership in widely divergent groups, each of which functions only with reference to a certain segment of his personality. . . .

There is little opportunity for the individual to obtain a conception of the city as a whole or to survey his place in the total scheme. Consequently he finds it difficult to determine what is in his own "best interests" and to decide between the issues and leaders presented to him by the agencies of mass suggestion. Individuals who are thus detached from the organized bodies which integrate society comprise the fluid masses that make collective behavior in the urban community so unpredictable and hence so problematical.

Although the city . . . produces a highly differentiated population, it also exercises a leveling influence. . . . This leveling tendency inheres in part in the economic basis of the city. . . . Progressively as cities have developed upon a background of [mass production of standardized products for an impersonal market], the pecuniary nexus which implies the purchasability of services and things has displaced personal relations as the basis of association. Individuality under these circumstances must be replaced by categories. When large numbers have to make common use of facilities and institutions, those facilities and institutions must serve the needs of the average person rather than those of particular individuals . . . the cultural institutions, such as the schools, the movies, the radio, and the newspapers, by virtue of their mass clientele, must necessarily operate as leveling influences. The political process as it appears in urban life could not be understood unless one examined the mass appeals made through modern propaganda techniques. If the individual would participate at all in the social, political, and economic life of the city, he must subordinate some of his individuality to the demands of the larger community and in that measure immerse himself in mass movements.

SOURCE: Louis Wirth, "Urbanism as a Way of Life," *American Journal of Sociology* 44 (1938): 1–24. Copyright 1938 by the University of Chicago Press. Reprinted by permission.

**Fig. 5.2** URBANISM AS A WAY OF LIFE. Wirth says that a modern urbanite does not owe allegiance to a single group but instead "acquires membership in widely divergent groups, each of which functions only with reference to a certain segment of his [or her] personality." One such group is the Military Order of the Louse, a veterans group, "so-named because many servicemen got lice while riding in boxcars during World War I. The women's auxiliary, the Cootiettes, started in 1930. Our main activities are assisting veterans and keeping alive the spirit of fellowship; our allegiance is to the government of the United States of America" (in Owens, 1975: n.p.).

city (dependent on inanimate energy sources) requires a centralized economic organization, a flexible kinship system, mass education, mass communication, and an achievement-oriented social-class system. By contrast, he says, a pre-industrial city (dependent on animate energy sources) requires face-to-face communication, rigid social differentiation by age and gender, and informal social controls based on kinship, religion, and social rank.

## Adding a Third Type: *Techno$chaft*

Call it postindustrial, postsuburban, or post-modern society. Or name it the World Informa-

tion Economy, the Global Village, the Third Wave, or *Techno$chaft* (so named by my San Francisco State students in "Mass Media and Society," Spring 1991). Whatever it's called, many theorists think it is a new form of social, spatial, and economic organization.

In general terms, *Techno$chaft* (or postindustrial society) is viewed as a type of society where wealth is based on the capacity to get, understand, and use information. One key difference between urban-industrial and postindustrial society is this: In *Gesellschaft*, manufacturing (particularly textiles, steel, and cars) dominates the economy; in *Techno$chaft*, global finance and electronic entertainment dominate the economy.

This shift from *Gesellschaft* to *Techno$chaft* is fa-

gemeinschaft    gesellschaft    techno$chaft

Fig. 5.3    *GEMEINSCHAFT, GESELLSCHAFT, TECHNO$CHAFT.* (Lisa Siegel Sullivan)

cilitated by information technologies. One result is that neither the shape of cities nor the range of a firm's business is inextricably tied to the physical location of factories, finance centers, and so on. Instead, there is a global urban system run, to a great extent, on information.

The case of the Italian clothing chain Benneton is instructive. It suggests that the global fashion business resembles electronic entertainment more than *Gesellschaft* manufacturing. Benetton was staggeringly successful in the mid-1980s because it operated thousands of shops as if

there's a kind of world uniform. There's a sort of "color of the week," and because of the media, that color sweeps the world very quickly. . . . Benetton's computer analysis shows what is selling in terms of type, price, and color of every Benetton item all over the world, every day. They dye 15 percent of their colors every day on the basis of the information they get that day. (Schwartz in Brand, 1987:240)

The Benetton world depends on borderless communication in a world of fading nations. Anthony Smith suggests why nations fade in *Techno$chaft:*

The whole history of the nation as a political unit of [hu]mankind has been predicated upon territoriality; the technology of printing came into being in the same era as the nation-state and both seem to be reaching the end of their usefulness in the era of the computer;

it is physically impossible to impose upon data the same kinds of controls that are imposed upon goods and paper-borne information. . . . (in Brand, 1987:239)

In this tantalizing (and disguised) hypothesis, Smith posits that technology is a key influence on political change: The rise of the nation-state and the rise of print occur at the same time, as do the fall of the nation-state and the rise of the computer, because computer data, unlike printed books, are essentially borderless and thus uncontrollable by sovereign states.

## HOW USEFUL ARE THE RURAL–URBAN TYPOLOGIES?

The anthropologist Margaret Mead, noted for her outspoken wit as well as her scholarship, once gave this explanation for migration from the countryside to cities: "At least 50 percent of the human race doesn't want their mother-in-law within walking distance." Mead's remark may tell us as much about rural-preindustrial life as the typologies do.

The typologies were constructed as tools for understanding the changes from rural-preindustrial to urban-industrial life in western Europe. But they remain very limited tools. Essentially, four kinds of criticism can be leveled at the typo-

**Table 5.2** Typologies of the Rural–Urban–Global Shift in Western Europe and North America

| Characteristics | Rural-Preindustrial Community (Gemeinschaft) | Urban-Industrial Society (Gesellschaft) | Global-Postindustrial Association (Technoschaft) |
|---|---|---|---|
| SPATIAL-GEOGRAPHIC | Cities organized around religious/public buildings, market centers. Symbols: church spires, forts, palaces. Urban places but no urban society. Close links to surrounding, immediate environment. Well-defined neighborhoods by ethnic/tribal group. | Cities organized around economic institutions, business/industry. Symbol: factory smokestacks. Urban society, dense settlements. Urban sprawl. Links to faraway places via communications and transport technology. | Cities organized around electronic communication. Symbol: skyscraper, temple of corporate finance and communications. Fragmented, collage cities. Continuous spatial restructuring. Shape of cities results from interplay of market forces, government policies, and community resistance. No single spatial pattern. Global urban system. "World cities" (e.g., Tokyo, New York City) play key roles. Sense of place fades. Time–space compression due to advanced information technology and firms' ability to use various spaces for various purposes. |
| ECONOMIC | Nonmarket economy: barter, exchange, or money exchange at a simple level. Wealth measured in land (or cattle, etc.), not money. Agricultural base. Relatively self-sufficient communities. Cottage, handicraft industries. Simple division of labor. Relative self-sufficiency. | Market economy. Cash nexus. Wealth measured in money, capital. Heavy manufacturing base. Interdependence at regional, national, international levels. Complex division of labor. Functional interdependence. | Late capitalism. Global interdependence. Agribusiness, transnationals, trading networks. "Compunications." Wealth based on ability to get and use information. Decentralization of production, centralization of control. Demassified, customized products. Flexible work practices. Heightened intercity competition for development. Information, communications, and service base. Power of market over cultural production. Growing gap between rich and poor. |

| Characteristics | Rural-Preindustrial Community (Gemeinschaft) | Urban-Industrial Society (Gesellschaft) | Global-Postindustrial Association (Techno$chaft) |
|---|---|---|---|
| SOCIOCULTURAL | Blood ties, extended family and kinship networks, neighborhood, friendship. Sense of community, belongingness. Face-to-face communication. Primary groups important. Tribal or ethnic cohesion. Homogeneity of culture, beliefs within tribal/ethnic group. Ascribed status. Religions, sacred explanations. | Blood ties relatively unimportant, individual as primary unit. Segmented roles. Social mobility. Heterogeneity. Urban, urbane culture. Mass communication. Secondary groups important. Alienation, anomie. Achieved status. Scientific, secular explanations. | Extended social networks. City as giant electronic screen or collage. Denationalized, world entertainment culture. Distinctions based on social status and taste all-important. Multiple viewpoints. "Reality" negotiated between social groups. Fragmentation and eclecticism. Acceptance of deep chaos in urban process. Gemeinschaft-like groups remain. Plural systems of knowledge. An aesthetic that celebrates cultural differences and quick changes. |
| POLITICAL | Traditional authority. Sacred traditions. Some experts (e.g., priests) with monopoly over knowledge, but generally widely shared knowledge base. Informal sanctions. Repressive law. Lack of contracts. Dominance by traditional religious/political elites. Family background, connections important. | Legal/rational authority. Secular traditions. Knowledge gap between experts and laypersons. Dominance by merchants, capitalists. Power elites. Occupations and professions among important interest groups. Bureaucracy. Restitutive law, contracts. Merit as principle of advancement rather than family background. | Corporate power dominates. Nation-state fades. Preeminence of professional-scientific-technical personnel. Meritocracy. Bureaucratic state. Democracy of consumers rather than citizens. Possibilities for both centralization and decentralization of political knowledge. |

logies. These deal with their major hypotheses, empirical evidence, analytical rigor, and contemporary relevance.

The rural–urban typologies have unique aspects, but they share a basic assumption: that people think, feel, behave, and organize their activities differently in rural and urban cultures. (These differences, in general terms, are outlined in Table 5.2, with one addition: alleged differences in Techno$chaft.) Further, the theoretical constructs assume that modern urban-industrial life requires or inevitably leads to particular forms of urban personality structure, social organization, and economic-political institutions.

## Untested Hypotheses

In 1951, Louis Wirth said that the hypotheses embedded in the typologies had not been tested in the light of empirical evidence (in Hauser, 19657:506–507). Unfortunately, Wirth's criticism stands to the present day.

## Contrary Evidence

Existing empirical evidence, however, does call into question the major hypotheses. Wirth himself drew attention to the U.S. city as a mosaic of local cultures, maintained by social isolation. In his study of Chicago's Jewish ghetto (1928:284–287), he noted that many *Gemeinschaft*-like groups (e.g., French Canadians, artistic rebels, hobos) had their own distinct type of dominant personality and moral code.

The work of George M. Foster goes to the heart of the matter, questioning the assumption that urban and rural modes of life are fundamentally different. Anthropologist Foster (1965) finds many so-called urban personality traits in rural society. According to Foster, peasant societies have an "image of limited good." That is, the good life is seen as finite and nonexpandable, and an individual can progress only at the expense of others. Cooperative behavior among peasants is perceived as dysfunctional to community stability. The result is that "extreme individualism is chosen over cooperation in preserving peasants' security," discouraging any changes in the status quo (Foster, 1965:310). Indeed, Foster finds that peasants typically express distrust of others, friendlessness, and suspicion of people outside the family. Such an orientation does not lead to the mechanical solidarity or the caring-sharing community that Durkheim and Tönnies envisioned. Rather, it leads to structural and psychological atomism.

Other writers (e.g., Banfield and Banfield, 1958; Talese, 1992) support Foster's vision of preindustrial communities as fiercely competitive, uncooperative, and contentious. In addition, some scholars (e.g., Springborg, 1986) claim that relationships in many ancient societies were contractual, not based on love or kinship. In light of such evidence, Tönnies's conception of *Gemeinschaft* seems a rather romantic vision of a past that never was.

If Foster and others find indifference and friendlessness in the rural countryside, other researchers find so-called rural personality traits in the city. The fieldwork of Oscar Lewis is illustrative. Anthropologist Lewis studied the "citification" of peasants in Mexico over a number of years. One such rural emigrant, Jesús Sanchez, had lived for over twenty years in a Mexico City slum tenement when Lewis interviewed him again, along with his four children. Their autobiographical statements, recorded by Lewis in *The Children of Sanchez* (1961), show them to be living refutations of Wirth's urban personality type; they are not uncaring, utilitarian, or blasé.

The thrust of Lewis's research is that there is no such thing as a typically urban personality. He shows that city dwellers have different responses to city life. Lewis (1967) argues that Wirth's key variables (large size, high density, and heterogeneity) are *not* the crucial determinants of urban personality or urban social life. Lewis advocates studying the varied social areas or neighborhoods in a city, not the city as a whole, in order to understand the various urban personali*ties*.

Sociologist-planner Herbert Gans ([1962] 1982) did study one neighborhood: an Italian-American working-class community in Boston. There he found an "urban village" based on social intimacy, not alienation and loneliness.

## Deterministic Assumptions

This brings up a related criticism of the typological tradition: its determinism. The typologies leave no room for varied cultural adaptations to urban-industrial life. Instead, they assume that urbanization and industrialization are such powerful processes that they stamp out cultural and ideological differences.

Yet many examples show that differing cultural traditions do count heavily in people's adaptations to urban life. In addition to Oscar Lewis's research in Mexico, there are other examples of differential responses to urban life from other continents. In Uganda, for instance, middle-class Ganda tribespeople work in the capital city of

## Front-page News from *The Budget*

**SEYMOUR, MISSOURI**

Ozark Menn. Church

June 2—Visitors Sun. were Arvan Weaver's niece and family, Warren and Judy Kurtz from Pine Grove, Pa. Four college students who had seen the Delbert Ramers at a McDonald's in Springfield decided to accept the invitation to come to church. They had dinner at Delbert's in the afternoon.

Putting another coat of sealer on the gym floor were Emery and Lavern Ropp, Mylon Overholt, Harley Miller, and Andy Miller. This was the second coat.

Our weather has been very changeable. One morn. it was 35 degrees but warmed up nicely and a lot of hay was made. Gardens are finally beginning to grow after the rains.

We had a church cleaning and a work day at the gym, getting ready for a wedding soon, of Loyal and Melrose.

Pre. David Miller went in to Byler Buildings after hours. While he was working the code to get in, he missed the last number of the burglar alarm, therefore, the alarm went off, not only at Byler Buildings, but also at the police station. He tried calling someone at Jamco Builders, but the answering service went on, with Murray Schrock trying to talk over it. Not being able to understand Murray, David ran back to Jamco, all the while trying to remember how to turn of the burglar alarm. In the meantime, owner Steve Burk called the police station, telling them no one needed to come out. The police, not recognizing Steve's voice, said they were coming anyhow, as it could have been a burglar calling them. Murray said if the police come, he is leaving. David teasingly told him if he left he would tell the police, "There goes the burglar!" Things soon calmed down and they all had a good laugh over it.

Many are preparing to leave for the ministers' meeting in Michigan.

—Mrs. Will Overholt

**HONEY BROOK, PA.** June 2nd 3 van loads of the Esh descendants went out to Buffalo Valley to mow to trim the Esh graveyard where my great-great-grandfather Shem Esh is buried. He died on May 7, 1839. As long as I can remember my parents, uncles and aunts and some of the cousins went out once a year to mow that graveyard. . . .

May 31st Paul James, son of Paul and Naomi Zook of Gap, had a bike accident down at Faith Mission Home, Va. He lost control going down over a hill. His neck and 6 vertebra are broke. Pauls went down on Monday.

. . . May 23rd Fannie, 99-yr-old widow of the late Daniel B. Stoltzfus (Bom), died at the Fairmount Home. The children were taking turns caring for her until it was almost too much for them. She was only at the home 2 or 3 weeks. She had a lot of descendants. It was a large funeral.

—Mrs. Benvel J. Stoltzfus

**Fig. 5.4** NEWS OF ONE *GEMEINSCHAFT*-LIKE GROUP. *The Budget*, published weekly since 1888, serves Amish-Mennonite communities throughout the Americas. Its June 9, 1993, edition, published in Sugarcreek, Ohio, consists of twenty-four pages. Here is a sample, taken from the twenty news reports (and three death notices) that comprise the front page.

Kampala, but they try to live in surrounding rural areas so that they can raise their own subsistence crops. This arrangement permits strong continuity between rural and urban environments (Southall and Gutkind, 1957). In Timbuktu, Mali (Miner, 1953), and Cairo, Egypt (Abu-Lughod, 1961), researchers found strong kinship relationships, not anonymity, superficiality, and transitory social associations, as Wirth predicted. In the sprawling city of Bangkok, Thailand, to cite another example, traffic seems death-defying to foreigners. Since 1945, Bangkok's population has mushroomed (and the UN estimates that it will reach over 10 million by the year 2000). The streets are packed with people and noisy vehicles. Despite this apparent chaos, Bangkok works rather harmoniously. A Thai architect–city planner thinks he knows why: Bangkokites were once water people. For centuries they lived on canals, now filled in. But the people still live like water people. They drive their cars and trucks as they used to drive river boats, accommodating to drivers and pedestrians as they once did on the canals. According to Mr. Jumsai, "Water people adapt to the flow of the current. They go with the forces of nature, not against." This sense of accommodation—literally and figuratively going with the flow—pervades the social fabric of

Bangkok, where overseas Chinese and other ethnic minorities live without apparent friction, unlike the inhabitants of so many cities in South Asia.

Lastly, there is the example of the Japanese-run factory. The factory has come to symbolize urban-industrial-capitalist life. In Western literature and social science, it has long stood for worker alienation and the loss of human feeling between employers and employees. But some Japanese factories (including some Japanese-run factories in the United States) do not fit this image; instead, they are familylike. According to some analysts, Japanese familylike factory relations reflect Japan's feudal past when landlords felt paternalistically responsible for their peasants. Others say that the concept of loyalty (to the family, the employer, etc.) pervades Japanese culture, including industrial relations.

These examples—Japanese familylike factories, Thai traffic patterns, and Ugandan residential patterns—suggest that we cannot make gross generalizations about *the* nature of city life or *the* personality of urbanites. In short, running a factory, beating the traffic, and living in crowded spaces are common features of urban-industrial life. But the responses to these constants may be different.

Of course, we should not forget the eastern European proverb: "'For example' is no proof." That is, for every example of how culture mediates a group's adaptation to urban-industrial life, a determinist could respond, "Hey, just wait. It's only a matter of time. Eventually, societies with similar economic systems will resemble each other (converge) in their basic institutional structures and world views." This is the core of **convergence theory.**

To be evenhanded, there is a great deal of evidence pointing to convergence. Here are a few examples:

1. A Spanish sociologist laments that young urbanites in Spain are catching up with other Western Europeans, becoming "a nation of narcissists, concerned mainly with the cult to the body, to comfort, to consumption, to money" (de Miguel in Riding, 1991:4).
2. Industrial cities as different as Detroit, Brussels, and Kiev face "the same economic forces throughout the world, with much the same results," according to the director of Johns Hopkins University's Institute for Policy Studies (in Raymond, 1990:A4). Increasing global economic interdependence, decreasing importance of national borders, and widespread use of communications technologies are leading to similar urban challenges, including unemployment, residential segregation by social class, and decaying housing.
3. Cross-cultural data show that the same occupations rank high or low in social esteem in all urban-industrialized societies. (Chapter 10 details this point.)
4. Cross-cultural data also suggest that the definition and expectations of the family are changing throughout the urban-industrial and postindustrial worlds. For one thing, government, professional experts, and business are taking over traditional family functions, including financial support and emotional warmth. Here is a stark case from Japan, a society once known for its extended family ties: A Tokyo company, Japan Efficiency Corporation, is in the rent-a-family business. Mainly older couples pay (typically more than $1,200 for a three-hour "family visit") for professional stand-ins to play the roles of children and grandchildren.

Such examples lead followers of Durkheim to reaffirm his sense of evolutionary development. In Durkheim's view, increases in the specialization of function *inevitably* lead to particular forms of social solidarity.

No matter which side of the convergence–cultural adaptation debate one finds more convincing at the present time, there are other serious criticisms of the typologies. These concern their contemporary relevance and their analytical rigor.

## Contemporary Irrelevance

First, let's consider their relevance in the contemporary world. A rural speck today—whether in Nepal or Mexico—is hardly a self-sufficient island. Satellites, transistor radios, and international trade agreements provide direct links between countryside and city. Even remote villages exist within a global political economy.

So, if rural communities are tied to far-flung nations as well as to nearby cities, what rural–urban contrasts make sense today? Should we expect to find meaningful differences in people's attitudes and behavior, depending on their rural or urban residence? Scholars disagree here too. One view, called the *massification thesis,* holds that rural people in advanced industrial societies become indistinguishable from their city cousins because of mass media, mass education, and other influences that break down rural isolation and diffuse urban culture into the countryside. Another view is that appreciable rural–urban differences persist even in advanced industrial societies (Glenn and Hill, 1978). However, as the new information superhighway replaces many Route 66s, my hunch is that more romantics than social scientists will find apprecible urban–rural differences.

The contemporary relevance of the typologies can be questioned on still other grounds. The nineteenth-century typology builders assumed that European patterns of change would be universal. But this pattern—the nearly simultaneous rise of big cities, industrialism, and capitalism—is not being repeated in many poor countries. Hence attitudes and behavior assumed to be associated with urbanization in Western Europe (and North America) may not characterize poor societies now undergoing urbanization.

## Jumbled Variables

This brings us to the problem of analytical rigor. The typologists did not separate the key variables in their hypotheses on urbanization and social change. Which variable—urbanization, industrialization, or capitalism—supposedly leads inevitably, invariably, and necessarily to urbanism as a way of life? The typologies do not specifiy. Rather, they assume that these three processes go hand in hand. But individualism, to take just one supposed trait of the urban person-

ality, may not be a necessary ingredient of urbanization per se. For example, in Japan, a post-industrial society, group loyalty and collective responsibility, not individualism, are highly valued.

This is a serious criticism of the typologies: They make too much of the supposedly fundamental differences between rural and urban traits. The assumption that modern urbanites have greater faith in science than in religion for controlling events merits special attention in this regard. If that assumption is correct, how can we explain the mass suicide and murder of over 900 Americans who followed the command of their spiritual leader, Jim Jones, to die in Guyana? One explanation was offered by evangelist Billy Graham: "It was the work of Satan." This explanation and the events at the People's Temple in Jonestown occurred in 1978, not in 1378. Thus the differences between so-called urban (industrial) and rural (preindustrial) personalities do not seem all that clear.

*To conclude:* The rural–urban typologies are limited tools for understanding the shift from rural-preindustrial to urban-industrial life. First, they have never been systematically tested. They remain *articles of faith* based more on historical imagination than on scientific research. Second, they are *deterministic.* The typological tradition comes out of a nineteenth-century Darwinian worldview of unilinear, one-way evolution. It cannot account for significant differences within preindustrial communities or industrial societies. Third, the typologies are *ethnocentric.* They assume that what happened in western Europe—particularly the hand-in-hand development of urbanization, industrialization, and capitalism—will happen universally. This has not been the case in much of the world. China, for instance, is industrializing more rapidly than it is becoming urbanized: 46.5 percent of China's national income in 1990 was produced by industry, but the majority of China's labor force (60 percent) work in agriculture ("China's divided economy" 1991:A6) Fourth, they rest on a dubious assumption: that the transformation from agricultural to industrial life requires, or inevitably leads to, a radical change in the nature of human personality. To begin with, they make too much of the differences between city and country, between traditional community and modern society. The distinguished anthropologist Clifford Geertz put it this way: "Stark 'great divide' contrasts between 'modern' and 'premodern' societies, the one individualistic, rational, and free of tradition, the other collectivistic, intuitive, and mired in it, look increasingly mythical, summary, and simple-minded" (1994:3).

Instinctively, we may feel that the sense of community is not the same in the Athenian polis and the American metropolis. We sense that life in a tribal village and medieval London are somehow different. Of course, there *are* differences between everyday life in a polis and a metropolis. But it is dangerous to attribute the differences to urbanization alone. The effects of industrialization, cultural values, and other variables have to be carefully unscrambled when assessing the ruran–urban shift in various societies. So far, this has not been done. Instead, theorists have accomplished only what poet William Carlos Williams advised against:

> to make a start
> out of particulars
> and make them general, rolling
> up to the sum, by defective means.
>
> (1953:11)

## ANOTHER LOOK

Looking back on the ties that bind, one basic theme emerges: Theorists fundamentally disagree on the nature of urbanization and urbanism. Their disagreements are not rooted in either their disciplinary backgrounds or their research methods. For example, two anthropologists (Robert Redfield and Oscar Lewis) studied the same Mexican village using the same method (fieldwork) but came to different conclusions about the nature of rural life. Similarly, theorists do not agree on the nature of urban life. All of these disagreements do stem from differences in (1) *levels of analysis,* (2) *theoretical orientations,* or (3) *attitudes toward "progress."*

1. *Levels of analysis.* Tönnies, Durkheim, and Spengler are macro-level theorists interested in the broad sweep of change from rural to urban society. Hence they focus on entire social systems in their analysis of urbanization and urbanism. Louis Wirth, investigating the urban personality, uses the entire city as his unit of analysis. Other theorists, notably Lewis, argue that neither entire social systems nor the city as a whole are proper units for studying social life or human personality. Lewis claims that large numbers, high density, and heterogeneity are not crucial determinants of either urban social life or the urban personality because both occur in smaller universes—families, neighborhoods, and so on. Thus, Lewis advises using smaller units of analysis to study the urbanization process and urbanism. Using micro-level analysis, as Lewis proposes (and Herbert Gans carried out in Boston), theorists often find many ways of life coexisting within the same city, not a single urban way of life.

2. *Theoretical orientations.* Structural-functionalists and many (but not all) Marxist-oriented scholars pay little attention to cross-cultural differences in their analysis of modern urban life. They think that, in the long run, technological and economic imperatives will render cultural differences insignificant. This determinism is rejected by theorists who insist that values, cultural traditions, and particular historical conditions can influence social organization in important ways. Thus structural-functionalists (e.g., followers of Durkheim) and many Marxist-oriented theorists tend to view urbanization in capitalist Western Europe and North America as a single, unitary process with similar effects on human personality; others tend to stress the different forms and meanings that urbanization and urbanism have taken.

3. *Attitudes toward "progress."* Do urban-industrial society (*Gesellschaft*) and/or postindustrial society (*Technoschaft*) represent human liberation and "progress"— or human enslavement and regression? Here thinkers profoundly disagree. In one camp are thinkers and activists who agree with poet Robinson

Jeffers's rejection of "progress": "I don't think industrial civilization is worth the distortion of human nature, and the meanness and loss of contact with the earth, that it entails." Similarly, Mahatma Gandhi became convinced that people could flower only in small communities bound by ties of vision and service.

The late French theologian-historian Jacques Ellul despaired of *The Technological Society* (1965) in which life is a disconnected set of activities. Post–World War II playwrights, notably Samuel Beckett and Eugene Ionesco, seem to share this vision, portraying discombobulated wanderers staggering around on a barren stage in a senseless universe.

In a second camp are a range of thinkers who believe that the technology and modern attitudes associated with *Gesellschaft* helped to free people from the shackles of tradition, enslavement or serfdom, scarcity, superstition, and parochialism. These include Karl Marx, who disdained the "idiocy of rural life"; inventor Buckminster Fuller, who suggested that people can evolve and transform their environment by using new technologies; political scientist Barrington Moore, who wrote that technological progress brings changes in social structure that provide the "prerequisites of freedom" (in Lasch, 1991:43); and conservative sociologist Robert Nisbet, who thought that the idea of progress is the single most important idea in Western history. This view is held by most liberals who envision a world progressively redeemed by human reason from poverty and ignorance (e.g., Frankel, [1955] 1968).

But another camp, one we might call the Third Way, disagrees with both extreme pessimists and optimists. Proponents point to the failure of *Gesellschaft* science and reason to eliminate poverty or provide both individual freedom and community, but they think it is possible to build social systems that are at once high-tech, democratic, and ecologically sound. For example, Roy Morrison (1991) describes Mondragon (a network of worker-owned and -operated cooperatives in the Basque region of Spain involving more than 21,000 workers) as a communitarian alternative to the capitalist, growth-oriented model of progress. Theodore Roszak argues that "deurbanizing" the world—scaling down the size and power of cities and placing cities in a balance with rural society—will serve the needs of both *Person/Planet* (1977–1978), and Murray Bookchin (1982) looks to societies based on "ecological wholeness."

Attempting to integrate insights from these opposing camps seems like a worthy cause. On closer inspection, however, it looks more like an impossible dream. No synthesis can occur, for proponents clash on core issues such as the nature of rural life and the impacts of capitalism and urbanization.

## KEY TERMS

**Collectivity** A group with common ends, but not common kinship origins. Examples: social science professors, computer networkers, and owner-workers of cooperative business.

**Community** A concept with many meanings, often used without precise definition. It can refer to a traditional community in the sense of *Gemeinschaft;* a group that shares only a territorial area; or a group that shares values and culture without a common territory (e.g., an occupational group).

**Convergence theory** Macro-level social theory that predicts that, over time, advanced industrial societies will develop similar traits despite their cultural or ideological differences in order to fulfill similar functions.

**Cosmopolis** From the Greek, meaning "world city." A cosmopolitan person is one whose identification and involvement are with a larger social universe than the local community.

**Counterculture** A group of people whose beliefs, symbols, attitudes, and values oppose those of the dominant culture. In the United States, 1960s hippies and 1990s streetwise slum youth are considered to be countercultural groups.

**Division of labor**   Social differentiation by work specialization or occupational role.

**Gemeinschaft-like**   A quality describing some close-knit religious, occupational, ethnic, and common interest groups (e.g., the Amish; Moonies; Hasidic Jews; God's Little Acre mobile home park in Apache Junction, Arizona; many Native American tribes; San Francisco's gay and lesbian community; a Marine battalion) existing within *Gesellschaft*. Members of a *Gemeinschaft*-like group share values, meanings, and goals, and they maintain kinlike, face-to-face relationships within their groups.

**Ideal type**   A mental construct used as a heuristic device to describe, compare, and test hypotheses. An ideal type is not meant to correspond exactly to any particular case in the observable world; rather, it is designed as a tentative model. Two or more ideal types form a classification scheme or typology. Examples: *Gemeinschaft, Gesellschaft, Technoschaft*.

**Mechanical and organic solidarity**   Durkheim's contrasting types of social solidarity. Mechanically solid societies are based on similar values, traditions, kinship, and a simple division of labor; organically solid societies are based on a complex division of labor requiring cooperation among heterogeneous people. Organic solidarity is so named because, in Durkheim's view, it is similar to the human body, in which specialized organs have to function interdependently if the entire organism is to survive.

**Polis**   From the Greek, usually translated as "city-state." A self-sufficient, small-scale political unit. It was not much like a modern nation-state, and it was much more than a city.

**Social cohesion**   Integrated group behavior resulting from social bonds or social forces cementing members over time. To achieve it, group members accept the group's goals and standards of behavior.

**Subculture**   A group of people who define themselves as different from the dominant culture in terms of some standards of behavior and values but who do not constitute an entirely different culture. Occupation, ethnicity, age, sexual orientation, religion, and social background can be bases for subcultures. In the United States, the Marines, circus performers, teenagers, and Mormons are considered subcultural groups. But the Amish and Hopi are considered separate cultures, not subcultures.

**Technoschaft**   A form of social, spatial, and economic organization based on information. Synonym: *postindustrial society*. Contrasts: *Gemeinschaft, Gesellschaft*.

**Urbanism**   Presumed patterns of social interaction and culture that result from the concentration of large numbers of people in small physical areas. The concept is also used to convey the idea that in advanced industrial societies, urban values, culture, and modes of social organization have spread even to rural areas.

## PROJECTS

**1. The division of labor.** Using historical materials and current U.S. Department of Labor data, compare and contrast the range of occupations in the Athenian polis, a medieval European town, and a modern American city. Do your findings support Durkheim's dichotomy between a relatively simple division of labor in a mechanicaly solid society and a complex division of labor in an organically solid society?

**2. Urbanism as a way of life: the view from Hollywood.** Whether or not mass-media productions reflect or create social reality is much debated. Either way, we can assume that a mass medium is an important conveyor of social values and images. In terms of urban life, do commercial movies present images that reinforce or contradict Wirth's concept of urbanism as a single way of life? To investigate this question, view several films (examples: *Taxi Driver, Manhattan, Wall Street, Salaam Bombay, The Godfather, Drugstore Cowboy, Saturday Night Fever, Longtime Companion, Crimes and Misdemeanors, Blue Collar, Atlantic City, Tin Men, My Beautiful Laundrette, Dim Sum, Falling Down, Do the Right Thing, The Dollmaker, Crossing Delancey*) and analyze their content in terms of Wirth's notions of (a) the superficial, transitory character of urban social relations and (b) competition and formal control mechanisms as substitutes for bonds of kinship and common values.

## SUGGESTIONS FOR FURTHER LEARNING

Few topics in social science and the humanities have drawn more ink than the concept of community. Countless works deal with the theme. A good starting place is the discipline of sociology because the concept of community is a fundamental or "unit-idea" of sociological thought. Classic works on community include Emile Durkheim, *The Division of Labor in Society* (New York: Free Press, [1893] 1964); Karl Marx, *Das Kapital* (New York: Modern Library, [1867] 1936); Claude-Henri de Saint-Simon, *On the Reorganization of European Society* (1814); Georg Simmel, *Philosophy of Money* (London: Routledge and Kegan Paul, [1900] 1978); Ferdinand Tönnies, *Community and Society* (New York: Harper & Row, [1887] 1963); and Auguste Comte, *The Positive Polity* (New York: Burt Franklin, [1851–1854] 1966). Essays of the German school (Weber, Simmel, Spengler) and the Chicago school (Park, Wirth, Redfield) appear in Richard Sennett's reader, *Classic Essays on the Culture of Cities* (New York: Appleton-Century-Crofts, 1969). See also the chapter on community in Robert A. Nisbet, *The Sociological Tradition* (New York: Basic Books, 1966).

For a look at preindustrial U.S. cities and towns, see sections of David R. Goldfield, *Cotton Fields and Skyscrapers: Southern City and Region, 1607–1980* (Baton Rouge: Louisiana State University Press, 1982), and Eric H. Monkkonen, *America Becomes Urban: The Development of U.S. Cities and Towns, 1780–1980* (Berkeley: University of California Press, 1988).

Day-to-day life in a traditional community is perhaps best described by artists. Among the most moving accounts is Ermanno Olmi's remarkable film, *The Tree of Wooden Clogs* (1978). In telling the story of peasant life in Italy around the turn of the twentieth century, Olmi captures the ethos of *Gemeinschaft* and the ironies of its alleged social cohesion and bonds of friendship. Other excellent evocations of preindustrial rural life can be found in historian Emmanuel Le Roy Ladurie's dramatic history of a town in southern France during the Inquisition, *Montaillou* (New York: Braziller, 1978); Camara Laye's *The African Child: Memories of a West African Childhood* (London: Fontana, 1962); and Robert Flaherty's pioneering documentary film, *Nanook of the North* (1922).

Day-to-day life in a modern subculture—gay pre–World War II New York City—is chronicled by George Chauncey in *Gay New York: Gender, Urban Culture, and the Making of the Gay Male World, 1890–1940* (New York: Basic Books, 1994). Called a "pioneering work of scholarship," it shows that before World War II, New York City had a large, communal gay world.

Are there imperatives of urbanism, as Louis Wirth argued? Or are certain urban patterns connected to a particular kind of urban development—capitalist development? That is the question posed by Martin King Whyte and William L. Parish in *Urban Life in Contemporary China* (Chicago: University of Chicago Press, 1984). Their research concentrates on the decade of the Cultural Revolution (1966–1976). They note that some tendencies may be universal. For example, "even with a regime of relative income equality, the prestige hierarchy of occupations remained relatively undisturbed, and as elsewhere, that hierarchy placed mental labor on top and manual labor at the bottom" (362). Further, they argue that Chinese urbanites focused concern on their family and native place but, for many historical reasons, did not develop any sense of urban community (366).

The video *Recuerdos de mi barrio* (1993) (available in Spanish or English from The Center for Latin America, University of Wisconsin–Milwaukee) shows why rural–urban migration in Cali, Columbia, in the 1970s was significantly different from that in many other areas: City officials there recognized spontaneous settlement as the solution to housing shortages.

The shift from self-sufficient rural community to modern urban society is the theme of many artworks. A vivid account of the rural–urban shift in France is found in the novels of Honoré de Balzac, a conservative, aristocratic writer who mourned the passing of traditional community and despised bourgeois capitalism. Novelist Chinua Achebe's work, *Things Fall Apart* ([1959] 1974), offers a sensitive inside look at the rural–urban shift in Nigeria. Gaston Kaboré's ninety-four-minute, award-winning film from Burkina Fasso in West Africa, *Zan Boko* (1988), focuses on the impact of city expansion on rural communities (available in Mossi and French with English subtitles from California Newsreel, San Francisco). Orson Welles's film *The Magnificent Ambersons* (1942), based on a Booth Tarkington novel, depicts the impact of industrialization, particularly the automobile, on a small American town and the consequent changes in social structure.

In *All That Is Solid Melts into Air: The Experience of Modernity* (New York: Penguin, [1982] 1988), political scientist and urbanist Marshall Berman considers the writings of Marx, Goethe, and others who contributed to the modernist consciousness. Berman notes that one of Marx's images of modernity—"all that is solid melts into air" (from the *Communist Manifesto*)—is the inspiration for poet Yeats's famous line, "Things fall apart, the center does not hold." Note that Chinua Achebe's novel about the shift from *Gemeinschaft* to *Gesellschaft* in Nigeria is also entitled *Things Fall Apart*.

A group's struggle to retain communitylike features within modern society is portrayed in many fine documentaries. *The Amish: Not to Be Modern* (Filmmakers Library, New York, 1985) shows that this *Gemeinschaft*-like group has preserved many rural traditions, such as that of fathers and sons husking corn. How the Amish adapt technology, prosper financially, and hold firm to most religious practices is described in Donald B. Kraybill's *The Riddle of Amish Culture* (Baltimore: Johns Hopkins University Press, 1989).

How one culture in the United States tries to live in harmony with nature—instead of conquering it—is a theme of Pat Ferrero's compelling film, *Hopi: Songs of the Fourth World* (fifty-eight minutes, New Day Films). The film depicts the Hopi's *Gemeinschaft*-like existence within *Gesellschaft*. In the PBS video series *Millennium* (1992) and its accompanying book *Millennium:*

*Tribal Wisdom and the Modern World* (New York: Viking Penguin, 1992), anthropologist David Maybury-Lewis says that serious consideration of tribal ways of life can lead people in modern society to think critically about living in harmony with nature and rehumanizing current economic systems. He comments that "in traditional societies, people are valuable; in modern society, things are the valuables." In *A Weave of Time* (1987), anthropologist John Adair documents fifty years of Navajo history, including changing customs and attitudes among generations of the same family.

The late anthropologist Barbara Myerhoff's field work among urban Hasidic Jews is highlighted in Lynne Litman's film, *In Her Own Time* (1985). The film is particularly moving because it suggests Myerhoff's personal dilemmas: faith or rationality, primacy of the group or the self. During the filming, Myerhoff discovered that she was terminally ill. While drawn to the community and spirituality of the Hasidim, she was uncomfortable with their restrictions and conformity. In a related vein, Chaim Potok's novels focus on the pull between staying in a *Gemeinschaft*-like community and joining the secular world of *Gesellschaft* for self-fulfillment. In *The Chosen* (New York: Penguin, [1966] 1970), for example, a teenage boy slated to succeed his father as head of a religious community, the Hasidic Jews, wants to study psychology rather than sacred texts.

Social scientists are not alone in constructing evolutionary typologies (e.g., the rural–urban shift). Various philosophers and spiritual leaders see a shift from one societal form of organization to another. Indian religious leader Sri Aurobindo described *The Human Cycle* (Pondicherry, India: Sri Aurobindo Ashram, [1916–1918] 1949) as a transition from the Age of Individualism and Reason to the Subjective Age and later the Spiritual Age. In a similar vein, Pierre Teilhard de Chardin wrote about *The Future of Man* (New York: Harper & Row [1959] 1964), which describes five phases of development, culminating in the "noosphere," or thinking sphere, which results from social ties. In "An Evolutionary Perspective on the Environmental Crisis," *Fields Within Fields* 13 (1974):18–30, John B. Calhoun views seven revolutions in consciousness, starting with Traditional and Agricultural and moving on up to the Scientific-Exploitive stage that would evolve into a communications-electronic revolution. He predicts that by 2018 we will reach the last stage: "compassionate-systems." In *At the Edge of History: Speculations on the Transformation of Culture* (New York: Harper & Row, 1971), William Irwin Thompson postulates four phases: tribal community, agricultural society, industrial civilization, and scientific-planetary civilization. Interestingly, the last phase is much like the first phase, only on a global scale.

The third type—post-*Gesellschaft, Techno\$chaft,* postmodernism—is the subject of geographer David Harvey's wide-ranging *The Condition of Postmodernity* (Oxford: Blackwell, 1989). An important contemporary urban theorist, Harvey links what happens in cities to macropatterns of political-economic change. In particular, see Chapter 4, "Postmodernism in the City: Architecture and Urban Design," which argues that postmodernism cultivates a concept of "the urban fabric as necessarily fragmented . . . and 'a collage' of current uses. . . . [P]ostmodernists design rather than plan" (66). For a discussion of the close relationship of economics to culture in post-*Gesellschaft* society, see F. Jameson, "Postmodernism, or the Cultural Logic of Late Capitalism," *New Left Review* 146 (1984):53–92. It is also the subject of *Global Dreams: Imperial Corporations and the New World Order* (New York: Simon and Schuster, 1994) by Richard J. Barnet and John Cavanagh. This excellent study continues Barnet's long-time interest in the global reach of corporations.

Les Blank's ethnographic films (available from Flower Films, El Cerrito, Calif.) celebrate the persistence of community within society. Among the studies of *Gemeinschaft*-like groups are *Ziveli: Medicine for the Heart,* a documentary about Serbian-American communities made in association with anthropologist Andrei Simic (1987, fifty-one minutes, color) and *Spend It All,* about the bayou people in the Cajun country of southwestern Louisiana (1971, forty-one minutes), in which communal tradition is reflected in shared food and music.

Individuals lost in the modern world without community or spirituality is a common Hollywood theme. For instance, in Michael Tolkin's *The Rapture* (1991), Sharon, the telephone-operator heroine, is shown as lonely and longing for faith in a secular, scientific age. *The Serial* (1980) satirizes religious cults, communes, sex orgies, and other attempts to find community in suburban San Francisco.

Novelist Rosellen Brown says that U.S. movie audiences hunger for connectedness, "for a love beyond expediency, for a life in which an individual can still see her shadow." In her opinion, *Fried Green Tomatoes* (1992) is a movie about women who "hang together in an unspoken conspiracy of affection and concern" and serves to satisfy that hunger much more, say, than Oscar-winning *Thelma and Louise,* which focuses on "glamorous, desirable women." Jonathan Berman's 1993 movie, *Shvitz* (Yiddish for "sweat"), is a quick immersion into the lost culture and community of the male steam parlor. Before most homes had bathtubs, going to the *shvitz* was a weekly big-city ritual for male immigrant Jews. The steambaths were a democratic institution: factory pressers, doctors, lawyers, and gangsters sweated, schmoozed, and noshed together. As Gerald Nachman, the *San Francisco Chronicle*'s critic put it, the pre-Nautilus *shvitzers'* "idea of a good workout is bending over to tie their shoelaces."

Are the nations of the world becoming more alike? See Walter Gillis Peacock et al., "Divergence and Convergence in International Development: A Decomposition Analysis of Inequality in the World System," *American Sociological Review* 53 (1988):838–852.

## REFERENCES

Abu-Lughod, Janet. 1961. "Migrant adjustment to city life: The Egyptian case." *American Journal of Sociology* 67:22–32.

Achebe, Chinua. [1959] 1974. *Things Fall Apart.* Greenwich, Conn.: Fawcett.

Banfield, Edward, and L. F. Banfield. 1958. *The Moral*

*Basis of a Backward Society.* New York: Free Press.

Bookchin, Murray. 1982. *The Ecology of Freedom: The Emergence and Dissolution of Hierarchy.* Palo Alto, Calif.: Cheshire.

Brand, Stewart. 1987. *The Media Lab: Inventing the Future at MIT.* New York: Viking.

"China's divided economy." 1991. *New York Times* [national edition] (December 18):A6.

Durkheim, Emile. [1893] 1964. *The Division of Labor in Society.* New York: Free Press.

Ellul, Jacques. 1965. *The Technological Society.* New York: Knopf.

Foster, George. 1965. "Peasant society and the image of limited good." *American Anthropologist* 67:293–315.

Frankel, Charles. [1955] 1968. *The Case for Modern Man.* Boston: Beacon Press.

Gans, Herbert. [1962] 1982. *The Urban Villagers: Group and Class in the Life of Italian-Americans.* New York: Free Press.

Geertz, Clifford. 1994. "Life on the edge." *New York Review of Books* (April 7):3–4.

Gergen, Kenneth J. 1991. *The Saturated Self: Dilemmas of Identity in Contemporary Life.* New York: Basic Books.

Glenn, Norval D., and Lester Hill, Jr. 1978. "Rural–urban differences in attitude and behavior in the United States." Pp. 12–20 in Jacqueline Scherer, ed., *Annual Editions.* Guilford, Conn.: Dushkin.

Goode, William. 1957. "Community within a community: The professions." *American Sociological Review* 22:194–200.

Hauser, Philip M. 1967. "Observations on the urban–folk and urban–rural dichotomies as forms of western ethnocentrism." Pp. 503–517 in Philip M. Hauser and Leo F. Schnore, eds., *The Study of Urbanization.* New York: Wiley.

Kahler, Erich. 1957. *The Tower and the Abyss.* New York: Braziller.

Kamm, Henry. 1978. "Life in Bangkok: River tradition makes it work." *New York Times* (November 19):9.

Kitto, H. D. F. 1951. *The Greeks.* Baltimore: Penguin.

Lasch, Christopher. 1991. *The True and Only Heaven: Progress and Its Critics.* New York: Norton.

Lewis, Oscar. 1961. *The Children of Sanchez.* New York: Random House.

———. 1967. "Further observations on the folk–urban continuum and urbanization with special reference to Mexico City." Pp. 491–503 in Philip M. Hauser and Leo F. Schnore, eds., *The Study of Urbanization.* New York: Wiley.

Miner, Horace M. 1953. *The Primitive City of Timbuctoo.* Princeton, N.J.: Princeton University Press.

Morrison, Roy. 1991. *We Build the Road as We Travel.* Santa Cruz, Calif.: New Society.

Owens, Bill. 1975. *Our Kind of People: American Groups and Rituals.* San Francisco: Straight Arrow Books.

Polanyi, Karl, Harry W. Pearson, and Conrad M. Arensberg. 1957. *Trade and Market in the Early Empires: Economics in History and Theory.* Glencoe, Ill.: Free Press.

Raymond, Chris. 1990. "Social scientists examine common challenges facing industrial cities around the world." *Chronicle of Higher Education* (July 11):A4.

Riding, Alan. 1991. "Politics? the generation gap yawns." *New York Times* [international edition] (June 17):A4.

Roszak, Theodore. 1977–1978. *Person/Planet.* Garden City, N.Y.: Doubleday.

Sjoberg, Gideon. [1960] 1965. *The Pre-Industrial City.* New York: Free Press.

Southall, Aidan, and Peter C. W. Gutkind. 1957. *Townsmen in the Making: Kampala and Its Suburbs.* Kampala, Uganda: East Africa Institute of Social Research.

Spengler, Oswald. [1918] 1962. *The Decline of the West.* New York: Knopf.

Springborg, Patricia. 1986. "Politics, primordialism, and orientalism: Marx, Aristotle, and the myth of the *Gemeinschaft.*" *American Political Science Review* 80:185–211.

Stone, I. F. 1979. "I. F. Stone breaks the Socrates story." *New York Times Magazine* (April 8):22.

Talese, Gay. 1992. *Unto the Sons.* New York: Knopf.

Tönnies, Ferdinand. [1887] 1963. *Community and Society.* New York: Harper & Row.

Weber, Max. [1906] 1960. "Capitalism and rural society in Germany." Pp. 363–385 in H. H. Gerth and C. Wright Mills, trans. and eds., *From Max Weber.* New York: Oxford University Press.

Williams, William Carlos. 1953. *Paterson.* London: Peter Owen.

Wirth, Louis. [1928] 1956. *The Ghetto.* Chicago: University of Chicago Press.

———. 1938. "Urbanism as a way of life." *American Journal of Sociology* 44 (July):1–24.

CHICAGO COURT BUFFS. "They call us the buffs. We're not lawyers but we watch—very closely—federal trials every day. We debate the cases and analyze the lawyers' performances. Most of us are retired, and this gives our minds a stretch. One buff puts out a daily paper summarizing our opinions. Our 'clubroom' is the twenty-third-floor corridor at the courthouse. Every year the federal judge holds a Christmas party for us. We have a kind of bond." (Kathy Richland)

# CHAPTER 6
# Metropolitan
# Community

Back to the Land?
From Frostbelt to Sunbelt
Interpreting the Population Trends

ANOTHER LOOK

All those lonely people . . . Strangers every-where, going who knows where. Nowhere people. Lonely crowds, hearing only the sounds of silence. People who don't care about other people . . .

That is a popular image of life in the big city. As a friend from a small town in Texas asked when she moved to a major **metropolis,** "Don't people here know we're all in the same cotton field together?"

Many popular images, including this one of lonely crowds in the metropolis, have some grounding in everyday experience. Yet this view of urbanites as isolated and unfeeling needs to be qualified. City dwellers aren't as disconnected from one another as many images would lead us to believe.

Also, the image of the rural, small-town past—where like-minded people cared deeply for one another in a well-ordered, stable community—is rather idyllic, existing more in theory than in reality. Still, that cozy, imagined world is compelling, especially for those of us who have lived in lonely crowds. How humane the ideal of traditional community seems: a way of life built on close social bonds, friendship, mutual caring, and personal security. But recall, too, the other face of traditional life. How many of us today would choose to submit to authority in the form of a mother-in-law or a hereditary ruler? How many of us would want to spend our whole lives interacting mainly with blood relatives? As Margaret Mead implies, there is another and *less attractive face of community:* distrust of outsiders, lack of privacy, conformity to convention and authority, and adherence to tradition. In addition, both social and geographic mobility are very limited in traditional community. This feature seems especially unattractive for the majority of us who would have been unfortunate enough to be born

serfs, slaves, and underlings rather than land-lords, princesses, and rulers.

Many contemporary voices bemoan the loss of community and seek to reestablish it. Some advocate a rejection of Western individualism and democratic tradition, substituting a religious way of life for modernism or postmodernism. The late Iranian leader, Ayatollah Khomeini, exemplifies this approach. Others want to establish a sense of we-ness within advanced technological societies, looking to support groups, cohousing settlements, or worker cooperatives as vehicles for creating community.

Is it only in TV's make-believe town of Cicely, Alaska, that people can have both personal freedom and close social ties? Does *Northern Exposure's* Cicely reflect a new American dream—the enjoyment of a sense of community and individuality simultaneously? We will return to various types of community seekers after examining what is called, rightly or wrongly, *metropolitan community.*

## SOCIAL CEMENT IN THE METROPOLIS

V. S. Naipaul, whose novels deal with poor countries emerging from a tribal or caste tradition into an uncertain modernity, says, "I feel no nostalgia for the miserable security of the old ways." For most people in modern society, "the miserable security of the old ways" is not even an option. Urbanism may not be a single way of life, as Wirth theorized, but it certainly does entail constant change, not the continuity of traditional community. Institutions and traditions that once promoted a sense of personal security, however miserable, no longer fulfill that function for many urbanites or suburbanites.

What, then, helps to bind contemporary people in the American metropolis? Not much, warns Harvard economist and Clinton cabinet member Robert Reich (1991a, 1991b). He believes that the top fifth of U.S. income earners are disengaging from (and losing interest in) the fate of the bottom four-fifths. The elite 20 percent may be charitable, Reich says, but their generosity typically supports institutions that serve or educate people like themselves—symphonies, private hospitals, museums, elite universities, and so on—not social services for the poor. Further, the rich tend to privatize their residential space, often living in guarded or gated economic enclaves. Indeed, by 1992, as many as 300,000 Californians were "forting up"—that is, living in walled, private neighborhoods (Blakely in Schreiner, 1992:A1). The result is an "us" versus "them" mentality. Physically and psychologically separate, the top 20 percent feels little sense of community with or responsibility for "them"—the bottom 80 percent.

Successful Americans, Reich concludes, are gradually seceding from the union. He says that this secession is speeded by the federal government's shift of responsibility for many public services to state and local governments, which are already financially strapped and often unable to provide good services. Public services (e.g., public parks, playgrounds, police) deteriorate even more as the rich withdraw their funds, switching to private services such as health clubs, golf clubs, spas, and hired security guards. (According to current estimates, the number of private security guards in the United States now exceeds the number of public police officers by about 2 to 1.)

Reich says that even more than a ZIP code and private tennis clubs separate the successful elite: they "inhabit a different economy from other Americans." Typically, this elite of "symbolic analysts" (who analyze or manipulate words, numbers, or visual images in their work as ad executives, research scientists, corporate executives, lawyers, software engineers, etc.) is linked by jet, modem, and other electronic media to people in world headquarters cities and resort centers but retains few ties to the activities of the 80 percent. Following this logic, a corporate executive in New York City is more involved with and at home with the world marketplace and acquaintances in Tokyo and the European Union than with the local public school or homeless people in the next county. In other words, the notion of "hometown" is losing both its emotional and its economic clout.

*To conclude:* Reich echoes a familiar theme: the breakdown of communal feeling in cosmopoli-

tan, highly specialized society. As we saw in Chapter 4, cosmopolitanism, the privatization of formerly public services (e.g., education), and increasing specialization were associated with the fall of the Greek polis centuries ago. And, as Chapter 5 details, a host of thinkers theorize that both urbanites and suburbanites in *Gesellschaft* tend to relate to one another on the basis of the cash nexus, not community ties. Now Reich adds more factors—income level and global work role—that separate people in the contemporary metropolis, thereby short-circuiting emotional and economic interdependence locally.

So, once again, we ask: What, if anything, helps to bind contemporary urbanites together? We get few clues from popular culture. Many films set in New York City —Martin Scorsese's *Goodfellas* (1990) and *Taxi Driver* (1976), Oliver Stone's *Wall Street* (1987), and Spike Lee's *Do the Right Thing* (1989), for example—depict the nation's corporate nerve center as corrupting and alienating. Violence, dog-eat-dog exploitation, interethnic mistrust, and intraethnic betrayal are presented as normal. Even in Woody Allen's love letter to *Manhattan* (1979), the main characters seem like aliens struggling to find affection in a lonely world. These movies show few forces or institutions—family, neighbors, religious groups, friends, ethnic subcommunities, and so on—that effectively provide emotional or financial support.

What movies like *Manhattan* and *Do the Right Thing* do not—perhaps cannot—portray is an unseeable, abstract force that ties people together economically (not emotionally): functional interdependence. *How* and at *what level* this works is a matter of current debate.

## METROPOLITAN COMMUNITY: ALIVE OR EXTINCT?

### One View: Metropolitan Division of Labor

Some theorists stress the functional interdependence that stems from the complex division of labor. This perspective, rooted in Emile Durkheim's ideas about organically solid society (Chapter 5), focuses on population density, interpersonal communication, and functional differentiation as factors cementing members of a metropolitan community. Among others, Robert Park (1916) and Ernest Burgess ([1923] 1925), creator of the concentric zone model of urban growth; Roderick D. McKenzie (1933); Amos Hawley (1950); and geographer Brian Berry and sociologist John Kasarda (1977) are associated with this perspective; all are urban ecologists who, like biological ecologists, focus on a population's adaptation to its environment. (Chapter 15 contains a more detailed discussion of urban ecology.)

We who live in cities or suburbs may not realize it, but we depend on absolute strangers for a wide range of goods and services. For example, unless you grow your own food, limit travel to places where your feet can take you, entertain yourself without mass media, fix a broken toilet (without calling a plumber from the Yellow Pages), receive no government benefits, and buy nothing that must be paid for in money, you depend on countless anonymous people to sustain your daily existence. Indeed, we are so interdependent and specialized that we need one expert to find another expert! This is clear to anyone suffering from a rare illness. Finding a specialist to diagnose and treat the ailment requires the advice of other specialists. With the continuing expansion of knowledge and the "expertization" of almost everyone, we are becoming increasingly dependent on the skill and good will of strangers just to survive.

Here we should pause for a few notes on terminology. *Population core* is synonymous with **central city**. The term *central city* is not synonymous with *inner city* or *center city*. The central city is—or was, due to recent changes, as we shall soon see—seen as central because (1) all goods into and out of the region come through this city and (2) it organizes the economic activities of its surrounding hinterland. The term *suburb* is synonymous with *hinterland* and **outside central city**.

The central city and its suburbs are the two basic components of a metropolitan area or metropolitan community. At the local level, a complex network of mutually sustaining activities links (or once linked) people in the population core and its suburbs.

In the urban ecologists' view, the commuting pattern is the key indicator of metropolitan interdependence. The U.S. Census Bureau agrees; it makes the journey-to-work pattern between a city and its surrounding suburbs the primary measure of metropolitan community. Thus, from this viewpoint, a metropolitan area is essentially an *integrated labor market*, measured by the number of people who live in the suburbs and commute to the central city for work.

How, then, do urban ecologists explain the massive exodus from U.S. central cities to suburbs, starting after World War II, that has transformed many metropolitan areas? They begin by looking at the interplay of ecological factors, known by their acronym, *POET: P*opulation, social *O*rganization, *E*nvironment, and *T*echnology. Their explanation for individuals and corporations relocating to U.S. suburbs centers on changes in transportation and communication technology. In particular, they point to the mass production and affordability of the private automobile as the key factor in suburban growth (e.g., Berry and Kasarda, 1977). As we shall discuss shortly, their explanation does not go unchallenged by the new urban theorists.

*To conclude:* Following Durkheim, urban ecologists stress functional interdependence in modern society based on the the complex division of labor. They see society *naturally* tending toward equilibrium or balance. Parts of a social system, like organs of a human body, fit together and run smoothly until some external disruption occurs; then societies, like bodies, adapt to the change. In their analysis of metropolitan life, urban ecologists focus on ecological factors and ignore or underplay social psychological factors (e.g., attitudes) and political factors, including the role of the state.

## Alternative View: New International Division of Labor ("Needle")

Dissenters don't deny that functional interdependence is important, but they put it in a very different context: the *new* international division of labor (or *Needle*, an acronym coined by San Francisco State student Erica Perkins, suggesting that people are knit together by the thread of global specialization). This view is associated with the so-called new urban theorists, a group of interdisciplinary social scientists including David Harvey (1985), Manuel Castells (1983), and Joe R. Feagin (1988). New urban theorists draw insights from diverse disciplines (geography, sociology, economics, planning, political science, cultural studies) and theoretical traditions (e.g., world systems theory and neo-Marxism to postmodernism).

New urban theorists think that the global capitalist economy is the abstract glue that cements people worldwide, albeit very unequally. Indeed, they theorize that "every major dimension of city life today is related to the shifts produced by changes in investment deriving from a hegemonic, global system of capital" (Gottdiener, 1987:77). One event serves to illustrate their view of borderless interdependence: On October 19, 1987, the U.S. stock market collapsed; the two immediate causes of the market tumble were news that (1) West Germany's central bank had raised its lending rate and (2) the U.S. trade deficit had increased.

Unlike urban ecologists, new urban theorists tend to incorporate political and cultural factors into their analyses, paying special attention to the influence of political individuals and organizations—citizens' groups, multinational managers, real-estate developers, and so on—on metropolitan outcomes. In this view, the impact of the *global* capitalist economy on *local* development, federal and local government policies, and local political coalitions—not population increase, new technologies, and other ecological variables (as the urban ecologists think)—best explains spatial and social change in metropolitan areas (Gottdeiner and Feagin, 1988).

## Urban Ecologists versus New Urban Theorists: A Case Study

The case of U.S. suburbanization illustrates some major differences between urban ecologists and new urban theorists. Very briefly, urban ecologists claim that the automobile was the key factor in suburban development. New urban theorists disagree. They argue that technology played only one part, for decentralization to the hinterland started before the introduction of the automobile. Instead of technology, they focus on the *political decision-making context* that resulted in the dominance of the auto over alternative transit forms (e.g., rail mass transit), as well as the particular actors that shaped the auto-centered transport system in the United States.

Finally, urban ecologists think that the highly specialized division of labor, new technologies, and increased population density spurred suburban growth. New urban theorists point to a different set of incentives and forces, including the following: *labor force considerations* (e.g., corporate owners and managers chose to relocate in the suburbs to control labor militancy in central cities); *national and local government intervention* (e.g., post–World War II progams to build suburban freeways, provide low-interest loans to suburban home builders, and subsidize defense-related industries that located in the suburbs); and the *role of political-economic players* (e.g., real estate speculators and developers) in the promotion of growth. In this view, the automobile and other technological innovations are important but only as a *means*, not a cause, of suburbanization (Gottdiener, 1985, 1994).

*To conclude:* New urban theorists see metropolitan shifts as part of larger processes with local repercussions—global capitalism and government intervention. In their view, these are the major forces shaping metropolitan areas, and they are not natural or neutral (i.e., they do not serve everyone's interests equally). However, local outcomes are not entirely determined by these macro-level processes; individuals and organizations (grass-roots citizens' groups, real-estate developers, etc.) can have important local impacts. Urban ecologists, by contrast, see metropolitan shifts as results of technological change (e.g., new communications technologies) and shifts in social organization (e.g., mass production, consumers' ability to pay for cars).

Now we turn from this theoretical debate to a related practical issue: how to measure a metropolitan area. This sounds rather unimportant and exceedingly boring. It is not unimportant.

## Measuring Functional Interdependence

At present, measurement is based on the urban ecologists' concept of functional interdependence. The journey-to-work pattern between a central city and its surrounding suburbs is probably the most common measure of metropolitan interdependence. Yet, using this measure, we conclude that many areas now called metropolitan are far from functionally interdependent: *In 1990, twice as many people in America commuted from suburban residence to suburban job as commuted from suburb to central city.* This decentralization has reached the point where most urbanists now believe that "the central city is no longer essential to the economic functioning of a metropolitan area" (Frey and Speare, 1988:19).

## The Need for New Concepts

What is the implication here? That *the very concept of metropolitan area as an urban core with dependent suburbs is outdated.* In other words, many suburbs have become independent of their mothercities. But official record keepers have not yet come to grips with this spatial shift. The U.S. Office of Management and Budget (OMB), originator of the metropolitan area concept, initiated a project to review present concepts for the 2000 census (Forstall, 1991), and the Council of Professional Associations on Federal Statistics is sponsoring a seminar that asks, "Should the metropolitan concept be eliminated?" (Fitzsimmons, 1995). Meanwhile, OMB and the U.S. Census Bureau retain the metropolitan area as a core concept. In part, this may reflect data collection problems. According to two highly respected demographers, some commuting data used by the Census Bureau in 1980 were nearly twenty years old because commuting data "require considerable time to compile" (Frey and Speare, 1988:23).

The metropolitan area concept may not describe present realities. But it offers a standardized measure and the promise of comparable data to scholars, planners, and so on.

Predictably, both theoretical and political disputes will accompany any process to reconceptualize the nature of metropolitan community. So will policy disputes. We can expect groups representing the interests of cities to resist the notion of *in*dependence between cities and "their" suburbs. For example, the National League of Cities (NLC), an advocate for more than 1,400 member cities, argues that cities and suburbs are *inter*dependent. In the NLC's view, "metropolitan areas are a single regional economy" (Ledebur and Barnes, 1992:12). Further, the NLC claims that "cities and suburbs have a common and essential stake in their shared economies. Growing disparities between these jurisdictions erode and eventually undermine the vitality of the regional economy and, hence, the welfare of both cities and suburbs." Is there any evidence that, as the NLC puts it, "the economic fate and fortunes of cities and suburbs are inextricably intertwined" (Ledebur and Barnes, 1993:4)? That depends on *how* interdependence is measured: The NLC abandons the more common measure of city–suburban interdependence—commuting patterns—in favor of changes in per capita incomes of cities and suburbs, reasoning that city–suburban incomes "tend to rise and fall together" (1992:15). Specifically, they say that in the largest seventy-eight U.S. metropolitan areas from 1979 to 1989, "For every dollar increase in central city income, suburban incomes increase by $1.12. Conversely, for every increase of $1.12 in suburban income, central city income increases by one dollar."

## Metropolitan Statistical Area (MSA)

To standardize the measurement of a metropolitan area, OMB developed the concept of a **Metropolitan Statistical Area (MSA).** As its name implies, the MSA is not a political unit; like many entities, it is only a geostatistical creation (Table 6.1). It is used as a uniform area for data gathering and analysis.

**Table 6.1** Geographic Entities of the 1990 and Other Recent U.S. Censuses

| | Number of Geographic Entities | | | | |
|---|---|---|---|---|---|
| | Decennial Censuses | | 1987 Censuses | | |
| | 1980 | 1990 | Economic | Agriculture | Governments[1] |
| **Legal/administrative entities** | | | | | |
| United States | 1 | 1 | 1 | 1 | 1 |
| States and statistically equivalent entities | 57[2] | 57[3] | 55[d] | 53 | 51 |
| State | 50 | 50 | 50 | 50 | 50 |
| District of Columbia | 1 | 1 | 1 | — | 1 |
| Outlying areas | 6[2] | 6[3] | 4[4] | 3[5] | — |
| Counties and statisticallfy equivalent entities | 3,231 | 3,248 | 3,221 | 3,179[6] | 3,042 |
| Minor civil divisions (MCD's) | 30,450 | 30,386 | — | — | 16,691 |
| Sub-MCD's | 265 | 145 | — | — | — |
| Incorporated places | 19,176 | 19,365 | 6,776[7] | — | 19,200[8] |
| Consolidated cities | — | 6 | — | — | 25[9] |
| American Indian reservations | 277 | 310 | — | — | — |
| American Indian entities with trust lands | 37 | 52 | — | — | — |
| Alaska Native villages (ANV's) | 209 | See ANVSA | — | — | — |
| Alaska Native Regional Corporations (ANRC's) | 12 | 12 | — | — | — |
| Congressional districts | 435 | 435 | — | — | — |
| Voting districts (VTD's) | 36,351 | 148,872[10] | — | — | — |
| School districts | 16,075 | 16,000[E] | — | — | 14,271 |
| Neighborhoods | 28,381 | — | — | — | — |
| ZIP Codes | 37,000 | 39,850[E] | 31,000[E] | 31,000[E] | — |
| **Statistical entities** | | | | | |
| Region | 4 | 4 | 4 | — | 4 |
| Divisions | 9 | 9 | 9 | — | 9 |
| Offshore areas | — | — | 7[11] | — | — |
| Metropolitan areas | | | | | |
| Standard metropolitan statistical areas (SMSA's) | 323 | — | — | — | — |
| Standard consolidated statistical areas (SCSA's) | 17 | — | — | — | — |
| Metropolitan statistical areas (MSA's) [including Puerto Rico] | — | 268 | 265 | — | 265 |
| Consolidated metropolitan statistical areas (CMSA's) | — | 21 | 21 | — | 21 |
| Primary metropolitan statistical areas (PMSA's) | — | 73 | 73 | — | 73 |
| Urbanized areas (UA's) | 373 | 405 | — | — | — |
| Alaska Native village statistical areas (ANVSA's) | See ANV | 217 | — | — | — |
| Tribal jurisdiction statistical areas (TJSA's) | — | 17 | — | — | — |
| Tribal designated statistical areas (TDSA's) | — | 19 | — | — | — |
| County subdivisions | 5,827 | 5,903 | 433 | — | — |
| Census county divisions (CCD's) | 5,512 | 5,581 | — | — | — |

(continued)

**Table 6.1** *(continued)*

| | Number of Geographic Entities | | | | |
| --- | --- | --- | --- | --- | --- |
| | Decennial Censuses | | 1987 Censuses | | |
| | *1980* | *1990* | *Economic* | *Agriculture* | *Governments[1]* |
| Unorganized territories (UT's) | 274 | 282 | — | — | — |
| Other statistically equivalent entities | 41 | 40 | — | — | — |
| Special economic urban areas (SEUA's) | — | — | 433[12] | — | — |
| Census designated places (CDP's) | 3,733 | 4,423 | 44[13] | — | — |
| Balance outside of MA's | — | — | 34[14] | — | — |
| Census tracts | 43,691 | 50,690 | — | — | — |
| Block numbering areas (BNA's) | 3,423 | 11,586 | — | — | — |
| Block groups (BG's) | 156,163 | 229,192 | — | — | — |
| Tabulated parts | 197,957 | 363,047 | — | — | — |
| Enumeration districts (ED's) | 102,235 | See BG | — | — | — |
| Blocks | 2,473,679 | 7,017,427 | — | — | — |
| Tabulated parts | 2,545,416 | — | — | — | — |
| Traffic analysis zones (TAZ's) | 160,000[E] | 200,000[E] | — | — | — |

— Not applicable

E Estimated

[1] No governments [*sic*] data are published or tabulated for statistical entities.

[2] Includes American Samoa, Guam, Northern Mariana Islands, Puerto Rico, Trust Territory of the Pacific Islands, U.S. Virgin Islands.

[3] Includes American Samoa, Guam, Northern Mariana Islands, Palau, Puerto Rico, U.S. Virgin Islands.

[4] Includes Guam, Northern Mariana Islands, Puerto Rico, U.S. Virgin Islands.

[5] Includes Guam, Puerto Rico, U.S. Virgin Islands.

[6] Data for Alaska's then 23 boroughs and census areas were aggregated into 5 entities statistically treated as county equivalents. No separate data were provided for independent cities, most counties coextensive with incorporated places, and a few other counties and statistically equivalent entities.

[7] Includes only those incorporated places with at least 2,500 population, except for three smaller places.

[8] Consolidated governments.

[9] Municipal governments.

[10] Includes only eligible areas participating under Public Law 94-171.

[11] Data were tabulated for 7 offshore areas—AK, CA, LA, TX, Atlantic, Northern Gulf of Mexico, and Pacific—which were treated as statistical equivalents of counties.

[12] Includes only selected minor civil divisions with at least 10,000 population in eight northeastern states.

[13] In agreement with the State of Hawaii, the Census Bureau does not recognize the city of Honolulu, which is coextensive with Honolulu County, for purposes of statistical presentations. Instead, the State delineates, and the Census Bureau provides data for, CDPs that define the separate communities within Honolulu County.

[14] Data for those portions of counties in the six New England States that were not included in some metropolitan area were aggregated, and these areas were treated as the statistical equivalents of places.

SOURCE: U.S. Bureau of the Census, *Maps and More: Your Guide to Census Bureau Geography* (Washington, D.C.: Government Printing Office, 1992, rev. 1994).

Introduced in the 1950 census (in a slightly different form) and modified several times (e.g., in 1983 from Standard Metropolitan Statistical Area [SMSA] to MSA), the general concept of a metropolitan area has remained constant: a large population center or "nucleus" (central city) together with its adjacent, socially and economically integrated communities (outside central city or suburban area). In other words, the concept is based on a parent–child relationship: The "mother" (the Greek root of *metro*polis) dominates her dependents (hinterland, sphere of economic influence, or suburbs), which could not exist on their own.

Figure 6.1 displays the component parts of an MSA for which census data are readily available: MSA, county, central city, urbanized area, place, minor civil division, **census tract,** block group or enumeration district, and block. Not illustrated but available since 1992, for a fee, are data for user-defined units (e.g., neighborhoods, school attendance areas, business zones) from the U.S. Census Bureau's User-Defined Areas Program (UDAP).

Before describing the criteria used to define an MSA, we should note how the U.S. Census Bureau defines and operationalizes some rather ambiguous terms, such as *urban* and *rural*. Here are some useful census definitions to keep in mind:

*Census tract*  Small, relatively permanent statistical subdivisions of a county delineated for all metropolitan areas and other densely populated counties. When first delineated, they had between 2,500 and 8,000 persons. They are designed to be homogeneous with respect to population characteristics such as living conditions and economic standing.

*Central city*  The MSA's core—the city (or cities) around which an MSA is formed. It must meet minimum population standards.

*Outside central city*  Every place in the MSA minus the central city.

*Rural places*  All places not defined as urban. Rural places are subdivided into rural-farm and rural-nonfarm categories.

*Urban places*  Three kinds of places are considered urban: (1) any incorporated municipality with at least 2,500 people; (2) the densely settled fringe, often unincorporated areas; (3) an unincorporated place with at least 2,500 people located outside an urban fringe area.

*Urbanized areas*  A subcategory of urban places. An urbanized area consists of a city with at least 50,000 people plus its adjoining urban fringe.

These census categories do not solve all the problems of classification. For instance, a farming community of 3,000 people is classified as an urban place, which can be very misleading. But at least the categories are standard so that uniform data can be collected.

Now, back to the MSA. Except in New England and Alaska, an MSA consists of *an entire county or a group of contiguous counties* that contain (1) at least one central city with at least 50,000 inhabitants (or "twin cities" with a combined population of at least 50,000) or (2) *an urbanized area* surrounding the central city with a population of at least 50,000 and a total metropolitan population of at least 100,000 (or 75,000 in New England). *Counties surrounding the central city are included in an MSA if they meet certain criteria of "metropolitan character" and socioeconomic integration with the central city.* These criteria are based on high population density or high level of commuting to the core. These criteria also show that the U.S. Census Bureau defines the metropolitan area as an integrated labor market: "the smallest area that is large enough to contain the workplaces of most of the people who reside in it, and the residences of most of the people who work in it" (Heilbrun, 1974:21).

A county contiguous to the central city's county must meet criteria of metropolitan character and integration to be included in the MSA. The criteria have changed over the years, but commute patterns and population density remain key indicators of a metropolitan system. Using Figure 6.1, for example, here is how to determine the extent of the metropolitan area: If a county surrrounding Linn County, home county of the central city of Cedar Rapids, has either (1) 50 percent of its workers commuting to the urban core and a density as low as twenty-five persons per square mile *or* (2) 15 percent commuters with a density of fifty persons per square mile and other evidence of metropolitan character, the county would be included in the MSA.

Note that *the entire county is the basic political unit of an MSA, except in the New England states and Alaska.* (For historical reasons, New England's MSAs are composed of cities and towns, which have more political significance there than counties. As a result, most New England MSAs are smaller in land area than those in the rest of the United States [Frey and Speare, 1988:23].) The

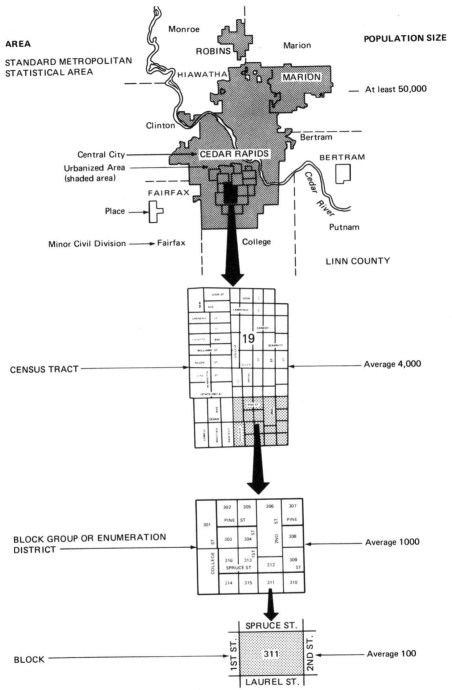

**Fig. 6.1** COMPONENTS OF A METROPOLITAN STATISTICAL AREA. An MSA is an integrated economic and social unit with a large population center, the central city. This chart illustrates the hierarchical relationship among units within the MSA. Since 1992, U.S. Census data have been available for each of these components, plus many used-defined components such as ZIP codes and neighborhoods. (Adapted from U.S. Bureau of the Census, *Census Geography* [October 1978])

minimum population standard for New England's central cities is 75,000, not 50,000. There are also alternative county-based metropolitan areas defined since the 1970s called *New England County Metropolitan Areas (NECMAs)*, which are more similar to MSAs in the rest of the United States. In Alaska, there are no counties; census divisions are used for defining MSAs.

Because metropolitan areas are defined on the basis of (presumed) economic and social interdependence—not political ties—MSAs can and do cross state lines. Interstate MSAs are common in the Northeast and Midwest but rare in the Far West.

Also, metropolitan systems change over time. MSA boundaries shift with economic growth or restructuring. For example, before 1963, Solano County, California, was included in the San Francisco–Oakland metropolitan area; in 1963 it became part of a new two-county metropolitan area as movers, working at newly created jobs or retiring there, stopped commuting to the Bay Area in large numbers.

Over time, the number of MSAs has changed. In the 1970 census, there were 243 metropolitan areas (then called SMSAs) in the United States and 4 in Puerto Rico, for a total of 247. In 1990, there were 264 MSAs in the United States and 4 in Puerto Rico, for a total of 268. In 1992, 9 new MSAs were added, including Rocky Mount, North Carolina. In 1994, based on population estimates, Hattiesburg, Mississippi, was added.

## Consolidated Metropolitan Statistical Area (CMSA) or Megalopolis

Popularly, a supermetropolitan area—a large metropolitan complex with at least 1 million in population—is often called a **megalopolis**. The U.S. Census Bureau calls it a **Consolidated Metropolitan Statistical Area (CMSA)**.

A CMSA's component areas are called **Primary Metropolitan Statistical Areas (PMSAs)**. A county or group of counties qualify as a PMSA if (1) local opinion supports separate recognition for a county or group of counties that demonstrate relative independence within the CMSA or (2) the county or group was recognized as a metropolitan area on January 1, 1980, and local opinion supports its continued recognition. For example, Solano County, California (mentioned in the previous section), is part of the Vallejo–Fairfield–Napa PMSA, one of six PMSAs that make up the nation's fourth largest CMSA, San Francisco–Oakland–San Jose. Planners predict that formerly rural Solano County will be the link connecting the Sacramento Valley to the Bay Area in less than twenty years, resulting in a new megalopolis of over 9 million people.

Population continues to concentrate in the nation's megalopoli. *As of 1988, about one-quarter of the U.S. population lived in the seven largest CMSAs:* New York, Los Angeles, Chicago, San Francisco, Philadelphia, Detroit, and Boston.

## Rural and Micropolitan Areas

Most Americans—about 79.4 percent—live in metropolitan areas as defined in 1992 (Forstall and Fitzsimmons, 1993:1). This percentage has grown enormously over the decades of the twentieth century.

There are, however, other Americas: (1) nonmetropolitan, very sparsely settled rural areas and (2) **micropolitan areas**—G. Scott Thomas's term (1990) for nonmetropolitan small towns of at least 15,000 population, located in a county of at least 40,000 residents (including the town). In recent years, nonmetropolitan America has captured the imagination of radio and TV writers, giving us Garrison Keillor's Lake Wobegon, Minnesota, and *Northern Exposure*'s Cicely, Alaska, a fictional community of 851 quirky individuals who possess a postmodern sensibility of separate but equal realities.

But in real life, nonmetropolitan America is dying out. For a period in the early 1970s, rural areas grew faster than metropolitan areas, but this **counterurbanization** (*decreasing* size, density, and heterogeneity) was short-lived. By 1990, "The American small town, which has long occupied a revered place in the nation's history and mytholo-

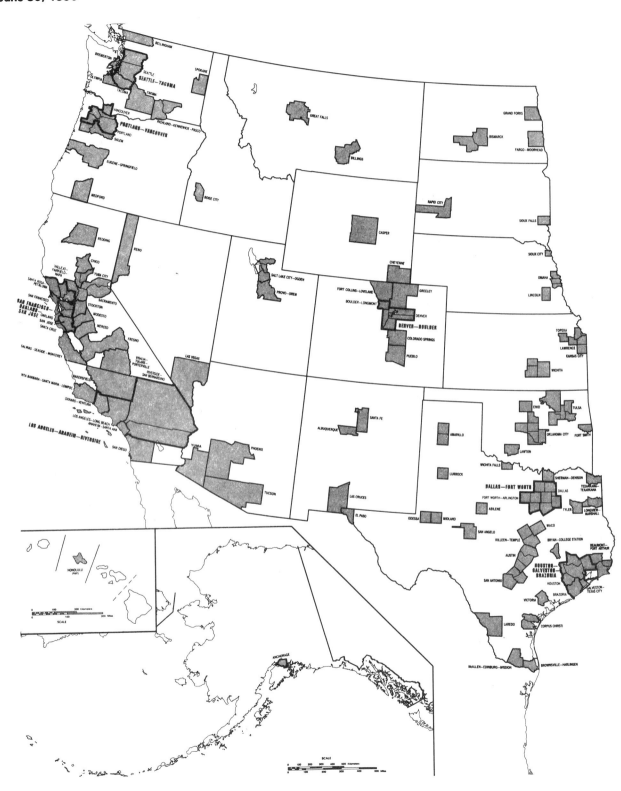

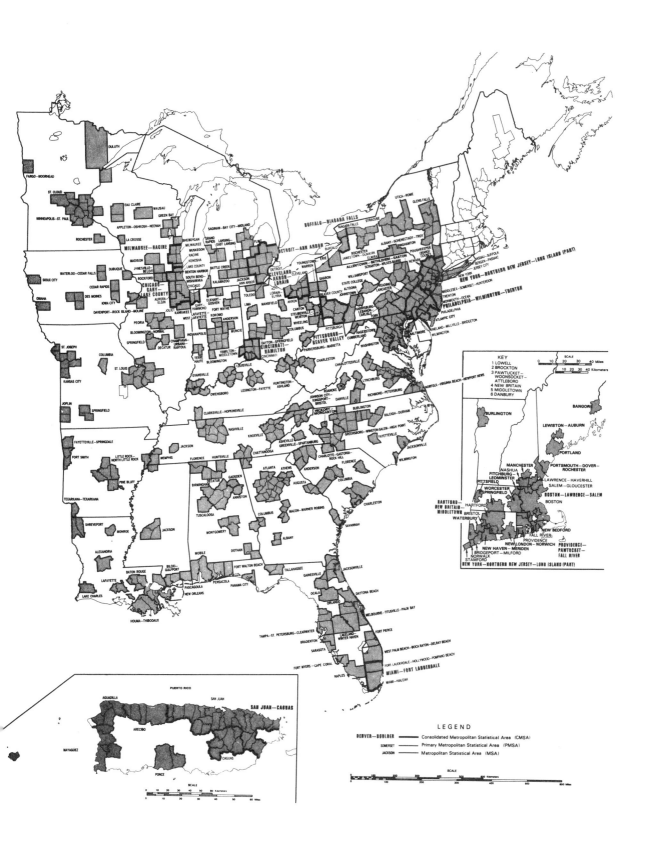

KEY
1 Lowell
2 Brockton
3 Pawtucket—
  Woonsocket—
  Attleboro
4 New Britain
5 Middletown
6 Danbury

SCALE
0  10  20  30  40 Miles
0  10  20  30  40 Kilometers

LEGEND

DENVER—BOULDER ━━━━━ Consolidated Metropolitan Statistical Area  (CMSA)

SOMERSET ───── Primary Metropolitan Statistical Area  (PMSA)

JACKSON ───── Metropolitan Statistical Area  (MSA)

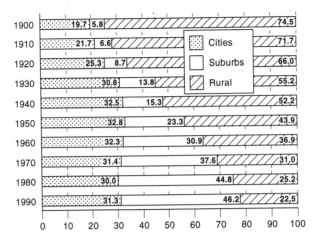

**Fig. 6.3** THE RURAL–URBAN SHIFT, 1900–1990. In 1900, almost three out of four people in the United States lived in rural areas. By 1980, the situation was reversed; three out of four people lived outside rural areas. (U.S. Bureau of the Census)

gy, is becoming something of a museum piece" (Johnson, 1990:A10). The reason is not cultural: Norman Rockwell's sentimental picture of small-town America still seems to dominate the popular imagination, crowding out darker counterimages, such as Sherwood Anderson's grotesques of *Winesburg, Ohio* (1919); Sinclair Lewis's provincial, drab, small Midwestern *Main Street* (1920); and David Lynch's hidden world of depravity beneath the blissful small-town exterior in the movie *Blue Velvet* (1986). Rather, their demise is primarily economic: "In an economic sense, a lot of these little places just aren't needed anymore" (Beale in Johnson, 1990:A10).

A few numbers show the population decline in rural America. As Figure 6.3 shows, at midcentury, about 44 percent of the U.S. population lived in small towns and on farms. By 1990, this proportion had declined to less than 23 percent.

Still, the sentimental attachment remains. More Americans prefer to live in small towns than in any other place.

Various polls confirm the long-standing American antimetropolitan bias. For example, a 1989 Gallup poll asked respondents if they would rather live in a city, suburb, small town, or farm.

Small towns were the top choice, favored by 34 percent; only 19 percent preferred a city.

As of 1989, about 15 million persons were living the apparent dreams of so many Americans. According to G. Scott Thomas (1990), that was the combined population of the 219 micropolitan areas in the United States. Idaho had the largest proportion of micropolitan residents (35 percent), followed by New Mexico (32 percent).

Residents of micropolitan and metropolitan areas differ in several ways. In general, metropolitan dwellers go to school longer and earn more money. In the vast majority of micropolitan areas (208 out of 219), per capita income fell below the national average in 1985 (Thomas, 1990). Micro areas tend to be less racially and ethnically diverse than MSAs.

### Where Are We Headed?

Will new communications and transport technologies reverse the population decline in rural America, allowing people to telecommute or to commute via high-speed trains? Or will most Americans soon be living in a handful of giant

CSAs with 10 to 50 million inhabitants? Which future is it—or are we headed in both directions?

True, we can't forecast the future with certainty. However, we have no rational choice but to attempt to anticipate it. Before looking ahead to alternative futures—ranging from a high-tech rural society and supercities to cities in the sky—let us reexamine where we have been, this time focusing on major population shifts and the transformation of community life in the United States.

## POPULATION SHIFTS

Looking back, we see how rapidly the United States was transformed from a collection of farms and small towns into a metropolitan nation. A few numbers will illustrate this shift from rural to urban and then to metropolitan life.

### From Rural to Urban

In 1790, only 5.1 percent of the U.S. population lived in urban places. By 1850, this number had increased to only 15 percent.

The year 1920 was a landmark. For the first time in the nation's history, more Americans lived in urban centers than in rural areas. However, urban growth was uneven. Very large cities grew faster than smaller ones due to the centralization of industry there. This pattern of centralization of people and industry is important because it set the pattern of urban settlement from 1920 to 1970. Indeed, even after thirty years of regional decentralization, the pattern of centralization was still apparent in 1970: 45 percent of the nation's population lived on 15 percent of the land area in the continental forty-eight states. Further, this small core produced much more than its share of economic wealth and power. Those people living on 15 percent of the land generated 55 percent of the national income and "a far higher proportion of the higher levels of economic decision making" (Morrill, 1978:435). So, the pattern set by 1920 held in 1970: a significant degree of economic concentration in which the largest cities generated the greatest wealth.

### From Urban to Suburban and Postsuburban

The year 1920 also marked the start of another long-standing trend: the movement *away* from central cities. Just as the United States became an urban nation in 1920, suburbs started growing at a faster rate than central cities. By 1970, more people lived around U.S. cities than within them.

This major population shift—from central city to outside central city—has various names: *suburbanization, metropolitanization,* and *urban sprawl.* Whatever it is called, it happened quickly. In fact, the transformation of America from an urban to a suburban nation took place in only fifty years (1920–1970), much faster than the rural–urban shift. By 1970, the United States was a metropolitan nation. The majority of people—140 million, or 70 percent—lived within metropolitan areas. More important, of this population, the majority (76 million) lived *outside* central cities.

Out-migration from central city to outside central city began in the nineteenth century. Streetcars and railroads made suburban areas more accessible to the well-to-do and socially prestigious groups. Suburban development did not boom, however, until after World War II. Between 1950 and 1970, suburbs grew from 30 million to 76 million residents. As the new urban theorists remind us, this massive population shift was encouraged by a host of federal government programs, ranging from a $2 billion-a-year highway construction program to Federal Housing Administration (FHA) and Veterans Administration (VA) mortgage guarantees. Such federal support led to a suburban housing boom, permitting a mass exodus from central cities by white, middle-class, and some working-class Americans.

Starting in the late 1960s, Americans moved to a new kind of outside central city location: *technoburb, edge city,* or *postsuburbia.* Whatever it's called, it is neither a traditional city nor a suburb. As detailed in Chapter 7, this new form is a culturally diverse, economically viable, multicentered region (such as Orange County, California) that reflects various societal trends in production and consumption.

a

**Fig. 6.4**  DISAPPEARING MAIN STREETS, RURAL UNITED STATES. No McDonald's here! Rural towns often feature non–fast food eateries such as (*a*) Arco, Idaho's "Fit as a Fiddle Calf-a." But video rentals seem ubiquitous, available in almost every nook and cranny of the United States, including (*b*) nonmetropolitan McCrae, Georgia. Although most Americans prefer them as the best places to live, small towns are disappearing for economic reasons. In years to come, however, telecommuters may repopulate some (particularly scenic) parts of the rural countryside. ([*a*] *Arco Advertiser;* [*b*] Judy Ireland)

## Back to the Land?

For a brief moment in the early 1970s, many rural places once regarded as "nowhere" became "somewhere." Entirely rural counties—not adjacent to metropolitan areas and having no urban places—were the fastest-growing areas (Morrison, 1978). But this reversal of the long-term trend toward metropolitanization was short-lived.

Theorists disagree on why this back-to-the-land movement happened at all. Some call it a "rural renaissance" (Frey, 1990:10–11). Others attribute the deconcentration to technological and structural factors, particularly improvements in communications technologies, decentralization of employment, a growing elderly population living on pensions, and the spread of retirement communities.

In the near future, another rural renaissance—based primarily on high-speed communications—might take hold, bringing numerous people, particularly professionals in hi-tech fields (computer programmers, for example) back to the land. Telecommuting could lower

b

employer and employee rent costs, reduce city traffic, make life less stressful for the rural refugees, and boost employee morale. Then again, telecommuting from the rural countryside may further isolate people socially and remove them from community life. New rural dwellers may also discover what many suburbanites have already found out: There is no place to hide; random violence, fear, drug abuse, hate, and pollution know no regional or national boundaries.

## From Frostbelt to Sunbelt

Another important population shift, starting about 1950, concerns interregional migration.

Popularly, this shift is called the move from Frostbelt to Sunbelt. Some call it the shift from *Rustbelt* (symbolizing the **deindustrialization** that transformed many northern factories into rusted-out plants) to *Gunbelt* (symbolizing the postwar growth of defense-related centers in the South and West).

Before 1950, people moved from the economically depressed southern states to northern industrial cities. In the 1950s, this pattern was reversed; population began flowing *to* the South and the West. By 1990, the majority of Americans—55 percent—lived in the South and West (Barringer, 1990:A16).

By the 1970s, the Sunbelt (the broad band of southern states from Florida to southern California) had taken the lead in population growth. A sunnier climate had some impact, but more important were jobs and economic expansion. Private business decisions and federal government policies encouraged the massive migration. Gigantic post–World World War II industries spread to the Deep South, Texas, southern California, and throughout the Sunbelt. Leading the list of new or expanded Sunbelt industries were oil and gas extraction, electronics, agribusiness, aerospace, and defense-related production. After World War II, the federal government spent billions of dollars to provide infrastructure (highways, irrigation projects, etc.) to the Sunbelt and to support the newly established defense-related industries there.

Yet, the Snowbelt–Frostbelt distinction may not be as useful as was once thought. Noyelle and Stanback (1984:222) indicate that the profound economic transformation of most U.S. cities is a complicated, often ambivalent process in which "many Snowbelt cities have clearly held their own." Further, they note that many key economic resources, such as banking and finance, didn't flow to the Sunbelt. For example, from the early 1960s to the early 1980s, "the share of deposits in the 40 'top 250' commercial banks headquartered in the nation's money centers (New York, Chicago, Los Angeles, and San Francisco) has grown from roughly 30 percent to over 50 percent" (228). Of these four cities, only Los Angeles is a Sunbelt city.

### Interpreting the Population Trends

What do all these internal migrations—from Frostbelt to Sunbelt, urban to suburban to post-suburban, metropolitan, and supermetropolitan—add up to? The picture is muddy. On the one hand, more Americans and new immigrants chose the Sunbelt than other areas during the 1980s: From 1980 to 1987, the Sunbelt accounted for two-thirds of the nation's population growth. On the other hand, as the then director of the U.S. Bureau of the Census commented, "Population shifts can be shifty. . . . Not all the sunshine is in the sunbelt" (Keane, 1985:6). For example,

Alaska had the highest growth rate of any state—24 percent—during the 1980 to 1984 period. Many headquarters functions, such as banking and finance, have remained largely in the biggest population national centers, the majority of which are non-Sunbelt cities: New York, Chicago, Los Angeles, and San Francisco. And as economic restructuring continues in postindustrial America, the Frostbelt–Sunbelt geographical distinction may become less important than other distinctions, such as Logan and Molotch's city types (Chapter 4).

Several other population trends are noteworthy:

1. *More footloose Americans.* Mainly elderly and extremely elderly retirees (age eighty-five and up, whose numbers have nearly tripled in the past quarter-century), the footloose can take their pensions, Social Security, and other nonwage income to the Florida sun, the Oregon seaside, or the daughter's spare room; they don't need to consider job opportunities when moving.

2. *More immigrants.* About 7 to 9 million legal and illegal immigrants in the 1980 to 1990 decade represent as much as 40 percent of the decade's population increase. Immigrants came primarily from Mexico, the Caribbean, and Asia and settled in southwestern MSAs. This trend signals a shift with political, social, and economic implications. For one, the U.S. Census Bureau predicts that by 2020, the United States will be slightly less female (down from 51.2 percent in 1994 to 50.9 percent in 2020), mainly because immigration tends to be largely male. In addition, due to immigration and population growth, people of Latino descent will become the largest minority (up from 9.7 percent of the population in 1993 to 15.7 percent in 2020).

3. *More supermetropolitanization.* As of 1990, for the first time in U.S. history, a majority of people (50.2 percent) lived in CMSAs. About 90 percent of the 1980 to 1990 population growth in the United States took place in CMSAs. The New York metropolitan area remained the nation's biggest (over 18 million

people), and the Los Angeles CMSA, with a population of about 14.5 million, held the runner-up spot.

4. *Bicoastalism.* Both population and income growth in the 1980s centered on MSAs around the Pacific and Atlantic coasts. California was the biggest population winner; it captured nearly one-quarter of the country's total population growth—and matching congressional clout. However, recession and defense cutbacks in the post–Cold War economy hurt California MSAs in the early 1990s proportionately more than MSAs in the Middle West. Still, by 2020, the Census Bureau expects California to be the biggest population gainer, increasing to 47.9 million people from 29.9 million in the early 1990s.

5. *Continued suburbanization.* This trend has remained constant since 1920. The fastest-growing counties in the United States lie on the outer rims of MSAs.

*One prediction:* By the year 2005, the number of telecommuters is expected to triple—to about 15 million people. Many will work at home, but others may work in small, neighborhood satellite offices. Since the first such telecommute center was established near Honolulu in 1989, the concept has spread not only throughout the United States but to towns near Vienna, Austria, and Berlin, Germany. This trend will probably spur further deconcentration of population, particularly around edge cities, in rich nations globally.

## ANOTHER LOOK

Industrialization, urbanization, and capitalism transformed West European and U.S. cities, changing the nature of urban space, work, and human relationships. Decades later, new communications technologies and the restructuring of the world economy once again are transforming metropolitan life. Bigness (supermetropolitanization) and sprawl (continuing population deconcentration out from the urban core) reflect these technological and organizational innovations.

Growth patterns such as bigness and deconcentration may be neither inevitable nor desirable. Land use patterns reflect human decisions and values. For instance, Americans tend to see the single-family home in a low-density suburb as ideal for children's growth, but the French tend to idealize big-city apartment life as healthy for their children's development. Further, suburbanites tend to see an expansive green lawn as a symbol of healthy living, while urban critics see it as an ecological outrage and a waste of time and energy.

Most Americans now live *in* metropolitan areas but *outside* central cities. Did they move to the suburbs in a vain quest for community? Do particular neighborhoods (or ZIP code clusters) in cities and suburbs represent *Gemeinschaft*-like communities? Are so-called edge cities, techno-burbs, or postsuburbs new type of communities, typical of *Technoschaft?* We turn to such questions in Chapter 7.

## KEY TERMS

**Census tract**   A small subdivision of a city within an MSA, devised by the U.S. Census Bureau to help tabulate and analyze census data. On the average, a census tract contains about 4,000 people.

**Central city**   The population center of an MSA, containing at least 50,000 people (or twin cities with a combined population of at least 50,000). This is not to be confused with the popular terms *center city* or *inner city.*

**Consolidated Metropolitan Statistical Area (CMSA)** U.S. Census Bureau term used to refer to regions comprising more than one MSA that are closely related socially and economically. A CSA always includes two or more contiguous MSAs that meet specific criteria of size, urban character, integration, and contiguity of urbanized areas. One of the constituent MSAs must have a population of at least 1 million people, and at least 75 percent of the population of each MSA must be classified as urban.

**Counterurbanization** In an urbanized society, the process whereby the proportion of nonmetropolitan residents increases relative to the proportion of metropolitan residents and cities become less dense, less heterogeneous, and smaller.

**Deindustrialization** The process of job shifting in the economy from manufacturing to services/information and the accompanying "outsourcing" of manufacturing jobs to other, lower-wage countries. In the United States, the general process has resulted in the demise of high-wage manufacturing jobs in older industrial cities like Detroit, Michigan, and Youngstown, Ohio, and the creation of lower-wage service jobs.

**Megalopolis** Popular term for a supermetropolitan area (Greek: *mega* = big) or CMSA, an urban complex with at least 1 million in population.

**Metropolis** A big city that dominates the surrounding area economically, socially, and culturally. From the Greek, meaning "mother city."

**Metropolitan Statistical Area (MSA)** As defined by the U.S. Census Bureau, a contiguous territorial unit economically and socially integrated around a central city or twin cities containing at least 50,000 people. The entire county in which the central city is located is always included in the MSA. (In New England, cities and towns are used instead of counties.)

**Micropolitan area** Not a U.S. census term. As defined by G. Scott Thomas, a single county with at least 40,000 residents, including the population of the core city, which has at least 15,000 residents, or any independent city with at least 15,000 residents. Using this definition, there were 219 micropolitan areas in the mid-1980s, including Hilton Head Island, South Carolina; Carson City, Nevada; and Selma, Alabama.

**Outside central city** Every place in the MSA minus the central city.

**Primary Metropolitan Statistical Area (PMSA)** A major component of a Consolidated Metropolitan Statistical Area (CMSA). A county or group of counties recognized as a separate MSA or any additional county or counties recognized by local opinion if it meets certain population and commuting criteria. There are four levels of PMSA, according to total population: level A—MSAs of 1 million or more; level B—MSAs of 250,000 to 1 million; level C—MSAs of 100,000 to 250,000; level D—MSAs of less than 100,000.

## PROJECTS

**1. Metropolitan areas** Using U.S. census data, look at the changes over time in your own or a nearby MSA. Did the population grow or decline since 1950? Did the number of counties in the MSA remain the same? In 1960 and 1990, what percentages lived in the central city and outside central city? What factors account for the demographic changes (or lack of change)?

**2. CMSAs** In the 1980s, 90 percent of U.S. population growth happened in metropolitan areas of more than 1 million people. Why?

## SUGGESTIONS FOR FURTHER LEARNING

American community life is a continuing, lively subject in both the arts and social sciences. A good introduction to the sociology of community is Roland L. Warren and Larry Lyon, eds., *New Perspectives on the American Community*, 5th ed. (Chicago: Dorsey, 1988). There are several selections by the so-called new urban theorists, including Manuel Castells, as well as classics in the field by Tönnies, Weber, Simmel, and Wirth.

In the popular arts, television in the early 1990s presented contrasting visions of neighborhood and small community, ranging from nostalgia in *The Wonder Years* to the morally bankrupt individuals with no sense of community in *Twin Peaks*.

For a strong argument that the small town in America is not the polar opposite of urban society but instead is permeated by the culture and politics of mass society, see Arthur J. Vidich and Joseph Bensman, *Small Town in Mass Society* (Princeton, N.J.: Princeton University Press, [1958] 1968).

Studies of *Gemeinschaft*-like communities within urban-industrial or industrializing societies include Charles Nordhoff's observations of utopian communities in nineteenth-century America, *The Communistic Societies of the United States* (New York: Dover, [1875] 1966); Benjamin Zablocki's study of the Bruderhof, *The Joyful Community* (Baltimore: Penguin, 1971); Barbara

Grizzuti Harrison's personal account and history of the Jehovah's Witnesses, *Visions of Glory* (New York: Simon and Schuster, 1978); and William M. Kephart's analysis of seven *Extraordinary Groups* (New York: St. Martin's Press, 1987), which include the Amish, the Gypsies, and followers of Father Divine. Of special note is Jacquelyn Dowd Hall et al., *Like a Family: The Making of a Southern Cotton Mill World* (New York: Norton, 1987); interviewees use the imagery of family to describe their own social relationships in a mill village.

*Gemeinschaft*-like qualities within *Gesellschaft* are suggested by many other observers, both artistic and academic. For example, three motion pictures focus on working-class Italian-American families. Two—*Bloodbrothers* (1978) and *Saturday Night Fever* (1977)—show kinship relations as emotionally suffocating and devastating to individual expression. (Using political scientist Ken Jowitt's typology, the Manero family typifies "ethnics" as opposed to "civics," or, to use another dichotomy, "locals," not "cosmopolitans.") In contrast, *Moonstruck* (1987) highlights the love and affection that a sense of community provides within the Italian-American working class. From a different perspective, William H. Whyte depicts the loss of individualism to corporate values, both in managerial work and in home life; see *The Organization Man* (New York: Simon and Schuster, 1956).

Can new communities be constructed with democratic decision-making structures, ecological awareness, and communitarian social relations? Some think so. In *We Build the Road as We Travel* (Santa Cruz, Calif.: New Society, 1991), Roy Morrison tells the story of the Mondragon cooperatives in the Basque region of Spain. Started by a parish priest and a few students in the early 1950s, the network has grown to employ some 21,000 people. They have developed their own nongovernmental social welfare and educational systems, as well as businesses. In the United States, Rancho Linda Vista, 35 miles north of Tucson, Arizona, is a communally-owned, close-knit community. What has held it together for over twenty years? "Art has kept us together," says one resident painter.

The commune movement is alive, although its numbers have fallen since a generation ago. See *The 1990/1991 Directory of Intentional Communities: A Guide for Intentional Living* (Evansville, Ind.: Fellowship for Intentional Community and the Communities Publications Cooperative, 1991).

Organizations interested in telecommuting include the Oakland, California–based Institute for Study of Distributed Work and the Bay Area Telecommuting Development Program, a project sponssored by the Metropolitan Transportation Commission (MTC) in the Bay Area.

## REFERENCES

Anderson, Sherwood. 1919. *Winesburg, Ohio.* New York: Huebsch.

Barringer, Felicity. 1990. "Census data show sharp rural losses." *New York Times* (August 30):A1+.

Berry, Brian, and John Kasarda. 1977. *Contemporary Urban Ecology.* New York: Macmillan.

Burgess, Ernest. [1923]. 1925. "Growth of the city." Pp. 47–62 in Robert E. Park, Ernest W. Burgess, and Roderick McKenzie, eds., *The City.* Chicago: University of Chicago Press.

Castells, Manuel. 1983. *The City and the Grassroots.* Berkeley: University of California Press.

Feagin, Joe R. 1988. *Houston—The Free Enterprise City.* New Brunswick, N.J.: Rutgers University Press.

Fitzsimmons, James D. (U.S. Census Bureau). 1995. Personal phone communication. May 2.

Forstall, Richard L. (U.S. Census Bureau). 1991. Personal phone communication. August 1.

Forstall, Richard L., and James D. Fitzsimmons. 1993. "Metropolitan growth and expansion in the 1980s." Technical working paper No. 6 (April), Population Division, U.S. Bureau of the Census. Washington, D.C.

Frey, William H. 1990. "Metropolitan America: Beyond the transition." *Population Bulletin* 45 (July).

Frey, William H., and Alden Speare, Jr. 1988. *Regional and Metropolitan Growth and Decline in the United States.* New York: Russell Sage Foundation.

Gottdiener, M[ark]. 1985. *The Social Production of Urban Space.* Austin: University of Texas Press.

———. 1987. *The Decline of Urban Politics.* Newbury Park, Calif.: Sage.

———. 1994. *The New Urban Sociology.* New York: McGraw-Hill.

Gottdiener, M., and Joe R. Feagin. 1988. "The paradigm shift in urban sociology." *Urban Affairs Quarterly* 24 (December):163–187.

Harvey, David. 1985. *The Urbanization of Capital.* Baltimore: Johns Hopkins University Press.

Hawley, Amos. 1950. *Human Ecology.* New York: Ronald Press.

Heilbrun, James. 1974. *Urban Economics and Public Policy.* New York: St. Martin's Press.

Johnson, Dirk. 1990. "Population decline in rural America: A product of advances in technology." *New York Times* [national edition] (September 11):A10+.

Keane, Dr. John G. 1985. "Our cities: Trends and times." Address to U.S. Conference of Mayors, Anchorage, Alaska (June 18).

Ledebur, Larry C., and William R. Barnes. 1992. *City Distress, Metropolitan Disparities and Economic Growth.* Washington, D.C.: National League of Cities.

———. 1993. *"All in It Together": Cities, Suburbs, and Local Economic Regions.* Washington, D.C.: National League of Cities.

Lewis, Sinclair. 1920. *Main Street.* New York: Harcourt.

McKenzie, Roderick D. 1933. *The Metropolitan Community.* New York: McGraw-Hill.

Morrill, Richard L. 1978. "Fundamental issues concerning future settlements in America." Pp. 431–440 in James W. Simmons and L. S. Bourne, eds., *Systems of Cities: Readings on Structure, Growth, and Policy.* New York: Oxford University Press.

Morrison, Peter A. 1978. "The current demographic content of national growth and development." Pp. 473–479 in James W. Simmons and L. S. Bourne, eds., *Systems of Cities: Readings on Structure, Growth, and Policy.* New York: Oxford University Press.

Noyelle, Thierry J., and Thomas M. Stanback, Jr. 1984. *The Economic Transformation of American Cities.* Totowa, N.J.: Rowman & Allanheld.

Orwell, George. 1949. *1984.* New York: Harcourt, Brace.

Park, Robert. 1916. "The city: Suggestions for the investigation of human behavior in the urban environment." *American Journal of Sociology* 20 (March):577–612.

Reich, Robert B. 1991a. "The secession of the successful." *New York Times Magazine* (January 20):16+.

———. 1991b. *The Work of Nations: Preparing Ourselves for 21st Century Capitalism.* New York: Knopf.

Sale, Kirkpatrick. 1976. *Power Shift: The Rise of the Southern Rim and Its Challenge to the Eastern Establishment.* New York: Vintage.

Schreiner, Tim. 1992. "Suburban communities 'forting up.'" *San Francisco Chronicle* (September 21):A1+.

Thomas, G. Scott. 1990. *The Rating Guide to Life in America's Small Cities.* Buffalo, N.Y.: Prometheus.

INTERCONNECTIVITIES AS "VIRTUAL COMMUNITIES." A patron at an electronic café communes in cyberspace with strangers via an electronic network. Many regulars consider themselves members of virtual communities. (Deborah Mosca)

# CHAPTER 7
# Making
# Connections

## SEARCHING FOR COMMUNITY,
## OR NEW HOUSES

Millions of Americans voted with their cars between 1950 and 1970, moving from the urban core to the suburbs. This mass exodus from the central city meant that by 1970 more Americans lived around cities than within them.

What kinds of people were these migrants? What kind of life did they lead once they got to the suburbs? A host of social critics thought they knew.

## Diatribes Against "Suburbia"

Shortly after the mass exodus from central city to suburb began after World War II, social critics looked at "**suburbia**," and here is what they saw:

Boring couples with small children, spending Saturday picking crabgrass out of their lawns.

Ugly, poorly planned tract developments called Merry Meadows or Happy Acres, high-sounding names that masked cheap construction and dull lives.

A land of joiners and conformists.

Frenetic participation in meaningless activities.

And the unflattering portrait continues. *The Man in the Gray Flannel Suit* (1955) rushes to catch his 6:43 A.M. commuter train, leaving his frustrated wife behind in *The Split Level Trap* (1960) with their 2.2 children. After she tries to fix *The Crack in the Picture Window* (1956), she goes to her neighbor for the morning kaffee klatsch. In a few hours, it's time to chauffeur the kids to their swimming lesson and then pick up her husband, *The Organization Man* (1956), at the commuter train. The couple dines on frozen pot pies and rushes off to a Republican Club meeting. As they reach the *Point of No Return* (1949) on this day-in, day-out routine, the husband starts to drink too much and his wife quietly goes ga-ga.

That was the stereotype of the suburbs: a vast wasteland. This negative image dominated novels and even so-called empirical studies in the 1950s.

With little evidence but much venom, most of the supposed social science studies in the 1950s crucified the suburbs. John Keats's antisuburban study, *The Crack in the Picture Window* (1956), is exemplary. According to Keats, the Drones typify the spiritual malaise and materialism of sub-

urbia. John and Mary Drone decorate their shoddily built, look-alike tract home in Rolling Knolls with plastic reproductions of high art. Further, the Drones live in a "jerry-built, homogeneous, postwar hell that destroys individualism":

When all dwellings are the same shape, all dwellers are squeezed into the same shape. Thus, Mary Drone in Rolling Knolls was living much closer to 1984 than to 1934, for she dwelt in a vast communistic barracks. This communism, like any other, was made possible by the destruction of the individual. In this case, destruction began with obliteration of the individualistic house and self-sufficient neighborhood, and from there on, the creation of mass-produced human beings followed as the night the day. (61)

To Keats and numerous other critics, suburbia was the American nightmare, not the American dream. It symbolized middle-class mediocrity and conformity.

Who were these critics who painted such a devastating picture of suburban life? Why did they attack with such venom? It is significant that the (negative) suburban image was the work of a small segment of Americans: urbane, upper-class white intellectuals. Overwhelmingly, the critics were well-educated WASP males; they lived either in the rural countryside or the major metropolitan centers, not in the suburbs.

These elite critics fell into two major categories, both tinged with romanticism. Some critics of suburbia looked backward, glorifying a rural past. Either they dreamed of recapturing Tönnies's vision of *Gemeinschaft* (people living in harmony with nature and one another in a tight-knit community) or they idealized Thomas Jefferson's American dream (a rural nation populated by self-sufficient, individualistic gentlemen farmers). Jefferson thought that democratic traditions needed to be nourished in the soil of yeoman farmers' fields.

It is Jefferson's ideal that underlies the most influential attack on suburbia, William H. Whyte's best-seller, *The Organization Man* (1956). Whyte's analysis of "The New Suburbia: Organization Man at Home" is one of the few empirically grounded studies of the 1950s, and his treatment of suburban Park Forest, Illinois, is more evenhanded than other critics' wholesale antisuburban tracts. Yet, on balance, Whyte concludes that the group tyrannizes the individual: "group immersion" equals "imprison[ment] in brotherhood" (404). Whyte's verdict, then, is that the price of a tight-knit community is tyranny of the individual, a price too high to pay.

If Whyte looked back to self-sufficient communities, other critics of suburbia looked forward to an imagined urban future. In this romantic vision, cities would be centers of high culture, social order, and true sophistication. Contemporary cities, these critics bemoaned, were disorderly and barbaric.

To both kinds of romantics (the traditionalists and the futurists), suburbia was a dismal failure. Neither countryside nor city, the suburbs seemed to combine the worst features of both.

This antisuburban literature has a familiar ring, for the same themes run throughout American intellectual history. Indeed, the antisuburban diatribes of the 1950s echo the antiurban harangues of earlier times. In both cases, members of the traditional WASP elite led the attack. They seem to have been reacting to an alien presence in ther midst that threatened their most cherished American dreams.

Comparing the antisuburban diatribes to the antiurban attacks of the 1880s, we can see what fears these social critics shared. In the late nineteenth century, upper-crust, educated WASPs worried that the immigrant "mobs" would destroy "their" cities and American high culture. Such literary figures as novelist Henry James did not hide their disdain for the lower-class ethnics streaming into New York City. To James, they represented the first stage of "alienism." Patrician James also criticized the newly rich business tycoons, the "vulgar rich," for their bourgeois values. (He especially disliked the tycoons who made their fortunes in American cities and then deserted them for the "non-descript excrescences" of fashionable suburbs.") What James feared was the spread of both alien traditions: mass culture and bourgeois values. Similarly, Whyte and other antisuburban critics in the 1950s found fault with mass culture and bourgeois values, this time symbolized by a new

mass migration: the move to the suburbs. But this time the "aliens" weren't lower-class ethnics; they were members of the white new middle class of corporate America.

*To conclude:* Lurking behind the 1950s critique of suburbia is the specter of George Orwell's nightmare world of *1984.* There, mass-produced people live in authoritarian **mass society.** Critics like Keats and Whyte feared that mass society, symbolized by suburbia, would destroy individualism. (There is a certain irony here, for according to Durkheim, Tönnies, and others in the typological tradition, individualism can flourish only in urban-industrial society.) These fears were fueled by the Cold War vision of the (former) Soviet Union, depicted—like suburbia—as the quintessence of conformity.

### The Myth of Suburbia

When the dust started settling on the newly paved roads of tract homes, social scientists began to paint a more complex portrait of suburban life. Post-1950s studies show that life beyond the city limits is hardly a wasteland of drab conformity and dreary, look-alike lives.

By the 1960s, researchers had dropped the label *suburbia.* It was, they inferred, a myth. Suburbs do not look alike, nor do their inhabitants share a lifestyle. Instead of homogeneity, the 1960s studies revealed a variety of suburban types: from enormously wealthy to middle income and dirt poor; Democratic and Republican; and from high- to low-density communities. Some urbanists (e.g., Schnore, 1963) distinguished suburbs on the basic of function: (1) residential bedroom suburbs, (2) industrial-manufacturing suburbs, and (3) mixed residential-industrial suburbs. Whatever their function, few fit the 1950s stereotype of suburbia. Take, for example, Levittown.

### Levittown

Constructed by a single developer in the late 1950s, Levittown, New Jersey, is a bedroom suburb outside Philadelphia. (Residents later changed its name to Wilingboro.) From the outside, it could have served as a model for Keats's dread "Rolling Knolls," home of the Drones. But from the inside, as Herbert Gans's monumental study of *The Levittowners* (1967) documents, this mainly working-class and lower-middle-class suburb does not fit the stereotype of suburbia.

Sociologist Gans lived in Levittown during its first years, gathering data as a participant-observer on the new suburb's way of life and politics. He found that the generally young residents were not marked by crushing conformity and homogeneity. What he did find, among other things, was that "by any yardstick one chooses, Levittowners treat their fellow residents more ethically and democratically than did their parents and grandparents. They also live a 'fuller' and 'richer' life" (1967:419).

Gans notes that there were no extremes in Levittown. Most residents were neither rich nor poor. The middle-income population was a result of the developers' key decision: to build houses in the $12,000 to $15,000 price range (1950s dollars). In essence, this one decision by the builders (Wiliam J. Levitt, his father, and his brother) determined who lived there and what kinds of groups developed in the new community. (*Note:* When various Levittowns, including one on Long Island, were built in the late 1940s and early 1950s, racial discrimination was open and legal in the United States. Levitt refused to sell to African-Americans because he feared losing potential white home buyers. He told the *Saturday Evening Post* in the mid-1950s that "as a company, our position is simply this: we can solve a housing problem or we can try to solve a racial problem. But we cannot combine the two.")

Yet there was a limited range of occupations, mainly in the technical and service areas. In addition, people came from various white ethnic backgrounds and, after a court order and some original homeowners' reselling houses to them, some African-Americans.

Most Levittowners saw their homes as the center of their lives. But, Gans noted, they were much more "in the world" and less parochial than their ethnic or WASP grandparents or parents.

According to Gans, there was little evidence in Levittown of what Whyte and others so feared: tyranny of the majority over the individual. Levittown neighbors did apply peer pressure to conform in minor ways (say, to keep the front lawn trimmed), but this did not lead to sameness of thought and action.

In general, Gans (1967:417–420) found that the young Levittowners did not resemble Whyte's and Keats's suburbanites. They were neither fearsome "apathetic conformists" nor frightful "organization men." Nor did they resemble the residents of upper-class, prestigious suburbs.

*To conclude:* Was Levittown a community? No, according to Gans,

It was not an economic unit whose members were dependent on each other for their livelihood, and it was not a social unit for there was no reason or incentive for people to relate to each other as Levittowners on any regular or recurring basis. And Levittown was clearly not a symbolic unit, for the sense of community was weak. (1967:chap. 7)

Then what was it? In Gans's view, Levittown was "only a loose network of groups and institutions . . . an administrative-political unit plus an aggregate of community-wide associations within a space." Levittowners did not come to find a sense of community; they came to carry on old ways of life in new houses. Which is what the newcomers did. They "re-created old life styles and institutions on new soil." Sociologist and planner Gans concludes that social planners shouldn't waste their time trying to re-create something that never existed in the first place: the cohesive community.

Gans's study of Levittown—plus other early social science studies of more affluent suburbs such as Princeton, New Jersey (Sternlieb, Borchell, and Saglyn, 1971), and poor suburbs like East St. Louis (Bollens, 1961)—suggest that *suburbanism is no more a single way of life than is urbanism*. Communities on the city's rim may share a label—*suburb*—but not a way of life. In other words, unlike Gertrude Stein's proverbial rose, a suburb is not a suburb is not a suburb. And, moving beyond Stein's rose, a suburb may no longer be sub-anything.

## Taking the Sub out of Suburban

Suburbs, as historian Lewis Mumford stated so succinctly, originally were "a collective effort to live a private life" ([1938] 1970:215). To be sure, modern suburbs—first on the outskirts of eighteenth-century London, then on the fringes of U.S. industrial cities in the late nineteenth century—housed the rich and powerful. Indeed, these strictly segregated (by class and function) bedroom suburbs of substantial houses on tree-lined lots have been called "bougeois utopias," blending ideas of "property, union with nature, and family life" (Fishman, 1987:15).

However, by the twentieth century, the dream of a suburban life reached beyond the elites to the middle and working classes. It is Los Angeles—"Autopia," as architectural historian Reyner Banham ([1971] 1976:chap.11) calls it—that best represents the fulfillment of the American Dream: money, speed, freedom, mobility, and a single-family suburban home. Los Angeles, the quintessential suburban metropolis of the twentieth century, is a seventy-square-mile area of "limitless horizontality" (Baudrillard, [1986] 1989:52) bound by a network of freeways and "shaped by the promise of a suburban home for all" (Fishman, 1987:15).

This metropolitan form, developed in the 1920s and 1930s, features a complex mix of urban, suburban, and rural spaces. Its basic unit is the decentralized suburb, or what we could call the "California Dreaming" utopia—in contrast to the "bourgeois" utopia. In the California Dreaming utopia, offices, shopping, services, and industries (formerly concentrated in the industrial city's core) are dispersed throughout the suburban area.

By 1945, suburbs were no longer satellites of Los Angeles. Instead, as historian Robert Fishman observes, "The suburb now becomes the heartland of the most rapidly expanding ele-

ments of the late twentieth century economy" (1987:16). The image of the suburb as a borderland (Stilgoe, 1989)—a privileged zone between city and country—became superseded by what Fishman calls a "posturban era" in which "high tech research centers sit in the midst of farmland and grass grows on abandoned factory sites in the core." Fishman then wonders, "As both core and periphery are swallowed up in seemingly endless multicentered regions, where can one find suburbia?" He answers his own rhetorical question as follows: The movement of houses, industry, and commerce to the outskirts has created

perimeter cities that are functionally independent of the urban core. In complete contrast to the residential or industrial suburbs of the past, these new cities contain along their superhighways all the specialized functions of a great metropolis—industry, shopping malls, hospitals, universities, cultural centers, and parks. With its highways and advanced communications technology, the new perimeter city can generate urban diversity without urban concentration. (1987:17)

The basis of this new city, Fishman says, is "the invisible web of advanced technology and telecommunications that has been substituted for the face-to-face contact and physical movement of older cities" (17).

To distinguish this new peripheral city from dependent, suburban bedroom communities, Fishman dubs it a **technoburb.** Others call this new city or zone **postsuburbia,** a form organized spatially around many distinct, specialized centers (Kling, Olin, and Poster, 1991) or an **edge city** (Garreau, 1991), which has 5 million square feet or more of leasable office space (the workplace of *Techno$chaft*); has 600,000 square feet or more of leasable retail space; has more jobs than bedrooms; is seen by locals as one place; and was a bedroom community or cow pasture as recently as the early 1960s. Lastly, this new type of settlement is also called **cyberbia,** a science fiction–sounding term that evokes an image of people connected by high-tech electronic communications.

Whatever it's called—*perimeter city, technoburb,*

*postsuburbia,* or *edge city*—it has become the center of most Americans' lives, replacing traditional categories of urban, rural, or suburban areas. *(Driving) time,* not space, determines its fluid boundaries: how long it takes to reach work, shopping, college, and so on by car conveniently. Although much maligned—as unsuited to current family patterns (in the 1990 census, only about 25 percent of the U.S. population fit the nuclear family stereotype), environmentally inefficient, and/or designed mainly by traffic engineers (Calthorpe, 1993)—car-based suburbs are not disappearing.

## The Transformation of Milpitas, California, 1954–1994

Post–World War II Los Angeles pioneered the technoburb. But this postsuburban form now exists in many hi-tech areas, typically near research universities—from Boston's Route 128 (MIT) and North Carolina's Research Triangle (Duke, University of North Carolina, North Carolina State University) to Salt Lake City's "Bionic Valley" (University of Utah) (Rogers and Larsen, 1986).

A brief history of Milpitas, California, located in northern California's Silicon Valley, the hi-tech complex near Stanford University, illustrates one place's swift transformation. In less than three decades, Milpitas ("little cornfield" in Spanish) evolved from a semirural community to a working-class suburb to a multicultural technoburb.

During World War II, only 600 people lived in semirural Milpitas. It didn't become a city until 1954. One year later, it was transformed into a residential-industrial suburb when the Ford Motor Company closed its assembly plant in industrial Richmond (about 50 miles north in the Bay Area) and opened a new plant there. Virtually all Ford auto workers moved with their new plant to Milpitas in 1955. Two years later, sociologist Bennett M. Berger interviewed 100 Ford workers and their spouses. As he documented in *Working-Class Suburb* ([1960] 1971), these auto workers and their wives were apparently unaffected by their move from industrial city to suburb; they

didn't take on the habits, attitudes, and aspirations of the middle class when they became suburban homeowners.

During its early years, Milpitas was the butt of wisecracks by David Letterman and Bob Hope, perhaps because "the local fragrance was a gagging mix of sewage and drainage ditch water" or perhaps because "the city's night life was an adult drive-in theatre across the road from the Ooh La Lodge Motel" (Tessler, 1989:A2). Then, the jokes turned sour. Over 2,400 workers lost their jobs in 1983, when the Ford plant closed as a result of "excess small car capacity, loss of domestic market share to Japanese auto imports, and serious financial problems" (Hansen, 1986:1).

Yet, by the mid-1980s, Milpitas was transformed anew; the once blue-collar city joined upscale Silicon Valley. It developed 24 industrial parks, 23 retail-professional centers, and 120 manufacturing plants (largely electronics). Its households had the highest income growth in the Bay Area—over 60 percent—from 1980 to 1987, averaging $46,867. And a $100 million giant shopping mall opened in 1994 on the very site of the former Ford assembly plant in Milpitas.

*To conclude:* As the head of the Milpitas Chamber of Commerce noted, "You can live here, work here, play here. It's a complete community. You can even die here. We have senior citizen centers" (in Tessler, 1989:A2). This sentiment sums up the new technoburban reality. Milpitas originated on the suburban periphery of another urban core (in this case, San Jose). Then it broke away economically and socially. Now, like other postsuburban developments, Milpitas is much more than a *sub-*urb. It is something relatively new: a conglomerate of residences, technologically advanced industries, services, and information processing.

## ZIP Codes as Neighborhoods

Conscious, perhaps touchy, about its former reputation, Milpitas launched a public relations campaign to change its image. Starting in 1989, the mayor worked hard "to let people know this is not a one-gas-station town anymore. It's upscale. My address is as good as the next guy's" (in Tessler, 1989:A2).

Address, as Milpitas's mayor implies, has important symbolic value. For example, Fox Network television's popular series of the early 1990s, *Beverly Hills 90210*, crams a great deal of information about its characters into an address: a five-digit ZIP code. Why? Because, like it or not, in the United States your ZIP code symbolizes much more than a postal zone. As market researchers were quick to see, a ZIP code represents the social status, values, even political beliefs of a neighborhood. Journalist Michael J. Weiss puts it this way: "You are where you live." Maybe not to your mother, but to people who want to sell you things and ideas, your ZIP code has become "a yardstick by which your lifestyle is measured" (Weiss, 1988:xi). A related notion, one long recognized by social scientists, may be a better motto: "In the eyes of others, you are what you buy." (The eminent sociologist Max Weber, among others, based his ideas of social status on shared consumption patterns or lifestyles, as detailed in Chapter 10.)

Blending U.S. census data, market research, and consumer surveys, analysts can predict a great deal about the consumption patterns, political preferences, and social backgrounds of residents in a ZIP code. The creator of one market research system goes as far to say this: "Tell me someone's zip code, and I can predict what they [*sic*] eat, drink, drive—even think" (Robbin in Weiss, 1988:1).

Here are some examples from Weiss's book, *The Clustering of America* (1988). Some "empty-nesting" suburbs (where postwar baby boomers have left, leaving aging parents) resemble the original Levittown; they are tract home communities such as ZIP code 08619 (Mercerville, New Jersey) or ZIP code 44221 (Cuyahoga Falls, Ohio). Residents of these Levittown-type communities tend to be older (primary age range: fifty-five and up), work at white-collar jobs, support fiscally conservative candidates, drive American cars, and read *Golf Digest*. In contrast, empty-nesters in ZIP codes 66205 (Mission, Kansas City,

Kansas) and 06430 (Fairfield, Connecticut) have a different profile; they also tend to be older (primary age range: forty-five to sixty-four), work at white-collar jobs, travel by cruise ship, live in single-unit housing, and support fiscally conservative candidates. But these folks have somewhat higher incomes and different tastes; they drive Mercedes and BMWs, buy natural cereal, and read the *New Yorker*.

Based on data Weiss uses, we can assume that Milpitas residents (ZIP codes 95035 and 95036) bought Ford Escorts when it was a working-class suburb. Now its white-collar technoburbanites buy Toyota Tercels in higher numbers.

This computer-driven market research tool is called PRIZM (an acronym for Potential Rating Index for Zip Markets) by its developer, Jonathan Robbin, a social scientist turned entrepreneur (Box 7.1). Its original use was to target audiences for Robbin's marketing company, Claritas. There is no use, for example, in advertising Ford pickup trucks in a Volvo neighborhood.

PRIZM is a for-profit, entrepreneurial tool geared to delivering potential buyers to sellers. But it has much wider applications, both practical and scholarly. Practically speaking, if you're moving to an unfamiliar place, it can help you select new neighbors and preferred neighborhood activities: singles bars, bowling alleys, ranch houses with teenagers, gas chain saws, novellas (Spanish soap operas), CB radios, college basketball games, health food stores, conservative politics, union meetings, cafés, funky brownstones, fast food, or Alice's unique restaurant. If you work as a fund-raiser or door-to-door magazine salesperson, it can assist you to pinpoint potential donors to the local symphony or subscribers to *Ebony*. (PRIZM contains much more cultural and economic information about individuals than the decennial U.S. census. But data collected by the Claritas Corporation and other such marketeers are proprietary; scholars do not have free or easy access to them.)

What's interesting to social scientists about PRIZM is its approach to the study of community and metropolitan differentiation. Essentially, it divides the nation's 36,000 ZIP codes into forty neighborhood types or "lifestyle clusters." Ac-

FROM SUBURBIA TO CYBERBIA, 1950s–1990s: A PHOTO ESSAY.

In the 1950s, Dublin, California, had a population of 1,000 ("most of them cows") plus "15 gas stations, six supermarkets, two department stores and a K-Mart." By 1973, when Bill Owens profiled Dublin in his book *Suburbia*, the San Francisco suburb was a fast-growing, lower-middle- and middle-income community. By 1990, it had grown to over 23,000 people, and its residents' household incomes also grew, up 54 percent in the period 1980–1987 to $47,705. According to Joel Garreau (1991:436), Dublin, together with three other East Bay cities on the Interstate-680 corridor, constitute an Edge City. Others call it *postsuburbia* or *cyberbia*. (Bill Owens)

Few walnuts remain in Walnut Creek, California (1990 population: 60,569), now a postsuburban development or edge city. It is located only a few miles from Dublin on the I-680 corridor and about one hour from San Francisco by Bay Area Rapid Transit (BART). (Deborah Mosca)

The Walnut Creek Arts Center, festooned with flags. According to Joel Garreau (1991:443), in edge cities, flags are often added to overcome sterility and to suggest "animated space." (Victoria Sheridan)

Residents of edge cities often feel quite separate socially and politically from nearby central cities. Cyberbanites Larry and Gail Brawn, both computer analysts, put it like this: "About twice a year we get to San Francisco. We live here, work here, go out to the movies and restaurants here. We shop here, and go to the doctor and vet here. When our spaniel Ginger got bowled over by Chui, our big dog, we took her to the vet in Walnut Creek and he told us to use hydrotherapy. Luckily, we had this Jacuzzi in our backyard." (Deborah Mosca)

cording to Weiss, PRIZM represents a new way of looking at the United States: *not as fifty states but as forty neighborhood types,* "each with distinct boundaries, values, consuming habits and political beliefs." Each neighborhood type, Weiss says, has a particular personality, described by names such as "Towns and Gowns," "Norma Rae–Ville," "Bohemian Mix," "Black Enterprise," and "Shotguns and Pickups" (Figure 7.1).

Weiss says that new neighborhood types emerge every decade. From 1970 to 1980, there were eight new clusters and eight that disappeared, reflecting many changes both in demographics and in tastes. He expects eight new types to develop in the 1990s, including: "Urban Independents" (households of unmarried couples, stepfamilies, and single parents living in quiet city areas); "Minority Achievers" (well-off Hispanic and Asian immigrants who arrived in the 1980s and joined the financially successful); "Sunbelt Industries" (communities built around new factories, such as Spring Hill, Tennessee); and "Gentrification Chic" (neighborhoods once down at the heels, now trendy, such as Washington, D.C.'s Capitol Hill).

The forty neighborhood types are also ranked in terms of status, from highest to lowest. Ranks, called *ZQs* (Zip Quality), are based on *residents' household income, home value, education, and occupation.* At the top of the status ladder is ZQ 1, "Blue Blood Estates," followed by ZQ 2, "Money and Brains" and ZQ 3, "Furs and Station Wagons." The lowest-status neighborhood is ZQ 40, "Public Assistance"; this rank mirrors the low social esteem of welfare recipients in the United States (Welfare recipients rank at the bottom of occupational prestige rankings, as detailed in Chapter 10.)

According to Weiss, "neighborhoods separated geographically can be virtually identical in lifestyle." Take, for example, ZIP codes 08540 (Princeton, New Jersey), 20007 (Georgetown in Washington, D.C), 94301 (Palo Alto, California), and 75205 (Park Cities in Dallas). Geodemographically, all are classified as ZQ 2, "Money and Brains" neighborhoods. In any ZQ2 neighborhood, you can expect to find ultrasophisti-

cated, well-heeled, college-educated people who buy specialty wines and classical recordings. Clearly, if you like to hunt, fish, listen to CB radio, and watch the roller derby, this is not the neighborhood for you. One implication here is that *Americans, known for their propensity to move, do not really move; instead, they merely go to and from the same neighborhood,* say, from New York's Greenwich Village (10014) to San Francisco's Haight-Ashbury (94117) to Washington, D.C.'s Dupont Circle (20036) to Chicago's Lincoln Park (60614) and Cambridge, Massachusetts (02139), all "Bohemian Mix" neighborhoods.

The forty neighborhood types are neither evenly nor randomly distributed over space. Some types ("Norma Rae–Ville," "Downtown Dixie–Style," "Tobacco Roads") are regional; others are coastal ("New Melting Pot"). Similarly, retirement communities ("Gray Power," "Golden Ponds") are primarily concentrated in the Sunbelt.

*To conclude:* Residents of the highest-status ZQ neighborhoods are the very people that Robert Reich (1991a) describes in "The Secession of the Successful"—the top 20 percent working mainly as symbolic analysts and living in aesthetically pleasing neighborhoods, often protected by electronic gates or private guards. Typically, these residents are white, conservative or moderate in their politics, well paid, and college educated.

Does—or can—this financially successful elite feel a sense of community with the bottom 80 percent? Weiss thinks not. He offers this explanation: Most Americans have a narrow "bubble of consciousness" that allows only a close circle of acquaintances inside; these acquaintances tend to live in ZQs near their own socioeconomic level (1988:268). Moreover, Weiss claims that "people who live 3,000 miles apart yet share the same neighborhood type have more in common with each other than with those people who live only three miles away" (6). In other words, *birds of a feather not only flock together, they exclude all others from their consciousness.* This implies that reaching across barriers—of status and neighborhood, income, education, ethnic differences, political and social preferences—is rare.

Box 7.1

## PRIZM'S FORTY AMERICAN NEIGHBORHOOD TYPES (RANKED BY ZQ AND REGROUPED ON THE BASIS OF SEVERAL CRITERIA, INCLUDING URBAN–SUBURBAN RESIDENCE)

| Name/Rank | Thumbnail Demographics | Some High-Usage Products | Percent of U.S. Population | Sample Neighborhoods | Median House-hold Income (MHI) | Percent of College Graduates in 1987 |
|---|---|---|---|---|---|---|
| **Highest income, mainly white, suburban households** | | | | | | |
| ZQ1 Blue Blood Estates | Super-rich, politically conservative suburbs | *New York Times*, Mercedes, skiing | 1.1 percent | Beverly Hills, Calif. (90212); Lake Forest, Ill. (60045) | $70,307 | 50.7 percent |
| ZQ3 Furs and Station Wagons | New money, politically conservative executive bedroom communities | *Forbes*, *Gourmet*, country clubs | 3.2 percent | Plano, Tex. (75075); Reston, Va. (22091) | $50,086 | 38.1 percent |
| ZQ5 Pools and Patios | Aging, upper-middle-class suburbs, politically moderate/conservative | *New Yorker*, Mercedes, health clubs | 3.4 percent | Kettering, Ohio (45429); Fairfield, Conn. (06430) | $35,895 | 28.2 percent |
| ZQ13 Gray Power | Upper-middle-class, politically conservative retirement communities | *Golf digest*, Lincoln Continental, country clubs | 2.9 percent | Sun City, Ariz. (85373); Danville, Va. (24541) | $25,259 | 18.3 percent |
| **High income, mainly white, urban** | | | | | | |
| ZQ2 Money and Brains | Ultrasophisticated, politically moderate/conservative, posh in-town elegant apartments, swank townhouses of well-off academics, managers | *New Yorker*, *Gourmet*, classical records, Mercedes | 0.9 percent | Georgetown, Wash., D.C. (20007); Grosse Point, Mich. (48236) | $45,798 | 45.5 percent |
| ZQ4 Urban Gold Coast | Upscale, liberal/moderate, high-rise renters | Tennis, *New York Times*, *Atlantic Monthly*, Mercedes | 0.5 percent | Upper West Side, Manhattan, New York City (10024); Rincon East, San Francisco, Calif. (94111) | $36,838 | 50.5 percent |

(continued)

Box 7.1 *(continued)*

| Name/Rank | Thumbnail Demographics | Some High-Usage Products | Percent of U.S. Population | Sample Neighborhoods | Median House-hold Income (MHI) | Percent of College Graduates in 1987 |
|---|---|---|---|---|---|---|
| **Affluent to comfortable income, mainly outside central cities, some ethnics** | | | | | | |
| ZA6 Two More Rungs | Upper-middle-class, college-educated, politically liberal/moderate, fringe city neighborhoods of apartments and white ethnic families and singles | Golf, *New York Times*, Mitsubishis | 0.7 percent | Skokie, Ill. (60076); Fort Lee, N.J. (07024) | $31,263 | 28.3 percent |
| ZQ8 Young Suburbia | Upper-middle-class, child-rearing suburbs | Swimming pools, home computers, *Skiing, Golf*, Toyota vans | 5.3 percent | Eagan, Minn. (55124); Pleasanton, Calif. (94566) | $38,582 | 23.8 percent |
| ZQ9 God's Country | Upscale exurban, conservative boom towns | Investment property, target shooting, *Ski*, sporty Saabs | 2.7 percent | Aspen, Colo. (81611); Plainsboro, N.J. (08536) | $36,728 | 25.8 percent |
| ZA10 Blue-Chip Blues | Most affluent blue-collar households, politically moderate, postwar suburban subdivisions | Racquetball, unions, *Golf, Skin Diver*, Chevrolet Sprints | 6 percent | Mesquite, Tex. (75149); Taylor, Detroit, Mich. (48180) | $32,218 | 13.1 percent |
| ZQ14 Black Enterprise | Mainly African-American, politically liberal, upper-middle and middle-class inner suburbs | Unions, malt liquor, *Essence, Ms.*, Cadillac Sevilles | 0.8 percent | Capitol Heights, Md. (20743); Cranwood, Cleveland, Ohio (44128) | $33,149 | 16.0 percent |
| ZQ16 Blue-Collar Nursery | Middle-class, mainly conservative, white, child-rearing towns | Campers, toy-sized dogs, Tupperware, *Mother Earth News*, Ford EXPss | 2.2 percent | Magnolia, Houston, Tex. (77355); Richmond, Mich. (48062) | $30,077 | 10.2 percent |
| ZQ17 New Homesteaders | Middle-class exurban, conservative, mainly white boom towns | Overnight camping, country music, environmental organizations, *Sunset, Harper's Bazaar*, Chevrolet Sprints | 4.2 percent | Yuma, Ariz. (85364); Redding, Calif. (96001) | $25,909 | 15.9 percent |

## Affluent to comfortable income, mainly single or childless

| | | | | | | |
|---|---|---|---|---|---|---|
| ZQ7 Young Influentials | Yuppie inner-ring, apartment/condo, politically moderate suburbs | Racquetball, *Sunset*, VW Cabriolets | 2.9 percent | North Side, Atlanta, Ga. (30339); Westheimer, Houston, Tex. (77603) | $30,398 | 36.0 percent |
| ZQ11 Bohemian Mix | Culturally bohemian, politically liberal, racially mixed, inner-city neighborhood | Classical music, *New Yorker*, *Harper's*, Alfa Romeos, Saabs | 1.1 percent | Greenwich Village, New York City (10014); Lincoln Park, Chicago, Ill. (60614); Haight-Ashbury, San Francisco, Calif. (94117) | $21,916 | 38.8 percent |
| ZQ15 New Beginnings | Middle-class, politically moderate, fringe-city neighborhoods, single and divorced apartment dwellers | Backpacking equipment, *Rolling Stone*, *Scientific American*, Mitsubishis | 4.3 percent | Englewood, Colo. (80110); Park Place, Houston, Tex. (77061) | $24,847 | 19.3 percent |

## Midscale city districts or midsize, middle-class towns and suburbs

| | | | | | | |
|---|---|---|---|---|---|---|
| ZQ12 Levittown, U.S.A. | Middle-class, mainly white, politically moderate suburban towns | Golf, ale, *Golf Digest*, *Barron's*, Mercury Marquises | 3.1 percent | Donelson, Nashville, Tenn. (37214); Cuyahoga Falls, Ohio (44221) | $28,742 | 15.7 percent |
| ZQ18 New Melting Pot | Middle-class, new immigrant, white-collar, politically moderate, ethnic singles and families | Health clubs, *New York Times*, *New Yorker*, Chevrolet Impalas | 0.9 percent | Geary St., San Francisco, Calif. (94121); Rogers Park, Chicago, Ill. (60660) | $22,142 | 19.1 percent |
| ZQ19 Towns and gowns | Middle-class, mainly white singles, white-collar, politically conservative college towns | Tennis rackets, folk music, *Modern Bride*, Mercury Sables | 1.2 percent | State College, Pa. (16801); Ithaca, N.Y. (14850) | $17,862 | 27.5 percent |
| ZQ20 Rank and File | Aging factory suburbs with middle-class, politically moderate, blue-collar, racially mixed couples in row houses | | 1.4 percent | Meriden, Conn. (06450); Fairview, Milwaukee, Wisc. (53219) | $26,283 | 9.2 percent |

*(continued)*

Box 7.1 (continued)

| Name/Rank | Thumbnail Demographics | Some High-Usage Products | Percent of U.S. Population | Sample Neighborhoods | Median Household Income (MHI) | Percent of College Graduates in 1987 |
|---|---|---|---|---|---|---|
| ZQ21 Middle America | Middle-class, blue-collar, politically moderate suburban towns | Motorcycles, mail-order catalogues, *Grit*, *Saturday Evening Post*, Plymouths and Chevrolets | 3.2 percent | Hagerstown, M.D. (21740); Elkhart, Ind. (46514) | $24,431 | 10.7 percent |
| ZQ22 Old Yankee Rows | Middle-class, politically moderate, row house areas of families and singles | Bowling, Christmas clubs, *New York Times*, *Self*, Mercurys | 1.6 percent | Bayonne, N.J. (07002); Melrose Park, Ill. (60160) | $24,808 | 11.0 percent |
| **Downscale urban and suburban areas** | | | | | | |
| ZQ28 Single City Blues | "Poor people's bohemia," of racially mixed singles, low-salaried, politically moderate city neighborhoods in multiunit housing | Skiing, New Wave music, *Harper's*, *Atlantic Monthly*, Mitsubishis | 3.3 percent | Mount Rainier, Md. (20712); southeast Portland, Ore. (97214) | $17,926 | 18.6 percent |
| ZQ31 Norma Rae–Ville | Lower-income, racially mixed, politically conservative mill towns | Chewing tobacco, watching professional wrestling, *Ebony*, *National Enquirer*, Pontiacs and Chevrolets | 2.3 percent | Dalton, Ga. (30720); Burlington, N.C. (27215) | $18,559 | 9.6 percent |
| **Mainly urban working class** | | | | | | |
| ZQ27 Emergent Minorities | Mostly African-American, politically moderate, lower-class, largely neglected neighborhoods with high unemployment, decaying projects | African-American contemporary music, malt liquor, *Jet*, *Ebony*, Chevrolet Novas | 1.7 percent | Anacostia, Washington, D.C. (20020); Rimpau, Los Angeles, Calif. (90019) | $22,029 | 10.7 percent |

| Cluster | Description | | Activities/Media | Location | Income | |
|---|---|---|---|---|---|---|
| ZQ32 Smalltown Downtown | Industrial inner-city areas, politically moderate, predominantly white families and singles | 2.5 percent | Gospel music, watching professional wrestling, *Southern Living, True Story,* Isuzu and Chevrolet Chevettes | Joplin, Miss. (64801); East San Diego, Calif. (92105) | $17,206 | 10.0 percent |
| ZQ34 Heavy Industry | Lower-working-class urban area, politically moderate, aging ethnic families and singles | 2.8 percent | Bowling, watching auto racing, *The Star, Modern Bride,* AMCs | Hamtramck, Detroit (48212); New Bedford, Mass. (02860) | $18,325 | 6.5 percent |

**Middle- to lower-income small towns**

| Cluster | Description | | Activities/Media | Location | Income | |
|---|---|---|---|---|---|---|
| ZQ23 Coalburg and Corntown | Midwestern middle-class small towns, politically moderate, mainly white, blue-collar families | 2.0 percent | Hunting, canning jars, *4 Wheel & Off Road,* AMC Eagles | Red Wing, Minn. (55066); Oil City, Pa. (16301) | $23,994 | 10.4 percent |
| ZQ24 Shotguns and Pickups | Lower-middle-class crossroads villages, mainly white, politically conservative families | 1.9 percent | Gas chain saws, *Grit, 4 Wheel & Off Road,* AMC Eagles | Zanesville, Ohio (43701); Molalla, Ore. (97038) | $24,291 | 9.1 percent |
| ZA25 Golden Ponds | Middle-class rustic towns of politically moderate, mainly white retired couples | 5.2 percent | Truck-mounted campers, toy-sized dogs, *True Story, Audio,* Dodge Diplomats | Cape May, N.J. (08204); Ocala, Fla. (32670) | $20,140 | 12.8 percent |
| ZQ26 Agribusiness | Middle-class farming and ranching communities, politically conservative, mainly white families | | Hunting, motorcycles, *Grit, Mother Earth News,* AMC Eagles | Clarion, Ohio (50525); Blackfoot, Idaho (83221) | $21,363 | 11.5 percent |
| ZQ29 Mines and Mills | Eastern lower-middle-class mill towns, politically moderate, mainly white families | 2.8 percent | Bowling, watching professional wrestling, *Grit, Popular Mechanics,* Chevy Spectrums | Sebring, Ohio (44672); Monessen, Pa. (15062) | $21,537 | 8.7 percent |

*(continued)*

Box 7.1 (continued)

| Name/Rank | Thumbnail Demographics | Some High-Usage Products | Percent of U.S. Population | Sample Neighborhoods | Median House-hold Income (MHI) | Percent of College Graduates in 1987 |
|---|---|---|---|---|---|---|
| ZQ33 Grain Belt | Low-income, small family farms concentrated in the Midwest, northern Plains. Some communities in poverty, politically moderate, mainly white families | Gas chain saws, canning jars, *Grit*, *Hunting* | 1.3 percent | Early, Iowa (50535); Butte, Neb. (68722) | $21,698 | 8.4 percent |
| **Rural poverty areas** | | | | | | |
| ZQ30 Back-Country Folks | Downscale rural and remote towns, politically moderate, mainly white families | Hunting, compact pick-up trucks, *True Story, Soap Opera Digest*, Dodge Diplomats | 3.4 percent | Dothan, Ala. (36301); Larose, La. (70773) | $19,843 | 8.1 percent |
| ZQ35 Share Croppers | Downscale, racially mixed, politically conservative southern hamlets in the Old Confederacy | Chewing tobacco, hunting, *Southern Living, Hunting*, Dodge Diplomats | 4.0 percent | Plains, Ga. (31780); Oak Hill, W.Va. (45656) | $16,854 | 7.1 percent |
| ZQ38 Tobacco Roads | Southern farm towns, politically conservative, mainly African-American families | Malt liquors, pipe tobacco, *Grit, Ebony*, Pontiac Bonnevilles | 1.2 percent | Sparta, Ga. (31087); Belzoni, Miss. (39038) | $13,227 | 7.3 percent |

| | | | | | |
|---|---|---|---|---|---|
| ZQ39 Hardscrabble | Isolated areas, politically moderate, mainly white families | Chewing tobacco, power boats, *Southern Living*, Hunting, AMC Eagles | 1.5 percent | Bonneville, Ky. (41314); Chinle, N.M. (86503) | $12,874 | 6.5 percent |

**Urban poverty neighborhoods**

| | | | | | |
|---|---|---|---|---|---|
| ZQ36 Downtown Dixie–Style | Downscale, politically liberal southern areas in transition, racially mixed singles and single-parent families | Soul and jazz music, *Ebony, Jet*, Isuzus | 3.4 percent | Selma, Ala. (36702); Galveston, Tex. (77550) | $15,204 | 10.7 percent |
| ZQ37 Hispanic Mix | Nationwide inner-city, politically moderate, low-wage, mainly Hispanic singles and families | Watching boxing, malt liquor, *New York, New York Times*, Mitsubishis | 1.9 percent | East Los Angeles, Calif. (90022); Hoboken, N.J. (07030) | $16,270 | 6.8 percent |
| ZQ40 Public Assistance | America's poorest inner-city areas, mainly African-American singles and single-parent families | Malt liquor, burglar alarms, *Essence, Jet*, Chevrolet Novas | 3.1 percent | Watts, Los Angeles, Calif. (90002); Hyde Park, Chicago, Ill. (60653) | $10,804 | 6.3 percent |

SOURCE: Adapted from Michael J. Weiss, *The Clustering of America* (New York: Harper & Row, 1988).

a

**Fig. 7.1** WHAT ZQ IS THIS? In the PRIZM system, each of forty neighborhood types is assigned a Zip Quality rank based on median value of home, residents' household income, education, and occupation. (*a*) "Blue Blood Estates," ZQ1, the highest-ranked neighborhood type, is characterized by super-expensive homes like this one in San Francisco's Pacific Heights section. (*b*) "Urban Gold Coast," ZQ4, is an area of sophisticated, affluent renters named for Chicago's Gold Coast, where this apartment house is located. (*c*) "Bohemian Mix," ZQ11 neighborhoods, are inner-city areas with liberal, racially mixed, culturally bohemian lifestyles with a high percentage of college graduates. (*d*) "Blue Collar Nursery, ZQ16, is a mainly white, middle-class, child-rearing area. (*e*) "New Melting Pot," ZQ18, is home to new immigrant, white-collar, middle-class, ethnic families and singles. (*f*) "Shotguns and Pickups," ZQ24, by contrast, is a rural crossroads village characterized by ceramic bird collections, dusty pickups, and support for legislation protecting U.S. jobs. ([*a–e*] Deborah Mosca; [*f*] Tim Teninty)

As a historian so nicely phrased it, "Walls and gates assume a world of strangers" (Leed, 1991: 18). In contemporary society, the barriers may be literal, (e.g., gated communities) or figurative (e.g., communities that erect an invisible wall against the lower middle class via zoning ordinances).

This brings us back to the two-sided face of community. To live near people one has "more in common with" or feels "comfortable with" usually means to live near people like oneself. To some, this is an ideal. For example, the St. Johnsbury, Vermont's, Preface to the Town Plan suggests that people *need* "spiritual unity" and need to pass on "*the* basic cultural inheritance." But whose inheritance? Only in a homogeneous community is there one agreed-on culture. This brings us to the other face of community: parochialism and insularity. In other words, the price of feeling a sense of we-ness and community with members of a small group is estrangement from people unlike those in the group.

b

Questions of democracy also arise. In a small community, the possibility of the majority's tyranny over the minority looms large. There is also the problem of scale: "Democratic" decisions at the micro-level can be restrictive, even oppressive, to outsiders and harmful to the society as a whole. For instance, is it democratic if a group of 2,000 or 20,000 keep people unlike themselves out of the neighborhood (by passing restrictive zoning regulations or by prohibiting children, for example), thus ensuring homogeneity?

There seem to be no easy answers to these questions. In fact, some believe that we are doomed to live either without individual freedom and a broad outlook in local community or without close bonds in cosmopolitan society. Can any community—aside from Cicely, Alaska, the fictional creation of TV's *Northern Exposure*—

meet the dual challenge of (1) encouraging personal freedom and openness to new ideas, and (2) providing intimacy and cohesive social bonds?

## Placeless, Faceless Communities: Interconnectivities

There are a few "places" that don't identify "residents" as members of either high- or low-status ZIP codes. These places may be instrumental in forging a new sense of we-ness among people of different ages, status positions, and tastes. To some, these "communities" meet the challenge: They guarantee freedom and provide intimacy.

"Residents" may be shut-ins, geographically

c   **Fig. 7.1**  (*continued*)

d

e

f

distant folks, students, or people sharing a particular interest (chess, conspiracy politics, etc.). At any rate, growing numbers of such residents spend hours daily communicating on computer bulletin boards with people they've never seen or met in any traditional manner. Students and faculty have a particular interest in the Internet, the network of electronic networks. Some think that the Internet is becoming "the academy of the 1990s" (DeLoughry, 1994:A25). In 1994, social scientists could choose from among more than 2,000 Internet discussion groups with colleagues and exchange information that is "at least six months ahead of journals and conferences, and certainly books" (Pantelidis in DeLoughry, 1994:A25).

Do such groups of electronic pen pals constitute a community? After all, social relationships carried on by impersonal technologies seem to be an oxymoron, like "standard deviation" or "jumbo shrimp." Yet personal computers promote a new sort of interconnectivity that is both placeless and faceless. People meet in cyberspace—a keyboard-connected computerland of shared information and inner secrets.

That is just what members of the WELL do. The WELL, an acronym for Whole Earth 'Lectronic Link, is a computer conferencing system born in 1986. Members can join over 100 ongoing computer conferences or news groups, each with a host/ess and a list of topics ranging from gardening to politics. The WELL office in Sausalito, California, hosts a monthly party, and subscribers organize Sunday brunches.

Most users agree that the WELL is a virtual community—"a place that's no place." One subscriber says, "The WELL is just like any other community, but it's easier to park." Another says, "I'm staring at a computer screen. But the feeling really is that I'm 'in' something: I'm some'where'" (in Moore, 1990:19–20). Another, who runs a couples conference on the WELL, says that people share their secrets and problems electronically: "There is real intimacy on the WELL" (Flower, 1994).

But critics are not so sure. For one, Internet surfer Clifford Stoll (1995) claims that there is a significant difference between virtual and real communities: Only in real communities is there a sense of responsibility to fellow members.

*To conclude:* "Human identity," philosophizes architect Christian Norberg-Schulz "is to a high [*sic*] extent a function of places and things" ([1979] 1984:21). He argues that individual identity and physical environment have been linked for centuries. But if the human identity–physical place relationship existed historically, it is being changed, perhaps destroyed, by computers and telecommunications. Indeed, "the digitization of the entire world," as reporter John Markoff (1994) calls the global spread of electronic media, may change the very definitions of "human identity" and "place."

Various observers, ranging from psychologists (e.g., Gergen, 1991), sociologists, and communications theorists to historians and hard-to-pigeonhole thinkers (notably the late Marshall McLuhan), insist that electronic media affect social relationships and human identity in deeply significant ways. For example, John Markoff and Katie Hafner, authors of *Cyberpunk* (1991), find an emerging sense of community among many computer networkers. Others stress the impact of television in changing our feeling of connectedness. Sociologist Joshua Meyrowitz puts it this way: Americans live in a *"19-inch neighborhood"* (1985:8). Television allows people to "pay more attention to, and talk more about, fires in California, starvation in Africa and sensational trials in Rhode Island than the troubles of nearly anyone except perhaps a handful of close family, friends and colleagues." In other words, Meyrowitz thinks that television gives viewers a *wider but shallower* sense of community. Interactive telecommunications—teleconferencing, most notably—can bring students from Moscow, Idaho, together with peers in the Russian capital on an ongoing (and surprisingly intimate) basis. Ever-increasing numbers of people spend hours "together" on the WELL or the Internet. These exchanges of ideas depend on having unique e-mail addresses, not similar ZQs or lifestyles. Indeed, in this setting, the concepts of local—and national—addresses become meaningless.

# SOCIAL NETWORKS

## A Structural Approach to Community

Although millions of people already navigate the worldwide information highway (and millions more "drive" onto the highway annually), most Americans do not belong to electronic networks. Yet, excluding hermits, people are not isolated; they belong to social networks. Analyzing these networks is another approach to studying how contemporary people maintain a sense of connection.

Network theory, pioneered by Elizabeth Bott (1957), is associated with the work of sociologists Barry Wellman (1979), Mark Granovetter (1973), and Claude Fischer (1982). It is based on four interrelated premises:

1. *Gesellschaft* and *Technoschaft* are *not* socially "disorganized" (as Tönnies and early urban theorists thought); modern institutions and processes, particularly the highly specialized division of labor and physical and social mobility, are tools for individual freedom.
2. People are involved in a "web of group affiliation" (Simmel, [1922] 1955), with varying intensities and degrees of stability.
3. Social structure is not spatially bounded in contemporary life.
4. Social networks play a variety of roles, from helping people to find jobs, spreading gossip, and offering social support and friendship to bridging the gap between different social worlds.

To illustrate this perspective's basic concepts, consider one of your networks, say, your friendship or work network. First, put yourself at the center of the network (called an *egocentric* network because you are at the center). Then try to determine your network's *range* (from narrow to wide, depending on the number of direct contacts you have within the network ), its *stability* over time, and its *density* (from close-knit to loose-knit; density is the proportion of actual connections among network members compared with the possible number of connections if all members were connected to the entire network). Next, look at the nature of the social ties. Are they *single-stranded* (one-dimensional, as in the case of you and a bank teller, who interact only about a banking transaction) or *multistranded* (multidimensional: say, you and the bank teller interact in many roles—you raise children together as mates, play soccer, and care for your aged aunt together)? Are the ties *strong*, as in warm friendships with reciprocity, emotional intensity, and frequent contact, or *weak*, as in acquaintanceships that are peripheral and less intense?

Network analysts offer the following kinds of insights based on their empirical studies:

1. *Ubiquity.* Most people, whether urban or suburban or rural, maintain close social ties with people outside their own households.

2. *Number and kinds of ties.* Rural dwellers have no more close social ties than urbanites or suburbanities; all have about the same number of close bonds. However, the *kind* of involvement differs: People in small towns and nonmetropolitan areas are more involved with kinfolk; urbanites and suburbanites are more involved with nonkin friends.

3. *Homogeneity.* Close associates tend to be similar in age, income level, religious preference, education, marital status, and occupational level. However, some groups tend to have more heterogeneous networks than others in terms of ethnicity and religion (ethnoreligion). For example, Laumann (1973) found that urban Protestants were more likely to be in networks that were occupationally alike but ethnoreligiously much more mixed than either Catholics or Jews.

4. *Strength of weak ties.* Weak ties are very useful; they can bridge diverse networks. Typically, strong ties are forged with people of similar backgrounds. While strong ties may provide emotional security, they can limit opportunities. For example, Boston's Italian-American "urban villagers" studied by Gans ([1962] 1982) had such strong ties in the West End and so few weak ties outside the close-knit circle that they missed

out on valuable information carried by weak ties, including political gossip about the city's plans to tear down their neighborhood (Granovetter, 1973).

5. *Strength of strong ties.* In general, urban villages—low-income, ethnic city neighborhoods such as Boston's former West End and a Mexican shantytown studied by Lomnitz (1977)—are characterized by strong ties; they tend to function more as subcommunities than do upper-income, more ethnically heterogeneous neighborhoods. In such parochial (rather than cosmopolitan) urban enclaves, strong ties provide an important support system where residents routinely exchange tools, resources, and favors. However, Gans is careful not to romanticize the West End's distinct working-class subculture. He says that the area was "not a charming neighborhood of 'noble peasants' living in an exotic fashion . . . and overflowing with a cohesive sense of community"; rather, it was a "run-down area of people struggling with the problems of low income, poor education, and related difficulties" ([1962] 1982:16).

6. *Mobility.* Both geographic and social mobility are heavily influenced by social ties. Most often, job seekers find employment information and get chosen over others with the same qualifications for a job because they have connections (the "who you know" factor) through weakly tied persons. In terms of geographic mobility, close ties play a key role in the creation of ethnic neighborhoods via "chain migration" (MacDonald and MacDonald, 1964). Chain migration happens when prospective movers get survival information and jobs in a new place arranged for them by closely tied previous migrants, normally kinfolk or coethnics. One study of several hundred migrants found that over half (51 percent) migrated with relatives and that all but 17 percent had relatives waiting for them upon arrival (Choldin, 1973). Once in the new place, migrants depended on relatives rather than coworkers or friends for help.

7. *Single-stranded ties.* A person's neighborhood is not the only warm nest for birds of a feather. As Louis Wirth and many others have suggested, shared interests bring the flock together too. A shared interest is often the basis for a single-stranded tie, resulting in only minimal mutual responsibility. In some cases, it is the foundation for what might be called "communities of *extremely* limited liability." (Sociologist Morris Janowitz coined the term *community of limited liability* in 1952. He meant that a local community today resembles a corporation: Neither has total liability for its members.) Members—if we can even call them by such a name—of a community of extremely limited liability have very limited expectations of one another, but they maintain regular social interaction. Here are some examples:

a. For fifteen years, a group of commuters took the 7:27 A.M. train into Chicago and the 6:02 P.M. back to suburban Whiting, Indiana on Monday through Friday. This group hosted retirement parties for "members" on the train, celebrated the end of the workweek together, and carried on running conversations about their lives, all—and only—on the train.
b. Members of twelve-step groups offer communal support focused on a particular need, say, avoiding alcohol, gambling, overeating, or cocaine.
c. People who pray or study Scripture together—the most common type of limited-liability community in the United States—support one another without requiring enduring commitment.

Interestingly, these groups complement (rather than clash with) deep-seated American values of individualism and personal growth. Such groups demand little but give participants a sense of feeling good about themselves (Wuthnow, 1994).

*To conclude:* Many people—from members of cousins' clubs, church groups, Lions, sororities, and street gangs to corporate officers, politicians, parents paying for their children's prestigious schools, and drug dealers—understand the importance of social networks. But *networking* became a buzzword and a verb only in the 1980s. The late Yippie (Youth International Party) Jerry Rubin of Chicago 1968 renown (as a protester

**Fig. 7.2**   A COMMUNITY OF EXTREMELY LIMITED LIABILITY. Dogs cavort at an off-leash dog park in Berkeley, California, while their human companions schmooze. In some ways, the park is like a neighborhood bar; most human visitors are regulars, arriving at about the same time of day and talking to the same people. (Barbara Cohen)

outside the Democratic National Convention) became famous for a second fifteen minutes when he turned networking into a yuppie tool; he sponsored parties in New York City where business cards could be exchanged and weak ties forged. Such alternative structures also represent one attempt to break down (or through) "old-boy networks" that typically excluded women and ethnics.

Understanding how social networks operate is relevant to a range of practical and theoretical pursuits—from getting a job or exchanging food stamps (Stack, 1975) to gaining access to power and resource capital without "connections" (Goldenberg, 1987:106–108).

## WHAT NEXT?

### Grand Dreams and Grandiose Schemes

Technoburbs, megalopoli, and electronic nowhere networks. These are some responses to urban growth in the past thirty years.

What about the next thirty years? Here we enter a mind-boggling realm where proposals range from cities floating in space to cities below the Earth and sea. In this arena, old concepts may take on new meaning. Imagine, for example, "commuting" daily from Los Angeles to Boston. It might take only twenty-one minutes by a passenger train powered by pollution-free magnetic levitation. Gerard K. O'Neill, professor emeritus of physics at Princeton University, was working on this idea at the time of his death in 1992.

O'Neill envisioned even grander technological projects. It may sound like science fiction, but he wrote that it is "almost inevitable" that humans will "breakout" from Earth, creating permanent colonies in space that could house up to 10,000 people. And what would life be like in these orbiting cities? O'Neill seems to suggest that present patterns of social life will continue, simply transferred to a space colony. (Yet, studies of people in closed, isolated environments, such as submarine crews, show that boredom and cabin fever are common, producing conflict among members. So we should not expect merely to transfer earthly behavior to skyward, closed cities.)

While O'Neill touted *The High Frontiers: Human Colonies in Space* (1977), others look to a Jules Verne vision: cities beneath the sea. Jacques Cousteau and Edouard Albert, for instance, proposed building an artificial island that would be a leisure town just off the coast of Monaco. Others, like Hidezo Kobayashi, envision a marine civilization with underwater urban structures.

At present, cities below and above the Earth are only a twinkle in the visionaries' eye. But even if they remain just a twinkle, the potential of such space-age cities may spur our collective imagination to redesign earthbound settlements. Likewise, imaginings of the future—from cultural historian William Irwin Thompson's (1978) vision of new "metaindustrial" villages and smaller, decentralized, symbiotic cities and Richard Register's (1987) carless "eco-city" to Robert Reich's (1991a) two-tier society, composed of the successful 20 percent and the unsuccessful 80 percent, to some socialist-feminist visions of a classless, gender-equal society (e.g., Kuhn and Wolpe, 1978)—shake our most basic assumptions about what is and what ought to be. Essentially, visionaries, whether scholars, mystics, science fiction writers, or artists, are moralists; they comment on good and evil in the present while presenting alternatives for the future. Long may

the imaginers live to enliven our sense of possibility! As a congressperson put it, "Unless we try to visualize what is beyond the horizon, we will always occupy the same shore" (Brown, 1993:B2).

## ANOTHER LOOK

For a change, theorists seem to agree on a basic point: Urban-industrial-capitalist society is too big, too specialized, and too heterogeneous to promote a sense of community except within smaller subcommunities. But on the question of what to do about this situation, if anything, consensus breaks down.

Differences in ideology and historical perspective are the basis of dissent over questions of modern community. Decentralists like William Irwin Thompson think that communications technology permits a return to a smaller-scale, more humane village life without the parochialism of preindustrial communities. In this view, the global village is possible without reinventing what Marx called the "idiocy of rural life." Centralists, on the other hand, tend to be prourban. Those in the Marxist tradition look to the radical restructuring of economic and political institutions as the precondition for reconstituting a sense of community by abolishing inequality and oppression. Ultraconservatives argue that secular modern urbanites cannot handle freedom, democracy, and advanced technology; a return to benevolent, authoritarian, religious rule is one answer for them. Other conservatives wish for a Jeffersonian past. Meanwhile, numerous philosophers are skeptical about whether *any* form of human social organization—urban, suburban, or rural—can encourage both personal freedom and intimate social bonds.

Theory aside, there seems to be a growing recognition that members of the global community share common concerns, perhaps a common fate. Since Hiroshima and Chernobyl, an understanding of the destructive power of technology—destruction that cannot be contained by political borders—combined with the spread of a global economy and culture have alerted us to our interdependence. This situation is reflected in language. *Afghanistanism* was once a term newspaper editors used to refer to the preference for stories about faraway, exotic places over hard-hitting, close-to-home news. That term disappeared almost overnight in 1980 when Soviet troops marched into Afghanistan, and no term has replaced it. Perhaps this signals the idea that no place on earth is now so remote as to deserve our ignorance or lack of concern.

## KEY TERMS

**Cyberbia** A postsuburban human settlement in an information-based, electronic (cybernetic) society.

**Edge city** Joel Garreau's (1991:chap. 1) term for any place outside the central city that contains the following: (1) at least 5 million square feet of leasable office space, which is more than downtown Memphis; (2) at least 600,000 square feet of leasable retail space—the equivalent of a fair-sized mall; and (3) more jobs than bedrooms. In addition, these places (4) were merely bedroom communities or semirural places as recently as the early 1960s but now (5) are seen by the local population as one place that "has it all"—jobs, shopping, and entertainment.

**Mass society** An imprecise term, used in the sense of *Gesellschaft*. Usually viewed as large-scale, urban-industrial society characterized by loss of traditional community ties, dependence on mass (instead of face-to-face) communications, and impersonal social relations.

**Postsuburbia** A relatively new spatial form, pioneered in Los Angeles in the 1920s and 1930s and developed elsewhere after World War II, characterized by a complex, decentralized mix of urban, suburban, and rural space and a mix of residents in terms of class and ethnicity.

**Suburbia** Negative stereotype of the suburbs created by social critics in the 1950s, connoting ugliness,

tacky construction, middle-class mediocrity, and conformism.

**Technoburb** A perimeter city or zone, perhaps as large as a county, that is functionally independent of the central city and can generate urban diversity without urban concentration; it is made possible by technologically advanced industries. Its residents meet their work, housing, and other needs in their immediate surroundings. The term was coined by Robert Fishman, author of *Bourgeois Utopias*.

## PROJECTS

**1. ZIP codes as communities.** First, walk through two residential neighborhoods that appear, on the surface, to represent different neighborhood types or ZQs. Record—but do not judge—what you see: Alfa Romeos, motorcycles, pickup trucks, private security, tricycles, single-family, large houses on tree-lined streets, condos, multiunit apartments, the *New York Times* on the doorstep, ale bottles, toy-sized dogs, remnants of TV dinners, imported French wine bottles and/or freeze-dried coffee jars in the curbside recycle container. Then, using U.S. Census of Population and Housing census tract and block data and precinct voting records (plus any proprietary data you can find, perhaps in a business library, organized by ZIP codes, such as Claritas's PRIZM, CACI/Source Products, Fairfax, Virginia), check out the residents' median income, ethnic background, presidential voting records, home value, and occupations. Based on the information you've collected, in what ZQ would you place the two neighborhoods?

**2. Neighborhoods as communities.** Do people in your city's neighborhoods feel a sense of community? Choose two neighborhoods and try to find out how residents perceive and feel about social relationships there. Construct a short questionnaire, including background questions on age and ethnicity, and on the use of neighborhood facilities. Administer the questionnaire to residents, perhaps a nonrandom sample of twenty persons. Are there differences between respondents in the two neighborhoods concerning their social relationships? If so, why might this be? (*Note:* Don't generalize on the basis of your nonrandom sample. That is, avoid all claims about what "people" say or do; report only what your *respondents* say or say they do.)

**3. Social networks.** Choose two novels and trace the social networks of the main characters in each. Are their relationships close or loose-knit, multi- or single-stranded? Do their webs of affiliation differ? If so, what difference does it matter to the story and to the characters' feelings?

## SUGGESTIONS FOR FURTHER LEARNING

The social science literature concerning suburbanization has mushroomed since the 1960s. Of particular interest are some recent studies focusing on the suburbanization of people of color. Generally, studies find wide variation among metropolitan areas in terms of minority suburbanization. In *Washington, D.C.: Inner City Revitalization and Minority Suburbanization* (Philadelphia: Temple University Press, 1987), Dennis E. Gale looks at how racial-ethnic changes have affected local politics. John R. Logan explores "Fiscal and Developmental Crises in Black Suburbs: The Case of Philadelphia" in *Business Elites and Urban Development*, ed. Scott Cummings (Albany: State University of New York Press, 1987). Logan concludes that the racial problems of the central cities are not solved by the "opening up" of the suburbs but that problems such as job and housing discrimination resurface outside the central city. In addition, he argues, black suburbs suffer from a narrow corporate tax base and are "ultimately more dependent on state and federal largesse to balance their budgets."

David Harvey contends that suburban growth served an extremely political purpose. In his major study, *The Urbanization of Capital* (Baltimore: Johns Hopkins University Press, 1985), geographer Harvey argues that suburbanization was but one "bourgeois response" to the ghetto riots in the 1960s; the aim was to disperse potential revolutionaries who were highly concentrated in cities.

Suburban growth and community is one topic of David Nasaw's *Going Out: The Rise and Fall of Public Amusements* (New York: Basic Books, 1993). The author, a professor of history and American studies, argues that by the 1960s, many suburban whites feared going downtown, and a vibrant urban culture—filled with roller coasters, picture palaces, carnivals, and baseball diamonds—was replaced by packaged entertainment and shopping in sterile suburban malls and theme parks. He says that post–World War II racial integration of urban public spaces played a major role in destroying whites' feeling of supremacy, the factor that he claims was the cement of mass white audiences.

James Howard Kunstler calls contemporary suburbs *The Geography of Nowhere* (New York: Simon and Schuster, 1993). His devastating critique recalls earlier diatribes against suburbia except that his main criticism concerns the domination and alteration of nature. In *From Where We Stand* (New York: Knopf, 1993), Deborah Tall draws a distinction between suburban *landscaping* and nature's *landscape*. F. Herbert Bormann, Diana Balmori, Gordon T. Geballe, and Lisa Vernegaard argue in *Redesigning the American Lawn* (New Haven, Conn.: Yale University Press, 1993) that lawns in one suburb are identical to lawns in another, thereby destroying a sense of place.

History professor Barbara Kelly revisits a Levittown on Long Island in *Expanding the American Dream: Building and Rebuilding Levittown* (Albany: State University of New York Press, 1993). She found that the early Levittown of two basic styles —small Cape Cods and ranch-style houses—has become much less architectually uniform due to extensive remodeling.

Are suburbanites happier than urbanites? Filmmakers disagree. Independent videomaker Jane Wilcox taped the daily lives of five suburban Long Beach, California, families and secretly made a fantasy track of possible private thoughts of the well scrubbed. Her work, *The Secret Thoughts and Interior Lives of Our Finest American Products*, is available via the underground video network. *Suburbia*, a cult classic film by Penelope Spheeris, shows another side of paradise: punkers who take over gutted houses in suburban Los Angeles. Lawrence Kasdan's 1992 film, *Grand Canyon*, reframes the issue, reinforcing Robert Reich's notion of the growing chasm between rich and poor in the United States. Tim Burton's fantasy film, *Edward Scissorhands* (1990), looks at suburbanites' reaction to a sweet outsider.

An ethnographic study of an upper-middle-class suburb near New York City (population: about 16,000) argues that suburbanites fear disorder and thus avoid interpersonal conflict. In *The Moral Order of a Suburb* (New York: Oxford University Press, 1988), M. P. Baumgartner claims that these suburbanites produce a superficially peaceful community that—below the surface—seethes with unresolved tensions.

Thirty-five years after William Whyte's *The Organization Man* (New York: Simon and Schuster, 1956), Paul Leinberger, a son of one of the original "organization men," and Bruce Tucker published their study *The New Individualists: The Generation After the Organization Man* (New York: HarperCollins, 1991). They claim that while their parents valued consumption, sociability, and a sales mentality, today's generation values creativity, subjectivity, and the artistic.

Chadds Ford, an elite suburb in Pennsylvania and home of painter Andrew Wyeth, is the focus of John D. Dorst's *The Written Suburb* (Philadelphia: University of Pennsylvania Press, 1989). Dorst argues that the suburb's institutions devote great energy to creating a historical identity for the site.

By the early 1990s, scholarship (most of it interdisciplinary) on the new postsuburban form or technoburb started exploding into print. Rob Kling, Spencer Olin, and Mark Poster, eds., *Postsuburban California: The Transformation of Orange County Since World War II* (Berkeley: University of California Press, 1991), is much more than a case study of the form; it develops four central themes—postsuburban spatial organization, information capitalism, consumerism, and cosmopolitanism—to explain the development of the new form. Contributors come from a variety of backgrounds, including demography, history, sociology, computer science, and the law. The impact of new communications technology on restructuring communities, perhaps creating what Marshall McLuhan calls a *global village*, is explored in Manuel Castells, *The Informational City* (Oxford: Blackwell, 1989).

In *The Next American Metropolis* (Princeton, N.J.: Princeton Architecture Press, 1993), architect Peter Calthorpe argues against suburbs and for "neotraditional," small-town grids. Laguna West, a master-planned community outside Sacramento, California, uses his neotraditional principles.

Those interested in telecommuting as a partial answer to transport hassles, congestion, and air pollution will be interested in following work-near-home practices. For example, people can drive a few miles to a telecommuting center in Riverside, California; this center, a satellite office, is financed by businesses and public agencies. Or they can use groupware (software that ties electronic mail to a central memory, assisting people in different locations to work together).

## REFERENCES

Banham, Reyner. [1971] 1976. *The Architecture of Four Ecologies*. New York: Penguin.

Baudrillard, Jean. [1986] 1989. *America*. London: Verso.

Berger, Bennett. [1960] 1971. *Working-Class Suburb*. Berkeley: University of California Press.

Bollens, John, ed. 1961. *Exploring the Metropolitan Community*. Berkeley: University of California Press.

Bott, Elizabeth. 1957. *Family and Social Network*. London: Tavistock.

Brown, George E., Jr. 1993. "Technology's dark side." *Chronicle of Higher Education* (June 30):B1–2.

Calthorpe, Peter. 1993. Interview with Terry Gross on *Fresh Air*, KQED-FM (July 14), 1:05 P.M. PST.

Choldin, Harvey. 1973. "Kinship networks in the migration process." *International Migration Review* 7:163–176.

DeLoughry, Thomas J. 1994. "For the community of scholars, 'being connected' takes on a whole new meaning." *Chronicle of Higher Education* (November 2):A25+.

Fischer, Claude S. 1982. *To Dwell Among Friends: Personal Networks in Town and City*. Chicago: University of Chicago Press.

Fishman, Robert. 1987. *Bourgeois Utopias: The Rise and Fall of Suburbia*. New York: Basic Books.

Flower, Joe. 1994. Comments at "Media After Convergence: Pacific Perspectives." Joint Conference sponsored by The Freedom Forum Pacific Coast Center and The Freedom Forum Media Studies Center at Columbia University in the City of New York. November 4, Oakland, Calif.

Gans, Herbert. [1962] 1982. *The Urban Villagers: Group and Class in the Life of Italian-Americans*. New York: Free Press.

———. 1967. *The Levittowners*. New York: Random House.

Garreau, Joel. 1991. *Edge City: Life on the New Frontier*. New York: Doubleday.

Gergen, Kenneth J. 1991. *The Saturated Self: Dilemmas of Identity in Contemporary Life*. New York: Basic Books.

Goldenberg, Sheldon. 1987. *Thinking Sociologically*. Belmont, Calif: Wadsworth.

Gordon, Richard E. [1960] 1961. *Split Level Trap*. New York: Random House.

Granovetter, Mark. 1973. "The strength of weak ties." *American Journal of Sociology* 78 (May):1360–1380.

Hansen, Gary B., with Marion T. Bentley and Matthew T. Nussbaum. 1986. "Two years later: A follow-up survey of the labor force status and adjustment of workers displaced by the 1983 Ford San Jose assembly plant closure." Unpublished paper (April). Business and Economic Development Services, Utah State University.

Janowitz, Morris. 1952. *The Community Press in an Urban Setting*. Chicago: University of Chicago Press.

Keats, John. 1956. *The Crack in the Picture Window*. Boston: Houghton Mifflin.

Kling, Rob, Spencer Olin, and Mark Poster, eds. 1991. *Postsuburban California: The Transformation of Orange County Since World War II*. Berkeley: University of California Press.

Kuhn, Annette, and AnnMarie Wolpe, eds. 1978. *Feminism and Materialism*. London: Routledge and Kegan Paul.

Laumann, Edward O. 1973. *Bonds of Pluralism*. New York: Wiley.

Leed, Eric J. 1991. *The Mind of the Traveler: From Gilgamesh to Global Tourism*. New York: Basic Books.

Lomnitz, Larissa Adler. 1977. *Networks and Marginality: Life in a Mexican Shantytown*. New York: Academic Press.

MacDonald, John S., and Leatrice D. MacDonald. 1964. "Chain migration, ethnic neighborhood formation and social networks." *Milbank Memorial Fund Quarterly* 42:343–397.

Markoff, John. 1994. "The Frontiers of New Media." Speech delivered at "Media After Convergence: Pacific Perspectives." Joint Conference sponsored by The Freedom Forum Pacific Coast Center and The Freedom Forum Media Studies Center at Columbia University in the City of New York. November 4, Oakland, Calif.

Markoff, John, and Katie Hafner. 1991. *Cyberpunk: Outlaws and Hackers on the Computer Frontier*. New York: Simon and Schuster.

Marquand, John P. 1949. *Point of No Return*. Boston: Little, Brown.

Meyrowitz, Joshua. 1985. "The 19-inch neighborhood." *Newsweek* (July 22):8.

Moore, Judith. 1990. "The way of the WELL." *Monthly* (January):19–21.

Mumford, Lewis. [1938] 1970. *The Culture of Cities*. New York: Harcourt Brace Jovanovich.

Norberg-Schulz, Christian. [1979] 1984. *Genius Loci: Towards a Phenomenology of Architecture*. New York: Rizzoli.

O'Neill, Gerard K. 1977. *The High Frontier: Human Colonies in Space*. New York: Morrow.

Register, Richard. 1987. *Ecocity Berkeley: Building Cities for a Healthy Future*. Berkeley, Calif.: North Atlantic.

Rogers, Everett M., and Judith K. Larsen. 1986. *Silicon Valley Fever: Growth of High-Technology Culture*. New York: Basic Books.

Schnore, Leo F. 1963. "The socio-economic status of cities and suburbs." *American Sociological Review* 28 (February):76–85.

Simmel, Georg. [1922] 1955. *Conflict and the Web of Group Affiliations*. Trans. Kurt Wolff and Reinhard Bendix. New York: Free Press.

Stack, Carol. 1975. *All Our Kin: Strategies for Survival in a Black Community*. New York: Harper & Row.

Sternlieb, George, Robert W. Burchell, and Lynne Sagalyn, with Richard M. Gordon. 1971. *The Affluent Suburb*. New York: Dutton.

Stilgoe, John R. 1989. *Borderland: Origins of the American Suburb, 1820–1939.* New Haven, Conn.: Yale University Press.

Stoll, Clifford. 1995. *Silicon Snake Oil: Second Thoughts on the Information Highway.* New York: Doubleday.

Tessler, Ray. 1989. "Milpitas outgrows the jokes." *San Francisco Chronicle* (February 14):A2.

Thompson, William Irwin. 1978. *Darkness and Scattered Light.* Garden City, N.Y.: Doubleday, Anchor.

Weiss, Michael J. 1988. *The Clustering of America.* New York: Harper & Row.

Wellman, Barry. 1979. "The community question: The intimate networks of East Yorkers." *American Journal of Sociology* 84 (March):1201–1231.

Whyte, William H. 1956. *The Organization Man.* New York: Simon and Schuster

Wilson, Sloan. 1955. *The Man in the Gray Flannel Suit.* New York: Simon and Schuster.

Wuthnow, Robert. 1994. *Sharing the Journey: Support Groups and America's New Quest for Community.* New York: Free Press.

# PART III
# Pluribus versus Unum

*Richard Steven Street*

*Dorothea Lange*

# CHAPTER 8
# Movin' On

Americans are always moving on.
It's an old Spanish custom gone astray,
A sort of English fever, I believe,
Or just a mere desire to take French leave,
I couldn't say. I couldn't really say.
But when the whistle blows, they go away.
Sometimes there never was a whistle blown,
But they don't care, for they can blow their own
Whistles of willow-stick and rabbit-bone,
Quail-calling through the rain
A dozen tunes but only one refrain,
"We don't know where we're going, but we're on
  our way!"

Stephen Vincent Benet, "Prelude" to *Western Star*

Movin' on is what Americans do all the time. Outsider Alexis de Tocqueville spotted this restlessness as far back as the 1830s: "An American will take up a profession and leave it, settle in one place and soon go off elsewhere." Indeed, nearly one-half of the U.S. population moved from one residence to another in just four years (1985–1989).

Today, moving to the big city—or away from it—is no big deal. A rural Texan can go to Houston and a New Yorker can move to Booneville, California, or Tokyo without feeling totally cut off from family and familiar things. In the United States, Japan, and other mass societies, McDonald's and CNN reach into the backwoods.

Only a tiny minority of rural Americans, including some French-speaking Cajuns living on the edge of Louisiana's bayous, are unfamiliar with urban life. For most Americans, urbanism is a way of life even if they live in Podunk: "The attitudes, behaviors, and cultural patterns of rural areas of the United States are dominated by urban values, urban attitudes, and urban life-styles" (Palen, 1987:12).

Urban culture is spreading worldwide. With the near-global diffusion of Coca-Cola and faxes, farmers outside San Salvador or Kiev would not feel totally out of place in today's cities. How different were the experiences of earlier generations of migrants! Imagine what Tevye the milk-man in *Fiddler on the Roof* might have felt, up-rooted from his East European shtetl and rerooted in New York City, trying to adjust to the rhythms of urban-industrial life.

## MIGRANT EXPERIENCES IN THE UNITED STATES

### The Old Migration

According to iconoclast Gore Vidal, "history is nothing more than the bloody record of the migration of tribes. When the white race broke out of Europe 500 years ago, it did many astounding things all over the globe" (1992:56). One astounding thing it did was to establish settlements in the Americas.

English, Dutch, and other western European settlers came to North America to live on farms and build colonial cities in the seventeenth and eighteenth centuries. Blacks from Africa arrived shortly after the English settlement at James-town, Virginia, in 1619. But it was not until the era of rapid industrialization that mass immigration took place. From the 1840s to the 1910s, about 35 million Europeans fled their plots of land, villages, and *Gemeinschaft*-like communities to resettle in U.S. cities. They came from all over Europe—Sweden, Germany, Ireland, Southern and Eastern Europe. They came from Japan and China too, first to work on the railroads and perform hard labor. Many, perhaps one-third, of all western European immigrants had no intention of staying forever. About one-third of Italian im-migrants, for instance, worked hard for years, scrimped and saved up to buy land in Italy, and then returned "home" (Wyman, 1993).

Mainly peasants and rural folk, most immi-grants were ill-prepared for urban life. They were the uprooted—from rural rhythms, tradi-tional ways of life, and often family. Some were led to believe that they would find streets paved with gold in the New World. Instead, many met hostility and discrimination—or racism, in the case of the Japanese and Chinese.

"No Irish Need Apply" signs greeted Boston's Irish in the 1850s when they searched for work, and ethnic stereotypes were nearly universal. Old-stock Americans accused the "foreign ele-ment" of having "animal pleasures" and a "pig-sty mode of life."

Fear was often pervasive in the nineteenth cen-tury. There was fear of cheap immigrant labor; fear of "inferior races" overwhelming white Anglo-Saxon Protestant (**WASP**) culture; fear of Papism and an international economic conspir-acy; and fear of the unknown.

In 1882, the Chinese Exclusion Act effectively ended Chinese immigration. By the 1920s, all im-migration to the United States was drastically curtailed by new restrictive legislation; the "im-migrant hordes," as critics called them, were shut out.

### Internal Migration

In the 1920s, when immigration from abroad came to a halt, another large-scale migration be-gan: an internal U.S. population shift. Once again the cities served as entry points for rural people—this time, black and white Americans. In terms of numbers, the most significant inter-nal movement was the migration of African-Americans out of the South and into northern and western cities. Between 1910 and 1970, over 6.5 million African-Americans left the South. Of those who remained, many also moved—from rural areas to cities. Today, the majority of African-Americans live in cities.

Since World War I, two kinds of forces have worked to move Americans from the country-side to the city: push and pull. Economic and natural forces (e.g., dust storms) pushed some off

a

**Fig. 8.1** ELLIS ISLAND, GATEWAY TO THE UNITED STATES. (*a*) The Promised Land: European immigrant women and children arrive at Ellis Island, off New York City, around 1907. (*b*) Immigrant Museum: Ellis Island, the first stop for millions of newcomers between 1892 and 1924, is again open to crowds, this time as a museum run by the National Park Service. The museum opened in 1990 in the restored main building. ([*a*] Museum of the City of New York; [*b*] Deborah Mosca)

the land and pulled others into urban areas, more precisely, into what Burgess called the *zone of transition* (Zone II). Southern dirt farmers, displaced by mechanized agriculture or beset by constant poverty, sought economic survival in cities. During the 1930s, Oklahoma whites (disparagingly called "Okies") moved westward when the Dust Bowl engulfed their land.

By World War II, large numbers of people were moving geographically, hoping to move up socially too. Southern blacks and rural whites were drawn to war-related industries in the North and West. Puerto Ricans moved to New York City seeking jobs. Chicanos (Mexicans and Mexican-Americans) and other Latinos in the Southwest came to western cities. Today, most Latinos, like most African-Americans, live in cities.

## The New Migration

New immigrants overwhelmingly trace their heritage to Asia or Latin America. As Figure 8.3 shows, in the years 1981 to 1990, over 88 percent of all legal newcomers were non-European. (But in 1991, for the first time in over twenty years, European immigrants topped the list of newcomers. The greatest number—56,839—came

b                                    **Fig. 8.1**   (*continued*)

from the former Soviet Union, reflecting changed U.S. immigration rules regarding Christians and Jews suffering religious persecution.)

The new migration started in the 1960s after U.S. immigration laws changed. From 1968 to 1990, about 14 million people immigrated to the United States (10 million legally and approximately 4 million illegally).

While old immigrants were mainly penniless European peasants, new non-European immigrants had a variety of backgrounds, from "first generation millionaires and top-flight engineers and scientists . . . to destitute refugees and undocumented workers" (Espiritu and Light, 1991:42). Some newcomer groups, particularly from India and Taiwan, tend to be predominantly college-educated, high-status, urban professionals (Table 8.1).

Even amid economic recession and high rates

of unemployment, 810,635 legal immigrants settled in the United States in one year, 1992; more than 704,000 legal newcomers came the year before (*Los Angeles Times*, 1993:A6). In addition, an estimated 200,000 to 300,000 illegal immigrants risked suffocation, drowning, disease, and virtual enslavement to come through the so-called Golden Door annually. California is the chief destination for many newcomers, both legal and illegal: A total of 336,663 foreign nationals made their home in California in 1992, and the state's population rose about 2.2 percent a year from 1980 to 1992, a rate higher than that of India or Indonesia (Kershner, 1993a:A1).

What brings these newcomers in such great numbers—numbers that rival those of some of the peak years of the 1900 to 1910 decade, when a record 8.2 million European immigrants arrived at Ellis Island? Not unemployment or destitu-

a

b

**Fig. 8.2** THE PEOPLE LEFT BEHIND. Badlands, dust storms, and rural poverty pushed people off the land in the 1930s, and the hope of economic survival pulled many to the city. (*a*) Dust storm, Cimarron County, Oklahoma, 1936. (*b*) Rural poverty near Wadesboro, North Carolina, 1938. (*c*) Southern sharecropper family. (Library of Congress: [*a*] Arthur Rothstein; [*b*] Post Wolcott; [*c*] Walker Evans)

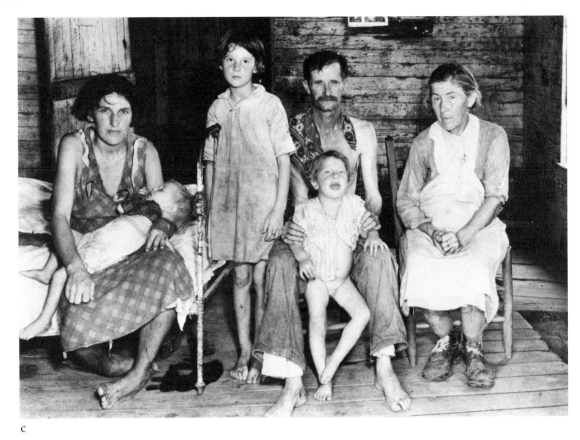

c

**Fig. 8.2**  (*continued*)

tion. Generally, people at the bottom of the income distribution in the sending country do not migrate; they lack the resources. (There are important exceptions, notably those who pay off their illegal passage by enslaving themselves for years to smuggling gangs.) Both push and pull factors—religious persecution and political upheaval in the homeland, changed U.S. immigration laws, low-wage industrial jobs in the United States associated with global economic restructuring, and family reunification—contribute to the new immigration. In addition, a few come to commit acts of terrorism in the receiving country. But, according to Portes and Rumbaut, the basic

reason for the new migration is hope: "the gap between life aspirations . . . and the means to fulfill them in the sending countries" (1990:12).

Most new immigrants, including undocumented workers, come from cities and settle in cities, particularly the largest ones. Since the 1960s, from one-quarter to one-third of all immigrants settled in just a handful of cities: New York (which remains the preferred site of arrival) and Los Angeles, Chicago, or Miami. This spatial concentration of immigrants is linked to economic and political factors, particularly the global restructuring of work that dislocates people in their home countries and creates a demand for

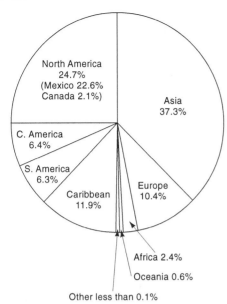

North America
24.7%
(Mexico 22.6%
Canada 2.1%)

Asia
37.3%

C. America
6.4%

S. America
6.3%

Caribbean
11.9%

Europe
10.4%

Africa 2.4%

Oceania 0.6%

Other less than 0.1%

**Fig. 8.3** NEW AMERICANS.
NOTE: It is estimated that about 200,000 persons enter the United States illegally annually. (SOURCE: U.S. Immigration and Naturalization Service)

**Fig. 8.4** GIVE ME YOUR TIRED, YOUR POOR . . .
Historically, European immigrants came to the United States to escape famine, political oppression, landlessness, and religious persecution. This tradition continues in the twentieth century. Nazi Germany's most renowned emigrant, Albert Einstein, is shown here taking the oath of citizenship with his stepdaughter in a Trenton, New Jersey, courtroom, October 1, 1940. (Peter C. Marzio, National Archives)

them across national borders in large headquarters' cities such as New York and Los Angeles.

Still, new immigrants are settling in small towns too. Take, for example, Garden City, Kansas. Literally in mid-America (it lies halfway between the Atlantic and the Pacific), Garden City is "a cow town in the short grass and sand-sage prairie of southwest Kansas" (Sontag, 1993:1). Its Main Street and downtown buildings reflect the recent influx of immigrants from Mexico and

Southeast Asia, many of whom work at a local meatpacking plant, a tortilla factory, a Laotian market renting Thai videos, and a Vietnamese-run karaoke bar. Remarking on this multiculturalism, a Garden City schoolteacher says, "We've become a little New York City in the land of Dorothy, Toto and Auntie Em" (in Sontag, 1993:1).

## Some Impacts of the Newcomers

If current population trends continue, so-called minorities will be the numerical majority in the

**TABLE 8.1** Immigrants' Employment, 1985–1987

| All U.S. Workers | Immigrants |
|---|---|
| 24% Managerial/professional | 25% |
| 31% Technical, sales, administration | 16% |
| 12% Production, craft, and repair | 12% |
| 16% Operators and laborers | 22% |
| 13% Service occupations | 20% |
| 3% Agriculture | 5% |

SOURCE: Vlae Kershner, "Calculating the Cost of Immigration: It Saps State Funds, but Helps Farms, Business," *San Francisco Chronicle* (June 23, 1993):A6.

Box 8.1

## A POTPOURRI OF MIGRANT MEMORIES

### The Uprooted

Over 56 million immigrants walked through the "Golden Door" from 1820 to 1991. Inside the United States, millions more migrated from South to North and from East to West. How did they feel about their old lives and new starts? Here are some remembrances.

### Dreams of America

Sitting in nineteenth-century Plotzk or Kiev, what did future emigrants think life in America would mean? Mary Antin, an East European Jewish immigrant who arrived in 1889, gives us an inkling:

America was in everybody's mouth. Businessmen talked of it over their accounts; the market women made up their quarrels that they might discuss it from stall to stall . . . children played at emigrating; old folks shook their sage heads over the evening fire, and prophesied no good for those who braved the terrors of the sea . . . all talked of it, but scarcely anyone knew one true fact about this magic land. (Antin, 1899:11)

### Stark Realities

Once here, "this magic land" turned into something else: sweatshops, tenements, and discouragement. Social reformer Jacob Riis describes a typical situation in New York City's seventh ward around 1890:

There were nine in the family: husband, wife, an aged grandmother, and six children; honest, hard-working Germans, scrupulously neat, but poor. All nine lived in two rooms, one about ten feet square that served as parlor, bedroom, and eating-room, the other a small hail-room made into a kitchen. . . . That day, the mother had thrown herself out of the window, and was carried up from the street dead. She was "discouraged," said some of the other women from the tenement. ([1890] 1970:41)

### From Dust Bowl to Peach Bowl

When the Dust Bowl hit during the Depression, some farmers in the Southwest traded their land for a Ford and headed west. They arrived in California hungry and broke, eating "tater stew so thin you could read a magazine right through it." Soon the Dust Bowl refugees were part of the Peach Bowl, wandering the open highways as migrant field labor.

The Dust Bowl refugees' plight has been celebrated in song and story. John Steinbeck's saga, *The Grapes of Wrath* ([1939] 1972), follows the Joad family to California, which did not turn out to be the promised land after all.

### Harlem: Seventh Heaven

At age sixteen, Malcolm X took a railroad job, mainly to visit Harlem. Here is how he remembers his first look at "This world . . . where I belonged":

Up and down along and between Lenox and Seventh and Eighth Avenues, Harlem was like some technicolor bazaar . . . combed not only the bright-light areas, but Harlem's residential areas from best to worst, from Sugar Hill up near the Polo Grounds, down to the slum blocks of old rat-trap apartment houses, just crawling with everything you could mention that was illegal and immoral. Dirt, garbage cans . . . drunks, dope addicts, beggars. Sleazy bars, store-front churches with gospels being shouted inside, "bargain" stores, hockshops, undertaking parlors. Greasy "home-cooking" restaurants . . . barbershops advertising conk experts. Cadillacs, secondhand and new . . . Harlem was Seventh Heaven! (Haley and Malcolm X, [1964] 1966:74–76)

### Forced Migration

This haiku by Sankuro Nagano reflects the irony of the Japanese-American internment camp experience in the land of "freedom":

> Against the New Year sky,
> Beyond the fence flutters
> The Stars and Stripes
> (in Hosokawa, 1969:359)

### Aztec Heritage of Migration

After Mexico City, Los Angeles is the largest Mexican city in the world. As the capital of *La Raza*, says Stan

Steiner, Los Angeles "is to the Mexicans what Boston has been to the Irish and New York City has been to the Jews" (1970:141). The heart of Los Angeles's Chicano population is the barrio (Spanish, originally meaning "neighborhood," later "native quarter" under colonial rulers). The barrio is a city within a city— a collection of urban villages, each with its own character, shrines, village patriarchs, gangs, and history.

Actor-movie director Luis Valdez (*La Bamba*) says that Mexicans have a long tradition of migration, one that is rooted in the legend of the founding of Mexico: The sun and war god of the Aztec's ancestors forecast that if his people migrated south, they would establish a powerful kingdom. According to Valdez,

In that march [the sun and war god] prophesied that the children would age and the old would die, but their grandchildren would come to a great lake. In that lake they would find an eagle devouring a serpent, and on that spot they would begin to build a great nation. The nation was Aztec Mexico. (in Steiner, 1970:130)

Of more recent migrations, Valdez syas that "we put our old history on wheels of jalopies. Culture of the migrants! It is nothing but our Aztec heritage of migrations, mechanized" (132).

### Freedom, Work, Family, and Hope

America's cities remain the most popular destination of the world's recent immigrants. What are the chief pulls? Here is what a few new immigrants say:

Bryony Schwan, born in Zimbabwe:

Coming to this country, I was amazed at the political freedom, the ability to speak out—that's why I wanted to become a U.S. citizen.

Le Xua, a political refugee from Vietnam:

I loved my country and didn't want to leave my motherland, because my ancestors are buried there and also because I had to leave my brothers and sisters behind. But living conditions . . . became impossible. . . . So we came here for freedom, but we also found that life is easier here than it was in Vietnam.

Mariya Kovaleva, a Pentecostal Christian from Ukraine:

We felt like we couldn't practice our faith because people discriminated against us. . . . [I]n the United States . . . we can go to church and practice our religion without discrimination. (in Holmstrom, 1992:10–11)

Roda Mohammed, political refugee from Somalia:

Before, in Mogadishu, I was just happy if my sisters would not be killed. Now [that we are all in America], one can be a teacher and another a model. I have high hopes for all of them. (interviewed on *All Things Considered*, National Public Radio, July 3, 1992)

ten largest cities in the United States within one generation. In the United States as a whole, guestimates are that by 2089, the majority of Americans will trace their heritage to groups other than white Europeans. This demographic shift is happening sooner in California: by 2003, **ethnic** and racial *minorities* will constitute a *majority* of the state's population. What this means for politics, culture, and everyday urban life is not clear. The response of urban institutions and groups is one important factor, particularly in hard economic times. Much also depends on the political leadership developed within ethnic communities and possible coalitions or conflicts.

Nationwide, two things are already clear. First, more voters and politicians are listening to groups lobbying to restrict immigration. Often, the anti-immigration voices cross liberal–conservative lines. Second, the recent influx of Asian and Latino immigrants has changed the long-standing bipolar model of race relations in the United States, away from black and white to much more complex multiethnic models. For example, Latinos will number 39 million by 2010, surpassing African-Americans as the nation's largest minority if current immigration levels continue (Passel and Edmonston in Barringer, 1992:E2).

## FROM ELLIS ISLAND TO LAX

### Adjustments to Urban Life

Few generalizations can be made concerning migrants' responses to urban life in the United States. Some felt lost in the American city, overwhelmed with longing for the structure and order of rural life, whether in the Old Country or the American countryside. Others relished the fast tempo, the opportunities to get ahead, and the chance to break away from domineering in-laws.

Such factors as ethnic background, religion, social class, the health of the local and global economy, and time of arrival in the city influence how migrants respond to U.S. urban life. For instance, eastern and southern Europeans arriving before 1920 came at the "right" time. At least some of these uprooted rural folk, or their children, could begin at the bottom of the socioeconomic ladder and move up as the country grew economically and prospered. In other words, the American dream did in fact work for many of these early immigrant families. Starting in the slums and sweatshops pictured in Jacob Riis's 1890 photos, many children or grandchildren of the European immigrants moved up and out. But those who arrived in the city at a later date, especially Appalachian whites and African-Americans from the South, came at the "wrong" time. Social mobility has been more difficult in recent decades due to structural changes in the economy, technological innovation, and—in the case of blacks—institutionalized racism. Unskilled jobs, once the point of entry for moving up, now tend to be dead ends. Few, if any, janitors become corporate board members.

African-Americans faced overwhelming obstacles. Their chances for economic advancement and social equality after 1920 were limited by segregation and discrimination, exclusion from many labor unions, and chronic injustice—all legal until the 1950s and 1960s. Desegregation laws, civil rights acts, affirmative action, and oth-er public policies aimed at creating equal opportunities have not yet significantly improved the life chances of most African-Americans. Like Native Americans and Latinos, they remain disproportionately poor and outside the mainstream of the U.S. economy.

Some scholars, notably William Julius Wilson (1978, 1987), argue that class—not race or racism—is now the key variable explaining African-American and Latino impoverishment. Wilson says that the mass of African-American workers constitute a permanent "underclass" due to changes in the macro-economic structure, particularly deindustrialization. But others (e.g., Bullard and Feagin, 1991) name race or racism, not class, as the *major* contributor to black poverty. And some scholars seem to vacillate on which is more important, class or race/ethnicity. For example, in 1981, sociologist Stephen Steinberg wrote a book whose title announced his viewpoint: *The Ethnic Myth.* At that time, Steinberg said that "class difference is far more important than the fact of ethnic difference" (170). A decade later, he had second thoughts. In 1992 Steinberg named "racism, which, still pervades the occupational world, especially in the service sector" (744), as a key factor in the making of the African-American underclass. Many respected social scientists agree, including political scientist Andrew Hacker (1992). Cornel West stated this viewpoint most succintly in his book title: *Race Matters* (1993).

To illustrate the role that ethnicity can play in immigrants' adjustment to urban America, let's look at two sets of newcomers, old migrants to New York City who entered through Ellis Island and new migrants to Los Angeles, many of whom landed at Los Angeles Airport (LAX). First, the old immigrants: Irish Catholics and East European Jews.

### Irish Catholics and East European Jews in New York City

The Irish started arriving after a potato famine in the Old Country during the 1840s. Waves of Russian, Romanian, and other East European Jews flocked to the New World after 1881; many were refugees, victims of pogroms like the one that struck Tevye's village in *Fiddler on the Roof*.

According to a descendant of Irish Catholic immigrants, Senator Daniel Patrick Moynihan (in Glazer and Moynihan, 1963), the Irish brought from rural Ireland certain habits of mind that influenced their reaction to U.S. city life: experience with mass politics; suspicion of legal niceties; indifference to proprieties such as not stuffing ballot boxes; a capacity for political bureaucracy; a preference for informal over formal political institutions; and pride in taking orders from a chain of command (starting with an oligarchy of stern elders). These qualities, Moynihan says, were easily transferred from the Irish countryside to U.S. city politics. Eventually, they led to Irish control over machine politics from the early 1870s to the 1930s in New York City and elsewhere. However, this political power didn't lead to control in the private business sector or to a push for social change. According to Moynihan, "the Irish did not know what to do with power once they got it" (in Glazer and Moynihan, 1963:229). Hence, they were "immensely successful" in politics, "but the very parochialism and bureaucracy that enabled them to succeed [there] prevented them from doing much with government" or using their political base to gain economic power.

The experience of the East European Jews was very different. Unlike the Irish in Ireland, East European Jews had long been a minority group within a larger hostile culture. While the Irish and many other immigrant groups came to America with one culture, "the Jews came with two, and frequently more than two cultures" (Sherman, 1965:122–123). Thus the Jews didn't need to get used to minority group status, which sapped so much of the energy of other immigrant groups.

Further, the East European Jews had chosen a "loose pattern for their collective existence" (Howe, 1976), whereas the Irish community tended to be more clannish. Most immigrant Jews wanted to keep their separate cultural life. At the same time, they did not depend on their ethnic ties to enter American social and economic institutions; this they did on an individual basis.

While the Irish Catholics used their communal experience in the sphere of city politics, the East European Jews channeled their energies into the professions and business (although most first-generation immigrants were manual laborers and factory workers). The Jews had long been dependent on the sufferance of potential pogrom makers and Jew haters. Working for themselves—not joining the corporate bureaucracy—meant that they didn't have to depend on "the good will or personal reaction of a person who may not happen to like Jews. . . . The American Jew tries to avoid getting into a situation where discrimination may seriously affect him [or her]" (Glazer, 1958:140).

Other important ethnic differences also affected the response of the two groups to U.S. urban life. For one thing, by the turn of the twentieth century, political dissent—especially socialism—had become a "vigorous strand within [Jewish] immigrant life" (Howe, 1976:287). For various reasons, this didn't happen in the Irish-American community. For another thing, the two groups developed into distinct subcultures based on world views, values, and religious doctrines. The East European Jewish subculture, as Glazer and Moynihan put it, is "secular in its attitudes, liberal in its outlook on sexual life and divorce, positive about science and social science," and passionate about education. Irish Catholics, by contrast, remain religious in their outlook, resist liberalized sexual mores, and strongly feel the "tension between moral values and modern science and technology" (1963:298).

These differences show up in many areas, from choice of occupation to participation in civic activities. For instance, the Jews' positive attitude toward modern science is reflected in the fact that "new disciplines such as psychoanalysis, particularly in New York, are . . . largely staffed by Jews" (Glazer and Moynihan, 1963:298).

One might think that over the generations these differences would become less important and that the values of the two groups would grow more alike. Not so, say Glazer and Moyni-

**Fig. 8.5**   THE LOWER EAST SIDE. (*a*) Hester Street: East European Jews lived on New York City's Lower East Side, the city's most densely populated area in the 1890s. One of the neighborhood's most crowded spots was Hester Street, where almost anything could be purchased from pushcarts and where new arrivals would line up, waiting for employers looking for cheap labor. Joan Micklin Silver's sentimental film about the assimilation process, *Hester Street* (1975), focuses on two young Russian Jewish immigrants' different adjustments to New York City in 1896: one rejects the past, the other rejects the present. (*b*) 97 Orchard Street: Once a six-story tenement that housed immigrants straight off the boat, this building is now part of the Lower East Side Tenement Museum. Scholars are trying to identify each of its approximately 7,000 residents from 1863 to 1939, including waves of Germans, East European Jews, Sephardic Jews, Irish, and lastly, Italians in the 1920s. The project is one of relatively few *urban* historic preservations amid preserved log cabins, antebellum mansions, and other rural sites. ([*a*] Library of Congress; [*b*] Martin Gorosh)

han. They argue that over the passing decades, the values and attitudes of Irish Catholics and East European Jews have grown farther apart.

Looking at five ethnic groups in New York City—the Irish, East European Jews, Puerto Ricans, Italians, and African-Americans—Glazer

and Moynihan conclude that race and ethnicity are significant, often independent, variables affecting city life. In their estimation, "Ethnicity is more than an influence on events; it is commonly the source of events. Social and political institutions do not merely respond to ethnic interests; a

b

great number of institutions exist for the specific purpose of serving ethnic interests" (1963:310).

Note that a number of distinguished social scientists disagree with Glazer and Moynihan, at least for white ethnics. Herbert J. Gans, for one, thinks that race and ethnicity are no longer important determinants of social life and politics for most whites (Euro-Americans). Gans's views will be detailed in the next chapter. First, let's consider two groups of new immigrants in Los Angeles and another group of immigrants who transformed Miami: the Cubans.

## Chicanos and Koreans in Los Angeles

According to two political scientists:

Los Angeles is a concept, an idea of what is both right and wrong about urban living; a commodity to be sold in the circuit of capital; a youthful vision that teases our desire for immortality; and a smothering, hot nightmare of social gridlock. But perhaps most of all, the City of Angels is an unsettling vision of our future. (Riposa and Dersch, 1992:vii)

A significant part of that future concerns immigrants.

In terms of tracking immigrants, future researchers have an advantage over us. By 2020, analysts will have a better idea of how various new immigrant groups adjusted to life in the Los Angeles metropolitan area. Now we can look only at a freeze frame of new immigrants in the new immigrant mecca.

In population, Los Angeles is the second largest city in the United States, located in a sprawl-ing county that encompasses 4,070 square miles. After New York City, it is also America's second *world city*: a city that has become like an entire world. Los Angeles is the new Ellis Island or, as UCLA urban geographer Edward W. Soja puts it, "the only place on earth where all places are."

Soja notes an irony: Los Angeles has long been ignored as bizarre or exceptional, but paradox-ically, "more than any other place," Los Angeles has "become the paradigmatic window through which to see the last half of the twentieth centu-ry" (1989:221). Writing about the globalization of Los Angeles, Soja continues:

Los Angeles has become an entrepot [warehouse] to the world, a true pivot of the four quarters, a congeries of east and west, north and south. And from every quar-ter's teeming shores have poured a pool of cultures so diverse that contemporary Los Angeles represents the world in connected urban microcosms, reproducing *in situ* the customary colours and confrontations of a hun-dred different homelands. (1989:223)

Los Angeles's diverse and colorful "pool of cultures" representing "the world" is recent. In-deed, in just one decade, 1980 to 1990, Los An-geles experienced a population transformation. In 1980, the Los Angeles metropolitan area was mainly white, or "Anglo." By 1990, the U.S. cen-sus shows that there were no ethnic majorities: the city was about 40 percent Hispanic, 37 per-cent non-Hispanic white, 13 percent African-American, and 10 percent Asian. Spanish is the primary foreign language spoken there, but within the Los Angeles Unified School District, some 160,000 students speak more than ninety languages, from Afrikaans and Amharic to Urdu, Yoruba, and Yiddish.

Central to understanding Los Angeles's new status and its rapid transformation are two con-nected factors: (1) its role in the world economy and (2) massive immigration. Following in New York City's footsteps, Los Angeles is emerging as a *headquarters city* (Logan and Molotch's term; see Chapter 4): a command post of the inter-national economic system. New immigrants—semi- and unskilled labor plus professionals and

managers—are attracted to jobs in Los Angeles's headquarters economy of manufactured prod-ucts, services, and financial goods. This mix of high- and low-income jobs has social and spatial impacts: a bipolar income distribution and resi-dences segregated into rich and poor areas.

Los Angeles's role of headquarters city or **global city** (Sassen's term, 1991) has been evolv-ing for years. Edward Soja notes that for most of the twentieth century, Los Angeles has been one of the most "superprofitable industrial growth poles in the world economy." In the decade 1970 to 1980, the region's total population grew by 1,300,000 and the number of nonfarm wage workers increased by 1,315,000, making the Los Angeles region "the world's largest job ma-chine," a position it continued to hold in the 1980s (192). By 1987, southern California, a five-county urban region centered on the city of Los Angeles, had a regional economic product larger than the gross national product of all but ten countries (Soja, 1989:191).

The Los Angeles region was the world's larg-est "job machine" up to the late 1980s. That was before the end of the Cold War and massive un-employment in defense industries, economic re-cession, earthquakes, wildfires, riots, an upsurge in the rate of serious crime, and the loss of tourist dollars hit the area particularly hard. Still, Los Angeles has been the most common U.S. destina-tion for both Mexicans and Koreans.

*Chicanos* First, let's consider Mexican immi-grants in Los Angeles, starting with the name game: There is no agreement on which name to use—Hispanic, Latino, or Chicano—and the dis-tinction is not always clear. Here I use *Chicanos* to mean only Mexicans and Mexican-Americans. (The broader term *Latinos* refers to Latin Ameri-cans in the United States of any national or racial background. *Hispanic* is the federal government's term, referring to the language community of Spanish-speaking people from all racial/ethnic backgrounds. Hence, Cuban-born singer Gloria Estefan is Latina and/or Hispanic. The late Arizona-raised farmworkers' organizer, Cesar Chavez, was Chicano, Latino, and/or Hispanic.

Spanish heritage, Filipino-born, Stanford University sociologist Francisco Ramirez is Hispanic but not Chicano or Latino.)

In Los Angeles, the community of Chicanos is composed of old-timers as well as newcomers. At the time of the U.S. war with Mexico (1846–1847), there were at least 80,000 Mexicans in territory that the United States later annexed, probably 20,000 of these in California. In the decade 1970 to 1980, the city of Los Angeles's Chicano population increased 57.3 percent as a result of immigration from Mexico (compared with only a 5.5 percent increase in the city's total population). By 1990, there were 925,141 Chicanos in Los Angeles.

In one year, 1987, 21 percent of all Mexican immigrants chose Los Angeles as their stateside destination. In part, this choice is a matter of high wages attracting poor workers. Employers actively recruited Mexican workers to fill low-wage jobs in the United States at various times in this century, particularly when Mexico was undergoing agricultural underemployment or factory unemployment. Traditionally, emigration from Mexico has appealed particularly to young, propertyless males with a growing family (Massey, 1987:1373, 1399). But recently, more female immigrants from Mexico have come to Los Angeles as cheap labor, filling jobs in the expanding low-wage industrial sector (Morales and Ong, 1991).

Mexican migration to the Los Angeles region is also a matter of preexisting social networks or "migration chains": older migrants from the same Mexican community link newcomers to jobs with U.S. employers and labor contractors (Massey, 1987:1374). For low-wage workers without money, college education, or technical skills —and over 70 percent of Chicanos were low-wage workers in the late 1980s—migration chains are the most important factor in determining where to locate. (In contrast, professionals depend much less on the help of ethnic-based migration chains. No national group is composed only of professionals and their kin, but a few, such as East Indian immigrants, have high percentages of professionals; they tend to rely more on their own skills than on migration chains, and they tend to

disperse spatially, both within a metropolitan area and within the country as a whole [Portes and Rumbaut, 1990:41, 33]. For example, in Los Angeles, the high-income, highly educated Iranian population is widely dispersed [Sabagh and Light, 1985].)

Once in Los Angeles, how have Mexican-Americans been treated? Historically, they met pervasive and blatant hostility from police, discrimination by employers and public officials, and paternalism by Anglo church leaders. During World War II, ethnic hatred erupted in the so-called Zoot Suit Riots in 1942 and reerupted in 1943 when aggression against young Chicano males by sailors and military police resulted in a reign of terror. The Los Angeles sheriff justified Chicanos' mass arrests by saying that their "desire to kill, or at least let blood" was an "inborn characteristic" (in Steiner, 1970:233). Further, Chicanos were barred from learning trades in defense plants and faced discrimination in public schools. Symbolizing the dominant white attitude toward them, Chicanos were allowed to swim in public pools only on days just prior to pool cleaning (Daniels, [1990] 1991:chap.12).

Since the 1940s, some blatant forms of economic oppression and cultural discrimination have been mitigated, but the Chicano community in Los Angeles still suffers from "its generally disadvantaged status" (Daniels, [1990] 1991:317) and negative stereotypes. For example, during the riots following the trial of four white policemen for the beating of a motorist, Rodney King, when live television cameras showed people looting, KABC anchor Paul Moyer asked the on-the-spot reporter, "Tell me, do these people look like illegal aliens?" The reporter responded, "Yes, they do, Paul." This image of Chicanos as lawless aliens—who can be detected merely by looking at them—is not countered by positive media images. On the contrary: Except for civil disturbances, Chicanos and other Latinos—who compose nearly one-quarter of California's residents—are nearly invisible in the mass media (Reynolds, 1992:12).

Media neglect adds to Chicano and Latino frustration and anger. According to a law professor at Stanford University, these groups see themselves as a "forgotten" population (Lopez in Espinosa, 1992:1).

Beginning with modest resources and social origins and facing discrimination, most Chicanos have few chances to "make it" by two common routes: working at a high-paid, professional-managerial job or owning a business. The proportion of Chicanos in professional-managerial jobs is low, and Mexico is the primary source of immigrant cheap labor in the United States. In 1990, the poverty rate among Mexican-Americans nationwide soared to 28 percent.

To date, Chicanos in Los Angeles have not participated fully in politics or education. Only a handful hold local elected office. They also have a low participation rate in education: In 1980 only 3 percent of Los Angeles's Chicanos over twenty-five years old had completed four years of college, and only 21.3 percent had completed high school. In part, this reflects the persistent use of Spanish among Chicanos, who tend to live in ethnic enclaves (barrios) such as East Los Angeles and have access to widespread Spanish-language media. Perhaps this also reflects a lack of organization directed to social change. For example, Chicano parents long thought that the Anglo-run parochial school system was racist and physically abusive toward their children, but rarely did they join protest groups or sue the Catholic archdiocese. In 1982, some of them did organize and sue, but during the 1980s and early 1990s, more showed their dismay in a mass exodus from Catholicism, converting mostly to evangelical sects run by Latino ministers (Davis, 1992:338).

Ironically, the election of conservative Republican businessman Richard Riordan as Los Angeles's mayor in 1993 may usher in an era of Latino political empowerment. In a plot twist worthy of Scott Turow, it turns out that the Catholic Church's cardinal in Los Angeles, Roger Mahony (once known as "Red Roger" for his advocacy on behalf of illegal immigrants and farm workers), has forged a close working relationship with Riordan, an Irish-American millionaire who helped the Los Angeles Catholic diocese professionalize its business management (Critser, 1993:4). A Riordan–Mahony alliance in gov-ernment may mean a deeper Chicano voice and vote.

Chicano community organizations fight discrimination, disadvantage, and exploitation in various ways. Some, like the Mexican-American Political Association (MAPA) and the United Mexican American Students (UMAS), use legal tactics to protect community members. Other organizations, notably gangs, use extralegal tactics. According to Martín Sánchez Jankowski, chair of the Chicano/Latino Policy Project at the University of California at Berkeley, gangs represent a form of local patriotism: "the gang member's strong identification with his community is . . . an expression of his patriotism toward his neighborhood and the lower-class ethnic groups who live there" (1991:199–200). Chicano gangs in Los Angeles, Jankowski says, provide a *Gemeinschaft*-like brotherhood; many members are kinfolk or treat one another like family. Pepe, a seventeen-year-old, told sociologist Jankowski that the Royal Dons, his gang, served the community—and themselves:

A lot of people from outside this community wouldn't understand, but we have helped the community whenever they've asked us. . . . [T]he community doesn't mind that we do things to make some money and raise a little hell because they don't expect you to put in your time for nothing. Just like nobody expects guys in the military to put in their time for nothing. (1991:47)

Jankowski notes that gangs in ethnic, poor communities—whether Chicano, Irish, or Jamaican—open up an avenue of upward mobility to low-income young males and provide rites of passage to adulthood, much as the Little League does for boys in more affluent neighborhoods. For Chicanos in ethnic enclaves such as East Los Angeles, gangs are a source of solidarity. Gangs reinforce a distinct ethnic identity and social networks, and they help impoverished newcomers cope with a complex environment.

*To conclude:* At present, the vast majority of Chicanos in Los Angeles are not being acculturated or assimilated. In part, this situation reflects the unique position of Chicanos: More than any other immigrant group, Chicanos can hold on to their ancestral culture because modern communications and geographical proximity enable them to maintain close ties with their country of origin, Mexico. Indeed, some observers predict that Chicanos may evolve into a bicultural, bilingual culture. For one, David Hayes-Bautista, a third-generation Chicano and former head of the Chicano Studies Research Center at the University of California at Los Angeles, predicts that in 100 years Chicanos will not have assimilated in the classic sense; they will still feel Chicano (in Mydans, 1991:A8). And in part, the Chicanos' lack of incorporation into the mainstream reflects their position in general: Most remain a "them" to mainstream Americans—separate and less than equal. As one journalist put it, Mexican-Americans are a group "without a ladder" (Suro, 1992:A1).

Chicano poet Rodolfo Gonzales writes that many Mexican-Americans feel

Lost in a world of confusion
Caught up in the whirl of an Anglo society,
Confused by the rules, Scorned by attitudes
Suppressed by manipulations, And destroyed by
    modern society.

(in Steiner, 1970:240–241).

In this situation, we can predict that Chicano ethnicity will not only survive but thrive, acting as a "valuable tool for the protection or enhancement of status" (Espiritu and Light, 1991:45).

On the surface, Chicanos and Koreans in Los Angeles have a different past and a different probable future. But they share more than what is readily apparent, including mass migrations related to the global economy.

**Koreans**  Los Angeles is now home to the largest Chicano and Korean communities in the United States. Unlike Mexican migration, this happened quickly for Koreans. A handful of Koreans, mostly farm workers, lived in California by World War I, but massive emigration started only in the mid-1960s. These newcomers were mainly middle-class urbanites; about 70 percent of Korean immigrants in Los Angeles came with college degrees in the 1960s (Takaki, 1989:437),

and many were doctors, teachers, and other professionals.

Emigrants left their homeland of South Korea for various push reasons, including military dictatorship, political and religious repression, few educational opportunities, very high population density, and economic dislocation. Sociologists Ivan Light and Edna Bonacich argue that Korean emigrés were pushed out for another reason:

Emigration from South Korea to the United States in the late 1960s and 1970s was causally connected to Korea's involvement in world capitalism. In particular, the economic and political consequences of Korea's role as a producer of cheap manufactured exports led to the dislocation and discontent of certain classes. Those who emigrated derived from these dislocated classes. (1988:124)

In terms of pulls, Korean emigration is intimately tied to U.S. immigration policy. Before 1965, Korea and other Asian countries came under restrictions that started with the Chinese Exclusion Act of 1882; the 1965 immigration law overturned the anti-Asian regulations and dramatically increased Asian immigration to the United States.

Once in Los Angeles, how have the Koreans been treated? That depends mainly on their occupation. Liquor store owners, grocers, and other merchants in South Central Los Angeles were a target of hatred by other minorities during the Rodney King riots. Further, many professionals found limited job opportunities, in part due to cultural and economic discrimination by whites. One survey found that only 35 percent of Korean professionals in Los Angeles were able to enter professional occupations there (Takaki, 1989:440). Seung Sook Myng Lee's story is common: A pharmacist in Korea for ten years, she could not take the licensing exam in California and became a knitting-machine operator in a Los Angeles garment factory, locked into a low-wage job. Others had difficulty getting employment outside the Korean community due to racial discrimination and language barriers.

Most Korean immigrants were not shopkeepers in Korea, but once in America, many opened small businesses. Why? Observers offer different reasons. Some draw a parallel here between self-employed Koreans and other ethnic minorities who cluster in self-employed small businesses rather than large corporations, such as Jews in New York City; in both cases, self-employment serves as a shield against job discrimination by non-coethnics. Other analysts believe that this occupational choice is related to Korean culture, particularly the Confucian ethic of hard work, close-knit families, and inner-directedness. Still others say that they were pushed into self-employment for various reasons, including the lack of professional opportunities noted above. Whatever the reasons, it is ironic that Koreans "had left white-collar jobs in a modernized economy in Korea and had become old-fashioned shopkeeping capitalists in America" (Takaki, 1989:442).

According to *Immigrant Entrepreneurs: Koreans in Los Angeles 1965–1982*, a study by sociologists Ivan Light and Edna Bonacich (1988:24), once in the United States, Korean immigrants have the motive, money, education, and ethnic resources to open and run small business enterprises. Indeed, when these sociologists conducted their content analysis in 1982, the extent of Korean small business ownership in Los Angeles was remarkable: The Yellow Pages of the Korean phone directory listed 4,266 Korean-owned businesses in Los Angeles County. Further, Koreans tend to hire coethnics, so that "about 62 percent of employed Koreans in Los Angeles County were either self-employed or employees of Korean-owned firms, mostly service and retail proprietorships" (1988:3–4).

Typically, entrepreneurial minorities tend to settle in large urban areas that offer close proximity to markets and workers (Portes and Rumbaut, 1990:33), and Koreans are no exception. Typically, Koreans opened small businesses inside the city of Los Angeles, the region's core, at the moment of "white flight." The city of Los Angeles was a slow-growth area compared to the four adjacent counties in the metropolitan area. From 1960 to 1980, the white population of the city of Los Angeles decreased from 71.9 to 44.4 percent, reflecting increased residential segrega-

tion of whites from African-Americans, Asians, and Latinos. White proprietors were abandoning inner-city ghetto neighborhoods, leaving a retail niche for Koreans. It was this void that Korean businesses filled, and many Koreans located their small businesses in ethnic enclave economies such as "Koreatown," a superblock of highly visible, concentrated immigrant entrepreneurship.

Generally, immigrants who own their own businesses earn much more than immigrants who work for wages (Portes and Rumbaut, 1990:73). Thus in most people's minds, it follows that Korean entrepreneurs are more independent than Chicano wage laborers. But Light and Bonacich suggest a different reality. They argue that although many Koreans own their own businesses, they are still economic pawns: "Koreans came to the United States as cheap labor," and "Korean immigrant entrepreneurship was a disguised form of cheap labor utilization by U.S. capitalism" (1988: 27).

How can it be that Korean business owners in Los Angeles are mere pawns? First of all, Light and Bonacich say, Koreans arrive with different expectations and experiences than U.S. workers. For one thing, South Korea has the longest workweek of all industrial nations—nearly 55 hours—almost 41 percent longer than that of the United States (Wolff, Rutten, Bayers, and the World Rank Research Team, 1992:146). Koreans expect to work very long and very hard each day for relatively little money, and they do not expect labor unions or government agencies to protect them. And, much more than the national average, Korean shopkeepers depend on the unpaid labor of spouses and children to earn their living. It is not unusual for Korean small businessmen and their wives to work six days a week without one day of vacation for eight or nine years in order for their children to get ahead. Korean wage laborers work just as long and hard. For example, Jung Sook Kim sewed clothing in a factory while her husband sold fruits and vegetables eleven hours a day in a store owned by a fellow Korean. She said that she came to the United States for "a better life" but found only "work, work, work" (in Takaki, 1989:445). Second, big corporations subcontract work at lower labor costs to small Korean garment factories and firms. Third, Korean small businesses (e.g., service stations, liquor stores, groceries, and real-estate offices) are often franchise businesses located in low-income, ghetto neighborhoods—considered risky both financially and physically by corporate executives. Thus large U.S. corporations that sell the franchises take no risk but penetrate markets that would otherwise be closed to them. In addition, franchisers gain from Korean family members' unpaid labor. In all these ways, Light and Bonacich argue, Korean small businesses provide profits for U.S. corporations.

In their business relations, Koreans—like other ethnic entrepreneurial groups before them—often find themselves in the potentially volatile position of **clientelistic hostility:** Clients of one ethnic group show hostility toward neighborhood vendors of another ethnic background. Spike Lee's 1989 movie, *Do the Right Thing*, dramatizes two instances of clientelistic hostility in the Bedford-Stuyvesant neighborhood of Brooklyn: (1) Sal, an Italian-American pizza parlor owner versus his African-American customers and (2) a Korean small businessman versus his African-American customers. When clients of one ethnic group feel slighted or demeaned by vendors of another ethnic group, contempt and hatred can lie dormant, waiting to explode. Such was the case in Koreatown in 1992. Relations between Korean shopkeepers and their African-American, Chicano, and other Latino clients in Los Angeles exploded, ending in the destruction of more than 2,500 Korean-owned stores during the Rodney King riots.

Light and Bonacich suggest another reason for clientelistic hostility: Ethnic entrepreneurial groups, including Koreans, "tend to draw a tight line around their realm of social responsibility. It ends at the boundary of their ethnic community. With the rest of the world they can act as ruthless competitors" (1988:435). In other words, *they divide the world into "us" and "them" on the basis of ethnicity.* The result, Light and Bonacich claim, is a society where ethnic division is encouraged but class division is ignored: "[B]ecause ethnic entrepreneurship, on the one hand, fosters cross-class

ethnic solidarities instead of cross-ethnic class solidarities, it helps to create an ethnically divided society. On the other hand, it inhibits the development of class conflict by fragmenting the working class along ethnic lines" (434–435).

In the end, Light and Bonacich (1988:435) believe that Korean immigrant entrepreneurs are themselves both victimized and victimizers. Driven from their homeland, suffering hardship, and working extremely long hours, they are "victims of world capitalism" who "help to perpetuate the system that created their own oppression" (435).

***Linkages?*** Earthquakes and mudslides in metropolitan Los Angeles became a metaphor for the region's shifting economic and cultural ground in the 1990s. National recession, the end of the Cold War (which brought a big loss of military-contracting jobs in the Los Angeles region), the civil unrest following the Rodney King verdict, and the loss of tourist dollars had far-reaching and negative impacts on Los Angeles's work force. The aerospace company Hughes Aircraft had been the largest industrial employer in southern California, but jobs in the aerospace industry declined by nearly a third from 1986 to 1992. Plant shutdowns in the 1980s meant unemployment for hundreds of thousands, including over 70,000 blue-collar workers in South Central Los Angeles, the area where the Rodney King uprisings began. (Squeezed by recession, Korean newcomers nationwide started leaving the United States. In 1980, only 2 percent returned to Korea; by 1990, 27 percent returned in a reverse migration.)

At first glance, Korean-Americans and Chicanos in metropolitan Los Angeles appear to share little, aside from vulnerablity to earthquakes and other natural upheavals. After all, they have nothing in common: language, culture, job skills, neighborhood, or educational background. In addition, their rates of business ownership differ widely: In 1980, business ownership as a percentage of group size was 9 percent for Koreans and 1.6 percent for Mexican-Americans nationwide. But perhaps the two seemingly disparate groups are linked. For example, Chicanos once held some of those approximately 70,000 now defunct jobs in South Central Los Angeles and shopped in Korean-owned stores. Moreover, if Light and Bonacich are correct, a significant irony connects Chicanos and Koreans: They share a basic economic relationship—both provide cheap labor for large U.S. corporations.

## THE NEED FOR NEW MODELS

Decades ago, Chicago became a lab for social theorists as European immigrants poured into the City of the Big Shoulders. Researchers at the University of Chicago constructed models charting the immigrants' adaptations to urban-industrial life. Louis Wirth wrote about *The Ghetto* ([1928] 1956) and how its eastern European Jewish residents dispersed over time. E. W. Burgess constructed his well-known zonal model of urban space, hypothesizing a link between immigrants' economic success and their assimilation over time. Burgess's notion of assimilation has been summed up as follows: "[European immigrants] came in, struggled hard, were discriminated against, lived in the ghetto. Eventually they climbed up, their children of the third generation went to a university, they joined the mainstream, and they are now Americans" (Portes in Coughlin, 1993:A11)

Does Burgess's model work for post-1965 immigrants from Latin America and Asia? Are new immigrants following the pattern of earlier immigrants, assimilating as they climb the ladder of economic success? A leading contemporary immigration researcher, Alejandro Portes, thinks not. Indeed, Portes and his colleagues say that at least one group of new immigrants—Cubans in Miami—are turning the old model on its head.

### Cubans in Miami

Just as Chicago once served as a laboratory for the study of eastern and southern European im-

migration, Miami has become a social lab for Latin American immigration. At the forefront of this scholarly interest in the new immigrants are Cuban-born sociologist Alejandro Portes and California-born anthropologist Alex Stepick. In their book *City on the Edge: The Transformation of Miami* (1993), Portes and Stepick say that the city has been transformed by Cuban newcomers, not the reverse: Instead of Cuban immigrants adapting to Miami, Miami adapted to the waves of Cuban immigrants. For example, instead of learning English and picking up American customs and *then* reaping political power and/or economic success—as many European immigrants did before them—Miami's Cubans *first* gained political and economic success and then began to adapt culturally.

As Portes and Stepick tell the city's story, Miami was a southern city founded in 1896. Unlike other U.S. cities of its day (which grew as centers of commerce or transportation or as central places), Miami had natural beauty on its side; it was developed as a tourist and retirement spot simply because it was a lovely site.

Then, in 1959, things started to change quickly. After the Cuban Revolution, groups of privileged Cubans fled to Miami. From 1959 to 1973, 500,000 Cuban refugees came to the city. Typically, these first Cuban immigrants were skilled, educated landowners or businesspeople. Some later moved out of Miami, but a large, occupationally diverse group remained—and prospered.

In large part, the first wave's prosperity was linked to a high degree of social cohesion (what Portes and Stepick call a "bounded solidarity") fueled by anti-Castro politics and a collective image of themselves as exiles waiting to return home. Many became successful in business and helped their compatriots. Some became bankers, granting "character loans" to fellow immigrants on the basis of their reputations alone (instead of the usual economic collateral).

In 1980, the second wave of over 100,000 Cuban immigrants came to Miami by boatlift. These immigrants, the so-called *marielitos* (named after the port of Mariel, Cuba), were less educated, less well-off financially, and less welcome (by both U.S. government officials and numerous first-wave Cubans). Many *marielitos* were black, and they faced prejudice and ostracism from some white Cuban exiles, African-Americans, and black Haitians.

According to Portes and Stepick, 1980 was a turning point for Miami: The *marielitos* arrived, Haitian immigration reached its high point, and African-Americans (many of whom considered themselves twice oppressed, by Cubans as well as by whites) rioted in Liberty City. In addition, the white power structure in 1980 was no longer sure that "they" (Cubans) would turn into "us" (Anglos). By this time, it was becoming clear that the immigrants would not fade into Miami's background and assimilate.

So far, Miami's Cubans have neither faded away nor melted in. Instead, they have maintained an ethnic enclave. And they have played key roles in mainstream politics and economics. Further, in a very short time, they have helped to transform Miami into a bicultural metropolis.

Some observers, including Stepick, claim that Miami is the most internationalized American city. Because in Miami, they say, the rules of the game for newcomers are not dictated by white Protestants. Instead, Miami has undergone a dramatic upsurge of biculturalism (Grenier and Stepick, 1992). Miami's home county, Dade County, is also at the forefront of bicultural issues, notably the effort (opposed by the organization called U.S. English) to include Spanish as well as English as a language of record for some city–county proceedings.

*To conclude:* The case of Cubans in Miami suggests that bicultural living can be an alternative to assimilation in U.S. cities. However, this model may have very limited application. First, there was a critical mass of Cubans and other Spanish speakers; by 1990 metropolitan Miami was 49 percent Hispanic. Second, the first wave of Cubans —united by political ideology and self-image —brought "cultural capital" (education, particular attitudes, and social know-how; see Chapter 10 for a detailed discussion of this concept) that enabled them to surmount many obstacles typically faced by immigrant groups. In other words, Miami may represent a unique case.

Finally, a word on Miami's biculturalism. It is important to note that racial and ethnic tension have not disappeared in Miami. Quite the contrary: "Biculturalism for Latinos has not brought multiculturalism for all ethnic groups . . . [l]east of all for black people" (Zukin, 1993:477).

## ANOTHER LOOK

According to the United Nations' "State of World Population Report," about 2 percent of the world's population—roughly 100 million people—have crossed their country's borders to become international migrants (British Broadcasting Corporation, 1993). Most migration occurs from one poor country to another, but migratory pressures in rich nations are increasing as "the growth of a global economy has emphasized rather than reduced inequality between nations" (in Robinson, 1993:All).

In coming years, demographers predict even greater mass migrations globally. Given economic hard times globally, we can predict that some newcomers to rich, receiving countries will be greeted with distrust or a racist backlash. European nations already face deadly anti-immigrant sentiment, and in the United States many groups seek to limit immigration.

Regarding scholarly work, there is an ongoing debate about immigrants' adjustment to urban America. On the one hand, some theorists see *cultural characteristics* as the primary reason why one group makes it or lags behind. In this view, factors such as family structure, moral values, and attitudes toward time and education lie behind a group's success or failure. Glazer and Moynihan's work, *Beyond the Melting Pot*, and research in the "culture of poverty" tradition exemplify this view. On the other hand, some theorists focus on *structural factors* such as the immigrants' social class backgrounds and role in the global economy. Light and Bonacich's study of Korean immigrant entrepreneurs is exemplary.

Shall never the twain meet? Are structuralists and culturalists doomed to talk past each other? As we shall see in the next chapter, there are fledgling attempts to merge the two traditions of culture and structure, notably by a group of researchers at the University of Chicago headed by sociologist William Julius Wilson.

## KEY TERMS

**Clientelistic hostility**  Hostility triggered by a situation in which neighborhood small businesses are owned by members of one ethnic group and shoppers come from other ethnic groups. Examples: Sal and his Italian family-owned pizza parlor in New York's Bedford-Stuyvesant area, where clients were typically African-American, in Spike Lee's movie, *Do the Right Thing;* animosity toward Korean merchants by other people of color in New York City and Los Angeles.

**Ethnic**  Refers to people with a sense of group identity different from that of other subgroups within a society. Ethnicity can be based on secular or sacred identity, national ancestry, race, or religious background (and, in some observers' view, sexual orientation).

**Global city**  Sociologist Saskia Sassen's term for New York, London, and Tokyo—cities that share comparable economic and social structures as command posts in the sector of international finance and advanced business services in the international economy. Synonym: *headquarters city* (Chapter 4).

**WASP**  Acronym for **W**hite **A**nglo-**S**axon **P**rotestant.

## PROJECTS

1. **Ethnicity.** Determine the two largest ethnic groups in your community. Find out when each group first settled there, where they lived, what work they did, and what institutions they built (e.g., churches, newspapers, private schools, clubs). Trace the changes over time from their arrival until today. Do members of each group cluster together in residential sections? What areas do they live in? What kinds of jobs do they hold now? Are their institutions still viable?

2. **Family history.** Use available research tools—including oral histories of relatives, genealogy charts, library documents, archival materials, and family diaries—to establish your family's ethnic history and consciousness. If Native American, where is your family rooted? If not Native American, when did they arrive here? What type of work did they do upon arrival in this country? What is their occupational profile today? Have family members spread out geographically? If they spoke another language, can your generation speak this language? Are there any regular gatherings (e.g., annual family reunions)? What distinctive ethnic traditions are retained by you? Do most of your friends come from your ethnic background? In what ways, if any, do you feel set apart from members of other ethnic groups?

3. **Immigration, past and present.** Compare and contrast attitudes toward "old" immigrants in the early 1900s and "new" immigrants in the 1990s. Using the method of content analysis, examine the positions and logics of a range of social and political groups (e.g., Dillingham's Immigration Commission, industrialists, labor unions, old-stock patriots, liberals, church and ethnic groups) toward immigrants. Next, analyze the rhetoric describing newcomers (e.g., fear- or hate-filled epithets, terms of endearment).

## SUGGESTIONS FOR FURTHER LEARNING

A growing number of museums are celebrating the immigrant experience. Among the most exciting is the Ellis Island Immigrant Museum, the building where 12 million immigrants landed, now restored.

On New York City's Lower East Side, one tenement where many immigrants first lived is preserved as part of the Lower East Side Tenement Museum. The museum, which gives tours of the restored 1863 tenement, offers a variety of walking tours of the Lower East Side, exhibits and services, including a genealogy service. On the West Coast, the Japanese American National Museum opened in Los Angeles in 1992; its first exhibit documented the experiences of *Issei* pioneers (first-generation immigrants from Japan) from 1885 to 1924. In the Midwest, the Immigration History Research Center at the University of Minnesota in Minneapolis has storerooms of materials on European immigration, including the business records of the Swiss-Italian Sausage Factory in San Francisco and all back issues of the Ukrainian-American newspaper, *Svoboda*.

For an overview of the history of the old immigration to America and immigrants' lives once they settled in the country, see *A Nation of Nations: The People Who Came to America as Seen Through Objects, Prints, and Photographs at the Smithsonian Institution* (New York: Harper & Row, 1976), edited by Peter C. Marzio of the Smithsonian Institution. This handsomely illustrated and designed volume contains short, readable, and frank essays by members of the Smithsonian staff, plus a useful bibliography.

Perhaps the most widely read book on the history of the mass migrations in the nineteenth century remains Oscar Handlin's *The Uprooted* (Boston: Little, Brown, 1952), an impressionistic account with relatively little empirical evidence. Handlin focuses on the loss of the Old World peasant community and the sense of alienation resulting in a new individualism. He makes few distinctions between differential adjustments to urban life among various European immigrant groups.

Scholarly study of the immigrant experience is enhanced by a series published by Arno Press (New York). Multivolume series on the experience of Italian-Americans, the American Catholic tradition, the Puerto Rican experience, the Chicano heritage, and the Chinese and Japanese in North America include literary chronicles as well as social science and personal accounts. Arno Press also publishes two series, called The American Immigration Collection (seventy-four books) and The Reports of the Immigration Commission, popularly known as the Dillingham Reports. This forty-one-volume series, originally published between 1907 and 1910, provides fascinating clues to the legislation enacted between 1917 and 1924 that closed America's gates to immigrants. The Dillingham Reports presented what they felt to be scientific proof of the inferiority of eastern and southern Europeans.

Personal memoirs of immigrants include Mary Antin, *From Plotzk to Boston* (Boston: Clarke,

1899), and Thomas C. Wheeler, ed., *The Immigrant Experience: The Anguish of Becoming American* (New York: Pelican, [1971] 1977). Selections include "A Chinese Evolution" by Jade Snow Wong; "Italians in Hell's Kitchen" by Mario Puzo; and "Norwegians on the Prairie" by Eugene Boe. Sociologist Charles C. Moskos, Jr., recalls his Greek-American family and childhood in Chicago and Albuquerque, New Mexico, in "Growing Up American," *Society*, January–February 1977, pp. 64–71.

One effort to preserve the history of ethnic immigrants in the Boston area is a project under the direction of Carla B. Johnston that has produced a five-tape oral history, a film, and a book that stress the value of the rich ethnic mix of Somerville, Massachusetts.

Internal migration of African-Americans and whites from the South to the North from 1900 to 1950 is detailed in Neil Fligstein's *Going North* (New York: Academic Press, 1981). He concludes that after 1930, the chief reason for both black and white migration north was the transformation of cotton agriculture from a labor-intensive, tenant economy to a capitalist, machine-oriented economy.

In *The Promised Land: The Great Black Migration and How It Changed America* (New York: Knopf, 1991), Nicholas Lemann focuses on African-American migration from the South to Chicago since the 1950s. It describes the impact of the War on Poverty by following specific families north from the sharecropper culture of the Mississippi Delta, creating a tale of three cities: Clarksdale, Mississippi; Washington, D.C.; and Chicago. Among other things, it shows that scholars can influence government policy: University of Chicago sociologists Richard Cloward and Lloyd Ohlin actively contributed in the effort to alleviate ethnic tensions in Chicago and the nation. Author and scholar Gary Wills deems this book "indispensable" for understanding recent African-American history. He puts Taylor Branch's *Parting the Waters* (New York: Simon and Schuster, 1988) in the same category.

Painter Jacob Lawrence chronicles the African-Americans' exodus from the South to northern cities after the World War I. His "Migration Series," a cycle of sixty paintings finished in 1941 when he was twenty-three, traveled to nine U.S. cities in the mid-1990s. A handsome catalog of the traveling exhibition is *Jacob Lawrence: The Migration Series* (Washington, D.C.: Rappahannock Press, 1993).

The plight of rural migrants is told in the works of John Steinbeck, particularly *The Grapes of Wrath* (New York: Viking, [1939] 1972). The movie version of Steinbeck's novel of the Joad family, starring Henry Fonda, appeared in 1940. In his autobiographical account, *Black Boy* (New York: Signet, [1937] 1963), Richard Wright relates his hopes when heading north on a train for Chicago: "With ever watchful eyes and bearing scars, visible and invisible, I headed North, full of a hazy notion that life could be lived with dignity" (285). Wright's early memories of life in Mississippi include the escape from the home of an uncle who had just been lynched by a white mob.

*Harlem on My Mind: Cultural Capital of Black America, 1900–1968* (New York: Random House, 1968) is a compilation of photos and news stories from the life and times of Harlem, including articles on the poetry of social protest in the 1920s, the lure of northern industry to southern blacks, and other aspects of urban black culture.

Michael J. Piore examines the rise of migration from Latin America and the Caribbean to the United States, as well as the process that brought waves of European immigrants to America and blacks to northern cities, in *Birds of Passage* (New York: Cambridge University Press, 1979). Alejandro Portes and Rubén G. Rumbaut's *Immigrant America: A Portrait* (Berkeley: University of California Press, 1990) concentrates on post-1965, non-European migration, paying attention to theory as well as numbers.

In the early 1990s, global migration and transnational identities became popular topics in many disciplines and interdisciplines, from anthropology, ethnic studies, and literary theory to film studies. See, for example, Karen McCarthy Brown's *Mama Lola: A Vodou Priestess in Brooklyn* (Berkeley: University of California Press, 1992). Brown, a professor of sociology and anthropology of religion, traces five generations of voodoo priesthood in Mama Lola's family, from Haiti to Brooklyn, and the mix of Catholic, French, and West African influences in the practical religion of voodoo. See also Maxine L. Margolis, *Little Brazil: An Ethnography of Brazilian Immigrants in New York City* (Princeton, N.J.: Princeton University Press, 1993), which examines the mainly middle-class 80,000 to 100,000 immigrant community in the New York metropolitan area; Constance R. Sutton and Elsa M. Chaney, eds., *Caribbean Life in New York City: Sociocultural Dimensions* (New York: Center for Migration Studies of New York, 1987, 1992); Gay Wilentz, *Binding Cultures: Black Women Writers in Africa and the Diaspora* (Bloomington: Indiana University Press, 1992); Ron Kelley, Jonathan Friedlander, and Anita Colby, eds., *Irangeles: Iranians in Los Angeles* (Berkeley: University of California Press, 1993); and Nina F. Schiller, ed., *Towards a Transnational Perspective on Migration: Race, Class, Ethnicity, and Nationalism Reconsidered* (New York: New York Academy of Sciences, 1992).

Several journals explore immigrant communities and the flow of cultures across national borders. See, in particular, *Public Culture* and *Diaspora: A Journal of Transsnational Studies.*

Organized around the themes of immigration and migration, Wesley Brown and Amy Ling, eds., *Imagining America: Stories from the Promised Land* (New York: Persea Books, 1991), is a multicultural anthology of twentieth-century American fiction. The volume includes short stories by Leslie Marmon Silko, Sandra Cisneros, Alice Walker, and Kim Yong Ik. In his novel, *what the hell for you left your heart in san francisco* (The Philippines: n.p. 1988), Bienvenido N. Santos presents an account of Filipino life in the United States at the beginning of the third wave of immigration (1971–1986). Immigrants fresh from Vietnam, the Caribbean, Europe, Sri Lanka, India, and other places people the short stories of Bharati Mukherjee's collection, *The Middleman* (New York: Grove Press, 1988). In *The Joy Luck Club* (New York: Ivy Books, 1989), novelist Amy Tan tells a tale of four Chinese-born mothers and their American-born daughters, reflecting on cultural and generational conflicts with a sense of tragicomedy. Al Santoli's *New Americans: An Oral*

*History. Immigrants and Refugees in the U.S. Today* (New York: Viking, 1988) shows how a range of New Americans—Guatemalan children who watched army helicopters gun down their friends, Eritreans who looked like human skeletons, and a Polish labor organizer electroshocked by Polish police, among others—are remaking themselves in the United States.

The despair of Los Angeles is captured by Luis J. Rodriguez in his memoir, *Always Running—La Vida Leca: Gang Days in L.A.* (Willamantic, Conn.: Curbstone, 1993). He describes a youth of near-homelessness and grinding poverty, combined with discrimination against Spanish-speaking children by public schools, all factors that led to his embracing gang life. The film *Menace II Society* (1993) opens with a shocking murder of Korean grocery store owners in Los Angeles and ends with the death of a teenager in the ghetto. In between, it shows what Allen and Albert Hughes, twenty-one-year-old twins who directed the movie, call the ghetto: "a concrete Vietnam" where "People kill over money, women, turf."

People on the borders of two nations live in a special human environment. In *Border People: Life and Society in the U.S.–Mexico Borderlands* (Tucson: University of Arizona Press, 1994), history professor Oscar J. Martinez analyzes the common ground shared by borderland people. For other scholarly research on U.S.–Mexican border people and border cities, see the University of Arizona Press and publications by the University of Arizona Mexican American Studies and Research Center in Tuscon.

In *A Mixed Race: Ethnicity in Early America* (New York: Oxford University Press, 1993), Frank Shuffelton brings together essays suggesting that U.S. culture has been multicultural from the beginning, arising out of a mix of interactive ethnic cultures. In *Racially Mixed People in America* (Thousand Oaks, Calif.: Sage, 1992), Maria P. P. Root and her coauthors look at the biracial and multiracial experience and try to recover the "multiracial past."

Several chapters in Gerry Riposa and Carolyn Dersch, eds., *City of Angels* (Dubuque, Iowa: Kendall/Hunt, 1992), concern immigration, ethni-city, and interethnic relations. The editors introduce Los Angeles as "the most studied city in the United States." If so, it promises to be even more studied: A group of social scientists redesigning undergraduate courses at UCLA seek to make Los Angeles a laboratory for many new, issue-oriented courses.

Films and video that depict new immigrants' adjustment to urban America include *Between Two Worlds: The Hmong Shaman in America* (Siegel Productions, Chicago, 1985), which captures the experiences of Hmong refugees, transplanted from mountain farming villages in northern Laos to high-rise tenements in Chicago and other cities. *Becoming American* (New Day Films) follows a preliterate tribal farm family from Laos to refugee camps in Thailand and their new home in Seattle. This documentary records their culture shock, community prejudice, and their gradual adaptation to urban life.

Journalist Robert Scheer's essay "The Jews of Los Angeles" in *Thinking Tuna Fish, Talking Death* (New York: Hill and Wang, 1988) is a fascinating study of some descendants of East European Jews that Irving Howe wrote about in *World of Our Fathers: The Journey of the East European Jews to America and the Life They Found and Made* (New York: Simon and Schuster, 1976).

Numerous feature films capture aspects of migration and ethnic life. The rhythms of preindustrial life for turn-of-the-century peasants in northern Italy, eventually kicked off the land, are portrayed in Italian director Ermanno Olmi's masterpiece, *The Tree of Wooden Clogs* (1978). Charlie Chaplin's silent film classic *The Immigrant* (1917) contrasts the promise and pain of immigration through the character of the baggy-trousered Little Tramp. In *Avalon* (1990), filmmaker Barry Levinson traces the saga of the Krichinskys, an immigrant family from Eastern Europe that settles in Baltimore and eventually is pulled apart by prosperity, suburbia, and television. Franco Brusati's *Bread and Chocolate* (1974) is a poignant satire about an Italian immigrant in Switzerland who wants to assimilate so badly that he dyes his hair blond. *El Norte* (1983) tells the story of a brother and sister fleeing for their lives from Guatemala. Their American dream brings them to southern California in Gregory Nava's poignant yet unsentimental epic. In *The Apprenticeship of Duddy Kravitz* (1974), actor Richard Dreyfuss portrays Duddy's struggle to make it as a second-generation Jew in Montreal. Joan Micklin Silver's *Hester Street* (1975) gives a sentimental glimpse of Lower East Side immigrant life in New York City around the turn of the twentieth century. Her film *Crossing Delancey* (1988) takes place in contemporary New York City, focusing on a third-generation immigrant's pull between total assimilation and strong ethnic identification. Wayne Wang's *Eat a Bowl of Tea* (1989) and Peter Wang's *A Great Wall* (1986) deal with Chinese-American adjustments and readjustments to urban America.

Rap music often reflects the rage of people who feel disenfranchised. One song, rapper Ice Cube's "Black Korea" (1991), has a prophetic ring. Recorded before the burning of Los Angeles's Koreatown in 1992, it warns Korean merchants to show more respect to African-Americans or face the possibility that their stores will be burned down. The San Francisco–based group Consolidated espouses an angry political agenda that ranges from antiracism, antisexism, and anticapitalism to militant vegetarianism. Hear their funky album, "Friendly Fascism" (1991).

## REFERENCES

Antin, Mary. 1899. *From Plotzk to Boston*. Boston: Clarke.

Barringer, Felicity. 1992. "As American as apple pie, dim sum or burritos." *New York Times* [national edition] (June 31):E2.

Benet, Stephen Vincent. 1943. *Western Star*. New York: Farrar & Rinehart.

British Broadcasting Corporation. 1993. *Newsdesk*, KALW-FM (July 6).

Bullard, Robert D., and Joe R. Feagin. 1991. "Racism and the city." Pp. 55–76 in M. Gottdiener and Chris G. Pickvance, eds., *Urban Life in Transition*. Urban Affairs Annual Reviews, vol. 39. Newbury Park, Calif.: Sage.

Coughlin, Ellen K. 1993."Miami a unique sociological laboratory, researchers on immigration find." *Chronicle of Higher Education* (September 1):A6+.

Critser, Greg. 1993. "Will Riordan be good for L.A.'s Latinos?" *San Francisco Examiner* [This World section] (July 4):8+.

Daniels, Roger. [1990] 1991. *Coming to America: A History of Immigration and Ethnicity in American Life*. New York: Harper Perennial.

Davis, Mike. 1992.*City of Quartz: Excavating the Future in Los Angeles*. New York: Vintage.

Espinosa, Suzanne. 1992. "'Forgotten' Latinos fight to dispel misperceptions." *San Francisco Chronicle* (July 20):A1.

Espiritu, Yen Le, and Ivan Light. 1991. "The changing ethnic shape of contemporary urban America." Pp. 35–54 in M. Gottdiener and Chris G. Pickvance, eds., *Urban Life in Transition*. Urban Affairs Annual Reviews, vol. 39. Newbury Park, Calif.: Sage.

Glazer, Nathan. 1958. "The American Jew and the attainment of middle-class rank." Pp. 138–146 in Marshall Sklare, ed., *The Jews: Social Patterns of an American Group*. Glencoe, Ill.: Free Press.

Glazer, Nathan, and Daniel Patrick Moynihan. 1963. *Beyond the Melting Pot*. Cambridge, Mass.: MIT Press.

Grenier, Guillermo, and Alex Stepick, eds. 1992. *Miami Now! Immigration, Ethnicity, and Social Change*. Gainsville: University Press of Florida.

Hacker, Andrew. 1992. *Two Nations: Black and White, Separate, Hostile, Unequal*. New York: Scribner.

Haley, Alex, and Malcolm X. [1964] 1966. *The Autobiography of Malcolm X*. New York: Grove Press.

Holmstrom, David. 1992. "The new Americans." *Christian Science Monitor* (June 17):9–12.

Hosokawa, Bill. 1969. *Nisei: The Quiet Americans*. New York: Morrow.

Howe, Irving. 1976. *World of Our Fathers: The Journey of the East European Jews to America and the Life They Found and Made*. New York: Simon and Schuster.

Jankowski, Martín Sánchez. 1991. *Islands in the Street: Gangs and American Urban Society*. Berkeley: University of California Press.

Kershner, Vlae. 1993a. "California leads in immigration—and backlash." *San Francisco Chronicle* (June 21):A1+.

———. 1993b. "Calculating the cost of immigration: It saps state funds, but helps farms, business." *San Francisco Chronicle* (June 23):A1+.

Light, Ivan, and Edna Bonacich. 1988. *Immigrant Entrepreneurs: Koreans in Los Angeles, 1965–1982.* Berkeley: University of California Press.

*Los Angeles Times.* 1993. "Rise in legal immigration to U.S. in '92." *San Francisco Chronicle* (December 14):A6.

Massey, Douglas S. 1987. "Understanding Mexican migration to the United States." *American Journal of Sociology* 92 (May):1372–1403.

Morales, Rebecca, and Paul Ong. 1991. "Immigrant women in Los Angeles." *Economic and Industrial Democracy* 12 (February):65–81.

Mydans, Seth. 1991. "They're in a new home, but feel tied to the old." *New York Times* [national edition] (June 30):A8.

Palen, John. 1987. *The Urban World,* 3rd ed. New York: McGraw-Hill.

Portes, Alejandro, and Rubén G. Rumbaut. 1990. *Immigrant America: A Portrait.* Berkeley: University of California Press.

Portes, Alejandro, and Alex Stepick. 1993. *City on the Edge: The Transformation of Miami.* Berkeley: University of California Press.

Reynolds, Barbara. 1992. "For media decision-makers, urban problems are old news." *EXTRA!* (July–August):12.

Riis, Jacob. [1890] 1970. *How the Other Half Lives: Studies Among the Tenements of New York.* New York: Dover.

Riposa, Gerry, and Carolyn Dersch, eds. 1992. *City of Angels.* Dubuque, Iowa: Kendall/Hunt.

Robinson, Eugene. 1993. "U.N. calls mass migrations global problems." *San Francisco Chronicle* (July 7):A1+.

Sabagh, Georges, and Ivan Light. 1985. "Emergent ethnicity: Iranian immigrant communities." Grant application, National Science Foundation.

Sassen, Saskia. 1991. *The Global City: New York, London, Tokyo.* Princeton, N.J.: Princeton University Press.

Sherman, C. Bezalel. 1965. *The Jew Within American Society: A Study in Ethnic Individuality.* Detroit: Wayne State University Press.

Soja, Edward W. 1989. *Postmodern Geographies: The Reassertion of Space in Critical Social Theory.* London: Verso.

Sontag, Deborah. 1993. "New immigrants test nation's heartland." *New York Times* [national edition] (October 18):1.

Steinbeck, John. [1939] 1972. *The Grapes of Wrath.* New York: Viking.

Steinberg, Stephen. 1981. *The Ethnic Myth: Race, Ethnicity, and Class in America.* Boston: Beacon Press.

———. 1992. "Occupational apartheid." *The Nation* (December 9):744+.

Steiner, Stan. 1970. *La Raza: The Mexican Americans.* New York: Harper.

Suro, Roberto. 1992. "Mexicans come to work, but find dead ends." *New York Times* [national edition] (January 19):A1+.

Takaki, Ronald. 1989. *Strangers from a Different Shore: A History of Asian Americans.* New York: Viking Penguin.

Vidal, Gore. 1992. "Monotheism and its discontents." *The Nation* (July 13):1+.

West, Cornel. 1993. *Race Matters.* Boston: Beacon Press.

Wilson, William Julius. 1978. *The Declining Significance of Race: Blacks and Changing American Institutions.* Chicago: University of Chicago Press.

———. 1987. *The Truly Disadvantaged: The Inner City, the Underclass, and Public Policy.* Chicago: University of Chicago Press.

Wirth, Louis. [1928] 1956. *The Ghetto.* Chicago: University of Chicago Press.

Wolff, Michael, Peter Rutten, Albert F. Bayers III, and the World Rank Research Team. 1992. *Where We Stand: Can America Make It in the Global Race for Wealth, Health, and Happiness?* New York: Bantam.

Wyman, Mark. 1993. *Round Trip to America.* Ithaca, N.Y.: Cornell University Press.

Zukin, Sharon. 1993. Review of *City on the Edge,* by Alejandro Portes and Alex Stepick. *Contemporary Sociology* 22 (July):477–479.

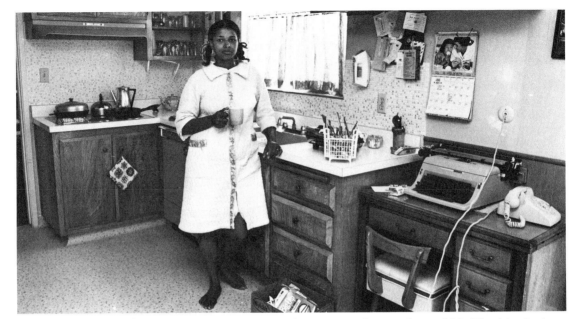

"I enjoy the suburbs. They provide Girl Scouts, PTA, Little League, and soccer for my kids. The thing I miss most is black cultural identity for my family. White, middle-class suburbia can't supply that. Here the biggest cultural happening has been the opening of two department stores." (in Owens, 1975:n.p.)

# CHAPTER 9
# Identity Crisis

## WORLDWIDE ETHNOSCAPES

### Global Identity . . .

Ever dream of writing the great American novel or directing the great American movie? Too bad, bad timing. Sensitivity to differences in ethnicity, race, gender, and class makes it difficult to even define an *American* novel or movie. Besides, an emerging genre may be taking their place: the global artwork. Global novels and movies leap across national boundaries; they include sophisticated characters from various cultures who happen to collide, typically in world cities such as New York, Bombay, and London. These artworks mirror supranational *Techno$chaft* where cosmopolitans commune in a global village. The movies of Jim Jarmusch (*Night on Earth*, 1992), James Ivory (*Heat and Dust*, 1983), and Stephen Frears (*My Beautiful Laundrette*, 1985) exemplify the genre.

Not surprisingly, many global writers and film-makers are themselves exiles or "shufflers." They shuffle between cultures, like English-Pakistani screenwriter Hanif Kureishi (*My Beautiful Laundrette*, 1985) and French director Louis Malle. Malle, at home in *Atlantic City* (1981), *Alamo Bay* (1985), *Calcutta* (1968), or Paris, embodies a citizen-of-the-world identity: Boundaries of ethnicity, nationality, race, and religion are of secondary importance at best. Implicitly, citizens of the world reject the **insider-as-insighter doctrine,** whereby members of a group claim a monopoly of knowledge unavailable to "outsiders."

### . . . versus the Pull of "Lesser Loyalties"

Simultaneously, there are powerful, some say primordial, forces antagonistic to global identity. Novelist and essayist V. S. Naipaul calls them "disruptive, lesser loyalties—of region, caste, and clan."

The flames of "lesser loyalties" have burned bright in recent years. In the United States, in cities from Miami to Los Angeles, ethnic and economic hatred exploded in riots or uprisings. Globally, in the former Yugoslavia and Soviet Union, onetime neighbors became enemies fighting to preserve tribal, religious, cultural, and / or ethnic communities. Between 1989 and 1994, ethnic conflict sparked record-high migrations of refugees: Over 23 million people—1 in every 114 people in the world—were uprooted and forced to move elsewhere (Darnton, 1994), and 26 million more people became refugees within their own countries (United Nations High Commissioner for Refugees, 1993).

During just one year, 1993, anti-Semites blamed Jews for either capitalism or communism in Russia, Hungary, and France. In Burundi, Hutus massacred Tutsis, and vice versa. In Germany, violence against "outsiders" ("them") led to the deaths of Turks and Vietnamese, the burning of refugees' homes, and the return of Gypsies (or Roma, as they call themselves), against their wishes, to Romania. In Romania, Roma were lynched, burned, and kicked to death by "Gypsy Skinners," a hate group modeled on the Ku Klux Klan. And so on.

The case of Germany's neo-Nazis illustrates how a search for community can be the flip side of hatred for outsiders. German neo-Nazis hope to create a Fourth Reich, a "pure race" German state without "outsiders" (that is, devoid of Jews, foreigners, and capitalists), ruled by a Nazi dictatorship. In other words, they seek an oxymoron: a modern *Gemeinschaft*. (Hitler used the same myth of racial purity as an ideal; the 1936 film *The Triumph of the Will* exhorts Germans to respect the cornerstones of *Gemeinschaft*: blood, land, and friendship.)

In Germany and other nations of Europe, hatred of the outsider may reflect an identity crisis. Some observers think that this crisis of identity is encouraged by "a lethal mix of unemployment, humiliation, and resentment that gave rise to the Nazis" in the 1930s (Whitney, 1992:A1). As one Italian put it, "European identity is in crisis. A white continent is becoming multicultural and multiethnic" (in Simpson, 1992:A10). In addition, extremists and nationalists blame foreigners and Jews for all that is wrong because they seek easy answers to complex problems: "In a complex world, where nothing seems clear-cut anymore, some people lap [neo-Nazism] up. All their questions find simple answers" (Bernd Wagner in Protzman, 1992:A4). The result is that "Whether in Birmingham, Frankfurt, Florence or Marseilles, third-world communities have become the target of simmering xenophobia and occasional racist violence" (Riding, 1991:3).

Ethnic and religious loyalties will probably prevail in many parts of the post–Cold War world. For example, in the Central Asian Republic of Tajikistan, formerly part of the Soviet

Union, the chief cleric predicts a key role for religion in shaping the region's future: "Our people have believed in Islam for thirteen hundred years. And Islam is ninety per cent of our culture and tradition, so you can't separate something religious from something national" (in Wright, 1992:75).

Ethnic loyalties may prevent subordinate groups from coming together around common economic interests. So argues sociologist Orlando Patterson. In his book *Ethnic Chauvinism,* (1977), Harvard professor Patterson chided both black power and white ethnic movements for celebrating a "tyranny of the lesser loyalties." Fifteen years later, Patterson says that ethnic particularism is helping to tear nations apart. (Patterson in Raymond, 1992:A12). He might have added that ethnic chauvinism can tear apart neighborhoods too, as in the Bosnian case of unspeakable brutality: "ethnic cleansing."

A major funder of university education in eastern and central Europe, George Soros, advocates an "open society" as an antidote to ethnic chauvinism. In an open society, he says, "no dogma has a monopoly, . . . the individual is not at the mercy of the state, . . . [and] minorities and minority opinions are tolerated if not respected" (1993:16). Soros, a Hungarian-born Jew, recounts that he learned the urgency of establishing an open society "at an early age when I nearly ended up in a gas chamber on account of my ethnic origin."

### Civics versus Ethnics

Political scientist Ken Jowitt (1992) draws a distinction between two types of identity in the world today: civics versus ethnics. (This distinction is similar to Soros's open society versus closed society and Tönnies's *Gesellschaft* cosmopolitanism versus *Gemeinschaft* localism.) Those who identify as civics, Jowitt says, stress the individual; those who identity as ethnics stress the group. In addition, civics stress the ability to view the world critically; ethnics see the world

divided into us (insiders) and them (outsiders). That is, *civics are inclusive, ethnics are exclusive.* For example, Jowitt distinguishes between South African Nelson Mandela as a civic because all ethnic groups are welcomed into his group, the African National Congress (ANC), and Zulu Chief Mangosuthu Gatsha Butalezi as an ethnic because only Zulus can become members of his Inkatha Freedom Party. Dozens of twentieth-century leaders—from Hitler, the Ayatollah Khomeini and Rabbi Meir Kahane to Elijah Mohammed and David Duke—symbolize the primacy of ethnic over civic identity.

According to Jowitt, a conflict between civics and ethnics is now a major feature of politics almost everywhere, including the United States. He fears a "Tower of Ethnic Babel" where ethnicity becomes *primary:* An individual's identity is first and foremost white, or Shia Muslim, or Pacific Islander, and so on. Jowitt fears that the United States, "the one nation indivisible, is being multiplied and divided."

It is in U.S. cities, Jowitt notes, that movements of ethnic rage combine with economic frustration to produce a boiling cauldron. If so, did this replace the proverbial "melting pot"?

### WHAT HAPPENED TO THE U.S. MELTING POT?

"These States," wrote poet Walt Whitman, "are the amplest poem. Here is not merely a nation, but a teeming nation of nations." A nation of nations—that was the vision: a great **melting pot,** a fusion of all immigrants into a new American. "Here," proclaimed naturalized American Jean de Crèvecoeur in 1782, "individuals of all nations are melted into a new race of man." Thus from the very beginning, America was viewed as a new nation—a nation unlike all others that would fuse people of different origins into one people.

But this ideal waned over the generations. When European Catholic and Jewish immigrants came in massive waves, many old-stock WASPs wondered whether the melting pot was possible —or desirable. By the 1880s and 1890s, several reactions to the immigrant tide had surfaced.

One reaction came from upper-crust WASPs: the founding of ancestral associations such as the Daughters of the American Revolution (DAR) in 1890. During the 1890s, some thirty-five hereditary, historical, and patriotic associations were formed as these old-stock WASPs searched for their roots (Baltzell, 1964).

Old-stock Americans also took direct action: trying to shut the floodgates. The American Protective Association (1886) and other groups aimed at restricting immigration were formed by those calling themselves "native Americans." Liberal reformers had another approach: turning "them" into "us." Schools, military academies, sports clubs, and settlement houses became vehicles for **assimilation,** not **acculturation.** Their goals: to inculcate the "American way of life" and to "Americanize" the immigrants.

Another reaction was to deny that some immigrant groups were capable of being assimilated. The San Francisco School Board, for instance, declared in 1905 that it would segregate Japanese children to prevent white children from being "affected by association with pupils of the Mongolian race" (in Hosokawa, 1969:86).

By 1908, when Israel Zangwill's play *The Melting Pot* appeared on Broadway, the Chinese had already been barred from further immigration; the Japanese in California were officially classified as "aliens ineligible to citizenship"; blacks were segregated and denied civil rights; upper-class WASPs were busy finding their roots; and millions of Catholic and Jewish immigrants lived and died in unsanitary, overcrowded, oppressive urban slums. Still, Zangwill's play was a great success. It celebrated "the great Melting Pot where all the races of Europe are melting and reforming! . . . The real American has not yet arrived. His is only in the Crucible. I tell you—he will be the fusion of all races, the coming superman" (1909:37–38).

## Race, Ethnicity, and Minority Groups

Today the American ideal of the melting pot has disappeared. In its place is **multiculturalism.**

What exactly are *race* and *ethnicity?* Slippery terms—social labels that humans pin on themselves and others. Such labels are far from universal. For instance, in the early 1960s, the U.S. State Department sent a light-skinned African-American scholar to West Africa as an ambassador; Africans viewed him as white, not black.

Labels do change. Here are a few examples: Local whites first classified Mississippi Delta Chinese as blacks, then reclassified them as whites (Loewen, 1988). The 1930 U.S. census classified white persons of Mexican birth or ancestry in the group called "other races"; in 1940, they were reclassified as "white." Some whites now call themselves Euro-Americans.

Human beings also create new racial-ethnic categories. For instance, the Nazis deemed the Japanese "honorary Aryans" during World War II, and *mestizo* is a term rooted in Cortez's conquest of Mexico (Carrasco, 1992).

Neither geneticists nor social scientists agree on what constitutes a race or an ethnic group. Generally, *race* refers to members of a group who see themselves—and whom others see—as having specific physical traits that set them off as different. (Racist *ideology* links race to *non*physical traits such as morality and intellect.)

**Census Definitions** The 1990 U.S. census recognizes the following major racial groups:

1. Whites.
2. Blacks (African Americans).
3. American Indians, Eskimos, and Aleuts.
4. Asians and Pacific Islanders.

Note that racial categories have changed dramatically since 1960, reflecting the recognition of new social identities. In 1950 and 1960, the U.S. Census Bureau recognized only two groups:

**Fig. 9.1** TURNING "THEM" INTO "US." Through Americanization classes, like this one at the Barrett Plant, Chicago, in 1919, reformers taught immigrants the "American way of life" and the English language. (Chicago Historical Society)

white and nonwhite. In 1970, it still recognized only two groups, renamed "White" and "Negro and other races." In 1980, there were fifteen designations, including "White," "Black," Japanese, and "Other," plus a separate category for Hispanics (who can be of any race or national ancestry). By 1990, there were twenty-five categories, including "Other."

To date, the U.S. census does not recognize biracial or multiracial persons. Historically, persons of mixed racial parentage are classified by the U.S. Census Bureau according to the race of the nonwhite parent, and "mixtures of races other than white" are generally "classified according to the race of the father" (U.S. Census Bureau,

1972: Appendix B-6). This definition reaffirms what Andrew Hacker reported in *Two Nations* (1992a): There is a hierarchy of color in America, and for whites, whiteness is highly prized over color. Thus however they define themselves, the countless numbers of persons who are offspring of white mothers and African-American fathers (including San Jose State professor Shelby Steele, a leading spokesperson against affirmative action, and Lani Guinier, a leading proponent of critical race theory) are viewed as African-American; the social definition of biracial is not available. For the 1990 census, people who identify as biracial—say, Japanese and white—were forced to circle either one of those two categories or "Other Race." A Berkeley, California–based organization, the Multi-Ethnic Interracial Student Coalition (known as Misc.) is trying to get the U.S. Census Bureau to add multiracial categories to the census.

The federal government's Office of Management and Budget (the agency that sets policy on gathering federal statistics) began a review of its racial and ethnic classifications in 1994. It was responding to demographic change and political pressure: (1) increased numbers of interracial marriages (0.4 percent of all U.S. marriages in 1960 to 2.2. percent in 1992), and (2) complaints by groups displeased by their current classification, particularly Arab-Americans, Hawaiian Islanders, and multiracial people. (Politically speaking, ethnic and racial reclassification is a can of worms. For example, the proposed multiracial category faces stiff opposition from some established ethnic groups who fear that it might reduce their counts in the U.S. census. Other groups lobbied to drop *all* classification by race or ethnicity.)

***Peoplehood***   Most generally, the term *ethnicity* connotes a "consciousness of kind," a sense of peoplehood (*eth* is the Greek root for "people"). This is a subjective belief; an objective blood relationship may or may not exist. According to the eminent German sociologist Max Weber, an ethnic group holds a subjective belief in its "common descent because of similarities of physical type or of customs or both, or because of memories of colonization and migration" ([1921] 1968:389). In Weber's definition, the defining element of an ethnic group is *the sharing of an identity based on a shared history*. Hence African-Americans, Amish, Hopis, and Italian-Americans are considered ethnic groups. But what about many others—for instance, persons with a multi-racial or multiethnic background—Vietnamese–African–Americans or Jewish Cuban Americans? It all depends on how individuals define themselves and how the larger society defines them.

***Who's a "Minority"?***   Changes in racial and ethnic consciousness are reflected in language. Take, for instance, the term **minority.** After World War I, *minority* referred to European national groups— Serbs, Latvians, Czechs, and other groups involved in the peace Treaty of Versailles. By the 1930s and 1940s, the term designated ethnic and racial groups in the United States.

It was Louis Wirth (Chapter 5) who first tried to define and comprehensively type U.S. minorities. In 1945, Wirth said that a minority is a group of people that is "singled out from the others in the society in which they live for differential and unequal treatment and who therefore regard themselves as objects of collective discrimination" (1945:347). Note that *Wirth makes no specific mention of race, ethnic background, religion —or numbers.* Instead, he emphasizes social oppression: minorities-as-victims. Using Wirth's definition, gays and lesbians, people in wheelchairs, and people weighing over 350 pounds, among other groups, qualify as minorities.

How minorities are defined is no small issue. For one thing, big money is at stake. Various governmental agencies set aside funds specifically for minority groups. The city of New Orleans, for example, earmarked about 20 percent of its $300 million budget in 1988 for minority-owned businesses. In a controversial ruling, Louisiana lawmakers defined the state's 200,000 to 300,000 Cajuns as a minority, thus qualifying them for these "minority set-asides." A Cajun spokesperson argued that his people had suffered cultural discrimination historically, particularly repression in the exercise of their French language, and that some had been enslaved or indentured. Thus according to Wirth's definition, the Cajuns qualify as a minority. But many in Louisiana felt that calling Cajuns a minority is a bad joke, mocking affirmative action programs in general and the discrimination and economic hardship faced by the state's 1 million African-Americans in particular.

Clearly, there is no agreed-on definition of *minority*. Some Americans use the word as Wirth intended: as a social-psychological badge of discrimination. Some use the word interchangeably with *people of color,* a term that returned to favor in the 1980s. Others use it to mean an economically disadvantaged ethnic group. Now many social scientists refer to groups once called minorities as *subcultures* or *subcommunities,*—that is, groups defining themselves as different from other groups and from the dominant culture in terms of world view and/or lifestyle. In this usage, there is a sense of difference—but not of discrimination or oppression.

## From Minority to Majority

However defined, *the term "minority" has nothing to do with numbers.* In many cities—including New York, Miami, Gary, Washington, Honolulu, El Paso, New Orleans, Chicago, Atlanta, and Baltimore—so-called minorities have become numerical majorities.

Such is also the case in many California cities, including Los Angeles, Oakland, Milpitas (Chapter 7), and "Everyone's Favorite City"—San Francisco. At the very least, this demographic development affects political coalitions and public school curricula. For whites, it may also affect deep-seated psychological assumptions. As one educator put it, "For 200 years we've had an idea that this is a European country with little pockets of minorities. The next generation in California is going to do away with that" (in Erlich, 1990:16).

Does this shift in many cities—from numerical majority to minority—mean that whites will consider themselves just one among many groups? An official of California Tomorrow, a San Francisco–based population research center, doesn't answer this question but notes that "as this state becomes more Hispanic and Asian, it will test whether we can peacefully change from a European-dominated society with minorities to a world society where everybody is a minority" (Butler in McLeod, 1991:A7).

In some cases, violence has accompanied the arrival of new ethnic groups. Such was the case in 1989 when five Southeast Asian children were gunned down by Patrick Purdy in a Stockton, California, schoolyard. More often when people of color move in, whites pull up stakes, not an AK-47. According to the director of the Center

for California Studies, "Some [white] people see immigrants as a threat. That's why you get white flight; that's why you get segregated cities. They don't want to deal with immigrants or minorities" (Lustig in McLeod, 1991:A7).

## A Clash of Values: White Ethnics versus WASP Superculture

Of course, American whites are far from homogeneous in culture. One division that remains important is WASP versus white ethnic.

Years ago Michael Novak, a spokesperson for white ethnic consciousness and a descendant of Slovak immigrants, wrote that white ethnics had been made to feel stupid, backward, and immoral by what he calls the WASP *superculture* in America. In *The Rise of the Unmeltable Ethnics,* Novak describes and contrasts white ethnic working-class culture and WASP superculture, so called because he feels it has tried to overwhelm and stamp out competing ways of life:

The WASP home cherishes good order, poise, soft voices, cleanliness . . . [such a home] offers culture shock to non-WASPs. Decorum and self-control. Tight emotions. . . . To the WASP, the direct flow of emotion is childish; his acculturation requires cognitive control. . . . The WASP way—the almost universal industrial way of the modern age—is to put a harsh rein upon the impulses of man's animal nature . . . and to order him docilely to produce. It is a life geared to action, to "changing history," to progress. (1971:179, 180, 185)

Working-class white ethnic homes, Novak (1971:26) says, are just the opposite, and the people in them don't share WASP values or goals. Noise, family get-togethers, and emotionality typify white ethnic home life. And instead of seeking to change history, white ethnic males see the world as a tough, violent place where hard work, family discipline, and gradual self-development are the routes to moderate success. To the women, the world outside remains "mainly unchangeable."

Other observers agree that family and neighborhood are centers of working-class ethnic life. And some, like Jane Jacobs, celebrate the vitality of such neighborhoods. She finds ethnic neighborhoods to be alive with activity, especially the sidewalks. Here is how she describes the "intricate sidewalk ballet" on her stretch of Hudson Street in New York City, a scene that not only animates the city but, she says, helps keep its residents safe:

When I get home after work, the ballet is reaching its crescendo. This is the time of roller skates and stilts and tricycles, and games in the lee of the stoop with bottletops and plastic cowboys; this is the time of bundles and packages, zig-zagging from the drug store back over ot the butcher's; this is the time when teenagers, all dressed up, are pausing to ask if their slips show or their collars look right; this is the time when beautiful girls get out of MG's; this is the time when the fire engines go through; this is the time when anybody you know around Hudson Street will go by. (1961:52)

Urbanist Jacobs idealized the New York City street as a place made safe by having everyone's "eyes on the street"—people watching and watching over one another while they talk, flirt, play, and so on. No one could mistake Jacobs's description of her ethnic neighborhood for a portrait of a middle-class WASP street scene.

WASPs like Richard Brookhiser (1991) might feel uncomfortable on Hudson Street. Brookhiser, a senior editor at the conservative *National Review,* thinks that what made America great—and what can save it—are basic WASP values, which he defines as self-control, reserve, conscience, antisensuality, hard work, determination not to waste time, success, and civic-mindedness. Perhaps that is what "traditional values" mean to WASPs —but not necessarily to working-class white ethnics or people of color.

## Once Again, the Entanglement of Race/Ethnicity and Class

For many white working-class ethnics, a life centered on family and neighborhood remains a deeply held value. Amid turbulence, even chaos, home and family can represent the comfort of an "island of homogeneity floating in a heterogeneous sea" (Muschamp, 1993:30). Take, for example, life in Canarsie, a Brooklyn, New York, neighborhood of mainly second- and third-generation Italians and Jews. There, neighborhood stability, particularly home and children, is highly valued; "alternative lifestyles" find little support. According to sociologist Jonathan Rieder, working-class whites of Canarsie experienced the period between 1960 and 1980 as a time of "danger and dispossession—culturally and internationally, but especially racially" (1985:1, 4). White workers often see themselves as victims, "the objects of others' will" —of reverse discrimination, of bureaucrats, of liberal social policies, and of the values of so-called cultural elites.

In Canarsie and similar neighborhoods, residents often find themselves in the "immediate line of fire" (Wilson in Wilkerson, 1992:A12). Typically, racial tension often shows up first and more intensely in such neighborhoods, for residents have fewer resources and escape valves than upper-middle-class whites. Here is a classic example: When the Irish took over the public schools in Boston and Cambridge in the first part of this century, Harvard University families moved their children out of public schools and started private ones. By 1962, only one out of over fifty members of the Harvard Graduate School of Education had children in Cambridge public schools (Binzen, 1970:49–50).

An observer from Mars might wonder why working-class whites and blacks don't recognize their common interests. After all, they often reside in side-by-side communities and share similar hopes. Such is the case in two Chicago blue-collar communities: white Mount Greenwood and black Roseland. Both are "churchgoing, workaday neighborhoods made up of people who put in overtime to pay the bills, who curse drugs and dandelions with equal indignation and who dream of a better life and maybe even college for their children" (Wilkerson, 1992:12). Yet, they are separated by two miles and by a gulf of fear and suspicion. Their worlds rarely intersect. They live as if on different planets. Sociologist William Julius Wilson thinks that "if you could get these [black and white working-class people] to recognize their common interests, it would go a long way toward alleviating racial hostility" (in Wilkerson, 1992:A12).

## The Grand Canyon

Countless observers have tried to understand the social psychological gulf between African-Americans and whites, what has been called the "American dilemma." Let's consider a few of their ideas.

One view is that permanent racism is the root of the grand canyon between blacks and whites (Bell, 1992). If so, what is at the root of racism? Here there is wide disagreement. Author Gore Vidal traces white racism to the Bible: "As descendants of Ham, blacks are forever accursed. . . . Racism is in the marrow of the bone of the true believer. For him [or her], black is forever inferior to white" (1992:55). Novelist James Baldwin had another explanation. He claimed that whites created the image of a lustful, lazy, stupid "nigger" to embody the very traits that whites cannot tolerate within themselves. Other analysts think that racism is essentially about power: White elites promote a racist ideology in order to help maintain poor whites' perception of their own superiority over subordinate groups such as African-Americans and Latinos; this ideology prevents poor people of color and poor whites with common class interests from making common cause. The upshot: white elites maintain their power, even if few in number (Cash, 1941). Others think that racism is chiefly motivated by psychological sentiments internalized in childhood, not by rational self-interest (Sears and Allen, 1984).

Whatever the underlying causes of racism, sociologists Robert D. Bullard and Joe R. Feagin (1991) say that there are two types: individual racism and institutionalized racism. *Individual racism* takes many forms, including a person's attempt to drive a black family out of a white neighborhood by burning a cross in the yard.

*Institutionalized racism* refers to organizational actions that carry out discriminatory practices, such as real estate agents' steering black families away from white areas. They argue that in both the North and the South, "the modern American city has its roots in well-institutionalized racism" by whites against blacks which is reflected in racially segregated housing, schools, and jobs (1991:72).

Political scientist Ira Katznelson (1981) offers a contrasting view, one based on capitalism and class. He argues that U.S. workers in major industrial cities act on the basis of class solidarity at work but on the basis of ethnic and territorial affinities at home. In Katznelson's view, this sharply divided consciousness—between the politics of work and the politics of community—is a divide-and-conquer tactic that has served to protect the core arrangements of capitalism. This pattern, he says, started in the post–Civil War era when workers were mobilized politically into labor unions at work and into city machines at home. Big city machines (Chapter 13) used divide-and-rule tactics to pit ethnic group against ethnic group, thereby diffusing or coopting the energies of the working class. Additionally, new government services were delivered to citizens in their communities, not their workplaces. The result, according to Katznelson, is that the U.S. urban political system produced "a working class unique in the West: militant as labor, and virtually nonexistent as a collectivity outside the workplace" (1981:71).

From another angle, sociologist Erving Goffman's study *Stigma* (1963) offers an approach to social identity that can be adapted to better understand black–white relations. Goffman says that a stigmatized individual is one who is disqualified from full social acceptance by so-called normals (people whose identity is accepted). Disqualification may be based on perceived character blemishes, physical deformities, or "the tribal stigma of race, nation, and religion." Normals "believe the person with a stigma is not quite human." Based on this assumption, normals "exercise varieties of discrimination, through which [they] effectively, if often unthinkingly, reduce the life chances" of the stigmatized individual. Then "normals construct an ideology which rationalizes their animosity and also explains the stigmatized person's supposed inferiority" (1963:4, 5). Although Goffman doesn't mention them, we can interpret various historic public policies, including the Chinese Exclusion Act of 1882 and racial segregation in U.S. public schools, as outgrowths of such stigmatizing ideologies.

Political scientist Andrew Hacker suggests how the stigma of blackness operates in the United States. In his book *Two Nations: Black and White, Separate, Hostile, Unequal* (1992a) and in a radio interview about the book (1992b), Hacker says that an African-American "bears the mark of slavery. Even after emancipation . . . blacks continued to be seen as an inferior species." According to Hacker, African-Americans are still treated as a "subordinate caste." Hacker supports this conclusion with stark examples, including this one about dental hygiene, an occupation that has one of the smallest percentages of blacks: "White people just don't want black fingers in their mouths. If that isn't racism, tell me what is" (1992b).

Hacker claims that few whites ever think about "how membership in the major race gives them power and privileges." Yet the greatest privilege any American can have is being white because "no matter how degraded their lives. . . . [whites] can never become black."

Just how important is it to be white in America? Hacker's experiment suggests that it's very important—to whites: He asked his white college students in New York City to put a price tag on having their white skin taken away and becoming black. On average, the white students thought that they should be indemnified $1 million—annually—for the loss of their whiteness.

Successful, educated, affluent African-Americans —professors, government officials, corporate managers, and so on—are not immune to discrimination. Quite the contrary. For instance, in 1991, 21 percent of high-income African-Americans were rejected for bank home loans, while low-income whites were rejected only 14 percent of the time (Documentary Consortium,

1992). In public places blacks often suffer hate crimes, avoidance, police harassment, or verbal epithets—solely because of their skin color (Feagin, 1991). A poignant story told by the distinguished Harvard scholar Henry Louis Gates, Jr., is on point:

I often find myself moving into upper-middle-class white neithborhoods, and the first thing I do when I move into a neighborhood is to check in with the police and introduce myself. "Hi. I am Doctor Gates. I go away often and I was wondering if there are any security precautions I should take during vacations." But of course that's not it. It's that sooner or later someone is going to see this Negro in a car and ask what he is doing there. I do it so often and they see this face. I've lived in all-white neighborhoods in Durham, N.C. and in Ithaca, N.Y., and now in predominantly white Lexington, Mass. I think it's disgusting to feel that you have to do that. (1992:48)

Gates's experiences and many social research studies suggest that in America a person's skin color—specifically blackness—remains an important, perhaps *the most important*, characteristic of the person, whatever the content of his or her character or station in life. Sadly, the United States has no monopoly on this color fixation.

## SYMBOLIC ETHNICITY

Arguably, race and ethnicity are the most widely written-about topics in America. That is a testament to their continuing centrality to the nation's conscience. Yet some scholars argue that many grand- and great-grandchildren of European immigrants (i.e., third- and fourth- generation white ethnics) may be characterized by **symbolic ethnicity**; that is, their ethnic identity may be more symbolic than real. Some claim that European ethnicity today—being Polish-American or Italian-American, for example—bears little relation to the ancestral European heritage. Instead, they say, white ethnic identity is more of a political and psychological defense mechanism against a lack of opportunities (e.g., Yancey, Ericksen, and Juliani, 1979).

Sociologist-urban planner Herbert J. Gans (author of *The Urban Villagers* and *Levittown*, discussed earlier), goes further, saying that "ethnicity is largely a [white] working-class style" (1979:3). Likewise, he claims that white "ethnic" political activity focuses on working-class issues, not ethnic ones. In fact, Gans says, working-class and lower-middle-class white ethnics often banded together in pan-ethnic coalitions, not narrow ethnic ones. According to Gans, these white pan-ethnic political coalitions developed most readily in conflicts over racial issues. Further, Gans notes that white ethnicity can serve as a convenient euphemism for antiblack endeavors or for political activities that have negative consequences for blacks (4).

By the third generation, most white ethnics have friends outside the ethnic group, depend little on fellow ethnics, and work for companies where ethnic ties are either irrelevant or not very relevant. (Note that third-generation white ethnics are aided by the "strength of weak ties," detailed in Chapter 7.) In other words, ethnicity is not central to their lives.

## Feelings and Food

By the third generation, ethnicity may not remain *central* to white ethnics, but, Gans argues, third-generation white ethnics do continue to see themselves as ethnics—whether they define ethnicity in terms of religion or national ancestry. This ethnicity expresses itself as a *feeling*—a feeling of being Italian or Polish or Jewish—that is primarily shown in nostalgia for the Old Country, pride in tradition, a desire to return to an imagined past, the practice of ceremonial holidays, and consumption of special foods.

Symbolic ethnicity, in my view, is often reinforced by a perceived need to fight negative stereotypes. For example, *fra noi,* a newspaper serving Chicagoland's Italian-American community, usually contains several articles (e.g., Gambino, 1992) about anti-Italian bigotry based on popular myths about the alleged links between organized crime and Italians, thus reminding coethnics of their collective image.

Gans concludes that among European immigrants, "symbolic ethnicity should become the dominant way of being ethnic by the time the fourth generation . . . matures into adulthood" (1979:16). We might add that even symbolic ethnicity seems problematic for some groups. Take, for example, U.S. Jews. Since the mid-1960s the small American Jewish population (about 5.5 million in 1990) has been eroding due largely to interfaith marriage: In one generation, the rate of Jewish intermarriage increased more than five times—from 9 percent before 1965 to 52 percent after 1985. And, once Jews intermarry, their children seldom identify as Jewish (Steinfels, 1992:156).

My hunch is that Gans's prediction of symbolic ethnicity as a dominant mode for European ethnics will hold true for some non-European immigrant groups too. Here is my hypothesis: Symbolic ethnicity will become the dominant way of being ethnic for *any* fourth-generation immigrant group with either of two key characteristics—(1) relatively high outmarriage rates, such as Koreans (Kitano and Chai, 1982) and Chinese (Kitano and Yeung, 1982) or (2) heavy representation in professional-technical occupations, such as Filipinos and East Indians (Portes and Rumbaut,1990:19–20). The logic is this: Both outmarriage and professionalization tend to blunt ethnic identification. People in professional-technical occupations rarely come from urban villages or tight ethnic communities, and outmarriage tends to create new cultural patterns. Peter Wang's semiautobiographical film, *A Great Wall* (1986), exemplifies one Chinese family's symbolic ethnicity. In the film, the father (a Silicon Valley computer professional born in China) takes his American-born Chinese wife and teenage son to Beijing for a visit to his sister and her family. A "great wall" of cultural difference—language; attitudes toward achievement, privacy, and parental authority, for instance—separates the two families. When the family returns to California, the father trades jogging for Chinese physical exercises (a form of symbolic ethnicity), but no one in the family makes his or her Chinese heritage a central feature of daily life.

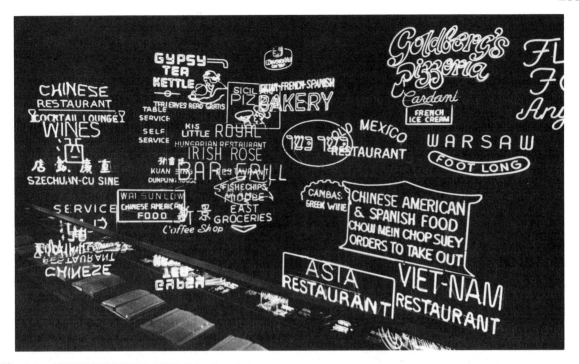

**Fig. 9.2** AMERICAN DIET: ETHNIC POTPOURRI. According to a National Restaurant Association survey, in the United States, Italian food is the most popular ethnic cuisine, followed by Chinese and Mexican food. In retail stores, ethnic-accentuated food is hot stuff. For example, salsa outsold ketchup by $40 million in 1992. According to a market researcher, "The taste for salsa is as mainstream as apple pie these days" (in O'Neill, 1992:B1). (Peter Garfield)

## THE STEWPOT

For some, ethnicity is mostly symbolic. But the persistence of racial and ethnic communities suggests that America is a **stewpot**—sometimes boiling over with anger, frustration, and hate—not a melting pot. After the turmoil in Los Angeles in the spring of 1992, some called it a boiling pot.

The Pennsylvania Amish and some groups have remained aloof and unassimilated by choice. But many groups, particularly African-Americans, had no choice. Speaking specifically about African-Americans, the late Supreme Court Justice Thurgood Marshall put it this way in 1987: "If the United States is indeed the great melting pot, the Negro either didn't get in the pot or he didn't get melted down."

At various historical periods, many non-WASP groups have been victims of discrimination, racism, or violence. Today, some argue that discrimination extends to some groups with WASP members too. Now let's take a closer look at some groups in the stewpot.

### Native Americans: The Unassimilated

In Rapid City, South Dakota, the office of the weekly *Lakota Times* is festooned with baseball pennants. There's one for the "Cleveland Indians" and others for the "Pittsburgh Negroes," the "Kansas City Jews," and the "San Diego Caucasians." Beneath the pennants is this sign: "Now you know how Native Americans feel" (Johnson, 1991:A10). Responding to such feelings, several media organizations have dropped nicknames that Native Americans consider offensive, using instead such terms as "Atlanta baseball team."

But new names don't change the Native Americans' bleak economic situation. As of 1990, Native Americans in the United States—numbering nearly 2 million persons, about one-half living in cities and one-half on reservations—remain the poorest ethnic group in the nation. In 1990, the median household income of the Navajo, the second largest Native American group, was $9,901; over 45 percent of the Navajos lived below the U.S. poverty line. The Pine Ridge Reservation, home of the Lakota-Oyate (called the Sioux by white settlers) in South Dakota's well-named Badlands, had the sad distinction of being the nation's poorest community in 1990; U.S. census data show that 63.1 percent of the 9,902 residents lived in poverty.

Whether in cities or on reservations, Native Americans suffer from high rates of unemployment, suicide, alcoholism, car accidents, and diabetes. In addition, the economic future for many is limited; in 1988, Native American eighth graders were also less likely to enter a college preparatory high-school program than any other ethnic group in the United States.

Official U.S. government policy toward the first Americans has been assimilationist, but the policy has not worked: "Hardly any community or tribe has wholly disappeared since the end of the days of conquest by warfare, genocide, or disease" (Sturtevant, 1976:22). Forcibly removed from their ancestral homes, robbed of schooling in their tribal languages and sent off to Bureau of Indian Affairs schools, and overwhelmed by white migrants, many Native Americans still retain their distinctive cultures.

Officially, the federal government vowed to assimilate Native Americans into the mainstream of American culture. Yet they weren't granted citizenship until 1924. And by 1994, more, not fewer, nations were recognized by the U.S. government: There were 545 federally recognized tribes.

The unique plight of the first Americans can be summed up as follows:

All elements in the American population either decided to leave their native country (which implies some dissatisfaction and thus readiness to adjust to a new environment) or else were violently wrenched from their homes and sent into slavery across the ocean, leaving no choice but adjustment and assimilation. But Indians are not like this at all. They are members of societies that remained in their native country, where they were invaded, conquered, and overwhelmed by foreigners. (Sturtevant, 1976:22)

Today, as Figure 9.3 suggests, Native American cultures may be undermined or overwhelmed by more subtle means: television.

However, there are some signs that Native American culture has not been totally overwhelmed. One is a flourishing, tribally controlled college in those same South Dakota Badlands: Oglala Lakota College. Chartered in 1971, the college follows a philosophy expressed in its motto: *Wa Wo Ici Ya*, a Lakota expression translated as "We can do it ourselves."

## African-Americans and Hispanics: Permanent Underclass?

Blacks from Africa first arrived in the English colonies in 1619. They were considered indentured servants who could work off their bonds after a period of time. This situation quickly changed, and by the mid-seventeenth century, the enslaved black population in the South increased. Northerners in colonial America also held slaves, mainly as house servants and farm workers.

The forced migration of black Africans to the fields and cities of the colonies and the early migration of British and European settlers to North America were inextricably linked: "They were both undertaken primaily in the hope of securing a better life—for whites" (Greene, 1976:89). Yale historian David Brion Davis goes further, arguing that the very notion of "the American dream" was originally made possible by the availability of enslaved labor: "From the early West India trade of the northeastern colonies to the cotton exports that helped pay for northern

**Fig. 9.3**  GENERATION GAP. In an Alaskan village, a Yupik renders a seal while her granddaughter watches TV. (Paul Souders)

railroads and industrialization, America's economy depended largely on slave labor" (1992:14).

From colonial days and the plantation South to the present, much has changed. African-Americans now have citizenship and civil rights. Most live in urban areas, not rural places. And yet, as victims of long-standing racism and economic discrimination, they are consigned as a group to lower socioeconomic status and marginalized.

Housing segregation is one measure of African-American marginalization. U.S. census data from 1990 show that about 30 percent of African-Americans live in virtual racial isolation. (That is, they live in neighborhoods that are at least 90 percent black.) Some analysts (e.g., Patterson and Winship, 1992:A17) say that most blacks *choose* to live separately from whites and that housing seg-

regation in itself is no problem. Others, including Douglas Massey, a leading analyst on migration and housing segregation, say that this pattern of residential immobility based by race harms African-Americans because "residential mobility [which they lack] is a major avenue of social mobility" (in Kilson and Bond, 1992:A16).

The fate of city dwellers at the bottom of the social ladder—particularly African-Americans and Latinos—has been questioned by many social scientists. William Julius Wilson's controversial and influential studies, *The Declining Significance of Race* (1978) and *The Truly Disadvantaged* (1987), argue that, primarily, it is structural changes in the metropolitan economy (e.g., deindustrialization, suburbanization of blue-collar work, and the consequent reduction in the pool of African-American marriageable men)—not a culture of poverty, not immigration policy, and not racism—that created a huge black "underclass." (The term *underclass* generally refers to the urban impoverished [particularly African-Americans and Latinos] who are chronically jobless and welfare dependent. Radicals prefer the word *lumpenproletariat,* a harsher term used by Marx to describe "the reserve army of the unemployed.")

Wilson, an African-American sociologist at Harvard University, maintains that class is more important than race in determining blacks' life chances due to these structural changes. He is not alone. Historian Jacqueline Jones (1992) says that by the late 1980s, historical and economic processes had created a multitude of "underclasses," and that these people were not necessarily black or residents of northern cities. New immigrants from Latin America, China, and Southeast Asia, as well as Appalachian white migrants, she notes, often faced the same prejudice as blacks from would-be employers, landlords, and public officials. She concludes that "black traits" that whites disliked most—presumed laziness, violent proclivities, welfare-seeking, unreliability, shiftlessness, lack of ambition—were associated more with lower-class position than with race.

Yet Wilson (among others) is now rethinking the question of the urban underclass. As a result of research he directed at the Urban Poverty and Family Life Project in Chicago from 1985 to 1989, Wilson now says that *no one factor explains why some disadvantaged groups are more likely to join the underclass than others* (in Raymond, 1991:A12). The Chicago researchers focused on 2,490 inner-city residents—1,177 African-Americans, 458 Puerto Ricans, 474 Mexicans, and 381 whites—and investigated their work and family experiences, friendship networks, marriage and children, and use of welfare; they also looked at structural reasons for joblessness such as automation. Researchers found a combination of structural and cultural factors that account for the rise of chronic poverty among African-Americans, including the following: living in the poorest neighborhoods among unemployed people (thereby cutting off "weak ties," dis-

cussed in Chapter 7, to job leads), racial discrimination, generally positive attitudes toward welfare, lack of access to automobiles, the presence of a sole adult in the house (preventing the sharing of child-care duties), and plant shutdowns.

The upshot, Wilson says, is that the mass of poor and poorly trained African-Americans have little hope or chance of escaping poverty and low status. Years earlier, Glazer and Moynihan came to the same conclusion. In 1963, they wrote that blacks and Puerto Ricans in New York City were a "submerged, exploited, and very possibly permanent proletariat" (299).

*To conclude:* The notion that large groups of citizens may be permanently poor goes against the American grain. As Tocqueville long ago observed, Americans will endure poverty and even servitude, but not fixed class differences. In the past, different standards of life were made tolerable either by the idea of equal opportunity for advancement or by the American dream of upward mobility through a sweaty brow and a pinch of luck. All were reassured that they too could move up socially and economically. This assumption provided hope for generations of Americans. But now this assumption is widely questioned as (1) both blue and white-collar jobs disappear from the United States. and (2) the gap between rich and poor grows wider. Still, countless Americans continue to "dream up and blame down" (Teninty, 1992).

## Making It: Japanese-Americans

Some ethnic groups prospered against all odds. Japanese-Americans are a case in point. The Japanese have met prejudice, discrimination, and racism—"the denial on racist grounds of the right to naturalization, the denial in the areas where they largely lived of the right to own land or enter certain professions, and eventually complete exclusion" (Hosokawa, 1969:xi). At the outbreak of World War II, about 110,000 Japanese-Americans living on the West Coast were evacuated from their homes and put behind barbed wire in "war relocation camps," a

a

**Fig. 9.4** THE CRIME WAS ANCESTRY. (*a*) A Japanese-American child in Los Angeles awaits transportation to World War II "relocation centers" like Manzanar. (*b*) Manzanar. Today, almost nothing remains of the 500-acre living area except a cemetery, stone guard houses with graffiti, and a plaque at the camp near Death Valley where 10,000 Japanese-Americans were incarcerated for the duration of World War II. The plaque, placed by the California Department of Parks and Recreation in cooperation with the Manzanar Committee and the Japanese American Citizens League, is difficult to read because it has been defaced. It says:

In the early part of World War II, 110,000 persons of Japanese ancestry were interned in relocation centers by executive order no. 9006 issued on February 19, 1942. Manzanar, the first of ten such concentration camps, was surrounded by barbed wire and guard towers containing 10,000 persons, the majority being American citizens. May the injustice and humiliation suffered here as a result of hysteria, racism and economic exploitation never emerge again.

(*c*) When Japanese-Americans on the West Coast were evacuated to relocation camps, their businesses were taken over by whites. ([*a*] Library of Congress; [*b*] Tim Teninty; [*c*] National Archives)

IN THE EARLY PART OF WORLD WAR II, 10,000 PERSONS
OF JAPANESE ANCESTRY WERE INTERNED IN RELOCATION
CENTERS BY EXECUTIVE ORDER NO. 9066, ISSUED ON
FEBRUARY 19, 1942.

MANZANAR, THE FIRST OF TEN SUCH CONCENTRATION
CAMPS, WAS BOUNDED BY BARBED WIRE AND GUARD
TOWERS, CONFINING 10,000 PERSONS, THE MAJORITY
BEING AMERICAN CITIZENS.

MAY THE INJUSTICES AND HUMILIATION SUFFERED HERE
AS A RESULT OF HYSTERIA, RACISM AND ECONOMIC
EXPLOITATION NEVER EMERGE AGAIN.

CALIFORNIA REGISTERED HISTORICAL LANDMARK NO. 850

PLAQUE PLACED BY THE STATE DEPARTMENT OF PARKS
AND RECREATION IN COOPERATION WITH THE MANZANAR
COMMITTEE AND THE JAPANESE AMERICAN CITIZENS
LEAGUE, APRIL 14, 1973.

b

c

**Fig. 9.4** (*continued*)

euphemism for concentration camps. Many of their urban businesses were taken over by whites, and their rural land was confiscated.

Yet, since the war, the Japanese-American community, a tiny minority group (1990 population: 847,000, constituting 11.7 percent of the total Asian population and less than one-third of 1 percent of the total U.S. population), has prospered economically and escaped ghettoization. For instance, Japanese-Americans tend not to live in racial isolation from whites, and 48 percent of Japanese-Americans aged twenty to twenty-four were enrolled in college in 1980, far exceeding the enrollment rate for whites (24 percent). Some scholars think that traditional Japanese culture and values have much to do with it. First-generation Japanese-Americans (*Issei*) came from a culture in which "diligence in work, combined with simple frugality, had an almost religious imperative, similar to what has been called 'the Protestant ethic' in Western culture," and psychologically, the *Issei* carried with them an "achievement orientation" (Petersen in Hosokawa, 1969:495). Such values were transmitted from *Issei* to *Nisei* (the second generation in America) and to succeeding generations by strong family ties and culture.

Some scholars dispute this cultural explanation. They suggest that Japanese emigrants started off with economic advantages: They tended to be skilled, literate nonpeasants whose technological know-how gave them a chance to grab onto the ladder of success (e.g., Ideda, 1973).

Will Japanese-Americans retain their distinctive culture? Probably not. The outmarriage rate is high. For example, in Los Angeles County, the U.S. center of Japanese-American population, the outmarriage rate is above 50 percent for the third and subsequent generations (Daniels, [1990]1991: 353). Furthermore, Japanese-Americans are moving out of "Japantowns" in big cities such as San Francisco.

Since the 1980s, Japanese-Americans have often been called part of an Asian "model minority." This stereotype is based partially on facts—for example, Japanese-Americans *are* more likely than whites to go to college in the United States,

and the average Japanese-American household had a median income of $40,537 (in constant 1990 dollars) in 1980, higher than whites' median income—but it obscures a great deal (e.g., Chinese women working for illegally low wages in garment sweatshops; a 12.2 percent poverty rate for the Asian and Pacific Islanders in 1990, compared with 8.8 percent for non-Hispanic whites). For Japanese-Americans in particular, the "model minority" label hides discomfort, fear of hate crimes, discrimination, and violence fueled by Japan bashing in America.

## Gays and Lesbians: An Ethnic-like Group?

The idea that there is such a thing as a "gay identity" is fairly recent, probably dating to the mid-1970s (Epstein, 1987:10). At that time, gays and lesbians came to see themselves as a legitimate and stigmatized minority, an ethnic-like group deserving the same legal protections against discrimination, defamation, and hate crimes as ethnic groups.

Whether or not gays and lesbians constitute a ethnic group is much debated. Some conservative religious groups and politicians see homosexuals as "deviants" who "violate human nature," reject "family values," and have an unacceptable "alternative lifestyle," not as members of an ethnic group.

Nonetheless, many gay communities act like ethnic groups. And before AIDS started to decimate them, gay male communities often resembled ethnic urban villages. (Typically, lesbians spread out more geographically but maintain strong support networks.) For example, San Francisco's Castro district in the late 1970s was a gay urban village—a spatially segregated and culturally distant ghetto—of some 25,000 to 30,000 gay men. It contained about 150 gay institutions ranging from bars, political clubs, newspapers, churches, and singing groups to a business association (FitzGerald, [1981] 1987:27).

Politically speaking, gays act like highly organized ethnic groups in many big cities. In San Francisco, to continue the example, "gays and

**Fig. 9.5**   GAY PRIDE. Activists at Gay Pride Day in San Francisco, June, 1992. (Deborah Mosca)

lesbians can claim the highest level of electoral mobilization, representation, and political assimilation in the city's political system" (DeLeon, 1992:30). Indeed, gay and lesbian clout has changed city politics. According to Manuel Castells, "the gay community transformed the local political system, making it very difficult for conservatives [particularly business interests] to control the city, and creating an alternative power base relying on neighborhood associations, public workers' unions, and oppressed ethnic communities" (1983:168–69).

In recent years, AIDS has taken a devastating toll on gay male communities throughout the nation. For example, in San Francisco, a survey taken in the late 1980s indicated that as many as 50 percent of gay men had been exposed to the AIDS virus. Thus for thousands, living with AIDS has replaced gay institution building. Yet, the city's contribution to AIDS patients as of June 1990—nearly $25 million in city funds (much more than federal and state contributions of $15.6 million), plus funds from community groups, nonprofit organizations, and businesses (DeLeon, 1992:190) —reflects local commitment to the gay community or communities. (Paralleling many nationality-based ethnic groups, the "first-wave" and "second-wave" gay immigrants distinguish between themselves on the basis of generation, manners, and style. But they show an opposite pattern: Second-generation gay organizations, such as ACTUP and Queer Nation, tend to be less establishment oriented and more confrontational than first-generation groups; in contrast, second-generation, nationality-based ethnic organizations, such as the Japanese American

Citizens League, tend to be hyperpatriotic and distance themselves from the previous generation [Kitano and Daniels, 1988].)

## Multiculturalism

*"Who controls the present controls the past."* This truism—that history is written by dominant groups—is not always true in multicultural America. Since the 1960s, more textbooks and artworks have come to reflect the views of the once vanquished or still subordinated. Two key processes influenced this new outlook: (1) the arrival of millions of non-European immigrants who brought with them a great variety of cultures and languages, and (2) social movements, particularly civil rights and women's rights, which alerted the nation to the separate and often unequal condition of many Americans.

While some scholars applaud so-called multiculturalists for expanding the historical vision, others blame them for helping to "disunite" America. The late Allan Bloom led the conservative attack on "the new [multicultural] curriculum" in his best-seller, *The Closing of the American Mind* ([1987] 1988:380). Bloom argues that multiculturalism is based on cultural relativism, a wrongheaded philosophy because human nature remains the same. Bloom's antidote? The Great Books approach, "in which a liberal education means reading certain generally recognized classic texts" (344), such as those of Plato and Shakespeare. Some liberals, notably historian Arthur M. Schlesinger, Jr., joined the conservative outcry against multiculturalism. In *The Disuniting of America* (1991), Schlesinger reveals his fear that ethnocentric chauvinists and academic hustlers will manipulate students' emotions and preach romantic notions of separatism. Meanwhile, radical critics charge that Bloom is sexist, antidemocratic, and elitist. Further, radicals suggest that both liberals and conservatives tend to confuse cause and effect. They say that multiculturalists did not *cause* the disunity of the United States; rather, fragmentation happened because

so many Americans were denied protection and resisted oppression. Finally, a variety of observers want to broaden the definition of multiculturalism. They argue that differences in regional background, class, religion, age, and gender identity are important cultural differences, neglected in the contemporary discussion of multicultures, which spotlights only ethnic-racial identity (e.g., Rodriquez, 1993).

*Columbus: Hero or Villain?* To write history is to construct, not merely record, reality. To *rewrite* history from the viewpoint of the vanquished—not the victors—can change the meaning of events and thus lead to heated controversy. Take one example: the transformation of Christopher Columbus. The year 1992 marked the five-hundredth anniversary of Columbus's arrival in the Americas. In many U.S. cities, this event was marked by celebrations, for conventional histories revere Columbus as the symbol of a triumphant European civilization: the hero who "discovered" America. But revised histories tell a different story. For example, *1492–1992: The Legacy of Columbus* (Zinn, 1991); *The Conquest of Paradise: Christopher Columbus and the Columbian Legacy* (Sale, 1990); *Dangerous Memories: Invasion and Resistance Since 1492* (Golden, 1992); and *Stolen Continents: The Americas through Indian Eyes Since 1492* (Wright, 1992) depict Columbus as an antihero who destroyed native cultures. Influenced by such revised thinking, some U.S. cities decided not to celebrate Columbus Day. In Berkeley, California, for example, a task force compared commemorating Columbus Day to "celebrating the massacre of thousands of indigenous people" because "Columbus was the person who began the genocide of Americans" (Curl in Rostler, 1992). Berkeley now celebrates October 12 as Indigenous Peoples Day.

No doubt as the United States becomes more colorful and multicultural, there will be more debates, even battles, over whose version of history to teach. Public schools are already a battleground.

To understate the case, college professors are

divided on multiculturalism. Some fear politicization of the traditional European-American–based curriculum ("the canon") and the breakdown of common discourse centered on "generic humanity." Others applaud the addition of new voices with new interpretations, arguing that U.S. colleges have long been politicized—promoting a narrow white European male view at the expense of subordinate groups such as people of color and women. Typically, conservatives fear what they call "political correctness" and the fragmentation of knowledge more than too narrow a vision; radicals fear what they call "Eurocentric monoculturalism" and "educational oppression" more than Balkanization. Often, liberals, wishing to make some curriculum changes without changing academe's deep structure, suffer the deepest personal pangs as epithets such as "racist" or "elitist" are thrown around on campuses.

Is it possible to celebrate heterogeneity *and* to retain the notion of "one nation, indivisible"? Opinions differ. Apparently, the Tennessee State Senate thinks so. Aware that they represent people of many faiths, not only Christians, the senators opened a session with an Islamic prayer. But a French academic, echoing Ken Jowitt's distinction between civics versus ethnics, thinks not: "Do we want to protect the rights of individuals or those of communities? We cannot have both" (in Brett, 1992:A37). (Historically, the French government has sponsored cultural homogeneity, not multiculturalism. Practically, this means that schools become the main vehicle for turning Algerian, Vietnamese, Senegalese, and other immigrants into Frenchmen and Frenchwomen; they do this by treating immigrants as individuals, not members of communities.)

Separatists of all colors, creeds, and pocketbooks—from white supremacists and black nationalists to wealthy folks living in gated communities protected by security guards—have chosen isolation or abandoned hope. Yet others hope to build multicultural understanding. How? Not through laws: Laws can break down barriers, but they cannot build bridges. Coming to terms with blood and beliefs may take a large dose of what the distinguished Bengali philosopher-artist Rabindranath Tagore (1861–1941) called "unity consciousness."

And it may take powerful artworks to help us to cross the bridge. Anna Deavere Smith's theaterpieces are just such works. In *Fires in the Mirror*, Stanford drama professor Smith acquaints us with twenty-six people—including Angela Davis, a Hasidic Jewish housewife, and the Reverend Al Sharpton—by drawing on their verbatim comments about emotionally charged events in Crown Heights, Brooklyn, New York: an African-American child's death in a car accident, a riot, and a retaliatory killing of a Hasidic Jewish student. In her theaterpiece about the Los Angeles riots and their aftermath, *Twilight: Los Angeles, 1992* (1993), Smith gives us an intimate acquaintance with very complicated conflicts involving Latinos, African-Americans, Koreans, whites, and police. She becomes the people she interviewed—from Rodney King's aunt and former Police Chief Daryl Gates to former Black Panther leader Elaine Brown and truckdriver Reginald Denny. As a whole, her work suggests that we need to discover our social glue. This theme runs through the words of Denny, beaten to near-death and then saved by people who saw the beating on TV. In the hospital, Denny awakens from unconsciousness, perhaps metaphorically as well as literally. Surrounded by urban strangers who saved his life and thinking about other total strangers who stuck by him, including helicopter pilots, Denny says, "There's a weird common thread in our lives." Smith helps viewers to take a step across the cultural abyss and to feel the common thread. At the same time, she faithfully represents the deep differences among her characters without judging them.

Also, scholarship can cross, even redefine, boundaries. One groundbreaking book is the first volume of Martin Bernal's *Black Athena:The Afroasiatic Roots of Classical Civilization* (1987). Bernal argues that Afroasiatic influences on classical Greece were systematically suppressed since the 1900s—mainly for racist reasons. Another is a provocative literary study, *Was Huck Black? Mark Twain and African-American Voices* (1993). Author Shelley Fisher Fishkin, a professor of American studies, suggests that Mark Twain

**Fig. 9.6** POLITICAL PLURALISM, 1950. Billboards in front of the Lower Manhattan Republican Club shows that a "balanced ticket" in New York City at that time meant white ethnic pluralism—from WASP and Irish to Jewish and Italian. (Museum of the City of New York)

based much of Huck's character and language on a black child he met in the 1870s. Her finding is important for many reasons, not least because Twain's *Huckleberry Finn*, published in 1884, is at the center of the American literary canon. Tracing Huck Finn's voice to a black source suggests that "African-american [*sic*] voices have helped shape what we have thought of a mainstream American literature" (Fishkin in Winkler, 1992:A6). Many literary scholars think that Fishkin's study is a major step in the emerging recognition of the overlap and interplay between ethnic cultures in the United States.

*To conclude:* Recognizing, even celebrating, ethnic differences brings back the enduring issue of community: insiders versus outsiders. As a *Newsweek* columnist phrased it, "You can't have the old enriching differences without some of the old prejudices" (Will, 1979:116). In other words, cultural identity wears two faces. One is proud and strong, giving a sense of special belonging to individuals and a rich variety to urban life. It gives the Dutch-Americans of small-town Pella, Iowa, and the former residents of Boston's Italian-American West End a sense of community. But the other side is ugly, glowering with misunderstanding and hate. And it is in cities, which bring together heterogeneous individuals, where both faces of cultural pluralism are so prominently displayed.

## ANOTHER LOOK

In a nation considered democratic and modern, positions assigned at birth—such as ethnic status—are supposed to count for little. But this is just not the case. Persistent inequalities still exist among ethnic groups, and our life chances are significantly influenced by the ethnic group into which we are born. This runs counter to democratic theory.

True, ethnicity is largely symbolic for some people today. Cosmopolitan citizens of the world (who tend to be affluent, college-degreed, idea workers) typically have more in common than with each other than with fellow ethnics or coreligionists, whether they live in New York City, London, or Tokyo.

Yet for many others, ethnicity remains significant, even primary. This, too, runs counter to classical social theory. Tönnies, Durkheim, and Marx, among others, suggested that kinship and blood relations are not key factors in the social organization of capitalist, mass society. Marx, for one, believed that ethnic ties would be replaced by bonds of social class in capitalist society. But so far, at least, ethnicity remains one of the strongest ties that bind throughout the globe, often coexisting and competing with cosmopolitanism. Moreover, whole nations are coming apart, apparently along ethnic lines. So, we see two opposing trends: (1) religious community, ethnic brotherhood and sisterhood, and ganglike organizations growing in strength, anchoring those adrift in a worldwide search for identity and meaning, and (2) many citizens coming together on the basis of supranational and cross-ethnic concerns—toxic waste in the global environment, space exploration, and workplace safety, to name just a few. Thus from Quebec, Northern Ireland, northern Italy, and Basque Spain to the former Yugoslavia and Soviet Union, India, Iraq, South Africa, and Sri Lanka, *Gemeinschaft*-like, communal loyalties compete with a *Techno$chaft* identification in a global village.

These are unsettling or exciting times, depending on your pessimism-optimism score. Or may-be both. In general, social conservatives are pessimistic about race relations, believing that "tribal" or ethnic feelings run so deep that they may be primordial, a part of "human nature." In this view, individual responsibility (not government programs such as affirmative action) and personal values are key components of good race-ethnic relations. Historically, liberals have been more optimistic, counting on public programs to level the playing field for the disenfranchised. But their mood took a dark turn in the Reagan–Bush era and the economic recession of the early 1990s. Many agree with Blanche Wiesen Cook (1992) that "race is where Americans have put their hate marbles." Growing numbers of liberals support political scientist Andrew Hacker's grim assessment: There is endemic racism in the United States. In contrast, radicals tend to think that liberals are obsessed with race—using race rather than social class to explain many U.S. events, including the Rodney King riots (which some radicals call a "rebellion") in Los Angeles. They tend to criticize liberals such as Hacker for minimizing government and corporate policies that perpetuate poverty and racism.

Wherever you score on the optimism–pessimism scale, remember: We may be approaching the end of an era. If so, we can expect to see breakthroughs in social theory. Meanwhile, it pays to be humble. In recent years, social scientists failed to foresee momentous changes affecting migration, race, and ethnicity, ranging from civil unrest in Los Angeles, the fall of the Berlin Wall, and the disintegration of the former Soviet bloc to "ethnic cleansing" in Bosnia, Rwanda, and elsewhere.

## KEY TERMS

**Acculturation**  A process by which one culture is modified through contact with another. Many subcultural differences are retained in the process.

**Assimilation**  (1) The merging of dissimilar subcultures into one common culture or (2) the absorption of one group by another, whereby the absorbed group loses its prior distinctiveness.

**Ethnicity**  A "consciousness of kind" or sense of peoplehood based on a subjective sense of community. Ethnicity can be based on national, racial, or religious background or, according to Max Weber, the sharing of a common identity based on a shared history.

**Insider-as-insighter doctrine**  The principle that only members of a group can truly understand that group's experiences due to their privileged access to knowledge. Otherwise stated: "You have to be one to know one" (whatever "one" is—female, Polish, dancer, soldier, etc.). Generally rejected by social scientists and journalists.

**Melting pot**  Process by which a unique American supposedly emerges from the blending together of immigrants with dissimilar backgrounds. Contrast: **stewpot.**

**Minority**  In the 1920s, this term referred to European national groups seeking self-determination after World War I (e.g., Latvians). In the 1930s, it referred to ethnic and racial groups in the United States. Sociologist Louis Wirth emphasized social oppression (minorities as victims) in his 1945 definition of minority groups.

**Multiculturalism**  Two connotations, depending on the user's ideology: (1) the celebration of pluralism or heterogeneity in a society where ethnic and other minority groups retain their cultural identity in a stewpot or (2) the fragmentation and breakdown of shared culture into groups based on race, ethnicity, age, gender and so on.

**Stewpot**  My term, rejecting the idea that the United States is a true melting pot. It implies that ethnic groups retain important social, economic, and/or cultural distinctions.

**Symbolic ethnicity**  Sociologist Herbert J. Gans's term for a voluntary ethnic involvement emphasizing identity—the *feeling* of being Italian, Japanese, or Jewish, for example—which expresses itself in various symbolic ways, particularly a nostalgic allegiance to the immigrant culture, ceremonial holiday celebrations, and special foods. Contrast: ethnicity as an important, taken-for-granted part of everyday life that is involuntary, public, and communal.

## PROJECTS

1. **"We Can All Get Along."** Rodney King's post-1992 riot/rebellion words have a hopeful ring. But growing numbers of people worldwide—from Bosnia's Serbs and Rwanda's Hutus to Sri Lanka's Tamil Tigers, Algeria's religious fundamentalists, and America's Posse Comitatus—are eschewing the goal of ethnic-racial and/or religious harmony. Using archival materials and electronic resources (e.g., Internet news groups), analyze the appeal and rationales of separatists. First, try to determine the number and kinds of separatist movements worldwide today. Second, choose three groups and determine their ideologies, paying special attention to their definitions of "outsiders." Third, analyze the members of the three groups in terms of relevant factors (e.g., occupation, gender, educational background, age, ethnicity). Do patterns emerge? If so, construct a typology of separatist groups.

2. **Ethnic-based institutions.** Historically, what ethnic-based institutions—newspapers, social clubs, marriage brokers, soccer clubs, churches, and so on—existed in your city or a nearby large city? How many remain viable today? Try to establish whether these organizations are central or peripheral to people's lives by interviewing readers, club members, and so on.

3. **Assimilation versus separation.** What do people lose and gain from leaving behind their cultural heritage (e.g., language, values) and joining—or attempting to join—the mainstream? First, examine what novelists and essayists say. Here are a few whose writings touch these issues: Richard Rodriguez, Richard Wright, V. S. Naipaul, Aaron Wildavsky (on his view of biblical personages), Jessica Hagedorn, Amy Tan, Chaim Potok, and Chinua Achebe. Then, if possible, interview a variety of newcomers and old-timers in terms of American immigration. Why and when did some "Americanize" their surnames? By the third generation, have some taken back their former surnames or created new first or last names as symbols of ethnicity? What value clashes occur in a family between the first

generation born and raised in the United States and their parents born outside the United States?

## SUGGESTIONS FOR FURTHER LEARNING

The literature on race and ethnicity in the United States and worldwide is voluminous. Studies range from a general work, Roger Daniels's *Coming to America: A History of Immigration and Ethnicity in American Life* (New York: Harper Perennial, [1990] 1991), to highly specialized monographs, such as Moshe Semyonov and Noah Lewin-Epstein's *Hewers of Wood and Drawers of Water: Noncitizen Arabs in the Israeli Labor Market* (Ithaca, N.Y.: ILR Press, Cornell University, 1987). Among the numerous studies of a particular ethnic group, see Illsoo Kim's *New Urban Immigrants: The Korean Community in New York* (Princeton, N.J.: Princeton University Press, 1981). For an overview of the scholarly literature, see J. Milton Yinger, "Ethnicity," *Annual Review of Sociology* 11 (1985):151–180.

For an example of changing definitions of race, see James W. Loewen, *The Mississippi Chinese: Between Black and White,* 2nd ed. (Prospect Heights, Ill.: Waveland Press, 1988). The 1,200 Delta Chinese came to the state of Mississippi about 1869 as sharecroppers. Originally classed with blacks, they are now viewed as essentially "white."

Martin Scorsese's films show that ethnicity remains important in many U.S. neighborhoods. In *Goodfellas* (1990), the film's key character, Henry Hill, was denied privileged status ("made man") in the Sicilian gang organization because his father was not Sicilian. *Italianamerican* (forty-eight minutes; made in 1974, released in 1990) is a documentary portrait of his parents, Charlie and Catherine Scorsese, who remember the hardships they encountered in establishing new lives in the United States.

Ethnicity may also play a role in life expectancy. Generally, nonwhite ethnic groups have shorter life expectancies. See Kyriacof C. Markides and Charles S. Mindel, *Aging and Ethnicity* (Newbury Park, Calif.: Sage, 1987), for trends in aging within various ethnic populations.

According to Michael Ignatieff, ethnic conflict is often driven by what Freud called the "narcissism of minor differences." That is, basically similar populations make much out of small differences that set them apart in a search for identity. In *Blood and Belonging: Journeys into the New Nationalism* (New York: Farrar, Straus & Giroux, 1994), he argues that conflicts between Serbs and Croats in the former Yugoslavia and between working-class Catholics and Protestants in Northern Ireland—who are more alike in terms of customs, language, political culture, and shared memories than any other groups—exemplify such narcissism.

An important work of scholarship in the multiculturalism debate is the first volume of Martin Bernal's projected four-volume series *Black Athena: the Afroasiatic Roots of Classical Civilization* (New Brunswick, N.J.: Rutgers University Press, 1987). In the first volume, Bernal, a professor of government at Cornell, argues that ancient Egyptian civilization was essentially African but that racist tendencies in nineteenth-century classical studies led to the denial of the influences of ancient Egypt and Phoenicia on classical Greek civilization for 150 years.

For a novel that reveals the spread of U.S. culture to other cultures, see Haruki Murakami, *Dance Dance Dance* (New York: Kodansha International, 1993). The narrator of the book, a citizen of Tokyo, idolizes Clint Eastwood and snacks at McDonald's or Dunkin' Donuts.

For a review essay of books dealing with multiculturalism, ethnic identity, and/or education, see Andrew Hacker, "Trans-National America," *New York Review of Books*, November 22, 1990, pp. 19–24.

Many see a seething cauldron in the United States, not a melting pot. Historian Arthur Schlesinger, Jr., argues on "What's American?" an audiotape (May 1992, Common Ground), that the "cult of ethnicity" could be dangerous. From a different angle, Ben J. Wattenberg sees a melting pot that is "alive, flourishing, expanding." Wattenberg, a fellow at the conservative American Enterprise Institute, concedes the existence of ethnic animosities but accentuates the upbeat idea that "In America everything is possible" in the

PBS video *The First Universal Nation* (June 1992).

In his video (First Run Features, 1991) and book *Blood in the Face* (New York: Thunder Mouth's Press, 1990), James Ridgeway examines one part of the seething U.S. cauldron: the racialist far right. He argues that the far right provides small-town America with "an interpretive framework with which to understand what was taking place" (e.g., farm foreclosures) behind the chaos of the times (1990:8). According to Ridgeway, white racists, such as the Aryan Nations, address "the fear and anger" of a large and growing group of Americans who feel that conventional politics offer them no hope. The book (1990:94) contains an excerpt from one of the racialist movement's key works, William Pierce's *The Turner Diaries* (1978); often compared with Hitler's *Mein Kampf*, it is a futuristic novel describing a group of whites who blow up FBI headquarters and start an all-out race war, thus establishing white supremacy in the United States.

In *The Rage of a Privileged Class* (New York: HarperCollins, 1993), journalist Ellis Cose reports on the anger of well-educated, successful African-Americans based on what they see as white racism. Cose quotes former New York City Mayor David Dinkins agreeing with a comment he heard: "A white man with a million dollars is a millionaire, and a black man with a million dollars is a nigger with a million dollars."

Stanford drama professor Anna Deveare Smith's powerful theaterpieces, *Fires in the Mirror* and *Twilight* (about the 1992 Los Angeles chaos) are in a class by themselves. Smith's extraordinary work combines social science interviews with an artistic sensibility to produce an understanding of the multiple realities of racial, ethnic, and class conflicts. *Fires in the Mirror* has been presented on PBS's *American Playhouse* (1993); it is also available on two audiocassettes (Bantam Doubleday Dell Audio, 1993) and in book form (New York: Doubleday, Anchor, 1993).

Donald Young's landmark book, *American Minority Peoples: A Study in Racial and Cultural Conflicts in the United States* (New York: Harper, 1932), pioneered the concept of minority peoples in America. Interestingly, Young did not link Europe's minorities (resulting from World War I) to America's minorities.

That "history is a battleground" is a point made by Deborah Lipstadt in *Denying the Holocaust: The Growing Assault on Truth and Memory* (New York: Free Press, 1993). In this case study of people who fabricate history, she traces the movement of Holocaust deniers.

In *America Revised: History Schoolbooks in the Twentieth Century* (Boston: Little, Brown, 1979), Pulitzer Prize winner Frances FitzGerald tells how Columbus has become a "minor character" in U.S. history as history gets remade in accord with the changing fashions and prejudices of the era. Ward Churchill's *Fantasies of the Master Race: Literature, Cinema and the Colonization of American Indians* (Monroe, Me.: Common Courage Press, 1992) is a pointed examination of "culture and genocide" in the 500 years since the arrival of Columbus. That history is written by the victors —not the vanquished—is a central point of the Oscar-winning Argentine film *The Official Story* (1985). History from the viewpoint of the vanquished is put forward in Michael Apted's documentary film *Incident at Oglala* (1992), an inquiry into the case of Leonard Peltier, an American Indian Movement activist convicted of killing two FBI agents in a shootout on the Pine Ridge reservation in 1975.

In *Loose Canons: Notes on the Culture Wars* (New York: Oxford University Press, 1992), Henry Louis Gates, Jr., says that in a world divided by nationalism, sexism, and racism, the way to rise above these divisions is to forge a civic culture that respects people's cultural similarities and differences. In *A Different Mirror: A History of Multicultural America* (Boston: Little, Brown, 1993), a professor of ethnic studies at Berkeley, Ron Takaki, answers the conservative critics of multiculturalism.

Allan Bloom, Dinesh D'Souza, and Roger Kimball are associated with a disapproving voice toward political correctness and (what they consider the excesses of) multiculturalism. *New York Times* reporter Richard Bernstein joins the chorus with *Dictatorship of Virtue: Multiculturalism and the Battle for America's Future* (New York: Knopf, 1994).

Many volumes focus on enhancing multicultural awareness. See Don C. Locke, *Increasing Multicultural Understanding* (Newbury Park, Calif.: Sage, 1992). In *Paul Robeson Jr. Speaks to Ameri-*

*ca* (New Brunswick, N.J.: Rutgers University Press, 1993), Robeson says that the controversy about multiculturalism is "at the heart of a profound ideological struggle over the values of American culture and the nature of U.S. civilization." Robeson, the son of the civil rights activist, actor, and singer, claims that "the inability of melting-pot liberalism to accommodate racial diversity along with ethnic diversity is the primary cause of racial conflict on predominately white campuses."

Betty Jean Craige argues that there are two types of multiculturalists: *globalists* (who promote public awareness of human diversity and "weaken the dominant culture by reducing national loyalty") and *ethnic preservationists* (who promote distinct cultural identities and "weaken the dominant culture by refusing to blend into it"). Both types, she says, have the potential for "ideologically disuniting the nation" and redefining the notion of "patriotism." See her article "Multiculturalism and the Vietnam Syndrome," *Chronicle of Higher Education*, January 12, 1994, p. B3.

On June 12, 1967, the U.S. Supreme Court ruled unanimously that laws barring racial intermarriage in sixteen states were unconstitutional. By the early 1990s, there were about 1 million interracial couples in the United States. Noting a biracial baby boom that started in the late 1960s, Maria P. P. Root, ed., *Racially Mixed People in America* (Newbury Park, Calif.: Sage, 1992), looks at the social and psychological adjustment of multiracial people as well as contemporary marriage patterns. Since 1988, college students on various campuses have formed mixed-race associations to discuss identity issues and political objectives. For example, there is a group at the University of California at Berkeley, the Multi-Ethnic Interracial Student Coalition, known as "Misc." There are also at least twenty chapters of a San Francisco–based group, the Association of Multi-Ethnic Americans.

Ellen K. Coughlin explains how "Conflicts over Census Categories [of race and ethnicity] Mirror Struggles in Society at Large" in *Chronicle of Higher Education*, March 24, 1993, p. A8. In this short review article, Coughlin discusses a report by the U.S. General Accounting Office that gives some history on the changes in 1990 categories.

Some groups maintain multiple identities. See, for example, "Cuban Jewish Women in Miami: A Triple Identity," a paper presented by Hannah R. Wartenberg at the eighty-third annual meetings of the American Sociological Association, Atlanta, Georgia, August 1988.

Moves toward a pan-ethnic identity are the subject of many recent studies. For an analysis of the emergence in the 1960s of an Asian-American consciousness, see Yen Le Espiritu, *Asian American Panethnicity: Bridging Institutions and Identities* (Philadelphia: Temple University Press, 1992). She notes that a new pan-ethnic identity came about, in large measure, for a political reason: strength in numbers. See Felix M. Padilla, *Latino Ethnic Consciousness* (South Bend, Ind.: Notre Dame University Press, 1985), for a discussion of the development of a collective identity among Puerto Ricans and Mexican-Americans in Chicago. For a discussion of the evolution of a "supratribal" identity among native Americans, see Stephen Cornell, *The Return of the Native* (New York: Oxford University Press, 1988) and *American Indian Ethnic Renewal* (New York: Oxford University Press, 1993).

In contrast, *Raising Black Children* (New York: Plume, 1993) by two African-American psychiatrists, Alvin F. Poussaint and James P. Comer, recognizes separate identity. The book is geared to child-rearing issues facing black children because, Poussaint says, "Parents ask, 'How do I raise a healthy black child in this racist society'?"

Taylor Branch begins his award-winning book, *Parting the Waters: America in the King Years, 1954–1963* (New York: Simon and Schuster, 1988), with the maxim that "race shapes the cultural eye—what we do and do not notice." In his history of the civil rights movement, Branch also pays close attention to class divisions within the black community. In his article "The Uncivil War," *Esquire*, May 1989, pp. 89–156, Branch analyzes the interethnic struggle between "two minorities of longstanding mutual empathy" who have in common "a history of cyclical swings between cultural separatism and assimilation"—African-Americans and Jews.

Richard Rodriguez's autobiography, *Hunger of Memory* (New York: Bantam, 1982), and commentaries on PBS's *MacNeil/Lehrer NewsHour* describe the heavy price of "making it" by assimilating into mainstream, middle-class America. Rodriguez's TV essays often speak to questions of multiculturalism, which he defines in class and regional terms as well as in terms of ethnic-racial categories.

Of special interest is a book with long-forgotten photographs by Ansel Adams and commentary by John Hershey: John Armor and Peter Wright's *Manzanar* (New York: Times Books, 1988). It documents the daily life of the Japanese-Americans who were taken at gunpoint to live in tar paper internment camps during World War II. In *Farewell to Manzanar* (Bantam: New York, [1973] 1985), Jeanne Wakatsuki Houston and James D. Houston give an account of one Japanese-American family's survival at Manzanar.

Pessimistic assessments of race relations in America have been on the ascendancy in recent years. Andrew Hacker's *Two Nations* (New York: Scribner, 1992), mentioned in the chapter, is exemplary. See also Derrick Bell's *Faces at the Bottom of the Well: The Permanence of Racism* (New York: Basic Books, 1992). Former Harvard Law School professor Bell argues that the United States is a racist country, and that blacks are worse off and more subjugated than at any time since slavery.

No ordinary museum, the Museum of Tolerance in Los Angeles features hands-on exhibits dealing with racial discrimination in the United States and atrocities all over the world. Sponsored by the Simon Wiesenthal Center, the museum opened in 1993 with a "Whisper Gallery" where visitors see and hear a variety of ethnic slurs from a video screen. Another exhibit encourages visitors to exchange places with people of different races to promote empathy.

## REFERENCES

Baltzell, E. Digby. 1964. *The Protestant Establishment: Aristocracy and Caste in America*. New York: Random House.

Bell, Derrick. 1992. *Faces at the Bottom of the Well: The Permanence of Racism*. New York: Basic Books.

Bernal, Martin. 1987. *Black Athena: The Afroasiatic Roots of Classical Civilization*. Vol. 1, *The Fabrication of Ancient Greece, 1785–1985*. New Brunswick, N.J.: Rutgers University Press.

Binzen, Peter. 1970. *Whitetown USA*. New York: Vintage.

Bloom, Allan. [1987] 1988. *The Closing of the American Mind: How Higher Education Has Failed Democracy and Impoverished the Souls of Today's Students*. New York: Simon and Schuster, Touchstone.

Brett, Patricia. 1992. "To French scholars, 'le politiquement correct' is a symptom of America's social breakdown." *Chronicle of Higher Education* (June 17):A37–38.

Brookhiser, Richard. 1991. *The Way of the WASP: How It Made America, and How It Can Save It, So to Speak*. New York: Free Press.

Bullard, Robert D., and Joe R. Feagin. 1991. "Racism and the city." Pp. 55–76 in M. Gottdiener and Chris G. Pickvance, eds., *Urban Life in Transition*. Urban Affairs Annual Reviews, vol. 39. Newbury Park, Calif.: Sage.

Carrasco, David. 1992. "The Spanish conquest." Audiotape. Boulder, Colo.: Alternative Radio.

Cash, W. J. 1941. *The Mind of the South*. New York: Vintage.

Castells, Manuel. 1983. "Cultural identity, sexual liberation and urban structure: The gay community in San Francisco." Pp. 138–170 in *The City and the Grassroots*. Berkeley: The University of California Press.

Chicago Religious Task Force on Central America. 1992. *Dangerous Memories: Invasion and Resistance Since 1492*. Chicago: Chicago Religious Task Force on Central America.

Churchill, Ward. 1992. *Fantasies of the Master Race: Literature, Cinema and the Colonization of American Indians*. Monroe, Me.: Common Courage Press.

Cook, Blanche Wiesen. 1992. Convention coverage with Robert MacNeil. PBS (July 13).

Coughlin, Ellen K. 1992. "Following Los Angeles riots, social scientists see need to develop fuller understanding of race relations." *Chronicle of Higher Education* (May 13):A10–11.

Daniels, Roger [1990] 1991. *Coming to America: A History of Immigration and Ethnicity in American Life*. New York: Harper Perennial.

Darnton, John. 1994. "Refugee crises growing trend worldwide." *San Francisco Chronicle* (August 8):A1+.

Davis, David Brion. 1992. "The American dilemma." *New York Review of Books* (July 16):13–17.

DeLeon, Richard Edward. 1992. *Left Coast City: Progressive Politics in San Francisco, 1975–1991.* Lawrence: University Press of Kansas.

Dinnerstein, Leonard, Roger L. Nichols, and David M. Reimers. [1979] 1990. *Natives and Strangers: Blacks, Indians, and Immigrants in America,* 2nd ed. New York: Oxford University Press.

The Documentary Consortium. 1992. "Your loan is denied." *Frontline,* PBS (June 23, 1992).

Epstein, Steven. 1987. "Gay politics, ethnic identity: The limits of social constructionism." *Socialist Review* 93–94 (May–August): 9–54.

Erlich, Reese. 1990. "Learning from Fremont: Suburban educators face tough new teaching problems in a district where students speak 80 languages." *San Francisco Examiner, This World* (March 11):15+.

Feagin, Joe R. 1991. "The continuing significance of race: Antiblack discrimination in public places." *American Sociological Review* 56 (February):101–116.

Fishkin, Shelley Fisher. 1993. *Was Huck Black? Mark Twain and African-American Voices.* New York: Oxford University Press.

FitzGerald, Frances. [1981] 1987. *Cities on a Hill: A Journey through Contemporary American Cultures.* New York: Simon and Schuster, Touchstone.

Gambino, Richard. 1992. "Political killing field: Presidency's path perilous indeed." *fra noi* (September):5+.

Gans, Herbert J. 1979. "Symbolic ethnicity: The future of ethnic groups and cultures in America." *Ethnic and Racial Studies* 2 (January):1–20.

Gates, Henry Louis, Jr. 1992. Comments in "Special report": "Race: Our dilemma still." *Newsweek* (May 11):48.

Glazer, Nathan, and Daniel Patrick Moynihan. 1963. *Beyond the Melting Pot.* Cambridge, Mass.: MIT Press.

Goffman, Erving. 1963. *Stigma.* Englewood Cliffs, N.J.: Prentice-Hall.

Golden, Renny. 1992. *Dangerous Memories: Invasion and Resistance Since 1492.* Chicago: Chicago Religious Task Force on Central America.

Greene, Jack P. 1976. " 'We the People'—the emergence of the American nation." Pp. 84–95 in Peter C. Marzio, ed., *A Nation of Nations: The People Who Came to America as Seen Through Objects, Prints, and Photographs at the Smithsonian Institution.* New York: Harper & Row.

Hacker, Andrew. 1992a. *Two Nations: Black and White, Separate, Hostile, Unequal.* New York: Scribner.

———. 1992b. Interview with Terry Gross on *Fresh Air,* KQED-FM (March 30).

Handlin, Oscar. 1952. *The Uprooted.* Boston: Little, Brown.

Holmstrom, David. 1992. "The new Americans." *Christian Science Monitor* (June 17):9–12.

Hosokawa, Bill. 1969. *Nisei: The Quiet Americans.* New York: Morrow.

Ideda, Kiyoshi. 1973. Review of *Japanese Americans: Oppression and Success,* by William Petersen. *Social Forces* 51 (June):499.

Jacobs, Jane. 1961. *The Death and Life of Great American Cities.* New York: Vintage.

Johnson, Dirk. 1991. "Paper gives a voice to Plains Indians." *New York Times* [national edition] (September 19):A10.

Jones, Jacqueline. 1992. *The Dispossessed: America's Underclasses from the Civil War to the Present.* New York: Basic Books.

Jowitt, Ken. 1992. Speech given at the at Commonwealth Club, San Francisco. KALW-FM.

Katznelson, Ira. 1981. *City Trenches: Urban Politics and the Patterning of Class in the United States.* New York: Pantheon.

Kilson, Martin, and George C. Bond. 1992. "Marginalized blacks." *New York Times* (May 17): A16.

Kitano, Harry H. L., and Lynn Chai. 1982. "Korean interracial marriage." *Marriage & Family Review* 5:75–89.

Kitano, Harry H. L., and Roger Daniels. 1988. *Asian Americans: Emerging Minorities.* Englewood Cliffs, N.J.: Prentice-Hall.

Kitano, Harry H. L., and Wai-Tsang Yeung. 1982. "Chinese interracial marriage." *Marriage & Family Review* 5:35–48.

Loewen, James W. 1988. *The Mississippi Chinese: Between Black and White,* 2nd ed. Prospect Heights, Ill.: Waveland Press.

Marzio, Peter C., ed. 1976. *A Nation of Nations: The People Who Came to America as Seen Through Objects, Prints and Photographs at the Smithsonian Institution.* New York: Harper & Row.

McLeod, Ramon G. 1991. "The challenge posed by state's ethnic mix." *San Francisco Chronicle* (February 26):A7.

Muschamp, Herbert. 1993. "Things generally wrong in the universe." *New York Times* [national edition] (May 30):sec. 2:30.

Mydans, Seth. 1991. "They're in a new home, but feel

tied to the old." *New York Times* [national edition] (June 30):A8.

Novak, Michael. 1971. *The Rise of the Unmeltable Ethnics.* New York: Macmillan.

O'Neill, Molly. 1992. "New mainstream: Apple pie and salsa." *New York Times* [national edition] (March 11):B1.

Owens, Bill. 1975. *Our Kind of People: American Groups and Rituals.* San Francisco: Straight Arrow Books.

Patterson, Orlando. 1977. *Ethnic Chauvinism: The Reactionary Impulse.* New York: Stein and Day.

Patterson, Orlando, and Chris Winship. 1992. "White poor, black poor." *New York Times* (May 3):A17.

Portes, Alejandro, and Rubén G. Rumbaut. 1990. *Immigrant America: A Portrait.* Berkeley: University of California Press.

Protzman, Ferdinand. 1992. "German attacks rise as foreigners become scapegoat." *New York Times* [national edition] (November 2):1, A4.

Raymond, Chris. 1991. "Results from a Chicago project lead social scientists to a rethinking of the urban underclass." *Chronicle of Higher Education* (October 30):A9+.

———. 1992. "Controversial Harvard U. sociologist relishes his role as a maverick." *Chronicle of Higher Education* (March 4):A8–12.

Riding, Alan. 1991. "France sees integration as answer to view of immigrants as 'taking over.'" *New York Times* [national edition] (March 24):3.

Rieder, Jonathan. 1985. *Canarsie: The Jews and Italians of Brooklyn Against Liberalism.* Cambridge, Mass.: Harvard University Press.

Rodriquez, Richard. 1993. Comments on San Francisco's KQED-FM Forum (December 17).

Rostler, Suzanne. 1992. "Columbus day leaves Berkeley calendars." *Berkeley Voice* (January 16):1.

Sale, Kirkpatrick. 1990. *The Conquest of Paradise: Christopher Columbus and the Columbian Legacy.* New York: Knopf.

Schlesinger, Arthur M., Jr. 1991. *The Disuniting of America: Reflections on a Multicultural Society.* Knoxville, Tenn.: Whittle Direct Books.

Sears, David O., and Harris M. Allen, Jr. 1984. "The trajectory of local desegregation controversies and whites' opposition to busing." Pp. 123–151 in Marilynn B. Brewer and Norman Miller, eds., *Groups in Contact: The Psychology of Desegregation.* New York: Academic Press.

Simpson, Victor L. 1992. "Winds of hatred blow across Europe." *San Francisco Chronicle* (November 11):A10.

Smith, Anna Deveare. 1992–1993. *Fires in the Mirror.*

Broadway theaterpiece, PBS-TV, *American Playhouse* (April 1993); audiotapes, Bantam Doubleday Dell Audio); book, New York: Anchor Doubleday.

Soros, George. 1993. "Bosnia and beyond." *New York Review of Books* (October 7):15–16.

Steinfels, Peter. 1992. "Debating intermarriage, and Jewish survival." *New York Times* [national edition] (October 18, 1992):A1+.

Sturtevant, William C. 1976. "The first Americans." Pp. 4–23 in Peter C. Marzio, ed., *A Nation of Nations: The People Who Came to America as Seen Through Objects, Prints, and Photographs at the Smithsonian Institution.* New York: Harper & Row.

Teninty, Tim. 1992. Personal conversation. Berkeley, Calif.

United Nations High Commissioner for Refugees. 1993. "The state of the world's refugees—the challenge of protection." New York: United Nations.

U.S. Bureau of the Census. 1972. *1970 Census of Population: General Social and Economic Characteristics: United States Summary.* Appendix. Washington, D.C.: Government Printing Office.

Vidal, Gore. 1992. "Monotheism and its discontents." *The Nation.* (July 13):1+.

Weber, Max. [1921] 1968. *Economy and Society.* Vol. 1. Totowa, N.J.: Bedminister Press.

Whitney, Craig R. 1992. "East Europe's frustration finds target: immigrants." *New York Times* [national edition] (November 13):A1+.

Wilkerson, Isabel. 1992."The tallest fence: Feelings on race in a white neighborhood." *New York Times* [national edition] (June 21):12.

Will, George. 1979. "Wagons in a circle." *Newsweek* (September 17):116.

Wilson, William Julius. 1978. *The Declining Significance of Race: Blacks and Changing American Institutions.* Chicago: University of Chicago Press.

———. 1987. *The Truly Disadvantaged: The Inner City, the Underclass, and Public Policy.* Chicago: University of Chicago Press.

Winkler, Karen J. 1992. "A scholar's provocative query: Was Huckleberry Finn black?" *Chronicle of Higher Education* (July 8):A6–8.

Wirth, Louis. 1945. "The problem of minority groups." Pp. 347–372 in Ralph Linton, ed., *The Science of Man in the World Crisis.* New York: Columbia University Press.

Wolff, Michael, Peter Rutten, Albert F. Bayers III, and the World Rank Research Team. 1992. *Where We Stand: Can American Make It in the Global Race for*

*Wealth, Health, and Happiness?* New York: Bantam.

Wright, Robin. 1992. "Report from Turkestan." *New Yorker* (April 6):53–75.

Wright, Ronald. 1992. *Stolen Continents: The Americas Through Indian Eyes Since 1492.* Boston: Houghton Mifflin.

Yancey, William. L., Eugene P. Ericksen, and Richard N. Juliani. 1976. "Emergent ethnicity: A review and reformulation." *American Sociological Review* 41 (June):391–402.

Zangwill, Israel. 1909. *The Melting Pot: A Drama in 4 Acts.* New York: Macmillan.

Zinn, Howard. 1991. *1492–1992: The Legacy of Columbus.* Audiotape. Boulder, Colo.: Alternative Radio.

# PART IV
# Rules of the Game

*Douglas M. McWilliams*

Richard Hedman; revised by Lisa Siegel Sullivan

# CHAPTER 10
# Social Ladders

"All people are created equal." That's what children learn in U.S. schools.

But growing up, we begin to realize that some people are more equal than others. Looking around town, we may notice that some people live in big houses on tree-lined streets, while others inhabit shacks by the railroad tracks. On prime-time television, we watch dramas in which people with badges of authority—police shields, white hospital coats, security clearance tags—wield power over those who don't. We may come across novelist F. Scott Fitzgerald's famous statement to Ernest Hemingway: "The very rich are different from you and me."

Before reaching voting age, most of us sense that—rhetoric and the Declaration of Independence aside—all people are not born equal and don't grow up equal. Most of us sense these inequalities in America—between rich and poor, powerful and powerless, socially esteemed and socially shunned. But rarely do we examine the *social* bases of these differences. Why? Because we haven't been taught to do so. Primary- and secondary-school textbooks rarely refer to inequalities that are linked to social factors. Hence, many Americans end up believing that existing disparities result from personal failure or bad luck.

Why is it that some Americans have more of the good things in life than others? How do occupation and other social structural variables affect a person's life chances? This chapter explores these questions. It looks at the influence of class, status, power, gender, age, religion, race, and ethnicity on a person's place in the social hierarchy. First, it outlines two general theoretical approaches to equality and inequality: the perspectives of Karl Marx and Max Weber. Next, it looks at some conceptual updates to Marx and Weber. Then it examines social hierarchies in metropolitan America today.

This chapter, then, deals with the larger societal patterns that influence the games urbanites play. The following chapter focuses on the micro level of analysis—face-to-face social interaction—and it concludes by demonstrating the virtue of combining macro and micro perspectives to gain a more complete understanding of urban social organization.

## TWO WAYS OF LOOKING AT SOCIAL STRATIFICATION: MARX AND WEBER

The topic of **social stratification** (the process by which individuals and groups rank each other in a social hierarchy, from the Latin *strata*, meaning "layers") has occupied social thinkers for thousands of years. Over the millennia, many explanations have been offered to justify a society's inequalities and to explain why some possess more valuables (money, prestige, material goods, knowledge, power, etc.) than others. In the case of India, inequalities between **castes** (rigid social divisions based on status ascribed at birth) are justified by Hindu scriptures linking one's present position in the social hierarchy to one's past lives. In other religious belief systems, one's current position on the social ladder is tied to faith, good works, or divine providence.

With the birth of modern social science in nineteenth-century Western Europe came new, nonreligious explanations for social inequality. Particularly important were the theories of Karl Marx and Max Weber. Before discussing their theories in detail, however, we should note that pseudoscientists were not far behind scientists in explaining human inequity. Some claimed that intellectual superiority was related to skull size or body shape. Others proclaimed that criminals had particular physical characteristics. The most famous of all pseudoscientific explanations for social inequality was social Darwinism. This ideology justified inequality on biological grounds as part of "natural selection." In 1911, the distinguished anthropologist Franz Boas assaulted social Darwinism and the idea of social evolution in general, arguing that there were no significant innate differences between racial or national groups (Degler, 1991:chap. 3).

Recently, however, Darwinism (social and biological) returned as an explanation for inequalities in America. Highly controversial—indeed incendiary—studies claim that (1) different races have different brain sizes and hence different intelligence quotients (Rushton, 1994), or (2) I.Q.s vary with race and ethnicity, leading to a polarization between smart, affluent elites and unintelligent poor people in the United States (Herrnstein and Murray, 1994), or (3) the United States is in economic and political decline because the least intelligent and most politically apathetic part of the population outbreed the intelligent and rich segment (Itzkoff, 1994). Critics call these studies pornographic psuedo-science, not social science, charging that their authors use bad data, misuse statistics, depend on wrongheaded notions of both race and intelligence, make unwarrented conclusions, start from a conservative bias and agenda, and record little more than social prejudice.

Today in many countries—including Brazil, Haiti, and Pakistan—gross inequality exists, including modern slavery. Usually, the justification is economic: the chains of debt. (As the song about coal miners puts it, "I Owe My Soul to the Company Store.") According to some estimates, India and Pakistan keep up to 35 million people in bondage due to indebtedness. In Brazil, over 16,000 people were enslaved in the early 1990s. Mainly, landowners bound their cheap laborers by forcing them to run up unpayable debts at company stores. In the United States, laborers smuggled in from China are lured by stories of streets lined with gold; those who escape the immigration authorities typically end up as indentured servants to organized gangs, working seven days a week for over fourteen hours a day to pay off their $30,000 passage (NBC, 1993).

Over the millennia, then, inequality has been justified on various grounds, notably biology, religion, special skills, and economics. Were he alive, this would not surprise philosopher Jean-Jacques Rousseau. In the eighteenth century, Rousseau wrote that "the strongest is never strong enough to always be master, unless he transforms his strength into right, and obedience into duty." In other words, those atop the social ladder need an ideology to legitimize their top spot. Ideologies of inequality, like alchemy, can help transmute might into right and special interests into the "common good."

We now turn to the theories of social inequality put forward by two nineteenth-century social scientists, Marx and Weber. Their ideas remain important—and controversial.

## Living on the Cusp

The German philosopher Hegel once wrote, "The owl of Minerva flies at dusk," meaning that wisdom appears at certain historical times: the approaching end of one era and the start of another. We seem to be living in such interesting times, the shift from modern to postmodern, or *Gesellschaft* to *Techno$chaft*.

In the nineteenth century, two German social thinkers, Karl Marx and Max Weber, lived at another such historical moment. Both witnessed the rapid rise of industrial cities, the rural–urban shift, and the changing social relationships that industrialization and urbanization brought. Profoundly influenced by these changing times, first Marx and then Weber formulated theories to describe and explain the bases of social stratification in different historical settings.

## Marx and Weber: No Specifically Urban Theory

The models of Marx and Weber remain the leading theories of social stratification today. Often they are viewed as competing models. But in important ways, the two intellectual giants agreed. Indeed, Weber's model can be seen as an extension of Marx's model, as well as an alternative to it.

Neither Marx nor Weber (nor Durkheim, for that matter) developed a specifically urban theory. They both viewed the modern city as a *dependent* variable, dependent on—not independent of—its larger context: a bureaucratic, industrial capitalist, state-centered society (Saunders, 1981:12). Marx analyzed Western European history, capitalism, and capitalist societies, not cities per se (Katznelson, 1992:45). Weber, after visiting America in 1904, commented that U.S. cities

**Fig. 10.1**   KARL MARX AND MAX WEBER. (Marx, Radio Times Hulton Picture Library; Weber, Alfred Weber Institut für Sozial und Staatswissenschaften der Universität, Heidelberg, Germany)

"served as a metaphor for capitalist modernity" (in Katznelson, 1992:10).

Marxist thinkers ignored the city for more than a century after Friedrich Engels published his 1845 portrait of Manchester, England (Chapter 4). But Marxists' inattention to cities took a U-turn by the 1970s. Indeed, Marxist-inspired theorists led to nothing less than an explosion of urban theory. Their theorizing was so different from conventional wisdom that some call it a paradigm shift.

New urban theory, most notably put forward by Henri Lefebvre in suburban Paris, David Harvey in Baltimore and Oxford, and Manual Castells in Berkeley, reinvigorated urban studies by stirring up controversy and focusing on a different set of issues. These new urban theorists concentrate on the following issues: the interplay

between local policies and state power; the role of class conflict in social change; the production of urban space, and the connections between the global system of production-consumption-exchange and the function of cities in poor and rich countries.

Many non-Marxists have been influenced by the new paradigm. This is ironic: For the first time in this century, Marxist-inspired theories moved from the left margin to the mainstream in many American universities at the very time that nations calling themselves "Marxist" or "socialist" began to repudiate Marxism. As one wag put it after the fall of the Berlin Wall, "The only Marxists left teach at Berkeley or work in Havana!"

Now let's consider Marx's and Weber's general ideas about social inequality in capitalist-urban-industrial society. Then we'll look at a few conceptual updates that draw inspiration from Marx or Weber.

## Marx and the Concept of Class

[T]he "first and only" time her grandmother [the wealthy Mrs. Peabody, member of a distinguished upper-class New England family] ever slapped [her granddaughter Marietta Endicott Peabody Tree] was when, as a young girl, Marietta referred to an acquaintance as "very middle class." After the slap came these stern, grandmotherly words: "There are no classes in America—upper, lower, or middle. You are never to use that term again." (Birmingham, 1968:340)

Pulitzer Prize-winning journalist J. Anthony Lukas once remarked that "America's dirty little secret is not sex. It is not power. Nor is it success. America's dirty little secret is class. It remains a secret even to some of its most cruelly treated victims." Noting a *New York Times* survey that found that one-quarter of all Americans don't consider themselves as belonging to any class at all, Lukas concluded, "To most of us, class is something only Germans with beards write about" (1978:9).

Most likely, Lukas was referring to one famous bearded German: Karl Marx. But he might have been noting another: Max Weber. Both Karl Marx (1818–1883) and Max Weber (1864–1920) insisted on the crucial importance of class in determining a society's system of individual rights and privileges. Both thought that one's class position was a key to one's life chances. Yet the name of Weber, a political liberal in his own time, is not well known to most Americans. In contrast, Marx is widely recognized, and to put it mildly, his ideas on social class have been unpopular among most Americans. At various times in U.S. history, even to be suspected of being a Marxist has spelled disaster for college professors, artists, high government officials, and others in numerous walks of life. Some lost their jobs, their friends, even their lives (by suicide) for real or suspected ad-

herence to Marxism. Woody Allen's film *The Front* (1976) dramatizes the plight of a Hollywood screenwriter blacklisted during the McCarthy era of the 1950s.

Why have Marx's ideas been considered alien and un-American? Why, even after the fall of Soviet-style Communism, are Marxist ideas still viewed as dangerous by so many Americans? Why is the concept of class "America's dirty little secret"? What did Marx think brought about social and political inequalities? And why do his ideas still fascinate scholars and activists today, over 100 years after he sat in London's British Museum painstakingly working them out? Before we can begin to answer these questions, a little background on Marx's thought is called for.

As noted in Chapter 5, Marx was one of many European theorists trying to make sense out of what was going on in his own time. Most theorists—Marx, Durkheim, Tönnies, and so on—agreed on what they saw: rural folk streaming into the industrial cities to work in the expanding factory system. . . . The nature and meaning of work were being transformed. But Marx had a unique slant on these events. To Marx, these changes signaled a historical event that became central to his analysis of history: the emergence of a new class of people, a mass of urban workers who controlled neither their work process nor their working conditions. He called this class of urban propertyless workers the **proletariat**.

According to Marx, the proletariat was one of two major social divisions or classes to result from the development of capitalism. The other new class he called **capitalists** or the **bourgeoisie**: urban-based, propertied people who determined what the proletariat produced, how they produced it, and what wages they were paid. Capitalists pay workers less than the value they produce—and pocket the difference. This is the root of capitalist exploitation. Yet, workers don't realize they are being exploited, and often capitalists themselves are unaware that they are exploiters. They attribute their profit to their own cunning, their investment in technology, their management skill, and so on. Further, Marx wrote, the structures of capitalism lead to human beings becoming alienated—from themselves, from the products of their labor, and in the end, from their nature as human beings.

To Marx, the development of medieval cities and mercantile capitalism in Western Europe were inextricably linked. Marx's choice of the word *bourgeoisie* denotes this linkage, for a *bourg* is literally a town; thus a bourgeois is an urbanite.

Very briefly, Marx reasoned as follows. Both the proletariat and the bourgeoisie developed out of the transformation from feudal to capitalist society between the sixteenth and nineteenth centuries in Western Europe. As this historical shift proceeded, self-sufficient peasant economies died out. In their place arose city-based economies controlled by merchants and bankers, increasingly dependent on trade and commerce. The growth of mercantilist cities in medieval Europe, starting in the 1500s, marked the expropriation of rural people. According to Marx, *the separation of the peasant from the soil was the basis of the whole capitalist process.* As rural people were separated from the land and uprooted to work in urban manufacturing, they came under the domination of the bourgeoisie. Now the urban workers had no land, no wealth—nothing except their labor, which they sold to factory owners. Living at a subsistence level with no public welfare system or unions to represent them, workers had few bargaining chips against their employers. In this situation, capitalist factory owners could set the wage scale and working conditions to suit their own class interests—specifically, the maximization of profit. Inevitably, the class interests of the proletariat would conflict with those of the bourgeoisie; the owners of capital wanted to maximize profit, not the welfare of their workers.

Up to this point, Marx's analysis of history doesn't seem very controversial. Marx's contemporaries of varying ideologies described the process of social change (e.g., from *Gemeinschaft* to *Gesellschaft)* in much the same way that Marx viewed the shift from feudal to capitalist society. (That these descriptions of the rural–urban shift transcended ideology is indicated by a footnote to history: Marx's favorite novelist was a French conservative, Honoré de Balzac [1834, 1833] 1946)

who mourned the passing of French aristocratic society but chronicled its demise in terms Marx thought brilliant.)

Marx did not invent the concept of class. It dates at least to ancient Rome, when people were ranked in six social divisions according to their wealth. Nor was Marx the first to recognize the existence of classes; many historians before him had used the concept. Then why are his ideas on social class considered un-American by so many?

First, Marx defined **class** in a way that *linked economic control to social domination.* Marx's logic was as follows. The nature and beliefs of human beings depend on what they produce and how they produce it. A person's social class is determined by his or her relationship to the **means of production** (inputs such as raw materials and tools, which produce or add to things of value in his or her society. These inputs include land in feudalism and factory machines in industrial capitalism). Class depends on how much the individual owns or controls of the means of production. By extension, Marx reasoned, those who own or control the means of production in a society also control the social organization of production. Thus, *classes are not—repeat,* not— income groups. Class is much more than an economic position; it also denotes the social relations that grow out of the way a society organizes its economy (e.g., private or collective ownership of the technology in use).

To a non-Marxist, "**capital** is just a thing (a machine, for example) or a sum of money. For a Marxist, that thing or that sum of money is only the facade for a social relation of domination: the machine has the mysterious power to compel people to obey 'its' rhythms, the money makes people dance to its tune" (Heilbroner, 1978:35). Under what Marx called the capitalist **mode of production** (the productive and social arrangements under capitalism, including the private ownership of the means of production), to be a capitalist or bourgeois ensures social as well as economic domination.

Second, Marx maintained that human history could be understood best as a continuing struggle among classes for domination and control over scarce resources. It is this idea—inherent class conflict—that has traditionally gone against the American grain. American ideology stresses the opposite idea: harmony among social classes. The assumption of class harmony is captured in a favorite saying by laissez-faire economists: "A rising tide lifts all boats," meaning that economic prosperity and growth help rich and poor alike.

Conventional widsom in the United States holds that workers' interests and the interests of business and industry are allied, not antithetical. The classic statement of this position came from "Engine Charlie" Wilson, head of General Motors in the 1950s: "What's good for GM is good for America." To a Marxist, this kind of thinking is, in itself, a form of capitalist domination. The concept of **hegemony**—cultural leadership or domination—helps to explain why. According to Italian Marxist Antonio Gramsci ([1932] 1975:235), the masses do not have to be held in check by laws or police power because they accept a basic but false notion: that the dominant class represents the general interest of the nation, not its own class interest.

However, many Americans have been questioning the long-assumed harmony of interests between workers and owners. Most probably, their suspicion of conventional wisdom was jogged by the news of (or personal experience with) real-world events: Wall Street scandals, savings and loan vandals, tax breaks for U.S. multinationals relocating jobs offshore, corporate restructuring, and so on. *New York Times* analyst Louis Uchitelle reports that shared anxiety over the changing economy gives rise to class consciousness: "an awareness among millions of Americans that they occupy the same unsteady boat, even if they are doing well in high-paying jobs" (1994:A6). This "anxious class," numbering in the millions, are those who "cannot count on having their jobs next year or next month and those whose wages have stagnated or lost ground to inflation" (Reich in Uchitelle, 1994:A6). Indeed, in 1995, *Newsweek* announced that instead of a rising tide lifting all boats, "A Rising Tide Lifts the Yachts" (1995:62D). The gap be-

tween rich and poor had widened so much that the United States led the industrialized world in its inequality of income. (Specifically, the share of wealth owned by the top 1 percent of U.S. households climbed from 20 percent in the mid-1970s to 35.7 percent in 1989.) Still, the notion of a "class war" remains unpopular in America. So does Marx's idea that some are rich and powerful because others are poor and powerless. Instead of a class enemy, such as owners of capital and multinational corporations, Americans tend to direct their anger at "government, immigrants, and the poor, among others" (Uchitelle, 1994:A6).

Finally, what has seemed so alien about Marx's views are his predicted outcomes of the class struggle between bourgeoisie and proletariat, the haves and have-nots. According to Marx, inherent contradictions within capitalism between the **forces of production** (e.g., the technology in use) and the **social relations of production** (e.g., private ownership of the technology in use) would work themselves out in a dialectical process and lead to a new form of society. He believed that the proletariat would develop a subjective **class consciousness**, realizing that they share an objective class situation (long hours, little pay, no control over their work process, domination by another class). Ultimately, Marx thought, workers would act as a class to wrest control from the bourgeoisie. To Marx, this was inevitable. He wrote in "The Communist Manifesto" in 1848, a year marked by revolutions in Europe:

The essential condition for the existence, and for the sway of the bourgeois class, is the formation and augmentation of capital; the condition for capital is wage-labour. Wage labour rests exclusively on competition between the labourers. The advance of industry, whose involuntary promoter is the bourgeoisie, replaces the isolation of the labourers, due to competition, by their revolutionary combination, due to association. The development of Modern Industry, therefore, cuts from under its feet the very foundation on which the bourgeoisie produces and appropriates products. (in McLellan, 231)

*To conclude:* Marx used one measure of social stratification: class. For Marx, class denotes social

Box 10.1

## SOCIAL THEORIST AS POLITICAL PAMPHLETEER: "THE COMMUNIST MANIFESTO"

### Section 1: Bourgeois and Proletarians

The history of all hitherto existing society is the history of class struggle.

Freeman and slave, patrician and plebeian, lord and serf, guild-master and journeyman—in a word, oppressor and oppressed, stood in constant opposition to one another . . . .

The modern bourgeois society that has sprouted from the ruins of feudal society has not done away with class antagonisms. It has but established new conditions of oppression, new forms of struggle in place of the old ones.

Our epoch, the epoch of the bourgeoisie, possesses however, this distinctive feature: it has simplified the class antagonisms. Society as a whole is more and more splitting up into two great hostile camps, into two great classes directly facing each other: Bourgeoisie and Proletariat.

From the serfs of the Middle Ages sprang the chartered burghers of the earliest towns. From these burgesses the first elements of the bourgeoisie were developed.

The discovery of America, the rounding of the Cape, opened up fresh ground for the rising bourgeoisie . . . .

The feudal system of industry, under which industrial production was monopolized by closed guilds, now no longer sufficed for the growing wants of the new markets. The manufacturing system took its place. The guild-masters were pushed on one side by the manufacturing middle class; division of labour between the different corporate guilds vanished in the face of division of labour in each single workshop.

Meantime the markets kept ever growing, the demand ever rising . . . . The place of manufacture was taken by the giant, Modern Industry, the place of the industrial middle class, by industrial millionaires, the leaders of whole industrial armies, the modern bourgeois. Modern industry has established the world-market, for which the discovery of America paved the way. This market has given an immense development to commerce, to navigation, to communication by land. This development has, in its turn, reacted on the extension of industry; and in proportion as industry, commerce, navigation, railways extended, in the same proportion the bourgeoisie developed, increased its capital, and pushed into the background every class handed down from the Middle Ages.

We see, therefore, how the modern bourgeoisie is itself the product of a long course of development, of a series of revolutions in the modes of production and of exchange.

Each step in the development of the bourgeoisie was accompanied by a corresponding political advance of that class. An oppressed class under the sway of the feudal nobility, an armed and self-governing association in the medieval commune; here independent urban republic (as in Italy and Germany), there taxable "third estate" of the monarchy (as in France) . . . , the bourgeoisie has at last, since the establishment of Modern Industry and of the world-market, conquered for itself, in the modern representative State, exclusive political sway. The executive of the modern State is but a committee for managing the common affairs of the whole bourgeoisie . . . . The bourgeoisie has subjected the country to the rule of the towns. It has created enormous cities, has greatly increased the urban population as compared with the rural, and has thus rescued a considerable part of the population from the idiocy of rural life . . . .

Modern industry has converted the little workshop of the patriarchal master into the great factory of the industrial capitalist. Masses of labourers, crowded into the factory, are organized like soldiers. As privates of the industrial army they are placed under the command of a perfect hierarchy of officers and sergeants. Not only are they slaves of the bourgeois class, and of the bourgeois State; they are daily and hourly enslaved by the machine, by the overlooker, and, above all, by the individual bourgeois manufacturer himself.

Source: Marx in David McLellan, ed., *Karl Marx: Selected Writings* (New York: Oxford University Press, 1977), pp. 222–227. Copyright © 1977 by David McLellan. Reprinted by permission of Lawrence & Wishart Ltd.

as well as economic domination (or dependence). His model of social stratification is like a pyramid where people are ranked on the basis of their ownership or lack of ownership of the productive means in their society. At the top of the pyramid are the bourgeoisie, a small number of people who control most of the society's wealth and power. In the middle of the pyramid are strata that Marx felt would eventually be eliminated by capitalistic advances (e.g., small business owners, termed small or *petty* bourgeoisie). The bottom layer of the pyramid broadens out to include the vast majority of people who have neither wealth nor power.

For Marx, power and wealth are two sides of the same coin under capitalism. Those who control the means of production control the society's social relations. Thus, the bourgeoisie controls not only the mechanical process of production but also the dominant ideas of the time and the governmental processes.

Marx's vision of a new society—based on social equality, not inequality; based on a sense of community rooted in labor, not ethnicity, nationality, or religion—has provided inspiration for revolutionary movements throughout the world. It has also provoked feelings of fear, distrust, hatred, and cynicism in many places, including countries that once called themselves Communist or socialist. In the United States, most Americans reject the notion of class struggle as the primary vehicle for social change.

## "Dream Up, Blame Down"

Another reason that Marx's ideas have been unpopular in the United States is that to many people, America represents the land of opportunity. In their minds, it is the place where a poor child can sell matchsticks on the corner and climb the ladder to success, as in the Horatio Alger stories of the nineteenth century. That is the **American dream**—self-made men and women, rugged individualists reaching the top by working hard and smart, playing by the rules, and having a pinch of good luck. Horatio Alger's

images of upward social mobility and an open class system have dominated American thought. Hence it is not surprising that historically Americans have tended to *"dream up and blame down"* (Teninty, 1992); that is, Americans tend to blame those below them on the social ladder for their lack of success while dreaming of reaching the top rung themselves.

A 1990 Gallup national random sample poll found that the majority of respondents (60 percent) consider themselves to be middle-class, whether they are dyemakers or doctors. Another poll puts the number at 85 percent who define themselves as middle-class (Cooke, 1992). To a neo-Marxist, the fact that so many Americans either deny the existence of class or see themselves as middle-class indicates how powerful the wealthy few really are: They have succeeded in binding the weak by the chains of their own ideas.

A neo-Marxist might accuse poor, powerless people who think they're middle-class of living in self-deception (or, as Marx called it, **false consciousness**). In rebuttal, a non-Marxist might tell the rags-to-riches stories of a Ross Perot, Steve Jobs, or Bill Clinton. The non-Marxist might point out that in 1992, Bill Gates, Microsoft's founder—not a Rockefeller—was the richest person in the United States, and that the richest person in the world was a Tokyo economics professor-turned-realtor. In addition, a non-Marxist might cite statistics showing the chance for upward social mobility in America: a child whose father is in the bottom 5 percent of income earners has one chance in twenty of making it into the top 20 percent of income-earning families (Solon, 1992). However, a neo-Marxist would use the same data set to show the opposite trend—the *lack* of intergenerational upward mobility in the United States: that same child has a 40 percent chance of staying poor or near-poor (Solon, 1992). The neo-Marxist might also reexamine the list of wealthy people in the United States, pointing out that there are many who inherited their wealth, including sixteen DuPonts, twelve Mellons, five Gettys, and three Rockefellers on the Forbes 400 list of the richest people in America in 1990 (Senneker, 1990).

## Marx, the Inescapable Critic

However one evaluates Marx's ideas, they are inescapable. Marxists and non-Marxists alike are still engaged in sorting out what he "really" meant and what application Marx's ideas have to the contemporary world. Critics and followers debate his political message of revolutionary action (is it applicable to postindustrial societies?); his assumptions about human psychology (can they account for people's drives to power? even under socialism, won't individuals try to reassert domination in the name of virtue, sex, or bureaucratic efficiency, if not wealth?); his consistency (is there an "early" Marx concerned with issues of alienation and a "late" Marx concerned with "laws" of capitalism?); and his views on history (is it wholly determined by structural factors, as he implies in some passages of his work, or is it dependent on the revolutionary consciousness of the proletariat, as he implies in other passages?). Contemporary Marxists, whom I call *neo-Marxists*, don't agree among themselves on these and many other points. Some even hold that the enemy is no longer capitalism but rather bureaucracy. They argue that bureaucracy— whether capitalist or socialist—is an instrument of domination and exploitation (Howard, 1978). As we shall soon see, this is not a new idea; Max Weber had the same notion.

If even those who consider themselves in the Marxist tradition question his ideas and view of human history, why do Marx's ideas continue to enthrall scholars, Marxist and non-Marxist alike? Economist Robert L. Heilbroner offers the following explanation: "The reason for the magnetism that Marx [still] exerts . . . is that Marx had the luck, combined of course with the genius, to be the first to discover a whole mode of inquiry that would forever belong to him. . . . I refer to Marx the inventor of critical social science, who 'critiqued' economics . . . . Marx invented a kind of social 'criticizing'—that is, subjecting the social universe to a particular sort of questioning" (1978:33).

By the late 1980s, many conservatives were celebrating the death of Marxist thought in the

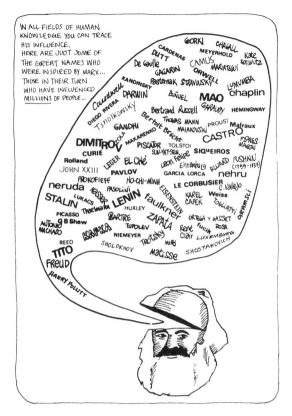

**Fig. 10.2**  MARX, THE INESCAPABLE. (Rius, *Marx for Beginners* [New York: Pantheon, 1979], p. 35. English translation © 1976 by Richard Appiganesi. Originally published in English in Great Britain by Writers and Readers Publishing Cooperative. Reprinted by permission of Pantheon Books, a Division of Random House, Inc.)

Soviet bloc, the so-called "socialist" nations (nations that most neo-Marxists consider bureaucratic, state-capitalist societies, not socialist or Communist). Yet, Marx's ideas remain central to social science, particularly to urban studies. Why? According to Heilbroner's argument, Marx continues to influence theorists "not because he is infallible" but rather because "he is unavoidable" for anyone who asks questions "about the nature of our thinking about society." "Sooner or later all such inquiries," Heilbroner says, "bring one to confront Marx's thought, and then one is compelled to adopt, confute, expand, escape from, or come to terms with the person who has defined the very task of critical social inquiry itself" (1978:33).

## Weber's View of Social Stratification: Class, Status, Power

Max Weber was one of the most distinguished social inquirers who found Marx inescapable. He skillfully applied Marx's historical method, and his ideas on social stratification were influenced by Marx's previous work.

Weber did not refute Marx's notions on social stratification. Rather, he expanded on them. In fact, much of Weber's political sociology can be viewed as an attempt to "round out" Marx (Gerth and Mills, 1958:47).

Like Marx, Weber made capitalism a central theme in his scholarly work, calling it "the most fateful force in our modern life" (Weber, [1904–1905] 1958:17). Weber viewed Western capitalism as unique because of its rational, bureaucratic form. That is, it is organized on the basis of pursuit of profit by rational calculation; it uses rational techniques, such as the legal separation of personal property from corporate property; and it depends on bureaucratic organization. According to Weber, this particular Western form of capitalism—"rational bourgeois capitalism"—linked profit making with the bureaucratic organization of the economy and high technology.

Weber and Marx agreed on the paramount importance of capitalism in modern life. They did not, however, share the same interpretation of capitalist institutions. Specifically, Marx saw capitalism as irrational in terms of meeting human needs. Weber viewed capitalist institutions, especially bureaucracy, as the epitome of rationality and efficiency. In fact, it was this ever-increasing movement toward bureaucratic efficiency and rationality that struck Weber as problematic; while efficient, it would inevitably lead to the depersonalization of the individual.

Weber agreed with Marx that under capitalism there is a class struggle between haves and have-nots. But unlike Marx, he did not make class struggle the central dynamic of his work. Instead, the bureaucratization of everything, which went hand in hand with the development of capitalism in the West, was Weber's primary concern.

Weber felt that Marx did not go far enough. Agreeing with Marx that capitalism separates the peasant from the soil and the propertyless urban masses from the means of production, he extended the analysis. *Bureaucratic organization separates all people from their labor*—the scientist from the means of inquiry, the soldier from the means of violence, and the civil servant from the means of administration.

In brief, Marx and Weber had very different views of what was inevitable. To Marx, the "dictatorship of the proletariat" and socialism were inevitable. To Weber, only the "disenchanted garden" of rational calculation was inevitable, and it would lead to the depersonalization of the individual through efficient bureaucratic management. Much more pessimistic than Marx, Weber commented that "for the time being, the

**Fig. 10.3** WEBER'S VIEW OF BUREAUCRACY: EFFICIENT BUT DEADLY. (Richard Hedman)

dictatorship of the [corporate and government] official and not that of the worker is on the march" (in Gerth and Mills, 1958:50). Thus while Marx looked forward to a socialist future in which people would control their work process and their lives, Weber felt that socialism (with its own bureaucracy) would be just another system for enslaving the individual.

Weber also felt that Marx's theory of history, with its emphasis on class struggle, was too one-dimensional. In his view, there were other important factors, especially the meanings that people brought to their situation.

Similarly, Weber felt that Marx's approach to social stratification was too simplified. For Weber, the economic order (class) was crucial to the social ranking process. But Weber contended that other institutional orders—the military, religion, politics, law, and so forth—were also important. All of these institutional orders were interrelated, but they were also separate and distinct. In his essay "Class, Status, Party" ([1922] 1958), Weber identified three interrelated but distinct social orders that influence a person's social rank:

1. The economic order (class).
2. The prestige order (status).
3. The political order (power).

**Class** Weber thought that those sharing the same position in the economic order (class) also share similar "life chances" or market position. They can expect similar opportunities for income, material goods, living conditions, and personal life experiences.

Researchers in the Weberian tradition usually determine class position by some measure of income and wealth. They see class as a series of graded income groups. Some define these as upper class, upper middle, middle, working, and the poor. Others pay attention to strata within one class, such as layers in the working class: self-employed, skilled workers, nonskilled in peripheral industries, marginally employed, and supervisors.

Applying Weber's notion of class as shared life chances, what do we find? First, the life chances of poor and rich Americans are not equal. Literally, the poor die younger. Specifically, there are class differences in mortality among adults twenty-five to sixty-four years old: In 1986, there were 16 deaths for every 1,000 white males with family incomes of less than $9,000. In contrast, there were 2.4 deaths for every 1,000 white males with incomes of $25,0000 or above (Pear, 1993:A1). Further, in 1986, lower-income people of any race died of heart disease at higher rates (2.3 times higher) than upper-income people. (*Note:* Being poor *and* Latino or African-American makes the odds worse. Here are a few grim statistics: African-American males in New York's Harlem are less likely to live to the age of sixty-five than men in Bangladesh, one of the world's poorest nations [McCord and Freeman, 1990]. African-Americans die more than six years younger than whites, and the gap between the life expectancy of whites and African-Americans is growing [Hilts, 1990:A1]. Latinos suffer rates of diabetes, tuberculosis, certain cancers, and lead poisoning that are much higher than the rates for non-Latino whites.) In sum, there is a health gap between affluent and poor in the United States, and this class gap has greatly widened—"more than doubled," according to a government epidemiologist —for three decades.

Similarly, the poor in the United States have unequal chances of obtaining decent housing and education. In brief, the poor—and especially poor African-Americans—are more likely than affluent people of all races to live in substandard conditions. The poor are much less likely to be enrolled in institutions of higher learning; this is especially important because higher education is viewed as the stepping stone to upward mobility. The poor are more likely to be victims of personal crimes of violence than the rich. For the same money, the poor often get shoddier merchandise and fewer groceries than the affluent. The poor often pay almost 10 percent more for an equivalent used car than middle-income shoppers ("Used cars," 1978:F17). In brief, a person's chances of obtaining a higher education, standard housing, and personal safety are directly tied to his or her economic position (class, in Weber's terms).

Perhaps most chilling is the plight of the poor—and vulnerable—as human guinea pigs. In 1993, the U.S. government revealed that from the 1940s to the mid-1970s, government agencies conducted or underwrote secret, potentially deadly experiments on many unknowing subjects. Most subjects "were drawn from the ranks of society's dispossessed, either by virtue of their race, age, income, or intelligence" (Healy, 1994:1). For example, cancer patients in Cincinnati (most of them poor and African-African) got "treatments" laced with radiation, Inupiat Eskimos in Alaska ate caribou that had absorbed radioactive debris, and children at a school for the mentally retarded in Massachusetts were given radioactive iron and calcium in their breakfast cereal that was served up by researchers at MIT (Healy, 1994:1). A physician and professor at Brown University, a critic of the so-called therapeutic radiation experiments conducted without permission, noted sarcastically, "For some reason, rich white people were deprived of all this wonderful research" (Egilman in Wheeler, 1994:A6).

*To conclude:* Millionaire novelist Tom Clancy once called members of Congresss failures because "if $120,000 a year is the best job you've ever had, you haven't really done much." Here the best-selling author reveals how much his value system is tied to the class system, as defined by Weber, and to what Wirth called the *pecuniary nexus.* Clancy's comment suggests that in America, people are judged by the numbers on their paycheck, not the number of good deeds completed or beautiful poems created.

Data based on Weberian measures of class affirm a related point: Class position makes a difference in determining what a person can expect to get out of life in America. As we shall see shortly, we come to the same conclusion if we use neo-Marxist measures of class.

**Status** In Weber's view, the status order of prestige is related to the economic order (class) but separate from it. People who share the same position in the hierarchy of prestige share a similar lifestyle. They display similar symbols of consumption and respectability. PRIZM's ZQ clusters, discussed in Chapter 7, draw their inspiration largely from this insight.

Taking some contemporary American examples, a high-prestige group might share the following symbols: knowledge of languages long dead, like Latin or Greek; worn Persian carpets; subscriptions to the *New Yorker* or the *New York Review of Books;* refined tastes in modern art and French wine; classical record collections; tennis rackets; a television set outside the living room; homes or apartments at a "good address"; membership in exclusive social clubs; and old school ties to elite educational institutions. A lower-prestige group would share different symbols, perhaps a framed diploma; metal venetian blinds; transparent plastic furniture covers; a "wall system" without books; an aquarium; homes in tract developments; bowling balls; a knowledge of home repair skills; copies of *Family Circle* or *Reader's Digest;* a television set in the living room; and ties to high-school buddies.

In other words, different status groups live in different "taste cultures" (Gans, 1974). A shared taste culture gives people a sense of belonging to the same kind of community. And according to Weber, status groups are communities; people in similar status groups see themselves as having common interests and tastes. (On this point, Weber and Marx differed. Marx felt that class members would recognize their common class interests. Weber thought that a person's objective economic position would not necessarily lead him or her to feel a sense of community with others who share that same position.)

Following Weber's analysis, then, we can predict (correctly) the following: Members of similar status groups tend to marry each other. They tend to enjoy the same kinds of cultural events and display similar symbols of consumption. They listen to similar radio stations. A case in point is National Public Radio (NPR). An audience survey found that "over one-half of all public radio listeners live in PRIZM's top four socioeconomic neighborhoods in the U.S." (Liebold, 1988:n.p.). In other words, people with high incomes, professional jobs, and many years of education make up the majority of public-radio lis-

**Fig. 10.4** WHO LIVES HERE? Not members of a lower-status group. The cathedral ceiling and stone fireplace; grand piano, oil painting in the living room, and harp in the dining room; lack of a visible television set and understated elegance indicate that this is an architect-designed home (not part of a tract development) inhabited by professionals. (Richard J. Sanders)

teners. The majority of NPR listeners live in the highest-ranking ZQ neighborhoods: "Blue Blood Estates," "Money and Brains," "Furs and Station Wagons," "Pools and Patios," and "Young Influentials."

Occupational groups, Weber noted, are also status groups. And in America, the work one does is probably the single best indicator of a person's relative prestige. (This was not always so. In *Gemeinschaft*, the best indicator of prestige is the social esteem of one's family. "Who is your father?" was an all-important query to a marriage-minded person in eighteenth-century Boston. But individual leisure activities and residential neighborhood—not family nor occupation—may be the crucial status markers in *Techno\$chaft*

or postindustrial society. If so, when adult strangers fall into conversation, the familiar "What do you do for a living?" will be replaced by "What are you into?" and "What's your ZIP code?")

Sociologists in the structural-functional tradition of Durkheim argue that the relative prestige of different occupations is essentially the same in all complex societies. Thus in *Gesellschaft* societies, we should expect to find the same occupations at the top of the status ladder and the same occupations at the bottom. This is because all complex societies face similar "functional imperatives." To get these tasks accomplished, advanced technological societies organize themselves in similar ways (Table 10.1).

Briefly, the structural-functional argument is

**Table 10.1** Occupational Prestige Rankings in the United States

| Occupational Title | Prestige Score |
|---|---|
| Member, president's cabinet | 89 |
| State governor; federal department head | 85 |
| U.S. Supreme Court justice | 84.5 |
| Nuclear physicist | 80 |
| Physician | 78 |
| College professor | 78 |
| Physician | 86 |
| Mayor of a larger city | 75 |
| Priest | 73 |
| Department head, city government | 70 |
| Electrical engineer | 69 |
| City manager | 66 |
| Computer programmer | 51 |
| Reporter on a daily newspaper | 47 |
| Receptionist | 39 |
| Service station manager | 37 |
| Artist or performer | 36 |
| Migrant worker | 14 |
| Cleaning woman in private home | 13 |
| Garbage collector | 13 |

SOURCE: Adapted from Donald Treiman, *Occupational Prestige in Comparative Perspective*. Copyright © 1977 by Academic Press, 318–329. Reprinted by permission of Academic Press and the author.

as follows. Social differentiation "inherently implies stratification. Specialization of functions carries with it inherent differences in the control over scarce resources, which is the primary basis of stratification." These resources—skill, knowledge, authority, property—function together to "create differential power. . . . Thus, the division of labor creates a characteristic hierarchy of occupations with respect to power exercised" and "this power leads to special privilege" (Treiman, 1977:5). So, in this view, power, privilege, and prestige become intertwined. A comprehensive study of occupational prestige worldwide (fifty-five countries) supports the view that there is indeed "a single, worldwide occupational prestige hierarchy" (Treiman, 1977:5–6).

In the United States, random sample polls show almost identical prestige rankings for occupations since the 1940s. In general, as Table 10.1 shows, professional, non-manual jobs rank much higher than service jobs and manual labor (Nakao and Treas, 1990).

The same pattern holds in high-tech societies worldwide. Heads of state and other high government officials such as ambassadors; doctors; university professors; physicists, and mayors of large cities occupy rungs at the top of the status ladder. At about the middle are the following occupations: professional athlete, advertising writer, television cameraperson, and police officer. At the bottom of the ladder are garbage collectors, contract laborers, shoe shiners, and recipients of public assistance. According to an international survey, agricultural gatherer is the least socially esteemed occupation worldwide (Treiman, 1977:Appendix A).

These occupational prestige rankings suggest a connection between the status order (prestige), the political order (power), and the economic order (class) in a complex society. That is, occupations that are prestigious are often highly paid and socially powerful. Yet as Weber pointed out, this is not necessarily the case. His third dimension of social stratification—the power order—is related to but separate from class and status.

*Power*   For Weber, a person's position in the power order is determined by the amount of control he or she has over politics and administration. This includes the exercise of formal and informal power. Elected officials and bureaucrats, for example, have formal power that goes with their office. Whoever becomes president of the United States or a member of the board of directors of AT&T has authority stemming from that position.

Soldiers, gang leaders, would-be revolutionaries, lobbyists, and bank presidents know that power also comes from either the barrel of a gun and/or the control over an organization's purse strings. Instinctively, Elaine Brown, the first woman to lead the Black Panthers, understood both formal power and informal power (**influence**). In *A Taste of Power* (1992), Brown reports that she began her initial address to several hundred Black Panther party officials in 1974 like this: "I have control over all the guns and all the money of this party.

Box 10.2

## TWO APPROACHES TO SOCIAL STRATIFICATION

### Dimensions of Stratification

**Karl Marx**

*One dimension: class*

A person's relationship to the means of production determines how much wealth he or she will have and thus the lifestyle he or she will be able to afford. The class that owns or controls the means of production also controls the ideas in that society.

**Max Weber**

*Three dimensions*

1. Class—shared life chances.
2. Status—shared lifestyle, social esteem, prestige.
3. Political power.

Class, status, and power do not necessarily coincide. For example, members of political elites can be lower-class or low in social esteem.

### Concept of Class

A concept combining economic and social relations. A class is composed of individuals who share a situation in terms of their relation to the ownership of the means of production. *Classes are not income groups.* Nor are classes occupational groupings (e.g., two people may both be engineers, but one may be a propertyless employee and the other may be the owner of a large firm). In a capitalist system, there are owners of capital (bourgeoisie) who live off profits; landowners who live off rents; and wage laborers (proletariat) who live off wages. Under capitalism, society is split into two great classes: bourgeoisie and proletariat. Class conflict is the key to understanding history.

Basically, class is an economic concept. A class is composed of people who share a common situation in terms of the market (what goods and services they can afford to buy) and similar life chances. Class divisions are based on property relations: property owners and the propertyless. Class struggles begin in an urban economy, where a credit market operates, and is developed by a small, powerful group (plutocracy).

### Concept of Status

Marx didn't use this concept to differentiate people. He assumed that those with economic power also held social and political power in capitalist society. He also thought that under capitalism, ideas and culture were produced by the ruling class (the capitalists or the bourgeoisie) in its own interests.

Status is not necessarily determined by or linked to class. Both propertied and propertyless people may belong to the same status group. Those who share a similar status tend to share a similar lifestyle (e.g., belong to the same kinds of clubs, display similar symbols of their station in life). In modern society, occupation is the single best indicator of status group.

### Using Marx or Weber: What Difference Does It Make?

Using Marx's unidimensional approach, a social scientist tends to find a rather cohesive elite holding economic (and thus political) power in a city or nation.

Using Weber's three-dimensional approach, a social scientist tends to find a more pluralistic and open system in which wealth, power, and prestige are unequally distributed.

There will be no external or internal opposition I will not resist and put down. I will deal resolutely with anyone or anything that stands in the way."

*To summarize:* Weber outlined three dimensions by which people rank and socially differentiate one another: class, status, and power. Each represents a distinct social order, They are functionally interrelated, but in Weber's analysis they don't necessarily coincide. Hence, a person may enjoy high status but wield little political power. Or a low-status person without property could conceivably have great political clout. In other words, Weber felt that Marx's approach was too one-dimensional because noneconomic institutions are also important in determining where one fits in the social hierarchy.

## CONCEPTUAL UPDATES

### The American Class Structure

Long after their deaths, Marx and Weber remain the theorists whom others debate, refute, and update—but not discard. One leading contemporary theorist, sociologist Erik Olin Wright, draws mainly on Marx to reconceptualize the nature of class in advanced capitalist society.

According to Wright and Martin (1987:7), three forms of exploitation are crucial in advanced capitalist societies: exploitation based on (1) ownership of *capital* assets (which yield profits); (2) control of *organization* assets (which come from supervising others), and (3) ownership of *skill* assets such as valuable talents and credentials (e.g., a Ph.D. or law degree). These types of exploitation correspond to the relationships between (1) capital versus labor, (2) manager versus workers, and (3) expert versus nonexpert.

Wright's typology of classes in advanced capitalist societies has undergone several revisions (1989, 1987 1985). However, it retains Marx's basic assumption: Class depends on the ownership (or nonownership) of the means of production. Hence Wright divides people into owners and nonowners. But Wright expands Marx's criterion

for class membership by incorporating the other two types of exploitation mentioned above: (2) control over organizational assets, operationalized as supervision of employees or control of labor power, and (3) ownership of skill assets, operationalized as having a professional, technical, or managerial job. (The presumed percentage of each class in the United States is noted in parentheses.)

### Owners

1. *Bourgeoisie.* Self-employed and employ (i.e., they purchase the labor power and control the labor of) more than ten employees. (1.8 percent)
2. *Small employers.* Self-employed and employ at least two persons in their business. (6.0 percent)
3. *Petty bourgeoisie.* Self-employed or own a substantial part of the business in which they work; they have no employees, so they neither buy nor control the labor of others. (6.9 percent)

### Nonowners (Wage Laborers)

4. *Managers.* Not self-employed. They merely sell their own labor to the bourgeoisie; they do not employ others, but they do make policy decisions about their organization, whether or not they supervise others. (12.4 percent)
5. *Supervisors.* Not self-employed but sell their own labor to the bourgeoisie. They do not employ others; they supervise others without making policy decisons about the workplace. (13.7 percent)
6. *Nonmanagerial experts.* Not self-employed. They sell their labor to capitalists; they do not make policy decisions about their workplace and do not supervise others; they do have professional, technical, and managerial occupations. (3.4 percent)
7. *Workers.* Not self-employed. They have only their own labor to sell to capitalists; they do

not make policy decisions and do not have professional, technical, or managerial occupations. (39.9 percent)

Under Wright's typology, then, the owner of a dress factory with twenty-five employees is a bourgeois (or bourgeoise, if female). A college professor is a nonmanagerial expert. A dry cleaner with three employees is a small employer. A vice president of a major bank is a manager. A self-employed jeweler or trucker with no employees is a petty bourgeois. A nursing administrator in a hospital is a supervisor. A file clerk, bridge toll taker, or auto assembler is a worker.

Note that there is *no middle-class category* in Wright's typology. To Wright (1985), the middle classes are truly in the middle—not in terms of income but in terms of relations of exploitation: They are part exploiter, part exploitee. They occupy "contradictory locations within class relations," sharing some traits with both bourgeoisie and proletariat. For instance, middle managers in a big organization do not own capital but, as managers, they exploit others on the basis of their organizational assets, and they are also exploited by capitalists.

Using these criteria, Wright finds inequalities based on class position. For one thing, education helps managers and supervisors earn much more money than workers as a group. Managers and supervisors get about $1,169 for each increment to education; income returns to workers with the same increments to education are much less—$655 (Wright, 1978).

*A final note on class structure in the United States:* One does not have to be a follower of Marx or Wright to recognize growing inequalities in America. Generally speaking, radicals, conservatives, and liberals agree that the gap is widening between rich and poor and between high- and low-status people. Here are just a few indicators. According to data from the Center for Budget and Policy Priorities, the after-tax incomes of America's richest families—the top 1 percent—more than doubled in the 1977 to 1988 period. In 1990, the richest 1 percent of the U.S. population had an after-tax income that virtually equaled the total income of the bottom 40 percent: "This means that 2.5 million Americans accrued the same income as did 100 million of America's poorest" (Coffin, 1991:1). Similarly, as conservative economist Milton Friedman points out, there is a growing income gap among employed workers in the United States:

In 1979, college-educated workers earned 47 percent more, on average, than those with just high-school education. Today [1991] the gap is 67 percent. Ten years ago, the chief executive officers of the nation's 300 largest companies made, on average, 20 times what the typical manufacturing worker made. Now the multiple is 93 to 1. (in Coffin, 1991:1)

Further, white households held ten times as much *wealth* as African-Americans and eight times as much wealth as Latinos in 1991, according to a 1994 U.S. Census Bureau report. Median household *income* for whites is about 60 percent higher than African-American income and 30 percent higher than Latino income. Nationally, the 1989 median household income was $31,435 for whites and $19,758 for African-Americans (Barringer, 1992b:A1).

What is the meaning of all these numbers? In a word, polarization. During the 1980s the rich got richer, the poor got poorer, and the chasm between them increased. Conservative analyst Kevin Phillips calls the 1980s a capitalist blowout where "the truly wealthy, more than anyone else, . . . flourished under Reagan" (1990:26). Perhaps for the first time in U.S. history, most young adults look ahead to having less—not more—than their parents in real and symbolic terms: money, skill credentials, home ownership, and fulfillment of the American dream.

Should this growing inequality be reduced? That depends on your ideology. Meanwhile, while scholars debate, government officials talk, and some citizens take to the streets or talk radio, the public schools of LaCrosse, Wisconsin, are trying a novel approach: integrating primary-school students by social class. Formerly, students attended neighborhood schools, which tended to be segregated on the basis of income. Starting in the 1990s, the children of affluent parents are bussed across town to working-class areas, and

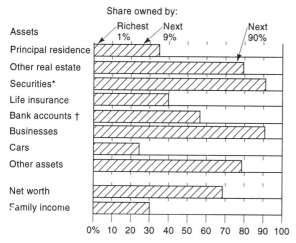

* Includes stocks, bonds and trusts.
† Includes all deposits in checking, savings and other accounts.

**Fig. 10.5** WHO OWNS WHAT ASSETS, 1989. According to the Federal Reserve, the gap between super-rich families (top 1 percent) and everyone else widened during the 1980s: In 1983, the richest 1 percent held 31 percent of the total net worth of U.S. families; by 1989, their share had increased to 37 percent. The share of the next richest 9 percent decreased from 35 percent in 1983 to 31 percent in the same time period. The share of the vast majority—the remaining 90 percent—decreased 1 percent, from 33 percent in 1983 to 32 percent in 1989. (Federal Reserve)

vice versa. Although the plan met resistance when first introduced, it has gained in popularity among students, teachers, and parents, who praise its mutual benefits.

## Cultural Capital

Alex, one of four *Sisters* (1992) in the NBC-TV series who live in Winnetka (a ZQ1 suburb on Chicago's North Shore), explains the difference between her plumber boyfriend and herself:

> "When I hear 'porcelain', I think Limoges, and he thinks American Standard."

Knowing that Limoges is a type of French porcelain china or that American social scientists pronounce Weber as "Vay-bear" (and not like the backyard barbeque grill) does not earn you a place in Paradise. Your ability or inability to discuss the virtues of a Manet versus a Monet painting is not a comment on the content of your character. But, like it or not, showing your familiarity (or lack of it) with these symbols is a badge of status, high or low.

High-status culture is the vehicle that allows a high-status group to maintain its cohesion and set itself apart from other societal groups (Dimaggio and Mohr, 1985:1233). Having competence in and participating in a society's high-status culture (its behaviors, habits, and attitudes) gives a person a great deal of **cultural capital.**

According to French social scientist Pierre Bourdieu ([1979] 1984), cultural capital includes the general cultural background, language competence, and behaviors that are passed from one generation to the next. He argues that upper-class children grow up with much different cultural capital than working-class ones. Specifically, socially advantaged parents typically transmit socially advantaged cultural capital to their offspring—who then become socially advantaged children. Schools plays an important role too: Schools systematically devalue the attitudes and behaviors of working-class children and reward the cultural capital of upper-class students. In these ways, Bourdieu says, cultural capital becomes a vehicle through which class and status hierarchies are maintained and reproduced.

Cultural capital is more important in *Gesellschaft* and *Technoschaft* than in *Gemeinschaft*. Why? Because high-tech societies depend more on democratic practices and merit promotion than family ties.

Theorist Bourdieu draws inspiration from Max Weber. Indeed, his concept of cultural capital draws primarily on Weber's ideas of status and lifestyle. Essentially, Bourdieu argues that taste —not class—is the key differentiator of people in modern times. True, Bourdieu says, different classes do tend to have different tastes, and class backgrounds tend to mold taste. But taste can be *learned* by mastering the symbols. In other words, people can re-create themselves by gaining cultural capital.

Bourdieu also expands on Marx. Just as Marx thought that capital yielded income profit, Bourdieu thinks that cultural capital yields *symbolic profit*: being seen by others as having good taste or distinction. In other words, a degree from Stanford or Brown, a living room with a Kazakh carpet on a hardwood floor, and a slim body all confer social esteem. Capital in the arena of culture gives symbolic profits—the conferring of prestige.

Symbols of good taste do not emerge from all strata in the population. Quite the contrary. Cultural capital reflects the culture of the dominant class. George Bernard Shaw instinctively understood this concept. In Shaw's 1913 play, *Major Barbara*, Undershaft, a millionaire munitions maker, proclaims that he will not give Greek teacher Adolphus Cusins part of his business. Why? Because Cusins brings no capital with him. Cusins counters, saying, "What! no capital! Is my mastery of Greek no capital? Is my access to the subtlest thought, the loftiest poetry yet attained by humanity, no capital? My character! my intellect! . . . are these no capital?" Later in the play, Cusins suggests that cultural capital and machine guns are not very different in the war of rich against poor: "As a teacher of Greek I gave the rich man an intellectual weapon against the poor man."

One study of cultural capital by DiMaggio and Mohr (1985) finds that familiarity with and interest in high culture does directly affect both educational and marital outcomes for men and women. They reject conventional assertions that women's attainment is based on more particularistic and diffuse qualities (e.g., physical attractiveness) than men's. Indeed, they say that "the most important finding of our separate analyses for men and women is the great similarity in the effects of cultural capital between genders" (1254) In terms of mate selection, for instance, they find that both men and women "desire intimacy based on cultural similarity," not transactions in which "goods" (e.g., attractiveness and earnings) are exchanged.

Now, let us reconsider the battle over multi-culturalism outlined in the previous chapter. Using Bourdieu's concept of cultural capital and Gramsci's concept of hegemony, we can construct the following hypothesis: *Because multiculturalism democratizes the content of cultural capital (by including symbols from subordinate groups), it dilutes the hegemony of the dominant class and thus will be fought with vehemence by the dominant class and its representatives.* This hypothesis predicts that some language variants (e.g., so-called Black English) and class or status-coded symbols (e.g., creating Spanish lyric music or rap songs; knowing how to find a flea market bargain) will be devalued by keepers of the "canon."

## STUDIES OF URBAN SOCIAL STRATIFICATION IN THE UNITED STATES

American social scientists generally adopt the Weberian approach when investigating how U.S. cities are socially stratified. But—and this is important—researchers in this tradition have not kept Weber's categories of class and status separate. Instead, they have joined class and status into a single concept: **socioeconomic status (SES)**. A person's SES is determined by a composite measure based on three variables: (1) income, (2) education, and (3) occupation. The rationale behind this composite measure is that the three variables tend to covary in complex societies, which means that high-skill occupations require a high level of education and are highly rewarded in terms of income.

What difference does it make if a researcher uses SES or separate measures of class and status? For one thing, SES ignores what Marx meant by class. It does not distinguish between owners and controllers of capital (including managers, large stockholders) and those who have little or no control over other people's work and social lives. For another thing, essentially SES is synonymous with prestige (the status order) exclusively. Consequently, studies that use SES as their indicator of social rank ignore what Weber originally meant: that class, status, and power (the three dimensions of stratification) are separate and distinct, although interrelated. And of course, using SES as an indicator of social stratification ignores class and the consequences of class. This is an ironic twist, for many American scholars who criticize Marx for being too one-dimensional turn out to be equally at fault. The difference is that most American scholars use status rather than class as their one dimension of social rank.

There are other problems with making status the only measure of social stratification. Most important, it assumes that status concerns are of paramount importance to everyone in America. Yet as many studies (e.g., Form and Stone, 1957) suggest, this is not the case. Blue-collar workers, for example, seem to be less interested in social respectability and prestige than in working conditions and monetary rewards.

*To conclude:* The concept of SES is not neutral. Using SES (rather than measures of status and class) as a filter through which to see the social system of American cities helps to perpetuate the notion that classes don't exist in America.

Once again, what you see depends on how you look at it. Remembering that what is defined as empirical evidence depends on what researchers already believe, let's review some leading studies on urban social stratification in America. We begin with an influential series of studies that established the pattern of research for future generations: the Yankee City series by social anthropologist W. Lloyd Warner and his associates.

## Yankee City: Lifestyles in a New England Town

Beginning in 1930, W. Lloyd Warner and his research group studied the system of social ranking in a small New England town they called "Yankee City." (The actual city was Newburyport, Massachusetts, which then had a population of about 17,000.) To do this, Warner developed two techniques that set the research pattern for future researchers of urban social stratification. Both techniques were designed to measure what Warner called "social class." He defined

social class as "two or more orders of people who are believed to be, and are accordingly ranked by the members of the community, in socially superior and inferior positions" ([1941] 1963:36). That's exactly what Weber meant by status. Thus Warner's techniques to measure class actually measure status.

Warner determined that Newburyport had six separate social strata (actually, status groups), each with its own particular lifestyle. He identified the following strata and the percentage of townspeople in each: upper upper (1.4 percent), lower upper (1.6 percent), upper middle (10 percent), lower middle (28 percent), upper lower (33 percent), and lower lower (25 percent). Thus most people in Yankee City were in the two lowest status groups (58 percent).

## Jonesville: A Typical Town, and How Its People Justify Inequality

Warner studied a small town near Chicago, dubbed "Jonesville" because it was considered to be a typical American community. Since it seemed to be representative, Warner used this town (actually Morris, Illinois) as a laboratory in which to look at status hierarchies in America.

What did Warner find in this typical American town? First, he found what he had found in Newburyport: six distinct status groups, each with its own particular lifestyle. Most people in Jonesville lived at the "level of the common man," or what others term the "middle class." Above the level of the common man is a layer divided into two parts and "crowned by an elite, and the one below [is] filled with a mixed old American and ethnic proletariat. . . . The highest crust is rewarded with deference; the lowest, often with ridicule, pity, or scorn" ([1949] 1964:23).

Second, Warner found that the status system of inequality in Jonesville (and, by extension, America) operates according to two competing logics: "1) All men are equal and 2) Some men are superior in status, others inferior" ([1949] 1964:293). These two contradictory propositions support the following practices and beliefs that he found typified Jonesville:

1. People in Jonesville rank skilled jobs above less skilled jobs.
2. Being a self-made person is good, but even better is to be born wealthy.
3. Recipients of public welfare are lowest on the social ladder.
4. People exposed to higher education are thought to be superior.
5. People can move up or down the status ladder, principally by accumulating money and transforming it into socially approved symbols: educational advancement; marrying up; learning the proper social skills, such as speech patterns; and joining the right churches and clubs ([1949] 1964:294–296). [*Note:* Today, we would say that such people possess cultural capital.]

How can the acceptance of inequality in Jonesville be reconciled with the American ideal of equality? Warner says that the shared belief in the American dream (the idea that anyone who works hard can make it to the top) is the key. The American dream provides "the moral code which enforces the rules of social mobility by insisting that all able [people] who obey the rules of the game have 'the right' to climb" ([1949] 1964:297).

Furthermore, Warner sees the American dream as a very functional belief. Without it, "there would be little or no movement between the classes [status groups]." He concludes that there is no fixed social rank order in Jonesville—or American cities generally. Rather, there is a "system of open classes [again, status groups]" ([1949] 1964:297).

Clearly, this is one person's vision, filtered through particular ideological assumptions and research techniques. Other researchers might (and did) paint a different community portrait of so-called typical American towns. (For one, see Thernstrom [1965] for a different look at Yankee City). Writing about another typical town, called Middletown—in reality, Muncie, Indiana—the Lynds ([1929] 1956) found a fairly rigid class system in operation.

*To conclude:* The composite measure of SES, based on income, education, and occupation, blurs Weber's distinctions. It also raises status to paramount importance and serves to perpetuate the notion that classes don't exist in the United States. This distortion of Weber's original meaning began with W. Lloyd Warner's influential series of urban studies, which set the pattern of research for future scholars. In their studies of Yankee City and Jonesville, Warner and his associates stated that they were studying class. In actuality, as we have noted, they studied what Weber meant by status. Warner found inequality in Yankee City and later in Jonesville. He also found that the American ideal of equality and the practice of inequality were rationalized by a deep-seated belief in the American dream of social mobility. However, cartoonist Jules Feiffer offers a more savage explanation: envy. Feiffer's buttoned-down cartoon executive says this: "If I didn't have envy, I wouldn't have power and I wouldn't be envied by everybody else whose sense of purpose motivates them to compete with me and climb to the top. Trust envy. It makes the system work" (1993:5).

## Studies of Particular Strata in the City

Warner and his associates looked at the entire social system in an American city. Other researchers focus on a particular stratum. *Hard Living on Clay Street* ([1973] 1991) by Joseph T. Howell is one example. It focuses on a white working-class neighborhood in Washington, D.C. Using participant-observation, Howell paints a portrait of two distinct types of blue-collar families: "hard living" and "settled" families, all migrants from the South.

Howell notes that the hard living families cope with everyday life in one way, the settled families in another. Generally, the lifestyle of the hard living families is characterized by heavy drinking, marital instability, tough and profane manners, political alienation, strong individualism, rootlessness, and a present time orientation

(Howell, [1973] 1991:263–264). Meanwhile, the settled families attend church regularly, have roots in the community, stay away from liquor, hold politically conservative ideas, have refined manners, and are concerned with their reputations. In the settled families' eyes, the hard living folk are "white trash." In popular terms, the difference between the two groups is often expressed by the following dichotomy: the "respectable" poor (settled) and the "disreputable" poor (hard living).

Howell's study raises several issues pertinent to our discussion of status and class. First, it suggests that two different status groups live side by side. The settled and hard living families, both in the same economic position, do not share a set of symbols, attitudes, or values. Thus Howell may call his research a study of a working-class neighborhood, but he is really dealing with two status groups residing as neighbors.

Second, Howell's portrait of blue-collar families suggests that people in the same objective economic situation don't necessarily react in similar ways. To a Marxist, the reaction of the settled families might indicate false consciousness about their "real" class situation. To a follower of Warner, however, the settled families' more cautious and refined lifestyle shows the power of belief in the American dream. Many children from settled families went to college; no children from hard living families did so, and most didn't even finish high school. The settled families, concerned with what others thought of them and with social respectability (status concerns), were indeed more upwardly mobile than the hard living families. As I discuss in the following chapter, the same objective situation (in this case, being part of the urban working class or proletariat) can be interpreted subjectively in different ways, and people's interpretation of their situation influences their behavior.

Finally, Howell doesn't suggest it, but his study indicates that class and status are more significant variables than race in explaining social behavior. In many important ways, the hard living folks on Clay Street resemble the African-American streetcorner men observed across town hanging out at *Tally's Corner* (Liebow, 1967).

Like Howell, many researchers analyze the lifestyles or life chances of poor Southerners re-rooted in northern cities (e.g., Liebow, 1967; Gitlin and Hollander, 1970; Kornblum, 1974). Some focus on white working-class communities, such as Brooklyn's Canarsie (Rieder, 1985) and Greenpoint–Williamsburg (Susser, 1982). Some describe the inner-city communities of Chicano youth (Horowitz, 1983).

Others investigate the other end of the social ladder: the rich, prestigious, and/or powerful. One such account is *Philadelphia Gentlemen* (Baltzell, 1958). This study, now more than a generation old, found two strata or layers of elites in Philadelphia: the social aristocracy, at the very top of the social ladder, and the achieving elite, just below. Together, these two strata made up Philadelphia's upper class. While there was no single lifestyle among this class (in both Marx's and Weber's sense of the term), their associations promoted a sense of class solidarity. For example, they tended to belong to the same highly esteemed social clubs, to have inherited wealth, and to have prestigious occupations (or be married to those who did). While not completely homogeneous, Philadelphia's upper class contained no African-Americans and just a sprinkling of people with southern European or Jewish backgrounds; otherwise, it was mainly WASP.

The finding that Philadelphia's upper class was almost exclusively WASP raises some complicated issues. For instance, to what extent do race, ethnicity, and religion affect a person's life chances? Is race or class background a better predictor of a person's position on the social ladder? Are some cities more egalitarian than others? What role does local culture play in determining a person's lifestyle? These are not easy questions to answer. Few researchers have asked questions in this way. Consequently, little data are available. Further, the data that do exist lend themselves to varying interpretations. With these methodological and ideological problems clearly in mind, we now examine the effects of several variables on a person's social rank: race, religion, sex, and age.

## OTHER VARIABLES INFLUENCING SOCIAL RANK

Historically, U.S. researchers have focused on status as the key dimension of social stratification. Where do such factors as race and ethnicity, religion, sex, and age fit into this model? How are they related to class, power, and status? The answers are far from clear-cut.

### Race and Religion

As American cities go, Salt Lake City, Utah, is most unusual. Settled by Mormons in the nineteenth century, the city (as well as the MSA and the state of Utah) are dominated by Mormon influence. Perhaps in no other U.S. city are the lines between church and state less clear. The church is a major landowner, business owner, and media controller, owning two television stations and sixteen radio stations ("Newspaper," 1991:A5). Yet, Salt Lake City is becoming less homogeneous. Estimates differ, but in 1980, about 60 percent of Salt Lake City's population was Mormon; by 1990, this had decreased to less than 50 percent. Newcomers include significant Greek Orthodox and Irish Catholic populations.

The first non-Mormon to be elected mayor of Salt Lake City (an Italian-American Catholic and Democrat in Republican, conservative Utah) says, "We're not quite Greenwich Village, but we've gone from a small-town mentality to a much more cosmopolitan community with a far greater global perspective" (in Johnson, 1991: A13). One of Salt Lake City's most cosmopolitan assets is a high level of literacy in Spanish, Korean, Swedish, and other international languages. This language literacy stems from religious practice backed up by educational opportunity: Mormons send young adults as short-term missionaries throughout the world. When these missionaries return home, they possess conversational ability that serves them well in the global economy. Also, Brigham Young University, a Mormon university in Utah (with nearly 30,000 students), offers over fifty languages—from Afrikaans and Hindi to Mayan, Tagalog, and Welsh.

Salt Lake City's recent history indicates that being part of the global economy can help to forge a new, more cosmopolitan identity— diversity in terms of politics, religion, and culture. Indeed, much has changed since the late 1970s, when many non-Mormons, particularly the city's handul of African-Americans, complained of discrimination (Ivins, 1978). At that time, few modern U.S. cities of its size were so dominated by a single religious group, especially a church that traditionally assigned blacks and women to a separate and lower place in heaven, as well as on earth. But less than fifteen years later, two non-Mormons, both Democrats and one a Lebanese-born woman, had been elected mayor. In addition, Salt Lake City was named by *Fortune* magazine as the best place in the country for companies to locate in 1990.

In most U.S. cities, the effects of race, religion, and ethnicity on a person's life chances or lifestyle are difficult to assess and disentangle. Religious and ethnic discrimination is often subtle and hard to measure. How does a researcher gather data on prestigious clubs that refuse admittance to blacks, Jews, or Catholics? How many marriages take place between ethnic group members and WASPs? How often do people in supervisory positions select people from similar ethnic or religious backgrounds when they have a heterogeneous field to choose from? Evidence is scarce.

### Ethnicity, Religion, and Region

Why is it that people unlike ourselves are not merely different but are typically viewed as lower on the status ladder? Is this habit of mind rooted in fear of the unknown? Or ethnocentrism? I do not know the answer, if indeed there is one. At any rate, most of us rank nearly everything, from neighborhoods and colleges to diet colas and cars, in terms of higher and lower status. Like it or not, Americans rank ethnic, regional, and religious groups on a status ladder too. (Table 10.2).

Who ranks at the top of the ladder? When American adults were asked in two polls (1964 and 1989) to rank the social standing of various ethnic, religious, and regional groups in the United States on a scale of 9 (highest rank) to 1 (lowest rank), white Americans born in the United States ranked even higher than "people of my own ethnic background."

As Table 10.2 shows, Americans will rank even a fictitious ethnic group, Wisnians. Although 61 percent of the 1,537 respondents in a national sample survey said that they could not rank the group, Wisnians got a relatively low ranking from the 39 percent who did. The director of the survey guesses that "people probably thought that if they were foreign-sounding, and they'd never heard of them, they couldn't be doing too well" (in Lewin, 1992:A10).

The ranking of ethnic, religious, and regional groups can change over time. For example, African-Americans, Jews, Japanese, Russians, Chinese, and Latin Americans all climbed the status ladder during the 1964 to 1989 period. It is unclear why, just as the reasons for ranking some groups above or below others—say, Chinese below Japanese—remain obscure.

Looked at from a different angle, religion (or lack of one) appears to be a fairly good predictor of education and income, two often used measures of stratification. Interestingly, the most comprehensive random sample of religious preference ever collected, reported in *One Nation Under God* (Kosmin and Lachman, 1993), reveals significant differences among denominations and between believers and nonbelievers. For example, 4.7 percent of Jehovah's Witnesses, 6.9 percent of Pentecostals, 20 percent of Roman Catholics, 36.3 percent of agnostics, and 46.7 percent of Jews graduated from college. There are significant differences in annual median household income too: Unitarians, $49,500; Disciples of Christ, $39,300, Episcopalians, $39,200, Jews, $36,700; agnostics, $33,300; Roman Catholics, $27,700; Pentecostals, $19,400.

**Table 10.2** The Ladder of Public Opinion: Where Some U.S. Groups Stand

| Group | 1989 | 1964 |
|---|---|---|
| Native white Americans | 7.03 | 7.25 |
| People of my own ethnic background | 6.57 | 6.16 |
| British | 6.46 | 6.37 |
| Protestants | 6.39 | 6.59 |
| Catholics | 6.33 | 6.36 |
| French | 6.07 | 5.73 |
| Irish | 6.05 | 5.94 |
| Swiss | 6.03 | 5.50 |
| Swedes | 5.99 | 5.41 |
| Austrians | 5.94 | 5.06 |
| Dutch | 5.90 | 5.60 |
| Norwegians | 5.87 | 5.48 |
| Scotch | 5.85 | 5.73 |
| Germans | 5.78 | 5.63 |
| Southerners | 5.77 | 5.25 |
| Italians | 5.69 | 5.03 |
| Danes | 5.63 | 5.20 |
| French Canadians | 5.62 | 5.08 |
| Japanese | 5.56 | 3.95 |
| Jews | 5.55 | 4.71 |
| People of foreign ancestry | 5.38 | 4.84 |
| Finns | 5.34 | 5.08 |
| Greeks | 5.09 | 4.31 |
| Lithuanians | 4.96 | 4.42 |
| Spanish-Americans | 4.79 | 4.81 |
| Chinese | 4.76 | 3.44 |
| Hungarians | 4.70 | 4.57 |
| Czechs | 4.64 | 4.40 |
| Poles | 4.63 | 4.54 |
| Russians | 4.58 | 3.88 |
| Latin Americans | 4.42 | 4.27 |
| American Indians | 4.27 | 4.04 |
| Negroes* | 4.17 | 2.75 |
| "Wisnians"† | 4.12 | — |
| Mexicans | 3.52 | 3.00 |
| Puerto Ricans | 3.52 | 2.92 |
| Gypsies | 2.65 | 2.29 |

*The term *Negroes* was used in the 1964 survey and kept in 1989 to conform with the earlier terminology.

†A fictitious group, the Wisnians, was added in 1989.

Source: National Opinion Research Center, 1989, in the *New York Times* [national edition] (January 8, 1992):A10.

## Ethclass

To what degree does ethnicity or religion divide members of the same class? For instance, do upper-class Irish Catholics have more social contacts with lower-class Irish Catholics than with upper-class WASPs? Who knows? Few studies deal with this intersection of ethnicity and social class, called **ethclass**.

Sociologist Milton Gordon, originator of the term *ethclass*, says that birds of our feather—the people we can relax with and feel at home with—are "likely to be of the same ethnic group *and* social class" (1978:135). Yet, ethclass may have limited application. If Herbert Gans is correct, ethnicity becomes mainly symbolic for many whites by the fourth generation in America; how useful, then, is the concept of ethclass?

Clearly, we need much more evidence before we can decide. We might begin by looking more closely at ZQ neighborhoods, one important place where birds of a feather flock together. For example, in the predominantly white, super-rich "Blue Blood Estates" (ZQ1), does an upper-class Japanese-American family feel more at home with its non-Japanese-American neighbors than with coethnics who live, say, in ZQ 11, "Bohemian Mix"?

There is not much data on these questions, but there is abundant information that African-Americans in U.S. cities have different—and unequal—life chances, lifestyles, and power. The Kerner Commission summarized the mountain of data succinctly in 1968: "Our nation is moving toward two societies, one black, one white—separate and unequal." Decade laters, the number of black elected officials had increased dramatically, and high-school graduation rates for African-Americans had doubled (Vobejda, 1992). But, as Harvard University professor Henry Louis Gates, Jr., pointed out, black America itself consists of at least two societies—separate and unequal

[T]he black middle class has never been larger. It has quadrupled since 1967, and it doubled during the nineteen-eighties alone. Never before have so many blacks done so well. And never before have so many blacks done so poorly. Forty-six per cent of black children live in poverty. (The figure for white children is sixteen per cent.) The black underclass has never been larger. (Blacks make up twelve per cent of the nation's population but fifty per cent of the nation's prisoners.) . . . the realities of race no longer affect all blacks in the same way. (1994:7–8)

In other words, class disparities *within* the "black community" grew wider in the last generation. While some African-Americans made economic advances, many more suffered poverty, unemployment, shorter life expectancies, and low-prestige.

These facts are undisputed. But how are we to interpret them? The traditional interpretation has been that racial discrimination is the key factor in limiting African-Americans to low-prestige and low-paid work. This interpretation is now under heavy attack. The scholarly work of William Julius Wilson, a University of Chicago sociologist, is indicative of this changing interpretation. When Wilson published the book *Power, Racism and Privilege* in 1973, he paid little attention to class. By 1978, he had changed his mind. In *The Declining Significance of Race* (1978:150), Wilson argued that "class has become more important than race in determining black life-chances in the modern industrial period." Wilson's argument is essentially this: Economic and technological change (the rapid growth of the corporate and government sectors, for instance) has led to a segmented labor market. This has served to solidify class differences between (1) a huge African-American underclass (created originally by discrimination and oppression) that is poor and poorly trained and (2) a much smaller group of well-educated, affluent, and privileged African-Americans who are experiencing many job opportunities.

Recent data seem to confirm Wilson's and Gates's idea that economic divisions *among* African-Americans are widening with time: The percentage of high-income (over $50,000) African-American families more than doubled from 1967 to 1990, while that of African-American families at the lowest income level (earning less than $5,000) grew by 50 percent. In 1990, more than one African-American family in nine earned less than $5,000 per year (Barringer, 1992a:A7).

One implication of Wilson's work is that the poor underclass—whether they live on Clay Street or hang out at Tally's Corner—share a fate. This fate is based on their class position, whether white, black, or brown.

Wilson is rethinking his vision of class and race (Chapter 9). Now he thinks that both structural factors (e.g., deindustrialization) *and* cultural factors (e.g., racial discrimination, the lack of two people in the house to share child-care duties) account for the increasing poverty of African-Americans.

Wilson's work has already stimulated other scholars. Perhaps the complicated issues concerning the relative importance of race, ethnicity, religion, and class in determining an American urbanite's life chances, lifestyle, and power will be a major research topic in this decade. Hopefully, this will be the case, for much work on these complex and ideologically loaded issues is sorely needed.

## Gender

Abundant statistical data testify to the increasing participation of women in the labor force, declining fertility rates, and many other topics. However, little attention has been paid to women in social stratification studies. There are reasons. Until quite recently, women were considered as appendages of their husbands; they were assumed to adopt the status and privileges of the men they married. With singlehood or divorce and full-time paid work becoming a way of life for more and more women, this assumption is changing. For example, Simpson, Stark, and Jackson (1988) conclude that working wives in the United States do not simply borrow their class identity from their husbands; increasingly, women's class identification has to do with such factors as union membership, self-employment, and work in a pink-collar occupation.

Also, social scientists themselves didn't pay attention to the variable of gender. Like medical

research, most studies of urban social stratification ignored women. In others, theorists treated women as a lower-status group, not recognizing the differences among subgroups. Thus much research and theory are needed on gender stratification and differential life chances for men and women.

However, there is also much that is known. We know that gender stratification and sexual harassment transcend economic and political systems. Judging from a report by the International Labor Organization ("Sex Harassment," 1992:C1+), sexual harassment against women in the workplace seems to be the norm, not the exception, in some industrial countries. For example, the study says that 58 percent of Dutch women and 74 percent of British women reported sexual harassment at work. Further, according to a study of ninety-nine nations published by the Population Crisis Council, women do not have full equality with men anywhere in the world, and women are "poor, powerless and pregnant" in the vast majority of nations (Camp, 1988). In the former Soviet Union, the majority of women work at low-paid blue-collar jobs; women professionals tend to be stuck at the lowest levels in their fields. In Israeli collective agricultural settlements (*kibbutzim*), the pioneer women started as equals, but even in this socialist milieu there is sexual inequality.

Why sexual inequality exists in the *kibbutz*—founded on the ideals of a small, classless society with economic, social, and political equality for all members—is a matter of some debate. But the point here is that sexual stratification exists and is a continuing feature of modern societies, whatever they call their economic-social system—capitalist, welfare state, socialist, or mixed. In other words, sexism is an international and intereconomic phenomenon.

## Women in Cities

As recently as 1975, women in the social science literature of cities were "part of the furniture," that is, simply there but barely noticed (Lofland,

1975:144). Since then, howver, there has been an explosion of research dealing with women in cities. This research deals with a wide range of issues, including the following: how the city has both "enhanced and constricted women's lives" and why "the experience of men and women in American cities is quite significantly different" (Stimpson, 1981:ix). But there seems to be no central focus to this research. Instead, research about women in cities is "as broad and as eclectic as the fields of urban studies and planning" (Wekerle, 1981:186).

Since there is no representative research about women in cities, let's look at a few studies that suggest the broad range. First, studies of women's work and family roles. In *City Women in America* (Lopata, Miller, and Barnewolt, 1986:57) the authors report that women remain segregated in a relatively few female-dominated occupations that are marked by "low pay and restricted mobility opportunities."

Second, studies of ethnic women. One such study, *Japanese American Women: Three Generations 1890–1990* (Nakano, 1990), documents the experiences of first-generation "picture brides" who entered marriages (in absentia) around a century ago with Japanese immigrants to America; then the brides sailed to Hawaii or the West Coast to join husbands they had never met. In the 1920s, some first- and second-generation Japanese-American women found work in sewing factories, one of the few jobs available to them in cities. By the third generation, *Nisei* women were fulfilling many traditional expectations, such as caring for elderly parents, but "they were also in a state of transition, easing out of some of the constraining aspects of the traditional mold" (200).

Third, divided cities—divided into men's spaces and women's spaces. For example, Dolores Hayden's *The Grand Domestic Revolution* (1981) documents the history of educated, white women's struggles in America to trade mansions for women-centered home design and community planning. Inspired by Susan B. Anthony's call to arms—"Away with your man-visions! Women propose to reject them all, and begin to dream dreams for themselves"—

Hayden explores many visionary schemes for emancipating women by transforming individual housework and/or child care into communal activities, including two from the 1860s: Harriet Beecher Stowe's model Christian neighborhood (where ten to twelve families would share a laundry and bakehouse) and Melusina Fay Peirce's attempts to organize her neighbors in Cambridge, Massachusetts, into cooperative housekeeping associations and kitchenless houses.

Fourth, the journey to work and residential choice. Because so many U.S. women now work outside the home and have primary responsibility for childcare and housework, they seek to minimize their time-wasting commute by living near the workplace. This constrains women's residential—and employment—choices as several studies show (e.g., Rutherford and Wekerle, 1988).

Finally, macro-level studies. Suzanne Mackenzie's article, "Women in the City" (1989), is exemplary. It traces the connections between gender restructuring and urban restructuring in the 1970s and 1980s. For one thing, Mackenzie notes that in North America, women became the fastest-growing group in the expanding self-employed sector, including home-based work (e.g., garment industry production). "Restructuring," she states, "was leading to the creation and expansion of an informal economy, that social space where people combined the resources of their homes and communities with networks of casual work to develop survival strategies"(116).

## Age

Given the work of Marx, Weber, Bourdieu, and Gans, it is not news that people's tastes differ by class or status group. But often we forget that age and gender also affect taste. Take, for example, listeners to National Public Radio (NPR). A comprehensive analysis of NPR listeners (1988) found that classical music and opera appeal more to women than to men; jazz appeals most to younger men (twenty-five to thirty-four years old); and information programs appeal primarily to listeners aged thirty-five to forty-four.

**Fig. 10.6** TOO YOUNG OR TOO OLD. Many in America face age discrimination. But some elders find new careers instead of rocking chairs. Edna W. Newman, for one, starting working as a disc jockey in her mid-seventies and became manager of WMRF, a radio station at the Daughters of Israel Geriatric Center in West Orange, New Jersey. (Barbara London)

It is also not news that both sexism and ageism exist in many societies. But structurally, there is an important difference between these two "isms": Sexism seems to surpass the boundaries of economic and social systems; ageism seems to be most prevalent in societies that define human value in terms of economic productive capacity. That is, the more a society believes that "you are what you do," the more the very old and the very young (the economically unproductive) will tend to be devalued.

In the United States, the specter of the old-age home haunts many who see themselves being relegated to the sidelines. Even in Japan, where family obligations traditionally meant taking care of one's parents, many older people face the twilight years bathed in darkness. Japanese movie-maker Yasujiro Ozu sensitively portrays the plight of an old couple whose children see them as a burden in *Tokyo Story* (1953).

Not hired because they're "too old" or forced to retire, stripped of social roles that give meaning to their lives, and often pushed aside, the old may be called *senior citizens*, but they're often treated as less than equal citizens. As the life expectancy in advanced industrial countries continues to increase, what will happen to people in their not so golden years?

Young people also receive unequal treatment. In some cases, American customs or laws presumed to protect children have served to deny them civil rights. In other cases (e.g., widespread exclusion from juries), young adults face discrimination. New York City became the first city in the United States to attack discrimination against young people in public places; since 1993, shops, restaurants, and movie theaters that ban children can be fined up to $100,000.

The specific consequences of age stratification for young and old include economic discrimination, age stereotyping, and territorial segregation (Johnson and Kamara, 1977–1978). In other words, old and young have a common plight.

## ANOTHER LOOK

Scholars and citizens agree that inequality exists. And, no matter how inequality is defined—by access to money, information, prestige, or power —most believe that the inequality gap between those who have and don't have is growing wider.

But *why* inequalities exist (and the parts that gender, race, ethclass, status, power, and religion in maintaining or perpetuating inequality) is a matter of continuing controversy. At the urban level, *how* a researcher goes about studying inequalities has less to do with disciplinary background than ideology. And *what* the researcher finds—an open system characterized by social mobility or a more rigid system of small, exclusive elites and social immobility—depends mainly on the theoretical orientation of the researcher. Specifically, those using the concept of status tend to find an open system; those using the concept of class tend to emphasize the rigidity of the social hierarchy. A subtle and immeasurable influence on researchers may also be present: fear—of change in the basic nature of the society and the economy. After all, why should we expect urbanists to be free from values about equality?

Those desiring to reduce inequality don't agree on how to do it. Programs of equal opportunity, not equal results, have been the liberals' mainstay, together with tax policies and public assistance. Marx had another solution—the creation of a classless society. Weber held out little hope of any solution, believing that even under socialism, people would be oppressed and de-

personalized by a common enemy: bureaucratic organization. Others have pointed to the rise of a new class, not predicted by Marx: scientists and technicians, intellectuals and professionals. This new class, it is often argued (e.g., Gouldner, 1979), shares a more important form of capital than money—culture—and it is increasingly gaining power and demanding autonomy. Bourdieu calls this important badge of distinction *cultural capital.*

Unsurprisingly, scholars disagree on who comprises the much-talked about middle class. Weberians see it as an income range that reflects what market basket of goods and services a group can buy in the market. Wright see it as a class that is both exploiter and exploited. But to many who once thought that they were in it and now wonder, the middle class may represent "a point of view more than an income range. It may be rooted in an attitude that its members control their economic destiny: they can provide for the necessities of life, build savings, and provide for future needs" (Nordheimer, 1992:A1).

Meanwhile, researchers have failed to disentangle the factors that influence collective inequalities, including sex, race, ethnicity, class, religion, and age. Ethnic and sexual stratification have been particularly neglected as independent factors that help determine who gets what out of life.

## KEY TERMS

**American dream**   The idea, many say myth, that any individual in the United States can climb the ladder of success if he or she works hard, plays by the rules, and has a pinch of luck. For many, owning a single-family, detached suburban home symbolizes the realization of the dream.

**Bourgeoisie**   (plural noun) Literally, "people who live in towns or cities" (bourgs). In Marx's analysis of social stratification, the bourgeoisie is the class that owns the means of production and thus controls the social relations of production under capitalism. The class opposing the bourgeoisie is the proletariat.

**Capital**   To orthodox economists two types, physical—all useful assets (except unimproved land and natural raw materials) used to produce goods and services and human—people's knowledge, skills, and energies, which can be used to produce goods and services. To Marx, capital is more than money or machines; it masks a social relation of domination.

**Capitalists**   In Marxist analysis, synonym for *bourgeoisie.*

**Castes**   Rigid social divisions based on status ascribed at birth. A caste system is typified by lack of social mobility; it is a closed class system. The classic example is traditional India, where Brahmins constitute the highest caste and the Harijans (untouchables) constitute the lowest caste.

**Class**   As used by Karl Marx, class position in the social hierarchy is determined by one's relationship to the means of production (ownership or nonownership). As used by Max Weber, class is determined by one's market position. A group of people who share a similar relationship to the means of production (Marx) or market position (Weber) are members of the same class.

**Class consciousness**   Sense of belonging to and identifying with a particular social class. This awareness is accompanied by a sense of solidarity with other individuals in the same class and by the feeling that one's own interests are tied to the position of the class as a whole.

**Cultural capital**   French sociologist Pierre Bourdieu's term for language competencies, attitudes, behaviors, and general familiarity with the culture and symbols of a particular class or status group. Contemporary high-status symbols include a preference for books of poetry over Harlequin novels.

**Ethclass**   Sociologist Milton Gordon's term for the intersection of class and ethnicity in determining a person's identity and assimilation. Example: a middle-class Puerto Rican probably feels more kinship with a middle-class Italian than with a lower-class Puerto Rican.

**False consciousness**   In Marxist analysis, the sense of belonging to or identifying with a social class to which one does not belong objectively.

**Forces of production**   In Marxist analysis, the technological, economic, and knowledge base of a society. It is one component of the mode of production (together with the social relations of production).

**Hegemony**   A term used by the late Italian Marxist Antonio Gramsci, meaning cultural leadership or domination.

**Influence**   Informal power. Unlike formal power, influence is rooted in such factors as money, guns, organization (e.g., lobby groups, political parties), and personal charisma.

**Means of production**   In Marxist analysis, inputs such as raw materials and tools that produce (or add to) things of value in a society. These inputs include land in feudalism and factory machines in industrial capitalism. Marxists maintain that the dominant class owns or controls the means or production.

**Mode of production**   To Marx, (1) the forces of production plus (2) the social relations of production. Together, these two components shape a society. Thus, the slave mode, the feudal mode, and the capitalist mode of production are different types of social forms.

**Power**   In Weber's analysis, one dimension of social stratification that can be independent of the economic and prestige orders. Power is the ability to force others, even if they resist, to carry out your policies. The political order consists of administrative-bureaucratic and elected positions in the corporate and governmental spheres.

**Proletariat**   Marx's term for urban propertyless workers who, he felt, stood in opposition to the owners of the means of production (the bourgeoisie or capitalists) who exploited them in industrial capitalist society. One member of this class: a prole (slang) or proletarian.

**Social relations of production**   In Marxist analysis, how people involved in production relate to each other and to the surplus that they collectively produce. Under capitalism, the social relations of production are the relations between the people who produce the surplus (workers) and those who decide how it should be appropriated (capitalists).

**Social stratification**   The process by which individuals and groups rank each other socially and differentiate each other in a hierarchy. From the Latin term *strata* ("layers", singular: *stratum*). Caste and class societies are socially stratified.

**Socioeconomic status (SES)**   A composite measure based on income, education, and occupation that combines class and status to determine a person's or group's place on the social ladder.

**Status**   One of Weber's three dimensions for ranking members of a society. Status is based on the prestige or social esteem that others in the society accord a person. It is a position in the social structure that, according to Weber, carries with it a certain lifestyle.

## PROJECTS

**1. Attitudes on class.** To investigate how some people in your community view the social structure and their place in it, construct a questionnaire and administer it at various sites in the community. You might ask the following questions: Do classes exist in America? How do you define yourself (upper class, upper middle, middle, lower middle, working class)? Does everyone in the United States have an equal chance to lead a long life and to get a good job? The questionnaire should be short but include background information on each respondent, including occupation (or job title) or lack of one (retired, unemployed). When examining responses, see how many respondents list themselves as middle class and how many of these are in the U.S. census categories of professional or managerial workers. What attitudes do your respondents hold toward class?

**2. Social status.** Replicate Warner's study of the distribution of housing in Jonesville in your community. Where are the fine houses located? Where do people with high-status occupations live? Is there a concentration of high-status homes in a particular neighborhood or neighborhoods?

**3. Taste differences.** Try to determine who reads and listens to what in your area. The first step is to determine if you can get access to data, perhaps from ad agencies or radio stations and newspaper circulation departments, that show the ethnicity, gender, age, and income of lis-

teners, readers, and viewers of different media. If you can, choose a few program or article categories (e.g., sports, rap, soap operas, comic strips, international news, classical music) and try to establish differences, if any, in readership, listenership, or viewership. If there are differences, why might these exist?

**4. Wealth: interpreting data on median net worth.** Family wealth (net worth) is based on assets (e.g., cars, stocks, bonds, equity in real estate, bank accounts, antique rugs, rare baseball cards) minus debts (e.g., home mortgage, credit card balances, loans). According to the U.S. Census Bureau in 1994, the typical American household lost about 12 percent of its wealth (almost $5,000) between 1988 and 1991. Lost jobs and falling home values meant that people dipped into personal savings and borrowed from other assets during the economic recession.

Overall, African-Americans and Latinos with the same incomes as whites in the United States are poorer than whites because they tend to have a much lower net worth (i.e., fewer assets and higher debts). For example, in 1991 the median *wealth, not income,* of white households was $44,408—nearly ten times that of African-American households ($4,604) and over eight times that of Latino households ($5,345).

How might these data be interpreted by the theorists discussed in this chapter? Discuss two or more interpretations of these data.

## SUGGESTIONS FOR FURTHER LEARNING

For a comparison of Marx's, Durkheim's, and Weber's thought, see Anthony Giddens, *Capitalism and Modern Social Theory* (London: Cambridge University Press, 1971). This book, which is not for beginners, contains an excellent chapter, "Fundamental Concepts of Sociology," which considers Weber's notions of class, status, and party.

Controversial French theorist (some say visionary) Jean Budrillard thinks that social class analysis is unnecessary for understanding postmodern society (*Techno$chaft*). See his *For a Cri-*

*tique of the Political Economy of the Sign* (St. Louis: Telos Press, 1981) and an essay by Dean MacCannell and Juliet Flower MacCannell, "Social Class in Postmodernity," in *Forget Baudrillard?* ed. Chris Rojek and Bryan S. Turner (London: Routledge, 1993), pp. 124–145.

American economist Thorstein Veblen detailed the lifestyles of various status groups in *The Theory of the Leisure Class* (New York: Macmillan, 1899) and popularized the term *conspicuous consumption*. Veblen, who taught for a time at the University of Chicago, was concerned, as Weber was, with the growth of rationality in modern life. Veblen advocated a society run by scientists and engineers (technocrats) instead of businesspeople. Another economist, John R. Commons, had ideas that paralleled those of Weber. In *Institutional Economics: Its Place in Political Economy* (New York: Macmillan, 1934) and *The Economics of Collective Action* (New York: Macmillan, 1950), he deals with various forms of power—moral, economic, and physical—and shows how they are linked together in property relationships.

More recently, the premier social analyst of French culture, Pierre Bourdieu, has attempted to rethink Max Weber's opposition between class and status groups in *Distinction: A Social Critique of the Judgement of Taste* (Cambridge, Mass.: Harvard University Press, [1979] 1984). This important book is "very French," as Bourdieu himself says, in its examples and form. But his examples can be adapted easily to the United States. His statistical charts, based on survey data, reveal great differences in aesthetic dispositions and consumption practices among class and status groups in France. For example, Table 17 (p. 184) shows the yearly spending by teachers, professionals, and industrial and commercial employers in 1972; it reveals that industrial and commercial employers pay over 37 percent of their annual spending on food, while professionals spend less than 25 percent. French university and secondary school teachers do 12 percent of their yearly spending on presentation (clothes, hairdressing, toiletries, etc.), much less than professionals spend (over 22 percent).

A board game designed and produced by political scientist Bertell Ollman is called "Class Struggle." Paralleling Marx's views on class, it pits capitalists against workers. Other game players include small-business people, students, and professionals.

Highly readable, Barbara Ehrenreich's *Fear of Falling: The Inner Life of the Middle Class* (New York: Harper Perennial, 1990) looks at the professional middle class (and its cultural capital), which she says is deeply anxious and insecure.

Literature dealing with social stratification is varied. It ranges from the classic American dream tales of upward social mobility by Horatio Alger, including *Ragged Dick* and *Mark, the Match Boy* (New York: Crowell-Collier, 1962), and John P. Marquand's portrait of upper-class life in Boston, *The Late George Apley* (Fort Lee, N.J.: Little, 1937), to Jack London's socialist outrage, expressed in his story of class oppression, *The Iron Heel* (New York: Macmillan, 1907). The effects of race on life chances are vividly portrayed in Claude Brown's autobiographical account, *Manchild in the Promised Land* (New York: Signet, 1965), and in the novels of Ralph Ellison, Richard Wright, and James Baldwin. Ellison's *Invisible Man* (New York: Signet, 1953) listens to records of Louis Armstrong playing and singing "What Did I Do to Be So Black and Blue?" sitting in his Harlem basement with 1,369 lights—to convince himself that he really exists in a world where people refuse to see him.

The concept of class is rarely dealt with head-on by Hollywood. English professor and social critic Benjamin DeMott, author of *The Imperial Middle: Why Americans Can't Think Straight About Class* (New York: Morrow, 1990), says that "class movies" like *White Palace* (1990), *Pretty Woman* (1990), *The Bonfire of the Vanities* (1990), *Working Girl* (1988), and *Driving Miss Daisy* (1989) don't deal responsibly with class because they obfuscate the realities of class, particularly the power associated with the upper class.

Here is a sampler of films and video productions, from varying ideological points of view, that deal with the themes of class and status. In *American Dream* (1991), documentary filmmaker Barbara Kopple examines a heartbreaking struggle that pits family members against one another: a walkout at the Hormel meat-packing plant in Austin, Minnesota. Union members pay a high price for defying their employer and their own international union by continuing their strike. Oscar-winning Sally Field portrays a southern textile worker in *Norma Rae* (1979), a liberal film based on a real-life event: a successful unionization effort in a southern mill town. Its view of the world is liberal, not radical. *Metropolitan* (1990) shows a very different scene—the preppie-debutante scene of New York City. Class difference is the driving force of *Pretty in Pink* (1986), a film that asks the old question: Can a young woman from the wrong side of town fall in love and marry the rich kid? (Old-time radio buffs can hear an earlier version of this question on the soap opera *Our Gal Sunday*.) A feature-length classic from the Marxist perspective is Henry Bieberman's *Salt of the Earth* (1953). Bieberman, one of the "Hollywood Ten" producers blacklisted during the McCarthy era, weaves together themes of class, ethnic, and sexual oppression around the incident of a miners' strike in the Southwest. Fritz Lang's classic silent film *Metropolis* (1927) presents a different ideological message: that workers (representing the "hands") and their bosses (representing the "head") each have a distinct place in society, but that to work smoothly together, both should be joined by human feeling, or "heart"; the film can be interpreted as a defense of rigid social stratification under capitalism. On the other hand, Stanley Kramer's Western, *High Noon* (1952), can be interpreted as presenting a contrary message. Critic Pauline Kael called *High Noon* a kind of civics lesson in which the frontier Western town represents a "microcosm of the evils of capitalist society" (*Kiss Kiss Bang Bang* [New York: Bantam, 1969], p. 349).

Among the many films that treat topics of racial, ethnic, and gender stratification are the comedy *Trading Places* (1983) and Robert Mulligan's drama *To Kill a Mockingbird* (1962), which deals with small-town prejudice against African-Americans. *Menace II Society* (1993), codirected by Allen and Albert Hughes, is a grim tale of a young African-American man growing up in a poverty-stricken area of Los Angeles. *Blue Collar*

(1978) is director Paul Schrader's hard-hitting drama that shows how auto workers are divided against one another on the basis of race, ethnicity, and dreams of upward mobility. Michael Moore's *Roger and Me* (1989) contrasts the life of Roger Smith, head of General Motors, with the lives of working-class people in Flint, Michigan, after the GM plant closings. Its sequel, *Pets or Meat?* (1992), contains a scene not for the squeamish: a snake swallowing a live rabbit, whole—which seems to symbolize filmmaker Moore's view of the relation between GM and its workers.

Ageism and the loss of roles in old age are sensitively portrayed in Japanese director Yasujiro Ozu's *Tokyo Story* (1953). This film also shows that stratification by age and isolation of older people are international phenomena.

For a guide to the veritable explosion of research on women in the city, see Deborah Husted, *Women and Urban America: A Selected and Multidisciplinary Bibliography of Materials Since 1960* (Monticello, Ill.: Vance Bibliographies, 1988).

Several TV productions are noteworthy in depicting themes of differential life chances and lifestyles. The NBC series *I'll Fly Away* (1992–1993), shown on PBS in 1994 and 1995, tells the stories of an African-American housekeeper, Lily, and her family and the family of her white employer, Forrest Bedford (perhaps ironically named for Nathan Bedford Forrest, a distinguished Confederate general and head of the newly formed Ku Klux Klan in 1866), during the battle for civil rights in the South. *The Jewel in the Crown*, referring to India, the British Empire's crown jewel, is a complex dramatic portrait of the last days of the British raj. This outstanding 1984 British production reveals both subtle and blatant forms of discrimination based on class, status, power, and ethnicity.

Thanks to the federal government's Works Progress Administration in the 1930s, the themes of class, status, and power decorate the walls of many city buildings, including Coit Tower in San Francisco. Many artists were supported throughout the Depression by WPA projects. In Canada, a social commentary on the role of railroad barons is painted on the walls of buildings in Revelstoke, British Columbia; the murals satirize the entrepreneurs who helped construct the town.

For works about social stratification in poor countries or among low-income people in rich countries, see Arthur D. Murphy and Alex Stepick, *Social Equality in Oaxaca [Mexico]: A History of Resistance and Change* (Philadelphia: Temple University Press, 1991); Joe T. Darden, Richard Child Hill, June Thomas, and Richard Thomas, *Detroit: Race and Uneven Development* (Philadelphia: Temple University Press, 1987); and Paul Willis, *Learning to Labor: How Working Class Kids Get Working Class Jobs* (New York: Columbia University Press, 1981).

## REFERENCES

Baltzell, E. Digby. 1958. *Philadelphia Gentlemen: The Making of a National Upper Class.* New York: Free Press.

Balzac, Honoré de. [1834] 1946. *Père Goriot* and *Eugénie Grandet.* New York: Random House.

Barringer, Felicity. 1992a. "Rich–poor gulf widens among blacks." *New York Times* [national edition] (September 25):A7.

———. 1992b. "White–black disparity in income narrowed in 80's, census shows but gap remained large and grew in Midwest." *New York Times* [national edition] (July 24):A1+.

Birmingham, Stephen. 1968. *The Right People: A Portrait of the American Social Establishment.* Boston: Little, Brown.

Bourdieu, Pierre. [1979] 1984. *Distinction: A Social Critique of the Judgement of Taste.* Trans. Richard Nice. Cambridge, Mass.: Harvard University Press.

Brown, Elaine. 1992. *A Taste of Power: A Black Woman's Story.* New York: Pantheon.

Camp, Sharon. 1988. "Poor, powerless and pregnant." Washington, D.C.: Population Crisis Committee.

Caplovitz, David. 1963. *The Poor Pay More: Consumer Practices of Low-Income Families.* New York: Free Press.

Coffin, Tristam. 1991. "Hard facts on the American economy." *Washington Spectator* (February 1):1–2.

Cooke, Alistair. 1992. "Letter from America: 50 years ago." National Public Radio, KALW-FM, San Francisco (December 14).

Degler, Carl N. 1991. *In Search of Human Nature.* New York: Oxford University Press.

DiMaggio, Paul, and John Mohr. 1985. "Cultural capital, educational attainment, and marital selection." *American Journal of Sociology* 90 (May):1231–1257.

Feiffer, Jules. 1993. Cartoon. *San Francisco Examiner* [This World section] (February 21):5.

Form, William H., and Gregory P. Stone. 1957. "Urbanism, anonymity and status symbolism." *American Journal of Sociology* 62 (March):504–514.

Gans, Herbert. 1974. *Popular Culture and High Culture.* New York: Basic Books.

Gates, Henry Louis, Jr. 1994. "The black leadership myth." *New Yorker* (October 24):7–8.

Gerth, Hans H., and C. Wright Mills, eds. and trans. 1958. *From Max Weber: Essays in Sociology.* New York: Oxford University Press.

Gitlin, Todd, and Nanci Hollander. 1970. *Uptown: Poor Whites in Chicago.* New York: Harper & Row.

Gordon, Milton M. 1978. *Human Nature, Class, and Ethnicity.* New York: Oxford University Press.

Gouldner, Alvin W. 1979. *The Future of Intellectuals and the Rise of the New Class.* New York: Seabury.

Gramsci, Antonio.[1932] 1975. *Letters from Prison: Antonio Gramsci.* Ed. Lynne Lawner. New York: Harper Colophon.

Hayden, Dolores. 1981. *The Grand Domestic Revolution.* Cambridge, Mass.: MIT Press.

Healy, Melissa. 1994. "U.S. used poor, sick for testing radiation." *San Francisco Examiner* (January 9):1+.

Heilbroner, Robert L. 1978. "Inescapable Marx." *New York Review of Books* (June 29):33–37.

Herrnstein, Richard J., and Charles Murray. 1994. *The Bell Curve: Intelligence and Class Structure in American Life.* New York: Free Press.

Hilts, Philip J. 1990. "Life expectancy for blacks in U.S. shows sharp drop." *New York Times* [national edition] (November 29):A1+.

Horowitz, Ruth. 1983. *Honor and the American Dream.* New Brunswick, N.J.: Rutgers University Press.

Howard, Dick. 1978. *The Marxian Legacy.* New York: Dutton.

Howell, Joseph T. [1973] 1991. *Hard Living on Clay Street: Portraits of Blue Collar Families.* Garden City, N.Y.: Doubleday, Anchor.

Itzkoff, Seymour W. 1994. *The Decline of Intelligence in America: A Strategy for National Renewal.* Westport, Conn.: Praeger.

Ivins, Molly. 1978. "Mormon action on blacks promises impact on Utah." *New York Times* (June 18):1+.

Johnson, Dirk. 1991. "Prosperity must make room for diversity in Utah." *New York Times* [national edition] (August 25):A13.

Johnson, Gregory, and J. Lawrence Kamara. 1977–1978. "Growing up and growing old: The politics of age exclusion." *Journal of Aging and Human Development* 8:99–110.

Katznelson, Ira. 1992. *Marxism and the City.* New York: Oxford University Press.

Kornblum, William. 1974. *Blue Collar Community.* Chicago: University of Chicago Press.

Kosmin, Barry A., and Seymour P. Lachman. 1993. *One Nation Under God: Religion in Contemporary American Society.* New York: Harmony.

Lewin, Tamar. 1992. "Study points to increase in intolerance of ethnicity." *New York Times* [national edition] (January 8):A1+.

Liebold, Linda K. 1988. "Audience 88: A comprehensive analysis of public radio listeners." Washington, D.C.: Corporation for Public Broadcasting.

Liebow, Elliot. 1967. *Tally's Corner: A Study of Negro Streetcorner Men.* Boston: Little, Brown.

Lofland, Lyn H. 1975. "The 'thereness' of women: A selective review of urban sociology." Pp. 144–170 in Marcia Millman and Rosabeth Moss Kanter, eds., *Another Voice: Feminist Perspectives on Social Life and Social Science.* Garden City, N.Y.: Doubleday, Anchor.

Lopata, Helena Znaniecki, Cheryl Miller, and Debra Barnewolt. 1986. *City Women in America: Work, Jobs, Occupations, Careers.* Vol. 1. New York: Praeger.

Lukas, J. Anthony. 1978. Review of *Chance and Circumstance. New York Times Book Review* (June 11):9+.

Lynd, Robert S., and Helen Merrell Lynd. [1929] 1956. *Middletown.* New York: Harcourt, Brace & World.

Mackenzie, Suzanne. 1989. "Women in the city." Pp. 109–126 in Richard Peet and Nigel Thrift, eds., *New Models in Geography: The Political-economy Perspective.* Vol. 2. London: Unwin Hyman.

McCord, Colin, and Howard P. Freeman. 1990. "Excess mortality in Harlem." *New England Journal of Medicine* (January 18):173–177.

McLellan, David, ed. 1977. *Karl Marx: Selected Writings.* New York: Oxford University Press.

Nakano, Mei. 1990. *Japanese American Women: Three Generations 1890–1990.* Berkeley, Calif.: Mina Press.

Nakao, Keiko, and Judith Treas. 1990. "Occupational prestige in the United States revisited: Twenty-five years of stability and change." Paper presented at the annual meetings of the American Sociological Association (August), Washington, D.C.

*NBC News.* 1993. (May 24), 5:44 P.M. PDT.

"Newspaper calls Mormon church an $8 billion-a-year enterprise." 1991. *San Francisco Chronicle* (July 1):A5.

Nordheimer, Jon. 1992. "From middle class to jobless: A sense of pride is shattered." *New York Times* [national edition] (April 13):A1+.

Pear, Robert. 1993. "Wide health gap, linked to income, is reported in U.S." *New York Times* [national edition] (July 8):A1+.

Phillips, Kevin P. 1990. "Reagan's America: A capital offense." *New York Times Magazine* (June 17):26+.

Rieder, Jonathan. 1985. *Canarsie: The Jews and Italians of Brooklyn Against Liberalism.* Cambridge, Mass.: Harvard University Press.

Rushton, J. Philippe. 1994. *Race, Evolution, and Behavior: A Life History Perspective.* New Brunswick, N.J.: Transaction Books.

Rutherford, Brent, and Gerda Wekerle. 1988. "Captive rider, captive labor: Spatial constraints and women's employment." *Urban Georgraphy* 9 (1988):116–137.

Saunders, Peter. 1981. *Social Theory and the Urban Question.* London: Hutchinson.

Senneker, Harold, with Dolores Lataniotis. 1990. "The richest people in America: The Forbes 400." *Forbes* (October 22).

"Sex harassment a global problem." 1992. *San Francisco Chronicle* (December 1):C1+.

Simpson, Ida Harper, David Stark, and Robert A. Jackson. 1988. "Class identification processes of married, working men and women." *American Sociological Review* 53 (April):284–293.

Solon, Gary. 1992. "Intergenerational income mobility in the United States." *American Economic Review* 82 (June):393–408.

Stimpson, Catharine R., 1981. Preface, Pp. ix–x in Catharine R. Stimpson, Elsa Dixler, Martha J. Nelson, and Kathryn B. Yatrakis, eds., *Women and the American City.* Chicago: University of Chicago Press.

Susser, Ida. 1982. *Norman Street: Poverty and Politics in an Urban Neighborhood.* New York: Oxford University Press.

Teninty, Tim. 1992. Personal conversation. Berkeley, Calif.

Thernstrom, Stephan. 1965. "'Yankee City' revisited: The perils of historical naiveté." *American Sociological Review* 30 (April):234–242.

Treiman, Donald J. 1977. *Occupational Prestige in Comparative Perspective.* New York: Academic Press.

"UAW chief calls Carter ineffective." 1978. *San Francisco Chronicle* (July 20):12.

Uchitelle, Louis. 1994. "Changing economy spawns 'anxious class.'" *San Francisco Chronicle* (November 21):A6.

U.S. Bureau of the Census. 1977. *Social Indicators 1976.* Washington, D.C.: Government Printing Office.

"Used cars: The poor get poorer." 1978. *New York Times* (June 18):F17.

Vobedja, Barbara. 1992. "Census figures show more blacks graduating." *San Francisco Chronicle* (July 24):2.

Warner, W. Lloyd, and associates. [1941] 1963. *Yankee City.* One volume, abridged. New Haven, Conn.: Yale University Press.

———. [1949] 1964. *Democracy in Jonesville: A Study in Quality and Inequality.* New York: Harper Torchbooks.

Weber, Max. [1904–1905] 1958. *The Protestant Ethic and the Spirit of Capitalism.* New York: Scribner.

———. [1922] 1958. "Class, status, party." Pp. 180–195 in Hans H. Gerth and C. Wright Mills, eds. and trans. *From Max Weber: Essays in Sociology.* New York: Oxford University Press.

Wekerle, Gerda R. 1981. "Women in the urban environment." Pp. 185–211 in Catharine R. Stimpson, Elsa Dixler, Martha J. Nelson, and Kathryn B. Yatrakis, eds., *Women and the American City.* Chicago: University of Chicago Press.

Wheeler, David L. 1994. "An ominous legacy of the atomic age." *Chronicle of Higher Education* (January 12):A6–7.

Wilson, William Julius. 1973. *Power, Racism and Privilege.* New York: Macmillan.

———. 1978. *The Declining Significance of Race: Blacks and Changing American Institutions.* Chicago: University of Chicago Press.

Wright, Erik Olin. 1978. "Race, class and income inequality." *American Journal of Sociology* 83 (May): 1368–1397.

———. 1985. *Classes.* London: Verso.

Wright, Erik Olin, Uwe Becker, Johanna Brenner, Michael Burawoy, Val Burris, Guglielmo Carchedi, Gordon Marshall, Peter F. Meiksins, David Rose, Arthur Stinchcombe, and Philippe Van Parijs. 1989. *The Debate on Classes.* London: Verso.

Wright, Erik Olin, and Bill Martin. 1987. "The transformation of the American class structure, 1960–80." *American Journal of Sociology* 93 (July):1–29.

Walker Evans

# CHAPTER 11
# Discovering the Rules

Pedestrians push their way pell-mell through a busy intersection. Subway riders grab the first empty seat they see. Bar patrons sit in a quiet corner to avoid conversation. Automatic teller machine (ATM) users look bored as they await their turn in silence. Or so it may seem at first glance. But appearances are often deceiving, especially in the case of face-to-face encounters with urban or suburban strangers.

This chapter looks behind some of those appearances. It focuses on everyday, routine activities of urban life—walking down a busy street in the CBD, riding public transportation, meeting people in a bar. Looking closely at such ordinary activities is not easy precisely because they are so ordinary. We tend to take them for granted and not subject them to analysis. After all, what adult in America thinks twice about the proper way to ride a subway or walk down a city street? We know how to accomplish these tasks without thinking! In other words, these actions seem natural.

Here I treat these "natural" behaviors as curious, problematic, and not at all natural. It is as if we are visitors in a strange, exotic country, prepared to suffer culture shock from exposure to a totally unfamiliar way of life. But geographically, we don't have to move anywhere. Instead, we'll be "traveling" along familiar city streets and perhaps making some startling discoveries.

My aim is to illuminate how routine social interaction takes place and why it happens as it does. As a guide on this mystery tour of the familiar, we will draw upon the insights of sociologists, social psychologists, and anthropologists.

## TAKING A FRESH LOOK AT THE FAMILIAR

In studying urban **social interaction,** we are mostly studying ourselves—our friends and families, work mates, and fellow students—or groups of people about whom we have already formed some opinion. For this reason, it is harder to examine ourselves with detachment than it is to study a foreign culture; we hold fewer preconceived notions and moral judgments about "proper" behavior patterns in faraway lands.

Suspending these assumptions long enough to see our own culture objectively is difficult. That is one reason why anthropologists have tended to scrutinize other cultures, not their own. It is also one reason why foreigners have provided some of the most astute observations about American culture.

Although it is difficult, taking a fresh look at familiar surroundings can be enlightening. Anthropologist Horace Miner (1956) and community activist Beverly Slapin (1990) examine parts of their own society using a trained eye, tongue in cheek, and active funnybone (Box 11.1). How many of us could so dispassionately record our

own rites, such as the "ritual fasts to make fat people thin and ceremonial feasts to make thin people fat" or the "Sacred Yuppie Jogging Ceremony"? It takes discipline and humor to look at ourselves as if *we* are the curious beings.

### Pedestrian Behavior

Since that is our mission—to look closely at the everyday activities of people in urban places—let's begin with an impressive but usually unnoticed feature of city life: the large numbers of total strangers that urbanites encounter daily. Standing on a busy streetcorner in San Francisco's CBD, for instance, my students counted 4,000 passersby within one hour. On one midtown block in Manhattan, New York City, some 38,000 pedestrians pass by on an average weekday (Whyte, 1974).

It is also impressive that pedestrians move in and around the CBD smoothly, with few scuffles or other incidents. But we take this for granted. Does anyone applaud the fact that pedestrians actually reach their destination without knocking each other down or holding up traffic? No, we just expect it.

We also expect that when we step off a busy streetcorner, we'll reach the other side of the street without mishap. Upon reflection, however, crossing a busy street is no small accomplishment. Three or four hundred strangers may be marching toward you; armies of unknown people are edging up from behind, all walking at different speeds; cars may be careening into your path; broken glass or dog excrement may be lying in wait. In this potentially dangerous battlefield, crossing the street now seems like a high-risk venture, not a routine activity.

Why is it, then, that crossing the street is such a common event? Because we expect that other pedestrians will follow the "rules of the game" and be competent game players. Like so many everyday activities, street crossing is governed by rules that are widely shared within any culture. These culturally shared rules (**norms**) are often implicit and hidden, but they exist nonetheless. If

Box 11.1

## STRANGE TRIBAL RITES REVEALED!

### "Body Ritual Among the Nacirema"
### by Horace Miner

[The Nacirema] are a North American group living in the territory between the Canadian Cree, the Yaqui and Tarahumare of Mexico, and the Carib and Arawak of the Antilles . . . .

According to Nacirema mythology, their nation was originated by a culture hero, Notgnihsaw, who is otherwise known for two great feats of strength—the throwing of a piece of wampum across the river Pa-To-Mac and the chopping down of a cherry tree in which the Spirit of Truth resided.

Nacirema culture is characterized by a highly developed market economy that has evolved in a rich natural habitat. While much of the people's time is devoted to economic pursuits, a large part of the fruits of these labors and a considerable portion of the day are spent in ritual activity. The focus of this activity is the human body, the appearance and health of which loom as a dominant concern in the ethos of the people. . . .

The fundamental belief underlying the whole system appears to be that the human body is ugly, and that its natural tendency is to debility and disease. Incarcerated in such a body, man's only hope is to avert these characteristics through the use of the powerful influences of ritual and ceremony. Every household has one or more shrines devoted to this purpose. The more powerful individuals in the society have several shrines in their houses, and, in fact, the opulence of a house is often referred to in terms of the number of such ritual centers it possesses.

. . . The focal point of the shrine is a box or chest, which is built into the wall. In this chest are kept the many charms and magical potions without which no native believes he could live. These preparations are secured from a variety of specialized practitioners. The most powerful of these are the medicine men, whose assistance must be rewarded with substantial gifts. . . .

. . . In the hierarchy of magical practitioners, and below the medicine men in prestige, are specialists whose designation is best translated "holy-mouth-men." The Nacirema have an almost pathological horror of, and fascination with, the mouth, the condition of which is believed to have a supernatural influence on all social relationships. Were it not for the rituals of

the mouth, they believe that their teeth would fall out, their gums bleed, their jaws shrink, their friends desert them, and their lovers reject them. . . .

In conclusion, mention must be made of certain practices that . . . depend upon the pervasive aversion to the natural body and its functions. There are ritual fasts to make fat people thin and ceremonial feasts to make thin people fat. Still other rites are used to make women's breasts larger if they are small, and smaller if they are large. General dissatisfaction with breast shape is symbolized in the fact that the ideal form is virtually outside the range of human variation. A few women afflicted with almost inhuman hypermammary development are so idolized that they make a handsome living by simply going from village to village and permitting the natives to stare at them for a fee.

. . . Our review of the ritual life of the Nacirema has certainly shown them to be a magic-ridden people. It is hard to understand how they have managed to exist so long under the burdens they have imposed upon themselves. SOURCE: Horace Miner, "Body Ritual Among the Nacirema," *American Anthropologist* 58 (1956):503–507. Reproduced by permission of the American Anthropological Association from the *American Anthropologist*, 58 (3), 1956, and the author. Copyright 1956 by the American Anthropological Association.

### "Caucasian American Religion, Ceremonies, and Beliefs"
### by Beverly Slapin

There were many different beliefs among the Caucasian American people. Some of them were strange, and some were humorous. Caucasian Americans believed in a supernatural power. They needed it for success in making money and in warfare. For some Caucasian Americans, this supernatural power could be called on in times of great stress. For instance, if a Caucasian American male stubbed his toe or lost in a baseball pool, he was often heard to yell, "Jesus Christ!" (jee'-sus-kryst').

Caucasian American ceremonies were usually of a

religious nature. Some ceremonies were for young Caucasian Americans to show their courage by going through torture.

One of the most bizarre of their rituals, the Sacred Yuppie Jogging Ceremony, involved holy footwear emblazoned with the legend "Nike" (Ni-kee), assumed to be the name of one of their gods. This leg-end, along with its symbol, was found on many items of their clothing, mostly footware. These artifacts were involved with their early morning "jogging" (jog'-ging) ceremony, thought to be the only ritual in which they attempted to demonstrate their oneness with nature.

SOURCE: Beverley Slapin, *Basic Skills Caucasian American Workbook* (Berkeley, Calif.: Oyate). 1990. Reproduced by permission of Beverly Slapin.

they didn't, the simple act of crossing a busy street would be impossible.

In the United States, most children learn explicit rules for being good pedestrians: "Cross on the green; wait on the red," "Look both ways before crossing," "Keep your head up," and "Watch out for open manhole covers." Other rules are not made explicit. For example, how many of us are aware that we follow definite walking patterns? Pedestrians can take any path to get across a busy street, but they don't. Looking at films of people walking down a midtown Manhattan street one block from Times Square, Michael Wolff (1973) found several interesting walking patterns, including the following:

1. In low-density pedestrian traffic, walkers detour from their original path to avoid bumping into another person; after the other person passes, the walkers return to their original path.
2. In high-density pedestrian traffic, there's no room to step completely around an oncoming walker. Thus, to accommodate people coming in the opposite direction, pedestrians use a range of almost imperceptible actions. One maneuver, used especially to avoid bumping into members of the same sex, is the "step-and-slide" (39). Here, a person slightly angles the body, turns the shoulder, and takes a tiny side step.

Now, what happens if a person is a bad or incompetent pedestrian? Usually, dirty looks or sharp words follow. If, for example, a person doesn't execute the step-and-slide maneuver in dense traffic and thus jostles another pedestrian, the jostled party might say something like "Whatsamatter, ya blind?" Such comments suggest that the jostler violated the rules of the game.

To discover people's expectations about routine activities, like walking down the street, researchers try deliberately to break the rules of the game. That's the way Wolff gathered his data. He designed an experiment which aimed at purposefully disrupting routine behaviors. For instance, his experimenters would stay on a straight-line collision course with an oncoming pedestrian. Cameras hidden from view recorded the surprised and shocked reactions of the oncoming pedestrians to this unexpected behavior.

What Wolff concluded from the experiment in New York City is that *cooperation, not competition* ("Each person for himself"), *is the general rule shared by pedestrians*. They expect that others will look around and notice who is coming toward them. And they expect that other pedestrians will cooperate to avoid contact and inconvenience to the other (Wolff, 1973:40).

It turns out, then, that appearances are deceiving; few pedestrians push pell-mell through a busy intersection. Instead, they avoid collision courses, estimate what moves and countermoves to take, and monitor the immediate environment for problems. And all within a nanosecond!

Few studies of pedestrian behavior exist. Luckily, two are gems: William H. Whyte's "The Skilled Pedestrian" ([1988] 1990) and "New York and Tokyo: A Study in Crowding" (1978). In the first study, Whyte talks about New York walkers the way Hemingway described bullfighters—as

**Fig. 11.1**   WHY DON'T THEY KNOCK EACH OTHER DOWN? The rule of pedestrian behavior is cooperation, not competition. (Brack Brown)

people showing grace under pressure: "With the subtlest of motions they signal their intentions to one another—shift of the eyes, a degree or so off axis, a slight move of the hand, a wave of a folded newspaper" (60).

Whyte's comparative study of New York and Tokyo deals with the pedestrian environments of two of the world's largest cities. He concludes that, despite cultural differences, New York and Tokyo pedestrians act a great deal alike:

1. New Yorkers and Tokyoites are highly skilled pedestrians. "They navigate adroitly."
2. Both walk fast. Whyte notes that people in big cities walk faster than people in smaller cities, and this holds true worldwide. The reason is unclear. One social psychologist (Milgram, 1970) thinks that the fast pace in very large cities is related to "stimulus overload," a bombardment of stimuli that apparently encourages people to speed up to seek relief. Others (e.g., Cranz, 1978) maintain that the stimulus

overload encourages people in very large cities to walk faster so that they can take advantage of more stimuli that the city offers.
3. Both cooperate to avoid collisions, but "Tokyo's pedestrians are in a class by themselves." The scene that Whyte paints of apparent chaos at a major subway station in Tokyo is instructive:

By all accepted density standards [Shinjuku subway station] is a manifest impossibility. . . . [A]t the rush hours, when the pedestrian traffic reaches an intensity unmatched anywhere, the scene appears chaotic. But it isn't. Somehow, people sort themselves out and for all the density the pedestrian speeds remain quite high; indeed, it is at rush hour that one sees the most running. By rights, people should be bumping into each other all over the place. They don't seem to. . . . [Furthermore, it seemed that] a good many of the pedestrians were rather stimulated by the challenge, and perhaps a bit pleased with themselves. (Whyte, 1978:8–9)

If we think inductively, these micro observations by Whyte and Wolff suggest certain hypotheses about city life:

1. *Crowding in one's immediate physical presence positively affects how one behaves.*

This hypothesis is all the more interesting because the effects are not in the expected direction. That is, it is widely believed that crowding is bad for people, that it can debilitate them psychologically. Yet, pedestrians in crowded situations seem to cooperate and, as Whyte's impressions of Tokyo suggest, even to enjoy themselves. (*Note:* Shinjuku station was the target of a [foiled] nerve gas attack on May 6, 1995. Had it succeeded, real chaos might have ensued, and at least 10,000 persons would have died. What impact such terrorism is having on Shinjuku pedestrians is not clear.) Further, in crowded situations urbanites don't seem nearly as indifferent to the needs of others as Wirth implies they should be in "Urbanism as a Way of Life" ([1938] 1969).

2. *Mutual trust—not distrust—is the norm in urban public places.*

That trust, not distrust, is the norm is indicated by people's reactions to violations of trust (e.g., following a collision course while walking down the street): surprise and disbelief. If distrust were the norm, pickpockets could not operate on a busy street. Pedestrians would clutch their valuables. If bumped into, they would assume an evil intent (not incompetence) and call for help.

These hypotheses fit into a larger theoretical framework. According to the late sociologist Erving Goffman, pedestrian traffic codes constitute one of many sets of ground rules that "provide the normative bases of public order" (1971:5). This means that social order in a crowded city can be maintained only if people don't aggress against one another. Rules (norms) help people adjust to each other's behavior and know what to expect of each other. This allows undisrupted interaction between strangers.

*To conclude:* Here are two discoveries (or, more precisely, hypotheses) we have made on this short trip down city streets:

1. *Routine interaction in public places embodies unspoken but widely shared understandings or rules.* These rules are not usually brought to conscious awareness by members of the culture. If someone violates the rules, others react with disbelief or disapproval.
2. *Shared social understandings are the basis of public order.* Without such rules or norms, other people's actions would be unpredictable and thus frightening or threatening; people would hardly be confident that their own routine goals (like walking to the store) could be reached. If the cement of public order—mutual trust—crumbled, a city would be a battlefield where every stranger constituted a potential threat.

*A note on mass violence:* Anarchists and revolutionaries understand that distrust and disruption can unglue the cement of public order. As a founder of the Order, a white racist Christian organization (that murdered Jewish talk show host Alan Berg in 1984), told the FBI, he hoped for "anything that would disrupt society in America" so that he would be able to "gather up his army of men and strike against the system, that being the U.S. government" (in Ridgeway, 1990:91). Indeed, after the Oklahoma City bombing, security in all U.S. federal buildings nationwide was beefed up, and Internal Revenue Service employees in San Francisco were advised to suspend the norm of trust: "Get in the habit of regularly looking around your area for anything suspicious" (IRS, 1995). Thus, the April 19, 1995, Oklahoma City bombing—and the March 12, 1995, Tokyo subway poison-gas attack—not only killed human beings in two cities; these acts threatened, at least momentarily, the norm of trust upon which modern cities everywhere are anchored.

Terrorist violence anywhere is uniquely chilling because it is an attack on social structure as well as individuals. Still, it is important to note that fear and anger may not be the only reactions to mass violence. Many people—far beyond those who were personally harmed by the terrorism in Oklahoma and Japan—shared a sense of outrage. This collective outrage, as the eminent sociologist Durkheim ([1895]1982) wrote long ago, can forge a stronger sense of social solidarity.

## Subway Behavior

On American city streets, it is a common understanding that pedestrians will keep their heads up, scan the environment, and adjust their behavior according to the needs of others. Do the same rules apply below the city streets, on subways?

Just as in the case of walking on the city streets, most of us are unaware that there are rules for riding public transportation—until somebody violates them. That is, riding a bus or subway is such a routine activity that we take it for granted. As ethnomethodologist Harold Garfinkel puts it, familiar settings (like subways) are full of "'seen but unnoticed,' expected background features" (1967:36).

Again, our task is to bring these background features into the foreground; our approach, as before, is to treat the familiar as unusual and problematic. In this way we are doing **ethnography**—that is, studying a community's culture by participant-observation. Our job is to decode the verbal and nonverbal messages that people send each other and to describe behavior appropriate to the situation (e.g., riding a subway).

Appropriate behavior is culturally relative. What is appropriate behavior in one culture may be out of place in another. Take, for instance, train behavior. Traveling by train (third class) through Greece, one could expect some variation on the following scene: passengers sharing whatever food and wine they have with strangers in their compartment; babies nursing at their mothers' breasts; chickens squeezed in the compartment and noisily peeping; smugglers trying to peddle their wares; and people sleeping amid the commotion. This is not what Americans expect to find when they board Amtrak. On U.S. trains, one expects to be casually noticed by other passengers but left alone.

The same is true of American subways. Subway riders expect to be treated with what Erving Goffman calls **civil inattention**. To be civilly inattentive, "one gives to another enough visual notice to demonstrate that one appreciates that the

other is present (and that one admits openly to having seen him), while at the next moment withdrawing one's attention from him so as to express that he does not constitute a target of special curiosity or design" (Goffman, 1963:84).

Civil inattention takes various forms. Researchers who conducted participant-observation in Boston and New York City subways found that some riders bury their heads in a newspaper. Others stare into space, look straight ahead without expression, or daydream (Levine, Vinson, and Wood, 1973).

Under certain circumstances, the general rule of civil inattention on subways can be suspended. Subway riders may smile or show openness to others they consider nonthreatening. This category includes children and matronly, middle-aged housewives. That middle-aged women—who look like housewives—constitute no threat is a revealing insight into our culture.

Civil inattention also comes into play when choosing a seatmate in the subway car. People tend to grab the first empty seat they see. But there is another consideration, especially for women: Which potential seatmate looks least threatening? People look for self-contained persons who show civil inattention. When choosing among equally self-contained and civilly inattentive persons, riders tend to sit down next to members of their own sex. This observation qualifies the first impression that subway riders sit in the nearest vacant seat. It also raises fascinating questions about trust levels between the sexes.

What purposes does civil inattention serve? Civil inattention is one device urbanites use "for immunizing themselves against the personal claims and expectations of others" (Wirth [1938] 1969:153). It may also serve as a mechanism of social control, keeping potentially dangerous situations from happening. When strangers aren't sure of each other's intentions, civil inattention helps to promote privacy and to maintain public order. In other words, the rule of civil inattention functions to "protect personal rights and to sustain proper social distance between unacquainted people who are temporarily placed together" (Levine et al., 1973).

**Fig. 11.2** CIVIL INATTENTION IN THE NEW YORK SUBWAY. Photographer Walker Evans captures the vacant faces associated with proper behavior on public transport. (*Many Are Called* by Walker Evans, introduction by James Agee. Copyright © 1966 by Walker Evans. Reprinted by permission of Houghton Mifflin Company)

What happens if civil inattention fails to sustain proper social distance? Sometimes authorities impose explicit rules. Such is the case in Cairo, Egypt. Cairo's subway system, completed in 1987, sets aside the first car of each train for women only to help protect them from the constant peril of male sexual harassment. (*Note:* This policy has its local critics who fear that gender segregation humiliates women, treating them as weak and subordinate.)

## Eavesdropping: Urbanites as Spies

Bystanders may pretend to be civilly inattentive —by reading a newspaper, for example—to cover up a common covert activity: eavesdropping. In a subway car, elevator, restaurant, gym, or other place where people congregate, a person may appear totally uninvolved, all the while listening intently to strangers' conversations. Why?

Perhaps eavesdropping soothes the troubled soul; it allows us to peek into other people's lives and problems without taking any responsibility for them. And it is a low-risk, no-cost activity. Besides, overheard stories can rival soap operas for tantalizing plots. Whatever the reasons for covert listening, the fact is that people do eavesdrop. This suggests that Wirth's ([1938] 1969) "uncaring urbanite" may not be that blasé after all.

Walker Evans, photographer of people on subways (and people in rural poverty; see Chapter 2), once advised us all to engage in relatively safe urban activities that can teach us something, including eavesdropping: "Stare, pry, listen, eavesdrop. Die knowing something. You are not here long."

## Bar Behavior

Within any culture, proper social distance varies with the social context. In America, strangers keep their distance on subways. But they don't in a bar. The bar is one setting where the proper social distance is considerably less than in a subway.

In a bar, the general rule of civil inattention is suspended. Whereas idle glances on a subway show that a person is closed to social interaction, researchers have found that the same kinds of glances in a bar demonstrate a person's openness. In a bar, almost no patrons bury their heads in a newspaper or book. But if they do, this gesture can serve to open conversation, not close off the possibility, as in a subway. As Sherri Cavan observed while researching her ethnography of bar behavior, *Liquor License*: "A middle-aged woman was sitting by herself, thumbing through a large book of Steinberg cartoons. A man sitting at the other end of the bar came over, asked her what she was looking at and then joined her" ([1966] 1973:144). In other words, what might ensure civil inattention in the subway or other settings can be an overture for social interaction in a bar.

If a person enters a tavern alone and wishes to remain alone, he or she will usually sit at the bar, not an empty table, and will sit in a particular way. According to Cavan, the solitary drinker—who is not open to social interaction—shows the intention to stay closed off by minimizing the physical space he or she occupies. Typically, a man will "sit with his forearms either resting on the edge of the bar, or flat on the bar before him, his upper torso hunched slightly forward over the bar, with all of his drinking accoutrements (drink, cigarettes, change, ashtray, and the like) contained within the area before him" ([1966] 1973:144–45). This posture serves to protect the solitary drinker from eye contact with others (one signal of openness in a bar).

As in many urban settings, what's deemed proper behavior differs for males and females. Mary Jo Deegan points out in "The Meet/Meat Market Ritual" (1989:48) that singles bars are more open to heterosexual women as participants than more "male-defined" drinking places such as cocktail bars. Yet women in singles bars rarely initiate conversation with a male stranger.

Why? Because, according to Deegan, "In general, women who frequent singles bars are generally supportive of traditional male–female relationships. . . . Women uninterested in maintaining these traditional rituals [e.g., responding to male overtures rather than initiating social interaction] do not attend these bars" (1989:44).

*To conclude:* When people enter a bar, they are expected to be sociable, not civilly inattentive. If they don't want to be sociable, they have to send body language signals for privacy (in subways, it's the opposite; people have to send signals for openness). But the solitary drinker is the exception in a bar, for "sociability is the most general rule in the public drinking place. Although the bar is typically populated primarily by strangers, interaction is available to all those who choose to enter" (Cavan, [1966] 1973:143).

Why is it that in most urban public settings, civil inattention serves to limit contact among strangers while sociability is the norm in bars? Cavan thinks this norm is associated with the idea that bars aren't really serious places. Instead, they are considered a setting for a time out from life's important concerns. Thus, she argues, what might seem threatening or dangerous in a more serious place appears nonthreatening in a bar (Cavan, [1966] 1973:154).

## ATM Behavior

Waiting in line seems to be a quintessentially urban experience, at least in the United States. Sometimes we speak to total strangers. Waiting to see the Dallas Cowboys or the Grateful Dead, fans often chat with strangers; shared enthusiasm in an "aficionado line" can create a momentary bond of communality and trust (Gasich, Hamilton, Leung, Steele, Van Ploeg, 1989:25).

More often, however, people avoid social interaction with strangers in line. This is particularly the case if money is involved. A prime example is ATM behavior.

By 1990, Americans used bank automatic teller machines (ATMs) an average of 11,400 times

**Fig. 11.3** QUEUING BEHAVIOR. Normally, waiting in line is not fun. But there are exceptions, such as "afi-cionado lines" and lines where bus riders can lean on sculpture, as in Seattle's Fremont section. (Harvey Bragdon)

each minute. And typically, patrons wait in line before transacting business. What do they do while waiting? What they *don't* do is talk to each other. As one observer puts it, "What we do at ATMs is engage in a very private act—intercourse with our money in public. . . . Comrades in ATM lines must not speak. In the sidewalk temple of money, it's crude to draw attention to the intimate commercial transaction going on nearby, in plain sight" (Mandel, 1988:A4). Besides, it may be unwise to draw attention, as danger and easy money sometimes go hand in hand: There is one ATM robbery for every 2 to 3 million transactions nationwide, and the targets of ATM crimes tend to be the most vulnerable, in-

cluding the elderly and frail (Halstuck, 1991:A1, A16).

## EVERYDAY GAMES AND DRAMAS

Looking at people in various urban public places —streets, subways, bars, ATMs—it is clear that the rules of the game (norms) and the roles people play (e.g., bar patron, subway rider, pedestrian) help to structure individual behavior, perceptions, even emotions. But to what extent? How much freedom do urbanites have to change the rules of the game? To create new **roles** in the drama of everyday life? Or to play old roles in a new way? Here, social theorists disagree.

## Whose Games Do We Play?

Thus far in Part III, we have drawn connections between what people do and what society expects them to do. We noted that whether in a bar or on city streets, people usually follow rules that they didn't construct, although they may be unaware that rules even exist. We also discussed the impact of macro social structures on individual behavior, particularly noting the effect of class and status on people's actions. For example, various community studies show that what appear to be personal choices—what part of town one lives in, what style of house one chooses—are heavily influenced by one's social rank in the community.

Most sociologists and anthropologists agree that social structure (including norms, roles, and social ranks) shapes individual identity and behavior. But they debate the *degree* to which people have freedom to invent new games or play by their own rules.

Theorists who focus on the larger patterns of social structure (**macro-level social analysis**) tend to stress the degree to which people follow society's rules. Marxists, for example, maintain that a person's class and class interests are most important in determining attitudes and behavior. Marx thought that what people produce and how they produce it determines a society's norms, morality, ideology, and individual consciousness: "Life is not determined by consciousness, but consciousness by life" ([1859] 1977:164).

Non-Marxists also point to the great impact of social structural variables on individual behavior. For example, Peter L. Berger (1963) writes that even in the most private games people play—courtship and marriage—the couple doesn't invent the game "or any part of it." The rituals (from dating to meeting the family, from holding hands to making love) are socially set. The couple merely decides that they will play the game with each other and not with other possible partners. Sociologist Berger says that Amer-

icans may believe that love is an "irresistible emotion that strikes where it will." Yet, upon deeper investigation, it turns out that "the lightning shaft of Cupid seems to be guided rather strongly within very definite channels of class, income, education, racial and religious background" (35). In other words, macro theorists of varying orientations point to the determining role that social structure plays in molding individual actions and thoughts.

**Micro-level social analysis**, on the other hand, tends to stress the freedom individuals have to negotiate the rules and improvise new acts. Symbolic interactionists, for example, do not deny that people act within the framework of their society and its rules, but these social psychologists maintain that "human beings are active in shaping their own behavior. Such structural features as social roles, social classes, and the like [do] set conditions for human behavior and interaction, but do not cause or fully determine the behavior and interaction" (Manis and Meltzer, 1978:7). Symbolic interactionists see individual behavior as part of a complex process in which people are constantly modifying their own actions in relation to other people's behavior and their interpretations of what's happening. In this view, people are not programmed, mindless robots. Instead, people themselves give meaning to situations and act accordingly: "the features (structures) of society are maintained and changed by the *actions* of people, and are not autonomous, or self-regulating. . . . Human behavior is an elaborate process of interpreting, choosing, and rejecting possible lines of action. This process cannot be understood in terms of mechanical responses to external stimuli" (Manis and Meltzer, 1978:7, 8).

Other social theorists interested in micro processes also stress the active role people play in molding their own behavior. Whatever their theoretical orientation (e.g., **symbolic interactionism, ethnomethodology**), most micro theorists emphasize two points:

1. People have choices about how to act.
2. People bring different meanings to the same event.

Hence, they argue, we must try to understand other people's meanings (i.e., the actors' subjective point of view) if we are to understand their behavior.

This debate over how much freedom people have to make up their own rules is essentially one of degree, not of kind. Both macro and micro theorists acknowledge that social structure and social organization provide the framework within which people act and give meaning to events. The difference is that macro theorists tend to see people as prisoners of society's rules, whereas micro theorists tend to focus on people's ability to push back (or build anew) the prison walls. (*Note:* The simple micro–macro distinction can't capture the variety of approaches to the study of society. For instance, Max Weber examined the development of meaning at the macro level, and commentators on Erving Goffman's work suggest that his micro studies are essentially analyses of social structure.)

Before discussing how micro and macro levels of analysis can be combined to study urban behavior, we turn to several useful concepts developed by micro theorists. These concepts—the **definition of the situation** and the **presentation of self**—deal with the same basic point: that social interaction, customs, and beliefs are often problematic.

## "The Definition of the Situation" (Thomas)

Reality, like beauty, exists in the eye of the beholder. The same object or event can have different meanings for different people, and "the degree of difference will produce comparable differences in behavior" (McHugh, 1968:8). That is the essence of social psychologist W. I. Thomas's classic statement on the subjective quality of reality: "If men [and women] define situations as real they are real in their consequences" (1928:572).

Thomas's statement points out that there are multiple realities, not just one reality. Perhaps this is most evident when cross-cultural social interaction takes place. For instance, as detailed

in Chapter 16, North Americans, who converse at a distance of about 12 inches, are considered cold and distant by Latin Americans; Latin Americans, who hold head-to-head conversations, are considered pushy and aggressive by North Americans. The potential consequences are misunderstanding, discomfort, and even prejudice or fist fights.

Here are two examples of multiple realities and their potential consequences.

1. George wines and dines LaDonna at the fanciest restaurant in town for weeks. She fantasizes about marrying him. Then George tells her, "I love you." Before LaDonna reacts to these ambiguous words, she must decide what they mean—to him. She asks herself, "Is his concept of love the same as mine? Is he just giving me a line? Will his love smother me? How many others does he love?" And so on. How LaDonna reacts to George's declaration of love (from planning a wedding to saying farewell) depends on what meanings she thinks George attaches to it.

2. In the early 1970s, a civil rights group in Syracuse, New York, showed two photographs to a group of white, suburban, middle-class church members. In each photo, a male teenager, dressed casually, was running down the street. There was only one significant difference between the two teenagers: One was African-American; the other, white. Respondents in this experiment were asked to describe what each teenager in the photos was doing. The range of responses was as follows, in order of times mentioned:

   a. *White teenager running down the street.* (1) Good Samaritan running to help a needy person (perhaps a car accident victim); (2) hurt child running home for help; (3) jogger or Little Leaguer out for exercise.

   b. *African-American teenager running down the street.* (1) thief running from the police or making a fast getaway; (2) looter during an urban riot running toward a store to rob it; (3) curious spectator running to watch a fire or an accident.

When presented with the profile of their responses, church members were shocked. For in large measure, they did share a definition of the situation—in this case, one they themselves labeled racist. Yet a few in the group did not attribute negative (indeed, criminal) meanings to the black teenager's behavior. Why did a minority of the group attribute normal behavior (curious spectator) to the black's gesture of running? An interesting research question. But that was not the experimenters' concern. Their concern focused on the potential real-life consequences of the majority's shared understanding: racist stereotypes that can bring psychological—and physical—harm to African-Americans. Their goal was to change the majority's definition of the situation.

From the symbolic interactionist point of view, these examples—words of love, gestures of running—show that stimuli have no inherent meaning. By themselves, words, gestures, symbols, and objects are meaningless; only people make them meaningful. Symbolic interactionists do not claim that people are free to attribute any meaning at all to an event or a symbol. To the contrary, they emphasize that meanings are socially derived through interaction. Hence, in America, people share the assumption that a star-spangled cloth flying at halfmast on a long pole means that someone important has died. If they see a woman in a long white dress with a veil, they assume she is being married.

What, then, is the special relevance of this social psychological concept—the definition of the situation—to urban life? It helps to explain why social order in the modern metropolis is so much more fragile than in traditional rural communities. When groups and individuals share a common definition of the situation, the basis for social order exists. Shared understandings of what is normal, proper, and good behavior characterize *Gemeinschaft* communities. In contrast, *Gesellschaft* and *Techno$chaft* societies are typified by heterogeneous populations with plural belief systems. For instance, Americans have different definitions of the situation concerning the supernatural and paranormal (Table 11.1).

More important for human relations, African-American and white American definitions of the racial situation are worlds apart. Here are just a few examples:

1. A poll conducted in 1993 found that African-American and white high-school students live in "two different worlds," having "different views, expectations, and experiences." For instance, "to the African American students, affirmative action means opportunity. To the Caucasian students it means reverse discrimination" (Krouse in Moore, 1993:B8).
2. A *New York Times*/WCBS News poll in 1990 found that 29 percent of African-American New Yorkers polled believe or think it possible that the U.S. government created the AIDS virus as a plot to infect African-Americans ("AIDS 'Plot,'" 1992:A22).
3. A National Opinion Research Center survey in 1990 found that a majority of whites polled think that African-Americans and Hispanics are more likely than whites to be lazy, violence prone, less intelligent, and less patriotic than whites ("Whites," 1991:A15).

What lies behind such negative stereotypes and racist attitudes? Researchers don't have a single explanation. But one thing is clear: People do not share a single definition of the situation.

It is in the modern metropolis that people are

---

**Table 11.1**   Multiple Realities

*Nationwide poll question:* "Which of the following do you believe in? UFOs, angels, devils, astrology, ghosts, and/or witches?"

*Percentage expressing belief in:*

| | |
|---|---|
| UFOs | 57% |
| Angels | 54% |
| Devils | 39% |
| Astrology | 29% |
| Ghosts | 11% |
| Witches | 10% |

SOURCE: Gallup Poll, "Surprising Number of Americans Believe in Paranormal Phenomena" (Princeton, N.J.: Gallup Organization, June 15, 1978). Copyright © 1978 by Gallup Poll. Reprinted by permission.

unlikely to share the same definition of the situation and, consequently, are unlikely to react similarly to the same event or stimulus. This situation lends itself to social disruption and conflict.

Let's apply this fairly abstract point to a practical problem: what to teach in a public high school. Imagine that you are a member of a neighborhood group in Oakland, California; the group is concerned with what teenagers are learning in social studies courses. Besides yourself, the following neighborhood people show up at the first meeting to discuss what should be taught: astrologers and astrophysicists; gays and straights; Chinese-Americans, whites (WASPs and ethnics), Chicanos, African-Americans, Native Americans, and Sikh-Americans; housewives, HIV-positive mothers, and women executives; New Agers and old-timers; welfare recipients, car mechanics, lawyers, and a self-proclaimed hedonist; Marxist community organizers, tax protesters, John Birch Society and ACLU members; advocates of appropriate technology, environmentalists, and an oil refinery executive; and atheists, Protestants, Catholics, Jews, Muslims, and Hindus.

Given this diversity, conflicts over what to teach surface immediately. The astrologer insists that students be taught that the position of the stars governs their lives. "Hooey," shouts the astrophysicist, advocating instruction in scientific methods to measure social phenomena. Some Chicanos want a bilingual program; others don't. A Marxist community organizer claims that the social science text ignores the key variable in American life—social class—while the John Bircher thinks it is laced with anticapitalist propaganda. A coalition—People United Against Racism—protests that the text is Eurocentric, ignoring all but Western European cultural contributions. The environmentalist dislikes the text because it advocates unlimited growth, and the oil company executive says that "kids should learn that without growth, there is no more prosperity." Gays question how the subject of marriage is treated in the required text. Meanwhile, the car mechanic worries that her child can't even spell the word *environment*. A feminist casti-

gates the text for its sexist neglect of women in U.S. history, but a lawyer thinks the book gives a "realistic" assessment of American history. And so it goes (Figure 11.4).

## Social Order Amid Multiple Realities

Given these varied social backgrounds, concerns, ideologies, and stocks of knowledge, it seems a miracle that any collective action can take place. Yet it usually does. How is social order possible in a milieu of multiple realities? The nineteenth-century sociologist, Emile Durkheim answered this important question by taking for granted that people conform to society's rules because they were taught to do so as children and because they benefit from assuming that others will also conform. Durkheim's stance is a structural-functional one, emphasizing the process by which people internalize norms and conform to them.

But other theorists have different answers. Philosopher Alfred Schutz (1967) argues that (1) individuals in the same culture share the belief that they can put themselves in one another's shoes and understand how another person could view their behavior; this allows for the development of empathy and understanding; and (2) this empathy and understanding allow people to transcend their personal experience and exchange perspectives through social interaction. Through the exchange of perspectives, Schutz thinks, people can question the rules they learned as children. Thus, they can help make or unmake the rules which create social order.

Erving Goffman (1959) might answer the question "How is social order possible?" in the following way. People hold different definitions of the situation, but they still have working agreements that help maintain order. This "working consensus," as Goffman calls it, may conceal wide disagreements among participants in any social interaction. But the working consensus is like a contract that states: If you support my act, I'll support yours; and if we cooperate, we'll all get our everyday tasks accomplished. Thus when

**Fig. 11.4** DEFINING THE SITUATION. (Lisa Siegel Sullivan)

people enter the physical presence of others, they take each other's behavior into account (even if no verbal communication occurs). They constantly modify their own behavior in order to act properly in a given situation. Acting properly reduces vulnerability, risk, and embarrassment. It is also less time-consuming than making up the rules from scratch every time people interact. In this way, social order is upheld.

We now turn to Goffman's ideas on how people try to impose their definitions of reality on others. He contends that we present ourselves in certain ways, trying to control or manage the impressions others have of us.

## "The Presentation of Self" (Goffman)

Erving Goffman explores "the little interactions that are forgotten about as soon as they occur." He microscopically examines "the little salutations, compliments and apologies" (e.g., smiles and "I'm sorry") that "serious students of society never collect." He finds "empty" gestures "perhaps the fullest of all." In short, his domain is "the slop of social life."

Goffman's examples of "the slop of social life" are taken mainly from urban society, but he is not usually classified as an urbanist. And rarely are his micro studies mentioned in the context of urban studies. This is unfortunate, perhaps one casualty of the dubious distinction between things urban and otherwise.

Goffman has been dubbed the "Woody Allen of American sociology" because he so powerfully unravels the fragile fabric of everyday life (Winkin, 1988). Similarly, he has been labeled the "Kafka of our time" because, like the great Czech writer, he "communicates so vividly the horror and anguish—as well as some of the absurd comedy— of everyday life" (Berman, 1972:1). His world, like Kafka's, is peopled with ordinary individuals— clerks, bureaucrats, shoppers—doing ordinary things. But in Goffman's hands, this ordinary world becomes extraordinary and complex.

In Goffman's vision, just getting through the day—standing in a bus line, greeting friends and acknowledging strangers, entering a repair store, and engaging in similar routine activity—is full of ritual, perhaps magic. In his view, this ritual process is worth exploring because it reveals the fragility and complexity of social behavior, particularly urban behavior.

Essentially, Goffman's vision is a theatrical one. He presents the everyday world as a theater in which we all act out roles and give performances in ongoing plays. His imagery is drawn from the stage. Hence, a person (in its first dictionary meaning, from *persona)* is a mask. Brief encounters in urban places are treated as masked rituals. Individuals are always "on" (as in "on stage"), performing and creating their roles. This theatrical model of social behavior recalls Shakespeare: "All the world's a stage and all the men and women merely players."

To Goffman, when we play roles and interpret other people's performances on the stage of everyday life, we wear masks or ritual faces. Our ritual faces aren't who we "really" are—but who we "really" are doesn't much matter. What does matter is the image we want the audience (ob-

servers) to have of our performance. Our masks allow us to manipulate our appearances and save face before others. That is what we do, according to Goffman, hundreds of times each day; we have an unspoken understanding with our audience whereby all of us role players agree to conduct ourselves to maintain our own face and the faces of other participants in the scene. Thus for Goffman, most routine social interaction in urban settings is nothing more than the effort to control the impression we make on others (*impression management*). We manage these impressions to keep up appearances and win acceptance from the audience. We want our audiences to accept our appearance—our performance— because it is on the basis of our appearance (and inferences about it) that they will react to us.

How we present ourselves, Goffman maintains, depends on the impression we want to make on a particular audience. We choose a role from our repertoire of identities; we put on one of our many faces, depending on our intent and our audience. Thus, we don't play the same part in front of all our audiences—family, strangers, colleagues, and so on—because "urban life would become unbearably sticky for some if every contact between two individuals entailed a sharing of personal trials, worries, and secrets. Thus if a man wants to be served a restful dinner, he may seek the service of a waitress rather than a wife" (1959:49).

Con artists are experts in impression management. Take, for example, "Alexi Indris-Santana," a supposed twenty-one-year-old Princeton University sophomore. College admission officers believed his background to be "unique and impressive": a self-educated ranch hand with a dying mother. Nearly three years passed before Alexi was unmasked, totally by chance, as a thirty-two-year-old fugitive from the law. Meanwhile, he had performed flawlessly in front of difficult audiences (Barron, 1991:C19). But his repertoire of characters did not end there. Two years later, the same man was accused of stealing more than $50,000 in gems from a Harvard University museum where he worked as a cataloger ("Man," 1993:A7). In another real-life drama, recorded in Wendell Harris, Jr.'s, biographical film,

*Chameleon Street* (released in 1991), a professional impostor performed thirty-six successful surgeries in Detroit, served many clients successfully as a civil rights attorney, and posed as a *Time* magazine interviewer—all without any formal training. How did Doug Street, the real chameleon, play these roles so successfully for fourteen years? Filmmaker Harris says that Street read voraciously, enough to dupe even trained professionals. His prison psychiatrist answered that Street could "intuit what a person needed and become that need."

Demeanor, dress, and speech are important props in managing impressions. Collegians who want to impress teachers as good students avoid appearing inappropriate, say, wearing a bathing suit or snoring through a political science class. Likewise, a young lawyer may wear a wedding band and horn-rimmed glasses to give the jury the impression of stability and maturity. (In one episode of the TV series *L.A. Law*, actor Harry Hamlin was "accessorized" by "wardrobe engineers" in this manner.) Men interested in dressing for successs should avoid a bow tie, says image consultant John T. Molloy (1988:115), because "it creates the impression of being unpredict-

able." And women who want to hide their authority from men could choose the Annie Hall look: an outsized jacket, shirt, and hat with a skirt or slacks. This look, made famous by actress Diane Keaton, exudes the nonthreatening charm of "helpless cuteness" (Lurie, ([1981] 1983:228–229).

How do we present ourselves in urban public or semipublic places? In ways that will appear proper to those around us, Goffman says. This serves to avert real or potential danger and embarrassment and to get the resuits we want.

If, however, a person feels that things aren't normal—that "something is up"—he or she may put on a performance to conceal the sense that something is wrong. Sometimes these acts can be pathetic: "Witness the vain and painful effort of someone sitting beside an obstreperous drunk on public transportation; witness the effort of the individual to act as if the drunk were either not there or not a special point of concern, in either case not something to cause his seatmate to appear to be anything but a person in a situation in which all appearances are normal and nothing is up" (Goffman, 1971:271).

For women in American cities, ordinary walk-

**Fig. 11.5**   URBAN PERFORMANCE. Ordinary walking down the street may be a put-on, designed to avoid embarrassment and control the audience's impressions. (E. Barbara Phillips)

ing may entail a "put-on," a performance designed to show that nothing is up. For instance, as a woman walks past a group of men on their lunch hour sitting on the pavement watching the world (and especially women) go by,

her face becomes contorted into a grimace of self-control and fake unawareness; her walk and carriage become stiff and dehumanized. No matter what they say to her, it will be unbearable. She knows that they will not physically assault her or hurt her. . . . What they will do is impinge on her. They will use her body with their eyes. . . . They will make her ridiculous, or grotesquely sexual, or hideously ugly. Above all, they will make her feel like a thing. (Tax in Goffman, 1971:272)

In this urban world of strangers, then, the woman walking down the street is not what she appears to be; she is trying as best she can to avoid embarrassment by managing the impressions that her audience has of her.

Such everyday encounters—a woman walking by an audience that may not support her act, a man trying to maintain a normal appearance while sitting next to a potentially disruptive drunk, people averting their eyes from each other on subways—are Goffman's primary focus. More precisely, he is concerned with how these social encounters are structured. And Goffman thinks that the most significant factor in this pattern of social interaction is "the maintenance of a single definition of the situation . . . expressed . . . and sustained in the face of a multitude of potential disruptions" (1959:254).

At this point, we return to some shared definitions of the situation—those working agreements, usually unspoken, that hold in a milieu of multiple realities—urban society.

## WALKING THE TIGHTROPE

### Minimizing Involvement, Maximizing Social Order

Urban society presents a Janus-like face: freedom and anarchy. One side offers freedom for individuals to choose from among alternative realities. The other portends danger: that the social order will break down from conflict over what's proper or right (normative conflict). That urbanites do take collective action and are not in constant conflict with each other suggests that some rules or norms, some shared definitions of the situation, still hold in this milieu of multiple realities. Throughout this chapter, we have seen indications that such norms exist. On the city streets, for instance, pedestrians cooperate so that they can all reach their destinations.

Below city streets, people appear civilly inattentive while they ride the subway. But here again, the implications are two-sided. The very norms that protect personal privacy and limit involvement with strangers (e.g., civil inattention) also promote the indifference so often attributed to urbanites. "I didn't want to get involved" is a common reason given by people who walk away from fellow human beings in trouble in urban public places. Yet the norm of noninvolvement may be highly situational. According to a study of *The Unresponsive Bystander* (Latané and Darley, 1970), urbanites are less likely to intervene in emergency situations if a crowd is nearby. Latané and Darley suggest that in a crowd, each individual assumes that someone else will take responsibility. Thus what appears to be indifference is really something else: a "diffusion of responsibility." This argument again points to numbers as a variable in urban social behavior. Further, it calls into question Wirth's notion that urbanites are indifferent, blasé, and uncaring.

*To conclude:* Urbanites seem to walk a tightrope. On the one hand, to get through the day, they cooperate with strangers. On the other, they maintain distance from them. Norms of behavior in public places provide guidelines on the proper degree of intimacy or noninvolvement (not the specific behaviors) expected there. According to one hypothesis, "urbanites seek to minimize involvement and to maximize social order" (Karp, Stone, and Yoels, 1977:110). In this view, urbanites have a common understanding, a common definition of the situation, that permits routine social interaction to take place. That is, they agree to cooperate to the extent that daily public life can go on. At the same time, they agree to protect their personal space by limiting the intensity of their involvement with strangers.

The *mini-max* hypothesis suggests that the quality of urban social behavior can best be understood by combining seemingly opposite ideas: "intimate anonymity," "public privacy," and "involved indifference." These descriptions seem schizoid. Yet they indicate the precarious balancing act that urbanites perform many times daily.

## CONSTRUCTING SOCIAL REALITY

Some norms of public behavior, such as civil inattention, seem to work to everyone's benefit. But this doesn't mean that all such rules are so mutually beneficial. A question posed by Erving Goffman focuses on this point.

In *Relations in Public*, Goffman comments that people's immediate surroundings—their homes and offices, for example—are viewed as their possessions, as part of their "fixed territory" (1971:288). People assume that these fixed territories will be free of danger, like a safe haven, for "the individual's sense of privacy, control and self-respect is tied to the dominion he exerts over his fixed territories." Now, what happens when someone's fixed territory is damaged by people who don't share the same standards of care? That is what occurred to the president of Columbia University, Grayson Kirk, when 150 student demonstrators occupied his office for six days in 1969. When Kirk returned to his office, he found cigarette butts and orange peels covering his rug, plus other remnants of the occupation. Looking around at this sight, he turned to reporters and asked, "My God, how could human beings do a thing like this?" But Goffman asks other questions:

The great sociological question, of course, is not how could it be that human beings would do a thing like this, but rather how is it that human beings do this sort of thing so rarely. How come persons in authority have been so overwhelmingly successful in conning those beneath them? (1971:288n.)

With these questions, Goffman hints that we can't really understand how the rules work without looking at both the process (micro focus) and the structure (macro focus) of social interaction. That is, people may be active agents in creating new performances, but they create them within a cultural, political, and historical context.

## The Public Definition of Reality

In urban society—characterized by multiple realities—competing individuals and groups are constantly struggling to transform their own definition of reality into the public definition of reality: a world of ready-made, taken-for-granted meanings, attitudes, feelings, and thoughts. As the student demonstrators' behavior indicates, this ready-made world of meanings is neither unchanging nor unchangeable. Meanings are open to constant negotiation and reinterpretation. At the same time, there are widely shared assumptions about how social interaction should take place at a particular historical moment. These shared assumptions (definitions of reality) are not simply there; they are generated by social processes and molded by power relations, class structures, and other social structural features.

**Table 11.2** Widely Shared Definitions of Reality

| | |
|---|---|
| Economic sector | Owners of manufacturing firms have the right to decide what product to make and how much to pay their workers (with a minimum wage floor). Competition is a good thing. |
| Political sector | Government and politics are so complicated that most Americans can't understand what's going on. |
| Aesthetic sector | Men and women who weigh 350 pounds are not physically attractive. |
| Social sector | Having a large family—ten children—is a strain on the parents and a burden on society. |

We don't all have an equal chance of getting others to accept our definition of reality: "He who has the bigger stick has a better chance of imposing his definitions of reality" (Berger and Luckmann, 1967:109).

Now we turn to a discussion of black street-corner men, one group of Americans who don't have big sticks (power, authority, wealth, high status, control over or access to mass media). Consequently, they have less chance of imposing their definitions of reality on other groups. In telling their story, Elliot Liebow demonstrates the power of applying both micro and macro levels of analysis to the study of urban social behavior.

## COMBINING MICRO AND MACRO ANALYSIS TO STUDY SOCIAL BEHAVIOR

### Case Study: *Tally's Corner*

Anthropologist Liebow recorded the daily, routine activities of twenty-four black men who hung out around a corner, Tally's Corner, near a carry-out restaurant in Washington, D.C. He talked with them on the street and accompanied them to their haunts: their homes, pool halls, neighborhood stores, and sometimes courtrooms. Liebow was an outsider for many reasons (race, religion, occupation, residence, manner of speech), but he participated in their lives as well as observing them. (Indeed, he reports that his marginality was disadvantageous in some ways but partially offset by the fact that "as an outsider, I was not a competitor" [1967:251]). His data are drawn from observing the actions of the men—unskilled construction workers, busboys, menial workers, and the unemployed, from their early twenties to their mid-forties.

A casual observer might think that the street corner men are hanging out because they're lazy, irresponsible, seeking instant gratification, or present-time oriented. They are wrong, says Liebow. And here is how he came to this conclusion.

To understand why the men hang out on the street corner, why they work at the jobs they do—or quit—and why they hold the attitudes they do, Liebow moves from the micro level (the street corner) to analyze larger social patterns that shape their lives (macro level). In so doing, he demonstrates that the men's jobs and self-concepts are molded by their place in the class and status system.

To begin with, the jobs the street corner men could get—parking attendant, janitor, counter-man, stock clerk, and the like—are generally dead ends. What janitor ends up at a white-collar job in the building he or she cleans? More important, all available work is low-paid and low-status. Liebow notes that neither society nor the street corner man who perform these jobs thinks they're worth doing and worth doing well: "Both employee and employer are contemptuous of the job. The employee shows his contempt by his reluctance to accept it or keep it, the employer by paying less than is required to support a family" (1967:58).

Thus these men are trapped in work that offers no prestige, little money, no chance for advancement or interesting opportunities, and little else. More prestigious work is closed to them. They lack the education (most went to inferior schools), and they don't have a network of friends and contacts that upper-middle-class people routinely develop by going to the right schools. Finally, they belong to a minority group, one that has experienced racial discrimination in employment and opportunities for training in highly paid trades.

In short, these are men without a future. And they know it.

Not having a future affects even the most intimate sphere of their lives: relationships with friends and lovers. Given the street corner men's structural situation, "friendship is easily uprooted by the tug of economic or psychological self-interest or by external forces acting against it." Friendships are very meaningful to the street corner men, but they are often threatened by routine crises that more affluent people don't face constantly.

Only by looking at the ways social structure impinges on the street corner men's lives, Liebow implies, can we make sense of their seeming refusal to work (Box 18.2) and their treatment of friends and lovers. Liebow concludes that the key factor in these men's lives is not psychological but rather social structural: the inability to earn a living and support their families. Behind their attitude toward their work and themselves is society's evaluation that they are worthless.

If Liebow had stopped his analysis at the micro level of face-to-face interaction on the street corner, he could not have made the connections between personality and social structure. Nor could he have shown so powerfully that the way these men define their situations grows out of the values, sentiments, and opportunities provided by the larger society.

## ANOTHER LOOK

Being urban involves playing games and following rules we didn't create. Yet, as the symbolic interactionists emphasize, urbanites can break the rules or help create new ones.

Of course, breaking the rules means taking risks. These risks can be minor or life-endangering. To break the unspoken rule of sociability in a bar by slighting a stranger may earn a person nothing more than a dirty look. But who knows? Perhaps this anonymous person believes himself to be the Devil and responds with a stab of his pocket knife. Similarly, college students who stage a live-in at the president's office may risk jail, expulsion from school, or long-term surveillance as "troublemakers."

The other side of this coin is that rule-breaking behavior (deviance from norms) can lead to new definitions of reality and social change. In the students' case, their actions could contribute to a general reconsideration of the proper relationship between students and authority figures.

People seem to accept injustice as long as they think it is inevitable or grant it moral authority. India's untouchables, for instance, have accepted their low status because they assume they are being punished for acts committed in previous reincarnations (Moore, 1978). If, however, people

think that an injustice is unnatural, they often rise up against it. Once again, this illustrates W. I. Thomas's dictum and demonstrates the link between beliefs and social action.

*Most of the time, most of us don't break the rules.* The rules provide comfort and security. They serve to reduce potential risk, physical or psychic. This is especially true in urban public life. Urbanites are surrounded by people whom they know nothing about—where they are coming from or where they are going, literally and figuratively. It's easier to conform, and we expect others to do the same.

This is what many general rules—civil inattention, for instance—are all about: risk avoidance. Indeed, much of urban public behavior can be understood as attempts to avoid risk. This stands in contrast to everyday encounters in rural, small-scale societies. In the Greek polis, citizens knew each other on sight. There was no wide diversity in their definitions of the situation. They could reasonably predict one another's behavior. In this milieu, urban public life could thrive.

Can urban public life survive, let alone thrive, in postindustrial society? That seems to be *the* question. Have we put such a high premium on maintaining social order and personal privacy that we avoid the promise of city life: new experiences, learning from people unlike ourselves? Will those who can possibly afford it retreat to private spaces (the home with its room-size television and communications system) or moatlike separation, well protected from the risky arena of urban streets and gatherings? Or can we create a new urban public life that offers growth opportunities for all?

Many observers hope so, and numerous visionaries think they know the way to enrich city life. Their solutions depend mainly on their ideologies and their levels of analysis: radical changes in the rules of the game, or transforming lower-class individuals into middle-class citizens, or decentralizing public institutions and promoting community control (Sennett, 1970; Whyte [1988] 1990).

However we evaluate these proposals to enrich urban public life, one point is clear: The way people interact at the face-to-face level cannot be divorced from larger patterns of social structure. Micro meets macro, intersecting at the carry-out street corner and every other urban public place.

# KEY TERMS

**Civil inattention**  Erving Goffman's term, referring to a general rule (norm) of urban social interaction. It occurs when "one gives to another enough visual notice to demonstrate that one appreciates that the other is present (and that one admits openly to having seen him), while at the next moment withdrawing one's attention from him so as to express that he does not constitute a target of special curiosity or design."

**Definition of the situation**  W. I. Thomas's term, referring to the idea that objective reality is less important than people's subjective interpretation of events, objects and actions. His famous statement "If men define situations as real they are real in their consequences" suggests that the same action or event can hold various meanings for various people, and that people will respond differently to the same action or event, depending on the meaning they attach to it.

**Ethnography**  A study of a group of people or a community using fieldwork methods (participant-observation, in-depth interviewing) to describe the behavior and attitudes of the people under study. Ethnographers focus on actors' subjective meanings and definitions of the situation.

**Ethnomethodology**  A movement or "school" in sociology led by Harold Garfinkel. Ethnomethodologists (from the Greek: *ethno*, "people"; *meth*, "a way of doing things") study the unspoken, tacit rules and agreements that govern ordinary, everyday activities. Often, their method is to break the rules, making background expectancies inoperative, to understand commonsense knowledge.

**Macro-level social analysis**  Analysis of social structural features (class structure, discrimination patterns, educational institutions, etc.) that mold an entire society.

**Micro-level social analysis**  Analysis of interpersonal processes that mold everyday social interaction.

**Norms**  Rules of the game; standards of right and wrong behavior that are shared by a group or society. Norms change over time and vary from culture to culture.

**Presentation of self**  Erving Goffman's term, referring to the self-conscious attempt a person makes to control the impressions that other people have of her or him.

**Role**  The performance of expected rights, obligations, and behaviors associated with a person's status. To "play a role" is to act according to expected, pre-established behavior patterns. Role is inseparable from status, for status is a collection of rights and duties, and role is the performance of those rights and duties.

**Social interaction** (face-to-face)  Encounters that happen any time two or more people come into each other's physical presence, thereby exerting reciprocal influence on each other's behavior. Verbal communication is not necessary for social interaction to take place.

**Symbolic interactionism**  A theoretical perspective within sociology that focuses on micro-level processes of social interaction. Symbolic interactionists pay special attention to the meanings people attach to events and behavior and the ways in which they communicate meanings (via words, gestures, and other symbols).

# PROJECTS

**1. Classroom behavior, micro level.** Few students subject what goes on in the classroom to objective analysis because it is such a routine, familiar activity. That is the goal of this project: to analyze the rules of the classroom game. Observe three classes with different teachers and examine such features as the following: Who sits where? Who initiates discussion? What do people wear? What are they talking about? What is the manner and style of speech used (vocabulary, tone, loudness)? Who negotiates possible disagreements? What happens if some disruption occurs? On the basis of your preliminary observations, formulate at least two hypotheses about classroom behavior.

Now, do a second round of observations—this time, testing your hypotheses. If, for instance, you posit that teachers tend to pay more attention to students sitting near them than to students farther away (e.g., in the back of a large classroom), count the number of times eye contact is maintained with each group, as well as other indicators of attentiveness (e.g., responsiveness to questions from each group). If you hypothesize that female students are more likely to speak up in class than male students if the teacher is female, then compare and contrast the number of times women speak in various classes taught by males and females. Depending on your hypotheses, you may want to note indicators of restlessness (coughs, slouched body posture), lack of interest in the class (side conversations, newspaper reading, falling asleep), or control mechanisms (assigned seat arrangements, attendance taking, etc.). Reexamining your data, what general rules for classroom behavior do you find?

**2. Classroom behavior, macro level.** The purpose of this project is to reexamine data collected in Project 1 in light of larger social contexts. For example, do the class size, teaching format, and interpersonal dynamics of the class reflect the power and status patterns of the larger society? Do the age, sex, race, and academic rank of the professor seem to affect students' response or teachers' style? Is the classroom a setting for democratic participation or a training ground for hierarchical organization? What authority relationships do students take for granted?

**3. Breaking the rules: making the background expectancies inoperative.** Urbanites generally display trust—not distrust—to strangers. Test the existence of this norm by the following experiment: Board a city bus and ask the driver if this bus passes a certain street that you want. After receiving an answer, ask again, "Does it really pass this street?" Continue this line of questioning (e.g., "Are you sure?"). What is the bus driver's reaction? (And your own?)

**4. Presentation of self.** Think about a social occasion that you attended recently (say, a party) at which there were people previously unknown to you. How did you present yourself? What clothes did you wear? What information did you reveal about yourself to these strangers? What impressions did you want them to have of you? How did you go about managing these impressions? Finally, in your terms, was it a successful performance?

**5. Definitions of the situation.** Pick a contemporary issue with wide-ranging consequences (e.g., immigration, gun control, affirmative action). Using archival materials, interviews, and media resources (e.g., Internet chat groups), try to better understand the range of attitudes and feelings about the issue and the bases on which people or groups disagree (e.g., religion, rural or urban residence, political ideology, years of education, gender, marital status, ethnicity).

## SUGGESTIONS FOR FURTHER LEARNING

For an introduction to urban social life from a symbolic interactionist view, see Candace Clark and Howard Robboy, eds., *Social Interaction*, 3rd ed. (New York: St. Martin's Press, 1988). Several articles and books discussed in this chapter (e.g., Horace Miner's "Body Ritual of the Nacirema."

For a primer on how to conduct qualitative field work, John Lofland's *Analyzing Social Settings* (Belmont, Calif.: Wadsworth, 1971) offers detailed instructions on intensive interviewing, participant-observation, and analysis of data. For a first-person account of doing fieldwork, see the methodology section of Elliot Liebow's *Tally's Corner*.

Micro studies in urban social interaction include several works by Canadian-born sociologist Erving Goffman. See especially the "weird but brilliant light," as one reviewer called it, that he sheds on "normal appearances" in *Relations in Public: Microstudies of the Public Order* (New York: Basic Books, 1971).

Seeing ourselves reflected through the eyes of an outsider (and a good observer) is often instructive. British author Adam Nicholson offers this advice to his compatriots in "Shopping Around" the Trumbull Shopping Park in Connecticut: "Always have a guide in the U.S.; it's a much more foreign place than you think." In his book of essays, *On Foot* (New York: Harmony Books, 1990), Nicholson remarks that the shopping mall, "a climate-controlled cocoon," is "the new heart of the New World (there are now more shopping malls in the States than either post offices or secondary schools)" where "occupants turn away from the world outside towards a neat and unfrightening vacuum . . . where people go for long walks in the most comforting landscape they know" (89).

Drinking places have been much studied by ethnographers. Aside from Sherri Cavan's study of urban bars, *Liquor License* (1966), see Mary Jo Deegan's essay, "The Meet/Meat Market Ritual," in *American Ritual Dramas: Social Rules and Cultural Meaning* (New York: Greenwood Press, 1989), in which she discusses four structural codes—class, sex, bureaucracy, and commodified time—that she considers fundamental patterns for action in one urban setting: a singles bar. For an ethnography of a bar-related occupation, see anthropologists James P. Spradley and Brenda J. Mann's *The Cocktail Waitress: Women's Work in a Man's World* (New York: Wiley, 1975). William H. Whyte's delightfully irreverent documentary film, *The Social Life of Small Urban Spaces* (1979), shows, *inter alia*, people drinking (and schmoozing, people-watching, and eating) in plazas, pocket-sized parks, and other urban settings.

Laurence Marshall Carucci, Michael Brown, and Lynne Pettler's *Shared Spaces* (New York: SAMS Press, 1989) is one of the few published studies dealing with ethnic differences in microspace. Specifically, the authors look at bars and churches, investigating how people interact in some Mexican, Polish, German, Irish, "American," Italian, Greek, and Serbian bars and churches in Chicago. The study was conducted while the authors were graduate students at the University of Chicago. Their writing style is turgid at best, but the theoretical frameworks and diagrams are useful to researchers exploring ethnicity's role in shaping social-spatial behavior.

For a look at how "public privacy" is constructed, see Laud Humphrey's study of homosexual males' behavior in public bathrooms, *Tea-*

*room Trade* (Chicago: Aldine, 1970), and David Karp's study of people in pornographic bookstores and movie theaters, "Hiding in Pornographic Bookstores: A Reconsideration of the Nature of Urban Anonymity," *Urban Life and Culture* (now named *Urban Life*) (1973):427–451. Works by Robert Sommer and Edward Hall discuss the spatial dimensions of constructing public privacy (Chapter 16).

Paul Ekman provides some clues on how people maintain normal appearances while acting deceitfully in his highly readable book, *Telling Lies: Clues to Deceit in the Marketplace, Politics, and Marriage* (New York: Norton, 1985). Psychologist Ekman warns that "there is no sign of deceit itself—no gesture, facial expression, or muscle twitch," but he describes clues in speech, voice, body, and facial expression that happen because liars "usually do not monitor, control, and disguise all of their behavior." For a vision of the world as nearly nothing but appearances—the world as masked ball—see Tom Wolfe's cynical novel *The Bonfire of the Vanities* (New York: Farrar, Straus & Giroux, 1987).

Many occupations use clothing as a prop to impress audiences. How-to-dress manuals, such as John T. Malloy's *New Dress for Success* (New York: Warner, 1988), offer tips on how to appear efficient and reliable.

Various studies—on pedestrian behavior, poolroom behavior, subway behavior, and so on—are collected in Arnold Birenbaum and Edward Sagarin, eds., *People in Places: The Sociology of the Familiar* (New York: Praeger, 1973). The introduction to the essays is especially useful; it weaves together the concerns of symbolic interactionists with the concerns of such theorists as Freud, Marx, and Weber. Globe-trotting novelist and essayist Paul Theroux discovers an alien land on his New York City "Subway Odyssey," *New York Times Magazine*, January 31, 1982, p. 20+. He notes that it is "beat up with patches of beauty, like a cityscape in China or India." Theroux writes that "as a New York City subway passenger, you are like [T. S. Eliot's] J. Alfred Prufrock—you prepare a face to meet the faces that you meet." Walker Evans's series of subway photographs were taken in the late 1930s but remained unpublished until 1966. In this collection, *Many Are Called*, Evans advised viewers to "stare. It is the way to educate your eye, and more. Stare, Pry, Listen, Eavesdrop. Die knowing something. You are not here long."

Psychologist Ervin Staub, of the University of Massachusetts, has made a life's work of studying the role of the bystander in aiding or preventing acts of evil. Inspired by people who intervened to save him from the Nazis, Hungarian-born Staub studied factors that make people more likely to come to someone's aid. He examines bystanders at the micro level, such as a case in 1993 where passersby saw but ignored Sidney Brookins, a man in Minneapolis, who lay dying for two days in 1993, and at the macro level, such as whole nations that avoided intervening in the Balkans. After the Rodney King riots, Staub was commissioned by a California police agency to design a training program that would encourage officers to intervene when a colleague employs too much force.

For a look at the ways in which people present themselves in public places, see Lyn Lofland's *A World of Strangers: Order and Action in Urban Public Space* (Prospect Heights, Ill.: Waveland Press, 1985).

New York University offers "Aesthetics of Everyday Life," a course that helps students to look at New York City through the eyes of an anthropologist. Topics range from office decor in corporations to notions of modesty in various communities.

Akira Kurosawa's great enigmatic film *Rashomon* (1951) gives an acquaintance with multiple realities. This Japanese film (later copied in Hollywood, with an American setting, and called *The Outrage*) portrays a double crime, variously interpreted by three participants and a witness. What really happened? Kurosawa doesn't say.

Numerous visions of urban encounters are found in art. Franz Kafka's story "The Metamorphosis" (of Gregor Samsa from a clerk to a gigantic insect) deals with the alienation and anonymity of urban life. Gritty movies of the 1970s often presented a vision of mean city streets. This mood is exemplified in *Taxi Driver* (1976): An angry cabbie, embittered by what he sees of human cruelty in New York City, buys a gun and begins to kill the crooks and pimps he despises. But movies like Paul Mazursky's *An Unmarried Woman* (1978) depict the big city as a place where strangers can connect and partake of a rich cultural heritage. *When Harry Met Sally* (1989) showcases a quintessential urban act: eavesdropping.

A classic work combining macro and micro approaches to the study of urban social interaction is Elliot Liebow's *Tally's Corner: A Study of Negro Streetcorner Men* (Boston: Little, Brown, 1967). A secondary analysis of micro studies, written from a symbolic interactionist perspective, is David A. Karp, *Being Urban: A Social Psychological View of City Life*, 2nd ed. (New York: Praeger, 1991).

## REFERENCES

"The AIDS 'plot' against blacks." 1992. *New York Times* (May 12):A22.

Barron, James. 1991. "Princeton says 'con artist' is foiled." *New York Times* [national edition] (February 28):C19.

Berger, Peter L. 1963. *Invitation to Sociology: A Humanistic Perspective*. Garden City, N.Y.: Doubleday, Anchor.

Berger, Peter L., and Thomas Luckmann. 1967. *The Social Construction of Reality*. Garden City, N.Y.: Doubleday, Anchor.

Berman, Marshall. 1972. Review of *Relations in Public*, by Erving Goffman. *New York Times* (February 27):sec. 7, 1–18.

Cavan, Sherri. [1966] 1973. "Bar sociability." Pp. 143–154 in Arnold Birenbaum and Edward Sagarin, eds., *People in Places: The Sociology of the Familiar*. New York: Praeger.

Cranz, Galen. 1978. Personal interview, June 29. Berkeley, Calif.

Deegan, Mary Jo. 1989. "The meet/meat market ritual." Pp. 31–50 in *American Ritual Dramas: Social Rules and Cultural Meanings*. New York: Greenwood Press.

Durkheim, Emile. [1895] 1982. *Rules of Sociological Method*. New York: Free Press.

Garfinkel, Harold. 1967. *Studies in Ethnomethodology*. Englewood Cliffs, N.J.: Prentice-Hall.

Gasich, Mimi, Leslie Hamilton, Jacqueline Leung, Alyson Steele, and Kathryn Van Ploeg. 1989.

"Queuing behavior." Unpublished paper for Sociology 150, Stanford University.

Goffman, Erving. 1959. *The Presentation of Self in Everyday Life.* Garden City, N.Y.: Doubleday, Anchor.

———. 1963. *Behavior in Public Places.* New York: Free Press.

———. 1971. *Relations in Public: Microstudies of the Public Order.* New York: Basic Books.

Halstuk, Martin. 1991. "Alarming rise in crimes at ATMS." *San Francisco Chronicle* (December 4):A1+.

Internal Revenue Service. 1995. "San Francisco District Safety Bulletin—Bomb Threats." (May 4). San Francisco: IRS.

Karp, David A., Gregory P. Stone, and William C. Yoels. 1977. *Being Urban: A Social Psychological View of City Life.* Lexington, Mass.: Heath.

Latané, Bibb, and John Darley. 1970. *The Unresponsive Bystander: Why Doesn't He Help?* New York: Appleton-Century-Crofts.

Levine, Janey, Ann Vinson, and Deborah Wood. 1973. "Subway behavior." Pp. 208–216 in Arnold Birenbaum and Edward Sagarin, eds., *People in Places: The Sociology of the Familiar.* New York: Praeger.

Liebow, Elliot. 1967. *Tally's Corner: A Study of Negro Streetcorner Men.* Boston: Little, Brown.

Lurie, Alison. [1981] 1983. *The Language of Clothes.* New York: Vintage.

"Man who once posed as orphan arrested for stealing gems." 1993. *San Francisco Chronicle* (May 114):A7.

Mandel, Bill. 1988. "ATM rites and rituals for our time." *San Francisco Examiner* (October 14):A4.

Manis, Jerome G., and Bernard N. Meltzer. 1978. *Symbolic Interaction: A Reader in Social Psychology.* Boston: Allyn & Bacon.

Marx, Karl. [1859] 1977. "The German ideology." Pp. 159–191 in David McLellan, ed., *Karl Marx: Selected Writings.* New York: Oxford University Press.

McHugh, Peter. 1968. *Defining the Situation.* New York: Bobbs Merrill.

Milgram, Stanley. 1970. "The experience of living in cities." *Science* (March 13):1461–1468.

Miner, Horace. 1956. "Body ritual among the Nacirema." *American Anthropologist* 58 (June): 503–507.

Molloy, John T. 1988. *New Dress for Success.* New York: Warner.

Moore, Barrington, Jr. 1978. *Injustice: The Social Bases of Obedience and Revolt.* New York: Pantheon.

Moore, Teresa. 1992. "Black and white youths 'in 2 different worlds'." *San Francisco Chronicle* (January 1):B8.

"Perspectives." 1993. *Newsweek* (May 17):23.

Ridgeway, James. 1990. *Blood in the Face.* New York: Thunder's Mouth Press.

Schutz, Alfred. 1967. *Collected Papers.* Ed. Maurice Natanson. The Hague: Martinus Nijhoff.

Sennett, Richard. 1970. *The Uses of Disorder: Personal Identity and City Life.* New York: Knopf.

Slapin, Beverly. 1990. *Basic Skills Caucasian Americans Workbook.* Berkeley, Calif.: Oyate.

Thomas, William I., and Dorothy Swaine Thomas. 1928. *The Child in America.* New York: Knopf.

"Whites retain negative view of minorities, a survey finds." 1991. *New York Times* [national edition] (January 10):A15.

Whyte, William H. 1974. "The best street life in the world." *New York* 15:26–33.

———. [1988] 1990. *City: Rediscovering the Center.* New York: Doubleday, Anchor.

———. [1988] 1990. "The skilled pedestrian." Pp. 56–67 in *City: Rediscovering the Center.* New York: Doubleday, Anchor.

Whyte, William H., assisted by Margaret Bemiss. 1978. "New York and Tokyo: A study in crowding." Pp. 1–18 in Hidetoshi Kato, ed., *A Comparative Study of Street Life.* Tokyo: Research Institute for Oriental Cultures, Gukushuin University.

Winkin, Yves, ed. and trans. 1988. *Les Moments et leurs hommes* by Erving Goffman. Paris: Editions du Seuil.

Wirth, Louis. [1938] 1969. "Urbanism as a way of life." Pp. 143–164 in Richard Sennett, ed., *Classic Essays on the Culture of Cities.* New York: Appleton-Century-Crofts.

Wolff, Michael. 1973. "Notes on the behavior of pedestrians." Pp. 35–48 in Arnold Birenbaum and Edward Sagarin, eds., *People in Places: The Sociology of the Familiar.* New York: Praeger.

# PART V
# Who Runs This Town?

Bill Owens

City Hall protest. (Suzanne Coshow)

# CHAPTER 12
# The Skeleton of Power

"Who runs this town?"

That sounds like a simple question, but it's deceptive. And as with most questions worth asking, serious observers answer in different ways.

Political scientists, lawyers, and public administrators often approach this question by examining a city's legal structure. This is because, as President Franklin D. Roosevelt once said, "structure is government." Knowing what cities and city officials can do legally is vital to understanding who runs any town.

But a city's legal structure reveals only a small part of the story. Local politics takes place within a larger context of public and private institutions. First, knowing how a city fits into the web of intergovernmental relations—spinning out from Washington, D.C., sometimes bypassing the state capital, and weaving its way down to City Hall —is important for understanding who and what run U.S. towns. Second, understanding the networks of informal power and influence may be more important, perhaps crucial, in figuring out who has the ability to get things done. For instance, Chicago's city charter contains no mention of party bosses or ethnic voting blocs. Nor does it refer to the influence of global corporations, nationwide religious groups, organized crime, street gangs, and other interest groups on public policy. Yet these individuals and organizations can be key actors in city politics. Thus both formal and informal power structures—at both the micro and macro levels—need to be examined before any conclusions are reached about who runs any town.

This chapter looks at the public institutional framework of local government. It investigates such questions as these: How are cities legally organized? What power and formal authority do city officials have? How do cities interact with other units of government in the U.S. federal system? The next chapter deals with the other aspect of power: extralegal structures. It examines informal networks of power and influence, mainly from a historical perspective. Then Chapter 14 examines contending views of how community power and influence have worked in U.S. cities since World War II.

First, a word about the name of the game— power. Like love, truth, beauty, and other abstract concepts, power can be defined in a hundred ways. Here, power means the ability to force an individual or group to do something,

even if they resist. Ultimately, power is rooted in the threat of force or the actual use of coercion. People from urban Kigali, Rwanda, to suburban Long Island, New York, understand that the accepted balance of power can be upset by anyone brandishing a lethal weapon. Even a ten-year-old—with a gun, stones, brick, or machete—can become powerful. (In the United States, arrests of people under eighteen for violent crime rose 47 percent from 1988 to 1992, according to FBI statistics. This upsurge in violence crosses boundaries of geography, class, and race.)

Power can be distinguished from authority and influence. By **authority,** we mean legitimate power: power used in such a way that people see it as legitimate. By influence, we mean informal power, sometimes based on persuasion. Chicago gangster Al Capone, both powerful and influential (but lacking in authority), understood the difference: He once said, "You can get much farther with a kind word and a gun than you can with a kind word alone."

We begin with an overview of governmental power and authority. In particular, we examine the role that citizens think government should play in their lives.

## THE SCOPE OF GOVERNMENT

"That government which governs least governs best." Jefferson's saying reflects the deep distrust many Americans feel toward government at any level, no matter who runs it. Fear of excessive government and centralized, faraway authority is a recurrent theme in U.S. history, rooted in the Jeffersonian ideals of liberty and small government.

### Government's Limited Scope

For ideological reasons, the scope of government in the United States is smaller and weaker than that of any other major country in the world today. In France, England, and Sweden, for in-

**Table 12.1**  Tax Revenues for Selected Countries

| | Tax Revenues, 1989 | |
|---|---|---|
| Country | Total ($bil.) | Per Capita ($) |
| United States | 1,522.2 | 6,119 |
| Australia | 88.6 | 5,269 |
| Austria | 51.8 | 6,805 |
| Belgium | 67.7 | 6,813 |
| Canada | 196.9 | 7,501 |
| Denmark | 52.9 | 10,314 |
| Finland | 44.0 | 8,867 |
| France | 421.4 | 7,503 |
| Greece | 18.0 | 1,795 |
| Ireland | 12.8 | 3,629 |
| Italy | 328.8 | 5,716 |
| Japan | 893.8 | 7,260 |
| Luxembourg | 3.4 | 9,017 |
| Netherlands | 103.0 | 6,936 |
| New Zealand | 16.5 | 4,931 |
| Norway | 41.4 | 9,790 |
| Portugal | 15.9 | 1,624 |
| Spain | 130.9 | 3,343 |
| Sweden | 106.5 | 12,537 |
| Switzerland | 56.3 | 8,381 |
| Turkey | 22.9 | 416 |
| United Kingdom | 306.0 | 5,349 |
| West Germany | 452.7 | 7,304 |

NOTE: Covers national and local taxes and Social Security contributions.

SOURCE: Adapted from U.S. Bureau of the Census, *Statistical Abstract of the United States 1992* (Washington, D.C.: Government Printing Office, 1992), Table 299, p. 186.

stance, government is expected to regulate the extent and nature of physical growth and to oversee the general health and welfare of its citizenry. And, as Table 12.1 shows, many countries collect much more revenue per capita to pay for such services. But the dominant ideology in the United States assigns as much responsibility as possible to the private rather than the public sector.

The scope of the public sector at all levels— federal, state, and local—increased dramatically in this century as America changed from a country of farms and small towns to a metropolitan nation. Yet, governments still operate in a climate generally hostile to them. And since a series of "gates"—Watergate, Koreagate, Irangate, and so on—an atmosphere of public cynicism prevails. Trust in government at all levels has been steadily declining since the 1960s. This mood is captured in a news columnist's comment about Congress: "The crime rate in Congress is probably higher than in downtown Detroit" (Newfield in Bogart, 1980:5).

For decades, groups have attacked big government and big spending. At the local level, California's Proposition 13 (the Jarvis–Gann initiative), passed in 1978, is often named as the harbinger of a nationwide revolt against "tax-and-spend" government. This initiative amended the state's constitution in a way that reduced property taxes, by nearly one-half, and restricted their future growth. Since many local government services are funded by the property tax, Proposition 13 effectively limited the expansion of local government services.

Why did the tax revolt happen first in California? Analysts point to a specific demographic reason—suburban growth (which provided " a demographic base for a selectively expanding conservatism")—plus the state's "involvement in competitive trade with Asia's industrial-technological sector" (Edsall and Edsall, [1991] 1992:137). Sociologist Harvey Molotch adds an often overlooked factor: skyrocketing property values. Molotch (1990:183) says that California's rising property values fueled rising property taxes: "the cutbacks blamed on Proposition 13 (including draconian budget decreases for public hospitals, paramedics, coastal protection and a proliferation of user fees for services formerly free) were due to wealth creation, rather than wealth erosion." Still, it didn't feel that way to homeowners, especially older ones on fixed incomes. On paper, their homes increased in value, but they couldn't eat or spend the profits unless they sold their homes. Thus, older homeowners, not corporate business, spearheaded Proposition 13 as a security blanket for their future.

California's cities were the first—but not the last—to feel the fiscal pinch. Taxpayers' rebellions occured in many states. Joblessness played a part: Between July 1979 and November 1982, for instance, over 3.6 million jobs disappeared in the private manufacturing sector in the United States—for a loss of nearly one out of every seven jobs in manufacturing (Edsall and Edsall, [1991] 1992:200).

In this economic climate, voters elected conservative political leaders. No new taxes! Reduce government spending! Privatize! These messages became rallying cries. They formed the centerpiece of Margaret Thatcher's Conservative government in Great Britain (1978–1990) and of the Reagan and Bush administrations (1980–1992).

Shortly, we will look at how federal anti–tax-and-spend policies affect cities. First, let's examine the impact of state policies on local government.

To begin with, the fiscal pinch became the fiscal crisis in many states. From the late 1970s on, downsizing was in. Due to circumstances beyond their borders (e.g., economic recession that cut into tax receipts), local governments in many states faced agonizing choices in "cutback management." In California, the revenue shortfall was especially serious. By 1993, California's legislators warned that there wasn't enough in the public coffers to fund adequately both law enforcement and education. Meanwhile, some who had opposed Proposition 13 some fifteen years earlier crowed that the chickens had come home to roost.

## Paradoxical Attitudes Toward Government

Attitudes toward government are often paradoxical. On the one hand, voters may desire limits on government's growth. On the other, they look to government to solve many issues of collective concern. In other words, "While people wish that government's powers were less, they expect it to do more" (Gottdiener, 1987:38).

In the case of California, two analysts of Proposition 13 conclude that "the people wanted something for nothing": "tax relief without dismantling the structure of public service built up over 30 years of expansion" (Sears and Citrin,

[1982] 1985:v). In other words, California's voters wanted lower taxes and more public services—simultaneously.

## Public–Private Sector Relationships

Even in spheres where American government is expected to act (either as problem solver, distributor of resources and benefits, or regulator), it is assumed that public policy will be made in conjunction with private group interests. Often private interests play a significant, some say dominant, role in public decision making. At the local level, for example, real-estate brokers and large land developers have a significant impact on zoning decisions, and private business influences urban redevelopment plans. Similarly, professional organizations, unions, and corporate officials are generally consulted on policies affecting their interests. Often such groups initiate policy proposals.

The political philosophy that underlies these public–private sector relations is rooted in classical liberalism and pluralist democracy. The dominant ideology holds that government reflects the individual citizen's wishes through group representation, and that government does not serve any one group's interest more than another's. Hence, under the theory of pluralism or interest-group democracy, government should act as a broker, balancing private interests.

## The Proper Role of Local Government

The dominant U.S. ideology holds that local government should act as a forum in which competing private interests negotiate and come to an accommodation that serves the entire community's interest. In this view, government is supposed to be a facilitator of private economic activity, not an obstacle. Thus private enterprise expects local government to set the stage for their activities by providing infrastructure (such as streets and sewers), maintaining police and fire protection, supporting a good business climate, and regulating certain activities to prevent chaos and quackery (e.g., land use regulations, public health standards).

To protect their citizens' welfare and to prevent untrammeled competition, local governments today have varying degrees of authority to intervene and regulate private business—by granting health permits to restaurants, construction permits to builders, and so forth. Clearly, the granting or withholding of such benefits can mean economic life or death to private entrepreneurs. Given these economic stakes, we could predict that local politics cannot be separated from economics. This close connection between political power and potential profit should be kept in mind when analyzing who runs any town.

*To conclude:* Local governments provide a number of services and goods for collective consumption and individual betterment, ranging from well-maintained roads to legal entitlements to make money. Various groups are concerned when their interests are at stake, whether they involve getting sewer hookups for a suburban housing development or a neighborhood day-care center. Local government is at the center of competing demands for its scarce resources. It can't fund all the projects proposed. It can't award more than one contract to build a new school or give everyone a license to operate a taxi. And in hard economic times, such as the recessionary 1990s, it may not be able to pay both its police officers and its paramedics. In this milieu, there are bound to be conflicts of interest, opportunities for corruption, and attempts to manipulate or persuade the public via the mass media.

## Local Political Environments

Local communities don't answer the normative question "What *should* government do?" in the same way. Some communities expect—and expect to pay for—only minimal public services. Others demand a higher level of services and more of them. Thus, the local political environment is a key factor in analyzing the scope of local government.

According to neoconservative "public choice" theorists (e.g., Peterson, 1981), people rationally choose a local political environment. For instance, when a woman chooses a particular place to live, she chooses one bundle of services over another. If she doesn't like the particular service bundle, she can vote with her car. Others disagree, saying that residential choices are due either to "forced choice," "dumb happenstance" (Molotch, 1990:195), or shared lifestyles (e.g., Weiss, 1988). Whatever their motivation for choosing one community over another, people do live in cities and suburbs that offer different services.

The following typology applies only to suburbs, classifying them according to their attitude toward economic development:

1. *Aggressive.* Suburbs that aggressively compete for business or industrial activities. Types pursuing this strategy: (1) older, close-in suburbs suffering from problems similar to those of their central city (e.g., fiscal pressure, stagnating income) and (2) newer, more prosperous suburbs.
2. *Regulatory.* Suburbs that adhere to regulations believed to be in the public interest and that are considered more important than development per se. Type pursuing this strategy: those with attractive land that can choose which development they want.
3. *Cooperative.* Suburbs that are moderately pro-development. Type pursuing this strategy: stable, established communities.
4. *Retentive.* Suburbs that want to retain existing businesses and industries. Type pursuing this strategy: old, stable suburbs of mixed residential-commercial activity.
5. *Reactive.* Suburbs that have no formal policy on economic development but react case by case. Type pursuing this stragegy: developed suburbs. (Pelissero and Fasenfest, 1988).
6. *Antidevelopment.* Suburbs that oppose economic development. Types pursuing this strategy: ecology-minded and/or upper-income suburbs.

According to the developers of this five ideal-type classification (I added the sixth type), the values of local elected officials in the suburbs they studied "shaped the particular mix of policies followed in each suburb" and determined the suburban community's approach to development" (Pelissero and Fasenfest, 1988:11).

Whether city or suburb, population size and mix, the values of local elected officials, and attitudes toward economic growth influence the local political environment. So does the level of tax resources available. For instance, relatively homogeneous, residential, upper-status suburbs (e.g., "Blue Blood Estates," "Furs and Station Wagons") do not need to promote economic growth or mediate among conflicting interests. Large, heterogeneous cities, on the other hand, often seek to juggle conflicting interests.

## CITIES AS CREATURES OF THEIR STATE

In the United States, cities are entirely creatures of their state governments. This stems from a decision made by the republic's founding fathers; they made no mention of cities in the United States Constitution. Instead, they granted the states the right to create or not to create all local jurisdictions, including cities.

When the states did create cities, they kept legal power over them. Hence, it is the fifty state legislatures that decide how city governments are structured.

### General Law Cities and Charter Cities

States grant legal powers to their creatures—the cities—in two different ways. Some states establish the general powers of city governments in state law; these are called **general law cities.** Other states spell out the powers of a city in a charter approved by the legislature; these are called **charter cities.**

Charters granted to cities by their states vary in content, but most describe the form, composition, powers, and limitations of city officials. To illustrate, a city **charter** might state that the city

council will be elected every four years; have one representative from each of ten districts; and have authority over personnel, zoning, parks, and budgeting.

An important variation is the **home rule** charter. Under home rule provisions in a state constitution, the precise definition of city powers is left up to the city voters, within limits set by the state constitution. About 75 percent of large U.S. cities operate under home rule provisions. About half of the states provide for home rule in their state constitutions, and about a dozen more allow home rule through legislation.

Charters can be revised, but voters usually greet revision with yawns. However, New York City was forced to revise its charter in 1989 after the U.S. Supreme Court ruled that the city's top government body, the Board of Estimate, was unconstitutional because it violated the principle of one person, one vote. New Yorkers approved a complete overhaul of municipal government, eliminating the Board of Estimate, a unique legislative–executive hybrid that exercised more power than the City Council.

### Dillon's Rule

When a legal question arises concerning the extent of power granted by a state to a city, the courts have traditionally ruled against cities. In other words, the courts narrowly construe city powers. This narrow construction of city powers is based on **Dillon's rule,** named for Iowa State Judge John F. Dillon, who published a leading treatise on municipal law.

What difference does it make if states legally control cities and if the courts narrowly interpret city powers? A great deal. Dillon's rule means that "a city cannot operate a peanut stand at the city zoo without first getting the state legislature to pass an enabling law, unless, perchance, the city's charter or some previously enacted law unmistakably covers the sale of peanuts" (Banfield and Wilson, 1963:65).

Because cities can do only what state legislatures expressly permit them to do (or what is "fairly implied" or "indispensable"), city **charters** often describe city powers in painstaking detail. Here is one illustration from the former city charter of Nashville, Tennessee:

In the event any regular member of the Fire Department above the rank of pipeman or ladderman, shall be temporarily absent from his duties without pay, because of illness or disability the chief of the Fire Department, subject to the approval of the Mayor, shall designate any regular member of the Fire Department from a lower rank to perform the duties of such member during his absence. . . . (in Banfield and Wilson, 1963:65)

Even under home rule charters (whereby cities can amend charters without going back to the legislature), cities are far from independent. They are still bound by the law of their state. And the state is omnipotent. In a 1923 case involving the city of Trenton and the state of New Jersey, the U.S. Supreme Court ruled that a state has the legal power to eliminate cities altogether, even against the will of the city's residents.


## CHANGING RELATIONSHIPS

### State Legislatures and City Interests

The posture of a state legislature is important to the cities of that state. Unfortunately for cities, state legislatures have generally adopted negative stances toward their cities—boxing them in with narrow grants of legal power and voting new power grudgingly.

City politicians have long felt victimized by their state legislatures. But the villains in the piece changed as the nation's population shifted from rural to urban to suburban locations. Specifically, before 1962, U.S. cities faced state legislatures dominated by rural, and usually antiurban, interests. By 1960, almost 70 percent of the U.S. population was urban, but about one-third of the states still had very large proportions of their population in rural areas. Further, before

1962, most state legislatures did not have the one person, one vote rule. Usually state legislative districts were drawn so that rural voters could elect more than their proportional share of representatives. For example, before 1962, only 11 percent of Californians (mainly from rural areas) could elect a majority of members of the California State Senate (Murphy and Rehfuss, 1976:28–49). Beginning with a landmark Supreme Court case in 1962, *Baker* v. *Carr*, an ongoing process of **reapportionment** has been under way. This court decision required one person–one vote, and it has led to a redrawing of electoral district lines so that the population in all legislative districts is substantially equal.

Since *Baker* v. *Carr* in 1962, rural domination of state legislatures has generally been reduced. But suburbs, not cities, have been the major benefactors. Demographics helps to explain why. By 1970, the U.S. population was roughly one-third urban, one-third suburban, and one-third rural or small town, with a slight suburban dominance. So the irony is this: State legislatures were reapportioned to ensure one person, one vote at the very time when population was shifting to the suburbs. Thus reapportionment generally did not significantly benefit big cities. It did benefit suburbs and hurt rural areas (Lehne, 1972).

In the 1970s, a new suburban–rural—and antiurban—coalition emerged in many states, replacing the historic rural, antiurban coalition. This new antiurban coalition continues to vote against legislation designed to meet big-city problems. Welfare is a case in point. In New York State, suburbs contain fewer welfare recipients than New York City. Reapportionment served to stiffen rural–suburban resistance to increased welfare benefits that would have gone to residents of New York City.

Antiurbanism escalated in the 1980s. By 1990, budget deficits had mounted in state capitals. California, Michigan, Ohio, Illinois, and several other populous—and suburban—states were faced with serious revenue shortfalls; they made drastic cutbacks in welfare and education, program cuts that adversely affected more urbanites than suburbanites.

## Suburbs versus Cities

Distinguished urban historian Richard C. Wade calls suburbanization "the most important fact of American social and political life" since 1945 (1982:20). A number of analysts agree, noting a related fact: the emergence of two separate—and unequal—communities in the United States, suburbs and cities.

Many suburbanites feel disconnected from and fearful of urban poverty, street crime, and other conditions facing their city neighbors. This emotional apartheid can start very young. For instance, student research teams in my classes at San Francisco State found in 1986, 1988, and 1990 that children in suburban San Francisco held extremely negative views of the city. Although over 80 percent of the preteenage respondents had never visited San Francisco, they characterized the city as the home of crime, grime, and slime. The vast majority had nothing positive to say about San Francisco, a city that most international tourists name as their favorite U.S. city.

Perhaps it is no accident, then, that Branson, Missouri—not San Francisco—is (after Orlando, Florida) the most popular vacation destination by car in the United States. As a *New York Times* reporter puts it, "the astounding growth of this squeaky-clean, virtually all-white, middle-of-nowhere Mecca is a revealing slice of America." One tourist at Branson's Elvis-A-Rama and glitzy country music theaters revealed why he vacationed there rather than in Los Angeles: "There's no smog blowing down from the hillsides. There's no graffiti.There are no gangs. I'm not prejudiced, but it's nice to be someplace where everyone speaks English" (in Applebome, 1993:B1).

In the past generation, it has become clear that suburban voters not only feel separate from city folk, they are also unwilling to fund public programs that could possibly turn cities around. This attitude is expressed in such vivid terms as "the War against the Cities" (Davis, 1993). I call it the "moating and malling of suburban America" or the "Yes, you *can* run and hide" syndrome. Whatever it's called, it describes suburban antiurbanism.

What lies behind this suburban antiurbanism? Analysts disagree. Mike Davis (1993) sees race and conservative politics as the keys. According to Davis, a conservative coalition in Congress unites suburban and rural representatives in both major political parties against any federal reinvestment in big cities dominated by minorities. He goes further, charging that all major candidates for president in 1992 may have acted "in cynical concert to exclude a subject [from their debates] that had become mutually embarrassing—cities": "The word 'city' now color-coded and worrisome to the candidates' common suburban heartland—was expunged from the exchanges. Thus the elephant of the urban crisis was simply . . . conjured out of sight" (3). Davis concludes that the 1992 presidential election means that "the big cities, once the very fulcrum of the political universe during Franklin Roosevelt's presidency, have been demoted to the status of a scorned and impotent electoral periphery" (3).

In more prosaic language, public opinion analyst William Schneider also attributes suburban antiurbanism to conservative ideology. Writing about "The Dawn of the Suburban Era in American Politics," Schneider claims that "a major reason people move out to the suburbs is simply to be able to buy their own government. These people resent it when politicians take their money and use it to solve other people's problems, especially when they don't believe that government can actually solve those problems" (1992:38).

I think there is another important factor: widespread pessimism about the future. Perhaps for the first time in U.S. history, citizens seem resigned to diminishing expectations and urban decline. This feeling is rooted in global shifts that affect people in suburbs, cities, and rural areas, albeit differently. Historically—and for good reason—after World War II, Americans were optimistic: They had rising expectations for the national economy and their own fortunes. They expected that their children would live with more, not less, than they had. Even without having heard of Burgess's hypothesis, they understood that moving *out* to the suburbs meant moving *up*, and literally millions of white middle-class and working-class Americans left town. But by the 1970s and early 1980s, global economic restructuring hit home. Once secure and relatively high-paid jobs in manufacturing moved to cheaper labor areas. Few high-paid jobs replaced them. White-collar workers, including top managers, also felt insecure as companies merged, and they found themselves unemployed or "rightsized" out of work. Consequently, for ever-increasing numbers, future prosperity seemed dreamlike. By the early 1990s, people were asking, *America: What Went Wrong?* (Barlett and Steele, 1992) As a University of Michigan director of consumer surveys put it, "People are satisfied today if they can keep their incomes and living standards from declining" (Curtin in Uchitelle, 1993:sec. 4, 1). In sum, downward mobility is knocking at the door.

What does this have to do with suburban anti-urbanism? Probably a great deal. During boom times, it is easier to have compassion for—or at least neutrality toward—strangers and people unlike oneself. During gloomy economic times, the politics of resentment can grip the heart and purse, widening the gulf between "us" and "them." The newly insecure assign blame to someone or something for their falling fortunes. In this milieu, many flee to the suburbs rather than fight what they see as irreversible urban decline, especially dangerous streets.

Liberals would say that the well-off blame the victims. Conservatives would say that the well-off rightly blame those who have not helped themselves but prefer to live off government giveaways. Radicals would say that it is ironic: A group of better-off people blame those at the bottom of the social ladder instead of the structures of capitalism that tend to impoverish them both.

We should remember that the term *suburb* covers many types of communities beyond the city rim: poor white suburbs, African-American suburbs, older industrial suburbs, mixed-use suburbs, rich residential suburbs, Mexican and Central American suburbs (e.g., Huntington Park outside Los Angeles), and at least one Chinese-American suburb (Los Angeles's Monterey Park, whose population is more than half Chinese, mainly immigrants from Hong Kong and Tai-

wan). Still, in general, suburbanites do tend to be middle-class, mainly white, property owners. Furthermore, suburbanites do tend to be better off economically than their central city neighbors, and this inequity increased in the 1980 to 1990 decade: In 1980, the per capita income of central city dwellers was 90 percent of those in the suburban ring; by 1990, it had decreased to 59 percent (Caraley, 1992).

Given that the future portends less, not more, property-owning suburbanites seek to hold the line economically. This condition make them very tax sensitive. The upshot is suburban hostility to both government and cities. This hostility coincides with two recent sociospatial developments that have important political consequences:

1. Since 1990, suburban residents are a majority in many states (including the nation's largest, California).
2. Many suburbanites live in edge cities or post-suburbia, settlements that are no longer dependent economically and socially on the urban core.

In brief, scarcity—not familiarity—breeds contempt. Fear can also breed secession from the union—not of South or Sunbelt from North and Rustbelt but of suburbs from urban core. With little hope for a more prosperous future and with no sense of community with their urban neighbors, suburbanites are not anxious to share their tax dollars with urban strangers.

Yet, ironically, many suburbs share city-type problems. As John V. Lindsay, then mayor of New York City, said prophetically more than two decades ago, "You can't wall in the city's problems." Affluent suburban counties around New York City face congestion, drugs, crime, expensive housing, garbage mounds, air pollution, and other so-called urban problems. Further, as Table 12.2 shows, both urban and suburban households are touched by crime. Nonetheless, few suburbanites apparently see a common future with their urban neighbors. Nor do those seeking high political office. In 1992, no presidential candidate spoke to specifically urban issues.

**Table 12.2**   Households Touched by Crime, 1981 and 1989, and by Characteristic, 1989

| | 1981 | | 1989 | | | | | | |
|---|---|---|---|---|---|---|---|---|---|
| | | | | *Percent Touched* | | | | | |
| *Type of Crime* | *Number (1,000)* | *Percent Touched* | *Number (1,000)* | *Total\** | *White* | *Black* | *Urban* | *Suburban* | *Rural* |
| Total† | 24,863 | 30.0 | 22,652 | 23.7 | 23.1 | 27.8 | 29.6 | 22.7 | 16.9 |
| Violent crime | 4,850 | 5.9 | 4,478 | 4.7 | 4.6 | 5.4 | 6.1 | 4.2 | 3.6 |
| Rape | 165 | 0.2 | 104 | 0.1 | 0.1 | 0.1 | 0.2 | 0.1 | 0.1 |
| Robbery | 1,117 | 1.3 | 967 | 1.0 | 0.8 | 2.2 | 1.8 | 0.7 | 0.4 |
| Assault | 3,890 | 4.7 | 3,591 | 3.8 | 3.8 | 3.6 | 4.4 | 3.5 | 3.2 |
| Theft | 17,705 | 21.4 | 15,905 | 16.7 | 16.6 | 17.0 | 20.3 | 16.5 | 11.6 |
| Burglary | 6,101 | 7.4 | 4,557 | 4.8 | 4.3 | 7.9 | 6.7 | 3.9 | 3.7 |
| Motor vehicle theft | 1,285 | 1.6 | 1,825 | 1.9 | 1.7 | 3.2 | 2.9 | 1.8 | 0.7 |

NOTE: A household is considered "touched by crime" if during the year it experienced a burglary, auto theft or household theft or if a household member was raped, robbed, or assaulted, or a victim of personal theft, no matter where the crime occurred. Data based on the National Crime Survey.

\*Includes other races not shown separately.

†Types of crime will not add to "total" since each household may report as many crime categories as experienced.

SOURCE: Adapted from U.S. Bureau of the Census, *Statistical Abstract of the United States 1992*, 112th ed. (Washington, D.C.: Government Printing Office, 1992), Table 299, p. 186.

So, if you add a mixture of economic recession, fear for personal safety on city streets, and tense race relations to long-standing cynicism about government, what have you got? A recipe for a volatile brew. Depending on your ideology and optimism-pessimism quotient, you see either the new survival of the fittest, creative challenges, or the war of all against all.

*A final note:* When issues are not framed as urban–suburban issues, suburbanites seem to follow the Golden Rule. Take health care, for example. A national random sample poll in 1993 revealed that a majority of respondents (including a majority of suburbanites) would be willing to pay higher taxes if everyone were covered (Utley, 1993).

*To conclude:* U.S. cities are creatures of state law. States can grant or take away powers from cities at will. State legislatures spell out city powers in general laws or charters. In some states, cities are granted considerable discretion to determine their own structures and powers under home rule charters, but even home rule cities are far from independent. Furthermore, cities have

been under the domination of state legislatures, historically controlled by rural interests and anti-urban attitudes. Demographic shifts and reapportionment reduced rural domination. But ironically, suburbs—not cities—gained the most influence and power from these changes. Unhappily for cities, suburban dominance, combined with economic hard times and fiscal austerity, led to a new and grimmer round of anti-urbanism.

## Local Governments in a Global Society: "Taking Responsibility for the Sky"

"All politics is local." This maxim of the late speaker of the U.S. House of Representatives, Tip O'Neill, means that local interests mold national political issues. Closing a naval base, for example, may be influenced by the local unemployment rate and the clout of the district's congressperson .

But there is another sort of local politics, and it

works in reverse: It starts locally and spreads. For instance, the city council of Irvine, a city in postsuburban Orange County, California, passed legislation restricting chlorofluorocarbons (CFCs) in the city. The anti-CFC ordinance raised the cost of some goods for local residents and caused hardships for some businesses. Indeed, as the *New Yorker*'s "Talk of the Town" columnist put it, "From a realist's point of view, Irvine's action seems almost unnatural; it's idealistic, even quixotic, for little Irvine to take responsibility for the sky" ("Notes," 1989:37). So why did they do it? According to the columnist, the idea of locality takes on renewed importance as global problems feel overwhelming, and the price of political awareness is often a feeling of helplessness:

[Government] leaders seem to fear that if they admit that a situation is lethal and out of control they will lose their authority. . . . It may be that authority . . . can . . . be recovered only on a local level, and that this is why local politics has acquired new significance. . . . The Irvine City Council did not claim that its one action would solve the ozone depletion situation, but it did acknowledge that it is no longer helpless. It examined its own contribution to the destuction of the ozone, asked, "If not us, who?" and heard the answer "No one."

Not a prairie fire but at least a flashlight, the action of Irvine illuminated the actions of other localities. Indeed, many other little places from Berkeley, California, and Suffolk County, New York, to Japan's Shiga Prefecture have taken responsibility for the sky . . . and the earth . . . and the water . . . and their fellow beings. In Palo Alto, California, for instance, city employees are reimbursed for business travel by bicycle, and the city requires large employers to provide showers for bicyclists. In Detroit, 125 teenagers and young adults worked with local residents to rehabilitate houses and march against crack houses as part of a Green Cities project. Recycling of glass and newspaper occurs in countless urban areas. Berkeley, California, sends technical assistance to a sister city in Central America. Two communities, one in Japan and the other in

Siberia, even have a "sister lake" relationship; they jointly study the flight of birds that migrate to and from their areas ("Sister Lakes," 1986:8).

*To conclude:* Local actions—from passing anti-pollution and gun control ordinances to conducting muncipal foreign policy—have wider political significance. Such local deeds encourage collective action, and they signal local resistance to the power of the nation-state (Kirby, 1993).

## FORMS OF CITY GOVERNMENT

As suggested, the first step in understanding how cities (including suburban cities) work is to clarify the city–state relationship. The second step entails understanding how a city's internal government is structured.

Getting something done in a city takes know-how and *know-who*. Who has the authority to condemn an unsafe building? What bureaucrat can grant a permit to hold a rally in the park? Can the mayor fire the school superintendent who has ordered the closing of the high school for his own birthday? Knowing whom to go to and how to get something done begins with an understanding of a city's governmental form.

Most city governments fall into one of three categories: the mayor–council form, the council–manager form, and the commission form. (In New England, town meetings also exist; they are used mainly by cities with less than 10,000 population and exclusively by cities with fewer than 100,000 inhabitants.) Large U.S. cities generally have a mayor–council form. Some smaller cities also follow this model. However, many smaller and medium-size communities, particularly metropolitan suburbs that grew up in this century, have a city council–manager form. Here a city manager, appointed by the **city council** and accountable to that legislative body, plays a key leadership role, and the elected mayor is less important. Finally, some cities have a commission form of government in which elected commissioners act collectively as the city council and individually as heads of city departments.

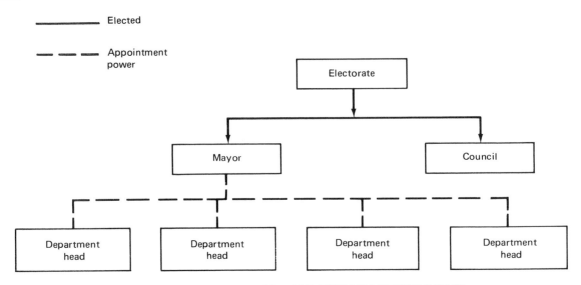

**Fig. 12.1**   THE MAYOR–COUNCIL FORM OF GOVERNMENT.

## Mayor–Council Form

The **mayor–council form** is the most common form of city government in the United States. It is also the predominant form in large cities. The organization chart in Figure 12.1 shows that under this form of government, mayors typically have appointment power—that is, they can appoint department heads. They do not have this power in council–manager cities. The organization chart also shows that the mayor and city council are elected independently. The mayor's independent elected status and significant appointment power indicate that under the mayor–council form, mayors have important executive powers. Other factors, not revealed on the organization chart, contribute to the mayor's role as executive leader. These may include the ability to intervene directly in the conduct of city government operations, to veto the city's budget, and to initiate legislation.

## Council–Manager Form

Consider Figure 12.2. The fact that the mayor is in a box, somewhere off in left field, is a signifi-

cant feature of the **council–manager form** of government. Under this form, which is common in many medium-size American communities, the mayor has much less power and authority than in a mayor–council government. The important actor in this fairly recent form of government is the **city manager,** appointed by the city council, as Figure 12.2 indicates. Usually the manager serves at the pleasure of the elected city council and can be removed at any time if a majority of councillors so decide. The city manager, in turn, typically has the power to hire and fire heads of city departments. He or she is also responsible for preparing the city budget, developing policy recommendations for the council's action, and overseeing city government.

In many cities, the city manager draws a bigger salary than the mayor or council members (who may be part-time or amateur administrators). Further, the city manager has a larger personal staff and more control over the flow of information than the mayor or councillors. This combination of professional expertise and access to and control over information gives city managers informal power beyond what is revealed in organization charts.

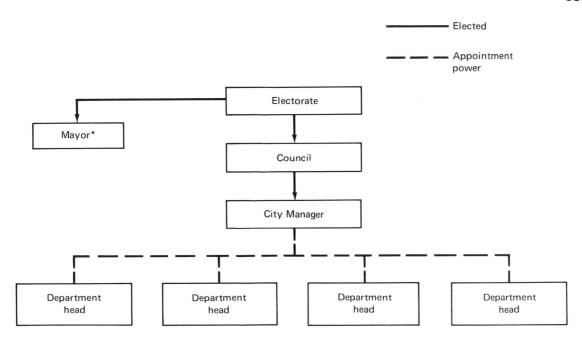

* Independently elected or appointed from
among the council members

**Fig. 12.2**  THE COUNCIL–MANAGER FORM OF GOVERNMENT.

## Commission Form

Under the **commission form** of government, voters elect a relatively small number of commissioners, who play a dual role as legislators and executives. Commissioners approve legislation and also head the city's departments.

The commission form was introduced in Galveston, Texas, following a flood in 1900 that "left both the city and its finances underwater" (Abrams, 1971:57). Today, no U.S. city with a population over 500,000 operates under this form—for good reasons. As Figure 12.3 shows, there is no strong executive leader. Power is exercised collectively by the city commissioners—the parks commissioner, police commissioner, and so on. Historically, this ideal of collective leadership has resulted in lack of coordination and government by amateurs.

*To conclude:* Few cities today use the commission

form; the mayor–council structure predominates in the larger cities; and council–manager governments are most commonly found in medium-size cities and suburbs. Why is the council–manager form so attractive to medium-sized communities and so unattractive to large cities? To understand this, some background is necessary.

The city manager plan was initiated in Staunton, Virginia, in 1908. It spread slowly throughout the nation up to the 1940s. After World War II, the council–manager form became widespread in medium-size communities, especially upper-income, white suburbs. Generally speaking, these suburbanites thought that the council–manager form would ensure professional, businesslike government and guard against something defined as inefficient, unprofessional, and corrupt: big-city politics. According to two long-time observers of governmental structure, council–manager governments seem best suited

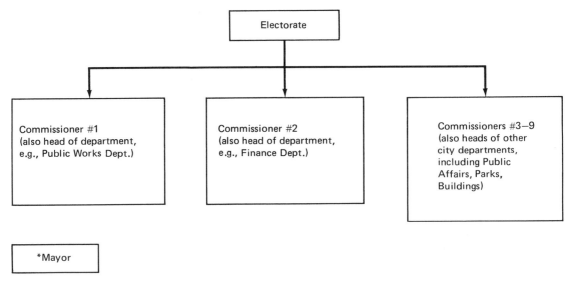

* Usually appointed from among commissioners.

**Fig. 12.3**   THE COMMISSION FORM OF GOVERNMENT.

to "relatively homogeneous white-collar communities where the political representation of diverse interests is not an important factor" (Bollens and Schmandt, 1970:116). Thus, ordinarily we shouldn't expect to find a city manager running a city composed of various ethnic groups and a significant blue-collar population. Typically, mayors operate in cities that mediate among diverse interests, not cities that seek primarily to create pleasant living conditions.

## ORGANIZATION OF CITY GOVERNMENTS

### Mayors, Strong or Weak

In cities with mayor–council governments, the **mayor** is popularly considered to be the head of city government, the responsible official with whom the local buck stops. But as the song says, "It ain't necessarily so." Often a mayor is powerless to improve bus service, create jobs for the unemployed, or reorganize the delivery of city services. The following exchange before a congressional committee between then U.S. Senator

Abraham Ribicoff (D.-Conn.) and then mayor of Los Angeles, Sam Yorty, is instructive:

*Senator Ribicoff:* As I listened to your testimony, Mayor Yorty, I made some notes. This morning you have really waived authority and responsibility in the following areas: schools, welfare, transportation, employment, health, and housing, which leaves you as head of a city with a ceremonial function, police, and recreation.
*Mayor Yorty:* That is right, and fire.
*Senator Ribicoff:* And fire.
*Mayor Yorty:* Yes.
*Senator Ribicoff:* Collecting sewage?
*Mayor Yorty:* Sanitation; that is right.
*Senator Ribicoff:* In other words, basically you lack jurisdiction, authority, responsibility for what makes a city move?
*Mayor Yorty:* That is exactly it. (U.S. Senate Hearings, 1966–1967:774)

In this exchange, Senator Ribicoff seems to blame Mayor Yorty for "waiving" responsibility. But in fact, Yorty never had the responsibility. In Los Angeles, as in many cities, mayors have limited powers, making them weak chief executives. Nonetheless, as outgoing San Francisco Mayor Dianne Feinstein warned her successor, "Anytime there's trouble, whether [the] Muni[cipal] [Railway] breaks down or someone is cited for double parking, they all come to you. There is no Teflon with this job" (1988:5).

Under the weak mayor–council arrangement, the city council or independent administrative boards dominate city decision making. Further, mayors (either strong or weak) have no authority to control many independent units of government within their political boundaries (e.g., school districts), as we shall soon see.

In weak-mayor governments, administrative boards or commissions exercise power independently of the mayor (who typically appoints members and can remove them). This arrangement serves to broaden the base of political participation. Indeed, city boards are often appointed with a keen eye on local power blocs. In San Francisco, for example, members of appointed boards reflect the city's ethnic and cultural pluralism. They are composed of a mix of African-Americans, whites, Latinos, Asian-Americans, single parents, labor unionists, real-estate brokers, gays and lesbians, environmentalists, and so forth.

Weak or strong, mayors often have little discretion over city money. In San Francisco, for example, the mayor controls only about 30 cents out of every budget dollar. The rest has to be spent on programs mandated by federal and state government, such as health care and jails.

## Hyperpluralism and Government by Bureaucrats

A weak-mayor form of government is attractive to many citizens because it can lead to government responsive to diverse interest groups. But does it lead to responsible government? No, say many political scientists. Frederick Wirt makes a strong case for the idea that its costs outweigh its benefits. Political scientist Wirt (1971:114) argues that the price paid for decentralized, fractioned power in a pluralistic city is an inability to formulate and implement long-range public policy:

When successful policy outcomes rest neces-sarily upon the agreement of so many disparate private groups and public authorities, the power of one component to block any action is magnified. Over time, consequently, only minor policy adjustments are possible.

According to Wirt, the result of so many disparate actors playing the political game is hyperpluralism. Having too many (*hyper*) different decision points and too many groups with veto power (*pluralism*) paralyzes public policymaking. The result, Wirt says, is non–decision making.

In the absence of strong executive leadership and the presence of disparate competing factions, who runs a heterogeneous U.S. city? According to Wirt, the bureaucrats take over. He claims that the result is a "government by clerks": long-staying, professional civil servants who were never elected and thus can't be recalled. They may be regulated by professional norms of service and efficiency, but they're not accountable to the citizenry. The growing strength of municipal unions further erodes city executives' power and authority. Max Weber (Chapter 10) predicted what some call the *bureaucratic phenomenon*—the rise and expansion of rational but fearsome bureaucratic administration and politics.

More than a generation ago, many studies of big-city politics found decisionmaking there hopelessly fractionated (e.g., Sayre and Kaufman, 1960). Today, some wonder if there are any solutions to unresponsive bureaucracies, proliferating and competing interest groups, weak control over public employees, and dwindling fiscal resources. The title of one study of city politics sums up this viewpoint: *The Ungovernable City* (Yates, 1977). But others disagree. Some, like Osborne and Gaebler (1992), argue that bureaucracies can become responsive and communities can be empowered if only the entrepreneurial spirit is introduced. And still others, as we shall see in the next chapter, have a different slant altogether. They claim that it doesn't matter if bureaucrats or bosses run the town; neither is accountable to the citizens, and neither has the interests of most citizens in mind. Among other things, what is needed, they say, is more citizen participation and grass-roots organizing.

*To conclude:* The formal structure of government limits leadership. Weak mayors have a hard time providing executive leadership and gathering resources to meet urban needs. Even strong mayors, who have more authority to meet some urban needs, can't control many key policy areas that have an impact on the quality of life in their cities. Nonetheless, mayors—weak or strong—bear the brunt of public dismay when trouble occurs. As New York City's former mayor, John V. Lindsay, once bemoaned: "the Board of Education and its empire [which I am not authorized to control] cannot continue to travel in its own orbit. . . . No matter how many asbestos walls are put between me and the Board of Education, at the end I get the blame if there's trouble" (in Hentoff, [1967] 1969:162).

Given their limited legal power, weak mayors must use informal powers to push through their programs. These include the power to persuade,

Box 12.1

## WHAT MAKES A MAYOR STRONG OR WEAK

### Legal Structure

**Strong**

1. Mayor–council plan, which grants the mayor the following powers in the city charter:
   a. A four-year term of office with possible reelection for many terms
   b. Power to appoint and remove city commissioners and/or department heads at will
   c. Power over the city budget (e.g., the right to submit an executive budget or have veto power over items in the budget)

**Weak**

1. Council–manager or commission form of government, with only a ceremonial role for the mayor
2. Mayor–council plan, in which the city charter limits the mayor's power in the following ways:
   a. A short term of office (e.g., two years)
   b. Commissioners and department heads not subject to the mayor's authority (e.g., commissioners appointed by the city council, agency heads protected by civil service)
   c. Little or no authority over budget matters

### Local Government Context

1. State constitution and/or general laws and/or city charter provisions do not significantly limit city authority
2. City performs many important local government functions

1. State constitution and/or general law and/or city charter provisions limit city authority significantly
2. Other layers of government (county, special districts, etc.) perform many important local government functions

### Personal Power and Influence

1. An effective political organization (e.g., a well-oiled political macine)
2. Strong support from powerful local interests, such as the financial/business community or labor

1. A weak or substantially nonexistent political organization
2. Lack of support from powerful local interests

the support of public opinion, and, in some cases, the influence that comes from controlling a well-oiled political machine. Box 12.1 outlines some factors that make a mayor weak or strong.

## THE CONTEXT OF LOCAL GOVERNMENT

We have hinted at one reason why mayors are unable to govern effectively: They can't control other units of government. Both strong and weak mayors operate in the context of a fragmented metropolis and a global economy.

### Fragmentation of the Metropolis

"God must have loved cities" because "[She or] He made so many of them." So comments a political scientist on the enormous number of local governments in the United States (Schultze, 1974:229). As Table 12.3 shows, in 1987 there were 19,200 municipalities alone and a total of 83,186 local government units in the nation. To further complicate matters, local government is organized in a crazy quilt pattern of separate and often overlapping types.

To unravel the intricacies of this crazy quilt, some basic vocabulary is necessary. **Municipality** is the U.S. Census Bureau's term for general-purpose units of local government. Cities are general-purpose governments—that is, they un-dertake a variety of functions and provide a range of services. Hence, by definition, cities are municipalities. Towns, townships, and boroughs are also municipalities. Other units of local government—separate from municipalities—include school districts, other special districts, and counties. *Fragmentation, proliferation,* and *Balkanization* are terms often used to refer to this pattern of local government.

This is the way the crazy quilt of local government is patterned within an MSA: Cities and other municipalities lie within the boundaries of a county. Within city boundaries (and often extending beyond them) are school districts and various other special districts that are independent of the city. Each unit of government—county, city, special district, school district—is a separate legal entity. This is important for analyzing how local government operates.

### Special Districts

**Special districts** are the most widespread type of local government, and their number keeps growing. As Table 12.3 shows, as of 1987, there were 29,532 special district governments, an increase of about 1,450 since 1982 (U.S. Bureau of the Census, 1992:278).

They are set up to serve either a single purpose (e.g., sewage treatment, housing-community development, hospital services, or fire protection) or several purposes, such as sewage and water provision.

**Table 12.3**  Number of Local Governments in the United States, 1942–1987

|  | *1942* | *1957\** | *1967* | *1977* | *1987* |
|---|---|---|---|---|---|
| Local governments | 155,067 | 102,341 | 81,248 | 79,862 | 83,186 |
| Country | 3,050 | 3,050 | 3,049 | 3,042 | 3,042 |
| Municipal | 16,220 | 17,215 | 18,048 | 18,862 | 19,200 |
| Township and town | 18,919 | 17,198 | 17,105 | 16,822 | 16,691 |
| School district | 108,579 | 50,454 | 21,782 | 15,174 | 14,721 |
| Special district | 8,299 | 14,424 | 21,264 | 25,962 | 29,532 |

*Adjusted to include units in Alaska and Hawaii, which adopted statehood in 1959.

SOURCE: Adapted from U.S. Bureau of the Census, *Statistical Abstract of the United States 1992,* 112th ed. (Washington, D.C.: Government Printing Office, 1992), Table 448, p. 278.

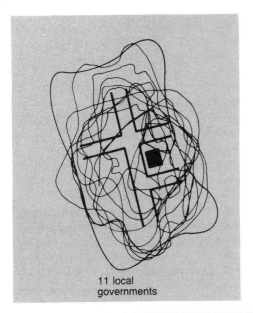

11 local
governments

**Fig. 12.4** OVERLAPPING SPECIAL DISTRICTS. The location of special district boundaries in one unincorporated portion of Portland, Oregon, 1967. (From John C. Bollens and Henry J. Schmandt, *The Metropolis,* 3rd ed. [New York: Harper & Row, 1975], p. 47. Based on information from the Portland Metropolitan Study Commission. Reprinted by permission of John C. Bollens)

Directors of special districts are not accountable to city or county government officials because special districts are totally separate legal entities. Their boundaries do not necessarily conform to those of any other local government unit. Often they overlap the boundaries of the city and each other.

The existence of independent, overlapping special districts can create problems for the coordination of public services. Figure 12.4 illustrates this problem. It shows an unincorporated area of Portland, Oregon, in which eleven separate special districts provide various services to area residents. None of the boundaries of these special districts are contiguous. Some residents live within the borders of one district but just outside the borders of another. Each of the eleven districts has its own governing body, which is total-

ly separate from all other local government units. Uncoordinated services can result if sewer district supervisors use Plan A for digging ditches while water district supervisors use Plan B for supplying water.

Many states have attempted to limit the proliferation of special districts and to consolidate existing ones. These efforts have met with only limited success.

Why are special districts so popular? The main reason is that special districts are separate from other local governments and thus are not subject to their debt limits. Special districts can issue bonds or borrow money after other local governments have reached the legal limits of their borrowing authority. For example, residents who want more sewers in a city that has already reached its debt limit might form an independent sewer district. The new special district could sell bonds to finance the sewer construction, unrestricted by the city debt limit. Also, districts can be drawn around a functional area, regardless of local government boundaries. A mosquito abatement district may cover the swampy part of three cities.

## Counties (Including Urban Counties)

Historically, the **county** has proved to be a very stable unit of government; its boundaries have generally remained unchanged for decades. For this reason, the county is used by the U.S. Census Bureau as the basic unit of the MSA.

In rural areas where there are no incorporated cities, county government acts as the general-purpose local government; typically, it regulates land use, licenses businesses, and provides police and fire protection. In urban areas, cities usually take over the basic general-purpose local government functions for their residents. In urban areas, counties serve as the general-purpose local government only for the unincorporated territory that lies within them. Counties also may provide some services to the residents of cities within their boundaries. For example, frequently the county operates libraries within both cities and unincorporated areas.

In recent times, a new spatial-demographic entity has emerged: the **urban county.** This term is used in various ways. It may refer to (1) a county that has assumed comprehensive authority over governmental functions, as in the case of Dade County, Florida (Miami's county); (2) any county with a large, dense population, giving it the characteristics of a city; or (3) a county that meets specified population size and legal power requirements to be eligible for certain federal funds.

Urban counties will probably become increasingly important. Recognizing this, some states have passed legislation that treats urban counties essentially as cities.

## The State's Role in Urban Affairs

Apart from their formal legal power, states exert power and authority over cities in many ways. For example, state programs operate within a city's boundaries, and cities may have little or no influence on these programs. Highway construction is illustrative. A state-funded highway can dramatically affect local land use, industrial location, and housing. Yet those cities through which it passes have no voice in determining its route.

The level of state involvement with urban issues varies widely. After the War on Poverty and other Great Society programs of the 1960s, statehouses were often bypassed by federal grants directly to city halls or neighborhood groups, thus decreasing state clout over their cities. However, some states (e.g., New Jersey) have taken an active role, creating institutions to deal with their cities.

*To conclude:* City governments are only one of several units of local government. Counties, school districts, and other special districts also exist, often performing citylike functions. In MSAs, there is a crazy quilt of fragmented and overlapping municipalities, counties, school districts, and other special districts. Some states also play a significant role in local affairs.

## Areawide Planning Efforts

In theory, the variety and vast array of decentralized local governments ensure citizens a democratic voice in matters that directly affect their lives. In practice, however, things are quite different.

For one thing, voters have little or no control over the most widespread of all local governments: the special district. Critics charge that supervisors of special districts often put special interests (particularly private business) or technical concerns above the public interest. Theodore W. Kheel, for one, argues that the Port Authority of New York and New Jersey (a multistate special district) is dominated by the interests of its corporate bondholders. In effect, Kheel says, the Port Authority serves the rich and is indifferent to the needs of people in the New York City area ([1969] 1971:443–449).

For another thing, many local issues, particularly land use and economic growth policies, have areawide effects. If City A permits a large chemical factory to locate there, nearby cities can be affected (by pollution, new transport patterns, etc.). But the affected cities have no say in the matter. Thus the crazy-quilt pattern of fragmented local government appears to give metropolitan residents the worst of both worlds: little democratic control and lack of coordinated policies.

Pushed largely by federal government requirements or incentives, most MSAs have established some kind of metropolitanwide planning organization. These organizations, called either a **council of governments (COG)** or an **areawide planning organization (APO),** are strictly voluntary and advisory. Local governments are not legally required to follow their recommendations. Consequently, COGs operate on good will. And sometimes good will runs smack into a fiscal crunch or seious political disagreement. The case of a large COG, the Association of Bay Area Governments (ABAG), is instructive. ABAG is the land-use planning agency for the nine-county San Francisco Bay Area, and by some accounts, it is "one of the Bay Area's most powerful lobbying groups" (Fimrite, 1993:A11). Besides conducting research and advising on water quality, and other matters, ABAG sets mandates for low-income housing. In 1992 and 1993, three cities, saying that they did not have the resources to comply with the housing guidelines, pulled out.

Do COGs represent the wave of the future for interlocal cooperation and areawide coordination? Not likely. To date, most have been little more than intergovernmental talk shows: Views are expressed, but nothing much happens—unless if the going gets rough. Then, cities and other local governments walk out.

## CHANGING GOVERNMENTAL STRUCTURES AND PATTERNS

### Broad Regional Government?

"We have outgrown our governments" (Osborne and Gaebler, 1992:246). That seems to be a popular opinion nowadays, except with conservatives, local officials—and voters.

Years ago, a leading population analyst forecast that by the year 2000, over 80 percent of the U.S. population would live in twenty-eight urban regions–concentrated, large, continuous zones of relatively high density. He thought that the present fragmentation of local government would be unable to handle these "huge webs of urbanization" (Pickard, 1977). He then asked: How can rational policies be achieved for entire urban regions that are politically fragmented, socially atomized, and economically complex? His answer: broad regional government.

Broad regional government may be a rational response to governmental fragmentation. However, it doesn't appear to be politically acceptable, at least in the United States. In Barcelona, Spain, a metropolitan government (made up of thirty-two mayors from a range of political parties) is responsible for planning, transport, and environmental services. But in the United States,

even regional agencies for one function—say, public transit—are suspect. The head of a Metropolitan Transportation Commission committee in the Bay Area thinks that "turf wars" stymie regional planning. He says that anyone who thinks politicians in Oakland, San Francisco, and the surrounding suburban cities will agree to unify the Bay Area's eighteen competing transit systems "is smoking marijuana" (in Demoro, 1985:4).

Neoconservatives raise another objection. Because they assume that small governments are more responsive to citizens' preferences than big, bureaucratic ones, they prefer fragmentation to centralized governments.

Political scientist Gregory R. Weiher (1991:195) holds a diametrically opposed view. He says that the present system of fragmented local government is *anti*-democratic. "The American model of democracy," he argues, "requires a citizenry in which social groups are not radically isolated from one another"; yet, "the system of urban jurisdictional boundaries" sponsors segregation of many kinds: "whites from blacks, lower income groups from the middle class, religious groups from one another." Thus, in his view, fragmentation is an instrument of antidemocracy.

At the present time, there are some strong regional agencies (e.g., Portland's Metropolitan Services District) and regional land-use planning organizations. There is even one umbrella-type agency that is essentially an areawide planning and coordinating agency: the Metropolitan Council of the Twin Cities, Minneapolis–St. Paul, area. It has an innovative tax-sharing formula whereby the region shares some of the tax revenue from new development (Bollens and Schmandt, 1982:373).

But there is no broad-based regional government in the United States. If broad regional government is such a hard sell, how will public services be delivered to metropolitan and megalopolitan residents? Most likely, by muddling through. Thus far, public services have been provided via a combination of traditional responses, minor adaptations, and innovative experiments.

## Traditional Responses and Minor Adaptations

On the more traditional side, residents of the urban fringe (unincorporated areas near a municipality that have urban service needs) are getting such urban services as police and fire protection in various ways: (1) by incorporation, thus creating a new municipality; (2) by contracting with the county or a nearby municipality for services; (3) by annexation; and (4) by forming special districts. Each of these techniques has its own problems and prospects.

**Incorporation** creates yet another local government, thereby adding to local fragmentation. Further, if its county is already financially strapped, the newly incorporated city can deprive the county of needed revenue. Contracting for services allows urban fringe residents to keep their highly valued rural environment, but at whose expense? Some observers feel that under contracting arrangements city residents pay more than their fair share because residents of unincorporated areas don't pay for large capital investments (jails, firehouses, etc.) or for training city employees.

The problem of coordinating special districts has already been noted. Recall also that the number of special districts has grown enormously since the 1950s, resulting in even more fragmentation of the metropolis.

**Annexation** is the only traditional response that doesn't lead to an increased number of local governments. Annexation results in political integration rather than metropolitan government. However, since it requires boundary changes, annexation is not feasible in many MSAs, where most land is already incorporated into municipalities.

To cope with disputes over annexation, incorporation, and special district formation, some states have set up boundary commissions. So far, they have helped somewhat to check the further proliferation of local governments, but they have had little success in reforming the existing crazy quilt of local governments in the metropolis.

## Innovative Experiments

On the more innovative side, the most ambitious proposals—broad regional government and a single, unified metropolitan government (called a *one-tier* or *one-level* government)—are just plans on a drawing board. But four models of structural change plus one entrepreneurial framework for delivering public services are currently in operation.

To date, the most ambitious effort at structural change in North America is Toronto, Canada's, federated or consolidated metropolitan government. Toronto established a "two-tier" **federation** in 1953. It consists of a single, areawide government as the first tier and the preexisting local governments as the second tier. The newly created metropolitanwide first tier, called the *Municipality of Metropolitan Toronto* or *Metro*, is governed by representatives from the preexisting governments: Toronto's municipal government plus twelve suburban governments. Metro has jurisdiction over the entire metropolitan area. It has power over many important urban functions: property assessment, water supply, sewage disposal, mass transit, health services, welfare, administration of justice, arterial roads, parks, public housing, redevelopment, and planning. Under Toronto's two-tier plan, some functions were retained by local governments while others were shared with Metro. For instance, Metro maintains reservoirs and pumping stations, but the second tier of local governments handles the distribution of water to their residents.

Short of federation, there is another model of structural change: the comprehensive urban county plan. Operating in Dade County (Miami), Florida, since 1957, a two-tier government gives the county government a powerful and integrating role over an area of 2,054 square miles and twenty-seven municipalities. Among its functions, the comprehensive urban county government is authorized to promote the entire area's economy, own and operate mass transit systems, construct expressways, provide uniform health

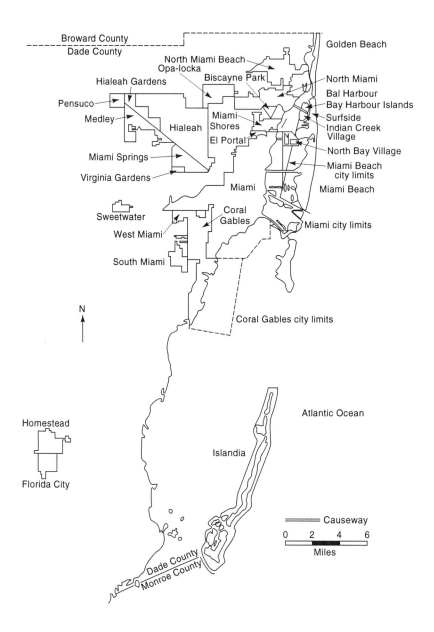

**Fig. 12.5** METROPOLITAN DADE COUNTY. In its early years, "Metro," the metropolitan government in Dade County, Florida, faced opposition, even "torment" (Bollens and Schmandt, 1982:328). It also faced a continuing struggle between the county and municipalities, the two levels of government. By the 1990s, however, residents of Dade County had turned their attention from government structure to less abstract issues, such as racial and ethnic tension, changing demographics, hurricane disaster relief, and high crime rates. (Metro-Dade County Planning Dept., 1994)

and welfare services, and maintain central records and communication for fire and police protection (Figure 12.5).

City–county consolidation is another technique. It is a one-government, not a two-tier, approach. Usually this type of governmental reorganization consists of the total or substantial merging of the county government with the largest city (or all municipalities) within its boundaries. Since World War II, there have been four major city–county consolidations: Baton Rouge–East Baton Rouge Parish (the parish is Louisiana's equivalent of the county) in 1947; Nashville–Davidson County, Tennessee (1962); Jacksonville–Duval County, Florida (1967); and Indianapolis–Marion County, Indiana (1969).

A more moderate type of institutional change is the formation of metropolitanwide special districts, either single or multipurpose in nature. The owner of the World Trade Center in New York City, the Port Authority of New York and New Jersey, is such a special district, one that crosses state as well as municipal boundaries.

## Privatization of Public Services

Government's contracting out to private firms is neither new nor experimental. Wells Fargo Bank horseback riders, known as the Pony Express, delivered the mail west of the Mississippi on contract to the U.S. government. More recently, milions of private employees have worked in defense-connected industries on government contracts.

What is new at the local level is the growth and range of privatization (also called *privatism*). In the Reagan era, many communities faced tax revolts, cutbacks in federal funds, shrinking tax collections due to economic recession, and fiscal austerity—but continuing demands for services —all at the same time! Localities turned to "entrepreneurial government" as a way to meet the challenges, contracting with private firms for services or entering partnerships with businesses. At least seventy-five communities in fifteen states, mainly new suburbs and cities hard pressed for revenue, contracted with private

companies to provide protection against fire. In Philadelphia, private companies or nonprofit organizations operate golf courses, homeless shelters, parking enforcement, vehicle repair, and convention centers. Phoenix, Arizona, turned over building and grounds maintenance, building security, janitorial services, landfill operations, bus system operation, garbage collection, street maintenence, and street sweeping to private enterprise. Chelsea, Massachusetts, contracted with Boston University to run its public-school system; school districts in many communities received free TV equipment and news broadcasts from Whittle Communications in exchange for getting a captive audience for their commercials. Newark, New Jersey, reduced its payroll from 10,000 to 4,000 between 1980 and 1988 by turning over programs dealing with AIDS and homelessness to the private sector. Other cities sold museums to private businesses under leaseback arrangements or contracted out the running of jails and prisons.

The story of Ecorse, Michigan, is instructive. In the 1950s, this small industrial town downriver from Detroit boomed. However, "by the early 1980s the ripple effect from plant closings, cutbacks and concessions threatened to swamp Downriver" communities, including Ecorse (Darden, Hill, Thomas, and Thomas, 1987:42). By 1986, its fortunes sank. Ecorse became the first U.S. city to go into receivership. The court told an expert on city finance to close Ecorse's gap between revenue and expenditures. What the expert did was to privatize. He contracted out garbage pickups, public works, animal control, and other services. Within five years, the $6 million city deficit had been turned into a $100,000 surplus (Marshall, 1991:1).

Privatization boosters include President Clinton and many so-called New Democrats. This suggests that in one generation, Americans had changed their expectations of government. In 1968, Robert Kennedy ran for president on a liberal platform, arguing that government was an instrument for the public good. In 1992, the three major candidates for president—Republican, Democrat, and United We Stand—seemed to share the belief that government was the enemy.

## The Report Card

Are these innovations success stories or not? Opinions differ widely. Most observers think that Toronto's two-tier government has made substantial strides toward rational policymaking for the metropolis. Scholars give a C or C+ to Dade County's comprehensive urban county plan. One assessment points to considerable instability in the relationship between the urban county government and preexisting municipal governments, as well as continuing fiscal and administrative problems. Two political scientists conclude that the Dade County two-tier arrangement suffers from continuing rivalry between the county and cities fror the allegiance and control of their citizenry (Bollens and Schmandt, 1982: 331). Meanwhile, observers note that government structure is not a burning issue for Dade Countians; they are much more interested in less abstract issues such as jobs, crime, and racial-ethnic tension.

City–county consolidations face great opposition, usually from outlying residents, who must approve the consolidation by popular vote, but sometimes from central city residents, who also must approve the change. As for the most moderate structural reform, the metropolitanwide special district, it has made significant gains in dealing with pressing metropolitan needs but is limited to one or a few functions. Further, like special districts that are not metropolitanwide, it is criticized for its nonaccountability to the people it serves.

Privatization has vocal supporters—and detractors. Boosters praise its cost savings, efficiency, and accountability. David Osborne, a member of President Bill Clinton's transition team, and Ted Gaebler, a former city manager, are its best-known supporters. They claim that privatization, one piece of their bigger plan for "reinventing government," can help produce caring as well as efficient government.

Detractors disagree for a host of reasons. Neoconservative thinkers don't want to *re*invent government; they seek to *dis*invent government. James Q. Wilson, for example, wants less bureaucracy and says, "You can have less bureau-

cracy only if you have less government" (in Winnick, 1993:A17). Some liberal critics call contracting out a union-busting strategy designed to weaken or destroy public employee unions by wringing concessions from them. Further, they note, governments are a major employer of so-called minorities; shrinking government jobs has a disproportionately negative impact on people of color and women. Others fear that if public schools and prisons are turned over to for-profit agencies, there will be less accountability to all citizens and less, not more, choice and opportunity for those at the bottom of the social ladder. Critics warn that private prisons and private jails threaten civil rights, leaving prisoners with less protection against brutality and arbitrary discipline (Lekachman, 1987) and not guaranteeing "customers" the rights of citizens. In addition, they oppose mixing public purpose with private business. They object to forcing students to listen to TV commercials in class in exchange for the provision of TV equipment and news broadcasts. And they cite instances where private fire departments left nonsubscribers' homes burning while fighting fires at subscribers' homes (Tolchin, 1985:13). Others warn of opportunities for a new kind of bossism, whereby the contract bidding process could degenerate into "pinstripe patronage" (Bertuol in Marshall, 1992). Finally, radical scholars and activists wonder who wins the most under privatization. A group of English and U.S. public policy researchers say that "the profit motive may be a powerful incentive, but it is not easily harnessed to achieve publicly defined policy objectives" (Barnekov, Boyle, and Rich, 1989:227); they conclude that the payoffs of privatization rarely trickle down to economically depressed communities but instead serve narrow private interests. Harvard scholar Elaine Bernard (1993) goes further; she says that privatism is part of a conscious effort by business to decrease public expectations of government and thereby limit more progressive options.

On balance, it appears that the current crazy quilt of local government is being patched up with bits and pieces. There is no whole new cloth.

Why have efforts to reform local government structure met with so little success? First, many interest groups correctly perceive that major structural changes would not be in their narrowly defined self-interest. Suburbanites, for example, tend to oppose any reform that links their future to the fiscal and political problems of their nearby city. African-American and Latino leaders in big cities often oppose metropolitanwide government because they could lose their recently won power in some central cities. Northern Democrats tend to resist metropolitanwide government because Republicans form a numerical majority in the MSA as a whole but not in the central city. Second, structural reform is hard to sell to voters. By contrast, metropolitanwide special districts can be established either without a popular vote or by state law requiring a popular majority in the entire area. Federation, comprehensive urban counties, and city–county consolidations usually require popular majorities in all of the municipalities involved, a very difficult consensus to obtain.

*To conclude:* Scholars don't agree on how metropolitan politics should be structured. One group, the centralists or consolidationists, claims that there are too many local governmental units to provide efficient, effective, and responsible government. Their solutions are centralized metropolitan or even broad regional government. Another group holds that government is not decentralized enough to provide responsive government. Their solutions are community control or neighborhood government. Finally, still another group thinks that the present system works well and is highly desirable because it allows citizens to maximize their choices in the consumption of public goods (e.g., through choice in housing location). This group has no proposed solutions because it doesn't define fragmentation as a problem.

Whatever scholars propose about metropolitan politics, citizens dispose in the end. And proposed reforms of any sort inspire yawns or fear —fear of more bureaucracy, more expense, less control, or changes in the balance of local power. Thus, the chances of reshaping local government seem dim.

## THE FEDERAL ROLE IN URBAN AFFAIRS

Even without structural reorganization, local government priorities and programs have changed dramatically since the New Deal. Corporate business decisions had significant impacts on localities (e.g., where to locate a new office, where to invest or disinvest), and they will be discussed in Chapters 14 and 15. Here, let's focus on another important external agent of change: the federal government. Federal officials have pushed (critics say forced) cities to rethink their programs with a variety of incentives, penalties, and mandated duties.

We now turn to a brief history of federal expansion in local life. It is divided into two eras: 1930s to 1950s and 1960s to 1992.

### Expansion of Federal Involvement in U.S. Life, 1930s–1950s

Since the 1930s, the federal government has been playing a larger role in U.S. life. The expansion of federal involvement in the economic and social life of the country has significantly affected metropolitan politics, both directly and indirectly. This means that the question "Who runs this town?" can't be answered without reference to the federal government.

It was during the Great Depression of the 1930s that the role of the federal government in American life began to grow. Amid the bread lines and competing ideologies of the time (ranging from radical proposals to redistribute wealth and power, technocratic manifestos to let scientists and engineers run government, and hate campaigns blaming African-Americans and Jews for economic distress, to demagogic appeals for fascist-type rule), President Franklin D. Roosevelt's New Deal administration moved decisively to maintain social order and economic security. (Radical critics say that it worked to *save* capitalism; conservative critics, to *end* capitalism.) Millions of Americans, assumed to be "temporarily poor" during the Depression, were provided some form of social security through New

Deal programs. Many functions once handled privately (by family, charities, etc.) or not at all were assumed by the federal government.

According to urban historian Richard C. Wade, the growth of federal power under the New Deal "developed out of the intractability of 25 percent unemployment, a stagnating economy and the desperation of millions" (1982: 21). New Deal programs did not take over state and local rights; "those governments simply had no capacity to meet even the most immediate relief needs, much less to plan for the future." The New Deal added programs that provided a safety net, such as a minimum wage, unemployment insurance, and Social Security. It also offered major assistance to *middle*-class citizens via such programs as the Federal Housing Administration's below-market-rate mortagages and the Federal Deposit Insurance Corporation, guaranteeing modest bank savings.

Subsequently, during World War II and after, the role of the federal government kept growing. (As might be predicted, so did the role of private interests that sought some of the growing state's resources.) Most citizens accepted the centralized system in Washington, D.C., and new programs served new needs, such as the GI Bill of Rights for returning service personnel. Meanwhile, the "temporarily poor" didn't disappear, and the national interest of a world power was translated into the need for defense industries located throughout the country and efficient transport links. Soon federal funds flowed into and around the nation's small towns as well as big cities. At the same time, modern technology and corporate business organization expanded significantly, and the Springdales of the nation—small towns and hamlets—found themselves in the midst of a mass society (Vidich and Bensman, [1958] 1968). As a result, decisions made in faraway federal agencies and corporate headquarters affected the lives of Americans in cities and rural areas, whether they realized it or not.

Federal policies don't have to be labeled "urban" to affect urban life. Indeed, many federal programs not so designated have changed the fabric of the metropolis as much as, or more than, funds earmarked for cities. Let's take a look at

two such post–World War II programs: housing and transportation.

## How Federal Policy Affected Postwar Housing and Transportation

*Housing*  Beginning with the New Deal, the federal government has pursued policies intended to strengthen financial institutions that provide mortgage money for housing, particularly single-family, detached houses. For instance, the Federal Housing Administration (FHA) was created in the midst of the Depression, when millions of homeowners were defaulting on mortgage payments because they were out of work, housing construction was at a virtual standstill, and banks were going bankrupt. The FHA was established to provide mortgage insurance to protect lenders (banks) against the risk of default on long-term, low-down-payment mortgage loans. The FHA contributed to a gradual recovery of the home finance industry during the 1930s, and then it spurred the massive post–World War II suburban housing boom. Other federal housing credit institutions (e.g., the Federal National Mortgage Association, called Fannie Mae) helped to create a national secondary mortgage market so that housing construction funds can flow freely into growth areas.

What impact did these federal housing policies have on cities and suburbs? An enormous impact. By stimulating suburban growth, federal programs underwrote the exodus of white middle-class residents from central cities. In so doing, they helped to cement metropolitanwide housing patterns of economic and racial segregation.

*Transportation*  Similarly, the billions of dollars poured into highway construction by Congress after World War II had a broad impact on the metropolis. The new interstate highway system, funded 90 percent with federal money, allowed commercial and industrial enterprises to move out of their central city locations and relocate in the suburbs. These location decisions by private business contributed to the erosion of the central city's tax base and to its financial stagnation.

*To conclude:* Whether intended or not, national policies not specifically urban have helped to change the shape and character of cities since World War II. In particular, federal policies opened up the suburbs, spurred regional growth in Sunbelt cities where new defense-related industries were generously supported, and provided the infrastructure (roads, airports) for private business to serve a national and global mass market. Cities, legal creatures of the state, increasingly became economically and socially tied to the national and international political economy.

## From Federalism to the New Federalism, 1960s–1992

In the 1960s, the number of federal programs aimed specifically at the metropolis rose dramatically. So did funding levels. Not surprisingly, the size and number of federal agencies that implement urban-oriented programs followed suit.

A cabinet-level agency, the Department of Housing and Urban Development (HUD), was established by the administration of President Lyndon B. Johnson in 1965 specifically to address urban needs. A year later, the Department of Transportation (DOT) was set up, increasing the national government's already active role in financing urban transit. Other cabinet-level departments expanded their urban programs as part of LBJ's Great Society. New programs, including the controversial War on Poverty, channeled funds directly to cities or urban community groups.

These were the days of Head Start, Job Corps, Vista, Model Cities, Foster Grandparents, Legal Services, Community Action, and so on. To liberals, these Great Society programs represented a step in the right direction: government intervention to provide equal opportunity for all citizens. To radicals, these programs represented govern-

ment's attempt to keep cities calm and coopt the poor by throwing out a few crumbs instead of attacking the capitalist structures that put people in poverty. To conservatives, these programs represented "a ragbag."

When President Richard M. Nixon started his second term in 1972, he proposed a New Federalism. He promised to take powers away from the federal government and give authority and flexibility to the state and local governments. The showpiece of Nixon's New Federalism was **general revenue sharing,** a program that came with few strings. Funds could be used to finance nearly any local government's program. (Before the fifteen-year revenue sharing program ended in 1987, $85 billion was distributed to 39,000 cities and towns, where the money was spent to purchase a variety of products and services, from flowers to fire trucks.)

President Nixon and his successor, Gerald Ford, did not destroy LBJ's Great Society, but they did change its course. While keeping up the level of federal spending for local programs, they redirected funds away from "the Democratic big-city heartland in the Northeast toward the urban South and West" (Davis, 1993:15).

The numbers tell the story of federal expansion. In one decade—1969 to 1979—federal outlays to state and local governments quadrupled to $85 billion, much of it being spent in cities (U.S. OMB, 1978:175). In percentage terms, cities' dependence on federal aid for their general revenue grew from 4 percent to 14 percent from 1965 to 1980. Big cities such as New York, Chicago, and Los Angeles depended on the federal government for nearly 17 percent of their general revenue (Burchell, Carr, Florida, and Németh, 1984:169).

Then, the Reagan–Bush "revolution" changed all that. President Ronald Reagan introduced *his* New Federalism in his 1981 State of the Union Message. Underpinned by the conservative ideas of Milton Friedman, Reagan's New Federalism decentralized many federal activities to states and local governments, assuring that, in Reagan's words, "these programs will be more responsive to both the people they are meant to help and the people who pay for them."

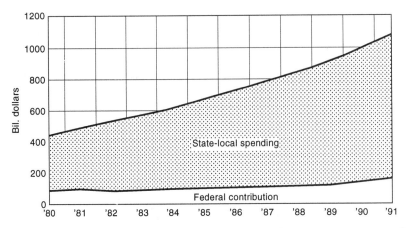

**Fig. 12.6**  THE FALLING FEDERAL CONTRIBUTION TO STATE AND LOCAL SPENDING, 1980–1991. (U.S. Bureau of the Census, *Statistical Abstract of the United States 1982–1983* [Washington, D.C.: Government Printing Office, 1983])

***New Tasks, Less Money***  However, instead of sustaining the level of federal funds flowing to state and cities, the Reagan and Bush administrations slashed the funding of federally financed, locally administered programs. Many federal grants-in-aid for education, public works, mass transit, and housing were cut or cut out. From 1980 to 1992, federal dollars spent on U.S. cities declined by 59 percent (Harpers Index, 1992:9). As one observer put it, "Washington has given the states new tasks but less money" (Tolchin, 1990:1). As Figure 12.6 shows, state and local spending increased while the federal contribution decreased during the Reagan–Bush years.

(By early 1995, the situation started to change. A Republican-led Congress joined many governors and mayors in a rebellion against "unfunded federal mandates": programs or regulations imposed by the federal government that require local and state governments to pay the costs of compliance out of their own pockets. Governors and mayors had long complained that unfunded federal mandates—in categories ranging from transportation, Medicare, and the environment to dog-kennel conditions—were costly burdens. For instance, in 1992 the state of

Ohio spent over $260 million for federally mandated programs, and New York City spent about $475 million of its own revenue to comply with the Clean Water Act, the Clear Air Act, and five other federal laws. Some governors had tried to reverse the trend. California's governor, for one, asked the federal government to contribute $2.3 billion to the state's bills for the cost of illegal immigrants. At the same time, consumer advocates and environmentalists warned that the public welfare and the natural environment would suffer if local officials could disregard state and national regulations.)

Cutbacks in federal aid were accompanied by stagflation, high interest rates, and bad economic times. This combination of hard times and budget cuts left localities tax-starved and defunded. More than half of the state and city governments in the United States faced "serious financial shortfalls" by 1990 (Hinds with Eckholm, 1990:1). Urbanist George Sternlieb of Rutgers University opined that "we don't have New Federalism, we have New Feudalism, where every community fends for itself with a hodgepodge of responsibilities and taxing powers" (in Hinds and Eckholm, 1990:A11). Worst-case budget scenarios became commonplace. For example, hundreds of patients and doctors jammed into San Francisco's City Hall to complain that more cuts to health clinics would endanger lives. The next day, hundreds of children and parents went to City Hall to complain that more library cuts would endanger the literacy of the next generation. Competition for scarce funds between libraries and health clinics was so fierce that one advocate for health care drove home his cause like this: "Dead people can't read books" (in Sandalow, 1993:1).

Severe cutting, even gutting, of cities' social programs raised critical voices to a fever pitch. Liberal reporter Bob Scheer called local government the "garbage can of American politics," left to pick up the pieces of "problems that the federal and state governments have failed to adequately deal with" (e.g., crime, drugs, disoriented vets) while "their tax base is pared to the bone" (1993:1).

*To conclude:* Starting with the New Deal, the federal government has been heavily involved in a wide range of urban programs, from child nutrition and law enforcement to community development. Cities lobby Congress intensely for programs through both nationwide organizations and individual lobbyists (Farkas, 1971). Political scientist John Mollenkopf (1983) points out in his study of urban legislation from 1933 to 1980 that when Republicans have national control, they redirect money away from central cities to the suburbs and newer metropolitan areas of the Sunbelt. Further, Republicans have restructured intergovernmental aid—by channeling it through states and block grants, for instance—to ensure that voters in central cities had the least possible influence. Thus the balance between city and suburban political power started shifting mightily to the suburbs in 1972 with Nixon's general revenue sharing. By 1992, more than one-half of U.S. cities were saddled with major service burdens and limited options. In a time of economic decline, they faced decreased federal and state aid, state prohibitions against raising local taxes, and widespread suburban antiurbanism. No major presidential candidate in 1992—Republican,

Democrat, or United We Stand—addressed these issues. This neglect of urban issues would not surprise urban historian Richard C. Wade. Ten years earlier, he noted that the country's political and social power had been permanently reallocated, completing the "suburban captivity of American politics" (1982:21).

## THE QUESTION RECONSIDERED: WHO RUNS THIS TOWN?

Federal regulations, state laws, areawide planning suggestions, special district decisions, county legislation, neighborhood requests. This list suggests that cities are not masters of their own fate. Instead, they are just one layer of government operating within a web of government—some call it a marble cake—of overlapping and intersecting layers.

To attain one's political goals, knowledge of the formal structures of government is essential. Knowing who's in charge in this governmental maze—who to blame, where to go for an authorization, where to protest a decision—is the first step in getting something done in city politics.

Here is a case study of one citizens' group that successfully worked its way through the maze of political structures. It highlights the necessity of appreciating the complexities of government's formal organization. It also shows that any meaningful response to the question "Who runs this town?" must take into account the web of government reaching from Washington, D.C., to the neighborhood day-care center.

### Case Study: What Bananas Learned About the Formal Structure of Government

The sign over a small building in Berkeley, California, reads BANANAS. No fruit is for sale there. Instead, on the front porch lie ice-cream containers, fabric remnants, and wood scraps, all ingredients for children's play projects.

Inside the building, organized chaos prevails.

**Fig. 12.7** BANANAS. This Berkeley, California, group of women learned their way around governmental structures. After years of hard work, they got what they wanted. (Cathy Cade)

A dozen women are answering phones and giving information about day care as actively as stockbrokers tell their clients about hot prospects. Parents and children stream into and out of the information area. A social service worker answers the "Warm Line," a precrisis counseling service for parents with day-care needs. What's going on here? The name says it all: Bananas, a multipurpose community service, helps to prevent parents from "going bananas" by providing various kinds of assistance with their preschool children.

Bananas didn't happen overnight. It grew out of years of frustration, organizing, and political struggle. The program director had gained some prior political experience during her fight to organize an employees' union on the University of California–Berkeley campus. Staff members learned by personal experience. Their first lesson was how to deal with and through governmental structures. To a significant degree, Bananas exists today because it learned this lesson.

In 1972, a small group of women—Bananas—became concerned that Berkeley had no place where parents could get information to help to set up play groups for preschool children. This nonhierarchically structured group had no money or community support, but they did have energy and commitment to their cause. They began to organize information assistance to parents, children, and day-care providers. After four years of hard work, they began to deal with city officials, trying to get government support for their activities.

In the process, they discovered whom to approach ("know-who") to get their project moving. Here are some of the lessons they learned.

1. *Find out who makes the decisions in city government.* Berkeley has a council–manager form of government. The city manager has the final word under this system, and negotiations for funding were carried on directly with him. Bananas didn't deal with the mayor. The specific budget recommendation ($18,477 in 1978) came from the city manager, since his office prepares the city budget.

2. *Find out what the city is authorized to fund.* There is no prohibition in Berkeley against using taxpayers' money for day-care activities. If there were, Bananas would have had to seek funding elsewhere.

3. *Find out what government agencies have an interest in the activity (and how they relate to city government).* Berkeley, like other towns, exists in a web of governments. Bananas had to learn the structure regarding child care. At the level closest to home is the Berkeley Unified School District, a special district run by an elected school board. The board, which is not accountable to city government, was often in disagreement with city officials. Since the school district provides child care for about 1,000 preschool children in the schools, it is an interested party in regard to other day-care activities in the community. Bananas dealt with the school board, not the Berkeley City Council, to coordinate information and referral activities.

Bananas also dealt with another interested party: the Berkeley Parks and Recreation Department. This city department administered a voucher system, paying low-income and working mothers a stipend for day care. Bananas staff members worked with the Parks and Recreation Department on a daily basis to refer voucher recipients to appropriate day-care centers.

Yet another interested party was the county. Alameda County, in which Berkeley is located, was operating day-care-related programs. The county's Social Services Department administered a federal program giving child-care vouchers to eligible recipients. When Bananas felt that the county was not taking full advantage of the voucher program, they pressed for wider benefits. To accomplish this, they went to the County Board of Supervisors, not the Berkeley City Council.

Bananas also dealt with a state-mandated regional center for child care, a clearinghouse agency for so-called special-needs children. To provide clear guidance to parents, Bananas had to go to this regional planning organization for information.

Then there is the state of California. It, too, is involved in child care. The state subsidizes certain types of day care for children with special needs. Bananas learned about the direct aid the state could provide to their clients.

Indirectly, through the county programs, Bananas was involved with federal funding. They also found out that the then Department of Health, Education and Welfare (now two cabinet-level departments, Health and Human Services and Education) provided direct funding to a few special day-care operations.

So, who runs this town? Bananas moved through the governmental maze to find out. At the level of formal structure, they discovered—often the hard way—that power and authority in their area of concern, child care, were shared by different layers of government and several city bureaucracies.

Eventually, Bananas got what they wanted, but not before they learned how informal networks of power operate. That is a theme we pick up in Chapters 13 and 14.

## ANOTHER LOOK

Citizens and scholars agree that the role of government at all levels has increased dramatically during their lifetimes. They disagree—sometimes violently—on whether this is desirable, necessary, or inevitable in mass society.

Concerning local government, American traditions have favored fragmented authority and power. While many political scientists (particularly liberals) describe the current crazy quilt of local government as irrational and inefficient, voters have not supported major structural change. Particularly in gloomy economic times, voters have turned their attention elsewhere: how to get more or the same (services) for less (taxes)—at the same time. Some hope that contracting out of public services will be an answer to the tax crunch, but critics think that privatization is frought with possibilities for inequity, corruption, and even a new sort of bossism.

Meanwhile, observers wonder if local governments—whatever their structure—matter much in a global society. To public choice theorists (e.g., Tiebout, 1956; Peterson, 1981), locality does remain important because people choose a particular place to live so that they can choose among bundles of services. But others say that people's residential choice is not dictated by such market logic. Furthermore, critics argue that local politics can no longer meet the burdens citizens place upon it: "Capital flight, industrial restructuring, fiscal crises, the powers of higher levels of government, and the autonomy of bureaucrats" combine to hem in local governments and render them powerless to manage the quality of community life (Gottdiener, 1987:21).

Perhaps, but at the same time there are local officials and ordinary citizens who reject powerlessness. Some practice spirited acts of nonviolent resistance by taking responsibility for their fellow beings and a small piece of the sky. Others, using the rhetoric of populist rebellion, form private armies and stockpile weapons against what they fear or hate: faraway, big government and urbanism as a way of life. Between these two reactions to powerlessness lies a chasm of difference—and direction. In my view, one looks backward to the values of a (real or romanticized) frontier past and the other accepts (for better and worse) the urban present and looks forward to the urban future.

More than a generation ago, two social scientists predicted that there would be an enduring battle between these two orientations. In *Small Town in Mass Society* ([1958] 1968), Arthur J. Vidich and Joseph Bensman observed that some small farmers and rural town dwellers resist "perhaps irreversible" trends toward *Gesellschaft* values. They cautioned that the defeat of ruralism in the United States could lead to a populist backlash based on rural hostility and defensiveness:

Populist democracy [identified with grass-roots democracy and "Americanism"] may become the basis for new social movements which could subvert the foundations of the present by holding to romanticized images of the past. An organized nativistic movement based partly on a xenophobic isolationism could shelter . . . defensive populists [and] a variety of other groups whose resentments are less crystallized but which could find a focus in some form of nativism. ([1958] 1968:346)

This populism had its origins in an earlier democratic ideology but, as Vidich and Bensman warned, it could go sour and become nativistic, antidemocratic, and quasi-totalitarian (346).

If some accommodation is not worked out between self-defined populist patriots who uphold "traditional" values and modernists who uphold urban values of heterogeneity, tolerance, and cosmopolitanism, we can predict that power—not authority—will prevail. Perhaps that is why Vidich and Bensman ended their community study with a plea to avoid a direct confrontation between the opposing orientations.

## KEY TERMS

**Annexation**  The addition of territory to a unit of government. Annexation usually involves a city's adding adjacent land to meet the problems of metropolitan expansion.

**Areawide planning organization (APO).**  See **Council of governments.**

**Authority**  Power used in such a way that people see it as legitimate.

**Charter**  The basic law of a local governmental unit that defines its powers, responsibilities, and organization. State constitutional or statutory provisions specify the conditions under which charters will be granted.

**Charter city**  A city whose powers are defined by a charter from the state. Contrast **general law city.**

**City council**  The policymaking and, in some instances, administrative board of a city. City councils are typically unicameral bodies.

**City manager**  A professional administrator, appointed by the city council, in a council–manager form of government.

**Commission form of government**  A form of city government in which both legislative and executive powers are exercised by commissioners. Not to be confused with a city commission. Features include (1) the concentration of legislative and executive power in a small group of commissioners elected at large on a nonpartisan ballot; (2) the collective responsibility of the commission to pass ordinances and control city finances; (3) the individual responsibility of each commissioner to head a city department; and (4) the selection of a mayor from among the commissioners, effectively reducing that office to one of largely ceremonial functions.

**Council–manager form of government**  A form of city government in which the city council appoints a professional administrator, the city manager, to act as the chief executive. With variations from city to city, the essentials of this plan are (1) a small council of five or seven members elected at large on a nonpartisan ballot, with power to make policy and hire and fire the manager; (2) a professionally trained manager, with authority to hire and fire subordinates, who is responsible to the council for efficient administration of the city; and (3) a mayor chosen separately or from within the council, but with no executive functions.

**Council of governments (COG)**  A voluntary organization of municipalities and counties concerned with areawide problems in a metropolitan area.

**County**  A major local government subdivision of the state. Counties may perform a variety of local government functions, including provision of welfare and social services, administration of libraries, and repair and maintenance of roads. Counties are typically governed by boards of supervisors or county commissioners. In rural areas, counties usually act as the general-purpose local government. In urban areas, they act as the general-purpose government for unincorporated territory and provide some services to residents of both unincorporated and incorporated areas within them.

**Dillon's rule**  A rule enunciated by Iowa Judge John F. Dillon, a nineteenth-century authority on municipal corporations, stating that a municipal corporation (such as a city) can exercise only those powers expressly granted to it by state law, those necessarily implied by the granted powers, and those essential for the purposes of the organization. If any doubt exists, it is to be resolved against the local unit in favor of the state.

**Federation**  An approach to municipal governmental reorganization that assigns areawide functions to an areawide or metropolitan government and leaves local functions to existing municipalities. Example: Toronto's Metro government.

**General law city**  A city created pursuant to the general law of the state in which it is located rather than under a charter.

**General revenue sharing**  An approach to the transfer of federal funds to lower levels of government—states and general-purpose local governments. Under general revenue sharing, states and local governments may use federal monies as they decide; there are no strings attached. This contrasts with program-related monies.

**Home rule**  Power vested in a local government, such as a city, to craft or change its charter and manage its own affairs, subject to the state constitution and the general law of the state. Under home rule, state legislative interference in local affairs is limited.

**Hyperpluralism**  The belief of some political scientists that city governments suffer from too many (hyper) private groups and public authorities playing the political game, which results in the paralysis of urban policymaking and the consequent bureaucratic takeover of political functions.

**Incorporation**  The formation of a new city from previously unincorporated territory. State law specifies how new cities are to be incorporated.

**Mayor**   The titular head of city government. The degree of a mayor's legal authority varies. In mayor–council governments, there are strong and weak mayors. In council–manager governments, the city manager runs the city's day-to-day affairs.

**Mayor–council form of government**   A form of city government in which the mayor is elected to serve as the executive officer of the city and an elected council serves as the legislative body.

**Municipality**   The U.S. Census Bureau's term for general-purpose units of local government other than counties. Municipalities include cities, towns and townships, and boroughs.

**Reapportionment**   Redrawing of legislative district lines so that representation in elected government bodies is proportional to the actual population. In 1962 the U.S. Supreme Court ruled in *Baker* v. *Carr* that representation had to be on a one person, one vote basis.

**Special district**   An independent unit of local government established to provide one or more limited functions, such as water. Special districts are usually created to meet problems that transcend local government boundaries or to bypass taxation and debt restrictions imposed upon local units of government by state law.

**Urban county**   (1) A county with responsibility for providing urban services for incorporated or unincorporated areas within its borders, or (2) a county where there is a substantial and densely settled population, giving it the character of a city, or (3) a county that meets specific criteria enabling it to receive certain federal funds.

## PROJECTS

1. **City government**. Determine the legal structure of the city in which you live or that of one nearby. Is it a general law or a charter city? If a charter city, is it a home rule charter city? Next, determine the form of the city government: mayor–council, council–manager, or commis-

sion. What are the major commissions, boards, departments, and agencies of the city?

2. **Local government context**. Examine the various layers of government, of which your city (or a nearby one) is just one. For instance, what kind and how many special districts lie within the city? What are significant state and federal involvements in the city? How have cutbacks at the federal and / or state levels in the past decade affected local services?

3. **Privatization**. If a nearby city has turned over public services to private contractors, analyze the impacts. Has privatization been cost-effective and efficient? Are customers happy with the service providers? Are there complaints, and if so, what kinds?

## SUGGESTIONS FOR FURTHER LEARNING

Neoconservatives Edward Banfield and James Q. Wilson's classic on the topic, *City Politics* (New York: Vintage, 1963), is dated, but it contains a clear and readable explanation of state–city relations and formal city structure. M. Gottdiener's *The Decline of Urban Politics: Political Theory and the Crisis of the Local State* (Newbury Park, Calif.: Sage, 1987) argues against neoconservative definitions and explanations.

In *The Fractured Metropolis: Political Fragmentation and Metropolitan Segregation* (Albany: State University of New York Press, 1991), Gregory R. Weiher argues that local government is far from democratic. In his view, it serves mainly parochial interests and is meant to avoid diversity in order to protect local advantage. He says that "the creation of local government in a great many cases is not a manifestation of a desire by citizens to be closer to or more involved in the democratic life of their society, but, on the contrary, a sign that they wish to blunt, deflect, and isolate themselves from democratic processes. The creation of local government is, in fact, an act of anti-government" (184).

For a theory of national state–city relations in Western societies, see Ted Robert Gurr and Desmond S. King, *The State and the City* (Chicago: University of Chicago Press, 1987). In their conclusion, "Futures for Post-Industrial Cities," the politicial scientists assert that "the state and city have become so interdependent that national officials who try to extricate government from responsibility for cities do so at great cost to the cities aned great poltiical risk to the state and their own administrations" (207–208).

What role should the federal government play in the economy? Accounts differ, mainly on ideological grounds. For a spirited defense of the idea that the federal government should "take a more creative part in our economy" in order to put "the country back on the road to real economic growth," see Felix Rohatyn, "What the Government Should Do," *New York Review of Books*, June 25, 1992, pp. 26–27. Liberal banker Rohatyn counsels that "both private business and local government will need [the federal government's] active help to carry out the investment and development that should be understaken if we are to have economic growth and social cohesiveness at home and be competitive internationally." For a conservative view, see E. S. Savas, former Assistant Secretary at HUD during the early Reagan years, *Privatizing the Public Sector: How to Shrink Government* (Chatham, N.J.: Chatham House, 1982).

What do city managers do? What are the values of city management? For a look at the history and practice of the council-manager form of government, see H. George Frederickson, ed., *Ideal and Practice in Council–Manager Government* (Washington, D.C.: International City Management Association, 1989).

In *Intergovernmental Relations in the American State: The Johnson Presidency* (Austin: University of Texas Press, 1989), David M. Welborn and Jesse Burkhead identity shifts in federal–state–local relationships since the nation's beginnings. They describe the nationalization of U.S. politics, whereby states play a subordinate role.

The National League of Cities, established in 1924 by and for reform-minded state municipal leagues, represents more than 1,300 cities; it keeps member cities informed on national poli-

cies that have local impact and undertakes research and analysis on policy issues that affect cities. NLC publishes a number of directories, including *Women in Municipal Government* and an annual *Directory of City Policy Officials,* as well as publications useful to scholars and policymakers, including the weekly *Urban Affairs Abstracts.* The National Conference of State Legislatures produces a number of reference works, including *Reforming State–Local Relations: A Practical Guide* (1989) and *State–Local Fiscal Indicators* (1990).

Are city manager governments more effective than strong mayor–council forms? Kathy Hayes and Semoon Chang find no apparent difference between them. See "The Relative Efficiency of City Manager and Mayor–Council Forms of Government," *Southern Economic Journal* 57 (July 1990):167–177.

The Academy for State and Local Government is a foundation sponsored by a number of nonprofit organizations, including the U.S. Conference of Mayors. Its International Center in Washington, D.C., publishes a monthly newsletter, *Public Innovation Abroad,* designed to "promote the international exchange of practical experience in dealing with common problems at the state, county and city levels of government."

The Washington, D.C.–based Conference on Alternative State and Local Policies, founded in 1975, provides, in its own words, "a national forum to assist progressives in developing strategies for change." Its publications range from books on state and local tax reform to legislative briefs and policy memos.

The impact of economic restructuring on local governments is the subject of numerous scholarly works. For a discussion of the causes and consequences of private business disinvestment in central cities, see Robert W. Burchell, James H. Carr, Richard L. Florida, and James Németh, *The New Reality of Municipal Finance: The Rise and Fall of the Intergovernmental City* (New Brunswick, N.J.: Rutgers Center for Urban Policy Research, 1984). For an argument that localities can create more "progressive" policies, see Pierre Clavel and Nancy Kleniewski, "Space for Progressive Local Policy: Examples from the United States and the United Kingdom," in *Beyond the City Limits: Urban Policy and Economic Restructuring in Comparative Perspective*, ed. John R. Logan and Todd Swanstrom (Philadelphia: Temple University Press, 1990), pp. 199–234.

Do privatization and public–private partnerships work? For a ringing endorsement, see David Osborne and Ted Gaebler, *Reinventing Government: How the Entrepreneurial Spirit Is Transforming the Public Sector* (Reading, Mass.: Addison-Wesley, 1992). For critiques, see Ray Forrest, "The Privatization of Collective Consumption," pp. 169–195, and Gregory D. Squires, "Partnership and the Pursuit of the Private City," pp. 196–221, both in *Urban Life in Transition*, vol. 39 of Urban Affairs Annual Reviews, ed. M. Gottdiener and Chris G. Pickvance (Newbury Park, Calif.: Sage, 1991). For a comparative study, see Timothy Barnekov, Robin Boyle, and Daniel Rich, *Privatism and Urban Policy in Britain and the United States* (New York: Oxford University Press, 1989).

For a look at local government in Great Britain, see Martin Loughlin, David M. Gelfan, and Ken Young, eds., *Half a Century of Municipal Decline, 1935–1985* (London: George Allen & Unwin, 1985). The contributors focus on land-use planning, housing, and social welfare. Several articles deal with managing decline rather than growth.

## REFERENCES

Abrams, Charles. 1971. *The Language of Cities.* New York: Viking.

Applebome, Peter. 1993. "Heedless of scorners, a g-rated Las Vegas booms in the Ozarks." *New York Times* [national edition] (June 1):B1+.

Banfield, Edward C., and James Q. Wilson. 1963. *City Politics.* New York: Vintage.

Barlett, Donald, and James B. Steele. 1992. *America: What Went Wrong?* Kansas City: Andrews and McNeel.

Barnekov, Timothy, Robin Boyle, and Daniel Rich. 1989. *Privatism and Urban Policy in Britain and*

the United States. New York: Oxford University Press.

Bernard, Elaine. 1993. "On creating a new party." Alternative Radio, Boulder, Colo. (April 2).

Bogart, Beth. 1980. "Corruption is in the system." *In These Times* (February 20–26):5.

Bollens, John C., and Henry J. Schmandt. 1970. *The Metropolis*, 2nd ed. New York: Harper & Row.

———. 1982. *The Metropolis*, 4th ed. New York: Harper & Row.

Burchell, Robert W., James H. Carr, Richard L. Florida, and James Németh, with Michael Pawlik and Felix Barret. 1984. *The New Reality of Municipal Finance: The Rise and Fall of the Intergovernmental City.* New Brunswick, N.J.: Center for Urban Policy Research, Rutgers University.

Caraley, Demetrios. 1977. *City Government and Urban Problems.* Englewood Cliffs, N.J.: Prentice-Hall.

———. 1992. "Washington abandons the cities." *Political Science Quarterly* 107 (Spring):1–30.

Darden, Joe T., Richard Child Hill, June Thomas, and Richard Thomas. 1987. *Detroit: Race and Uneven Development.* Philadelphia: Temple University Press.

Davis, Mike. 1993. " Who killed L.A.: The war against the cities." *CrossRoads* 32 (June):2–19.

Demoro, Harre W. 1985. "Super transit agency called 'impractical'." *San Francisco Chronicle* (October 18):4.

Dillon, John F. 1911. *Commentaries on the Law of Municipal Corporations*, 5th ed. Vol. 1, sec. 237. Boston: Little, Brown.

Edsall, Thomas Byrne, with Mary D. Edsall. [1991] 1992. *Chain Reaction: The Impact of Race, Rights, and Taxes on American Politics.* New York: Norton.

Farkas, Suzanne. 1971. *Urban Lobbying.* New York: New York University Press.

Feinstein, Diane. 1988. "Mayors' tips for the new mayor." *San Francisco Chronicle* (January 9):A5.

Fimrite, Peter. 1993. "Alameda drops out of regional agency." *San Francisco Chronicle* (May 19):A11.

Gottdiener, M. 1987. *The Decline of Urban Politics: Political Theory and the Crisis of the Local State.* Newbury Park, Calif.: Sage.

Harper's Index. 1992. *Harper's Magazine* (July):9.

Hentoff, Nat. [1967] 1969. "A mayor speaks on the bureaucracy." Pp. 161–165 in Leonard I. Ruchelman, ed., *Big City Mayors.* Bloomington: Indiana University Press.

Hinds, Michael de Courcy, with Erik Eckholm. 1990. "80's leave state and cities in need." *New York Times* [national edition] (December 30): A1+.

Kheel, Theodore W. [1969] 1971. "The Port Authority strangles New York." Pp. 443–449 in David M. Gordon, ed., *Problems in Political Economy: An Urban Perspective.* Lexington, Mass.: Heath.

Kirby, Andrew. 1993. *Power/Resistance: Local Politics and the Chaotic State.* Bloomington: Indiana University Press.

Lehne, Richard. 1972. *Reapportionment in the New York State Legislature: Impact and Issues.* New York: Municipal League.

Lekachman, Robert. 1987. *Visions and Nightmares: America After Reagan.* New York: Macmillan.

Marshall, Jonathan. 1991. "Troubled cities put services out to bid." *San Francisco Chronicle* (June 3): 1+.

Mollenkopf, John. 1983. *The Contested City.* Princeton, N.J.: Princeton University Press.

Molotch Harvey. 1990. "Urban deals in comparative perspective." Pp. 175–198 in John R. Logan and Todd Swanstrom, eds., *Beyond the City Limits: Urban Policy and Economic Restructuring in Comparative Perspective.* Philadelphia: Temple University Press.

Murphy, Thomas P., and John Rehfuss. 1976. *Urban Politics in the Suburban Era.* Homewood, Ill.: Dorsey.

"Notes and comment, the talk of the town." 1989. *New Yorker* (October 9):37.

Osborne, David, and Ted Gaebler. 1992. *Reinventing Government: How the Entrepreneurial Spirit Is Transforming the Public Sector.* Reading, Mass.: Addison-Wesley.

Pelissero, John P., and David Fasenfest. 1988. "A typology of suburban economic development policy." Paper delivered at the annual meetings of the American Political Science Association, Washington, D.C.

Peterson, Paul E. 1981. *City Limits.* Chicago: University of Chicago Press.

Pickard, Jerome P. 1977. *Report to the Federal Commission on Population Growth and the American Future.* Washington, D.C.

Riordan, William L. [1906] 1963. *Plunkitt of Tammany Hall.* New York: Dutton.

Sandalow, Marc. 1993. "S.F.'s $188 million deficit will force tough choices." *San Francisco Chronicle* (May 17):A1.

Sayre, Wallace, and Herbert Kaufman. 1960. *Governing New York City: Politics in the Metropolis.* New York: Russell Sage.

Scheer, Bob. "S.F. soaking up nation's troubles." *San Francisco Examiner* (June 27):A1.

Schneider, William. 1992. "The suburban century begins." *Atlantic Monthly* (July):33–44.

Schultze, William A. 1974. *Urban and Community Politics.* North Scituate, Mass.: Duxbury.

Sears, David O., and Jack Citrin. [1982] 1985. *Tax Revolt: Something for Nothing in California.* Cambridge, Mass.: Harvard University Press.

"'Sister lakes': mainly for the birds." 1986. *Public Innovation Abroad* 10 (August):8.

Tiebout, Charles. 1956. "A pure theory of local expenditures." *Journal of Political Economy* 64 (October):416–424.

Tolchin, Martin. 1985. "Towns turn to private companies to fight fires." *New York Times* [national edition] (July 28):13.

———. 1990. "States take up new burdens to pay for 'new federalism'." *New York Times* [national edition] (May 21):A1.

Uchitelle, Louis. 1993. "Three decades of dwindling hope for prosperity." *New York Times* [national edition] (May 9):sec. 4, 1.

U.S. Bureau of the Census. 1992. *Statistical Abstract of the United States 1992,* 112th ed. Washington, D.C.

U.S. Office of Management and Budget (OMB). 1978. *Special Analyses of the Budget of the United States Fiscal Year 1979.* Washington, D.C.: Government Printing Office.

U.S. Senate. 1966–1967. *Federal Role in Urban Affairs.* Hearings before the Subcommittee on Executive Reorganization of the Committee on Governmental Operations, 89th and 90th Cong., 2nd sess.

Utley, Garrick. 1993. *NBC Nightly News* (May 15), 5:45 P.M. PST.

Vidich, Arthur J., and Joseph Bensman. [1958] 1968. *Small Town in Mass Society: Class, Power and Religion in a Rural Community.* Princeton, N.J.: Princeton University Press.

Wade, Richard C. 1982. "The suburban roots of the new federalism." *New York Times Magazine* (August 1):20+.

Weiher, Gregory R. 1991. *The Fractured Metropolis: Political Fragmentation and Metropolitan Segregation.* Albany: State University of New York Press.

Weiss, Michael J. 1988. *The Clustering of America*. New York: Harper & Row.

Winnick, Louis. 1993. "Al Gore's misguided mission." *New York Times* [national edition] (September 7):A17.

Wirt, Frederick M. 1971. "The politics of hyperpluralism." Pp. 101–125 in Howard S. Becker, ed., *Culture and Civility in San Francisco*. New Brunswick, N.J.: Transaction Books.

Yates, Douglas. 1977. *The Ungovernable City*. Cambridge, Mass.: MIT Press.

*Thomas Nast*

"Let us prey." (Thomas Nast)

# CHAPTER 13
# Bosses, Boodlers, and Reformers

Urban politics is a drama. It is played out against a backdrop of legal, institutional structures. A tidy organization chart would show these structures in a series of boxes: the mayor or city manager, followed by the city council and department heads, boxed in at the center of a mosaic of governments from Washington, D.C., down to the local board of education.

But what the organization chart doesn't show lies at the heart of the drama—patterns of influence. The two are inseparable. Formal structure

**Fig. 13.1** ORGANIZATION CHART. Charts show only how formal structures operate. They can't reveal how informal influences affect city politics. (Richard Hedman)

is the skeleton of politics. Informal structures breathe life into the body politic. Getting something done in a city, whether having an ordinance passed or starting a government-funded program, requires *acquaintance with* structures of influence as well as *knowledge about* government.

Influential private institutions, from multinational corporations to local banks, "make critical decisions that determine the well-being of urban communities. They provide jobs and housing, influence land use patterns, affect air and water pollution, and determine a multitude of the matters of great moment to urban dwellers" (Judd and Swanstrom, 1994:xiii–xiv).

Structures of influence can operate *extra*legally or *il*legally. PACs (political action committees), PTAs (parent–teacher associations), and PBAs (police benevolent associations) exemplify legal organizations that seek to influence public policy *extralegally*. That is, citizens accept such groups as legitimate actors in the political process, but they are not mentioned in city charters or the U.S. Constitution.

Other organizations operate illegally, some-times in opposition to elected officials, sometimes in tandem with them. In the Americas, Columbian drug lords' private armies and the revolutionary Peruvian El Sendero Luminoso (Shining Path) represent powerful, illegal groups that influence through intimidation and violence. In addition, organized crime holds sway across the world, from the *yakuza* in Tokyo to the so-called Russian Mafia in L'vov, Ukraine. Perhaps the most notorious structure of influence operating in tandem with government officials is Sicily's *sistema del potere*: the power structure or system. In the towns of Sicily, "almost everything is explained with the phrase 'sistema del potere'. . . . The chiefs of the Sicilian sistema personally choose the subcontractors on most major public works projects. . . . According to law enforcement authorities in Rome and Palermo, the public purse is now one of the largest sources of income for the Mafia" (Viviano, 1993:A1, A10). And, according to a secret French government report, the Cosa Nostra (often called Mafia in Europe) is a worldwide business outfit with annual business dealings estimated at $20 billion

(Viviano, 1993:A11). Few public governments command such resources—or loyalty.

Thankfully, history is not destiny. Yesterday's institutions need not be tomorrow's fate. In western Sicilian towns, for example, citizens' groups have organized the Anti-Mafia Coordinating Association. In Los Angeles, two important gangs made peace after the Rodney King riots in the South-Central area. In Italy, a web of scandal implicating the power elite, from past presidents to top executives, has also brought widespread demands to stop the way "politicians run Italy as a jigsaw of fiefs" (Cowell, 1993:A1).

Still, today's systems of influence can, in part, be understood by looking at the historical context. Here we focus on extralegal influences on U.S. urban politics. So, let's begin by looking back to a time in the United States when bosses and **machine** politics ran most of the nation's cities. Over time, most of these old-style machines ran out of steam, but newer-style machines are still alive. This chapter traces these changes in local politics and suggests reasons for the changes. It begins with a discussion of an uniquely American institution: the city political machine. For decades, bosses and their machines provided the power and energy to get things done.

## THE CITY POLITICAL MACHINE

Beginning after the Civil War, virtually all U.S. cities at one time or another were dominated by a political machine. In some cities, machines rose and fell in a few years, succeeded by other machines or reform governments. In others, a machine retained power for generations. Today, with some notable exceptions such as Chicago, only fragments of the great old machines remain. So-called reform governments have replaced most of them, and new forms of coalition politics have arisen. As one writer puts it, "One gets a sense of the excitement of the paleontologist in searching through the fossils of American party machines" (Schultze, 1974:177).

Yet, the old machine, which generally ran out of steam, is a political model that has present-day applications, In many large and small U.S. cities, politics is organized on a machinelike basis or has surviving elements of party machinery. For instance, many cities have ward-size bosses who act like the old machine bosses.

A colorful cast of characters revved up the old machines and kept them oiled: men like cigar-chomping Tammany leader George Washington Plunkitt in New York City and Chicago's Richard J. Daley, a man of many malapropisms. Another set of actors and actresses helped to smash the machines: reformers or, as the bosses called them, *goo-goos*.

## A Bunch of Crooks or Friend of the Poor?

In the 1870s, political satirist Thomas Nast drew devastating cartoons depicting New York City's Boss Tweed and his Tammany Hall (the Democratic party machine) Ring of machine operatives. One cartoon (shown at the beginning of this chapter) shows the Tweed Ring feasting on the corpse of New York City, strewn with the bones of law, liberty, justice, and the city treasury. Standing on a cliff crumbling in a political storm, the Tammany "vultures" intone pseudoprayerfully, "Let us prey." Nast's cartoons helped to fix one image of machine bosses that persists in the American mind: corrupt, incompetent characters concerned primarily with taking money from the public treasury to feather their own nests. But there is also a contradictory image that remains in the American imagination: the city machine as friend—even family—to the poor and powerless, particularly lower-class white ethnics. This vision can be found in much popular literature that romanticizes the city boss. In Edwin O'Connor's novel *The Last Hurrah* (1956), for instance, Boston's Mayor Jim Curley is portrayed as the warm-hearted protector of the city's Irish in the late nineteenth century.

Which image more nearly approximates the reality? Before deciding, let's look at how machines work, what services the old machines provided, and what forces led to their general extinction.

## How City Machines Work

Whether past or present, city machines are highly structured, hierarchical organizations with no pretense to an individualistic mentality. In fact, party discipline and organizational loyalty fuel the machine.

Controlling votes is the name of the machine game. The machine is goal-oriented, and its goal is getting nominees elected to public office. It is organized to achieve this goal. A cadre of loyal party workers (and a core of voters) is held together by a mixture of material rewards and psychic benefits, including personal recognition, jobs, and a sense of community. This loyal cadre is part of a highly disciplined party hierarchy headed by a single executive or board of directors (Greenstein, 1964).

Typically, the hierarchically structured machine has a bottom rung in charge of mobilizing the votes of a single **precinct** (the basic unit of voting and party organization in the United States). Machine precinct captains are responsible to **ward** captains or bosses. At the top is a central committee composed of ward bosses and the central boss. Loyalty, trust, and discipline bind the lower and upper levels together.

At the street level, where voters deal with machine operatives, contacts are face-to-face and unbureaucratic. This lack of red tape and bureaucratic rigidity were appealing features to immigrants in the nineteenth and twentieth centuries. These newcomers feared or could not understand city hall, settlement houses, and private charities that were supposed to be tending to their needs. Tammany Hall leader George Washington Plunkitt boasted that he could get clothing and temporary shelter to fire victims in his New York City ward very quickly—before they froze to death—while the city and private organizations could not.

In dealing with constitutents, machines are informal. But internally, they run like an army or a business. Here is a British scholar's comment about late-nineteenth-century city machines:

An army led by a council seldom conquers: it must have a commander-in-chief, who settles disputes, decides in emergencies, inspires fear or attachment. The head of [the machine] is such a commander. He dispenses places, rewards the loyal, punishes the mutinous, concocts schemes, negotiates treaties. He generally avoids publicity, preferring the substance to the pomp of power. . . . He is a Boss. (Bryce, 1889, vol. 2:109)

Sitting "like a spider, hidden in the midst of his web," the Boss recalls another publicity-shy figure: the Godfather. The fictional Don Corleone in *The Godfather* (Puzo, [1969] 1973) is a commander-in-chief, running an organization resembling an old-style machine.

Once in control of a city, a machine fueled its engine in numerous ways:

1. It gained control of patronage jobs. Chicago's Mayor Richard Daley (head of the Cook County Democratic machine) personally controlled at least 25,000 jobs.
2. It decided who got city contracts, often padded to permit healthy profits for machine supporters. For example, Boss Tom Pendergast of Kansas City ran three businesses that relied on city contracts, including a wholesale liquor firm that sold to retail outlets that stood to lose their liquor licenses if they didn't buy supplies from his firm (Gist and Fava, 1974:457).
3. It gave insiders a chance to speculate in real estate by profiting from advance tips on city action (Box 13.1).
4. It granted special favors (e.g., zoning variances) for a bribe to the machine.
5. It got kickbacks from recipients of city contracts.
6. Sometimes it got pocket money from blackmail of persons threatened with criminal prosecution by machine-controlled city attorneys.

*To conclude:* The city machine is an informal structure of influence and power that never appears in a city's charter or organization chart. It is an organization that mobilizes votes and distributes the benefits of office to supporters. Internally, the city machine is held together by trust and discipline. It combines rational goals with brotherly loyalty. Like an army or a business, it is based on strict discipline and hierarchy. But machines deal with their constituents in a non-bureaucratic, personal manner. Its power and influence in the city are based on the services it provides.

## What Services Machines Provide(d)

Getting some help with the rent or a job down at city hall. Maybe some graft, what Plunkitt called "honest graft," or otherwise. These don't seem to be big benefits to get from a city machine. Yet when all the thousands of small favors and economic assists are totaled, they add up to a major urban social service: an informal welfare system.

It is important to remember that city machines rose to prominence in the nineteenth century as hundreds of thousands of European immigrants, mostly poor and unskilled, poured into the nation's cities. These immigrants had few support networks. Family members and friends were frequently left behind in the Old Country. Private charities and churches were ill-equipped to deal with all the immigrants' daily needs, and there were almost no government welfare programs. In this context, the old machine functioned as a personal deliverer of services, without layers of bureaucracy.

Like family, the machine could be counted on. It could bail you out of jail, get you a job when work was hard to find, supply you with free railroad passes, remember you with a gift for your wedding, and generally help you when you needed help. And at Christmas time, there was food. Chicago's renowned social reformer and Hull House director, Jane Addams, records that the alderman from her ward, Johnny Powers, the famed "Prince of Boodlers" (grafters), personally delivered ten tons of turkeys and ducks, shaking each voter's hand as he greeted them with a "Merry Christmas" (Addams, [1898] 1972:14).

The old machine also served as a vehicle of economic assimilation for immigrants. This kind of assimilation promoted upward mobility, but it allowed white ethnic immigrants to keep their ethnic identities. Indeed, city machines fostered ethnic identity, not cultural assimilation. This is ironic, for even opponents of machine corruption thought that at least machines were doing something good: ladling the immigrants into the melting pot (Stead, 1894). But to the contrary, machines encouraged the stewpot. They used "ingenious techniques for capitalizing upon ethnic and racial heterogeneity" (Lowi, 1968:v). One technique involved settlement patterns. In Chicago, for example, the Irish tended to reside on the South Side. This housing pattern was encouraged by the machine, for the Irish could then be controlled by a ward boss of their own ethnic background and also become a voting bloc.

To most people living in a city's ward, machine politics meant ethnic politics. And ethnic politics provided a way to climb the economic ladder for white ethnics, who were generally barred by class and ethnic prejudice from advancing through jobs in commerce and industry.

The career of George Washington Plunkitt, long-time Tammany boss in New York City, shows how the machine provided opportunities for at least a few lower-class white ethnic males. Plunkitt started out as a butcher's assistant in a working-class Irish ward. He rose through the ranks of the Tammany machine, becoming the master of "honest graft" (Box 13.1).

Now, let's take a look at two well-oiled, efficient machines. Operating almost 100 years apart, the Tweed Ring controlled New York City from 1866 to 1871, and the Daley machine controlled Chicago politics from 1955 until Daley's death in 1976—and beyond. These brief case studies give a flavor of the bosses and the forces that promoted them.

## Case Study: New York City's Tweed Ring, 1866–1871

Most often, political scientists point to Tammany Hall boss William Tweed and his Tweed Ring as exemplars of corrupt machine rule (e.g., Mandelbaum, 1965; Callow, 1966). Some assert that Tweed (who never ran for mayor) and his ring (the mayor, city controller, some aldermen, numerous operatives) stole as much as $200 million from the public treasury in five years.

Box 13.1

---

## HOW THE MACHINE WORKED

### "Practical" Advice from George Washington Plunkitt, Tammany Hall Politician

#### On Controlling Votes

There's only one way to hold a district; you must study human nature and act accordin'. You can't study human nature in books. . . . If you have been to college, so much the worse for you. . . . To learn real human nature, you have to go among the people, see them and be seen, I know every man, woman, and child in the Fifteenth District, except them that's been born this summer—and I know some of them, too. I know what they like and what they don't like, what they are strong at and what they are weak in, and I reach them by approachin' at their right side. . . . For instance, here's how I gather in the young men. I hear of a young feller that's proud of his voice. . . . I ask him to come around to Washington Hall and join our Glee Club. He comes and sings, and he's a follower of Plunkitt for life.

What tells in holdin' your grip on your district is to go right down among the poor families and help them in the different ways they need help. I've got a regular system for this. If there's a fire in Ninth, Tenth, or Eleventh Avenue, for example, any hour of the day or night, I'm usually there with some of my election district captains as soon as the fire-engines. If a family is

burned out I don't ask whether they are Republicans or Democrats, and I don't refer them to the Charity Organization Society, which would investigate their case in a month or two and decide they were worthy of help about the time they are dead from starvation. I just get quarters for them, buy clothes for them . . . and fix them up till they get things runnin' again.

Another thing. I can always get a job for a deservin' man. I make it a point to keep on the track of jobs, and it seldom happens that I don't have a few up my sleeve ready for use.

#### On "Honest Graft"

There's an honest graft, and I'm an example of how it works. I might sum up the whole thing by sayin': I seen my opportunities and I took 'em. Just let me explain by examples. My party's [the Democrats] in power in the city, and it's goin' to undertake a lot of public improvements. Well, I'm tipped off, say, that they're going to lay out a new park at a certain place. I see my opportunity and I take it. I go to that place and I buy up all the land I can in the neighborhood. . . . Ain't it perfectly honest to charge a good price and make a profit on my investment and foresight? Of course, it is. Well, that's honest graft.

---

---

Tweed was a huge man with uncouth manners, and he spent money conspicuously. Since he had been a man of modest means before rising through Tammany's ranks, he was often attacked as a vulgar crook, a plunderer. Cartoonist Thomas Nast was a particularly effective and vicious assailant, depicting Tweed as a vulture.

There is little doubt that Tweed was corrupt. It is also true that New York City's debt rose rapidly under Tweed, about $31 million in two years. And construction projects sponsored by

Tweed—particularly the ornate courthouse near City Hall (the setting for many movie trials, including *Kramer vs. Kramer*)—were scandalously expensive.

But before passing judgment on Tweed, consider his social context and the sources of contemporary criticism. First, many of Tweed's critics came from educated and wealthy WASP backgrounds. Thomas Nast is a case in point. In his cartoons, Nast often depicted lower-class Irish as apes. He was distressed to see power in "his" city pass into the hands of people he considered ill-mannered and unpolished: Irish Catholic immigrants, mainly poor and uneducated. It is noteworthy that Nast did not use his poison pencil to caricature WASP robber barons like John Jacob Astor, who enjoyed warm working relationships with the bosses and who were hardly paragons of virtue. Indeed, the robber barons' unscrupulous wealth-getting techniques —stock manipulation, price fixing, false advertising—and profits from political corruption made the taking of public boodle pale by comparison. Thus Nast's attacks on the Tweed Ring seem to be based more on class, ethnic, and religious bias than on righteous indignation against corruption per se.

Second, it isn't clear that the Tweed Ring was really a machine at all. The standard interpretation of the machine (e.g., Mandelbaum, 1965) depicts it as a tight-knit organization based on greed and personal gain, with little regard for the public interest. Those who interpret the machine in this way, seeing it essentially as a system of organized bribery operating without a sense of the public good, point to the Tweed Ring's ability to dominate virtually every aspect of New York City's political life. But an alternative view of the Tweed Ring holds that tight-knit machines didn't emerge until much later in the nineteenth century, when business entrepreneurs needed stable city governments to provide the proper climate for long-term business investments (Shefter, 1976).

Whether or not it was a tight-knit machine, the Tweed Ring did have substantial impact on New York City, then undergoing rapid change. It pressed a range of school, hospital, and public works projects; obtained reforms to protect city teachers' job security; and established much-needed public baths (Hershkowitz, 1978:348). The Ring provided jobs for lower-class laborers before government employment or unemployment programs existed. It changed the bias of the New York City Parks Commission, which had previously concentrated funds in Central Park to benefit upper-class residents, and diverted funds to smaller parks that met the needs of lower-class immigrants. It secured a new city charter in 1871

that centralized city government and reduced government fragmentation (and, not incidentally, made the machine's work easier). This charter reform represented a more efficient way of reviewing budgets than the former structure, in which each city department presented an independent budget to the state legislature.

Finally, Tweed, who died in jail a broken man in 1878, may have been much maligned by history. Recent scholarship suggests that the extent of the Tweed Ring's corruption was far less than was previously believed (Hershkowitz, 1978).

Thus the ledger sheet shows that Tweed and his Ring were both a bunch of crooks and a friend to the poor. They were something else too: a friend of the rich, especially the rising class of entrepreneurs, whose fortunes grew during the post–Civil War period of rapid industrialization and urbanization. The Tweed Ring didn't challenge the fundamental interests of the new entrepreneurs. Nast and other aristocrats may have hated Tweed and his lower-class ilk, but the machine bosses weren't antibusiness. Nor were they radical in their politics. Tweed's Ring worked comfortably and often closely with the robber barons. In fact, when Tweed was being prosecuted in 1871 for corruption, John Jacob Astor and five other millionaires signed an affadavit attesting to Tweed's good character, swearing that he never stole a cent from the New York City treasury. Financier Jay Gould (who once boasted that he could hire one-half of the working class to kill the other half) paid Tweed's $1 million bail.

## Case Study: The Daley Machine in Chicago, 1955–1976 and Beyond

People called Richard J. Daley many names: king maker (for his support of John F. Kennedy for president in 1960); fascist pig (for his role at the Democratic National Convention in 1968); a damn good mayor (even the beacon of Republican sentiments, the *Chicago Tribune*, supported his later mayoral campaigns); and simply Boss. Observers dispute the wisdom of his policies, but they agree that Mayor Daley had clout. And Daley's clout, extending far beyond Chicago, was based on his leadership and control of the Cook County (Chicago) Democratic Party machine, the nation's last full-blown, old-style machine.

In many ways, Daley resembled the bosses of the nineteenth century more than most of his urban contemporaries, so-called reform mayors like New York City's John V. Lindsay. Like so many Chicago machine politicians before him, Daley came from a lower-class, Irish immigrant family. He grew up in the Bridgeport section of Chicago, an Irish-American neighborhood, and he never moved away. A devoutly religious and old-fashioned family man, Daley didn't try to be refined or polished. Chicagoans delighted in his malapropisms (e.g., "Together we must rise to ever higher and higher platitudes"). Yet despite his rough edges, Harvard-educated presidential nominees and corporate business executives paid him court at city hall. The reason: He had clout, power, and influence based in a well-oiled machine.

Daley didn't create Chicago's machine. It grew out of the economic crisis of the 1930s (Gosnell, [1937] 1968:8). The machine was consolidated during the 1930s and 1940s but weakened by Daley's predecessor. In the 1950s, at a time when machines in New York City and other places were withering away, Daley refueled the machine by making adaptations, promoting internal reforms, and attracting federal funds to the city.

Under Daley's leadership, the day-to-day activities of Chicago's ward bosses remained much as they had been for decades. A ward boss's typical evening consisted of the following types of work: talking to a black building manager seeking a reduction in the $20 per month rodent extermination charge in his building; listening to two precinct captains who were asking for forty-two garbage cans; counseling a female computer programmer who thought she was being mistreated by her supervisor; and speaking to a Polish-American truck driver who was looking for work. In each case, the ward boss said that he would see what he could do (Rakove, 1975:122).

The following story, recounted by a *New York*

*Times* reporter, exemplifies how the Daley machine worked at the street level: A secretary was robbed at knifepoint en route home. The next day, she returned to the crime scene, hoping to retrieve her beloved red suede purse. She asked a city garbage crew that was passing by if they had seen the purse. The crew chief said yes, it was in the truck—along with several tons of garbage. The crew chief phoned his foreman, who phoned the precinct captain, who ordered the truck driven to a vacant lot. There the entire load of garbage was dumped out until the purse was found. Then the precinct captain took the woman and her leather purse to a friend's dry-cleaning shop, where the purse was cleaned without charge. After all this, the secretary was driven to her place of work. Two years later, in 1975, she voted to reelect Richard J. Daley as her mayor (Malcolm, 1986:20).

As central boss, Daley spent part of each workday in activities that helped his reelection and ensured machine control. One observer reports:

By two o'clock [Daley]'s back behind his desk and working. One of his visitors will be a city official unique to Chicago city government: the director of patronage. He brings a list of all new city employees for the day. The list isn't limited to the key employees, the professional people. All new employees are there—down to the window washer, the ditch digger, the garbage collector. After each person's name will be an extract of his background, the job, and most important his political sponsor. Nobody goes to work for the city, and that includes governmental bodies that are not directly under the mayor, without Daley's knowing about it. (Royko, 1971:23)

Daley wanted to see every name on the list because the individual became much more than an employee: "he joins the political Machine, part of the army numbering in the thousands who will help win elections. They damn well better, or they won't keep their jobs" (Royko, 1971:23).

What drove Daley and his ward bosses to devote so much time and energy to people's personal problems? To larger issues affecting city life? For many, the motive was payoffs and jobs. Daley himself was never accused of enriching himself at the public trough, but relatives and

**Fig. 13.2**  MAYOR RICHARD J. DALEY. Chicago's late mayor was largely responsible for reviving his city's CBD in an era of suburban decentralization. Under his aegis, Sears built the world's tallest building on the CBD's fringe. (*Chicago Tribune* photo)

friends were found on the city payroll. For others, there were some of the same motives that impel people in other walks of life: ego satisfaction, power, success. But not fame—for most ward bosses remain unknown to the public. Nor ideology—Chicago's machine operatives are essentially pragmatists, not ideologues. They may share many concerns of the liberal wing of the Democratic party, but they don't seek to implement a particular political platform. Instead, they seek to win elections, provide services, and act as power brokers between conflicting ethnic and interest groups. One ward boss summarized his

philosophy as follows: "Don't make no waves" and "Don't back no losers" (Neistein in Rakove, 1975:11).

In terms of substantive policies, the Daley machine encouraged large-scale business in the city. For example, to sweeten the pot for the giant Sears corporation, seeking to build a headquarters, the city agreed to pay more than $1 million to relocate sewer lines for the proposed building (O'Connor, 1975:139). The Sears building, still the world's tallest, is only one of many built during Daley's rule. Daley's record on housing construction, however, is another and controversial story. Daley's machine effectively blocked dispersal of low-income, racially integrated housing. This led to an even higher concentration of African-Americans in virtually segregated neighborhoods. Chicago remains the North's most racially segregated city to this day.

In terms of internal organization, the Daley machine adjusted to the city's changing ethnic composition, in particular to the increase in African-American and Hispanic communities. Widening the patronage net from old-line ethnic group supporters, the Daley machine reached political accommodation with the late William Dawson, a member of Congress who ran a tight-knit black submachine on Chicago's South Side. As one political scientist and Daley insider summarized:

The machine co-opts those emerging leaders in the Black and Spanish-speaking communities who are willing to cooperate; reallocates perquisites and prerogatives to the Blacks and the Spanish-speaking, taking them from ethnic groups such as the Jews and Germans, who do not support the machine as loyally as their fathers did; and ostracizes or punishes those aspiring Black politicians who will not cooperate. (Rakove, 1975:16)

But the era of the African-American tight-knit submachine was short-lived. African-Americans had long cooperated with (or were coopted by) the machine, seeing no viable alternative. But President Reagan's commitment to cut back the welfare state and changing demographics in Cook County rewrote the rules of the game. Then a remarkable grass-roots movement of over 200 organizations—from church groups to POWER (a coalition of African-Americans, whites, and Latinos organized as People Organized for Welfare and Employment Rights)—focused African-American disaffection from the machine. By 1982, a voter registration drive in the African-American community (one slogan: "Praise the Lord, and register") signaled a growing political consciousness and nonmachine participation in the political life of the city (Kleppner, 1985). Meanwhile, for a host of reasons, the citywide machine was creaky. Daley's political machine started declining before his death in 1976, and in

1983 antimachine candidate Harold Washington (originally a product of the Dawson submachine) was elected the city's first African-American mayor and the city's first reform mayor in fifty years. Some observers (Margolis, 1987:A14) were sounding the machine's death knell.

Is the Chicago machine dead? Not quite. At least not yet. After Harold Washington died in office during his second term, Daley's son Richard M. Daley was elected and reelected mayor. *Newsweek* ("Conventional Wisdom," 1990:4) called young Daley a "genius at creating [his] own dynasty." Even so, the future of Chicago's machine is far from assured, for the Chicago governed by Rich Daley is not the growing, prosperous city his father ruled. By the 1980s, the "city that works" didn't. A *Chicago Tribune* headline trumpeted, "Fewer Firms, Fewer Jobs, Less Revenue" (Longworth, 1981:1). Chicago experienced disinvestment, deindustrialization, a net loss of 123,500 jobs between 1972 and 1981 (Moberg, 1984:6), "fiscal crises affecting virtually all public services, and exacerbation of tensions along racial, ethnic, and class lines that have historically divided this city of neighborhoods" (Squires, Bennett, McCourt, and Nyden, 1987:3). Although some business leaders spoke fondly of the "good old days" under Mayor Daley (the city's central power broker), no amount of patronage or turkeys—the kinds of goodies that machines can offer their loyal followers—makes such structural challenges disappear.

Conventional wisdom is that in many cities this mismatch—between goodies available and goodies needed—did the bosses in years before: during FDR's New Deal in the 1930s. But not in Chicago. As one wag commented, "Chicago is America's museum, where old ways are on display" (Will, 1984:92). Yet by the early 1990s, the times were changing, even in Chicago. Taxpayers demanded higher-quality services and lower tax bills; city officials feared the out-migration of working-class homeowners. "Son of Boss" privatized a range of former patronage jobs, including janitorial services, tree stump removal, and parking ticket enforcement. (Critics of privatization claim that African-American city workers have been hardest hit because they hold a disproportionately large number of jobs amenable to privatization: service and maintenance jobs.) According to political scientist Paul Green, Daley's privatization shows that "the taxpayer is more important than the payroller" (in Mahtesian, 1994:A3). This attitude probably signals the end of old-style bossism.

Shortly, we'll discuss why most city machines fell decades ago. First, let's explore why they rose.

## Why Machines Rise

Muckraking journalist Lincoln Steffens once asked a New York City boss, "Why must there be a boss, when we've got a Mayor and a council . . . " The boss broke in, "That's why. It's because there's a mayor and a council and judges and a hundred other men to deal with" (Steffens, 1931:187).

Sociologist Robert Merton ([1958] 1968) offers a more theoretical approach to the reasons behind the machine's existence, one from the structural-functional perspective. Merton holds that a persistent social structure must perform some positive functions inadequately fulfilled by other structures or else it would cease to exist. He argues that machines fulfill latent functions unmet by other institutions, including the following: humanized, personalized welfare for the poor; direct, centralized contact for big business interests; jobs and social mobility for ethnic newcomers and others who cannot move up (socioeconomically) in business and industry; and protection for various illegal activities run by those excluded from legal opportunity structures. In brief, it serves the needs of the poor and certain interest groups, especially business.

Conflict-oriented theorists hold a different view of machines. They agree that machines provided services to the poor—and to wealthy entrepreneurs—but they argue that these needs could have been met in other, more radical ways. According to this perspective, the Tammany Hall machine in the nineteenth century was a conservative force, preying on the poor and helping to preserve the structure of poverty inherent in capitalist enterprise (Knauss, 1972). That is, the machine diffused or coopted the energies of the lower class—which, in European countries, was calling for revolutionary answers to poverty, not help with the rent. In this view, the Daley machine is comparable to a colonial empire, ruling white ethnic groups by a combination of divide-and-rule tactics and relegating most Irish-Americans, as well as African-Americans and Spanish-speaking people, to the position of the "submerged majority" (Knauss, 1972:90).

These two interpretations do not stand in total contradiction. Rather, their emphases differ. So do their taken-for-granted assumptions about the nature of politics in the United States. Both note the machine's latent functions but disagree on who really benefited from their rule.

## Why Machines Fall

The logical extension of the structural-functionalist argument on the rise of machines is this: Machines fall when they no longer serve needed functions or when other institutions evolve to fulfill the same functions. Thus according to this analytic framework, machines have gradually withered away because of long-term macro-level changes affecting cities. The following reasons are usually advanced for the old machine's widespread demise in the twentieth century:

1. *The scope of government increased.* Fewer people depended on city machines for favors and rewards as government began supplying welfare services. Also, party machines couldn't offer as many goodies when various reforms took hold (e.g., the rise of a civil service, merit-based bureaucracy that cut into patronage jobs).
2. *Competing institutions (besides government) grew in strength.* Labor unions and single-issue groups gained influence and power at the expense of political parties and their machines.
3. *Business interests no longer found the machine useful.* As the scope of the federal government

expanded in the twentieth century, and as corporate business expanded its operations throughout the nation's cities, big business could deal with the centralized federal regulatory commissions (such as the Interstate Commerce Commission), many of which they helped to establish. At the city level, some local business leaders were in the forefront of government reform, realizing that good-government reformers would sponsor policies in their interests (e.g., efficient government) and that the bosses had become a liability to them.

*To conclude:* Old-style machines withered away because of macro-level changes in American society that affected cities: the growth of big government, which supplied social services, and the expansion of big business, which wanted to deal with centralized control at the federal level. The machine's unique functions were gradually taken over by rival institutions. In most cities, old machines were replaced by newer, more streamlined models of government.

## LOCAL GOVERNMENT REFORM

Long-term societal changes in U.S. life, especially the growth of corporate business and the expanded role of the federal government, were accompanied by vigorous municipal reform efforts that contributed to the fall of machines. It is unlikely that reformers could have smashed city machines on the strength of their ideas alone, but the combination of historical forces undermining the machine and articulate, organized reformers desiring its demise led to a reform agenda.

So-called good government reformers, or "goo-goos," emerged in the latter part of the nineteenth century as a response to machine politics, immigration, industrialism, and rapid urbanization. The successes and failures of these reformers explain much of the variation in local government forms today. For example, before the reform movement, virtually all local governments had a mayor–council form. The wide-

spread council–manager form in medium-size and smaller communities today is a direct outgrowth of the goo-goos' efforts.

## The Goo-Goos: A Disparate Lot

Leaders in the movement to reform municipal government, a movement dating roughly from the 1890s through the Progressive Era to 1917, had motives as mixed as their backgrounds. Some were like college-educated Jane Addams, a settlement-house worker distressed by urban poverty and social isolation in the city. Addams viewed reform as one way to get city government to meet the desperate needs of the people who came to her Hull House in Chicago. There were muckraking journalists too, like Lincoln Steffens, who exposed *The Shame of the Cities* (1904); they sought to control urban crime, graft, vice, and political corruption. There were professors of political science and public administration, who wanted to extend administrative norms of behavior (rationality and efficiency) to the political sector, particularly to the executive branch; they supplied a stream of efficiency-oriented proposals to reform-minded commissions (Schick, [1973] 1974:14). And there were other academics, including sociologists at the University of Chicago, who wanted to re-create the conditions of a small-town community within the metropolis and to stem what they considered social "disorganization."

What groups provided the good-government movement with its principal strength and fundamental purpose—middle-class reformers, professionals, or business groups? This is a subject of lively debate among scholars (Kennedy, 1971; Stave, 1972; Brownell and Stickle, 1973).

Since the words and thoughts of the reformers are preserved in their writings, it's possible to get a sense of what they believed they were doing. But many scholars advise going beyond the reformers' words and focusing instead on the practice of reform to get a better perspective on the movement and the reformers' purposes. For one, historian Samuel P. Hays (1964) notes that the reformers described themselves as just plain folks interested in morality, rationality, and efficiency in city government. But, Hays claims, this was hardly the case. According to Hays, most reformers were WASPs from upper-income business or professional backgrounds.

In Hays's view, the disparate lot of reformers had a rather self-serving purpose that united them, whether they were conscious of it or not: the centralization of decision making. Doing business at the ward level was simply not what the business and professional people wanted; their world was cosmopolitan, not based in their neighborhood community.

Furthermore, Hays contends, the reformers' manifest goal—government by trained professionals—meant that nonprofessionals would be shut out of city government. In effect, this meant that minorities, immigrants, and members of the lower class would be excluded from the city politic. In other words, the latent function of the reform thrust for businesslike, efficient government was to consolidate power in the hands of upper-middle and upper-class WASP elites.

## Thrusts of the Reform Movement

The municipal reform movement had several interconnected thrusts. First, it attempted to make machine government difficult or impossible. Second, it tried to make elected officials more accountable to voters. Third, it sought to make government less political and more businesslike. Fourth, it tried to stamp out industrial disorder and movements considered dangerous and anti-American. Each thrust led to a set of specific measures.

To make machine politics more difficult, reformers supported **direct primaries** (in which voters, not the machine bosses, select candidates); nonpartisan elections; and citywide, at-large elections (rather than ward or district elections, which, in theory, increased the clout of ward bosses). To make local government officials more responsive to citizen demands, reformers pushed the **initiative, referendum,** and **recall**—

measures aimed at giving citizens more direct say either in proposing and deciding on legislation or in removing officials thought to be insensitive or corrupt.

To "take politics out of government" and make it more "efficient," the reformers sponsored measures to change the form of local government and to professionalize government. To separate politics from administration, they pushed the council–manager form of government. To take the "spoils" out of office, they wanted civil service merit examinations for local government service. This would not only cut patronage possibilities but also provide job security for bureaucrats, who couldn't be dismissed when a new faction gained control of city hall. To increase the efficiency of city government, they supported professional education in public administration and city planning.

Finally, reformers founded a number of private institutions aimed at "Americanizing" the children of immigrants. These included settlement houses, the YMCA, and the Playground Association of America. Reformers also used the public schools to inculcate values of patriotism, obedience, and duty. It was in the 1880s, for instance, that saluting the flag was introduced into grammar schools (Tyack, 1974). These reform efforts at citizenship training and patriotism grew out of mixed motives: humanitarianism and/or an urge to turn "them" into "us," thus preserving the dominant WASP culture in the face of immigrant, non-Protestant religious beliefs and southern and Eastern European cultural traditions.

That many reformers acted out of ethnic prejudice and class interests is suggested in the comments of Andrew D. White, a Progressive reformer and the first president of Cornell University, in 1890:

The work of a city being the creation and control of the city property, it should logically be managed as a piece of property by those who have created it, who have a title to it, or a real substantial part in it [and not by] a crowd of illiterate peasants, freshly raked in from the Irish bogs, or Bohemian mines, or Italian robber nests. . . . (in Banfield and Wilson, 1963:153)

What White and many other Progressive reformers sought to prevent was a city ruled by a "proletariat mob" (in Banfield, 1961:213). They also wanted to prevent the rise of "anti-Americanisms," particularly socialism, anarchism, and syndicalism. It is an interesting and almost forgotten fact that one "ism"—municipal socialism—was a serious competitor to the reform movement. Between 1900 and the start of World War II, Milwaukee, Berkeley, and other cities elected socialists to the city council or the mayoralty. The Industrial Workers of the World (the Wobblies [Chapter 1]) also presented radical alternatives to good government reform measures (Stave, 1975).

*To conclude:* Beginning at the end of the nineteenth century and gathering momentum in the early twentieth, a disparate lot of reformers—ranging from settlement house workers and journalists to professors of public administration and business people—called for reforms in city politics. Their major goals were: (1) to make machine politics difficult or impossible, (2) to make elected officials more accountable to voters, and (3) to make government more businesslike and less political. This group of reformers, mainly members of the new middle and upper classes (professionals and expansionists from business, labor, and agriculture) wanted to adapt the new urban-industrial society to meet their own needs. They chose government reform to do it. In place of the personalized, ward-level, somewhat representative government under the machine, they urged efficiency-minded, professional, centralized city government. One latent function of their agenda was to wrest control of the nation's cities from those they considered unprofessional and uncouth: lower-class white ethnics.

## How Successful Were the Reformers?

Many structural changes desired by the good-government reformers were instituted in American cities, particularly medium-size and smaller cities. For instance, the council–manager form of government is a direct outcome of the goo-goos'

efforts. But reformers never completely gained control over city governments, and the larger, more heterogeneous cities were especially difficult for reformers to reshape.

At this point, we should ask: What difference did reform make in the actual day-to-day operations and policies of city governments? Scholars are not in total agreement here. One well-regarded study points out that, in general, the more a city government was reformed, the less responsive it became to the needs of different racial and income group constituencies in the city (Lineberry and Fowler, 1967). Another study of urban politics argues that the machine controlled and manipulated the lower-class vote, but the reformers reduced and trivialized it (Greenstone and Peterson, 1973). Yet another study finds that, in the long run, government structure matters very little when it comes to city taxing and spending policies (Morgan and Pelissero, 1974:1005). Most assessments conclude that good-government reform led to lower voter turnouts, less diversity in the class and ethnic composition of city government, and less responsive and representative government (Hawkins, 1971:93–99).

Only the most naive goo-goos thought that municipal reform would end patterns of influence, and indeed it has not. Even in completely reformed governments, trained professionals do not develop value-neutral policies without regard to their political consequences.

*A final note about reformed governments and their critics:* A reevaluation of Progressive-era reforms comes from two contemporary would-be reformers: David Osborne and Ted Gaebler, authors of *Reinventing Government* (1992). In their view, municipal reforms (e.g., civil service merit systems, criteria for awarding government contracts) did limit graft and corruption. At the same time, they say, these reforms resulted in government bureaucracies that undermined effective government: "In making it difficult to steal the public's money, we made it virtually impossible to manage the public's money. In attempting to control virtually everything, we became so obsessed with dictating how things should be done . . . that we ignored the . . . results. The product was government with a distinct ethos: slow, inefficient, impersonal" (14). Osborne and Gaebler's alternative? "Entrepreneurial government," suitable "from schoolhouse to statehouse, city hall to the Pentagon." This new type of government, they argue, would encourage competition rather than monopoly; emphasize mission, not rules; decentralize authority; meet customers' needs; and "steer more than row."

Weber (Chapter 10) thought that bureaucracy was deadly but efficient. Osborne and Gaebler think it deadly and inefficient. What's clear to them is that bureaucratic governments today just don't fit a fast-paced, postindustrial world where "customers" demand high quality and choice in a marketplace of niches, not mass markets. What's not clear to their critics is how to avoid turning government *by* entrepreneurs into government *for* entrepreneurs. Without rules and professionalization, how can "honest graft, " as Plunkitt called it, and the plunder of public funds be controlled?

## BOSSES AND MACHINES: AN UPDATE

With notable exceptions like Chicago, the old machines were broken by a combination of the goo-goos' reform efforts and macro-societal factors such as the rise of rival institutions. But fragments of the machines remain. In many cities, a hundred little amenities of life can depend on the clout of ward-level bosses: how many times a week garbage is collected, who gets a new construction job, or how brightly the street lights shine. However, political patronage suffered a sharp blow in 1990: the Supreme Court ruled 5 to 4 that the use of partisan political considerations as the basis for hiring, promoting, or transferring most public employees was unconstitutional. This ruling prevents a mayor from reserving camp counseler jobs in the park system or nonpolicy jobs in the sanitation department, for example, for his or her supporters.

In short, good-government reform didn't completely do away with time-honored patronage jobs or other benefits that politicians can dis-

pense to supporters. Despite civil service merit exams, nonpartisan elections, and other reforms, who you know—or who you can get to—still counts in city politics. One modern development is noteworthy: the newer machine. The newer machine derives its power base from nonelected office: the city's bureaucratic administration. It doesn't depend on loyal ward bosses or city councillors who deliver votes or give out turkeys at Christmas.

## Robert Moses, Newer-style Boss

The newer machine and how it works are best exemplified by one man and the empire he built: Robert Moses's New York City. A lifelong bureaucrat and appointed official, Moses never served as mayor of the nation's largest city. Yet it was Moses—not the mayors, city planners, professorial consultants, or Democratic party heads —who shaped modern New York City's total urban environment. From the 1930s to the late 1960s, Moses molded a city and its sprawling suburbs. And his influence didn't stop there: "In the twentieth century, the influence of Robert Moses on the cities of America was greater than that of any other person" (Mumford in Caro, 1975:12).

How Moses, hardly a household name, built his empire and used his power to shape a city in his own vision is a tale well told by Robert A. Caro in *The Power Broker: Robert Moses and the Fall of New York* (1975). The following quick study of Moses is based on Caro's Pulitzer Prize–winning book.

Robert Moses (1899–1981) started his long career in 1909, during the era of municipal reform. A passionate idealist with imagination, iron will, determination, arrogance, and dreams, he worked for the good-government organization in New York City as a specialist in civil service reorganization. He argued for the idea that jobs and promotions should be awarded on the basis of merit, not patronage. He spent the years 1914 to 1918 in the administration of New York City's reforming mayor: one year devising a public personnel sys-

**Fig. 13.3**   ROBERT MOSES, POWER BROKER. Operating behind the scenes, Moses shaped most of the development of highways, bridges, parks, beaches, and related infrastructure for the New York City area, as well as massive redevelopment projects and housing construction. (Copyright © Arnold Newman.)

tem and another three years fighting to get it adopted. He battled with the city's appropriations unit, the Board of Estimate, which was "dominated by one of the most corrupt political machines the United States had ever known" (Caro, 1975:4), to replace patronage with civil service. By 1918, Moses had made such a nuisance of himself that Tammany Hall decided to crush him—and it did. Caro reports that at the age of thirty, with his civil service personnel system papers being used as scrap paper, "Robert Moses, Phi Beta Kappa at Yale, honors man at Oxford, lover of the Good, the True and the Beautiful, was out of work and, with a wife and two small daughters to support, was standing on a line in the Cleveland, Ohio, City Hall, applying for a minor muncipal job" (1975:5).

According to Caro, Robert Moses spent the rest of his life using that same iron will, determination, and imagination in another way: to amass power. He wanted power to transform his ideas into reality. And Moses was successful.

Moses sat atop an empire built on the bureaucracies of New York City parks, urban renewal, and highway programs. The immensity of his power and his empire is suggested by a few statistics: Since 1931, seven bridges linking the island boroughs of New York were built: "Robert Moses built every one of those bridges." Between 1945 and 1958, the New York City Housing Authority built 1,082 buildings: "no site for public housing was selected and no brick of a public housing project [was] laid without his approval." Moses built every superhighway in New York

City except one. He built Shea Stadium and decided what factories, stores, and tenements
would be razed for urban renewal. He was the
dominant force behind two huge private housing
developments in Manhattan and the Bronx.

More important, for over thirty years, Moses
established the priorities of what got built in the
New York metropolitan region. This had a vast
impact on "not only the physical but also the
social fabric of the cities, on the quality of life
their inhabitants led" (Caro, 1975:7–8).

How did Robert Moses become America's
greatest builder—of roads, parks, hospitals,
schools, urban renewal sites, and even sewers
(whose design and site he approved)? He used
an institution still in its infancy when he came to
it in the 1930s: the public authority. Public authorities supposedly are entities outside governmental bureaucracies. Their members are appointed for long terms, which, in theory,
insulates them from politics. They were institutions thought to be not only outside but above
politics. But under Moses, public authorities—
the Triborough Bridge Authority, New York's
Housing Authority, Parks Authority, and so
forth—were political machines "oiled by the lu-
bricant of political machines: money. Their
wealth enabled Moses . . . to exert a power that
few political bosses in the more conventional
mold ever attain" (Caro, 1975:17).

*To conclude:* Robert Moses was a political boss,
newer style. Using the public authorities as his
power base, he became "the locus of corruption
in New York City" (although personally, he was
honest in financial matters). Giving out contracts
and commissions (for public relations, insurance,
building contracts, etc.), Moses replaced graft
with legal benefits.

## The Local–National Connection

*Act locally. Fund nationally.* That might be the slogan for a range of new-style political "bosses"
and their groups. For instance, in the 1994 election for the U.S. House of Representatives, Republican candidates ran on a *national* platform

(Newt Gingrich's Contract with America), and
many candidates raised more money from out-
of-state donors than in-district contributors.
And, ironically, some ultraright local or state
"militia" leaders use short-wave radio and the
Internet to organize and fund-raise across state
lines while advocating county-level government
(and resisting, sometimes violently, selected state
and federal laws).

Here, in more detail, are two examples that
illustrate the impact of national groups on local
politics: the Christian Coalition and Emily's List.
The conservative Christian Coalition was created
in 1989 from the mailing lists used by the unsuccessful presidential candidate Pat Robertson. By
1993, it claimed 350,000 members with 750 local
chapters and an annual budget of $8 to $10 million (Sullivan, 1993:34). Using grass-roots tactics
combined with national fund-raising, Robertson
and his generals aim to raise "an army who
cares." Their motto: "Think like Jesus. Lead like
Moses. Fight like David. Run like Lincoln" ("Perspectives," 1993:23). At political-activism sessions they "train people to be effective—to be
elected to school boards, to city councils, to state
legislature and to key positions in political parties." Robertson's overall goal? In his words, to
be "THE MOST POWERFUL POLITICAL ORGANIZA-
TION IN AMERICA" by the year 2000 (in Sullivan,
1993:34). Unlike city political machines, the
Christian Coalition is deeply ideological, ce-
mented by a desire to halt what they perceive to
be the decline of traditional values.

Also ideologically based, but in direct opposition to the Christian Coalition, is a group dedicated to helping Democratic, prochoice women
win political office: Emily's List, an acronym for
*Early Money Is Like Yeast* . . . (it makes the
dough rise). Ellen Malcolm founded this organization in 1985. By the end of 1992, the group had
24,000 members and gave $200,000 from its cam-
paign chest to 171 state and local candidates. According to founder Malcolm, Emily's List pays
close attention to local races "because this is exactly what the Christian Coalition is doing" (in
Friedman, 1993:65).

Do Robertson and Malcolm represent a new
kind of boss, one suited to the electronic super-

highway that makes Washington, D.C., just a nanosecond away from Seattle or Yuma? Both wield influence over armies of workers. But if they do run machines, Boss Tweed and Boss Daley would hardly recognize their style and ideological commitment.

## ANOTHER LOOK

America made a unique contribution to urban politics: the city machine. In general, theorists agree that the machine was a product of its times, rising in an era of rapid industrialization and urbanization and falling in an era of national expansion. But theorists disagree on the costs and benefits of this institution, which was based on networks of influence and power rather than legitimate authority. Disagreements center on who benefited most, and the answers depend on the scholar's theoretical orientation. Social scientists who stress the idea of harmony in the social system (structural-functionalists) say that the city machine served the needs of various social groups, and when it could no longer serve these needs, it sputtered out. But conflict theorists have a different interpretation. They say that the old machines served the interests of the rising class of business people more than it served the poor, and it ran out of steam when the business interests found new and better ways to serve their needs. Further, conflict-oriented scholars argue that the city machines served an important latent function: By providing some benefits to a few ethnics, they diverted the lower classes from seeking more radical alternatives to their plight.

The good-government reform movement is also variously interpreted. Some scholars see the movement as a progressive step toward efficiency and rationality in local government. Others view it as a power grab by professionals and entrepreneurs to control the cities, preventing the "unwashed proletarian mob" from taking power.

On one point scholars agree, whatever their theoretical orientation, discipline, or political ideology: No type of structural reform has succeeded in doing away with informal networks of

influence. Neoconservatives like Nathan Glazer and Pat Moynihan point to whole bureaucracies in New York City's reform government that exist mainly to serve ethnic interests. In an update to *Beyond the Melting Pot* (1979:ix), they write that "ethnicity and race dominate the city, more than ever seemed possible in 1963." Liberal scholars often point to the widening net of influence, as the next chapter details. Radicals tend to focus on behind-the-scenes dealings by elites that influence city policymaking and on arrangements in capitalist cities that serve the interests of land developers and corporate business more than those of poor ethnic groups. Once again, while they agree that informal networks count in city politics, they disagree on how these networks operate and who they benefit most. That is the subject to which we now turn.

## KEY TERMS

**Direct primary**   Selection of candidates to run in an election by direct vote of the electorate rather than selection by a party committee or another back-room method.

**Initiative**   An electoral device by which interested citizens can propose legislation through petitions signed by a specified number of registered voters (usually 5–15 percent). The initiative process bypasses local elected officials. If passed, an initiative becomes law without being considered by the local governing body.

**Machine**   A political organization to mobilize votes and distribute the benefits of office to its members.

**Precinct**   The basic unit of political party organization in the United States. Cities and counties are divided into precinct polling districts, each containing from 200 to 1,000 voters.

**Recall**   A provision permitting removal of elected officials before the expiration of their terms if the electorate so votes in a special recall election. It was introduced by reformers as a device to increase the accountability of local elected officials.

**Referendum**  An electoral device that permits citizens to decide directly upon proposed legislation. A proposed bill is placed on the ballot and voted on directly by the electorate. Their decision is binding on the local governing body of the jurisdiction in which the referendum took place.

**Ward**  The political division of a city for the purpose of electing members to the city council (or board of aldermen). In cities where there are district elections, each ward elects one representative to the local governing body of the city.

## PROJECTS

1. **Biography of a boss.** What kind of people were the bosses? Were there any women among them? Select a famous (or infamous) city boss from material in the Suggestions for Further Learning and do a biographical sketch. What social and economic context set the stage for the boss's reign? What was his ethnic identity and his power base? Can you determine the sources of his money and power? With what concrete activities is the boss associated? What finally happened to him? Relate the facts of the boss's life to some of the theoretical material in this chapter on how machines worked and the functions they served.

2. **Machines.** The shadow of old machines lives on in more subtle forms today. One area in which machinelike structures are likely to exist is the delivery of social services to low-income groups. Test this hypothesis for a community near you by examining a social service program. Can you identify a strong, bosslike figure or figures in the program who dominate decision making (e.g., who is hired and where grant money goes)? Is there an ethnic basis of power in the system? What latent and manifest functions do the program(s) serve?

3. **Reformers.** Examine the local political reform movement in one city. Examine political histories to determine what group(s) were active in charter revision or other political reform activities. What groups are currently active in local government reform? Determine the social bases of the groups—past and present—and their

agendas. What do they say about their own motives? Are there alternative explanations for their political behavior?

## SUGGESTIONS FOR FURTHER LEARNING

The scholarly literature about urban politics has changed greatly in the past several decades, so much so that many texts are being totally rewritten rather than revised. Dennis R. Judd and Todd Swanstrom's *City Politics: Private Power and Public Policy* (New York: HarperCollins, 1994) is a case in point. Yet few of the new texts mention, let alone discuss at length, *global* influences on local decisions (e.g., location decisions by multinational corporations, international trade agreements).

For a historical look at urban bosses and the way they operated, see Harold Zinc's *City Bosses in the United States* (Durham, N.C.: Duke University Press, 1930); it remains a classic in this genre. Bruce M. Stave's *Urban Bosses, Machines, and Progressive Reformers* (Lexington, Mass.: Heath, 1972) has selections by contemporary observers, both criticizing the bosses (e.g., Jane Addams, Lincoln Steffens) and defending them (George Washington Plunkitt), as well as classic political science and sociological interpretations (e.g., the works of Samuel Hays and Robert Merton). William L. Riordan's *Plunkitt of Tammany Hall* (New York: Dutton, [1906] 1963) contains the personal reflections of a Tammany Hall politician.

A standard negative interpretation of Boss Tweed and the Tweed Ring can be found in Seymour Mandelbaum, *Boss Tweed's New York* (New York: Wiley, 1965). In contrast, Leo Hershkowitz, in *Tweed's New York* (Garden City, N.Y.: Doubleday, Anchor, 1978), depicts Tweed as a victim of the older New York City elite, which disliked him as much for his involvement with Catholic (largely Irish) voters and politicians as for his graft. For those truly interested in Tweed, nearly 6,000 pages of legal and financial records have been brought together on microform, with a printed guide by Leo Hershkowitz, in *Boss Tweed in Court: A Documentary History* (Bethesda, Md.: University Publications of America, 1990).

E. L. Doctorow's *The Waterworks* (New York: Random House, 1994) takes place in New York City just as the Tweed Ring starts to come apart in 1871. McIlvaine, Doctorow's journalist narrator in the novel, says this about the Ring: "They were nothing if not absurd—ridiculous, simpleminded, stupid, self-aggrandizing. And murderous. All the qualities of men who prevail in our Republic." Indeed, the amoral spirit of New York City pervades the novel. According to historian Simon Schama, Doctorow's "New York of then and now and ever is a place imprisoned in thuggish corruption, where the police conspire with, rather than against, crime; a lair of vampire capitalism, a warren of alleys crawling with the urchin 'street rats' who subsist on the refuse of the city's wants and needs, darting beneath the wheels of indifferent carriages, vending the news, loitering at the edge of scummy saloons" ("New York, Gaslight Necropolis," *New York Times Book Review,* June 19, 1994, p. 31).

A novel romanticizing the political machine in Boston is Edwin O'Connor's *The Last Hurrah* (Boston: Little, Brown, 1956). Political scientist Steven P. Erie infers that O'Connor's idea of why the machine fell was backward.

Machinelike organizations have also suffered in recent years. For example, in San Francisco's Chinatown, the once dominant Chinese Six Companies (Chinese Consolidated Benevolent Association) had great influence from 1882 to the 1970s. Its influence waned by the 1980s, in part due to the rise of governmental social service agencies. For details, see Steven A. Chin's reporting in the *San Francisco Examiner* (November 1993).

Mayor Richard J. Daley and his machine are best described in Milton Rakove, *Don't Make No Waves . . . Don't Back No Losers* (Bloomington: Indiana University Press, 1975). Rakove, a political scientist who spent years as a participant-observer of the Chicago machine, shows how the machine was organized, what values its members held, and what it did. His book contains case study material describing the actual interactions between ward politicians and their constituents. It does not particularly praise Daley, but it does not condemn him. Critical treatments of the Daley machine include Len O'Connor's *Clout* (New York: Avon, 1975), Mike Royko's *Boss* (New York: Signet, 1971), Eugene Kennedy's *Himself: The Life and Times of Mayor Richard J. Daley* (New York: Viking, 1978), and William J. Grimshaw's *Bitter Fruit: Black Politics and the Chicago Machine, 1931–1991* (Chicago: University of Chicago Press, 1992) .

*Jack Gance,* the hero of Ward Just's novel (Boston: Houghton Mifflin, 1989), works for the Chicago political machine before going to Washington. One reviewer noted that author Just has "an ear for the idiom of corruption, the offhand way 'sweet deals' are made by the machine."

Concerning the Chicago machine, Kenneth R. Mladenka found that even before 1975, Chicago's machine did not trade services for votes. In "The Urban Bureaucracy and the Chicago Political Machine: Who Gets What and the Limits to Political Control," *American Political Science Review* 74 (1980):991–998, Mladenka reports that "the urban [professionalized] bureaucracy is the major actor" in the process of who gets what vital public services. In *Rainbow's End: Irish-Americans and the Dilemmas of Urban Machine Politics, 1840–1985* (Berkeley: University of California Press, 1988), Steven P. Erie says that it was not the birth of the welfare state under FDR but rather the cutbacks of the welfare state under Reagan that did Chicago's machine in.

"Unfortunately, [Robert Moses] will have a double epitaph: 'He was the man who built New York' and 'He was the man who strangled Red Hook and killed substantial parts of the Bronx.' " That was the assessment of the president of the Triborough Bridge and Tunnel Authority, Robert Moses's last power base, on the occasion of Moses's birth centenary in 1988. Moses remains a controversial figure long after his death in 1981. Architecture critic Allan Temko calls him a "brilliant and ruthless czar of public works, who for 40 years was virtually a law unto himself." Robert A. Caro's *The Power Broker: Robert Moses and the Fall of New York* (New York: Vintage, 1975) is a massive dissection of how Robert Moses masterminded much of the physical development in New York City—bridges, beaches, parks, housing projects, and such colossal developments as the United Nations building and Rockefeller Center. In telling Moses's story, Caro provides unparalleled insight into the way political power at the local level operates. In *All that Is Solid Melts into Air: The Experience of Modernity* (New York: Simon and Schuster, 1981), Marshall Berman puts Moses's construction of the Cross-Bronx Expressway into a macro context: "So often the price of ongoing and expanding modernity is the destruction not merely of 'traditional' and 'pre-modern' institutions and environments but—and here is the real tragedy—of everything most vital and beautiful in the modern world itself. Here in the Bronx, thanks to Robert Moses, the modernity of the urban boulevard was being condemned as obsolete and blown to pieces, by the modernity of the interstate highway" (295). For a look at "The World That Moses Built" (1989), see the PBS episode of *The American Experience*; the video details the execution of Lincoln Center, Jones Beach, and other Moses projects.

In *The City Builders: Property, Politics and Planning in London and New York* (Cambridge, Mass.: Blackwell, 1993), Susan S. Fainstein analyzes the creators of the urban built environment, particularly realty developers, planners, and community leaders and their advisors.

One of Frank Capra's social-message films, the classic *Mr. Smith Goes to Washington* (1939), depicts a back-room political boss and businessman at the federal level, Jim Taylor (head of the Taylor machine in the U.S. Senate), being countered, somewhat unsuccessfully, by a righteous and moral opponent. Movie critic Robert Sklar comments in *Movie-Made America* (New York: Random House, 1975) that "once Capra's heroes begin their open struggles with wealth and power, they find themselves unable to triumph by asserting their strength and involving their alliances. [The political bosses] are simply too wealthy and powerful" (211).

## REFERENCES

Addams, Jane. [1898] 1972. "Why the ward boss rules." Pp. 10–15 in Bruce M. Stave, ed., *Urban Bosses, Machines, and Progressive Reformers.* Lexington, Mass: Heath.

Banfield, Edward C. 1961. *Urban Government.* New York: Free Press.

Banfield, Edward C., and James Q. Wilson. 1963. *City Politics.* New York: Vintage.

Brownell, Blaine A., and Warren E. Stickle, eds. 1973. *Bosses and Reformers: Urban Politics in America, 1880–1920.* Boston: Houghton Mifflin.

Bryce, James. 1889. *The American Commonwealth.* New York: Macmillan.

Callow, Alexander B., Jr. 1966. *The Tweed Ring.* New York: Oxford University Press.

Caro, Robert A. 1975. *The Power Broker: Robert Moses and the Fall of New York.* New York: Vintage.

"Conventional wisdom." 1990. *Newsweek* (April 2):4.

Cowell, Alan. 1993. "Broad bribery investigation is ensaring the elite of Italy." *New York Times* [national edition] (March 3):A1+.

Friedman, Jon. 1993. "The founding mother." *New York Times Magazine* (May 2):50+.

Gist, Noel P., and Sylvia Fleis Fava. 1974. *Urban Society.* New York: Crowell.

Glazer, Nathan, and Daniel Patrick Moynihan. 1979. *Beyond the Melting Pot: The Negroes, Puerto Ricans, Jews, Italians, and Irish of New York City,* 2nd ed. Cambridge, Mass.: MIT Press.

Gosnell, Harold F. [1937] 1968. *Machine Politics: Chicago Model.* Chicago: University of Chicago Press.

Greenstein, Fred I. 1964. "The changing pattern of urban party politics." *Annals of the American Academy of Political and Social Science* 353:1–13.

Greenstone, J. David, and Paul E. Peterson. 1973. *Race and Authority in Urban Politics: Community Participation and the War on Poverty.* New York: Russell Sage.

Hawkins, Brett. 1971. *Politics and Urban Policies.* Indianapolis: Bobbs-Merrill.

Hays, Samuel P. 1964. "The politics of reform in municipal government in the Progressive era." *Pacific Northwest Quarterly* 55:157–169.

Hershkowitz, Leo. 1978. *Tweed's New York.* Garden City, N.Y.: Doubleday, Anchor.

Judd, Dennis R., and Todd Swanstrom. 1994. *City Politics: Private Power and Public Policy.* New York: HarperCollins.

Kennedy, David, ed. 1971. *Progressivism: The Critical Issues.* Boston: Little, Brown.

Kleppner, Paul. 1985. *Chicago Divided: The Making of a Black Mayor.* De Kalb: Northern Illinois University Press.

Knauss, Peter R. 1972. *Chicago: A One-Party State.* Champaign, Ill.: Stirpes.

Lineberry, Robert P., and Edmond P. Fowler. 1967. "Reformism and public policies in American cities." *American Political Science Review* 3:701–716.

Longworth, R. C. 1981. "Fewer firms, fewer jobs, less revenue." *Chicago Tribune* (May 11):1.

Lowi, Theodore J. 1968. "Foreward to the second edition: Gosnell's Chicago revisited via Lindsay's New York." Pp. v–xviii in Harold F. Gosnell, *Machine Politics: Chicago Model.* Chicago: University of Chicago Press.

Mahtesian, Charles. 1994. "No room for patronage in new Chicago." *San Francisco Sunday Examiner and Chronicle* (May 8):A3.

Malcolm, Andrew H. 1986. "Study sees Chicago as a divided city." *New York Times* [national edition] (October 5):A16.

——. 1986. "Daley, 10 years gone, remains 'the mayor'." *New York Times* [national edition] (December 21):A20.

Mandelbaum, Seymour. 1965. *Boss Tweed's New York.* New York: Wiley.

Margolis, Jon. 1987. "Chicago's 'machine' no longer invincible." *San Francisco Examiner* (April 5): A14.

Merton, Robert. [1958] 1968. "Manifest and latent functions." Pp. 731–738 in *Social Theory and Social Structure.* New York: Free Press.

Moberg, David. 1984. "Will neighborhood jobs win 'war' for Washington?" *In These Times* (May 2–8):6.

Morgan, David R., and John P. Pelissero. 1974. "Urban policy? Does political structure matter?" *American Political Science Review* 74 (December):999–1006.

O'Connor, Edwin. 1956. *The Last Hurrah.* Boston: Little, Brown.

O'Connor, Len. 1975. *Clout.* New York: Avon.

Osborne, David, and Ted Gaebler. 1992. *Reinventing Government: How the Entrepreneurial Spirit Is Transforming the Public Sector.* Reading, Mass.: Addison-Wesley.

"Perspectives." 1993. *Newsweek* (May 17):23.

Puzo, Mario. [1969] 1973. *The Godfather.* New York: Fawcett World.

Rakove, Milton. 1975. *Don't Make No Waves . . . Don't Back No Losers.* Bloomington: Indiana University Press.

Riordan, William L. [1906] 1963. *Plunkitt of Tammany Hall.* New York: Dutton.

Royko, Mike. 1971. *Boss.* New York: Signet.

Schultze, William A. 1974. *Urban and Community Politics.* North Scituate, Mass.: Duxbury.

Shefter, Martin. 1976. "The emergence of the political machine: An alternative view." Pp. 14–44 in Willis D. Hawley, Michael Lipsky, Stanley B. Greenberg, J. David Greenstone, Ira Katznelson, Karen Orren, Paul E. Peterson, Martin Shefter, and Douglas Yates, eds., *Theoretical Perspectives in Urban Politics.* Englewood Cliffs, N.J.: Prentice-Hall.

Shick, Allen. [1973] 1974. "Coming apart in public administration." *Maxwell Review* 10:13–24.

Squires, Gregory D., Larry Bennett, Kathleen McCourt, and Philip Nyden. 1987. *Chicago: Race, Class, and the Response to Urban Decline.* Philadelphia: Temple University Press.

Stave, Bruce M., ed. 1972. *Urban Bosses, Machines, and Progressive Reformers.* Lexington, Mass.: Heath.

——. 1975. *Socialism and the Cities.* Port Washington, N.Y.: Kennikat.

Stead, W.T. 1894. *If Christ Came to Chicago: A Plea for the Union of All Who Love in the Service of All Who Suffer.* Chicago: Laird & Lee.

Steffens, Lincoln. [1903] 1904. *The Shame of the Cities.* New York: P. Smith.

——. 1931. *The Autobiography of Lincoln Steffens.* New York: Harcourt, Brace.

Sullivan, Robert. 1993. "An army of the faithful." *New York Times Magazine* (April 25):32+.

Tyack, David. 1974. *The One Best System: A History of American Urban Education.* Cambridge, Mass.: Harvard University Press.

Viviano, Frank. 1993. "How Mafia rules its empire." *San Francisco Chronicle.* (May 20):A1+.

Will, George F. 1984. "A devil of a town." *Newsweek* (February 13):92.

Bill Owens

# CHAPTER 14
# Getting Things
# Done

If Boss Tweed were alive today, he would find a much expanded political arena. Typically, old-style machines were based on coalitions of white ethnic immigrants, business interests, and boodlers. Today the range of political players is broader. On the local scene are such additional groups as municipal employee unions, gays and lesbians, feminists, race-based organizations, multilocational corporations, and a host of single-issue lobbyists (tax revolters, environmentalists, prolifers, pro-choicers, nude- beach proponents, historic preservationists, and so forth). All represent legal, private, or nonprofit organizations, acting informally and extralegally—that is, without specific mention in the city charter.

In addition, another set of players makes its will known without a vote on the city council:

people and groups engaged in illegal activities. These include street gangs, computer hacker rings, organized crime, terrorists or freedom fighters (depending on where you stand), and international drug cartels. Many have muscle; all have their own agendas.

Throughout the world, few, if any, places seem to be exempt from corruption. But some nations, cities, and neighborhoods operate in a *culture of corruption*. For example, Haiti under the Duvaliers was known as one of the world's great kleptocracies. In China "almost all journalists are on the take now" (Kristof, 1993:A4). In Italy, over 2,500 members of the country's leadership, including over 100 politicians, were implicated in a corruption scandal that threatened to bring down the national government in 1993. To get something done in Lagos, Nigeria, presumes an understanding of the widespread system of payoffs and "dash" (tips or bribes). In the United States, links between labor unions, organized crime, and politicians were exposed by the Department of Justice in the 1960s. In some United States neighborhoods, residents and small business owners get protection from gang members or racketeers, not the police. And kickbacks from government contracts, although illegal, remain standard operating procedure in countless places.

How do people figure out whom to trust in this jam-packed scene of extralegal and illegal groups, not to mention civil servants and elected officials? How do they find one another, let alone work together, for mutual benefit? How can ordinary citizens participate in public decision making? What impact are these varied new players having on community power relations? And how can any group get what it wants without going bananas? We now turn to these questions.

## COALITION POLITICS

Past or present, people representing varied interest groups in the city join together in alliances, trying to secure benefits that local government can dispense. What contractor will get the bid for a new building? Which neighborhood will get the building? What kinds of services will be dispensed there? Which people will get the jobs created by the new building? Such specific concerns are often the objects of intense political struggle fought out in the arena of coalition politics. In this arena, several rules of the game are commonly understood: "you help me and I'll help you" and "politics makes strange bedfellows."

In Tweed's New York City, political battles were fought over which neighborhoods got public baths, what jobs went to the Irish or other ethnic groups, and who got the lucrative contract to plaster the new courthouse. Graft and ethnic politics played a major role in determining who got what from the city treasury. Today ethnic politics remains a key factor and graft has not been eliminated, even in the most reformed governments. But now groups and individuals also seek a bigger share of the *legal* benefits available from municipal government. And single-issue groups seek government's help in furthering their aims, whether they be no smoking in local stores or setting up a women's health center.

From Tweed's day to the present, the players and issues may have changed, but the game remains the same. Whether old machine, reform government, or issue-oriented politics in a reform context, groups compete for scarce resources by organizing coalitions. These coalitions are informal and extralegal; they have no formal standing in the city's legal structure.

## Case Study: The Fight over Yerba Buena

One battle in San Francisco over who got what—and what share—of public resources illustrates the nature of coalition politics. This battle is meticulously described in *Yerba Buena: Land Grab and Community Resistance in San Francisco* (1973) by city planner Chester Hartman. Hartman's book, a prime source of the following study, details the complex nature of coalition building and the stakes involved in the bitter contest over land use. Richard DeLeon's study, *Left Coast City: Progressive Politics in San Francisco 1975–1991* (1992), updates the Yerba Buena story. In addition, political scientist DeLeon draws a contrast between the city's pro-growth coalition of real-estate developers and labor unions that first pushed Yerba Buena forward and the city's more recent (and atypical) slow-growth coalition of "three Lefts" —liberalism, environmentalism, and populism —that came together in the mid-1980s to limit physical development of the city. Here let's focus on the pro-growth coalition that put together the Yerba Buena project.

Yerba Buena is an 80-acre parcel of land adjacent to San Francisco's CBD. In Burgess's model, it is part of the Zone-in-Transition. It was the focus of an intense political struggle in the late 1960s and 1970s, for it was the proposed site of a comprehensive redevelopment program.

Once, Yerba Buena had thrived. After the San Francisco earthquake in 1906, the Southern Pacific Railroad located its main terminal there, bringing with it a cluster of luxury hotels, warehouses, and light manufacturing plants.

But by the mid-1960s, Yerba Buena was in decline. As Chapters 4 and 15 describe in detail, macro-societal trends changed the face of the city. Manufacturing activity declined; white-collar work increased; new technologies made the railroad obsolete for many purposes; and the composition of the city's population was changing. These economic and demographic forces took their toll on Yerba Buena. By the 1960s, most of its warehouses had been abandoned for new ones near port, airport, or suburban locations. Manufacturing had declined. Few goods and people came into the city by train. The residential population of the area consisted of elderly, single, lower-class men and a mixture of ethnic families. Most residents were poor, without power or prestige. They lived in the old luxury hotels, which had long since become residential hotels, offering cheap accommodations in very faded elegance. Many residents were clients of welfare and social service agencies.

Change for the area seemed inevitable. But what kind? And in whose interests? One answer was aggressively pursued by the local government agency responsible for urban renewal and redevelopment, the San Francisco Redevelop-

ment Agency (SFRA), and a coalition of interest groups it helped to put together. This constellation of interests proposed a convention center complex—the Yerba Buena Center. Their plan included a convention center, tourist hotels, a sports arena, office buildings, and a parking garage. It was to be a joint venture of private and public resources. The SFRA would clear the lands; the city and private developers would build the center; city bonds would underwrite some publicly owned parts of the center.

Private business groups formed the backbone of the coalition put together by the SFRA. Why did they support it? Traditional political stakes were involved: economic gain, jobs, and a variety of other benefits.

First, private economic gain. Several long-established local business groups viewed the proposed Yerba Buena Center as a boon. The San Francisco Convention and Visitors' Bureau was in the forefront of the pro–Yerba Buena forces. Composed of tourist-oriented businesses, the bureau wanted a convention complex for obvious reasons. Visiting conventioneers would eat in their restaurants, patronize their clubs and bars, and buy "I Got My Crabs at Fisherman's Wharf" T-shirts in their stores. Likewise, the local Hotel Owners' Association envisioned conventioneers packing their hotels. The Chamber of Commerce thought a convention center would be generally good for business. These pro–Yerba Buena Center commercial interests did not stand idly by or just make rhetorical statements about the benefits to the city from such a project. They funded studies "proving" how much San Francisco would benefit from the proposed center; lobbied elected city officials to give necessary approvals; and actively intervened in project planning.

Second, jobs. The proposed construction of a massive new physical complex was attractive to the building trades unions, and thus they joined the pro–Yerba Buena coalition. At times, when the project was stalled, they mobilized support in the form of street demonstrations.

Third, a host of other benefits. Different versions of the Yerba Buena plan reflected efforts to woo a wide range of other interest groups. An Italian cultural center was proposed by the city's

Italian-American mayor to get support from San Francisco's influential Italian-American community. A civic light-opera center was added to the plan in an attempt to appeal to the local social elite, who wanted such a cultural facility. Plans for parking garages were expanded and shifted closer to a nearby department store; a high-level executive of the store served as head of the Redevelopment Commission (the appointed body in charge of the SFRA) and as a member of the corporate board that would run the parking garages.

In short, a pro–Yerba Buena Center coalition came together around self-interest. Members of the alliance sought different resources and benefits: money, jobs, cultural facilities, and other perquisites for themselves. They didn't define this as selfish. In their minds, what they wanted for themselves made a good, livable city.

This pro–Yerba Buena Center coalition had enough clout to move ahead with the project. The local mass media added their influence in the form of editorials and news stories, stressing the benefits to the city as a whole from a convention site. By 1966, the SFRA had obtained a federal grant to acquire land, relocate the residential occupants, and demolish buildings.

Then a reaction set in. Neighborhood residents, mostly poor and elderly, fought to stop what they saw as a land grab. Some residents, seasoned in the labor struggles of the 1930s, established an organization called Tenants and Owners in Opposition to Redevelopment (TOOR) to represent and protect neighborhood interests. TOOR demonstrated against the proposed convention center, appealed to the city government to stop it, and filed a lawsuit to block the project. In their view, the Yerba Buena Center would destroy the neighborhood they had long called home. If development did take place, they demanded fair treatment: construction of subsidized housing they could afford, located in the same neighborhood or nearby; social services and open space; and a voice in planning how their future neighborhood would be built.

When it started, TOOR hardly seemed a threat. It had little clout, especially against the well-staffed pro–convention center coalition. About

all it did have, according to grizzled ex-labor leader George Wolff, who led TOOR, was a sense of injustice: "It was a good beef." Armed with a "good beef," neighborhood residents fought hard to preserve their turf. But alone, without allies, a sense of moral outrage was a weak weapon.

TOOR, staffed by several politically astute radicals who lived in the neighborhood and representing a group of ethnically diverse poor and elderly persons, initially found an ally in a very different group: environmentalists. These people (mainly young professionals who lived far from Yerba Buena) opposed the project on ecological and aesthetic grounds. They feared that high-rise buildings in Yerba Buena would destroy the city's low-density land use and offbeat charm. They didn't want more cars to come into the city and add to air pollution. Housing and social services—the Yerba Buena residents' main concern—was not the environmentalists' key issue. But since both the environmentalists and TOOR wanted to stop the Yerba Buena project, they made common cause.

This improbable coalition between the poor and elderly and the affluent and young was joined at one point by another group: disgruntled taxpayers. The proposed Yerba Buena project was going to be very expensive, and a portion of the development was to be financed by city-backed bonds. City officials, with rosy projections, told taxpayers that the bonds would be paid off at no cost to the city. But the taxpayers' group feared that the convention center could be a financial disaster and that the city would have to raise property taxes in order to repay its bonds. Moreover, the taxpayers' group resented the fact that the city had not submitted the bond issue to voter approval. They felt that this was illegal as well as immoral. So, another temporary alliance was struck with the neighborhood residents by yet another group that opposed the convention center (some taxpayers)—but for very different reasons.

Eventually the original pro–Yerba Buena coalition found itself under attack on several fronts. Sued in federal court for illegal displacement of the residents, vilified before officials of the De-

**Fig. 14.1** REDEVELOPMENT: FOR WHAT? FOR WHOM? These were concerns underlying the struggle between competing coalitions for or against San Francisco's proposed Yerba Buena Center. (Michael Schwartz)

partment of Housing and Urban Development, and lambasted at city hall, they came to a standstill. For a while.

Then a complex deal was struck between the city and TOOR. Essentially, TOOR obtained funding for housing projects in exchange for an end to litigation. Thereafter, TOOR sided with the city against its former allies, the environmentalists and fiscal opponents of the convention center.

What was the eventual outcome of the struggle? As is so frequently the case in politics, neither TOOR and its sometime allies nor its op-

ponents totally won or lost. The pro–Yerba Buena Center coalition won to the extent that the major outlines of its proposal were kept intact. However, TOOR won significant accommodations. New, low-rent housing units had been built by the late 1970s, including Wolff House (named for TOOR's leader, who died during the struggle), which now houses former residents of the Yerba Buena area. Relocation benefits and social services were improved too.

TOOR's sometime allies got the city to undertake environmental-impact analyses, scale down the size of the parking garages, and increase the amount of public open space in the project area. And the taxpayers' group won in the sense that it persuaded the city to reduce the amount of the bond issue and hence the city's potential fiscal liability.

From another angle, Yerba Buena's story is part of a larger saga: economic restructuring in central cities, global economic recession, and competition in the global marketplace. In the late 1980s, property values for luxury office space in San Francisco plummeted. Again and again, Yerba Buena's chief developer, Olympia & York (the Toronto-based real-estate empire builder and largest commercial property taxpayer in New York City), downscaled its deal with the SFRA. In the end, O&Y committed to build only one instead of three office towers. (The city had counted on O&Y's building three office towers and collecting $68 million from them; the money was to be spent on a state-of-the-art arts center, a park, a children's center, etc.) By 1992, O&Y was struggling to survive under bankruptcy protection. Meanwhile, the project was unfinished. As a longtime city resident said when he looked at the land that had housed poor men before 1966 and remained empty, "The Good Lord will call me home before this ever gets done" (in Bishop, 1992:A10).

This case study illustrates some important points about urban politics. First, informal power arrangements are the key to understanding how things get done. Nothing in the city charter of San Francisco or any other city deals with the role that private interest groups or citizens' action associations play in policymaking. Yet such groups are leading actors in the process of policy formation. Nor does the city charter or the organizational chart of city government indicate the relative influence of neighborhood residents versus opposing groups or the possibility of increasing that influence by coalition building. These are matters of informal power and influence.

Second, the Yerba Buena struggle illustrates that in U.S. cities, by and large, it is private interests that mold the plans of proposed projects. Government units, such as redevelopment agencies, act as power brokers to resolve conflicts among competing private groups.

Third, successful political outcomes can result from effective coalition-building efforts. In most cases, a rather strange mix of political actors can find themselves making common cause. In Yerba Buena, for a time, labor unions and business interests joined forces to promote the proposed convention center; the elderly poor, led by neighborhood radicals, were aligned for a while with liberal, socially esteemed environmentalists and fiscal conservatives. This array of forces on either side came together on a single issue; it was not a broad-based coalition of a multi-issue nature, which is much more difficult to put together or sustain.

Finally, the Yerba Buena case shows that in politics, few things happen overnight. Participation in coalition politics can lead to anxiety for people with short time lines, low frustration levels, and a distaste for conflict. Moving a project forward or trying to stop it takes patience, wits, organizational talent, energy, imagination, and perseverence. Often it also takes money, access to the mass media, endless strategy meetings, and hard bargaining. Some players in the game of politics command more resources than others by virtue of their social and economic position, their personal characteristics, and their occupational role. However, while players don't start with equal resources, even the most well organized and powerful groups (in the Yerba Buena case, economic elites and government officials) sometimes reach political accommodation with less powerful groups having fewer resources.

The Yerba Buena struggle leads us to consider broader questions about the nature of community power. We now turn to this ideologically loaded issue.

## COMMUNITY POWER

According to most U.S. civics texts, local decision making is a broadly participatory effort. Almost everyone, the texts imply, has a chance to express strongly held views; then consensus emerges, reflecting the public interest. The Yerba Buena case study suggests that this conventional textbook version of how decisions are made is rather ide-alized. How can we better understand the local decision-making process? What theoretical frame-work best fits the actual practice? Researchers have been investigating these questions for de-cades, and they don't agree.

Community power research in America began with a few participant-observer studies in the 1920s and 1930s, after the reform movement had gained a foothold in many large and small U.S. cities. The most influential work of this period was produced by Robert S. and Helen M. Lynd, professors of sociology and social philosophy. Their landmark studies *Middletown* ([1929] 1956) and *Middletown in Transition* (1937) traced the day-to-day life of a typical small midwestern ur-ban community (Muncie, Indiana, never identi-fied by name by the Lynds). In Middletown, the Lynds found that government was "enmeshed in undercover intrigue and personalities" (1937: 322) that operated mainly behind the scenes. The Lynds concluded that voters were apathetic and that "experts" (doctors, intelligence testers, etc.) were starting to displace the authority of the judi-cial system. Further, according to the Lynds, government in Middletown was becoming an "adjunct to the city's dominant interests," partic-ularly business (1937:chap. 24).

After World War II, community power re-search attracted numerous investigators, mainly those working in the sociological and social an-thropological traditions. Later, starting in the 1960s, a new spate of studies appeared, largely in response to those in the 1950s. These studies, mainly conducted by political scientists, chal-lenged both the methodologies and the findings of the earlier studies. By the mid-1970s, re-searchers turned their attention to one issue they considered crucial: the physical restructuring of communities, or "urban renewal." Since that time, theorists have been trying to join micro to macro concerns. For instance, they ask: Do macro-economic processes determine urban poli-cies or merely constrain them? What is the con-nection between the attempt to control urban space and the attempt to dominate the larger so-ciety? What is the role of the nation-state in ur-ban growth or decline? How do public govern-ment and private business decisions interact to affect cities? Given national politics and the inter-national mobility of capital, do local political leaders have some room to move or are they es-sentially powerless in the struggle to shape the future of their cities?

Let's look at the ways these community power researchers answer the question "Who runs this town?" We pay special attention to competing models of community power: the elitist versus the pluralist model plus a newer model of urban political economy: the city as growth machine.

## The Elitist Model

"Who runs this town?" According to Floyd Hunter, a relatively small, cohesive economic elite. Many sociologists (e.g., Baltzell, 1958) agree with this **elitist model.** Hunter's seminal study *Community Power Structure* ([1953] 1963) found that in "Regional City" (Atlanta, Georgia), a rath-er small group of rich and/or socially pres-tigious local influentials controlled the city's de-cision making. These influentials, Hunter says, shared similar values and weren't, for the most part, accountable to the public.

How did Hunter arrive at his conclusions? To identify Regional City's influentials, Hunter used the method of **reputational analysis**. First, he compiled a long list of people who might exer-cise power in Atlanta. From various sources, Hunter constructed a preliminary list of 175 names. Second, he selected a panel of people to judge the names on the list; these judges were balanced in terms of ethnicity, religion, age, oc-cupation, and sex. Those people receiving top ratings from the judges left Hunter with a short list of 40 names. Finally, he conducted personal interviews with all those on the short list accessi-ble to him (27 persons), asking them to identify the most influential people in the city. From their replies, Hunter reached this conclusion: The community power structure of Atlanta was dom-inated by top executives in banking, finance, commerce, and insurance. There were also some lawyers, industry executives, and socially promi-nent persons, but they were far fewer in number.

**Fig. 14.2** ELITIST MODEL. Floyd Hunter argues that a small elite makes virtually all the important decisions in urban politics. (Richard Hedman)

Interestingly, the smallest number of influentials came from the sectors of government and labor.

After establishing that Atlanta was run by a small group of business and professional people, Hunter explored the interaction among these elites. Here he used another research technique: **sociometry,** a method for studying small-group interaction—who interacts with whom. By tracing what committees the top 40 participated in, what corporate boards they sat on, and what social clubs they belonged to, Hunter concluded that the most influential people in Atlanta interacted very closely. As one interviewee told Hunter: "there are 'crowds' in Regional City—several of them—that pretty well make the big decisions. There is the crowd I belong to (the Homer Chemical crowd); then there is the First State Bank crowd, the Regional Gas crowd, the Mercantile crowd, the Growers Bank crowd, and the like" (in Hunter, [1953] 1963:77).

These "crowds," according to the people Hunter interviewed, were primarily responsible

for making fundamental city decisions, such as the decision to undertake urban renewal in the downtown area. These decisions were made by informal consensus of the economic elites. Formal government decision makers, including the mayor, were only peripheral actors until the stage of implementation was reached.

In general, subsequent studies of community power that use Hunter's reputational method have come to the same conclusion: The elitist model most closely approximates the reality of community power and decision making.

The implications of Hunter's research were upsetting to those who saw city political processes (and American politics in general) as a participatory process that promoted the public interest rather than narrow private interests. Hunter's model—that elites ran the city of Atlanta and largely determined the fate of over 300,000 inhabitants (the city's population when he studied it)—led to more studies of community power and a competing model: the **pluralist model.**

**Fig. 14.3** PLURALIST MODEL. Pluralists argue that urban politics is characterized by the representation of various interests in the community, not the domination of a cohesive elite. (© 1976 Richard Hedman)

## The Pluralist Model

"Who runs this town?" According to a Yale political scientist's influential study, published in 1961, community power is not held by a small, cohesive economic elite. Rather, power is shared among different local elites. Investigating *Who Governs?* (1961) in New Haven, Connecticut (population then 150,000), Robert Dahl found that power in the city is broadly diffused. Decision makers in one issue area, such as education, weren't influential in another, such as urban redevelopment. Thus Dahl concluded that pluralist democracy works at the urban level.

How did Dahl arrive at his findings? To identify community influentials, he employed **deci-sion analysis:** observation and analysis of a political system (also termed *issue* or *event analysis*). This technique focuses on the actual decision-making process. Dahl chose three key local areas —education, urban redevelopment, and nominations for political office—and looked at decisions in each issue area made over a period of about a decade. From interviews with participants in the decisions, news accounts, written records, and observations, Dahl determined who initiated successful proposals or who successfully vetoed someone else's policy alternative. Then Dahl judged that those with the greatest proportion of successes in making public policy were the most influential leaders in New Haven.

Dahl determined that leadership in New Haven was more specialized than Hunter had found in Regional City. In Hunter's Atlanta, there was a set of interlocking relationships between a small financial-commercial elite that was influential in essentially all major decisions. That is, the banker or manufacturer who had a major say in redevelopment decisions also influenced education and party nomination decisions. By contrast, in New Haven, Dahl found a specialization of influence: "With few exceptions any particular individual exerts a significant amount of direct influence in no more than one of the three issue areas studied" (1961:181). Thus, he deduced that New Haven was not monolithic in its power structure. Rather, it was pluralistic. Diverse groups, each with its own sphere of influence, ran New Haven.

Dahl also found diversity among the leaders. They came from various class, white ethnic, and religious backgrounds. (Dahl didn't describe their race; presumably all were white.) No one stratum of society, he argued, produced leaders in different issue areas.

Yet Dahl did not claim that the groups in New Haven shared power equally. Still, in his view, "New Haven [was] a republic of unequal citizens —but for all that a republic" (1961:220).

## The City-as-a-Growth-Machine Model

Dahl recognized land development as one important area of urban politics. Indeed, he celebrated New Haven's mayor as an entrepreneur of redevelopment. But Dahl did not made urban growth central to his analysis. By contrast, Hunter did; he noted that, among Atlanta's top leaders and underprofessionals, the highest-priority issue in 1950 and 1951 concerned land use: the Plan of Development (a plan for annexing unincorporated areas to Regional City).

Starting in the mid-1970s, community power research shifted away from Dahl's pluralist model and Hunter's elitist model to urban political economy models. Yet in the tradition of Hunter, the recent models put urban growth politics at center stage (Logan and Zhou, 1989:461).

Community power studies in the newer urban political economy tradition constitute variations on a general theme: growth-oriented urban alliances. Some theorists think that the private sector forms the basis of urban renewal support (e.g., Stone, 1976; Friedland, 1983), others think that "political entrepreneurs" build pro-growth coalitions out of conflicting interests (Mollenkopf, 1983:19). Some analysts argue that business elites are internally divided and depend on the state to coordinate their various interests (O'Connor, 1973). Others think that large businesses work together to ensure their general prosperity (Whitt, 1986). Some use the concept of *urban regime* (e.g., Stone, 1989; DeLeon, 1992), acknowledging that local governments alone can't mobilize and coordinate the necessary resources to govern and bring about results; therefore, business leaders typically play a vital role in a city's informal governing coalition: "Governments wants business investment, but businesses also want government cooperation" (Stone, 1991:290).

In general, theorists of growth-oriented urban alliances share the following premises: (1) local government officials must sustain growth to maintain local services and fiscal well-being, and (2) local business firms get involved in local politics to help their profitability, such as increasing the value of their property. So, both local officials and business have an interest in urban growth, and this mutual interest leads to their working together in a pro-growth coalition (Fleischmann and Feagin, 1987:208). In addition, these theorists think that (3) local politics counts; it is not merely a reflection of larger macroeconmic forces, and (4) local political leadership makes a difference in determining which cities get what.

Now, let's look more closely at one variant of the general model: the **growth machine model.** Sociologist Harvey Molotch first published his model in 1976. It was later amplified in *Urban Fortunes* (1987), a prize-winning book by Molotch and his coauthor and fellow sociologist John R. Logan.

First, research methods. Unlike Hunter or Dahl, Logan and Molotch rely primarily on historical and social science research studies. In-

**Fig. 14.4** CITY-AS-A-GROWTH-MACHINE MODEL. According to Logan and Molotch, local entrepreneurs, not economic imperatives or a wide variety of interest groups, are primarily responsible for the shape of cities. These businesspeople actively promote growth in their own interest. (Lisa Siegel Sullivan)

stead of conducting original research, they use other people's case studies, often reanalyzing the original data and offering new interpretations.

Now, substance. According to the city-as-a-growth-machine model, "The desire for growth creates consensus among a wide range of elite groups, no matter how split they might be on other issues" (Logan and Molotch, 1987:50–51). Logan and Molotch note that even pluralist studies of community power, such as Banfield's (1961) study of Chicago, also find that elites agree on one central issue: Urban growth is good. Numerous community power studies from a host of perspectives, including studies of U.S. southern border cities (D'Antonio and Erickson, 1970), Dallas and Fort Worth (Melosi, 1983), and Atlanta at two points in time (Hunter, 1953, 1980) also find that elites were united on growth policy.

Logan and Molotch reject both pure economic logic and natural geographic factors as key shapers of cities. Instead, they say that "the activism of entrepreneurs is, and always has been, a critical force in shaping the urban system, including the rise and fall of given places" (1987:52). In the nineteenth century, U.S. communities—or primar-

ily their development elites—competed among themselves for growth stimuli, particularly government-funded transportation infrastructure (e.g., railroad routes) and government-supported institutions such as colleges and prisons. In frontier towns, "growth entrepreneurs" were mainly professionals, but law, medicine, and pharmacy quickly became sidelines. These individuals made their money as town developers.

Chicago's William Ogden was "perhaps the most spectacular case of urban ingenuity." Ogden came to the Windy City in 1835 and succeeded in becoming Chicago's mayor, great railway developer, and owner of much of its finest real estate. He was also the organizer and first president of the Union Pacific Railroad. Using his business and civic roles, Ogden was able to make Chicago "the crossroads of America, and hence the dominant metropolis of the Midwest. Chicago became a crossroads not only because it was 'central' (other places were also in the 'middle') but because a small group of people (led by Ogden) had the power to literally have the roads cross in the spot they chose." Ogden himself became wealthy out of the deals that resulted from this marriage of government activity and land sales (Logan and Molotch, 1987:53–54).

In more recent times, Logan and Molotch note, entrepreneurs still make a difference. For instance, in 1956, Colorado leaders convinced President Eisenhower to link Denver to Salt Lake City by an expensive mountain road, thus removing the threat that Cheyenne, Wyoming, would become the Western crossroads. Thus Logan and Molotch reject deterministic economic or geographic explanations of how cities rise in the nation's hierarchy. Rather, they point to the all-important role of a city's entrepreneurs who make things happen.

To make things happen, cities try to create a "good business climate." A first-rate opera or ballet company may subtly enhance a city's growth potential. Low taxation and "cooperative" government set a good mood. But some ingredients are crucial for a good business climate: "There should be no violent class or ethnic conflict" (Logan and Molotch, 1987:60), and perhaps most important, the local public attitude should be pro-growth.

In terms of the organization of the growth coalition, Logan and Molotch (1987:62) comment that those who spend their time and money participating in local affairs are those who have the most to gain or lose in land-use decisions: "Local business people are the major participants in urban politics, particularly business people in property investing, development, and real estate financing." Businesspeople's interaction with public officials, including their financial support of campaigns, gives them what others (e.g., Stone, 1981) call *systemic* power. Local newspapers and other monopolitic business enterprises are also tied to metropolitan growth, although they are not directly involved in land use.

Since much of the private sector's effort to achieve growth involves government, "local growth elites play a major role in electing local politicians," 'watch dogging' their activities" (Logan and Molotch, 1987:63). Key players include politicians, the local newspaper publisher, leaders of utilities, and transportation bureaucrats, both public and private. Auxiliary players have less of a stake in growth but still play a role

in promoting or maintaining it: universities, symphony orchestras, professional sports teams, organized labor, self-employed professionals and small retailers, and corporate capitalists. Some of these groups support growth because of what they will gain in rent; some stand to receive other financial profits.

Local growth is sold to different groups on different grounds—jobs, attraction of tourist dollars, enhancement of civic pride, and so on. But, Logan and Molotch argue, many of these claims are phony. Take, for instance, the appeal to workers—that growth "makes jobs." In their view, local growth does not make jobs, but it does distribute them: "In any given year, the United States will see the construction of a certain number of new factories, office units, and highways—regardless of where they are put. . . . [Short of introducing draconian measures,] a locality can only compete with other localities for its share of newly created U.S. jobs" (Logan and Molotch, 1987:89)

(Here we could add a related issue that fits into Logan and Molotch's schema: pitting one city against another to keep existing jobs. For example, General Motors announced that it would close some of its plants in the early 1990s. Ypsilanti, Michigan, and Arlington, Texas, both sought to keep their GM plants open, offering incentives such as tax abatements to sweeten the pot. Eventually, GM opted to close its Willow Run plant in Ypsilanti and keep its Arlington plant open. Ypsilanti sued GM, basically because GM had received tax breaks for years on the understanding that it would keep Willow Run open. Thus although spatial barriers may mean less and less, differences among places remain important to investors, resulting in heightened intercity competition.)

Who actually wins the most from urban growth? Logan and Molotch say that governments are mobilized to intensify land uses for private gain—rent and other profit. In most cases, they say, local growth is "a transfer of wealth and life chances from the general public" to what they call the *rentier groups* (a term generally used to mean groups that live off of government securities or other dividends but used by

Logan and Molotch to specify people who profit from rents of buildings and land) and their associates" (1987:98).

## COMPARING THE MODELS

Logan and Molotch, Dahl, and Hunter disagree on the role and degree of involvement of the business community in local government. For Dahl, professional politicians determine government decisions, while business executives and professionals make their mark in civic organizations. For Hunter, a commercial-financial elite informally sets basic policy, later implemented by government officials. For Logan and Molotch, local business is the major participant in urban politics, but local business and local government make good marriage partners because both are interested in growth and need one another.

All the model makers are trained social scientists committed to scientific rigor, accuracy, and honesty. How, then, could they arrive at such different conclusions about who runs this town?

### Why the Theorists Disagree

In the case of Dahl and Hunter, one possibility is that the towns themselves are different, and that their findings reflect significant variations between Atlanta and New Haven. However, this explanation falls apart in light of subsequent restudies of the two towns. On the one hand, a restudy of New Haven found that a big-business ruling elite is in control (Domhoff, 1977). On the other hand, a restudy of Atlanta found that a series of competing coalitions exists (Jennings, 1964). Evidently, the power structures of Atlanta and New Haven aren't as different as scholars' perceptions of them.

In other words, what you see depends on how you look at it. Here are the bases for the researchers' disagreements:

1. *Differences in disciplinary perspectives.* Logan and Molotch are trained in sociology but draw

freely on ideas rooted in geography, economics, and history. Their focus on informal elites and big winners and losers in urban growth (in terms of race and class) reflects their sociological perspective. Hunter was trained in sociology and anthropology; he emphasized social structure and social class in his analysis of community power. Instead of giving weight to the formal machinery of government, he focused on informal social networks (*crowds*). In fact, he argued that formal decision makers were brought into policymaking only after the real decisions had been made in the private sector. In contrast, political scientist Dahl emphasized the importance of formal government structure. He did not take a close look at informal decision making. Consequently, official position (e.g., mayor) plays a much more important part in Dahl's analysis of power structures than in Hunter's work.

2. *Differences in research methods.* Since Logan and Molotch rely on other researchers' empirical studies, which employed a variety of research methods, their differences with both Hunter and Dahl do not lie here.

The elitist–pluralist debate has centered largely on this issue. Hunter's critics charge that his reputational method leads to the identification of a relatively small economic elite. Critics say that if you ask "Who are the top leaders in this town?" you will find that there is a small, cohesive leadership. In addition, critics charge that Hunter confuses the reputation for having power with the substance of power. The fact that knowledgeable people think an individual exercises power is not proof; it is only hearsay evidence. Thus Hunter and those who hold an elitist model of power are accused of lack of rigor in their methods of research.

By the same token, Dahl's critics charge that decision (or event) analysis is misleading; it leads to the identification of a pattern of broader participation in decision making than actually exists. Critics of pluralism argue that Dahl's decision analysis neglects a whole dimension of power: the ability to keep issues out of the decision-making arena altogether (Bachrach and Baratz, 1962). For example, a study that defines the issue as the decision makers did might conclude that, in the 1940s, the major issue in a southern town was fluoridation of the water supply—that is what decision makers there might have said. Of course, this would overlook the fact that schools in that town were entirely segregated or that racial discrimination existed; these were not issues for the local policymakers. In other words, decision analysis can't investigate nondecisions, those that never reach the public stage (e.g., the decision to keep schools segregated). Further, Dahl's critics say that his choice of decisions to investigate—political nominations, public education, and urban redevelopment—narrowed the field of political activity and neglected broader private sector decisions. Finally, critics point out that Dahl gave little specific information on the decisions he studied, so that readers must take his conclusions on faith.

It is noteworthy that subsequent community power studies using Hunter's reputational technique tend to find elitist patterns of local power, while studies using Dahl's decision analysis tend to find pluralist patterns of local power. This suggests an implicit bias in the research techniques.

Logan and Molotch use neither the case study approach nor reputational or decision analysis. Instead, they draw on a range of research studies from various perspectives and disciplines, often reinterpreting the authors' findings.

3. *Differences in theoretical orientation.* Logan and Molotch start from a viewpoint that puts individuals, not abstract market forces or macroeconomic imperatives of the larger system, at center stage: "All capitalist places are the creations of activists who push hard to alter how markets function, how prices are set, and how lives are affected." This point of view distinguishes them from both the mainstream ecological paradigm of Burgess and the structuralism of neo-Marixan urbanists, which, in their view, are too deterministic. They also reject Dahl's pluralism. Focusing on local elites who try to make money from urban development, Logan and Molotch argue that growth is often portrayed falsely by these elites as beneficial to all when, in actuality, both the advantages and disadvantages are unevenly distributed. In tone, they are close to Hunter.

Hunter assumes that inherent conflict exists between social classes, that the interests of the few (the crowds of economic elites) run counter to the interests of the many. It follows, then, that the elites rule in their own interest against the interests of the citizenry. Hunter rejects the notion that government is neutral, a mere negotiator among interest groups representing a wide spectrum of the population. By contrast, in *Who Governs?* Dahl takes social stability for granted. Consequently, he does not explore the measures that ensure social continuity (e.g., lack of information, threat of coercion). Conflict-oriented theorists criticize Dahl and pluralists generally for assuming that a political consensus exists and that this consensus works to everyone's benefit. This assumption of social harmony, critics say, prevents pluralists from studying how and in whose interests this alleged consensus is maintained. On the other hand, pluralists attack Hunter and conflict-oriented theorists generally for looking for conflict based on social class differences and therefore finding it.

4. *Differences in levels of analysis.* Both Dahl and Hunter deal with cities as cities, not as centers of larger metropolitan areas. Hunter did discuss the ties of Atlanta's influentials to the federal government and foreign interests, but both Hunter and Dahl focused on the city level. Thus their differences cannot be accounted for by the level of analysis they used. Indeed, both scholars have been criticized for restricting their discussion of community power to the micro level. In his restudy of New Haven, Domhoff (1977) argues that community power in that city cannot be understood if it is not placed in a macro-political context. Domhoff believes that a national network for urban policy planning exists, and that New Haven's suburban ruling class (which Dahl thought had withdrawn from city politics) has become part of this national network, dominating the politics and culture of the central city via decision making at the national level. Similarly, sociologists Vidich and Bensman insist that community politics cannot be understood except in the context of national life. In their study *Small Town in Mass Society*, Vidich and Bensman claim that "almost all aspects of [small-town life in upstate New York] were controlled by external

forces over which [townspeople] had little control; the idea of democratic self-determination had no basis in fact" ([1958] 1971:320). As we shall see in a case study of Caliente, a small town in the western desert (Chapter 15), life-and-death community decisions are often made in places far from the community.

Logan and Molotch focus on "place-based" (local) elites, but unlike both Hunter and Dahl, they consistently link local development to national policy. Their macro–micro linkage results from their theoretical orientation: non-Marxist urban political economy.

5. *Differences in political ideology.* Logan and Molotch attempt to construct a "sociology of urban property relations" (1987:13). Paying great attention to human agents in urban growth, they reject various forms of what they deem determinism. Specifically, they reject the notion that city space is a mere reflection of larger processes under capitalism, particularly capital accumulation and the reproduction of social classes. Logan and Molotch infer that meaningful participation is extremely limited. Here they would agree with both Dahl and Hunter.

Both Dahl and Hunter found relatively small numbers of people participating in community decision making. In both cases, the top leadership represented about 1/100th of the city's population. Also, they agreed that the top leaders work with a second level of minor decision makers (Dahl called them *subleaders* and Hunter called them the *understructure*), but that a very small group effectively made major decisions. Thus their findings do not seem too different. The major difference between Hunter and Dahl lies in the interpretation of their data. And their interpretations stem from normative assumptions about how democracy *should* work.

Hunter implied that something was rotten in Atlanta; local government practice didn't live up to democratic ideals. In his view, it is not proper for a small economic elite to make decisions, for he assumes that the interests of elites are not the interests of the citizenry as a whole. Hunter ([1953] 1963:239) found that most people are apathetic about politics because they're not consulted about decisions that affect their lives. Further, he found that people disadvantaged by the status quo are not an articulate group and can't make their demands known. However, Hunter didn't accept the elitist community power structure as inevitable or legitimate. He offered proposals, based on his community organization background, to bring about wider participation in local politics and to make pluralism really work.

Dahl, on the other hand, was more pessimistic when he wrote his New Haven study. He thought that the masses should not be full participants in the political process because they are the "apolitical clay" of the system (1961:227). He believed that it was better for this inert mass of clay to remain inert. People—including scholars—change their minds over the years. (Dahl has since become a member of the Democratic Socialist Organizing Committee, an organization committed to ideals closer to Hunter's proposals than to interest-group pluralism.) But in the 1950s, Dahl thought that democracy's health is best preserved by depending on the competence and standards of political elites. For this reason, some observers claim that *pluralism* is misnamed; it should be called *democratic elitism* (Bachrach, 1967).

Some critics suggest that by putting his stamp of approval on New Haven's power structure, Dahl was guilty of "ideological spleen" (Phillips, 1971–1972:85). That is, he wrote off the mass of citizens without examining why they're apathetic or ill-informed. Others charge that Hunter was too optimistic about the common people ever being full participants in the political process.

To pluralists like Dahl, government promotes the general welfare, not special interests, and market forces primarily shape cities. To followers of Hunter's elitist model, business elites are the prime mover; government follows their lead. To Logan and Molotch, entrepreneurs primarily shape cities in their own interest, within a context of economic and political forces; local government also seeks growth, for different reasons, so business and government are natural allies.

Interestingly, conservative and liberal social scientists who look at cities tend to see pluralistic power structures, whereas radical social scientists tend to see elitist systems of power. Similarly, decentralists tend to view community power as highly concentrated; centralists tend to see a dispersion of power.

*To conclude*: Over the decades, the study of community power has attracted a variety of scholars, including those who are not often considered urbanists (e.g., Dahl and Hunter, the Lynds, and W. Lloyd Warner before them). Why? The microcosm of the city provides a testing ground for democratic theory in general. Perhaps this is the key to understanding the long-standing debate between elitists and pluralists.

Scholars engaged in the continuing debate over the nature of community power are dealing with an age-old normative question: "Who should govern?" Pluralists find that current decision makers—professionals, experts, members of the well-educated upper middle class, and a few lower-status people—run things in a rational, efficient, and evenhanded manner. Their rule ensures social order. Critics of pluralism, on the contrary, find that local decision makers are members of elite groups who make decisions with their own interests in mind, interests that conflict with those of groups denied access to policymaking, particularly lower-class and lower-status people. Hunter and those using the elitist model are far less concerned with questions of efficiency and rationality in government than are the pluralists; the elitists stress issues of equality and equal representation of everyone's interests. Between these two perspectives lies a chasm of difference.

## CITIZEN POLITICS

### Citizen Participation

Stein Rokkan once said that "votes count but resources decide." All three models of community power support this view. Neither Logan and Molotch, Dahl, nor Hunter give much attention to voters' choices as determinants of local politics.

Likewise, neither the pluralist, elitist, nor city-

as-a-growth-machine models find that great numbers of local citizens participate in decision making. In fact, even though the political arena may seem infinitely more crowded than in Boss Tweed's day, community power researchers of all ideological stripes find that *only tiny minorities of the population play the game of city politics.*

Pluralists assume that these actors, while small in number, represent a diversity of groups and interests. Further, they assume that political leaders don't serve the interests of one group more than those of another. Pluralists point to the following individuals or groups as participants in the political process, either formally or informally: (1) government officials, both elected and appointed; (2) government bureaucrats; (3) business executives and business-oriented organizations (e.g., Chamber of Commerce); (4) organized labor; (5) political parties; and (6) special-interest groups and single-issue groups (e.g., Association for the Education of the Mentally Retarded, local garden clubs).

Radical critics of pluralism reject the idea that the power of the local garden club can be equated with the power of corporate institutions. They say that, for example, to equate the PTA with Mobil or IBM is to ignore the message of George Orwell's *Animal Farm* (1954): "All animals are equal . . . but some are more equal than others." Further, they point to the millions of dollars that big lobbies spend annually, dollars that ensure access to policymakers at the very least and serve to make the "level playing field" a myth. In 1991 and 1992, for example, political action committees (PACs) spent $205 million in contributions to politicians nationwide; almost $189 million was dished out to candidates for Congress (Table 14.1).

Amid the race riots of Watts, Los Angeles, and other urban conflagrations in the 1960s, a number of activists and political theorists tried to change the rules of the political game. Their goal was to make the less equal a bit more equal, to bring new players into the arena of politics. More specifically, they sought to broaden the structures of influence and power to include those whom Dahl and Hunter agreed didn't participate in local policymaking: the poor and near-poor, the powerless, racial minorities, and the

**Table 14.1** The Top 10 Political Action Committee Spenders, 1991–1992 (in millions, rounded to the nearest hundred thousand dollars)

| | |
|---|---|
| Teamsters | $11.8 |
| American Medical Association | 6.3 |
| National Education Association | 5.8 |
| National Rifle Association | 5.7 |
| National Association of Realtors | 4.9 |
| Association of Trial Lawyers of America | 4.4 |
| American Federation of State, County, and Municipal Employees | 4.3 |
| United Auto Workers | 4.3 |
| National Congressional Club | 3.9 |
| National Abortion Rights Action League | 3.8 |

SOURCES: Federal Election Commission; *Newsweek*, May 24, 1993, p. 6.

socially unesteemed. What they called for was *citizen participation*.

But exactly who should participate? How much power should people long excluded from politics now have in making public policy? What would the stirring slogan "Power to the People" mean in practice? These questions stirred controversy and fear in the 1960s.

Since that time, the focus of citizen participation has shifted, suggesting that the stakes are big when there is a proposed change in the political rules. Here is a brief history of events and movements that had an impact on urban politics.

In the early 1960s, the civil rights movement mobilized large numbers of African-Americans, many of whom had never before voted or participated in more active forms of public policymaking. Typically, these new political players came from lower-class backgrounds and had lifestyles that differed from those of traditional decision makers. Many people wondered how these new players would use their potential for political power.

*"Maxfeas"* In 1964, Congress passed the War on Poverty program put forward by President Lyndon B. Johnson. Then the debate over how "the people" would exercise their power heated up, for no one could predict how newly politicized African-Americans and others long excluded

from the political process would use their resources. Under the War on Poverty program, the federal government mandated a rather vague provision for the "maximum feasible participation of the poor" in community action programs ("maxfeas" for short). This meant that poor people were supposed to participate in the planning and execution of community action programs. However, members of Congress and mayors alike had few hints that maxfeas would be taken seriously. When there was a surge of energy and militant action by the poor in many cities, mayors and other traditional political actors were taken by surprise. And they were not happy. Some local officials developed ingenious methods of dealing with citizen participants, especially militant ones. Often they sent out what Tom Wolfe (1971) calls the *flak catchers*, low-level bureaucrats whose job entailed calming the militants down and catching their flak. Meanwhile, when the new political participants tried to secure social changes in their own interests, they were called a host of names, including "un-American."

The exact intent of Congress in mandating maxfeas is not clear. But one thing is clear: Congress did not intend that the opportunity extended to the poor and powerless should upset the traditional balance of power at the urban level. Members of Congress complained, threatening to veto funds for the War on Poverty. Big city Democratic mayors complained to the national Democratic administration, threatening to do something if funds weren't redirected away from community groups and funneled back to them.

By the late 1960s, the War on Poverty had been reduced to a holding action. Vietnam gripped the nation and the federal purse; some activists switched from antipoverty to antiwar efforts, and critics raged against the program. Mayors and members of Congress had been stung by the unintended consequences of the maxfeas provision for citizen participation. Even the War on Poverty's sponsor, President Johnson, accused the program of being run by "sociologists and kooks." And the omnipresent Daniel Patrick Moynihan, wearing his professorial hat, argued that maxfeas was based on *Maximum Feasible Misunderstanding* (1969). The political backlash

**Fig. 14.5** STARTING YOUNG. Citizen participation can mean attending a political rally, voting, lobbying, bringing a lawsuit, e-mailing a comment to city hall, rioting, and/or running for office. (Deborah Mosca)

against "too much participation" by the "wrong kinds of people" served to emasculate the antipoverty program, and President Richard M. Nixon dismantled it during the early 1970s. (Several War on Poverty programs, however, still exist, notably Head Start.)

Looking back, people involved in the 1960s attempts at citizen participation have mixed feelings. Some feel that it was a time of exciting social change. Others wonder if it was a cruel hoax, perpetuating political and economic inequality under the guise of equal opportunity.

Today, participation in politics for some citizens is a spectator activity (voting, putting a bumper sticker on the car). For others, it is more involving: e-mailing the mayor, giving money to a candidate, joining a group with political goals. And for a very few, participation means running for political office, leading a protest, sponsoring a recall campaign, and/or committing an act of civil disobedience or terrorism.

### Dark Shadows

By the mid-1990s, many Americans felt left behind to wallow in a swamp of discontent. Momentous changes had touched people's daily lives—the reorganization of the economy, deindustrialization, a communications revolution, transnational interdependence, social movements, and so on. But instead of a reasoned, modulated public conversation over choices in a time of change and widespread fear of personal (and national) decline, there were loud noises: bombs bursting in air, the fever-pitched voice of *The Snarling Citizen* (Ehrenreich, 1995), and the cocked guns of a paramilitary counterculture dreaming *Warrior Dreams* (Gibson, 1994). Alienated, some stopped voting. Facing postmodern society, some looked back to a romanticized rural past, just as Tönnies had done in his dislike for modern society. Others took to talk radio or the Internet, blaming "them" (female executives, people of color, gays, environmentalists, animal rights supporters, politicians, Jews, etc.) for their own loss of affluence, status, and hope. And a few, perhaps inspired by Travis Bickel, the fictional Vietnam vet in Martin Scorcese's *Taxi Driver* (1976), used violence to cleanse the cities of "scum."

Surprisingly, liberals, radicals, and ultrarightists identified a common enemy of citizen participation: globalism. Not surprisingly, they disagreed on how to respond to its challenge.

Liberals feared that effective citizen participation had become meaningless in a global economy. Ralph Nader, for one, warned that officers of the World Trade Organization, the successor to the General Agreement on Tariffs and Trade (GATT), and other international organizations would govern world trade without input from local or state governments, let alone citizen groups. The upshot, Nader says, is that citizen participation is being replaced by autocracy: Faceless, unelected bureaucrats sit in secret administrative tribunals in faraway places, deciding key issues.

Radicals are divided. Some stress the importance of nonviolent local action; others reason that citizen input à la Nader has little impact on international capitalism. Meanwhile, ultrarightists put a different spin on globalism: They fear a "satanic" conspiracy aimed at establishing a one-world government that, they claim, is run by evil Jewish bankers, Bolsheviks, the Federal Emergency Management Agency, and the United Nations. Their solution: the primacy of county-level government, property rights, and the right to

bear arms. Critics denounce them as paranoid fanatics or latter-day Ku Klux Klansmen (i.e., white Christian males who seek easy answers to complex processes that serve to lower their social position). Scholars (e.g., Kazin, 1995) note that their brand of right-wing populism runs deep in American history.

Meanwhile, economic conservatives are not much concerned with the possible ramifications for citizen participation in the global economy. Traditionally, they have preferred the market to decide who gets what.

At the same time, people of varying stripes look to new forms of citizen participation. One tool for broadened participation, used by the Danish government, is the *consensus conference*. Ordinary citizens of varying backgrounds deliberate on technology policy such as genetic engineering, an area long dominated by academic and business elites. Another tool is—or may be—electronic communication.

## Electronic Democracy?

By the 1970s, the term *citizen participation* had vanished from the political vocabulary. Recently, this term has resurfaced—with a new twist. Now, often as not, it refers to participation in public-access computer networks. In Santa Monica, California, to take one example, citizens can gain access to city information and services via computer modem. Started in 1989, Santa Monica's Public Electronic Network (PEN) has been used by city residents about 1,500 times a week for computer conferences on public issues, e-mail, electronic bulletin boards of city information, and on-line forms. The enhancement of a sense of local community was one of its original objectives (Creighton, 1992).

Do wired city halls constitute a step toward electronic democracy? Do electronic town meetings signal wider citizen participation? Or are they just new ways of fooling Jane and John Q. Public into believing they have a real voice—when they have but a faint whimper? Assessments and hopes differ. Speaking about PEN, a professor of communications at the University of Southern California says that the electronic network does not encourage people to participate if they are not already involved in city government (Dutton in Figallo, 1992). Others point out that an electronic network has serious drawbacks for public decision making. First, computer conferences take a great deal of time—some call it a *time sink*. Second, computer conferences can, and often are, dominated by a very small number of users. Third, so-called electronic town meetings have come under heavy attack as undemocratic; often one person does all the talking—the leader.

The technology for widespread citizen participation is not in question. Interactive video, e-mail, computer conferencing, and other means for citizen input already exist. What remains problematic are the *ends* to which this powerful technology will be put. For example, in 1985 French students used MiniTel, a national computer system, to organize successful protests against unwanted educational changes. The government of Singapore uses information technology (IT) to track transportation use and many other aspects of citizens' lives. Scientists exchange information quickly among their peers worldwide, thus bypassing traditional gatekeepers such as journal editors. A high-tech gay group in the United States, calling itself Digital Queers, uses computer technology for grass-roots organizing; on-line communication "provides [gay] people with a way of coming out of the closet more easily, without being seen" (Signorile in Tuller, 1994:A11). Two large national organizations, the League of Women Voters and Project Vote Smart, sponsored an Internet election trial in 1994, and the California World Wide Web server is expected to become a model for reporting national elections. In the coming decade, many issues relevant to electronic democracy will bear close monitoring, including privacy, pseudoparticipation, and manipulation of the many by the few.

*To conclude:* Can a superhighway be a vehicle for citizen participation? Some think so, if the road is electronic. For example, in 1993 the Rome-based Transnational Radical Party had 40,000 members from 75 nations who exchange opinions, plan strategy, and decide on policies on the

Internet. Also, through its connection to the Internet, Amnesty International mobilizes its members to bring pressure on governments to release political prisoners. The Institute for Global Communications' computer network encourages users to work together on environmental and peace issues by dialing up locally and acting globally.

Now participation includes mass action (demonstrations, riots), class action (lawsuits), talk radio, and computer conferencing on the Internet. Using one or more of these techniques, new players have entered the local and international political arenas.

From the 1960s on, other events changed political participation in the United States. Most notably, numerous subcommunities organized around particular interests, forming such varied groups as the Italian-American Anti-Defamation League, the Homeless Coalition, the Montana Militia, the Black Panthers, the Gray Panthers, and Queer Nation. Rarely were these new game players greeted with enthusiasm or grace by traditional community decision makers. In some cases, repression, threats, and even murder accompanied the struggle for citizen politics. On the other hand, so did political accommodation. Voting rights were made secure for African-Americans through grass-roots organizing. The number of African-Americans and Latinos who held elected office in cities with populations of over 50,000 grew from zero in 1960 to 30 in 1986. (However, as Hatfield [1989: D1] notes, in 1989, fewer than 15,000 of the nation's 504,404 national, state, and local elected officials were Latino, Asian, or African-American, although they constituted about 25 percent of the population.) Women ran successfully for political office in communities throughout the nation; in 1985, 14,672 women served as mayors and municipal council members (U.S. Bureau of the Census, 1992:Table 434). Day-care centers were funded by cities in response to demands from community groups like Bananas. And so on.

Picket the mayor's office, e-mail the city manager, bring a lawsuit in federal court, lobby the bureaucrats, bad-mouth the opposition, go on a hunger strike, get elected to the city council, convince the Chamber of Commerce, take out an ad in the newspaper, leak a juicy tale to the press, bribe a housing inspector, seize the bulletin boards, mau-mau the flak catchers, organize the grass roots, build a coalition, terrorize a neighborhood, riot, ask the ward boss, and threaten to move a factory out of town to a cheaper place, taxwise. These are some of the methods urbanites have used in the game of local politics to get what they want.

What methods work best? That depends on the circumstances; there is no easy or single answer. Moreover, the methods people use to reach their political goals depend on who they think runs the town. Those who side with Hunter in the community power debate might think that talking to bureaucrats in order to get their proposal enacted is a waste of time. Those who side with Dahl might lobby the functional experts on a particular issue. Those who see the city as a growth machine might figure out how their project fits in with the community's economic development and then rally support from members of a pro-growth coalition.

When trying to change the distribution of local governmental resources, most groups in America work within the existing political system, either by lobbying, organizing, bringing lawsuits, or finding—and pushing—the levers of power. This brings us back to Bananas, the day-care service group encountered in Chapter 12.

## Case Study Continued: How Bananas Learned Who Runs This Town and Got Some Things Done

Terrorists play by their own rules. But other groups trying to reach their political goals have to understand the rules of the game. Bananas had to learn about formal government structure before they knew whom to approach. That learning process was accompanied by some important lessons in the structure of influence. Here is a summary of what Bananas learned.

Over the course of several years, as Bananas provided services welcomed by the community and built credibility, they found that they could work with members of the Ron Dellums machine. And Bananas found that things got done

when Dellums called a state assemblyman, who in turn talked to a Berkeley City Council member and a county supervisor about space for a daycare center. In the past, Bananas had asked, written memos, talked, demonstrated, and lobbied. Now it took only a few phone calls from the right people to bring action. According to Bananas member and initial program director Arlyce Curry (1978), the group could never have gotten funding from the city of Berkeley or accomplished many of its goals without the backing of the Dellums machine.

*Political lesson 1.* The city machine (or at least its shadow) lives on, even in the most reformed governments. Not the Tweed Ring of yesteryear or a Richard J. Daley–like version—but a shadow model. In Berkeley, California (population about 120,000), there is a shadow machine that includes elected officials in the city of Berkeley, the neighboring city of Oakland, the county government, the state assembly, and the U.S. House of Representatives. That is, a group of Democratic party politicians—ranging from the city and county to the state and national levels—works closely together on issues of common concern. Congressman Ronald Dellums (D.-Calif.) is an influential member of this group, often referred to locally as the "Dellums machine."

The so-called Dellums machine doesn't look much like the old machine. It lacks strict discipline and hierarchical structure. Its goal is not spoils; its members press a particular political agenda and share an ideological perspective. But it does work to mobilize votes and dispense benefits.

*Political lesson 2.* In local government, there is usually more than one coalition; a group trying to obtain something can work with several coalitions. As in many cities, Berkeley politics has various coalitions. Aside from the Dellums group, there is the Berkeley Democratic Club (a group of more middle-of-the-road liberals than members of the Dellums machine). Bananas didn't deal with the Democratic Club for several years. But as this group gained more seats on the city council (and the Dellums-supported group lost seats), Bananas found that it had to work with another ally.

*Political lesson 3.* Ethnicity and race are important factors in city politics; compromise among different ethnic groups often entails conflict. To-day Bananas is a multiracial group. But it began as a mainly white group that splintered from a biracial day-care organization. The split between African-Americans and whites centered on jobs and services: who would work at the day-care centers and which community (African-American or white) would receive more services. For some time, tempers ran high as the African-American-dominated group charged racism and Bananas's staff accused them of racial power plays. Mean-while, the African-American-dominated group received city funds for day care and Bananas didn't. As Bananas appealed to a broader constit-uency and became known as a resource for other day-care groups (including a Chicano group that Bananas helped to obtain city space), it gained credibility. Finally, after five years of grass-roots organizing, a new Berkeley city manager, himself an African-American, decided to mediate be-tween the two groups. After about six months of negotiations, the city's day-care budget was split, half going to the African-American-dominated group and half to Bananas. Later, Bananas ex-panded its membership and became a multira-cial group.

*Political lesson 4.* Never underestimate the power of goodwill and mutual aid. Bananas alone was weaker than Bananas supported by a range of community interests: single parents, feminists, day-care center operators, and com-munity service agencies.

*Political lesson 5.* Adaptability increases the chances of survival in changing times. In times of recession and near-broke local government, funding from private and nonprofit sources be-comes crucial. As government funding cutbacks hit hard, Bananas scrambled for funds to keep its doors open. Along with nearly 200 other groups, Bananas applied to the Gulf & Western Founda-tion, a nonprofit foundation, for financial aid. It won a three-year, $135,000 grant to strengthen its resources and add staff in 1983. A decade later, Bananas was still alive and very active.

In short, Bananas learned the facts of commu-nity political life by personal experience. Mem-bers of the group spent years of hard work learn-ing how to accomplish their goals. Understanding the informal power structure of the city was a major element in their eventual success.

## ANOTHER LOOK

Urban politics, using either peaceful methods of compromise, negotiation, and back-room deals or more militant techniques of confrontation and intimidation, is a process that determines who gets what from the public purse. The history of U.S. cities shows that both formal and informal power structures are used and manipulated by people seeking public resources.

The way groups play the political game de-pends on how they think it works. And the way scholars describe the structure of community power depends on their research methods, politi-cal ideology, level of analysis, theoretical orienta-tion, and intellectual discipline. The debate be-tween pluralists and elitists illustrates once again that what you see depends on how you look at it.

It is also noteworthy that scholars do agree on one point: The number of people involved in making key decisions affecting a city's distribu-tion of resources is very few, relatively speaking. Is this good or bad? Here scholars disagree. Some fear hyperpluralism and the consequent government by bureaucrats. Others are more frightened by the notion that small elites control the quality of urban life. Still others suggest that the issue is essentially false, for the whole idea of local control is a mere illusion; key decisions af-fecting cities are no longer made there, for the growth of big business and big government has changed the nature of politics. In this view, sig-nificant decisions with political impact—where a new company will locate and pay taxes, how much federal aid the city will get, and so on—are made far away from the city, with little citizen participation.

## KEY TERMS

**Decision analysis**   A research technique, associated with Robert Dahl, used to gain an understanding of how a political system works. It involves the observation and analysis of decision making and the actors involved in making decisions. The decision analyst attempts to find out who made important decisions and how they were made by observing events directly, analyzing historical records, and interviewing participants in the decision (e.g., urban renewal project sites).

**Elitist model of community power**   A model, associated with Floyd Hunter, that describes urban politics as dominated by a relatively small, cohesive elite, primarily from the private business sphere.

**Growth machine model**   A model, associated with sociologists Harvey Molotch and John Logan, that describes urban politics as dominated by a local pro-growth coalition of of businesses, commercial landowners, and rentiers (persons with a fixed income from stocks and bonds or persons who profit from rents); government agencies are also key actors in the politics of growth.

**Pluralist model of community power**   A model, associated with Robert Dahl, that describes urban politics as pluralistic in terms of the individuals or groups represented in decision making, with no one dominant group.

**Reputational analysis**   A research technique, associated with Floyd Hunter, used to gain an understanding of how a political system works. It involves surveying the opinions of knowledgeable persons in the community about who makes key decisions.

**Sociometry**   The study of the network of relationships among members of a group. The patterns of interaction in a group can be presented diagrammatically, using a sociogram.

## PROJECTS

1. **Community power.** Do a reputational study of power in your community. The simplest form might consist of having professors at your college or university list the most influential people in the community. More time-consuming and more valuable studies would involve surveys of several different types of "knowledgeables" and/or use of an expert

panel with follow-up interviews, asking those who score high on the list to identify powerful actors in the community.

2. **Community power.** Do a decisional study in your community. A simple approach would be to analyze who participated in two or more issues, based on newspaper coverage of the issues. Content analysis of news articles could be supplemented by one or more of the techniques used by Dahl: interviews, direct observation (e.g., attending sessions of formal decision-making bodies), and examination of historical records.

3. **Community power.** Pick two cities already studied by community power researchers (e.g., San Francisco, Philadelphia, New York, Boston, Chicago, Atlanta) and examine the researchers' findings. Did the researchers come to similar conclusions? If not, why? Which of the three models seems to best fit the data for each city?

## SUGGESTIONS FOR FURTHER LEARNING

For a case study of coalition politics, see two books by Chester Hartman, *Yerba Buena: Land Grab and Community Resistance in San Francisco* (San Francisco: Glide, 1973) and *The Transformation of San Francisco* (Totowa, N.J.: Rowman and Allanheld, 1984). City planner Hartman provides details on a complex battle between downtown groups and neighborhood residents over a large-scale redevelopment project.

The classic statement of the elitist model of community power is Floyd Hunter's *Community Power Structure* (New York: Anchor, [1953] 1963). The classic opposing statement from the pluralist perspective is Robert Dahl's *Who Governs?* (New Haven, Conn.: Yale University Press, 1961).

For case studies of community power in the pluralist tradition, see Roscoe C. Martin, Frank Munger et al., *Decisions in Syracuse: A Metropolitan Action Study* (Bloomington: Indiana University Press, 1961); Linton C. Freeman, *Patterns of Local Community Leadership* (Indianapolis: Bobbs-Merrill, 1968); and Wallace S. Sayre and Herbert Kaufman, *Governing New York City* (New

York: Russell Sage, 1960). For case studies in the elitist tradition, see Ritchie P. Lowry's study of "Micro City" (Chico, California), *Who's Running This Town?* (New York: Harper & Row, 1965); August E. Hollingshead's study of Morris, Illinois (studied also by W. Lloyd Warner and named "Jonesville"), *Elmstown's Youth* (New York: Wiley, 1949); and C. Wright Mills's study of a midwestern city of 60,000 people, "The Middle Classes in Middle-Sized Cities," *American Sociological Review* 11 (1946): 520–529.

For the theory underlying the newer community power models and case studies using these concepts, see Harvey Molotch, "The City as a Growth Machine: Toward a Political Economy of Place," *American Journal of Sociology* 82 (1976): 309–330; John Mollenkopf, "The Postwar Politics of Urban Development," *Politics and Society* 5 (1976): 247–295; Clarence N. Stone, *Regime Politics: Governing Atlanta, 1946–1988* (Lawrence: University Press of Kansas, 1989); and William G. Domhoff, *Who Rules America Now? A View for the '80s* (Englewood Cliffs, N.J.: Prentice-Hall, 1983). In *The Contested City* (Princeton, N.J.: Princeton University Press, 1983), John H. Mollenkopf gives a history of national urban programs and their implementation in San Francisco and Boston. He argues that during times of economic and political crisis, such as the New Deal and Lyndon B. Johnson's Great Society, "political entrepreneurs" reshape coalitions that bring in the less powerful or previously unrepresented. In "Local Business Leaders and Urban Policy: A Case Study," *Insurgent Sociologist* 14 (1987):33–56, Nancy Kleniewski concludes that in Philadelphia, the impetus for urban renewal came from both political interests and economic interests who interrelated in a pro-growth coalition. Also see Adolf Reed, Jr., "The Black Urban Regime: Structural Origins and Constraints," in *Power, Community, and the City: Comparative Urban and Community Research*, vol. 1, ed. M. Smith (New Brunswick, N.J.: Transaction Books, 1988).

In "Organizational Ties and Urban Growth," in *Networks of Power: Organizational Actors at the National, Corporate, and Community Levels*, ed. Robert Perrucci and Harry R. Potter (New York: Aldine de Gruyter, 1989), pp. 97–109, J. Allen

Whitt critiques both network analysis and Molotch's city-as-a-growth-machine thesis.

M. Gottdiener addresses what he considers *The Decline of Urban Politics* (Newbury Park, Calif.: Sage, 1987), focusing on the role of the "local state." In Chapter 5, Gottdiener evaluates the differences between power elitists and pluralists and reviews current debates within neo-Marxism relating to community power.

For a look at New York City in the 1980s, see John Hull Mollenkopf, *A Phoenix in the Ashes: The Rise and Fall of the Koch Coalition* (Princeton, N.J.: Princeton University Press, 1993), and Chris McNickle, *To Be Mayor of New York: Ethnic Politics in the City* (New York: Columbia University Press, 1993). Mollenkopf argues that Mayor Ed Koch gave "new patronage" to community service providers and put together a pro-growth coalition with the corporate elite and land developers. McNickle says that when mayoral candidates so often sound alike, they distinguish themselves by their image. To be mayor of New York City, he says, "requires a leader who can reconcile the competing visions the city's ethnic groups hold of the metropolis, at least in sufficient measure to win the confidence of a majority."

While the United States continues to be a colorful global stew pot, its elected officials remain decidedly pale—and male. Nonetheless, according to University of Houston political scientist Richard Murray, quoted in Bill Turque, "Breaking an Ole Boy Network," *Newsweek*, June 19, 1989, p. 39, women are perceived to be not only kinder as managers but also more honest than men: "women are less likely to have their hand in the tray." Various organizations, including the National Organization for Women (NOW), the National League of Cities, and women's political caucuses can provide up-to-date numbers of office holders.

V. S. Naipaul brings an outsider's fresh eyes to Atlanta in *A Turn in the South* (New York: Knopf, 1989). The Trinidad-born, Oxford-trained novelist and nonfiction writer notes a dichotomy between political and economic power in Atlanta: African-Americans hold elected positions, but the economic power is all white. "The great encircling wealth and true power of white Atlanta," he says, lie in suburban Atlanta, which "could get by quite well without the black-run city center." Thus novelist-essayist Naipaul implicitly agrees with political scientist Clarence Stone's assessment of Atlanta's power structures.

A series of six documentary films was inspired by Robert and Helen Lynd's 1929 and 1935 studies of *Middletown*. Produced by Academy Award winner Peter Davis, the films explore both the continuity and change in Muncie, Indiana. The films, released in 1982, range from 60 to 120 minutes each and focus on various aspects of the community, including Muncie's mayoral race, "The Campaign." Study guides are also available from the distributor, First Run/Icarus Films, in New York City.

For a historical examination of anti-government groups, see Michael Kazin, *The Populist Persuasion: An American History* (New York: Basic Books, 1995). See also *Warrior Dreams: Paramilitary Culture in Post-Vietnam America* (New York: Hill and Wang, 1994); author James William Gibson says that the fall of Saigon and the start of *Soldier of Fortune* magazine, both in 1975, underpin a paramilitary counterculture among some white American males. This suggests that the paramilitary ultraright was in place years before federal actions at Waco, Texas, and Ruby Ridge, Idaho, the two events commonly thought to be catalysts for its rise.

Sherry Arnstein describes the experience of citizen participation in the federal Model Cities program and develops her model of participation in "A Ladder of Citizen Participation," *Journal of the American Institute of Planners* 35(1969): 16–24. From the viewpoint of the 1990s, participants in the Free Speech, feminist, and antiwar movements assess *Berkeley in the '60s*, Mark Kitchell's 1990 documentary film, shown on PBS's *P.O.V.* and in commercial movie theaters.

An off-Broadway play by Oyamo, *I Am a Man*, produced in 1993 by New York City's Working Theatre, is a gripping look at one form of participation in the political process: a strike for better working conditions and equal pay. The drama centers on T. O. Jones, the leader of the Memphis sanitation workers, who staged a wildcat strike in 1968.

Radicals and liberals were rethinking the concept of citizen participation in the 1980s. A series of books gives a sense of the authors' point of view: Carl Boggs, *Social Movement and Political Power: Emerging Forms of Radicalism in the West* (Philadelphia: Temple University Press, 1986); Harry C. Boyte, Heather Booth, and Steve Max, *Citizen Action and the New American Populism* (Philadelphia: Temple University Press, 1986); and Harry C. Boyte and Frank Riessman eds., *The New Populism* (Philadelphia: Temple University Press, 1986).

A tongue-in-cheek work of New Journalism satirizing community participation and the anti-poverty programs is Tom Wolfe's "Mau-Mauing the Flak Catchers," in *Radical Chic and Mau-Mauing the Flak Catchers* (New York: Bantam, 1971), which describes how San Francisco poverty groups (African-American, Chicano, and Samoan) confronted minor government officials in a ritualized manner in order to rip off poverty program money.

## REFERENCES

Bachrach, Peter. 1967. *The Theory of Democratic Elitism: A Critique*. Boston: Little, Brown.

Bachrach, Peter, and Morton S. Baratz. 1962. "The two faces of power." *American Political Science Review* 56:947–952.

Baltzell, E. Digby. 1958. *Philadelphia Gentlemen*. Glencoe, Ill.: Free Press.

Banfield, Edward C. 1961. *Political Influence: A New Theory of Urban Politics*. New York: Free Press.

Bishop, Katherine. 1992. "San Francisco feels developer's fall." *New York Times* [national edition] (May 24):A10.

Caplow, Theodore. 1980. "Middletown fifty years after." *Contemporary Sociology* 9:46–50.

Creighton, Kathleen. 1992. Computer conference, the WELL (November 30), 9:36 A.M.+.

Curry, Arlyce. 1978. Personal interview with Dick LeGates, Berkeley, Calif. (July 21).

Dahl, Robert. 1961. *Who Governs? Democracy and Power in an American City*. New Haven, Conn.: Yale University Press.

D'Antonio, William V., and Eugene C. Erickson. 1970. "The reputational technique as a measure of community power: An evaluation based on comparative and longitudinal studies." Pp. 251–265 in Michael Aiken and Paul E. Mott, eds., *The Structure of Community Power.* New York: Random House.

DeLeon, Richard Edward. 1992. *Left Coast City: Progressive Politics in San Francisco, 1975–1991.* Lawrence: University Press of Kansas.

Domhoff, G. William. 1977. *Who Really Rules? New Haven and Community Power Reexamined.* New Brunswick, N.J.: Transaction Books.

Ehrenreich, Barbara. 1995. *The Snarling Citizen: Essays.* New York: Farrar, Straus & Giroux.

Figallo, Cliff. 1992. Computer conference, the WELL (December 16):8:21 A.M.+.

Fleischmann, Arnold, and Joe R. Feagin. 1987. "The politics of growth-oriented urban alliances: Comparing old industrial and new Sunbelt cites." *Urban Affairs Quarterly* 23:207–232.

Friedland, Roger. 1983. *Power and Crisis in the City: Corporations, Unions and Urban Policy.* New York: Schocken.

Gibson, James William. 1994. *Warrior Dreams: Paramilitary Culture in Post-Vietnam America.* New York: Hill and Wang.

Hartman, Chester. 1973. *Yerba Buena: Land Grab and Community Resistance in San Francisco.* San Francisco: Glide.

Hatfield, Larry D. 1989. "Minorities: Large numbers, little clout." *San Francisco Examiner* (August 13):D1.

Hunter, Floyd. [1953] 1963. *Community Power Structure: A Study of Decision Makers.* New York: Doubleday, Anchor.

———. 1980. *Community Power Succession.* Chapel Hill: University of North Carolina Press.

Jennings, M. Kent. 1964. *Community Influentials: The Elites of Atlanta.* Glencoe, Ill.: Free Press.

Kazin, Michael. 1995. *The Populist Persuasion: An American History.* New York: Basic Books.

Kristof, Nicholas D. 1993. "4 years after Tiananmen, the hard line is cracking." *New York Times* [national edition] (June 1):A1+.

Logan, John R., and Harvey Molotch. 1987. *Urban Fortunes: The Political Economy.* Berkeley: University of California Press.

Logan, John, and Min Zhou. 1989. "Do suburban growth controls control growth?" *Amercian Sociological Review* 54:461–471.

Lynd, Robert S., and Helen M. Lynd. [1929] 1956. *Middletown.* New York: Harcourt, Brace & World.

———. 1937. *Middletown in Transition.* New York: Harcourt, Brace & World.

Melosi, Martin. 1983. "Dallas–Fort Worth: Marketing the metroplex." Pp. 162–195 in Richard M. Bernard and Bradley R. Rice, eds., *Sunbelt Cities: Politics and Growth since World War II.* Austin: University of Texas Press.

Mollenkopf, John Hull. 1983. *The Contested City.* Princeton, N.J.: Princeton University Press.

Moynihan, Daniel Patrick. 1969. *Maximum Feasible Misunderstanding.* New York: Free Press.

Nader, Ralph. 1993. Remarks on the *MacNeil/Lehrer NewsHour*, PBS (December 14), 5–6 P.M. PST.

O'Connor, James. 1973. *The Fiscal Crisis of the State.* New York: St. Martin's Press.

Orwell, George. 1954. *Animal Farm.* New York: Harcourt, Brace & World.

Phillips, E. Barbara. 1971–1972. "You've repossessed my bootstraps, so brother, can you spare a dime?: The liberal paradigm of political economy in theory and practice." *Maxwell Review* 8:59–95.

Stone, Clarence N. 1976. *Economic Growth and Neighborhood Discontent: System Bias in the Urban Renewal Program of Atlanta.* Chapel Hill: University of North Carolina Press.

———. 1981. "Community power structure—a further look." *Urban Affairs Quarterly* 16:505–515.

———. 1989. *Regime Politics: Governing Atlanta, 1946–1988.* Lawrence: University Press of Kansas.

———. 1991. "The hedgehog, the fox, and the new urban politics: Rejoinder to Kevin R. Fox." *Journal of Urban Affairs* 13:289–297.

Tuller, David. 1994. " 'Digital queers' flying high in cyberspace." *San Francisco Chronicle* (January 7):A11.

Turque, Bill, with Ginny Carroll. 1989. "Breaking an ole boy network." *Newsweek* (June 19):39.

U.S. Bureau of the Census. 1992. *Statistical Abstract of the United States 1992*, 112th ed. Washington, D.C.: Government Printing Office.

Vidich, Arthur, and Joseph Bensman. [1958] 1971. *Small Town in Mass Society: Class, Power, and Religion in a Rural Community.* Garden City, N.Y.: Doubleday.

Whitt, Allen J. 1986. "The local inner circle." *Journal of Political and Military Sociology* 14 (Spring):115–125.

Wolfe, Tom. 1971. "Mau-mauing the flak catchers." Pp. 117–184 in *Radical Chic and Mau-Mauing the Flak Catchers.* New York: Bantam.

# PART VI
# Space and Place

*Allan Jacobs*

# CHAPTER 15
# Metropolitan
# Form and Space

For the tourist, a city proudly presents its unique and shiny face—its Fisherman's Wharf, Eiffel Tower, or Bronx Wildlife Conservation Center (formerly the Bronx Zoo). Typically, tour buses with oversize windows bypass a city's black eyes, such as the South Bronx and a waste-disposal center (popularly called the garbage dump).

Geographers may be interested in the unique features of a city, asking how and why they happen to be there. David Harvey's inquiry (1989b) into the building of Sacré-Coeur, the grandiose church atop Paris's Montmartre, is exemplary. But, in addition, geographers look for patterns in city form and space.

Walking around San Francisco and looking at the city's edges, an astute observer might notice the following spatial features:

1. Residences of affluent and poor people segregated in different areas.
2. Lumberyards located outside the central business district (CBD).
3. Shops offering specialty items or services, ranging from Nigerian wood carvings and evangelical religious books to income tax assistance, all situated in commercial areas.
4. Sprawling shopping malls, with hundreds of parking spaces, set in edge cities or postsuburbia.

These observations can be used to generate hypotheses (scientifically testable statements of relationship) about metropolitan form and space. Here is one hypothesis: People and activities are not randomly distributed throughout a city or metropolis. To the contrary, specific spatial patterns exist, influenced by such factors as the mix of commodities and services produced there. This hypothesis is confirmed by geographers who measure spatial patterns and theorize about why they take the forms they do.

But the concept of space is not the exclusive province of geographers. Indeed, after years of neglect, space is a hot topic in social theory and philosophy.

## BRINGING SPACE BACK IN

In terms of its theoretical importance, space rivaled the spotted owl; it was almost extinct by the mid-twentieth century. Practical, political, and theoretical concerns—the seeming annihilation of space by time and a global economic system incorporating a "geographical nihilism"

(Smith, [1984] 1991:177), to name just two—had marginalized the concept of space.

Then, starting in the 1970s, space was brought back into social theory in a big way. (Likewise, it returned to popular consciousness, thanks to such events as Earth Day.) Now influential thinkers in a range of disciplines and hybrids (e.g., geography, city planning, economic sociology, and cultural theory) point to space as a key to understanding modern social, political, and economic life.

## Henri Lefebvre's Influence

Henri Lefebvre, a major intellectual figure in France (and a one-time Parisian taxi driver), played a key role in reviving the interest in space. A daring and creative thinker, Lefebvre developed a "theory of space, and he introduced into urban discourse the analysis of the state, and the role of the political in shaping people's dispositions about the city" (Katznelson, 1992:96). His work influenced David Harvey and Manuel Castells, major contributors to the new urban paradigm.

According to Lefebvre, space will soon play a preeminent role in modern societies. In his influential and demanding book *The Production of Space*, philosopher-urbanist-activist Lefebvre says that the effects of space may be observed on all planes—from the "arrangement of surfaces in a supermarket" to the "ordering of 'flows' within nations or continents" ([1974] 1991:412. Most important, Lefebvre says, we should be concerned "with space on a world scale." In his view, only by generating or producing a space can groups, classes, ideas, values, and political systems be recognized. For Lefebvre, space is much more than a built environment; it is also a force of production and an object of both consumption and political struggle (Katznelson, 1992:98).

This chapter draws on a number of disciplines and hybrids to better understand spatial patterns among and within cities. It begins with a discussion of the system of cities: how cities are arranged in relation to each other. Then it examines the internal structure of the city: how spatial patterns are arranged within the modern U.S. city and its surrounding area.

## THE SYSTEM OF CITIES

### Central Place Theory

Why is a city located at point A rather than at point B? Why are there so few big cities and so many small towns in a regional landscape?

Geographers have been asking such questions at least since 1826, when the German economic geographer Johann von Thunen published *Isolated State* ([1826] 1966). More than 100 years later, another German geographer, Walter Christaller, developed the most comprehensive model: **central place theory** (Figure 15.1). This model suggests that "a hierarchy of places will develop wherein a few large cities dominate more small cities, leading, ultimately, to a dense network of evenly spaced trade center towns that serve the local population" (Hudson, 1985:11).

Christaller's theory attempts to demonstrate a relationship between the number, importance, and distance of cities from one another within a geographical area or region. It deals with two key variables: city *importance* (roughly measured by population size) and *distance* to other cities and urban communities.

Christaller's theory is this: A *central place* (a centrally located city or urban community) provides goods and services to people living in the surrounding region, commonly called a *hinterland.* A hierarchy of goods and services is available (ranging from the lowest to the highest order of services available), depending on the importance or population size of the city. Central places of the lowest order (small towns) serve only a nearby area. Central places of a higher order (larger towns and cities) serve a roughly hexagonal area covering a larger surrounding region; this region might contain several lower-order central places. Finally, a large, region-serving city serves a roughly hexagonal area

around it that might contain many other lower-order central places.

Central place theory conceives of cities as part of a regional landscape, not as self-sufficient economic entities. Various commodities and services must be exchanged. Some items will be "exported" from the city, such as banking services or manufactured goods. These will be exchanged for food and other things that the city "imports."

Traditionally, central place theorists use two measures to determine the level of economic interchange between a city and its outside world—**hinterland** and **range.** A ciy's hinterland is the surrounding area to which a city (central place) provides goods and services. A city's range is conceptualized as the area from which persons travel to the central place to purchase a service or merchandise, such as a baseball game or gasoline, offered there.

### Does Central Place Theory Work?

Unsurprisingly, Christaller's theory works best under the conditions that his model assumes: flat land areas with a uniformly distributed population and a relatively unspecialized economy. Thus in places like Iowa in the 1930s where these conditions existed, there was an observable hierarchy of cities: many hamlets, fewer villages, and many fewer towns.

According to geographer John C. Hudson, central place theory is "correct in its basic predictions" (1985:12). But, he notes, the theory is "silent about how such a system might come about."

Hudson breaks the silence. Starting in the 1850s, Hudson says, railroad companies played an important role as deliberate designers of the settlement system on the prairies and plains of North America. For instance, in North Dakota, Hudson finds that "entire line-chains of towns were planned, quite deliberately, by those with enough money and influence to make their plans a reality." Thus the system of cities on the Great Plains resulted primarily from the railroads' actions to serve their own interests—not from nat-

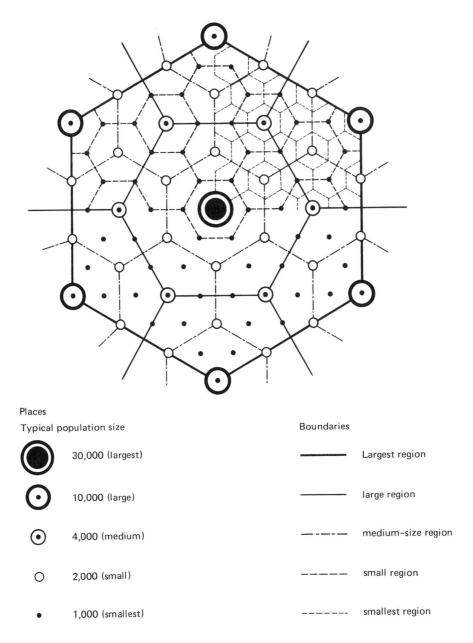

Places

Typical population size

30,000 (largest)

10,000 (large)

4,000 (medium)

2,000 (small)

1,000 (smallest)

Boundaries

———————— Largest region

———————— large region

—·—·—·— medium–size region

— — — — small region

- - - - - - smallest region

**Fig. 15.1** CHRISTALLER'S CENTRAL PLACE THEORY. According to economic geographer Walter Christaller, the largest central place in the region illustrated (population: 30,000) is the most important market center for a large hexagonal region around it. Progressively smaller central places lie at the center of a system of smaller hexagonal market regions within the main market region. (Walter Christaller, *Central Places in Southern Germany* [Englewood Cliffs, N.J.: Prentice-Hall, 1966], p. 66. Copyright 1933 by Gustav Fisher Verlag Jena. Reprinted by permission)

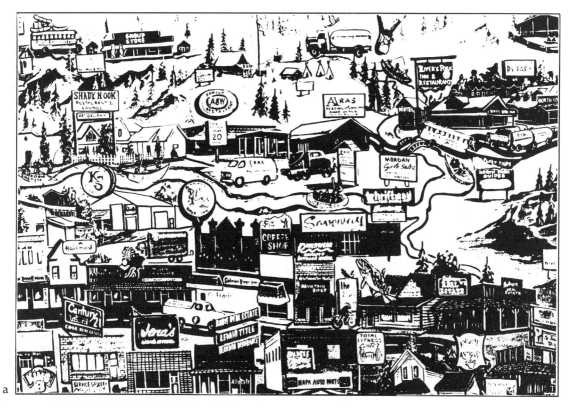

**Fig. 15.2** ELECTRONIC RETAILING. TV home shopping networks and the Internet play havoc with the concept of range. Instead of shopping nearby, (*a*) a consumer in Salmon, Idaho (population: about 3,000), where big retail outlets don't exist, as this poster by Jerry Grusell shows, and (*b*) a Chicagoan (who is pressed for time, snowed in, or tired out) can get many goods and services—from exercise equipment and high-fashion clothes to psychic advice—from home. (Tim Teninty)

ural evolution or chance. Nonetheless, the Plains' settlement pattern does match the predictions of central place theory.

But does central place theory predict settlement patterns *outside* agricultural regions? Does it explain where cities will be located in postindustrial society? In a word, no.

Central place theory does not explain the urban hierarchy in a global economy. To understand why, let's look at Iowa again, this time in the 1990s. First, the state's economy is no longer unspecialized; its top exports in 1990 were industrial machinery and computer equipment ("Internet," 1991:4). Second, Iowa's hinterland is the world. In 1990, Iowa's products were exported to

fourteen countries and territories. Iowa is typical, not an exception. Throughout the United States, millions of urban and suburban jobs depend on exports. In California, for example, economists estimate conservatively that one in twelve jobs is related to international trade (Eckhouse, 1989:B1).

In other words, city systems in postindustrial economies like the United States are unlike those in southern Germany in the 1930s, when Christaller conducted his research. One big difference is that *the American economy today is dominated by large, multilocational firms.* Geographer Allen Pred (1977:99) notes that between 1960 and 1973, the number of domestic and foreign jobs controlled by the 500 largest U.S. corporations

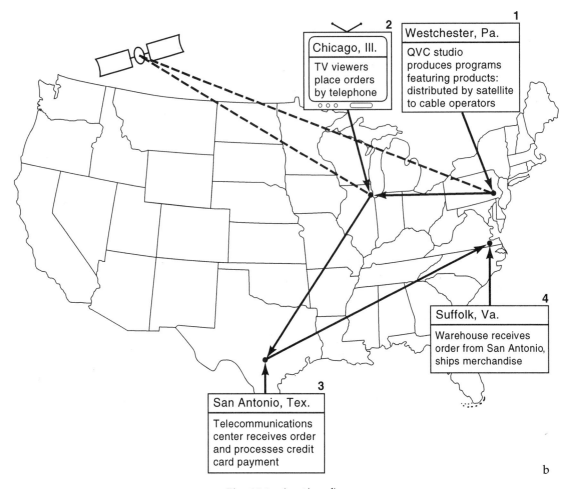

**Fig. 15.2**   (*continued*)

grew more than 68 percent—to a total of 15.5 million. Most of these corporations, Pred observes, are multilocational, carrying on their activities in more than one place. When he published his findings in 1977, multilocational business firms in the San Francisco–Oakland–San Jose Bay Area controlled jobs in 234 other metropolitan centers in the United States and Canada. The supermarket chain Safeway, for example, has its headquarters in the San Francisco Bay Area, but it employs people in hundreds of localities; by 1992, Safeway employed 104,900 people worldwide (Koenig, 1993:D11).

A second difference concerns the *internationalization of hinterlands*. Christaller's model assumes

regional hinterlands. Today, firms cross national boundaries so often that many sectors in the "American economy" are not American anymore. Fast-food franchisers like McDonald's are the most visible planetary enterprises. But many businesses have a global reach. For example, Baker & McKenzie, the world's largest law firm in 1993, employs 1,640 lawyers in 32 countries. This group, nicknamed "McFirm," is not an American firm with foreign offices. Rather, it is an international firm with attorneys representing 45 nationalities; most of these attorneys live outside the United States (Feder, 1993:1). Furthermore, the Internet, a global web of computer networks, is becoming a vast marketplace that makes national (as well as city, suburban, and state) boundaries easy to ignore. Big and small companies troll the Internet for new customers. According to the Internet's program manager, in April 1993 there were 6,545 commercial users on the Net; one year later, the number had more than doubled—to 14,154 commercial users (in Lewis, 1994:3–6).

A third difference concerns *the growth of government intervention*. Christaller's model assumes relatively little government influence on business' location decisions. Now, however, state and local officials often play a key role, lobbying private corporations to locate in their state or city. For example, after California's governor personally phoned the president of a toy company in Denmark, the state legislature changed tax laws affecting non-U.S. companies, and a team of state–local, private–public officials promised over $7 million in assistance with marketing and roads if the company located outside San Diego. It did (Reinhold, 1993:1).

Lastly, *Christaller's model wrongly predicts the role of the biggest city, populationwise, in a system of cities*. If the model were correct, the largest city in a system of cities—in the United States, New York City—would contain the headquarters of the nation's largest business corporations. To the contrary, in the 1970s only one-quarter of the 500 largest U.S. corporations were headquartered in New York City (Pred, 1977). By 1989, New York had only 59 headquarters of the top 500 (Sassen, 1991:171). (Note, however, that even if firms locate their headquarters outside major cities, "they continue to be dependent on the specialized services and financial firms concentrated in major cities" [Sassen, 1991:171].)

*To conclude:* In the national or global economy, central place theory neither explains nor predicts how the system of cities works. As Paul Kantor puts it, "The reorganization of the national economy by multilocational corporations has decisively redefined the economic functions of cities and unleashed wholly new patterns of urban development" (1988:170). In the postindustrial age, Kantor continues, *"From the perspective of corporate managers, cities are usually interchangeable; from the perspective of those who live in the cities, they are economically dependent."*

Yet a key assumption behind central place theory still holds: Cities can't exist if residents do nothing but take in each other's laundry. That is, there must be economic interaction and exchange between a city and the world outside if the city is to stay viable. This remains the case for twentieth-century supercities, just as it did for urban specks in a rural world some 5,000 years ago. To paraphrase poet John Donne, no city is an island. Cities and their hinterlands are interdependent in terms of economic functions. Christaller, of course, assumed that hinterlands would depend essentially on a nearby central place. In effect, geographer Allen Pred reconceptualizes the notion of hinterland, suggesting that the nation and the world can be a central place's hinterland.

## Classifying Cities by Function

Two geographers, Chauncy Harris and Edward Ullman (1945:7), pioneered the effort to classify cities by function. They reasoned that cities fall into three types:

1. Cities as *central places* (performing comprehensive services for a surrounding area; these cities tend to be evenly spaced throughout the region).
2. *Transport cities* (performing "break-of-bulk" services; these cities tend to be arranged in linear patterns along rail lines and at seacoasts).
3. *Specialized function cities* (performing one service, such as mining or recreation, for large areas).

Harris and Ullman did not think that a city would engage in only one function. Rather, they thought, most cities would represent a combination, and the relative importance of each factor would vary from city to city. New York City, for instance, was seen as a principal center for wholesaling and retailing (central place type), a great port (transport type), and a manufacturing center (specialized function type).

## New Spatial Models

Essentially, central place theory and functional classification sought to answer these questions: "What types of economic functions will occur in a city of a given size, and how does this city relate to its hintereland?" Recent theory addresses a different question: Where does a city (or metropolitan region) with a particular production-consumption profile fit into a national or world system of cities?

Starting in the 1970s, social theorists in Europe and North America have been trying to understand the impact of large-scale changes on the organization of metropolitan space. Generally, theorists point to the following shifts to explain why a world urban system exists: (1) *economic restructuring*, the transformation from manufacturing to services-information and deindustrialization in so-called advanced economies; (2) *the new international division of labor* ("Needle" [Chapter 4]); and (3) *the internationalization of capital*. A variety of social scientists—geographers David Harvey (1982), Doreen Massey (1984), and Neil Smith ([1984] 1991); sociologist-planner Manuel Castells (1989); political sociologist Sharon Zukin (1988); urban planner Saskia Sassen (1988); and political scientist–development specialist Michael Peter Smith ([1987] 1989), to name just a few—have been writing about the world urban system. They do not always agree on major issues, including this key question: Is space a mere reflection of social forces or an independent element of social life? Nevertheless, these urban theorists tend to share a vocabulary and a multidisciplinary approach, called the *political economy perspective* or the *new urban paradigm*.

Two models based on this new urban paradigm were reviewed in Chapter 4: the new international division of labor (Needle) and Logan and Molotch's typology of U.S. cities. Now let's consider a composite model that focuses on the global network of cities. This composite model parallels the work of Manuel Castells and John Mollenkopf, discussed at some length in Chapter 18.

## The Global Network of Cities

What follows is a brief summary of the political economy model of the global network of cities. This summary is based primarily on ideas from two sources: Michael Peter Smith and Joe R. Feagin's introduction to *The Capitalist City* ([1987] 1989) and Saskia Sassen's *The Global City: New York, London, Tokyo* (1991), a book that has been called "a central text for understanding the future of the post-modern, post-socialist, post-industrial world" (Watson in Coughlin, 1994:A8).

First, a note about these authors. Scholars who think about global **systems of cities** tend to criss-cross disciplinary lines. Feagin is exemplary, as noted in Chapter 2. But Sassen is in a class by herself. She is a one-person model of globalism and interdisciplinarity: Now a U.S. citizen, Sassen, a professor of urban planning at Columbia University in New York City, was born in Holland, grew up in Buenos Aires, studied in Rome, earned a Ph.D. in economics and sociology in the United States, and then studied philosophy in France. She has given major speeches to varied groups, including the Modern Language Association, the American Museum of Natural History, big-city mayors, and the American Political Science Association. She travels widely but considers one global city—New York City—home. Let us now turn from Sassen's global-interdisciplinary background to her global-interdisciplinary perspective on cities (which she shares with Smith and Feagin).

According to Sassen, Smith, and Feagin, modern capitalism is a global network of both corporations and cities. At the top of the global urban hierarchy are *first-tier* cities (also called *world command* or *global* cities) such as Tokyo, London, and New York. First-tier or global cities have "extraordinary concentrations of top corporate decision-makers representing financial, industrial, commercial, law and media corporations" (Smith and Feagin ([1987] 1989:3), and they perform central place functions at the global level (Sassen, 1991:169). These global cities are the brains of the global economy.

Spatially, the transnational corporate web is

grounded in global cities. Global cities themselves constitute a system, particularly in terms of international finance, investment, and real estate markets. This means that what Sassen calls *transnational spaces*—spaces outside the control of any state or national government—exist within first-tier cities. (For example, neither the state of New York nor the U.S. government can control the wages or working conditions of the employees of New York City–based multinational corporations who work in Mexico or other offshore locations.) Socially, it means that the world economy has created a two-tier class structure inside global cities: People who live there are almost exclusively highly paid professionals in financial and "producer services" (e.g., lawyers, accountants, ad executives) or low-wage workers (e.g., janitors and truck drivers who ensure the smooth functioning of the financial and producer service sectors).

But only a handful of cities are first-tier cities. Most cities occupy niches lower down in the world urban hierarchy. For example, there are *specialized command cities* (which concentrate the headquarters of a particular industry, such as rubber companies in Akron, Ohio), *divisional command cities* (which concentrate major divisions of top firms, such as oil companies in Houston), *specialized manufacturing cities* (e.g., car manufacturing in Birmingham, England), *state command cities* such as Brasilia, Islamabad, and Washington, D.C., and many *difficult-to-classify cities* that perform diverse economic and state functions (e.g., Mexico City, Singapore, and São Paulo). All these cities are interconnected through an organizational web of transnational corporations and their suppliers.

*To conclude:* The political economy model or new urban paradigm assumes that corporate and city networks are inextricably intertwined in a capitalist world market. In this model, the top 500 to 1,000 multinational corporations "have created an integrated, worldwide network of production, exchange, finance and corporate services arranged in a complex hierarchical system of cities (Feagin and Smith, [1987] 1989:6).

We now move from the political economy model of how cities relate to one another in a world system to an examination of spatial patterns *within* North American cities. The key questions here are these: How are cities internally structured? Why are they structured in this particular way?

## THE INTERNAL STRUCTURE OF CITIES

Fancy houses, skyscrapers, public housing, factories, and warehouses. What part of town are they in? As we hypothesized at the beginning of this chapter, they are not located just anywhere by chance.

To determine exactly where they are located requires empirical investigation. It means going out and observing what facilities do or do not exist in different locations.

In our effort to understand how people and their various activities are distributed over space, we do not have to start from scratch. Since the 1920s, social scientists have collected data and constructed models that attempt to describe and explain patterns of urban space. First, let's look at the three classic models of the **internal structure** of the U.S. industrial-capitalist city: the concentric zone model, the sectoral model, and the multiple nuclei model.

### Classic Models of U.S. Cities

***Burgess's Concentric Zone Model***   University of Chicago sociologist Ernest W. Burgess pioneered the systematic study of the North American city's internal structure. In the 1920s, he developed a model of internal city structure and urban growth: the so-called Burgess **concentric zone model** or hypothesis. This model grew out of Burgess's fascination with a remarkable city at a remarkable time. Early in this century, Chicago —the laboratory for the **Chicago school of sociology**—was a city in transition. The population change in the city over a very short period of time was noteworthy. In 1880 the emerging metropolis had about 500,000 inhabitants. Ten years later, the population had more than doubled.

Chicago was (and remains) a city of ethnic diversity. By 1920, there were large communities of Czechs, Italians, Eastern European Jews, Swedes, Germans, Irish, Italians, Lithuanians, Poles, and increasing numbers of African-Americans (4.1 percent of the population at that time).

The Windy City resembled a vast collection of urban villages, each having its own churches, social clubs, politicians, newspapers, welfare stations, schools, and restaurants. Alongside this ethnic diversity was prejudice, especially against the newer immigrants from southern and Eastern Europe, and a desire to residentially segregate the foreign stock.

As Chicago's population increased, these urban villages or enclaves (enclosed territories) grew, contracted, or shifted. Burgess was impressed with the great differences among various city neighborhoods and tried to make sense of the spatial patterns and cultural life in these communities. He speculated that there was a pattern to the way these neighborhoods grew or shifted, just as there was in plant and animal communities (Park, Burgess, and McKenzie, 1925:47–62). This theoretical framework—that cities, like plant and animal communities, have a characteristic organization and develop territorially as a result of competition for space—is called **urban ecology** or, more broadly, *human ecology*.

Urban ecologists are concerned with the study of the spatial distribution of people and institutions in cities. This distinctive perspective originated with members of the Chicago school, particularly Robert Park and Ernest W. Burgess, and it is continued today by urban ecologists such as geographer Brian J. L. Berry and sociologist John Kasarda (1977). Key concepts in this perspective include competition for a place in urban space, residential segregation, **invasion,** and **succession.** Implicit hypotheses in urban ecology include the following:

1. Cultural changes in a city are correlated and reflected in changes in spatial, territorial organization.

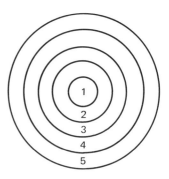

**Fig. 15.3** BURGESS'S CONCENTRIC ZONE MODEL OF THE U.S. CITY. 1 = CBD; 2 = wholesale and light manufacturing; lower-class residential; 3 = working-class residential; 4 = middle-class residential; 5 = commuter's zone.

2. There is an intimate relationship between the social and moral order in a city and physical space, between physical distance and social distance, and between residential proximity and social equality.

Urban ecologists investigate the interrelationships between physical space and the social order at three levels: neighborhood, city, and region.

Working from the perspective of urban ecology, Burgess developed and refined a zonal model. The city can be conceived as a series of concentric circular zones of typical combinations of land use (Figure 15.3). This model was derived from empirical research through inductive reasoning processes. Yet, as noted in Chapter 3, Burgess worked from a theoretical framework (urban ecology), so that the concentric zone model is a product of both inductive and deductive reasoning processes.

Here is what Burgess says about his model: "In the growth of the city we have differentiated the series of concentric zones which is one way of indicating as the city expands outward from its center, how each successive zone tends to encroach upon the further outlying zones" (Burgess and Bogue, 1964:11). Burgess saw the city as containing five successive zones. Zone I is the center of business and civic life. Zone II surrounds Zone

I; it is the Zone-in-Transition, where "areas of residential deterioration caused by the encroaching of business and industry from Zone I" are found. It is a district of rooming houses, slums, and artists' colonies. Zone III contains duplexes or two-family housing where immigrants and second-generation families (the children of immigrants) live. Zone IV houses "small businessmen, professional people, clerks, and salesmen," who live in apartments and shop at neighborhood shopping centers. Zone V consists of a ring of bedroom suburbs (Burgess, [1923] 1925:114–123).

This zonal model doesn't just describe spatial patterns; it contains an implicit hypothesis on the relationship of urban space to social order. Burgess thought that physical location and people's social background are connected in city space. Taking one example—family type—Burgess noted that Zone I (the Central Business District) is mostly a "homeless men's region"; Zone II is "the habitat of the emancipated family"; Zone III is "the natural soil of the patriarchal family transplanted from Europe"; Zone IV provides "the favorable environment for the equalitarian family"; and Zone V is "without question the domain of the [female-centered] family" ([1923] 1925: 114–123).

What, then, is the relationship between physical location and social background? The model postulates an inverse relationship between central location and an urbanite's socioeconomic status (SES). That is, the higher up on the social ladder, the farther the person lives from Zone I. Thus the zonal model hypothesizes that where people live depends on their position on the social ladder.

If this hypothesis is correct, we should be able to predict changes in urban residence patterns. For one thing, we should expect a relationship between social mobility and physical space. Thus, we could predict that as people move up the social ladder, they move out from the city center. Many urban ecology studies conducted in the 1920s showed that this was indeed the case. Immigrant groups first settled in Zone II, the Zone-in-Transition, and moved to outlying zones as they moved up socioeconomically. Then other new migrants to the city would replace the groups that moved up—and out. Such was the succession of residential movements in the city.

A classic illustration of succession is found in Lowell and other textile mill towns of nineteenth-century Massachusetts. First the English, then the Irish after them, then the Czechs and central Europeans, and finally Italians, Poles, and other Southern and Eastern European immigrants resided near the CBD. Over the generations, as each group moved up the SES ladder (say, from unskilled worker to skilled laborer to first-line supervisor and perhaps to manager), its residence moved farther out. As one group moved up and out, its homes were sold or rented to a group below them on the social ladder. And thus various groups succeeded one another on the same plots of ground. (*Note:* By the late 1980s, Lowell was a *former* mill town, but new groups, including 20,000 Cambodians, were living near the CBD.)

The zonal model contains another hypothesis that concerns urban growth. It postulates that cities and towns tend to expand radially from their CBD.

All the hypotheses contained in the zonal model grow out of one basic assumption: that economic competition is the chief organizing agent of human communities. Darwin thought that competition in the struggle for existence is the key variable in the organization of animal communities. Burgess thought that economic competition played a similar role in human affairs and believed that it was expressed in terms of a struggle over space.

According to Burgess, people and business activities tend to be separated into rather homogeneous subareas of a city, and this segregation into so-called natural areas is part of the competition for space. That is, these homogeneous natural areas are not planned but result from the workings of the self-regulating economic market (Adam Smith's "invisible hand," mentioned in Chapter 3).

To Burgess, then, market forces are the key determinants of a city's internal structure. On this point, most urban land economists and urban geographers agreed with Burgess. Many still do. Others developed different models of city structure, however, including two important competing models.

**Hoyt's Sectoral Model**   In the 1930s, real-estate economist Homer Hoyt looked at the residential patterns of 142 cities. As Hoyt organized his data, he observed spatial patterns that didn't fit Burgess's model. Here were Hoyt's main criticisms of the concentric zone model:

1. The retail shopping center, not the financial center, is the central point in most cities.
2. The wholesale and light manufacturing zone adjoins the CBD but does not encircle it.
3. Heavy industry tends to follow river valleys and river fronts, bays or deep tidal basins, or outer belts. New transportation technology is the key factor here, for it is no longer necessary for industry to locate in a concentric pattern close to the center of the city.
4. Working-class people tend to locate near industry. However, factories *do not* form a concentric circle around the CBD; neither do the workers' homes.
5. High-rent areas do not form a complete circle around the outer edge of the city.
6. Commuter housing takes the form of scattered, isolated communities; it is not a zone at all. (1939:17–23)

Hoyt's data did more than conflict with Burgess's hypothesis. They suggested an alternative model of the industrial city: a **sectoral model.** This model, pictured in Figure 15.4, describes U.S. cities as organized in wedges of activity moving outward from the city center, particularly along rail lines, roads, trolley tracks, and other transportation corridors.

Hoyt found that the rent structure of housing also tended to be organized by sectors, not zones. Thus rents along a transport line moving out from the center of the city were often similar. A high-rent wedge might start near the center of the city and follow an exclusive boulevard out to the city's edge. A low-rent wedge might follow the railroad corridor.

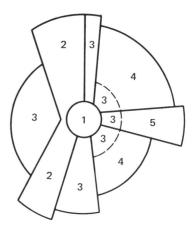

**Fig. 15.4**   HOYT'S SECTORAL MODEL OF THE U.S. CITY. 1 = CBD; 2 = wholesale and light manufacturing; 3 = lower-class residential; 4 = middle-class residential; 5 = upper-class residential. (Adapted from Chauncy Harris and Edward L. Ullman, "The Nature of Cities," *Annals of the American Academy of Political and Social Science* 242:Fig. 5, p. 13. Copyright by the American Academy of Political and Social Science, 1945. Reprinted by permission of the publisher and Chauncy Harris)

**Harris and Ullman's Multiple Nuclei Model**   Geographers Chauncy Harris and Edward L. Ullman (1945) developed another model of urban form that departs significantly from both the concentric zone and sectoral models. They based their so-called **multiple nuclei model** on the idea that cities develop not one but many nuclei (centers) of activity (Figure 15.5).

According to Harris and Ullman, four factors cause the development of multiple nuclei:

1. Certain activities need specialized facilities (e.g., a port needs a waterfront).
2. Similar activities tend to cluster together (e.g., financial institutions group together on Wall Street in New York City).
3. Some unlike activities are not compatible (e.g., an auto-assembly plant and an entertainment district would not be good neighbors).
4. Certain activities cannot compete financially for the most desirable sites (e.g., lower-class housing and warehousing cannot afford to locate in high-rent districts).

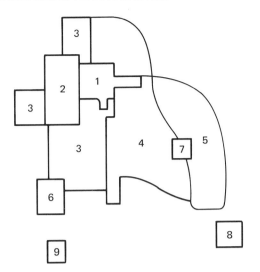

**Fig. 15.5** HARRIS AND ULLMAN'S MULTIPLE NUCLEI MODEL OF THE U.S. CITY. 1 = CBD; 2 = wholesale and light manufacturing; 3 = lower-class residential; 4 = middle-class residential; 5 = upper-class residential; 6 = heavy manufacturing; 7 = outlying business district; 8 = dormitory suburb; 9 = industrial suburb. (Adapted from Chauncy Harris and Edward L. Ullman, "The Nature of Cities," *Annals of the American Academy of Political and Social Science* 242:Fig. 5, p. 13. Copyright by the American Academy of Political and Social Science. Reprinted by permission of the publisher and Chauncy Harris)

## How Useful Are the Classic Models?

The three models of urban form and growth may shed some light on spatial patterns in some cities. But over the years, critics have raised the following criticisms of their usefulness:

1. *No general model is possible.* No city is so neatly organized that it totally fits some theoretical model. Physical features such as hills and lakes serve to distort expected spatial patterns.
2. *The models are time-bound and place-bound.* The models, constructed between the early 1920s and mid-1940s, apply to only some North American cities in the era of industrial capitalism; they cannot explain or predict spatial pat-

terns in postindustrialism. Nor do they explain or predict urban land use outside of Western Europe and North America, which evolved in ways that have little to do with market forces. For example, the spatial development of Lagos, Nigeria, Brasilia, Brazil, and New Delhi, India, was influenced by political, military, and symbolic factors (e.g., colonialists' desire for social control, imperial or nationalist pride).
3. *The models neglect noneconomic values.* The classic models are based on economic logic; they overlook sentiment, local culture, social movements, and politics as influences on spatial patterns.

First, let's focus on the last major criticism: the models' economic bias. From different angles, Walter Firey, Gerald Suttles, and Mike Davis all argue that the models are economistic. Other critics say that politics affects land use and that this major factor is missing from the models. Next, let's look at two other possible paths to understanding city space: (1) social area analysis, an approach to studying urban growth and differentiation that implies a critique of the classic models, and (2) computer modeling as a method of describing and generalizing about urban space. Finally, let's look at a recent spatial model of metropolitan space.

### Firey's Critique: The Classic Models Are Too Deterministic
One important critic of the classic models, sociologist Walter Firey (1947), argues that city land-use patterns are not based purely on deterministic, economic considerations. He claims that such nonrational factors as sentiment and symbolism influence city shape.

Looking around Boston, Firey noted that actual land use didn't fit the patterns predicted by any of the classic models. For instance, old churches and the Boston Common (a public park) are located on very expensive land, and low-density eighteenth-century redbrick buildings stand on Beacon Hill, a high-status, high-rent residential district. If the models were correct, none of these should have been standing;

**Fig. 15.6** LOCAL CULTURE IN "EVERYONE'S FAVORITE CITY." San Francisco's strong identity is based on a rich local culture that includes streets named for Jack Kerouac, Isadora Duncan, and other local writers and artists; colorful neighborhoods ranging from the Haight-Ashbury and North Beach to Chinatown; a large public park with a bandshell, boating, and bison; hundreds of restaurants; parades celebrating cultural diversity; professional sports teams; romantic songs memorializing its bridges and cable cars; homes of the very wealthy and infamous, and many more internationally recognized features. (Phillip Adam, © 1989)

they would have been torn down to make way for higher-density uses in the economic competition for space.

Firey concluded that the classic models couldn't account for noneconomic considerations: people's sentimental attachment to urban landmarks, whether their existence made economic sense or not. He rejected several notions inherent in the classic models: (1) that physical space can be divorced from cultural values; (2) that land use blindly follows some sort of Darwinian economic

imperative; and (3) that people passively accept whatever the market dictates. Many recent events offer support for Firey's views. Consider, for example, the "save Grand Central Terminal" movement in New York City and numerous instances where historic-preservation societies have saved buildings from the wrecker's ball.

To correct for the economic determinism of the human ecologists' classic models, Firey called for an approach he termed *cultural ecology*. This approach, in contrast to urban ecology, would take into account specific cultural and historical factors 's influencing a city's land-use patterns.

### Suttles's Critique: Local Culture Counts

Sociologist Gerald D. Suttles (1984) agrees with Firey: The classic models left cultural values out. But Suttles thinks that Firey himself didn't give culture its due. According to Suttles, Firey treated culture as a kind of leftover—an intangible residue whose effects were found only when deviations from expected economic outcomes occurred to upset zonal or sectoral patterns. By contrast, Suttles wants to make local culture an integral element of cultural ecology, not a mere residual factor.

By *culture* Suttles means everything from what people put in their museums to what they write on their T-shirts. And, Suttles says, some cities have "alot [sic] of local culture": "songs that memorialize their great streets or side streets, homes once occupied by the famous or infamous, a distinctive dialect or vocabulary, routine festivals and parades that selectively dramatize the past, novels, dirty lyrics, pejorative nicknames, special holidays, dead heroes, evangelical moralists, celebrated wastrels, and so on" (1984:284).

Cities with a great deal of local culture, Suttles posits, tend to have a strong self-image, replete with icons of entrepreneurial success and ethnic mobility, historic districts, corporate images, and representations of civic life (Figure 15.6). We might add that a city's sports team and its larger-than-life players bestow identity. For instance, when the Raiders moved out of Oakland, California, local residents fought for years to bring them back—partly for economic reasons, but mainly for reasons of civic identity.

It may seem bizarre, but urban traffic accidents can be a mark of local culture too. New York City, for instance, has a highly unusual pattern of car victims: In the United States as a whole, the fatal victim of a city traffic accident is six times more likely to be a driver or a passenger than a pedestrian; in New York City, about 50 percent of the victims are pedestrians. Why? The head of the city transportation department's safety division offers this explanation: "There's a lot of challenging going on out there, cars challenging pe-

destrians and pedestrians challenging cars . . . the cars usually win" (Friedman in Wald, 1993:1). In other words, one of New York City's traffic problems may be "that it is filled with New Yorkers" (Wald, 1993:1).

For a variety of reasons, including newness, many cities remain "nonentities." Suttles does not name any such nonentity, but Gertrude Stein did. In a famous putdown of Oakland, her one-time hometown, she remarked, "There is no there there."

Recognizing local culture as part of the objective realm and integrating it into the ecological approach, Suttles argues, may help to explain some aspects of city life. For one thing, he suggests, we can better understand why some places resist land redevelopment while other cities do not.

### Davis's Update: The Ecology of Fear

Mike Davis (1992) sees Burgess's ecological model as a tribute to social Darwinism. To Davis, author of *City of Quartz: Excavating the Future in L.A.* ([1990] 1992), Burgess's model is a "combination of half-moon and dart board . . . [that] represents the five concentric zones into which the struggle for the survival of the fittest (as imagined by Social Darwinists) supposedly sorts urban social classes and housing types" (1992:3).

Davis offers his own zonal model, remapping the zones not of Chicago but of post-1992 riot-torn Los Angeles. Davis keeps such factors as class and race, but adds what he calls a "decisive new factor" in understanding the ecology of Los Angeles: fear. Fear, he says, is eating the soul of the city, and different groups cope by adopting "security strategies and technologies according to their means."

Davis thinks that a new species of spatial enclave is emerging in Los Angeles: *social control districts (SCDs)*. These districts, found in Burgess's Zones I and II, include *abatement districts* (e.g., a prostitution abatement zone), which extend traditional police power over industries and behaviors deemed "noxious"; *containment districts* (e.g., the core's "homeless containment district"), which "quarantine potentially epidemic social problems"); and *enhancement districts* (e.g., drug-free zones), which add legal penalties to crimes committed near public institutions.

Outside the inner rings, Davis suggests that some "overclass" Los Angeles neighborhoods are moving to exclude the underclass. He foresees that "electronic guardian angels" will protect upwardly mobile Anglos while consigning the underclass to "community imprisonment."

What does this add up to? In Davis's view, a militarization of the landscape. Zone I—the Downtown Core—is a Fortress comprehensively monitored by video. This comprehensive surveillance constitutes "a virtual *scanscape*—a space of protective visibility that increasingly defines where white-collar office workers and middle-class tourists feel safe Downtown" (Davis, 1992:5) Davis predicts that video monitoring of Zone I workplaces will become "linked with home security systems, personal 'panic buttons,' car alarms, cellular phones, and the like, in a seamless continuity of surveillance over daily routine" (5).

Zone II in Burgess's model, inspired by Chicago, was the zone-in-transition. In Davis's model, it is the "halo of barrios and ghettos" that surround Los Angeles's fortified core. This tenement zone is "the most dangerous zone" of Los Angeles. Nearby MacArthur Park, once the crown jewel of the city park system, is now a "free-fire zone where crack dealers and street gangs settle their scores with shotguns and uzis" (Davis, 1992:6) Many bungalows in the zone look like prison cells—or cages—where "working-class families must now lock themselves in every night" (7).

In Zone III (Burgess's zone of working men's homes), Davis sees a vast network of watchful neighbors providing a "security system that is midway between the besieged, gun-toting anomie of the inner ring and the private police forces of more affluent, gated suburbs" (1992:13). The danger here, he says, is that thousands of citizens become police informers under the official slogan "Be on the Lookout for Strangers," and this "inevitably stigmatizes innocent groups." In Zone IV of Davis's Los Angeles, there are many gated communities resembling a "fortified honeycomb, with each residential neighborhood now encased in its own walled cell" (15).

Here, as in Zone V (wealthy neighborhoods on the distant metropolitan frontier; Burgess's commuter zone), "mini-citadels" are inhabited by more and more "geron[to]crats," the "ruling class of aged, Anglo Baby-boomers, living in 'security-patrolled villages'." Beyond Zone V lies the "Toxic Rim," a "zone of extinction," where polluting industries and disasters waiting to happen are being located.

Does Davis see a way out of this "bad dream"? Yes, maybe. He thinks it is theoretically possible (but practically difficult) to avoid "mega-city apocalypse" by reversing American urban decay with massive new public works (Davis, 1992:20).

*To conclude:* Davis, Firey, and Suttles all reject the purely economic logic of the classic models. Firey and Suttles add sentiment and local culture as influences on city space. Davis adds political and social factors, particularly repression and monitoring by the overclass of the underclass. In his theorizing about unplanned city growth, Burgess shared an evolutionary bias toward social change with conservative thinkers. Yet Burgess and his University of Chicago sociology colleagues were concerned with social reform too. In the 1930s, the Department of Sociology organized a project to bring "community development" to Chicago's near North Side slums; this project produced new notions of self-help and citizen participation (Janowitz, 1967:viii). Nearly seventy years later, Davis implicitly rejects Burgess's conservative theoretical bias, but he shares Burgess's hope that nonviolent urban reform can stop the "dystopic tendencies" operating in cities.

**Other Critiques: Politics Counts**   In Davis's Los Angeles, the "natural order" is far from natural: Social control and surveillance stabilize class and race relations; inequality and fear become accepted as natural; razor-wire substitutes for white picket fences and electronic cameras replace dogs named Spot. Ideologically, then, there is a chasm between Burgess's model and Davis's update.

In large part, this ideological chasm reflects political changes in the United States. When Burgess first published his zone model in 1923, market forces did play a major role in determining what was located where in U.S. metropolitan space, so it is no wonder that he viewed city form as a result of Darwinian struggles for space. But since that time, the so-called invisible hand of the market has been greatly mitigated by government intervention. Here are a few examples of government programs and policies that affect the price and use of land in metropolitan space: local zoning laws; federal–local urban renewal; federal loans to small businesses; housing subsidies (e.g., federal low-interest mortgages, public-housing projects, federally and state-funded roads and tax write-offs for certain types of construction, and local rent control); public investment in mass transit, sewers, schools, and other infrastructure; the placement of a city garbage dump; and the closing of a military base.

*To conclude:* Burgess published his concentric zone model in a time of limited government. This may account for his neglect of political factors in the struggle for urban space. (The two other classic models—Hoyt's sectoral model and Harris and Ullman's multiple nuclei model—came later, but they too pay no attention to politics as a force in city shape.) But there were individuals, as much as twenty years before Burgess published his model, suggesting that politics affected land use. Muckraking journalist Lincoln Steffens, for one, exposed the corruption of local government by business, calling it *The Shame of the Cities* ([1903] 1904). To Steffens, local business meddled with the "self-regulating" market because "in a country where business is dominant, businessmen must and will corrupt a government which can pass laws to hinder or help business" ([1931] 1937:299). And by the time Burgess published his model, the municipal reform movement had often succeeded in limiting the influence of urban political machine bosses who, like Boss Tweed, regularly intervened in the market of supply and demand for political ends (Chapter 13).

Today most urban theorists recognize that a variety of players can influence governmental land use decisions. In the United States, this recognition, together with the expansion of government's role in urban life, underlies a new model of urban land use. Before turning to this new model, however, let's look briefly at two other approaches to investigating urban growth: (1) social area analysis and (2) computer modeling.

## Social Area Analysis: A Method of Investigating Urban Growth and Differentiation

While Firey and Suttles fault the classic models for leaving out cultural variables, others criticize Burgess, Hoyt, and Harris and Ullman for neglecting societal variables. These critics point out that the classic models treat the city as if it were an island, adrift from its larger society.

One approach—social area analysis—attempts to look at city form and space as a product of societal forces. Social area analysis (technically, the term refers to a method of investigation developed by sociologists Eshref Shevky and Wendell Bell) starts from a basic premise: Urban growth and differentiation result from changes in the organization of society.

Specifically, these investigators argue that groups in society tend to segregate themselves on the basis of *social rank, family type,* and *ethnicity and race.* Shevky and Bell measure social rank by an index of occupation and education; family type by several measures, including type of residence, age of children, and wife's status in the labor force; and ethnicity / race by the proportions of African-Americans and other segregated populations in the census tract.

According to social area analysis, as a city becomes more complex and heterogeneous, areas within the city become more homogeneous (in terms of social rank, family status, and ethnicity). One study of the Chicago metropolitan area using Shevky and Bell's basic approach found this generally to be the case. Chicagoans do live among people like themselves in terms of class, race, ethnicity, and point in the life cycle (Rees, 1970).

Few disagree with the underlying premise of social area analysis: that changes in the socioeconomic organization of society have spatial effects. But the Shevky–Bell model has been questioned on both theoretical and empirical grounds. Specifically, critic Janet L. Abu-Lughod

(1969) found that one of its measures of change—social rank—accounts for most of the variation in city structure and that another measure—family type—is culture bound and inapplicable to other social systems, such as that of Egypt.

## Computer Models of Urban Structure

No computer model of urban structure has yet gained wide acceptance. Still, computer models are being used to map a variety of projects, including alternative urban futures. One, developed by University of California–Berkeley professors, called the *California Urban Futures Model*, attempts to predict how cities in the Bay Area might expand in the next two decades given different sets of conditions.

## NEW PERSPECTIVES ON METROPOLITAN SPACE

Perhaps we live at "dusk" (the historical moment between the end of one era and the beginning of another), a moment that Hegel thought would encourage clear vision, even wisdom. That may explain the burst of urban theory in America and Western Europe starting in the 1970s.

## The Political Economy Model or New Urban Paradigm

One new approach to city spatial structure, referred to in earlier chapters, is called the *new urban paradigm* or, alternatively, the *political economy model*. It stresses the role of power in the allocation of urban land. Unlike Burgess's model, it assumes that both economic and political power, not economic competition in a "free enterprise market," are key determinants of who gets what in city space. It assumes that such factors as the social class system, social conflict and the nonneutral role of government influence the spatial patterns of U.S. cities.

The political economy paradigm is rooted in Marxist thought, and initially the model was championed by neo-Marxists. Geographer David Harvey's *Social Justice and the City* (1973) and urbanist Manuel Castells's *La Question urbaine* (*The Urban Question: A Marxist Approach* [1977]) are usually credited as seminal studies. But very quickly—by the early 1980s—more and more mainstream social scientists began to see the urban world through the lens of the political economy model. For example, Logan and Molotch are not Marxists, but they share some of the model's basic assumptions and apply them in their prize-winning and influential book *Urban Fortunes* (1987) (Chapter 4).

Now let's take a brief look at the ideas of David Harvey and Manuel Castells, two contributors to the new paradigm. Although they disagree with one other on some key points, both link the city to broader patterns of global restructuring and both draw on Marx's ideas. In addition, both are international figures whose ideas, teaching, research, and personal identities cross many borders.

*David Harvey* In a time when many, if not most, academics inhabit disciplinary cubbyholes, British geographer David Harvey stands out as a transnational, Renaissance-like person. Formerly a professor in the United States and holder of the Halford MacKinder Chair of Geography at Oxford University, he has written about topics as far afield as Nietzsche's images of destruction and creation (1989a), the history of the Sacré-Coeur Basilica in Paris (1989b), and housing investment in the United States and Great Britain (1982). Here we'll focus on just a few of his ideas, mostly developed in his groundbreaking book, *Social Justice and the City* (1973).

Working within the framework of Marx's work on capitalist accumulation, Harvey asks how any particular urban spatial pattern came to exist. He rejects benign biotic processes and Darwinian competition as determinants of city space. Rather, he says, capitalist city spatial patterns result from social conflict, class struggle, political-economic competition, and capitalism's need to accelerate development. The key element in shaping and reshaping capitalist cities, he thinks, is capitalist production. In his view, urban space is constantly being restructured under capitalism as a joint result of government policies (e.g., tax rates set by localities) and private firms' location decisions (which are influenced by capitalism's need for accelerated development). He sees capitalist production as the key element in the shaping and reshaping of cities.

Some mainstream theories, he notes, do describe and predict land use in the Western capitalist city. For example, Alonso's bid rent theory (Chapter 2) correctly predicts what happens to poor folks: They end up in slums on high-priced land near the city center—where they can least afford to live. But Harvey wants more than *description*. He calls for change—change in the underlying conditions that promote such unjust (in his view) outcomes. His *prescription*: eliminate ghettos. How? By doing away with "competitive bidding for land use" and replacing it with a "socially controlled urban land market and socialized control of the housing sector" (Harvey, 1973:127). In other words, Harvey thinks that people made up the political rules for the economic system (including the rules determining land rents and values) in the first place, and that people can change them.

As Harvey sees it, people can remake the political-economic rules, but capitalism's circulation process frames the rules and affects urban spatial processes. Here is his logic: The capitalist system produces more commodities than can be used or consumed. Faced with these crises of overproduction, capitalists prefer investing in commodities than in fixed capital (e.g., office buildings) because they stand to earn higher profits. But they will invest in fixed capital when there is an overaccumulation or surplus of capital. After World War II, a time of overaccumulation in the United States, capitalists (buoyed by government policies such as road building and Veterans Administration loans to home buyers) used their surplus capital to fund suburban development. This illustrates the circle that capitalists seek to complete: putting money into circulation as investment and returning this money as money *plus profit*. Suburbanization, deindustrialization, gentrification,

urban redevelopment, and reorganization of the urban hierarchy are a few of the processes that occur as "part of a continuous reshaping of geographical landcapes" by capitalist forces. According to Harvey, the built—and rebuilt—landscape of cities and suburbs thus has more to do with capitalist profitability than with efficiency or people's needs.

***Manuel Castells*** Spanish-born, French-trained, Berkeley professor Manuel Castells shares Harvey's viewpoint: People can change the rules of the game. In fact, he sees the city as a theater of action where organized groups and social movements try, often successfully, to change the rules in their own interest. As an example, Castells notes the gay movement's success in reorganizing neighborhood space in San Francisco. Not only was the gay social movement successful in reallocating physical and social space, but it also changed the political landscape, becoming an important force in San Francisco (Castells, 1983:337).

But, like Harvey, Castells see urban land allocation as much more than an expression of local political action. Both look to broad societal forces, particularly market forces, class struggles, and government policies, as key influences on spatial patterns in capitalist cities.

According to Castells, cities and world regions are being transformed by the combined impact of a technological revolution and the restructuring of capitalism. In addition, he says, the transformation of the modern state plays a role in changing spatial patterns. For example, in Castells's view, the "rise of a technologically-oriented warfare state has a definite suburban form on the fringes of the large metropolitan areas in expanding regions. . . . Militarization, high-technology development, and suburbanization seem to be closely related processes, in the specific conditions of the U.S., and as a consequence of the policies associated with the rise of the warfare state" (1989:306). In the warfare state, Castells expects cities to become more internally segregated, not only socially but also culturally and functionally (306).

Castells calls his theorizing part of a *techno-*

*economic paradigm* (1989:350). Yet the name may mislead, for Castells is not a determinist; he believes that human actions—setting up a worldwide network of local governments, active citizen participation, for example—can "master the formidable forces unleashed by the revolution in information technologies" and lead to new sociospatial structures, reintegrating time and social space.

*To conclude:* The acceptance of the political economy model by mainstream social science is ironic, indeed doubly so. First, mainstream social scientists in the United States had not even discussed Marx's ideas for decades, let alone embraced them. In the 1920s, Park and Burgess dismissed Marx's ideas as either "irrelevant or wrong" (Abu-Lughod, 1991:234). At the height of the Cold War in the 1950s, only the rarest, most deviant social scientist assigned Marx to college students. Yet acceptance of the political economy model came very quickly in the late 1970s and early 1980s, when the Cold War was still hot enough to make Marxist ideas suspect. Second, growing acceptance within academia of the Marxist-inspired political economy model came at the same time that U.S. and British voters veered toward Reaganomics and Thatcherism, conservative calls for a return to "free market" economics (a synonym for capitalism). So in the 1980s, in at least in two postindustrial Western nations, there was a mismatch between popular consciousness and theoretical understanding: Just as urbanists revised or rejected Burgess's views of the free market, national administrations in the United States and Great Britain revived those very ideas.

True, some say that the political economy model is not comprehensive. For example, it does not account for recent conflicts over multicultural curricula or other conflicts based on identity and culture, not economics. But currently, there is no competing model that liberal or conservative social scientists offer for understanding urban spatial structure in postindustrial society. The model described below is not an ideological competitor; it lies squarely in the radical tradition. For the moment, then, this new urban paradigm has the ideological field all to itself.

## The Multinucleated Metropolitan Region Model

Dissatisfied with existing appoaches to spatial restructuring, M. Gottdiener set out in the 1970s to study the relationship between *Late Capitalism* (Mandel, [1972] (1987) and deconcentration: the absolute increase of population and density of social activities in areas outside traditional city regions and population centers (Gottdiener, 1985:9) His goal was to better understand the "sprawling, polynucleated nature of metropolitan growth" (1985:vii) in the United States. Although Gottdiener distances himself from the models of Lefebvre, Castells, and Harvey, he has been influenced by their work. Indeed, his model can be viewed as a modification, not a rejection, of the political economy approach. We need not detail the differences among the models here, except to point out that Gottdiener's vision is more oriented to the "transformation of social relations" and the role that the state (government) plays in sociospatial patterns.

In a nutshell, here is Gottdiener's thinking: Besides people, so much industry, banking, and industry, and so many corporate headquarters, had moved to U.S. suburban areas by the 1970s that these areas were transformed into centers of metropolitanwide activities. This process of becoming an urbanized region is called *deconcentration*, and the new space it produces is called a **multinucleated metropolitan region.** Orange County in southern California is an example of this *qualitatively new form of settlement space* (Gottdiener, 1985; Gottdiener and Kephart, 1991).

Nothing like Orange County has ever happened in urban history. According to sociologists Gottdiener and George Kephart, this new spatial form means that the traditional concept of the city is now obsolete: "urban life is now organized in metropolitan regions composed of polynucleated and functionally differentiated spaces . . . that are neither suburbs nor satellite cities; rather, they are fully urbanized and independent spaces that are not dominated by any central city" (1991:34). Yet, these new decentralized counties have the "economic vitality and cultural diversity formerly associated with the traditional central city" (Kling, Olin, and Poster, 1991:9).

Postsuburban Orange County, one of twenty-one such regions in the United States, is polynucleated; there is no dominant urban center, and about 70 percent of its population live outside its three largest cities. Further, Orange County employs about 1 million people; a majority works in the information sector. Orange County offers the full array of services associated with urban life, but it is not an urban center. It is "a sociospatial form of late capitalism" (Gottdiener and Kephart, 1991:34).

Using a sample of twenty-one counties like Orange County (i.e., multinucleated, highly urbanized counties adjacent to traditional urban centers), Gottdiener and Kephart try to assess what factors account for the growth of such postsuburban centers. On the basis of their comparative analsyis, they conclude that high technology is the primary base of economic growth in many counties, but not all. Nor can the growth in services alone account for the emergence of the multinucleated economy. In their view, many social forces—"military-related spending in the permanent war economy, the growth in high technology, the robust real estate market, racism, the flight of the white industrial working class to the hinterland, the construction of traditional (non-high-technology) manufacturing plants, the hypertrophic expansion of service-related industries, and new arrangements in the corporate business structure—have all combined" to produce this new settlement space (52).

Retail life in Orange County and other multinucleated metropolitan regions is dominated by enclosed shopping malls, highlighting the "core cultural value of consumerism." (Kling et al., 1991:9). (*Note:* The man who pioneered the design of shopping malls in the early 1940s, architect Victor Gruen, included public cultural facilities as well as retail stores in his original plans. Developers perverted his plans, and later Gruen denied that he was the father of the "malling of America.")

*To conclude:* The multinucleated metropolitan region model attempts to rethink urban spatial patterns in light of the interplay of macro-level changes, particularly shifts in the organization and structure of information technology, the economy, and the political system. Like the political economy model, which it complements, it rejects the premises of the classic models.

## WHERE PEOPLE LIVE

### How Race and Ethnicity Affect Housing Patterns

Melting pot? Stewpot? Witches' brew? Which food metaphor best symbolizes the situation of multiethnic American cities? The answer depends on many factors, including the ethnic/racial composition of the city. As noted in Chapter 9, some groups did melt into the dominant culture; others were partially assimilated; some rejected the dominant culture altogether as a matter of choice; and still others were hardly affected.

One way of measuring the degree to which an ethnic or racial group has blended into the dominant culture is to examine that group's housing pattern over time. Housing patterns—segregation or dispersion, for example—are not the only measure of assimilation. (Intermarriage rates are another key measure.) But residential patterns often indicate larger patterns of social mobility and/or lack of social mobility and acceptance.

Before moving on, a few words about the measurement of residential segregation are appropriate. By now, it should come as no surprise that researchers use various indexes to measure racial segregation, and that different measures yield different results. One widely used measure is the **index of dissimilarity.** This measures the distribution of white and nonwhite (synonymous with "Negro" when used in a landmark 1965 study by the Taeubers) households among census blocks. A *census block* (not census tract, which tends to have a lower score for similarity) can have a score from 0 to 100: the higher the number, the higher the level of racial segregation. The index of dissimilarity looks at the population of a racial

**Table 15.1**  Indexes of Dissimilarity for the Ten Most Segregated and Least Segregated Metropolitan Areas: United States, 1980 and 1990

| *1980* | | *1990* | |
|---|---|---|---|
| *Metropolitan* | *Index of Dissimilarity* | *Metropolitan Area* | *Index of Dissimilarity* |
| *Most Segregated* | | *Most Segregated* | |
| Bradenton, Fla. | 91 | Gary, Ind. | 91 |
| Chicago, Ill. | 91 | Detroit, Mich. | 89 |
| Gary, Ind. | 90 | Chicago, Ill. | 87 |
| Sarasota, Fla. | 90 | Cleveland, Ohio | 86 |
| Cleveland, Ohio | 89 | Buffalo, N.Y. | 84 |
| Detroit, Mich. | 89 | Flint, Mich. | 84 |
| Ft. Myers, Fla. | 89 | Milwaukee, Wis. | 84 |
| Flint, Mich. | 87 | Saginaw, Mich. | 84 |
| Ft. Pierce, Fla. | 87 | Newark, N.J. | 83 |
| West Palm Beach, Fla. | 87 | Philadelphia, Pa. | 82 |
| *Least Segregated* | | *Least Segregated* | |
| El Paso, Tex. | 49 | Charlottesville, Va. | 45 |
| Columbia, Mo. | 49 | Danville, Va. | 45 |
| Victoria, Tex. | 49 | Killeen, Tex. | 45 |
| Charlottesville, Va. | 48 | San José, Calif. | 45 |
| Clarksville, Tenn. | 48 | Tucson, Ariz. | 45 |
| Colorado Springs, Colo. | 48 | Honolulu, Hawaii | 44 |
| San José, Calif. | 48 | Anaheim, Calif. | 43 |
| Anaheim, Calif. | 47 | Cheyenne, Wyo. | 43 |
| Honolulu, Hawaii | 46 | Ft. Walton Beach, Fla. | 43 |
| Fayetteville, N.C. | 43 | Clarksville, Tenn. | 42 |

NOTE: These indexes are based on block group data and pertain to persons reporting white or black as their race.

SOURCE: Adapted from Reynolds Farley and William H. Frey, "Changes in the Segregation of Whites from Blacks," *American Sociological Review* 59 (1994): 33.

group in an entire city and asks this question: To make every census block in the city mirror the racial makeup of the city as a whole, what percentage of each group would have to move to another block? Thus the index of dissimilarity is a measure of *absolute* segregation (Table 15.1). Another index measures *relative* segregation: the **index of exposure**. This index measures the proportion of people in a neighborhood sharing the same ethnic/racial background. Often it is used as a stand-in for measuring positive interaction between racial groups; the assumption here is that physical proximity to people from other racial/ethnic groups promotes positive interaction and empathy. (This is a big, and often incorrect, assumption. Anecdotal evidence [Phillips, 1992–1993] from several racially mixed high schools and colleges in the Bay Area suggests the oppo-

site: Physical closeness without specific programs to increase sensitivity can lead to negative interaction, increased isolation of racial/ethnic groups, and misunderstanding.)

Now, let's consider the contrast between the housing patterns of Dutch immigrants and their families in Kalamazoo, Michigan, and African-American migrants to Chicago over a period of time. Families with Dutch surnames spread throughout Kalamazoo between 1873 and 1965. They did not stay grouped together in one area.

Contrast the Dutch pattern of housing dispersion in Kalamazoo to the pattern of African-American housing segregation and concentration in Chicago. Dutch immigrants in Kalamazoo dispersed as they moved up the socioeconomic ladder and became Americanized. There was no residential area of the city from which they were systematically excluded. Conversely, Chicago's African-Americans were systematically excluded from some sections of the city and did not, as a group, climb the socioeconomic ladder. Thus, in 1970, Chicago's African-Americans remained highly segregated and concentrated in a small **ghetto** area near the center of the city (as predicted by Alonso's bid rent theory). Moreover, this pattern extended to metropolitan Chicago. In 1970, almost 50 percent of Chicago's suburbs with more than 2,500 inhabitants had no black residents; only two had more than 50 black residents. By 1980, the total African-American population of Chicagoland's suburbs had increased—from 3.6 percent in 1970 to 5.6 percent in 1980 (Herbers, 1981:1). However, interpreting the meaning of this small increase is problematic, for much of the suburbanization increase occured in older, close-in industrial areas, not in such suburb-like areas as "Pools and Patios" or "Young Suburbia." In farther-out suburban counties, such as McHenry County (which experienced a population growth of over 32 percent during the decade), African-Americans constituted a minuscule presence, one-tenth of 1 percent of the population in 1980. Similarly, in farther-out suburban DuPage County, African-Americans made up 1.6 percent of the population. What we have in Chicagoland, then, is the continuation of a metropolitanwide pattern identified by Berry and Kasarda (1977:21–52): the segregation and concentration of blacks.

In fact, this pattern of African-American exclusion from suburbs is nationwide. In 1977, America's suburbs were about 94 percent white. In 1990, the suburbs were about 84 percent white (U.S. Bureau of the Census, 1990:Table 6) and about 87 percent non-African-American (U.S. Bureau of the Census, 1992:Table 3, p. 33). Thus, with some exceptions (mainly low-income, older African-American suburbs such as East Palo Alto, California), the United States retains a pattern of "chocolate cities and vanilla suburbs" (Farley, Schuman, Bianchi, Colasanto, and Hatchett, 1978; Farley, Steeh, Jackson, Krysan, and Reeves, 1994). Further, applying indices of dissimilarity and exposure to 1980 census data from fifty-nine metropolitan statistical areas, population researchers at the University of Chi-

cago note that "blacks remain less suburbanized than other minority groups." Even in suburbs, "black segregation remains quite high." These researchers, Massey and Denton, conclude that "inner-city blacks display the highest levels of segregation observed for any [ethnic] group in any [city or suburban] locale" (1988:622).

In brief, then, compared with Asian-Americans and Latinos, African-Americans remain highly concentrated in central cities (Massey and Denton, 1988:621). Within those areas, they experience high levels of spatial isolation, particularly in northwestern and midwestern cities. (Massey and Denton note that Asian-Americans were the least segregated and most suburbanized minority in 1980.)

Is this continuing pattern of African-American housing segregation and concentration mainly a matter of racial discrimination? Many think so. Population researchers Massey and Denton, for instance, say that their research shows that "black suburbanization is completely unrelated" to socioeconomic factors (e.g., occupational status and household income), contextual factors in the metropolitan area (e.g., housing inflation, employment growth), or compositional factors (e.g., population characteristics of the central city and suburbs). In other words, Massey and Denton conclude that in the process of spatial assimilation, there are "strong penalties for being black": "Two decades after the Civil Rights Act of 1968, which, in theory, banned racial discrimination in the sale and rental of housing, blacks have still not achieved equal access to housing in American cities or suburbs" (1988: 622). Quite simply, say Massey and other coauthors (Gross and Shibuya), "the real cause of concentrated black poverty [is] racial segregation," not segregation by class (1994:443).

In the case of Chicago, the late Mayor Richard J. Daley did not hide his racism. He believed that it was right to keep blacks out of established white ethnic neighborhoods because they "didn't keep their yards clean, and the neighborhoods went to hell and that kind of thing" (Erlichman in Scheer, 1979:8).

But many observers think housing segregation is much more complicated, involving issues of social rank as well as race. For Berry and Kasarda (1977:22), the key to understanding the virtual isolation of metropolitan Chicago's African-Americans is neighborhood status:

Since blacks as a group are considered of lower status by many whites and, in large concentrations, are associated with residentially undesirable areas, the arrival of large numbers of blacks reduces a neighborhood's rank in residential status hierarchy for whites . . . . Because neighborhood status is so affected by racial change, areas that attract large concentrations of blacks are typically unable to retain white residents. . . .

Berry and Kasarda's findings in Chicago support what researchers found in other U.S. cities: If whites can possibly afford to do it, they will live with those of their own social rank and race. For those familiar with the Burgess model and social area analysis, this should come as no surprise. Both hypothesize that in urban society, people will sort themselves out by social background variables. Burgess and Park thought this sorting-out process happened in an unplanned fashion, creating natural areas. And before the Great Depression, they charted the shift of ethnic neighborhoods in Chicago, using the terms **invasion** and **succession** to describe some of the sorting and sifting.

Since the University of Chicago researchers first used these terms to describe residential urban change, studies in Chicago and elsewhere have documented the process. They tend to find a period of "penetration," in which a few minority-group families buy into a residential area. This period is followed by the "invasion," in which a substantial number of their group follows.

Neighborhood invasion is sometimes accompanied by block busting, a tactic practiced by unscrupulous real-estate speculators. In a typical block-busting situation, the speculator comes into a white neighborhood and warns residents that "they" (nonwhites) are going to move in very quickly. White residents are led to believe that their property values will drop sharply as the area becomes "undesirable." These scare tactics may stimulate panic selling at artificially low prices. Then the block buster can purchase the houses cheaply and resell them to minority buyers at inflated prices.

As this scenario suggests, invasion and succes-sion are not always natural processes. Race baiting, rezoning, and bank redlining (refusal to grant loans in areas around which red lines have been drawn) are examples of conscious, planned responses by individuals and institutions that often intervene in the trickle-down, invasion-succession model.

*To conclude:* "American apartheid" is what a leading population researcher calls the pattern of racial separation between whites and African-Americans in the United States (Massey, 1990). If so, how did this pattern evolve? Some think that race (and class) segregation in the United States is a by-product of conscious policy decisions by local political actors who engage in local protectionism (e.g., Smith, 1988:10). Generally, scholars estimate that economic factors (low social class or socioeconomic status) account for only 10 percent of African-American residential racial segregation in U.S. cities (Sorenson, Taeuber, and Hollingsworth, 1975). And what accounts for the other 90 percent? "The remainder is due to [negative] racial attitudes which in the United States have continued to distort the spatial structure of American cities" (Abu-Lughod, 1991:260). In Chicago, the most racially segregated big city in the United States, these patterns date back at least to World War I. Here is what the Chicago Real Estate Board wrote in its April 1917 *Bulletin:*

The Committee recognizes that a great immigration of negroes have arrived . . . in Chicago, and that some feasible, practicable and humane method must be devised to house and school them. . . . The Committee is dealing with a financial business proposition and not with racial prejudice, and asks the cooperation of the influential colored citizens. Inasmuch as more territory must be provided, it is desired in the interest of all, that each block shall be filled solidly and that further expansion shall be confined to continuous blocks, and that the present method of obtaining a single building in scattered blocks, be discontinued. (in Helper, 1969:25)

Ironically, then, at the very time when Burgess theorized that economic competition under-pinned urban growth and that "natural" areas resulted from urban differentiation, realtors openly sponsored policies that foiled the market's so-called natural processes. Later, after World War II, it was federal policy that foiled the market. As mentioned in Chapter 12, billions of tax dollars supported highway construction and suburban home loans. Whether intended or not, these popular government programs—paid for by white and nonwhite taxpayers alike—hardened the pattern of residential apartheid: Large numbers of returning non-Hispanic white vets took advantage of Veterans Administration loans, buying homes in the new suburbs. Meanwhile, other vets were discouraged or, in many cases, prevented (by covenants or negative attitudes) from buying suburban homes. Once again, private and public policies intervene in natural processes, helping to shape local character.

## What People Live In

Aided by Lucille Ball and Desi Arnaz's 1950s film *The Long, Long Trailer* and other negative stereotypes of the era, mobile homes got a bad rep and a bad rap. Typically, they were portrayed as ticky-tacky housing for lower-income people of questionable taste and habits.

By the 1980s, both the name and the image had changed. Renamed "manufactured housing," the homes appealed to a broad spectrum of buyers—retired folks, middle-income families, and others. (The vast majority was not mobile at all; 90 percent had no wheels.) Indeed, one out of every four new homes sold in the 1980s was a manufactured house (Malthus, 1993). In 1992, over 210,000 manufacturered homes were sold in the United States; their average price, $28,000 in 1992 dollars (Einstein, 1993:B1), made them attractive.

Years ago, trailer parks down by the railroad tracks were common. Now, more often than not, they are well-kept subdivisions with names like Forest Crest Estates.

## How Age Affects Housing Patterns

Just as people sort themselves out by social rank, family status, and race/ethnicity, they group themselves by age. At different points in their life cycle, individuals may seek out different neighborhoods. For instance, as a middle-income woman goes through life, in her twenties she may reside in a singles area near the heart of the city, later move to a suburban house to raise children and commute to work, and, after the children grow up, move to a city apartment. In Weiss's (1988) terms, she started in ZQ11, "Bohemian Mix," or ZQ18, "New Melting Pot"; moved to ZQ12, "Levittown," ZQ6, "Two More Rungs," or ZQ8, "Young Suburbia," and moved again to ZQ15, "New Beginnings," or ZQ4, "Urban Gold Coast." Years later, she may move again, perhaps to ZQ13, "Gray Power."

Understanding the population characteristics of neighborhoods and towns in terms of age (and family structure) is essential to informed policymaking. It would make no sense to locate daycare centers in the heart of a retirement colony or playgrounds where there are no children. It would make sense to locate board-and-care homes for the very elderly in places with high concentrations, such as Los Angeles County, California (where the the greatest *number* of people over eighty-five—85,427, or 1 percent of the county's population—resided in 1990), and Smith County, Kansas (where the highest *percentage* of residents over eighty-five—5.2 percent, or 265 out of 5,078—lived in 1990).

The population pyramid is a convenient device for presenting information about a community's age composition. Figure 15.7 shows pyramids for two different kinds of communities in terms of age. Pyramid A is top-heavy, illustrating that most neighborhood residents are middle-aged or older. Pyramid B bulges out at the bottom, revealing the relatively large number of children in the neighborhood.

Pyramid-type diagrams can be used to display various characteristics of a population, including sex, income, family composition, occupation, and marital status. Interestingly, new categories (added in the 1980 and 1990 decennial U.S. censuses) will permit more refined data analysis and pyramid building. Of special interest is a category added under household living arrangements and family styles: partner/roommates—unrelated and unmarried adults of the opposite sex, forming two-person households.

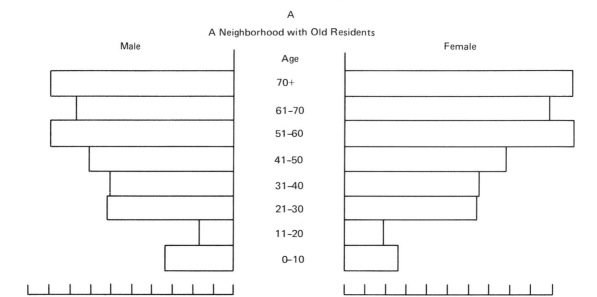

## A
### A Neighborhood with Old Residents

Male       Age       Female

Percentage of total population

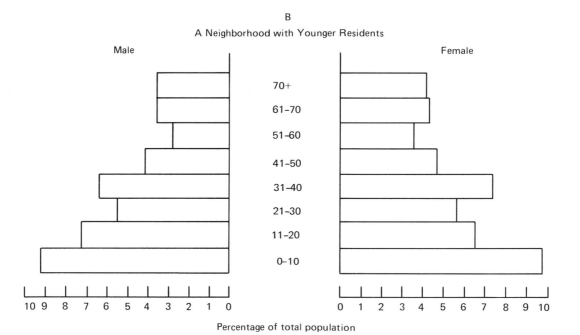

## B
### A Neighborhood with Younger Residents

Male       Age       Female

Percentage of total population

**Fig. 15.7** POPULATION PYRAMIDS OF TWO NEIGHBORHOODS WITH DIFFERING AGE STRUCTURES, DISAGGREGATED BY SEX.

Population pyramids are useful for looking at a given population at one moment in time, say, 1990. But they are static; they don't reveal how the population characteristics of a community may change over time. For this kind of data analysis, a dynamic study is required. The uses of a dynamic study can be illustrated by examining an important trend occurring in many American cities today: gentrification.

## Gentrification

A dynamic study of a neighborhood located in Burgess's Zone III might show the following breakdown by social rank over time: 1970: 90 percent working class, 5 percent middle class, 5 percent upper middle class; 1980: 80 percent working class, 5 percent middle class, 25 percent upper middle class; 1990: 40 percent working class, 10 percent middle class, and 50 percent upper middle class. These data indicate that the neighborhood is undergoing **gentrification** (from the English *gentry*, the class immediately below the nobility). That is, people of higher class and status "invaded" a working-class area, renovating existing homes. This is not what the invasion-succession model predicted. In fact, gentrification represents the opposite process, one we might call *trickle-up*. Some theorists call this process *reinvasion.*

Gentrification has occurred in many American cities that have charming inner-city houses. In Washington, D.C., for instance, the now fashionable and expensive Georgetown section was primarily a lower-status area until World War II.

Some observers applaud this development. They say that gentrification brings back the white middle and upper middle classes to the city, thereby upgrading the housing stock and increasing the tax base. Stanford professor Richard Muth, for one, believes that "all of us consumers will benefit" by gentrification (in Hartman, Keating, LeGates, and Turner, et al, 1982:27).

But an important question remains: Where will those gentrified out of their homes go? A reporter put it this way: "In Washington, a burst of

investment and energy transforms Capitol Hill, an old run-down neighborhood, into a prized antique. . . . Nearby, a 30-year-old woman who grew up in the neighborhood finds she cannot afford to live near her mother, and must move to a suburban apartment, although she works nearby" (Wald, 1987:4–7).

Displacement of low-income people, pushed out of their homes by affluent people, is often one outcome of gentrification. But a less obvious effect concerns jobs: Gentrification can mean that housing for the well-off displaces jobs for the poor: "In Manhattan, which may have the most intense pressures for housing in the nation, the city is watching its manufacturing industries . . . being literally squeezed out by residential lofts" (Wald, 1987:5).

Theorists using the political economy paradigm approach gentrification from another angle. They say that investment capital moved out of U.S. central cities in the 1950s and into suburbs, where profit rates were higher. Later, when inner cities deteriorated, a "rent gap" resulted, and capital returned to earn higher profits. The big winners in this process, they say, are the owners of capital; the big losers are the displaced urban poor (Smith and LeFaivre, 1984).

So, what is to be done? Should public policy slow down or speed up gentrification? That is a normative issue, a question of values—not a question that can be answered by looking at data.

Up to this point, we have treated housing patterns as if they existed in isolation. Now we will examine patterns of industrial and commercial activity in cities and suburbs that influence housing and many other land uses.

## ECONOMIC ACTIVITIES IN METROPOLITAN SPACE

After streets and roads (which consume the largest amount of a city's space), housing is usually the most widespread land use. Commercial and industrial activities take up far less space, about 10 percent combined (Murphy, 1974:311, 379).

Although economic activities don't take up much room, relatively speaking, they greatly influence what kinds of housing exist in a city (rooming houses, mansions, slums, etc.) and what kinds of people live there.

## Central Business District (CBD)

The downtown or **central business district (CBD)** is the key commercial area in most modern U.S. cities. This area is much more than a physical place. It is a symbol of a city's cultural vitality as well as of its economic well-being. It may evoke numerous images: skyscrapers, hustle-bustle, street musicians, high fashion, litter, big department stores, and/or empty streets after the offices close. Following Walter Firey's remarks about people's sentimental attachment to landmarks, we could hypothesize that a run-down CBD has subtle psychological effects on urbanites. But beyond these difficult-to-measure effects, the CBD serves basic economic functions. Its major functions are (1) the retail selling of goods and services for profit and (2) the performance of office and financial activities for a city and its hinterland.

As in central place theory, exchange plays a key role in understanding the importance of the CBD in America. Exchange of goods, services, and information requires social interaction, and intensely developed areas like the CBD permit convenient, face-to-face interaction. For example, tens of thousands of corporate and financial workers are concentrated in a small physical area on New York City's Wall Street.

How can a CBD be precisely defined and delimited? The U.S. Census of Retail Trade (1976:Introduction) provides some guidelines. This U.S. Census Bureau publication describes the CBD as "an area of very high land valuation; an area characterized by a high concentration of retail businesses, offices, theatres, hotels, and 'service' businesses; and an area of high traffic flow." Ordinarily, the CBD follows existing census tract boundaries, consisting of one or more whole census tracts. To delimit CBDs more pre-

cisely, geographers have mapped and measured a variety of things: building heights, traffic flows, employment in retail trade, land values, and residents' perceptions of the CBD (Murphy, 1974: 347–352). Such studies find that land values peak close to the center of the CBD. They also show that land uses within the CBD change as distance from this point of peak land value increases. For example, the proportion of land devoted to retailing declines as one moves out from the point of highest land value.

Land uses vary in vertical space too. Moving upward from the ground floor of buildings in the CBD through successive stories, offices increase while retailing declines (Murphy and Vance, 1954a, 1954b).

After World War II, CBDs changed as technology and the economy evolved. White-collar and service industries gained in importance as the United States moved to a postindustrial economy. Retail sales activities in the CBD declined as suburbs drew downtown department store customers; the big stores tended to decentralize rather than expand in the CBD. Further, new communications technologies made it possible to communicate quickly without face-to-face interaction. All these changes meant that firms once clustered in the CBD became free to move, even to offshore locations. Thus an insurance company in Boston can maintain a symbolic presence downtown but also have back offices in far-flung suburbs or in Ireland. The company can interact with customers and companies by the Internet, fax, or telephone instead of face-to-face; it can store its data anywhere and retrieve them instead of storing them in the CBD.

Time was when a fancy downtown address meant a great deal in terms of status. This was particularly true for stockbrokers. America's best-known street—Wall Street—was the quintessential "good" address. But now, with global finance, brokers do business from St. Louis to the corner of Last Chance Gulch and Sixth Street in Helena, Montana. New York City's share of employment in the securities industry reflects this shift, dropping from 50 percent in 1970 to 30 percent in 1992 (Solomon, 1993:43).

Since the 1950s, many CBDs in the United

States have been on a roller-coaster ride, surging with expansion, dipping with vacant buildings in an overbuilt downtown, and sometimes resurging. By the mid-1980s, new office buildings, retail stores, and people poured into many downtowns. Even in some Rust Belt cities like Cleveland, the CBD comeback was "phenomenal" (Edelstein in Schmidt, 1987). But this expansion was short-lived: By the early 1990s, increased white-collar unemployment, new federal tax laws, a worldwide economic slowdown, and a sagging national economy spelled trouble for many CBDs. For instance, in April 1993, the office vacancy rate in Dallas's CBD was 39.1 percent (Pinder, 1993:F5).

Even in the best of times, however, a vibrant CBD is not an equal opportunity employer. CBD jobs tend to be white-collar and pink-collar (female-dominated jobs such as secretarial work), but many urbanites needing work are qualified for blue-collar work—and most of that work has moved outside of town to suburban locations or outside of the country. So, there is often a bad fit in the CBD (and the entire central city) between workers wanted (white-collar) and workers available (blue-collar). Typically, the hardest hit by this mismatch are low-income African-Americans, who are systematically excluded from suburbs by class and racial segregation.

## Decentralized and Multicentered Commercial Activities

Starting after World War II, commercial activities in the United States were increasingly located *outside* the central city. By the 1970s, a new spatial entity took form: a postsuburban zone. As detailed earlier in this chapter, Orange County, California, exemplifies this entity; it is organized around "many distinct, specialized centers rather than a traditional city center surrounded by industrial and residential areas (Kling et al., 1991:6). Some describe this decentralization as a shift in spatial patterns: from "milk in a bottle" to "spilled milk" (Fainstein, Gordon, and Harloe, 1992:5).

More recently, decentralization has gone global. Practically, this means that employees answering the 800 computer helpline number or processing claims for an insurance company in Iowa might be in Dublin, Ireland. Indeed, over 400 U.S. companies have decentralized some back-office functions to Ireland alone.

## Manufacturing

**Manufacturing** consists of (1) transforming raw materials into new products and (2) assembling component parts into new products such as cars This transformation usually takes place in a factory or mill. Indeed, the "dark satanic mill" and factory smokestack once symbolized a city's economic lifeblood. Now, in the postindustrial economy, manufacturing in the United States has declined relative to the service and information sectors. In the 1950s, about 33 percent of all U.S. workers held manufacturing jobs; with deindustrialization, the proportion plummeted to 17 percent by 1991 (Barlett and Steele, 1992:18). By 1991, almost 10 million more people worked in the service sector than in manufacturing, and nearly as many people held government jobs as manufacturing jobs.

With economic restructuring, however, a global assembly line now exists, and it stretches from the *maquiladoras* near the U.S.–Mexican border to the prison workshops of China and from the sweatshops of Los Angeles to the redesigned auto plants in Tennessee.

## ANOTHER LOOK

"Have economic logic. Will travel." That could be the motto for the early theorists concerned with the shape of urban space in Europe and North America. Economic assumptions underlie the classic models of urban form and space, and they cross-cut disciplines and political ideologies.

Central place theorists use economic logic to

deduce that there is a system of cities, a functionally interdependent urban hierarchy. Theorists who classify cities by function also assume economic interdependence. Durkheim (Chapter 5) does the same. The U.S. government bases its definition of the metropolitan statistical area on the notion of an integrated labor market (Chapter 6). Urban ecologists build a theoretical framework around the idea that human communities develop spatially as a result of economic competition, and that industrial cities are structured internally by market forces.

Even critiques of central place theory and the classic models assign a major role to economic forces in shaping the modern city. Allen Pred's critique of central place theory doesn't refute its basic assumptions. Instead, Pred updates Christaller's theory to fit advanced technological, capitalist economies. Pred suggests that a city's hinterland in the postindustrial era doesn't stop at hexagonally shaped borders but often extends past regional, even national, boundaries. In Walter Firey's critique of Burgess's, Hoyt's, and Harris and Ullman's models of city structure, economic factors are not denied. However, Firey says that people do not live by the exchange of bread alone, and that noneconomic factors such as sentiment and symbolism should be added to the models. And even those like Lewis Mumford (Chapter 4), who think that religion and art can, and indeed have, historically determined human settlement patterns, say that unrestricted economic competition has shaped the modern U.S. city.

Newer models and perspectives on urban and metropolitan space—the political economy model, the multinucleated metropolitan region model, Davis's ecological update—add such factors as state intervention, grass-roots social movements, and overwhelming fear to the mix of influences on space. But all respect the role that money and investment capital play in spatial patterns.

Thus theorists from many disciplines agree that macro-level economic factors have influenced, even determined, the shape and form of urban-industrial space. But they do not agree on whether or not this unplanned growth and de-

velopment of modern cities has been good or bad for people who live in them. That is, the theorists of urban form describe the same processes affecting urban spatial growth and differentiation but prescribe varied solutions for changing the modern metropolis. This situation should sound familiar, for nineteenth-century theorists (Marx, Tönnies, Durkheim) described the rural–urban shift in similar ways. But they too prescribed different solutions to what they viewed as the ill effects accompanying that shift.

The design of new cities, of course, depends on what people think is wrong with the old ones. In part, the next chapter deals with this issue. It also suggests how micro-level factors affect urban space and how micro- and macro-level forces together shape urban space.

## KEY TERMS

**Central Business District (CBD)**  A North American term indicating the heart of the industrial city; commonly referred to as "downtown." The U.S. Census Bureau defines the CBD as an area of very high land valuation characterized by a high concentration of retail businesses offices, theaters, hotels, and service businesses and marked by high traffic flow.

**Central place theory**  Economic geographer Walter Christaller's 1933 theory, which holds that a hierarchy of central places (cities) evolves to serve surrounding hinterlands. The smallest central places, offering a limited range of goods and services, serve relatively small, hexagonal-shaped areas, while the largest central place in a region has a wide range of goods and services available and a much larger hinterland containing many smaller and intermediate central places.

**Chicago school of sociology**  A school of thought developed at the University of Chicago that attained its greatest prestige in the late 1920s and early 1930s. Sociologists Ernest W. Burgess and Robert E. Park were leading members of the school. The urban ecology perspective developed by the Chicago school shaped subsequent thinking about cities.

**Concentric zone model**  A model of the internal structure of the city, developed by Chicago school sociologist Ernest W. Burgess in the 1920s, that conceptualized cities as organized in a series of concentric zones radiating out from the city center. Each zone tended to have a different population type and a different set of land uses and functions. Immigrant ethnic groups, according to Burgess, initially tended to settle close to the center of the city and gradually moved out toward the periphery as they became assimilated.

**Gentrification** The process whereby members of a higher-income and higher-status group move into a neighborhood occupied by lower-income, lower-status persons. When this "trickling up" occurs, the neighborhood will be physically improved but many of the former residents displaced. This process reverses the filtering-down process whereby one group moves up the socioeconomic ladder and another group, lower on the ladder, moves into the housing left behind.

**Ghetto** A section of a city, often rundown and/or overcrowded, inhabited chiefly by a minority group that is effectively prevented from living in other areas because of prejudice or economic barriers. Historically, the word was first used in medieval Venice to refer to the place where armaments were kept; later, this arsenal area became the Jewish quarter of Venice. Over time, *ghetto* became a synonym for the area where Jews were forced to live in isolation by law or custom.

**Hinterland** In central place theory, the area adjacent to and dependent on an urban center. This term once referred to the backcountry or the area in back of the coastal region. Today it refers to the urban sphere of influence or trade area, which may be global in scope.

**Index of dissimilarity.** A measure of *absolute* racial segregation in housing citywide. It measures the distribution of white and nonwhite households among census blocks. Each census block can have a score from 0 to 100; the higher the number, the higher the level of racial segregation. The index looks at the population of a racial group in an entire city, asking this question: To make every census block in the city mirror the racial makeup of the city as a whole, what percentage of each group would have to move to another block?

**Index of exposure.** A measure of *relative* racial segregation in housing. It measures the proportion of people sharing the same ethnic/racial background in a neighborhood. Often it is used as a stand-in for measuring positive interaction between racial groups, the assumption being that physical proximity to people from other racial/ethnic groups promotes positive interaction and empathy.

**Internal structure of the city** The location, arrangement, and interrelationships between social and physical elements within a city.

**Invasion and succession** Terms that describe the process of social change in cities. These terms fit into a theoretical model that sees successive social groups competing for and succeeding one another in a given physical area. Invasion describes the entrance into an area of a new class or group and the resulting displacement of certain other classes or groups of existing residents. The process may, however, involve an amalgamation of the invasion types with the resident types. Succession describes the order, in a series of territorial occupations, as one group in an area is forced out or replaced by another.

**Manufacturing** Transforming a substance into a new product. Assembly of component parts is also considered manufacturing if the new product is not a building (a structure or other fixed improvement).

**Multinucleated metropolitan region** Neither city nor suburb, a new spatial form with many specialized centers characterized by enclosed shopping malls, usually a conglomerate of high-tech industry, services, and information processing. Examples include Orange County, California and Suffolk County, New York.

**Multiple nuclei model** A model of the internal structure of the city developed by geographers Chauncy Harris and Edward L. Ullman. In their view, a city has more than one nucleus. Thus not only the CBD, but also a port, a university, or an industrial area, may act as the center around which activities are organized.

**Range** A term in central place theory referring to the zone or tributary area around a central place from which persons travel to the center to purchase the good (service or merchandise) offered at that place. Theoretically, the upper limit of this range is the maximum possible radius of sales. The lower limit of the range is the radius that encloses the minimum number of consumers necessary to provide a sales volume adequate for the good to be supplied profitably from the central place. Today electronic retailing and catalog shopping make the concept obsolete for many goods and services.

**Sectoral model**   A model of urban growth developed by real estate economist Homer Hoyt in the 1930s. The model holds that classes of land use tend to be arranged in wedge-shaped sectors radiating from the CBD along major transportation corridors.

**System of cities**   A term describing how cities of different sizes and functional types are interdependent and economically interrelated in systematic ways. Pre-1970s literature on system of cities describes the specialization of functions among cities (in Europe and North America mainly) and how they interact; post-1970s literature focuses on the global urban hierarchy.

**Urban ecology**   The study of the spatial distribution of people and institutions in cities from a distinctive perspective, originated by members of the Chicago school of sociology, particularly Ernest W. Burgess and Robert E. Park.

## PROJECTS

1. **Postsuburbia**. Compare and contrast any five postsuburban counties in the United States (e.g., Prince Georges, Maryland; Fairfax, Virginia; Gwinnett/De Kalb, Georgia; Orange, California; Du Page, Illinois; Contra Costa, California; Oakland, Michigan; Montgomery, Pennsylvania; San Mateo, California; Fairfield, Connecticut; Norfolk, Massachusetts; Broward, Florida; Monmouth, New Jersey; Santa Clara, California) with five industrial cities. Using U.S. census data, look for the annual county employment growth by sector (e.g., manufacturing, land development, finance, service), demographic data (e.g., total population, size of the largest place in 1980 and 1990), and socioeconomic characteristics (e.g., race/ethnicity, median family income, poverty rate, unemployment rate). What features do the postsuburban counties share? Are some more like industrial cities than bedroom communities, the old stereotypical suburb?

2. **Age–sex pyramids**. Review Figure 15.7 and the discussion of age–sex pyramids. Obtain

the volume *U.S. Census of Population and Housing*, which contains census tract information for your community. Skimming the age characteristics in the city, select one census tract that has a high concentration of older residents and one that has a high concentration of young children. If any other census tracts stand out as having unusually nonuniform distributions of population by age or sex, you may want to include them as well. Construct age–sex pyramids for each census tract similar to those in Figure 15.7. Construct some plausible hypotheses about the areas based on the census data alone. Finally, visit the two census tracts. Do your observations seem to support your hypotheses?

## SUGGESTIONS FOR FURTHER LEARNING

Urban geography texts reveal how much the discipline's boundaries have expanded—or blurred. In Truman A. Hartshorn, *Interpreting the City: An Urban Geography*, 2nd ed. (New York: Wiley, 1992), the subject matter ranges from the origin of cities and central place theory to ethnicity in the city and intrametropolitan industrial and wholesale space. Likewise, in *A Social Geography of the City* (New York: Harper & Row, 1983), David Ley discusses topics ranging from urban form and national political culture to consumption in a livable city. He includes a most interesting account of the time-geography approach to urban activity patterns in the chapter "The City of Mind and Action."

A comprehensive introductory text on urban geography on one continent is Maurice Yeates, *The North American City*, 2nd ed. (New York: Harper & Row, 1989). The ecological approach to urban spatial analysis is explored in Brian J. L. Berry and John D. Kasarda, *Contemporary Urban Ecology* (New York: Macmillan, 1977).

Leslie J. King includes updates of the theory in *Central Place Theory* (Beverly Hills, Calif.: Sage, 1984). Key writings on the system of cities and the urban hierarchy are collected in Larry S. Bourne and James W. Simmons, eds., *Systems of*

*Cities* (New York: Oxford University Press, 1978). In Paul C. Cheshire and Alan W. Evans, eds., *Urban and Regional Economics* (Cheltenham: Elgar, 1991), contributors discuss the urban hierarchy, central place theory, industrialization of industry and aspects of the Reagan–Thatcher legacy in regional development.

Key writings on the internal structure of the city are collected in Larry S. Bourne, ed., *The Internal Structure of the City*, 2nd ed. (New York: Oxford University Press, 1982). This anthology also deals with other topics in urban studies including urban imagery, policy issues, and futurism.

Unfortunately, the works of many important social theorists are not easily accessible. Foremost in this category is Marx's *Capital* (*Das Kapital*). However, in *Marx's Kapital for Beginners* (New York: Pantheon, 1982), David Smith and Phil Evans present his key ideas in a sophisticated and funny comic book. It includes a discussion of Marx's concepts of overproduction, the accumulation of capital, and circuits of capitalist circulation, which play an important role in the political economy paradigm. The profound-but-dense-and-difficult category includes the shapers of the political economy paradigm: Henri Lefebvre, *The Production of Space* (Cambridge, Mass.: Blackwell, [1974] 1991), and Manuel Castells's writings. For a readable "translation" of their ideas, see Ira Katznelson, *Marxism and the City* (New York: Oxford University Press, 1992), chap. 3. Also in this category is Allen Pred's out-of-print *Making Histories and Constructing Human Geographies* (Boulder, Colo.: Westview Press, 1990). Geographer Pred attempts to reformulate social theory and to merge historical study, human geographical inquiry, and social analysis. Pred concludes that "each place has its own sites of confrontation, its own spaces of struggle, its own arenas of contention, even if the contested issues are embedded in nonlocally based power relations and geographically extensive processes. Such conflicts cannot escape intersecting with unique local historical geographies" (232–233). He ends with a call for a "new critical social science that—whatever its practical implications—is as sensitive to the construction of human geographies as it is to the making of histories."

In *Metropolis: From the Division of Labor to Urban Form* (Berkeley: University of California Press, 1988), Allen J. Scott disputes the existence of a postindustrial society, suggesting that Castells's notion of a new information processing mode of economic organization is "utterly wrong" (7).

For a discussion of ideas that underpin the multinucleated metropolitan region model of space, see Rob Kling, Spencer Olin, and Mark Poster, eds., *Postsuburban California: The Transformation of Orange County since World War II* (Berkeley: University of California Press, 1991). For ideas underlying the political economy model from a geographical viewpoint, see Richard Peet and Nigel Thrift, eds., *New Models in Geography: The Political-Economy Perspective*, 2 volumes (London: Unwin Hyman, 1989). Also see issues of *Antipode*, a radical geography journal, published in February, May, August, and November, and the *International Journal of Urban and Regional Research*, published quarterly.

Gentrification and redevelopment in central cities are among the topics discussed in J. John Palen and Bruce London, eds., *Gentrification, Displacement and Neighborhood Revitalization* (Albany: State University of New York Press, 1984). In *Building American Cities: The Urban Real Estate Game*, 2nd ed. (Englewood Cliffs, N.J.: Prentice-Hall, 1990), Joe R. Feagin and Robert Parker deal with gentrification, as well as with decentralized urban growth and developers, bankers, and speculators (whom they call "shapers of American cities"). A documentary film directed and narrated by Nora Jacobson, *Delivered Vacant* (1992), follows Hoboken, New Jersey's mid-to-late 1980s transformation from working-class area to gentrified condo colony. The *New York Times* critic Vincent Canby called it "something of an urban epic showing that "time wounds all heels." Many real-estate developers, seen in the mid-1980s wheeling and dealing, went bankrupt by 1990, and their properties were auctioned off.

Starting before World War I, Chicago was the lab for urban sociology and geography in the United States, and the literature on the city's sociospatial structure continues to be rich. For an addition to the analysis of its residential segregation, see Arnold R. Hirsch, *Making the Second Ghetto: Race and Housing in Chicago, 1940–1960* (New York: Cambridge University Press, 1985). Hirsch looks at various ways of blocking racial integration in the city, ending in a ghetto supported by government action.

University of Pennsylvania sociology professor Douglas S. Massey and his former colleagues at the University of Chicago continue the tradition of scholarship in racial residential segregation. In *American Apartheid: Segregation and the Making of the Underclass* (Cambridge, Mass.: Harvard University Press, 1993), he and coauthor Nancy A. Denton look at the ways in which housing segregation of African-Americans has differed from the segregation of other ethnic groups, and they review the factors leading to spatial isolation.

In *The Culture of Cities* (Cambridge, Mass.: Blackwell, 1994), Sharon Zukin argues that cities are saved not only by economic structures and political institutions, but also by culture, which includes art and buildings.

Originally a series of muckraking newspaper articles, next a book, and then an hour-long PBS video, Donald L. Barlett and James B. Steele's *America: What Went Wrong* (Kansas City: Andrews and McMeel, 1992) presents data from a number of sources (e.g., bankruptcy filings, Internal Revenue Service records, interviews with workers) to support its basic point: that the state (the federal government) and large corporations have changed the rules of the game in the global economy to favor the powerful and affluent. Easy-to-read graphs—on plant closings in the United States and jobs shifted to Mexico since 1965, for example—and a breezy style make the data very accessible.

## REFERENCES

Abu-Lughod, Janet L. 1969. "Testing the theory of social area analysis: The ecology of Cairo, Egypt." *American Sociological Review* 34:198–212.
———. 1991. *Changing Cities: Urban Sociology*. New York: HarperCollins.
Barlett, Donald L., and James B. Steele. 1992. *America:*

*What Went Wrong?* Kansas City: Andrews and McMeel.
Berry, Brian J. L., and John D. Kasarda. 1977. *Contemporary Urban Ecology*. New York: Macmillan.
Burgess, Ernest W. [1923] 1925. "Growth of the city." Pp. 47–62 in Robert E. Park, Ernest W. Burgess, and Roderick McKenzie, *The City*. Chicago: University of Chicago Press.
Burgess, Ernest W., and Donald J. Bogue, eds. 1964. *Contributions to Urban Sociology*. Chicago: University of Chicago Press.
"Canada, Japan to export markets for Iowa manufacturers." 1991. *Global View* (June):4.
Castells, Manuel. [1972] 1977. *The Urban Question: A Marxist Approach*. Cambridge, Mass.: MIT Press.
———. 1983. *The City and the Grassroots: A Cross-Cultural Theory of Urban Social Movements*. Berkeley: University of California Press.
———. 1989. *The Informational City: Information Technology, Economic Restructuring and the Urban-Regional Process*. Cambridge, Mass.: Blackwell.
Christaller, Walter. [1933] 1966. *Central Places in Southern Germany*. Trans. C. W. Baskin. Englewood Cliffs, N.J.: Prentice-Hall.
Coughlin, Ellen K. 1994. "The emergence of the 'global city.'" *Chronicle of Higher Education* (January 5):A8–9.
Davis, Mike. 1992. "Beyond *Blade Runner:* Urban control the ecology of fear." *Open Magazine Pamphlet, No. 23.* Westfield, N.J.: Open Media.
———. [1990] 1992. *City of Quartz*. New York: Vintage.
Eckhouse, John. 1989. "1 in 15 jobs in state related to exports." *San Francisco Chronicle* (March 4):B1+.
Einstein, David. 1993. "Housing industry finds a new star." *San Francisco Chronicle* (September 30): B1+.
Fainstein, Susan S., Ian Gordon, and Michael Harloe. 1992. *Divided Cities: New York and London in the Contemporary World*. Oxford: Blackwell.
Farley, Reynolds, Howard Schuman, Suzanne Bianchi, Diane Colasanto, and Shirley Hatchett. 1978. "Chocolate city, vanilla suburbs: Will the trend toward racially separate communities continue?" *Social Science Research* 7:319–344.
Farley, Reynolds, Charlotte Steeh, Tara Jackson, Maria Krysan, and Keith Reeves. 1994. "The causes of continued racial residential segregation: Chocolate city, vanilla suburbs revisited." *Journal of Housing Research* 4:1–38.
Feder, Barnaby J. 1993. "The unorthodox behemoth of law firms." *New York Times*, business section [national edition] (March 14):1.
Firey, Walter. 1947. *Land Use in Central Boston*. Cambridge, Mass.: Harvard University Press.

Gottdiener, M. 1985. *The Social Production of Urban Space.* Austin: University of Texas Press.

Gottdiener, M., and George Kephart. 1991. "The multi-nucleated metropolitan region: a comparative analysis." Pp. 31–54 in Rob Kling et al., eds., *Postsuburban California: The Transformation of Orange County since World War II.* Berkeley: University of California Press.

Harris, Chauncy, and Edward L. Ullman. 1945. "The nature of cities." *Annals of the American Academy of Political and Social Science* 242:7–17.

Hartman, Chester, Dennis Keating, and Richard LeGates, with Steve Turner. 1982. *Displacement: How to Fight It.* Berkeley, Calif.: Legal Services Anti-Displacement Project.

Harvey, David. 1973. *Social Justice and the City.* Baltimore: Johns Hopkins University Press.

———. 1982. *The Limits to Capital.* Chicago: University of Chicago Press.

———. 1989a. *The Condition of Postmodernity.* Cambridge, Mass.: Blackwell.

———. 1989b. "Monument and myth: The building of the basilica of the Sacred Heart." Pp. 200–228 in David Harvey, *The Urban Experience.* Baltimore: Johns Hopkins University Press.

Helper, Rose. 1969. *Racial Policies and Practices of Real Estate Brokers.* Minneapolis: University of Minnesota Press.

Herbers, John. 1981. "Census finds more blacks living in suburbs of nation's largest cities." *New York Times* [national edition] (May 31):1+.

Hodge, Gerald. 1965. "The prediction of trade center viability in the Great Plains." *Regional Science Association, Papers and Proceedings* 57:87–118.

Hoyt, Homer. 1939. *The Structure and Growth of Residential Neighborhoods in American Cities.* Washington, D.C.: Federal Housing Administration.

Hudson, John C. 1985. "Plains country towns." *Mosaic,* (Fall):11–15

International City Managers Association. 1963. *Municipal Year Book.* Washington, D.C.: ICMA.

"Internet: International Network on Trade, Inc." 1991a. *Global View* 2 (June):1.

Jakle, John, and J. A. Wheeler. [1969] 1972. "The Dutch and Kalamazoo, Michigan: A study of spatial barriers to acculturation." *Tijdschrift Voor Economische en Sociale Geografie* 60:249–254.

Janowitz, Morris. 1967. "Introduction." Pp. vii–x in Robert E. Park, Ernest W. Burgess, and Roderick McKenzie, *The City.* Chicago: University of Chicago Press.

Kantor, Paul, with Stephen David. 1988. *The Dependent City: The Changing Political Economy of Urban America.* Glenview, Ill.: Scott Foresman/Little, Brown.

Katznelson, Ira. 1992. *Marxism and the City.* New York: Oxford University Press.

Kling, Rob, Spencer Olin, and Mark Poster, eds. 1991. *Postsuburban California: The Transformation of Orange County Since World War II.* Berkeley: University of California Press.

Koenig, David. 1993. "Big employers got bigger." *San Francisco Chronicle* (April 19):D11.

Lefebvre, Henri. [1974] 1991. *The Production of Space.* Trans. Donald Nicholson-Smith. Oxford: Blackwell.

Lewis, Peter H. 1994. "Getting down to business on the net." *New York Times* [national edition] (June 19): sec. 3, 1+.

Lohr, Steve. 1994. "Can e-mail cachet = jpmorgan @park.ave?" *New York Times* [national edition] (June 6):A1+.

Malthus, David. 1993. *All Things Considered,* KQED-FM (June 26).

Mandel, Ernest. [1972] 1987. *Late Capitalism.* Trans. Joris DeBres. London: Verso.

Massey, Doreen. 1984. *Spatial Divisions of Labour: Social Structures and the Geography of Production.* London: Methuen.

Massey, Douglas S. 1990. "American apartheid: Segregation and the making of the underclass." *American Journal of Sociology* 96 (September): 329–357.

Massey, Douglas S., and Nancy A. Denton. 1988. "Suburbanization and segregation in U.S. metropolitan areas." *American Journal of Sociology* 94 (November):592–626.

Massey, Douglas S., Andrew B. Gross, and Kumiko Shibuya. 1994. "Migration, segregation, and the geographic concentration of poverty." *American Sociological Review* 59:425–445.

Murphy, Raymond E. 1954. *The Central Business District.* Chicago: Aldine.

———. 1974. *The American City: An Urban Geography,* 2nd ed. New York: McGraw-Hill.

Murphy, Raymond E., and James E. Vance, Jr. 1954a. "A comparative study of nine central business districts." *Economic Geography* 30:301–336.

———. 1954b. "Delimiting the CBD." *Economic Geography* 30:189–222.

Park, Robert E., Ernest W. Burgess, and Roderick McKenzie. 1925. *The City.* Chicago: University of Chicago Press.

Phillips, E. Barbara. 1992–1993. Interviews with students at high schools in Berkeley and Albany, California, and San Francisco State University, Stanford University, and Contra Costa College.

Pinder, Jeanne B. 1993. "Downtown's empty feeling." *New York Times* [national edition.] (May 9):F5.

Pred, Allen. 1977. *City Systems in Advanced Economies.* New York: Wiley.

Rees, Philip H. 1970. "The factorial ecology of Chicago: A case study." Pp. 319–394 in Brian J. L. Berry and Frank E. Horton, eds., *Geographic Perspectives in Urban Systems.* Englewood Cliffs, N.J.: Prentice-Hall.

Reinhold, Robert. 1993. "Humbled by mean recession, California fights for its jobs." *New York Times* [national edition] (December 19):1+.

Sassen, Saskia. 1988. *The Mobility of Labor and Capital: A Study in International Investment and Labor Flow.* London: Cambridge University Press.

———. 1991. *The Global City: New York, London, Tokyo.* Princeton, N.J.: Princeton University Press.

Scheer, Robert. 1979. "Ehrlichman talks about Nixon." *San Francisco Chronicle* (May 30):8.

Schmidt, William E. 1987. "U.S. downtowns: No longer downtrodden." *New York Times* [national edition] (October 11):1.

Shevky, Eshref, and Wendell Bell. 1955. *Social Area Analysis.* Berkeley: University of California Press.

Smith, Michael Peter. 1988. *City, State, and Market: The Political Economy of Urban Society.* New York: Blackwell.

Smith, Michael Peter, and Joe R. Feagin, eds. [1987] 1989. *The Capitalist City: Global Restructuring and Community Politics.* Cambridge, Mass.: Blackwell.

Smith, Neil. [1984] 1991. *Uneven Development.* Cambridge, Mass.: Blackwell.

Smith, Neil, and Michele LeFaivre. 1984. "A class analysis of gentrification." Pp. 43–63 in J. John Palen and Bruce London, eds., *Gentrification, Displacement and Neighborhood Revitalization.* Albany: State University of New York Press.

Solomon, Jolie, with Seema Nayyar. 1993. "West of Wall Street." *Newsweek* (May 24):42–43.

Sorenson, Annemette, Karl E. Taeuber, and Leslie J. Hollingsworth, Jr. 1975. "Indexes of racial residential segregation for 109 cities in the United States, 1940 to 1970." *Sociological Focus* (April): 125–142.

Steffens, Lincoln. [1903] 1904. *The Shame of the Cities.* New York: McClure Phillips. (Originally published in 1903 as seven articles in *McClures' Magazine*)

———. [1931] 1937. *The Autobiography of Lincoln Steffens.* New York: Harcourt, Brace.

Suttles, Gerald D. 1984. "The cumulative texture of local urban culture." *American Journal of Sociology* 90 (September):283–304.

Taeuber, Karl, and Alma Taeuber. 1965. *Negroes in Cities.* Chicago: Aldine.

Thunen, Johann Heinrich von. [1826] 1966. *Isolated State [Der Isolierte Staadt].* Trans. Carla M. Wartenberg. Ed. and introduction by Peter Hall. Oxford: Pergamon.

U.S. Bureau of the Census. 1976. *Census of Retail Trade, 1972.* Vol. 2: *Area Statistics.* Washington, D.C.: Government Printing Office.

———. 1990. *1990 Census of Housing, General Housing Characteristics, United States.* CH-1-1. Washington, D.C.: Government Printing Office.

———. 1992. *Current Population Reports P20–464: The Black Population in the United States: March 1991.* Washington, D.C.: Government Printing Office.

Wald, Matthew L. 1987. "Managing gentrification: A challenge to the cities." *New York Times* [national edition] (September 13):sec. 12, 4–7.

———. 1993. "Traffic deaths in New York say a lot about New Yorkers." *New York Times* [national edition] (May 9):1.

Weiss, Michael J. 1988. *The Clustering of America.* New York: Harper & Row.

Zukin, Sharon. 1988. *Loft Living: Culture and Capital in Urban Change.* New Brunswick, N.J.: Rutgers University Press.

Stephen Hender

# CHAPTER 16
# A Sense of Place

Ebenezer Howard's Garden City
Megastructures or Ministructures?
Postnationalist Architecture

ANOTHER LOOK

How important is a sense of place? Important enough for presidents-elect to evoke it. When William Jefferson Clinton rode by bus into Washington, D.C., for his inauguration on January 17, 1993, he started from Monticello, home of his namesake, President Thomas Jefferson. For many Americans, Monticello calls to mind past glories and American heroes. (Not to all, however. Elaine Brown [1993], onetime head of the Black Panthers, called Clinton's journey from Monticello an affront to African-Americans because Jefferson kept slaves there.) And coming to Washington in this style—by bus, not by limousine, and by retracing President Jefferson's route to his inauguration—President Clinton symbolized his own long journey that began in Hope (Arkansas). As presidents and lesser politicians know, identification with place can have a subtle emotional impact on citizens.

Physical settings can have mind-boggling effects as well. Consider the case of Carlos Castaneda. As an anthropology graduate student at UCLA, Castaneda set out to do fieldwork among the Yaqui Indians. Once there, he became drawn into the mystical reality of his informant, a sorcerer named Don Juan. At one point, Don Juan suggested that he find his "own spot" on the floor of the cabin where they were staying. Puzzled, Castaneda tried to respond to this strange request. "I had to feel all the possible spots," Castaneda reports in his field notes. "I covered the whole floor. . . . I deliberately tried to 'feel' differences between places." As he continued, Castenada "saw" two spots on the floor that appeared to glow and shimmer. When he approached one spot, he felt nauseous and afraid; the other one made him feel exhausted. Later, he heard Don Juan talking and laughing above his head and woke up. "You have found the spot," Don Juan told him (Casteneda, 1968: 29–30, 34).

Castaneda's extraordinary experience illustrates two themes that run throughout this chapter:

1. The sense of place can have a powerful, even magical, impact on us—often at the unconscious level.
2. People perceive and attach meaning to physical space in various ways.

These themes complement a macro-level theme of Chapter 15, namely, that city form and space reflect a society's economic and social structures.

This chapter, then, is about how people perceive and use space. It begins with a discussion of general perception and spatial perception. Next, it examines views about the effects of the physical environment on human behavior. Then it moves to close encounters in space: What happens if a man tries to invade a woman's personal space or if outsiders enter your turf? After reviewing the findings of environmental psychology—a subdiscipline devoted to the study of behavior / environment—the chapter considers the principles that architects, landscape architects, urban designers, and planners use to shape urban space. Finally, it turns to dreams: grand dreams of creating new cities.

## PERCEPTION: FILTERING REALITY

We have seen that one person's reality is another's fantasy. People in the same city have different cognitive maps (Chapter 2). Radicals, liberals, and conservatives can look at the political economy and see very different realities (Chapter 3). Figure 16.1 indicates why people disagree on what's real. It shows that perceptual data are processed through three reality filters: cultural, social, and psychological. It implies that the way we filter perceptual data determines how we construct "objective" reality.

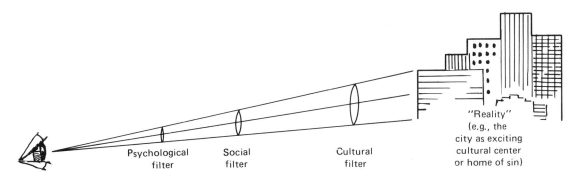

**Fig. 16.1** THREE FILTERS OF REALITY. Sense data pass through cultural, social, and psychological filters before becoming "objective" reality in our minds.

## Cultural Filters

Reflecting on how culture transforms physical reality—what is there—into experienced reality, American anthropologist Dorothy Lee says:

[T]he universe as I know it or imagine it in the Western world is different from the universe of the Tikopia, in Polynesia. It follows . . . that I feel differently about what I see. As I look out of my window now, I see trees, some of which I like to be there, and some of which I intend to cut down . . . the Dakota Black Elk Indian, however, saw trees as having rights to the land, equal to his own. (1959:1)

Lee also notes that we perceive behavior within the conceptual framework of our own culture: "When I throw a ball, do I perform an aggressive causal act, as my culture predisposes me to believe? Or does the ball leave my hand, as the Greenland Eskimo puts it, or do I merely actualize the ball's potential to move, as the Navaho would have it" (1959:2)?

Others suggest that what we see (and feel) depends on what language we speak. According to the Sapir–Whorf hypothesis (named for its developers, anthropologist Edward Sapir and amateur language fancier Benjamin Whorf), language does much more than reflect culture; it molds our world view and thoughts. In this view, people's conception of reality is significantly determined by the categories available to them in their language. For instance, Hopi Indians have no tenses in their language, nor do they have nouns for times or days. The Sapir–Whorf hypothesis suggests that as a result, Hopis see the world in terms of dynamic, ever-changing motion. By contrast, English speakers see the world in terms of linear progression; for them, seconds, hours, and years mark the "reality" of time passing by. English speakers also tend to see events as having a beginning, a middle, and an end; they define things as past, present, or future. This way of viewing the world is foreign to a Hopi speaker.

Language and other elements of culture (including the objects we produce and the beliefs we hold) provide the context in which we perceive reality. Within that broad cultural context, there are often subcultural meanings too. For instance, gyrating wildly on a disco dance floor may be perceived as harmless fun by some, perhaps most, Americans, but not by members of a religious community that equates dancing with evil.

Who is to say which cultural or subcultural reality is "true"? Or, as anthropologist Lee (1959:2) asks, "Are they all true, all different facets of the same truth?"

## Social Filters

Social identity also helps to shape the reality people perceive. Consider, for example, a common scene of pedestrians and shoppers along Chicago's opulent "Magnificent Mile" at Christmas time. The meanings observers attach to this bustling scene—and what they actually see—can differ with social background. All a child might see in this morass of sense data are the stuffed toys in the store windows. A journalist might focus on an unusual or a paradoxical event, perhaps a bag lady sifting through the garbage amid the affluence. Meanwhile, the bag lady sees none of this affluence as she searches through the garbage containers for something to eat.

It follows that *what we see and how we distort features of the urban environment are conditioned by who we are.* One classic study, "They Saw a Game" (Hastorf and Cantril, 1954), documents the importance of the perceivers' social and academic affiliations in the selective perception of a college football game. Surveying fans of both teams, researchers found that they actually saw very different games.

### Psychological Filters

Finally, we filter information through our own particular needs, memories, feelings, past experiences, and present concerns. Thus a starving Bosnian might focus on food scraps lying on the ground, whereas a well-fed member of Congress touring refugee camps might not notice them.

Psychoanalysts also point to the role that fantasies, myths, and long-forgotten experiences play in perceiving reality. How these operate is a matter of debate, but it is generally acknowledged that the unconscious mind can have powerful effects on a person's thoughts and acts. Sigmund Freud first became aware of the power of the unconscious in 1882; later he called this *psychic reality.*

*To conclude:* How we construct reality depends partially on chance—the culture into which we're born and raised and the language we speak; partially on our social location and identity; and partially on our psychic history and present concerns. Thus what our senses pick up from the environment and translate into "objec-tive reality" constitutes a highly selective process of perception.

## PERCEIVING THE BUILT ENVIRONMENT

Billboards, tombstones, buildings, highways, and everything else people construct form the **built environment.** The built environment serves both functional and symbolic purposes. For instance, an apartment building at a "good address" is more than a shelter; it is a symbol of the residents' status. As an essayist of metropolitan life puts it, "Nothing succeeds like address" (Lebowitz, [1974] 1978).

### Architecture as Symbolic Politics

Buildings offer clues to the values of the people who built them. Political scientist Harold Lasswell (1979) argues that many American buildings reflect one of the society's central concerns: power. In Lasswell's view, architecture makes a political statement, expressing the values of a society's dominant elites.

Normally, the built environment sends another message, one of social order. Order turns into chaos, however, when bombs explode buildings. For example, when the World Trade Center's sub-basements were blasted in 1993, there was "chaos. Turbulence on a global scale. A feeling Virginia Woolf once described in her diary as 'things generally wrong in the universe'" (Muschamp, 1993c). Death traps all, the federal building in Oklahoma City, buildings in South-Central Los Angeles, Waco, and Sarajevo stand as symbols of social glue that has come unstuck—or a new world disorder in the making.

Architecture speaks in different voices, depending on who's listening. When French radicals occupied the Basilica of Sacré Coeur in Paris in 1971—100 years after the Paris Commune's attempt at self-government—they attacked the church atop Montmartre as a symbol: the betrayal of revolutionary ideals and the rise of reactionary movements (Harvey, 1989). Similarly,

**Fig. 16.2** FORTRESS AMERICA. The fortress-like Pentagon in suburban Washington, D.C., symbolizes U.S. military might. (U.S. Army photograph)

when an angry mob destroyed the U.S. embassy building in Pakistan's capital of Islamabad in 1979, it was not commenting on the artistic merit of a widely acclaimed architectural triumph. Rather, the mob attacked the building as a symbol of foreign power.

Most often, architecture reflects the voices of the powerful. In America this means that big cities reflect the look of the corporate culture, not of local cultures. Indeed, the *New York Times* architecture critic Herbert Muschamp argues that "the chaos that erupted [in 1992] in South-Central Los Angeles was caused in large part by the lack of integration between the homogenized culture of corporations and developers and the culture of

minority neighborhoods." Then, noting that it is widely reported that efforts to rebuild Los Angeles have failed, Muschamp (1993c:30) asks a series of questions about power and culture: "Do inner city neighborhoods want to be remade in the image of corporate culture? Must success always look like a Marriott Hotel? A Kmart? A cluster of glass high-rises? Or are we prepared to acknowledge that, for integration to occur, the corporate culture must also be remade?"

When the weak become more powerful, meanings attached to buildings can change. For example, before the Chinese revolution in 1949, pagoda-like buildings in Beijing's Forbidden City symbolized the grace and power of China's rul-

a

**Fig. 16.3** HOW BUILDINGS SPEAK TO US. "Our architecture reflects us, as truly as a mirror," said Louis Sullivan, the inventor of the skyscraper. As objects, buildings can represent the values of a culture—in tall church spires, factory smokestacks, or skyscrapers housing corporate headquarters and banks. Buildings send different messages to different audiences too. (*a*) Once part of the Forbidden City in Beijing, this former temple, a symbol of grace and imperial power under China's former rulers, is now a people's museum. (*b*) Downtown Chicago, with its steely majesty and industrial power, combined with a curlique bit of fantasy, a parking garage. (Galen Cranz)

b

**Fig. 16.4** MONUMENT TO MEMORY. The United States Holocaust Memorial Museum in Washington, D.C., evokes the horror of the Nazi death camps of the 1940s where 11 million human beings—6 million Jews and 5 million others, including people deemed "handicapped," Jehovah's Witnesses, gays, Polish intellectuals, and Roma (Gypsies)—were killed in a coldly systematic way. On April 19, 1993, during the week of the museum's opening, a Roper poll revealed that memory can be faulty: *Over one-third of U.S. adults in the random sample survey thought the Holocaust may not have happened* (22 percent thought that it was possible that the Holocaust never happened; another 12 percent did not know if it was possible that it happened). A follow-up poll by Roper's rival, the Gallup Organization, found that asking the question in a different way (specifically, without a double negative) may lead to different responses. Even so, nearly one out of five Gallup respondents indicated some doubt that the Holocaust occurred. (Alan Gilbert. Courtesy of the United States Holocaust Memorial Museum)

ing dynasties. Today the same buildings represent the former rulers' exploitation of the peasants' resources and labor.

If economic change occurs in a society, buildings themselves can reflect the transformation. Take, for example, an industrial wasteland in Culver City, California, on Los Angeles's edge. Architect Eric Owen Moss is reshaping Culver City's empty factories (abandoned when employers shifted blue-collar jobs to Mexico or other cheaper labor sites offshore) into a postindustrial workplace of media-based industries. Moss creates "areas where information is pooled. The result is an architectural analogy to the climate of mental exchange that nurtures businesses based on information" (Muschamp, 1993a:32). Here we have an architect—a *symbolic analyst,* to use Robert Reich's term ([1991] 1992; Chapter 6)—shaping his artistic vision of the present: the shift from manufacturing to information and services. Similarly, Paul Knox (1991), a professor of urban affairs and planning at Virginia Polytechnic Institute and State University, argues that the contemporary architecture of metropolitan Washington, D.C., reflects a new capitalist order. He says that the built environment in a decentralized arena of production, linked by global communication networks, is now marked by a postmodern aesthetic of playfulness, combinations of styles, and designs that differentiate social classes (as predicted by Bourdieu [Chapter 10]).

And sometimes buildings are shaped as monuments to the past. The United States Holocaust Memorial Museum in Washington, D.C., which opened in 1993, is one such monument to memory (Figure 16.4). According to critic Muschamp, the building itself and the exhibits inside are so compelling that their emotional impact is shattering. Muschamp says that "a place is a form of knowledge. James Freed's design arises from that pivotal idea" (1993b:sec. 2:1). Architect Freed immersed himself in the built environment of Hitler's Final Solution, and some images remained unforgettable, particularly the observation towers (reminding prisoners of their total lack of control) and the brick ovens with steel

bands placed around them "when the ovens threatened to explode from overuse." Freed absorbed these forms into his building "as if he could distill their meaning in a ritual of recollection." The result, says Muschamp, " is an architectural vocabulary that is partly symbolic, partly abstract": "Images of confinement, observation, atrocity and denial surface and recede within the building's hard industrial forms: expanses of brick wall bolted with steel, floating glass bridges engraved with the names of devastated cities, lead pyramids clustered into sentry-box rooflines" (1993b:32). This museum, Muschamp concludes, is "a place quarried from the memory of other places."

## Las Vegas, Nevada

Sometimes the built environment sends messages that are far from subtle. Such is the case of Las Vegas, Nevada, a gambling and pleasure spot supreme. In the words of Tom Wolfe, Las Vegas is "the only town in the world whose skyline is made up neither of buildings, like New York, nor of trees, like Wilbraham, Massachusetts, but signs" (1977:7). Indeed, Las Vegas buildings are little more than concrete sheds with neon signs, including a restaurant shaped like a duck—which is actually one huge sign. Architect Robert Venturi and his colleagues ([1972] 1977) call this "duck and shed" architecture. They say that these extreme forms of advertisement are functional to the local economy.

That is, Las Vegas depends on persuading transient consumers to stop and spend money. In addition, the unlikely blend of architectural styles at gambling casino-hotels like Caesar's Palace—Italian Renaissance, neoclassical, modern, and early Christian tomb—are very functional, for they appeal to the fantasies of a diverse clientele.

In Las Vegas, the built environment doesn't let you forget where you are. True, a building (and population) boom in the 1980s attracted a number of financial-service companies and large non-

Box 16.1

## SIGNS, SEX, AND SHOW BUSINESS

### The Las Vegas Story

Las Vegas is the only town in the world whose skyline is made up neither of buildings, like New York, nor of trees, like Wilbraham, Massachusetts, but signs. One can look at Las Vegas from a mile away on Route 91 and see no buildings, no trees, only signs. But such signs! They tower. They revolve, they oscillate, they soar in shapes before which the existing vocabulary of art history is helpless. I can only attempt to supply names—Boomerang Modern, Palette Curvilinear, Flash Gordon Ming-Alert Spiral, McDonald's Hamburger Parabola, Mint Casino Elliptical, Miami Beach Kidney. Las Vegas' sign makers work so far out beyond the frontiers of conventional studio art that they have no names themselves for the forms they create. Vaughan Cannon, one of those tall, blond Westerners, the builders of places like Las Vegas and Los Angeles, whose eyes seem to have been bleached by the sun, is in the back shop of the Young Electric Sign Company out on East Charleston Boulevard with Herman Boernge, one of his designers, looking at the model they have prepared for the Lucky Strike Casino sign, and Cannon points to where the sign's two great curving faces meet to form a narrow vertical face and says:

"Well, here we are again—what do we call that?"

"I don't know," says Boernge. "It's sort of a nose effect. Call it a nose."

Okay, a nose, but it rises sixteen stories high above a two-story building. In Las Vegas no farseeing entrepreneur buys a sign to fit a building he owns. He rebuilds the building to support the biggest sign he can get up the money for and, if necessary, changes the name. . . . In the Young Electric Sign Co. era signs have become the architecture of Las Vegas. . . . Men like Boernge, Kermit Wayne, Ben Mitchem and Jack Larsen, formerly an artist for Walt Disney, are the designer-sculptor geniuses of Las Vegas, but their motifs have been carried faithfully throughout the town by lesser men, for gasoline stations, motels, funeral parlors, churches, public buildings, flophouses and sauna baths.

Then there is a stimulus that is both visual and sexual—the Las Vegas buttocks decolletage. This is a form of sexually provocative dress seen more and more in the United States, but avoided like Broadway message-embroidered ("Kiss Me, I'm Cold") underwear in the fashion pages, so that the euphemisms have not been established and I have no choice but clinical terms. To achieve buttocks decolletage a woman wears bikini-style shorts that cut across the round fatty masses of the buttocks rather than cupping them from below, so that the outer-lower edges of these fatty masses, or "cheeks," are exposed. I am in the cocktail lounge of the Hacienda Hotel, talking to managing director Dick Taylor about the great success his place has had in attracting family and tour groups, and all around me the waitresses are bobbing on their high heels, bare legs and decolletage-bare backsides, set off by pelvis-length lingerie of an uncertain denomination. I stare, but I am new here. . . . On the streets of Las Vegas, not only the show girls, of which the town has about two hundred fifty, bona fide, in residence, but girls of every sort, including, especially, Las Vegas' little high-school buds, who adorn what locals seeking roots in the sand call "our city of churches and schools," have taken up the chic of wearing buttocks decolletage step-ins under flesh-tight slacks. with the outline of the undergarment showing through fashionably.

SOURCE: Tom Wolfe, *The Kandy-Kolored Tangerine Flake Streamline Baby* (New York: Bantam, 1977), p. 8. Copyright © 1963, 1964, 1965 by Thomas K. Wolfe, Jr. Copyright © 1963, 1964, 1965 by New York Herald Tribune, Inc. Reprinted by permission of Farrar, Straus and Giroux, Inc.

gambling businesses to Las Vegas. But no one familiar with U.S. urban culture could mistake its pleasure domes for a center of manufacturing or high finance. "The Strip," as part of Route 91 in Las Vegas is called, is legendary for its glitzy gambling casinos.

Las Vegas has a distinctive sense of place, one that some term "pleasure zone architecture," "roadside eclecticism," and "commercial vernacular" (Venturi, Scott Brown, and Izenour, 1977),

**Fig. 16.5** FANTASYLAND. Las Vegas appeals to fantasies of fortune, fun, and folly by lifting tourists out of everyday reality. (Tim Teninty)

and others call a destructive "highway extravaganza" (Blake, 1979). Most U.S. cities are far less distinctive—or bizarre, depending on your taste. Nonetheless, most people feel a sense of place wherever they live because they invest the natural and built environment with meaning and sentiment.

## DOES ENVIRONMENT DETERMINE BEHAVIOR?

Will youngsters growing up amid the tall signs and desert sands of Las Vegas be significantly different from those raised in snowy, tree-lined Wilbraham, Massachusetts? Do bad housing conditions produce bad people?

The extent to which the natural and built environments affect behavior is a question of persistent debate. One view maintains that environment determines behavior. At the very least, it states, the natural and built environments play a key role in determining behavior. Britain's Lord Manny Shinwell speaks eloquently for this point of view—**environmental determinism**—in describing his own background. Born in 1884 (and interviewed by R. W. Apple in 1979, at age ninety-five), Shinwell grew up in Glasgow, Scotland's, notoriously squalid Gorbals slum, where people "lived in three-story tenements, with one

lavatory on each landing for three families. Filthy black smoke poured in when you opened the windows. There was every opportunity to become a criminal, and even the best of us emerged from it as hardened agitators and rebels."

Shinwell did not become a criminal. But he did emerge as an agitator and rebel of sorts. A school dropout at age eleven, he read voraciously, got out of the Gorbals, went on to play a leading role in the nationalization of England's coal mines, and become a combative orator in the British Parliament for forty-eight years.

Shinwell's story raises difficult questions. Was it the filthy smoke pouring in and the crowding or was it the poverty and social conditions in the Gorbals that influenced residents' behavior? This is hard to sort out, for bad physical conditions often go hand in hand with low income and low status. If a teenager living in a deteriorated tenement commits robbery or murder, we can't conclude that the physical environment determined such behavior. After all, not all people who live in the same physical environment, like the Gorbals, become criminals. This fact supports critics of physical environmental determinism. Critics argue that cultural and psychological variables have more influence on behavior than does physical environment. This dilemma of interpretation can be illustrated by examining one notoriously bad physical environment: the Pruitt-Igoe public housing project in St. Louis, Missouri.

### Case Study: Pruitt-Igoe

Before its demolition in 1974, Pruitt-Igoe symbolized the worst kind of urban environment. The massive project covered 57 acres and contained 33 slab construction buildings, each with 2,762 apartments on 11 stories. It was designed originally to house about 10,000 people, whites living in the Igoe portion and African-Americans living in the Pruitt portion. A Supreme Court decision barred this racial segregation, and the project became racially integrated.

When Pruitt-Igoe opened in 1954, it won praise as an exciting advance in low-income housing. A decade later, it was the subject of

**Fig. 16.6** PRUITT-IGOE HOUSING PROJECT. St. Louis, Missouri's vast low-income residential complex was praised initially for its architecture but came to symbolize bad design and social disaster. Built in 1954, it was demolished just twenty years later by the U.S. Department of Housing and Urban Development. (U.S. Department of Housing and Urban Development)

worried commission reports as a social disaster area. By the mid-1960s, it was occupied entirely by poor blacks, mainly on welfare and disproportionately living in large, female-headed households. By the early 1970s, federal officials had given up on Pruitt-Igoe. The entire project was dynamited and totally demolished in 1974 (Figure 16.6). Reviewing the sad history of Pruitt-Igoe, an environmental determinist would have a ready explanation for its failure: bad physical design. Pruitt-Igoe was very large and very densely settled. Each high-rise was identical to the next. The project had virtually no open space, elevators that stopped only on some floors, easily broken windows, and other poor design features. To a physical determinist, social disaster was predictable, for the project design spelled trouble.

In contrast, a critic of physical determinism would point out that physical design was the least of the problems at Pruitt-Igoe. In a housing project with a large number of poor children, juvenile delinquency and vandalism could be anticipated no matter how well designed it was. Further, as long as tenants were unemployed, without ownership rights in their residence, and conscious of their "bad address," hopelessness and hostility could be expected.

Who's right? One perceptive commentator argues that there is no right answer in the debate about environmental determinism because it is based on faulty assumptions. Galen Cranz, a sociologist of spatial behavior at Berkeley's School of Architecture, believes that both environmental determinists and their critics are on the wrong track. Cranz (n.d.) says that there is a reciprocal relationship between the built environment and human behavior. The built environment affects behavior but, at the same time, it reflects broader social, economic, and political forces. In her view, people receive messages about the social meaning of their world from many sources—verbal, nonverbal, and environmental. Usually these varied sources transmit similar messages, only in different symbolic forms. Cranz calls this *redundancy.*

Applying the redundancy concept to the Pruitt-Igoe case, we would note how verbal, nonverbal, and environmental sources sent the same message to poor African-American residents:

You are inferior beings. This message was reinforced in subtle and not so subtle ways—waiting in line for welfare checks, being subjected to police surveillance, discriminated against in jobs, and so forth. Residents could hardly avoid knowing that the larger society devalued them as low-status, low-income persons, for the message was all around them. In the mass media of the 1950s and early 1960s, for instance, few African-Americans appeared in any role; those visible few were most often cast as bad people or losers. So Pruitt-Igoe's prison-like physical design merely confirmed the larger society's negative attitude toward them. Over and over, in various forms, the message of inferiority went out. Redundancy.

Perhaps Winston Churchill had the final word. When he reopened the House of Commons after World War II, he said: "We shape our buildings and then they shape us."

## THE SPIRIT AND ENERGY OF PLACE

### Genius loci

According to novelist Lawrence Durrell (1969: 156), it is not buildings that shape human identity. Rather, it is "the spirit of place."

What is the *spirit* of place? According to philospher and architectural historian Christian Norberg-Schulz ([1979] 1984:5), ancient Romans thought that there is a "spirit of place" or guardian spirit of the locality (*genius loci*) that gives life to people and places, accompanying them from birth to death and determining their character. These Romans, Norberg-Schulz says, believed that they should come to terms with the guardian spirit of the locality because survival depended on having a good relationship with the place in both the physical and the psychic sense.

### Feng shui

In some cultures, a good relationship with place is all-important. Such is the case in traditional

Chinese culture. Today, many home builders, business owners, city planners, and interior decorators are influenced by *feng shui*—that is, the "feel of a place."

Literally, the words *feng shui* (pronounced "fung sway") mean "wind" and "water." Figuratively, the technique is based on the idea that there are currents of invisible energy that flow in certain directions, just like the energy flows of wind and water.

*Feng shui* aims at ensuring that all things are in harmony with their surroundings (Walters, 1988:8). Ninth-century scholar Yang Yun-sung originally codified the principles of *feng shui*. He drew inspiration from the harmonious, undulating hills and meandering rivers around Gwelin in southwest China, a spectacularly scenic region celebrated by centuries of Chinese poets and painters.

Today, many people dismiss *feng shui* as mere superstition. But others, particularly in Hong Kong, Vietnam, and other parts of the world where the Chinese have been influential, still plan houses and villages based on the principles of *feng shui*. In the San Francisco Bay Area, for example, it is not unusual for a *feng shui* expert to suggest the "perfect direction" of a business (ensuring prosperity) or the "perfect arrangement" of a home (creating happiness and tranquility). According to *feng shui* principles, a bend in the river outside a hotel might help the hotel's financial success. A house's entrance door must open inward in order to attract good energy, or *ch'i* (the same term used by acupuncturists to describe the body's flow of vital energies).

*To conclude:* Do the spirit and energy of place remain defining elements of human experience? Or have technology and social reorganization destroyed the traditional importance of place? There is no one answer. As suggested in Chapter 7, what Joshua Meyrowitz (1985) calls the "19-inch neighborhood"—TV—has replaced a sense of place for many people. Others surmount space and place (and time zone differences) by meeting friends on electronic highways called *bulletin boards*. Indeed, e-mail bonding replaces coffee klatsches and pickup basketball in some ZIP codes. At the same historical moment, however, numerous other persons, from East Timor and

Bosnia to southern Africa, are sacrificing their lives for inches of ancestral land invested with political, religious, tribal, or ethnic significance.

It is safe to say that in *Technoschaft*, the spirit of place does not play a defining role in most people's lives. Indeed, there may be much less of a spirit of place, particularly for members of electronic networks. Why? Because computers, faxes, and other "instruments of instant artificial adjacency" are creating "Cyberbia": an "ageographical city" that is "visible in clumps of skyscrapers rising from well-wired fields next to the Interstate; in huge shopping malls . . . surrounded by swarms of cars; in hermetically sealed atrium hotels cloned from coast to coast; in uniform 'historic' gentrifcations . . . in the clouds of satellite dishes pointed at the same geosynchronous blip" (Sorkin, 1992:xi).

Still, tourism is arguably the biggest (legal) business in the world. This suggests that the experience of place remains of keen interest.

## EXPERIENCING PERSONAL SPACE

How people experience space depends on their reality filters and on the kind of space they occupy. Here we focus on two types of occupied space: personal and social.

A leading environmental psychologist, Robert Sommer (1969:viii), uses the term **personal space** in two ways: to describe (1) "the emotionally charged zone around each person, sometimes described as a soap bubble or aura, which helps to regulate the spacing of individuals" and (2) "the processes by which people mark out and personalize the spaces they inhabit." Personal spaces are those we consider ours.

### Personal Space as Protective Bubble

We treat our bodies and that invisible bubble surrounding our bodies as the most private, inviolate territory. It is ours; we own it. All societies have rules about touching the bodies or invading the body territories of others. In the United States, for instance, "affectionate bodily contact

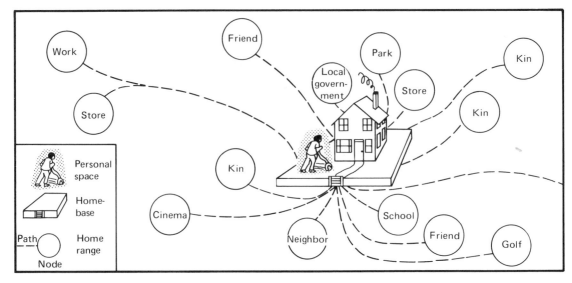

**Fig. 16.7** IMMEDIATE PHYSICAL ENVIRONMENT. People tend to see their personal space, home base, and home range as inviolate territories or "defensible space." (J. D. Porteous, "An Organizing Model of Territoriality in an Urban Setting," in *Environment and Behavior: Planning and Everyday Urban Life* [Reading, Mass.: Addison-Wesley, 1977], p. 29. Copyright © 1977 by J. Douglas Porteous. Reprinted by permission)

is almost completely taboo among men" (Parsons, 1951:189).

What happens if another person tries to break our bubble by invading it? That depends. We may withdraw and move away; we may get hostile; we may do nothing. Researchers find that one key variable in people's reactions to the invasion of personal space is sex. Conducting experiments on Los Angeles beaches, researchers found that men can routinely invade women's personal space, but the reverse is not acceptable. The researchers offer two different explanations: (1) women are simply more sociable than men, or (2) women can't prevent their space from being invaded because, in general, their social status is lower than that of men (Skolnick, et al., 1977:307–316).

How big is a person's bubble? That depends too. Bubble sizes vary from culture to culture. Not knowing this could lead to misunderstanding, even trouble. That is one reason U.S. embassy officials receive training in what anthropologist Edward T. Hall (1959) calls **proxemics**: the study of how people in different cultures use intimate space, particularly for social interaction such as conversation.

Hall, a pioneer in the study of personal space,

illustrates why proxemics is important for cross-cultural understanding: "In Latin America the interaction distance is much less than it is in the United States. Indeed, people cannot talk comfortably with one another unless they are very close to the distance that evokes either sexual or hostile feelings in the North American." The result, Hall says, is that "when they move close, we withdraw and back away. As a consequence they think we are distant or cold, withdrawn and unfriendly. We, on the other hand, are constantly accusing them of breathing down our necks, crowding us, and spraying our faces" (1959:164).

Nonverbal communication may be equally misunderstood. Hall (1966) recounts a personal experience that illustrates the point. While waiting for a friend in an empty hotel lobby in Washington, D.C., Hall seated himself in a solitary chair. He expected any stranger to leave him alone. Yet, a stranger entered the lobby and stood so close to Hall that he could hear him breathe. Hall moved slightly to signal his annoyance with body language. The stranger only moved closer. But Hall would not abandon his post. He thought, "Why should I move? I was here first." Moments later, a group arrived to join his "tormentor." It was then that Hall realized, from gestures and language, that the stranger was an Arab. Later, Hall described the scene to an Arab colleague, who helped him understand what had happened: "In Arab thought I had no rights whatsoever by virtue of occupying a given spot; neither my place nor my body was inviolate! For the Arab, there is no such thing as an intrusion in public. Public means public."

The size of a person's inviolate sphere of privacy varies with the surroundings, the social importance of the person, and other characteristics such as age. Each culture has implicit rules about the proper spatial distance in particular situations. In America, a person who invades another's body territory—even for a specific purpose, such as asking directions—usually acknowledges the intrusion by saying "Excuse me."

### Personalizing Our Space: Home Territories

Home territories are "areas where the regular participants have a relative freedom of behavior and a sense of intimacy and control over the area" (Lyman and Scott, [1967] 1970:92). They are spaces in which we feel safe and comfortable. Home territories consist of home base (the home and its immediate surroundings) and home range (places where a person feels safe and a sense of belonging).

***Home Base***   "Home," writes an urban designer, "is a haven in the turbulent seas of life. It embodies the familiar, it is the place we feel most comfortable in, where we know better than anywhere else what will happen. Home is bound up with our identity. We instinctively rise to its defense when it is attacked or threatened" (Appleyard, 1978b:1). Or as the English say, "A person's home is his [or her] castle."

Meanings attached to home pass through cultural, social, and psychological filters. In the United States, the meaning of home base varies with social class and status. Two research studies illustrate these differences. A study of Pruitt-Igoe found that the most important function of home to tenants was house-as-safe-haven (Rainwater, 1966). The study suggests that lower-class, low-status tenants lived in a world of perceived

**Fig. 16.8**   HOUSE AS SYMBOL. A residence is often sold on the basis of status appeal, not function. In this ad, which appeared in the *New York Times,* the high status of present and former occupants (governor of New York State, "Famous NY Entertainers"), seclusion (5+ wooded private acres, closest neighbor 23 acres), and zip code (the "richest zip code in U.S.") are the selling points of this very expensive property.

threat: crime and vandalism, health hazards, verbal abuse, and so on. To them, home represented a retreat. By contrast, to upper-class, high-status groups, home also symbolizes their social position. Striving young executives in the San Francisco Bay Area frequently choose mock-colonial homes that conspicuously display their stability and wealth; more established professionals tend to choose less showy, better-designed homes (Werthman, 1965).

Living spaces are more than devices for sending messages to others about who we are or wish to be. Homes are also symbols of the way we perceive ourselves. According to architect Claire Cooper, "The furniture we install, the way we arrange it, the pictures we hang, the plants we buy and tend are expressions of ourselves, all are messages about ourselves that we want to convey back to ourselves." She calls this "house-as-symbol of self" (1976:36).

Through their homes, people often tell themselves one thing, outsiders another. In most American homes, for instance, the living room doesn't look lived in. There are no cookie jars, coats lying around, or papers strewn about. If guests are expected, it is usually the living room that is cleaned up, while unkempt bedrooms or other private spaces are left as is. In France, upper-status families often have a special room for entertaining—the parlor, whose perfect appearance usually contrasts to the messier private spaces. Similarly, Japanese-American families in northern California often present a conventional image to their neighbors by their front-yard landscaping; for their own enjoyment, they use a rear, hidden-from-view Japanese garden (Appleyard, 1978a).

Increasingly, makeshift homes are becoming symbols of something else: permanent homelessness. Although it may seem to be an oxymoron, increasing numbers of homeless persons are constructing homes or home-like boxes and shacks. These structures—made of orange crates, refrigerator shelving, or other leftovers—are called the "architecture of despair" by Margaret Morton, a photographer who has been documenting the structures in New York City. According to Morton, they reflect "the profound need to create a sense of home, no matter how extreme the circumstances" (in Brown, 1993:18). Such "spontaneous settlements" like Bushville in New York and Mud Flats in Miami are reminiscent of the "no-tech" shantytowns in poor countries, such as Rio de Janeiro's favelas and bamboo riverside huts in Dhaka, Bangladesh (Rapoport in Brown, 1993:18). All these makeshift dwellings may or may not qualify as examples of what J. B. Jackson (1984:85) calls *vernacular architecture.* (Jackson, an influential voice in landscape studies, says that vernacular dwellings suggest something "traditional": "the dwelling of the farmer or craftsman or wage earner." But, makeshift street architecture is "built with local techniques, local materials, and with the local environment in mind," all characteristics of vernacular architecture.) Whichever they are, they are much more than shelter. They are symbols of people's inventiveness and, at the same time, seemingly permanent poverty.

***Home Range*** Beyond home base lies home range, that area in which a person feels a sense of belonging or perhaps ownership. As noted in the next section, public territories (social space) are often converted into the home range of individuals or social groups.

The extent of a person's home range varies with age, social standing and background, and personal disposition. Children tend to have the narrowest home ranges. Very young children may perceive a one-block area around home as home range. For older children, home range is often equated with their neighborhood. For some adults, too, home range consists of little more than their neighborhoods. This is often the case with immigrants who arrive in large cities speaking no English. One students told me that his mother had not left San Francisco's Chinatown since her arrival from China in 1949. This suggests that residents of homogeneous ethnic neighborhoods have a stronger sense of home range than residents of more heterogeneous neighborhoods and/or more fear of the world beyond the neighborhood.

For other adults, the workplace is a home territory. A person can invest his or her office with

**Fig. 16.9** CITY SLEEPER. Throughout the world, homeless people construct shelters out of oddments. San Francisco architect Donald MacDonald has another idea: building compact, clean, low-cost shelters called "city sleepers." (Josh Freiwald)

the symbolic meaning of home base—inviolate territory and safe haven. For instance, when a sportscaster in Fresno, California, was interrupted in the television studio—on the air—by a (toy) gun-toting man, he was first petrified, and then angry: "It's just like somebody coming into your home—it's just a gross, gross violation of one's privacy," he said afterward (Cotta in Massey, 1987:A3).

The most dramatic example of workplace-as-safe-haven is a government's embassy building. Traditionally and by international accord, any government's embassy anywhere in the world is considered inviolate territory; an embassy building symbolizes the honor and security of a nation. Thus in 1979, when the U.S. embassy in Teheran, Iran, was invaded and hostages were taken, many Americans reacted as if their own homes had been threatened.

The drama of Teheran and the little everyday experiences of discomfort when someone moves "too close" indicate that we invest physical space with symbolic meaning, and that these meanings can have a powerful impact on our feelings and actions. This impact may be intensified when territorial encroachment occurs.

## Privatization of Domestic Public Space

Before industrialization and urbanization in Europe, there was little distinction between domestic public and private space. In medieval French homes, for example, "all-purpose rooms were the rule, in aristocratic, peasant, and artisan dwellings alike" (Olsen, 1986:101). Then, first among noble households and gradually among households lower on the social ladder came "privacy in sleep; privacy in eating; privacy in religious and social ritual; finally, privacy in thought" (Mumford, 1961:285). In other words, domestic privacy largely replaced communality.

In terms of privacy, many observers draw a parallel between the home and the city, suggesting that "the city is the home writ large." That is, instead of using public space, urbanites (at least those who can afford to do so) retreat into their safe havens called home.

## EXPERIENCING SOCIAL SPACE

Social space consists of public territories that, officially at least, offer equal access to all. Individuals generally feel that they do not control the use of social space, although they have free access to it. As discussed more fully in Chapter 11, Americans tend to maximize their privacy and mini-mize their involvement with strangers in social space.

## Public Space as Symbol

Tiananmen Square in Beijing, China, is the largest public space on earth. On its southwestern corner stands a Kentucky Fried Chicken, reputedly the largest KFC in the world in terms of sales. But, for most of us, neither of these factoids defines Tiananmen Square. Instead, thanks to CNN, most adults worldwide associate this monumental public space with the events of June 3/4, 1989: the Chinese army's lethal attack on peaceful dissidents.

To China's leaders, Tiananmen Square symbolizes the smashing of a "serious counterrevolutionary rebellion." To most others, the square symbolizes the crushing of the spirit of democracy. Either way, the world's largest social space is much more than 100 acres of land; it is a place full of meaning—even for most of us who have never been there.

## Colonizing Social Space

Officially, streets, public beaches and parks, and other public territories are open to all. In practice, these social spaces often become colonized or expropriated into some group's home territory. At that point, the invisible borders of this private "turf" may be defended against invaders. "Streets are most vulnerable to colonizing in this manner" and "streets become unofficial home areas to all those groups who require relatively secluded yet open space in which to pursue their interests or maintain their identities" (Lyman and Scott, [1967] 1970:95).

Sometimes the transformation of public territory into private turf reflects a strong sense of community. If so, rigid divisions between insiders and outsiders—us and them—can occur, resulting in hostility or territorial terror. This is the case in Boston. "The tourist who makes a wrong turn," says a Boston news reporter, "can find himself in another Boston—a city of 'turf,' of neighborhoods to avoid, of hostile graffiti. This Boston . . . is a place where . . . race affects the places blacks can drive, work and play" (Husock, 1979:32–34). In Boston, African-Americans generally avoid the city's beaches, located in South Boston (a poor, white, Irish neighborhood and the scene of beachfront confrontations).

Even a small urban space can become privatized, sometimes with deadly consequences. In 1987, a man was shot to death in San Francisco over a parking space; it had been "reserved" by members of a local gang as a sacred shrine to a murdered gang member.

## Street People's Turf

Panhandlers and the homeless stake out a sidewalk or doorway in many cities. Then they privatize or colonize their territory, discouraging spatial invasion by other street people or "respectable types."

Generally speaking, street musicians, pretzel peddlers, and newspaper hawkers add liveliness and color to urban space. So few complain about their privatizing public space. But public reaction to the homeless is another story. The homeless can make passersby uncomfortable, either because their presence reminds "respectable types" of the existence of poverty in the midst of affluence or because their appearance and / or behavior can be unpredictable or frightening. Ironically, a dog or another companion animal may cut through a passerby's fear, guilt, or disgust, thus narrowing the social and physical distance between passerby and homeless and reestablishing a sense of humane and human encounter (Figure 16.10).

Homeless women tend to be barely visible to mainstream society. Thanks to Elliot Liebow, however, we can gain insight into some of their lives. In *Tell Them Who I Am* (1993), Liebow introduces us to about twenty (mainly white and middle-aged or older) homeless women in suburban Washington, D.C. As one reviewer puts it, to read this urban ethnography

is to begin to see what it's like, day in and day out: the spare, cold breakfasts after nights of too little sleep; the desolate feeling of having to be out on the street at 7 a.m. every day, no matter what; the painful sloughing off of prized possessions; the jealousies and moments of grace among people thrown together by sheer, unhappy circumstance. (Coughlin, 1993:A8)

(As noted earlier, urban anthropologist Liebow illuminated another nearly invisible segment of society, at least to middle-class whites: poor African-American males congregating at *Tally's Corner* [1967] in Washington, D.C.)

## Streets

Most urbanites use social space daily because they walk or ride down city streets. After observing street behavior in New York City and Tokyo, William H. Whyte (1978:14–16; [1988] 1990: chaps. 4, 6) concludes that people like somewhat crowded streets. This observation flies in the face of assumptions made by many planners and architects who, in Whyte's view, "overscale" and design megastructures that bury streets in underground concourses or put streets "up in the air in glass-enclosed walkways." According to Whyte, the result is loss of the vital friction of social space, loss of activity and liveliness. He says that

mile after mile, Tokyo's streets are consistently more interesting than [those in the United States]. Mixture is one reason. The Japanese do not use zoning to enforce a rigid separation of uses. Instead, they encourage different uses, side by side and upward—shops, showrooms, pachinko parlors, offices all mixed together and with glass-walled restaurants rising one on top of another—three, four, and five stories up. ([1988] 1990:89)

*To conclude:* Whether human territoriality is genetically programmed or culturally learned is a matter of much debate, particularly among sociobiologists and sociologists. In either case, people do display a sense of territoriality. Human ecologists from Park, Burgess, and McKenzie (1925) to Hawley (1950) use the concept of territoriality in

**Fig. 16.10** PRIVATIZING PUBLIC SPACE. Animals often serve as props for the homeless. Dogs, in particular, seem to encourage contributions from passersby and discourage spatial invasion by other street people. (Brack Brown)

their analysis of urban communities, paying particular attention to territorial invasion of one ethnic group by another. In recent years, social scientists have paid increasing attention to personal as well as social space, focusing on their symbolic meanings to individuals and social groups.

This current focus—on the symbolic uses of space, on the meanings people attach to home territories and public territories—can be viewed as an implicit critique of the classic models of urban space. The work of Sommer, Hall, Appleyard, and Whyte, among others, suggests that nonrational, noneconomic factors influence people's perception and use of space. Shades of Walter Firey, Gerald Suttles, and Mike Davis!

## Policy Implications

What are some policy implications that follow from these insights about human spatial behavior? Psychologist Robert Sommer (1969) argues that an understanding of how people perceive and use space is fundamental to intelligent design of the built environment. His studies of various intimate and public environments—from homes for the elderly to the Los Angeles airport—suggest that even very minor rearrangements of things in space can affect people's behavior. For instance, Sommer visited a hospital where the chairs were arranged in such a way as to make cleaning the floors easy but conversation among patients impossible. A slight shift of the furniture gave patients a chance to converse freely. Sommer's ideas about space have particular significance for those displaced from their home base and home range: people who live in total institutions, such as hospitals and jails. Institutionalized people have little control over their personal space. The psychological implications of feeling powerless to control one's immediate environment are suggested in the following account of a schizophrenic as she neared recovery in a hospital: "To the stupefaction of the nurse, for the first time I dared to handle the chairs and change the arrangement of the furniture. What unknown joy to have an influence on things; to do with them what I liked" (in Sommer, 1969:83).

Increasingly, design professionals are drawing on the work of Sommer and other students of the environment in order to better shape the spaces in which we live, work, and play. Apple Computer in Silicon Valley, California, to take one example, redesigned its work spaces, replacing the open-plan cubicles with private spaces for computer designers and common areas for informal meetings. This arrangement reflects what some call the spirit of Silicon Valley: "quiet informality combined with intense commitment" (Markoff, 1993:F7).

Design professionals are also becoming aware that what is important to them, such as subtle nuances in building design, may be relatively unimportant to people who have to use those spaces. For instance, a user study of a low-income housing project found that tenants would have preferred better maintenance service and less subtle architecture. And they would have preferred larger kitchens—the typical social gathering place for residents—and smaller living rooms (Cooper, 1975).

In many other cases, however, there is a wide gap between what planners think people need and what people want. William Whyte's caustic comments about the planned disappearance of lively streets suggest this gap. Other defenders of the lively street, particularly Jane Jacobs (1961), have a large popular following, but to date, their impact on planning and public policy has been limited.

## ENVIRONMENTAL PSYCHOLOGY

Environmental psychology deals with the relationships between human behavior and the physical environment, both natural and built. Theorists and researchers in this subdiscipline commonly are trained as psychologists, but other behavioral scientists call themselves environmental psychologists as well. Researchers tend to focus on rather limited kinds of human behavior, particularly people's perception of the environment and the environment's impact on their actions and emotional states.

## Key Concepts and Research Thrusts

Environmental psychologists have no single model for studying behavior–environment relationships. They work from mechanistic models, cognitive models, or behavioral models (Heimstra and McFarling, 1978:7–8). But researchers do share a vocabulary, including the following concepts (Ittelson et al., 1974):

1. *Cognition.* How people assign meaning to the world around them and make sense out of their environment or personal space: (1) the moving bubble around our bodies and (2) the process of personalizing immediate space.
2. *Crowding, overcrowding.* A large number of persons gathered closely together in limited space.
3. *Dominance behavior.* How people react in situations of inequality.
4. *Perception.* How people perceive or become aware of their environment.
5. *Privacy.* Freedom from the presence or demands of others.
6. *Sensory adaptation.* How people adapt to the environment, particularly under conditions of stress or sensory overload.
7. *Territoriality.* How people identify, possess, feel safe in, and/or defend space.

Long before researchers called themselves environmental psychologists, they conducted behavior–environment studies. Such studies followed no plan but rather "proceeded in fits and starts depending upon local interest and the availability of funds" (Sommer, 1969:8). Over the years, large corporations funded basic research on people's reactions to temperature, light, color, and sound. They also supported applied research, including studies of light intensity in factories, carpeting in hospitals, and background music in offices. One landmark in applied research, funded by plumbing suppliers, is the work of Alexander Kira and his Cornell colleagues, *The Bathroom: Criteria for Design* ([1966] 1976). This eight-year study may evoke snickers from the uninitiated (or perhaps win the infamous Golden Fleece Award from former Senator William Proxmire, had it been federally funded), but Kira's findings have serious implications for environmental design. For example, Kira's work shows that most standard bathroom equipment is difficult for the disabled and elderly to use with ease. This leads to a sense of helplessness

and frustration. The implication here is that redesign of basic household equipment could decrease their feeling of powerlessness.

One particularly important area of applied research concerns institutional settings, such as hospitals, offices, schools, and college dorms. Sommer's research, mentioned earlier, suggests that institutional decisions about space are often made with little knowledge of users' behavior. Environmental studies can make clear the impacts of various alternatives—open or partitioned offices, secluded or centrally located nurses' stations, movable or stationary school desks—on people's emotional states and patterns of social interaction.

We should remember, however, a basic point sometimes downplayed or overlooked by environmental psychologists: *Spatial arrangements reflect power arrangements.* This means that users' needs and institutional needs may be in direct conflict. How space is arranged may reflect the need of people in charge to maintain control or to provide services efficiently rather than humanely. For instance, schoolchildren may prefer to have movable rather than stationary desks. But teachers may find the constant rearrangement of their pupils disconcerting. Similarly, secluded nurses' stations in hospitals may isolate nurses from one another, patients, and visitors. This arrangement may be considered functional in the minds of hospital administrators, for it makes "time-wasting" chit-chat difficult. Even minor rearrangements of space, then, may entail changes in the structures of power and authority.

## Rats, Chickens, and People

"It is interesting," says Robert Sommer, "that more is known about animal than about human spatial behavior" (1969:12). Much research has been done on the way animals adapt to shared space. We know, for instance, a great deal about the connections between the crowding of rats and their disoriented behavior, about the crowding of chickens and their decreased egg laying, about the territoriality of captive animals and their strengthened dominance orders. Laboratory animals do react to crowded conditions by competing for space and by developing certain pathologies. But what about the human animal? How do high density and crowding affect us? And what about people in captive spaces like total institutions: Do they develop a stronger sense of territoriality?

Michelson (1976) has reviewed studies of crowding in various environments, including prisoner-of-war camps, slave ships, densely populated cities such as Hong Kong, and housing units with more than 1.01 persons per room (the U.S. Census Bureau's definition of "overcrowded"). He finds their conclusions ambiguous and mixed. The basic problem is that crowding tends to go hand in hand with other factors, such as powerlessness and low status. If, for instance, prisoners of war are psychologically disoriented, how can it be shown that crowding is the key variable leading to their disorientation? Perhaps other factors—isolation from the familiar, lack of control over space, and so on—may be more important than density.

Indeed, some studies suggest that crowding is less important for people than other conditions. Baldassare (1979) concludes that crowding has no measurable impact on residential well-being and minimal effects on social interaction. He thinks that most humans can avoid "social overload" by organizing their activities and space. Yet those who lack the social power to control their space—the disabled, the poor, and children, for instance—may be more affected by residential crowding. Another study finds that schoolchildren in Toronto who live in crowded housing units learn less well than those who don't. However, further analysis suggests that the presence or absence of someone in the room is a key factor in the child's learning, not crowding per se (Michelson, 1976:158).

Concerning territoriality, one important study suggests that caged people do react like caged animals. In this study of schizophrenic patients on a psychiatric ward, psychologists found that territoriality was important in the patients' behavior. For instance, patients who exhibited a strong sense of territoriality were more likely to win in confrontations with other patients that occurred within their territory. Territoriality helped to define the social hierarchy of the ward (Esser et al., 1970).

After a review of the literature on density and crowding, Krupat ([1985] 1989:112) reaches the following conclusion: High-density living in cities does not cause social pathology. Further, he critiques what he calls the "urban stressor approach"—research that focuses on crowding, density, noise, pollution, and commuting to work, as bad stressors. He suggests that the urban stressor approach subtly biases our image of the city, overlooking the idea that high input levels are preferred by some people with certain personalities (126).

Some researchers go further. In their article "Crowding Studies and Urban Life—A Critical Review" (1975), sociologists Fischer, Baldasarre, and Ofshe totally discredit the notion that increased numbers of persons and density lead to social pathologies. Indeed, recent research presented at the 1994 conference of the Social Science History Association claims that villages—not cities—were often the scenes of violence in earlier times, particularly during the Middle Ages in Europe and in the early nineteenth century in the United States. These new studies contradict the view that violence is part and parcel of dense urban industrial centers. Joan McCord, a past president of the American Society of Criminology, notes that the recent research should "undermine the basic claim that the city, with its anonymity and crowding, is in and of itself the factor in causing violence" (in Butterfield, 1994). Others, including Eric H. Monkkonen, professor of American urban history at the University of California at Los Angeles, thinks that cities are a civilizing influence—not a factory for crime.

*To conclude:* Behavior–environment studies are problematic for several reasons. In most cases, people are not captive animals like laboratory rats; leaping from conclusions about rats or chickens to the way humans react is unjustified. Further, the notion that persons in authority (such as hospital administrators and office managers) are unaware of users' needs may be naive. Ken Kesey's portrayal of Big Nurse in *One Flew*

*Over the Cuckoo's Nest* (1962) illustrates the point. Consciously or unconsciously, Big Nurse manipulated mental patients by exercising control over their space. True, patients may have felt more comfortable, secure, and powerful in other kinds of spaces. However, it does not follow that Big Nurse or other authority figures will modify spatial arrangements under their control on the basis of behavior–environment research findings. Their need to maintain authority may conflict with people's need to control their space. And like so much else in urban life, those with power, authority, or high status have more ability to control their space than those without these resources.

This brings us to a more thorough exploration of the design of urban spaces. What assumptions or theories underlie the thinking of those who shape the spaces we live in: building architects, landscape architects, planners, interior decorators, and other design professionals?

## SHAPING SPACE

### Design Principles

When men and women receive their degree in architecture from Harvard University, they rise at the graduation ceremonies and a university official pronounces them qualified "to shape the space in which we live." This pronouncement makes design professionals sound like value-free technicians, which, of course, they are not.

Those deemed qualified to shape urban space—architects, licensed interior decorators, planners, and other design professionals—learn to think in a certain way about the physical world. This way of thinking is called *design.*

What is design? According to architect-designer Christopher Alexander, design is "the process of inventing physical things which display new physical order, organization, form in response to function" (1964:1). In his early theoretical work, *Notes on the Synthesis of Form,* Alexander states that "every design problem begins with an effort to achieve fitness between two en-

tities: the form in question and its context" (1964:15). However, a physical form is part of a whole ensemble of components, and one design objective (e.g., using the most appropriate material for each part of a building) may conflict with another design principle (e.g., using uniform materials for an entire project). Achieving "fitness" between form and context is particularly difficult when the context is obscure. This is the case when architects and planners try to design an entire new city.

What constitutes a good fit between form and context? According to Alexander, that's hard to define. Perhaps it is easier to see what constitutes a bad fit. For instance, we know there is a bad fit if a seesaw in a children's playground is designed with dangerously sharp edges.

Of course, design questions involve value judgments. Most important, whose values will be served? Consider, for example, one of eight purposes of urban design outlined by Paul D. Spreirigen: "To make the city humane" (1965:68–69). That seems a noble purpose, but what does it actually mean? To urban designers (who are usually trained as architects initially but who concentrate on large-scale design issues), it may mean the razing of a densely settled area they consider a slum. This may seem inhumane, however, to residents of a densely settled neighborhood who happen to like it there. Such was the case with Boston's West End, as Herbert Gans fully describes in *The Urban Villagers* ([1962] 1982).

In other words, designing urban spaces is not a value-neutral process. Perhaps it was the growing awareness of this fact that led Christopher Alexander to depart from his original scientific-rational approach to design and to embark on a new course, one that rejects many established design principles and does not pretend to be value-free.

Modern city planning and urban design, Alexander maintains, are based on an unfortunate model—the city as a tree: a rigid, abstract structure that lacks complexity and contains no overlapping structures. He argues that "it is this lack of structural complexity, characteristic of trees, which is crippling our conceptions of the city"

([1965] 1978:382). In his view, a city is not a tree; a city should be designed with ambiguity, overlap, and multiplicity of aspect.

In 1977, Alexander and his colleagues at Berkeley's Center for Environmental Structure published a seminal work on city design calling for a new way of designing for complex social systems. They developed what they call *A Pattern Language* (Alexander, Ishikawa, Silverstein, Jacobson, Fiksdahl-King, and Angel, 1977). The "language" consists of some 250 elements that the authors think should be considered in the design process. Alexander and his colleagues don't pretend to be value-free. Instead, they call for a participatory, process-oriented, dynamic structuring of symbolic and functional patterns in environmental design. Here is a small sample of their design principles:

1. *On home and work.* "The artificial separation of home and work creates intolerable rifts in people's inner lives. . . . Concentration and segregation of work leads to dead neighborhoods" (1977:52).
2. *On communal space.* "Give every institution and social group a place where people can eat together [because] without communal eating, no human group can hold together" (699, 697).
3. *On institutional scale.* "To make the political control of local functions real, establish a small town hall for each community of 7000, and even for each neighborhood" (240).
4. *On access to ideas and services.* "Allow the growth of shop-size spaces around the local town hall, and any other appropriate community building. Front these shops on a busy path, and lease them for a minimum rent to ad hoc community groups for political work, trial services, research, and advocate groups. No ideological restrictions" (244).
5. *On the importance of multipurpose, communal places.* "Somewhere in the community [create] at least one big place where a few hundred people can gather, with beer and wine, music, and perhaps a half-dozen activities, so that people are continuously criss-crossing from one to another (446).

This sample reveals that Alexander and his colleagues represent a new attitude to architecture and planning—an alternative to mainstream ideas and practices that stress functional order and the separation of contexts within city space. Clearly, Alexander is a decentralist, trying to mold the physical environment to meet what he considers human needs for small-scale community and activity. He is also an integrator, trying to bring together in space various activities that people enjoy or need for survival.

In recent years, Alexander has been designing widely accepted, comfortable, traditional office furniture that seeks to "humanize the rooms where we spend our working lives" (in Ketchum, 1989:B4). But Alexander's theories remain controversial, particularly his insistence on what might be called *messy order*, such as criss-crossing functions in space. *A Pattern Language* sent ripples through many architectural and design schools. Still, it hasn't had much impact on the built environment. Given the radical restructuring of social life that it implies, this is not surprising.

Designing an attractive, functional city is the goal of many a planner or designer, even if few get the chance. Architects, on the other hand, design buildings. What are their goals? According to one architect, "We try to design buildings that are orderly, economical, and pleasing" (McLaughlin, 1962). Of course, what is orderly, economical, or pleasing depends on one's taste and values. To architect-designer Christopher Alexander, tree-like order in a building or city is deadly. Large-scale environments, which might be economical, bring high social costs in the long run. And aesthetic pleasure, Alexander would argue, comes not from having everything in its separate place, but from interlacing varied human activities.

*To conclude:* Most design professionals do not make explicit the values underlying their work. Christopher Alexander is an exception to that rule. He makes numerous unsubstantiated statements about the nature of human beings (e.g., "All people have the instinct to decorate their surroundings" [1977:1147]). Yet he does not hide his ideology. He stresses the need for community and communalism, the need for people to create and re-create their own environments, and the need to learn from various aspects of the city. He likes small, family-owned grocery stores, places where urbanites can watch the world go by, and elevated places as city landmarks. Most of all, he wants to enrich the city by breaking it into "a vast mosaic of small and different subcultures, each with its own spatial territory, and each with the power to create its own distinct life style . . . so that each person has access to the full variety of life styles in the subcultures near his [or her] own" (1977:50).

Alexander's vision of decentralized subcommunities is not widely shared in the design professions. Nor is it economically probable if current dominant values don't change. But his ideas may have an important impact on the postindustrial cities of America. And his explicit ideology is a refreshing antidote to the falsely value-free rhetoric of so many design professionals.

## Designing the Natural Environment

*Landscape* and *architecture* may seem contradictory, but together they reflect the goal of landscape architecture: to shape the natural environment, just as the architect molds the built environment. Frederick Law Olmsted, the profession's pioneer, coined the term *landscape architecture* in 1858.

Olmsted, the developer of Central Park in New York City, had specific ideas about parks. He wanted to keep rural nature in a close relationship to the industrial cities growing up in post–Civil War America. This would relieve the anxiety of urban life, Olmsted thought. Parks would also strengthen the sense of community within large cities. Where else, he asked, could over 50,000 people come together "with an evident glee in the prospect of coming together, all classes represented . . . each individual adding by his mere presence to the pleasure of all others?" (in Glaab and Brown, 1976:234).

Olmsted's influence stretched from New York City's Central Park and the boulevards of Chicago to San Francisco's Golden Gate Park. He inspired a park and boulevard movement in the late nineteenth century, and he provided the ideology for reshaping the industrial city.

Assessments of Olmsted's work vary. According to two urban historians, Olmsted was more instrumental than anyone else in reshaping "for the better the way in which American cities were to grow" (Glaab and Brown, 1976:233). Critics, on the other hand, argue that Olmsted and the designers and planners he inspired were antiurban and aristocratic in their approach to parks. Their aesthetically pleasing, grand getaways from soot and noise, it is argued, did nothing to relieve the urban anxiety rooted in poverty and social conflict.

However Olmsted's work is judged, he left an indelible stamp on the natural environment of American cities. Indeed, one could reasonably claim that the natural and built environments of U.S. cities today are, to a significant degree, the handiwork of two impassioned men: Olmsted, who developed Central Park in the nineteenth century, and Robert Moses (master builder or destroyer of living communities, depending on your viewpoint), who controlled Central Park and much else in mid-twentieth century New York City (Chapter 13). It is interesting to note that neither was an elected political official.

Today landscape architects rarely have a chance to reshape huge pieces of urban space or to impose their ideologies on an entire city, let alone a nation. Instead, most do the following kinds of work: landscape planning and assessment (e.g., evaluating the suitability of land for a new national park); site planning (e.g., analyzing a proposed hospital site to assess the fit between the form of the natural environment and the building); and/or landscape design (i.e., super gardening—selecting plants and materials).

Landscape architects (almost named *rural embellishers* by Olmsted) are not the only professionals concerned with the natural environment. Increasingly, urban designers and city planners are devoting attention to working with, rather than against, nature. Ian McHarg, a leading advocate of "design with nature," thinks that designers generally neglect the natural environment in their decisions, say, about highways: "In highway design, the problem is reduced to the simplest and most commonplace terms: traffic, volume, design speed, capacity, pavements, structures, horizontal and vertical alignment" ([1969] 1971:31). These considerations, McHarg adds, are then filtered through a purely economic cost-benefit model, driving out noneconomic values such as damage to wildlife.

## THE IMAGE OF THE CITY

### Making the City Observable

Urban designers try to make the city observable. What does that mean? "Making the city observable," says one urban designer, "means making the plethora of public information public" (Wurman, 1971:8). It means making clear visually the patterns of the city.

Kevin Lynch developed specific ideas about the visual image of the city (Figure 16.11). Lynch (1960) classifies the contents of a city's image that are associated with physical forms into five main elements: paths, edges, nodes, districts, and landmarks. In Lynch's scheme, paths are the channels along which an observer moves: streets, transit lines, railroads, canals. Edges are linear breaks in the continuity of the city: shores, walls, railroad cuts, edges of development. Districts are the medium-to-large sections of the city having some common identifiable character that an observer may mentally enter. Nodes are strategic spots in a city: intensive loci to and from which people travel. Landmarks are reference points that the observer does not enter.

One of Lynch's main interests is the **imageability** of a city: that quality of the urban landscape that evokes a strong image in the mind of anyone who observes it. Imageability is "that shape, color, or arrangement which facilitates the making of vividly identified, powerfully structured, highly useful mental images of the environment" (Lynch, 1960:9). Lynch is concerned with a city's imageability, or heightened visi-

bility, because he found in his research that people feel most comfortable in city space when they can recognize its overall patterns. Lynch's work has influenced urban designers throughout the world. The design of Ciudad Guyana in Venezuela, for example, was inspired by his ideas.

### The View from the Road

Roads and streets take up most of the U.S. city's space. For that reason alone, they are worth special attention. In addition, "public streets are the primary determinants of the form of the city . . . the routes, and the physical environment along them, are the initial and dominant experience of the city for all people" (Wurman, 1971:35).

Road watching can be, perhaps should be, a delight. In fact, Kevin Lynch and his colleagues, Donald Appleyard and John R. Myer (Appleyard et al., 1964), say that the highway is a work of art. Hence, they want to make each journey an artistic experience for drivers and passengers. How? By designing highways that give people a sense of the rhythm and continuity of the road.

*To conclude:* Apparently, people need to recognize and make coherent patterns out of their physical surroundings. To Kevin Lynch, it is the job of the city planner and urban designer to make the city's image more recognizable, vivid, and memorable to the city dweller. Clear images, Lynch believes, give people emotional satisfaction, an easy framework for communication, and personal security. To architect-designer Christopher Alexander, coherent patterns of environmental structure are also crucial, but he would design them in a more complex, subtle way: via overlapping and criss-crossing functions in space. Both design theorists emphasize the social and psychological impact of urban forms on city dwellers' well-being.

## GRAND DESIGNERS

A city can be considered an art form—a special art form that reflects the builders' belief system

**Fig. 16.11** LYNCH'S ELEMENTS OF THE CITY IMAGE. (Paul D. Spreirigen, *Urban Design: The Architecture of Towns and Cities* [New York: McGraw-Hill, 1965], pp. 50–51. Copyright © 1965 by the American Institute of Architects. Reprinted by permission)

and values. Villages constructed by the Dogon tribe in Mali, West Africa, reveal the imprint of their values and cosmology. The tribe feels indissolubly connected with the cosmos and its timeless rhythms, and the physical layout of the Dogon village reflects this belief. Each building stands in a particular relation to the sun, and the granary building (symbol of the world system) is constructed with invariant male–female parts (Griaule, 1965). A Dogon community is a work of artistic symmetry and cosmic vision; it is a symbolic representation of the tribal universe. Similarly, the ancient city of Babylon was more than a city; it was a vision of heaven on earth.

Heaven on earth—or at least a better society—has been a perennial interest of philosophers, artists, and city planners. Often the ideal city transcends the dominant ideas of the society that produced it. Like artists, visionary planners suggest solutions to problems only dimly understood in their own time. Thus in the twelfth century, European visionaries designed cities of God on earth amid war and strife. In the nineteenth century, utopian socialists designed classless communities amid the evolution of industrial capitalism.

Here I focus on only a few grand designers. This brief survey is intended to indicate the range of visions and the sources from which they sprang: patriotism, profit and philanthropy, paternalism, pure aesthetics, ideology, religious ardor, and utopian dreams.

## Pierre-Charles L'Enfant's Washington, D.C.

Major Pierre-Charles L'Enfant was a grand designer inspired by the vision of America as a new society. L'Enfant, a young French infantryman, came to America to fight in the Revolutionary War.

For several years after the war, the new national government moved from place to place, debating alternative sites for the nation's capital. Badly divided, Congress finally decided on a new location on the Potomac River, and George Washington himself rode along the wild, swampy 80-mile general location, choosing the precise site where Washington, D.C., now stands. Meanwhile, L'Enfant was instructed to do general survey work on the new site. Interpreting this charge very liberally, he plunged ahead, with remarkable results.

On one design point, L'Enfant was adamant. The new capital was not to be a gridiron city, with parallel streets running at right angles to one another. While practical, the gridiron lacked the grandeur L'Enfant thought appropriate to a capital city. Thomas Jefferson, a designer as well as a philosopher and future president, approached L'Enfant with his own proposal: a checkerboard city with alternate squares left in open space. L'Enfant responded that such a grid concept was "tiresome and insipid." L'Enfant won.

Today Washington reflects L'Enfant's grand design. There is a wheel-like arrangement of streets running off a central spoke, long malls with vistas, broad diagonal avenues bearing the names of the original thirteen colonies, and major public buildings arranged in a federal triangle.

## Utopian Visionaries

In America, utopian visions existed from the very beginning. Indeed, to some, America itself was utopia: the New World, a chance to create paradise on earth. The names of colonial towns—New Haven, Connecticut, and New Hope, Pennsylvania, to name only two—convey this idealism.

Early utopians were inspired by religious visions. Generally, they set up small, intentional communities. Most often they were Protestant separatists breaking away from established sects, such as the United Society of Believers, popularly called the Shakers. The oldest communistic society in the United States, the Shakers, set up a parent community in 1792 at Mount Lebanon on the border of Massachusetts and Connecticut.

In the nineteenth century, religiously inspired utopian communities flourished from Oneida,

New York, to the frontier of the Midwest. But there was also a new development: the growth of secular utopian visions. Some were translated from paper blueprints into actuality.

One of the most famous is Robert Owen's experiment at New Harmony, Indiana. Owen, a rich industrialist turned utopian entrepreneur, came to the United States from Scotland in the 1820s to introduce a new system of society that would remove the reasons for conflict among individuals. Utopian socialist Owen (like his French contemporary Charles Fourier) believed that large cities around industrial areas were unhealthy and that the best alternative was a small, self-sufficient community. In such a community Owen hoped to promote a noncompetitive, wholesome way of life based on socialism and education.

Owen designed an architectural model of his ideal community: a square-shaped arrangement that would contain between 800 and 1,200 people. Inside the square were to be public buildings, while families would live on three sides and children over three years of age would live on the fourth side. Outside the square were to be manufacturing facilities, stables, farm buildings, and agricultural land.

The design plan of New Harmony was never realized. Instead, Owen and his followers moved into a village formerly occupied by another utopian sect. The hopes for New Harmony were not realized either. The dream of utopian socialism was quickly shattered by internal dissent.

Still, the failure of New Harmony did little to dampen the spirits of other communitarian experiments in the mid-nineteenth century. Dozens of other communities, both religious and secular, were established. One of the longest lived was John Humphrey Noyes's community of radical Protestants in Oneida, New York. Their imposing Mansion House still stands, and descendants of the original Oneida community still conduct tours, explaining to visitors how the system worked. Of special interest, guides say, is the Oneida community's theory and practice of communism in human relationships as well as material goods (via "complex marriage" and the dissolution of the nuclear family).

## Company Towns: Lowell, Massachusetts, and Pullman, Illinois

New Harmony and Oneida exemplify the search for a radically new and better social order through communitarian socialist ideals. Planned manufacturing towns were inspired by different motives: profit, paternalism, and/or reform in the interest of softening class antagonism.

Lowell, Massachusetts, is the most famous example of early planned manufacturing towns. Built by Frances Cabot Lowell in the early nineteenth century, it was the model for dozens of other New England mill towns.

Realizing that he would need abundant cheap labor to run his water-powered textile mills, Lowell set out to attract workers, mainly New England farm girls, to his town. And disturbed at the horrific social conditions in English factory towns that he had visited, Lowell set out to improve the workers' lot. The result: Lowell, Massachusetts, a planned town. It was laid out physically to fit the social order Lowell envisioned. Textile mills lined the river, flanked by a canal. Between them was housing for America's first female labor force—boarding houses operated much like convents (Chapter 18). A main road linked the manufacturing and housing areas to other urban activities.

About a half-century later, cities privately built by industrialists reached their zenith in Pullman, Illinois. George M. Pullman, the railroad sleeping-car magnate, decided to consolidate his manufacturing activities and housing for his workers at a 4,000-acre site about 12 miles south of Chicago. Designed by an architect and a landscape engineer, the town of Pullman was meant to be a model industrial community. When it went into operation in 1881, the town presented a strong contrast to the crowded, unsanitary tenements of industrial cities. There were neat row houses, a shopping center, an elegant theater, a hotel, a church, a school, and a host of cultural institutions (excluding bars or brothels). By the early 1890s, the population had reached about 12,000 Pullman workers and their families—living in Pullman-owned homes.

Why did George Pullman build such a town? In part, he had a great deal of imagination; he was an environmental determinist of sorts and thought that miserable urban conditions led to workers' "costly vices." And in part, he hoped his planned community "would soften the bitter antagonism which wage earners often felt toward their employers, and would enable him to attract a stable and highly competent labor force; it would also earn 6 per cent on the money invested in it" (Glaab and Brown, 1976:237).

Did the town serve Pullman's ends? No. Paternalism or "benevolent, well-wishing feudalism," as it was often called in its own day, went against American democratic ideals. Labor violence, culminating in the Pullman strike of 1894, showed that workers' hostility toward their benevolent boss was not softened by decent housing or terraced front yards. Shortly after the strike, an Illinois court ruled that Pullman's company had no legal right to run the town. Eventually, Pullman got rid of the town, and it was annexed to Chicago.

Lowell and Pullman are striking examples of company towns with pretensions to design excellence. But they are part of a broader pattern. Similar experiments, much less grand in scale, include Kohler, Wisconsin (plumbing fixtures); Hershey, Pennsylvania (candy bars); and Gary, Indiana (steel).

## The City Beautiful Movement

Ironically, at the very time that Pullman's feudal dream of industrial community south of Chicago was being smashed by labor violence, events in the Windy City were to have a greater impact on the future of urban America. Chicago, the symbol of the rising industrial city, was chosen to host the quatercentenary of Columbus's discovery of America. This World's Fair of 1893/1894 (called the Columbian Exposition) marked the beginning of great interest in city planning and landscape architecture.

The Columbian Exposition was not just a typical fair; it was a brand-new city. Working from a design by Frederick Law Olmsted, Chicago architect-planner Daniel H. Burnham supervised the construction of what came to be called the White City (Figure 1.5). This monumental group of buildings, constructed on a plan, was set in an environment of green open space, grand boulevards, and an artificial lagoon on Chicago's South Side. By the time the fair closed in 1894, about 27 million people had attended. What they saw, in the words of one historian of American city planning, was

[an] enthralling amalgam of classic Greece, imperial Rome, Renaissance Italy, and Bourbon Paris, as impossible in the midwest as a gleaming iceberg would be in the Gulf of Mexico, yet somehow expressive of the boastfulness, the pretensions, the cultural dependence, the explosive energy, and the ingenious optimism of industrial America. . . . The millions gaped and admired and almost disbelieved that so much beauty and splendor had sprung up in Chicago, city of grain and lumber and meat, city of railroads and smoke and grime . . . the brilliant image of symmetrical edifices, colossal statues, and stupendous domes burned in memory long after the summer pilgrims had returned to their lackluster commercial cities, dreary mill towns, and homely prairie villages. (Scott, 1969:33)

After the Columbian Exposition, civic beautification organizations sprang up in many cities and the City Beautiful movement took hold. "Make no little plans," Burnham advised in 1912, for "they have no magic to stir men's blood. Make big plans; aim high in hope and work."

While the near-evangelical fervor of Burnham and his followers didn't lead to the total reshaping of American cities, his bold vision did have an impact. Today, touches of City Beautiful architecture and landscaping can be found throughout the United States, from Omaha and Buffalo to St. Louis, Seattle, and San Francisco. Perhaps even more important, Burnham and Olmsted's White City and Burnham's subsequent plan for Chicago's urban growth in 1909 signaled a new era: the growing acceptance of city planning as a legitimate tool for urban industrial America.

## Ebenezer Howard's Garden City

Visionary Ebenezer Howard (1898) combined socialist principles with romantic ideals to propose a new kind of planned community: the garden city. In the English reformer's vision, the best of the countryside and city could be combined by building small, rather self-sufficient communities limited to about 30,000 people, surrounded by permanent green belts. Around the turn of the twentieth century, Howard proposed that London be surrounded with cooperative communities where slum dwellers and people of all income groups would live and collectively own the land. The aim of these new towns was to motivate London slum dwellers to resettle willingly —without being forcibly displaced, as urban renewal in the United States has so often done— and to provide standard housing, as well as to "save" London by providing new parks, sewers, and so forth. When two garden cities were actually built in England, planners throughout the world became interested. Garden cities became fashionable in the United States after 1910. But many, like Forest Hills Gardens, New York (financed by the Russell Sage Foundation and designed by Frederick Law Olmsted, Jr.), became bedroom communities for affluent commuters, not cooperatively owned communities for all income groups, as Howard had proposed.

The garden city movement in the United States attracted noted urbanists, including Lewis Mumford. Yet Howard's ideas for stemming the slums and sprawl of industrial cities did not progress very far in the United States, given its traditions of private enterprise.

Despite Daniel Burnham's memorable phrase, big plans have never really stirred American blood—at least, not enough to totally rebuild or redesign cities. Instead, city planning has proceeded piecemeal. Private master builders (the Levitts of Levittown, for instance) and a few public builders (headed by the master builder (or destroyer) of them all, Robert Moses in New York City) did change the face of the metropolis in the twentieth century, but such efforts followed no overall plan. Why? Some observers point to deep-rooted American traditions of localism and the fear of federal government intervention as destructive of democratic ideals. This view is expressed by Wisconsin's former governor, Lee Dreyfus: "The federal government

should defend the shore, deliver the mail, and stay the hell out of my life" (in Ingalls, 1979:3).

Some Marxists have a different explanation. They claim that modern American cities grew in an unplanned way as a result of capitalism. They start from the basic assumption that "the mode of production, being the sum of productive forces and relations of production, influences the spatial and temporal organization of any environment indirectly—through the specific kinds of relationships that dominate a given society" (Gutnov, 1970:23–25). Thus "primitive society," they say, is characterized by structures based on a kinship system of houses branched around families. By contrast, in feudalism there is a closed circle of class-based relationships: Lords and ladies live in their castles, serfs work and live in their fields and villages, and merchants and artisans inhabit the towns. And, in monopoly capitalism, private property and corporate investment set "the broad parameters within which land and housing patterns emerge." One such land-use pattern is "corporate centralization"; it has brought "office development to major central cities, literally elevating the skylines" and a "bimodal distribution of development, in the center and in the outlying ring" of many U.S. cities such as Houston (Feagin and Smith, [1987] 1989:28, 29).

## Megastructures or Ministructures?

The tradition of grand design is alive and well in many parts of the world. The range of innovative ideas—from satellites in the sky to underwater structures—is suggested in Chapter 7.

Interestingly, some of the most critically acclaimed designers transcend borders with ease. For example, when Japanese architect Fumihiko Maki (who invented the term *megastructure* in the 1960s) won the equivalent of a Nobel Prize in architecture, he was cited by the jury for his fusion of East and West, as well as traditional and modern cultures. Jurors said that Maki creates "an architecture representing the age-old qualities of his native country while at the same time juxtaposing contemporary construction methods and materials" (in Temko, 1993:A5).

Here we focus on just two architect-visionaries. First, let's consider the ideas of Paolo Soleri, an architect-planner who has crossed both national and disciplinary boundaries. We also examine one criticism of Soleri's work: For all his futurism, he is reinventing not the wheel, but the tree. Then we take flight with the fanciful fantasies of Lebbeus Woods.

*A Blend of Architecture and Ecology*   Paolo Soleri (1969) advocates a new kind of city for the future. Soleri's dream is not easy to describe in words; linear, analytical thought is not his forte. Perhaps the best way to understand his vision is by looking at the plans for a Soleri-designed community, which he calls an **arcology:** the blend of architecture and ecology. An arcology is intended to place people in megastructures, making the land available for agriculture, work, and leisure.

In terms of design, Soleri's arcologies have one surface but many levels. Most extend below the ground and high in the air. They range from a massive arcology holding 500,000 residents on less than 2 square miles of land to an offshore community anchored to the continental shelf.

Despite their massive scale, Soleri says, his arcologies are "about miniaturization": creating a more intimate and less wasteful form of human spatial organization. The large spaces of the arcologies would be divided into large and small spaces to give inhabitants a sense of human scale.

Decades ago, Soleri and some of his followers began construction of an arcology for about 3,000 inhabitants at a remote desert site about 70 miles north of Phoenix, Arizona. Named Arcosanti, it is a prototype of futurist Soleri's vision.

Like most visionaries, Soleri has devoted followers and vocal detractors. One of the most interesting critiques of his work comes from Christopher Alexander. He finds the organic shapes of Soleri's futuristic cities to be organized on the old principle of the tree, complete with its rigid structure. Alexander rejects the city-as-tree plan as artificial. More important, Alexander makes a connection between city form and human personality. In his view, cities rigidly structured like trees help to create rigid, disciplined people. The city-as-tree may have been suitable for ancient Roman military camps because discipline and order were the values of those in charge. But the tree is not suitable for modern, pluralistic societies. In other words, Alexander finds a bad fit between tree-like cities and democratic contexts.

*A Synthesis of High Tech and Nature*   The models of architect Lebbeus Woods create a "fanciful world existing somewhere between the visions of Aldous Huxley and the Brothers Grimm—a world where high technology and nature, seemingly strange bedfellows, are synthesized" (Ingalls, 1991:B60). In Woods's drawings, pod-like structures float over Paris streets, trailing nets that shift with the wind. Buildings envisioned for underground Berlin shift with the earth's tectonic plates.

Woods, founder of the Research Institute for Experimental Architecture, wants to reinvent the world in all of its complexity. And he wants to replace hierarchy with *heterarchy,* a cybernetics concept referring to systems composed of networks of independent, autonomous parts. (In his view, hierarchical systems are composed of interdependent parts, and this interdependence robs the parts of their autonomy.) Practically, this means he highly values individualism, and he designs with this value in mind.

How does Woods concretize individualism? He makes the home a live-work lab where advanced electronic machines (computers, faxes, electronic musical instruments, etc.) are a focal point. By embracing these machines, he thinks, people can interact with other people, develop themselves, and understand the changing forces that animate the natural world.

## Postnationalist Architecture

Lille, France, is near the French entrance to the Channel Tunnel or "Chunnel." It is also the site of Euralille, a new and impressive $500 million, postnationalist project of public architecture financed by the European Union (EU). This mega-project celebrates cyberspace, not nationalism. In the words of a short-story writer, Euralille "looks and feels as if a lunar research station has crash-landed onto a small, respectable French market town. This is meant as a compliment" (Coupland, 1994:H45).

According to Euralille's master planner, the Dutch-born architect and Eurocitizen Rem Koolhaas (pronounced Cool House), "architecture reveals the deepest and sometimes most shocking secrets of how the values of a society are organized" (in Coupland, 1994:H45). Koolhaas incorporates into his work the structural processeses that he feels inform postmodern society, and he creates architectural metaphors for these processes, including the following: transnationalism, diversity, the obsolescence of physical space, centerless cities, deregionalization, deindustrialization, fragmentation, fluidity, and "drive-thru-ness" (Coupland, 1994:H45). For instance, in Koolhaaus's project, walls turn into doors, doors and walls disappear, and roads flow through structures.

## ANOTHER LOOK

Whatever grand designers dream up, people will undoubtedly continue to personalize their space. A spot of color here . . . a sentimental remembrance there . . . status symbols and territorial markings all around.

Still, no matter how creative we are in trying to control and personalize our space, we are limited by the larger social context. People who want to live in large communal groups, for example, can't do so if the housing stock is composed of small apartments. Social facts constrain individual action.

Theorists disagree on this: How much does the built environment influence human behavior? Does the physical environment merely reflect, or can it also create, social reality? Social scientist Harold Lasswell views architecture as a symbolic expression of a society's dominant values. So do architect Chris Alexander, novelist Lawrence Durrell, and neo-Marxist geographer David Harvey.

But design theorist Alexander goes a step further; he wants to create new physical forms in order to create new social patterns. Alexander argues that city form and space not only reflect values but also shape human action. In his view, a new society cannot be constructed on the cornerstones of old buildings. In fact, many visionaries share that idea.

Sociologists of the Chicago school (Park, Burgess) had a different perspective. As sociologists, they didn't focus on the design of buildings, but they did insist on the interrelationship of spatial forms and social processes, notably economic competition. Moreover, Park and Burgess were interested in reforming the industrial city, not remaking it. Their hope was to improve the physical environment in order to decrease what they considered "social disorganization." A strong emphasis on determinism, whether physical (Alexander) or socioeconomic (Park and Burgess), underlies much of this thought.

Meanwhile, other theorists implicitly reject physical determinism and the idea that bad physical environments produce social disorganization. Herbert Gans's work is illustrative. Gans says that living in what others might call a slum—such as Boston's West End—does not lead to social disorganization. Nor does moving to and living in suburban Levittown change people's behavior. Creating new buildings, even new institutions at the community level, had little impact on how Levittowners acted or felt. In other words, the extent to which space and place influence or mold behavior remains controversial. As on many other key issues, theorists do not share a vision.

Finally, micro meets macro in metropolitan space. The way people perceive, use, and interpret their environment is linked to their social-cultural being. And there is another important connection: Just as the command over space in a classroom or hospital reflects micro power relationships, the command over urban-suburban space reflects macro power relationships.

## KEY TERMS

**Arcology**   Architect Paolo Soleri's term, blending elements of architecture and ecology, to describe compact, self-contained futuristic cities, which he compares with the design of great ocean liners. Soleri's arcologies range from small projects like Arcosanti, an experimental community actually under construction in Arizona, to megastructures to replace New York City.

**Built environment**   As distinguished from the natural environment, it is everything that people have constructed.

**Environmental determinism**   The view that the built environment plays a determining, or at least crucial, role in shaping human behavior.

**Imageability**   Kevin Lynch's term describing the degree to which a city is visually legible or evokes a strong image in any observer's mind.

**Personal space**   As used by Robert Sommer, both the bubble around each person and the processes by which people demarcate and personalize the spaces they inhabit.

**Proxemics**   The study of how people in various cultures use space, especially for social interaction.

## PROJECTS

1. **Personal space.** How large are various people's protective bubbles? Test the size of their bubbles by breaking them—that is, by invading their space. Be sure to choose a range of people whose space you can invade: older and younger, authority figures, family and friends, men and women. At what distance do these various people seem to feel uncomfortable when you engage in a conversation?

2. **Uses of social space.** Observe how people use space. For example, select a social space, such as a park, and identify users and their behav-

ior. Are there any instances of expropriation or personalizing of social space?

3. **City planning.** What is the general design of the community in which you live? Is it what Christopher Alexander would call a tree? Or are there subtle, complex, overlapping functions in space?

4. **Utopia.** Design a city (in physical terms) that reflects your particular notion of a social-political-economic ideal way to live. Include the location of major institutions, living quarters, and basic economic activities.

5. **House as projected symbol of self.** Interview women, men, and children living in different ZIP code neighborhoods, trying to better understand what kinds of *dream houses* they choose. Develop an interview schedule so that you ask each respondent the same questions. A few possible questions: What type of home do you prefer—a single-family, detached dwelling; an apartment; a cohousing arrangement; or something else (please specifiy)? What should be the largest room—kitchen, living room, den, other (please specify)? Do you prefer a feeling of formality or informality? What colors would you choose for the kitchen? Then analyze the responses, paying special attention to possible patterns of difference.

6. **Defining *home*.** Using a combination of archival research and inteviews, determine how various religious, ethnic, and regional groups define *home*.

## SUGGESTIONS FOR FURTHER LEARNING

Some classics in the field of personal and social space are cited in the chapter itself, including the works of Robert Sommer on personal space and Edward T. Hall's studies of proxemics. To these should be added, in my view, the collected works of Erving Goffman, particularly *Relations in Public* (New York: Basic Books, 1971); *Encounters* (Indianapolis: Bobbs-Merrill, 1961); and *Asylums* (Garden City, N.Y.: Doubleday, 1961).

For a brief discussion with a useful typology of spatial territories (public, home, interactional, and body), see Stanford M. Lyman and Marvin B. Scott, "Territoriality: A Neglected Sociological Dimension," *Social Problems* 15 (1967):236–248. This article contains a section on the reactions of people who are systematically denied free territories, including body adornment and reorganization of psychic space (via drugs).

For a history and discussion of some of environmental psychology's unresolved issues, see Gary T. Moore, "Environment and Behavior Research in North America," Working Paper 85–11 (Milwaukee: Center for Architecture and Urban Planning Research of the University of Wisconsin, 1985). For a bibliography of the field, see Lenelis Kruse, *Environment and Behavior, Part II: An International and Multidisciplinary Bibliography, 1982–1987* (Paris: Saur, 1988).

Is there a relationship between environmental determinism, social Darwinism, and nineteenth-century imperial expansion? In their chapter, "Political Economy and Human Geography," in *New Models in Geography,* vol. 2 (London: Unwin Hyman, 1989), geographers Richard Peet and Nigel Thrift suggest that some nineteenth-century geographers justified Euro-American hegemony as the "natural, even god-given consequence of the superior physical environments of Western Europe and North America." See also Richard Peet's article, "The Social Origins of Environmental Determinism," *Annals of the Association of American Geographers* 75 (1985):309–333.

In *The Meaning of the Built Environment* (Beverly Hills, Calif.: Sage, 1982), Amos Rapaport focuses on users' meanings, not architects' understandings. He looks at everyday environments rather than at the lifestyles of the rich and famous.

The symbolism of physical settings concerns a wide range of scholars. For instance, the distinguished professor of the history of religions, Mircea Eliade, discusses the religious meaning of dwellings, which he sees not only as "machines for living" but also as "the universe that man constructs for himself by imitating the paradigmatic creation of the gods, the cosmogony," in his essay "The World, the City, the House," in *Occultism, Witchcraft and Cultural Fashions* (Chicago: University of Chicago Press, 1975). Archi-

tects Susanna Torre, Cynthia Rock, and Gwendolyn Wright look at the relationship between women's domestic space and traditional family roles in "Rethinking Closets, Kitchens, and Other Forgotten Spaces," *Ms.*, December, 1977. In *The Signature of Power* (New Brunswick, N.J.: Transaction Books, 1979), Harold Lasswell discusses the political symbolism of architecture.

Can people be happy and really human without green spaces and nature? No, according to sociobiologist Edward O. Wilson's *biophilia hypothesis.* Wilson's emerging hypothesis holds that humans have a genetically based need to affiliate with the natural world. In *The Biophilia Hypothesis* (Washington, D.C.: Island Press / Shearwater Books, 1993), editors Stephen R. Kellert and Edward O. Wilson do not want to forsake urban society; rather, they counsel nature's conservation for humans' psychological well-being.

The evocation of a sense of place is commonly the forte of visual and literary artists. In the film *Chalk* (1993), director Rob Nilsson offers a first-hand look at San Francisco's gritty Tenderloin district; Nilsson chose homeless people to play many of the movie roles. In an earlier film, *Northern Lights* (1979), Nilsson and codirector John Hanson vividly evoke a particular time and place: the landscape of desolate Dakota farmland around 1915 as Norwegian homesteaders struggle collectively to win against powerful interest groups (bankers, eastern grain dealers, and railroad tycoons). Mordecai Richler's stories of St. Urbain Street in Montreal are collected in *The Street* (Toronto: McClelland and Stewart, 1969). In *Look Homeward, Angel* (New York: Scribner, 1929), novelist Thomas Wolfe exalts Asheville, North Carolina, while Sinclair Lewis satirizes small-town American life in *Babbitt* (New York: Harcourt, Brace, 1949).

A sense of place is sometimes evoked by social scientists and historians. See, in particular, Jane Jacobs's description of New York City's Hudson Street in *The Death and Life of Great American Cities* (New York: Vintage, 1961) and Alan Trachtenberg's *Brooklyn Bridge: Fact and Symbol* (Chicago: Phoenix, [1965] 1979), which is accompanied by Walker Evans's photographs. In *Paris: A Century of Change* (New Haven, Conn.: Yale University

Press, 1979), architectural historian Norma Evenson traces changes in the City of Light as it outgrew its horse-and-carriage heritage. No ordinary tour, Paul Goldberger's *The City Observed: New York* (New York: Vintage, 1979) is a witty look at civic architecture.

In *No Sense of Place: The Impact of Electronic Media on Social Behavior* (New York: Oxford University Press, 1985), Joshua Meyrowitz weds concepts from Marshall McLuhan and Erving Goffman, claiming that the electronic media have restructured the relationship between place and space and demystified previously "backstage" areas.

Elliot Liebow's participant-observer study of homeless women, *Tell Them Who I Am* (New York: Free Press, 1993), may not be a ground-breaking work like his earlier *Tally's Corner: A Study of Negro Streetcorner Men* (Boston: Little, Brown, 1967). In the 1960s, Liebow's urban ethnography of African-American males caused a stir because, as reporter Ellen K. Coughlin (1993:A8) notes, "Mr. Liebow was a white man in a segregated society who got close to a group of black ghetto residents." She adds, "It also appeared at a time when white society was trying to understand the racial unrest exploding in its face." This recent study of a group of mainly white women without a home may be less controversial, but its conclusions will be debated. For example, Liebow argues that the only things that separate people with homes from the homeless are money and support from friends and family.

For accounts of home territories and defensible space, see Oscar Newman, *Defensible Space* (New York: Macmillan, 1972); Kenneth E. Read, *Other Voices: The Style of a Male Homosexual Tavern* (Chicago: Phoenix, 1980); and Sherri Cavan, *Liquor License* (Chicago: Aldine, 1966).

The symbolism of home base, home range, and social spaces can be seen in Claude Fregnac and Wayne Andrews, *The Great Houses of Paris* (New York: Vendome, 1979); David Hicks, *Living with Design* (New York: Morrow, 1979); and Paul Hirshorn and Steven Izenour, *White Towers* (Cambridge, Mass.: MIT Press, 1979), an account of a fast-food hamburger chain.

For studies of American city planners, architects, and landscape architects, see Thomas S. Hines, *Burnham of Chicago: Architect and Planner* (Chicago: Phoenix, 1979); John W. Reps, *The Making of Urban America: A History of City Planning in the United States* (Princeton, N.J.: Princeton University Press, 1965); and John Coolidge, *Mill and Mansion: A Study of Architecture and Society in Lowell, Massachusetts* (New York: Columbia University Press, 1942). For a comparison of how U.S. and European cities differ in terms of physical characteristics and architecture, see Wayne Attoe and Donn Logan, *American Urban Architecture: Catalysts in the Design of Cities* (Berkeley: University of California Press, 1989).

In *The Granite Garden: Urban Nature and Human Design* (New York: Basic Books, 1984), Anne Whiston Sprin argues that disregard for physical nature is the source of many urban environmental problems. Peter Nabokov and Robert Easton discuss Native Americans' reverence for the natural world and the organic environments they create in *Native American Architecture* (New York: Oxford University Press, 1989).

As *New Yorker* critic Brendan Gill once pointed out, America's leading authorities on urban life nearly always turn out to be learned amateurs—people like Frederick Law Olmsted and Jane Jacobs. An addition to this list is William H. Whyte. His years of scholarly labor about cities is published in *City: Rediscovering the Center* (New York: Doubleday, Anchor, [1988] 1990).

But beware: Amateurs, like experts, can make serious mistakes. In the case of the Sapir–Whorf hypothesis, Geoffrey K. Pullum, professor of linguistics and dean of graduate studies and research at the University of California at Santa Cruz, argues that Benjamin Lee Whorf, "Connecticut fire prevention inspector," published an amateur linguistics article in an MIT alumni publication. Whorf's article, Pullam claims, was reprinted widely—replete with its false claims intact! See Pullam's *The Great Eskimo Vocabulary Hoax and Other Irreverent Essays on the Study of Language* (Chicago: University of Chicago Press, 1991).

Public space and the shape of cities is the subject of debate in the fall 1986 issue of *Dissent*. In "Pleasures and Costs of Urbanity," Michael

Walzer distinguishes between "single-minded space" (e.g., zoned businesses, residential areas, and highways used by single-minded citizens characteristically in a hurry) and "open-minded space" (e.g., old central cities and other multipurpose spaces where people characteristically loiter). In "Take It to the Streets," Marshall Berman takes his cue from Marx, who argued that modern people lead a double life—one public, the other private; he argues that the most crucial form of open-mindedness is "openness to the urban underclass. This class of people is as old as urban life itself, and a recurrent heartache to people who care about cities." In "The Fall and Rise of Public Space," Michael Rustin traces U.S. concepts of space to capitalism: "Capitalism promotes a view of space as an alienable and private commodity. This also leads to a focus on individuals as opposed to corporate communities. Functions that were formerly undertaken in public become individualized and segregated" (489).

A series of essays, ranging from Langdon Winner's "Silicon Valley Mystery House" and Margaret Crawford's "The World in a Shopping Mall" to Michael Sorkin's "See You in Disneyland," are brought together in Michael Sorkin, ed., *Variations on a Theme Park: The New American City and the End of Public Space* (New York: Hill and Wang, Noonday, 1992). The authors see megamalls, zones of gentrification, pseudohistoric markets, and corporate enclaves as forms of a new sort of cityscape. The paradigm for all these places, they argue, is the theme park.

The architectural criticism of Herbert Muschamp is informed by social science insight and heightened by many felicitous turns of phrase. His columns in the Sunday *New York Times* are like mini-lectures by an inspired teacher.

For a joyful description of architecture as beautiful object and artifact of sociocultural history, see lawyer Philip M. Isaacson's *Round Buildings, Square Buildings, and Buildings That Wiggle Like a Fish* (New York: Knopf, 1988). For highly opinionated judgments on what buildings can and should be in terms of vitality and humaneness, see PBS's eight-hour-long episode series, *Pride of Place: Building the American Dream* (1986), and the accompanying book of the same name by Robert A. M. Stern (Boston: Houghton Mifflin, 1986).

The TV series is an architectural travelogue, with architect-scholar Stern as the tour guide, and it is probably the most ambitious TV series about U.S. architecture ever made.

Some utopian visions—and attempts to actualize them in the United States—are detailed in Charles Nordhoff, *The Communistic Societies of the United States* (New York: Dover, [1875] 1966); he includes a variety of religious and secular groups, including the Oneida community, the Amana Society, and noncommunistic colonies of Anaheim, California, and Vineland, New Jersey.

Part utopian, part pragmatic, cohousing is one response to single-parent families and two-income households. Pioneered in Denmark, a cohousing development, typically of twenty units, groups private houses around a central commons and shared kitchen, dining, and child-care facilities. More than that, it is a balanced way of community life. See Kathryn McCamant and Charles Durret, *Cohousing: A Contemporary Approach to Housing Ourselves* (Berkeley, Calif.: Habitat / Ten Speed Press, 1988).

For an update on New Harmony, Indiana, see architecture critic Ada Louise Huxtable, "A Radical New Addition for Mid-America," *New York Times*, September 30, 1979, sec. 2. She focuses on a handsome new building in Owens's dream town and its fit with the town's historic past.

John Brinckerhoff Jackson has been called America's most distinguished landscape historian. In *The Necessity for Ruins and Other Topics*, (Amherst: University of Massachusetts Press, 1980), Jackson argues that U.S. culture has a three-step formulation of its history: (1) the good old days, (2) a period of decay, and (3) the present, in whch the past is reconstructed according to current needs. In *Disovering the Vernacular Landscape* (New Haven, Conn., Yale University Press, 1984), he draws a distinction between the established landscape ("maintained and governed by law and political institutions, dedicated to permanence and planned evolution") and the vernacular landscape, "identified with local custom, pragmatic adaptation to circumstances, and unpredictable mobility."

Edward T. Hall, founder of proxemics, describes his own work as paralleling J. B. Jackson's studies on vernacular landscape. In *An Anthro-*

pology of Everyday Lifew: An Autobiography (New York: Doubleday, Anchor, 1992), Hall recalls architect Mies van der Rohe's comment—"God is in the details"—and says that he concentrates on understanding the details of everyday life: "It is the details of the rules underlying common behavior that govern the world" (xv).

Maxine Kumin's strong sense of place informs *In Deep: Country Essays* (New York: Viking, 1987). Poet, novelist, and critic Kumin writes from her "hardscrabble kingdom on a hill" in rural New Hampshire.

According to Richard P. Horwitz, "a highway lined with businesses—gas stations, motels, fast-food outlets, family restaurants, retail malls—all trimmed in asphalt and colored lights" is *The Strip: An American Place* (Lincoln: University of Nebraska Press, 1985). Wright Morris speaks of a sense of (typically American) place in *The Home Place* (Lincoln: University of Nebraska Press, 1968). He notes that the grain elevator is a monument to the Great Plains: "Anyone who was born and raised on the plains knows that the high false front on the Feed Store, and the white water tower, are not a question of vanity. It's a problem of being. Of knowing you are there" (76).

In *The Visual Elements of Landscape* (Amherst: University of Massachusetts Press, 1987), geography and landscape architecture professor John A. Jakle examines the aesthetic pleasure of landscape, including the act of sightseeing, a form of spontaneous, visual pleasure seeking.

According to reporter-novelist James Howard Kunstler, almost everything built in the last fifty years in the United States is

depressing, brutal, ugly, unhealthy and spiritually degrading: the jive-plastic commuter tract home wastelands, the Potemkin village shopping plazas with their vast parking lagoons, the Lego-block hotel complexes, the "gourmet mansardic" junk-food joints, the Orwellian office "parks" featuring buildings sheathed in the same reflective glass as the sunglasses worn by chain-gang guards, the particle-board garden apartments rising up in every meadow and cornfield, the freeway loops around every big and little city with their clusters of discount merchandise marts, the whole destructive, wasteful, toxic, agoraphobia-inducing spectacle that politicans proudly call "growth."

As this passage from his book, *The Geography of Nowhere: The Rise and Decline of America's Man-Made Landscape* (New York: Simon and Schuster, 1993), suggests, Kunstler has a gift for strong images but questionable generalizations.

In *People in Cities: The Urban Environment and Its Effects* (Cambridge: Cambridge University Press, [1985] 1989), environmental psychologist Edward Krupat examines images of the city, stress and crowding, and the impact of urban design on urbanites' behavior. His two concluding chapters present a comparative social psychological analysis of urban planning and design, including a discussion of the failure of Pruitt-Igoe in St. Louis.

Called by some the "master builder," Louis Sullivan believed that architecture is the true mirror of a nation's values: "As you are, so are your buildings. And, as your buildings, so are you." For an insight into Sullivan's career, see Robert Twombly, *Louis Sullivan: His Life and Work* (New York: Viking/Elisabeth Sifton Books, 1986).

In the film *City Limits* (National Film Board of Canada, 1971), best-selling author Jane Jacobs sparkles with insight on how city space might be used humanely. She likes the creative disorder of older neighborhoods, active streets, and well-used odds and ends of city space. Her book *The Death and Life of Great American Cities* (New York: Random House, Modern Library, [1961] 1992) was a seminal work when first published.

For a range of perspectives within the social sciences on space and place, see the journals published by professional associations, such as the American Sociological Association's *American Sociological Review*, and newer journals, including *Gender, Place and Culture: A Journal of Feminist Geography* (first issue, January 1994) and *Antipode*.

## REFERENCES

Alexander, Christopher. 1964. *Notes on the Synthesis of Form*. Cambridge, Mass.: Harvard University Press.

———. [1965] 1978. "A city is not a tree." Pp. 377–402

in Stephen Kaplan and Rachel Kaplan, eds., *Humanscape: Environments for People.* North Scituate, Mass.: Duxbury.

Alexander, Christopher, Sara Ishikawa, and Murray Silverstein, with Max Jacobson, Ingrid Fiksdahl-Kins, and Shlomo Angel. 1977. *A Pattern Language: Towns, Buildings, Construction.* New York: Oxford University Press.

Apple, R. W., Jr. 1979. "Britain's notable nonagenarians." *New York Times Magazine* (November 11):50+.

Appleyard, Donald. 1978a. "Environment as symbolic action." Working paper. Berkeley: Institute for Urban and Regional Development.

———. 1978b. "Home." Working paper. Berkeley: Institute for Urban and Regional Development.

Appleyard, Donald, Kevin Lynch, and John R. Myer. 1964. *The View from the Road.* Cambridge, Mass.: MIT Press.

Baldassare, Mark. 1979. *Residential Crowding in America.* Berkeley: University of California Press.

Blake, Peter. 1979. *God's Own Junkyard: The Planned Deterioration of America's Landscape,* new and updated ed. New York: Holt, Rinehart and Winston.

Brown, Elaine. 1993. Comments on *Talk of the Nation,* National Pubic Radio (August 26).

Brown, Patricia Leigh. 1993. "The architecture of those called homeless." *New York Times* [national edition] (March 28):A1+.

Butterfield, Fox. 1994. "A history of homicide surprises the experts." *New York Times* [national edition] (October 23):A10.

Castaneda, Carlos. 1968. *The Teachings of Don Juan: A Yaqui Way of Knowledge.* New York: Pocket Books.

Cooper, Claire. 1975. *Easter Hill Village.* New York: Free Press.

———. 1976. "The house as symbol of self." Pp. 435–449 in Harold M. Proshansky, William H. Ittelson, and Leanne G. Rivlin, eds., *Environmental Psychology.* New York: Holt, Rinehart and Winston.

Coughlin, Ellen K. 1993. "Author of noted study on black ghetto life returns with a portrait of homeless women: 25 years after 'Tally's Corner,' Elliot Liebow looks at another neglected part of society." *Chronicle of Higher Education* (March 31):A7–8.

Coupland, Douglas. 1994. "Rem Koolhaas, post-nationalist architect." *New York Times* [national edition] (September 11):H45.

Cranz, Galen. n.d. "Double talk: Redundancy as a way of conceptualizing the relationship between humans and their environment." Unpublished manuscript.

Durrell, Lawrence. 1969. *Spirit of Place: Letters and Essays on Travel.* Ed. Alan G. Thomas. New York: Dutton.

Esser, A.H., et al. 1970. "Interactional hierarchies and power structure in a psychiatric ward: Ethological studies of dominance in a total institution." Pp. 25–61 in S. J. Hutt and C. Hutt eds., *Behavioural Studies in Psychiatry.* Oxford: Pergamon Press.

Feagin, Joe R., and Michael Peter Smith. [1987] 1989. "Cities and the new international division of labor: An overview." Pp. 3–34 in Michael Peter Smith and Joe R. Feagin, eds., *The Capitalist City: Global Restructuring and Community Politics.* Cambridge, Mass.: Blackwell.

Fischer, Claude S., Mark Baldasarre, and Richard J. Ofshe. 1975. "Crowding studies and urban life—a critical review." *Journal of the American Institute of Planners* 41 (6):406–418.

Gans, Herbert. [1962] 1982. *The Urban Villagers,* updated and rev. ed. New York: Free Press.

Glaab, Charles N., and A. Theodore Brown. 1976. *A History of Urban America,* 2nd ed. New York: Macmillan.

Griaule, Marcel. 1965. *Conversations with Ogotemmeli.* London: Oxford University Press.

Gutnov, Alexei, et al. 1970. *The Ideal Communist City.* New York: Braziller.

Hall, Edward T. 1959. *The Silent Language.* Garden City, N.Y.: Doubleday.

———. 1966. *The Hidden Dimension.* Garden City, N.Y.: Doubleday.

Harvey, David. 1989. "Monument and myth: The building of the Basilica of the Sacred Heart." Pp. 200–228 in *The Urban Experience.* Baltimore: Johns Hopkins University Press.

Hastorf, Albert H., and Hadley Cantril. 1954. "They saw a game: A case study." *Journal of Abnormal and Social Psychology* 49:129–134.

Hawley, Amos H. 1950. *Human Ecology, A Theory of Community Structures.* New York: Ronald Press.

Heimstra, Norman W., and Leslie H. McFarling. 1978. *Environmental Psychology,* 2nd ed. Monterey, Calif.: Brooks/Cole.

Howard, Ebenezer. 1898. *Tomorrow: A Peaceful Path to Real Reform.* London: Sonnenschein.

Husock, Howard. 1979. "Boston, the problem that

won't go away." *New York Times Magazine* (November 25):32+.

Ingalls, Zoe. 1979. "The chancellor as governor: 'He's no longer an education man.'" *Chronicle of Higher Education* (November 19):3–4.

———. 1991. "An architect creates a fanciful world." *Chronicle of Higher Education* (October 30):B60.

Ittelson, William H., et al. 1974. *An Introduction to Environmental Psychology.* New York: Holt, Rinehart and Winston.

Jackson, John Brinckerhoff. 1984. *Discovering the Vernacular Landscape.* New Haven, Conn.: Yale University Press.

Jacobs, Jane. 1961. *The Death and Life of Great American Cities.* New York: Vintage.

Kesey, Ken. 1962. *One Flew over the Cuckoo's Nest.* New York: Viking.

Ketchum, Diana. 1989. "A renegarde architect designs for 'every man'." *New York Times* [national edition] (June 29):B1+.

Kira, Alexander. [1966] 1976. *The Bathroom: Criteria for Design.* New York: Viking.

Knox, Paul L. 1991. "The restless urban landscape: Economic and sociocultural change in the transformation of metropolitan Washington, D.C." *Annals of the Association of American Geographers* 81:181–209.

Krupat, Edward. [1985] 1989. *People in Cities: The Urban Environment and Its Effects.* Cambridge: Cambridge University Press.

Lasswell, Harold. 1979. *The Signature of Power.* New Brunswick, N.J.: Transaction Books.

Lebowitz, Fran. [1974] 1978. *Metropolitan Life.* New York: Fawcett Crest.

Lee, Dorothy. 1959. *Freedom and Culture.* Englewood Cliffs, N.J.: Prentice-Hall.

Liebow, Elliot. 1967. *Tally's Corner: A Study of Negro Streetcorner Men.* Boston: Little, Brown.

———. 1993. *Tell Them Who I Am.* New York: Free Press.

Lyman, Stanford M., and Marvin B. Scott. [1967] 1970. "Territoriality: A neglected sociological dimension." Pp. 88–109 in Stanford M. Lyman and Marvin B. Scott, *A Sociology of the Absurd.* Pacific Palisades, Calif.: Goodyear.

Lynch, Kevin. 1960. *The Image of the City.* Cambridge, Mass.: MIT Press.

Markoff, John. 1993. "Where the cubicle is dead." *New York Times* [national edition] (April 25):F7.

Massey, Steve. 1987. " 'Religious' gunman gets on TV." *San Francisco Chronicle* (December 5):A3.

McHarg, Ian. [1969] 1971. *Design with Nature.* Garden City, N.Y.: Doubleday, Natural History.

McLaughlin, Robert W. 1962. *Architecture: Creating Man's Environment.* New York: Macmillan.

Meyrowitz, Joshua. 1985. "The 19-inch neighborhood." *Newsweek* (July 22):8.

Michelson, William H. 1976. *Man and His Urban Environment.* Reading, Mass.: Addison-Wesley.

Mumford, Lewis. 1961. *The City in History.* New York: Harcourt, Brace & World.

Muschamp, Herbert. 1993a. "An enterprise zone for the imagination." *New York Times* [national edition] (March 14):sec. 2, 32.

———. 1993b. "Shaping a monument to memory." *New York Times* [national edition] (April 11): sec. 2, 1+.

———. 1993c. " 'Things generally wrong in the universe'. " *New York Times* [national edition] (May 30):sec. 2, 30.

Norberg-Schulz, Christian. [1979] 1984. *Genius Loci: Towards a Phenomenology of Architecture.* New York: Rizzoli.

Olsen, Donald J. 1986. *The City as a Work of Art:* New Haven, Conn.: Yale University Press.

Park, Robert E., Ernest W. Burgess, and R. D. McKenzie. 1925. *The City.* Chicago: University of Chicago Press.

Parsons, Talcott. 1951. *The Social System.* New York: Free Press.

Rainwater, Lee. 1966. "Fear and the house-as-haven in the lower class." *Journal of the American Institute of Planners* 32:23–31.

Reich, Robert B. [1991] 1992. *The Work of Nations: Preparing Ourselves for 21st-Century Capitalism.* New York: Vintage.

Scott, Mellier. 1969. *American City Planning.* Berkeley: University of California Press.

Skolnick, Paul, et al. 1977. "Do you speak to strangers? A study of invasions of personal space." *European Journal of Social Psychology* 7:307–316.

Smith, Michael Peter, and Joe R. Feagin, eds. [1987] 1989. *The Capitalist City.* Cambridge, Mass.: Blackwell.

Soleri, Paolo. 1969. *Arcology: The City in the Image of Man.* Cambridge, Mass.: MIT Press.

Sommer, Robert. 1969. *Personal Space.* Englewood Cliffs, N.J.: Prentice-Hall.

Sorkin, Michael, ed. 1992. *Variations on a Theme Park: The New American City and the End of Public Space.* New York: Hill and Wang, Noonday Press.

Spreiregen, Paul D. 1965. *Urban Design: The Architecture of Towns and Cities.* New York: McGraw-Hill.

Temko, Allen 1993. "S.F. visual arts center architect wins prestigious Pritzker prize." *San Francisco Chronicle* (April 26):A5.

Venturi, Robert, Denise Scott Brown, and Steven Izenour. [1972] 1977. *Learning from Las Vegas.* Cambridge, Mass.: MIT Press.

Walters, Derek. 1988. *Feng Shui: The Chinese Art of Designing a Harmonious Environment.* New York: Simon and Schuster, Fireside Book.

Werthman, Carl. 1965. *Planning and Purchase Decision.* Berkeley: Center for Planning and Development Research.

Whyte, William H. 1978. "New York and Tokyo: A study in crowding." Pp. 1–18 in Hidetoshi Kato, ed., *A Comparative Study of Street Life: Tokyo, Manila, New York.* Tokyo: Research Institute for Oriental Cultures, Gakushuin University.

———. [1988] 1990. *City: Rediscovering the Center.* New York: Doubleday, Anchor.

Wolfe, Tom. 1977. *The Kandy-Kolored Tangerine-Flake Streamline Baby.* New York: Bantam.

Wurman, Richard Saul. 1971. *Making the City Observable.* Minneapolis, and Cambridge, Mass.: Walker Art Center and MIT Press.

# PART VII
# Paying Their Way

*Lucy Hilmer*

John N. Ballator

# CHAPTER 17 PRODUCING, CONSUMING, EXCHANGING

Whatever their ideological differences, social theorists rank economic activities high on their list of factors that influence, perhaps determine, the fate of cities and nations. Recall, for example, the debate over the earliest cities: Economic assumptions underlie both the Childe thesis and the trade thesis of Jane Jacobs (Chapter 4); both assume that what people produce and exchange are prime determinants of human settlement patterns. Burgess's concentric zone hypothesis rests on another economic assumption, namely, that economic competition is the key determinant of land use. The U.S. government's MSA concept grow out of economic reasoning too; it uses the integrated labor market as the leading indicator of interdependence within a geographical area. Likewise, Logan and Molotch's typology of contemporary cities (Chapter 4) is based on socioeconomic logic, specifically, that cities play varied roles in the international division of labor. In other words, many agree with this observation by a geographer: "First of all, and most fundamentally, the city can be viewed as a focus of production" (Thrift, 1989:43).

This chapter focuses on some basic economic functions. It pays special attention to what most theorists think is the single most important factor in the growth or decline of metropolitan economies: the health of the global and national economies. (Jane Jacobs [1984] is a dissenter on this key point. Just as she turned conventional wisdom on its head about early cities, as discussed in Chapter 4, iconoclast Jacobs reverses the taken-for-granted economic relationship of cities to nations. Essentially, she argues that strong urban economies are the backbone and motor of the wealth of nations, not vice versa.)

At the outset, we should note two different phenomena related to economics and metropolitan life. First, there appears to be a serious mismatch between theorists' high ranking of economics as an influence on our fates and the general public's low interest (or literacy) in economics. Typically, in the United States, courses in economics are not required by secondary schools or colleges; bookstores devote more space to self-help and mysticism than to economics; and mass media do not provide in-depth debates on economic issues such as tax policy or the General Agreement on Tariffs and Trade (GATT), perhaps because economics seems so complicated or boring. This gap does not bode well for democratic participation. Second, as writer Douglas Coupland so nicely puts it,"the future is happening far faster than anybody ever thought it would" (1994:H45). Consider, for example, that *urban* economics did not even exist until 1965, when the first urban economics text appeared. Just one generation later, the subdiscipline of urban economics seemed woefully outdated. What

changed? The economic landscape and an appreciation that cities are part of a *global* economic system of producers, consumers, and exchangers. Not only can't mayors direct their economies, but "national governments have lost much of their power to direct their own economies" (Brecher, 1993:685). In large measure, this reflects the power of multinational corporations (MNCs). The U.S. government, for example, outlaws trading with nations defined as "enemies" (e.g., Cuba in the early 1990s), but it cannot stop American MNCs from trading illegally with those nations through the MNCs' non-U.S. subsidiaries.

## POLITICAL ECONOMY: A BEGINNING VOCABULARY

Let's begin with a basic vocabulary of political economy. Of course, economists don't agree among themselves any more than other social scientists do. Thus what's basic to one kind of economic analysis is peripheral to another or is rejected altogether. Consider, for example, the concept of the market of supply and demand. The self-regulating market mechanism is central to classical liberal economics. Most introductory textbooks look at the world through the filter of the competitive market. Yet many economists reject this basic assumption about how the world works. Indeed, some influential modern liberals view the market mechanism with suspicion or even disdain. For one, John Kenneth Galbraith has long argued that supply and demand no longer work to regulate the economy. In general, Galbraith (1968) says, business corporations manipulate the market to suit their own needs. In particular, the free market doesn't work at all to regulate oil prices. According to Galbraith (1979:3), the Organization of Petroleum Exporting Countries (OPEC) oil cartel has proved "inconveniently resistant to free market doctrine."

Other voices, from some unexpected corners, echo Galbraith's words. We might predict that Marxist economists would repudiate the market mechanism, and indeed they do. They argue that the American economy (and its subsystems of urban economies) are best understood in the framework of monopoly capitalism, not the competitive market system. But we might be surprised to find that even some conservatives question free market theory. Respected scholar Charles Lindblom, a professor of politics and economics at Yale who is considered a conservative, stirred great controversy a generation ago with his book *Politics and Markets* (1978). There he maintains that the emergence of large private corporations renders market doctrine obsolete. Essentially, Lindblom concurs with Galbraith; markets are necessarily manipulated by big business corporations in order to ensure economic stability and growth.

Yet market doctrine continues to enjoy widespread support among U.S. economists, particularly since the disintegration of the Soviet Union. And introductory economics texts in the mainstream, such as the fourteenth edition of Paul Samuelson and William D. Nordhaus's *Economics* (1992:45), contend that while markets are far from perfect, generally they still work effectively to answer the questions of who gets what and what goods are produced.

Once again, this shows that what you see depends on how you look at it. With this in mind, let's consider some concepts—first mainstream (classical and neoclassical), then alternative—that political economists use to explain how the world works.

## Supply, Demand, Price, and the Market Mechanism

Twin concepts—supply and demand—provide the cornerstones of classical and neoclassical economics, that body of thought associated with Adam Smith ([1776] 1970) and contemporary theorists such as Milton Friedman. The logic of supply and demand is as follows. In a market, or "free enterprise," economy, the **supply** of a particular good, such as automobiles, is assumed to be related to consumer demand. Why produce a car if no one will buy one? (An advertising campaign might, of course, persuade the public that

it needs a car or a second car, thus stimulating demand for the product.)

**Demand** for a product implies that consumers both want and will pay for it. Take car buying as an example of how supply and demand work. The number of cars that will be produced, the logic goes, depends on their cost. At $8,000, the demand for a new car will be great (assuming that there is gas to power it). As the **price** rises to $28,000, demand falls. As shown in Figure 17.1, a demand curve shows that the lower the price, the greater the demand. The demand curve slopes downward. This indicates the inverse relationship between the price of a good and the quantity of that good demanded by consumers. Economists often call this the *law of downward-sloping demand*.

Now, let's look at the supply side. How many cars will be produced at different prices? This information can be charted with a supply curve. Suppose, for example, that new cars are selling for $8,000. At that price, manufacturers do not want to supply any cars to the market; instead of making a profit, they would lose money. Car manufacturers would produce something else that yielded a higher profit. But they would be willing to produce about 5 million cars if the price were $13,000. As the price keeps rising, manufacturers are willing to supply increasing numbers of cars, as the supply curve in Figure 17.2 shows. This supply curve indicates that the higher the price, the more cars will roll off the assembly lines.

At some point, classical economic theory continues, a point of equilibrium between supply and demand will be reached. That is, there will be a price that satisfies both consumers and producers. In the case of cars, this equilibrium point can be found by putting the demand and supply curves together and noting the point at which they intersect. In the example here (Figure 17.3), the point of intersection is at a little less than $15,000. This represents the equilibrium price.

Above that price, the theory states, there will tend to be a surplus of cars on the market and hence a downward pressure on the price. Below the equilibrium price, there will tend to be a shortage of cars and hence an upward pressure

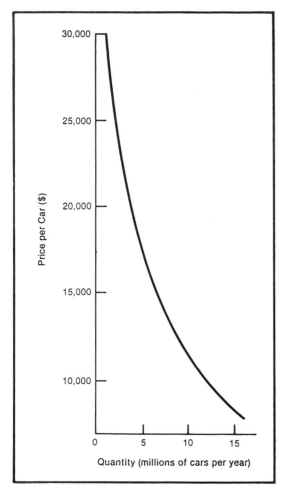

**Fig. 17.1** DEMAND CURVE. This curve for cars slopes downward, indicating that as the price increases, demand decreases.

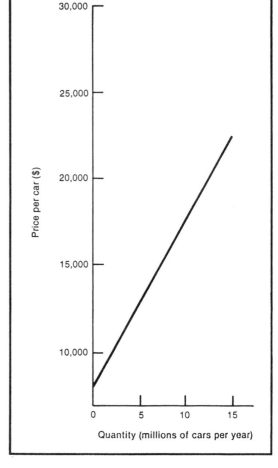

**Fig. 17.2** SUPPLY CURVE. This curve shows that the higher the price of cars, the more will be supplied to the market.

on the price. According to Samuelson (1964:63), the equilibrium price is the only price that can last for any length of time. This is because the equilibrium price "is that at which the amount willingly supplied and the amount willingly demanded are equal."

## Profit

A basic assumption underlies the above discussion of supply and demand. It is this: Suppliers attempt to maximize their profit while consumers attempt to maximize their well-being (utility).

What exactly is profit? According to Samuelson, **profit** is what "you have left over from the sale of product (your oranges, apples, bread, and manicures) after you have paid the other factor costs" (wages, interest, rent) (1964:181). Firms pursue different strategies to maximize profit. They may hire cheaper labor, employ more efficient managers, increase advertising, buy less expensive raw materials, expand markets, and so forth. Or they may relocate to areas,

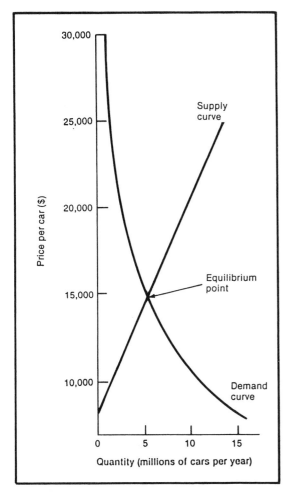

**Fig. 17.3** EQUILIBRIUM PRICE. The point at which the supply curve intersects with the demand curve is called the *equilibrium price* or *point*. This is the point at which the amount of a product produced and the amount demanded are the same.

ness Is to Increase Its Profits" (1970)—nothing else. Other economists, such as Lindblom and Galbraith, contend that modern corporations seek stability and growth as well as profit.

## Utility

Do individuals and households also try to maximize their gain? Yes, according to free market doctrine. Indeed, the assumption of the "rational, self-interested economic individual" (maximizing utility or well-being) is a key psychological assumption underlying classical liberal economics. As detailed in Chapter 3, liberal philosophers and political economists base their view of how the world works on this vision of human nature.

But this basic assumption is under suspicion, even attack. For instance, Harvey Leibenstein argues in *Beyond Economic Man: A New Framework for Microeconomics* (1976) that market doctrine is wrong; people don't follow the model of rationality attributed to them. Many feminist economists agree (Chapter 2). Despite such criticism, the model of rational economic behavior underlies conservative and liberal thought. Meanwhile, Marxists have a different perspective. They tend to emphasize the deception (via advertising, mass media, political rhetoric, etc.) used by dominant elites to control and confound members of the working class, making it difficult for them to even know what's in their best interest.

## Externalities

When something is produced—bits of information, chemicals, microchips—the production process can have external effects. These effects may benefit or penalize innocent bystanders. For example, if a chemical plant dumps waste into a river, the waste contaminates the river for everyone. This is called a *negative externality*. On the other hand, a *positive externality* can bring social benefits to members of the community. A new Metro station in Washington, D.C., may give an economic boost to surrounding shops. The bees

either at home or offshore, where labor and taxes are lower or antipollution regulations are minimal.

Is profit the only goal of private business firms? Here economists disagree. Some argue that business has a social responsibility to the community in which it operates. Nonsense, retorts the dean of economic conservatives, Milton Friedman. He says that the business of business is business: The "Social Responsibility of Busi-

from a flower nursery may pollinate the neighbors' gardens—all without cost to the neighbors. In other words, **externalities** (also called *spillover effects*) occur outside the market. An individual or a firm can benefit or hurt people without economic compensation or payment: "Externalities exist when private costs or benefits do not equal social costs or benefits" (Samuelson and Nordhaus, 1992:736).

Even the most rational, self-interested person may not be able to calculate the effect of externalities. What, for instance, is the impact of toxic wastes entering the groundwater of border towns in Mexico? Residents of suburban San Francisco claim that one negative externality of their nearby oil refineries is a much higher than average rate of cancer, and doctors suggest that babies on both sides of the U.S.–Mexican border are being born with severe birth defects due to toxic wastes in the water. Or consider the case of gambling in Atlantic City, New Jersey. The majority of urbanites there, including one pastor of a downtown church, voted for casino gambling in the 1970s. They reasoned that new hotels and gambling would bring jobs and an economic boost to the city's lagging economy. However, many have since changed their minds. Gambling brought an influx of prostitutes and purse snatchers to the downtown area. One result was a sharp decline in membership and attendance at central city churches. According to the downtown pastor (in Janson, 1979:20), worshippers fear being harassed or mugged.

Externalities, either positive or negative, are not distributed equitably. Factory smoke may pollute one part of the urban landscape and not another. Likewise, the benefits or costs of externalities are not randomly distributed. Indeed, many observers argue that negative externalities affect the powerless much more than the powerful. In *Unequal Protection: Environmental Justice and Communities of Color* (1994), sociologist Robert D. Bullard (1994) and others document toxic racism in many American cities. For example, in a 1-square-mile area of Los Angeles (with a majority population of African-Americans and Latinos), there are waste dumps, smokestacks, and toxic wastewater pipes; in the industrial corridor

of Louisiana, which is home to a largely African-American population, there is a "toxic gumbo" of carcinogens; and in Carver Terrace, an African-American subdivision in Texarkana, there are homes built on a toxic waste site of PCPs, arsenic, and creosote.

In many cases, contemporary governments intervene to control negative externalities such as toxic gumbo or dirty water. While critics often complain that some government regulations are too coercive, liberal economists say that "most people today agree that government is needed to curb some of the worst externalities created by the market mechanism" (Samuelson and Nordhaus, 1992:42).

## Equity

**Equity** refers to the fair or just allocation of something. What's considered fair, of course, is a matter of perspective. Consider the case of a gasoline shortage. Pure market theorists think it fair to allocate available gas by the price system. Those who can afford the product will pay the higher price; others will make substitutions or do without. Liberals think this unfair, preferring some kind of rationing system.

What's fair or equitable is filtered through a larger framework of justice, a normative theory. Take income distribution, for example. A market system often generates great income inequality. Is this situation fair? According to liberal economists Samuelson and Nordhaus, this is a question for politics and ethics, not economics: "Economics cannot answer questions of how much poverty is acceptable and fair" (1992:44). As we shall see shortly, Marxists economic thought makes no such sharp distinction between politics and economics.

## Efficiency

In mainstream economics, **efficiency** refers to "the absence of waste, or the use of economic resources that produces the maximum level of satisfaction possible with the given inputs and technology" (Samuelson and Nordhaus, 1992: 735). Classical and neoclassical theory holds that the market works—and works better than other economic systems—to produce efficiency: In a compettitve market, a business firm will find the cheapest way to produce a product—say, a gas range—by efficiently using land, labor, and other factors of production. If it doesn't, the theory holds, the company will not survive the competition.

Efficiency is usually measured by cost per unit of production. Thus if the Whiz Gas Range Company produces two stoves at a cost of $150 while the Flamethrower Company produces two comparable stoves at a cost of $75, then Flamethrower is considered twice as efficient as Whiz.

However, efficiency is not always easy to measure, particularly in the postindustrial economy. More and more people are working in the service and information sectors, where efficiency is no longer a matter of producing cheaper stoves. How can a public-school teacher's or public administrator's efficiency be measured when profit is not a goal and social benefit is hard to gauge with precision?

Today, governments intervene to remedy market inefficiences. For instance, in the United States, the federal government subsidizes public goods (e.g., national defense), counters monopolies (via antitrust law), and regulates negative externalties (e.g., antipollution laws). Local governments also intervene in markets; they provide public goods (e.g., community swimming pools) and regulate negative externalities (e.g., antismoking ordinances).

Finally, mainstream economists acknowledge that efficiency can conflict with equity. According to Samuelson and Nordhaus, "Even the most efficient market system may generate great inequality" (1992:43). They cite the example of the Irish potato famine of 1848 and 1849: "Queen Victoria's laissez-faire government let millions of Irish children, women, and men starve . . . when a fungus suddenly destroyed the potato crop." Similarly, economists Robert Heilbroner and Lester Thurow say that markets "allocate goods and services more effectively than other systems of rationing, particularly planning in one form or another," but they note that "the underlying distribution (or maldistribution) of income clashes with other standards of the public interest that we value more highly than efficiency" (1994:181).

## AN ALTERNATIVE VOCABULARY

Today a wide range of people reject both liberal and conservative perspectives on how the political economy does and should work. These include former Dominican priest Matthew Fox, goddess worshipper Starhawk, and the Hopi in the Southwest, all of whom reject notions of profit, efficiency, and utility, embracing instead a global reverence for the earth.

Here, let's focus on one alternative to conservative and liberal visions: Marxist political economy. Generally, Marxists argue that consumer sovereignty is a sham and that the public good can't result from each individual's pursuit of self-interest. Most neo-Marxists agree that unregulated MNCs or transnational corporations (TNCs) are "the world's most powerful economic actors" (Brecher, 1993:686).

Now let's examine several concepts that are central to the Marxist critique of the market mechanism and capitalism. Although brief, this discussion will indicate why Marxist analyses of the economy are so at odds with mainstream studies.

### Capital

To non-Marxists like Paul Samuelson and William D. Nordhaus (1992), **capital** is simply one input of production. (The other two are land and labor.) It consists of "durable produced goods that are in turn used in production. The major components of capital are equipment, structures, and inventory" (730). Capital goods include "machines, roads, computers, hammers, trucks, steel mills, automobiles, washing machines, and buildings" (20). The U.S. economy exemplifies

**capitalism** because (1) capital, or *wealth*, is primarily the private property of the capitalist, and (2) private markets are the prime vehicles used to allocate resources and generate incomes.

By contrast, to a Marxist, capital is not just a thing, like machines. It is much more. It is a social relation. Marxists think that the means of production in society, like machines, become capital when "they have been monopolized by a certain sector of society and used by that class to produce surplus value—that is, the income of the capitalist class (generally, profits, interest, and rent) that comes from the exploitation of another class" (Gurley, 1975:32). Thus for Marxists, capital is more than the means of production in society; it is the way in which these means are used. In this way, Marxist thought links economics to politics and social order. Thus to a Marxist, capitalism is not only an economic system based on private property; it is also a political and social system based on the domination and exploitation by capitalists of nonpropertied workers.

## Surplus Value

Business firms make a profit because they are efficient and compete successfully in the marketplace. Often, firms buy something (raw materials), fashion it into a manufactured good, and resell it for profit. Or they exchange goods for profit. Or they increase prices, which provides profits. That is how free market theorists explain profitability. Marxists have a different explanation.

To a Marxist, a key source of profit in capitalist economies derives from **surplus value**. What is surplus value and when does it arise? Marx's concept of surplus value may be explained in this way: "Surplus value arises when a capitalist purchases labor-power (the capacity for labor) at its value, employs the labor-power in a work process that he controls, and then appropriates the commodities produced. Surplus value is the difference between the net value of these commodities and the value of labor-power itself" (Gurley, 1975:33).

In this view, the secret of profit is human labor-power: "A worker sells his labor-power—his mental and physical capabilities—to a capitalist for its value, and the capitalist uses the labor-power to obtain commodities which have a value higher than that of the labor-power purchased" (Gurley, 1975:33). In a word, profit results from the exploitation of labor in the production sphere.

## Monopoly Capitalism

In nineteenth-century Great Britain and America, the characteristic economic unit was the small firm. Typically, many textile firms (like Lowell's factory in Massachusetts) or bakeries produced a small share of the total product available in the marketplace. Such firms often faced stiff competition from one another. This situation typified competitive capitalism.

Marxist scholars emphasize how much this situation has changed since the nineteenth century. The typical economic unit today, Paul Baran and Paul Sweezy write, is "a large-scale enterprise producing a significant share of the output of an industry, or even several industries, and able to control its prices, the volume of production, and the types and amounts of its investments" (1966:6). In other words, they contend, the typical economic unit in capitalist countries now has the attributes of a monopoly.

In their book *Monopoly Capital: An Essay on the American Social and Economic Order* (1966), Baran and Sweezy focus on one major theme: the ways in which profit or surplus—"the difference between what a society produces and the costs of producing it"—is generated and absorbed under monopoly capitalism. (*Note:* Marxist theorists don't equate profit and surplus. However, one form of profit, in their view, results from the private appropriation of surplus value.) They stress the critical role that technological innovation played in the development of a system composed of giant corporations that maximize profit and accumulate capital: **monopoly capitalism**. These corporate giants, Baran and Sweezy argue, are price makers: "they can and do choose what prices to charge for their products" (57). Price makers ban price cutting to reduce competition and remove "the dangerous uncertainties from the rationalized pursuit of maximum profits" (59). Often this takes the form of cartels that regulate prices and output. Or it takes the form of tacit collusion among business firms. In either case, the result, they claim, is clear: Competitive capitalism has faded away, replaced by monopoly capitalism. And they argue that the capitalist state (e.g., the U.S. government) actually functions to strengthen monopoly and regularize its operations.

The implications of Baran and Sweezy's critique of market doctrine are wide-ranging. For example, they contend that the Great Depression of the 1930s was not "the Great Exception" but rather the "normal outcome of the workings of the American economic system" (1966:240).

Without explicating their tightly reasoned, complex analysis of capitalist crises and monopoly capitalism, let us examine one issue of special relevance to urban America: automobilization. Writing on the history of monopoly capitalism, Baran and Sweezy (1966:244–245) pose an interesting question: Why did the second wave of auto production in the United States occur after World War II and not in the 1930s, when it would have led to a needed economic boom? After all, the technology existed. And people presumably needed more cars as much in the 1930s as in the 1940s. "The answer," they say, "is that in 1937 people did not have the required purchasing and borrowing power to get things started, while after 1945 they did. . . . We have here a classic case of quantity turning into quality." What they mean is that the post–World War II suburban boom generated a snowball effect, making shopping centers and other facilities either necessary or profitable. But even with these powerful stimuli and with defense spending increases, Baran and Sweezy (1966:246) say, unemployment grew. Their conclusion: "Surely, an economy in which unemployment grows even during the expansion phase of the business cycle is in deep trouble" (248).

## Late Capitalism

To economist Ernest Mandel ([1972] 1987:9), late capitalism is a further phase of monopoly capitalism (which he equates with imperialism) that started after World War II. Mandel says that late capitalism is typified by a centralization of capital: A few very large financial groups "dominate the economy of each capitalist country," and "these giant monopolies divide the world markets of key commodities between themselves" (594–595). In late capitalism, the MNC becomes the main form of capital.

## Social Structures of Accumulation

Starting in the late 1970s, a group of U.S. economists working in the Marxian tradition put forward a new approach to analyze the structure and development of capitalist economies and societies: the *social structure of accumulation (SSA)*. SSA refers to "the complex of institutions which support the process of capital accumulation. The central idea of the SSA approach is that a long period of relatively rapid and stable economic expansion requires an effective SSA" (Kotz, McDonough, and Reich, 1994:1).

For our discussion, what is most important about this approach is that it includes political and cultural institutions as well as economic ones. At the domestic level, these institutions may include such arrangements as the organization of work, the role of the state in the economy, and the type of race and gender relations. At the international level, these institutions may include financial, trade, and political environments.

*To conclude:* The view that economic life is inseparable from political and cultural life is a key assumption of Marxist thought. To Marx, at any historical time, people have a certain level of productive capacity. This capacity depends on the technology available to them (machines, tools, etc.), the natural environment (fertile or infertile land, water, etc.), and their own knowledge and skills. These Marx calls the *material forces of pro-*

*duction*. Marx believed that the material forces of production determine how people survive economically (for instance, in nomadic food gathering or industrial production). And, Marx thought, the material forces of production determine how people relate to one another socially in the process of producing and exchanging things and ideas (for instance, as master and slave, as capitalist and worker). Marx called these production and exchange relationships the *social relations of production*. Together, the material forces of production and the social relations of production (the economic base of society) mold what Marx called the *superstructure*: the way people think, their legal systems, their political and religious institutions, and their world views. In brief, Marx held that the dominant ideas and institutions of any society are determined by people's material being.

## The Informational Mode of Development

According to urban theorist Manuel Castells (1989), the restructuring of capitalism in the 1970s and 1980s, plus a technological revolution, are transforming the cities and regions of the world. The main process in this transition is not, he says, the shift from manufactured goods to services, but the "emergence of information processing as the core, fundamental activity," which conditions the production, distribution, management, and consumption processes. Indeed, Castells argues that "our economies should be characterized as information economies, rather than as service economies" (167).

How are these changes affecting cities and regions? Castells says that one result is this: High-level decision making is increasingly centralized in global cities such as New York, and organizational management is decentralized within major metropolitan areas.

Not all theorists agree with with Castells and Mandel. Some even reject the basic assumption that there is a postindustrial society. For one, geography professor Allen J. Scott (1988) doesn't think that there has been a fundamental shift away from industrial capitalism. Others disagree ideologically. For example, conservatives and liberal thinkers do not make such necessary and inevitable links between economics and social-political life. Yet most social scientists—whatever their ideological perspective—agree that the way people organize themselves economically and the productive forces available to them have a great impact on their lives. This applies to cities too. As two non-Marxist urbanists put it a generation ago, "economic forces are prime determinants of the ecological and physical structures of cities. Directly or indirectly, these factors influence the pattern of living as well as the social and governmental institutions of metropolitan complexes. Changes in the mode of production or of economic organization inevitably find reflection in metropolitan life" (Bollens and Schmandt, 1970:72).

## AN EMERGING VOCABULARY

### Restorative Economy and Sustainability

Just a decade or so ago, those preaching the end of industrialism were dubbed extremists. Now consumers are buying their books, if not all their ideas. Take, for example, Paul Hawken's *The Ecology of Commerce* (1993). Hawken, an apostle of socially responsible capitalism, warns that if we want to avert commercial and biological catastrophe, we must "end industrialism as we know it." How? Not by recycling burrito foil and tin cans. In his view, such measures do not go far enough; he warns that the planet's "carrying capacity" has already been surpassed Rather, he says, it is up to business to create a sustainable, restorative economy by ambitious measures that use market principles, not government mandates. These include creating incentives that will encourage businesses to make decisions on the basis of long-term ecological (and commercial) sustainability, not short-term (and short-sighted) gain. For example, he suggests that the price of a product should include the cost of cleaning up its wastes, such as plastic in automobiles.

Poet William Blake knew that what is unimaginable today can become conventional wisdom tomorrow. Perhaps notions like a biologically sustainable economy that restores nature as it goes may fall into that category. Meanwhile, former gardening company executive Hawken remains a visionary, kook, or alarmist, depending on your assessment of the planetary situation.

## THE ECONOMY OF METROPOLITAN AREAS

### Cities and MSAs in the National and Global Economies

"No city is an island." This truism can be illustrated at both the national and international levels.

First, the national level. America is one mass market for goods, information, and services. Corner bakeries no longer supply the bulk of bread for sandwiches in small-town America, and local authors do not publish the vast majority of high-school textbooks; regional and national corporations do.

Second, the international level. To a significant degree, there is a world market and system of cities; the globe is a single economic unit, not a collection of separate nations, let alone cities. As noted earlier, major corporations tend to be multinational and multilocational, producing and distributing their goods globally. Many "American" brand names—McDonald's, Levi's, IBM, and Coca-Cola, to name a few—are as familiar to people in Paris and Tokyo as to those in New York or Booneville (Figure 17.4). These MNCs salute no particular flag; their work forces, materials, and profits are transnational. For example, by the early 1990s, 80 percent of Coca-Cola's operating profits came from outside the United States (Cohen, 1991:C1) As the president of a major MNC put it (before it was acquired by AT&T, the world's largest telecommunications company): "We at NCR think of ourselves as a globally competitive company that happens to be headquartered in the U.S." (in Uchitelle, 1989:A1).

**Fig. 17.4** AMERICAN BRAND NAMES. McDonalds, Coca-Cola, and Levi's are internationally known brand names of American-identified MNCs. These golden arches are found in Kyoto, Japan. (Tim Teninty)

The international political economy and national policies affect metropolitan economies in different ways. Here are a few examples:

1. *International recession.* The drop in tourism due to recession hurt Tahoe City, California, more than Indianapolis, Indiana.
2. *Global politics.* The end of the cold war meant reductions in military contracts and personnel; these losses of funds and jobs adversely affected module production centers and innovation centers more than, say, retirement centers.
3. *Immigration.* Cuban immigration helped to transform Miami from a sleepy community

into an international boom town and a super-market for affluent Latin American tourists in the 1960s (Morganthau, 1980:36). As Chapter 8 details, by the 1990s, Miami's Cuban community had became a major economic and political force.

4. *International pacts*. The North American Free Trade Agreement (NAFTA) can lead to major shifts of manufacturing and consumption, which, in turn, can lead to new employment in some cities and unemployment in others. Already, *maquiladoras*, non-Mexican-owned plants located within 50 miles of the U.S. border, have transformed the Mexican landscape and socialscape.

How much a particular metropolitan area suffers or benefits during times of international or national economic change depends on many factors. Some of the most important factors are (1) the industry mix, (2) demographic and social factors, (3) geographic location, and (4) dependence on petroleum products and proximity to energy sources.

**The Industry (or Productive) Mix**   The degree to which a particular metropolitan area benefits or suffers from changes in the global and national economies depends partially on the mix of productive activities there. (*Note:* Economists use the term *industry mix*, but in my view, the term *productive mix* better captures the notion that services and information—not manufacturing—typify the U.S. economy today.) If the U.S. economy expands and household incomes rise, consumers tend to spend their additional money on cars and luxury items, not suntan lotion or dish towels. Hence metropolitan areas producing goods subject to elastic demand (cars, luxury items, durable goods) tend to benefit during times of national economic growth. But during hard times, when people make do by fixing up their old cars rather than purchasing new ones, these areas tend to suffer disproportionately. That is the meaning of the old saying, "Whenever the nation catches a cold, Detroit gets pneumonia." Reflecting recent realities, a more up-to-date saying might be: "When auto executives were slow to make smaller, less profitable cars and when international competition drove a better bargain, Detroit got the shaft."

Metropolitan areas that produce basic foodstuffs, computerized billing services, toilet paper, and other products with inelastic demand are not in favorable positions during growth periods. But they tend to suffer less during economic downturns. Why? Because people don't give up eating junk food during hard times. Nor do they cancel insurance policies or stop seeing movies.

Richmond, Virginia, is one city whose product mix cushions the effects of economic downturns. Tom Robbins explains why in his novel *Even Cowgirls Get the Blues*:

Richmond, Virginia, has been called a "depression-proof" city. That is because its economy has one leg in life insurance and the other in tobacco. During times of economic bellyache, tobacco sales climb even as other sales tumble. . . . Perhaps a cigarette gives an unemployed man something to do with his hands. . . . In times of depression, policy-holders somehow manage to keep up their life insurance premiums. . . . Perhaps they insist on dignity in death since they never had it in life. . . . (1976:38)

**Demographic and Social Factors**   A metropolitan area's ability to respond quickly to change (e.g., technological innovation) depends partly on its people. Cities with large proportions of unskilled, elderly, or narrowly trained people may suffer more in times of national economic slump than those with a highly adaptable labor force. In addition, one-industry towns with highly specialized workers face economic disaster if new technology makes their functions obsolete. This is what happened to the railroaders in a town called Caliente; as the case study later in this chapter details, the town suffered "Death by Dieselization."

**Geographic Location**   "Chicago is midway between the [New York] Stock Exchange and the Frontier." That is how literary critic Alfred Kazin (1970) explains Chicago's importance at the start of this century. It was, as Carl Sandburg memorialized in his hymns to the city, "Hog Butcher for the World" and "The Nation's Freight Handler." Today Sandburg would have to revise his lines because the stockyards have moved west. But Chicago's transport function remains important, and the world's busiest (or second-busiest, depending on whom you believe) airport is located there. (For other explanations of Chicago's importance between 1900 and 1920, see Chapter 1.)

With technological change, new national needs, or the discovery of some important natural resource, cities can gain or lose strategic importance. In the 1970s, for instance, small towns like Rock Springs, Wyoming, grew quickly as energy sources were extracted from the earth around them. Just as quickly, they can quickly lose their basic reason for existence and become ghost towns. Policymakers in Alaska fear that boom towns built around the oil pipeline may suffer that fate.

*Energy Needs* Availability of energy sources and easy access to transportation have played a major role in city growth for millennia. Early industrial firms, for instance, had to locate near available sources of energy, such as water power. Technological innovations—electricity, combustion engines, telephones, computers, and e-mail—brought changes in industrial, services-informational, and residential locations. In the process, some older urban-industrial areas in the United States became victims of change.

Energy shortages and rising energy costs are bound to have widespread but uneven effects. Many of these effects are still unclear. Will Rocky Mountain cities, located near important energy sources, mushroom in population? Will technological and organizational innovations—perhaps a long-charge electric car and home or nearby regional workstations—allow growing numbers of working mothers, juggling home and work duties, to commute short distances or to compute to work?

*To conclude*: Forces external to a city's or an MSA's control, such as the state of the nation, cannot be controlled by people in any one me-

tropolis. But the effects of national or global economic change can be cushioned somewhat by local policy. To cite one instance, a declining MSA dependent on a single industry might attempt to attract growth industries to its area. Or it might engage in massive retooling efforts for local workers. But no metropolitan area can change forces beyond its control. Whether they like it or not, cities are economic creatures of the nation and, increasingly, of the world.

## Basic and Nonbasic Sectors

All productive activities that help residents of an urban area earn a living constitute that area's **economic base**. These activities include manufacturing, retail trade, sales, tourism, information and services, professional and managerial work, clerical and construction work, and transport.

Once again, the notion that cities can't exist if local residents merely take in each other's washing becomes crucial in understanding how local economies work. Interaction and exchange between the city or MSA and the world beyond its boundaries are essential for continued existence.

Economists draw a sharp distinction between two types of economic activity: basic and nonbasic. **Basic goods and services** are those produced primarily for export out of the city or metropolitan area. Such goods and services constitute the export sector. Examples include TV productions and movies from the Los Angeles–Long Beach area, software designs from the Seattle area, and refrigerators from Amana, Iowa. (Tourism counts as a basic activity although its products—souvenir T-shirts, hotel rooms, restaurant meals, and so on—are bought or consumed on the spot, not literally exported.) **Nonbasic goods and services** are primarily produced for local consumption. These goods and services are produced for internal markets and constitute the local sector. Examples include beauty shops, restaurants, cleaners, gas stations, and dairies (Figure 17.5).

Most urban economists argue that a city's or an MSA's potential for economic growth de-

**Fig. 17.5** NONBASIC SECTOR. Garage sales, gas stations, beauty shops, and cleaners are part of an urban area's nonbasic economic sector. (Brack Brown)

pends on the strength of its export or basic sector. The rationale is as follows: Export goods bring money in from outside the urban area, money that finances the importing of goods that the urban area doesn't produce for itself. In addition, the logic goes, nonbasic activity is largely dependent on basic activity. For example, if a chemical plant closes and the majority of a city's workers become unemployed, they will no longer patronize local retail or service establishments (e.g., restaurants, furniture stores, hair stylists) to the same extent, and eventually these operations will contract or fold.

Years ago, conventional wisdom about the importance of the basic sector to a local economy was challenged by planner Hans Blumenfeld (1955:131). He argued that a strong nonbasic sector is the key to a strong local economy, not the

reverse. He contends that the nonbasic sector's efficiency is crucial for the operation of basic sector firms.

In either case, both positions rest on an implicit assumption: that cities are like nations, self-sufficient in certain productive activities and dependent on the outside world for others. For this reason, economists use international trade terms when discussing basic and nonbasic sectors. Thus an MSA is said to improve its *balance of payments* position if it can produce locally some product that it formerly imported. An MSA is said to enjoy a *comparative advantage* if it can produce a commodity more efficiently and more cheaply than another urban area.

## The Underground Economy

Some productive activities never get counted as part of the basic or nonbasic sector because they remain **underground**, or off the books. That is, not all income is reported for tax purposes. For instance, many household helpers, service personnel who receive tips, successful gamblers, laundromat managers, garage-sale holders, and drug dealers evade taxes (Figure 17.6). The Internal Revenue Service estimates that in one year, 1992, between $110 and $127 billion went unreported and unpaid (Trager, 1993:E1).

## Identifying Basic Sector Industries

How can the export or basic sector activity within a city or an MSA be identified? Mainstream economists use either (1) the employment base method or (2) input–output analysis.

*Employment Base Method* The **employment base method** of identifying basic sector industries compares local and national employment patterns. Here is a hypothetical example. In your city, about 6 percent of the labor force works in the food and kindred products industry, while

**Fig. 17.6**  THE UNDERGROUND ECONOMY. Billions of dollars go untaxed in the off-the-books economy. It is estimated that illicit drug trade profits alone account for about 2 percent of the GNP of the United States. (Lisa Siegel Sullivan)

the national average is less than 2 percent. Less than 1 percent of your city's labor force produces nonelectrical machinery, while the national average is over 2 percent. Thus we can assume that your city exports food products and imports nonelectrical machinery.

The employment base method can be used for either specific industries or major sectors of the economy (e.g., public administration, durable goods manufacturing, and nondurable goods manufacturing). Using U.S. census data, the percentage of the labor force employed in these sectors (and the national average for each sector) can be found. It is clear that a highly specialized area (like Silicon Valley for electronics or Washington, D.C., for public administration) will

show the greatest deviation from national employment patterns.

*Input–Output Analysis*  The employment base method gives a quick and rather simple view of a local economy's basic and nonbasic sectors. But it can't show the interconnections between local industries. Nor can it show how increases in one sector of the local economy will affect other sectors. For this kind of evaluation, an **input–output analysis** is needed. Input–output analysis works on the following assumptions: Every good or output produced (financial services, cars, public administration, etc.) requires inputs (labor, raw materials, etc.). If expansion occurs in one indus-

**Table 17.1** Input–Output Table Showing Interindustry Flows for a Hypothetical Region

| Industry Producing \ Industry Purchasing | 1. Agriculture and Extraction | 2. Manufacturing (light and heavy) | 3. Power, Communications, and Transportation | 4. Business, Finance, and Services | 5. Households | 6. All Others | Total Gross Output |
|---|---|---|---|---|---|---|---|
| | | | *(in thousands of dollars)* | | | | |
| 1. Agriculture and extraction | $200 | $300 | $100 | $500 | $300 | $200 | $1,600 |
| 2. Manufacturing (light and heavy) | 100 | 200 | 100 | 150 | 450 | 700 | 1,700 |
| 3. Power, communications, and transportation | 200 | 300 | 200 | 350 | 200 | 150 | 1,400 |
| 4. Business, finance, and services | 300 | 300 | 200 | 400 | 800 | 300 | 2,300 |
| 5. Households | 200 | 100 | 400 | 300 | 100 | 900 | 2,000 |
| 6. All others | 600 | 500 | 50 | 600 | 150 | 400 | 2,300 |
| Total inputs | 1,600 | 1,700 | 1,400 | 2,300 | 2,000 | 2,300 | 11,300 |

SOURCE: Adapted from Walter Isard, *Methods of Regional Analysis* (Cambridge, Mass., and New York: Technology Press of MIT and John Wiley, 1960), p. 312. Copyright © 1960 by the Massachusetts Institute of Technology. Reprinted by permission of the M.I.T. Press, Cambridge, Mass.

try, additional inputs will be needed; some will be obtained locally and others from outside the community. Those added inputs from within the local community will stimulate other local activity. These effects snowball; more inputs stimulate more local purchases—at restaurants, by retail outlets from wholesalers, and so forth. Using input–output analysis, these interindustry relations can be detailed.

Table 17.1 is a simplified input–output analysis of a hypothetical MSA. All economic activity is classified into six categories. Reading across the rows, we can see how much output was produced in each category and where this output went. Reading down the columns, we can see how much each category of economic activity consumed and where the inputs came from. Thus manufacturing consumed $1.7 million worth of total inputs: $300,000 from agriculture and extraction, $200,000 from manufacturing, and so forth. Total inputs to any category of economic activity equal total outputs. Consequently, manufacturing consumed $1.7 million in inputs and provided $1.7 million in outputs. This is a very simple input–output table.

Economists have constructed more sophisticated models to describe and predict interindustry flows within a larger region. Yet such models have not been very helpful to decision makers. Problems of data collection, the complexity of real-world transactions, and theoretical problems have so far limited the practical applications of input–output analyses (Figure 17.7).

## Case Study: Caliente

What happened to the town of Caliente illustrates many of the abstract notions mentioned above. As you read this case history, recall some of the factors that influence the state—if not the fate—of cities and MSAs: (1) the health of their labor market, their tax base, and the effectiveness of government support programs; (2) the productive mix, demographic and social factors, geographic location, and energy needs; (3) the basic–nonbasic sector distinction; (4) changes in the national economy; and (5) the international political economy.

In 1949 sociologist Fred Cottrell studied a small desert town he called Caliente. This town,

**Fig. 17.7** GARBAGE IN, GARBAGE OUT. Bad data are not improved by running them through a computer. (© 1976 Richard Hedman)

located in a county with little more than 2,500 people, had only one reason for existence: It serviced the steam engines as they moved between Salt Lake City and Los Angeles. When the diesel locomotive replaced the steam engine, Caliente's repair shops were no longer needed because diesel engines need less frequent servicing than steam engines. Geographically, Caliente was no longer strategic. This technological switch from steam resulted in "Death by Dieselization" (1951). For a city so dependent on one industry—railroading—the closing of the railroad shops and the permanent loss of railroad jobs meant the collapse of Caliente's economic base.

After the initial shock of disbelief, Caliente's residents tried to find a new economic base. As Cottrell (1972) says in his update on Caliente, several ventures were tried, including agriculture and tourism. Then fate took a strange turn. The federal government wanted to use land near Caliente to test atomic devices. At the time, the potential negative externalities of this project were largely unknown, and local citizens didn't protest this land use, for atomic testing would bring jobs. In fact, only a few jobs were created this way. Then, during the Korean War, when the primary source of tungsten was cut off, the government paid for a mill near Caliente's profitable deposit. Over time, however, the tungsten mine closed down, and the nuclear test site workers moved to housing closer to their work. So, despite its effort to find a new economic base, "the economic picture is bleak" (Cottrell, 1972:76).

Given this bleak picture, one might expect Caliente to shrivel up and become a ghost town. After all, not only did it lose its economic base, it lost much of its tax base: "the railroad tore down, gave away or abandoned much of its fixed structure. In turn it demanded and got a reappraisal that reduced Caliente's tax revenue" (Cottrell, 1972:78). And many other towns in the region did become ghost towns when they stopped exporting ore and thus could not pay for imported goods.

But Caliente did not die. It survived. It didn't exactly prosper, but it did survive. How? Initially by attempting to rebuild its export sector. Then

by government support for various projects, including a mill for tungsten, a rare metal whose supply was interrupted by international politics. And then by providing services to residents—education, nursing, parks, and so forth. But how do residents pay for these services? In large measure through railroad retirement benefits, state pensions, Social Security payments, and other government support programs.

Cottrell (1972:84) concludes that the income of most Caliente residents does not come from exporting goods to the market. Instead, it comes from sources outside the town "who pay Caliente people for doing things mostly for each other." In this sense, Caliente represents a national trend away from producing things and toward delivering consumer services.

In the long run, can Caliente survive with no export sector? Cottrell is dubious. At some point, decisions (which will be made by outsiders—state voters, mainly) will have to be made. When the physical structures of Caliente deteriorate, will the schools and hospitals be rebuilt? Or will the stores and streets and physical structures be allowed to be reclaimed by the desert? Whatever the decision, Caliente's fate will not be determined by local residents. This, of course, is not new for Caliente. Past decisions were also made by faraway decision makers: railroad managers and stockholders.

Caliente is far from a typical town. But its story does illustrate the growing importance of government support programs to improve the ill health of the town's tax base and labor market. It also indicates how little control a one-industry (specialized function) town has over its own fate, particularly when technological change renders its specialized function obsolete. Outsiders have always determined Caliente's fate; now they are state voters and government decision makers instead of private railroad managers.

Cottrell stresses the ironies concerning the American value of individualism and the belief in the market. The people of Caliente are rugged individualists, believers in the "American way" of the price system and progress. Fiercely independent in an interdependent world, some Caliente people suffered more than others for their beliefs: " 'good citizens' who assumed family and community responsibility are the greatest losers. . . . those who were—by middle class norms—most moral were the most heavily penalized" (Cottrell, 1951:360; 1972:68). Those who could pick up and leave the community—who owned no property there and had not sunk deep roots—"the nomads," suffered least. The final irony is that for all their rugged frontier individualism, these people on the desert "must listen ever more closely to the beat of a distant drummer to whose cadence they must march" (1972:85).

The small town of Caliente was created by outsiders for technological reasons. The site happened to be located at a point on the transcontinental railroad where steam engines needed to be serviced. Technology and lack of physical barriers dictated Caliente's location. Other towns like Caliente that have a relatively undiversified economy (one that produces only a narrow range of goods and services) can also find themselves in a shaky economic position, without much warning when and if technological change hits. The shutdown of a military base or a branch manufacturing plant of an MNC can spell economic disaster for local residents. And such decisions are made outside the local community—by outsiders. As the people of Caliente found out, local residents have little influence over location decisions that so vitally affect their lives and livelihoods.

*To conclude*: The case of Caliente's dependence on outsiders for its existence—both originally and now—is extreme. And the decision that originally created Caliente was not complicated. By contrast, business location decisions in the global economy are much more complex. Economically, producers of goods and services often maximize efficiency and profit by grouping or clustering together in dense settlements. Historically, this economic fact helps to explain the existence and development of cities. However, in a timeless, increasing borderless economy, many functions can be—and are—decentralized across metropolitan and global landscapes.

## ECONOMICS OF THE FUTURE

In the postindustrial, energy-conscious era, location decisions become very complex. Energy shortages and rising costs may force business firms and their workers to relocate. Increasing numbers of manufacturing firms move out of U.S. metropolitan areas altogether—and into the urban areas of China and Mexico or the techno-burbs of France. Firms that depend on electronic communications and fax machines, rather than oil, may scatter to the rural countryside. Large numbers of professionals and white-collar workers may communicate rather than commute to work. All such phenomena are affecting both global business and residential location patterns.

### International Trends and Policies

Without pretending to be clairvoyant, we can identify some trends that will affect the economic life of American cities. Here are a few; they are categorized as international, national, and regional, but it will become clear that these categories are often inseparable.

(1) *The political economy of oil*—what oil producers and U.S. MNCs do will affect the nation's cities. (2) *The income gap between rich and poor nations will widen.* Even more U.S. firms could leave U.S. metropolitan areas for overseas locations, where labor is cheaper and unions are either weak or banned. The world's poor nations could boycott some U.S. products made in metropolitan areas, affecting the export sector of local economies. Poor nations could band together and sharply increase the price of their raw materials, affecting American cities in various ways, depending on the products they produce.

### National, Regional, and State Trends and Policies

(1) *Energy:* When asked why U.S. troops were fighting in the oil-rich Persian Gulf, Secretary of

State James Baker replied simply, "Jobs." More than a decade earlier, some national policymakers had predicted energy's all-important role: "The most important determinant of the health of the nation's economy in the future is likely to be the health of its energy policy" (in Rattner, 1979:sec. 4: 1). Indeed, the Gulf War reminded American and Japanese citizens of oil's importance to advanced industrialized countries.

Energy crunches and national energy policies have different impacts on the nation's cities and regions. Cities in the "energy corridor" between Houston and New Orleans are in a very different position than Frostbelt cities.

Several other trends or policies bear close watch, particularly (2) *the ever-increasing reach of MNCs*, (3) *the level of federal government support programs*, (4) *the commitment to lower the national deficit*, and (5) *the increasing income gap between rich and poor in cities and suburbs*. All of these affect the fate of cities. The precise effects of these trends and policies remain debated and debatable. But one thing seems clear: Individual cities, postsuburban areas, and MSAs have little—and decreasing—ability to control their own fate.

## ANOTHER LOOK

Theorists agree on the importance of economic factors to the fate of cities. But they disagree on how the economy today really works—and how it could work better. The dean of free marketeers, Milton Friedman, looks to supply, demand, price, and the market mechanism to explain how the U.S. economic system should work. Generally, conservatives base their economic views on a psychological assumption: that individuals and business firms are rational, self-interested profit maximizers. They see the workings of the marketplace as a technical issue, not a moral one. Liberals like John Kenneth Galbraith point to the lack of equity in the conservative stance. If the poor cannot afford heating fuel in times of skyrocketing prices, should the market dictate that

they go cold while the rich don't? Liberals think not. Further, liberals tend to favor spending public money to retrain the U.S. labor force to meet the challenges of the world economy. For one, political economist Robert B. Reich, before being appointed to the Clinton cabinet, advocated retraining programs in his book, *The Work of Nations: Preparing Ourselves for 21st Century Capitalism* (1991). Also, liberals point to the problems of social disorder and political instability that might follow from a pure market doctrine. Thousands of cold, angry people might not shiver alone but rather start burning down cities in frustration or out of a feeling of relative deprivation. Marxists—now joined by strange comrades such as Charles Lindblom—reject the notion of market sovereignty. In their view, giant corporations manipulate the market, removing uncertainties from the pursuit of profits. Radicals do not expect government at any level—federal, state, or local—to change what they perceive as a gross imbalance between corporate power and citizen subordination.

Meanwhile, nations are becoming less important economically, even obsolete, in the global economy. Perhaps paradoxically, some theorists suggest that "cities will become the essential unit for thinking about the production, consumption, and exchange of commodities and the generation of wealth and jobs" (DeLeon, 1993:2).

Note that while theorists and politicians continue to debate economic issues, American citizens are experiencing a growing sense of powerlessness over their collective economic fates. Some turn inward to find their own souls via a series of therapies. Some consume things and show off symbols. Others downscale. And some tune out by turning on. Still others turn to collective answers—single-interest groups, party politics, or private militia.

Finally, there seems to be an enormous gap between *what is* (giant private corporations and big government) and what many think *should be* (smaller government, individualism). This gap between traditional American values and modern American institutions is not easily reconcilable, at least not without dismantling major institutions. This suggests the following irony: In an era of national and international markets, of worldwide economic interdependence, comes the cry for more self-sufficiency, more local autonomy. Seeing how this contradiction is worked out in the political and economic spheres awaits us.

## KEY TERMS

**Basic and nonbasic economic activities** (or **sectors**) The basic economic sector consists of goods and services produced primarily for export out of the community (exception: tourism-connected items such as hotel rooms). The nonbasic economic sector consists of those goods and services produced primarily for local consumption, such as garage sales and hair styling shops.

**Capital** A term with many denotations. To a non-Marxist, machines, factories and plants, and stores and stocks of finished and unfinished goods. To some Marxists, all of these *and* the way in which they are used (the social relationships of production). To Marxist economist Ernest Mandel ([1972] 1987:591), capital is "exchange-value which seeks a further accretion of value"; it first appears "in a society of petty commodity producers in the form of owners of money (merchants or usurers) who intervene in the market with the aim of buying goods in order to resell them at a profit."

**Capitalism** To a non-Marxist, an economic system in which capital or wealth is primarily the private property of capitalists (synonyms: *free enterprise system, profit system, price system*). To a Marxist, an economic-social-political system based on private property and the domination and exploitation by capitalists of non-propertied workers.

**Demand** The degree to which consumers want and will pay for a product. Demand curves illustrate that the higher the price of a good, the fewer the people who will be willing to buy it .

**Economic base** In orthodox economics, all activities that produce income for members of a community. In Marxist social thought, the productive forces of society and the social relations of production.

**Efficiency** Measured (by economists) by using a ratio of units of output to units of cost. The efficiency of a business firm is related to its profitability.

**Employment base method** A method for identifying basic sector activities by comparing local and national employment patterns.

**Equity** Fairness or justice in the distribution of something, such as benefits or burdens.

**Externalities** Spillover effects or indirect consequences—either positive or negative—to individuals or groups not directly involved in the action. Such spillovers occur outside the market so that those affected, for better or worse, neither pay nor receive payment for the activity. Externalities occur when private benefits or costs do not equal social benefits or costs.

**Input–output analysis** A method of measuring the interconnections between industries in a city, MSA, or region. It attempts to show how the growth or decline in one basic sector industry will affect other sectors or industries.

**Monopoly capitalism** A late stage of capitalism (following the commercial and industrial stages) identified by Marxist theorists. Baran and Sweezy characterize this stage as one in which the typical economic unit is the giant corporation and the problem faced by such a corporation is absorption of the surplus.

**Price** To market theorists, the financial cost of a good or service determined by the market of supply and demand. Marxist theorists stress the degree to which prices are fixed by cartels or large corporations under monopoly capitalism.

**Profit** To market theorists, the net income of a business firm after all expenses of production have been paid. To Marxist theorists, one form of profit derives from surplus value.

**Supply** The quantity of a good provided to the market at a given price. Supply curves slope upward, indicating that the higher the price, the more of the good will be supplied to the market.

**Surplus value** A Marxist concept, key to Marx's analysis of capitalism. He reasoned that business profits are based in the production sphere. This means that, in Marx's view, one source of profit is the exploitation of labor; that is, human labor power becomes the source of value that goes unpaid by the capitalist employer. If, for instance, a worker spends three hours in "necessary labor" (necessary to subsist) and three hours in "surplus labor" (the time in which the worker produces exclusively for the employer), the surplus labor time is the source of surplus value.

**Underground economy** Unreported and thus untaxed income. Examples include money from unreported restaurant tips, drug deals, house cleaning, babysitting, and nanny work. The Internal Revenue Service estimates that between $110 and $127 billion went untaxed in 1992. Synonyms: *off the books, under the table.*

## PROJECTS

1. **Basic sector.** Using the employment base method, try to determine what goods and services your community exports. Helpful data sources are U.S. Bureau of the Census publications, including the decennial census material (see, for instance, the *U.S. Census of Population* summary for national averages in some categories) and the *Census of Business* (selected services, retail trade, manufactures), which is published every five years.
2. **Masters of their own fate?** Interview various members of your community (including presumed decision makers such as elected and appointed officials; the unemployed; members of different occupational groups, students, etc.). Pose the following questions: (a) What are five or six important decisions or events that have affected the economic life of this community in the past decade? (b) Who was responsible for these decisions? Alternatively, what forces led to them? Note the patterns of response. For instance, do interviewees tend to name local decision makers or events? Do they draw links between what happened nationally and internationally (e.g., oil policies, government support programs, new technologies) and local economic life?

## SUGGESTIONS FOR FURTHER LEARNING

The first urban economics book published in the United States is Wilbur R. Thompson, *A Preface to Urban Economics* (Baltimore: Johns Hopkins University Press, 1965). Although a classic in the field, it is not recommended for beginners. For a more recent text, also in the mainstream, see Arthur Sullivan, *Urban Economics* (Homewood, Ill.: Irwin, 1993). For readable and iconoclastic interpretations, see Jane Jacobs's *The Economy of Cities* (New York: Vintage, 1976) and *Cities and the Wealth of Nations: Principles of Economic Life* (New York: Random House, 1984).

Many recent economic studies focus on the national and international economies, not on cities per se, but the connections between global and local economics are implied. In *The Great U-Turn: Corporate Restructuring and the Polarizing of America* (New York: Basic Books, 1990), two professors of political economy, Bennett Harrison and Barry Bluestone, attempt to explain how and why the United States moved from higher-wage jobs and greater equality in family incomes to lower-wage jobs during the 1970s and 1980s. They conclude that "the recent stagnation of American incomes and the rise of inequality have their origins in the growth in global competition and specifically in a distinctive array of business strategies adopted by American corporate managers to cope with the ensuing decline in corporate profitability" (xii). Although published more than twenty years ago, Richard J. Barnet and Ronald E. Muller's *Global Reach* (New York: Simon and Schuster, Touchstone, 1974), remains a valuable and highly readable study about the power of MNCs. Chapter 2, "From Globaloney to the Global Shopping Center," shows how "industry has transcended geography" and gives examples of the internationalization of finance capital. Barnet and John Cavanagh's update, *Global Dreams: Imperial Corporations and the New World Order* (New York: Simon and Schuster, 1994), paints a portrait of global corporations as they evolved since the 1970s. They claim that MNCs have replaced national power and dominate the fate of the world's economy and people.

In *The Global Marketplace* (New York: Macmillan, 1987), business writer Milton Moskowitz scrutinizes 102 MNCs, reporting on how each of these essentially stateless entities operates. For example, in the late 1980s, Philips was Holland's largest company, the third largest TV-set manufacturer in the United States, and the world's largest maker of light bulbs; the corporation employed 344,000 (50,000 in the United States), and its profits were estimated at $500 million. Topping his list of the 100 largest U.S. MNCs (American companies ranked by their foreign sales) are two oil companies (Exxon, 1; Mobil, 2), one information-computer company (IBM, 3), and two auto companies (Ford, 4; General Motors, 5).

For a very brief description of the explosion of Marxist studies and the theory of the capitalist city, see "The City of Theory," in Peter Hall, *Cities of Tomorrow* (Oxford: Blackwell, [1988] 1990). For an extended Marxist perspective on the global scene, see Joyce Kolko, *Restructuring the World Economy* (New York: Pantheon, 1988), which argues that reform on a national scale cannot begin to deal with the global economic crises in energy, trade, the monetary system, and so on. In *The Economic Crisis and American Society* (Princeton, N.J.: Princeton University Press, 1980), Manuel Castells presents a complex technical discussion of economic crisis in advanced capitalism; Chapter 3 contains a section on "The Crisis of American Cities." In "From City to Metropolis," David M. Gordon (a key figure in the elucidation of the SSA approach to capitalist development) theorizes that the patterns of urban development correspond to the three main stages of capital accumulation in advanced industrial countries: commercial, industrial, and corporate capitalism; the article is included in William K. Tabb and Larry Sawers, eds., *Marxism and the Metropolis: New Perspectives in Urban Political Economy* (New York: Oxford University Press, 1978). For a discussion of U.S. capitalism from a Marxist perspective, see also Ann Markusen, *Profit Cycles, Oligopoly, and Regional Development* (Cambridge, Mass.: MIT Press, 1985). The Union for Radical Political Economics (URPE) compiles reading lists from courses throughout the country dealing with radi-

cal analyses of economics; the list is distributed through its New York City office.

For a classic case study of a city and its relationship to its metropolitan region, see Edgar M. Hoover and Raymond Vernon, *Anatomy of a Metropolis* (New York: Doubleday, 1962).

The pioneer in economic base studies, Charles M. Tiebout, described the nature and uses of input–output analysis in *The Community Economic Base Study* (New York: Committee for Economic Development, 1962). For applications of input–output analysis, see *Metropolitan Challenge* (Dayton, Ohio: Metropolitan Community Studies, 1959) and the Association of Bay Area Government's "1987 Input–Output Model and Economic Multipliers for the San Francisco Bay Region" (Oakland, Calif., 1991). Recent developments and interpretations of input–output analyses can be found in a series of conference papers in John H. L. Dewhurst, Geoffrey J. D. Hewings, and Rodney C. Jensen, eds., *Regional Input–Output Modelling* (Brookfield, Vt.: Avebury, 1991). An application of the employment base method is found in Ezra Solomon and Zrko G. Bilbija, *Metropolitan Chicago: An Economic Analysis* (New York: Free Press, 1959).

One element in the nationalization of economic enterprise is the franchise—the fast-food restaurant, motel chain, and tax-preparation storefront, to name a few examples. For a look into this business, see Stan Luxenberg, *Roadside Empires: How the Chain Franchised America* (New York: Viking Penguin, 1985).

Both documentaries and Hollywood movies deal with themes of economic change and technology's impact on social life. Michael Moore's *Roger and Me* (1989) and its sequel, *Pets or Meat?* (1992), are comic, tongue-in-cheek—but ultimately tragic and radical—looks at Flint, Michigan's, attempt to survive General Motors's auto plant closings and deindustrialization. Orson Welles's film *The Magnificent Ambersons* (1942) depicts the economic and social impact on a small town of industrialization (particularly the automobile). Louis Malle's prize-winning documentary *Phantom India* (1968) contains a section on Calcutta that suggests the interrelationship between that city's present poverty and past history (e.g., the separation of jute fields and jute factories when partition of Bengal took place in 1947).

On the specific issue of energy, see Daniel Yergin, *The Prize: The Epic Quest for Oil, Money, and Power* (New York: Simon and Schuster, 1991); this important book was the subject of a PBS series in January 1993.

## REFERENCES

Baran, Paul A., and Paul M. Sweezy. 1966. *Monopoly Capital: An Essay on the American Economic and Social Order*. New York: Monthly Review Press.

Blumenfeld, Hans. 1955. "The economic base of the metropolis: Critical remarks on the 'basic–nonbasic' concept." *Journal of the American Institute of Planners* 21:114–132.

Bollens, John C., and Henry J. Schmandt. 1970. *The Metropolis: Its People, Politics, Economic Life*, 2nd ed. New York: Harper & Row.

Brecher, Jeremy. 1993. "After NAFTA: Global village or global pillage?" *The Nation* (December 6):685–687.

Bullard, Robert D., ed. 1994. *Unequal Protection: Environmental Justice and Communities of Color*. San Francisco: Sierra Club.

Castells, Manuel. 1989. *The Informational City: Information Technology, Economic Restructuring and the Urban-Regional Process*. Oxford: Blackwell.

Cohen, Roger. 1991. "For Coke, world is its oyster." *New York Times* [national edition] (November 21):C1+.

Cottrell, William Fred. 1951. "Death by dieselization: A case study in the reaction to technological change." *American Sociological Review* 16:358–385.

———. 1972. *Technology, Man, and Progress*. Columbus, Ohio: Merrill.

Coupland, Douglas. 1994. "Rem Koolhaas, postnationalist architect." *New York Times* [national edition] (September 11):H45.

DeLeon, Richard. 1993. Personal communication (December 24).

Friedman, Milton. 1970. "Social responsibility of business is to increase its profits." *New York Times Magazine* (September 13):32+.

Galbraith, John Kenneth. 1968. *The New Industrial State*. New York: Signet.

———. 1979. "Oil: A solution." *New York Review of Books* (September 27):3–6.

Gurley, John G. 1975. *Challengers to Capitalism: Marx, Lenin, and Mao*. San Francisco: San Francisco Book.

Hawken, Paul. 1993. *The Ecology of Commerce: A Declaration of Sustainability*. New York: HarperBusiness.

Heilbroner, Robert, and Lester Thurow. 1994. *Economics Explained: Everything You Need to Know About How the Economy Works and Where It's Going*. Rev. and updated ed. New York: Simon and Schuster, Touchstone.

Jacobs, Jane. 1984. *Cities and the Wealth of Nations: Principles of Economic Life*. New York: Random House.

Janson, Donald. 1979. "Atlantic City's clergy say casinos hurt churches." *New York Times* (September 2):1, 20.

Kazin, Alfred (narrator). 1970. *The Writer and the City*. Distributed by Chelsea Films.

Kotz, David, M., Terrence McDonough, and Michael Reich, eds. 1994. *Social Structures of Accumulation: The Political Economy of Growth and Crisis*. Cambridge: Cambridge University Press.

Leibenstein, Harvey. 1976. *Beyond Economic Man: A New Framework for Microeconomics*. Cambridge, Mass.: Harvard University Press.

Lindblom, Charles. 1978. *Politics and Markets*. New York: Basic Books.

Mandel, Ernest. [1972] 1987. *Late Capitalism*. Trans. Joris De Bres. London: Verso.

Mathews, Tom. 1979. "The angry west vs. the rest." *Newsweek* (September 17):31–40.

Morganthau, Tom. 1980. "Miami: Latin crossroads." *Newsweek* (February 11):36+.

Rattner, Steven. 1979. "Energy policy: An enigma surrounded by a riddle." *New York Times* (July 1):sec. 4, 1.

Reich, Robert B. 1991. *The Work of Nations: Preparing Ourselves for 21st Century Capitalism*. New York: Knopf.

Robbins, Tom. 1976. *Even Cowgirls Get the Blues*. Boston: Houghton Mifflin.

Samuelson, Paul A., and William D. Nordhaus. 1964. *Economics*, 14th ed. New York: McGraw-Hill.

Scott, Allen J. 1988. *Metropolis: From the Division of Labor to Urban Form*. Berkeley: University of California Press.

Smith, Adam. [1776] 1970. *The Wealth of Nations*. New York: Penguin.

Thrift, Nigel. 1989. "Introduction." Pp. 43–54 in Richard Peet and Nigel Thrift, eds., *New Models in Geography: The Political-Economy Perspective*. Vol. 2. London: Unwin Hyman.

Trager, Louis. 1993. "Underground economy costs billions in taxes." *San Franciso Examiner* (February 14):E1+.

Uchitelle, Louis. 1989. "Spread of US plants abroad is slowing exports." *New York Times* [national edition] (March 26):A1+.

"I really enjoy being here because it's my pleasure to help people. They'd have to fire me before I'd quit. I know I'm loved and vice versa." (in Owens, 1975:n.p.)

# CHAPTER 18
# Blue-Collar,
# White-Collar,
# Shirtless

In terms of people and their work in America, the old Chinese curse seems especially applicable: "May you live in interesting times." The next two decades promise to be interesting—and stressful—times as people continue adjusting to postindustrial society. For one thing, individuals are being forced to rethink their attitudes toward work because labor experts predict that there may never again be enough decently paid full-time work for the available workers in the United States or elsewhere. Indeed, sociologist Herbert Gans suggests that people in the "post-work society" should start thinking about a future "in which the full-time job is no longer the basic source of people's income, status, and self-respect" (1993:B3).

This chapter is about jobs and joblessness. It traces the great historical changes in the nature and meaning of work. First, it takes a peek at the post-work society. Then it looks backward: to preindustrial and early industrial times in Europe and North America. Next it returns to modern times, investigating worker alienation and dissatisfaction. It also examines differing occupational structures of some contemporary U.S. cities, probing what the changing types and locations of jobs implies for cities and city dwellers. Finally, it looks at those within MSAs who are unemployed and underemployed or who are employed full-time but can't make it economically: the metropolitan poor.

## THE POST-WORK SOCIETY

"What do you want to do when you grow up?" A first-grade teacher in Houston got the following answers from her six-year-old students: airline pilot, soldier, rock star, police officer, U.S. president, teacher, and doctor. Interestingly, none of these children said they wanted to collect bugs, travel to foreign lands, watch TV all day, or hike in the woods. All answered by naming *work-related* roles. Why? In the United States, people's identity has been tied traditionally to their work. Apparently these first graders had already absorbed the message: In large measure, you are what you do.

This situation is changing for a number of reasons—structural, social psychological, and moral. On the one hand, as the United States has moved from an industrial to a postindustrial so-

ciety, more people have less work, at least paid work, to do. By the time they grow up, these first graders may find that technology has changed the nature of much of the work they actually end up doing, giving them a great deal of time for leisure or unpaid work. Indeed, we could hypothesize that in postindustrial societies, the key question for a substantial portion of the population is no longer "What do you do?" (the question typical in *Gesellschaft* societies) but rather "What are you into?" That is, many are defining themselves in terms of their leisure interests, whether it be surfing, information surfing via computer, or collecting old beer cans.

Moreover, in the postindustrial society, many are finding that they *have* to define themselves in terms of their leisure activities if they wish to retain their dignity. Not everyone trained in a trade or an occupation is able to practice it. This phenomenon is rooted in structural and technological factors. For example, due to the new international division of labor, some industrial jobs moved offshore. Other jobs have been made obsolete by technological change. In West Virginia, for example, productivity per coal miner increased while mining employment dropped more than 50 percent from 1980 to 1990; this helps to explain the state's unemployment rate of 11.7 percent, the highest in the United States in 1993 (Toner, 1993:A8). And others attract too many prospective workers, causing a structural mismatch between jobs and people. For instance, twice as many persons graduated college with teaching credentials as there were available jobs in 1977 (Watkins, 1979:10). So, it's no surprise when a house painter turns out to have a Ph.D. in English literature. In a labor force that now hovers around 125 million persons, countless numbers of Americans are already doing work they never dreamed of doing in order to survive.

## THE HUMAN DIMENSION: WORK AND THE INDIVIDUAL

Traveling back a few hundred years in time and space to seventeenth-century London, we find the following situation: bakers requesting an increase in the price of bread. The bakers supported their request with the following information about their work setting and weekly costs:

Thirteen people there were in such an establishment: the baker and his wife, four paid employees who were called journeymen, two maidservants, two apprentices, and the baker's three children. Food cost more than anything else, more than raw materials and nearly four times as much as wages. Clothing was charged up, too, not only for man, wife, and children but for the apprentices as well. Even school fees were included in the cost of baking bread. (Laslett, [1965] 1971:1)

This image—of a world without complex machines or complex organizations—provides a striking contrast to that of a modern factory or office building. In preindustrial England, workers produced their bread and clothing without electricity or layers of bosses. They worked by hand, creating a finished product with co-workers who were family members or with whom personal ties were established. This small-scale, technologically simple world of work is a world we have lost. Before mourning its passing, however, recall its less romantic aspects. Work was hard and long. Children often started productive activity at age three or four, and women played a subordinate role. There was no worker's compensation or unemployment insurance and few occupational standards for health or safety. People died young.

First in England and then in continental Europe, the passing of the world of preindustrial work brought sweeping changes. Urbanization and industrialization changed where people lived, how they worked, how they related to one another, and how they related to the products of their labor.

## Lowell, Massachusetts: Working Conditions of America's First Female Labor Force

Let's return to one of the grand designer's cities, Lowell, Massachusetts (Chapter 16), to examine some characteristics of early industrial society.

Lowell illustrates what happened in the beginning phases of America's industrialization and urbanization processes: (1) the rural–urban shift, (2) the increasing scale and organization of work, and (3) the changing conditions and psychological meaning of work.

Lowell was one of America's first mill towns, named after the designer of a version of a power loom, Francis Cabot Lowell. Lowell devised a mill system in which raw fiber was manufactured into cloth under a single roof. Incorporated in the 1820s, the town of Lowell drew unmarried young women, daughters of Yankee farmers, to its mill jobs. Contrary to popular belief, it was young women—not men—who first worked in manufacturing during the period of early industrialization; they pioneered in the textile mills. Why? As Howe (1978:9) comments, "men's work" in the fields was considered more valuable and irreplaceable.

Young women came from the countryside and moved into company-owned boarding houses within walking distance of the mills. These women workers were kept under strict supervision by house mothers in their living quarters and by mill managers in their workplaces. Church attendance was compulsory, and an early curfew was enforced. Hence, the mill women—America's first female industrial labor force—exchanged countryside for city, family for house mothers and mill managers, and family concern for tight social control.

The mill women also exchanged self-paced work for labor discipline and small-scale work for large-scale industrial organization. No longer did they do chores with their family unit. Now they labored side by side with hundreds of strangers from other rural communities, each one doing a small part of the whole production process.

Writings by the mill workers themselves reveal mill working conditions: poor lighting, little ventilation, noise, overcrowding, long hours (80 hours a week), and low wages. One anonymous worker describes the rhythm of her workday: "Up before day, at the clang of the bell—and out of the mill by the clang of the bell—into the mill and at work, in obedience to that ding-dong of a bell—just as though we were so many living machines" (in Eisler, 1977:161).

## New England to the New South to Offshore: More Hard Times in the Mill

Factory conditions have changed a great deal since those early days in Lowell, Massachusetts. Ironically, however, textile manufacturing represents an important exception.

Hard times in the mills for men and women (and children) have been the norm, not the exception, since the first textile mill in America was established in 1791 in Pawtucket, Rhode Island: "The huge sprawling textile industry has a long, unhappy history of low wages, long hours, child labor, stretch-out and speed-up, company-dominated mill towns, chronic unemployment and instability" (Fowke and Glazer, [1960] 1961:69).

In the late nineteenth century, New England cotton mills started moving south to take advantage of cheaper labor. These textile mills built the New South. People from the back woods flocked into the mill towns of North Carolina and other southern states, attracted by the promise of a few dollars in their pocket every week. But soon the glamor wore thin, and local folk began singing the blues:

When I die don't bury me at all
Just hang me up on the spool room wall,
Place a knotter in my hand,
So I can spool my way to the Promised Land
I got the blues, got them Winnsboro cotton-mill
    blues. . . .

By the mid-1920s, the Piedmont (a region from southern Virginia through the central Carolinas and into northern Georgia and Alabama) had eclipsed New England as the world's primary producer of cloth and yarn (Hall, Leloudis, Korstad, Murphy, Jones, and Daly, 1987:xi). Still, wages stayed low, but the prices of shoes and food went up. When white workers followed organizers and joined unions, they were blacklisted. African-Americans had no chance to join

unions; the vast majority were excluded from textile jobs.

After World War II, more mills moved south. As a former *New York Times* White House correspondent explains it, "Yankee industrialists trooped happily down from the upcountry with their little factories and mills to find a promised land flowing with the milk and honey of tax breaks, free land, cut-rate utilities, and most importantly, a cheap, docile, undemanding and unorganized labor pool" (Wooten, 1979:10).

Not much had changed by the 1980s. In *Hard Times, Cotton Mill Girls*, Victoria Byerly gives this personal memoir of mill work in her hometown of Thomasville, North Carolina:

My work in the mill was turning the cuffs down on little girls' socks. It was the next person's job to pack them in plastic. I had to turn thousands of socks a day before I could make the production quota. Any less and I would be out of a job. Everyone arrived a few minutes early in the morning and cut lunch a few minutes short to be ready to go when the whistle blew. At the sound of the whistle it was a race with the clock as I stood using every part of my body to move rhythmically back and forth to keep the pace required for production. (1986:4)

Byerly's account of southern mill rhythms echoes the Lowell women workers' sentiments of much earlier decades.

One mill worker interviewed by Byerly, Johnny Mae Fields, expressed her feelings of being exploited and dehumanized in Kannapolis, a mill town where she worked: "Everyone is upset all the time, you know, weeping and gnashing teeth. . . . [The mill owner] is a businessman from the top of his head to his toes, and I don't think he cares what color you are, he just doesn't regard mill workers as human beings . . . you find people with long faces feeling like they're working too hard—too much for too little" (1986:6).

*Norma Rae* (1979) tells the story of the struggle to unionize a southern textile town in the 1970s. As the Oscar-winning film shows, hard times in the mill are still not gone and long forgotten. In the late 1970s, textile manufacturing was the South's dominant industry (accounting for about one-fifth of all jobs and $1.8 billion in annual sales), and it was the only major U.S. industry not significantly unionized (Conway, 1979).

Cotton mills remain important to the South's economy. For example, in North Carolina, the biggest employing state, there were 212,000 production workers with a payroll of about $365 million in 1987 (*1987 Census of Manufactures*, 1990: Table 2, Industry 2211). But after Norma Rae's struggle and Johnny Mae Fields's interview, major changes hit many southern mill towns, making hard times even harder. First, competition from offshore mills drove down wages even more. For example, in Kannapolis, the town where Johnny Mae Fields worked, mill workers were laid off and later rehired—at lower wages—to do one job: sew "Made in the USA" labels over Taiwanese labels (Byerly, 1986:7). Second, some runaway shops that moved south after the unionization of northern mills moved again, this time to nonunion locations offshore in East Asia and the Pacific Islands.

This is true of garment factories too. Ironically, many "Made in the U.S.A." labels are attached to garments "manufactured in foreign-owned factories by foreign workers" (Shenon, 1993:A1). In Saipan, for instance, workers contracted from China, the Philippines, and other Asian countries earn about half of the U.S. federal minimum wage and typically live eight to a room in barracks conditions much more cramped than those of the nineteenth-century mill women in Lowell, Massachusetts. According to *New York Times* reporter Philip Shenon, workers complain that they live in "virtual captivity" (1993:A6). In a nutshell, as the *New York Times* headlined its news story, "Saipan Sweatshops Are No American Dream."

Most Americans may be unfamiliar with the workers' exploitation; some call it "indentured servitude" or "slavery" (Shenon, 1993:A6). But anyone who visits a shopping mall will be familiar with the labels they make: "Over the last year, Arrow, Liz Claiborne, The Gap, Montgomery Ward, Geoffrey Beene, Eddie Bauer and Levi's have all made clothes on this palm-fringed island [in the northern Marianas] that is part of the American commonwealth in the Western Pacific" (Shenon, 1993:A1). This is no mom-and-pop operation either: In one year, 1992, about $279 million worth of wholesale clothing, "virtually all of it made by foreign labor," was shipped from Saipan to the United States.

**Fig. 18.1** THE MOBILITY OF CAPITAL. Money is homeless. Investment capital salutes no national, state, or local flag. All other things being equal, a mill, garment factory, or other enterprise will pick up stakes and relocate offshore if it can make products or provide services more profitably. (Richard Hedman)

## Modern Times

Unlike Saipan, the United States and other post-industrial societies have fewer and fewer people working in mills and factories. By 1970, about one-half of all job holders in the United States were working in the service-information sector. This bland statistic hides the shattered lives of individuals whose American dream became *Rusted Dreams* (Bensman and Lynch, [1987] 1988:1) when mills shut down:

Steve Szumilyas, Ron Turner, and Joe Smetlack worked together in a rolling mill at Wisconsin Steel on Chicago's Southeast Side. At 4 P.M. on Friday, March 28, 1980, Steve was working at the reheater furnace when his foreman came by with news that would shatter his world: the gates were being locked at the end of the shift; the mill was going down; 3400 steelworkers were out of a job.

Steve immediately phoned his buddies Joe and Ron (who were on vacation) to tell them what had happened. Then he went back to work, "like they asked me to," and finished out the shift.

In postindustrial society or *Techno$chaft*, more and more people work in fast-food franchises and offices, many of them factory-like in the sense that they are highly mechanized (Mills, 1951:chap. 9). Indeed, Barbara Garson (1988) calls much modern work—at McDonald's or the office—the "electronic sweatshop": Clerks are automated, and professionals are turned into clerks.

Yet whether office or factory, some significant similarities between work now and in earlier times still exist. Few people, then or now, produce things with their own tools; most workers do only a small part of the entire production process; and most work in hierarchically structured organizations.

Of course, there is great variety in the working conditions of Americans today. On the one hand, there is the skilled craftsperson who sees a job through from start to finish and the researcher who sifts data alone at her or his computer. On the other hand, there is the auto work-er who only attaches left-rear bumpers, the airline reservation clerk whose calls are monitored electronically by managers, the bureaucrat who writes memos for someone else's signature, and the McJobs waitress who takes orders from everybody.

Are people unhappy attaching left-rear bumpers or taking orders? If employed, do they feel lucky to have work, no matter how boring? Does the assembly line inevitably lead to meaninglessness because it breaks up jobs into tiny pieces, with each person performing a highly specialized task? Is high-tech office work dehumanizing? We now turn to such questions, noting how the structure and organization of work affect the individual's feeling about his or her work.

## Alienation

As societies shift from economies based on agriculture and small-scale cottage industries to relatively simple industrial economies (symbolized by Lowell, Massachusetts) or to more complex industrial organization, many changes take place in the nature of work.

Usually, the location, scale, type, and nature of work are transformed. First, the location of work (and residence) changes. In preindustrial economies, much work must take place on or near agricultural land. Without machine-powered transport and other advanced technology, people extract a living from their natural environment and live near it. Productive activities do not cluster in cities; they are decentralized in villages and small towns. Indeed, big cities were the exception in preindustrial Europe and America. In contrast, work activities in industrial societies arise in and cluster in urban areas. Raw materials, labor to transform them into a finished product, and transport to move them become concentrated in cities. Some scholars predict that

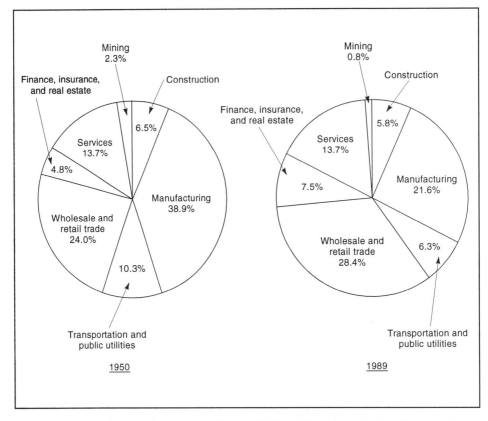

**Fig. 18.2**   PRIVATE INDUSTRY JOBS, EXCLUDING AGRICULTURE, 1950 and 1989. (Bureau of Labor Statistics)

much work will again become decentralized in the postindustrial society; they argue that fast transport and new communications technologies will permit many people to work and live in small towns and rural places.

Second, the type of work changes. In preindustrial societies, the majority of people are engaged in primary-sector activities—farming, mining, fishing, and other extractive activities. In industrial economies, secondary-sector activities—transforming raw materials into manufactured products—dominate. In postindustrial economies, tertiary-sector activities—services and information—dominate. That the United States is well into postindustrialism is indicated by a few statistics. Before 1980, American Telephone & Telegraph (AT&T), an information-based company, became the first U.S. company in the nation's history to have assets of over $100 billion. It also employed almost 1 million people, more than the nation's largest industrial firm, General Motors.

Third, the scale of work changes. The family farm or the thirteen-person bakery is no longer the typical production unit. Even the textile mills of Lowell are small by the standards of today's auto assembly plant.

Finally, the nature of work changes. In predindustrial societies, people do not have much mastery over nature, but they do exercise some control over their work process. In handicraft and cottage industries, for instance, artisans own the tools of their trade, have a tradition of craftsmanship, work at their own pace, and introduce some variation into their products. Compare that situation with modern industry, exemplified by the assembly line. The left-rear bumper attacher has no discretion over how or where to place the bumper on the car; the pace of work and the product are standardized, and "the care of tools and machinery is divorced from the pride of ownership" (Bendix, [1956] 1963:204). In modern industry, the worker has little control over the work process at any level—from macro decisions about what product will be made or how much it will cost down to decisions concerning the pace of work, the arrangement of work space, or what tools are used. These conditions of industrial labor produce standardized products efficiently. And according to many observers, they also produce alienated human beings—powerless people who feel estranged from their work and themselves.

Karl Marx was the first theorist to focus on alienating work. In the *Economic and Philosophic Manuscripts of 1844*, Marx began to investigate the concept of **alienation**, and his ideas have exerted a powerful influence ever since on Marxists and non-Marxists alike (Figure 18.3). In fact, the term *alienation* has entered the social scientist's general vocabulary, regardless of discipline or ideological bent. However, not all theorists agree with Marx on its definition or causes. According to Marx, alienation is not part of industrial production per se. It is inevitable only under a certain kind of social organization of industrial work—capitalist production.

Here is how he came to this conclusion. To Marx, human history proceeds in developmental stages: from primitive communities to slave states to feudalism and then to capitalist systems. Under European feudalism (the productive system preceding capitalism), serfs' labor was not seen as a commodity to be bought and sold in the marketplace; a paternalistic relationship operated between manor lord and serfs, with obligations recognized on both sides. Goods and services in the feudal system were produced mainly for personal use and local markets. Then, during the sixteenth century, a new mode of production began to undermine serfdom and the rural manor system of European feudalism: commercial

capitalism. As the new class of merchant capitalists grew, so did trade, market exchanges, and towns. Over the course of several hundred years, commercial (or mercantile) capitalism developed into industrial capitalism. By the mid-nineteenth century, the transformation to industrial capitalism was complete.

In Marx's view, it was this mode of production, capitalism, that inevitably led to the worker's alienation. For the first time in human history, people became wage laborers, selling their labor on the open market just like any other commodity. According to Marx, this transformed people into commodities, dehumanizing and depersonalizing them.

To illustrate how Marx viewed the process of alienation, let's return to the example of Lowell, Massachusetts. Marx would have viewed it something like this: Mr. Lowell buys the labor of young women, puts it to work, and treats it like any other tool of production (e.g., a machine). This labor force—or human labor power—then becomes the source of value to Mr. Lowell, just like any other machine. How? By producing surplus value. Workers in Lowell's mill put in a thirteen-hour day. But they produce enough to pay for their own food, shelter, and other needs in only four or five hours; this is necessary work time. During the remaining working hours, the worker produces a surplus product, over and above what she or he requires to meet personal needs. This surplus product is pure profit for the employer.

To Marx, private ownership of the means of production is the highest form of alienation. Marx reasoned as follows: Private ownership of the factories and other means of production results in the labor of the many being transformed into the capital of the few. It means that the very essence of human beings (*Homo faber*: people as producers)—the creative act of work—is transformed into a possession of someone else, the capitalist employer. In this way, what formerly belonged to human beings (the products of their labor) is taken away and "alienated" from them, the rightful owners. This leaves workers dispossessed. They own nothing—neither the tools of their trade nor the finished product. In the end,

Marx wonders: where does the product of the workingman's labour end up?

BY HIS LABOUR, A WORKER MAKES SOMETHING (CLOTH, MACHINERY, TYRES, BOOKS, HOUSES...). BUT THIS OBJECT, BY THE FACT OF REMAINING THE BOSS'S PROPERTY, TURNS <u>HEY PRESTO!</u> INTO MERCHANDISE (A <u>COMMODITY</u>)...

LABOUR OBVIOUSLY DOESN'T PRODUCE THINGS FOR THE IMMEDIATE BENEFIT OF THE WORKER WHO MAKES THEM. RATHER, IT IS GRIST FOR SOMEONE ELSE'S MILL...

Alienation begins with the worker being squeezed dry...

"...THE ALIENATION OF THE WORKER IS EXPRESSED THUS: THE MORE HE PRODUCES, THE LESS HE CAN CONSUME; THE MORE VALUE HE CREATES, THE LESS VALUE HE HAS... LABOUR PRODUCES FABULOUS THINGS FOR THE RICH, BUT MISERY FOR THE POOR. MACHINES REPLACE LABOUR, AND JOBS DIMINISH, WHILE OTHER WORKERS TURN INTO MACHINES..."

(Marx: "Manuscripts of 1844")

(This is how alienation makes its victims...)

ALIENATION NOT ONLY DEGRADES MAN, BUT ALSO DE-PERSONALISES HIM. WHAT CAN YOU EXPECT?

MARX STATES: THE BOSS IMPOSES THE KIND OF WORK, THE METHOD AND THE RHYTHM, BUT HE NEVER BOTHERS IF THE WORKER ENDS UP AS:

A mere appendage of flesh on a machine of iron...

(Marx)

**Fig. 18.3** ALIENATION À LA MARX. (Rius, *Marx for Beginners* [New York: Pantheon, 1978], p. 79. English translation © 1976 by Richard Appignanesi. Originally published in English in Great Britain by Writers and Readers Publishing Cooperative. Reprinted by permission of Pantheon Books, a Division of Random House, Inc.)

people become alienated not only from their own products but also from themselves. It is this process of capitalist industrial production that degrades and depersonalizes humans. Only capitalism's replacement by a new mode of production, socialism, can establish an unalienated relationship between worker and work.

Non-Marxists as well as Marxists have quarreled with Marx's interpretation of the causes of alienation as well as its potential cure. Most notably, sociologist Max Weber argued that the mode of production in modern society has little impact on alienation. In his view, bureaucracy, the state, and large-scale industrial organization are inherently alienating, whether capitalist or socialist. Following Weber, others argue that Chinese workers assembling autos or pushing pens in factory-like offices will become just as alienated from work and themselves as their counterparts in Lordstown or Washington. Given this premise—that bureaucracy and hierarchy are the real culprits, no matter who owns the means of production—the cures offered to end alienation range from ending hierarchy (Thayer, 1973) to living in voluntary simplicity within smaller, more self-sufficient communities (Satin, 1978) to building networks of worker-owned and -operated businesses (Morrison, 1991).

Much social research shows that inherently alienating tendencies do exist in the techniques of modern manufacturing and bureaucratic organization. For instance, a sociological study of textile work, auto assembly, print shops, and chemical plants by Robert Blauner (1964) contends that alienation is built into industrial work. Yet, Blauner argues, the organization of work can mitigate some of technology's effects. Technological imperatives of the auto industry may dictate a certain kind of work—fast and fragmented—but the reorganization of work (e.g., job rotation) may minimize some alienating features.

At the same time, a series of studies claims that modern work is not the outcome of autonomous technical processes. For one, Richard C. Edwards argues in *Contested Terrain* (1979) that the first large business corporations depended on hierarchical control over workers; this system of delegated authority made first-line supervisors

(foremen) into petty tyrants over workers, often beyond the control of their bosses. To curb the first-line supervisor's power, employers turned to another form of control: technical control, embedded in the design of production itself. Instead of obeying first-line supervisors, workers obeyed the dictates of the assembly-line process itself. In other words, the specific design of machines prestructured the work. First-line supervisors thus became mere enforcers of prestructured work (see also Noble, 1977). Edwards thinks that most industrial workers still work under this system but that modern companies, like IBM and Polaroid, use a more subtle system of control, *bureaucratic control*. Here, domination is also hidden—but it is not in the machines: "Supervisors and workers alike become subject to the dictates of 'company policy.' Work becomes highly stratified, and impersonal rules govern promotion." Other writers (e.g., Braverman, 1974) argue that modern work has been systematically degraded not only on the assembly line but also in clerical work, retail jobs, and the service trades.

Can work be made more fulfilling and less alienating? Many think that job enrichment and flextime can make a difference. Whether such programs actually humanize work is much debated. Many argue that they are empty gestures because work can't be humanized until attitudes toward authority and hierarchy outside of work change radically (Shrank, 1978).

Others think that workers' cooperatives may make a real difference. In Spain's Basque region, for instance, there is a network of more than 170 worker-owned and -operated cooperatives serving over 100,000 people in the town and surrounding area of Mondragon. Essentially, Mondragon is an experiment in social reconstruction through cooperative community based on cooperative entrepreneurship. It runs on several principles of democracy and self-management, including one member, one vote and the pursuit of *equilibrio*, a word meaning "balance" and "a vital process that harmonizes and balances a diverse and growing community of interests: those of the individual and the co-op, the particular co-op and the co-op system, and the co-op system and the community and environment" (Morrison, 1991:4). In the United States, a spate of workers' co-ops appeared in the 1960s and 1970s as part of larger social movements. By 1975, there were about 5,000 co-ops (Rothschild and Whitt, 1986:11) providing everything from cornbread and cheese to health care. In one case study, ethnographer Ann Arnett Ferguson (1991:112) concludes that the twenty members of the Wholly Grains bakery collective share two basic organizational principles: worker control and a minimal division of labor.

This brings us back to familiar challenges, encountered by the ancient Greeks as well as present-day societies: Can there be experts without gross social inequalities? Is it possible to have both extreme task specialization and democracy? Is most work doomed to be alienating and meaningless in the complex division of labor? The nineteenth-century French sociologist Emile Durkheim wrote about these issues from a different angle than his German contemporary Marx.

## The Anomic Division of Labor

Sociologist Emile Durkheim ([1893] 1966) theorized that, under normal conditions in organically solid society, the complex division of labor

**Fig. 18.4** THE CHEESEBOARD, A WORKERS' COOPERATIVE. Started in the 1960s by owner-workers, this bread and cheese shop in Berkeley, California, is still going strong. It offers age-based discounts, with consumers 100 years old getting free cheese. According to Steve Sucher, one of the owner-workers, "We pride ourselves on being the only bakery in the country to close on May Day." Some joke that they serve a body politic divided into radical minds and bourgeois stomachs. (Barbara Cohen)

would bring people together in a way that would make them feel interdependent (Chapter 5). However, Durkheim warned that under abnormal conditions an **anomic division of labor** could occur, disrupting social solidarity. If extreme specialization of function goes hand in hand with a decrease in communication between people doing different specialized tasks, then an anomic division of labor results. In this situation, individuals become isolated from each other, separated by lack of understanding. In turn, this lack of communication leads to a lack of rules that define and regulate relationships among individuals, each performing a specialized job.

Durkheim's example of the anomic division of labor was the conflict between management and labor during the early stages of industrialization. At that time there were few agreed-on rules governing their relationship. We might extend Durkheim's concept and apply it to other aspects of contemporary work. For instance, many workers now feel that their work is not only boring but meaningless. They don't see how their specialized task matters to the rest of society. Like characters in Charlie Chaplin's film *Modern Times* (1936), they feel like so many cogs in a machine. A bank clerk turned firefighter put it like this:

[T]he firemen, you actually see them produce. You see them put out a fire. You see them come out with babies in their hands. You see them give mouth-to-mouth when a guy's dying. . . . That's real. To me that's what I want to be. I worked in a bank. You know, it's just paper. It's not real. You're lookin' at numbers. But I can look back and say, "I helped put out a fire. I helped save somebody." It shows something I did on this earth. (in Terkel, 1975:589)

The anomic division of labor may be hastened in postindustrial society. The gaps between expert groups and lay publics are growing wider. Communities with common values and common goals are based increasingly on occupation. Such occupationally based communities—academics, doctors, race-car drivers, and so on—often discourage communication with outsiders by speaking and writing in esoteric jargon and monopolizing their expertise instead of sharing it widely. This trend does not bode well for a dem-

ocratic society. Nor does it encourage a sense of mutual interdependence.

*To conclude:* Industrial work, for disputed reasons, can lead to alienation from self, others, and the products of one's labor. Under certain conditions, industrial organization can also lead to an anomic division of labor in which people lack a feeling of mutual interdependence and believe that their work lacks social meaning.

In the United States, traditionally alienating work such as auto assembly has been fading away, eliminated by technological change and global competition. This means that more and more people are service and white-collar workers, producing paper, ideas, and services instead of manufactured goods.

Does it follow, then, that most work is becoming more satisfying in the postindustrial economy? Probably not, as Max Weber might have predicted. For Weber, Marx was right about the wage worker being separated from the products of his or her labor, but Marx did not go far enough. Weber thought that wage workers represented only one case of a universal trend toward bureaucratization. In other words, it is argued, when white-collar workers function in a bureaucratic system, they encounter a machine "as soulless as . . . machines made of iron and steel" (Simone Weil in Upjohn Institute, 1973:39). Already many white-collar workers in lower-echelon jobs complain of white-collar woes: boring, dull, routine jobs. Those with a college education and high expectations for self-fulfillment through work are particularly prone to high turnover and subtle forms of sabotage.

## Worker Satisfaction, Overwork, and Stress

Today's stressed administrative assistants, hoping they will not come down with repetitive motion sickness or other illnesses from word processing eight hours a day, are not in the same position as characters in a Charles Dickens novel who toiled from dawn to dusk for starvation wages. Nor are airline reservation clerks of the 1990s like the Lowell mill women of the 1840s,

**Table 18.1**  U.S. Census Bureau Occupation Classification System

**Executive, administrative, and managerial occupations**
1. Officials and administrators, public administration (e.g., CEOs)
2. Management-related occupations (auditors, buyers, etc.).
3. Officials and other administrators (e.g., public relations managers, education and health administrators; postmasters; funeral directors)

**Professional specialty occupations**
1. Engineers and natural scientists
2. Health diagnosing occupations
3. Health assessment and treating occupations
4. Teachers, librarians, and counselors
5. Other professional specialty occupations (e.g., sociologists, urban planners, photographers, clergy, reporters)

**Technicians and related support occupations**
1. Health technologists and technicians
2. Technologists and technicians, except health (e.g., air traffic controllers, airplane pilots, computer programmers)

**Sales occupations**
1. Supervisors and proprietors
2. Sales representatives, commodities, and finance
3. Other sales occupations (e.g., cashiers, news vendors, retail sales workers)

**Administrative support occupations, including clerical**
1. Computer equipment operators
2. Secretaries, stenographers, and typists
3. Financial records processing occupations
4. Mail and message distributing occupations (e.g., mail carriers)
5. Other administrative support occupations

**Private household occupations**
Examples: cooks, child care workers, household cleaners

**Protective service occupations**
1. Police and fire fighters

2. Other protective service occupations (e.g., sheriffs, guards)

**Service occupations, except protective and household**
1. Food service occupations (e.g., cooks, bartenders)
2. Cleaning and building service occupations (e.g., pest controllers, janitors)
3. Health and personal service occupations (e.g., dental assistants, baggage porters, hospital orderlies)

**Farming, forestry, and fishing occupations**
1. Farm operators and managers
2. Farm workers and related occupations (e.g., gardners, animal caretakers)

**Precision production, craft, and repair occupations**
1. Mechanics and repairers
2. Construction trades
3. Precision production occupations (e.g., precision textile and apparel machine workers)
4. Extractive occupations (e.g., miners, oil well drillers)

**Machine operators, assemblers, and inspectors**
1. Machine operators and tenders, except precision (e.g., paint spraying, motion picture projectionists, textile machine operators)
2. Fabricators, assemblers, inspectors, and samplers (e.g., welders, painters)

**Transportation and material moving occupations**
1. Transportation occupations
2. Motor vehicle operators
3. Rail and water transportation occupations
4. Material moving equipment operators

**Handlers, equipment cleaners, helpers, and laborers**
1. Construction laborers
2. Freight, stock, and material handlers (e.g., garbage collectors, stevedores)
3. Other handlers, equipment cleaners, helpers, and laborers

SOURCE: U.S. Bureau of the Census, *1980 Census of Population, General Social and Economic Characteristics, United States Summary* (Washington, D.C.: Government Printing Office, 1983), Appendix B, pp. 14–16.

closely supervised at home as well as in the workplace. Still, worker dissatisfaction remains widespread.

A generation ago, the *majority* of American workers reported that they were not satisfied with their work. Taking a look at *Work in America* (Upjohn Institute, 1973:16), a special task force found that only 43 percent of **white-collar** work-

ers and only 23 percent of **blue-collar** workers would choose to do similar work again (16). (The study's authors report that whether a worker would again choose the same work is the best single indicator of job satisfaction.)

In general, the U.S. Department of Health, Education, and Welfare (HEW) task force found that white-collar workers in the professional and technical category (as defined by the U.S. Census Bureau) reported higher levels of job satisfaction than did other groups. Interestingly, urban university professors were the single most satisfied occupational group surveyed; 93 percent said that they would do the same work again (1973:16). By contrast, auto-assembly workers were the least satisfied. The task force reports that only 16 percent would choose to redo the same work, and another study (Garson, 1973: 173) reports that no auto workers—0 percent— would choose the same work again. (*Note:* U.S. census categories have changed somewhat since the HEW task force collected its data. After the 1970 census, the Census Bureau dropped the categories of white- and blue-collar, farm workers, and service workers as the chief occupational divisions. It has never recognized the category **pink collar**, a popular term referring to jobs performed mainly by women such as housecleaning and waiting tables. Table 18.1 details U.S. census occupational categories now in use.)

Ironically, many of those desperately dissatisfied workers in the 1970s no longer have the option of doing the same work. Hundreds of thousands of auto workers, the most dissatisfied group, lost jobs during U.S. deindustrialization. Now, if they can find a job at all, it is likely to be just as unsatisfying—and lower paying.

While job satisfaction is down, stress and overwork are up. A Harris poll found that Americans think their work hours rose 20 percent while their leisure time fell about 32 percent between 1973 and 1988. This is particularly the case for working women. One study found that employed mothers, in addition to their work outside the home, do almost as much domestic labor as nonworking mothers (Kotz, 1988:17).

Neither the mental nor the manual laborer is immune to stress. Ten of the most stressful jobs, according to the National Institute on Workers Compensation, are the following: inner-city high-school teacher, police officer, miner, air-traffic controller, medical intern, stockbroker, journalist, customer service–complaint department worker, waitress, and secretary.

In general, job satisfaction is linked to type of work and occupational status. Specifically, mental laborers (like Reich's "symbolic analysts") are more satisfied than manual laborers. Further, job satisfaction is linked to social status; the higher the status of an occupation, the more satisfied are its practitioners. High pay and high job satisfaction also tend to go together. However, this relationship is unclear because most highly paid jobs also rank high in other characteristics valued by workers (e.g., social esteem, job autonomy, challenge of the work itself).

Why, then, is it that some relatively low-paid and low-prestige work does not produce job dissatisfaction? To illuminate this complex issue, let's examine two groups of very satisfied workers, one midway on the prestige ladder (daily journalists) and one near the bottom (garbage collectors).

## Brief Case Studies: Daily Journalists and Garbage Collectors

*Daily Journalists* With the exception of TV personalities, daily news reporters and editors have only a moderate amount of social esteem. Yet unlike most contemporary American workers, journalists working on local daily newspapers or

**Table 18.2**  The Most and Least Secure Jobs in the 1990s

| *Highest Unemployment Rates in 1990* | *Lowest Unemployment Rates in 1990* |
|---|---|
| Construction labor (18.1%) | Air-traffic controller (0.0%) |
| Construction helper (17.2%) | Supervisor, police and detective (0.0%) |
| Short-order cook (14.2%) | Pharmacist (0.2%) |

SOURCE: U.S. Bureau of Labor Statistics, 1990, in David Wallenchinsky and Amy Wallace, "High and Low Unemployment Rates," *San Francisco Chronicle* (May 15, 1991):B3.

television and radio newscasts enjoy their work. Indeed, one survey of journalists working in nonelite news organizations (i.e., organizations unlike the *New York Times* or national TV networks) reveals that less than 1 percent would choose not to do similar work again (Phillips, 1975). At the same time, most of these same journalists feel underpaid, and a considerable number dislike the bureaucratic organizations they work for. Then why are they so happy in their work?

The answers seem to be related to the nature of the work itself. One reason is that daily reporters and editors view their work as nonroutine. Another is that they feel mentally challenged by it, having a chance to be creative and to constantly learn. In addition, they perceive themselves as having a great deal of autonomy on the job. To a participant-observer, this may not seem the case at all, for journalists work within hierarchically structured organizations that, to an outsider, often suppress initiative. But the news workers themselves do not feel that they work under crushing constraints of bureaucratic, institutional, and stylistic pressures. They don't feel hemmed in—no time clocks to punch, no specific amount of work to do, and no absolute standards of performance. Instead, they tend to judge themselves by professional standards of inner quality controls. Finally, the craft of journalism promotes a sense of participation in events. Journalists feel that the stories they write, film, edit, or broadcast have some public impact. Thus it seems that craft-related factors (nonroutine work, political efficacy, participation in events, etc.) account for daily journalists' high level of job satisfaction.

What's fascinating is that the journalists' relative lack of alienation from work is not dependent on their social background. Whether young or old, people of color or white, conservative or liberal, married or single, female or male, professionally trained or not, they like their work (despite their cynical, hard-boiled image). Their positive attitude toward work and the society in which they work seems to grow out of the journalistic craft itself (Phillips, 1975).

**Garbage Collectors**  Journalists practice "clean" work (i.e., mental rather than manual labor), which they generally find intellectually stimulating. But what about those who do society's "dirty" work? One highly paid steel worker in Illinois says that "it's hard to take pride in a bridge you're never gonna cross, in a door you're never gonna open." For him, the problem isn't the fact that his work is dirty, but that he feels no sense of contributing to society, no sense of achievement (in Terkel, 1975:2).

The steel worker's comment suggests that the social meaning of work—not necessarily the work itself—is important for individuals. Empirical support for this assertion comes from a study of society's dirtiest work: garbage collection.

For more than ten years, sociologist Stewart E. Perry followed the history of an Italian-American cooperative of garbage collectors. By working their routes with them, talking, and visiting, Perry sought to answer some fundamental questions about the nature of work and worker satisfaction. What Perry (1978) found was a foul-smelling, back-breaking occupation, but one that did not necessarily alienate its practitioners. The men he studied, members of the Sunset Scavenger Company in San Francisco, were not dissatisfied with their work. Perry attributes the garbage collectors' positive attitude toward their dirty work to the collective ownership and policymaking of the company. A private corporation, Sunset is owned by the workers themselves. They collect dividends and actively participate in setting company policy. Of the 315 active partners at the time of Perry's study, all but 18 were still working the trucks, and the company's president received the same wage as the men on the trucks.

According to Perry, it is pride of ownership that accounts primarily for the garbage collectors' lack of alienation from work. As one scavenger told him, "a man walks through this yard here [at the Sunset Scavenger Company] and says, 'I own a piece of this; this is mine.'"

*To conclude:* These brief case studies raise theoretical issues important for the quality of urban life and the redesign of urban work. The case of the Sunset Scavengers suggests that no work—even society's dirtiest work—is inherently alienating; it implies that lack of control over work and/or lack of ownership are the roots of alienation. But the case of the journalists suggests a very different notion: that some work is intrinsically challenging and satisfying. Even if journalists work in hierarchically structured organizations, have little objective control over work, and share no monetary profits with the owners, they don't feel a sense of meaninglessness or powerlessness. Perhaps the *illusion* of control is key here, for to an outside researcher, the actual control exercised by daily journalists seems limited.

These issues remain unsettled. Few answers to the issue of job alienation are evident, although the number of thinkers about work (and the leisure time to think about it) has never been greater. Radical intellectuals, particularly Marxists, are going through a profound crisis of thought that turns primarily on the question of whether or not bureaucracy is inherently alienating. Ultraconservatives (e.g., de Lesquen and le Club de l'horloge, 1979) are returning to ideas best suited to a preindustrial, aristocratic society. Conservatives tend to believe that most people need close supervision and hierarchical control; this is what organization theorist Douglas McGregor (in Bennis, 1970) calls the *Theory X* of human behavior. In contrast, liberals tend to subscribe to what McGregor calls the *Theory Y* of human behavior: that work is natural and that most people will work hard if they have a chance to fulfill their human potential.

And yes, there is a *Theory Z*. Developed by UCLA professor William G. Ouchi, it refers to a participative management style common in Japan. A Theory Z company assumes "that any worker's life is a whole, not a Jekyll–Hyde personality, half machine from nine to five and half human in the hours preceding and following. Theory Z suggests that humanized working conditions not only increase productivity and profits to the company but also the self-esteem for employees" (Ouchi, [1981] 1982:165). A group of sociologists at Indiana University (Hodson, Welsh,

and Rieble, 1993) see positive benefits to workers from participation and team organization, but Theory Z remains very controversial. In the United States, Theory Z is criticized by radicals as a company-oriented philosophy masquerading as workplace democracy, inspiring employee loyalty without giving workers any real control. Further, recent decisions by the National Labor Relations Board make some aspects of Theory Z culture (e.g., employee committees) illegal. Finally, in Japan, the linchpin of Japan's system of employer–employee loyalty—lifetime employment—is falling victim to corporate layoffs and plant closings. As Japanese workers in factories and executive suites get *kata tataki* ("the tap on the shoulder"—that is, fired), Theory Z may not be far behind as a management ideology.

## LOCAL OCCUPATIONAL STRUCTURES

Let's shift now from the impact of work on the individual to its impact on an entire community. This means looking at the occupational structures of individual cities, suburbs, and post-suburban areas.

### The Relationship of Jobs to Social Climate and Governance

A community's occupational profile—that is, a snapshot of its employment mix—gives clues to its social character, its economic vitality, and even its recreational facilities. This kind of information is useful to scholars, policymakers, and potential investors. It can also be helpful in our everyday lives. For instance, suppose that you find yourself in the enviable position of being able to choose from among five equally attractive job offers in as many communities. How will you choose? For the sake of argument, let's say that you don't care about the city's physical climate, but you do care about its cultural-aesthetic facilities. The cultural climate you pre-fer, of course, depends on your personal tastes and background. But whatever scenes you favor (country music bars, soul food restaurants, body-building gyms, mega-malls, coffee houses with computers, union meetings, bowling alleys, etc.), you can get some idea if they exist by ex-amining a community's occupational profile. (You won't be able to get a total picture without sorting through additional data on the particu-lar kinds of goods and services produced in your potential hometown, but we'll return to that later.)

If an industry dominates a community, say, textiles or software design, it will be reflected in that area's social climate. But no table of census data can reveal the relationship between what a city or postsuburban area produces and how that place looks and feels. Only a thorough ground-ing in economic and cultural history can provide such insight (e.g., the textile industry's resistance to unionization, the computer professionals' preference for bicycling over bowling, and the lack of attention to city beautification in older auto-plant towns).

Also, the composition of a community's labor force has some bearing on its governmental structure. City council–manager government ap-pears more often in white-collar towns than in blue-collar towns. The employment mix also has some bearing on informal power structures. More specifically, we can expect different pat-terns of influence in textile-based Gastonia, North Carolina, and high-technology, profes-sional Menlo Park, California.

Returning to Logan and Molotch's typology outlined in Chapter 4, we can see that the occu-pational mix of a city has important, sometimes grave, implications for an urban area's vitality. For instance, without a massive conversion from war preparation to peacetime uses, an "innovation center" such as Silicon Valley in northern California suffers a much more severe economic downturn from the end of the cold war (and the drying up of defense contracts) than, say, a retirement center or a headquarters city.

## CHANGING U.S. EMPLOYMENT PATTERNS

In the 1950s, for the first time in human history, more people in a single nation were thinking about things, managing things, and communicat-ing about things than actually producing things. Most, but not all, theorists agree that this mo-mentous shift, made possible by advanced tech-nology, signaled the emergence of postindustrial society. (For a dissenting opinion, see Scott, 1988.) As discussed in other chapters, in the United States this transformation led to regional shifts (from Frostbelt to Sunbelt), intrametro-politan shifts (from central city to outside central city), and shifts from primary-sector economic activities (which provide the basic raw materials for existence, such as agriculture, fishing, min-ing, and forestry) and secondary-sector activities (which transform primary raw materials into fin-ished goods) to tertiary-sector activities (consist-ing of services, wholesale and retail trade, infor-mation processing, communication, utilities, finance, insurance, public services and govern-ment, real estate, and transportation).

Some effects of postindustrialism, combined with impacts of global restructuring, can be seen with the naked eye, notably abandoned factories dotting the inner-city landscape. But other im-pacts are invisible or harder to see; these include the decline in union membership and the rise in demand for highly skilled workers. Here, let's examine two of these hard-to-see phenomena: (1) temporary or contingent work and (2) dual cities.

### Contingent or Temporary Work

Not long ago, Apple Computer was praised by organizational theorists as a management model of caring and sharing. In Cupertino, its Silicon Valley headquarters, Apple provided on-site child care, a generous profit-sharing plan, and many other employee perks. By 1993, however, the company were paring, cutting down on full-time employees in a shaky economy. Over 20 percent of Apple's work force were temporaries or, in Appletalk, members of the "ring"—employees on short-term contracts without health or other benefits—not the "core."

The day of the forty-hour week with benefits has vanished for millions of Americans. Replacing full-time workers are consultants, flexible workers, temps, independent contractors, contingent workers, disposables, or throwaway workers. Whatever they're called, they are everywhere—from the university classroom and the health clinic to the factory and office. And their numbers are increasing: In 1982, about 25 percent of the jobs people found were either part-time or temporary; in 1992, the figure was about 50 percent (Kilborn, 1993:1). Some may prefer part-time or temporary work; for most, however, it is involuntary.

The United States holds the world's record for multiple job holders; in 1994, 7 million Americans (about 6 percent of the work force) held 15 million jobs (Uchitelle, 1994:1). A Harvard labor economist, Richard Freeman, thinks he knows why this trend of multiple job holding is increasing: The wages from one job are insufficient (in Uchitelle, 1994:1).

Indeed, few new temporary jobs pay as well as regular jobs. Nor do they come with regular benefits. Indeed, some fear—while others praise—the rise of a new class of cheap, temporary workers, particularly in manufacturing. From the corporate point of view, the creation of a two-tier wage system (where temps get $2 to $3 less per hour than permanent employees who work alongside them) is a boon to U.S. manufacturers. According to a spokesperson for the National Association of Temporary Services, "The temps, in effect, are earning wages that are competitive with worker pay in other countries," which, he infers, helps keep jobs in the United States (Steinberg in Uchitelle, 1993:A1).

The annual payroll for the temporary work force—for both elite (professionals or other highly skilled workers) and nonelite workers—is growing. In 1991, elite temps constituted 24 percent of the 1.15 million people who make up the total temporary work force; in 1981, they constituted 14 percent of the total.

Economists say that the U.S. recession of the 1990s speeded up the shift to temporary or contingent work. Most think that the shift is permanent. One analyst predicts that by 1998, the overall temp ranks will increase by 50 percent (Scott in Diesenhouse, 1993:F5).

The shift to temporary work brings up a host of political questions as well as psychological, sociological, and economic ones. For instance, will core employees parallel core countries in the world system; that is, will they try to control their rings (periphery) in a colonial-like manner? Will U.S. labor unions, already severely weakened by global restructuring and deindustrialization, lose even more clout? How will workers adjust to much more uncertainty and instability in their work lives? How will insecurity at work affect parenting and political participation? The answers await us.

## The Dual City

The term **dual city** comes from John Mollenkopf and Manuel Castells's 1991 book of the same name. But the concept is much older. In the Western world, it dates at least to Plato's *Republic:* "Any city, however small, is in fact divided into two, one the city of the poor, the other of the rich; these are at war with one another, and in either there are many smaller divisions, and you would be altogether beside the mark if you treated them all as a single State."

Mollenkopf and Castells say that contemporary New York is such a dual city. In their view, it is "a paradoxical mix of splendor and decay"—a city composed of two separate and unequal cities where slums flourish, homelessness increases, and ethnic hostility is rife amid sumptuous office blocks with a core of mainly white male professionals and managers.

New York City prospered during the 1980s, but not all residents shared the wealth. Instead, the authors claim, residents experienced increased income inequality. Who won and who lost the most? Mollenkopf and Castells state that "the higher the income of a stratum, the faster its income grew" during the 1977 to 1986 decade (1991:400). In contrast, the real income of the bottom 10 percent decreased by nearly 11 percent. As a result, the poverty rate in New York City jumped from 19 percent to 23 percent between 1977 and 1986. The authors conclude that the city experienced "social polarization," not just inequality: "the rich are becoming richer and the poor are becoming poorer in absolute terms" (401).

Nevertheless, they say, New York's social structure is so complex that it should not be reduced to a dichotomy between rich and poor. Instead, they note that two opposing forces dominate New York City's social structure: *corporate upper professionals,* who "constitute a coherent social network" and whose interests are directly linked to the development of the city's corporate economy, versus *the remaining social strata* (e.g., an army of clerical workers; low-skilled workers; immigrant manual workers, particularly Dominicans and Chinese; a middle class based in the public sector; those outside the formal labor force). They conclude that economic, cultural, and political polarization in New York City "takes the form of a contrast between a comparatively cohesive core of professionals in the advanced corporate services and a disorganized periphery fragmented by race, ethnicity, gender, occupational and industrial location" (Mollenkopf and Castells, 1991:402).

Does the dual city typify postindustrial cities? Mollenkopf and Castells suggest that it does. Further, they tie together the social, economic, spatial, and technological aspects of postindustrial society: "The dual city is the social expression of the emerging spatial form of postindustrial society, while the global city is its economic expression, and the informational city its technological expression" (1991:415). The dominant class in dual cities, and in the postindustrial era generally, they say, is "the managerial technocracy allied to the global financial elite." This class has a key resource: "exclusive access to the most important information" (415).

*To conclude:* According to Mollenkopf and Castells, the dual city is based on the dichotomy between the "organized center" and the "disorganized peripheries." Once again, we have a core and ring, this time Big Apple style. Interestingly, world-systems theory, Appletalk, and the dual city concept share an image: a dichotomy between core and periphery (ring) that describes polarization and inequality.

Baltimore's Mayor Kurt Schmoke acknowledges the existence of dual cities. In 1994 he said that "we are not suggesting that our entire city has the same problems as a Third World country but . . . there are sections of the city that are similar to the problems of less-developed countries" (in Friedman, 1994:A2). So did the Agency for International Development (AID), the foreign assistance arm of the U.S. government; in 1994, AID shifted its focus from poor countries like Bangladesh to poor American inner cities.

## The Dual Nation

The United States is showing the same two-tier pattern as New York City. Between 1983 and 1989, the net worth of the richest 1 percent of U.S. households increased from 31 percent to 37 percent of the national total. By 1989, the top 1 percent, consisting of 834,000 households, had a net worth of about $5.7 trillion; *this 1 percent was worth more than the bottom 90 percent of Americans, 84 million households, whose net worth was about $4.8 trillion* (Nasar, 1992:A1). (*Note*: The net worth of a household is what it owns, including real estate, stocks, savings accounts, and so on, minus what it owes, such as home mortgage, credit card debt, and loans. Typically, wealth is more concentrated than income.) By 1995, the United States was the most economically unequal industrialized nation.

This two-tier pattern also holds for non-Latino whites. California illustrates this economic polarization: In 1990, more than one in five African-Americans and Latinos were classified as poor, one in seven Asian-Americans were officially poor, but fewer than one in ten whites were classified as poor.

Furthermore, the number of children in poverty suggests a pattern of growing inequality. In one year—from 1990 to 1991—the number of California children living in poverty increased by 500,000, to a total of 2.2 million. The result: One in four California children lived in poverty in 1991 (McLeod, 1993:A19).

How could this increasing pauperization of children have happened in the most populous state of the United States, a rich core nation? Conservative analysts point to the rising number of single-parent families (who are much more likely to be poor than two-parent families) and the rising number of immigrants to California during the 1980s. Liberals tend to focus on the lack of conversion to a peacetime economy that hit California's military-defense industries particularly hard, plus stagnant wages for people in low-paying jobs. Radicals tend to look at two-tier cities and nations as economic, social, and spatial expressions of postindustrial capitalism.

## POVERTY IN METROPOLITAN AREAS

Poverty and unemployment dominate the life situation of many in the "disorganized peripheries." And, as big corporate employers continue to "downsize" or "rightsize," employees in the core are not immune to pink slips and long-term joblessness. Now let's take a closer look at the **unemployed,** the **underemployed**, and the full-time **employed** who still can't survive economically in the nation's MSAs: the metropolitan poor.

### Defining Poverty

Being poor in America is largely a question of definition—official government definition. That is, if the federal government's threshold for poverty changes, millions of people can be thrown out of poverty—or into poverty—on paper. For example, the Census Bureau's statistics for 1989 show an overall poverty rate of 12.8 percent, or 31 million people. But the former chair of a con-

gressional committee on hunger says that the threshold should be raised to include destitute people. If this were done, about 44 million—not 31 million—would be considered poor. Similarly, as noted in Chapter 2, some feminist economists think that today's poverty threshhold is ridiculously low because it neglects real needs, such as child care expenses.

The current federal definition of **poverty** is based on a Social Security Administration (SSA) index. This measurement system, which originated in the work of SSA employee Mollie Orshansky, was established in 1964. It has been revised slightly over the years and is adjusted annually for inflation. Currently, most analysts use the SSA poverty definition, an absolute standard of money income. Essentially, the SSA poverty threshold is calculated by determining subsistence food costs and multiplying that figure by the number of people in the household. Households with an income below the threshold are classified as poor. In 1993, the poverty threshold for a family of four, both farm and nonfarm, was $14,279. In 1977, the average threshold for a nonfarm family of four was $6,191. (The farm–nonfarm distinction is no longer used by the Census Bureau.) Some people think that the SSA definition, which does not count nonmonetary benefits as income, overestimates the extent of poverty in the United States (while critics say that the threshhold is much too low). Experimentally, the Census Bureau has tried measures that count nonmonetary benefits; using these measures substantially reduces the number of people in poverty.

Another federal agency, the Bureau of Labor Statistics (BLS), once used the "standard budget" as a measure to describe minimum subsistence levels and above. Standard budgets are normative estimates of living costs. They take into account such items as food, housing, clothing, personal and medical care, and transportation. The BLS (U.S. Department of Labor 1976a:83) made the following assumptions in calculating the costs for lower, intermediate, and higher budgets:

The lower budget family lives in rental housing without air conditioning . . . relies heavily on public transportation, supplemented, where necessary, by the use of an older car, performs more services for itself and utilizes free recreation facilities in the community. Compared with the intermediate budget, the life style in the high budget is marked by more home ownership, high levels of new-car ownership, more household appliances and equipment, and more paid-for services.

The BLS abandoned the standard budget concept after 1981. Why? According to a BLS spokesperson, the BLS let it go "because [the standard budgets] badly needed updating and there was no money in the [BLS] budget" (Hoyle, 1993). Perhaps. There may be another, more political reason: Using the BLS lower budget, many more persons—millions more—would be defined as poor or living at the subsistence level, and no administration gains public relations points from an increase in national poverty. In 1974, for example, the BLS figured the annual costs of a lower budget for a four-person family in a metropolitan area at $9,323; the poverty threshhold based on SSA standards for a family of four was figured at a little more than one-half of that figure—$5,038. Had the BLS measure been used, the number of people at or below the subsistence level would have greatly increased.

Some radical critics of government poverty measures maintain that the standard should be based on *relative* rather than *absolute* guidelines. These critics argue that being poor in America can be measured only in comparison with being rich. Following this logic, families earning less than a BLS higher budget standard would be classified as poor.

Some liberal critics say that the assumptions of the SSA are outdated. Because families today spend much more for housing, the formula should be based on housing, not food. Doing so would raise the poverty threshold about 50 percent.

Other critics think that nondollar measures should be included in measuring poverty. The National Academy of Sciences recommends that poverty be based on disposable income (the cash and *noncash* benefits left after a family pays essential expenses and taxes). Using this measure, there would be higher poverty rates for families

lacking health insurance and lower rates for families receiving public assistance. The Children's Defense Fund uses rates of immunization against preventable disease, infant mortality rates, and the incidence of malnutrition. Using these measures of health and well-being, it finds that the percentage of malnourished children is higher in the United States than in Somalia, where U.S. troops were dispatched to bring food to the starving (in Johnson, 1992:A12).

Social scientists John E. Schwarz and Thomas J. Volgy (1992) argue for different measures of minimum economic self-sufficiency because, they think, the SSA poverty line is much too low. Former president Jimmy Carter (1993) has a simpler measure: "Anyone who has a house now is considered rich [by those who don't]."

Using the the official yardstick, the SSA income threshold, how many Americans are poor? The nationwide total in 1978 was 24.5 million, or 11.4 percent of the population. In 1991, the nationwide total was 35.7 million, and the percentage had climbed to 14.2 percent of the population (U.S. Bureau of the Census, 1992: Table A). Here are a few breakdowns by age and race/ethnicity: In 1991, one in five poor persons was a child. The poverty rate for whites rose to 11.3 percent. For African-Americans, the poverty rate increased to 32.7 percent, and for Latinos, it rose to 28.7 percent. For Asian-Americans, the poverty rate also rose, to 13.8 percent in 1991.

*To conclude:* How poverty is defined and measured has serious economic and political consequences. If, for example, poverty statistics reflected cost of living differences, the flow of federal funds would increase to higher-cost areas, such as New York City, and decrease to lower-cost areas, such as Mississippi. Indeed, poverty statistics affected how at least $22 billion in federal money was distributed in 1994 for a variety of local programs, including child nutrition (Pear, 1994:A1).

## Who Are the Metropolitan Poor?

Where do the poor live? As has historically been the case, in 1991 the nonmetropolitan poverty rate (16.1 percent) was higher than that of metro-politan areas (13.7 percent). Also, as in the past, the poor were concentrated in metropolitan areas (75.1 percent). Within MSAs, the poverty rate in-side central cities (20.2 percent) was more than twice the rate outside central cities (9.6 percent).

Who are the poor? Disproportionately, they are African-American, Latino, Southeast Asian, female heads of families with no husband pre-sent, and children. According to the U.S. Census Bureau, in 1991 the poverty rate was 9.4 percent for whites not of Latino origin; 32.7 percent for African-Americans; 13.8 percent for Asians and Pacific Islanders; and 28.7 percent for people of Latino origin (of any race). More than one-third of female householders without husbands pre-sent (35.6 percent) lived below the poverty line. Among African-Americans, more than 50 per-cent of female householders without husbands present were officially poor. About 50 percent of both African-American and Latino-origin familes with a female householder and no husband pre-sent were below the poverty level in 1991 (U.S. Bureau of the Census, 1992:xiii). More than 30 percent of all Cambodian, Laotian, and Viet-namese households in the United States "lan-guish in poverty, giving Southeast Asians the highest rate of welfare dependency of any racial or ethnic group" (Dunn, 1994:A1).

How many persons work full time and still fall below the poverty level? In total, in 1991, over 2 million people. Despite popular stereotypes, "most poor people work for a living and do not live in inner-city ghettos" (Capistrano, 1992:6). According to Schwarz and Volgy, these are *The Forgotten Americans* (1992): the nation's 30 million working poor.

Before continuing, a few reminders on statis-tics are needed. First, as noted earlier, there is an active off-the-books, or underground, economy in the United States. This means that people—perhaps more than 6 million—earn cash but don't report it for income tax purposes. The im-plication is that many classified as unemployed and/or poor may not be. Second, census takers tend to undercount the urban poor. This has seri-ous results for cities, particularly for the distribu-tion of federal funds based on the number of persons below the poverty line. Finally, the method of measuring employment and unem-ployment probably needs revision. Sar Levitan, chair of a national commission on employment statistics, said years ago that they "come close to being straight random numbers" at the local lev-el (in Shabecoff, 1978:19). Since this is the level at which federal public employment funds are allo-cated, the numbers game is crucial to cities. Fur-ther, Levitan questions whether sixteen- and seventeen-year-olds who are full-time students and look for a job a few hours per week should really be counted as part of the labor force, which they still are. Meanwhile, the plaque on Levitan's office wall provides the proper cautionary note: "Statistics Are No Substitute for Good Judg-ment."

*To conclude:* In the early 1990s, the metro-politan poor tended to be (1) concentrated inside central cities rather than around them and (2) disproportionately female, African-American, Southeast Asian, and Latino. Children under the age of eighteen were at particular risk. In 1991, to take one year, 18.2 percent of white children, 45.4 percent of African-American children, and 40.1 percent of children of Latino origin fell below the poverty line. Furthermore, the percentage of chil-dren living in poverty increased faster in suburbs than in central cities or rural areas: From 1973 to 1992, the proportion of suburban children in poverty grew 76 percent, while that of central city children in poverty grew 56 percent and that of rural children in poverty grew 36 percent. Tufts University researchers J. Larry Brown and John T. Cook cite the following reasons for this increase: the transformation of the American economy, declining real wages, nonaffluent fami-lies' moving in relatively large numbers from central cities to suburbs, and suburban expan-sion into previously rural areas (in Associated Press, 1994:A7).

## Why Are They Poor?

Why did 36,734,000 people in the United States fall below the poverty line in 1993? Was it mainly bad luck? Bad families? Horrible housing? World conditions? It comes as no surprise that observers disagree on the causes and cures of poverty: As one reporter put it, some believe that the poor are poor because they "are oppressed (Jesse Jackson), lazy (Ronald Reagan) and seduced by the welfare state (Charles Murray). They have too many babies, and have them too soon (Daniel Patrick Moynihan). They need tax relief (Jack Kemp). They need our help (Bill Clinton). They need to help themselves (Bill Clinton, again)" (DeParle, 1993:E1).

In different eras, different notions dominate social thought. And some resurface, like old wines in new bottles. For instance, social Darwinism dominated poverty beliefs about eighty years ago. Briefly, social Darwinism held that those who reach the top of the economic ladder are the fittest, surviving and winning the struggle for existence. By implication, the poor are unfit. This idea has resurfaced in recent years with a new twist: the claim that poverty is linked to genetic inheritance. Exhaustive social research (e.g., Jencks, Smith, Acland, Bane, Cohen, Gintis, Heyns, and Michelson, 1972) shows that genes and IQ scores have relatively little effect on economic success. Still, whether social or biological, Darwinian theories of poverty die hard.

Another notion is rooted even more deeply in American thought: Anyone who works hard can succeed. In this view, anyone who wants a job can get one, work hard, and make it. Thus the poor are just lazy. The Horatio Alger stories in the period of rapid industrialization popularized this aspect of the American dream and strengthened the belief in the so-called Protestant work ethic. Again, much social research (e.g., Valentine, 1979) shows that most poor Americans prefer to work and "identify their self-esteem with work as strongly as do the nonpoor" (Goodwin, 1972:112). Recent studies point to the problem of low-paying, often unattractive work that rarely provides a long-term solution to welfare dependence (DeParle, 1994:A1). But social science findings have done little to change firm beliefs or prejudices. No matter what social scientists find, some will undoubtedly continue to believe that poor people are lazy people.

Currently, several different notions about the causes of poverty dominate academic and/or policymaking circles. Here is a brief summary of competing notions:

1. *Poverty as personal failure.* This view—that poverty is largely the result of personal failure and lower-class attitudes—is associated with political scientist Edward Banfield (1974). According to Banfield, certain psychological traits prevent the poor from changing their status. In brief, he argues that lower-class people lack typically middle-class attitudes about planning ahead, saving for a rainy day, and pursuing an education.

2. *Poverty as a culture, passed on from generation to generation.* This view, associated with the anthropologist Oscar Lewis, holds that the poor are present-time oriented and lack planning ability (as Banfield also says). But the reasons the poor act differently from the nonpoor have little to do with individual failure (as Banfield says) and much to do with the class-stratified, capitalistic societies they live in. Based on fieldwork in Latin America and the United States, Lewis (1964) argues that the poor lack the means to break the cycle of poverty. So they adapt as best they can—in a subculture set apart from other subcultures in capitalist society. This subculture—the **culture of poverty**—is transmitted from one generation to the next, making it nearly impossible to break the chains that bind.

3. *Poverty as a lack of opportunity.* This view, associated with liberals, holds that "the poor lack the skills and education to find employment in an automated society" (Campbell and Burkhead, 1968:626). Extending opportunities for the poor (without disturbing existing institutions) is the solution that follows from this stance, exemplified by the War on Poverty in the 1960s and programs such as Affirmative Action and so-called minority set-asides.

4. *Poverty as a result of racism or ethnic discrimination.* In this view, people of color are disproportionately poor because they have been systematically discriminated against in a variety of ways, both blatant and subtle, that limit

**Fig. 18.5** WHY DOES POVERTY EXIST? Theorists disagree. Radicals think that poverty is a structural feature of capitalism. Liberals say that poverty can be decreased within the existing institutional structure. Conservatives hold that poverty stems from personal failure and/or lower-class attitudes. (Margaret Bourke-White, *Life* magazine. © 1937 Time, Inc.)

opportunities. Being disadvantaged is expressed in myriad ways, from being turned down for a bank loan to being turned down for membership in exclusive clubs where business is done over dinner. Further, in this view, social isolation and/or or residential segregation, faced by many African-Americans and Latinos, cuts them off from job leads gained by weak ties. The solutions that follow from this position range from aggressive monitoring of institutions that discriminate (e.g., banks that redline) and enforcing antidiscrimination laws to changing the way

localities fund public schools (to provide better education for children in racially isolated and poor areas) and holding sensitivity training sessions.

5. *Poverty as a result of deindustrialization and technological change.* In this view, associated with neoliberals such as Robert Reich, American workers were thrown out of work as part of global shifts in production and new technologies. The solution that follows from this logic is worker retraining.

6. *Poverty as a structural feature of capitalism.* This view, held by Marxist-oriented scholars, holds

that under capitalism, some are poor because others are rich. In this view, the capitalist state helps capitalists to maintain power over wage workers and thus cannot be expected to intervene meaningfully to end poverty—for that would mean speeding capitalism's downfall.

Although it is possible to combine some of these views—say, poverty as lack of opportunity and racism—no synthesis of all these views is possible; they are too at odds with one another. But a study we've considered before, *Tally's Corner* (1967) by Elliot Liebow, does include aspects of both the structural and social psychological perspectives.

### Tally's Corner

The New Deal Carry-out shop is on a corner in downtown Washington, D.C. It would be within easy walking distance of the White House . . . if anyone cared to walk there, but no one ever does. . . . One block south of the Carry-out is a broad avenue which serves roughly to divide the Carry-out neighborhood from the downtown business and shopping district. (Liebow, 1967:17, 18)

It was here, in this Zone-in-Transition, African-American ghetto neighborhood that urban anthropologist Liebow did his participant-observation research. One of the first questions he asked was, "Why are these men hanging out on streetcorners?" Some might think there's a simple answer: They don't want to work. That's what a truck driver said when some of the men refused his offer of work: "These men wouldn't take a job if it were handed to them on a platter." Several streetcorner men did fit the truck driver's stereotype. Leroy preferred playing pinball to working at parking lots, and Sea Cat, "an excellent story teller," walked out on his job. Arthur, age twenty-eight, doesn't want to work. But Liebow found that most did work—at weekend or evening jobs—and thus they could hang out near the Carry-out shop during the day. Some of the streetcorner men were doing illegal work—hustling. Liebow thinks that this makes sense,

since the legal work available to the men is low-paying, low-status, and dead-end.

Liebow disputes notions that the poor are present-time oriented and can't plan ahead. To the contrary, "when Richard squanders a week's pay in two days it is not because he is 'present-time oriented,' unaware or unconcerned with his future. He does so precisely because he is aware of the future and the hopelessness of it all" (Liebow, 1967:66). Thus what may seem to others as a present-time orientation is interpreted by Liebow as a future-time orientation. The difference is that it is a future filled with trouble. He gives the following concrete example:

One day, after Tally had gotten paid, he gave me four twenty-dollar bills and asked me to keep them for him. Three days later he asked me for the money. I returned it and asked why he did not put his money in a bank. He said that the banks close at two o'clock. I argued that there were four or more banks within a two-block radius of where he was working at the time and that he could easily get to any one of them on his lunch hour. "No, man," he said, "you don't understand. They close at two o'clock and they closed Saturday and Sunday. Suppose I get into trouble and I got to make it [leave]. Me get out of town, and everything I got in the world layin' up in that bank? No good! No good!" (69)

The result of their structural situation, Liebow says, is a constant awareness of a troubled future. This discourages Tally and the other streetcorner men from putting money in the bank, sinking roots, committing themselves to a family or friends, and devoting their energies to a job, for all these commitments could hold them hostage.

### What Should Be Done About Poverty?

Some poor townsmen were sitting around discussing the vexing question of poverty. "Poverty is hell," one man said, "but I know how to remedy this evil. People should put all they own into a common pot so that there would be enough for everyone." Another man, Hershel by name, responded, "That is indeed a fine plan, but the question is how to carry it out. I suggest we divide the task. I'll get the endorsement of the poor. You can tackle the rich."

Folk tales, like this one from nineteenth century Russia (in Howe and Greenberg, 1954:615–616), often contain ideological visions. So do programs sponsored by government or private organizations that seek to end or hide poverty.

During the 1960s, federal, state, and local government responses to poverty were dominated by a liberal vision. This means that the policy thrust was toward increased funds for cities and programs aimed at widening economic opportunities. Such programmatic responses to poverty included the following: bilingual and adult education; Project Head Start, the Community Action Program, and other War on Poverty programs; the encouragement of "black capitalism" with small business loans and technical assistance; job training; fair employment practices and affirmative action laws; and incentives to encourage industries to relocate in economically depressed areas. Programs that potentially threatened to do more than increase economic opportunity, notably the Community Action Program of the War on Poverty (which some mayors viewed as a threat to their legitimate power), were usually short-lived (Phillips, 1971–1972). Among the liberal policies recommended over the years have been welfare reform, reduction of unemployment, and income-maintenance programs.

By the 1990s, homelessness and poverty in the United States had increased, not decreased, and the question was asked again: What is to be done? Some former poverty warriors despaired. For one, a former member of President John F. Kennedy's Council of Economic Advisers and Nobel Prize winner James Tobin declared utter ignorance in confronting the forces that affect poverty, such as drugs and guns: "Understanding them or prescribing remedies are outside my competence" (in DeParle, 1992:A13). Liberals maintained that "the paradox of poverty in a wealthy nation will continue until society makes greater efforts to provide all citizens with improved educational and economic opportunities as well as adequate income maintenance in times

of need" (Jencks and Peterson, 1991:v). Radical critics had long since dismissed liberal notions of equal opportunity and programs, claiming that the big winners of most so-called antipoverty programs are not the poor but the affluent: large corporations that run work training centers, university professors who conduct poverty research, consulting firms paid to evaluate poverty programs, and so on.

For different reasons, conservatives also dismiss liberal solutions to poverty. Edward Banfield (1974), Charles Murray (1984; Herrnstein and Murray, 1994), and other neoconservatives think that big government can't solve the problem of poverty and shouldn't try. Their alternative: Let the market mechanism of supply and demand, not government, regulate social problems. Conservatives and neoconservatives tend to favor removing regulations on the market so that it can work "properly." Hence, they suggest repealing minimum wage laws, reasoning that without a minimum wage, employers would hire more low-skilled people and unemployment would decrease. Murray (1993), for one, suggests ending welfare for single mothers on the assumption that poor women will rationally decide not to have children if government refuses to support them. Conservatives also press for laws favoring business expansion and tax reduction on the premise that money poured in at the top will filter down to the poor.

Radicals argue that pouring money in at the top doesn't help the poor. The economic pie may grow bigger, but the share for the poor remains the same (Kolko, 1962) or even decreases, as it did in the 1980s. They point out that since the 1980s, the income distribution in the United States has been growing more and more unequal. In 1989, the highest quintile (one-fifth) of households received 46.8 percent of the aggregate income; in 1979, this group received less—44.2 percent. This concentration of income was accompanied by lower shares going to the lowest and middle three quintiles (U.S. Bureau of the Census, 1990:5) Using another measure, the so-called Gini index or index of income concentration (which varies between 0, perfect equality, to 1, perfect inequality), income inequality is shown to have increased greatly between 1979 and 1989, indeed about twice as much as the change in the previous decade (U.S. Bureau of the Census, 1990:5). Radicals also point to the deceptive quality of government-sponsored antipoverty programs. They argue that job retraining programs, for example, may convince the public that something is being done to end poverty but, in reality, it is only preserving a system of structured inequality: capitalism. In the radical view, the idea of equal opportunity for advancement is false. It is equivalent to comparing a lottery ticket to a savings bond that always pays off. In the words of Simone de Beauvoir (1953), "any ticket may be the winning one, but only a tiny percentage of them actually do win." To end poverty, radicals argue, the institutional and class structure that perpetuates it must be changed—not just around the edges, as liberals would have it, but at its core: capitalist productive relations.

## ANOTHER LOOK

For individuals, on-the-job stress and meaninglessness remain serious issues. This holds true across occupational categories as well as national boundaries. For instance, in Japan, one survey reports that 25 percent of Japanese male and female respondents in business fear *karoshi*—death from overwork—and nine out of ten complain of too much job stress (Holman, 1991:A12). In the United States, some surveys show that the majority are dissatisfied with their work. And, according to the United Nations International Labor Organization, job stress afflicts workers worldwide (Dart, 1993:1).

Meanwhile, neither widespread worker dissatisfaction nor job stress is high on the political agenda. Instead, the clarion call in the United States and Western Europe is *jobs, job, jobs*. In 1993, headlines in the *New York Times* announced that "Youth Joblessness in New York City Soars to 40%, Worst on Record" and "Food Stamp Users Up Sharply, to 10.4% of the U.S., in Sign of Weak Recovery." Public officials propose retraining programs for the "deindustrialized" but fail to specify what kinds of jobs the displaced workers will be trained for. In this atmosphere, we cannot expect those with jobs to risk them by speaking out against on-the-job boredom, repression, stress, or low wages.

Unfortunately, there is little public debate concerning the probability that, along with a suburban single-family home, dignified, interesting, and well-paid work is becoming an impossible dream for more and more persons in America. What this means for long-term living standards, poverty rates, and the quality of life is another difficult but undebated question.

*A final thought on theory and practice:* In 1837, an anonymous contributor to the *Edinburgh Review* commented that "newspapers are perhaps the best representative, at any given time, of the real moral and intellectual state of the greater part of a population" (1837:197). Today, we might substitute "TV" for "newspapers." And what stories does TV tell us about the quality of work, the nature of poverty, and the route to success in metropolitan America? In numerous TV sitcoms, work is challenging and family-like, even fun. People "make it" by luck and pluck, not government assistance. These stories that we tell and retell ourselves avoid stark realities: Work is not fun for most Americans; over one-tenth of Americans receive food stamps; millions of people work full-time but remain poor; and millions more get welfare or subsidies of some sort (e.g., money for not growing a particular crop, cheap grazing rights on federal land, bailouts for savings and loan institutions). As the era of postindustrialism progresses, it will be interesting to watch TV portrayals of work, leisure, self-fulfillment, and poverty. Will the stories change? Stay tuned.

## KEY TERMS

**Alienation**   A widely used concept in social science, philosophy, and the humanities with various meanings. As used by Marx, who focused on labor, alienation is the process by which the worker is dispossessed of his or her product by the capitalist mode of production. Other theorists center on varying aspects of alienation: self-estrangement, meaninglessness, and powerlessness.

**Anomic division of labor**  According to Durkheim, an abnormal form of the division of labor that occurs when extreme specialization of tasks is coupled with a decrease in communication between individuals performing different specialized tasks. This leads to vague rules governing relationships between groups and lack of a sense of interdependence in organically solid society.

**Blue-collar**  A category of workers (as opposed to white-collar and service workers) formerly used by the U.S. Census Bureau but still popularly used. It includes automobile mechanics, assembly-line workers, transport operators, and nonfarm laborers.

**Culture of poverty**  Oscar Lewis's term, referring to his belief that the poor in capitalist societies possess and transmit to their children a distinct set of cultural-sociopsychological traits that sets them apart from the nonpoor. These characteristics, Lewis believed, are universal and include the inability to plan ahead, wife beating, and low levels of education and income.

**Dual city**  Any city divided in two—one part poor, the other rich. The term dates at least to Plato's *Republic*. In John Hull Mollenkopf and Manuel Castells' view, it is the social expression of the spatial form of postindustrial society.

**Employed**  As defined by the U.S. Census Bureau, an employed person is a civilian sixteen years of age and over who (1) did any work as a paid employee or worked fifteen or more hours as an unpaid worker on a family farm or in a family business or (2) had a job but did not work during the week that the census took a count due to illness, bad weather, vacation, industrial strikes, or personal reasons.

**Pink-collar**  Female-concentrated occupations such as clerical work, cashiering, bank teller jobs, nursing, elementary school teaching, private household work, and word processing–typing.

**Poverty**  A controversial term referring most often to lack of money and material possessions; some analysts include lack of power over decision-making processes. Most U.S. analysts use the Social Security Administration's measure of poverty, which establishes a threshold by calculating the subsistence food costs for a family of more than three persons and multiplying that figure by 3. Critics of this absolute standard of poverty argue that poverty is relative to wealth; hence, a relative, not an absolute, standard should be used.

**Underemployment**  Inadequate employment of three different types: (1) too few hours of work, (2) inadequate income level, and (3) mismatch of occupation and skills. Distinguished from *unemployment*.

**Unemployed**  As defined by the U.S. Census Bureau, a civilian sixteen years of age or older who was neither at work nor holding a job (but temporarily not working) or looking for work during the previous four weeks and available to accept a job.

**White-collar**  A category of workers (as opposed to blue-collar and service workers) formerly used by the U.S. Census Bureau but still used popularly. White-collar workers include the following: professional and technical workers (e.g., teachers, lawyers, radio operators); nonfarm managers and administrators (e.g., business executives); sales workers (e.g., retail sales clerks); and clerical workers (e.g., typists).

## PROJECTS

1. **Working: personal views.** How do people feel about the work they do? Interview people in your community who engage in different activities—professor, garbage collector, secretary, sales clerk, farm worker, doctor, and so forth. Try to find out if they would choose the same work again if they had a choice; what they like most about their jobs; what they would change about their working conditions; and what they dislike about their work.
2. **Temps.** Find out what jobs in your community are done by temporary or contingent workers. Analyze the breakdown using census occupational categories. For example, are most jobs executive, professional, and technical?
3. **Slavery and involuntary servitude.** What jobs, in what communities worldwide, tend to be performed by desperately poor people who are virtual slaves or prisoners? Do any enterprises in or near your community em-

ploy such labor? If so, do owners allow access to their employees by reporters or union organizers? What laws or organizations work to protect these workers? What rationales do governments or private employers use for perpetuating these working conditions? *Note: Before setting out on this research project, discuss it with local contacts who might assess any possible risks.*

## SUGGESTIONS FOR FURTHER LEARNING

Changes in contemporary work, workplaces, and wage structures in America, including the decline in relatively high-paid, semiskilled work and the decline in unionization, are the subject of many recent social science studies. See, for example, D. Stanley Eitzen and Maxine Baca Zinn, *The Reshaping of America: Social Consequences of the Changing Economy* (Englewood Cliffs, N.J.: Prentice-Hall, 1989), and two studies by Lawrence Mishel and Jared Bernstein: *The State of Working America* (Armonk, N.Y.: Sharpe, 1993) and *The Joyless Recovery: Deteriorating Wages and Quality in the 1990s* (Washington, D.C.: Economic Policy Institute, 1993).

How people feel about their work is the subject of a number of personal statements in literary, film, and interview forms. Ben Hamper captures the boredom of work at General Motors in his autobiographical *Rivethead: Tales from the Assembly Line* (New York: Warner, 1991). *Roger and Me* and *Pets or Meat?* Michael Moore's films about his hometown, Flint, Michigan, are Swiftian satires on work (and nonwork) at GM's Flint plant. Studs Terkel's *Working* (New York: Avon, 1975) presents dozens of people speaking about their work. Documentary photographer Milton Rogovin teamed up with oral historian Michael Frisch to produce *Portraits in Steel* (Ithaca, N.Y.: Cornell University Press, 1993), a book of photos of twelve steelworkers taken in 1976 and 1987 together with the subjects' own words about their lives during that period.

Some of America's most renowned literature focuses on issues of work and its alienating ef-

fects. Most notable is Arthur Miller's haunting indictment of the economic system that results in alienation, *Death of a Salesman*, in *Collected Plays* (New York: Viking, 1957). Fiction about work by contemporary American writers—including Ken Kesey, Joyce Carol Oates, Grace Paley, and John Updike—is collected by William O'Rourke in *On the Job* (New York: Vintage, 1977).

For a compilation of attitude scales used to measure job satisfaction, see John P. Robinson, Robert Athanasiou, and Kendra B. Head, *Measures of Occupational Attitudes and Occupational Characteristics* (Ann Arbor, Mich.: Institute for Social Research, Survey Research Center, 1969).

Work is the focus of a subfield within sociology: the sociology of occupations and professions. Within this subfield, there has been an outpouring of gender-based research since the mid-1960s. One groundbreaking study compares working men's and women's relative contributions to housework and child care: Arlie Hochschild with Anne Machung, *The Second Shift* (New York: Avon, 1989). It reveals that in about 80 percent of the two-career families studied, the majority of women accept the inequity of their doing the housework but tend to suffer frequent illness and exhaustion. In *Small, Foreign, and Female* (Berkeley: University of California Press, forthcoming), Karen Hossfeld looks at the interplay of race, class, and gender on the life chances of immigrant women working in Silicon Valley.

Women's work has been a recent concern of anthropologists too. For example, in *Sunbelt Working Mothers: Reconciling Family and Factory* (Ithaca, N.Y.: Cornell University Press, 1993), Louise Lamphere and her colleagues compare the experiences of Anglo and Chicano women working in clothing and electronics factories in Albuquerque, New Mexico.

Peter Laslett's *The World We Have Lost* (New York: Scribner, [1965] 1971) is a sociological history of preindustrial England. Lloyd Bonfield, Richard Smith, and Keith Wrightson eds., *The World We Have Gained* (Oxford: Blackwell, 1986), is a collection of essays published by Laslett's students and colleagues. The essays range across Western Europe from the thirteenth to the nineteenth centuries and deal with such topics as marriage, courtship, and occupational structures in late medieval and early modern times.

For a sociological analysis of management ideologies in the course of industrialization, see Reinhard Bendix, *Work and Authority in Industry* (New York: Harper Torchbooks, [1956] 1963). Bendix looks at the relations between employers and workers with—but not through—the eyes of those who have sought to defend and advance the development of industry. The book "deals with ideologies of management which seek to justify the subordination of large masses of men [and women] to the discipline of factory work and to the authority of employers."

How were the old mills as workplaces and as places on the early American landscape? Anthropologist Anthony F. C. Wallace examines the old mills and tenements in the Rockdale region south of Philadelphia in his brilliant account *Rockdale: The Growth of an American Village in the Early Industrial Revolution* (New York: Knopf, 1978). Tamara K. Hareven and Randolph Langenbach explore Manchester, New Hampshire's, old mills in *Amoskeag: Life and Work in an American Factory City* (New York: Pantheon, 1978), and Steve Dunwell writes of *The Run of the Mill* (Boston: Godine, 1978).

The culture of poverty and a critique of this perspective are found, respectively, in Oscar Lewis's work, particularly *La Vida* (New York: Random House, 1966), and Eleanor Burke Leacock, ed., *The Culture of Poverty: A Critique* (New York: Simon and Schuster, 1971).

Theories on the relationship of work and welfare from a radical perspective are presented by Frances Fox Piven and Richard Cloward, *Regulating the Poor* (New York: Vintage, 1971), in which they argue that welfare regulates both the poor and members of the labor force. A very different view of work and poverty is contained in Edward Banfield, *The Unheavenly City Revisited* (Boston: Little, Brown, 1974), now considered a classic statement of the conservative (or neoconservative) position.

Films dealing with work, welfare, and poverty include Charlie Chaplin's classic *Modern Times* (1936) and Paul Schrader's *Blue Collar* (1978). Frederick Wiseman's documentary *Welfare* (1975)

attacks the red tape and callousness of the welfare system, showing its effects on those who work in it as well as those who depend on it. For a portrayal of the rhythm of factory life in the late nineteenth century, see the opening scenes of *The Organizer* (1964), which creates the mood of modern industrial life as workers pour into the factory to the purr of machines. Barbara Kopple's award-winning film, *Harlan County, U.S.A.* (1976), shows the rhythm of work in the coal mines, as well as management–labor struggles and union problems in "bloody Harlan" County, Kentucky. A much broader attack, from a Marxist perspective, on the nature of poverty in modern society is found in *The History Book* (1975, produced for the Danish Government Film Office). The feature-length film *Salt of the Earth* (1954) intertwines three themes of exploitation from a radical perspective: management versus labor, Anglo versus Latino miners, and women's oppression by men. The film's director, Herbert J. Biberman, was one of the Hollywood Ten, blacklisted during the McCarthy era.

Economist-photographer Sebastião Salgado celebrates the heroism and dignity of anonymous working women and men, from coal miners in India to steel workers in France. One of his exhibits, "Workers: an Archeology of the Industrial Age," toured the United States from 1993 to 1995. An unusual monument to working-class heroes, mainly teenagers who lost their lives on whaling boats in far-flung places, can be found in New Bedford, Massachusetts's Seamen's Bethel; the walls are lined with marble tablets marking their contributions.

Work is an enduring theme in folk music. The song "John Henry" immortalizes the competition between human and machine that (apparently) took place in West Virginia; a statue in Summers County immortalizes the miner, not the machine. For an introduction to labor songs, listen to John Greenway, *American Industrial Folksongs* (Riverside 12-607) and *American History in Ballad and Song* (Folkways FH 5801), as well as a number of songs sung and played by Pete Seeger, especially *American Industrial Ballads* (Folkways FH 5251).

For views on the shift from the world of preindustrial to industrial work in Europe, see E. P. Thompson, *The Making of the English Working Class* (New York: Vintage, 1963), a classic work of scholarship sympathetic to the workers' struggle to nourish the tree of liberty. Herbert Gutman attempts to do for the U.S. working class what Thompson did for the first working class (in England) in his collection of essays, *Work, Culture, and Society in Industrializing America, 1815–1919* (New York: Knopf, 1976). This book has already been influential in giving a new interpretation of American labor history. For a very different perspective, see Neil J. Smelser, *Social Change in the Industrial Revolution* (Chicago: University of Chicago Press, 1959), which takes a structural-functionalist perspective on the development of class consciousness.

For the role of professionals in industrial and postindustrial society, see David F. Noble, *America by Design* (New York: Knopf, 1977), a study of the relationship between the engineering professions, technology, and corporate capitalism. Noble's central thesis is that engineers played a significant role in protecting capitalist corporations from technological disruption. Noble debunks the idea that technology is an automatic process and presents a case study of machine tools to support his point. See Alvin W. Gouldner, *The Future of Intellectuals and the Rise of the New Class* (New York: Seabury, 1979), for the argument that the professionals (e.g., scientists, administrators, intellectuals, and technicians) are now assuming critical influence in postindustrial society, a factor not predicted by nineteenth-century thinkers, including Marx. Indeed, Gouldner maintains that Marx was wrong when he theorized that the bourgeoisie would one day be overthrown by the workers, for culture is an important form of capital that Marx neglected. See also Pierre Bourdieu's work, discussed in Chapter 10, for views on cultural capital.

Charlie Chaplin was not the only artist to envision people as cogs in a machine in the machine age. This vision is reflected in the works of many painters, including Ferdinand Leger. Some see the architecture of the Bauhaus school, which is rational, efficient, and unadorned, as another response to technological advance. Ludwig Mies

van der Rohe's glass apartment building at 880 Lake Shore Drive in Chicago is one example of Bauhaus style. The Bauhaus Museum in Berlin contains a treasure trove of artifacts of the machine age.

A classic work on race, poverty, and social policy is Kenneth B. Clark, *Dark Ghetto* (New York: Harper Torchbooks, 1965). For more recent material, see Jonathan Kozol, *Savage Inequalities* (New York: Crown, 1991), and Christopher Jencks and Paul Peterson, eds., *The Urban Underclass* (Washington, D.C.: Brookings Institution, 1991).

How can unemployment be relieved? Surprisingly, some managers, politicians, and union leaders in Western Europe agree: a four-day, thirty-three-hour workweek with a reduction in salary. For up-to-date accounts of policies on joblessness, see the national press of various countries (e.g., Paris's *Le Monde*, Tokyo's *Asahi Shinbun*, and the *New York Times*).

## REFERENCES

Anonymous. 1837. *Edinburgh Review* 65:197.

Associated Press. 1994. "Child poverty soars in suburbs." *San Francisco Chronicle* (September 28): A7.

Banfield, Edward C. 1974. *The Unheavenly City Revisited.* Boston: Little, Brown.

Bendix, Reinhard. [1956] 1963. *Work and Authority in Industry.* New York: Harper Torchbooks.

Bennis, Warren. 1970. *American Bureaucracy.* Chicago: Aldine.

Bensman, David, and Roberta Lynch. [1987] 1988. *Rusted Dreams: Hard Times in a Steel Community.* Berkeley: University of California Press.

Blauner, Robert. 1964. *Alienation and Freedom: The Factory Worker and His Industry.* Chicago: University of Chicago Press.

Braverman, Harry. 1974. *Labor and Monopoly Capital: The Degradation of Work in the Twentieth Century.* New York: Monthly Review Press.

Byerly, Victoria. 1986. *Hard Times, Cotton Mill Girls: Personal Histories of Womanhood and Poverty in the South.* Ithaca, N.Y.: ILR Press.

Campbell, Alan K, and Jesse Burkhead. 1968. "Public policy for urban America." Pp. 577–647 in Harvey S. Perloff and Lowdon Wingo, Jr., eds.,

*Issues in Urban Economics.* Baltimore: Johns Hopkins University Press.

Capistrano, Robert. 1992. "The explosive economy of poverty; bland statistics belie the devastation and desperation of America's poor." *The Recorder* (May 14):6.

Carter, Jimmy. 1993. Remarks on *The Charlie Rose Show*, KQED-TV (July 15), midnight–1 A.M. PST.

Conway, Mimi. 1979. *Rise Gonna Rise: A Portrait of Southern Textile Workers.* Garden City, N.Y.: Doubleday, Anchor.

Dart, Bob. 1993. "U.N. report calls job stress global problem." *San Francisco Chronicle* (March 23):A1.

de Beauvoir, Simone. 1953. *America Day by Day.* New York: Grove Press.

Delaney, Paul. 1979. "The struggle to rally black America." *New York Times Magazine* (July 15):20+.

de Lesquen, Henry, and le Club de l'horloge. 1979. *La Politique du Vivant (The Politics of the Living).* Paris: Albin Michel.

DeParle, Jason. 1992. "At poverty conference, gloom and dashed hope." *New York Times* [national edition] (June 1):A13.

———. 1993. "An unfinished portrait of the poor." *New York Times* (December 26):E1.

———. 1994. "Welfare mothers find jobs easy to get but hard to hold." *New York Times* [national edition] (October 24):A1+.

Diesenhouse, Susan. 1993. "In a shaky economy, even professionals are 'temps'." *New York Times* [national edition] (May 16):F5.

Dunn, Ashley. 1994. "Southeast Asians highly dependent on welfare in U.S.; 30% of families get aid." *New York Times* (May 19):A1+.

Durkheim, Emile. [1893] 1966. *The Division of Labor in Society.* New York: Free Press.

Edwards, Richard C. 1979. *Contested Terrain: The Transformation of the Workplace in the Twentieth Century.* New York: Basic Books.

Eisler, Benita. 1977. *The Lowell Offering: Writings by New England Mill Women (1840–1945).* Philadelphia: Lippincott.

Ferguson, Ann Arnett. 1991. "Managing without managers: Crisis and resolution in a collective bakery." Pp. 108–132 in Michael Burawoy, Alice Burton, Ann Arnett Ferguson, Kathryn J. Fox, Joshua Gamson, Nadine Gartrell, Leslie Hurst, Charles Kurzman, Leslie Salzinger, Josepha Schiffman, and Shiori Ui, *Ethnography Unbound: Power and Resistance in the Modern Metropolis.* Berkeley: University of California Press.

Fowke, Edith, and Joe Glazer, eds. [1960] 1961. *Songs of Work and Freedom.* Garden City, N.Y.: Doubleday, Dolphin.

Friedman, Thomas L. 1994. "U.S. cities in trouble give foreign aid agency new life." *San Francisco Examiner* (June 26):A2.

Gans, Herbert J. 1993. "Scholars' role in planning a 'post-work society'." *Chronicle of Higher Education* (June 9):B3.

Garson, Barbara. 1988. *The Electronic Sweatshop: How Computers Are Transforming the Office of the Future into the Factory of the Past.* New York: Penguin.

Garson, G. David. 1973. "Automobile workers and the radical dream." *Politics and Society* 3:163–177.

Goodwin, Leonard. 1972. *Do the Poor Want to Work?* Washington, D.C.: Brookings Institution.

Hall, Jacquelyn Dowd, James Leloudis, Robert Korstad, Mary Murphy, Lu Ann Jones, and Christopher B. Daly. 1987. *Like a Family: The Making of a Southern Cotton Mill World.* New York: Norton.

Herrnstein, Richard J., and Charles Murray. 1994. *The Bell Curve: Intelligence and Class Structure in American Life.* New York: Free Press.

Hodson, Randy, Sandy Welsh, and Sabine Rieble. 1993. "Is worker solidarity undermined by autonomy and participation?" *American Sociological Review* 58:398–416.

Holman, Richard L. 1991. "Japanese voice work fear." *Wall Street Journal* (April 26):A12.

Howe, Irving, and Eliezer Greenberg, eds. 1954. *A Treasury of Yiddish Stories.* New York: Viking.

Howe, Louise Kapp. 1978. *Pink Collar Workers: Inside the World of Women's Work.* New York: Avon.

Hoyle, Kathy. 1993. Telephone conversation (July 14), Bureau of Labor Statistics, Washington, D.C.

Jencks, Christopher, and Paul E. Peterson, eds. 1991. Preface to *The Urban Underclass.* Washington, D.C.: Brookings Institution.

Jencks, Christopher, Marshall Smith, Henry Acland, Mary Jo Bane, David Cohen, Herbert Gintis, Barbara Heyns, and Stephan Michelson. 1972. *Inequality: A Reassessment of the Effect of Family and Schooling in America.* New York: Basic Books.

Johnson, Clarence. 1992. "One of 5 American children lives in poverty, studies say." *San Francisco Chronicle* (December 18):A12.

Kilborn, Peter T. 1993. "New jobs lack the old security in time of 'disposable workers'." *New York Times* [national edition] (March 15):1+.

Kolko, Gabriel. 1962. *Wealth and Power in America: An*

*Analysis of Social Class and Income Distribution.* New York: Praeger.

Kotz, David. 1988. "Feel overworked? More and more Americans do." *In These Times* (March 9–15):17.

Laslett, Peter. [1965] 1971. *The World We Have Lost.* New York: Scribner.

Lewis, Oscar. 1964. "The culture of poverty." Pp. 149–174 in J. J. TePaske and S. N. Fisher, eds., *Explosive Forces in Latin America.* Columbus: Ohio State University Press.

Liebow, Elliot. 1967. *Tally's Corner: A Study of Negro Streetcorner Men.* Boston: Little, Brown.

Marx, Karl. 1972. *Karl Marx: The Essential Writings.* Ed. Frederic L. Bender. New York: Harper & Row.

McLeod, Ramon G. 1993. "More children living in poverty in California." *San Francisco Chronicle* (June 11):A19.

Mills, C. Wright. 1951. *White Collar.* New York: Oxford University Press.

Mollenkopf, John Hull, and Manuel Castells, eds. 1991. *Dual City: Restructuring New York.* New York: Russell Sage Foundation.

Morrison, Roy. 1991. *We Build the Road as We Travel.* Santa Cruz, Calif.: New Society.

Murray, Charles. 1984. *Losing Ground: American Social Policy, 1950–80.* New York: Basic Books.

———. 1993 Remarks on *Eye to Eye*, CBS-TV (December 16), 9–10 P.M. PST.

Nasar, Sylvia. 1992. "Fed report gives new data on gains by richest in 80's." *New York Times* (April 21):A1+.

Noble, David F. 1977. *America by Design.* New York: Knopf.

Ouchi, William G. [1981] 1982. *Theory Z: How American Business Can Meet the Japanese Challenge.* New York: Avon.

Owens, Bill. 1975. *Our Kind of People: American Groups and Rituals.* San Francisco: Straight Arrow Books.

Pear, Robert. 1994. "Auditors say cutoff for poverty should rise in high-cost areas." *New York Times* [national edition] (August 5):A1.

Perry, Stewart E. 1978. *San Francisco Scavengers.* Berkeley: University of California Press.

Phillips, E. Barbara. 1971–1972. "You've repossessed my bootstraps, so brother, can you spare a dime?: The liberal paradigm of political economy in theory and practice." *Maxwell Review* 8:59–95.

———. 1975. "The artists of everyday life: Journalists, their craft, and their consciousness." Ph.D. diss., Syracuse University.

Porter, Russell B. [1937] 1969. "Speed, speed, and still more speed—that is Flint." Pp. 28–34 in Ray Ginger, ed., *Modern American Cities.* Chicago: Quadrangle.

Rothschild, Joyce, and J. Allen Whitt. 1986. *The Cooperative Workplace: Potentials and Dilemmas of Organizational Democracy and Participation.* New York: Cambridge University Press.

Satin, Mark. 1978. *New Age Politics, Healing Self and Society: The Emerging New Alternative to Marxism and Liberalism.* West Vancouver, B.C.: Whitecap.

Schwarz, John E., and Thomas J. Volgy. 1992. *The Forgotten Americans.* New York: Norton.

Scott, Allen J. 1988. *Metropolis: From the Division of Labor to Urban Form.* Berkeley: University of California Press.

Shabecoff, Philip. 1978. "Overhaul is urged in jobless figures." *New York Times* (July 16):19.

Shenon, Philip. 1993. "Saipan sweatshops are no American dream." *New York Times* [national edition] (July 18):A1+.

Shrank, Robert. 1978. *Ten Thousand Working Days.* Cambridge, Mass.: MIT Press.

Special Task Force to the Secretary of Health, Education and Welfare. 1973. *Work in America.* Cambridge, Mass.: MIT Press.

Terkel, Studs. 1975. *Working.* New York: Avon.

Thayer, Frederick C. 1973. *An End to Hierarchy! An End to Competition! Organizing the Politics and Economics of Survival.* New York: New Viewpoints.

Toner, Robin. 1993. "Striking coal miners fight to protect shrinking power." *New York Times* [national edition] (June 8):A8.

Uchitelle, Louis. 1993. "Use of temporary workers is on rise in manufacturing." *New York Times* [national edition] (July 6):A1+.

———. 1994. "Moonlighting plus: 3-job families on the rise." *New York Times* [national edition] (August 16):A1+.

W. E. Upjohn Institute for Employment Research. 1973. *Work in America: Report of a Special Task Force to the Secretary of Health, Education, and Welfare.* Cambridge, Mass.: MIT Press.

U.S. Bureau of the Census. 1973. *Census of Population: 1970.* Vol. 1, *Characteristics of the population.* Washington, D.C.: Government Printing Office.

———. 1979. *Current Population Reports.* Series P-60, No. 119: *Characteristics of the Population Below the Poverty Level: 1977.* Washington, D.C.: Government Printing Office.

———. 1990. *1987 Census of Manufactures: Industry Series. Weaving and Floor Covering Mills: Industries 2211, 2221, 2231, 2241, and 2273* (April). Washington, D.C.: Government Printing Office.

———. 1990. *Current Population Reports.* Series P-60,

No. 168: *Money Income and Poverty Status in the United States: 1989* (advance data from the March 1990 *Current Population Survey).* Washington, D.C.: Government Printing Office.

————. 1992. *Statistical Abstract of the United States: 1992.* Washington, D.C.: Government Printing Office.

U.S. Department of Health, Education and Welfare. 1976. "The measure of poverty." Technical Paper 18 (October 1). Washington, D.C.: Government Printing Office.

U.S. Department of Labor. 1976a. *BLS Handbook of Methods for Surveys and Studies,* Bulletin 1910. Washington, D.C.: Government Printing Office.

————. 1976b. *BLS Handbook of Labor Statistics,* Bulletin 1905. Washington, D.C.: Government Printing Office.

Valentine, Bettylou. 1979. *Hustling and Other Hard Work: Life Styles in the Ghetto.* New York: Free Press.

Watkins, Beverly T. 1979. "Number of college graduates in education drops 4 pct." *Chronicle of Higher Education* (July 9):10.

Wooten, James. 1979. "Southern conflict." *New York Times Book Review* (July 8):10+.

# CHAPTER 19
# Raising and
# Spending Money

Why do so many modern cities face financial trouble? In the United States, should the federal government bail out near-bankrupt cities?

This chapter provides a framework in which to consider such controversial questions. First, it looks at the impact of the international and national political economies on local revenue. Next, it outlines the U.S. system of local public finance—where money for local services comes from (including the system of fiscal federalism) and where it goes. Then it looks at fiscal crisis. Finally, it looks briefly at the politics of the local budgeting process.

This chapter reemphasizes the idea that cities exist within a complex, interdependent national and international system. This is important for understanding who gets what city services—and who finally pays for them.

## HOW GLOBALIZATION AFFECTS LOCAL FINANCE

Prosperous Orange County, California—the home of Disneyland and families with median incomes of nearly $46,000—seemed the envy of most public managers. Yet, this postsuburban county of 2.4 million persons declared bankruptcy in December 1994. Why? Essentially, because it had lost billions of dollars in its high-risk investment pool.

Orange County's experience is not the norm. Few U.S. counties and cities actually declare bankruptcy. Only seven local governments declared bankruptcy between 1960 and 1984 (ACIR, 1985:8). But cities in America and many parts of the world do experience severe financial woes. For example, in the early 1990s, Philadelphia teetered on the brink of insolvency, and New York City faced a budget gap of more than $2 billion. Even Tokyo sold off plots of land when it was strapped for money in the late 1970s.

Bridgeport, Connecticut, did file for bankruptcy in 1991. Its plight epitomizes "the struggle of many localities to balance revenues and expenditures in a changing federalist system and a volatile global economy" (Pammer, 1992:3). In other words, what local public services people get in Bridgeport (or Biloxi), and how much in taxes they pay for them, depend substantially on two factors outside of their control.

How do these two key factors—a volatile global economy and changes in the federal system—affect U.S. cities? To begin with, at the international level, a massive U.S. trade deficit can lead to a decline in U.S. exports. This is what happened in the 1980s. One result was increased urban unemployment, particularly in manufacturing. More urban unemployment, in turn, decreased the local tax base. Other international events have local impacts too. For instance, if Germany raises its interest rates, if Japan lowers its trade barriers, or if the European Union (EU) hits a downturn (which results in lowered demand for U.S. goods), people in Keokuk and Kenosha will feel the repercussions in terms of services and local taxes.

Next, at the national level, such events or processes as a mushrooming federal deficit, a decade of decreased federal aid to cities, changing types of federal aid, and recession can take a heavy toll on local finances. This is what happened in the 1980s and 1990s. From fiscal year 1969 through 1992, the federal government spent more than it took in on a yearly basis (Pammer, 1992:5) and thus depended on deficit spending. (Cities have fewer options than the federal government; they cannot borrow to finance operating deficits. Many slashed services and deferred maintenance on roads and other facilities.)

Not only did federal urban aid decrease nearly 50 percent in the 1980 to 1990 decade, but the *type* of financial grant changed, leaving local governments less discretion. Specifically, state and local governments favored a type of grant-in-aid called *general revenue sharing*; this program came with almost no strings attached so that cities and states could use the funds largely as they chose. But general revenue sharing was short-lived: Born in 1972, it died in 1985. By 1989 nearly 90 percent of total grant funds came in a number of very specific categorical programs—which leave little discretion to the grantees. For example, in 1989, there were approximately 340 grant programs, ranging from large grants to Medicaid ($33 billion) and Aid to Families with Dependent Children ($10.9 billion) to the relatively small grant of $34 million to the National Endowment for the Arts (Musgrave and Musgrave, 1989:485). Most (70 percent in 1989) categorical grants are *formula based*: that is, they are based on some mix of fair share allocation, need for the particular

service, and capacity to meet the need from locally raised revenues.

The nearly 50 percent decrease in federal urban aid, combined with national recession and
international trade deficits, meant that by 1990
hundreds of cities faced empty coffers or
worse—negative cash flow. In 1993, over 50 percent of the cities participating in the annual National League of Cities poll predicted that their
spending would exceed their revenues; a decade
earlier, only one-fourth reported deficit spending
(*Los Angeles Times*, 1993:A10).

Time was when states often rescued their own
creatures, the cities. However, by the early 1990s,
over one-half of the states faced serious budget
deficits and couldn't bail out local government
(Pammer, 1992:3). Indeed, the governor of California, the nation's largest state, turned the tables
on local governments: He shifted some local
taxes to the state level.

How do cities and states cushion global and
national impacts on tax capacity? Some develop
a municipal or state foreign policy. San Francisco
and San Jose, California, sent mayors to Asia to
drum up trade. The state of Iowa has a full-time
staff to attract international business to the state,
acting as its own Department of Commerce. Other places, both cities and counties, try to diversify
their economic bases (Cope, 1990).

## THE SYSTEM OF LOCAL PUBLIC FINANCE

### The Multitiered Context

Recall that local government in the United States
includes various political units: cities and other
municipalities; counties; towns and townships;
school districts; and nonschool special districts.
Depending on local practice, the same service
(the provision of water, for example) may be provided by different types of local government.
Further, a service provided locally in one state
may be provided elsewhere at the state level. For
these reasons, it is difficult to talk about typical

revenue and spending patterns of local government.

The total package of public services received
by city residents comes from local, state, and federal sources. A complex, multitiered governmental system collects revenue, provides public services, and returns some money for local use.
Why is it important which governmental unit
pays for what as long as city residents get the
public services they want? The answer to that
question seems obvious. It is not. The explanation requires a more in-depth understanding of
how a tax system works. Let us begin by looking
at different parts of the fiscal system: own source
revenue and fiscal federalism.

## WHERE LOCAL GOVERNMENT REVENUE ORIGINATES (1): OWN SOURCE REVENUE

Generally, urban public finance statistics refer to
*all* local government revenue or expenditures.
These include monies raised or spent by cities
and other municipalities, counties, towns and
townships, school districts, and nonschool special districts.

Table 19.1 indicates the revenue sources of all
governments, including local government. It
shows that in 1987, more than two-thirds (66.7
percent) of local government revenue came from
**own source revenue**—that is, money raised directly by local governments, primarily in the
form of taxes and charges. (By comparison, in
1975 and 1976, just over half—54.8 percent—
came from own source revenue.) In 1987, the remaining one-third (33.3 percent) came from **intergovernmental transfers**—that is, revenue
raised by another level of government (state or
federal) and returned to local governments. In
1990, the trend continued: Over 67 percent of
local government revenue came from own
source revenue (Tax Foundation, 1993:Table
A11).

## Types of Own Source Revenue

Local government relies most heavily on the **property tax.** (In contrast, the federal government relies mainly on the individual income tax and payroll taxes as major sources of revenue, while states rely heavily on sales and excise taxes.) For that reason, it deserves relatively extended discussion.

1. *The local property tax* (an annual tax on land and buildings based on their assessed monetary value; typically, the assessed value is less than one-half of the market value) accounts for the largest share of own source local government revenue in the United States. In 1983, to take one year, the property tax accounted for nearly one-half (46 percent) of local tax receipts. Yet (for various reasons, including problems in administering the tax), in fairly short order there has been both (1) a net decline in property tax collections and (2) a decline in the importance of the property tax for own source revenue. Less than a decade before, in 1975 and 1976, the property tax accounted for more than three-quarters (81.2 percent) of local government's own source revenue (U.S. Bureau of the Census, 1978:4)

Property tax rates vary widely from one jurisdiction to another. This variation reflects value differences, as well as differences in the strength of the tax base among communities. Some communities want—and are willing to tax themselves for—higher levels of service.

Long unpopular, the property tax is a common target of taxpayers' revolts. Whether or not the tax and the **tax rate** are fair is much debated. Conservatives tend to favor taxes based on benefit, not ability to pay (e.g., user charges and sales taxes). Liberals tend to prefer taxes based on ability to pay rather than benefit (e.g., individual and corporate income taxes). Many, perhaps most, observers think that the property tax is based on ability to pay, not benefit. But, according to the Musgraves (1989:429), the local property tax—the major form of wealth taxation in the United States—serves as only a rough approximation of ability to pay. Further, they argue that the property tax "may not be the best way to figure ability to pay." For this, they suggest a substitute: the "net worth tax," which "would have to be national rather than local in scope" (428, 430). If acted on, their proposal would change dramatically—indeed, revolutionize—the current tax system.

Another debate, mainly among academics, concerns the incidence of the property tax. (**Incidence** refers to who finally pays it.) At first glance, it seems as if a property owner bears the burden of the property tax. Simple, but not necessarily so. Those who ultimately pay the tax may not be the persons who pay it directly. For instance, if a jurisdiction raises the property tax rate, apartment building owners there must pay higher taxes. The incidence of the tax *appears* to fall on these owners. However, they may just pass on the increases to their tenants by raising rents.

Finally, it bears noting that some *state* governments have their eye on the local property tax. In California, for instance, the state shifted $2.6 billion in property taxes from local government to fund school districts and community colleges in 1993. Of the countries, Los Angeles County loses the most under this tax shift.

2. *User charges* are direct charges paid by the users of publicly provided services. Examples include bridge tolls, admission fees to the zoo, and metered parking. Virtually all local governments have some user charges.

Local governments have increased their dependence on user charges since the 1970s. This raises questions of equity and fairness. With user charges, the poor can be barred from going to the zoo or attending activities intended to be public. (When a public service or facility such as a museum or fire fighting is privatized, consumers no longer pay user charges; they pay a fee directly to the entrepreneur. But the issues of fairness and equity remain.)

3. *Sales tax* and *excise taxes* are paid by a buyer at the time of purchase that go to the local government. New York City, for one, relies heavily on a city sales tax. A sales tax (and user charges too) is a **regressive tax**, not a **progressive tax**. For

example, a student earning $5,000 and an entrepreneur earning $500,000 each pay the same amount of sales tax on a book or boots. For the student, that tax represents a much greater proportion of his or her income that it does for the entrepreneur. Indeed, available data point to the conclusion that lower-income people pay the heaviest sales taxes proportionate to their income.

4. The local *income tax* is based on earned income paid by local individuals or corporations to local government. The income tax is a direct tax based on the ability-to-pay principle, whereby the larger proportional tax burden is placed on individuals or firms whose capacity to pay is greater (i.e., it is progressive, not regressive). Generally, it is not a big revenue producer for local government. (But individual income taxes are the main revenue source for the federal government.)

5. *Miscellaneous sources* are such disparate taxes as Dade County, Florida's, restaurant tax (earmarked to provide rehabilitation for the homeless), Las Vegas's gambling tax, and San Francisco's hotel tax.

## Competition Among Jurisdictions for Own Source Revenue

Units of local government often compete for tax dollars, frequently in a highly destructive way. The reason involves the property tax and local government's dependence on it for raising revenue.

Cities want a strong **tax base**—that is, valuable real property (land and structures, both residential and commercial) subject to a city's taxing power. The higher the **assessed value** (the amount at which property is valued for tax purposes) of taxable real property, the stronger the tax base is.

A strong tax base is a relative matter. There is no dollar amount over or under which a tax base can be considered weak or strong. Rather, a tax base is considered strong if it can provide revenue for public services that residents need or

want (e.g., schooling, fire fighting, and police protection). For example, City A has a strong tax base, and City B has a weak tax base. Given the same demand by city residents for local services, City A will be able to provide more desired services and/or keep the tax rate (the ratio of the tax to the tax base) low. In contrast, City B must provide fewer services, have higher tax rates, or both.

This raises the question of what homeowners and businesses consider a reasonable tax burden. And it leads to the issue of why governments compete for property tax revenue. Many homeowners, faced with an ever-mounting annual tax bill as their assessed valuation rises with inflation, may grumble about what they consider an unreasonable tax burden. They may join tax revolts like California's successful Proposition 13 movement in 1979 or move to jurisdictions where the tax burden is lighter. Businesses may relocate to nearby jurisdictions or faraway islands where they either pay less tax for the same services or are promised tax breaks for locating there.

We should note several points concerning tax grumbles. First, despite what homeowners often believe, the average residence does not usually pay its own way. That is, the average homeowner's property tax pays only a portion of what it costs to provide public services for that dwelling and those who live in it. Second, business and commercial properties often pay more than their own way. "Clean" industries, particularly research and development activities, are especially attractive to localities because they generate relatively high tax revenue and require relatively few public services. But there is an important qualification here. Business and commercial properties often pay more than their own way *if they pay their full share*. In many cases, local taxpayers subsidize commercial-industrial property owners, real estate developers, and mineral companies because local governments allow them to evade property taxes. For tax purposes, many cities assess real estate at only a portion of its market value. According to citizen advocate Ralph Nader, billions of dollars are lost to the public purse annually due to underassessment. Further, Nader claims that large corporations withhold proper payments to governments and apply pressure on governments to "unjustifiably transfer public funds and privileges to corporate control" (1971:16). Nader calls this *corporate socialism.*

What happens if local government officials dare to enforce or even raise property taxes on business and industry? Often there is the risk of immediate retaliation. Industry's most effective weapon is the threat to move elsewhere if tax breaks or subsidies are not granted or continued. This threat can serve as the rationale to keep business and industry's tax burden comparatively low.

Why are taxes lower in some local political units than others? This involves the "fit" between the strength of the tax base and the services paid for from that tax base. Within a single MSA, for example, tax burdens are generally heavier in central cities than elsewhere. Years ago, this was because there was a better fit between demands for public services and fiscal resources to meet those demands in communities outside central cities. But today, many postsuburban communities have highly valued industrial and residential property; they may have a better fit between demand and resources than central cities.

This brings us back to the issue of why local governments compete for property tax revenue. Local governments want to keep tax burdens for residents as low as possible. Thus they compete to strengthen their tax base. A city may try to lure industry into the community by offering tax breaks or zoning variances. Frequently these efforts result in "beggar thy neighbor" outcomes. The experience of Irvine, California, in the 1960s provides a classic example. Located in southern California, Irvine provided numerous sites for commercial-industrial development but few for houses as it expanded in the 1960s. By attracting highly valued taxable industries and keeping its tax base strong, the city kept property tax rates for its relatively few homeowners low. The tax rate for commerce and industry also remained low. This development strategy, however, imposed negative externalities on Irvine's neighbors. Neighboring jurisdictions ended up paying

for Irvine workers' public services (such as schooling for its children) because the workers lived mainly in these other jurisdictions—which enjoyed none of Irvine's tax advantages. Later, under the settlement order of a lawsuit, Irvine permitted more housing construction. And by 1990, the city of Irvine, part of postsuburban Orange County, had a population of 110,330 residents, including more than 6 percent below the poverty level (Hornor, 1993:188).

## Central City versus Suburban Tax Bases

In general, central cities have higher tax rates than their surrounding communities. Faced with declining tax bases and escalating demand for services, central cities set higher tax rates than suburbs, which typically have fewer service demands and stronger tax bases. Thus within MSAs, taxes for similar local services or the level of local services (e.g., efficient or inefficient fire protection, regular or irregular garbage pickups) depend significantly on the community's tax base.

One result of the disparity between tax bases in central cities and their suburbs (as well as disparities among suburban communites) is this: Within MSAs, funds spent on education differ widely from community to community. In 1971, the California Supreme Court reacted to these disparities in its landmark, nationally important decision *Serrano* v. *Priest.* This decision held that the property tax system of financing public education violated the equal protection guarantees of the state constitution. The court stated that the amount of money available for a child's education should not depend on the amount of taxable real property located in his or her community. The court ordered the state legislature to devise a new system of financing public education. Since that decision, a number of state courts have found that school spending should not be based on the local property tax. But the struggle over more equitable school financing is far from settled; twenty-five states have faced lawsuits intended to make school spending more fair. Nowhere has the battle been rancorous than in

Texas, which has the nation's second largest public-school system (after California). The battle started in 1968 after Demetrio Rodriguez sued for more money for his own children and those of others in a poor school district in San Antonio. The differences in spending between rich and poor districts was not trivial in 1968, and it remains substantial: By 1992, spending on the 5 percent schooled in Texas's richest school districts averaged $11,801 per child, while spending on the 5 percent schooled in the poorest districts averaged $3,190 per child (Verhovek, 1993:A6).

One experiment in school funding bears special notice. In 1994, Michigan voters approved a plan to use sales and other taxes, not property taxes, to fund schools. Essentially, this plan came about after property owners (many of them older, without school-age children, or younger, with children in private school) were reluctant to pay higher property taxes. The Michigan plan will narrow the gap between rich and poor school districts by providing a minimum per student and by limiting spending increases by richer districts.

## Are Central Cities Bankrupt?

PHILADELPHIA NEARS BANKRUPTCY. Banner headlines like this have become common in recent years. But what does it mean to say that a city is broke?

A city may be unable to pay its bills for one or both of the following reasons: (1) costs increase (pay increases for public employees, higher prices for supplies) and/or (2) revenues decline (either in absolute terms or in relation to need). On the cost side, changes in demographic and physical conditions could mean increased expense. For instance, the number of people needing a local service such as a day-care center may increase. Or demands on a city for new services (e.g., the establishment of a rape-prevention service) may be made. On the revenue side, the city may suffer from a declining tax base or a general economic slump. Its legal powers to raise revenue may be curtailed, perhaps under a Proposition 13–type constitutional amendment. In

addition, it may gamble—and lose—on risky securities that promise high returns. In Ohio alone, municipalities lost at least $13 million in tax money in the early 1990s on bad investments in so-called mortgage derivatives (Wayne, 1994:1).

Due to deindustrialization, disinvestment, and deterioration, Rustbelt cities tend to be the most vulnerable to serious financial stress. (Many of these older industrial cities in the Northeast and Midwest fall into the category of have-not intergovernmental cities, which will be discussed shortly.) However, by the mid-1990s, some Sunbelt local governments were also vulnerable to fiscal woes. Bad investments, economic recession, military-base shutdowns, and defense cutbacks spelled financial hardships for scores of communities. Indeed, after disastrous losses in its investment funds, a postsuburban Sunbelt county—Orange County, California (Chapter 7)—declared bankruptcy on December 6, 1994; to date, this is the largest bankruptcy case involving a unit of government in the history of the United States.

If a local government finds itself in fiscal trouble, what should be done? Predictably, experts disagree, depending on their ideology. Typically, conservatives advocate belt tightening, laying off public employees, cutting services, and paying off the debt. Both conservatives and neoliberals consider contracting out services to private companies as cost-cutting measures. Liberals tend to see the root of the problem as decreased revenue sources and thus look to more or higher taxes, preferably the federal income tax, which is returned to localities via federal programs. Radicals tend to link urban fiscal crisis to large-scale economic trends associated with contemporary capitalism, particularly the flight of private capital to wherever it can bring the highest rate of return, including overseas or offshore.

## O'Connor's Fiscal Crisis Theory

As noted above, radicals don't see cities' financial crunch as a temporary aberration. Nor do they think it can be solved by more money (liberal solution) or belt tightening (conservative solution). Instead, radicals argue that the term *urban fiscal crisis* is misleading, for fiscal crisis at the urban level is merely a symptom of systemwide economic crisis under advanced capitalism.

Radical political economist James O'Connor has constructed a provocative theory that attempts to explain why capitalist countries like the United States are likely to be caught in a financial squeeze. In *The Fiscal Crisis of the State* (1973), O'Connor argues that the United States has moved into a new economic phase: advanced monopoly capitalism. He claims that in this phase of late capitalism, the state socializes more and more capital costs among its citizens but allows the social surplus (including profits) to be privately appropriated. This "socialization of costs and the private appropriation of profits," O'Connor argues, "creates a fiscal crisis, or 'structural gap,' between state expenditures and state revenues" (1973:9). Thus, even before New York City's near-bankruptcy in the mid-1970s, the slashing of federal aid to cities, and the long recession that has continued cities' financial binds into the 1990s, O'Connor predicts continuing fiscal crisis in the capitalist state. Why? Because government needs to maintain and expand vital services in order to seem legitimate—but cannot finance the services.

## Do Suburbs Exploit Central Cities?

O'Connor implies that the fiscal crisis of the cities can never be solved by giving them more money or letting the market decide who gets what services. That is a very controversial idea. So is his statement that "tax finance is (and always has been) a form of economic exploitation" (O'Connor, 1973:203), reflecting inequities in the class structure.

A further explanation of the fiscal plight of U.S. cities suggests another form of exploitation: that of cities by their surrounding metropolitan areas. Some urbanists claim that cities are in bad financial shape because their surrounding suburbs take unfair advantage of them. These observers point out that suburbanites use city streets, public buildings, and other urban amenities without paying taxes for them. John Kenneth Galbraith expresses this view in no uncertain terms: "It's outrageous that the development of the metropolitan community has been organized with escape hatches that allow people to enjoy the proximity of the city while not paying their share of the taxes" (in Shenker, [1975] 1977). Galbraith concludes colorfully, "Fiscal funkholes are what the suburbs are."

If Galbraith is right, what should be done to stop the exploitation of central cities by their suburbs? One suggested remedy is commuter taxes. Another is the creation of metropolitanwide government. Predictably, neither of these remedies has been popular with suburbanites. Other proposed remedies focus on the transfer of tax functions from local government to regional or higher levels.

*To conclude:* Whether or not suburbs are fiscal funkholes, as Galbraith claims, is a matter of debate. However, there is broad agreement that the match between fiscal resources and service demands within a metropolitan area is inequitable. Metropolitan tax sharing, adopted by Minneapolis–St. Paul, is one of many proposals to deal with fiscal equity within MSAs.

## WHERE LOCAL GOVERNMENT REVENUE ORIGINATES (2): FISCAL FEDERALISM

Chief Justice Oliver Wendell Holmes once remarked that taxes are the price of civilization. If so, all levels of government in the U.S. federal system compete to civilize us. Local, state, and federal governments all collect taxes from their constitutents. Each level places primary emphasis on different revenue sources, but each also tends to use sources employed by competing levels of government.

The three-tier system of revenue collection and distribution in the U.S. federal system is called **fiscal federalism.** The amounts and sources of revenue collected at each level (and redistributed from federal and state governments) for one year are shown in Table 19.1.

**Table 19.1**  Total Government Revenue by Source and Level by Government Fiscal Year 1990 ($millions)

| Source | Total | Federal | State | Local |
|---|---|---|---|---|
| Total revenue | $2,046,998 | $1,154,996 | $659,971 | $580,193 |
| Intergovernmental | a | 2,911 | 143,534 | 190,723 |
| From federal government | a | — | 134,926 | 18,449 |
| From state government | a | 2,911 | — | 172,274 |
| From local government | a | — | 8,607 | b |
| Revenue from own sources | 2,046,998 | 1,152,085 | 516,437 | 389,470 |
| General | 1,493,179 | 780,479 | 408,188 | 321,599 |
| Taxes | 1,133,886 | 632,267 | 310,561 | 201,130 |
| Property | 155,613 | — | 6,228 | 149,765 |
| Individual income | 572,524 | 466,884 | 99,279 | 9,563 |
| Corporation income | 117,073 | 93,507 | 21,751 | 1,815 |
| Sales and gross receipts and customs | 231,855 | 53,970 | 153,535 | 30,815 |
| Customs duties | 16,810 | 16,810 | — | — |
| General sales and gross receipts | 121,287 | — | 103,165 | 21,585 |
| Motor fuel | 33,120 | 13,077 | 20,639 | 664 |
| Alcoholic beverages | 9,223 | 5,753 | 3,400 | 279 |
| Tobacco products | 10,002 | 4,268 | 5,980 | 193 |
| Public utilities | 17,892 | 6,476 | 6,752 | 4,903 |
| Other | 23,521 | 7,586 | 12,743 | 3,192 |
| Motor vehicle and operators' licenses | 11,444 | — | 10,131 | 769 |
| Death and gift | 15,355 | 11,500 | 3,832 | 23 |
| All other | 30,021 | 6,406 | 15,238 | 8,378 |
| Charges and miscellaneous | 359,293 | 148,212 | 97,627 | 120,469 |
| Utility and liquor stores | 58,642 | — | 6,473 | 52,430 |
| Insurance trust | 495,176 | 371,206 | 101,776 | 15,441 |
| Employee retirement | 98,669 | 4,401 | 71,136 | 15,370 |
| Unemployment compensation[c] | 18,541 | 100 | 17,952 | 71[d] |
| Old-age, survivors, disability and health insurance | 361,684 | 361,684 | — | — |
| Railroad retirement | 4,352 | 4,352 | — | — |
| Other | 11,930 | 669 | 12,688 | — |

[a] To avoid duplication, transactions between levels of government are eliminated in the combined total.

[b] Transactions among local units of government are excluded.

[c] Relates to cooperative state-Federal programs administered by state employment security agencies, including regular and extended or supplemental programs.

[d] Washington, D.C., only.

SOURCE: The Tax Foundation, *Facts & Figures on Government Finance* (Baltimore: Johns Hopkins University Press, 1993), p. 13.

## State–Local Intergovernmental Transfers

Before 1929, state and local governments provided most public services within the intergovernmental system. Since the Great Depression of the 1930s, the federal government's share of public expenditures has grown, while the state and local governments' share has diminished.

How much do states give to their local governments, and where does the money go? In one selected year, 1989, states gave a total of over $153 billion in aid to local governments (U.S. Bureau of the Census, 1992:Table 470). Most of this aid was "restricted"; that is, it had to be spent on programs identified by the state government.

Historically, one program has received the largest percentage of state funds—highways. In 1954, highways received 51.6 percent of state money; in 1985, 62.7 percent (ACIR, 1987:59). Over time, the percentage of state funds for education has remained stable (1954, 10.6 percent; 1985, 10.3 percent), while outlays to housing and welfare decreased significantly from 1954 to 1985.

## Federal Transfers to State and Local Governments

The federal government, through its various agencies, transfers revenue to both state and local governments. During the 1960s and 1970s, federal grants-in-aid expanded about 1,500 percent: from $3.8 billion in 1957 to $61.4 billion in 1977 (Kantor, 1988:213). Much of this aid was given directly to cities, bypassing the statehouse. Then, as noted earlier, during the 1980 to 1992 Reagan–Bush administrations, some programs were ended (e.g., general revenue sharing) and others were cut drastically.

What enables the federal government to redistribute funds to lower levels? Primarily, revenue from the federal personal income tax. Since it was authorized in 1913, the income tax has become the single largest revenue producer for the nation.

## The Intergovernmental City

Due to economic decline (e.g., the abandonment of the core by private investors, a shrinking tax base, and loss of industry, retail trade, and people) and growing demands for public services, some cities grew dependent on federal and state intergovernmental transfers. A new term—**intergovernmental city**—refers to such places: older, economically declining industrial cities characterized by acute levels of federal and state revenue transfer, significant poverty-stricken populations in ill health, higher than average crime rates, and eroding tax bases (Burchell,

Carr, Florida, Németh, Pawlik, and Barreto, 1984). Among others, Newark, Cleveland, Baltimore, Louisville, Minneapolis, and Buffalo meet these criteria.

What happened to intergovernmental cities after "the dismantling of intergovernmentalism" that began with Reagan's 1982 budget? In their book, *The New Reality of Municipal Finance: The Rise and Fall of the Intergovernmental City* (1984:259), Burchell et al. say that federal cutbacks to state and local governments were felt most severely by distressed intergovernmental cities. Not only did declining urban areas "bear a disproportionate burden of rollbacks in federal aid, [but] many needy cities also lost substantial amounts of indirect revenues as entitlement programs for the poor and near-poor were curtailed." Further, the haves (nonintergovernmental cities) and the have-nots (intergovernmental cities) "adjusted in [their] own characteristic way: the non-intergovernmental city by slower service growth; the intergovermental city by service retrenchment" (345).

*To conclude:* Most scholars find that tax policies at local, state, and federal levels have not served to change the relative distribution of income and wealth in the United States. In part, this is due to regressive state-local taxes (although there is debate over the regressivity of the property tax). Further, state and local taxes are relatively inelastic compared with federal income taxes. (**Elasticity** refers to the "stretchability" of a tax. In an expanding economy, an elastic tax promotes higher tax receipts, but during a recession it brings in less revenue.) One implication here concerns the relative growth of different levels of government. Particularly in periods of economic growth, the federal level can be expected to expand its revenue bases faster than the state and local levels.

Another implication concerns government's role in the redistribution of income. This ideologically loaded issue has practical consequences. Liberal economists stress government's legitimate function in correcting the market distribution of income. Critics argue that this redistribution has not really happened. Conservatives argue that it should not happen; that is, government does not have the legitimate role of correcting the market distribution of income from affluent to poor. Radicals claim that the tax system, particularly the state and local system, ensures that the poor stay poor and the rich remain rich; conservatives argue that the government should not intervene to make the rich poorer; and liberals think government should intervene but don't agree on how effective tax policy has been in achieving income redistribution.

Finally, we return to our original questions: What difference does it make which revenue source is used? What difference does it make which level of government—national, state, or local—raises it? By now, the answers should seem complex, entangled with a host of political, socioeconomic, and moral concerns. And the answers are complex.

Cities exist within an interdependent system, buffeted by macro-level forces beyond their control. These include the health of the global and national economies, the movement of people and industry to more profitable areas inside the country or offshore, and structural changes in the economy. Yet cities must deal with many of these large-scale forces armed only with meager weapons, particularly meager in comparison with federal resources. Many older central cities, including New York, have tackled what are essentially national problems, such as poverty, by attempting to redistribute income from richer to poorer individuals via an extensive welfare system and low-cost university education. However, over time, these city policies helped to drive away middle-income people and businesses that feel overburdened by taxes. This exodus reduces the city's inelastic own source tax base even more. Attempts to raise city taxes to even higher levels only hasten the retreat of more people and industry. And so the cycle goes. In other words, the fiscal crisis of the cities is best understood in a much larger framework.

## ALLOCATING THE PUBLIC BUDGET

Once tax revenue wends its tortuous way to the public coffers, a drama unfolds: the annual ritual of allocating the budget. This process can be as complex as the mating ceremony of the giant elephant seal. To make the behind-the-scenes budgetary process more comprehensible, we turn to studies by scholars of urban public finance, public budgeting, political science, and policy analysis.

## The Politics of the Budgetary Process

Public budgeting may elicit groans or yawns. It does sound rather dry. Generally, it is not reported in the news media because it is a complex story to tell, because it happens behind closed doors (and thus is difficult to show on TV), and because it is what *New York Times* columnist William Safire calls a MEGO (My Eyes Glaze Over)—a bore to audiences. As a result, local news media give broad coverage to what mayors, county legislators, and other elected public officials do or say publicly, but they offer little reportage on the bureaucratic politics of public budgeting. This is unfortunate for citizens because budget making is a political process that can reveal a great deal about local priorities and power relations.

In fact, the core of local politics—who gets what from the public purse—is hammered out in the budgetary process. Will city revenue be used for day-care centers or a rape-prevention center? Will money be spent to spruce up sidewalks in affluent residential neighborhoods, plant trees in the CBD, or add a police officer to the force? In times of fiscal stress, which services will be sacrificed? These are the kinds of issues addressed in the budgetary process. Clearly, the answers have great impact on local residents.

Indeed, understanding the politics of budgeting is a key to understanding government. Aaron Wildavsky, a political scientist and public policy analyst, points out why in his influential book, *The Politics of the Budgetary Process* (1974). He says that a government budget

may be characterized as a series of goals with price tags attached. Since funds are limited . . . the budget becomes a mechanism for making choices among alternative expenditures. . . . If politics is regarded in part as a conflict over whose preferences shall prevail in the determination of . . . policy, then the budget records the outcomes of this struggle. (2–5)

He concludes that "in the most integral sense, the budget lies at the heart of the political process."

While Wildavsky analyzes the federal budgetary process, some of his insights are helpful in understanding local government budgeting as well. First, Wildavsky notes that budgeting is **incremental**. This means that "the largest determining factor in this year's budget is last year's budget" (1974:13). Second, Wildavsky points out that much game playing is involved in budgeting. For instance, in deciding how much money to request, government agency bureaucrats pick up cues from legislative and/or executive officials and then devise plans to get as much money as they can reasonably expect. They may play it straight, presenting a budget request already cut to the bone. They may pad their request, anticipating budget cuts. Or they may include items favored by those who review the budget as their lowest priority so that the reviewers won't eliminate funds for the bureaucrats' real concerns. In addition, a public agency may try to build and use constituencies that independently put pressure on legislators and executive officials to fund their pet projects.

As Wildavsky describes it, the federal budgeting process is fragmented, incremental, and highly specialized. Reacting to the apparent irrationality of such a decision-making system, reformers in the 1960s called for changes in the budget preparation process. Subsequently, reform measures (e.g., zero-based budgeting) were enacted at the federal level. All aimed to make the consequences of alternative spending policies clear and comparable on a cost basis. But Wildavsky thinks that any such efforts to bring rationality to budget making fly in the face of political exigencies and thus are doomed to failure.

Meanwhile, some of the ferment for budgetary reform reached local government. Various systems for greater rationality were instituted in many cities. But as one of Wildavsky's colleagues lamented while doing budget research, "I found myself working in the city of Oakland, California, where the total budget was small enough to have been a rounding error in the Department of Defense" (Meltsner, 1971:ix). Indeed, after Proposition 13 passed in 1979, Oakland and all cities in California were legally prevented from increasing their chief money raiser: the property tax. And, as federal support to the cities decreased in the 1980s, all the elaborate systems analysis techniques could not create something from nothing, especially money.

A study of the budgeting process in Cleveland, Detroit, and Pittsburgh found that rules for decision making are well established and seldom vary (Crecine, 1969). In Oakland, California, the first rule of thumb—"cut all increases in personnel"—lends support to Wildavsky's skepticism about rational budget making.

By the 1990s, the rules of the game had changed in Oakland and many other cities. According to the director of the Jesse M. Unruh Institute of Politics at the University of Southern California, the stages of budget cutting circa 1993 are these: "First, you cut some fat; you can always do that. Then you get into the bone, and that starts to hurt. The third stage, where we are now, is amputation. You can cut off a leg or an arm now, but do you do the same next year?" (Berg in Haeseler, 1993:1)

*To conclude:* The picture of municipal budgeting that emerges from various studies is not one of rationality, imagination, or intellectual debate. Instead, during "normal" times, budget matters are guided by historical precedent—the previous year's appropriations. During times of extreme fiscal stress, nearly all bets are off as employees are asked to take time off without pay and give back raises, taxes are increased, and services are amputated. As cities run out of quick fixes (e.g., renegotiating fringe benefits with unions, freezing police hires), they have to face further cost (and service) cutting or raise revenues.

Unlike the federal budgeting process (which is typified by real struggles over alternative spending policies), the municipal budgeting process is dominated by gloom over lack of revenue. There

**Table 19.2** City Government Revenue and Expenditures, U.S. Largest Cities, 1990 (New York City through Miami)

| Cities Ranked by 1990 Population | Total | General Revenue Total | Intergovernmental From State and Local Govts | Intergovernmental From Federal Government | Taxes Total | Taxes Property | Taxes Sales and Gross Receipts | Utility and Liquor Store Revenue | Gross Debt Out-standing |
|---|---|---|---|---|---|---|---|---|---|
| New York City, NY | $37,807 | $32,056 | $11,339 | $994 | $15,171 | $6,589 | $3,554 | $1,840 | $26,005 |
| Los Angeles, CA | 6,585 | 3,519 | 370 | 69 | 1,739 | 632 | 773 | 2,162 | 6,278 |
| Chicago, IL | 3,777 | 3,033 | 486 | 266 | 1,597 | 627 | 831 | 207 | 4,298 |
| Houston, TX | 1,702 | 1,296 | 26 | 31 | 692 | 376 | 296 | 227 | 3,611 |
| Philadelphia, PA | 3,380 | 2,587 | 459 | 152 | 1,588 | 311 | 34 | 558 | 3,796 |
| San Diego, CA | 1,296 | 1,087 | 129 | 66 | 348 | 138 | 186 | 131 | 1,406 |
| Detroit, MI | 2,021 | 1,517 | 560 | 113 | 522 | 182 | 50 | 157 | 1,450 |
| Dallas, TX | 1,120 | 812 | 19 | 19 | 475 | 278 | 184 | 101 | 1,570 |
| Phoenix, AZ | 1,115 | 958 | 226 | 88 | 317 | 117 | 185 | 112 | 2,062 |
| San Antonio, TX | 1,434 | 534 | 57 | 39 | 201 | 111 | 84 | 868 | 4,035 |
| San Jose, CA | 700 | 605 | 72 | 7 | 308 | 117 | 137 | 6 | 1,043 |
| Baltimore, MD | 1,865 | 1,655 | 741 | 61 | 640 | 437 | 45 | 48 | 1,257 |
| Indianapolis, IN | 892 | 866 | 186 | 71 | 388 | 314 | 16 | 8 | 953 |
| San Francisco, CA | 2,914 | 2,342 | 639 | 101 | 867 | 464 | 185 | 185 | 2,392 |
| Jacksonville, FL | 1,399 | 673 | 94 | 48 | 223 | 173 | 41 | 638 | 4,297 |
| Columbus, OH | 547 | 476 | 46 | 26 | 261 | 22 | 6 | 71 | 1,072 |
| Milwaukee, WI | 781 | 559 | 235 | 42 | 154 | 143 | 4 | 39 | 516 |
| Memphis, TN | 1,689 | 750 | 455 | 14 | 154 | 115 | 29 | 806 | 736 |
| Washington, DC | 4,323 | 4,080 | 73 | 1,234 | 2,310 | 727 | 674 | 52 | 3,423 |
| Boston, MA | 1,805 | 1,603 | 675 | 71 | 576 | 533 | 28 | 58 | 854 |
| Seattle, WA | 1,011 | 630 | 66 | 27 | 320 | 106 | 141 | 321 | 904 |
| El Paso, TX | 303 | 244 | 11 | 14 | 111 | 56 | 52 | 34 | 451 |
| Cleveland, OH | 677 | 521 | 57 | 73 | 268 | 50 | 3 | 156 | 713 |
| New Orleans, LA | 716 | 634 | 39 | 88 | 272 | 123 | 130 | 49 | 1,128 |
| Nashville-Davidson, TN | 1,547 | 916 | 169 | 14 | 455 | 261 | 162 | 591 | 2,331 |
| Denver, CO | 1,088 | 939 | 160 | 46 | 359 | 99 | 218 | 86 | 1,266 |
| Austin, TX | 1,033 | 534 | 55 | 9 | 170 | 103 | 63 | 453 | 3,188 |
| Fort Worth, TX | 501 | 401 | 30 | 50 | 191 | 130 | 57 | 56 | 942 |
| Oklahoma City, OK | 370 | 328 | 4 | 24 | 163 | 25 | 134 | 30 | 504 |
| Portland, OR | 441 | 392 | 53 | 20 | 205 | 144 | 30 | 44 | 639 |
| Kansas City, MO | 620 | 517 | 25 | 25 | 309 | 56 | 132 | 41 | 616 |
| Long Beach, CA | 740 | 573 | 65 | 33 | 153 | 67 | 71 | 166 | 749 |
| Tucson, AZ | 437 | 350 | 94 | 27 | 130 | 26 | 98 | 70 | 773 |
| St. Louis, MO | 645 | 513 | 31 | 43 | 287 | 36 | 120 | 30 | 709 |
| Charlotte, NC | 422 | 383 | 85 | 19 | 136 | 121 | 5 | 30 | 706 |
| Atlanta, GA | 801 | 680 | 95 | 70 | 209 | 113 | 64 | 62 | 1,069 |
| Virginia Beach, VA | 717 | 680 | 167 | 86 | 335 | 202 | 106 | 37 | 508 |
| Albuquerque, NM | 505 | 461 | 109 | 53 | 121 | 43 | 73 | 44 | 1,264 |
| Baton Rouge, LA | 386 | 350 | 23 | 18 | 172 | 53 | 108 | 3 | 766 |
| Oakland, CA | 503 | 476 | 49 | 26 | 202 | 100 | 60 | — | 1,110 |
| Pittsburgh, PA | 391 | 357 | 64 | 25 | 222 | 102 | 22 | — | 604 |
| Sacramento, CA | 327 | 272 | 27 | 614 | 143 | 45 | 84 | 19 | 309 |
| Minneapolis, MN | 730 | 584 | 134 | 31 | 190 | 147 | 34 | 24 | 1,980 |
| Tulsa, OK | 437 | 379 | 13 | 7 | 152 | 18 | 130 | 38 | 1,451 |
| Honolulu, HI | 1,095 | 1,018 | 50 | 66 | 387 | 302 | 54 | 77 | 805 |
| Cincinnati, OH | 640 | 400 | 61 | 39 | 220 | 37 | 4 | 54 | 231 |
| Miami, FL | 372 | 309 | 36 | 29 | 163 | 120 | 35 | — | 560 |

SOURCE: Adapted from U.S. Bureau of the Census, *Statistical Abstract of the United States 1992* (Washington, D.C.: Government Printing Office, 1992), Table 476, pp. 300–301.

| | Expenditure | | | | | | | | | |
|---|---|---|---|---|---|---|---|---|---|---|
| | General Expenditure | | | | | | | | | |
| Total | Total | Education | Housing and Community Development | Public Welfare | Health and Hospitals | Police Protection | Fire Protection | Highways | Utility and Liquor Store | Cities Ranked by 1990 Population |
| $37,630 | $31,292 | $7,040 | $2,287 | $5,803 | $3,378 | $1,760 | $743 | $867 | $3,985 | New York City, NY |
| 6,448 | 3,228 | 12 | 229 | — | 8 | 618 | 240 | 173 | 2,670 | Los Angeles, CA |
| 3,408 | 2,865 | 1 | 128 | 83 | 79 | 535 | 210 | 327 | 193 | Chicago, IL |
| 1,660 | 1,387 | — | 18 | — | 49 | 238 | 132 | 91 | 213 | Houston, TX |
| 3,498 | 2,579 | 16 | 137 | 191 | 246 | 305 | 114 | 65 | 652 | Philadelphia, PA |
| 1,080 | 868 | — | 78 | 1 | 1 | 137 | 57 | 53 | 172 | San Diego, CA |
| 1,946 | 1,458 | 3 | 41 | — | 91 | 287 | 78 | 131 | 259 | Detroit, MI |
| 989 | 785 | — | 12 | — | 16 | 141 | 72 | 87 | 121 | Dallas, TX |
| 1,348 | 1,153 | 4 | 57 | 1 | 2 | 153 | 79 | 152 | 174 | Phoenix, AZ |
| 1,687 | 688 | 1 | 28 | 5 | 16 | 96 | 59 | 59 | 988 | San Antonio, TX |
| 721 | 680 | — | 62 | — | — | 91 | 48 | 60 | 9 | San Jose, CA |
| 1,611 | 1,495 | 493 | 65 | 2 | 52 | 142 | 77 | 134 | 42 | Baltimore, MD |
| 952 | 899 | (Z) | 47 | 59 | 155 | 166 | 32 | 49 | 22 | Indianapolis, IN |
| 2,519 | 1,886 | 52 | 37 | 239 | 410 | 139 | 95 | 27 | 435 | San Francisco, CA |
| 1,396 | 695 | — | 37 | 13 | 29 | 74 | 48 | 33 | 672 | Jacksonville, FL |
| 597 | 486 | — | 5 | — | 20 | 88 | 57 | 41 | 111 | Columbus, OH |
| 649 | 551 | — | 43 | — | 10 | 114 | 56 | 46 | 34 | Milwaukee, WI |
| 1,587 | 717 | 372 | 8 | — | 14 | 63 | 53 | 18 | 814 | Memphis, TN |
| 4,513 | 4,142 | 674 | 247 | 672 | 443 | 276 | 98 | 124 | 86 | Washington, DC |
| 1,726 | 1,498 | 463 | 55 | 3 | 198 | 157 | 88 | 43 | 62 | Boston, MA |
| 945 | 546 | — | 23 | — | 11 | 71 | 48 | 61 | 346 | Seattle, WA |
| 293 | 233 | — | 5 | — | 12 | 42 | 19 | 113 | 49 | El Paso, TX |
| 708 | 501 | — | 45 | — | 16 | 114 | 57 | 40 | 207 | Cleveland, OH |
| 750 | 662 | — | 63 | 18 | 11 | 56 | 28 | 49 | 60 | New Orleans, LA |
| 1,505 | 843 | 263 | 6 | 12 | 66 | 54 | 33 | 29 | 629 | Nashville-Davidson, TN |
| 1,031 | 910 | — | 13 | 98 | 111 | 84 | 46 | 115 | 100 | Denver, CO |
| 1,012 | 541 | (Z) | 5 | 2 | 109 | 45 | 31 | 72 | 448 | Austin, TX |
| 501 | 389 | — | 6 | — | 9 | 49 | 31 | 37 | 92 | Fort Worth, TX |
| 371 | 315 | — | 8 | — | 1 | 47 | 38 | 28 | 49 | Oklahoma City, OK |
| 441 | 370 | (Z) | 28 | (Z) | 1 | 74 | 47 | 22 | 42 | Portland, OR |
| 571 | 496 | 24 | 8 | (Z) | 44 | 69 | 38 | 50 | 49 | Kansas City, MO |
| 775 | 583 | — | 62 | — | 13 | 81 | 53 | 23 | 191 | Long Beach, CA |
| 473 | 352 | — | 24 | 2 | 1 | 50 | 23 | 59 | 113 | Tucson, AZ |
| 607 | 529 | 1 | 21 | 7 | 43 | 89 | 29 | 16 | 29 | St. Louis, MO |
| 508 | 432 | — | 9 | (Z) | 2 | 34 | 26 | 55 | 72 | Charlotte, NC |
| 741 | 582 | 17 | 20 | 2 | — | 68 | 37 | 27 | 102 | Atlanta, GA |
| 679 | 643 | 293 | 5 | 13 | 17 | 39 | 19 | 79 | 13 | Virginia Beach, VA |
| 577 | 495 | — | 15 | 1 | 6 | 55 | 24 | 36 | 82 | Albuquerque, NM |
| 368 | 344 | — | 10 | 1 | 27 | 39 | 18 | 14 | 5 | Baton Rouge, LA |
| 523 | 482 | 2 | 52 | 1 | (Z) | 55 | 37 | 27 | — | Oakland, CA |
| 401 | 353 | — | 8 | (Z) | 7 | 42 | 36 | 40 | 14 | Pittsburgh, PA |
| 310 | 272 | (Z) | (Z) | — | 1 | 57 | 33 | 24 | 21 | Sacramento, CA |
| 716 | 621 | (Z) | 76 | — | 10 | 51 | 27 | 41 | 22 | Minneapolis, MN |
| 415 | 362 | — | 6 | — | 7 | 37 | 30 | 21 | 50 | Tulsa, OK |
| 909 | 726 | — | 71 | — | 8 | 96 | 40 | 40 | 182 | Honolulu, HI |
| 577 | 478 | — | 56 | — | 35 | 57 | 45 | 58 | 51 | Cincinnati, OH |
| 955 | 324 | (Z) | 22 | 1 | (Z) | 80 | 41 | 11 | — | Miami, FL |

**Table 19.3** Per Capita Direct General Expenditures of Local Governments in Selected Metropolitan Areas by Major Function, Fiscal Year 1983

| Area | Total | Education | Highways | Public Welfare | Health and Hospitals | Police Protection | Fire Protection | Interest on General Debt | All Other |
|---|---|---|---|---|---|---|---|---|---|
| Total, 75 major SMSAs | $1,374 | $538 | $63 | $87 | $105 | $85 | $42 | $64 | $390 |
| Anaheim–Santa Ana–Garden Grove, California | 1,316 | 583 | 67 | 95 | 27 | 86 | 48 | 53 | 357 |
| Atlanta, Georgia | 1,236 | 489 | 37 | 5 | 229 | 63 | 35 | 57 | 322 |
| Baltimore, Maryland | 1,269 | 515 | 153 | 1 | 60 | 82 | 44 | 62 | 352 |
| Boston–Lowell–Brockton–Lawrence–Haverhill, Massachusetts | 1,127 | 493 | 49 | 8 | 79 | 74 | 66 | 34 | 325 |
| Buffalo, New York | 1,699 | 618 | 105 | 217 | 96 | 62 | 37 | 81 | 482 |
| Chicago, Illinois | 1,253 | 532 | 65 | 12 | 49 | 102 | 46 | 70 | 378 |
| Cincinnati, Ohio–Kentucky–Indiana | 1,029 | 437 | 44 | 42 | 67 | 65 | 36 | 43 | 295 |
| Cleveland, Ohio | 1,416 | 527 | 59 | 98 | 159 | 95 | 53 | 59 | 365 |
| Columbus, Ohio | 1,130 | 459 | 46 | 78 | 61 | 72 | 43 | 75 | 295 |
| Dallas–Ft. Worth, Texas | 1,255 | 549 | 66 | 3 | 91 | 69 | 40 | 95 | 343 |
| Denver–Boulder, Colorado | 1,397 | 619 | 72 | 84 | 63 | 87 | 39 | 73 | 361 |
| Detroit, Michigan | 1,438 | 601 | 72 | 12 | 122 | 100 | 40 | 59 | 431 |
| Ft. Lauderdale–Hollywood, Florida | 1,335 | 431 | 76 | 2 | 255 | 123 | 39 | 37 | 273 |
| Hartford–New Britain–Bristol, Connecticut | 1,077 | 534 | 57 | 33 | 9 | 63 | 39 | 35 | 308 |
| Houston, Texas | 1,527 | 708 | 86 | 4 | 100 | 80 | 47 | 113 | 388 |
| Indianapolis, Indiana | 1,048 | 442 | 43 | 53 | 149 | 50 | 30 | 34 | 246 |

| | | | | | | | | |
|---|---|---|---|---|---|---|---|---|
| Kansas City, Missouri–Kansas | 1,164 | 473 | 84 | 4 | 78 | 80 | 36 | 78 | 333 |
| Los Angeles–Long Beach, California | 1,587 | 558 | 47 | 196 | 142 | 109 | 49 | 37 | 448 |
| Miami, Florida | 1,504 | 532 | 40 | 14 | 145 | 119 | 51 | 77 | 525 |
| Milwaukee, Wisconsin | 1,604 | 610 | 88 | 83 | 153 | 105 | 43 | 57 | 466 |
| Minneapolis–St. Paul, Minnesota–Wisconsin | 1,560 | 510 | 115 | 154 | 118 | 68 | 37 | 110 | 449 |
| Nassau–Suffolk, New York | 1,885 | 926 | 84 | 93 | 80 | 158 | 29 | 105 | 410 |
| Newark, New Jersey | 1,470 | 611 | 54 | 134 | 45 | 88 | 46 | 47 | 447 |
| New Orleans, Louisiana | 1,157 | 389 | 60 | 8 | 126 | 79 | 37 | 75 | 382 |
| New York, New York–New Jersey | 2,114 | 559 | 77 | 361 | 214 | 122 | 60 | 92 | 629 |
| Philadelphia, Pennsylvania–New Jersey | 1,224 | 477 | 44 | 57 | 71 | 82 | 24 | 73 | 395 |
| Phoenix, Arizona | 1,389 | 582 | 96 | 22 | 69 | 94 | 39 | 77 | 409 |
| Pittsburgh, Pennsylvania | 1,188 | 484 | 58 | 38 | 66 | 51 | 18 | 108 | 365 |
| Portland, Oregon–Washington | 1,363 | 637 | 67 | 9 | 28 | 71 | 65 | 61 | 424 |
| Riverside–San Bernardino–Ontario, California | 1,556 | 592 | 56 | 203 | 167 | 84 | 35 | 46 | 372 |
| Rochester, New York | 1,594 | 730 | 98 | 146 | 54 | 62 | 29 | 75 | 400 |
| Sacramento, California | 1,537 | 561 | 43 | 249 | 54 | 77 | 60 | 30 | 464 |
| St. Louis, Missouri–Illinois | 949 | 467 | 59 | 7 | 62 | 73 | 24 | 27 | 231 |
| San Antonio, Texas | 1,091 | 543 | 36 | 3 | 84 | 49 | 26 | 57 | 293 |
| San Diego, California | 1,391 | 553 | 47 | 146 | 161 | 70 | 33 | 31 | 350 |
| San Francisco–Oakland, California | 1,719 | 490 | 63 | 155 | 250 | 97 | 58 | 63 | 544 |
| San Jose, California | 1,577 | 657 | 72 | 139 | 170 | 79 | 51 | 33 | 378 |
| Seattle–Everett, Washington | 1,293 | 490 | 87 | 1 | 89 | 72 | 41 | 66 | 448 |
| Tampa–St. Petersburg, Florida | 1,126 | 444 | 50 | 15 | 82 | 82 | 31 | 48 | 374 |
| Washington, D.C.–Maryland–Virginia | 1,790 | 653 | 51 | 139 | 129 | 105 | 52 | 106 | 554 |

SOURCE: Adapted from The Tax Foundation, Facts & Figures on Government Finance (Baltimore: Johns Hopkins University Press, 1990), p. 300.

is little concern for substantive policy issues or much attention paid to citizens' views.

## Where Local Government Revenue Goes

What mix of local government activities gets funded via the incremental budgeting process? The largest slice of local funds goes to education. The remainder is divided among numerous services ranging from sewage to administration.

Table 19.2 shows how the largest cities in the United States raised and spent their money in the year ending June 30, 1990. This table, based on U.S. census data, reveals wide variations among cities—but beware of false comparisons: The table does not show per capita expenditures.

Of course, city government spending does not tell the whole story. Funds for some functions come from other local sources, such as school districts, and/or higher levels of government. Thus Table 19.2 shows zero expenditures in many cities for education and public welfare, but Table 19.3 shows that these functions are indeed financed in cities and throughout metropolitan areas (called SMSAs, not MSAs, in 1983 when these data were collected). In other words, the total package of public services received by a city or MSA's residents comes from local, state, and federal sources.

Predictably, the single most important determinant of spending level is the availability of money. But a number of other factors—political environment, income and age distributions of residents, and so forth—also help explain differences in spending levels and service mixes among urban communities.

*To conclude:* We all know people who claim to be committed to some cause, such as saving the environment. Yet their words and actions may not be closely linked. More than high-sounding phrases, the way people actually spend their time and money reflects their level of commitment and priorities. So it is with governments. A budget is a value statement reflecting the priorities and real commitments of a collectivity—or, theoretically at least, the majority's preferences.

Thus, whatever values taxpayers claim to hold can be measured against how much money they're willing to commit to these goals relative to others.

In the United States, local public finance reflects traditional commitments to locally controlled education and basic services such as sewers and water. But the local budget alone cannot reveal the total package of value preferences. For a more realistic assessment of what taxpayers both want and get in terms of public services, we have to examine the system of fiscal federalism: federal, state, and local expenditure patterns.

## ANOTHER LOOK

Ultimately, local public finance is tied to metropolitan, state, national, and global production and consumption, as well as local value preferences. How much is produced in a city, state, nation, and the world affects the public services citizens receive. The public goods and services citizens want to consume—and pay for collectively—reflect their values. How much surplus is available for public allocation determines the limits of public spending.

Theorists disagree on normative questions of political economy: What, if anything, should be done to encourage fiscal equity between central cities and their suburbs? Should the federal government take over all fiscal responsibility for welfare assistance via a national tax? In the interest of a truly equitable ability-to-pay tax, should the property tax be abandoned in favor of a net worth tax? Should the federal government decrease its involvement in traditionally local functions? Should government at all levels lower its voice and tighten its belt, letting the market decide who gets what services? The answers depend on the theorist's political ideology.

Even if policy analysts agree on the wisdom of a particular tax policy, it doesn't follow that their findings will have public policy impact. One example is sales taxes. Researchers have collected mounds of empirical evidence showing that sales

taxes are regressive, affecting the poor more than the affluent. However, unless those empowered to change tax policy want to do so, the evidence has little significance. In other words, theorists propose, others dispose.

## KEY TERMS

**Assessed value**   The amount at which real property (land and structures) is valued for property tax purposes. Frequently the assessed value of property is set at some fraction of the full market value, such as 25 percent.

**Elasticity**   A measure of the degree to which a revenue source will stretch as an economy expands or shrinks. It is expressed as a coefficient by dividing a percentage change in tax revenue by a percentage change in income.

**Excise tax**   A tax on the sale of a specified type of good, such as cigarettes, liquor, and gasoline. An excise tax, unlike a sales tax, is limited to specified items rather than applied across the board.

**Fiscal federalism**   The system of intergovernmental fiscal relations within the U.S. federal system in which different layers of government (federal, state, or local) collect and spend revenue.

**Incidence**   The final resting place of a tax after all shifting has occurred. A statement of tax incidence shows who finally pays the tax.

**Income tax**   A tax levied on individual and corporate income. Theoretically it is a progressive tax based on the ability-to-pay principle, whereby a larger tax burden is put on individuals or firms that have a greater capacity to pay.

**Incremental**   Refers to small units. Normally, public budgets are not constructed anew every year. Rather, they are incremental in nature; policy makers make small increases or decreases in some budget categories.

**Intergovernmental city**   In the United States, an older industrial city that is virtually dependent on federal and state transfers to provide routine public services because it suffers from economic decline (e.g., private

disinvestment; loss of industry, retail trade, and population) and growing demands for public services.

**Intergovernmental transfer**   A transfer of revenue from one level of government to another.

**Own source revenue**   Revenue raised by a jurisdiction directly from income sources that it controls, such as a local property tax.

**Progressive tax**   One in which the rate of the tax increases as the taxable base grows—for example, 5 percent tax on an income of $1,000, 8 percent tax on $5,000, and 25 percent tax on $30,000.

**Property tax**   A tax on real property: land and such improvements on land as housing and commercial-industrial buildings. The amount of tax paid is based on the assessed value of the property, and the tax rate is set by the jurisdiction.

**Regressive tax**   One in which the rate of the tax remains the same while the taxable base grows; the opposite of a progressive tax. Thus, the proportion of tax paid by a person earning $5,000 is greater than that paid by a person earning $25,000. Sales and excise taxes are regressive.

**Sales tax**   A tax based on a flat percentage of the selling price. It is paid at the time of sale by the purchaser, collected by the seller, and subsequently turned over to some level of government.

**Tax base**   For a community, the total assessed value of all real property within its borders. It also refers to the value at which a tax rate is applied to determine the tax owed. In property taxes, for instance, the tax base is the assessed valuation of real property.

**Tax rate**   The rate applied to the assessed value (in the case of the property tax) or to earnings (in the case of the income tax) for tax purposes.

**User charge**   A tax paid by the person who actually uses a publicly provided good. Examples include bridge tolls and admission fees to city museums.

## PROJECTS

1. **Local revenue sources.** Using census data, construct a pie chart of local government revenue sources for two different cities.

2. **Local expenditures.** Using census data, construct a pie chart of general expenditures for the same two cities.

3. **Comparison of revenue patterns.** Compare the data collected in Projects 1 and 2. Are there differences between the two cities in terms of own source revenue and intergovernmental transfers? Are there differences between the cities in terms of spending patterns? What hypotheses might you construct to explain any differences?

4. **The budgeting process.** Attempt to find out as much as you can about the budget-making process in your community. Using interviews with city officials, any relevant newspaper clippings, and informal talks with knowledgeable academics, try to determine who the major actors are and what interest groups seem to have some input into the budgeting process.

## SUGGESTIONS FOR FURTHER LEARNING

The leading text on urban public finance is Richard A. Musgrave and Peggy B. Musgrave, *Public Finance in Theory and Practice,* 5th ed. (New York: McGraw-Hill, 1989). While difficult, it does not presuppose a background in economics. For details on fiscal federalism and how formula-based and project grants are allocated, see Chapter 29, "The Structure of Fiscal Federalism."

Cities primarily dependent on federal and state government revenue to support local public services—so-called intergovernmental cities—are the focus of Robert W. Burchell, James H. Carr, Richard L. Florida, and James Németh, with Michael Pawlik and Felix R. Barreto, *The New Reality of Municipal Finance* (New Brunswick, N.J.: Rutgers University Press, 1984). This study traces the rise and decline of intergovernmental cities, which, for the most part, are large, partially deindustrialized Rustbelt communities. Such cities suffered disinvestment and eroded local tax bases during the period 1960 to 1980. Commenting on the aftermath of federal cutbacks to intergovernmental cities, the authors

conclude that "there is a basic realization that if cities have to go it alone, they indeed can. Further, in the long run, this might be the better way" (345).

The Tax Foundation, a unit of Citizens for a Sound Economy Foundation, publishes data files on diskettes and a hard-copy edition of *Facts & Figures on Government Finance* (Baltimore: Johns Hopkins University Press). The twenty-fifth edition of this book, published in 1990, contains a helpful glossary, as well as hundreds of tables on federal, state, and local government fiscal operations. Formerly biennial, the reference book is now published annually.

A book that has greatly influenced public policy analysis is Aaron Wildavsky, *The Politics of the Budgetary Process,* 2nd ed. (Boston: Little, Brown, 1974), an urbane and readable book. Wildavsky deals with public budgeting at the national level, but many games local budgeters play can be understood by the rules Wildavsky has decoded. Local budgeting is described in Arnold Meltsner, *The Politics of City Revenue* (Berkeley: University of California Press, 1971), an informed tour of the drab and frugal offices of city budgeteers in Oakland, California. Decades after Meltsner's book, the offices are still drab, some public services have been privatized (e.g., the art museum), and deep budget cuts have enforced frugality in providing public services.

In *Mayors and Money: Fiscal Policy in New York and Chicago* (Chicago: University of Chicago Press, 1992), Ester R. Fuchs examines why Chicago remained relatively stable fiscally, while cities with similar economic conditions (e.g., Houston) did not. She finds three interrelated factors: historical budget patterns, formal-legal arrangements with other units or levels of government, and the relative clout of interest groups and political parties. Both Martin Shefter's *Political Crisis/Fiscal Crisis: The Collapse and Revival of New York City* (New York: Columbia University Press, 1992) and John Hull Mollenkopf's *A Phoenix in the Ashes: The Rise and Fall of the Koch Coalition in New York City Politics* (Princeton, N.J.: Princeton University Presss, 1992) focus on other factors affecting fiscal policy, particularly political resources deriving from economic change.

# REFERENCES

Advisory Commission on Intergovernmental Relations (ACIR). 1985. *Bankruptcies, Defaults, and Other Local Government Financial Emergencies.* Washington, D.C.: ACIR.

———. 1987. *Significant Features of Fiscal Federalism.* Washington, D.C.: ACIR.

Burchell, Robert W., James H. Carr, Richard L. Florida, and James Németh with Michael Pawlik and Felix R. Barreto. 1984. *The New Reality of Municipal Finance: The Rise and Fall of the Intergovernmental City.* New Brunswick, N.J.: Rutgers University Press.

Cope, Glen Hahn. 1990. *Successful Economic Development: Meeting Local and Global Needs. Baseline Data Report.* Vol 23, no. 1. Washington, D.C.: International City–County Management Association.

Crecine, John P. 1969. *Governmental Problem Solving: A Computer Simulation of Municipal Budgeting.* Chicago: Rand McNally.

Hacker, Andrew, ed. 1965. *The Corporation Take-Over.* Garden City, N.Y.: Doubleday, Anchor.

Haeseler, Rob. 1993. "Bay counties hurting—tax shift latest blow." *San Francisco Chronicle* (August 3):A1+.

Hornor, Edith R., ed. 1993. *California Cities, Towns and Counties.* Palo Alto, Calif.: Information Publications.

Kantor, Paul, with Stephen David. 1988. *The Dependent City: The Changing Political Economy of Urban America.* Glenview, Ill.: Scott, Foresman/Little, Brown.

*Los Angeles Times.* 1993. "Survey finds no easing of cities' financial binds." *San Francisco Chronicle* (July 9):A10.

Malcolm, Andrew H. 1978. "Tokyo on the brink of bankruptcy, facing central government rule." *New York Times* (February 4):1.

Meltsner, Arnold. 1971. *The Politics of City Revenue.* Berkeley: University of California Press.

Meltsner, Arnold, and Aaron Wildavsky. 1970. "Leave city budgeting alone!: A survey, case study, and recommendations for reform." Pp. 311–358 in John P. Crecine, ed., *Financing the Metropolis: Public Policy in Urban Economics.* Beverly Hills, Calif.: Sage.

Musgrave, Richard A., and Peggy B. Musgrave. 1989. *Public Finance in Theory and Practice,* 5th ed. New York: McGraw-Hill.

Nader, Ralph. 1971. "A citizen's guide to the American economy." *New York Review of Books* (September 2):14–18.

O'Connor, James. 1973. *The Fiscal Crisis of the State.* New York: St. Martin's Press.

Pammer, William J., Jr. 1992. "The future of municipal finances in an era of fiscal austerity and economic globalization." Pp. 3–11 in *The Municipal Year Book 1992.* Washington, D.C.: International City–County Management Association.

Shenker, Israel. [1975] 1977. "Urban experts advise, castigate, and console the city on its problems." Pp. 5–10 in Roger E. Alcaly and David Mermelstein, eds., *The Fiscal Crisis of American Cities.* New York: Random House.

Tax Foundation. 1993. *Facts & Figures on Government Finance, 1993 edition.* Baltimore: Johns Hopkins University Press.

U.S. Bureau of the Census. 1978. *City and County Data Book 1977.* Washington, D.C.: Government Printing Office.

———. 1992. *Statistical Abstract of the United States 1992.* Washington, D.C.: Government Printing Office.

Verhovek, Sam Howe. 1993. "Texans reject sharing of school district wealth." *New York Times* [national edition] (May 3):A1+.

Wayne, Leslie. 1994. "Local governments lose millions in complex and risky securities." *New York Times* [national edition] (September 25):A1+.

Wildavsky, Aaron. 1974. *The Politics of the Budgetary Process,* 2nd ed. Boston: Little, Brown.

# FINALE
# To Be Continued

Imagine a huge blank wall.

"How boring is a blank wall," sigh the city council members. Moving quickly against boredom (and graffiti), they vote funds for 500 paintbrushes and truckloads of nonspray paint. Then they invite men, women, and children from each city block to transform a blank wall in the CBD into a giant mural about city life.

The idea spreads. Soon muralmania grips the nation's cities. People everywhere are painting city scenes on blank walls. "Cities grow curiouser and curiouser," sniff the urbanists. "This muralmania deserves our undivided attention," they decide. So, grant proposals are written— and funded.

The social scientists swing into action. An economist collects data on the time spent painting instead of working at paid employment and the consequent rise or fall in the GNP. Teams of participant-observers join paint crews in twenty-two selected cities. A political scientist studies the relationships that develop between city hall flaks and neighborhood block groups. A geographer charts the location of blank walls in small, medium-size, and large cities. A sociologist gathers data on the social backgrounds of those who paint skyscrapers and those who paint playgrounds. A mass communications researcher examines the impact of muralmania on prime-time TV programming. An organization theorist explores how paint crews divide their tasks. And on and on . . .

One year passes. Everywhere people are painting blank walls. Or they're talking about what's painted on walls that used to be blank. Throughout the nation, conferences on muralmania are held. Scholars present learned papers, including "Ethnic Styles of Depicting City Hall," "The Spatial Relation of City Murals to Transport Nodes," "How Paint Crews Handle Conflict on Scaffolds," and "A Cost–Benefit Analysis of Muralmania with Emphasis on Changes in Consumer Buying Patterns."

Meanwhile, political commentators reflect on the deeper meanings of muralmania. According to one radical pundit, "Muralmania presents a strong case against capitalism. Here we have nonalienated labor, working collectively in their own interest, to creatively humanize the cities. The lesson is clear: We can end alienation if we end capitalism." A liberal draws a different lesson: "Muralmania presents a strong case for equal opportunity. Given an equal chance to express themselves and a little on-the-scaffold training, all Americans—regardless of social background, color, or creed—can rise to the top rungs of the ladder." A conservative columnist doesn't agree, writing that "muralmania presents a strong case for letting the free market work without government interference. Responding quickly to consumer preferences, the market was responsible for providing gallons of paint at cheaper prices and for employing the jobless in paint factories. The message is self-evident: Keep the government out of running and regulating our lives, and the nation will prosper." Other voices are raised. A decentralist comments, "How beautiful is smallness. Muralmania presents a strong case for local community action. Just imagine what energy would be released through neighborhood government." A centralist, on the other hand, argues that "muralmania presents a strong case for central coordination and economies of scale. Without regional paint buying and the vast administrative effort that went into organizing paint crews, muralmania would have fizzled out." Clearly, muralmania has captured the nation's imagination. Amid the TV talk shows, editorials, parades, and block parties, social scientists continue their analysis. One team of content analysts carefully examines photos of all city scenes painted by all the people on all the cities' walls. Grounded—rather, flooded—in data, they construct a typology to make sense out of the infinite variety of urban images painted on once-blank walls. Seventy-five categories of images are devised. Here are just a few:

1. Types of people depicted by occupation (several thousand subcategories, taken from the U.S. Department of Labor's job title dictionary).
2. Types of people depicted by race (twenty-five subcategories, taken from the 1990 U.S. census).
3. Types of technology depicted by energy source (seventeen subcategories, including feet and hands, electronic, and appropriate).
4. Types of ideas expressed by symbols (ten subcategories, including religious, political, and economic).

After constructing this typology of urban images painted during muralmania, the social scientists look over data about the muralists themselves. Then, as is their bent, they construct numerous hypotheses. Here's one about differential perceptions of urban life: Big-city radicals tend to paint public buildings, while small-town conservatives tend to paint private homes and small businesses. During a coffee, tea, or frozen-yogurt break, the urbanists sit around and wax poetic. "Isn't it amazing," says one, "that each city speaks with a distinctive voice. Take Los Angeles and San Francisco, for example. Their murals have very different images. Frankly, I have never felt comfortable in L.A."

A colleague chides, "Really, you are so Bostonian! I bet you feel right at home in San Francisco. After all, it's an eastern look-alike. Its personality was created by enterprising Easterners bitten by the gold bug and out to strike it rich. It just doesn't feel like L.A., that space-age Autopia, that western Surfurbia to its south."

"Good grief," moans an aged urban theorist. "Your discussion of San Francisco and Los Angeles is disturbing. All my scholarly life, I've been searching for the fundamental forces that govern modern urban life. I have tried to discover the structures and institutions that underlie modern cities everywhere. Now you remind me of the vast differences between two cities, both located in the same outpost of postindustrial society, that state of the (imagi-)nation called California. Is there no hope of constructing a theory that can explain urban life and behavior in Los Angeles, San Francisco, Boston, Moscow, Beijing, and Keokuk, Iowa?"

Others chime in. One says, "An international team of 439 scientists recently announced the discovery of the top quark: the last of twelve subatomic building blocks now thought to constitute the material world. This finding is central to understanding the nature of time, matter, and the universe. But for us to search for the fundamental components of urban life—the City Quarks—seems less fruitful. In my view, no one (or even twelve) element can possibly explain how all cities work at any historical point in time. Neither can any one theory."

Another adds, "I agree. First off, what we label a 'city' is not a single beast. The name 'city' covers administrative capitals, commercial-trade centers, military garrisons, religious shrine settlements, and rather small trading posts. How can any single theory explain urban existence in these various kinds of cities? Clearly, being an urbanite in New York City and in Crescent City, California, is a qualitatively different experience. Furthermore, cities aren't single units. Take a big city like Chicago. It's got diverse neighborhoods. It's got urban villages and cosmopolitan corners. It's got bread makers in small shops and computer programmers in the Prudential Building. It's got folks like my grandparents, who came to the city from a Mississippi farm, and it's got my kids, who think that chocolate milk comes from chocolate-colored cows."

A political sociologist enters the discussion. "Yes, yes, Even so, some key concepts can help us to understand how cities work. These concepts concern underlying structures and institutions, whether they're experienced in people's heads or not. My candidates for key concepts include economic and social interdependence, specialization, and differentiation."

An anthropologist suggests that "population size and growth and population density could be added to the list. Of course, theorists since the ancient Greeks have pointed to the importance of population size and density for human relations. Now some anthropologists claim that there are such things as 'magic numbers' that influence, even determine, human behavior. Some even claim they have the exact number in the game. For instance, the magic number for hunter-gatherer bands is 25; over that, people risk conflict and fighting. In early villages, the magic number is 100; over that, villagers tend to split into two villages. And so on."

"Hmm," a skeptic wonders aloud. "This magic number business is a bit too deterministic for my taste." "Well," says the anthropologist, "I can show you evidence from 102 societies—including baboons and Bushmen—where the numbers work." The skeptic responds, "You can show me all the evidence you want. My intuition tells me it's plain nonsense."

The discussion heats up. At this point, one of the urbanists tries to lower the temperature level: "Colleagues, let us give our imagination free play. How might you explain how cities work to a person who had never seen or lived in one— say, an Aché tribesperson in Venezuela today?"

The first scholar answers, "I would use the analogy of the human body. Each organ of the body performs a particular function. The heart, for instance, pumps the blood through the human system, and the brain coordinates motor activity. Each organ is useless on its own. Organs function together in harmony, and together they form a living, organic system. This living system can't be described merely by talking about each separate organ because the body is more than the sum of its parts. It is the same with cities. The lifeblood of cities—goods, services, ideas—is circulated throughout the metropolitan system by networks of transport and communication. Managers and administrators, like the human brain, coordinate human activity. And just like the human body, the city is more than the sum of its parts. In addition, just as the body grows and becomes differentiated into specific organs and systems, cities grow more complex and become differentiated internally."

The second scholar answers, "Your analogy is elegant and simple to understand. That is why it is so seductive. Yet it lacks a certain dimension. It doesn't convey the possibilities for change and conflict. Someone once said that cities are places where unexpected things happen. Your metropolitan system-as-human-body metaphor neglects this sense of spontaneity. Also, human bodies have boundaries that everyone can see.

Cities don't. Where, for instance, do the boundaries of New York City begin and end? On a map, the political boundaries are clear. But the eyes and ears of the Big Apple stretch across the globe. In addition, the whole idea of a metropolitan system may be passé in postsuburban America. No, your metaphor is misleading. The metaphor of the city as a machine—with meshing gears and parts all working in harmony—suffers from similar shortcomings, in my opinion."

The third scholar answers, "Let me offer another metaphor from the world of biology. This is only fair, since Charles Darwin took his idea of the survival of the fittest from Herbert Spencer, a sociologist (who, incidentally, gave us the metaphor of society as a human body). I think the city is most like a single cell. Just as it is in the nature of cells in the body to pool their resources and to fuse when possible, I think it is in the nature of urban life for people to come together and join with each other in common activity whenever possible."

"Colleagues," a fourth injects, "I prefer to return to our empirical evidence for our metaphor. Murals all over this country show the city to be a swirl of nonagricultural activities. So I offer this image: the city as collage."

Another urbanist speaks up: "This discussion reminds me of old elephant stories. One person looks at the city and sees bodies and systems. Another sees single cells trying to fuse together. Still another sees a collage or a mosaic. Similarly, one searches for underlying structures and institutions. Another focuses on subjective meanings of city life. Still another seeks fundamental elements of city life everywhere. And some stick to the available evidence, while others depend on intuition. Each approach has its merits—and limits. The trouble is, they don't seem to lend themselves to synthesis. So, what is to be done?"

"No doubt some of us will continue to dissect small pieces of the urban scene," answers a plumber-turned-theoretician. She continues, "Some will focus on substantive issues—urban transport, terrorism, pollution, and so on. Some will explore particular parts of urban culture. Others will try to make the connections between the small pieces and the theoretical issues. Still others will try to merge theory and practice, applying their knowledge to improve the quality of urban life. Whatever we do, I hope we remember John Gardner's admonition: 'We must have respect for both our plumbers and our philosophers, or neither our pipes nor our theories will hold water.'"

Hopefully, all of us will continue the long search for knowledge by sharing our evidence and insights and by asking better questions. That is why we cannot say "The End." That is why we say instead, "To Be Continued . . ."

# Brief Biographies

Any list of notables is bound to dissatisfy some and to offend or outrage others. This relatively short list reflects my judgment of persons whose ideas, research, and/or actions have significantly contributed to urban theory or practice, either directly or indirectly. Thus I include Max Weber, Emile Durkheim, Karl Marx, and other macro-level social theorists because their conceptual frameworks have had an important impact on urban studies. Others, including Robert Moses and Frederick Law Olmsted, are known primarily as doers rather than thinkers, and their doings influenced the shape of modern urban America. Still others, such as Milton Friedman and John Kenneth Galbraith, are included because they represent points of view to be reckoned with.

Who is systematically underrepresented or excluded from this list? There are few behind-the-scenes urban policymakers. I would have liked to include Abraham Levitt and sons of Levittown, David Rockefeller of the Chase Manhattan Bank, and others whose decisions (e.g., suburban development, redlining of urban areas) have had enormous impact on twentieth-century urban America or on particular cities, but that is a list in itself. Also, there are few poets, artists, or writers of the city; a more complete listing would include Georgia O'Keefe, Woody Allen, Tom Wolfe, John Ashbery, Walt Whitman, Saul Bellow, Thomas Wolfe, Finley Peter Dunne, Frank Norris, and many, many more. Thus, this list is necessarily incomplete. It is merely a list of *some* notable contributors to the study or practice of things urban.

**Jane Addams** (1860–1935) College-educated, well-traveled social reformer. Founder of Chicago's Hull House in 1889, first president of the Women's International League for Peace and Freedom, and co-winner of the Nobel Peace Prize for 1931, Jane Addams started at Hull House and moved into a wider political arena of social reform. She helped to promote labor legislation, set up juvenile courts, sponsored municipal government reform, and agitated for women's suffrage.

**Christopher Alexander** (b. 1936) Innovative architect-designer whose book *A Pattern Language* (1977) summarizes an alternative vision of design: highly participatory and decentralized, with attention to symbolism and overlapping (nontree-like) structures.

**Edward R. Banfield** (b. 1916) Neoconservative urbanist best known for his controversial book *The Unheavenly City* (1968), which drew a storm of criticism from liberals and radicals for its gloomy view of human nature and government's ability to do much about urban problems. Earlier works include co-authorship of classic studies of city decision making: *Politics, Planning, and the Public Interest* (1955) and *City Politics* (1963). Banfield is currently Shattuck Professor of Urban Government at Harvard University.

**Ernest W. Burgess** (1886–1966) Formulator of the Burgess hypothesis. Burgess hypothesized that U.S. industrial cities are structured in concentric zones. Burgess was a principal figure in the University of Chicago's school of sociology and urban theory. *The City* (1925), coauthored with Robert E. Park and Roderick D. McKenzie, exerted a powerful influence on urban sociologists, geographers, economists, and other students of the city.

**Daniel Burnham** (1846–1912) Architect, city planner, and highly skilled propagandist for his own ideas, Burnham is best remembered for building according to a preestablished plan. He was the inspiration behind the Columbian Exposition Fairgrounds, called the White City, at the Chicago World's Fair of 1893. Later he devised the Chicago Plan of 1909, gaining business support for his notion of the City Beautiful. He has been called the predecessor of New York City's Robert Moses because of his obsession with highways and his policies, which led to the eviction of poor people in order to widen Chicago's thoroughfares. Burnham's vision is revealed in his quip: "Make no little plans. They have no magic to stir men's blood."

**Manuel Castells** (b. 1942) Spanish-born, French-trained, multidisciplinary urban theorist. Castells, who teaches at the University of California at Berkeley and at various universities throughout the world, is one of the leading contemporary analysts of the city. Influenced by Marx and twentieth-century French structural neo-Marxists, he attempts to link types of urban organization to forms of capitalism.

**V. Gordon Childe** (1892–1957) Australian-British archeologist whose thesis stressed the importance of environment (capable of producing an agricultural surplus), technology, and social structure (emergence of a governing elite) to the origin of cities in ancient Mesopotamia. He was Abercromby Professor of Prehistoric Archeology at the University of Edinburgh.

**Walter Christaller** (1893–1969) The developer of central place theory, Christaller published a seminal book, *Central Places in Southern Germany* (1933), describing the size, spacing, and number of so-called central places in a region.

**Robert Dahl** (b. 1915) Author of the influential study of urban decision making *Who Governs?* (1961), which presents a pluralist view of community power structure. Professor of political science at Yale University, Dahl joined the Democratic Socialist Organizing Committee (DSOC) in the late 1970s.

**Richard J. Daley** (1902–1976) Chicago's late mayor (1955–1976) and boss of the Cook County Democratic Party machine, often considered to be the last surviving old-style city machine in American politics. Daley was a second-generation Irish-American and self-made man who never moved from his small neighborhood house or lost his working-class accent and malapropisms. He was undisputed master of ethnic politics in Chicago during his tenure as mayor. However his various policies are interpreted, observers agree that Daley had political clout.

**Emile Durkheim** (1858–1917) Eminent French sociologist who asked a key question: How do individuals make up a stable, cohesive society? In his first book, *The Division of Labor in Society* (1893), Durkheim addressed this question by examining two forms of social solidarity: mechanical and organic. He theorized that in modern (organically solid) societies, social cohesion results from, or is expressed by, social differentiation (division of labor).

**Walter Firey** (b. 1916) Best known for his book *Land Use in Central Boston* (1947), in which he developed a theory of cultural ecology. Firey argued against the economic determinism of the classic models of urban spatial structure, contending that cultural values and symbolism play a significant role in the way cities are structured. He is professor of sociology at the University of Texas and a specialist in human ecology and regional planning.

**Milton Friedman** (b. 1912) The leading spokesperson for U.S. economic conservatives today. A pure market theorist, Friedman proposes market solutions to national and urban problems. He taught at the University of Chicago and is presently at the Hoover Institution at Stanford. His ideas reached a wider audience through his PBS series, *Free to Choose*.

**John Kenneth Galbraith** (b. 1908) A self-proclaimed "abiding liberal," Canadian-born Galbraith has long served as a member of Harvard University's economics department. He has produced numerous books, including *The New Industrial State* ([1967] 1971), and has played political roles, including ambassador to India during the 1960s. (Ironically, his ideological opponent, Daniel Patrick Moynihan, followed him at the New Delhi Embassy several years later.)

**Herbert Gans** (b. 1927) Author of *The Urban Villagers* (1962) and *The Levittowners* (1967), sociologist and city planner Gans disputes Wirth's notion that urbanism is a way of life. Currently, he is professor of sociology at Columbia University.

**Erving Goffman** (1922–1982) Called "the Kafka of our time" for his vision of routine encounters, Canadian-born sociologist Goffman is known for his dramaturgical model of social interaction: People present themselves or perform in various masks, depending on the audience and the impression they wish to manage. To Goffman, social interaction in public and semipublic places is guided by unspoken rules (norms) that help maintain public order.

**David Harvey** (b. 1935) A leading urban analyst, influenced by Marx's writings, concerned with the relationship of the built environment and the spread of industrial capitalism. He taught at Johns Hopkins for many years before becoming the Halford Mackinder Professor of Geography at Oxford University.

**Floyd Hunter** (1912–1992) Author of *Community Power Structure: A Study of Decision Makers* ([1953] 1963), a classic statement of the elitist model of community power, and an update, *Atlanta's Policymakers Revisited* (1979).

**Jane Jacobs** (b. 1916) Popularizer of unconventional ideas about cities and city planning. As a journalist and later editor of *Architectural Forum*, Jacobs grew increasingly critical of planning that destroyed communities, separated land uses, and rebuilt sterile areas. Her best-selling book, *The Death and Life of Great American Cities* (1961), presents an alternative view in which planners should protect neighborhoods, mix land uses, and pay attention to design details that matter to people. In *The Economy of Cities* (1970), she argues that the first cities led to agriculture, not vice versa. Presently she is an independent writer and iconoclast in Toronto.

**Henri Lefebvre** (1901–1991) French seminal thinker whose original work is wide-ranging, from urbanism and architecture to the production of space and dialectical logic. His writings influenced a generation of younger urbanists who brought space back into social theory.

**Oscar Lewis** (1914–1970) American anthropologist who did much of his work in urbanizing societies. A critic of Louis Wirth, he found that people adjust to urban life in various ways and that the city is not the proper unit for analyzing social life.

**Elliot Liebow** (1925–1994) Author of the classic *Tally's Corner* (1967), a study of black streetcorner men in Washington, D.C. Anthropologist Liebow hung out with the unskilled urban men and, based on his first-hand observation, drew a portrait of their social and work situations linking their way of life to macro-level social forces. In 1993, he published a study of homeless women in suburban Washington, D.C. Between books, he worked as a U.S. government bureaucrat.

**Kevin Lynch** (1918–1984) A key figure in urban design, Lynch invented a vocabulary that dominates urban design today. He was concerned with making cities more imageable so that their residents find them understandable and reassuring. After an apprenticeship with Frank Lloyd Wright, Lynch turned to teaching. His best-known work is *The Image of the City* (1960). He taught in the Department of Urban Studies and Planning at the Massachusetts Institute of Technology.

**Malcolm X** (1925–1965) Second in command of the Black Muslim movement in the United States during the early 1960s, he left the party after a policy disagreement with party leader Elijah Muhammad. He was believed to have been forming a new movement when he was assassinated in 1965.

**Karl Marx** (1818–1883) Revered by many, feared by some, and loathed by others, Marx's ideas are inescapable. Although his ideas have not been widely popular in the United States, he was known to Americans in the nineteenth century through his articles for the *New York Daily Tribune* between 1852 and 1862. Fur-

ther, Marxian concepts, particularly alienation, have become part of the working vocabulary of social scientists, whatever their attitude toward Marx's work. Marx's major writings include the early *The German Ideology* (1846) and the three-volume, magisterial *Capital* (1867, 1885, 1894).

**Robert Moses** (1888–1981) Master builder of U.S. cities, Moses used his base as head of public authorities in New York City to establish a new kind of political machine, lubricated by money but rooted in bureaucratic power instead of ward-level politics. He mobilized banks, contractors, labor unions, the mass media, insurance companies, and churches to shape the physical structure of New York City and social policies. He has been called the single most powerful man in New York and the chief influence on American cities in the twentieth century.

**Daniel Patrick Moynihan** (b. 1927) Democratic senator from New York and leading spokesperson for the neoconservatives, Moynihan formerly served as U.S. ambassador to India, urbanist at the Joint Center for Urban Studies at MIT and Harvard University, Nixon's policy advisor, and U.S. ambassador to the United Nations. A prolific writer, Moynihan is the author or coauthor of numerous urban studies, including *Beyond the Melting Pot* (1963), a study of five ethnic groups in New York City. His long-time interest in ethnicity extends to the international scene; in his book *Pandaemonium* (1993), polymath Moynihan reveals the qualities for which he is known: forthrightness, wit, and phrase-making ability (*benign neglect* was his term—his policy advice to the Nixon administration for certain social issues).

**Lewis Mumford** (1895–1990) A charter member of the Regional Planning Association of America in 1923 (whose studies influenced the eventual building of Radburn, New Jersey, and other greenbelt towns). With the publication of *The Culture of Cities* (1938), Mumford gained a worldwide reputation. In the course of writing more than twenty books, he came to represent a particular view of urban life and urban "solutions." In his own words, "the city should be an organ of love; and the best economy of cities is the care and culture of men. . . . Otherwise the sterile gods of power, unrestrained by organic limits or human goals, will remake man in their own faceless image and bring human history to an end."

**Richard and Peggy Musgrave** (married 1964) Coauthors of *Public Finance in Theory and Practice* (5th ed., 1989), the best-known urban public finance textbook. Migrants from Harvard University, they are now teaching at the University of California, Santa Cruz.

**James O'Connor** (b. 1930) A radical economist-sociologist who developed the theory of the *Fiscal Crisis of the State* (1973). O'Connor is presently professor of sociology at the University of California, Santa Cruz.

**Frederick Law Olmsted** (1822–1903) Pioneer American landscape architect. Olmsted was the moving force behind many projects to make the natural environment accessible to urbanites, including Central Park in New York City, before the era of Boss Tweed. Olmsted left his mark on countless American parks, waterfronts, and civic areas.

**Robert E. Park** (1864–1944) Member of the Chicago school of sociology and collaborator with Ernest W. Burgess in developing the ecological perspective on urban phenomena, Park was a news reporter and social reformer turned sociologist. He taught sociology at the University of Chicago from 1914 to 1933.

**Pericles** (ca. 490–429 B.C.) Led citizens of the Athenian polis to overthrow a ruling oligarchy in about 463 B.C. Under his democratic leadership, Greek culture flourished, producing what is often called the Golden Age of Pericles. His most famous speech, the "Funeral Oration," was given on the occasion of a funeral for soldiers who had died in the war between Athens and Sparta.

**Henri Pirenne** (1862–1935) Belgian economic historian who advanced a thesis tracing medieval European cities to the revival of commerce in the twelfth century.

**George Washington Plunkitt** (1842–1924) A cracker-barrel philosopher of machine politics. A lifelong Tammany Hall politician in New York City from the days of Boss Tweed until his death, Plunkitt gave a classic description and defense of the city machine, including "honest graft."

**Carl Sandburg** (1878–1967) Born in Galesburg, Illinois, to Swedish immigrants, Sandburg was a poet, Lincoln scholar, humanitarian, and newspaper writer. *The People, Yes* (1936) is often considered to be his epic. Sandburg's bold images of industrial cities are double-edged, noting both the promise and the problems they

portend. But in general, he celebrated urban industrial society and the countless Americans who created it.

**Adam Smith** (1723–1790) Known primarily for *An Inquiry into the Nature and Causes of the Wealth of Nations* (1776), considered the first comprehensive system of political economy. A professor at the University of Glasgow, he used the concept of the invisible hand, whereby the individual seeks personal gain and thus promotes the public interest. Smith viewed the world as a well-ordered, harmonious mechanism. His ideas lie at the base of laissez-faire economics.

**Robert Sommer** (b. 1929) Psychologist who observes how people actually use airports, classrooms, convalescent homes, and other spaces in order to provide guidance to architects and other design professionals. His study *Personal Space* (1969) is a seminal work on the way in which people relate to their immediate space. Currently, Sommer is professor of psychology at the University of California, Davis.

**Lincoln Steffens** (1866–1936) A muckraking journalist and antimachine crusader, Steffens authored a series of magazine articles in 1903 exposing *The Shame of the Cities*. He concluded that "the source and sustenance of bad government [are] not the bribe taker, but the bribe giver, the man we are so proud of, our successful businessman." Later in life, Steffens studied, wrote, and lectured in defense of the Russian Revolution. His autobiography is a notable literary contribution.

**W. I. Thomas** (1863–1947) Contributed the concept of "the definition of the situation" to social psychology. His best-known book (with Florian Znaniecki), *The Polish Peasant in Europe and America* (1918), details the connections between the individual's definition of the situation and his or her family and community background. For Thomas, the interrelationship of individual personality and social order was a key concern.

**Ferdinand Tönnies** (1855–1936) German sociologist who identified two contrasting types of society and mentality: *Gemeinschaft* (community) and *Gesellschaft* (society). Tönnies, like Marx, traced social development as an evolutionary transition from primitive communism and village-town individualism to capitalistic urban individualism and, in the future, to state socialism. Tönnies's concepts, although not original, have influenced generations of scholars.

**William Marcy Tweed** (1823–1878) Boss of the

New York City Tweed Ring from 1866 to 1871 and the symbol of a corrupt machine politician. Originally a chair maker and voluntary fireman, Tweed became an alderman (1852–1853), sat in Congress (1853–1855), and was repeatedly elected to the New York State Senate. In 1870, he was made commissioner of public works for the city. But his real power came informally as the grand sachem (head) of Tammany Hall, New York City's Democratic party machine. He was criminally and civilly indicted for various frauds and eventually jailed. After a brief escape to Cuba and Spain (1875–1876), he was recaptured and died in a New York jail while suits were pending against him for recovery of $6 million.

**Edward L. Ullman** (1912–1976) Together with Chauncy Harris, Ullman developed the multiple nuclei model of internal city structure, which holds that city space is organized around a number of independent centers of commercial, manufacturing, and residential activity. He taught geography at various universities, including the University of Washington and Harvard University.

**Samuel Bass Warner, Jr.** (b. 1928) Urban historian whose particular fascination is the interplay between social history and physical space. Among his books are *The Private City* (1968), which examines Philadelphia's society and physical form in the late eighteenth, mid-nineteenth, and early twentieth centuries, and *Streetcar Suburbs* (1962), which describes the social and physical dynamics of Boston's pre-automobile suburbs at the end of the nineteenth century. He is presently professor of history and social science at Boston University.

**W. Lloyd Warner** (1898–1970) With his research associates, social anthropologist Warner set the pattern of research for future generations with the *Yankee City* series, studies of urban social stratification. Warner developed two techniques for studying what he called social class, but he actually measured social status, not class. In general, Warner found that American cities have a "system of open classes" (that is, status groups).

**Max Weber** (1864–1920) A classic figure in the European liberal tradition whose sociological work ranged from the theory of bureaucracy and authority to the methodology of social science. His essays on *The Protestant Ethic and the Spirit of Capitalism* (1904–1905), *The City* (1921), and "Status, Class, Party" (1922) continue to stimulate debate even today. Rationalization of modern life was a theme in Weber's political sociology. He envisioned the dawn of an age in which bureaucracy would be like an "iron cage," reducing the individual's role within an ever-expanding network of management and control.

**William H. Whyte** (b. 1917) A social scientist by avocation instead of vocation. He is the author of *The Organization Man* (1956), an influential study of the ethics, ideology, and lifestyle of the "new middle class" that runs big business and public organizations. In the section on the organization man at home in the suburbs, Whyte details his fear that the norms of the suburb, like those of the corporation, violate the spirit of individualism.

**Louis Wirth** (1897–1952) Member of the Chicago school of sociology and disciple of Robert E. Park. He is best remembered for his classic essay, "Urbanism as a Way of Life" (1938), in which he argues that large size, heterogeneity, and high density in the city lead to a particularly urban way of life.

# Index